Contents

Portuguese azulejos
colour section following
p.216

Coastal Portugal colour
section following p.352

Port wine colour
section following p.536

D0994159

◀◀ Lisbon's Praça do Comércio ◀ High summer, Nazaré

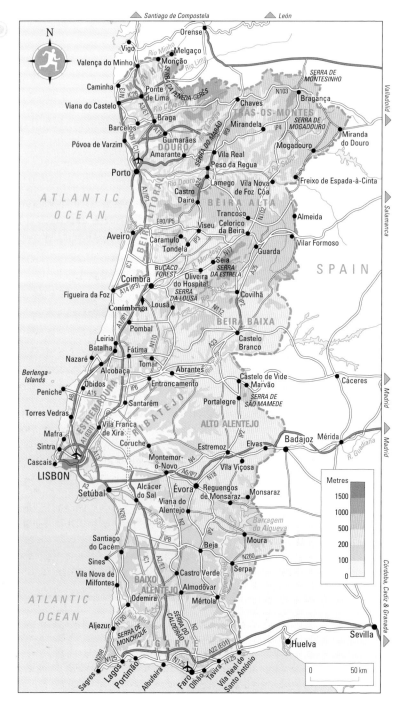

Introduction to

Portugal

Portugal is an astonishingly beautiful country. The rivers, forests and lush valleys of the centre and north are a splendid contrast to its contorted southern coastline of beaches, cliffs and coves, and even the arid plains of the Alentejo region are tempered by vast groves of olive, oranges, cork and vines. Spring comes early everywhere, when dazzling flowers carpet hillsides across the country, and summer departs late, with sea-bathing possible deep into the autumn. It's a country that demands unhurried exploration – indeed, Portuguese talk of their nation as a land of *brandos costumes* or gentle ways.

For so small a country, Portugal sports a tremendous cultural and social diversity. There are highly sophisticated resorts along the Lisbon and Estremaduran coast, as well as on the southern Algarve, upon which European tourists have been descending for fifty years. Lisbon itself, in its idiosyncratic way, has more than enough diversions to please city devotees – firmly locked into contemporary Europe without quite jettisoning its most endearing, rather old-fashioned, qualities. But in the rural areas – the Alentejo, the mountainous Beiras, or northern Trás-os-Montes – this is often still a conspicuously underdeveloped country. Tourism and European Union membership have changed many regions – most notably in the north, where new road-building scythes through the countryside – but for anyone wanting to get off the beaten track, there are limitless opportunities to experience smaller towns and hamlets that still seem rooted in earlier centuries.

Differences between the **north and south** are particularly striking. Above a roughly sketched line, more or less corresponding with the course

▲ Cork groves, Alentejo

of the Rio Tejo (River Tagus), the people are of predominantly Celtic and Germanic stock. It was here, in the north at Guimarães, that the Lusitanian nation was born, following the Christian reconquest from the North African Moors. South of the Tagus, where the Roman, and then the Moorish,

The Golden Age

For over a hundred years, in the period spanning the fifteenth to sixteenth centuries, Portugal was one of the richest countries in the world, an economic powerhouse that controlled a trading empire spreading from Brazil in the west to Macau in the east. It was Vasco da Gama's discovery of a sea route to India in 1498 that kick-started the **spice trade**, shooting Portugal – already doing well from **African gold** and **slavery** – into the top league of wealthy nations. Its maritime empire reached a peak during the reign of Manuel I "The Fortunate" (1495–1521), the so-called Golden Age that also produced Luís de Camões and Gil Vicente, two of Portugal's greatest writers, along with the new, exuberant Manueline architectural style. Portugal was to hit the jackpot again in the seventeenth century, when enormous gold reserves were discovered in Brazil, but changing markets and over-indulgence soon reduced its financial clout, and after the **Great Earthquake** of 1755 the country sank into economic obscurity. Nevertheless, the physical legacy of Portugal's empire remains in the surviving buildings and monuments of the Golden Age, such as Lisbon's **Torre de Belém** and **Mosteiro dos Jerónimos**, while **Portuguese** itself is the world's fifth most-spoken language.

civilizations were most established, people tend to maintain more of a Mediterranean lifestyle (though the Portuguese coastline is, in fact, entirely Atlantic). Life follows an easy pace, especially in the dog days of summer, when the sweltering heat restricts activity. **Agriculture** reflects this divide as well, with oranges, figs and cork in the south, and more elemental corn and potatoes in the north. Indeed, in places in the north the methods of farming date back to pre-Christian days, based on a mass of tiny plots divided and subdivided over the generations.

More recent events are also woven into the pattern. The 1974 Revolution, which brought to an end 48 years of dictatorship, came from the south, an area of vast estates, rich landowners and a dependent workforce; while the later conservative backlash came from the north, with its powerful religious

▶ Café Brasileira, Lisbon

Fact file

• Portugal is the most south-westerly country in mainland Europe; its only neighbour is Spain with which it shares one of the longest and most established borders in Europe.

• The country occupies an area of approximately 92,000 square kilometres with a surprisingly diverse landscape – from the steep mountains of the north to the arid plains of the Alentejo and the wetlands of the south-east coast. The entire coastline of 1,793km gives on to the Atlantic Ocean.

• Tourism is the country's largest industry, though the greatest proportion of the population works in agriculture. Twenty-six percent of land remains arable, with a further thirty-six percent made up of forests and woodland. Portugal's most important exports are textiles, wine, especially port from the north of the country, and cork – over fifty percent of the world's wine corks come from Portugal.

• Apart from brief periods of Spanish occupancy, Portugal has been an independent country since 1140. It became a republic in 1910 and is now a parliamentary democracy divided into eighteen regions, together with two autonomous regions (the islands of Madeira and the Azores). It joined the EU in 1986 and, despite rapid economic growth, remains one of the EU's poorest countries, with a GDP of around sixty-six percent that of the four leading European economies.

authorities and individual smallholders wary of change. But more profoundly even than the Revolution, it is **emigration** that has altered people's attitudes and the appearance of the countryside. After Lisbon, the largest Portuguese community is in Paris, and there are migrant workers spread throughout Europe and North America. Returning, these emigrants have brought in modern ideas and challenged many traditional rural values. New cultural influences have arrived, too, through Portugal's own immigrants from the old African colonies of Cape Verde, Mozambique and Angola, while the country's close ties with Brazil are also conspicuously obvious.

The greatest of all Portuguese influences, however, is **the sea**. The Atlantic dominates the land not only physically, producing the consistently temperate climate, but mentally and historically, too. The Portuguese are very conscious of themselves as a seafaring race; mariners like Vasco da Gama led the way in

Food from afar

Portugal's former status as an important trading nation has had a far greater influence on world cuisine than is often realized. The **tempura** method of deep-frying food was introduced to the Japanese by six-teenth-century Portuguese traders and missionaries, while the fiery curry-house mainstay **vindaloo** derives from a **vinho** (wine) and **alho** (garlic) sauce popular in Portuguese Goa. Indeed, the use of **chillis** in the East only began when the Portuguese started to import them from Mexico. **Bacalhau** (dried salt cod) – now a staple in diverse European countries and fashionable restaurants alike – started life as a way of preserving fish on board the Portuguese voyages of exploration; another, less exotic, Portuguese export is **marmalade** (although Portuguese **marmelada** is actually made from quince).

Despite this historic global culinary influence, however, it is only recent-ly that the Portuguese themselves have embraced foreign tastes. Pizza,

pasta and bland Chinese food are the best that most towns can muster, though you will find restaurants specializing in dishes deriving from Portugal's former colonies – keep an eye out for Angolan *mufete* (beans with palm oil and fish), chicken *piri piri* (chicken with chilli sauce), which originated in **Angola** and **Mozambique**, *caril de camarão* (shrimp curry) and *chamuças* (samosas) from **Asia** and **Brazilian** meals such as *feijoada* (pork and bean stew), *picanha* (sliced rump steak) and *rodizio* (barbecue meat buffet).

▲ Nossa Senhora dos Remedios, Lamego

the exploration of Africa and the New World, and such links long ago brought influences to bear upon the country's culture: in the distinctive music of fado, blues-like songs heard in Lisbon and Coimbra, for example, or the Moorish-influenced Manueline architecture that provides the country's most distinctive monuments.

This "glorious" history has also led to the peculiar national characteristic of *saudade*: a slightly resigned, nostalgic air, and a feeling that the past will always overshadow the possibilities of the future. The years of isolation under the dictator Salazar, which yielded to democracy after the 1974 Revolution, reinforced such emotions, as the ruling elite spurned influences from the rest of Europe. Only in the last three decades, with Portugal's entry into the European Union, have things really begun to change and the Portuguese are becoming increasingly geared toward Lisbon and the cities. For those who have stayed in the countryside, however, life remains traditional – often disarmingly so to outsiders – and social mores seem fixed in the past.

Where to go

The obvious place to start a visit to Portugal is the capital, Lisbon, which within its environs contains a selection of just about everything the country has to offer: historical monuments, superb beaches and the former royal retreat of Sintra, along with neighbourhood grill houses, hip nightclubs and traditional city quarters. Further north on the Rio Douro (River Douro), Porto is the country's second city and the economic heart of the nation, perhaps best known for its port wine lodges. It certainly beats to a faster work rhythm than the rest of the country but the city nevertheless retains an earthy, typically Portuguese welcome for outsiders.

These are the only cities of any size in Portugal, but the country's cultural and historical past is also reflected in vibrant smaller towns, especially the university towns of medieval **Coimbra** and Roman **Évora**, in the country's first capital of **Guimarães**, at the religious centre of **Braga**, in canalside **Aveiro** or historic **Viseu**. Other towns have a more idiosyncratic

▼ Rossio station, Lisbon

interest – in **Fátima**, Portugal has one of the world's most revered Catholic shrines, beautiful **Tomar** was headquarters of the Knights Templar, while **Guarda** boasts of being the highest city in Europe.

Elsewhere, some of the continent's most extraordinary **monuments** dominate entire towns – the monasteries, abbeys, convents and pilgrimage sites of Mafra, Alcobaça, Batalha, Lamego and others are all well visited. There are also great weekly and monthly **markets** – like those at Barcelos, Évora, Estremoz and Loulé – that are a throwback to earlier times and attract locals and visitors alike. **Nature**, meanwhile, provides the caves and dinosaur tracks of

▲ Lux, Lisbon

Estremadura, the iconic national forest of Buçaco, the surviving salt pans of the central coast, the ski fields near Covilhã and the various regional wine routes. But if Portugal has a natural emblem it is surely its famous **beaches**, the most alluring of which are in the **Algarve**, where you can still escape the crowds on the offshore islands around Tavira and along the west coast north of Sagres. Other less-developed (but more exposed) Atlantic beaches can be found up the entire west coast of Portugal, from the surfer hangouts of the Alentejo and Estremadura to the more traditional **Costa da Prata** resorts in the Beira Literal. Crowds are even thinner along the **Costa Verde** around Viana do Castelo, but by the time you are this far north the sea is decidedly chilly for much of the year.

The most dramatic and verdant inland scenery lies in the north around the sensational gorge and valley of the **Rio Douro** and in the mountainous natural parks of the Serra da Estrela, Peneda-Gerês, Montesinho, Alvão and Serra da Malcata. Some rural villages in northern **Trás-os-Montes** still live a startlingly traditional existence firmly rooted in subsistence farming. Touring the minor *serras*, especially in the **Beira** region, can also show you a largely untouristed side of the country, as can the wide-open plains of the flat southern **Alentejo**, scattered with some of Portugal's prettiest whitewashed villages. Finally, all along the border with Spain you'll find fortified border settlements, from **Valença do Minho** in the north to **Mértola** in the south, most of them complete with fantastic castles and many barely touched by tourism.

▼ Vineyards, Douro valley

When to go

A weather map of endless suns sums up the situation across the whole of Portugal in summer, certainly between June and September, when the only daytime variation across the country is a degree or two further up the scale from 30°C. In July and especially August (the Portuguese holiday month), the coastal resorts are at their busiest and prices correspondingly reach their peak. It's also a horribly hot time to tour the Alentejo or to expect to do much walking about cities, medieval towns and archeological sites. It's a few degrees cooler in mountain areas but there's little shade at altitude and, again, high summer is not an ideal time for hiking holidays.

With such a verdant landscape, it should be no real surprise that Portugal also has a fairly high level of **rainfall**. Most of it falls from November to March, though shifting weather patterns mean you can just as easily experience bone-dry winter months and downpours in May and June. The north of Portugal is particularly wet, and in the higher areas showers are possible more or less throughout the year. In central and southern Portugal, especially on the coast, it is mild all year round and, although it can be cloudy in winter, when the sun does break through it is delightfully warm.

Perhaps the best times of year to visit are in **spring** (ie, from February) – for the dazzling flowers – and early **autumn** (October), when the weather is warm but not too hot and the summer crowds have thinned out. Swimmers, however, should note that the official swimming season in Portugal lasts from the beginning of June to mid-September; outside these months, outdoor pools and river beach facilities close, while some hotels, restaurants, campsites and water parks only open from around Easter to September.

In **winter**, in the north things can get pretty cold, especially inland where snow is common along the mountainous border areas in January and February. But, if you don't mind the odd tourist facility being closed, then crisp, sharp sunshine makes winter a highly appealing time to visit the centre and south of the country. In Lisbon, Estremadura, the Alentejo and the Algarve there are dramatic reductions in hotel prices and, in February, the almond blossom lights up the countryside. This is the time when you'll see the country at its most Portuguese, with virtually no tourists around.

Average temperatures and rainfall

Daytime temperatures (°C) and average monthly rainfall (mm)

	Jan	Mar	May	Jul	Sep	Nov
Lisbon						
Max °C	14	18	22	27	25	17
Min °C	8	10	13	17	16	12
Rainfall	111	109	44	3	33	93
Porto (Costa Verde)						
Max °C	13	15	19	25	24	17
Min °C	5	7	10	15	14	8
Rainfall	159	147	87	20	51	148
Faro (Algarve)						
Max °C	15	18	22	28	26	19
Min °C	9	11	14	20	19	13
Rainfall	70	72	21	1	17	65

things not to miss

It's not possible to see everything that Portugal has to offer in one trip — and we don't suggest you try. What follows is a selective taste of the country's highlights: outstanding buildings and historic sights, natural wonders and vibrant events. They're arranged in five colour-coded categories, which you can browse through to find the very best things to see and experience. All highlights have a page reference to take you straight into the guide, where you can find out more.

01 **Évora** Page **491** • A UNESCO-protected university town complete with Roman temple, Moorish alleys and medieval walls.

03 Parque Nacional da Peneda-Gerês Page **430** • Hikers and bikers won't want to miss the trails that wind through the country's only national park.

02 Museu Gulbenkian, Lisbon Page **118** • One of Europe's greatest treasure chests of art and applied art, ancient to Lalique.

05 Monsanto Page **314** • The ancient hilltop settlement of Monsanto seems to grow out of the very rocks it's built upon.

04 Estádio da Luz, Lisbon Page **140** • Portugal's most famous stadium hosts top-class football matches throughout the season.

07 Pegadas dos Dinossáurios
Page **207** • On the dinosaur trail in Estremadura – see Portugal's 175-million-year-old sauropod tracks.

06 Bairro Alto, Lisbon Page
102 • The capital's big night out – touring the bars, clubs and restaurants of the funky Bairro Alto neighbourhood.

08 Corgo train line Page **448** • One of Portugal's great rides, the Corgo train line winds through spectacular gorges from Peso da Régua to Vila Real.

09 Olhão Page **556** • The Algarve's biggest fishing port is the departure point for boat trips to the sandbank islands.

10 **Ericeira** Page **174** • Lisbon's favourite beach retreat – and a noted surfers' hangout.

12 **Tram #28, Lisbon** Page **85**
• The capital's best tram route winds through all the historic districts.

11 **Valença** Page **415** • Explore this superb fortified town, located on Portugal's northern border with Spain.

13 **Velha Universidade, Coimbra** Page **235** • Portugal's third-largest city boasts its oldest and most prestigious university.

14 **Grutas de Mira de Aire** Page **206** • Daily tours explore the tunnels and caverns of the country's largest cave system.

15 Sintra Page **149** • The hilltop retreat near Lisbon is one of the most scenic in the country, surrounded by opulent palaces and country estates.

16 Vila Nova de Milfontes Page 537 • The Alentejo coast is a lot less developed than the Algarve, but every bit as attractive.

17 Coastline, Lagos Page **597** • Explore the extraordinary shaped rocks and grottoes by boat from the historic Algarve port of Lagos.

18 Tibães Page **399** • This barely visited monastery in the north is one of the oldest and most atmospheric buildings in the country.

19 Alcobaça Page **195** • The sculpted tombs of Dom Pedro and Inês de Castro dominate this glorious twelfth-century Cistercian monastery.

20 Fado Page **135** • Mariza, pictured, is one of the most critically acclaimed performers of Portugal's most famous musical genre.

21 Mosteiro Palácio Nacional de Mafra Page **177** • With 5200 doors and 2500 windows, this lavish palace-convent nearly bankrupted the country when it was built in the eighteenth century.

22 Ilha de Berlenga Page **184** • Tour the dramatic coastline by boat, or even stay the night – the Atlantic bird-sanctuary island is a real get-away-from-it-all destination.

24 **Alfama, Lisbon** Page **99** • A village in the heart of the capital, with streets so narrow and precipitous that few cars can enter.

23 **Citânia de Briteiros** Page **386** • Step back to pre-Roman times at the magnificent Celtic hill fort near Braga.

25 **Festa de São João** Page **338** • You can expect to be pounded with plastic hammers during one of the country's most important saint's days, especially in Porto.

26 Bom Jesus do Monte, Braga
Page **396** • Possibly Portugal's most photographed church, reached up a grand ornamental stairway.

27 Monsaraz
Page **507** • Many of the medieval houses in the fortified hilltop village of Monsaraz have been converted into atmospheric guest houses.

28 Feira de Barcelos
Page **399** • The country's liveliest and most colourful market shows that rural traditions are alive and well.

29 Óbidos
Page **185** • Picture-book walled town that was once the traditional bridal gift of Portuguese kings.

30 **Convento de Cristo, Tomar** Page **213** • Tomar's extraordinary "Convent of Christ" is the former headquarters of the Knights Templars.

31 **Museu de Arte Contemporânea de Serralves, Porto** Page **341** • Contemporary art in a wonderful building remodelled by Portugal's leading architect, Álvaro Siza Vieira.

32 **Pastéis de Belém** Page **125** • These delicious flaky custard tartlets have been made and served for over a century at the *Antiga Confeitaria de Belém*.

33 **Porto's riverfront** Page **337** • The historic riverside *bairro* of Ribeira is now a UNESCO World Heritage Site.

34 Rio Douro valley Page **361** • Take a boat trip from Peso da Régua up one of the loveliest river valleys in Portugal.

36 Guimarães Page **379** • The first capital of Portugal is a beguiling place of cobbled streets and historic buildings.

38 Conímbriga Page **240** • Vivid mosaics at the most important Roman site in Portugal.

35 Monte de Santa Luzia, Viana do Castelo Page **409** • There are superb views from the hilltop basilica over the northern resort of Viana do Castelo.

37 Parque Natural de Montesinho Page **471** • Bucolic unspoilt countryside dotted with traditional villages.

39 Serra da Estrela Page **296** • The highest mountains in Portugal conceal windswept uplands, remote villages and challenging hiking trails.

Basics

Basics

Getting there

There are regular direct flights to Lisbon, Faro and Porto, though travellers from outside Europe may find it cheaper to fly via London and arrange onward travel from there – in particular, there are no direct flights to Portugal from Australia or New Zealand. If you want to see some of France or Spain en route, or are taking a vehicle, there are various overland combinations of ferry, rail and road to consider, though these will nearly always work out pricier than flying. European rail passes might save you some money, but most of the major ones need to be purchased before you leave. Package holidays and tours can be good value, whether it's an Algarve beach holiday or escorted walking tour – and travel agents and specialist tour operators can also provide car rental, hotel bookings and other useful services.

Air fares are seasonal, with the highest – for flights from Europe or North America – in July and August and during school holidays (Easter, Christmas/New Year and some half-term breaks in May and October).

The **cheapest flights** from the UK and Ireland are usually with no-frills budget and charter airlines, especially if you're prepared to book several weeks (or months) in advance or chance a last-minute deal. Budget airline tickets are sold direct (by phone or online) on a one-way basis, and you may find the outward or return leg of your journey significantly more expensive depending on demand. Be aware, too, of airport taxes, which can occasionally work out more expensive than the flight itself. The flights also all have fixed dates, and are non-changeable and non-refundable, while return tickets with charter airlines may limit your stay to one month.

The major **scheduled airlines** are usually (though not always) more expensive, but tickets remain valid for at least three months (often a year) and have a degree of flexibility should you need to change dates after booking. You can cut costs by going through a specialist flight or discount agent, who may also offer charter flights, and special student and youth fares, plus a range of other travel-related services.

Flights from the US and Canada

The only direct non-stop services between **North America** and Portugal are from New

York (Newark) to Lisbon with Continental Airlines or Tap (around $1100–1600), or Toronto to Lisbon or Porto with SATA (around $1400). Flight time on both routes is seven to eight hours. From all other cities you'll need to get a connecting flight via New York or a European airport. If you want to fly to Porto or Faro, TAP can organize onward flights from Lisbon, while some of the European airlines, such as BA, Lufthansa and Air France, fly direct to Porto and/or Faro from their home hubs.

Indirect flights via a **European hub** can be $300 cheaper, though journey times are upwards of thirteen hours. All flights to Portugal from central USA and the West Coast involve changing planes, either in New York or in Europe. From the Pacific coast, expect to pay around about $300 on top of the New York fare. The fare will also depend in large part on connection times: you pay more for shorter waits.

From **Canada** to Portugal, most airlines route through New York or Europe. Indirect flight times from Montreal and Toronto to Lisbon are around 10–14 hours; 14–15 hours is the best you can hope for from Vancouver. From Vancouver, Toronto and Montreal via New York, high-season returns start at CDN$2000.

Another option is to take advantage of cut-price tickets between Canada or the US and London (from $700 return US East Coast, $1000 US West Coast; Toronto and Montreal to London from CDN$1000, Vancouver from

CDN$1200), with airlines like Virgin, American Airlines, British Airways and United, and then make your way from there, as the onward flight from London to Portugal can cost as little as US$150 return (see below for all the details).

Flights from the UK and Ireland

Flying to Faro, Lisbon or Porto takes two to three hours from airports around the **UK** and **Ireland**. Given the plethora of budget and charter airlines serving the Algarve – there are regular flights from numerous regional airports – Faro is generally the cheapest destination

and, even in high season, return fares under £100 are common (€250 from Ireland). Booking as early as possible – months in advance – is the key to a good price, occasionally as low as £3 return (before taxes). But even if you miss the best deals, you're unlikely to part with more than £150–200 for a return flight to Portugal. Of course, if you leave it too late, or want a fully flexible ticket with a scheduled airline, you could spend as much as £400.

Charter flights (usually to Faro) can also be very good value, especially for last-minute deals. However, these usually only operate in summer.

Fly less – stay longer! Travel and climate change

Climate change is the single biggest issue facing our planet. It is caused by a build-up in the atmosphere of carbon dioxide and other greenhouse gases, which are emitted by many sources – including planes. Already, flights account for around three to four percent of human-induced global warming: that figure may sound small, but it is rising year on year and threatens to counteract the progress made by reducing greenhouse emissions in other areas.

Rough Guides regard travel, overall, as a global benefit and feel strongly that the advantages to developing economies are important, as are the opportunities for greater contact and awareness among peoples. But we all have a responsibility to limit our personal "carbon footprint". That means giving thought to how often we fly and what we can do to redress the harm that our trips create.

Flying and climate change

Pretty much every form of motorized travel generates CO_2, but planes are particularly bad offenders, releasing large volumes of greenhouse gases at altitudes where their impact is far more harmful. Flying also allows us to travel much further than we would contemplate doing by road or rail, so the emissions attributable to each passenger become truly shocking. For example, one person taking a return flight between Europe and California produces the equivalent impact of 2.5 tonnes of CO_2 – similar to the yearly output of the average UK car.

Less harmful planes may evolve but it will be decades before they replace the current fleet – which could be too late for avoiding climate chaos. In the meantime, there are limited options for concerned travellers: to reduce the amount we travel by air (take fewer trips, stay longer!), to avoid night flights (when plane contrails trap heat from Earth but can't reflect sunlight back to space), and to make the trips we do take "climate neutral" via a carbon offset scheme.

Carbon offset schemes

Offset schemes run by **climatecare.org**, **carbonneutral.com** and others allow you to "neutralize" the greenhouse gases that you are responsible for releasing. Their websites have simple calculators that let you work out the impact of any flight. Once that's done, you can pay to fund projects that will reduce future carbon emissions by an equivalent amount (such as the distribution of low-energy lightbulbs and cooking stoves in developing countries). Please take the time to visit our website and make your trip climate neutral.

www.roughguides.com/climatechange

There are fewer charters and low-cost outfits flying to Lisbon and Porto, but shop around and flights can be as cheap as those to Faro if you buy your ticket early. Even within a few weeks of departure, you should be able to find a high-season seat for around £150–200. Airlines flying into Lisbon include BA/GB Airways (from Heathrow and Gatwick), Easyjet (from Luton), Monarch (from Gatwick), TAP (from Heathrow and Dublin, the latter code-shared with BMI), and Aer Lingus (from Dublin); while direct flights to Porto are also operated by BA/GB Airways (from Heathrow), TAP (from Heathrow) and Ryanair (from Dublin, Liverpool and Stansted). If direct flights are full, you are best off getting a cheap flight to Faro and travelling overland from there.

Flights from Australia and New Zealand

Although there are no direct flights from **Australia** or **New Zealand** to Portugal, airlines offer through tickets with their partners via European or Asian hubs. Whichever you choose, keep an eye on connection times; some, like the British Airways/Qantas combo, are slick and take under 26 hours, but others – usually cheaper – may see you twiddling your thumbs in a departure lounge for up to a day.

High-season returns from Australia to Lisbon average A$2500–3500, though rock-bottom deals can be found for around A$1700. Flying into London and buying a budget onwards ticket from there may work out cheaper. The lowest London fares start at about A$1700 return, though with a major airline it's more likely to be nearer A$2500 range, depending on your departure city.

High-season economy return fares from New Zealand to Lisbon are pretty stable, starting at around NZ$2500.

Trains

London to Lisbon by **train** takes at least 24 hours via the Channel Tunnel, and closer to forty hours if you use the cross-Channel ferry, both routes via Paris. It's usually more expensive than flying, too, even if you qualify for under-26 or over-60 discounts, or buy a **railpass** (see "Getting around", p.33).

The cheapest standard return fare over the Channel by **ferry** and with no couchette reservation in Spain is at least £200 and involves transferring stations in Paris (from Nord to Austerlitz). Tickets are valid for two months and allow stops anywhere along the pre-specified route; dates can be freely changed after booking. The quicker route from London Waterloo, using the Channel Tunnel's Eurostar train service, starts at £250 return, including obligatory seat reservations on the *TGV Atlantique* (from Paris Montparnasse to the Spanish border at Hendaye/Irún) and couchette on the overnight *Sud-Expresso* (from the border to Lisbon). Through tickets can be bought from one of the agents listed on p.31.

Buses

Eurolines (℗0870/514 3219, ⓦwww .nationalexpress.com) operates various services to Portugal, but it's a long journey (35–42hr depending on your destination) from the UK. There are at least two bus changes involved: one in France, the other in Spain. Buses leave on Tuesdays and Fridays from London Victoria: Lisbon and Faro cost £150/€210 return if booked at least four days in advance, and reductions are available for over-60s – tickets can be bought online or from any National Express agent.

If you want to combine Portugal with trips to other parts of Europe, consider a **Euroline pass.** The pass, which covers forty cities in Europe, is valid for either fifteen days (mid-Sept to May: £115 for under 26, £135 for over 26; June to mid-Sept £190 under 26, £225 for over 26) or thirty days (mid-Sept to May: £160 for under 26, £205 for over 26; June to mid-Sept £245 under 26, £300 for over 26).

Overland from Spain

Bus or train connections from Madrid, Málaga, Santiago de Compostela and Seville to Portugal are easy, with rewarding stops en route. Rail passes (see p.33) are valid on all the routes below, but you'll be liable for supplements on many trains. There are of course numerous other border road crossings, but if you're in a rental car remember to check whether you're covered to take the vehicle between countries.

From Madrid (Chamartin station), the overnight *Lusitânia Comboio Hotel* takes 10hr 30min to Lisbon, arriving in time for breakfast. The train has seats and couchettes and cabins complete with showers, plus restaurant, buffet bar and lounge. Prices start at €56 one-way, €89 return, for a second-class seat or €79 one-way, €126 return for the cheapest berth (four-bed cabin); there are also singles, doubles and *gran classe* cabins available. Change at Entroncamento in Portugal for Coimbra and Porto. Tickets can be bought at Chamartin, or through the Spanish (Ⓦ www.renfe.es) or Portuguese (Ⓦ www .cp.pt) railway companies' websites.

Another scenic route – the one taken by the *Sud-Expresso* from the French border at Hendaye/Irún – passes through San Sebastian and Salamanca, entering Portugal at Vilar Formoso in Beira Alta, and calling at Portugal's highest town, Guarda; change at Coimbra for Porto. Tickets for the entire 13hr Irún–Lisbon journey start at €65 one-way, €105 return (€92/148 for the cheapest six-bed berth), and again can be bought online.

From northern Spain, two trains a day connect Vigo in Galicia to Porto (around 3hr 30min), passing the border at Tuy/Valença on the River Minho, then following the river and coast down via Vila Praia de Âncora, Viana do Castelo and Barcelos.

From the great Andalusian cities of Granada, Córdoba and Seville in southern Spain you are well placed to get a bus to the border at Ayamonte/Vila Real de Santo António, for onward transport by bus or train along the Algarve coast.

By car and ferry

Driving the 2000km or so from the UK to Portugal, using the standard **cross-Channel services** or Eurotunnel (Ⓦ www.eurotunnel .com) through the Channel Tunnel, takes two full days. It's not a cheap option (factoring in the cross-Channel trip, tolls, overnight stops and meals), but it is a good way of seeing something of France and Spain on the way. The AA (Ⓦ www.theaa.co.uk) has a useful route-finder to help you plan your trip.

The best way of cutting down the driving time to Portugal is to catch a **ferry** to either Santander or Bilbao in northern Spain. Brittany Ferries (Ⓦ www.brittanyferries.co.uk) sails from Plymouth to Santander (two weekly; 19hr), and P&O Ferries (Ⓦ www.poferries .com) from Portsmouth to Bilbao (four weekly; 29hr). They are expensive services, and either route still leaves a six-to-eight-hour drive before you reach Portugal itself. Return fares including cabin accommodation to Santander start at £670 (though can be as high as £1200 in summer); to Bilbao fares start at £480 (summer £770).

Tickets can be bought direct from the ferry companies (at the ports, by phone or online), or from travel agents, and from online agents dealing with all operators, like Seaview (℡ 0870/571 1711, Ⓦ www.seaview.co.uk) and Direct Ferries (Ⓦ www.directferries.co.uk).

Package holidays and tours

Standard package holidays (available from any high-street travel agent) concentrate on the Algarve's beaches, with accommodation usually in large resort hotels or villas; note that some companies only take two-week bookings in high season. Summer prices start at around £350 per person (including flights) for a week's bed and breakfast at a modest hotel or villa near the beach, though you'll have to search hard; more usual for week-long

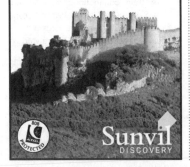

holidays is £400–700, including flights, with prices based on two people travelling together. In low season, last-minute deals can bring the cost of a week's or ten days' accommodation and flights into the £200–300 range.

Several companies also offer fly-drive holidays based around accommodation in historic manor houses and *pousadas* (upwards of £500 per person for a week, including flights and car), whilst others offer sporting holidays (mainly tennis and golf) and more specialized tours such as bird-watching, horse-riding, hiking, biking and wine tours. Summer golfing packages based in a three- or four-star hotel start at £500 a week, whilst other specialized holidays average £100–200 a day, depending on the style of accommodation. Most specialist tour operators should be able to arrange flights, insurance and car rental, and are flexible about extending flights, allowing you to indulge in some independent travel as well. The list of specialist operators below is of mainly smaller companies, directed towards arranging holidays for individuals.

Holiday and specialist tour operators

Abreu Tours ☎020/7313 2617, ⓦwww .abreu-tours.com. *Pousada* bookings, Douro cruises, tailor-made holidays and fly-drive packages.

Arblaster & Clarke ☎01730/893344, ⓦwww .winetours.co.uk. Sophisticated specialists offering Douro walks, wine tours and cruises.

ATG Oxford ☎01865/315678, ⓦwww.atg-oxford .co.uk. Stylish six-day walking trips through the Alentejo and Minho regions, staying at intimate three- and four-star hotels and manor houses from around £1600. There's an emphasis on fine food and prices are reasonable for the quality.

Caravela ☎0207 630 9223, ⓦwww.caravela.co.uk. TAP airline's touring arm covers most options, from luxury golfing packages in Lisbon region at a five-star hotel (including flights and car rental), to Douro river cruises, fly-drive *pousada* holidays and city breaks.

Destination Portugal ☎01993/773269, ⓦwww .destination-portugal.co.uk. Long-established, value-for-money agency offering flights and car rental, golfing breaks, personalized thematic tours (culture, history, wine) and accommodation bookings at four-star hotels, *pousada* and manor houses.

Equitour ☎0800 043 7942, ⓦwww.equitour.co.uk. Classic horse-riding breaks from £850 for a week, including flights to Lisbon, with optional trail riding. Accommodation is by the stables.

First Choice ☎0870/850 3999, ⓦwww.firstchoice .co.uk. Major charter holiday operator for the Algarve, Porto and Lisbon, mainly self-catering in villa complexes. Very good last-minute deals, especially in winter.

GreyPower Travels ☎00-351/229 448 839, ⓦwww.greypowertravels.com. Family-run tour operator based in Porto, specializing in group tours for over-55s for around £900 (but not including flights), with one-week programmes in northern Portugal and Galicia, the accent on history and culture.

Jonathan Markson Tennis ☎020/7603 2422, ⓦwww.marksontennis.com. Three-star apartment accommodation and intensive tuition at the Praia da Luz Ocean Club near Lagos for wannabee tennis stars – the week-long courses (around £750) include 15 hours of coaching.

Light Blue Travel ☎01223 568904, ⓦwww .lightbluetravel.co.uk. Upmarket Algarve operator combining a huge selection of villas and hotels for tennis packages based at Vale do Lobo Tennis Academy, with more mainstream villa and beach resort holidays.

Limosa Holidays ☎01263/578143, ⓦwww .limosaholidays.co.uk. Three-centre bird-watching in Alentejo, Algarve and Madeira (or Algarve only). There's some walking involved. Price (around £1100 for a week) includes flights, minibus transport and full board at modest local hotels and restaurants.

Longshot Golf ☎0870/609 0995, ⓦwww .longshotgolf.co.uk. One of the best golfing specialists, with the emphasis on three- and seven-day packages at top resorts in the Algarve and around Lisbon. Can also arrange car hire.

Magic of Portugal ☎0800/980 3378, ⓦwww .magicofportugal.co.uk. A build-your-own-holiday setup, with a good selection of moderately priced villas with pools, plus year-round golfing packages and self-drive tours.

Portuguese Affair ☎020/7385 4775, ⓦwww .portugueseaffair.com. High-quality but value-for-money villa and long weekend holidays in the Algarve, Alentejo, Costa Verde, Minho and Sintra. Also handles flights and car rental.

Pure Vacations ☎01227 264264 ⓦwww .purevacations.com/surf. Affordable week-long surfing holidays, with villa accommodation around Lisbon, Porto or the Algarve. Prices are with breakfast or half-board and include local transport and optional tuition, plus flight options.

Ramblers Holidays ☎01707/331133, ⓦwww.ramblersholidays.co.uk. Good-value one- and two-week walking trips in the eastern Algarve (based at Tavira), Alentejo, Lisbon, the Douro valley and northern parks, and options into Spain. The emphasis is on nature, and accommodation is in simple hotels. Several departures weekly throughout the year.

Rough Tracks ☏070/0056 0749, ⓦwww
.roughtracks.com. Relaxed point-to-point cycling
jaunts (5–6hr a day) in and around Gerês, and from
Lisbon to Faro, with accommodation in local pensions
and hotels. Prices are based on half-board and
exclude flights. Monthly departures between April and
July and from Sept to Nov.

Thomson Villas with Pools ☏0870/167 6548,
ⓦwww.thomson.co.uk. Vast selection of Algarve
villas (at Vilamoura, Albufeira, Silves and Carvoeiro) to
suit most budgets, which can be packaged online with
reasonably priced flights.

Travel Club of Upminster ☏01708/225 000,
ⓦwww.travelclubofupminster.co.uk. Long-
established family-run travel agency offering
accommodation in four- and five-star beach resorts as
well as villas in the Algarve.

Travellers Way ☏01527/559000, ⓦwww
.travellersway.co.uk. One-stop agency for quality
villa vacations throughout the country, golf and riding
holidays.

Airlines, agents and operators

Many **airlines** and **discount travel websites**
offer you the opportunity to book your tickets
online, cutting out the costs of agents and
middlemen. The websites listed below all offer
good deals and useful price comparisons.

ⓦwww.expedia.co.uk (in UK), ⓦwww.expedia
.com (in US), ⓦwww.expedia.ca (in Canada)
ⓦwww.lastminute.com (in UK)
ⓦwww.opodo.co.uk (in UK)
ⓦwww.orbitz.com (in US)
ⓦwww.travelocity.co.uk (in UK), ⓦwww
.travelocity.com (in US), ⓦwww.travelocity
.ca (in Canada), ⓦwww.zuji.com.au (in
Australia), ⓦwww.zuji.co.nz (in New Zealand)

Airlines

Aer Lingus ⓦwww.aerlingus.com
Air France ⓦwww.airfrance.com
Air New Zealand ⓦwww.airnewzealand.com
American Airlines ⓦwww.aa.com
bmi ⓦwww.flybmi.com
bmibaby ⓦwww.bmibaby.com
British Airways ⓦwww.ba.com
Continental Airlines ⓦwww.continental.com
easyJet ⓦwww.easyjet.com
First Choice Airways ⓦwww.air2000.com
flyBE ⓦwww.flybe.com
Lufthansa ⓦwww.lufthansa.com
Monarch Scheduled ⓦwww.flymonarch.com
Qantas Airways ⓦwww.qantas.com
Ryanair ⓦwww.ryanair.com

SATA ⓦwww.sata.pt
South African Airways ⓦwww.flysaa.com
TAP (Air Portugal) ⓦwww.flytap.com
Thomsonfly ⓦwww.thomsonfly.com
Thomas Cook Airlines ⓦwww.thomascook.com
United Airlines ⓦwww.united.com
Virgin Atlantic ⓦwww.virgin-atlantic.com

Agents and operators

STA Travel US ☏1-800/781-4040, Canada ☏1-
888/427-5639, UK ☏0870/1630 026, Australia
☏1300/733 035, New Zealand ☏0508/782 872.
Worldwide specialists in independent travel; also
student IDs, travel insurance, car rental, rail passes,
and more. Good discounts for students and under-
26s. ⓦwww.statravel.com.

ebookers UK ☏0800/082 3000, Republic of
Ireland ☏01/488 3507, ⓦwww.ebookers.com. Low
fares on an extensive selection of scheduled flights
and package deals.

North South Travel UK ☏01245/608 291,
ⓦwww.northsouthtravel.co.uk. Friendly, competitive
travel agency, offering discounted fares worldwide.
Profits are used to support projects in the developing
world, especially the promotion of sustainable tourism.

Trailfinders UK ☏0845/058 5858, Republic of
Ireland ☏01/677 7888, Australia ☏1300/780 212,
ⓦwww.trailfinders.com. One of the best-informed
and most efficient agents for independent travellers.

Rail and bus contacts

Busabout UK ☏020/7950 1661, ⓦwww
.busabout.com.

Eurolines UK ☏0870/5 808 080, Republic of
Ireland ☏01/836 6111, ⓦwww.nationalexpress
.com/eurolines.

European Rail UK☏020/7387 0444, ⓦwww
.europeanrail.com.

Europrail International Canada ☏1-888/667-
9734, ⓦwww.europrail.net.

Eurostar UK ☏0870/5 186 186, ⓦwww.eurostar
.com.

Rail Europe US ☏1-877/257-2887, Canada
☏1-800/361-RAIL, UK ☏0870/837 1371, ⓦwww
.raileurope.com/us.

ScanTours US ☏1-800/223-7226 or 310/636-
4656, ⓦwww.scantours.com.

STA Travel US ☏1-800/781-4040, Canada
☏1-888/427-5639, UK ☏0870/1630-026,
ⓦwww.statravel.com.

Trailfinders UK ☏0845/058/5858, Republic of
Ireland ☏01/677 7888, Australia ☏1300/780 212,
ⓦwww.trailfinders.com.

Walshes World Australia ☏02/9318 1044, New
Zealand ☏09/379 3708.

Getting around

Portugal is not a large country and you can get almost everywhere easily and efficiently by train or bus. Regional trains are often cheaper and some lines very scenic, but it's almost always quicker to go by bus – especially on shorter or less obvious routes. Approximate times and frequencies of most journeys are given in the "Travel details" section at the end of each chapter; local connections and peculiarities are pointed out in the text. You'll obviously have a great deal more flexibility if you drive and be able to see much more in a short trip, though it's worth bearing in mind that Portugal has one of the highest accident rates in Europe.

Trains

Comboios de Portugal (CP; enquiries on ☏808 208 208, ⓦwww.cp.pt) operates all trains. For the most part it's an efficient network with modern rolling stock, while there are some highly picturesque lines in the north that are among the country's best attractions, notably the Douro main line and the narrow-gauge Tâmega, Corgo and Tua branch lines. **Timetables** (*horários*) for all individual lines are available from stations and on the CP website, which has a good English-language version.

Most **train services** are designated Regionais (R) or Interregionais (IR), covering the country from Faro in the south to Valença do Minho in the north. Be aware that rural train stations can sometimes be a fair way from the town or village they serve – Portalegre station and town are 12km apart, for example. Intercidades (IC) are faster and more expensive services, connecting Lisbon to the main regional centres; while the modern, high-speed Alfa Pendulares (AP) trains run from Lisbon to Faro, and from Lisbon to Braga via Santarém, Coimbra, Aveiro and Porto. **Urban services** (*urbanos*) in Lisbon (to Cascais, Sintra, Setúbal and Vila Franca de Xira) and Porto (to Aveiro, Braga and Guimarães) provide a useful, cheap commuter link to local towns, while both cities also have an expanding underground **metro** system.

Rail passes

Although convenient, a **rail pass** for Portugal probably won't save you any money

unless you plan to travel extensively by train or are visiting the country as part of a wider European tour. With some passes, you will also be liable to pay supplements and seat reservations on intercity and Alfa Pendular services. However, CP's own **Bilhete Turístico**, available to anyone at major Portuguese train stations, is valid for first-class travel on all trains for seven days (£86/€120), fourteen days (£146/€205) or 21 days (£214/€300); under-12s and over-65s pay half-price.

All other rail passes have to be bought before leaving home. Anyone resident in the EU for at least six months can buy a **Eurodomino pass** (ⓦwww.raileurope.co.uk), allowing three to eight days unlimited rail travel in one calendar month. Prices for under-26s (second class) start at £37/€52 for three days, up to £80/€112 for eight days. Over-26s pay £42/£96 (€59/€135), or £76/137 (€107/192) for the first-class version. Travellers from outside Europe can buy the **Portuguese Railpass** (ⓦwww.raileurope.com), for any four days' unlimited first-class travel within fifteen days, for €106/US$135.

Unless you're travelling to Portugal by train, or also visiting Spain, the major pan-European rail passes tend not to be such good value. The **Inter-Rail Pass** (ⓦwww.raileurope.co.uk/inter-rail) is available to EU residents of at least six months standing. The passes cover 29 European and North African countries; Portugal is zoned with Spain and Morocco. Passes are available for one zone for sixteen days (under-26s £140/€196, over-26s £206/€288), two zones in 22 days (£200/€280, £285/€400), and all zones in one month (£277/€388, £393/€550).

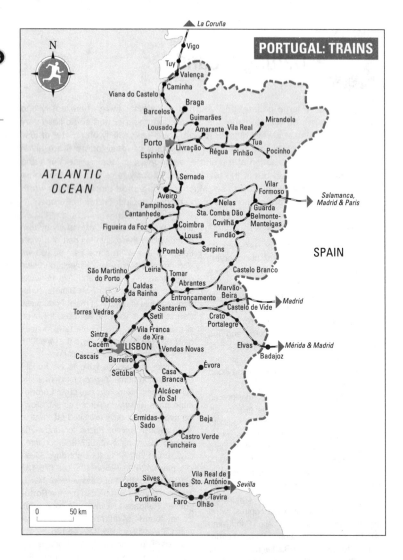

PORTUGAL: TRAINS

La Coruña

Vigo

Tuy

Valença

Caminha

Viana do Castelo

Braga

Barcelos

Guimarães

Lousado

Amarante Vila Real

Mirandela

Porto Livração Régua Pinhão Tua

Espinho Pocinho

ATLANTIC OCEAN

Sernada

Vilar Formoso

Aveiro

Salamanca, Madrid & Paris

Pampilhosa Nelas

Cantanhede Sta. Comba Dão Guarda Belmonte-Manteigas

Coimbra Covilhã

Figueira da Foz Lousã Fundão

Pombal Serpins

SPAIN

São Martinho do Porto Leiria Tomar Castelo Branco

Caldas da Rainha Abrantes Marvão-Beira

Óbidos Entroncamento Castelo de Vide

Torres Vedras Santarém Crato

Setil Portalegre Madrid

Sintra Vila Franca de Xira

Cacém LISBON Vendas Novas Elvas Mérida & Madrid

Cascais Barreiro Badajoz

Setúbal Casa Branca Évora

Alcácer do Sal

Ermidas-Sado Beja

Castro Verde

Funcheira

Vila Real de Sto. António Sevilla

Lagos Silves Tunes

Portimão Faro Tavira Olhão

N

0   50 km

Non-EU residents can buy a **Eurail Pass** (ⓦwww.raileurope.com), which allows unlimited first-class train travel in eighteen countries for a set period of between fifteen days (€580) and three months (€1634). Under-26s will save around thirty percent with a Eurailpass Youth, valid for second-class travel. A scaled-down version, the Eurail Selectpass, allows travel in up to five adjoining countries for between five days (€454) and fifteen (€816) days within a two-month period, while cheaper still, if you're travelling with up to five companions, is a joint Eurailpass Saver.

Tickets and reservations

Most visitors simply buy a **ticket** every time they travel; first-class is *primeira classe* or *conforto*, second-class is *segunda classe* or *turística*. Always turn up at the station with time to spare since long queues often form at the ticket office. However, at small, unstaffed regional stations you can just pay the ticket inspector on board. Major stations have credit-card ticket machines for purchasing long-distance IC or AP tickets (on the day of travel or up to thirty days in advance); and you can also buy IC and AP tickets on the CP website.

Fares are extremely good value, even on the most modern services. A typical regional journey, across the Algarve from Faro to Vila Real de Santo António, only costs around €5. The Lisbon-to-Porto route costs around €20 second class/€30 first class by Intercidade, or around €30/40 on the fastest Alfa Pendular service. It's cheapest on all services if you avoid travelling on Friday afternoons, Sunday afternoons, Monday mornings, national holidays and the day preceding a national holiday. There are fifty-percent **discounts** for children under 12 (under 4s go free), and thirty-percent for senior citizens (over-65s, ID required; ask for a *bilhete terceira idade*) and Euro 26 card-holders

– but discounts aren't given on AP trains, nor on some weekend IC trains. **Seat reservations** are obligatory on IC and AP trains, though they are included in the ticket price.

Buses

Buses connect almost all of the country's towns and villages, with services operated by a wide array of private companies. It can be a little confusing at times: at some bus stations you may find two or more companies running services to the same towns; conversely, buses going to the same destination may leave from different terminals. However, there is a national network of **express buses**, with Rede Expressos (Ⓦ www.rede-expressos.pt) offering a daily service to destinations right across the country – you can book tickets online or buy them at bus stations and ticket desks (often in cafés by the bus stop/station). Buying tickets in advance is a wise idea, but even in summer in tourist areas the day

Driving: a survivor's guide

Portugal's accident statistics are shocking (the worst per capita in the EU) and only a couple of days driving on Portuguese roads will tell you why. **Drink-driving** is rife, despite the strict laws and advertising campaigns: this is a country where motorway service stations have bars, and lorry drivers in roadside restaurants polish off a jug of wine with their lunch before getting back in their rigs. Sunday afternoons, after big family lunches, are considered particularly dangerous times to be on the roads. Reckless **overtaking** is the norm – across solid white lines, on blind corners, on hills, in crowded town centres – while on otherwise deserted motorways you'll need to check your mirror every few seconds to make sure someone isn't right up your exhaust pipe. Posted **speed limits**, meanwhile, are viewed by most drivers as minimum requirements. On bends in country roads, **oncoming vehicles** routinely approach down the middle (or even right on your side), so as not to lose any preciously acquired speed – and **speed bumps** are *always* dealt with by shifting across to the other side of the road rather than slowing down. "Right of way" is something of an alien concept – vehicles zoom across roundabouts without so much as a glance – while the use of **indicators** is in its infancy. **Parking** restrictions are treated with impressive disdain, with cars routinely left on corners and at pedestrian crossings, garage exits and bus stops. In addition, drivers are always happy to stop for a lengthy chat with passers-by or other drivers at traffic lights, thus blocking the road. It goes without saying that talking (illegally) on a hand-held **mobile phone** while driving is considered a basic motoring skill.

Despite all this, driving in Portugal is – paradoxically – less stressful than in most European countries. There's far less traffic for a start, while the locals take most things in their stride. There's relatively little road rage, and, surprisingly, the horn doesn't get much use (unless you're driving far too slowly for the liking of the car behind). And, of course, any mistakes you might make blend seamlessly into the general mayhem that is an average day out on the roads.

before is usually fine. **Fares** are good value: the Lisbon–Porto express route costs €15, Faro–Lisbon €16, Porto-Bragança €11. Under 4s travel free, under 12s half-price, and there are fifteen-percent **discounts** for under 26s and senior citizens over 65 with relevant identification.

Local and rural bus services go virtually everywhere you're likely to want to go, with the notable exception of some of the natural parks, like the Serra da Estrela, Serra de Malcata and Montesinho. However, services are often restricted to one or two departures a day, or geared towards school and market times – meaning early morning weekday departures, sometimes only during term times. Many local services are reduced – or non-existent – at weekends.

The local **bus station** – Rodoviaria or Camionagem – is usually the best place to check services and routes. Most companies have timetables posted in the ticket-office window and copies to give away, though outside the Algarve it's rare to find anyone who speaks English. Turismos often have bus timetables too, though you can't always count on them being up-to-date.

Driving

A massive EU-funded construction programme has improved roads right across the country – particularly in previously remote areas like Trás-os-Montes and Beira Alta – and what often appears to be a minor route on a map can turn out to be a new, beautifully engineered highway. But there are still plenty of winding, poorly maintained roads, especially in rural areas – and you can expect to encounter highway repairs, farm vehicles, roaming animals and locals laden with wood or produce on almost any countryside journey. Other than on city approaches and during rush hour, **traffic** is generally light, though as car ownership has increased dramatically in recent years so too has congestion. **Petrol** (*gasolina*) prices have also increased steadily and now almost match those in the UK (around €1.35 a litre); unleaded is *sem chumbo*, diesel *gasóleo*.

Most **main roads** are prefixed EN – Estrada Nacional – or just N, with the faster regional highways denoted as IP (Itinerário Principal) or IC (Itinerário Complementar).

On the whole, they are two-lane roads, with passing lanes on hills, though stretches near some towns and cities are dual-carriageway. The **motorway** (*auto-estrada*) network (prefixed with "A") comprises a central spine of four- or six-lane **toll roads** (signposted "Portagem") that links the Algarve with Lisbon, Porto, the main inland towns and the north. The tolls are considered expensive by the Portuguese, who tend to use the older routes where possible; driving up the A1 from Lisbon to Porto, for example, costs around €18 (though the east–west trans-Algarve A22 is currently free). However, it's always much quicker by motorway and, with some sections virtually deserted, they are a pleasure to drive. Incidentally, at the toll-gates don't drive through the lane marked "Via Verde" (an automatic debit-payment lane for locals), but use any lane with a green light above it – you pay in cash, or with Visa or Mastercard.

Traffic drives on the right: **speed limits** are 50kph in towns and villages (often enforced by tripped "Velocidade Controlade" traffic lights), 90kph on normal roads, and 120kph on motorways and inter-regional highways. Unless there's a sign to the contrary at road junctions (and there rarely is), vehicles coming from the right have **right of way** – it can be horribly confusing, but most drivers use something approaching common sense to interpret whose turn it is. Other **road signage** is also poor, particularly at roundabouts, city exits and highway access roads, where the signs you've been following simply dry up for no reason; often, too, there's little or no warning of turns at slip-roads and junctions; or destinations are often sign-posted in one direction and not the other. In addition, many roads keep their old designations when upgraded, so for example, the Vila Real–Chaves road, once the IP3, now a motorway, is also marked as the A24 and, just for good measure, as the E801 (a pan-European route).

Driving licences from most countries are accepted, so there's no need to get an international one before you leave. Many **car insurance** policies cover taking your car to Portugal; check with your insurer when planning your trip. However, you're advised to take out extra cover for motoring assistance

Distance Chart (kms)

	AVEIRO	BEJA	BRAGA	BRAGANÇA	CASTELO BRANCO	COIMBRA	ÉVORA	FARO	GUARDA	LEIRIA	LISBON	PORTALEGRE	PORTO	SANTARÉM	SETÚBAL	VALENÇA DO MINHO	VIANA DO CASTELO
AVEIRO																	
BEJA	380																
BRAGA	120	500															
BRAGANÇA	320	560	230														
CASTELO BRANCO	216	254	330	310													
COIMBRA	64	278	170	314	160												
ÉVORA	306	78	425	484	175	255											
FARO	499	152	620	697	390	455	215										
GUARDA	180	360	260	203	106	169	282	495									
LEIRIA	121	265	238	380	170	67	190	390	188								
LISBON	242	193	361	510	250	196	150	300	236	128							
PORTALEGRE	310	181	410	390	80	240	104	317	188	170	228						
PORTO	68	50	53	255	277	118	370	575	365	185	314	360					
SANTARÉM	185	195	310	450	169	138	118	300	281	70	79	145	254				
SETÚBAL	290	139	417	560	270	246	108	250	372	180	50	192	362	121			
VALENÇA DO MINHO	194	580	91	323	407	250	502	702	348	314	443	484	123	384	492		
VIANA DO CASTELO	140	524	49	280	355	194	448	648	295	261	390	434	71	331	440	53	
VILA REAL	185	512	107	138	264	207	440	661	160	271	403	344	117	340	450	198	155

in case your car breaks down, and **motoring organizations** like the RAC (@www.rac.co.uk) or the AA (@www.theaa.co.uk) can help. Alternatively, you can get 24-hour assistance from the Automóvel Clube de Portugal (@www.acp.pt), which has reciprocal arrangements with foreign automobile clubs.

If you're **stopped by the police** in Portugal, they'll want to see your personal ID or passport, driving licence, and papers for the car (including ownership papers if it's your own car). By law, you should also have a red warning triangle and a fluorescent yellow jacket in the car (provided in rental cars). It pays to be patient and courteous since the police can – and do – levy on-the-spot fines for speeding, parking and other offences. Pleading ignorance won't get you anywhere.

Parking

Many towns and beach resorts are now flooded with traffic, especially in summer, so you may find problems finding a central **parking space**. Some cities, like Coimbra, have park-and-ride schemes, while in Porto there are huge car parks at suburban metro stations. We've pointed out useful parking advice in the guide, and also highlight accommodation with private or easy parking. When **parking in cities**, do as the locals do and use the empty spaces pointed out to you. A tip of €0.50 to the man doing the pointing will pay them for "looking after" your car. **On-street parking** is usually metered, even in the smallest towns. The price varies, but averages €0.40 an hour, though it's generally free from 8pm until 8am the next morning on weekdays, on Saturday

afternoons and all day Sunday. **Garage parking** is always more expensive – up to €10 a day – but where it's available it is the most secure option.

Car and motorbike rental

Car rental is relatively inexpensive and usually cheapest of all arranged in advance through one of the large multinational chains (Avis, Budget, Easycar, Hertz, Holiday Autos or National, for example). Check their websites for competitive Internet deals and special offers. Otherwise, rental agencies (including local firms) are found in all the major towns and at the airports in Lisbon, Porto and Faro; details are given in the guide. Local rates start at €30–50 a day with unlimited mileage, theft cover and collision damage waivers. Minimum age for rental is 21, though up to and including the age of 24 you'll have to pay a supplement.

Collision **insurance** is vital, since without it you'll be liable for costs should the vehicle be damaged – and this includes even minor scratches, easily acquired down unmade tracks or in crowded car parks. Ensure that all visible damage on a car you're picking up is duly marked on the rental sheet. The standard supplement is CDW (Collision Damage Waiver), but even this often has a liability rate of up to €1000, though for an additional daily fee (Super CDW) you're completely covered, save for a small (usually €50) excess. These waiver charges soon add up (from around €10 a day on top of the car rental fee), but you can avoid all Super CDW and excess charges by taking out an annual insurance policy (from £51) with

Portugal's five best drives

The **N222** careers high above the south bank of Porto's greatest river, the Douro, before hugging the water as far as pretty Pinhão (see p.363).

Drive right across the highest mountains in Portugal, from Seia to Covilhã (see p.301), on the **N339**.

The trans-Trás-os-Montes **N103** snakes around northern Portugal's wildest terrain, skirting the Parque Natural de Montesinho (see p.477).

Take to the skies on the **N379-1**, which crosses the Serra de Arrábida mountains high above the Baia de Setúbal (see p.165).

Starting at Porto de Lagos, north of Portimão, and ending near the Spanish border at Alcoutim (see p.570), the scenic **N124** traverses the Algarve without passing a single beach resort.

Insurance4carhire.com, which also covers windscreen and tyre damage.

You can also rent mopeds, scooters and low-powered (80cc) **motorbikes** in many resorts, with costs starting at around €25 a day. You need to be at least 18 (and over 23 for bikes over 125cc) and to have held a full licence for at least a year. Rental should include helmet and locks along with third-party insurance. Helmet use is obligatory.

Car rental agencies

Avis US ℡ 1-800/230-4898, Canada ℡ 1-800/272-5871, UK ℡ 0870/606 0100, Republic of Ireland ℡ 021/428 1111, Australia ℡ 13 63 33 or 02/9353 9000, New Zealand ℡ 09/526 2847 or 0800/655 111, ⌨ www.avis.com.
Budget US ℡ 1-800/527-0700, Canada ℡ 1-800/268-8900, UK ℡ 08701/565 656, Republic of Ireland ℡ 09/0662 7711, Australia ℡ 1300/362 848, New Zealand ℡ 0800/283 438, ⌨ www.budget.com.
Europcar US & Canada ℡ 1-877/9406900, UK ℡ 0870/607 5000, Republic of Ireland ℡ 01/614 2888, Australia ℡ 1300/131 390, ⌨ www.europcar .com.
Hertz US ℡ 1-800/654-3131, Canada ℡ 1-800/263-0600, UK ℡ 020/7026 0077, Republic of Ireland ℡ 01/870 5777, Australia ℡ 08/9921 4052, New Zealand ℡ 0800/654 321, ⌨ www.hertz.com.
Holiday Autos US ℡ 0871/222 3200, Republic of Ireland ℡ 01/872 9366, Australia ℡ 1300/554 432, New Zealand ℡ 0800/144 040, ⌨ www .holidayautos.co.uk.
National US ℡ 1-800/CAR-RENT, UK ℡ 0870/400 4581, Australia ℡ 02/13 10 45, New Zealand ℡ 03/366 5574, ⌨ www .nationalcar.com.

Taxis

Travelling by **taxi** in Portugal is relatively cheap by European standards, and meters are used in towns and cities – an average journey across Lisbon or Porto costs around €6. Additional charges are made for carrying luggage (€1.50 per item), travelling at weekends or between 10pm and 6am (twenty percent more), and for calling a cab by phone (€0.75) – these charges are all posted inside the cab, so there shouldn't be any misunderstanding. You may have to rely on taxis more than you expect, since bus and railway stations are often some way removed from town centres, while in rural areas there may be no other way to reach your next destination. Outside town limits, the journey is usually charged by the kilometre – the driver should be able to quote you a figure for the trip.

Bicycles

Bicycles are a great way of seeing the country, though anywhere away from the coast – especially north of Lisbon and inland from the Algarve's beaches – is hilly, and you'll also find pedalling hard work across the burned plains of southern Alentejo. Several specialist outlets, plus hotels, campsites and youth hostels, rent bikes from €10–15 a day; the major ones are listed in the text. We also list specialist **cycle tour operators** on p.32.

Portugal's woeful road accident statistics mean that defensive riding is essential. Fitting a rear-view mirror to the handlebars is a definite advantage, as is reflective and fluorescent clothing (or sashes) at night. In general, it's best to assume that drivers will not obey road signs or regulations – just be prepared. Obviously, minor country roads have far less traffic to contend with, but locals know them backwards and so speeding – even around blind corners – is the norm. For more information on cycling abroad, contact the UK's national cycling organization, the **CTC** (℡ 0870/873 0060, ⌨ www.ctc.org .uk), though you'll have to join to access their tours and notes on cycling in Portugal.

Collapsible bikes can be taken for free on regional and interregional **trains** (ie, the slow ones), so long as they're dismantled and stowed in a bag or other cover. Otherwise, bikes can be taken on the Lisbon and Porto urban lines and regional trains from Coimbra – there's usually a small charge during the week, free at weekends. The CP website (⌨ www.cp.pt) has the latest details.

Accommodation

In almost any Portuguese town you can find a basic pension offering a double or twin room for €30 or under. The only accommodation that you're likely to find cheaper than this is a youth-hostel dorm or a simple room in a private home, while you can expect to pay more for accommodation in Algarve resorts in summer, in the mountains in the winter, or year-round in Lisbon where an average room is likely to cost €30–40. Moving upmarket, you're often spoilt for choice, with some wonderful manor houses (from €60) and a network of comfortable hotels known as *pousadas* (from €100), all at prices that beat the rest of Europe hands down. Even in high season you shouldn't have much of a problem finding a bed in most Portuguese regions. However, the best places in Lisbon and the Algarve are often booked up for days ahead. Advance reservations here are advised, especially if you're arriving late.

A *quarto duplo* has two single beds, and a *quarto casal* has a large double bed for a couple. A single room – *quarto solteiro* or *individual* – is a little cheaper, but almost always proportionately more expensive per person than if you were to share. Ask to see the room before you take it, and don't be afraid to ask if there's a cheaper one available (rooms without private bathrooms are often considerably less). In higher-graded hotels, you'll often get a better rate simply by asking, especially out of season or at the end of the day.

Lastly, a word of warning: between November and April, give or take a month, night time temperatures throughout Alentejo, the mountain Beiras and Trás-os-Montes can plummet to below freezing, and even along the coast temperatures of under 5°C are common. However, few pensions have any form of **heating** other than the odd plug-in radiator,

so check out the facilities before taking a room, or you'll find yourself wearing the entire contents of your luggage for the night. Similarly, in the height of summer check for a fan or air conditioning, as nights can remain very warm.

Private rooms and B&B

Rooms let out in private houses – **dormidas** or **quartos** – are most commonly available in seaside resorts, either advertised in windows or hawked at bus and train stations; the local turismo may also have a list of available rooms. Rates average around €20 for a double/twin, though on the Algarve in high season expect to pay up to twice as much. It's always worth haggling over prices, especially if you're prepared to commit yourself to a longish stay, but don't expect too much success in summer. Room quality and facilities vary greatly; some are no more than a

Accommodation price codes

All establishments listed in this book have been categorized according to the price codes outlined below. They represent the price for the **cheapest available double/twin room in high season** (ie, June to September, though some local variations apply). Breakfast is included, unless otherwise stated. For **youth hostels** we give the euro price for a dorm bed instead.

❶ under €35
❷ €36–50
❸ €51–70

❹ €71–100
❺ €101–140
❻ €141–200

❼ €201–250
❽ €251–300
❾ over €301

bed in a converted attic; others come with modern bathrooms, TVs and air conditioning. Always ask where the room is before you agree to take it – you could end up miles from the town centre or beach. Breakfast is not usually included.

Bed-and-breakfast (B&B) places on the UK model do exist, though are not widespread – owners tend to be foreigners living in Portugal, renting out rooms or cottages by the night for extra cash. Keep an eye out in turismos and cafés for business cards and flyers, particularly on the Algarve, in the Alentejo and the Beiras.

Pensions

Regular budget accommodation is in a **pensão** (plural *pensões*) or **residencial** (*residenciais*), officially graded in three categories and charging from €20–50 double, depending on season, location and facilities. They often occupy old, characterful buildings, sometimes with owners to match – at the cheapest end of the scale rooms rarely come with bathrooms or indeed much else other than the bed, a heavy and almost never used wardrobe, and perhaps a chair or table. More upmarket places will have modern en-suite rooms, plus TVs, heaters and air conditioning; the fanciest tend to style themselves an **albergaria** (inn). Breakfast is usually included, but don't expect much more than coffee, bread and preserves, and possibly some sliced ham and cheese. You'll also see some budget places to stay named as a *hospedaria* or *casa de hóspedes* – a cheap boarding house – though they are less common these days, tending to be either for pilgrims en route to Fátima, or distinctly dodgy dosshouses in red-light districts.

Hotels and inns

Hotels are all classified with one to five stars. A one-star hotel usually costs about the same as a higher-grade pension (around €40) and often doesn't show any notable difference in standards. At two- and three-star hotels, en-suite doubles cost up to €80 (though older establishments may have one or two cheaper rooms without en-suite bathrooms); many three-star places these days have air-conditioned rooms with cable/satellite TV, and even swimming pools, so they can be pretty good value. For rooms with all mod cons in four- and five-star hotels, you'll pay anything from €100 to €300, while the very fanciest places can pretty much charge what they like – boutique hotels in the Algarve like *Estalagem Vila Joya* or luxury hotels in Lisbon such as the *Lapa Palace* attract an international clientele paying top rates. An **estalagem** (plural *estalagems*) – an inn – is a cosier place of four- or five-star quality, often in a converted historic building or manor house. All hotels and inns serve breakfast, usually (though not always) included in the price. In one- and two-star hotels it tends to be continental-style; more substantial buffet breakfasts are provided at three-star places and up.

Pousadas

Pousadas de Portugal (☎218 442 001, ⓦwww.pousadas.pt) is a chain of over forty hotels that have either been converted from historic properties like old monasteries

---

Unusual places to stay

A former tuna-fishing village, *Vila Galé Albacora*, Tavira p.563

A monk's cell, *Convento de São Francisco*, Mértola, p.532

A queen's palace, *Pousada Dona Maria I*, Queluz, p.159

A count's country retreat, *Paço de Calheiros*, Ponte de Lima, p.426

A pigeon house, *Pombal, Quinta das Aveleiras*, Torre de Moncorvo, p.460

A sailing ship, *Navio Gil Eannes* hostel, Viana do Castelo, p.408

A port-wine estate, *Quinta de la Rosa*, Pinhão, p.370

A room within the city walls, *Residencial Santos*, Guarda, p.287

An island fort, hostel on Ilha Berlenga, p.184

A convent (with a snooker room in the cloister), *Pousada de Flôr da Rosa*, p.517

or castles or are located in dramatic countryside settings. They are scattered across the country, with particular concentrations in the Alentejo and the north, though there are only three on the Algarve (a fourth will open shortly) and none in Porto. While all make full use of the cloisters, chapels and other features of the original buildings, some are somewhat staid, with an old-fashioned elegance. Others, though, have been dramatically modernized by Portugal's top architects – the interiors of those in Alcácer do Sal, Tavira and Amares are stunning. Facilities and service are equivalent to those in four- and five-star hotels. Standard rooms as well as suites are available; there's almost always a swimming pool, lovely gardens and a good restaurant. We've covered most of the *pousadas* in the guide – particular Rough Guide favourites along with those mentioned above include those set in the castles at Óbidos, Estremoz and Setúbal, the convent and monastery conversions at Belmonte, Beja and Évora, and the beautifully sited properties at Manteigas (Serra da Estrela), Valença and Santa Luzia (Viana do Castelo).

Prices vary considerably depending on the season, day (more expensive Fri & Sat nights), location, size and position of the room, but expect to pay €145–225 in summer, or €95–160 in low season. Look out for last-minute deals on the website, plus seasonal promotions, especially for the over-60s, who receive good discounts most of the year. You can book by phone at individual *pousadas*, or through the central reservations number or online.

Rural tourism: country and manor houses

An increasingly popular mid-range alternative is to stay in a privately owned country or manor house, promoted under the banner of **Turismo no Espaço Rural** (TER). You may also encounter the following terms: "TR" or Turismo Rural (country houses); "TH" or Turismo de Habitação or Turihab (old manor houses and palaces); "CC" or Casas no Campo (simpler country houses); and "AT" or Agro-Turismo (farmhouses, often on working farms or wine estates). Properties vary from simple farmhouses offering just two or three rooms on a bed-and-breakfast

basis, to country manors, often dating from the sixteenth to eighteenth centuries and complete with period furnishings. *Quintas* or *herdades* are farm estate houses, and you can even stay in palaces (*palácios*), owned by Portuguese aristocrats who have allowed their ancient seats to become part of the scheme.

There are hundreds of properties available, all of which have been inspected and approved by the government tourist office. In terms of facilities, surroundings and atmosphere, they are often unbeatable value – **rates** start at around €60 a night, though the grandest places might charge up to €120 for a double/twin room, or a little more for self-contained apartments or cottages within the grounds (sleeping up to six). Large breakfasts are invariably included, while many will provide typical dinners made from local ingredients, sometimes accompanied by wine and other produce made on the estate. Others offer suitably rural activities like fishing, rambling, horse riding and wine-tasting.

Owners tend to join one of several marketing organizations (see list below), though you can of course book directly with the houses themselves (details in the guide) or via specialist holiday operators in your own country (see "Getting there" for details). Minimum stay requirements (up to three nights in some places) are more likely to be waived if you approach the establishments directly.

Country and manor house contacts

ANTER (Associação Nacional de Turismo no Espaço Rural), Rua 24 de Julho 1, 7000 Évora ☎ & ℻ 266 744 555. A wide choice of places, mainly from Lisbon southwards.

CENTER (Central Nacional de Turismo no Espaço Rural) ☎ 258 931 750, ⊛ www.center.pt. Umbrella organization handling reservations for Casas no Campo, Aldeias de Portugal, Solares de Portugal and the village tourism project in Peneda-Gerês. Mainly in Minho but also in and around the Douro Valley and Beiras, Trás-os-Montes, around Lisbon and Azores. Credit cards accepted.

Manor Houses of Portugal ⊛ www.manorhouses .com. Lists a wide range of manor houses, estate cottages, palaces, *quintas* and historic hotels.

Privetur ⊛ www.privetur.co.uk. Over 100 properties countrywide, including manor houses, *quintas*, cottages and farms.

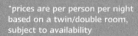

Villas

Virtually every area of the country – certainly near the coast – has some sort of **villa** or **apartment** available for rent, from simple one-room studios to luxurious five- or six-bed houses complete with garden and swimming pool. Holiday and specialist tour operators in your own country (see "Getting there") can provide full details of properties across Portugal, though note that in summer the best places are booked up months in advance. You can expect to pay at least €60 a night in high season for a two-person studio apartment, or up to €200 a night for a top villa – and the minimum rental period in summer is usually a week. Outside peak period you should be able to turn up and bag somewhere for the night for between 25 and 50 percent less – the local turismo will probably be able to help.

Youth hostels

There are around forty **youth hostels** (*pousadas de juventude*) in Portugal, affiliated to the international youth-hostel network. You'll need a valid membership card, available from your home-based youth-hostel association, or you can join on your first night at any hostel. Advance bookings are advised and can be made direct with the hostels or through the central reservations office or online (℡707 203 030, ⓦwww .pousadasjuventude.pt).

The hostels themselves are often on the basic side, but are all in good or convenient locations, most with kitchens and lounges. Some of the new ones – at the Parque das Nações in Lisbon and at Guimarães, for example – are extremely comfortable, while others now boast Internet facilities, cafés, bars or bike rental. The price for a **dormitory bed** varies according to hostel location and facilities, but runs from €7–16 in high season (basically July, August, Easter, Christmas and other public holidays), and €7–11 the rest of the year; over 25s pay €3 more a night. Many hostels also have simple double/twin or family **rooms** available, costing €25–30 without a private WC, €25–45 with. You'll usually also be able to hire sheets and blankets if necessary, and cheap meals are often available. The most expensive hostels are in Lisbon, Porto and on the Algarve.

Some rural hostels have a curfew (11pm or midnight), while the ones in Lisbon, Porto and the Algarve are open all hours. Among the **best hostels in Portugal** are those at Vilarinho das Furnas (in Peneda-Gerês National Park), Penhas de Saúde (in the Serra de Estrela – high season here, incidentally, is Oct–April), Areia Branca (on the beach, close to Peniche), Oeiras (on the seafront near Lisbon), Viana do Castelo (in an old sailing ship), Alcoutim (northeastern Algarve), and Guimarães, Lagos and Leiria (good buildings in historic towns).

Camping

Portugal has several hundred authorized **campsites**, many in very attractive locations and, despite their often large size (over 500 spaces is not uncommon), they can get extremely crowded in summer. The most useful campsites are noted in the text, and unless otherwise stated are open all year round. The **Roteiro Campista** (ⓦwww .roteiro-campista.pt) booklet detailing the country's campsites is available from most Portuguese tourist offices and from bookshops and newsstands; the website is also extremely useful.

Most of the larger campsites have spaces for campervans/RVs and caravans, and will also have permanent caravans and bungalows for rent. Charges are per person and per caravan or tent, with showers and parking extra; even so, it's rare that you'll end up paying more than €6 per person, although those operated by the **Orbitur** chain (ⓦwww .orbitur.pt) – usually with bungalows on site as well – are more expensive. The cheapest are usually the municipal sites in each town, often fairly central but usually very crowded.

A few sites require an **international camping card** and, if you're planning to do a lot of camping, it's a good investment. The card gives discounts at member sites and serves as useful identification: many campsites will take it instead of your passport, and it covers you for third-party insurance when camping. The card is available from most home motoring or cycling organizations and camping and caravan/RV clubs, or you can get a national card from the Federação de Campismo e Montanhismo de Portugal (ⓦwww.fcmportugal.com).

You're not allowed to camp in urban zones, in zones of protection for water sources, or less than 1km from camping parks, beaches, or other places frequented by the public. What this means in practice is that you can't camp on tourist beaches, which we don't advise anyway – we've had lots of reports of thefts. But with a little sensitivity you can pitch a tent for a short period almost anywhere else in the countryside. That said, camping outside official sites is prohibited in all Portugal's natural parks, in an attempt to reduce littering and fire damage.

US and Canada

Hostelling International-American Youth Hostels ℡ 301/495-1240, Ⓦ www.hiayh.org
Hostelling International Canada ℡ 1-800/663 5777, Ⓦ www.hihostels.ca

UK and Ireland

Youth Hostel Association (YHA) England and Wales ℡ 0870/770 8868, Ⓦ www.yha.org.uk
Scottish Youth Hostel Association ℡ 01786/891 400, Ⓦ www.syha.org.uk
Irish Youth Hostel Association ℡ 01/830 4555, Ⓦ www.irelandyha.org
Hostelling International Northern Ireland ℡ 028/9032 4733, Ⓦ www.hini.org.uk

Australia, New Zealand and South Africa

Australia Youth Hostels Association ℡ 02/9565-1699, Ⓦ www.yha.com.au
Youth Hostelling Association New Zealand ℡ 0800/278 299 or 03/379 9970, Ⓦ www.yha.co.nz

Food and drink

Portuguese food can be excellent and is nearly always inexpensive. Virtually all cafés and simple restaurants will serve you a basic meal for around €5–6, while for €15–25 you have the run of most of the country's establishments. Servings tend to be huge. Indeed, you can usually have a substantial meal by ordering a *meia dose* (half portion), or *uma dose* (a portion) between two. Meals are often listed like this on the menu and it's normal practice; you don't need to be a child. Lunch is usually served noon–3pm, dinner from 7.30pm onwards; don't count on being able to eat much after 10pm outside cities and tourist resorts. Snacks and small meals can be found throughout the day in bars, cafés and pastry shops. Useful words and terms are covered below, but for a full eating and drinking glossary see p.657.

The quickest way to get trampled to death is to come between the Portuguese and their lunch.

A Small Death in Lisbon, Robert Wilson

Although the Portuguese introduced many types of cuisine to a global market, foreign restaurants have yet to make much of an impression in Portugal outside Lisbon and the Algarve. Chinese establishments are the exception, though. Fast food, whilst popular with Portuguese youth and families, is – in town centres at least – conspicuous by its absence. Whilst McDonald's and company do now cover most of the country, they're mainly found on the outskirts of towns or in shopping centres.

Breakfast, snacks and sandwiches

For **breakfast** it's best to head to a café, a *pastelaria* (pastry shop) or a *confeitaria* (confectioners), where you'll be able to order a croissant, some toast (*uma torrada*; a doorstep with butter), a simple ham or cheese sandwich (*sandes*) or some sort of cake or pastry (see p.47). A *padaria* is a bakery, and any place advertising *pão quente* (hot bread) will usually have a café attached. For sandwiches (*sandes* or *sanduíches*), common fillings include cheese, ham, *presunto* (smoked ham) and *chouriço* (smoked sausage). *Sandes mistas* are a combination of ham and cheese; grilled, they're called *tostas*. Better places offer the same on wholewheat or rye – ask for a *tosta mista com pão caseiro* or *com pão integral*.

Classic Portuguese **snacks**, available throughout the day, include *croquetes* (deep-fried meat patties), *pastéis* or *bolinhos de bacalhau* (cod fishcakes), *iscas de bacalhau* (battered cod fishcakes with egg), *chamuças* (samosas), *bifanas* (a thin slice of grilled or fried pork on bread), and *prego no pão* (steak sandwich), which when served on a plate with a fried egg on top is a *prego no prato*. In the north you'll also find *lanches* (pieces of sweetish bread stuffed with ham) and *pastéis de carne* or *pastéis de Chaves* (puff pastries stuffed with sausage meat).

You may also see blackboard lists of dishes, or a sign reading **petiscos** or **comidas**, which are Portugal's answer to Spain's tapas. Usually served cold, these are little dishes that range from the simple and sublime to the truly unspeakable: not only prawns, sardines, snails, grilled octopus, marinaded chicken livers, *tremoços* (pickled lupin seeds) and *pimentos* (marinaded fried sweet peppers), but also *orelhas de porco* (crunchy pig's ears – nice if you like cartilage), and *túberos* (marinated boiled pig's testicles).

Restaurants and meals

Eating out is rarely expensive and many Portuguese enjoy daily lunches and weekend family evening meals at a restaurant. Standards are fairly uniform and price differentials usually depend on the restaurant location, decor and the way the food is presented rather than on the quality of ingredients. Indeed menus tend to be markedly similar wherever you go, certainly within each region.

Apart from straightforward **restaurants** (*restaurantes*), you could end up eating a meal in one of several other venues. A *tasca* is a small neighbourhood tavern, while a *casa de pasto* is a cheap local dining room usually with a set three-course menu, mostly served at lunch only. A *cervejaria* is literally a "beer house", more informal than a restaurant, with people dropping in at all hours for a beer and a snack. In Lisbon they're often wonderful tiled caverns specializing in seafood. Also specializing in seafood is a *marisqueira*, while a *churrasqueira* specializes in char-grilled meat, especially chicken, pork chops and sausages.

Wherever you eat, it's always worth taking stock of the **prato do dia** (dish of the day)

Vegetarian Portugal

Traditional Portuguese cuisine is tough on strict **vegetarians**, and egg dishes, salads and soups will be the main choices available on most menus. Virtually every meal ordered in a restaurant also comes with rice and salad. It's always worth asking whether a restaurant has a good cheese board (*tábua de queijos*): while some cheeses contain animal rennet (*coalho animal*), labels listing *cardo* (thistle flower rennet) among the ingredients are safe. In Lisbon, Porto and some parts of the Algarve, there are **vegetarian restaurants**, even macrobiotic ones, together with Chinese, Italian and Indian establishments where you should be able to put together a non-meat meal. Also, most towns have **health-food shops** where you can find cereal bars, gluten-free biscuits, organic dried fruit and the like, whilst for picnics you're spoiled for choice, with a wealth of fruit, bread, cakes and pastries widely available.

if you're interested in sampling local speciali-ties. The *ementa turística* is worth checking out, too – not a "tourist menu", but the set meal of the day, sometimes with a choice of two starters and two main courses, plus dessert and a glass of beer or a small carafe of wine. It can be very good value, though smarter restaurants sometimes resent the law that compels them to offer the *ementa turística*, responding with stingy portions and excessive prices.

The one thing to watch for when eating out in Portugal is the plate of **appetizers** placed before you when you take a table and before you order. These can be quite elaborate little dishes of seafood, cheese, sardine spread and *chouriço*, or can consist of little more than rolls and butter, but what you eat is counted and you will be charged for every bite. *Não quero isto* ("I don't want this") should get the waiter to take it away. When you want the bill, ask for *a conta* and make sure nothing is included that you haven't eaten, beyond the basic cover charge.

Restaurants listed in this guide have each been given a **price category**: inexpensive (less than €15), moderate (€15–25), expen-sive (€25–35), or very expensive (over €35). This is the price per person you can expect to pay for a three-course meal, or equivalent, including drinks. Obviously, in many restau-rants, the listing is only a guide to average costs, since you will almost always be able to eat more cheaply (choosing the *prato do dia*, skipping dessert) or more expensively (eating seafood, quaffing vintage port).

Dishes and specialities

Many meals start with one of Portugal's extraordinarily inexpensive **soups**. The thick vegetable *caldo verde* – a cabbage-and-potato broth, sometimes with ham – is as filling as dishes come, and at its best in the north. In the south the traditional mainstay is *sopa à alentejana*, a garlic and bread soup with a poached egg in it. Nearly all places do a basic *sopa de legumes* (vegetable soup), suitable for vegetarians.

Fish and seafood

On the coast, **seafood** is pre-eminent: crabs, prawns, crayfish, cuttlefish, squid, clams and huge barnacles are all fabulous

(most of it from the Algarve), while fish on offer usually includes hake (*pescada*), salmon (*salmão*, often farmed), bream (*dourada*), seabass (*robalo*), and – in the north – trout (*truta*). The most typical Portuguese fish dish is that created from *bacalhau* (dried, salted cod), which is much better than it sounds. It's virtually the national dish with reputedly 365 different ways of preparing it – served with boiled egg and black olives, made into a pie, char-grilled or cooked in a traditional copper *cataplana*, the list is endless. Almost every restaurant in the country boasts a *bacalhau* dish, and some cook little else. Perhaps the best to try are *bacalhau á bras* (fried with egg, onions and potatoes) and *bacalhau com natas* (baked in cream).

Grilled or barbecued **sardines** provide one of the country's most familiar and appetizing smells, and in the Algarve and elsewhere you should definitely try a *cataplana*, named after the wok-like lidded copper vessel in which it's cooked. The best *cataplanas* are made with seafood, as is *arroz de marisco*, a bumper serving of mixed seafood in a gloopy rice; *massa de peixe/marisco* is a similar dish but with noodles – *cataplanas*, *arroz* and *massa* dishes are usually served for a minimum of two people. Other seafood specialities include a **caldeirada de peixe**, basically a fish stew, and *açorda* (a rural bread stew traditionally made from stale bread mixed with herbs, garlic, eggs and whatever farmers found to hand), at its best served with shellfish. *Migas* is very similar, but is usually slightly drier. Look out too for *feijoada,* a rich stew made from beans, either with fish or meat.

Meat dishes

Simple grilled or fried steaks of beef, veal and pork are common, while chicken is enlivened by the addition of *piri-piri* (chilli) sauce, either in the cooking or provided on the table. **Meat** is usually at its best when barbecued (*no churrasco*). Also ubiquitous are *porco à alentejana* (pork cooked with clams), which originated, as its name suggests, in Alentejo, and *rojões* (chunks of roast pork, served with black pudding) from the north (mainly Minho and Douro). *Leitão* – spit-roast suckling pig – is distinctly Portuguese, too, at the centre of many a communal feast, particularly in

Beiras. It's either served sliced and cold, or – better – just off the coals. Roast kid (*cabrito*) is ubiquitous in mountain areas, while another Beiras speciality, *chanfana* (goat stew), is usually served in a traditional earthenware pot. Duck is usually served shredded and mixed with rice (*arroz de pato*); rabbit is served in rural areas (*a caçadora*, hunter's style, as a stew), and roasted quail (*cordoniz*) is often on the menu too.

However, steel yourself for a couple of special dishes that local people might entice you into trying. Porto's **tripas** (tripe) dishes incorporate beans and spices but the heart of the dish is still recognizably chopped stomach-lining; while *cozido à portuguesa*, widely served in restaurants on a Sunday, is a stomach-challenging boiled "meat" stew in which you shouldn't be surprised to turn up lumps of fat, cartilage or even a pig's ear. Other traditional dishes use pig's or chicken's blood as a base – the words to look for are *sarrabulho* and *cabidela* – though the addition of cumin, paprika and other spices can turn these into something quite delicious.

Accompanying nearly every dish will be **potatoes**, either fried in the case of most meat dishes or boiled if you've ordered fish. The distinction is less marked in tourist resorts on the Algarve and elsewhere, but trying to get chips to come with your grilled trout or salmon in a rural town simply invites incomprehension – fish comes with boiled potatoes and that's that. Most dishes are also served with a helping of rice and salad. Other vegetables occasionally make an appearance, though salads are more common. Any restaurant can certainly rustle up on request a mixed salad (*salada mista*) of lettuce, tomatoes, onions and olives.

For **dessert**, you'll almost always be offered either *salada da fruta* (fruit salad), fresh fruit, the ubiquitous Olá, Miko or Gelvi ice cream lists, *pudim flan* (crème caramel), *arroz doce* (rice pudding) or *torta da noz* (almond tart). The presence of home-made desserts on a restaurant's menu is a good indicator of how seriously they take their food, but no restaurant will have the range of cakes and pastries you'll find in a pastry shop (see below). Cheese is widely available, but is usually eaten as a starter when it is generally either the hard *queijo seco* (goat's or sheep's cheese) or cottage-cheese like *queijo fresco* (see box, p.50).

Pastries, cakes and sweets

Pastries (*pastéis*), buns (*bolinhos*), rolls (*tortas*), tarts (*tartes*) and cakes (*bolos*) are serious business in Portugal, at their best in *confeitarias* and *casas de chá* (tearooms), though you'll also find them in cafés and *pastelarias*. There are hundreds of local specialities, in many places known as *doces conventuais* ("convent desserts"), thanks to the gastronomic inspiration of nuns past.

Some particularly delightful confections include **pastéis de nata** (custard tarts), *queijadas de Sintra* (Sintra "cheesecakes", not that they contain any cheese), *palha de ovos* (egg pastries) from Abrantes, *bolo de anjo* ("angel cake", with a super-sweet fluffy topping), *mil-folhas* (big light millefeuille pastries nicknamed "Salazar" on account of the late dictator's puffed up self-importance), *bolinhos* made with beans (*feijão*), carrot (*cenoura*) or pumpkin (*chila*), *bolos de arroz* (rice-flour muffins), *suspiros* ("sighs" – meringues), and a range of almond biscuits and marzipan (*bolinhos de maçapão*) from the Algarve. The incredibly sweet egg-based *ovos moles* wrapped in wafers – most famously from Aveiro – are completely over-the-top, as are *pastéis de Tentúgal* (millefeuille rolls containing more *ovos moles*). Equally filling is *broa de mel* – a heavy but soft bread made from cornflour and honey, found mainly in the north. *Broa doce* is similar but contains dried fruit.

Markets and fruit

A **market** (*mercado*) is the best place to put together a picnic: fruit, dried fruit and vegetables, nuts, bread, smoked meat and cheese, olives, biscuits and cakes. Every town has its own market, usually open Monday to Saturday mornings, sometimes also in the afternoons. The choice is usually widest on Saturdays, while on Mondays fish can be difficult to find. Portuguese fruit is a particular joy, especially in the Algarve and the region around Alcobaça, though any market should turn up some excellent local produce (ask for *frutas da região*), usually given away by their smaller size and more battered appearance.

You may even find officially certified *biológico* – organic – produce, though it has yet to make much of an impact on mainstream food-buying habits.

In spring cherries are a delight, when you can also sample *anonas* from Madeira (sugar apples or sweetsops; there's a second harvest in Oct/Nov), plus strawberries and early apples and pears from Alcobaça. Particularly good summer fruits are melons, peaches and apricots, and exotics from the Algarve including Barbary figs, guavas and mangoes, plus *nêsperas* or *magnórios* (loquats or medlars, especially in June). The grapes arrive in late summer and autumn, especially black Moscatel and a welter of local white varieties. Pears, apples, plums and figs are also good at this time, including the long black figs called *bêberas* (don't eat the sap in the stem, which will blister your lips).

Winter is the time for citrus fruits, pomegranates, and immensely sweet *dióspiros* (persimmon or date-plums; tomato-like spheres with pulp like liquidized jam, eaten with a spoon). Winter and early spring is also the time for chestnuts (*castanhas*), which you can buy roasted from street vendors around the country. Available year-round are delicious finger-sized bananas from Madeira, and sweet and aromatic pineapples from the Azores.

Wines

Portugal is now an internationally recognized centre of vinicultural excellence, and the output from some of its regions – notably Alentejo, Bairrada, Dão, Estremadura, Ribatejo and the Douro – has garnered a strong following. Most wines are made in small cooperatives with local grape varieties, many peculiar to Portugal. The only disadvantage is that smaller farmers are not always well trained in using pesticides correctly, so overspraying can lead to residues.

Portuguese **wine lists** (ask for the *lista de vinhos*) don't just distinguish between *tinto* (red), *branco* (white) and *rosé*, but between *verde* ("green", meaning young, acidic and slightly sparkling) and *maduro* ("mature", meaning the wines you're probably accustomed to). You'll find a decent selection from

around the country in even the most basic of restaurants, and often in half-bottles, too. In humbler places, the house wine is served in jugs – and can be surprisingly easy to knock back.

Some of the best-known **maduros** are from the Douro region: Planalto is an excellent crisp white, while reds are always good if expensive. Red wines from the Dão region (a roughly triangular area between Coimbra, Viseu and Guarda, around the River Dão) taste a little like burgundy, and they're available throughout the country. Quinta de Cabriz from Carregal do Sal (near Viseu) is an excellent mid-range Dão red. The Alentejo is another area with a growing reputation – Reguengos and Monte Velho wines have the strength and full body typical of that region. Among other smaller regions offering interesting wines are Colares (near Sintra), Bucelas in the Estremadura (crisp, dry whites) and Alenquer from Ribatejo.

The light, slightly sparkling **vinhos verdes** – "green wines", in age not colour – are produced in quantity in the Minho. They're drunk early as most don't mature or improve with age, but are great with meals, especially shellfish. There are red and rosé *vinhos verdes*, though the whites are the most successful. Casal Garcia and Gato are the two labels you see everywhere; far better is Ponte de Lima and Ponte da Barca. For real quality, try the fuller strength Alvarinho from Monção and Melgaço, along the River Minho. Also worth seeking out are *vinhos verdes de quinta*, which are produced solely with grapes from one property (*quinta*), along the lines of the French chateaux wines: look for labels saying "Engarrafado pelo Viticultor (or Produtor)" and "Engarrafado na Propriedade (or Quinta)".

Otherwise, Portuguese **rosé wines** are known abroad mainly through the spectacularly successful export of Mateus Rosé, Saddam Hussein's favourite tipple before he was toppled. This is too sweet and aerated for most tastes, but other rosés – the best is Tavel – are definitely worth sampling.

Portugal also produces an interesting range of sparkling, **champagne-method wines**, known as *espumantes naturais*. They are designated *bruto* (extra dry), *seco* (fairly dry), *meio seco* (quite sweet) or *doce* (very sweet). The best of these come from the Bairrada region, north of Coimbra, though Raposeira wines – a little further north from near Lamego – are more commonly available.

Fortified wines

Port (*vinho do Porto*), the famous fortified wine or *vinho generoso* ("generous wine"), is produced from grapes grown in the vineyards of the Douro valley and mostly stored in huge wine lodges at Vila Nova de Gaia, facing Porto across the River Douro. You can visit these for tours and free tastings; see the *Port wine* colour section for all the details. Even if your quest for port isn't serious enough to do this, be sure to try the dry white aperitif ports, still little known outside the country.

Smoked meats and sausages

Traditionally, **pork** took pride of place in Portuguese cooking, attested to by prehistoric stone *porcas* – carvings of sows or boars – found in the north of the country. To last out the year, much of the slaughtered animal was preserved as smoked legs of ham and spiced sausages – *enchidos* ("stuffed things") or *fumeiros* ("smoked things"). Some *enchidos* have to be cooked, but many can be eaten raw and are great for picnics.

Alheiras, azedos and farinheiras These have their roots in the Inquisition, when Jews felt obliged to mimic the Catholic passion for sausages while avoiding pork, although nowadays most of them are far from kosher. *Alheiras* are based on bread and chicken, the best from Mirandela in Trás-os-Montes, and are served grilled or steamed. The superior *alheiras de caça* contain game fowl such as partridge. *Azedos* are a more meaty variant and a little sour, whilst *farinheiras* from Beira Baixa and Alentejo are more floury, and seasoned with paprika, wine or oranges. All need cooking.

Buchos and maranhos *Bucho* ("stomach"), from Trás-os-Montes, is Portugal's haggis, usually stuffed with pork, rice and bits of cartilage, and seasoned with wine and garlic. *Maranhos*, from Beira Baixa, are similar but contain goat's meat or mutton, tempered with garlic, wine, onion, parsley and mint.

Chouriço or linguiça The most common of the *enchidos*, eaten raw or grilled over flaming alcohol (*chouriço assado*). The best are from Alentejo, Guarda, Lamego, Montemor-o-Novo and Trás-os-Montes. The stuffing varies from coarsely chopped pieces of the less digestible parts of pigs to finer blends flavoured with herbs and wine (*chouriço de vinho*). *Chouriço doce*, served as a boiled starter, is a variant from Trás-os-Montes containing almonds, cinnamon and syrup.

Moiras A cross between *morcelas* and *chouriço*, famously from Lamego, made with wine and onion, and having a strong, bitter taste. Can be eaten raw but best cooked.

Morcelas or sangueiras Similar to black pudding, these are filled with blood and fat and have an intense aroma of cumin and cloves. Traditionally eaten with corn-flour polenta (*farinha de milho*), the best and least fatty are from Guarda.

Paio (or palaios, paínhos or paiolas) The largest pieces of meat go into these – *paio*, especially from Beira Baixa, contains a more or less solid chunk of prime smoked and seasoned ham, delicious on bread.

Presunto King of the *fumeiros* and Portugal's challenge to Parma ham: smoked leg of pork preserved in sea salt and cured for months or years, often found hanging in local *tascas* and *adegas*. Eaten as an appetizer in very thin slices, or as a stuffing for trout (*truta recheada com presunto*).

Salpicão Similar in quality to *paio* in that it contains prime meat rather than noses and trotters, virtually fat-free, and can be sliced like cured bacon. There are many varieties, variously seasoned with wine, salt, paprika, bay leaves, garlic or even orange peel. Eaten sliced with bread, or in stews and *feijoada*. Mainly from Beiras, Alentejo and Rio Douro.

Madeira (*vinho da Madeira*), from Portugal's semi-autonomous Atlantic island province, has been exported to Britain since Shakespeare's time – it was Falstaff's favourite drink, known then as sack. Widely available, it comes in four main varieties: Sercial (a light dry aperitif), Malvasia (very sweet, heavy dessert wine), Vermelho (a sweeter version of Sercial) and Boal or Malmsey (drier versions of Malvasia). Each improves with age and special vintages are greatly prized and priced. Also worth trying are the sweet white dessert wines (*moscatel*) from Setúbal, which – like port and Madeira – also come as yearly vintages. You can also drink them ice-cold as an aperitif.

Portuguese cheese

There's a huge range of regional Portuguese cheese, a sizeable quantity of which is still handmade (the label D.O.P. guarantees that it was made in its traditional area). A *queijo de cabra* or *cabreiro* is goats' cheese, sheep is *ovelha*, cow is *vaca*, while a mixture of these is *queijo de mixtura*. Hard cheese is *queijo de pasta dura*, soft is *de pasta mole*, cured is *curado* (not necessarily to maturity), and buttery is *amanteigado*.

Queijo Alentejano Small hard rounds of matured cheese (typically Alentejan) made from goat or sheep's milk, often referred to as *Queijo Seco* (dry cheese). They're curdled with thistle flowers (*cardo* or *coalha-leite*) instead of rennet, and pressed and turned daily for several months. Look for *Queijo de Nisa* from northern Alentejo (similar to Parmesan) and *Queijo de Serpa* from the south – strong, tart and available young (soft) or mature (hard).

Queijo da Serra (or Queijo Serrano) Unctuous, aromatic cotton-girdled beauty from the Serra da Estrela. It's not matured for long, and consequently has an almost liquid texture. The cloth simply keeps the cheese in one place, so don't try to slice it (at least in public): the traditional method is to cut out a hole on top and scoop up the contents by spoon.

Azeitão A gorgeous sheep's milk cheese from near Lisbon, which crumbles slightly when you cut it and has a pleasantly astringent taste.

Queijo de Ovelha Churra A hard cheese made with milk from the rugged sheep of southern Trás-os-Montes, especially around Vila Flôr. The soft, delicate flavour comes from the rennet used for coagulation. Stronger variants are sold in Alto Douro and Trás-os-Montes, cured with salt, olive oil and paprika.

Queijo Queimoso (or Picante) Rich and piquant (*queimoso* means "burning") mix of goat/sheep's milk, similar to Roquefort. The best is from the Serra da Gardunha in Beira Baixa. Less pungent is the paprika-covered *pimentão*, made from cows' milk.

Rabaçal Slightly tart cheese, a splendidly refined blend of sheep's milk and cows' milk, at its best from Ansião in the Serras de Penela, near Coimbra.

Queijo de Tomar Tiny semi-hard matured cheese from Ribatejo.

Queijo da Ilha de São Jorge The best of the Azores' acclaimed cows' milk cheeses, with a Swiss look and flavour. It's also the heaviest, weighing in at over 7kg; it's sold in wedges. *Queijo da Ilha Branca* is similar. There are other good cows' milk cheeses from the Minho.

Queijo fresco (or requeijão) *Queijo fresco* is strained, lightly pressed curds of cows' milk one or two days old, whilst *requeijão* is unpressed curds of sheep's milk, vaguely similar to cottage cheese. Both are neutral in taste.

Chèvre A recent introduction styled on the soft French cylindrical goats' cheeses, primarily from Ribatejo and Minho.

Flamengo *Flamengo* ("Flemish") is a direct copy of Dutch Edam, complete with the red wax. The best is *Limiano*, from Ponte de Lima in Minho. *Flamengo* is also industrially produced in rectangular blocks and sold sliced as *queijo em barra* or *queijo em fatias*.

Spirits (licor)

The national **brandy** is arguably outflanked by its Spanish rivals – which are sold almost everywhere – but the native spirit is available in two major labels (Macieira and Constantino), each with loyal followings. It's frighteningly cheap. Portuguese gin is weaker than international brands but again ridiculously inexpensive. Be warned that the typical Portuguese measure of spirits is equivalent to at least two shots in Britain or North America.

Local firewaters – generically known as aguardente – include *bagaço* (the fieriest, made from grapes), *aguardente de figo* (made from figs, with which it shares similar qualities when drunk to excess), *ginginha* (made from cherries), and the very wonderful *Licor Beirão* (a kind of cognac with herbs). In the Algarve, the best-known firewaters are *medronho*, made from the strawberry tree and which tastes a bit like schnapps, and *amarginha*, made from almonds. Other local spirits include *brandymel*, a honey brandy, *licor de bolota* (made from acorns) and *licor de ameixa* (a plum brandy).

Beer

Portugal's main **beer** (*cerveja*) brands, found nationwide, are Sagres and Super Bock, and you'll also see Cristal and Cintra, not that there's much to distinguish any of them. The standard beer in Portugal is a typical European-style lager (around five percent strength), but the main brands also offer a *preta* (black) beer – a kind of slightly fizzy lager-stout – as well as wheat- and fruit-flavoured and non-alcoholic versions, none particularly successful. International brand beers are also available in some bars, but are nearly always more expensive.

When drinking draught beer, order *um imperial* (or *um fino* in the north) if you want a regular glass, and *uma caneca* for half a litre. If you prefer bottled beer, ask for *uma garrafa*.

Coffee, tea and soft drinks

Coffee (*café*) comes black, small and espresso-strong (*uma bica* in the south, or simply *um café*); black, small but weaker (*um carioca*); small and with milk (*um garoto* in Lisbon and the south, *um pingo* in the north); or large and with milk but weak (*um galão*), often served in a glass. For white coffee that tastes of coffee and not diluted warm milk, ask for *um meia de leite*.

Tea (*chá*) is a big drink in Portugal (which originally exported tea-drinking to England) and you'll find wonderfully elegant tea houses (*casas de chá*) dotted around the country. It's usually served plain; *com leite* is with milk, *com limão* with lemon, but *um chá preta com limão* is tea with lemon rind. Herbal teas are known as *infusões*; most places have at least some bags. The most common are camomile (*camomila*) *cidreira* (lemon-balm), *tília* (linden) mint (*menta*), and *lúcia-lima* (lemon verbena).

All the standard **soft drinks** are available. Local varieties include the Tri Naranjus range of still fruit drinks and fizzy Sumol; both are loaded with chemicals. Healthier is fresh orange juice (*sumo de laranja*), which – rather surprisingly for an orange-producing country – can be awkward to find; adding the word *natural* or *fresca* should get you the real thing. If there is a juicer available, ask for it *da maquina* to get it freshly squeezed. *Sumo de limão* is lemonade.

Mineral water (*água mineral*) comes either still (*sem gás*) or carbonated (*com gás*), often from the northern Portuguese spas of Pedras Salgadas or Vidago. This is incredibly inexpensive in supermarkets, less so in tourist shops and restaurants.

The media

Foreign-language newspapers (including the European editions of British papers, plus the *International Herald Tribune*, *Le Monde* and the like) can be bought in the major towns, cities and resorts, usually the same day in Lisbon and much of the Algarve or a day late elsewhere. For an English-language view of what's happening in Portugal, the weekly *Portugal News* (⊛www.the-news.net) is widely available, while *The Resident* (weekly; ⊛www.portugalresident.com) – aimed at expats – has both an Algarve and a Lisbon edition.

The Portuguese press

The most established and respected Portuguese daily **newspapers** are the Lisbon-based, traditional *Diário de Notícias* (⊛www.dn.pt); the more independent *Público* (⊛www.publico.pt) and Porto's *Jornal de Notícias* (⊛www.jnoticias.pt). They have their uses for daily listings information (with good Friday supplements), even if you have only a very sketchy knowledge of the language. The stylish *Público* has the youngest feel, good for the arts, with fairly easy-to-read listings. *Expresso* is also good, with lots of meaty articles. The best-selling tabloid is the right-wing *Correio da Manhã* (⊛www.correiomanha.pt) and its rival, *24 Horas*. Business dailies *Diário Económico* and *Jornal de Negócios* will keep you up to date with economic issues. For fans of Portuguese **sport** (basically football), *A Bola* (⊛www.abola.pt), *O Jogo* and *Record* (⊛www.record.pt) cover the daily ins and outs of teams and players and include upcoming sports fixtures.

TV and radio

You're not going to escape the television in Portugal – there's scarcely a bar or a restaurant in the country that doesn't have one switched on. There are four domestic **stations** – the state-run RTP1 and 2: and the private channels SIC and TVI. The best is 2:, which is a mix of films from all over the world, National Geographic-style documentaries

and daily coverage of the arts. The other three channels are far more downmarket, heavy on gameshows, variety shows, reality TV, and imported or adapted American and British series. Films are nearly always shown in their original language (ie, subtitled rather than dubbed), while you also get a full diet of *telenovelas* (soaps), either Brazilian or home grown, which make for compelling if trashy viewing, even if you don't understand a word. The best news programming is on RTP1 (1pm and 8pm); for comprehensive weather forecasting, turn to TVI.

Most Portuguese households and businesses get their TV via **cable or satellite** subscription. Even in small two- and three-star *residenciais* and hotels you'll often get a couple of foreign-language channels (BBC World, CNN, Eurosport, MTV), while four- and five-star places usually offer a wider range plus pay-for movie channels.

Portugal has a plethora of national and local **radio stations**. RDP's Antena 1 is the most serious of the lot, mixing golden oldies and Portuguese music with news on the hour, Antena 2 has classical music, and Antena 3 has the best contemporary sounds and new Portuguese music. *Rádio Comercial* is the best of the independent stations, with alternative sounds especially in the evenings. Or with a short-wave radio you'll be able to tune into the BBC World Service (⊛www.bbc.co.uk/worldservice).

Festivals

Portugal maintains a remarkable number of folk customs, which find their expression in local carnivals (*festas*) and traditional pilgrimages (*romarias*). Some of these have developed into wild celebrations lasting days or even weeks and have become tourist events in themselves; others have barely strayed from their roots.

Every region is different, but in the north especially there are dozens of village festivals, everyone taking the day off to celebrate the local **saint's day** or the harvest, and performing ancient songs and dances in traditional dress for no one's benefit but their own. Look out for the great **feiras**, especially at Barcelos in the Minho. Originally they were simply markets, but as often as not nowadays you'll find a combination of agricultural show, folk festival, amusement park and, admittedly, tourist bazaar. Most towns also put on concerts, dances, processions and events throughout the year (but especially between June and September), while an increasing number of **music festivals** are held in Portugal, from jazz to electro.

The festival list is potentially endless and only the major highlights are picked out in the **festival calendar** opposite. Other local festivals and events are picked out in the guide, while for more details check with turismos or have a look at the websites of the various town halls (Câmara Municipal), which always carry news about forthcoming festivities: the addresses are usually in the following format, ⓦ www.cm-nameoftown.pt.

Among major **national events**, Easter week and the Santos Populares festivities associated with St Anthony (June 12/13), St John (June 23/24) and St Peter (June 28/29) stand out. All are celebrated throughout the country with religious processions. Easter is most magnificent in Braga (p.391), where it is full of ceremonial pomp, while the saints' festivals tend to be more joyous affairs. In Lisbon, during St Anthony (see p.136), the Alfama becomes one giant street party. In Porto, where St John's Eve is the highlight of a week of celebration (p.338), everyone dances through the streets all night, hitting each other over the head with leeks or plastic hammers.

Events calendar

January
6: Epiphany (*Dia de Reis*) The traditional crown-shaped cake *bolo rei* (king's cake) with a lucky charm and a bean inside is eaten; if you get the bean in your slice you have to buy the cake next year.

February
Carnaval Many areas now have Rio-like carnival parades, and Lisbon and towns in the Algarve are good destinations. But Carnaval has much older traditions steeped in spring-time fertility rites, and for a glimpse of what it was like before thongs and spangles, the masked merry-making of the **Entrudo dos Compadres** (p.369), near Lamego, is superb.

March/April
Easter Holy week (Semana Santa) religious processions in most places, most majestically in Braga, and at São Brás de Alportel in the Algarve (the **Festa das Tochas**). The **Festa da Mãe Soberana** in Loulé (Algarve) is one of the country's largest Easter festivals. Another good location is Tomar, where the floral crosses of the procession are ceremoniously destroyed afterwards.

May
Early May: Queima das Fitas The "burning of the ribbons", celebrating the end of the academic year, reaches its drunken apogee in Coimbra and other university towns.
3: Festa das Cruzes The "Festival of the Crosses" is the biggest annual event in Barcelos (Minho).
13: Fátima (*Peregrinação de Fátima*) Portugal's most famous pilgrimage commemorates the Apparitions of the Virgin Mary; also in October.
End of May (or early June), Corpus Christi *Vaca das Cordas* is a "running of the bull" ceremony in Ponte de Lima with roots in classical mythology (see p.423).

June

First weekend: Festa de São Gonçalo Prominent saint's day celebrations in Amarante (see p.358).

First week: Rock in Rio-Lisboa Europe's largest rock festival (an offshoot of the enormous Rock in Rio fest) is held in even years.

First two weeks: Feira Nacional da Agricultura Held at Santarém, for ten days from the first Friday, with dancing, bullfighting and an agricultural fair.

Santos Populares (Popular Saints) Celebrations in honour of Santo António (St Anthony, June 12–13), São João (St John, 23–24) and Pedro (St Peter, 28–29) throughout the country.

Arraial Pride Lisbon's increasingly popular gay pride event changes exact date and venue but has recently been held at Lisbon's Parque de Monsanto.

July

First week: Festa dos Tabuleiros Tomar's biggest and most spectacular procession only takes place every four years (next is 2007); see p.212.

First two weeks: Festa do Colete Encarnado Held in Vila Franca de Xira, with Pamplona-style running of bulls through the streets.

Festival de Ópera e Música Clássical Top performers grace Ponte de Lima's manor houses, parks and theatres; see p.424.

Sintra Music Festival Performances by international orchestras, musicians and dance groups in parks, gardens and palaces in and around Sintra, Estoril and Cascais. An offshoot of the festival are the "Noites de Bailado" – ballet, dance and opera in the Centro Cultural Olga Cadaval near Sintra train station.

Silves Beer Festival Local and international beers by the bucket load, plus live entertainment.

August

First week: Festival Sudoeste Much-heralded four-day rock, indie and electro music festival (with camping) held at Zambujeira do Mar (Alentejo coast).

First weekend: Festas Gualterianas The major festival in Guimarães has been held since the fifteenth century.

First weekend: Festa do Nossa Senhora da Boa Viagem Seafaring is celebrated at Peniche with religious processions by boat and on land.

Third weekend: Romaria da Nossa Senhora da Agonía Viana do Castelo's major annual religious celebration, plus carnival and fair (see p.408).

Jazz Numa Noite de Verão The "jazz on a summer night" festival at the Gulbenkian's open-air amphitheatre in Lisbon.

September

First week: Romaria de Nossa Senhora dos Remédios The annual pilgrimage in Lamego comes to a head at the end of the first week, though events start in the last week of August (see p.367).

Second & third weekends: Feiras Novas The "New Fairs" – a traditional festival and market – held in Ponte de Lima.

20: Festa de São Mateus A week's worth of celebrations in Elvas (Alentejo), including a huge religious procession plus the usual fairs and fireworks.

October

First two weeks: Feira de Outubro More bull-running and fighting in Vila Franca de Xira.

13: Fátima The second great pilgrimage of the year at Fátima.

November

First two weeks: Feira Nacional do Cavalo The National Horse Fair, held in Golegã (see p.219).

11: São Martinho Celebrations in honour of St Martin, with roots in pre-Christian harvest festivals: coincides with the first tastings of the year's wine, roast chestnuts and *Água Pé* – a weak wine made from watered-down dregs. At its most traditional in northern Trás-os-Montes, Beira Baixa (particularly Alcains), Golegã (see p.219), and Penafiel east of Porto.

December

24: Christmas (*Natal*) The main Christmas celebration is midnight Mass on December 24, followed by a traditional meal of *bacalhau*, turkey or – bizarrely in Trás-os-Montes – octopus.

31: New Year's Eve (*Noite de Ano Novo*) Individual towns organize their own events, usually with fireworks at midnight, and the New Year is welcomed by the banging of old pots and pans.

Sports and outdoor activities

Internationally famed for its top beaches, golf courses and tennis centres, Portugal also has an ideal climate for a variety of other outdoor pursuits including surfing, windsurfing, walking and adventure sports. Spectators can enjoy top-class football throughout the country, along with Portugal's own brand of bullfighting.

Adventure activities

The whole **outdoor activity** scene is rapidly expanding, with many areas now offering things like paragliding, abseiling, rap-jumping, rafting, canyoning, caving, and mountain-bike and 4WD expeditions. There's most scope in the mountain areas – notably the Serra da Estrela and Peneda-Gerês parks – and on the major rivers (Douro, Mondego and Zêzere), but many of the smaller natural parks and reserves also have local adventure outfits ready to show you the surroundings. We've picked out some of the best options in the text – it's always worth contacting operators in advance, since activities are sometimes only for groups (though individuals may be able to join in) and are always heavily subscribed at weekends and during summer holidays. Prices vary considerably, but you can expect to pay from €20 for a day's guided mountain-walking, or €50 for white-water rafting or canyoning. Check also with your insurance company to see if you are covered for such activities.

Beaches, river beaches and swimming pools

The Algarve, of course, has the country's most popular sandy beaches, many of them sheltered in coves – the sea is warmest on the eastern Algarve, and remains swimmable year-round if you're hardy. The west of the country faces the full brunt of the **Atlantic** and while there are some stupendous stretches of coastline you need to beware the heavy undertow and don't swim if you see a red or yellow flag. The EU blue flag indicates that the water is clean enough to swim in – sadly, not always the case – and that the beach has lifeguards. For a full

rundown of the country's best beaches, see the *Coastal Portugal* colour section.

An unsung glory of central and northern Portugal is its **river beaches** – you'll see signs (*praia fluvial*) everywhere directing you to quiet bends in the local river or to weirs or dramatic gorges. Often, the local municipality erects a summer bar (usually open June to September), and there are usually picnic and barbecue areas, and public toilets. Each sizeable (and not so sizeable) town also has a **swimming pool** (*piscina*), usually outdoors, and also only open from June to September. At indoor municipal pools (open all year) you may have to show your passport, and you'll have to wear a swimming cap.

Bullfighting

The Portuguese **bullfight** (*tourada*) is neither as commonplace nor as famous as its Spanish counterpart. In Portugal the bull isn't killed, but instead wrestled to the ground in a colourful and skilled display. As a result of the fight, however, the bull is usually injured and it is always slaughtered later in any case.

A *tourada* opens with the bull, its horns padded or sheared flat, facing a mounted *toureiro* in elaborate eighteenth-century costume. His job is to provoke and exhaust the bull and to plant the dart-like *farpas* (or *bandarilhas*) in its back while avoiding the charge – a demonstration of incredible riding prowess and elegance. Once the beast is tired the *moços-de-forcado*, or simply *forcados*, move in, an eight-man team dressed in "seven dwarfs" hats. Their task is to immobilize the bull. It appears a totally suicidal mission – they line up behind each other across the ring from the bull, while the front man shouts and gesticulates to persuade the bull to charge them. In theory, the front man leaps between the charging bull's horns while the rest grab hold and try to subdue it, but in practice it often takes two or three attempts, the first tries often resulting in one or more of the *forcados* being tossed spectacularly into the air.

The **bullfighting season** lasts from April to October, and there are weekly fights at the bullrings in Lisbon, Cascais and at Albufeira and Lagos on the Algarve. However, the great Portuguese bullfight centre is **Ribatejo**, where the animals are bred. If you want to see a fight, it's best to witness it here, amid the local aficionados, or as part of the festivals in Vila Franca de Xira and Santarém. Local towns and villages in the Ribatejo also feature bull-running through the streets at various of their festivals.

There is a small band of Portuguese bullfighters and fans, mostly in the town of Barrancos in southern Alentejo, who claim the Spanish model as their own and spent the 1990s defying the forces of law and order by publicly killing bulls in the ring. Their defiance has finally met with legal approval, allowing the practice in areas where this was traditional.

Football

Portuguese **football** has a long tradition and is the country's favourite sport, bar none. The exploits of the most famous Portuguese coach, Chelsea's Jose Mourinho, make headline news, while the national team came closest to glory in the 2004 European Championships, held in Portugal – they were beaten in the final by surprise winners Greece, though the real legacy was the construction of several excellent new stadiums, including the Estádio do Dragão in Porto and Benfica's Estádio da Luz.

The leading clubs, inevitably, hail from the country's big cities, Porto and Lisbon. Over the last decade, **FC Porto** has swept up every title available, including the national Superliga title (eight in twelve years, at the time of writing), the European UEFA Cup in 2003, and – its crowning glory – the Europe's Champions League title in 2004. Lisbon-based **Benfica** experienced a similar golden age in the 1960s, when Mozambique-born striker Eusébio was at his masterful height.

The other big team is **Sporting**, also from Lisbon, and these days usually the closest rivals to Porto.

Just about every Portuguese supports one of these three teams and, in the provinces, usually one of the lesser, local outfits as well. Of these, Boavista (Porto's second team), Sporting Braga and Guimarães are the most successful. Ticket prices for league matches depend on who's playing: a clash between two big names averages €15–40 depending on the seat location, whilst a game between a big name and a lesser-known team is about half that. The Superliga season runs from the end of August to mid-May, most matches being played on Saturdays and Sundays. Live televised matches are regular fixtures of most bars and restaurants, usually on Friday or Sunday evenings, often other days too.

Holiday sports and activities

Portugal is a year-round **golf** destination, though exclusivity is often the key word. Some of the country's finest hotels and villa complexes have golf courses attached, or have connections with a golf club, and undoubtedly the best deals are on special golf-holiday packages. Otherwise, green fees on 18-hole courses start at around €60, though multi-play packages and discounts are nearly always available. The Greater Lisbon area and the Algarve have the bulk of the courses: for more information consult a specialist tour operator or check out the excellent websites Ⓦwww.portugalgolf.pt and Ⓦwww.algarvegolf.net.

Many larger Algarve hotels also have year-round **tennis courts**. If you want to improve your game, the best intensive coaching is at the Vale do Lobo Tennis Academy (packages organized by Light Blue Travel Ⓦwww.lightbluetravel.co.uk) or the Praia da Luz Ocean Club near Lagos (Jonathan Markson Tennis Ⓦwww.marksontennis.com).

Horse-riding stables around the country offer one-hour or full-day rides, often on Lusitano thoroughbred horses. The main areas for tourist rides are Estoril and Sintra, the Algarve and the Alentejo, while the province of Ribatejo lies at the heart of Portugal's equestrian traditions. Prices start from around €20 for an hour's trek, rising to around €80–100 for a full day, which usually includes a picnic lunch. For details of *centros hípicos* (riding schools) in a particular area, contact the local tourist office.

The only **skiing** is in the Serra da Estrela (usually possible from December to February, sometimes March), though you wouldn't specifically travel to Portugal for it. The slopes lie just below the *serra's* highest point, Torre, with access easiest from Covilhã and Penhas da Saude. The lifts, ski school, and ski and snowboard rental are operated by Turistrela (☎707 275 707, ⓦwww.turistrela .pt); a day's gear rental starts at €25, lessons from €30, and you can also book reasonably priced ski packages. The year-round artificial run at **Ski Parque** (p.303), near Manteigas, is another option, and this also doubles as an outdoor activity and adventure centre.

Walking in Portugal's parks

Portugal only has one **national park** – the Parque Nacional Peneda-Gerês, in the Minho – but there are over thirty other **protected areas**, designated as *parques naturais* (natural parks), *reservas naturais* (natural reserves) or other specifications. You'll find them all listed and profiled on the website of the government's Instituto da Conservação da Natureza (ⓦwww.icn.pt – click on "Áreas Protegidas"). All the main parks, and many of the minor ones, are covered in the guide and between them account for some of Portugal's most dramatic landscapes – from the high-mountain scenery of the Serra da Estrela to the limestone caves of the Serras de Aire e Candeeiros, or the island hideaway of the Ilha Berlenga to the lagoons, dunes and marshes of the Ria Formosa.

Throughout the guide we've recommended **walks and hiking trails** wherever possible. All of the parks have information centres (contact details noted in the guide), and most promote trails and tours within their area. Marked walking routes are becoming more popular, but signage and trail maintenance are extremely patchy. English is rarely spoken, even at major information centres, making it difficult to find out about the status of routes, while there is a real paucity of proper walking maps (see "Maps" on p.68 for the best advice). Hiking in Portugal's highest mountains, the Serra da Estrela (see p.296), can be particularly disappointing; probably the most reliable place is the Peneda-Gerês national park (p.430).

Watersports

The biggest **windsurfing** and **surfing** destinations are Guincho and Praia Grande, north of Lisbon, though the winds and currents here require a high level of expertise. Ericeira on the Estramadura coast is another popular centre and frequently hosts pro competitions, as do Peniche in Estremadura, Espinho south of Porto (popular with bodyboarders), and Figueira da Foz near Coimbra. The west coast of the Algarve, around Sagres, is also excellent for surfers (see p.605). We've highlighted rental outfits and surf camps in nearly all these places, while a couple of good websites (in Portuguese) are: ⓦwww.beachcam.pt for surf-savvy weather and wave height forecasts and events, and ⓦwww.surfingportugal.com, home to the Federação Portuguesa de Surf, which organizes competitions.

Some adventure outfits offer **kayaking** in the *serra* rivers, though there's a more gentle introduction on the Rio Mondego, starting from Penacova (p.242), basically a half-day float trip downriver to Coimbra.

Scuba diving for beginners is best off Praia do Carvoeiro near Lagoa in the Algarve, where Tivoli Diving (☎282 351 194, ⓦwww.tivoli-diving.com) and Divers Cove (☎282 356 594, ⓦwww.diverscove.de) offer standard dives with equipment rental for around €40, plus night and wreck dives for experienced divers, and full PADI-accredited four-day Open Water courses (with tuition in English, from €400). On the west coast, conditions can be more trying, with a strong undertow, though there are more sheltered waters between Lisbon and Cascais. Experienced divers should appreciate the wrecked German U-1277 submarine off Matosinhos in the north of Portugal: contact Mergulhomania (ⓦwww.mergulhomania.com).

Shopping

Though most large towns in Portugal have at least one out-of-town shopping centre, in the majority of towns people still do much of their purchasing in traditional shops and markets. Old town centres look like they haven't looked for thirty years or more in the UK, with a butcher, a baker and a candlestick-maker on every corner, not to mention a florist, a grocer and a hardware store.

We've pointed out regional handicrafts, specialist shops and markets throughout the guide, but there's a general rundown below of things you'll see and might want to buy. The Lisbon and Porto accounts also have their own dedicated shopping sections. Specialist craft and souvenir shops might be able to arrange shipping home for you; otherwise, go to the local post office, where all kinds of insured, registered and signed-for services are available (see ⓦ www.ctt.pt, which has an English-language version).

Markets

A town's **mercado municipal** (municipal market) is the place to buy meat, fish, fruit, veg and bread. In larger towns they are open daily (not Sunday), usually from 7 or 8am until lunchtime; smaller towns might have a market just once or twice a week. Often, a town's regular market is supplemented by a larger weekly affair, sometimes at a different site in the open-air, where you'll also be able to buy clothes, shoes, ceramics, baskets, furniture, flowers, toys, tools and a million-and-one other things you never knew you needed. In the case of the great **weekly markets** at Barcelos (Minho; Thurs), Viana do Castelo (Minho; Fri), Ponte da Barca/Arcos de Valdevez (Minho; Wed), Carcavelos (Lisbon, Thurs), Estremoz (Alentejo; Saturday) and Loulé (Algarve; Sat), or the monthly markets at Évora (Alentejo, second Tues) and Santarém (Ribatejo; second/fourth Sun), these constitute a major reason to visit in the first place. The best **flea market** in the country is Lisbon's Feira da Ladra (Tues & Sat), just the place to buy a candelabra or a set of dusty postcards.

Mini-markets and supermarkets

In small villages and towns the **mini-mercado** (mini-market) is as convenient as convenience-shopping gets. **Super-mercados** tend to lie on the outskirts of towns – Intermarché, Pingo Doce, Jumbo, Continente.and Mini-Preço are the main supermarket names, selling pretty much everything you would expect (though choices can be more limited in out-of-the-way locations), while the pile-em-high German-owned Lidl is increasingly prevalent. In Lisbon (namely *Columbo*), Coimbra (*Forum*) and the Algarve (Guia's *Algarve Shopping* and Faro's *Forum*), the **mega-shopping centre** is king. Hugely popular and geared up for whole days out (with cafés, restaurants, cinemas and kids' entertainment), these giant malls tend to have hundreds of local and international shops and at least one supermarket.

Ceramics

Highest-profile souvenirs are probably ceramics of all kinds, from traditional *azulejo* tiles to elaborate figurines, cookware to sculpture. The virtual symbol of Portuguese tourism, the ceramic **Barcelos cockerel** (see p.401), perches on every tat-shop shelf. You can buy rustic, brown kitchen **earthenware** in every market and supermarket for just a few euros, but interesting regional variations include Barcelos' own brown-and-yellow pottery ware, black earthenware (from Tondela) and the almost Aztec-style patterns (Santa Comba Dão) typical of the Viseu region. Porches is the centre for the Algarve's pottery and ceramics, whilst Caldas da Rainha in Estremadura is probably the best-known

The Chinese Shop

There's scarcely a town in Portugal that doesn't have a *Loja Chinês*, a **Chinese-run emporium** selling everything under the sun. In many ways, they fulfil the same function as a "pound" or "dollar" shop, selling basic household items really cheaply – if you need two-dozen toilet rolls, a set of tupperware, fifty wine glasses or a washing-up bowl, this is where you come. But they are also good for dirt-cheap toys and electronics – all made in the Far East, guaranteed to break after a couple of hours – and for all those things you never knew you needed, like a Portuguese flag, a Star Wars light sabre or an alarm-clock shaped like a man on a toilet.

ceramics town – caricatured rustic **figurines** and floral- and animal-inspired plates and bowls have been produced here since the nineteenth century. Estremoz in the Alentejo has an even older heritage, and is also known for its elaborate figurines and its flower- and leaf-festooned pottery.

Carpets, rugs, blankets, tapestries, linen and lace

Hand-stitched **Arraiolos carpets** (from the town of the same name in Alentejo) have a worldwide reputation, and they cost a fortune, but there's nothing to stop you looking. **Tapestries** from Portalegre (Alentejo) have been known since the seventeenth century, and the *colchas* or **embroidered bedspreads** of Castelo Branco (Beira Baixa) for just as long – again, the high prices and lengthy ordering times mean these are unlikely spur-of-the-moment purchases for most visitors. Hand-woven woollen **rugs and blankets** are a more realistic buy, with particularly fine examples from Reguengos de Monsaraz (Alentejo) – you can hang them on a wall. Rustic woolly blankets (and fleece-lined slippers) also are a feature of the mountain villages of the Serra da Estrela – Sabugeiro has hundreds of them displayed in its souvenir shop windows. For embroidered **linen and lace** it's Vila do Conde (north of Porto) that is the best-known centre, though many other fishing towns – like Peniche and Nazaré in Estremadura – also have a strong bobbin lace tradition. The biggest and best pieces command high prices, but there's plenty of reasonably priced work available too.

Food and drink

Port wine is the most popular buy, with cheap run-of-the-mill stuff available in supermarkets or gathering dust above the salt cod in old-fashioned grocery stores. For specific names and vintages you need to have done your homework since a recent vintage (not yet ready to drink) starts at around €30, with the serious stuff commanding prices of €100 and upwards. The colour section tells you more about port, while visiting a lodge in Porto or along the Douro is by far the best way to immerse yourself in the subject. Don't miss a drink in the *solares* in Porto or Lisbon either, where you can sample individual glasses from hundreds of different varieties.

Virtually every region in Portugal produces **table wine**, often remarkably good. See p.49 for suggestions if you want to take home a bottle or two, while regional **wine routes** (past vineyards and estates open to the public) are well-signposted, particularly in the Alentejo, Ribatejo and Dão valley.

Taking food home is more problematic, depending on your country's importation laws, but no one is going to object to a bottle of **olive oil** – the best are now sold like wines, from single estates, particularly in the Douro, where production is an adjunct to the wine business. Other suggestions include a jar of mountain **honey** from the Serra da Estrela, or sealed packs of mountain **herbs and teas**, particularly from the Serra do Gerês. Portuguese **cheeses and hams** are excellent – there's a full rundown on pp.50–51 – but, again, to take them home you'll have to get them vacuum-packed (you can buy them like that at Lisbon airport).

Clothes, shoes and accessories

Portugal's textiles industry has traditionally been one of the most important in Europe,

Clothing and shoe sizes

Women's dresses and skirts

American	4	6	8	10	12	14	16	18
British	8	10	12	14	16	18	20	22
Continental	38	40	42	44	46	48	50	52

Women's blouses and sweaters

American	6	8	10	12	14	16	18
British	30	32	34	36	38	40	42
Continental	40	42	44	46	48	50	52

Women's shoes

American	5	6	7	8	9	10	11
British	3	4	5	6	7	8	9
Continental	36	37	38	39	40	41	42

Men's suits

American	34	36	38	40	42	44	46	48
British	34	36	38	40	42	44	46	48
Continental	44	46	48	50	52	54	56	58

Men's shirts

American	14	15	15.5	16	16.5	17	17.5	18
British	14	15	15.5	16	16.5	17	17.5	18
Continental	36	38	39	41	42	43	44	45

Men's shoes

American	7	7.5	8	8.5	9.5	10	10.5	11	11.5
British	6	7	7.5	8	9	9.5	10	11	12
Continental	39	40	41	42	43	44	44	45	46

and though this has suffered badly from cheap rivals from the Far East, you can still pick up brand-name seconds from many of Portugal's weekly flea markets (see p.59). For quality **designer clothes**, however, you have to head to Lisbon, particularly Avenida da Liberdade (for international names) or the Bairro Alto (for local cutting-edge styles). Fátima Lopes is the current style icon, and Ana Salazar is another leading name. Some of the larger shopping centres also have designer boutiques; indeed the giant centre at Alcochete is Europe's largest designer discount outlet. Leather goods have a fair reputation in Portugal, particularly **bags and shoes** (and belts and briefcases) – most big towns and shopping centres will have a decent selection, though a common complaint is that Portuguese shoe shops don't always stock the larger or wider sizes you might require. **Gold and silver** filigree work is notable – there are some fine shops in Lisbon and Porto – and you'll be able to pick up cheap, hippy-style jewellery at beaches along the Algarve, especially Albufeira.

Travelling with children

As Portuguese society largely revolves round family life, the country is very child-friendly and families will find it one of the easiest places for a holiday. The two main worries for parents in Portugal are cars – which don't always observe pedestrian crossings – and the strong sun. Keep young children covered up between 11am and 3pm, make them wear a hat, and always apply a high-factor sun screen. Be aware, too, that many castles and monuments are unrailed and may have very steep drops, while sea bathing – especially on the west coast – can be hazardous, with dangerous undertows. Cobbled town centres and stepped alleys are also difficult for anyone trying to sightsee with a toddler and a pushchair.

Most **hotels and pensions** can provide an extra bed or a cot (*um berço*) if notified in advance. There is usually no charge for children under six who share their parents' room (or under-3s in some of the stingier four- and five-star places), while discounts of up to fifty percent on accommodation for 6- to 8-year-olds are not uncommon. Baby-sitting and child supervision are available at most four- and five-star places, though you'll have to pay. However, many small hotels and pensions have their own restaurants, so provided your children are reasonable sleepers (and your baby monitor works!) you can at least stay on a budget and have dinner.

Children are welcome in all **cafés and restaurants** at any time of the day, irrespective of whether or not they sell alcohol. Indeed, waiters often go out of their way to spend a few minutes entertaining restless children; tots may even find themselves being carried off for a quick tour of the kitchens while parents finish their meals in peace. Highchairs (*cadeirinha de bebé*) are normally the clip-on-table variety. Specific child menus are scarce, though restaurants nearly all serve half portions (*meia dose*) as a matter of course – these are still too much for most children to finish, but the Portuguese often

simply order a *dose* or two between the family. Note, however, that restaurants rarely open much before 7.30pm, so kids will need to adjust to Portuguese hours; local children are often still up at midnight.

Specific changing facilities in restaurants, cafés and public toilets are largely non-existent, and when you do find them – such as in larger shopping centres – they are usually part of women's toilets only.

Fresh milk for **babies** (*leite pasteurizado*) is sold in larger supermarkets; mornings are best as it tends to sell out by mid-afternoon – *gordo* is full-fat, *meio-gordo* half-fat and *magro* skimmed milk. *Mini-mercados*, smaller shops and cafés generally only stock UHT, which is what most Portuguese kids drink. Nappies/diapers (*fraldas*) are widely available in supermarkets and pharmacies, as are formula milk, babies' bottles and jars of baby food – though don't expect the full range of (or indeed any) organic or salt-free choices you might be used to at home.

Most **museums, sights and attractions** don't usually charge for small children, while under 12s get in for half price. On public transport, under-5s go free while 5–11 year-olds travel half price on trains but pay full fare on metros and buses.

Travel essentials

Cinemas

To an English-speaking visitor's joy, films are almost always shown with the **original soundtrack** with Portuguese subtitles. Listings are in local newspapers or on boards placed somewhere in the central square of every small town; don't expect film names to be literal translations of the original – whoever's in that line of work seems to prefer titles based on Roget's entries for "fatal" and "dangerous". Screenings are cheap, with reduced prices at matinées and on Mondays. The website ⓦwww.7arte.net reviews and lists the latest releases.

Costs

Portugal remains one of the EU's least expensive destinations and you can live very cheaply here, especially if you steer clear of Lisbon and the Algarve, which are inevitably far more expensive.

The biggest single **cost** is usually accommodation – travelling out of season (when many hotels drop their prices) and with a companion (to share rooms) will always save you money. Unless you camp (with a night from around €5) or stay in a hostel dorm (from around €8 a night), you can expect to pay €10–15 per person per night for the cheapest accommodation.

Apart from accommodation, you could reasonably expect to survive on a daily budget of €25 if you're prepared to have a picnic lunch and a budget evening meal, though this won't leave much change for sightseeing or transport. Stretch to a budget of €40 per person per day, however, and you can easily afford two meals in modest restaurants, drinks in the evening, entry to a museum or two, and a bus or train ride – if you're just visiting Lisbon and the Algarve you can add twenty percent to these figures.

Eating out can be very cheap, and sometimes costs even less than putting together a picnic. You can always get a substantial basic meal for around €8, or €5–6 if you choose the day's set menu at the cheapest *tascas* and *adegas*. Dinner in the smartest of restaurants is unlikely to cost more than €20 a head. A bottle of house wine rarely comes to more than €7, and the same bottle in supermarkets might be three times cheaper, whilst a bottle or glass of beer in a bar is around €1. Museums and attractions are rarely more than €3 to enter. Even transport is not going to break the bank, especially since most distances are fairly short. Car-hire prices are low and petrol reasonable while public transport is good value. A second-class train journey from Porto to Lisbon, or Lisbon to the Algarve, for example, starts at €20, whilst the same journey by bus costs €16. Valued added tax (known as IVA, around twenty per cent), for most tourist-related services, is usually included in advertised prices, though some car rental outfits especially like to keep it separate to appear cheaper than they really are.

Crime and personal safety

By European standards, Portugal is a remarkably crime-free country – people really do still leave their cars and house doors unlocked in the country. However, there's the usual **petty theft** in the cities and larger tourist resorts, particularly in the form of pickpockets on public transport and in bus and train stations. Best advice is not too carry too much cash or valuables, and leave your passport in the hotel safe where possible. Drivers should never leave anything visible in the car (preferably, don't leave anything in the car at all). Violence directed at tourists is rare – if you are threatened, hand over your valuables and run. In an **emergency**, dial ☏112 for the police or an ambulance.

There are two main police forces: the metropolitan **Polícia de Segurança Pública** (PSP) and the more rural **Guarda Nacional Repúblicana** (GNR). Either handles incidents involving tourists; their contacts are given in

"Listings" throughout the guide. Most police officers in the Algarve speak some English, but elsewhere you can't count on it and since tourists can usually muster only a few basic words of Portuguese, confusion can easily arise. To this end, showing deference is wise: the Portuguese still hold respect dear, and the more respect you show a figure in authority, the quicker you'll be on your way.

If you do have anything stolen, you'll need to go to a police station – primarily to file a **report** (*formulário de participação de roubo*), which your insurance company will require before they'll pay out for any claims. Expect it to take ages.

Portugal is rarely a dangerous place for **women travellers** and you only need to be particularly wary in parts of Lisbon at night (around Cais do Sodré, at the top end of Avenida da Liberdade, on the metro and on the Cais do Sodré–Cascais train line), in the darker alleys near the river in Porto, and in streets immediately around train stations in the larger towns (traditionally red-light districts). If you are on your own or feel uncomfortable anywhere, you should be able to get around at night by taxi. On the whole, though, the country is formal to the point of prudishness.

Disabled travellers

Portugal is slowly coming to terms with the needs of travellers with **disabilities**, but you should not expect much in the way of special facilities. However, people are generally ready to help and will go out of their way to make your visit as straightforward as possible.

Lisbon, Porto and Faro **airports** have ramps, lifts and adapted toilets. You'll also find **ramped access** to some museums and public buildings, while adapted **WCs** can be found at some train stations and major shopping centres. Local turismos should be able to help plan your stay, but they don't always have staff who speak English. It's worth bearing in mind that many *pensões* and *residenciais* are located on the first floor and up and don't have lifts. However, most four- and five-star **hotels** have lifts, wheelchair ramps and specially adapted bedrooms and bathrooms, while many manor houses and farmhouses have guest rooms on the ground floor.

On **public transport**, wheelchair access is usually possible as far as the platform (even if you have to wait for someone to come with a key to start the lift, not always in working order), but getting from the platform on to the train can be difficult. Lisbon's metro is not recommended, either in terms of access or for the crowds that throng it at rush hour. Porto's metro is more accessible, though outside the centrally located underground stations, where platforms are at the same level as the train doors, getting on and off will require assistance. Self-drive vehicles with automatic gear-shifts are available from the larger car rental companies, and there are reserved disabled parking spaces across the country (though they are not always respected).

Portugal's old **town centres** – specifically their steps and cobblestone alleys – pose their own problems. However, a number of attractive medieval towns and villages have been rehabilitated as part of central Portugal's Aldeias Históricas scheme, which has also meant the construction of some smooth wheelchair-accessible pathways alongside the cobbles.

Addresses

Most **addresses** in Portugal consist of a street name and number followed by a storey, eg Avenida da República 34-3° (US, fourth floor). An "esq" or "E" (for *esquerda*) after a floor number means you should go to the left; "dir" or "D" (for *direita*) indicates to the right; *esquina* means corner or junction; R/C stands for *rés-do-chão* (ground floor). In rural areas, the address may simply consist of a house or building name followed by the area. *Apartado* followed by a number is a PO Box, not a physical address. In this guide, we've also used the following abbreviations: Av (for Avenida, avenue), Pr (Praça, square) and Trav (Travessa, alley).

Useful contacts

Access Travel UK ☎ 01942/888 844, ⓦ www
.access-travel.co.uk. Small tour operator offering
Algarve accommodation suitable for the disabled.
Holiday Care UK ☎ 0845/124 9971, ⓦ www
.holidaycare.org.uk. Publishes an information pack
about holidaying in Portugal.
**Secretariado Nacional Para a Reabilitação
e Integração das Pessoas com Deficiência**
ⓦ www.snripd.pt. The government organization
promoting awareness of, and help for, the disabled
in Portugal – the website features a nationwide
searchable database (under "Accessibilidade") for
fully and partially accessible public buildings, hotels,
restaurants, cafés, bars, transport facilities, etc.
Wheeling Around the Algarve Portugal ☎ 289
393 636, ⓦ www.player.pt. Accessible holiday
accommodation, transport (including adapted
cars), and sporting/leisure activities in the Algarve.
All facilities are personally inspected before
recommendation.

Electricity

Mains voltage is 220V, which works fine with
equipment intended for 240V. Plugs are the European
two round pin variety; adaptors are sold at airports,
supermarkets and hardware stores.

Entry requirements

EU citizens need only a valid passport or
identity card to enter Portugal, and can stay
indefinitely. Citizens of Canada, the US,
Australia and New Zealand do not need a
visa for stays of up to ninety days. Most other
nationals will have to apply for a **visa** from a
Portuguese embassy or consulate – there's a
full list at ⓦ www.min-nestrangeiros.pt/mne
/estrangeiro. Entry conditions can change,
however, so check the situation before leaving home on ⓦ www.eurovisa.info.

If necessary, an extension to your stay
can be arranged once you're in the country. Extensions are issued by the nearest District Police headquarters or the
Foreigner's Registration Service – Serviço
de Estrangeiros e Fronteiras (ⓦ www.sef.pt)
– which has branch offices in most major
tourist centres. You should apply at least
a week before your time runs out and be
prepared to prove that you can support
yourself without working (for example by
keeping your bank exchange forms every
time you change money). Extended stay

visas are also available through Portuguese
consulates.

Portuguese embassies and consulates abroad

Australia and New Zealand 23 Culgoa Circuit,
O'Malley ACT 2606 ☎ 02/6290 1733, ⓦ www
.consulportugalsydney.org.au; ⓔ embportcamb
@internode.on.net. Plus consulates in Sydney,
Melbourne, Brisbane, Adelaide, Darwin and Fremantle.
Canada 645 Island Park Drive, Ottawa K1Y 0B8
☎ 613/729-0883, ⓦ .www.embportugal-ottowa
.org; ⓔ embportugal@embportugal-ottawa.org.
Plus consulates in Vancouver, Montreal and Toronto.
Ireland Knocksinna House, 7 Willow Park, Foxrock,
Dublin 18 ☎ 01/289 4416, ⓔ embport@Dublin
.dgaccp.pt.
New Zealand Nearest embassy is in Australia
(see above). Consulates: PO Box 305, 33 Garfield
St, Parnell, Auckland ☎ 09/309 1454; and PO Box
1024, Suite 1, 1st floor, 21 Marion St, Wellington
☎ 04/382 7655.
South Africa 559 Leyds Street, Muckleneuk, 002
Pretória ☎ 02712 341 2340, ⓔ portemb@satis
.co.za.
UK 11 Belgrave Sq, London SW1 8PP ☎ 08700 005
6970, ⓔ london@portembassy.co.uk.
USA 2012 Massachusetts Avenue, NW, Washington
DC 20008 ☎ 202/328-8610, ⓔ embportwash
@mindspring.com. Plus consulates in New York,
Boston and San Francisco.

Gay and lesbian travellers

Though traditionally a conservative society,
Portugal has become increasingly tolerant
of homosexuality, at least in the cities and
in the Algarve. In more rural areas, however,
old prejudices are engrained and coming
out is still a problem for many. As there is no
mention of homosexuality in law, gays have
the same rights as heterosexuals by default
and the legal age of consent is 16. The best
contact is the Lisbon-based **Centro Comunitário Gay e Lésbico de Lisboa** (Rua de
São Lázaro 88 international ☎ 218 873 918,
Wed–Thurs 6–11pm, Fri & Sat 6pm–1am),
just north of Metro Martim Moniz. The
centre organizes events and can help with
information. It is run by ILGA whose comprehensive website (ⓦ www.ilga-portugal
.org) is in English and Portuguese. Another
good website is ⓦ www.portugalgay.pt.
The biggest scene is in Lisbon, which has a

number of gay bars and clubs, plus the gay-friendly *Anjo Azul* hotel (see p.89).

Health

Portugal poses few health problems for the visitor, and the worst that's likely to happen to you is that you might fall victim to an upset stomach.

As an EU country, Portugal has free reciprocal health agreements with other member states. EU citizens can simply show their **European Health Insurance Card** and passport at a health centre or hospital for treatment. The European Health Insurance Card replaced the old E111 form – to obtain one, enquire at a post office or check Ⓦ www.dh.gov.uk/travellers. Note, however, that you will need to pay for any treatment at any private hospital in Portugal.

No inoculations are required, though you'll want to make sure you're up to date with your **tetanus** jab. Tap water is generally safe to drink, although most visitors and indeed Portuguese prefer bottled water, especially in summer, and this is recommended if you have a sensitive stomach.

Otherwise, just use common sense: wash and peel fruit and vegetables, and avoid eating snacks that appear to have been sitting in display cabinets for too long. **Mosquitoes** can be a menace in the summer, especially in the Algarve, but – except for very rare and isolated cases – related illnesses are absent. Mosquito-repellent lotion and coils are widely sold in supermarkets and pharmacies. Take care to use a high-factor **sun cream** as the sun is extremely powerful.

For minor complaints go to a **farmácia** (pharmacy); most have a green neon cross outside. There's one in virtually every village and English is often spoken. Pharmacists are highly trained and can dispense drugs that would be prescription-only in Britain or North America. Generic drugs are widely available. Opening hours are usually Monday to Friday 9am to 1pm and 3 to 7pm, Saturday 9am to 1pm. Local papers carry information about 24-hour or nighttime pharmacies (*farmácias de serviço*) and the details are also posted on every pharmacy door. **Condoms** – *preservativos* – are widely available from street vending machines and in pharmacies

and supermarkets. In more rural places you may have to ask and the pharmacist will set out an array on the counter, in the best formal Portuguese manner.

In an **emergency**, dial ☏ 112 (free); the ambulance service (*ambulância*) is run by volunteers and is also free. A hospital is the first port of call; details are given in the "Listings" sections at the end of each major town or city account. Standards of care are perfectly adequate once you get past the waiting room, and cases are dealt with according to urgency. Basic **hospital treatment** is free for EU citizens, though you'll have to pay for X-rays, lab tests and the like. Contact details of English-speaking doctors can be obtained from British or American consular offices or, with luck, from the local tourist office or a major hotel; consultation fees average €20–30.

Insurance

Although EU health care privileges apply in Portugal, it's essential to take out a travel **insurance policy** before travelling to cover against loss, theft and illness or injury. Before paying for a new policy it's worth checking whether you're already covered: some all-risks home insurance policies may cover your possessions when overseas, and many private medical schemes include cover when abroad.

Even so, you still might want to contact a specialist travel insurance company, or consider the travel insurance deal we offer (see overleaf). A typical travel insurance policy usually provides cover for the loss of baggage, tickets and – up to a certain limit – cash or cheques, as well as cancellation or curtailment of your journey. Most of them exclude so-called dangerous sports unless an extra premium is paid: in Portugal this can mean scuba diving, windsurfing, trekking and kayaking. Many policies can be chopped and changed to exclude coverage you don't need – for example, sickness and accident benefits can often be excluded or included at will. If you do take medical coverage, ascertain whether benefits will be paid as treatment proceeds or only after you return home, and if there is a 24-hour medical emergency number. When securing baggage cover, make sure that the per-article limit – typically under £500/$750 and sometimes as little as £250/$400 – will cover your most valuable possession.

If you need to make a claim, you should keep receipts for medicines and medical treatment, and in the event you have anything stolen, you must obtain an official statement from the police (a *formulário de participação de roubo*); police stations are included in "Listings" throughout the guide.

Rough Guides has teamed up with Columbus Direct to offer you **travel insurance** that can be tailored to suit your needs. Products include a low-cost **backpacker** option for long stays; a **short break** option for city getaways; a typical **holiday package** option; and others. There are also annual **multi-trip** policies for those who travel regularly. Different sports and activities (trekking, skiing and so on) can be usually be covered if required.

See our website (Ⓦwww.roughguides insurance.com) for eligibility and purchasing options. Alternatively, UK residents should call ☎0870/033 9988; US citizens ☎1-800/749 4922; Australians ☎1-300 /669 999. All other nationalities ☎+44 870/890 2843.

Internet

Internet cafés can be found in the larger towns and resorts, most charging around €1.50–2.50 per hour. Nearly all of the larger post offices have Internet posts which you can access by credit card (around €3 per hour) or by buying a prepaid net card. Some turismos, municipal libraries (often in the town hall) and youth centres (*institutos da juventude*) offer half an hour's free access, while others make a charge. Wireless (wifi) access is increasingly available in bars, hotels and other public "hot-spots", though if you take your own laptop make sure you've got insurance cover and all the relevant adaptors for re-charging. See the guide for specific details of where to go to get online.

Portugal on the Internet

There's a lot of **information** about Portugal in English available on the Internet, and the websites listed below are a useful starting point, whether you want to find out local festival dates or the best wine vintages.

The country's newspapers all have their own websites too (see p.53), which, while in Portuguese, can be useful sources of information.

General sites

Ⓦ**www.algarvenet.com** A detailed site dedicated to the Algarve, covering everything from tourist sites to weather and shopping.

Ⓦ**www.bugbog.com** A "first point of call" website with a fine selection of images of Portugal (http://www.bugbog.com/gallery/portugal_pictures/portugal_pictures_door.html).

Ⓦ**www.maisturismo.pt** Search engine for hotels of all categories throughout Portugal, plus manor houses and other rural tourism choices.

Ⓦ**www.pai.pt** The Portuguese Yellow Pages. Telephone numbers can also be found through Ⓦwww.118.pt.

Ⓦ**www.portugal.org** The tourism site has a comprehensive, annually updated festival and events calendar as well as lists of other websites related to all things Portuguese.

Ⓦ**www.portugalvirtual.pt** Comprehensive directory of everything from hotels to shops, tourist sites and businesses.

Food and wine

Ⓦ**www.gastronomias.com** An encyclopedia of Portuguese gastronomy, with thousands of recipes organized by region, plus restaurant reviews and features on cheese and wine. Only some pages have English translations.

Ⓦ**www.infoportwine.com** An independent port wine site, with up-to-date practical advice and reviews for travelling along the Douro.

Ⓦ**www.ivp.pt** Everything you every wanted to known about port wine, from the official Instituto dos Vinhos do Douro e do Porto.

Ⓦ**www.vinhoverde.pt** The official site for *vinho verde*, with information (in Portuguese) about producers, labels, regional history and attractions.

Sport and leisure

Ⓦ**www.overpower.net** Website detailing windsurfing clubs and events.

Ⓦ**www.portugalgolf.pt** Provides a full rundown of all the country's golf courses.

Ⓦ**www.portuguesesoccer.com** Independent soccer magazine in English, with reports on games, fixtures and links to official club websites.

Ⓦ**www.sailing.org/sailingclubs/por.asp** The International Sailing Federation site has links to all Portugal's major sailing clubs.

ⓦ**www.surfingportugal.com** All the news and information (in Portuguese) you need for surfing in Portugal.

Culture

ⓦ**www.blitz.pt** Online Portuguese magazine on contemporary underground sounds, including interviews, concert reviews and music clips.
ⓦ**www.ipmuseus.pt** The Portuguese Museums Institute, with English version: info on over 100 museums, special events, and links to their websites.
ⓦ**www.ippar.pt** Instituto Português do Património Arquitectónico website (with English version) has lots on Portugal's historical buildings, including a calendar of events held in them.
ⓦ**www.min-cultura.pt** Ministry of Culture's site, with lists of events throughout the country including cinema, theatre, music and dance.
ⓦ**www.uc.pt/artes/6spp** Six centuries of Portuguese painting (in Portuguese only), with reproductions from most major artists' works.

Laundry

Small pensions don't really like you doing your **laundry** in your room, though as long as you're discrete you should be fine. Hotels generally have a laundry service, but it's usually pretty expensive. It's far better to take your clothes to the local *lavandaria* (there's at least one in every town), where you can get them washed, dried and even ironed at a very reasonable cost – you may have to come back the next day to pick them up. They usually charge by weight – a plastic-bag full of clothes shouldn't cost more than €7 or €8.

Living in Portugal

Most **EU citizens** who want to stay in Portugal, rather than just visit as a tourist, are not required to apply for a residence permit – their passport or ID is sufficient to allow them to stay indefinitely as employees, self-employed or students. However, you will need to register with various agencies if you are staying, to access health care etc, and will require a *numero de contribuinte* (social security number) to do just about anything else, from opening a bank account to settling an electricity bill. **Non-EU citizens** who want to extend their tourist stay must apply to the Serviço de Estrangeiros e Fronteiras (ask at the nearest police station or visit ⓦwww.sef .pt); to get a job, they must apply for a work permit before they enter Portugal. Wherever you are from, without a special skill you're unlikely to have much luck finding any kind of long-term **work**, especially without having mastered the language. Teaching English is a common route – there are language schools in every major town – and bar work might be a possibility on the Algarve.

Study and work programmes

AFS Intercultural Programs US ☎1-800/ AFS-INFO, Canada ☎1-800/361-7248 or 514/288-3282, UK ☎0113/242 6136, Australia ☎1300/131 736 or 02/9215 0077, NZ ☎0800/600 300 or 04/494 6020, international enquiries ☎+1-212/807-8686, ⓦwww.afs.org. Global UN-recognized organization running summer programmes to foster international understanding.
American Institute for Foreign Study ☎1-866/906-2437, ⓦwww.aifs.com. Language study and cultural immersion, as well as au pair and Camp America programs.

Mail

Post offices (*correios*) are normally open Monday to Friday 8.30am to 6pm, the smaller ones closing for lunch. Larger branches sometimes open on Saturday mornings, while the main Lisbon and Porto offices have longer hours. Offices are invariably understaffed, so you'll find it's quicker to buy stamps (*selos*) from coin-operated vending machines in streets or inside the offices, or from newsagents. Letters or cards should take three or four days to arrive at destinations in Europe, and seven to ten days elsewhere. *Correio azul* is the equivalent of airmail or first-class, and theoretically (but not always in practice) takes two or three days to Europe, five elsewhere.

You can have **poste restante** (general delivery) mail sent to you at any post office in the country. Letters should be marked "Poste Restante", and your name, ideally, should be written with your surname first, in capitals and underlined. To collect, you need to take along your passport – look for the counter marked *encomendas*. If you're expecting mail, ask the clerk to check for letters under your first name as well as surname. See also p.59 on having large items posted back to your home country.

Maps

Recommended are the waterproof and untearable Rough Guide Map: Portugal (1:350,000), Michelin's Portugal (1:400,000, #440), and Geo Centre's Euro Map Portugal and Galicia (1:300,000). Note, however, that on-going road building projects mean that many **maps** are quickly out of date. The big car hire companies in Portugal have an interest in keeping their maps as up to date as possible, though tend to be relatively small scale. Also in Portugal, the Portuguese National Tourist Office and the turismos in larger towns can also provide you with a reasonable map of the country (1:600,000), which is fine for everything except mountain roads. Similar maps and more detailed regional plans can be bought at most service stations in cities, larger towns and along major highways and at bookshops such as FNAC. Rough Guides also produces a map of Lisbon (marked with shops, bars, hotels and restaurants, local transport routes and the surrounding area). Michelin's Lisboa Planta Roteiro is the nearest to an A–Z of the city. For the Algarve, get a copy of the Rough Guide Map: The Algarve (1:100,000). For northern Portugal, the best is Turinta's North of Portugal map (1:250,000).

The Geocid website at ⊕http://geocid-snig .igeo.pt offers high-resolution satellite and aerial topographic images and innumerable maps of almost all of Portugal. For walking and hiking, the best maps are the 1:25,000 topographic plans belonging to the so-called "Série M888", produced by the Instituto Geográfico do Exército (⊕www.igeoe.pt). You can order them online from the Institute, or from shops in Portugal; see below. Just as useful are the institute's 1:50,000 "Série M782" plans. Sheets from either series cost €5.12.

Money

Portugal is one of the twelve European Union countries to use the **euro** (€). Euro notes are issued in denominations of 5, 10, 20, 50, 100, 200 and 500 euro, and coins in denominations of 1, 2, 5, 10, 20 and 50 cents and 1 and 2 euro. The coins feature a common EU design on one face but different country-specific designs on the other. No matter the design, all coins and notes can be used in the member states.

At the time of writing, the exchange rate was around €1.40 to £1 (€1=£0.71), or €0.78 to $1 (€1=$1.27). Up-to-the-minute rates are displayed at ⊕www.xe.com.

You'll find a **bank** (*banco*) or savings bank/building society (*caixa*) in all but the smallest towns. The major banks are Atlântico, Banco Espírito Santo, BPI, and Millennium (BCP); the main *caixa* is Caixa Geral de Depósitos. Standard opening hours are Monday to Friday 8.30am to 3pm, remaining open at lunchtimes when everything else is closed. In Lisbon and larger Algarve resorts, some banks may also open in the evening to change money, while others have installed automatic exchange machines for various currencies. Exchange bureaux (*câmbios*), which you'll find in Lisbon, Porto and the Algarve, tend to have longer working hours, closing on weekdays at around 6pm, and also open on Saturdays. Changing cash in banks is quick and easy, and shouldn't attract more than a €3 commission. However, it's unwise to carry all your money as cash, so consider the alternatives.

By far the easiest way to get money in Portugal is to use your bank debit card or credit card and a personal identification number (PIN) to withdraw cash from an **ATM** (known as a Multibanco). You'll find them in even the smallest towns, and also at petrol stations along major routes. Instructions are available in English, and the daily withdrawal limit depends on your bank or credit card company, usually €200 a day. The amounts withdrawn on debit cards are not liable to interest payments, though the transaction fee is usually at least £1, often more – your bank can advise on this. Currently only the Nationwide Building Society do not charge for this service. You'll also need to check with your domestic bank whether you can use your debit card directly in shops, etc, as not all systems are available in Portugal.

Credit cards can also be used over the counter, with MasterCard and Visa accepted just about everywhere, though as ever American Express is more restricted – we've noted hotels in the guide that don't accept plastic. Remember that all cash advances on credit cards are treated as loans, with interest accruing daily from the date of withdrawal; there may also be a transaction fee on top of this, typically around 2.75 per cent.

Travellers' cheques are not widely accepted, and can attract outrageous commission in banks (upwards of €13 per transaction). It might be worth considering them as a back-up if your plastic is lost, stolen or swallowed by an ATM, in which case be sure to keep the purchase agreement and a record of cheque serial numbers safe and separate from the cheques themselves. In the event that cheques are lost or stolen, most companies claim to replace them within 24 hours. The issuing company will expect you to report the loss immediately to the police, and to them.

You can also now load up traveller's cheques on prepaid cards; the Post Office and American Express also offer this service, along with some other companies. However you have to buy the cards (from around £10) and expect to pay cash withdrawal charges of around £1. Some companies also charge to load them in the first place, so they are not always good value.

Discounts and discount cards

A **Euro 26 card** (🅦www.euro26.org.uk, €13 for one year) is worth having for European residents under 26 – it'll get you free or reduced admission to many museums and sights, discounts on bus and train tickets (on distances over 90km), and reductions in numerous shops and restaurants, campsites and youth hostels, cinema tickets and some car rental. The card is available from USIT in Ireland (🅦www.usitnow.com), and in the UK from STA (🅦www.statravel.co.uk). The card is also sold in Portugal at post offices, youth hostels, and at branches of the Caixa Geral de Depósitos bank. Ask for a Cartão Jovem; you'll need a photo and your passport. Of much less use is an ISIC card (International Student Identity Card, 🅦www.isiccard.com), which is rarely accepted, even if you attempt an explanation in Portuguese.

Senior travellers in Portugal are also entitled to a range of benefits. Many sites and museums give generous discounts to over-65s and it is always worth showing your senior citizen's card or another form of ID when asking for tickets. On trains seniors get up to fifty-percent discounts if they ask for a *bilhete terceira idade*, and there's fifty-percent off a Bilhete Turístico rail pass (see p.33). Look out, too, for seasonal promotions for over-65s at the country's *pousadas* (see pp.41).

Opening hours and public holidays

Shops and businesses generally open from 9/9.30am until 12.30/1pm and 2.30/3pm until 6/7pm. Most also open on Saturday

Public holidays

January 1	New Year's Day (*Dia Um de Janeiro*)
Shrove Tuesday	February/March Carnival (*Carnaval*)
Good Friday	March/April (*Sexta Feira Santa*)
April 25	Liberty Day, commemorating the 1974 Revolution (*Vinte Cinco de Abril*)
May 1	Labour Day (*Dia do Trabalhador*)
Corpus Christi	End-May/early-June (*Corpo de Deus*)
June 10	Portugal Day (*Dia de Portugal*)
August 15	Feast of the Assumption (*Festa da Assunção*)
October 5	Republic Day (*Dia da Instauração da República*)
November 1	All Saints' Day (*Dia de Todos os Santos*)
December 1	Celebrating independence from Spain in 1640 (*Dia da Restauração*)
December 8	Immaculate Conception (*Imaculada Conceiçaõ*)
December 25	Christmas Day (*Natal*)

mornings, especially in towns and cities. Larger **shopping centres and malls** stay open seven days a week, often until 10pm.

Museums, churches and monuments usually open from 10am to 12.30pm and 2/2.30pm to 6pm, though the larger ones stay open through lunchtime. Almost all museums and monuments, however, are **closed** on Mondays (or Wednesdays for palaces), as well as on Christmas Day, New Year's Day, Good Friday and other public holidays. **Restaurants** tend to close one day a week, often Sunday or Monday.

On national **public holidays** (see list on p.70) almost everything is closed and transport services are much reduced (though tourist facilities – restaurants, tourist shops and the like – stay open). There are also endless local festivals and holidays when entire towns, cities and regions grind to a halt: for example June 13 in Lisbon and June 24 in Porto.

Phones

All **Portuguese phone numbers** have nine digits. Land lines start with a 2, mobiles with a 9. Numbers starting with 800 are free; 808 are local rate calls. To **call Portugal from abroad**, dial your international access number + 351 (country code) + 9-digit number. You can search for national phone numbers for free online at ⓦwww.118.pt; or call DQ (Directory Enquiries in English) on ☏760 506 070.

The cheapest way of making a call from a public telephone is with a **telephone card** (*carta telefónico*), available from post offices, newsagents, supermarkets and kiosks. The national operator is Portugal Telecom (ⓦwww.ptcom.pt), which issues its own cards for national and international use (various types and denominations, from

€5), though cards are also issued by several competitors. Locals often use the **phone cabins** found in post offices and in offices of Portugal Telecom, usually next door – tell the clerk where you want to call and pay afterwards. Most overseas phone companies provide **telephone charge cards**, allowing you to call from Portugal using a PIN number and have the bill charged to your home account or to a charge card. This might be convenient, but charges are higher than using a Portuguese phone card. Avoid making any calls from **hotel phones**, which always have very high charges. The **cheap rate** for national and international calls operates Monday to Friday 9pm to 9am, and all day weekends and holidays.

Portugal has one of the highest densities of **mobile phone** (*telemóvel*) use and ownership in the world. Most mobile phones bought in the UK and Ireland, Australia and New Zealand use GSM, which works in Portugal, though it's unlikely that a mobile bought for use in the US will work outside the States. Prices are coming down, but it's expensive to use your own mobile exclusively to make national and international calls in Portugal. You might be able simply to buy a replacement **SIM card** for your own phone, though this depends on the model, contract and service provider – Vodafone has shops all over Portugal, for example, including at Lisbon airport. Or, if you're coming for more than a couple of weeks, you could even **buy a phone** in Portugal – basic models cost as little as €30, with pay-as-you-talk tariffs running at around €0.30/minute.

Time

Portugal is in the same **time zone** as the UK, following GMT in winter. Clocks go forward

---

Useful telephone numbers

Calling home: international access code ☏00 + your country code + city/area code minus initial zero + number
Emergency services ☏112
International directory enquiries ☏177
International operator (for help with reverse-charge calls) ☏171
National directory enquiries ☏118
Time ☏12151
Weather forecast ☏12150

an hour at the end of March and back an hour at the end of October. If you're coming from France or Spain, turn your watch back one hour.

Toilets

Public toilets are neither numerous nor obvious, though a number of cities including Porto and Lisbon have installed French-style coin-operated automated toilets, usually in main squares. Cafés are handy in an emergency, though you'll have to order something first, and sometimes ask for the key (*por favor, a chave do banheiro*). The "facilities" at cheaper cafés and bars may leave you somewhat dazed. A sign reading *Sanita, Retretes, Banheiro, Lavábos* or *WC* will head you in the right direction, then it's *homens* or *cavalheiros* for men and *senhoras* or *mulheres* for women.

Tourist information

You can request a wide range of free brochures and maps from **ICEP Portugal** (the Portuguese trade and tourism agency) in your home country, or consult their website ⓦwww.portugal.org. Portugal's official tourism website ⓦwww.portugalinsite.com is another good place to start for basic country information.

In Portugal itself you'll find a **tourist office**, or turismo, in almost every town. Most are listed in the guide, with full opening hours and contact details. Note, however, that the official opening times are not always followed, particularly in more rural places where offices are short-staffed. At least one member of staff in each office will usually speak English in the main towns and resorts, though in out-of-the-way places this may not be the case – French may be an option. Some offices are extremely helpful and professional, others seem to treat your visit as an intrusion and will fob you off with whatever they think you want to hear. If you need specific information, persevere. They should be able to find help with a room (some will make bookings, others simply supply lists), and they often have useful local maps to supplement the ones in this book, leaflets that you won't find in the national offices and details of local events.

In addition, there's a national telephone enquiries service (☎808/781 212, Mon–Fri 8am–7pm), whose English-speaking operators give information about museums and their opening times, transport practicalities and timetables, hotels and restaurants (no prices given or bookings made), and hospitals and police stations, among other information. Calls are charged at local rates.

ICEP Portugal offices abroad

Canada 60 Bloor St West, Suite 1005, Toronto, Ontario M4W 3B8 ☎416/921-7376, ⓔicep .toronto@icep.pt.
Ireland 54 Dawson St, Dublin 2 ☎01/670 9133, brochure line ☎1800/943131, ⓔinfo@icep.ie.
UK Portuguese Embassy, 11 Belgrave Sq, London SW1 8PP ☎020/7201 6666, brochure line ☎0845/355 1212, ⓔtourism.london@icep.pt.
USA 590 Fifth Avenue, 4th Floor, New York, NY 10036-4702 ☎212/354 4403, ⓔtourism @portugal.org.

Guide

Guide

Lisbon and around

CHAPTER 1 # Highlights

* **Castelo de São Jorge**
Despite its bloody past, this makes a tranquil haven with dazzling views over the capital. See p.98

* **Alfama** Explore the city's oldest quarter, though be warned – getting lost here is half the fun. See p.99

* **Museu Nacional do Azulejo**
The splendid *azulejo* (tile) museum traces the history of this most Portuguese of art forms. See p.101

* **Bairro Alto** Don't miss a night out in Lisbon's "upper town", packed with vibrant bars, clubs and restaurants. See p.102

* **Mosteiro dos Jerónimos**
The magnificent Manueline monastery houses the tomb of Vasco da Gama. See p.111

* **Museu Gulbenkian** An awe-inspiring collection of priceless art and antiquities. See p.118

* **Antiga Confeitaria de Belém**
Enjoy a tasty custard tart in Belém's most traditional pastry shop-café. See p.125

* **Lux** Dance till dawn at one of Europe's coolest clubs. See p.132

* **Estádio da Luz** The country's finest sports arena, home of its most famous football club, Benfica. See p.140

* **Palácio National, Sintra** A splendid royal retreat in the summer residence of kings. See p.149

△ Castelo de São Jorge from the Baixa

Lisbon and around

There are few cityscapes as startling and eccentric as that of **Lisbon** (Lisboa). Built on a switchback of hills above the broad Tejo estuary, its quarters are linked by an amazing network of cobbled streets with outrageous gradients, up which crank trams and funiculars. Down by the river, the outstretched arms of a vast, Rio-like statue of Christ embrace one of the grandest of all suspension bridges and a fleet of cross-river ferries. For visitors, it's hard not to see the city as an urban funfair, a sense heightened by the brooding castle poised above the Alfama district's medieval, whitewashed streets, the fantasy Manueline architecture of Belém, the vibrant mosaics of the central Rossio square, and the adventurous contemporary architecture in the Parque das Nações. Gentler than any port or capital should expect to be, and defiantly human in pace and scale, Lisbon is immediately likeable.

For much of the last century, the city stood apart from the European mainstream, an isolation that ended abruptly with the 1974 Revolution and the subsequent integration into the European Community (now the European Union) just over a decade later. Over the past hundred years, central Lisbon's population has more than doubled to over a million, one tenth of all Portuguese, with numbers boosted considerably after the Revolution by the vast influx of **refugees** – *retornados* – from Portugal's former African colonies of Angola, Cabo Verde, São Tomé e Principe, Guinea-Bissau and Mozambique. The *retornados* imposed a heavy burden on an already strained economy, especially on housing, but their overall integration is one of the modern country's chief triumphs. Portuguese Brazilians and Africans have had a significant effect on the capital's culture, and alongside the traditional fado clubs of its Bairro Alto and Alfama quarters, Lisbon now has superb Latin and African bands and a panoply of international restaurants and bars.

The 1755 Great Earthquake destroyed many of Lisbon's most historic buildings. The Romanesque **Sé** (cathedral) and the Moorish walls of the **Castelo de São Jorge** are fine early survivors, however, and there is one building from Portugal's sixteenth-century Golden Age – the extraordinary **Mosteiro dos Jerónimos** at Belém – that is the equal of any in the country. Two major museums demand attention, too: the **Fundação Calouste Gulbenkian**, a combined museum and cultural complex with superb collections of ancient and modern art, and the **Museu Nacional de Arte Antiga**, which is effectively Portugal's national art gallery. The main contemporary highlight is the **Oceanário** (Europe's second-largest oceanarium) out at the **Parque das Nações** Expo site, and there are numerous smaller museums throughout the city too, but more than anything perhaps, it's the day-to-day

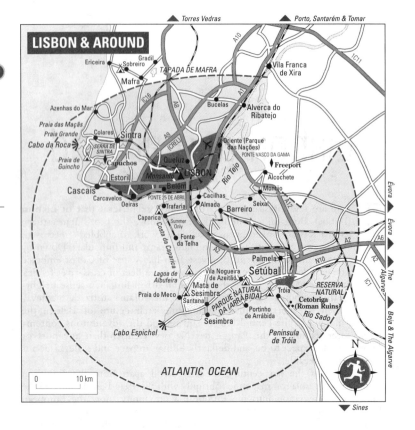

LISBON & AROUND

Torres Vedras

Porto, Santarém & Tomar

Ericeira
Gradil
Sobreiro
Mafra
TAPADA DE MAFRA
Vila Franca
de Xira

Azenhas do Mar
Bucelas
Alverca do
Ribatejo

Praia das Maçãs
Praia Grande
Colares
Sintra
Cabo da Roca
SERRA DE
SINTRA
Oriente (Parque
das Nações)
PONTE VASCO DA GAMA

Praia de
Guincho
Capuchos
Queluz
Rio Tejo
Freeport

Estoril
Monsanto
Belém
LISBON
Alcochete

Cascais
Carcavelos
Oeiras
PONTE 25 DE ABRIL
Cacilhas
Trafaria
Almada
Montijo

Caparica
Summer
Only
Barreiro
Seixal

Costa da Caparica
Fonte
da Telha

Palmela
N10

Lagoa de
Albufeira
Vila Nogueira
de Azeitão
Setúbal
RESERVA
NATURAL

Mata de
Sesimbra
Tróia
Cetobriga
(Roman Ruins)

Praia do Meco
Santana
PARQUE NATURAL
DA ARRÁBIDA
Rio Sado

Portinho
de Arrábida
Sesimbra

Cabo Espichel
Península
de Tróia

N

ATLANTIC OCEAN

0   10 km

Sines

Évora
Évora
The Algarve
Beja & The Algarve

life on display in the streets, avenues and squares that makes the city so enjoyable – from the shoe shiners of the Rossio to the multitude of Art Nouveau shops and cafés.

It would take a few days to do Lisbon justice, though it's better still to make the capital a base for a week or two's holiday, taking day trips and excursions out into the surrounding area. There's no need to rent a car; you can see almost everything by public transport. The beach suburbs of **Estoril** and **Cascais** are just half an hour's journey away to the west, while to the south, across the Tejo, are the miles of dunes along the **Costa da Caparica**. Slightly further south lies the port of **Setúbal**, featuring one of the earliest Manueline churches, and nearby is the resort of **Sesimbra** – a popular day trip for Lisboans. To the north is the Rococo **Palácio de Queluz** and its gardens, which you can see en route to **Sintra**, to the northwest, whose lush wooded heights and royal palaces make up Byron's "glorious Eden".

Lisbon

Physically, central **LISBON** is an eighteenth-century city: elegant, open to the sea and carefully planned. The description does not extend to its modern expanse, of course – there are suburbs here grim as any in Europe – but remains accurate within the old central boundary of a triangle of hills. This "lower town", the **Baixa**, was the product of a single phase of building, carried out in less than a decade by the dictatorial minister, the Marquês de Pombal, in the wake of the earthquake that destroyed much of central Lisbon in 1755.

The **Great Earthquake**, which was felt as far away as Jamaica, struck Lisbon at 9.30am on November 1 (All Saints' Day) 1755, when most of the city's population was at Mass. Within the space of ten minutes there had been three major tremors and the candles of a hundred church altars had started fires that raged throughout the capital. A vast tidal wave swept the seafront, where refugees were seeking shelter, and, in all, 40,000 of the 270,000 population died. The destruction of the city shocked the continent, prompting Voltaire, who wrote an account of it in his novel *Candide*, into an intense debate with Rousseau on the operation of providence. For Portugal, and for the capital, it was a disaster that in retrospect seemed to seal an age.

Before the earthquake, eighteenth-century Lisbon had been arguably the most active port in Europe. The city had been prosperous since Roman, perhaps even Phoenician, times. In the Middle Ages, as **Moorish** Lishbuna, it thrived on its wide links with the Arab world, while exploiting the rich territories of the Alentejo and Algarve to the south. The country's reconquest by the Christians in 1147 was an early and dubious triumph of the Crusades, its one positive aspect being the appearance of the first true Portuguese monarch **Afonso Henriques**. It was not until 1255, however, that Lisbon took over from Coimbra as the capital.

Over the following centuries Lisbon was twice at the forefront of European development and trade, on a scale that is hard to envisage today. The first phase came with the great **Portuguese discoveries** of the late fifteenth and sixteenth centuries, such as Vasco da Gama's opening of the sea route to India. The second was in the opening decades of the **eighteenth century**, when the colonized Brazil yielded both gold and diamonds. These phases were the great ages of Portuguese patronage. The sixteenth century was dominated by Dom Manuel I, under whom the flamboyant national architectural style known as **Manueline** (see box on p.214) developed. Lisbon takes its principal monuments – the tower and monastery at Belém – from this era. The eighteenth century, more extravagant but with less brilliant effect, gave centre stage to **Dom João V**, best known as the obsessive builder of Mafra, which he created in response to Philip II's El Escorial in Spain.

In the nineteenth and early twentieth centuries the city was more notable for its political upheavals – from the assassination of Carlos I in 1908 to the Revolution in 1974 – than for any architectural legacy, though the Art Nouveau movement made its mark on the capital. In the last two decades, however, Lisbon has once more echoed to the sounds of reconstruction on a scale not seen for two hundred years. The influx of EU cash for economic regeneration in the 1980s was followed by works associated with Lisbon's status as **European City of Culture** in 1994, its hosting of the **Expo** in 1998 and the **European Championships** of 2004. These events boosted the transport infrastructure,

80

LISBON

Parque da Bela Vista

Airport

Roma Metro

Campo Grande

Palácio Marquês de Fronteira

ACCOMMODATION

13ª da Sorte	M
Alegria	O
Amazónia	H
Avenida Alameda	E
Britania	I
Dom Carlos	G
Dom Sancho I	K
As Janelas Verdes	T
Lapa Palace	R
Lisboa Plaza	N
NH Liberdade	L
Miraparque	D
Portuense	P
Pousada de Juventude	B
Real Palácio	A
Ritz Four Seasons	F
Sana Classic Rex	C
Suíço Atlântico	Q
Veneza	J
York House	S

BARS & CLUBS

Armazém F	21
Estado Líquido	15
A Ginginha	12
Kapital	18
Kremlin	16
Lux	13

CAFÉS & RESTAURANTS

A Linha d'Água	3
Bela Ipanema	8
Bica do Sapato	17
Botequim do Rei	5
O Cantinho do Rato	7
Casanova	19
Centro de Arte Moderna	1
Coentrada	11
Deli Deluxe	20
Eleven	4
Os Tibetanos	10
Picanha	14
Portugália	6
Ribadouro	9
Versailles	2

Zoo

JARDIM ZOOLÓGICO (M)

Bus Station

Sete Rios Station

AV. DOS COMBATENTES

PRAÇA DE ESPANHA

Museu Gulbenkian

Centro de Arte Moderna S. SEBASTIÃO (M)

RUA DA BENEFICÊNCIA

AV. DE BERNA

Hospital

CAMPO PEQUENO (M)

ENTRECAMPOS (M)

Entrecampos Station

AVENIDA DA REPÚBLICA

Praça de Touros

CAMPO PEQUENO

Culturgest

R. DO ARCO DO CEGO

AREEIRO

AREEIRO (M)

AV. ALMIRANTE REIS

ALAMEDA (M)

ARROIOS (M)

PENHA DE FRANÇA

SALDANHA (M)

Museu Dr A. Gonçalves

PICOAS (M)

ESTEFÂNIA

PARQUE (M)

Pavilhão dos Desportos

Estufas

Parque Eduardo VII

Fundação

CAMPOLIDE

Aqueduto das Águas Livres

Amoreiras

RATO (M)

MARQUÊS DE POMBAL (ROTUNDA) (M)

AV. J. A. DE AGUIAR

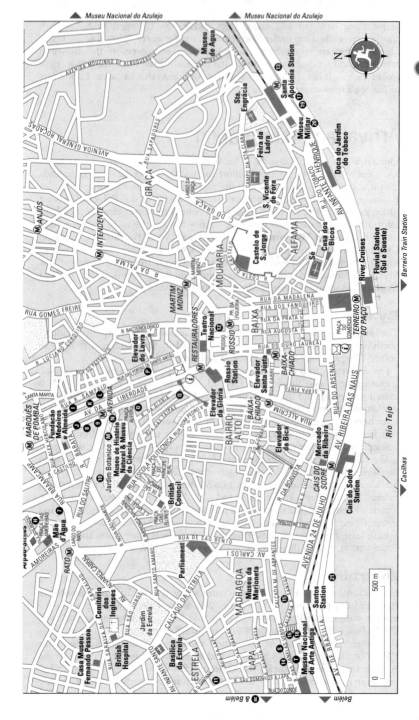

bequeathing new rail and metro lines and Europe's longest bridge – with another river crossing under construction to the north. The historic *bairros* (districts) and riverfront have also been given makeovers. If this non-stop rebuilding and renovation has somewhat diminished the erstwhile lost-in-time feel of the city, it has also injected a wave of optimism that has made Lisbon one of Europe's most exciting capitals.

Arrival and information

On arrival, the first place to head for is Rossio, the main square of the lower town, easily reached by public transport and with much of the city's accommodation within walking distance. On the western side of the adjoining Praça dos Restauradores is the main Portuguese tourist board in the **Palácio da Foz** (daily 9am–8pm; ☎213 463 314, ⓦwww.visitportugalinsite.com) – useful for information on destinations outside Lisbon – though the main Lisbon tourist office, the **Lisbon Welcome Centre**, is down by the riverfront in Praça do Comércio (daily 9am–8pm; ☎210 312 810/5, ⓦwww.visitlisboa.com) and can supply accommodation lists, bus timetables and maps. In summer, smaller "Ask Me" kiosks are dotted round town near the main tourist sights, such as on Rua Augusta and opposite Belém's Mosteiro dos Jerónimos.

By air

The **airport** (☎218 413 700, ⓦwww.ana-aeroporto.pt) is twenty minutes north of the city centre and has a tourist office (daily 8am–midnight; ☎218 450 660), ATMs, 24-hour exchange bureau and car rental agencies.

The easiest way into the centre is by **taxi** and, depending on traffic conditions, a journey to Rossio should cost €10–13. Note that you'll be charged €1.60 extra for baggage, and that fares are slightly higher between 10pm and 6am, at weekends and on public holidays. The tourist office at the airport also sells **taxi vouchers**, priced according to the zone or destination you are travelling to. The vouchers allow you to jump the queue for airport taxis and establish the cost beforehand, but otherwise they work out more expensive than normal rides.

Alternatively, catch the #91 **Aerobus** (every 20min, 7am–9pm; €3, free from the Welcome Desk for TAP passengers; ☎966 298 558), which departs from outside the terminal and runs to Praça do Marquês de Pombal, Praça dos Restauradores, Rossio, Praça do Comércio and Cais do Sodré train station. The ticket, which you buy from the driver, gives you one day's travel on the city's buses and trams. Cheaper **local buses** (#44 or #45, every 10–15min, 6am–midnight; €1.20) leave from outside the terminal to Praça dos Restauradores and Cais do Sodré station, though these are less convenient if you have a lot of luggage.

By train

International and most long-distance trains arrive at **Estação Santa Apolónia** (fares and timetable info on ☎808 208 208, ⓦwww.cp.pt), which is a fifteen-minute walk east of Praça do Comércio (and on the Gaivota metro line from 2007). Buses #9, #39, #46 or #90 run from **Santa Apolónia** to Praça dos Restauradores or Rossio. At the station there's a helpful information office (Wed–Sat 8am–1pm; ☎218 821 606) and an exchange bureau. Trains from the Algarve terminate at **Estação do Oriente** (☎800 201 820), 5km east of the centre at Parque das Nações, on the Oriente metro line, convenient for the airport and for the north or east of Lisbon. There are bus links to towns north and south of the Tejo from here and frequent services on to Santa Apolónia.

Local trains – from Sintra or Queluz – emerge right in the heart of the city at **Estação do Rossio** (☎213 433 747), a mock-Manueline complex with the train platforms an escalator-ride above street-level entrances, via **Sete Rios**, by the main bus station (see below). Services from Cascais and Estoril arrive at the other local station, **Cais do Sodré** (☎213 424 780), on the Caravela metro line – you can either walk the 500m east along the waterfront to Praça do Comércio or take any of the buses heading in that direction.

By bus

The main bus station is opposite the zoo at **Sete Rios** (metro Jardim Zoológico on the Gaivota line), 2.5km north of Rossio, which has an information office (6am–10pm ☎969 502 050) that can help with all bus arrival and departure details. You can usually buy tickets if you turn up half an hour or so in advance, though for the summer express services to the Algarve and Alentejo coast it's best to book a seat (through any travel agent) a day in advance. An increasing number of bus services also use the **Oriente** transport interchange at Parque das Nações on the Oriente metro line. See "Listings" for contact details for the other minor bus terminals.

By car

Driving into Lisbon can take years off your life, and if it's the beginning or end of a public holiday weekend, should be avoided at all costs. Heading to or from the south on these occasions, it can take over an hour just to cross the Ponte 25 de Abril, a notorious traffic bottleneck. **Parking** is also very difficult in the centre. Pay-and-display bays get snapped up quickly, and many unemployed people earn tips for guiding cars into available spaces (give a small tip – a euro should do it – to avoid finding any unpleasant scratches on your car when you return).

If you are driving, head straight for an official **car park**: central locations include the underground ones at Restauradores; Parque Eduardo VII; Parking Berna on Rua Marquês de Sá da Bandeira near the Gulbenkian; and the Amoreiras complex on Avenida Engenheiro Duarte Pacheco. Expect to pay around €8–10 per day. Wherever you park, do not leave valuables inside: the break-in rate is extremely high.

If you are **renting a car** on arrival for touring outside Lisbon, the best advice is to wait until the day you leave the city to pick it up; you really don't need your own transport to get around Lisbon. See "Listings" on p.39 for car rental companies and remember to leave plenty of time if returning your car to the airport: paperwork is time-consuming.

City transport and tours

Most places of interest are within easy walking distance of each other, though it's fun to use Lisbon's **public transport system** at some stage. As well as the tram, bus, *elevador* (funicular), ferry or metro, taxis are widely used and are among the cheapest in Europe. Although Lisbon ranks as one of the safer European cities it does have its share of pickpockets, so take special care of your belongings when using the metro and buses. If you want to see the city quickly, or just get a different view, consider taking a **tour** – we pick out the highlights below.

Public transport in the city is operated by **Carris** (☎213 613 078, ⓦwww .carris.pt). You can just buy a single **ticket** (*bilhete simples*) each time you ride, but it's much better value to buy one of the available **travel passes**. A **day pass** (*bilhete um dia*; €3.30) allows unlimited travel on buses, trams, *elevadores* and the metro until midnight of that day. For a **five-day pass** (*bilhete cinco dias*; €13) you will first need a *Sete Colinas Card* (Seven Hills Card; €0.50), which allows access to the electronic barriers on the metro. For longer stays, you will need a *Lisboa Viva Card* (€5), on which you can load a thirty-day pass (€25.50). Cards and passes are available at main metro stations, at kiosks next to the Elevador Santa Justa, and in Praça da Figueira, among other places.

If you're planning some intensive sightseeing, consider a **Cartão Lisboa** (Lisbon Card; €13.50 for one day, €23 for two, or €28 for three), which entitles you to unlimited rides on buses, trams, metro and *elevadores* and entry to around 25 museums, including the Gulbenkian and Museu de Arte Antiga, plus discounts of around 25 to 50 percent at other sights and attractions. It's available from all the main tourist offices, including the one in the airport.

The metro and local trains

Lisbon's **metro** – the Metropolitano – is the quickest way to reach outlying sights, including the Gulbenkian museum, the zoo, bus station and the Oceanarium. The most central metro stations are those at Restauradores, Rossio and Baixa-Chiado, all in Zone 1, and it is unlikely that you'll need to stray from the

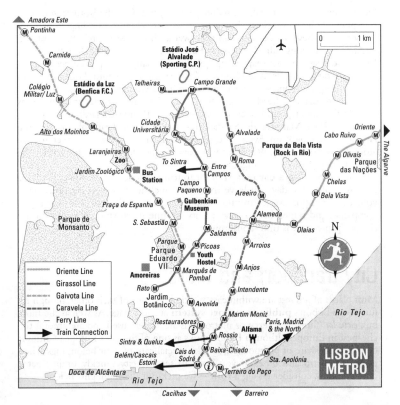

central zone. The **hours of operation** are daily from 6.30am to 1am and tickets cost €1.10 per journey (Zone 1), or €6.50 for a ten-ticket *caderneta* – sold at all stations. If you think you're going to use the metro a lot, buy a one-day pass as detailed above.

The local train line from **Cais do Sodré** station runs west along the coast to Belém (€1), or to Estoril and Cascais (€1.50 to either). Other local trains depart from the central **Rossio** station to Queluz (€1.10) and Sintra (€1.50 one way).

Trams, elevadores and buses

At the slightest excuse you should ride one of Lisbon's **trams** (*eléctricos*). Ascending some of the steepest gradients of any city in the world, the five tram routes are worth taking for the sheer pleasure of the ride alone. The best route is #28, which runs from Martim Moniz to Prazeres: try and get on at either terminal as the most interesting stretch – from São Vicente to the Estrela gardens via the Alfama and the Baixa – has become so popular that standing room only is the norm.

The three funicular railways and one street lift – each known as an **elevador** – offer quick access up to Lisbon's highest hills and the Bairro Alto (see box below for their routes). Otherwise, **buses** (*autocarros*) run just about everywhere in the Lisbon area, filling in the gaps to reach the more outlying attractions. Most trams, buses and *elevadores* run every ten to fifteen minutes throughout the day, from around 6.30am to midnight: stops are indicated by a sign marked *paragem*, which carries route details. Clubbers can take advantage of the *Madrugada* ("Dawn Service") **night buses**, which operate 12.30–5am. Most services run to and from Cais do Sodré station, and useful routes include the #201 (Belém via the docas) and the #208 (Parque das Nações).

Individual **tickets** (*bilhetes*, also known as BUCs, pronounced *books*) for buses, trams and *elevadores* can be bought on board (tram #15 has an automatic ticket

---

Tram and elevador routes

Trams

#12 runs from Praça da Figueira to Largo Martim Moniz via the Alfama.

#15 A modern "supertram" from Praça da Figueira to Algés via Belém; buy tickets in advance or take exact change for automatic ticket machines.

#18 from Rua da Alfândega via Praça do Comércio and Cais do Sodré to the Palácio da Ajuda.

#25 from Rua da Alfândega to Campo Ourique via Praça do Comércio, Cais do Sodré, Lapa and Estrela.

#28 from Largo Martim Moniz to Prazeres, via the Alfama, Baixa, Chiado, São Bento and Estrela.

Elevadores

Elevador da Bica: links Calçada do Coimbro in Barrio Alto to Rua da Boavista near Cais do Sodré station.

Elevador da Glória: links the Bairro Alto with the west side of Praça dos Restau-radores.

Elevador de Santa Justa: a lift, rather than a funicular, taking you from Rua do Ouro, on the west side of the Baixa, up to a walkway by the ruined Carmo church.

Elevador do Lavra: links Rua São José, just off Av da Liberdade, to the back of the Hospital de São José.

machine and does not issue change) and cost €1.20/€2.40 for zone 1/2. It's much cheaper to buy tickets in advance (either individually or in blocks of ten) from kiosks around the main bus terminals, such as in Praça do Comércio and Praça da Figueira. These cost €0.75 each and are valid for two journeys within a single travel zone or one journey across two travel zones. Punch the ticket in the machine next to the driver when you board. Travel passes (see p.84) are also valid on all buses, trams and *elevadores*.

Taxis

Lisbon's cream **taxis** are inexpensive, as long as your destination is within the city limits; there's a minimum charge of €2 and an average ride across town will cost around €8–10. Fares are higher from 10pm to 6am, at weekends and on public holidays. All taxis have meters, which should be switched on, and tips are not expected. Outside the rush hour taxis can be hailed quite easily in the street, or alternatively head for a **taxi rank**, found outside the stations, at Rossio, at the southern end of Avenida da Liberdade, and at Estação Fluvial – you can expect to queue during morning and evening rush hours. At night, your best bet is to ask a restaurant or bar to call a cab for you, or phone yourself (which entails an €0.80 extra charge): try Rádio Taxis ☎218 119 000, Autocoope ☎217 932 756 or Teletáxi ☎218 111 100.

Ferries

Ferries cross the Rio Tejo at various points, offering terrific views of Lisbon. The most useful and picturesque route is from **Cais do Sodré**, which runs passenger and car ferries to Cacilhas (every 5–10min, daily 5.30am–2.30am; €0.75). Another attractive route plies from **Belém** to Porto Brandão and Trafaria (every 30–60min, Mon–Sat 6.30am–11.30pm, Sun 7.30am–11.30pm; €0.75), from where you can catch buses to Caparica. Other commuter routes run from **Praça do Comércio** (Estação Fluvial) to Barreiro (for train connections to Palmela and the south; every 20–30min; €1.85) and to the satellite towns of Seixal and Montijo (every 30min; €1.65).

Tours

Public transport is good fun but can be crowded, so if you want more space or are pushed for time, it is worth considering one of the various organized tours of the city. The turismos have more information about any of the tours covered below.

Bus tours Carris (☎213 582 334, ⊚ www.carristur .pt) operates two open-top bus tours: the one-hour Circuito Tejo (hourly 9.15am–8.15pm; board-at-will day-ticket €14) takes passengers around Lisbon's principal sites, with clearly marked stops across the city; while the Olisipo tour (three departures daily; €14) departs from Pr do Comércio to Parque das Nações. Art Shuttle offers an upmarket minibus service which can take 2–8 people on three-hour city tours for €35 (May–Sept). Reservations on ☎800 250 251, ⊚ www.artshuttle.net.
River cruises Cruises up the Rio Tejo depart from Estação Fluvial (daily 11am & 3pm; 2hr; €20;

☎218 820 348). The price includes a drink and a bilingual commentary, with stops at Parque das Nações and Belém (tide permitting).
Tram tours Eléctrico das Colinas (Hills Tour; March–Oct hourly 9am–6pm; Nov–Feb departures at 11.30am, 2.30pm & 4.30pm; €17; ☎213 582 334) takes passengers on a ninety-minute ride in an antique tram from Praça do Comércio, around Alfama, Chiado and São Bento.
Walks Four themed two-hour guided walks are offered by Lisbon Walker (☎218 861 840, ⊚ www .lisbonwalker.com, €15), departing from outside café Martinho da Arcada (see p.127) at 10am and 5pm.

Accommodation

Hotel capacity has almost doubled since 1990 and Lisbon has no shortage of sumptuous places to stay, including historic buildings and palaces, along with numerous less exclusive options in and around the centre. Cheaper **guest houses** can be found on the streets parallel to Avenida da Liberdade, such as Rua das Portas de Santo Antão and Rua da Glória. The Baixa grid, including the more upmarket area of the Chaido, has a fair selection of places, too, though rooms in the Bairro Alto – handy for the nightlife – can be both hard to come by and noisy. The most atmospheric part of town, around the Alfama and the castle, has some very attractive choices, though prices here are higher. Many **hotels** are located outside the historic centre, particularly along Avenida da Liberdade, around Parque Eduardo VII and in the prosperous suburb of Lapa. Lisbon also has several **youth hostels**, including one right in the city centre and another out at the Parque das Nações, while the closest **campsite** is 6km west of the centre, with others sited close to regional beaches.

The airport information desk, or either of the tourist offices in town, will establish whether or not there's space at a city *pensão* or hotel. They won't reserve the room for you but will supply telephone numbers if you want to call yourself. Don't be unduly put off by some fairly insalubrious staircases, but do be aware that rooms facing onto the street can be unbearably noisy. Although air conditioning is standard in the better establishments, you'll have to rely on opening windows in cheaper places, which adds to the noise level. The humbler guest houses also often lack central heating, which can make them pretty chilly during the cool winter nights.

Between June and September, rooms can be hard to find without an **advance reservation** and prices are at their highest – though August can be less expensive as many people head for the beach. At peak times, be prepared to take anything vacant and look around the next day for somewhere better or cheaper. During the rest of the year you should have little difficulty finding a room, and can even try knocking the price down, especially if you're able to summon up a few good-natured phrases in Portuguese. Unless stated, all of the below include breakfast.

Baixa and Chiado

The following are marked on the Baixa and Chiado map on p.93.

Hotel Borges Rua Garrett 108 ☏213 461 951, ⓦwww.lisbonhotelborges.com A traditional three-star in a great position for Chiado's shops and cafés, though the rooms are very ordinary and the hotel often fills with tour groups. Also has triples. ❸

Hotel Duas Nações Rua da Vitória 41 ☏213 460 710, ⓦwww.duasnacoes.com. Classy, pleasantly faded, nineteenth-century hotel in the Baixa grid with a secure entrance and friendly reception.

Rooms, with or without bath, are simply furnished but comfortable and clean. ❸

Residencial Insulana Rua da Assunção 52 ☏213 427 625, ⓦwww.insulana.cjb.net On the top floor of an old Baixa building, above a series of shops, this decent *residencial* has smart en-suite rooms with satellite TV. The bar overlooks a quiet pedestrianized street. ❸

Hotel Lisboa Regency Chiado Rua Nova do Almada 114 ☏213 256 100, ⓦwww.regency-hotels-resorts.com. Stylish hotel designed by Álvaro Siza Viera – the architect responsible for

---

A room with a view (as long as you ask for one...)

Pensão Coimbra e Madrid, p.88
Hotel Lisboa Regency Chiado, p.87
Hotel Metrópole, p.88
Pensão Ninho das Águias, p.88

Solar dos Mouros, p.89
Hotel Príncipe Real, p.89
Pensão Londres, p.89

the Chiado redevelopment – with Eastern-inspired interior decor. The cheapest rooms lack much of a view, but the best ones have terraces with stunning castle vistas, a view you get from the bar terrace too. Rooms are not huge but are plush and contemporary. Limited parking available. ❻

Rossio, Restauradores and Praça da Figueira

The following are marked on the Baixa and Chiado map on p.93.

Hotel Avenida Palace Rua 1 de Dezembro ☎213 218 100, ⓦ www.hotel-avenida-palace.pt. Lisbon's grandest downtown hotel has an elegant nineteenth-century style with modern touches and very comfortable rooms sporting high ceilings, traditional furnishings and marble bathrooms. Artists Gilbert and George often stay here. ❽

Pensão Coimbra e Madrid Pr da Figueira 3-3° ☎213 424 808, ⓕ 213 423 264. Large, decently run (if faintly shabby) *pensão*, above the *Pastelaria Suiça*. Superb views of Rossio, Pr da Figueira and the castle from the street-honkingly noisy front-facing rooms. Others vary in attraction, so you might need to ask to see one or two before you make your choice. No credit cards or breakfast. ❶

Residencial Florescente Rua das Portas de Santo Antão 99 ☎213 426 609, ⓦ www .residencialflorescente.com. One of this pedestrianized street's best-value options, where many of the rooms are spick-and-span and come with TV, a/c and small bathroom. However, others are windowless and less appealing, and be prepared for street noise. Internet access on request. ❸

Residencial Gerês Calç da Garcia 6 ☎218 810 497, ⓦ www.pensaogeres.com. The beautifully tiled entrance hall sets the tone in one of the city's more characterful central guest houses, located on a steep side street just off the Rossio. The varying-sized rooms are simply furnished and all have TVs and showers. There's also internet access. No breakfast. ❸

Hotel Lisboa Tejo Rua dos Condes de Monsanto 2 ☎218 866 182, ⓦ www.evidenciahoteis.com. This historic Baixa townhouse has been given a superb makeover, and now combines bare brickwork with cutting edge design. Wood-floored rooms aren't huge but come with modems and mini bars, and downstairs is a boutiquey, Gaudí-inspired bar. ❺

Hotel Metrópole Rossio 30 ☎213 219 030, ⓦ www.almeidahotels.com. Very centrally located period hotel, with most of the comfortable rooms (as well as the airy lounge bar) offering superb views over Rossio and the castle. However, you pay for the location and the square can be pretty noisy at night. ❻

Hotel Portugal Rua João das Regras 4 ☎218 877 581, ⓦ www.hotelportugal.com. An amazing old hotel that has suffered from an appalling conversion; the high decorative ceilings upstairs have been chopped up under wall partitions. For all that, there are comfortable rooms, an ornate TV room and a fine *azulejo*-lined staircase. ❹

VIP Eden Pr dos Restauradores 18–24 ☎213 216 600, ⓦ www.viphotels.com; metro Restauradores. Compact studios and apartments sleeping up to four people, in the impressively converted Eden Theatre. Get a ninth-floor apartment with a balcony and you'll have the best views and be just below the rooftop pool and breakfast bar. All studios come with dishwashers, microwaves and satellite TV. Disabled access. ❺, larger apartments ❻

Alfama and Castelo

The following are marked on the Alfama and Castelo map on p.99.

Pensão Ninho das Águias Costa do Castelo 74 ☎218 854 070. Beautifully sited *pensão* in its own view-laden terrace garden on the street looping around the castle – this is one of the most popular budget options in Lisbon, so book well in advance. Climb up the staircase and past the bird cages. Rooms are bright but spartan, though avoid the dingy basement room. Those with private bath cost €5 more. No breakfast. ❷

Pensão São João de Praça Rua de São João de Praça 97-2° ☎218 862 591, ⓕ 218 881 378. Located immediately below the cathedral in a fine town house with street-facing balconies, this has bags of character even if it is slightly shabby. ❶, en-suite ❸

Sé Guest House Rua São João de Praça 97-1° ☎218 864 400, ⓕ 263 271 612. In the same building as the São João de Praça but more upmarket. Lots of bright African art, wooden floors throughout, bright, airy rooms with TVs and communal bathrooms, and friendly, English-speaking owners. ❹

Albergaria Senhora do Monte Calç do Monte 39 ☎218 866 002, ⓔ senhoradomonte@hotmail.com. Comfortable, modern hotel in a beautiful location, close to Largo da Graça, with views of the castle and Graça convent from its south-facing rooms – the more expensive rooms (❺) have terraces. Parking available or tram #28 passes close by. Breakfast served on a fine terrace. ❹

Solar do Castelo Rua das Cozinhas 2 ☎218 870 909, ⓦ www.heritage.pt. Boutique hotel in a historic eighteenth-century mansion abutting the castle walls on the site of the former palace kitchens, parts of which remain. Just fourteen bright, modern rooms cluster round a tranquil

Moorish courtyard, where breakfast is served in summer. **7**

Solar dos Mouros Rua do Milagre de Santo António 6 ☎218 854 940, ⊛www.solardosmouros.com. A tall, beautifully renovated town house done out in a contemporary style with its own bar. Each of the twelve rooms offers superb vistas of river or the castle and comes with CD player and a/c. There's plenty of modern art to enjoy if you tire of the view. **7**

Bairro Alto, Príncipe Real and around

The following are marked on the Bairro Alto map on pp.104–105.

Hotel Anjo Azul Rua Luz Soriano 75 ☎213 478 069, ⊛www.anjoazul.cb2web.com. This is the city's first exclusively gay hotel, in a blue-tiled eighteenth-century town house right in the heart of the nightlife. There are just twenty simple but attractive rooms, some with own bath and balconies. No breakfast but communal kitchen. **3**

🏃 **Hotel Bairro Alto** Pr Luís de Camões 8 ☎213 408 223, ⊛www.bairroaltohotel .com. Grand eighteenth-century building modernized into a fashionable boutique hotel. Rooms and communal areas still have a period feel – the lift takes a deep breath before rattling up its six floors – but modern flare appears in the form of DVDs in rooms, a rooftop café and swish split-level bar. **8**

Pensão Camões Trav do Poço da Cidade 38-1° ☎213 467 510, ☏213 464 048. In a great if noisy position, this small *residencial* has a mixed bag of rooms – some have a balcony, and the more expensive ones have a private bathroom. Breakfast provided April–Oct only. **2**

Casa de São Mamede Rua da Escola Politécnica 159 ☎213 963 166, ☏213 951 896. On a busy road, this superb seventeenth-century town house comes with period fittings, a bright breakfast room and even a grand stained-glass window. Rooms are rather ordinary but come with private bathroom and TV. **4**

Pensão Globo Rua do Teixeira 37 ☎213 462 279, ⊛www.pensaoglobo.com. Located in an attractive house with a bar/TV room, budget rooms are simple but clean and reasonably large (though those at the top are a little cramped; avoid those without windows). It's in a good location, near the clubs but in a quiet street. Best rooms have showers and views. No breakfast. **1**

Pensão Londres Rua Dom Pedro V 53 ☎213 462 203, ⊛www.pensaolondres.com. Great old building with high ceilings and pleasant enough rooms with satellite TV spread across four floors; the best ones have their own showers and fine city views. Also rooms sleeping 3/4. **3**

Pensão Luar Rua das Gavéas 101-1° ☎213 460 949, ⊛www.pensaoluar.com. Calm, polished interior and decently furnished rooms (with shower), though as this is the heart of the nightlife area, these can be somewhat noisy. Some are also much larger than others, so ask to see. **2**

Hotel Príncipe Real Rua da Alegria 53 ☎213 407 350, ⊛www.hotelprincipereal.com. Recently renovated, this small four-star sits on a quiet street just below the Bairro Alto. Just eighteen rooms, each with modern decor and some with balconies – best ones boast superb city views. Best of all is the top-floor suite with stunning vistas (**0**); other rooms **5**

Pensão Santa Catarina Rua Dr Luís de Almeida e Albuquerque 6 ☎213 466 106. In a quiet side street near the happening Miradouro de Santa Catarina, this simple little guest house has decent rooms and friendly owners. **2**

Lapa

To reach these hotels (marked on the general map of Lisbon on pp.80–81), take bus #40 or #60 or tram #25 from Pr do Comércio.

As Janelas Verdes Rua das Janelas Verdes 47 ☎213 218 200, ⊛www.heritage.pt. This discreet eighteenth-century town house is just metres from the Museu Nacional de Arte Antiga. There are well-proportioned rooms with marble-clad bathrooms, period furnishings, and a delightful walled garden with a small fountain where breakfast is served in summer. The top-floor library and terrace have stunning river views. **7**

Lapa Palace Hotel Rua do Pau de Bandeira 4 ☎213 949 494, ⊛www.lapapalace.com. A stunning nineteenth-century mansion in the heart of the Diplomatic Quarter, with lush gardens, health club and five-star facilities. Rooms – which cost around €430 a night – are luxurious, particularly within the Palace Wing, where the decor is themed from Classical to Art Deco. In summer, grills are served in the gardens by the pool. Disabled access. **9**

Residencial York House Rua das Janelas Verdes 32 ☎213 962 435, ⊛www.yorkhouselisboa.com. Installed in a seventeenth-century carmelite convent, rooms come with rugs, tiles and four-poster beds. The best are grouped around a beautiful interior courtyard, hidden from the street by high walls, where drinks and meals are served in summer. The highly rated restaurant is also open to non-residents. **6**

Alcântara

🏃 **Pestana Palace** Rua Jau 54 ☎213 615 600, ⊛www.pestana.com. See map on p.110. Set in an early twentieth-century palace full of priceless works of art, most of the spacious and contemporarily furnished rooms at this superb five-star hotel are in tasteful modern wings that stretch either side of luxuriant gardens. Prices start at about €430 a night. There are indoor and outdoor pools, a sushi bar, health club and restaurant. A superb buffet breakfast is served in the ballroom. ❾

Avenida da Liberdade and around

The following are marked on the map of Lisbon on p.80.

Residencial 13 da Sorte Rua do Salitre 13 ☏213 531 851, ⓦwww.trezedasorte .no.sapo.pt; metro Avenida. Translates as "Lucky 13", and it's certainly an attractive option in a good location. The en-suite rooms are spacious, well decorated, and have cable TV and fridges. No breakfast. ❸

Residencial Alegria Pr Alegria 12 ☏213 220 670, ⓦwww.alegrianet.com; metro Avenida. Great position, facing the leafy square, with spacious, spotless rooms with TVs, though front rooms can be noisy. ❸

Hotel Amazónia Trav Fábrica dos Pentes ☏213 877 006, ⓦwww.amazoniahotels.com. Spacious and modern three-star in a quiet part of town with a small outdoor pool. Top-floor rooms come with city views, some with balconies. All rooms have satellite TVs and minibars. There's a downstairs bar and restaurant, car parking and disabled access. Good value. ❺

Hotel Britania Rua Rodrigues Sampaio 17 ☏213 155 016, ⓦwww.heritage.pt. Designed in the 1940s by influential architect Cassiano Branco, this is a characterful Art Deco gem with huge airy rooms, each with traditional cork flooring and marble-clad bathrooms. The hotel interior, with library and bar, has been declared of national architectural importance. Breakfast charged as extra. ❻

Hotel Dom Carlos Parque Av Duque de Loulé 121 ☏213 512 590, ⓦwww.domcarloshoteis.com; metro Marquês de Pombal. Decent three-star hotel, with fair-sized rooms, all with bath, cable TV and minibar. There's also a downstairs bar with plasma TV screens. Garage parking. ❺

Residencial Dom Sancho I Av da Liberdade 202 ☏213 513 160, ⓦwww.dsancho.com; metro Avenida. One of the few inexpensive options right on the Avenida, set in a grand old mansion with high ceilings and decorative cornices – though the front rooms are noisy. The large en-suite rooms come with satellite TV and a/c. ❹

Hotel Lisboa Plaza Trav Salitre 7 ☏213 218 200, ⓦwww.heritage.pt; metro Avenida. Just off the Avenida, and in front of a theatre park, this bright,

polished, four-star hotel has marble bathrooms, bar, restaurant and botanical garden views from rear rooms. Limited disabled access. ❻

Hotel NH Liberdade Av da Liberdade 180B ☏213 514 060, ⓦwww.nh-hotels.com. Tucked into the back of the Tivoli Forum shopping centre, this Spanish chain hotel offers ten floors of modern flare. The best rooms have balconies facing the traditional Lisbon houses at the back. Unusually for central Lisbon, there's a rooftop pool. Also a bar and restaurant. ❻

Hotel Suíço Atlântico Rua da Glória 3 ☏213 461 713, ⓔh.suisso.atlantico@grupobarata.com; metro Restauradores. Tucked around the corner from the *elevador*, just off the Avenida, this provides standard mid-range accommodation. Rooms have showers, and some have a balcony overlooking the seedy Rua da Glória. The intriguing mock-baronial bar is the best bit. ❸

Pensão Portuense Rua das Portas de Santo Antão 151–153 ☏213 461 749, ⓦwww.pensaoportuense .com; metro Restauradores. Welcoming and good-value guest house just off the pedestrianized stretch. The rooms are all en-suite with TVs and a/c. ❸

Hotel Veneza Av da Liberdade 189 ☏213 522 618, ⓦwww.3Khoteis.com; metro Avenida. Built in 1886, the distinguishing feature of this former town house is an ornate staircase, now flanked by modern murals of Lisbon. The rest of the hotel is more ordinary, with standard en-suite rooms containing minibars and TVs. Parking. Breakfast charged as extra. ❹

Praça Marquês de Pombal and Saldanha

The following are marked on the map of Lisbon on pp.80–81.

Residencial Avenida Alameda Av Sidónio Pais 4 ☏213 532 186, ⓕ213 526 703; metro Parque or Marquês de Pombal. Very pleasant three-star *pensão* on a quiet side road, with air-con rooms, all with bath and park views. ❸

Miraparque Av Sidónio Pais 12 ☏213 524 286, ⓔmiraparque@esoterica.pt; metro Marquês de Pombal or Parque. An attractive building with a traditional feel overlooking Parque Eduardo VII. The reception can be a bit brusque, but there's a decent bar and restaurant, and all the spacious, if slightly old-fashioned, rooms come with TV. ❹

Hotel Real Palácio Rua Tomás Ribeiro 115 ☏213 199 500, ⓦwww.hoteisreal.com; metro Picoas or Parque. Though most of the rooms are in a bland modern extension, the best ones here are in the original seventeenth-century palace, with its own courtyard, now housing a café-bar. Five-star facilities include a health club and restaurant. ❼

Ritz Four Seasons Rua Rodrigo da Fonseca 88 ⏀213 811 400, ⓦwww.fourseasons.com; metro Marquês de Pombal. This vast modern building is one of the grandest and – at €340 a double – one of the most expensive hotels in Lisbon. Rooms are huge, with classy marble bathrooms, great beds and terraces overlooking the park, while public areas are replete with marble, antiques, old masters and overly attentive staff. There's also a fitness centre, spa, highly rated restaurant and internet facilities. Disabled access. Parking. ⑧

Sana Classic Rex Rua Castilho 169 ⏀213 882 161, ⓦwww.sanahotels.com; metro Marquês de Pombal. Smart hotel with in-house restaurant and small but well-equipped rooms, complete with TV, minibar and baths. The front rooms have large balconies overlooking Parque Eduardo VII. ⑥

Parque das Nações

Tryp Oriente Av Dom João II ⏀ 218 930 000, ⓦwww.tryporiente.solmelia.com; metro Oriente. This modern, four-star hotel is in an excellent location – three minutes by taxi from the airport or a short walk from Oriente station and the Parque's restaurants and bars. The rooms are comfortable, bright and spacious, many with sweeping views of the river Tagus and Ponte Vasco da Gama – better the higher up your room. Good off-season rates and special deals available. ④

Youth hostels

Lisboa Parque das Nações Rua de Moscavide 47–101, Parque das Nações ⏀218 920 890, ⓔliboaparque@movijovem.pt; metro Oriente. See Parque das Nações map on p.123. Five minutes walk northeast of Parque das Nações, towards the new bridge, this well-equipped modern youth hostel has eighteen four-bedded dorms and ten double rooms. There's also a pool table and disabled access. Dorms from €13, rooms ②

Pousada de Juventude da Almada Quinta do Bucelinho, Pragal, Almada ⏀212 943 491, ⓔalmada@movijovem.pt. On the south side of the Tejo – with terrific views back over Lisbon – this is not particularly convenient for sightseeing in the city (take a train from Entrecampos or Sete Rios to Pregal, the first stop after Ponte 25 de Abril), but is within striking distance of the Caparica beaches.

There are over twenty four-bedded dorms and thirteen twin rooms with their own loos, plus a games room, disabled access and internet facilities. Dorms from €16, rooms ②, apartments ③

Pousada de Juventude de Catalazete Estrada Marginal, Oeiras ⏀214 430 638, ⓔliboaparque @movijovem.pt. Set in an eighteenth-century sea fort overlooking the seapools in Oeiras, a beach suburb on the train line to Cascais – bus #44 from the airport passes. Reception open 8am to midnight. Four- or six-bedded dorms (€13) and simple twin rooms ① (or ② en-suite). Parking.

Pousada de Juventude de Lisboa Rua Andrade Corvo 46 ⏀213 532 696, ⓔlisboa@movijovem.pt; metro Picoas. See map on p.80. This is the main city hostel, set in a rambling old building, with a small bar (6pm–midnight) and canteen. Thirty rooms sleeping four or six (with shared bathrooms), or doubles with private shower rooms. There's also a TV room on the top floor, and breakfast is included in the price. Disabled access. Dorms €16, rooms ②.

Campsites

See p. 44 for details.

Parque Municipal de Campismo Estrada da Circunvalação, Parque Florestal de Monsanto ⏀217 623 100, ⑤217 623 105. The main city campsite – with disabled facilities, a swimming pool and shops – is 6km west of the city centre, in the expansive hilltop Parque de Monsanto. The entrance is on the park's west side. Bus #43 runs here from Pr da Figueira via Belém. Though the campsite is secure, take care in the park after dark.

Orbitur Costa de Caparica Av Afonso de Albuquerque, Quinta de Santo António, Monte de Caparica ⏀212 901 366, ⓦwww.orbitur.pt. In a good position a short, tree-shaded walk from the beach, this is one of the few campsites in Caparica open to non-members, but tents, caravans and bungalows are crammed in cheek by jowl. Facilities are good, including tennis courts and a mini market.

Orbitur Guincho N247, Lugar da Areia, Guincho ⏀214 870 450, ⓦwww.orbitur.pt. Attractive campsite set among pine trees close to Guincho beach, which is served by bus from Cascais. The site, with its own tennis courts, minimarket and café, also has bungalows and caravans for rent. Orbitur members get a ten-percent discount.

The City

Eighteenth-century prints show a pre-quake Lisbon of tremendous opulence, its skyline characterized by towers, palaces and convents. There are glimpses of this still – the old Moorish hillside of Alfama survived the destruction, as did

Belém – but it is the Marquês de Pombal's perfect Neoclassical grid that covers the centre, Europe's first great example of visionary urban planning. Giving orders, following the earthquake, to "Bury the dead, feed the living and close the ports", the king's minister followed his success in restoring order to the city with a complete rebuilding. The lower town, the **Baixa** – still the heart of the modern city – was rebuilt according to Pombal's strict ideals of simplicity and economy. In an imposing quarter of ramrod-straight thoroughfares, individual streets were assigned to each craft and trade, with the whole enterprise shaped by grand public buildings and spacious squares.

At the Baixa's southern end, opening onto the Rio Tejo, is the broad, arcaded **Praça do Comércio**, with its grand triumphal arch as well as ferry stations for crossing the river and tram terminus for Belém. At the Baixa's northern end – linked to the Praça do Comércio by almost any street you care to take – stands Praça Dom Pedro IV, popularly known as **Rossio**, the main square since medieval times and the only part of the rebuilt city to remain in its original place, slightly off-centre in the symmetrical design. Rossio merges with Praça da Figueira and Praça dos Restauradores and it is these squares, filled with cafés and lively with buskers, business people, and streetwise hawkers and dealers, which form the hub of Lisbon's daily activity. At night the focus shifts to the **Bairro Alto**, or upper town, high above and to the west of the Baixa, and best reached by funicular (the Elevador da Glória or Elevador da Bica) or by the great street elevator, the Elevador de Santa Justa. Between the two districts, halfway up the hill, is **Chiado**, Lisbon's most elegant shopping area. East of the Baixa, the landmark **Castelo de São Jorge** surmounts an even higher hill, with the **Alfama** district – the oldest, most fascinating part of the city with its winding lanes and anarchic stairways – sprawled below.

From Rossio, the main, palm-lined **Avenida da Liberdade** runs north to the city's central park, **Parque Eduardo VII**, beyond which spreads the rest of the modern city: the **Museu Gulbenkian** is to the north as is the zoo, bullring and the famous football stadia. No stay in Lisbon should neglect the futuristic oceanarium in the **Parque das Nações**, 5km to the east of the city centre, or the waterfront suburb of **Belém**, 6km to the west, which is dominated by one of the country's grandest monuments, the Mosteiro dos Jerónimos. En route to Belém lies Lisbon's other main museum, the **Museu de Arte Antiga**, close to the rejuvenated docks at **Alcântara**.

The Baixa

At the southern, waterfront end of the **Baixa** (pronounced *Bye-sha*), the **Praça do Comércio** was the climax to Pombal's design, surrounded by classical buildings and centred on an exuberant bronze of Dom José – the reigning monarch during the earthquake and the capital's rebuilding. The metro station (due to open 2007) is named **Terreiro do Paço**, after the royal palace (*paço*) that once stood on this spot – the original steps still lead up from the river. Ironically, Portugal's royals came to a sticky end in the square; in 1908, alongside what was then the Central Post Office, King Carlos I and his eldest son were shot and killed, clearing the way for the declaration of the Republic two years later. Nowadays the square is one of the city's main venues for New Year's Eve festivities.

At the western side of the square lies the **Lisbon Welcome Centre** (daily 9am–8pm), which acts as the tourist office as well as housing a café, internet centre, shops, restaurant and exhibition hall, all buried in a series of rooms between the square and neighbouring Rua do Arsenal, where there is another

Bairro Alto

Castelo

Alfama

Barreiro & River Cruises

Cais do Sodré

RESTAURADORES

Elevador da Glória

Palácio Foz

ABEP Cinema & Events Kiosk

TRAV. DE SANTO ANTÃO

JARDIM REGEDOR

RUA DE SANTO ANTÃO

MARTIM MONIZ

LARGO MARTIM MONIZ

R. F. E. FONSECA

R. DOM DUARTE

R. JOÃO DO OUTEIRO

R. DA MOURARIA

RUA DA PALMA

TRAV. DO ARCO DA GRAÇA

ARCO DA GRAÇA

RUA DA GRAÇA

Teatro Nacional Dona Maria II

LG. SÃO DOMINGOS

C. DE GARCIA

RUA B. QUEIROZ

RUA DA BETESGA

PR. DOM JOÃO DA CÂMARA

Rossio Station

São Domingos

R. DOM. DO ALEGRETE

R. DOM. DO ALEGRETE

Convento do Carmo

Elevador de Santa Justa

Rossio Station

LG. DUQUE CADAVAL

PRAÇA DOM PEDRO IV (ROSSIO)

ROSSIO

RUA DA PRATA

RUA 1 DE DEZEMBRO

C. DO CARMO

R. DA CONDESSA

TV. J. D. DEUS

RUA DO DUQUE

RUA DA OLIVEIRA

RUA NOVA DA TRINDADE

R. DA TRINDADE

LG. DO CARMO

LG. R. BORDALO PINHEIRO

TRAV. DO CARMO

R. SERPA PINTO

C. DO SACRAMENTO

PRAÇA DA FIGUEIRA

CHIADO

RUA GARRETT

Igreja dos Mártires

BAIXA-CHIADO

BAIXA-CHIADO

CALÇ. NOVA DE S. FRANCISCO

RUA IVENS

RUA CAPELO

R. ANCHIETA

RUA DO OURO (AUREA)

RUA DO CRUCIFIXO

RUA DA PRATA

RUA DA BETESGA

R. JOÃO DAS REGRAS

R. D. DUARTE

P. BORRATEM

R. DA MADALENA

RUA DOS CORREEIROS

RUA DOS DOURADORES

RUA DOS FANQUEIROS

RUA DA ASSUNÇÃO

RUA DOS SAPATEIROS

RUA AUGUSTA

RUA DA VITÓRIA

RUA DE S. NICOLAU

BAIXA

Teatro Nacional de São Carlos

Museu do Chiado

LARGO DA BIB. PÚBLICA

R. DES. FRANCISCO

RUA NOVA DO ALMADA

RUA DA CONCEIÇÃO

RUA DE SÃO JULIÃO

Câmara Municipal

RUA DO COMÉRCIO

Núcleo Arqueológico

R. DA PADARIA

R. DA MADALENA

R. DOS BACALHOEIROS

Santo António

Sé

Conceição Velha

RUA DA ALFÂNDEGA

R. DO V. MACHADO

RUA VITOR CORDON

RUA FERRAGIAL

RUA DO ARSENAL

PRAÇA DO MUNICÍPIO

Trams to Belém/Ajuda

Arco de Rua Augusta

Lisbon Welcome Centre

Statue of Dom José

PRAÇA DO COMÉRCIO

AV. DA RIBEIRA DAS NÁUS

AVENIDA INFANTE DOM HENRIQUE

TERREIRO DO PAÇO (2007)

Fluvial

Rio Tejo

R. DE SÃO MAMEDE

R. DO ALMADA

R. CORPO VELHO

RUA DAS PEDRAS NEGRAS

R. DE S. ANTÓNIO

Trams to Belém

CAFÉS & RESTAURANTS

A Berlenga	5
Bernard	15
Bom Jardim/ Rei dos Frangos	3
A Brasileira	14
Adega Santo Antão	2
Andorra	1
Associação Católica	18
Beira Gare	6
Casa do Alentejo	4
Celeiro	8
Confeitaria Nacional	11
João do Grão	12
Leão d'Ouro	7
Martinha da Arcada	17
Nicola	10
Suiça	9
Tão	16
Terreiro do Paço	19
Vertigo	13

ACCOMMODATION

Avenida Palace	D
Borges	J
Coimbra e Madrid	G
Duas Nações	L
Florescente	A
Gerês	C
Insulana	I
Lisboa Regency Chiado	K
Lisboa Tejo	H
Metrópole	F
Portugal	E
VIP Eden	B

0   100 m

THE BAIXA & CHIADO

△ Elevador de Santa Justa

entrance. North of Praça do Comércio, the largely pedestrianized Rua Augusta is marked by a huge arch, **Arco da Rua Augusta**, depicting statues of historical figures, including Pombal and Vasco da Gama. Beyond here you'll encounter buskers and street artists, banks and business offices, though this area was also the site of Lisbon's earliest settlement. Building work on the Banco Comercial Português at Rua dos Correeiros 9 revealed Roman fish-preserving tanks, a

Christian burial place and Moorish ceramics, which can be viewed from the tiny **Núcleo Arqueológico** (book in advance for visits, Thurs 3–5pm, Sat hourly 10am–noon & 3–5pm; free; ⊕213 211 700). Most exhibits can be viewed through glass floors or from cramped walkways during the thirty-minute tours.

Many of the streets in the Baixa grid take their names from traditional crafts and businesses once carried out here, such as Rua da Prata (Silversmiths' Street), Rua dos Sapateiros (Cobblers' Street), Rua do Ouro (Goldsmiths' Street, now better known as Rua Aurea) and Rua do Comércio (Commercial Street). Although the trades have largely disappeared, tiled Art Deco shopfronts and elaborately decorated *pastelarias* still survive here and there, while Rua da Conceição retains its shops selling beads and sequins.

At the western end of Rua de Santa Justa in the upper reaches of the Baixa, it's hard to avoid Raul Mésnier's **Elevador de Santa Justa** (daily 9am–9pm; ticket office above the entrance, €1.50), one of the city's most eccentric structures. Built in 1902 by a disciple of Eiffel, a giant lift whisks you 32m up the innards of a latticework metal tower before depositing you on a platform high above the Baixa. The exit at the top of the *elevador* – which leads out beside the Bairro Alto's Convento do Carmo – is below the rooftop café, which has great views over the city.

Rossio and Praça da Figueira

Rossio (officially Praça Dom Pedro IV) – at the northern end of the Baixa grid – is Lisbon's oldest square and, though shot through with traffic, remains the liveliest. The square itself is modest in appearance but its popular cafés are a good spot for tourists to find find their feet.

The square's single concession to grandeur is the **Teatro Nacional de Dona Maria II**, built along the north side in the 1840s. Here, prior to the earthquake, stood the Inquisitional Palace, in front of which public hangings, *autos-da-fé* (ritual burnings of heretics) and even bullfights used to take place. The nineteenth-century statue atop the central column is of Dom Pedro IV (after whom the square is officially named), though curiously it's a bargain adaptation: cast originally as Maximilian of Mexico, it just happened to be in Lisbon en route from France when news came through of Maximilian's assassination.

The **Igreja de São Domingos**, immediately to the east in Largo São Domingos, was where the Inquisition read out its sentences. It was gutted by a fire in the 1950s, but has now been fully restored. The road and square outside the church, at the bottom of Rua das Portas de Santo Antão, is a popular meeting place. The local African population hangs out on the street corner, while Lisbon's lowlife frequent the various **ginginha bars**, which specialize in lethal measures of cherry brandy. Resist the urge to eat the proffered cherry itself – they've been soaked in alcohol for years and provide a kick usually only available from expensive drugs. South, past the church, the street runs into **Praça da Figueira**, the square adjacent to Rossio. It contains some of the main city bus and tram stops and, like Rossio, is centred on a fountain and lined with shops.

The Sé and around

Lisbon's cathedral – the **Sé** (daily 9am–7pm; free) – stands stolidly on a slope overlooking the Baixa grid. Founded in 1150 to commemorate the city's reconquest from the Moors, it has a suitably fortress-like appearance, similar to that of Coimbra, and in fact occupies the site of the principal mosque of Moorish Lishbuna. Like so many of the country's cathedrals, it is Romanesque – and extraordinarily restrained in both size and decoration. The great rose window

△ Rossio, looking towards Convento do Carmo

and twin towers form a simple and effective facade, but inside there's nothing very exciting: the building was once splendidly embellished on the orders of Dom João V, but his Rococo whims were swept away by the earthquake and subsequent restorers. You need to buy tickets for admission to the Baroque **treasury** (Mon–Sat 10am–5pm; €2.50) with its small museum of treasures, including the relics of St Vincent, brought to Lisbon in 1173 by Afonso Henriques, having arrived in Portugal from Spain in a boat piloted by ravens. For centuries the descendants of these birds were shown to visitors but the last one died in 1978, despite receiving great care from the sacristan. Nevertheless, ravens are still one of the city's symbols. You can also access the thirteenth-century **cloister** (Mon–Sat 10am–6pm, Sun 2–6pm, €2.50). This is currently being heavily excavated, revealing the remains of a sixth-century Roman house and Moorish public buildings.

Opposite the Sé is the church of **Santo António** (daily 9am–7.30pm; free), said to have been built on the spot where the city's adopted patron saint was born. His life is chronicled in the neighbouring museum (Tues–Sat 10am–1pm & 2–6pm, Sun 10am–1pm; €1.20, free on Sun).

South to the river

Winding down south from the cathedral, towards the river, you'll find the church of **Conceição Velha** on Rua da Alfândega, severely damaged by the earthquake but still in possession of its flamboyant Manueline doorway. It's an early example of the style, hinting at the brilliance that later emerged at Belém. Five minutes walk further east, on Rua dos Bacalhoeiros, stands the curious **Casa dos Bicos** (Mon–Fri 9.30am–5.30pm; free), set with diamond-shaped stones. The building was built in 1523 for the son of the Viceroy of India, though only the facade of the original building survived the earthquake. It sees fairly regular use for cultural exhibitions; at other times, you can look round the remains of Roman fish preserving tanks and parts of Lisbon's old Moorish walls (demolished in the fifteenth century), which were excavated during renovation work in the 1980s.

On the riverfront just east of here, across the busy Avenida Infante Dom Henrique, lies the **Jardim do Tobaco** dockland development. Facing one of the broadest sections of the Tejo, there are fine views from the outdoor tables of its upmarket restaurants.

Up to the Castelo

From the Sé, Rua Augusto Rosa winds upward towards the castle, past sparse ruins of the **Teatro Romano** (57 AD), set behind a grille just off to the left at the junction of ruas de São Mamede and Saudade. The finds excavated from the site can be visited at the small adjacent **Museu do Teatro Romano** (entrance on Patio de Aljube; Tues–Sun 10am–1pm & 2–6pm; free), which has multimedia explanations about the theatre's history. Further up the hill you reach the **Igreja da Santa Luzia** and the adjacent **Miradouro da Santa Luzia**, from where there are fine views down to the river. Catch your breath here for the final push up to the castle, higher up the hill to the northeast. Signposts keep you on the right track as the roads wind confusingly ever higher.

Just beyond, at Largo das Portas do Sol 2, is the Fundação Espírito Santo Silva, home of the **Museu Escola de Artes Decorativas** (Ⓦ www.fress.pt; Mon–Sat 10am–5pm; €5), a seventeenth-century mansion stuffed with what was once the private collection of banker Ricardo do Espírito Santo Silva, who offered it to the nation in 1953. On display are some of the best examples of seventeenth- and eighteenth-century applied art in the country. Highlights include a stunning sixteenth-century tapestry depicting a parade of giraffes, beautiful carpets from Arraiolos in the Alentejo, and oriental quilts that were all the rage in the seventeenth century. The museum also has a courtyard café.

Over the road from the **terrace-café** in Largo das Portas do Sol, the views are tremendous – a solitary palm rising from the stepped streets below, the twin-towered facade of Graça convent, the dome of Santa Engrácia, and the Tejo beyond. **Tram** #28 runs from Rua da Conceição in the Baixa, past the Sé and Santa Luzia, to Largo das Portas do Sol. Coming from Rossio, **bus** #37 from Praça da Figueira follows a similar route, cutting off at Santa Luzia and climbing to one of the castle entrances.

The siege of Lisbon

A small statue of Afonso Henriques, triumphant after the siege of Lisbon, stands at the main entrance to the Castelo de São Jorge. It was an important victory and led to the Muslim surrender at Sintra. It was not, however, the most Christian or glorious of Portuguese exploits. A full account of the siege survives, written by one Osbern of Bawdsley, an English priest and Crusader, and its details, despite the author's judgemental tone, direct one's sympathies to the enemy.

The attack, in the summer of 1147, came through the opportunism and skilful management of Afonso Henriques, already established as "King" at Porto, who persuaded a large force of French and British Crusaders to delay their progress to Jerusalem for more immediate and lucrative rewards. The Crusaders – scarcely more than pirates – came to terms and in June the siege began. Osbern records the Archbishop of Braga's demand for the Moors to return to "the land whence you came" and, more revealingly, the weary and contemptuous response of the Muslim spokesman: "How many times have you come hither with pilgrims and barbarians to drive us hence? It is not want of possessions but only ambition of the mind that drives you on."

For seventeen weeks the castle and inner city stood firm but in October its walls were breached and the citizens – including a Christian community coexisting with the Muslims – were forced to surrender. The pilgrims and barbarians, flaunting the diplomacy and guarantees of Afonso Henriques, stormed into the city, cut the throat of the local bishop and sacked, pillaged and murdered Christian and Muslim alike. In 1190 a later band of English Crusaders stopped at Lisbon and, no doubt confused by the continuing presence of Moors who had stayed on as New Christians, sacked the city a second time.

Castelo de São Jorge

The impressively sited **Castelo** (daily: March–Oct 9am–9pm; Nov–Feb 9am–6pm; €3) is perhaps Lisbon's most splendid monument, an enjoyable place to spend a couple of hours, wandering amid the ramparts looking down upon the city. Beyond the main gates stretch gardens and terraces, walkways, fountains and peacocks, all lying within heavily restored Moorish walls. At first the Portuguese kings took up residence within the castle – in the *Alcáçova*, the Muslim palace – but by the time of Manuel I this had been superseded by the new royal palace on Terreiro do Paço. Of the *Alcáçova* only a much-restored shell remains. This now houses **Olisipónia** (daily 10am–1pm & 2–5.30pm), a multimedia exhibition detailing the history of the city. Portable headsets deliver a 35-minute commentary presenting aspects of Lisbon's development through film, sound and image, and while it glosses over some of the less savoury chapters of the past – such as slavery and the Inquisition – it's a useful introduction to the city. Built into the ramparts, the Tower of Ulysses contains a **Câmara Escura** (March–Oct 10am–1pm & 2–5.30pm, every 30min), a periscope focusing on sights round the city with English commentary – though the views are almost as good from the neighbouring towers.

Outside the castle complex but still within the castle's outer walls is the tiny medieval quarter of **Santa Cruz**, still very much a village in itself, with its own church, school and bathhouse. Just below the castle to the north and west sprawls the old **Mouraria** quarter, to which the Moors were relegated on their loss of the town. North of the castle, meanwhile, Calçada da Graça leads up to the Graça district and the **Miradouro da Graça**, which offers stunning views across the city.

Alfama

The oldest part of Lisbon, stumbling from the walls of the castle down to the Rio Tejo, **Alfama** was buttressed against significant damage in the 1755 earthquake by the steep, rocky mass on which it is built. Although none of its houses dates from before the Christian conquest, many are of Moorish design and the kasbah-like layout is still much as Osbern the Crusader described it, with "steep defiles instead of ordinary streets … and buildings so closely packed together that, except in the merchants' quarter, hardly a street could be found more than eight foot wide". In Arab-occupied times Alfama was the grandest part of the city, and

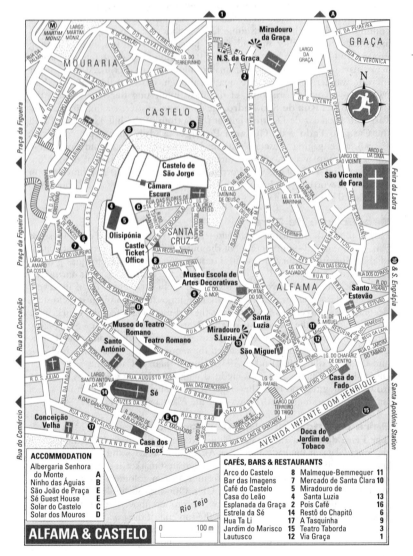

ALFAMA & CASTELO

0   100 m

continued to be so after the Christian reconquest, but following subsequent earthquakes the new Christian nobility moved out, leaving it to the local fishing community. Today, although an increasing number of tourist-orientated fado restaurants is in evidence, the quarter retains a largely traditional life of its own: you can eat at local prices in the cafés, the flea market (see below) engulfs the periphery of the area twice a week, and this is very much the place to be during the June "Popular Saints" festivals (above all on June 12), when makeshift cafés and stalls appear on every corner and there's music and partying until daybreak.

Ruas de São Miguel and São Pedro

The alleys and passageways are known as **becos** and **travessas** rather than **ruas**, and it would be impossible (as well as futile) to try and follow any set route. Life continues here much as it has done for years: kids playing ball in tiny squares and chasing each other up and down precipitous staircases; people buying groceries and fish from hole-in-the-wall stores; householders stringing washing across narrow defiles and stoking small outdoor charcoal grills. At some point in your wanderings around the quarter, though, head for the **Rua de São Miguel** – off which are some of the most interesting **becos** – and for the (lower) parallel **Rua de São Pedro**, the main market street leading to the lively Largo do Chafariz de Dentro, right at the bottom of the hill. Here you'll find the **Casa do Fado e da Guitarra Portuguesa** (daily 10am–1pm & 2–6pm; €2.50), an engaging museum outlining the history of fado and Portuguese guitar by way of wax models, pictures, sounds and descriptions of the leading characters and styles of this very Portuguese music. It's an excellent introduction to fado and worth seeing before you visit a fado house. There's also a good shop for fado CDs and a small café.

São Vicente de Fora

East of the castle, the name of the church of **São Vicente de Fora** (Tues–Sat 9am–12 noon & 3–6pm; free) – "of the outside" – is a reminder of the extent of the sixteenth-century city walls. Located where Afonso Henriques pitched camp during his siege and conquest of Lisbon, the church was built during the years of Spanish rule by Philip II's Italian architect, Felipe Terzi, its severe geometric facade an important Renaissance innovation. Through the cloisters, decorated with **azulejos**, you can visit the old monastic refectory, which since 1855 has formed the **pantheon of the Bragança dynasty** (Tues–Sun 10am–6pm; €4). Here, in more or less complete sequence, are the bodies of all Portuguese kings from João IV, who restored the monarchy, to Manuel II, who lost it and died in exile in England in 1932. Among them is Catherine of Bragança, the widow of Charles II who is credited with introducing teatime to the Brits. You can enjoy tea and other beverages at the monastery café, which has a roof terrace commanding superb views over the Alfama and the Tagus.

Feira da Ladra and Santa Engrácia

The **Feira da Ladra**, Lisbon's rambling and ragged flea market, fills the Campo de Santa Clara, at the eastern edge of Alfama on Tuesdays and Saturdays (9am–3pm). Though it's certainly not the world's greatest market, it does turn up some interesting things: oddities from the former African colonies, old prints of the country, and inexpensive clothes and CDs. Out-and-out junk – broken alarm clocks and old postcards – is spread on the ground above the church of Santa Engrácia, and half-genuine antiques at the top end of the *feira*. To get here, tram #28 runs from Rua da Conceição in the Baixa to São Vicente (see above), and bus #12 runs between Santa Apolónia station and Praça Marquês de Pombal.

While at the flea market, take a look inside **Santa Engrácia** (Tues–Sun: May–Oct 10am–6pm; Nov–April 10am–5pm; €2, free Sun 10am–2pm), the loftiest and most tortuously built church in the city. Begun in 1682 and once a synonym for unfinished work, its vast dome was finally completed in 1966. Since 1916, the church has been the **Panteão Nacional** housing the tombs of eminent Portuguese figures, including former presidents, the writer Almeida Garrett and Amália Rodrigues, Portugal's most famous fado singer. You can go up to the terrace and look down on the empty church and out over the flea market, port and city.

Museu Nacional do Azulejo

About 1.5km east of Santa Apolónia station on Rua da Madre de Deus is the **Museu Nacional do Azulejo** (Tues 2–6pm, Wed–Sun 10am–6pm; €3, free on Sun 10am–2pm), one of the most appealing of Lisbon's small museums. Installed in the church and cloisters of Madre de Deus, a former convent dating from 1509, the museum traces the development of tile-making from Moorish days to the present. This is a fascinating story (see feature on p.116) and the museum contains a hugely impressive collection of **azulejos** covering the main styles of tile from the fifteenth century to the present day. The church itself has a Baroque interior, installed after the earthquake of 1755, and it still retains striking eighteenth-century tiled scenes of the life of St Anthony. But most of the museum is set around the church cloisters, which house many more delights, including Portugal's longest *azulejo* – a wonderfully detailed 36-metre panorama of Lisbon, completed in around 1738 – and fascinating examples of the large *azulejo* panels known as **tapetes** (carpets).

Don't miss out on the opportunity of a drink in the lovely garden **café** at the museum. You can come here directly by bus: #104 from Praça do Comércio or #105 from Praça da Figueira.

Chiado

On the west side of the Baixa, stretching up the hillside towards the Bairro Alto, the area known as **Chiado** – the *nom de plume* of the poet António Ribeiro and pronounced *she-ah-doo* – suffered great damage from a fire that swept across the Baixa in August 1988. Many old shops in Rua do Crucifixo were destroyed, but following restoration their soaring new marble facades consciously mimic the originals.

Chiado remains one of the city's most affluent quarters, focused on the fashionable shops and old café-tearooms of the Rua Garrett. Of these, **A Brasileira**, Rua Garrett 120, is the most famous, having been frequented by generations of Lisbon's literary and intellectual leaders. The street's **Igreja dos Mártires** (Church of the Martyrs) occupies the site of the Crusader camp during the Siege of Lisbon. The church was later built on the site of a burial ground created for the English contingent of the besieging army. Music recitals are often held in the church; check the local press for details.

Just beyond, Rua Serpa Pinto veers downhill past the Teatro Nacional de São Carlos (the main opera house) to the **Museu do Chiado** (Ⓦwww.museudochiado-ipmuseus.pt, Tues–Sun 10am–6pm; €3, free on Sun until 2pm). In a stylish building, this incorporates the former Museum of Contemporary Art, whose original home was damaged in the Chiado fire. The new museum was constructed around a nineteenth-century biscuit factory, which explains the presence of the old ovens. The three floors display the work of some of Portugal's most influential artists since the nineteenth century. Highlights include the beautiful sculpture *A Viúva* (The Widow) by António

Teixeira Lopes and some evocative scenes of the Lisbon area by Carlos Botelho and José Malhoa. Look out also for the wonderful decorative panels by José de Almada Negreiros, recovered from the San Carlos cinema.

Around Cais do Sodré

A ten-minute walk west of the Baixa grid, along the riverfront or the parallel **Rua do Arsenal** (a road packed with shops selling dried cod, cheap wine, port and brandy) is **Cais do Sodré** station and metro, from where trains run out to Estoril and Cascais, and ferries cross to Cacilhas. It's not the most elegant of areas, but it's certainly full of character.

The **Mercado da Ribeira** (market Mon–Sat 6am–2pm) is located in the domed building on Avenida 24 de Julho, just opposite Cais do Sodré. This is Lisbon's main market, featuring an array of local characters selling fish and meat of all shapes and sizes, alongside tables full of fruit and vegetables. The upper level serves as a centre for regional arts and gastronomy and, though squarely aimed at tourists, the **Loja de Artesenato** (Sun–Thurs 10am–7pm, Fri & Sat 10am–10pm) specializes in art and crafts from Lisbon and the Tejo valley. The upper level also hosts exhibitions and live music at weekends (Fri & Sat 10pm–1am), from jazz to folk, and also has a fine restaurant (see p.129).

A short walk behind the market is the precipitous **Elevador da Bica** (entrance on Rua de São Paulo; Mon–Sat 7am–9pm, Sun 9am–9pm; €1.20), a funicular railway leading up to the foot of the Bairro Alto. Take a left at the top and then the second left down Rua M. Saldanha and you'll reach the **Miradouro de Santa Catarina**, where young buskers gather for the spectacular views over the city next to a handy drinks kiosk with outdoor tables.

Bairro Alto

By day, the narrow seventeenth-century streets of the upper town, or **Bairro Alto** – high above the central city, to the west of the Baixa – have a quiet, residential feel, with children playing and the elderly sitting in doorways. Two of the city's most interesting churches – the Convento do Carmo and Igreja de São Roque – are located on the fringes, as are some of the city's most bohemian boutiques, making the quarter well worth a morning or afternoon's exploration. At night, its character changes entirely, as it's here that you'll find many of the city's best bars, restaurants and fado clubs. Many of the Bairro Alto's most interesting thoroughfares lie west of Rua da Misericórdia, a confusing network of cobbled streets, whose buildings are often liberally defaced with grafitti. Traffic is restricted to residents only, and though dodgy characters offering hash still lurk on the corners round the market building on Rua da Atalaia, it's essentially safe at any time if you keep valuables out of sight.

You can approach the Bairro Alto on two amazing feats of engineering in the form of its funicular-like trams, originally powered by water displacement, and then by steam, until electricity was introduced. Most conveniently, the **Elevador da Glória** (daily 8am–midnight; €1.20), built in 1885, links the quarter directly with Praça dos Restauradores, departing from just behind the Palácio da Foz tourist office. The **Elevador da Bica** (see "Around Cais do Sodré" above) climbs up to Rua Loreto at the foot of the Bairro Alto. A third approach, by the **Elevador de Santa Justa** (see p.95), has its exit at the side of the Convento do Carmo.

From the Elevador da Glória to São Roque

The Elevador da Glória drops you at the top of the hill on Rua de São Pedro de Alcântara, from whose adjacent gardens there's a superb view across the city

Eça de Queirós

Halfway down the Rua do Alecrim, in the Bairro Alto, stands a bizarre statue of a frock-coated, moustachioed man who looks down with a rather bemused expression at the half-naked woman sprawled in his arms. The man is **Eça de Queirós** (1845–1900), who in a series of outstanding novels turned his unflinching gaze on the shortcomings of his native land; the woman is presumably Truth – the quality for which his work was most often praised during his lifetime.

While Eça's earliest novels, like *The Sin of Father Amaro* (1875 – recently modernized and made into an acclaimed Mexican film) and *Cousin Bazilio* (1878), reveal a clear debt to French naturalism in their satirical intent, his mature writings offer a more measured critique of contemporary Portuguese society. Novels like *The Illustrious House of Ramires* (1900) work by gradually building up a picture of decadence and inertia, through an assemblage of acutely observed vignettes tinged with a sardonic but always affectionate humour.

Eça's cosmopolitan outlook was a result of both his background and of the fact that he was extremely well travelled. Born out of wedlock, he was brought up by his paternal grandparents in the north of Portugal in an atmosphere of Liberal political ideas. At Coimbra University, where he studied law, he was part of a group of young intellectuals (known as the "Generation of 1870") dedicated to the idea of reforming and modernizing the country. His adult years were spent as a career diplomat and for much of the 1870s and 1880s he was in England, first as consul in Newcastle upon Tyne and then in Bristol.

Oddly enough, it was at Newcastle that Eça wrote much of his masterpiece, *The Maias* (1888), a complex portrayal of an aristocratic, land-owning family unable, or unwilling, to adapt to changing times. Focusing on three generations of male family members, Eça brilliantly conveys what he sees as a peculiarly Portuguese indolence and hedonism that inevitably acts as curb to good intentions – a condition that becomes a metaphor for the country's inwardness and lack of ambition.

The Maias – written while the author was staying in what is now the hotel *As Janelas Verdes* (see p.89) – is the Lisbon novel *par excellence*, conjuring up an extraordinarily powerful sense of place. The essential charm of the city is beautifully conveyed – whether the bustle of the Chiado, or the faded grandeur of the São Carlos Opera House (all places that have changed little over the last hundred years). Best of all is a description of a seemingly carefree day trip to Sintra, in which a mundane errand and a romantic assignation are poignantly interwoven in a way that reveals Eça at his subtle best.

---

to the castle. Immediately across the road is the **Solar do Vinho do Porto** (Port Wine Institute), a good place to stop and taste Portugal's finest tipple (see p.133), while a turn to the left from the *elevador* takes you downhill and round the corner to the **Igreja de São Roque** (daily 8.30am–5pm; free), in Largo Trindade Coelho. From the outside, this looks like the plainest church in the city, its bleak Renaissance facade (by Filipo Terzi, architect of São Vicente) having been further simplified by the earthquake. Nor does it seem impressive when you walk inside until you look at the succession of side chapels, each lavishly crafted with *azulejos* (some emulating reliefs), multicoloured marble, or Baroque painted ceilings.

However, the highlight of a visit is the **Capela de São João Baptista**. It was one of the most bizarre commissions of its age and, for its size, is estimated to be the most expensive chapel ever constructed. It was ordered from Rome in 1742 by Dom João V to honour his patron saint and, more dubiously, to requite the pope, whom he had persuaded to confer a patriarchate upon Lisbon.

GAY & LESBIAN

106	11
Bric-a-Brac Bar	7
Finalmente	12
Max	15
Purex	27
Sétimo Céu	21
Trumps	2

Casa Museu
Amália Rodrigues

0   100 m

N

▲ Estrela

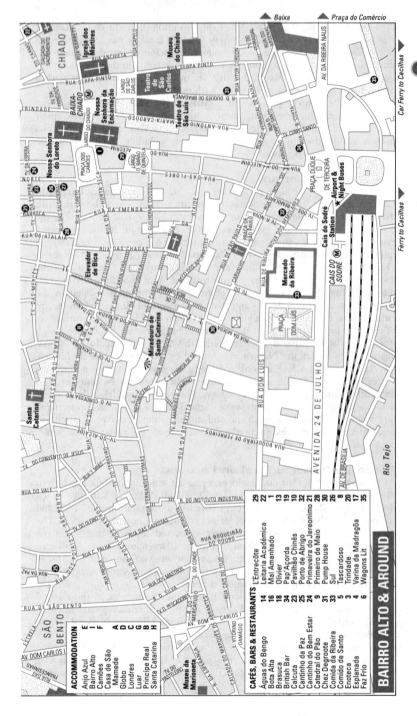

▲ Baixa   ▲ Praça do Comércio

Car Ferry to Cacilhas ▶

Ferry to Cacilhas ▶

CHIADO

Igreja dos Mártires

Museu do Chiado

Nossa Senhora da Encarnação

Teatro de São Carlos

Nossa Senhora do Loreto

BAIXA-CHIADO Ⓜ

Teatro de São Luís

Elevador de Bica

Miradouro de Santa Catarina

Santa Catarina

SÃO BENTO

Museu da Marioneta

Mercado da Ribeira

PRAÇA DOM LUÍS

Cais do Sodré Station

CAIS DO SODRÉ Ⓜ

Airport & Night Buses

PRAÇA DUQUE DE TERCEIRA

AVENIDA 24 DE JULHO

Rio Tejo

ACCOMMODATION

Anjo Azul	E
Bairro Alto	F
Camões	I
Casa de São Mamede	A
Globo	D
Londres	C
Luar	G
Príncipe Real	B
Santa Catarina	H

CAFÉS, BARS & RESTAURANTS

Águas do Bengo	29
Bota Alta	22
Brasuca	1
British Bar	13
Calcuta	18
Cantinho da Paz	34
Cantinho do Bem Estar	23
Catedral do Pão	25
Chez Degroote	24
Comida da Ribeira	9
Comido de Santo	31
Enoteca	33
Esplanada	5
Faz Frio	4
L'Entrecôte	14
Leitaria Académica	16
Mal Amanhado	18
Olivier	19
Pap'Açorda	10
Pavilhão Chinês	32
Porto de Abrigo	21
Primaveira do Jereonimo	28
Primeiro de Maio	30
Pump House	26
Sul	8
Tascardoso	20
Trindade	17
Varina da Madragõa	35
Wagons Lit	

BAIRRO ALTO & AROUND

Designed by the papal architect, Vanvitelli, and using the most costly materials available, including ivory, agate, porphyry and lapis lazuli, it was actually erected at the Vatican for the pope to celebrate Mass before being dismantled and shipped to Lisbon. Take a close look at the four "oil paintings" of John the Baptist's life and you'll discover that they are in fact mosaics, intricately worked over what must have been years rather than months.

Next to the church, the associated **Museu de São Roque** (Tues–Sun 10am–5pm; €1.50, free Sun) displays sixteenth- to eighteenth-century paintings and the usual motley collection of vestments, chalices and bibles bequeathed to the church over the centuries, including treasure from the Capela de São João Baptista.

Convento do Carmo

Further south, it's a couple of minutes' walk down to the pretty **Largo do Carmo**, with its outdoor café facing the ruined Gothic arches of the **Convento do Carmo**. Once the largest church in the city, this was half-destroyed by the earthquake but is perhaps even more beautiful as a result. In the nineteenth century its shell was adapted as a chemical factory but these days it houses the splendid **Museu Arqueológico do Carmo** (Mon–Sat: April–Sept 10am–6pm; Oct–March 10am–5pm; €2.50), whose miscellaneous collection is one of the joys of the city, housing many of the treasures from monasteries that were dissolved after the 1834 Liberal revolution. The entire nave is open to the elements, with columns, tombs and statuary scattered in all corners. Inside, on either side of what was the main altar, are the main exhibits, centring on a series of tombs of great significance. Largest is the beautifully carved, two-metre-high stone tomb of **Ferdinand I** while nearby, the tomb of **Gonçalo de Sousa**, chancellor to Henry the Navigator, is topped by a statue of Gonçalo himself, his clasped arms holding a book to signify his learning. Other noteworthy pieces include a fifteenth-century alabaster relief, made in Nottingham, and sixteenth-century Hispano-Arabic *azulejos*. There's also a model of the convent before it was ruined, an Egyptian sarcophagus (793–619 BC), whose inhabitant's feet are just visible underneath the lid, and, more alarmingly, two pre-Columbian mummies which lie curled up in glass cases, alongside the preserved heads of a couple of Peruvian Indians.

Praça do Príncipe Real and around

At the north end of Rua do Século, or a pleasant ten-minute walk uphill from the top of Elevador da Glória along Rua Dom Pedro V, lies the attractive **Praça do Príncipe Real**, one of the city's loveliest squares, laid out in 1860 and surrounded by the ornate homes of former aristocrats – now largely offices. The central pond and fountain is built over a covered reservoir that forms the **Museu da Água Príncipe Real** (Mon–Sat 10am–6pm; €1.50). Steps lead down inside the nineteenth-century reservoir where you can admire the water and view temporary exhibits from a series of walkways winding among the columns, often accompanied by ambient music.

From here it is a short walk along Rua Escola Politécnica to the classical building housing the city's natural science museums; alternatively take bus #15 or #58 from Cais do Sodré station. The **Museu de História Natural** (Mon–Fri 10am–1pm & 2–3pm, closed Aug; free) exhibits a rather sad collection of stuffed animals tracing the evolution of Iberian animal life, while the adjoining **Museu da Ciência** (Mon–Fri 10am–1pm & 2–5pm, Sat 3–6pm; closed Aug; €2.50) includes an imaginative interactive section amongst its otherwise pedestrian geological displays.

Beyond the museums lies the entrance to the enchanting **Jardim Botânico** (May–Oct Mon–Fri 9.30am–8pm, Sat & Sun 10am–6pm; Nov–April same hours until 6pm; €3), almost completely invisible from the surrounding streets. Portuguese explorers introduced many plant species to Europe and these gardens, laid out between 1858 and 1878, form an oasis of twenty thousand exotic plants from around the world – each one neatly labelled.

São Bento

São Bento, downhill and west from the Bairro Alto, was home to Lisbon's first black community – originally slaves from Portugal's early maritime explorations. However, the area today is best known for the Neoclassical parliament building, the **Palácio de São Bento** (or Palácio da Assembléia), originally a Benedictine monastery before the abolition of religious orders in 1834. It can only be visited by prior arrangement (☏213 919 000), though you get a good view of its steep white steps from tram #28, which rattles right by.

A little way uphill from here, Rua de São Bento 193 is the house where Portugal's most famous fado singer lived from the 1950s until her death in 1999. The house has been preserved as the **Casa Museu Amália Rodrigues** (Tues–Sun 10am–1pm & 2–6pm; €5), tracing the life and times of the daughter of an Alfama orange seller who became an internationally famous singer. Revered in her lifetime, her death resulted in three days of national mourning, and her record covers, film posters and everyday belongings are lovingly displayed here.

Estrela

Situated on another of Lisbon's hills, the district of **Estrela** lies 2km west of Bairro Alto – a thirty-minute walk or a short ride on tram #28 from Praça Luís de Camões in Chiado, or bus #13 from Praça do Comércio. Its main point of interest for the visitor is the **Basílica da Estrela** (daily 8am–12.30pm & 3–7.30pm; free), a vast domed church and *de facto* monument to late-eighteenth-century Neoclassicism. Opposite the church is the **Jardim da Estrela**, among the most enjoyable gardens in the city, a quiet refuge occasionally graced with an afternoon band. There's a pool of giant carp, too, and a café with outside tables.

Through the park and on Rua de São Jorge is the gate to the post-Crusader **Cemitério dos Ingleses** (English cemetery; ring loudly for entry) where, among the cypresses, lies Henry Fielding, author of *Tom Jones*, whose imminent demise may have influenced his verdict on Lisbon as "the nastiest city in the world".

A little uphill from here, the **Casa Museu Fernando Pessoa**, Rua Coelho da Rocha 16 (Mon–Wed 10am–6pm, Thurs 1–8pm, Fri 10am–6pm; free), was home to Portugal's best-known poet for the last fifteen years of his life (see box overleaf). The building is now a cultural centre containing a few of Pessoa's personal belongings, such as his glasses and diaries, and exhibits of artists who have been influenced by Pessoa. There's also Almada Negreiros' famous painting of the writer on display, depicting him in his distinctive spectacles and black hat.

From the stop in front of the Basílica da Estrela you can catch the #25 tram down the steep Rua de São Domingos à Lapa, getting off where the tram veers left into Rua Garcia de Orta. Here, you're only a five-minute walk from the Museu Nacional de Arte Antiga (see p.108); staying with the tram takes you to Praça do Comércio and back into the Baixa.

Fernando Pessoa

"Whether we write or speak or do but look
We are ever unapparent. What we are
Cannot be transfused into word or book."

Fernando Pessoa (1888–1935) is now widely recognized not just as Portugal's greatest poet of the twentieth century but as one of the major – and strangest – figures of European Modernism. Born in Lisbon, Pessoa spent most of his childhood in Durban, South Africa, where he received an English education and wrote his earliest poems – in English. He returned to Portugal in 1905 and spent most of his adult life working as a translator for various commercial firms. The rest of his time was devoted to literature. He founded a short-lived artistic magazine, *Orpheu*, in 1915 with fellow poet Mario de Sá-Carneiro, contributed to several other magazines, and rapidly became a conspicuous figure in the Baixa cafés where he wrote.

Much of Pessoa's work is concerned with the evasive nature of the self and, perhaps in recognition that personality can never be fixed, his work was created under a number of different identities, or "heteronyms". Each of his poetic alter egos had a fully worked out history, vision and style of their own – he even went so far as to have calling cards printed for his English heteronym, Alexander Search. By a marvellous piece of poetic serendipity, *pessoa* actually means "person" in Portuguese, a word that in turn derives from *persona* – the mask worn by Roman actors. Of the many heteronyms that Pessoa adopted, three were responsible for his finest poems. They are the nature poet, Alberto Caeiro; the classicist, Ricardo Reis; and the ebullient modernist, Álvaro de Campos. All three made their first appearance in 1914, and to some extent their histories intertwine with each other but with Caeiro regarded as the master by the other two. They share an obsessive introspection and a morbid fascination with interior and exterior reality that makes Pessoa one of the most telling of existential artists.

Pessoa died a year after the publication of *Mensagem* (Message), a series of patriotic and mystical poems dealing with Portuguese history. Written for a national competition (which he didn't win), this was the only volume of his Portuguese verse to appear during his lifetime. What he left was a large trunkload of manuscripts and typescripts, often in quite fragmentary form. These include the unclassifiable *Livro do Desassossego* (Book of Disquiet) written under the heteronym Bernardo Soares, a quasi-autobiography, consisting of aphorisms, anecdotes, and philosophical rumination, that has a directness and self-centredness that is both exhilarating and irritating by turns. It is in the piecing together and editing of these scraps of writing that the posthumous reputation of the enigmatic Pessoa has been built.

Museu Nacional de Arte Antiga

The **Museu Nacional de Arte Antiga**, Rua das Janelas Verdes 95 (Tues 2–6pm, Wed–Sun 10am–6pm; €3; Ⓦ www.mnarteantiga-ipmuseus.pt), Portugal's national gallery, is situated in the wealthy suburb of **Lapa**, a kilometre south of Estrela. To get here directly, take bus #40 or #60 from Praça do Comércio, or bus #27 or #49 on the way to or from Belém. It features the largest collection of Portuguese fifteenth- and sixteenth-century paintings in the country, European art from the fourteenth century to the present day and a rich display of applied art showing the influence of Portugal's colonial explorations. All of this is well displayed in a beautifully converted seventeenth-century palace, once owned by the Marquês de Pombal. The garden and café (hours as for museum) are worth a visit in their own right. The palace was built over the remains of the Saint Albert monastery, most of which was razed in the 1755 earthquake, although its beautiful chapel can still be seen today.

The Collection

The museum highlights ten "reference points" to guide you round the extensive collection. Principal highlight is Nuno Gonçalves's altarpiece for Saint Vincent (1467–70), a brilliantly marshalled composition depicting Lisbon's patron saint receiving homage from all ranks of its citizens, their faces looking remarkably modern. The other main highlight is Hieronymus Bosch's stunningly gruesome *Temptation of St Anthony* in room 57 (don't miss the image on the back, showing the arrest of Christ). Elsewhere, seek out the altar panel depicting the Resurrection by Raphael; Francisco de Zurbarán's *The Twelve Apostles;* a small statue of a nymph by Auguste Rodin and works by Albrecht Dürer, Cranach, Fragonard and Josefa de Óbidos, considered one of Portugal's greatest women painters.

The Oriental art collection shows the influence of Indian, African and Oriental designs derived from the trading links of the sixteenth century. There is inlaid furniture from Goa, Turkish and Syrian *azulejos*, Quing Dynasty porcelain and a supremely satisfying series of late sixteenth-century Japanese *namban* screens (room 14), showing the Portuguese landing at Nagasaki. The Japanese saw the Portuguese traders as southern barbarians (*namban*) with large noses – hence their Pinocchio-like features.

Museu da Marioneta

A kilometre east of the Museo Nacional de Arte Antiga, on Rua Esperança 146, lies the Museu da Marioneta puppet museum (Wed–Sun 10am–1pm & 2–6pm, €2.50, children €1.50). Contemporary and historical puppets from around the world are displayed in this former eighteenth-century convent and demonstrated in a well-organized museum. Highlights include shadow puppets from Turkey and Indonesia, string marionettes, Punch and Judy-style puppets, and faintly disturbing almost life-sized contemporary figures by Portuguese puppeteer Helena Vaz. There are also video displays and projections, while the final room shows Wallace and Gromit style plasticine figures and how they are manipulated for films.

Alcântara and Santo Amaro Docks

Loomed over by the enormous Ponte 25 de Abril suspension bridge, Alcântara has a decidedly industrial hue, with a tangle of railway lines, flyovers and cranes from the docks dominating the skyline. Nevertheless, the area is well known for its nightlife, mainly thanks to its dockside warehouse conversions that shelter cafés, restaurants and clubs. Parts of Alcântara are also getting a makeover under eminent French architect Jean Nouve, which should see some adventurous residential and commercial buildings to complement an enlarged cruise terminal.

The **Doca de Alcântara** remains the city's main docks with an increasing number of luxury cruise ships calling daily. After dark, its boat-bars and warehouse conversions come into their own, its clubs and bars attracting an older, more moneyed crowd than those of the Bairro Alto. By day, the dock's main attraction is the **Don Fernando II e Glória** frigate (℡213 620 010; Tues–Sun 10am–5pm; €3), built in India in 1843 and now a ship museum showing what sea life was like in the mid-nineteenth century.

A better bet by day is to head west to the more intimate **Doca de Santo Amaro,** nestling right under the humming traffic and rattling trains crossing Ponte 25 de Abril. This small, almost completely enclosed marina is filled with

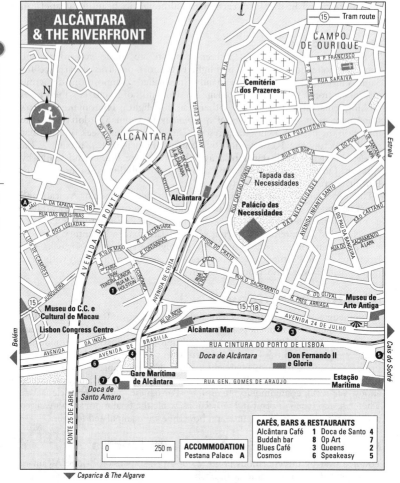

▲ *Parque de Monsanto*

ALCÂNTARA & THE RIVERFRONT

⎯⑮⎯ Tram route

CAMPO DE OURIQUE
R. P. FRANCISCO
RUA SARAIVA

Cemitéria dos Prazeres

ALCÂNTARA
RUA POSSIDÓNIO
RUA DO BORJA
R. DO POSS.
R. DE SANTANA À LAPA
Estrela ▶

Tapada das Necessidades

Alcântara
Palácio das Necessidades
SÃO CAETANO

R. DO PAU DA BANDEIRA
SACRAMENTO À LAPA

RUA DE ALCÂNTARA
PRIOR DO CRATO
RUA D. SACRAMENTO
R. DO OLIVAL
Museu de Arte Antiga

Ⓐ JAU C. DA TAPADA ⑱
RUA DAS INDUSTRIAS

R. PRES. ARRIAGA
AVENIDA 24 DE JULHO

⑮ Museu do C.C. e Cultural de Macau
Lisbon Congress Centre
Alcântara Mar
❷ ❸
Cais do Sodré ▶

◀ Belém

AVENIDA DA INDIA BRASÍLIA
RUA CINTURA DO PORTO DE LISBOA
Doca de Alcântara
Don Fernando II e Gloria
❺

❻
Gare Marítima de Alcântara
Doca de Santo Amaro
❼ ❽
RUA GEN. GOMES DE ARAÚJO
Estação Marítima

0   250 m

ACCOMMODATION
Pestana Palace **A**

CAFÉS, BARS & RESTAURANTS
Alcântara Café	1	Doca de Santo	4
Buddah bar	8	Op Art	7
Blues Café	3	Queens	2
Cosmos	6	Speakeasy	5

▼ *Caparica & The Algarve*

bobbing sailing boats and lined with tastefully converted warehouses. Its international cafés and restaurants are more pricey than usual for Lisbon, but the constant comings and goings of the Tejo provides plenty of free entertainment. Leaving Doca de Santo Amaro at its western side, you can pick up a pleasant riverside path that leads all the way to Belém (see opposite), twenty minutes' walk away.

Ponte 25 de Abril

Resembling the Golden Gate Bridge in San Francisco, the hugely impressive Ponte 25 de Abril was opened in 1966 as a vital link between Lisbon and the southern banks of the Tejo. Around 2.3km in length, the main bridge rises to 70m above the river, though its main pillars are nearly 200m tall. It was originally named Ponte de Salazar after the dictatorial prime minister who ruled Portugal with an iron fist from 1932 to 1968, but took its present name to mark the date of the revolution that overthrew Salazar's regime in 1974. You'll pass over it if you take a bus or train south of the Tejo.

Belém and around

It was from **Belém** (pronounced *Ber-layng*) in 1497 that Vasco da Gama set sail for India, and here too that he was welcomed home by Dom Manuel, "The Fortunate" (**O Venturoso**). Da Gama brought back with him a small cargo of pepper, but it was enough to pay for his voyage several times over. The monastery subsequently built here – the **Mosteiro dos Jerónimos** – stands as a testament to his triumphant discovery of a sea route to the Orient, which amounted to the declaration of a "Golden Age". Built to honour the vow Dom Manuel made to the Virgin in return for a successful voyage, it stands on the site of the hermitage founded by Henry the Navigator, where Vasco da Gama and his companions had spent their last night ashore in prayer. The monastery was partly funded by a levy on the fruits of da Gama's discovery – a five-percent tax on all spices other than pepper, cinnamon and cloves, whose import had become the sole preserve of the Crown. The Rio Tejo at Belém has receded with the centuries, for when the monastery was built it stood almost on the beach, within the sight of moored caravels and of the Torre de Belém, guarding the entrance to the port. This, too, survived the earthquake and is the other showpiece Manueline building in Lisbon.

Both monastery and tower lie in what is now a pleasant waterfront suburb, 6km west of the city centre. It is also home to a small group of museums, most of them set up by Salazar during the 1904 Expo, and to the historic café, *Antiga Confeitaria de Belém* (see p.125). You can get here by **tram** (signed Algés) – the fast supertram #15 runs from Praça da Figueira via Praça do Comércio (20min) – or by the Oeiras train from Cais do Sodré to Belém station. At Belém, a road train (*comboio turístico*) follows a 45-minute circuit (roughly hourly 10am–7pm, except 1pm, day ticket €3 includes 25 per cent reduction to Museu da Marinha) from the Mosteiro dos Jerónimos to the Museu dos Coches, returning on an uphill route.

When planning your trip keep in mind that quite a few of the sights at Belém are **closed on Mondays**.

Mosteiro dos Jerónimos

Even before the Great Earthquake of 1755 the **Mosteiro dos Jerónimos** (daily: June–Sept 10am–6.30pm, Oct–May 10am–5pm, restricted access Sat mornings and during Mass; free) was Lisbon's finest monument. Begun in 1502, and more or less completed when its funding was withdrawn by João III in 1551, the monastery is the most ambitious and successful achievement of Manueline architecture (see box on p.214) and is now a UNESCO World Heritage site. It is largely the achievement of two outstanding figures: **Diogo de Boitaca**, perhaps the originator of the Manueline style with his Igreja de Jesus at Setúbal, and **João de Castilho**, a Spaniard who took over the construction from around 1517.

It was Castilho who designed the **main entrance** to the church, a complex, shrine-like hierarchy of figures centred around Henry the Navigator (on a pedestal above the arch). In its intricate and almost flat ornamentation, it shows the influence of the contemporary Spanish style, *Plateresque* (literally, the art of the silversmith). Yet it also has distinctive Manueline features – the use of rounded forms, the naturalistic motifs in the bands around the windows – and these seem to create both its harmony and individuality. Just inside the entrance

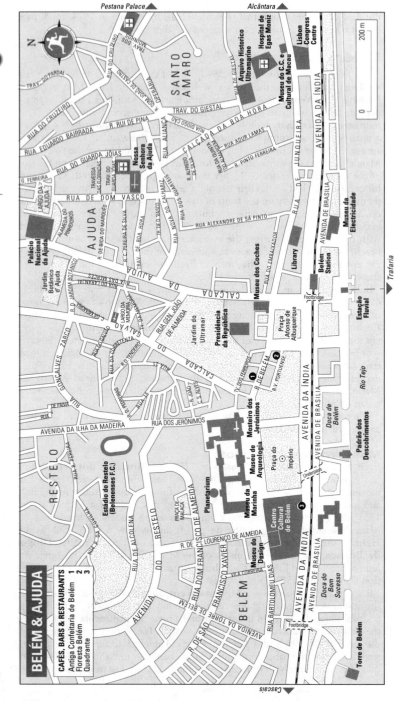

BELÉM & AJUDA

CAFÉS, BARS & RESTAURANTS

Antiga Confeitaria de Belém	1
Floresta Belém	2
Quadrante	3

lie the stone **tombs** of Vasco da Gama (1468–1523) and the great poet and recorder of the discoveries, Luís de Camões (1527–70).

The breathtaking sense of space inside the church places it among the great triumphs of European Gothic. Here, though, Manueline developments add two fresh dimensions. There are carefully restrained tensions between the grand spatial design and the areas of intensely detailed ornamentation. And, still more striking, there is a naturalism in the forms of this ornamentation that seems to extend into the actual structure of the church. Once you've made the analogy, it's difficult to see the six central columns as anything other than palm trunks, growing both into and from the branches of the delicate rib-vaulting.

Another peculiarity of Manueline buildings is the way in which they can adapt, enliven, or encompass any number of different styles. Here, the basic structure is thoroughly Gothic, though Castilho's ornamentation on the columns is much more Renaissance in spirit. So too is the semicircular apse, added in 1572, beyond which is the entrance to the remarkable double **cloister** (same hours as church; €4.50, free Sun 10am–2pm). Vaulted throughout and fantastically embellished, this is one of the most original and beautiful pieces of architecture in the country. Again, it holds in balance Gothic forms and Renaissance ornamentation and is exuberant in its innovations, such as the rounded corner canopies and delicate twisting divisions within each of the arches. These lend a wave-like, rhythmic motion to the whole structure, a conceit extended by the typically Manueline motifs drawn from ropes, anchors and the sea. In this – as in all aspects – it would be hard to imagine an artistic style more directly reflecting the achievements and preoccupations of an age.

In the wings of the monastery are two museums. The **Museu de Arqueologia** (Ⓦwww.mnarqueologia-ipmuseus.pt; Tues 2–6pm, Wed–Sun 10am–6pm; €3, free Sun morning), to the west of the main entrance, is housed in a Neo-Manueline extension to the monastery, added in 1850. It has a small section on Egyptian antiquities, but concentrates on relatively dull Portuguese archaeological finds, though there are a few fine Roman mosaics unearthed in the Algarve. Its temporary exhibits can be rewarding. Of more overall interest is the enormous **Museu da Marinha** (Tues–Sun: April–Sept 10am–6pm, Oct–March 10am–5pm; €3), with its entrance opposite the Centro Cultural de Belém, packed not only with models of ships, naval uniforms and a surprising display of artefacts from Portugal's oriental trade and colonies, but also with real vessels – among them fishing boats and sumptuous state barges – a couple of seaplanes and even some fire engines.

Torre de Belém

Still washed on three sides by the sea, the Tower of Belém, **Torre de Belém** (Tues–Sun: June–Sept 10am–6.30pm, Oct–May 10am–5pm; €3) stands 500m west of the monastery, fronted by a little park. Whimsical, multi-turreted and with a real hat-in-the-air exuberance, it was built over the last five years of Dom Manuel's reign (1515–20) as a fortress to safeguard the approach to Lisbon's harbour. Before the Great Earthquake shifted the course of the water, it stood virtually in the centre of the river. As such, it is the one completely Manueline building in Portugal, the rest having been adaptations of earlier structures or completed in later years.

Its architect, **Francisco de Arruda**, had previously worked on Portuguese fortifications in Morocco and the Moorish influence is very strong in the delicately arched windows and balconies. Prominent also in the decoration are two great symbols of the age: Manuel's personal badge of an armillary sphere (representing the globe) and the cross of the military Order of Christ, once the Templars, who took a major role in all Portuguese conquests. Though worth entering for the views from the roof, the tower's interior is unremarkable except for a "whispering gallery". It was used into the nineteenth century as a prison, notoriously by Dom Miguel (1828–34), who kept political enemies in the waterlogged dungeons.

Padrão dos Descobrimentos

Walking back along the waterfront, towards the monastery, you can't miss the **Padrão dos Descobrimentos** (Monument to the Discoveries; June–Sept Tues–Sun 9am–6.30pm, Nov–May Tues–Sun 9am–5pm; €2), an angular concrete building in the shape of a caravel which was erected in 1960 to commemorate the 500th anniversary of the death of Henry the Navigator. Henry appears on the prow with Camões and other Portuguese heroes. Within the monument is a temporary exhibition space, with interesting changing exhibits on the city's history. The entrance fee also gives lift access up to the top for some fine views of the Rio Tejo and Torre de Belém.

Centro Cultural de Belém, Museu do Design and Museu dos Coches

Across from the monument, on the western side of Praça do Imperio, an underpass leads to the **Centro Cultural de Belém** (Ⓦwww.ccb.pt), which puts on regular cultural exhibitions and concerts as well as hosting live entertainment over the weekend. There are plans to open a home for the Berardo Foundation's enormous contemporary art collection too, currently based in Sintra (see p.152). For the best views of the surroundings, drop into the café, whose garden esplanade overlooks the river and the Monument to the Discoveries.

The centre also houses the **Museu do Design** (daily 11am–8pm, last entry 7.15pm; €3.50), whose collection comprises design classics – furniture to jewellery – spanning the period from 1937 to today, which were amassed by former stockbroker and media mogul Francisco Capelo. Exhibitions are occasionally rotated, but there are usually chairs by Charles and Ray Eames and Phillipe Starck on display, plus 1970s bean bags, an amazing Joe Colombo Mini Kitchen, works by the Memphis Group and contemporary designs by Tomas Tavira and Álvaro Siza.

Northeast of here lies the leafy **Jardim do Ultramar** (daily 10am–5pm; €1.50), a green oasis with hothouses, ponds and towering palms – the entrance is on Calçada do Galvão. In the southeastern corner of the gardens lies the Portuguese President's official residence, the pink **Presidência da República** (closed to the public). If you are here on the third Sunday of the month, look out for the **changing of the guard** at 11am, along with the Cavalry Regiment's display of horsemanship on the area in front of Rua Vieria Portuense.

At the corner of Belém's other main square – Praça Afonso de Albuquerque, a few minutes' walk east from the monastery along Rua de Belém – you'll find the **Museu dos Coches** (Ⓦwww.museudoscoches-ipmuseus.pt; Tues–Sun 10am–6pm; €3, free Sunday 10am–2pm). Housed in the attractive former royal riding school, it contains one of the largest collections of saddlery and coaches in the world – heavily gilded and sometimes quite beautifully painted – along with historic sedan chairs, children's buggies and traps.

East to Ponte 25 de Abril

Heading back over the railway footbridge to the riverside from Praça Afonso de Albuquerque, past the ferry station, it is possible to walk the 2km along the relatively traffic-free gardens all the way from Belém to the Ponte 25 de Abril. En route is the extraordinary redbrick **Museu da Electricidade** (Tues–Fri & Sun 10am–12.30pm & 2–5.30pm, Sat 10am–12.30pm & 2–8pm; €3), an early twentieth-century electricity generating station with cathedral-like windows. The electricity museum's highlights include its original enormous generators, steam turbines and winches – all looking like something out of the science-fiction film *Brazil*. There are also temporary exhibitions.

North of the railway line, just beyond the high-tech **Lisbon Congress Centre** on the main Rua da Junqueira 30, it is another ten minutes' walk to the **Museu do Centro Científico e Cultural de Macau** (Tues–Sat 10am–5pm, Sun noon–6pm; €3). This museum is dedicated to Portugal's trading links with the Orient and its former colony of Macau, which was handed back to Chinese rule in 1999. There are model boats and audio displays detailing early journeys, and exhibits of Chinese art from the sixteenth to the nineteenth centuries, including an impressive array of opium pipes and ivory boxes.

Palácio Nacional da Ajuda

Tram #18 from Praça do Comércio, or bus #14 from central Belém or Calçada da Ajuda behind the Museu dos Coches, will take you to the hilltop **Palácio Nacional da Ajuda** (tours every 30min, Mon, Tues & Thurs–Sun 10am–4.30pm; €4, free Sun morning 10am–2pm). Started in 1802, the palace was incomplete when the royal family fled to Brazil to escape Napoleon's army in 1807, though what was completed was used as a royal residence after 1821. The decor was commissioned by the crashingly tasteless nineteenth-century royals, Dona Maria II and Dom Ferdinand, and like their Pena Palace folly at Sintra, it's all over-the-top aristocratic clutter. The richly ornate banqueting hall, however, is highly impressive; likewise the lift, which is decked out with mahogany and mirrors. The palace is also used for occasional concerts. Opposite the palace is the attractive **Jardim Botânico d'Ajuda** (Mon, Tues & Thurs–Sun 9am–dusk; €1.75), one of the city's oldest botanical gardens – a fine example of formal Portuguese gardening boasting some great views over Belém.

Avenida da Liberdade, Parque Eduardo VII and Amoreiras

To the north of the Baixa is the city's principal park – the **Parque Eduardo VII**. The easiest approach is by metro (to Marquês de Pombal or Parque) or bus (to Marquês de Pombal), though you could also walk up the main **Avenida da Liberdade** in about twenty minutes, which would give you the chance to make a couple of stops along the way. The bottom end of Avenida da Liberdade, just above metro Restauradores, has some of the city's nicest outdoor cafés, with esplanade tables in the green swathes that split the avenue. Running parallel, to the east, the pedestrianized Rua das Portas de Santo Antão is well known for the seafood restaurants that line it, waiters hovering by every doorway attempting to entice you in. Avenida da Liberdade ends in a swirl of traffic at the landmark roundabout of **Praça do Marquês de Pombal** (otherwise known as Rotunda).

Fundação Medeiros e Almeida

Once the Avenida da Liberdade was the exclusive address for some of Lisbon's most respected figures, and you can experience a taste of this opulence at the **Fundação Medeiros e Almeida**, Rua Rosa Araújo 41 (Mon–Sat 1–5.30pm; €5), set in the former home of art collector and industrialist António Medeiros

△ View from Parque Eduardo VII

(1895–1986). Parts of the house have been kept as they were when he lived there, while other rooms display his priceless collection of works, including 2000-year-old Chinese porcelain, an important collection of sixteenth- to nineteenth-century watches, and dazzling English and Portuguese silverware. There are sumptuous eighteenth-century **azulejos** in the Sala de Lago, a room also filled with bubbling decorative fountains.

Parque Eduardo VII

At the top of the avenue lies the formal **Parque Eduardo VII**. On the west side, at the northern end, are the **Estufas** (hothouses) (daily: April–Sept 9am–6pm, Oct–March 9am–5pm, Estufa Quente closes thirty mins earlier; €1.50), one *quente* (hot) planthouse and one *fria* (cool), filled with tropical plants, pools and endless varieties of palms and cacti. Concerts and exhibitions are occasionally held in the tile-fronted **Pavilhão dos Desportos** at the opposite side of the park. You can walk uphill to a viewpoint, which affords fine views over the city, and over the grassy hillock beyond (with its olive trees, lake and café) to the Gulbenkian museum (see p.118), or alternatively take bus #51, which runs from Belém to the museum via the top of the park.

Casa-Museu Dr Anastácio Gonçalves

Five minutes east of the park, near metro Saldanha, is the **Casa-Museu Dr Anastácio Gonçalves** (Ⓦwww.cmag-ipmuseus.pt; Wed–Sun 10am–6pm, Tues 2–6pm; €2), on Rua Pinheiro Chagas. Set in the Casa Malhoa, a Neo-Romantic building with Art Nouveau touches – such as its beautiful stained-glass window – the house was constructed for the painter José Malhoa in 1904 and retains many of its original fittings. It now holds the private art collection of ophthalmologist Dr Antastácio Gonçalves, Calouste Gulbenkian's doctor. When he died in 1964, Gonçalves left a collection not quite as sumptuous as Gulben-kian, but amongst his two thousand works of art are paintings by Malhoa himself, Chinese porcelain from the sixteenth-century Ming dynasty, and furniture from England, France, Holland and Spain dating from the seventeenth century.

Amoreiras and around

West of the park, up Avenida Engenheiro Duarte Pacheco, is Lisbon's post-modernist shopping centre, **Amoreiras** (daily 10am–midnight), a wild fantasy of pink and blue designed by Tomás Taveira in the 1980s, and sheltering ten cinema screens, sixty cafés and restaurants, 250 shops and a hotel. Most of the shops here stay open until midnight (11pm on Sun); the heaviest human traffic is on Sunday, when entire families descend on the complex for an afternoon out. To get here directly by bus, take the #11 from Rossio/Restauradores.

Rua das Amoreiras runs down to the delightful **Praça das Amoreiras**, dominated on its west side by the soaring wall of the **Aqueduto das Águas Livres**. Opened in 1748, the aqueduct stood firm during the 1755 earthquake, bringing a reliable supply of drinking water to the city for the first time. On the south side of the square the **Mãe d'Água** water cistern (Mon–Sat 10am–6pm; €2.50) marks the end of the line for the aqueduct, with the reservoir contained within a cathedral-like stone building with gothic lion heads. The water cistern now hosts occasional exhibitions and has great views from its roof. The entrance to the aqueduct itself is around a kilometre north of Praça das Amoreiras, at Calçada da Quintiha 6 in Campolide (bus #58 from Rossio; March–Oct daily 10am–6pm; €2.50). You can walk right over the 60-metre-high central section, which takes about fifteen or twenty minutes.

On the northeast side of Praça das Amoreiras, set in a former eighteenth-century silk factory, the **Fundação Arpad Siznes-Viera da Silva** (Mon & Wed–Sat noon–8pm, Sun 10am–6pm; €2.50) is a gallery dedicated to the works of two painters and the artists who have been influenced by them: the Hungarian-born Arpad Siznes (1897–1985) and his Portuguese-born wife Maria Helena Viera da Silva (1908–92). The foundation shows the development of both the artists' works, with Viera da Silva's more abstract, subdued paintings contrasting with the colourful, more flamboyant Siznes, whose *Enfant au cerf-volant* shows the clear influences of Miró, who was a friend of his wife.

Fundação Calouste Gulbenkian

The **Fundação Calouste Gulbenkian** is the great cultural centre of Portugal – and it is a wonder that it's not better known internationally.

Calouste Gulbenkian

Calouste Sarkis Gulbenkian was the Roman Abramovich of his era, making his millions from oil but investing in the world's best art rather than top footballers. Born of wealthy Armenian parents in Istanbul in 1869, he followed his father into the oil industry and became oil consultant to the Ottoman court. In 1911 he set up the Oil Petroleum Company, raking in 5 per cent of the company's vast profits, most of which he invested in England where he chose to live. During this time, his legendary art-market coups included buying works from the Leningrad Hermitage after the Russian Revolution of 1917. During World War II, his Turkish background made him unwelcome in Britain. Gulbenkian literally auctioned himself and his art collections to whoever would have him: Portugal bid security, an aristocratic palace home (a marquês was asked to move out) and tax exemption, to acquire one of the most important cultural patrons of the century. From 1942 to his death in 1955, he accumulated one of the best private art collections in the world. His dying wish was that all of his collection should be displayed in one place, and this was granted in 1969 – a century after his birth – with the opening of the Museu Calouste Gulbenkian. The museum continues to buy works of art with his funds to this day, much of it for the Centro de Arte Moderna, which was opened in 1984.

Located a few minutes' walk north of Parque Eduardo VII, the foundation is set in its own grounds, and features a museum whose collections take in virtually every great phase of Eastern and Western art – from Ancient Egyptian scarabs to Art Nouveau jewellery, Islamic textiles to French Impressionist paintings. In a separate building, across the park, the Centro de Arte Moderna concentrates largely on Portuguese works, touching on most styles of twentieth-century art.

Astonishingly, all the main museum exhibits were acquired by just one man, the Armenian oil magnate **Calouste Gulbenkian** (see box, above). Today, in the capital alone, the Gulbenkian Foundation runs an orchestra, three concert halls and two galleries. It also finances work in all spheres of Portuguese cultural life – there are Gulbenkian museums and libraries in the smallest towns – and makes charitable grants to a vast range of projects. To reach the main entrance of the complex, on Avenida de Berna, take bus #31 or #46 from Restauradores, #51 from Belém (not weekends), or the metro to Praça de Espanha or São Sebastião. The admissions desk of the museum has a schedule of current activities.

Museu Gulbenkian

The objects in the **Museu Gulbenkian** (ⓦ www.gulbenkian.pt; Av de Berna; Tues–Sun 10am–5.45pm; €3, combined ticket with Museu de Arte Moderna €5, free on Sun) aren't immense in number but each themed collection contains pieces of such individual interest and beauty that you need frequent unwinding sessions – well provided for by the basement **café-bar** and tranquil gardens.

It seems churlish to hint at highlights, but they must include the entire contents of the small **Egyptian room**, which covers almost every period of importance from the Old Kingdom (2700 BC) to the Roman period. Particularly striking are the bronze cats from 664–525 BC and the Head of Sestrostris III from the XIIth dynasty (2026–1785 BC). Fine **Roman** statues, silver, glass and intricate gold jewellery, along with coins from ancient **Greece**, come soon after. **Mesopotamia** produced the earliest forms of writing, and two cylinder seals – one dating from before 2500 BC – are on display, along with architectural sculpture from the Assyrian civilization. **Islamic arts** are magnificently represented by ornamented texts, opulently woven carpets, glassware (such as the fourteenth-century mosque lamps from Syria) and Turkish *azulejos*. There is some stunning fourteenth-century Syrian painted glass and some superbly intricate eighteenth-century silk coats from **Persia**. These are followed by remarkable illuminated manuscripts and ceramics from **Armenia**, porcelain from **China**, and beautiful **Japanese** prints and lacquer-work.

△ Lalique brooch Museu Gulbenkian

European art includes work from all the major schools, beginning with a group of French medieval ivory diptychs (in particular the six scenes depicting the life of the Virgin) and a thirteenth-century version of St John's prophetic *Apocalypse*, produced in Kent and touched up in Italy under Pope Clement IX. From fifteenth-century Flanders, there's a pair of panels by van der Weyden, and from the same period in Italy comes Ghirlandaio's *Portrait of a Young Woman*. The seventeenth-century collection yields two exceptional portraits – one by Rubens of his second wife, *Helena Fourment*, and Rembrandt's *Figure of an Old Man* – plus works by van Dyck and Ruisdael. Eighteenth-century works featured include a good Fragonard and a roll-call incorporating Gainsborough, Sir Thomas Lawrence and Francesco Guardi. Finally Corot, Manet, Monet, Degas and Renoir supply a good showing from nineteenth- to twentieth-century France.

Sculpture is poorly represented on the whole, though a fifteenth-century medallion of *Faith* by Luca della Robbia, a 1780 marble *Diana* by Jean-Antoine Houdon, and a couple of Rodins all stand out. Elsewhere, you'll find **ceramics** from Spain and Italy; **furniture** from Louis XV to Louis XVI; eighteenth-century works from **French goldsmiths**; fifteenth-century Italian bronze **medals** (especially by Pisanello); and assorted Italian tapestries and textiles, including a superb fifteenth-century red velvet parasol from Venice. The last room consists of an Art Nouveau collection, with 169 pieces of fantasy jewellery by **René Lalique**; look for the amazing bronze and ivory Medusa paperweight (1902) and the fantastical *Peitoral-libélula* brooch, half woman, half dragonfly, decorated with enamel work, gold, diamonds and moonstones.

Centro de Arte Moderna

The modern art centre embraces pop art, installations and sculptures – some witty, some baffling, but all thought provoking. Most of the big names on the twentieth-century Portuguese scene feature, including black and white panels by Almada Negreiros (1873–1970), the founder of *modernismo* (his self-portrait is set in the café *A Brasileira*); the bright Futurist colours of Amadeu de Sousa Cardoso, and Paula Rego (one of Portugal's leading contemporary artists; see box, below) whose *Mãe* (1997) is outstanding. There are subtle abstracts and

Paula Rego

Paula Rego (born 1935) shot to international prominence in 1990 when she was appointed as the National Gallery Artist in Residence in London, and she is now considered one of the world's leading figurative painters. Although she has spent most of her life in England – she married English artist Vic Willing – her formative years were spent in Salazar's Lisbon, where she was born. Her sheltered childhood was passed in the confines of a wealthy family home and she still feels bitter about the way her mother became a "casualty" of a society which encouraged wealthy women to be idle, leaving work to their servants. Her women are portrayed as typical of the servants of her childhood: stocky and solid. Other adults are usually viewed with the unsentimental eye of a child, and she avoids graceful forms, preferring hairy, bony yet powerful female figures. Power and dominance are major themes of her work; she revives the military outfits of post-war Portugal for her men and dresses many of her women like dolls in national costume. Several of her pictures convey sexual opposition, the result perhaps of a background dominated by the regimes of the Roman Catholic church and a military dictatorship. Her images are rarely beautiful, but are undoubtedly amusing, disturbing and powerful. Her work is often displayed at galleries and temporary exhibitions around Lisbon.

sculptures by American expressionist Arshile Gorky, and powerful photos by Fernando Lemos (1926). British artists also feature; most striking are the prostrate figure of a man, *Close II,* by Anthony Gormley and Bill Woodrow's wooden "War-head" sculpture. Next to the museum, don't miss the perennially popular self-service **restaurant** (see p.130).

Outer Lisbon

Few visitors explore anything of Lisbon beyond the Gulbenkian, unless for a trip to the Sporting or Benfica football stadiums. However, there is the **Praça de Touros** (bullring) at Campo Pequeno, the **Jardim Zoológico** (the city's zoo, around 2km north west of the Gulbenkian), and by the nearby **Palácio dos Marquêses da Fronteira** (a further 1km northwest of the zoo).

Praça de Touros

Built in 1892, the Praça de Touros do Campo Pequeno is an impressive Moorish-style bullring seating nine thousand spectators. The Portuguese *tourada* (bullfight) is neither as commonplace nor as famous as its Spanish counterpart, but as a spectacle it's marginally preferable, as here the bull isn't killed in the ring, but instead is wrestled to the ground in a genuinely elegant, colourful and skilled display. After the fight, however, the bull is usually injured and it is always slaughtered later in any case. Performances start at 10pm on Thursday evenings from Easter to September. The bullring also hosts visiting circuses and occasional events, while beneath it is an underground shopping and cinema complex. Tickets (from €15–75, depending on where you sit) can be bought from the ticket office (☏217 820 575) or from one of the ticket agencies listed on p.135.

Jardim Zoológico

The **Jardim Zoológico**, at Estrada de Benfica 158–160 (daily: April–Sept 10am–8pm, Oct–March 10am–6pm; €12, children under 12 €9; ⓦwww .zoolisboa.pt) has been greatly improved over recent years and makes for an enjoyable day out, especially if you have children. There's a small cable car (daily from 11am until 30min before closing time), which offers a fine aerial view of many of the enclosures, a reptile house (11am–30min before closing time), a boating lake and various animal "shows" – sealions, macaws and the like – as further diversions. Just by the entrance, the **Animax** amusement park (daily 11am–8pm) has further rides to shed parents of a few euros. Bus #31 links Restauradores with the Jardim Zoológico via Praça Marquês de Pombal, or simply take the metro to Jardim Zoológico.

Palácio dos Marquêses da Fronteira

Palace enthusiasts should make every effort to visit the seventeenth-century **Palácio dos Marquêses da Fronteira**, Largo de São Domingos de Benfica 1 (tours daily Mon–Sat: June–Sept at 10.30am, 11am, 11.30am & noon; Oct–May at 11am & noon; €7.50, gardens only €3; reservations advised ☏217 782 023), which is around twenty minutes' walk west from the zoo; bus #46 from Restauradores (via the zoo) also passes nearby. After the view of the bland housing development on neighbouring Rua de São Domingos de Benfica, the fantastic gardens of this small, pink country house, complete with topiary, statues and fountains, represent something of an oasis. Inside, there is period furniture along with more stunning *azulejos* dating back to the seventeenth century, with some particularly vivid ones showing the battles during the Restoration Wars with Spain.

Parque das Nações

Parque das Nações – the Park of Nations – the former Expo 98 site, 5km to the east of the city, remains a huge attraction for Lisboans who come here en masse at weekends – and it's also a popular riverfront residential area. The main highlight is the **Oceanário** (oceanarium), though there are plenty of other attractions, from water gardens to a cable car, as well as a diverse array of bars, shops and restaurants, many overlooking Olivais docks and the astonishing 17km-long Vasco da Gama bridge.

Oriente metro deposits you in the bowels of the **Estação do Oriente**, a stunning glass-and-concrete bus and train interchange designed by Spanish architect Santiago Calatrava. As you exit the station, head through the Vasco da Gama shopping centre to the main **Posto de Informação** (daily 9.30am–8pm; Oct–April until 7pm; ☎218 919 333, ⓦwww.parquedasnacoes.pt), which has details of current events. If you want to visit more than a couple of things, it may be worth buying a *Cartão do Parque* (€16.50, valid one month), which allows unlimited access to the main sights (including the oceanarium) and discounts at other attractions.

A **road train** trundles anticlockwise round the whole park (daily 10am–7pm, until 5pm from Oct–April, every hour; €2.50, children €1.50), starting and finishing in front of the Pavilhão Atlântico. From here, you can also **rent bikes** (from around €4/hr), a good way to get round the flat, traffic-free lanes. It is not too taxing, however, to walk to the principal attractions, especially if you take advantage of the cable car (see p.124).

Oceanário de Lisboa

At weekends in particular, hour-long queues to get in the futuristic **Oceanário de Lisboa** (daily 10am–7pm; €10; ⓦwww.oceanario.pt) are not uncommon, so it is worth getting here early. Designed by Peter Chermayeff, and resembling a set from a James Bond film, Europe's second-largest oceanarium contains around 8,000 fish and marine animals. Its main feature is the enormous central tank, the size of four Olympic-sized swimming pools, which you can look into from different levels to get close-up views of the sharks and rays. Perhaps even more impressive are the re-creations of various ocean ecosystems, such as the Antarctic tank containing frolicking penguins, and the Pacific tank, where otters bob about and play in the rock pools. These areas are separated from the main tank by invisible acrylic sheets, which give the impression that all the marine creatures are swimming together in the same space. On the darkened lower level, smaller tanks contain shoals of brightly coloured tropical fish and other warm water creatures. Find a window free of the school parties and the whole experience becomes the closest you'll get to deep-sea diving without getting wet.

The rest of the park

Children like the **Pavilhão do Conhecimento Ciência Viva** (Knowledge Pavilion for Live Science; ⓦwww.pavconhecimento.pt; Tues–Fri 10am–6pm, Sat & Sun 11am–7pm, last entry 1hr before closing; €6, children €3), which is run by Portugal's Ministry of Science and Technology (which shares the premises). There are permanent interactive exhibits here, including holograms, plus a cybercafé with thirty terminals offering free internet access. Behind the centre lies the **Jardim da Água** (Water Garden), crisscrossed by ponds linked by stepping stones, with enough fountains, water gadgets and pumps to keep kids occupied for hours.

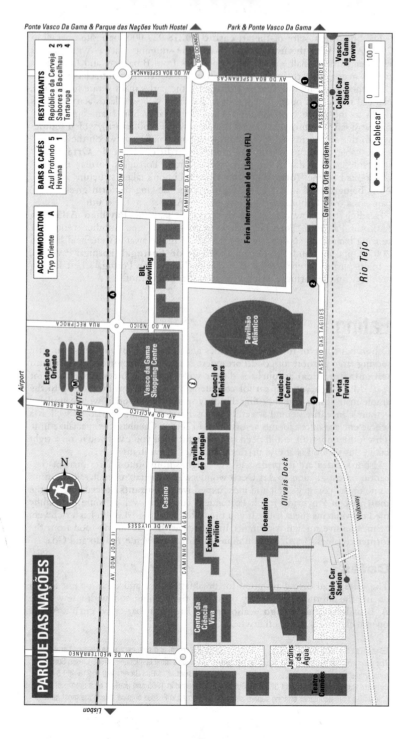

PARQUE DAS NAÇÕES

ACCOMMODATION	
Tryp Oriente	A

BARS & CAFÉS	
Azul Profundo	5
Havana	1

RESTAURANTS	
República da Cerveja	2
Sabores & Bacalhau	3
Tartaruga	4

Ponte Vasco Da Gama & Parque das Nações Youth Hostel ▲   Park & Ponte Vasco Da Gama ▲

Airport ▲

Lisbon ▼

N

Estação do Oriente

BIL Bowling

Vasco da Gama Shopping Centre

Casino

Exhibitions Pavilion

Centro da Ciência Viva

Jardins da Água

Teatro Camões

Pavilhão de Portugal

Council of Ministers

Oceanário

Nautical Centre

Pavilhão Atlântico

Feira Internacional de Lisboa (FIL)

Garcia de Orta Gardens

Vasco da Gama Tower

Cable Car Station

Porta Fluvial

Cable Car Station

Olivais Dock

Walkway

Rio Tejo

ORIENTE

AV. DE BERLIM

AV. DOM JOÃO II

RUA RECÍPROCA

AV. DO ÍNDICO

AV. DO PACÍFICO

CAMINHO DA ÁGUA

AV. DE ULYSSES

AV. DOM JOÃO II

AV. DE MEDITERRÂNEO

CAMINHO DA ÁGUA

AV. DO BOA ESPERANÇAS

AV. DO BOA ESPERANÇAS

PASSEIO DAS TAGIDES

PASSEIO DAS TAGIDES

PASSEIO DAS TAGIDES

- - - - ● Cablecar

| 0 | 100 m |

123

The brand-new, state-of-the-art **casino** (☎218 929 000) opposite opened in 2006. Along with the usual casino fodder, the stunning space – with its glass cylinder entrance hall – also hosts top shows from Broadway and London as well as major concerts in the performance hall, which has a retractable roof.

On the riverfront, the **Teatro Camões** is the park's main venue for theatre, classical music and opera. Beyond here, a narrow walkway leads across Olivais docks to the **cable car** (Mon–Fri 11am–7pm, Sat & Sun 10am–8pm; €3.50 one way, €5.50 return; children €1.80 one-way, €3.50 return), which shuttles you to the northern side of the park, with commanding views on the way.

The cable car drops you just beyond the **Jardim Garcia de Orta**, a leafy waterside garden displaying plant species from Portugal's former colonies, overlooked by the **Torre Vasco da Gama**, Lisbon's tallest structure at 145m. Now being turned into a hotel, the top floor viewing platform gives a 360° panorama over Lisbon, the Tejo and into the Alentejo to the south.

Heading back towards Olivais docks you'll pass the **Pavilhão Atlântico** (Atlantic Pavilion), Portugal's largest indoor arena and another venue for touring bands and sporting events; the MTV music awards were held here in 2005. Opposite stands the elegant **Pavilhão de Portugal** (Portugal Pavilion), a multi-purpose arena designed by Álvaro Siza Vieira, Portugal's best-known architect, and featuring a distinctive sagging concrete roof.

Eating

Lisbon has some of the best-value cafés and restaurants of any European city, serving large portions of good Portuguese food at sensible prices. A **set menu** (**ementa turística**) at lunch or dinner will get you a three-course meal for €10–13, though you can eat for considerably less than this by sticking to the ample main dishes and choosing the daily specials. **Seafood** is widely available – there's an entire central street, Rua das Portas de Santo Antão, as well as a whole enclave of restaurants across the Rio Tejo at Cacilhas that specialize in it. This is the only time you'll need to be careful what you eat if you're on a tight budget, as seafood is always pricier than other menu items.

Lisbon's **cafés** are its pride and joy, ranging from atmospheric turn-of-the-century artists' haunts to Art Deco wonders. The capital, naturally, also features some of the country's best and most expensive **restaurants**, specializing for the most part in a hybrid French-Portuguese cuisine, as well as some beautifully tiled **cervejarias** (beer halls). If you tire of the local food, Lisbon has a rich vein of inexpensive foreign restaurants, in particular those featuring food from the former colonies: Brazil, Mozambique, Angola, Cape Verde, Macão and Goa.

Cafés

The cafés listed below are good for breakfast, coffee and cakes or just a beer during the afternoon. Most stay open into the evening, too, with a few – like **A Brasileira** and **Vertigo** – also on the late-night bar-crawl circuit. All are open daily unless stated otherwise.

Baixa and Chiado

The following are marked on the Baixa and Chiado map on p.93.

Bernard Rua Garrett 104 ☎211 373 133. Old-style café with an ornate interior offering superb cakes,

ice cream and coffees, and an outdoor terrace on Chiado's most fashionable street. Closed Sun.

A Brasileira Rua Garrett 120 ☎213 469 547. Opened in 1905 and marked by a bronze of Fernando Pessoa outside, this is the most famous of Rua Garrett's old-style coffee houses. Livens up at night with a more youthful clientele swigging beer outside until 2am, though the interior is its real appeal.

Confeitaria Nacional Pr da Figueira 18 ☏ 213 424 470. Opened in 1829 and little changed since, with a stand-up counter selling pastries and sweets below a mirrored ceiling. There's a little side room for sit-down coffees and snacks and a few outdoor tables. Closed Sun Oct–April.

Nicola Rossio 24 ☏ 213 460 579. A former haunt of Lisbon's literary figures, dating back to the seventeenth century, this grand old place is not quite what it was following restoration, but is still a good stop for breakfast. Outdoor seats are always at a premium.

Suíça Rossio 96 ☏ 213 214 090. Famous for its cakes and pastries; you'll have a hard job getting an outdoor table here, though there's plenty of room inside – the café stretches across to Pr da Figueira, where the best tables are.

Vertigo Trav do Carmo 4 ☏ 213 433 112. An arty crowd frequents this bar-brick walled café with an ornate glass ceiling. Occasional art exhibits and a good range of cakes and snacks. Open until midnight.

Alfama and the eastern riverfront

The following are marked on the Alfama and Castelo map on p.99.

Café do Castelo Castelo de São Jorge. Set inside the castle walls, this offers good-value buffet lunches – all you can eat for around €8 – as well as drinks. Its outdoor tables are beautifully positioned under shady trees with peacocks for company. Inexpensive.

Miradouro de Santa Luzia Miradouro de Santa Luzia ☏ 218 863 968. Hilltop suntrap just below the viewpoint of the same name. Drinks and meals are slightly pricey but you pay for the views, which are fabulous.

Pois Café Rua São João da Praça 93–95 ☏ 218 862 497. With its big comfy sofas and laid-back ambience, walking into this Austrian-run café feels like going into someone's large front room. A friendly, young crowd, light meals and homemade snacks, including a great *apfelstrudel*. Recommended. Closed Mon.

Bairro Alto and Cais do Sodré

The following are marked on the Bairro Alto map on pp.104–105.

Catedral do Pão Rua Dom Pedro V 57C, Bairro Alto ☏ 213 224 358. Relaxed, ornate corner *pastelaria* where you can enjoy coffee and croissants.

Leitaria Académica Largo do Carmo 1–3, Bairro Alto ☏ 213 469 092. Tables in one of the city's nicest, quietest squares, outside the ruined Carmo church. Also does light lunches – the grilled sardines are hard to beat.

Wagons-Lit Estação Fluvial, Cais do Sodré. Simple café with lovely outdoor tables facing the river. A great place for a drink and popular with ferry commuters from the terminal next door.

Belém

Antiga Confeitaria de Belém Rua de Belém 90 ☏ 213 637 423. See map on p.112. Excellent tiled pastry shop and café, which has been serving superb *pasteis de Belém* (flaky tartlets filled with custard-like cream) since 1837; an unmissable place during a visit to Belém.

Parque Eduardo VII and northern Lisbon

The following are marked on the Lisbon map on pp.80–81.

Botequim do Rei Parque Eduardo VII. Tranquil park café by a little lake, with outdoor seats surrounded by geraniums. Closed Mon.

A Linha d Água Parque Eduardo VII. Glass-fronted café at the northern end of the park, facing a small lake. It's a fine spot to down a coffee or beer, and decent buffet lunches are served too.

Versailles Av da República 15A ☏ 213 546 340; metro Saldanha. A fine traditional café where a fleet of waiters circle the starched table-cloths beneath chandeliers.

Restaurants

There are hundreds of restaurants throughout the city, with concentrations in all the areas in which you're likely to be sightseeing. Restaurants in the **Alfama** and especially the **Baixa** are good for lunch as most have inexpensive set menus catering for local workers. In **Belém**, Rua Vieira Portuense, near the monastery, has a terrace of *tascas* and restaurants with outdoor seats that are always busy at lunchtime (those further from the monastery tend to be the best value). Out at the **Parque das Nações**, the riverfront Passeio das Tágides is one long line of moderately priced bars and restaurants specializing in international cuisine, from

Restaurants with best views

Associação Católica p.126	Bica do Sapato p.128
Casa do Leão p.128	Quadrante p.130
Teatro Taborda p.128	Eleven p.131
Jardim do Marisco p.128	

Israeli to Cuban. The *docas* at **Alcântara** also have a range of international restaurants, while the waterside places at **Doca do Jardim do Tobaco** and by **Santa Apolónia** station tend to specialize in upmarket Portuguese and fusion cuisine. By night the obvious place to be is the **Bairro Alto**, which houses several of the city's most fashionable restaurants, as well as plenty of other more basic value-for-money venues.

Options for **vegetarians** are somewhat limited in Lisbon, though *Celeiro* (p.126), *Tão* (p.127) and *Os Tibetanos* (p.131) are worth seeking out. Indian restaurants also offer good vegetarian options, as do some of the museum cafés, notably at the Centro de Arte Moderna at the Gulbenkian (p.130).

Restaurants listed are open daily for lunch and dinner, unless otherwise stated. Note that many are **closed** on Sunday evenings or Mondays, while on Saturday nights you should reserve a table for the more popular places. The listings below have been coded into four **price categories**: inexpensive (less than €15), moderate (€16–25), expensive (over €25), and very expensive (over €50) – the average price per person you can expect to pay for a two-course meal, including drinks.

Baixa

The following are marked on the Baixa map on p.93.

Adega Santo Antão Rua das Portas de Santo Antão 42. Very good value *adega* with a bit of local character: a bustling bar area and tables inside and out offering great grilled meat and fish. Closed Mon. Inexpensive.

Andorra Rua das Portas de Santo Antão 82 ☎213 426 047. Occupying a raised bit of the street, the *Andorra* specializes in *açorda* and *arroz de marisco*, plus fresh fish and steaks, served at its well-positioned outdoor tables. Good for people watching. Moderate.

Associação Católica Trav Ferragial 1. Go through the unmarked door and head for the top floor for this self-service canteen offering different dishes each day. The chief attractions are the low prices and the nice rooftop terrace with views over the Tejo. Open Mon–Fri noon–3pm. No credit cards. Inexpensive.

Beira Gare Rua 1° de Dezembro 5. Perennially buzzing snack-bar restaurant opposite Rossio station serving bargain stand-up Portuguese snacks or cheap meals night and day in the back diner. No credit cards. Inexpensive.

A Berlenga Rua Barros Queiróz 35 ☎213 422 703. A *cervejaria* with a window stuffed full of crabs and seafood. Early-evening snackers at the bar munching prawns give way to local diners eating meals chosen from the window displays. Moderate unless you choose the more pricey seafood.

Bom Jardim/Rei dos Frangos Trav de Santo Antão 11–18 ☎213 424 389. The "king of chickens" has branches on two sides of an alleyway connecting Restauradores with Rua das Portas de Santo Antão. It is the place for spit-roast chicken – a half one with fries costs about €7. Inexpensive.

Casa do Alentejo Rua das Portas de Santo Antão 58 ☎213 469 231. Extravagantly decorated building which is as much a private club dedicated to Alentejan culture as a mere restaurant. The courtyard is stunning, as is the period furniture, a perfect backdrop for sound Alentejan dishes such as *carne de porco à alentejana* (grilled pork and clams). Moderate.

Celeiro Macrobiótico-Naturista Rua 1° de Dezembro 65 ☎213 422 463. This health-food supermarket with basement self-service restaurant offers tasty vegetarian spring rolls, quiches and the like. Closes 8pm, and at weekends. Inexpensive.

João do Grão Rua dos Correeiros 220–228, ☎213 424 757. Established Baixa restaurant with an *azulejo*-covered interior, outdoor seats on a

△ Diners, *Bom Jardim*

pedestrianized stretch and reliable Portuguese food, including some fine rice dishes. Moderate.

Leão d'Ouro Rua 1° de Dezembro 105 ☎213 469 195. Very attractive *azulejo*-lined restaurant specializing in seafood (which can push the price up) and grilled meats. Get there early or reserve a table. Moderate.

Martinho da Arcada Pr do Comércio 3 ☎218 879 259. Beautiful restaurant in the arcade, little changed from the beginning of the twentieth century when it was frequented by writer Fernando Pessoa. Formal service and well-presented traditional Portuguese food, but you can always just call in for a coffee and *pastel de nata* in the attached stand-up café, or have less formal lunches at the outdoor tables under the arches. Closed Sun. Expensive.

Tão Rua dos Douradores 10 ☎218 850 046. Fashionable, very good value eastern-inspired vegetarian restaurant, with set meals from around €5. Tasty vegetarian sushi, risottos, grilled aubergines and salads. Closed Sun. Inexpensive.

Terreiro do Paço Pr do Comércio ☎ 210 312 850. Stylish restaurant right on the square, serving high-quality meat and fish dishes accompanied by wine in glasses the size of pumpkins. Intimate downstairs tables are separated by wooden screens, though upstairs is nicer, under a brick-vaulted ceiling. Saturday lunch specials feature *cozido* (boiled meat stews), while Sunday brunch concentrates on Portuguese specialities like *bacalhau* or *coelho* (rabbit). Closed Sun evening. Expensive.

The Sé, Alfama and Castelo and Doca Jardim do Tobaco

The following are marked on the Alfama and Castelo map on p.99.

Arco do Castelo Rua do Chão da Feira 25 ☎ 218 876 598. Cheerful place specializing in Goan dishes, like a tempting shrimp curry, Indian sausage and spicy seafood. Closed Sun. Moderate.

Casa do Leão Castelo de São Jorge ☎ 218 875 962. Couldn't be better sited, within the castle walls and with an outdoor summer terrace, offering a superb city view. Service is slick – this is rated one of the city's best restaurants – and the menu highlights classic Portuguese dishes such as *cataplana de cherne* (sea bass stew). Expensive.

Estrela da Sé Largo S. António da Sé 4 ☎ 218 870 455. Beautiful restaurant with wooden booths built in the nineteenth century for discreet trysts. It serves tasty dishes like *alheira* (sausage) and salmon as well as tapas. Closed weekends. Moderate.

Hua Ta Li Rua dos Bacalhoeiras 115 ☎ 218 879 170. Highly rated Chinese restaurant, particularly popular at Sun lunch when reservations are advised. There's good-value seafood (which pushes prices up to moderate) alongside all the usual Chinese dishes. Inexpensive.

Jardim do Marisco Av Infante Dom Henrique, Doca Jardim do Tobaco Pavilhão AB ☎ 218 824 240. Best positioned of the row of warehouse-restaurants in the Doca Jardim do Tobaco develop-ment. No prizes for guessing the speciality: the counter groans under the weight of crabs, giant prawns and shellfish. There's an upstairs terrace with great river views. Expensive.

Lautasco Beco do Azinhal 7 ☎ 218 860 173. There are tables in a pretty courtyard with fairy lights, making this a particularly romantic spot for a night out. The *cataplana* is recommended. Reservations advised. Closed Sun & Dec. Expensive.

Malmequer-Bemmequer Rua de São Miguel 23–25, at Largo de São Miguel ☎ 218 876 535. Charcoal-grilled meat and fish (try the sole) served

up amidst cheery, flowery decor. The set menu costs around €15. Closed Tues lunch & all day Mon. Moderate.

Mercado de Santa Clara Campo de Santa Clara, east of São Vicente de Fora ☎ 218 873 986. Above the old market building and by Feira da Ladra, this characterful restaurant offers award-winning cuisine and river views. It specializes in beef and meat dishes, though there's a small fish selection which can push it into the expensive range. Closed all day Mon and Sun evening. Moderate.

A Tasquinha Largo do Contador Mor 5–7. Considering its position, on the main route up to the castle, this lovely *tasca* has remained remark-ably unaffected by tourism, with a few tables in its traditional interior and a fine outdoor terrace. Closed Sun. Moderate.

Teatro Taborda Costa do Costelo 75 ☎ 218 879 484. Fashionable theatre café-restaurant with fine views from the terrace. The menu makes a change, offering fresh vegetarian dishes, Greek salads and the like. Open from 2pm, closed Mon. Moderate.

Via Graça Rua Damasceno Monteiro 9B ☎ 218 870 830. Unattractive new building but an interior offering stunning panoramas of Lisbon. Superbly cooked specialities include spider crab, clam *cataplana* and lobster. Closed all day Sun, and Sat lunch. Expensive.

Santa Apolónia

The following are marked on the Lisbon map on pp.80–81.

Bica do Sapato Armazém B, Cais da Pedra à Bica do Sapatas ☎ 218 810 320. Part-owned by actor John Malkovich and attracting Lisbon's glitterati, this is a very swish warehouse conversion with an outside terrace facing the river opposite Santa Apolónia. The menu features a long list of Portu-guese dishes given a modern twist. Closed Mon lunch & all day Sun. Expensive.

Casanova Loja 7 Armazém B, Cais da Pedra à Bica do Sapato ☎ 218 877 532. The modest *Casanova* offers pizza, pasta and crostini accom-panied by fine views from its outside terrace. It's phenomenally popular and you can't book, so turn up early. Closed all day Mon & Tues lunch. Moderate.

Deli Deluxe Av Infante Dom Henrique, Armazem B, Loja 8 ☎ 218 862 070. A modern deli with delectable cheeses, cured meats and preserves, though the riverside café-restaurant at the back is even more appealing. Outdoor seating and a range of goodies from croissants to speciality teas, yoghurts, bagels, salads and cocktails. At weekends, the set brunches from €8 are superb. Closed Mon. Moderate.

Chiado, Cais do Sodré and around

The following are marked on the Bairro Alto map on pp.104–105.

Chez Degroote Rua dos Duque de Bragança 4 ☎213 472 839. Romantic spot in a tastefully restored town house, with soaring ceilings and shuttered windows. Specialities include various beef dishes and some great starters. It's popular with a gay clientele but not exclusively so. Closed Sun. Moderate.

A Comida da Ribeira Mercado da Ribeira ☎210 312 600. Upstairs in the market building, this is a very popular lunch spot – get here early to beat the rush. Well-priced regional dishes and superb value lunch buffets. Inexpensive.

L' Entrecôte Rua do Alecrim 121 ☎213 428 343. The place to eat steaks washed down with fine wines. There's a relaxed, informal atmosphere in the spacious, wood-panelled interior. Set menus are around €15, though it's easy to spend more if you wade through the a la carte menu. Closed Sat & Sun lunch. Expensive.

Porto de Abrigo Rua dos Remolares 16–18 ☎213 460 873. Old-style tavern-restaurant serving market-fresh fish at reasonable prices; the *arroz de polvo* (octopus rice) and garlicky shrimps are superb. Closed Sun. Moderate.

Bairro Alto and around

The following are marked on the Bairro Alto map on pp.104–105

Águas do Bengo Rua do Teixeira 1 ☎213 477 516. African music restaurant owned by Angolan musician Waldemar Bastos. The menu features unusual-for-Lisbon tropical dishes – like chicken cooked in palm oil – and there's seafood too, though, this can push your dinner into the expensive category. If you're lucky and he's about, Waldemar will play a tune or two. Dinner only, closed Mon and winter. Moderate.

Bota Alta Trav da Queimada 37 ☎213 427 959. This attractive old tavern with quirky, boot-themed decor (its name means "high boot") attracts queues for its large portions of traditional Portuguese food. It's always packed and the tables are crammed in cheek by jowl; try to get there before 8pm. Closed Sun. Moderate.

Brasuca Rua João Pereira da Rosa 7 ☎213 220 740. Well-established Brazilian restaurant in a great old building downhill from the Bairro Alto. Dishes include a good *feijoada moqueca* (chicken and bean stew) and *picanha* (slices of garlicky beef). Closed Mon from Nov–April. Moderate.

Calcuta Rua do Norte 17 ☎213 428 295. Very popular Indian restaurant at the foot of the Bairro Alto, with modern decor and a largely young clientele. Lots of chicken, seafood and lamb curries, tandooris, good vegetarian options and a reasonable set menu. Closed Sun. Moderate.

O Cantinho do Bem Estar Rua do Norte 46. The decor borders on the kitsch, with fake chickens and a tiled roof over the kitchen, but the "canteen of well-being" lives up to its name with friendly service. Rice dishes and generous salads are the best bet; the passable house wine comes in ceramic jugs. Closed Mon. Moderate.

Comida de Santo Calç Engenheiro Miguel Pais 39 ☎213 963 339. Rowdy, late-opening Brazilian restaurant serving cocktails and classic dishes. Expensive.

Esplanada Pr do Príncipe Real ☎962 311 669. Glass pavilion in the square with outdoor seats under the shady trees. Great for lunch, as it does a good range of pizzas, quiches and vast wholemeal sandwiches. Inexpensive.

Faz Frio Rua Dom Pedro V 96 ☎213 461 860. A traditional restaurant, replete with tiles and private cubicles, serving huge portions of *bacalhau*, seafood paella and other daily specials. Closed two weeks in late August. Moderate.

Mal Amanhado Rua Alegria 54A ☎213 433 381. Steeply downhill towards Avenida da Liberdade, this bustling local serves superb dishes such as *migas*, mixed fried fish and pork kebabs from around €10. Recommended. Closed Sat lunch and all day Sun. Inexpensive.

Olivier Rua do Teixeira 35 ☎213 421 024, ⊛www.restaurante.olivier.com. The most talked about restaurant amongst Lisbon foodies with an excellent value set menu of €30 offering quality modern Portuguese cuisine. Expect starters from cherry tomato kebabs with feta, crab guacamole or game sausage; mains such as scallops a la crème or roast pork with honey and rosemary; and divine desserts including chocolate coulant with ice cream and fruit coulit. Reservations recommended. Evenings only. Closed Sun. Expensive.

Pap Açorda Rua da Atalaia 57–59 ☎213 464 811. Famous restaurant attracting arty celebrities who enjoy the agreeable surroundings of a dining room converted from an old bakery, now hung with chandeliers. *Açorda* – the house speciality – is a sort of bread and shellfish stew, seasoned with fresh coriander and a raw egg. Reservations recommended. Closed Sun & Mon. Expensive.

A Primavera do Jerónimo Trav da Espera 34 ☎213 420 477. This tiny place neatly crams in a couple of dozen diners, a bar and a kitchen area and a very long menu, overseen by the owner and his daughter. *Azulejos* inscribed with Portuguese proverbs dot the walls, while the mid-priced, home-cooked Portuguese dishes are highly rated (as newspaper reviews on the walls testify). Reservations advised. Closed Sun.

Primeiro do Maio Rua da Atalaia 8 ☎213 426 840. Buzzing *adega* with good-value dishes of the day and sizzling meat and fish specials. Closed Sat lunch & all Sun. Moderate.

Sul Rua do Norte 13 ☎213 462 449. Jazzy, split-level wine bar and restaurant – the 'round table' in the lower mezzanine is ideal for large groups. Dishes include chicken kebabs, risotto and *bife na pedra* (steak cooked on a stone). Mains start at around €16. Closed Mon. Expensive.

Trindade Rua Nova da Trindade 20 ☎213 423 506. Huge vaulted beer hall-restaurant – the city's oldest, dating from 1836 – with some of Lisbon's loveliest *azulejos* on the walls. It specializes in shellfish, though other dishes are also good, as is the beer. There's a patio garden. Moderate.

São Bento, Lapa and around

Unless otherwise stated, the following are marked on the Bairro Alto map on pp.104–105.

Cantinho da Paz Rua da Paz 4, São Bento ☎213 969 698. Near the parliament building, this offers excellent Goan dishes such as shark soup, prawn curry and some vegetarian options. It's on a side street just off tram route #28. Moderate.

Coentrada Rua de São Domingos à Lapa 100, ☎213 928 860. Mon–Fri noon–3pm. See Lisbon map, pp.80–81. Set in the former Palácio dos Condes de Monte, this stylish restaurant serves quality Portuguese lunches. Tables are also set out in the lovely old courtyard surrounded by *azulejos* and below the palace bell tower. Mon–Fri lunches only, open evenings and weekends for groups of over 40. Expensive.

Picanha Rua das Janelas Verdes 47, Lapa ☎213 975 401. See Lisbon map, pp.80–81. Just up from the Museu de Arte Antiga, with an intimate, ornately tiled interior, *Picanha* has multi-lingual service and specializes in *picanha* (thin slices of beef) accompanied by black-eyed beans, salad and potatoes. Great if this appeals to you (as that's all they do) and for a fixed-price of around €14 you can eat as much of the stuff as you want. Closed Sat & Sun lunch. Moderate.

Varina da Madragoa Rua das Madres 34, ☎213 965 533. Once the haunt of Nobel Prize for Literature winner José Saramago, and it's easy to see why he liked it: a lovely, traditional restaurant with grape-embellished *azulejos* on the walls and a menu featuring superb Portuguese dishes such as *bacalhau*, trout and steaks. Closed Sat lunch and all day Sun & Mon. Moderate.

Alcântara and the docks

The following are marked on the Alcântara and the docks map on p.110.

Alcântara Café Rua Maria Luísa Holstein 15, Alcântara ☎213 637 176. Elite designer bar-restaurant blending industrial and modern architecture. One of the city's trendiest in decor and clientele. Dinner and drinks only, until 3am. Expensive.

Cosmos Armazém 15, Doca de Santo Amaro ☎213 972 747. Daily noon–4am. Relatively inexpensive for these parts, with pasta, pizza or salads from around €8, and plenty of outside seating facing the marina. After midnight the inside is cleared for dancing til the small hours. Inexpensive.

Belém

The following are marked on the Belém map on p.112.

Floresta Belém Pr Afonso de Albuquerque 1. One of the best-value places on this stretch, attracting a largely Portuguese clientele, especially for weekend lunches. Great salads, grills and fresh fish inside or on a sunny outdoor terrace. Closed Sun evening. Moderate.

Quadrante Centro Cultural de Belém ☎213 612 400. Good-value self-service food (salads, sandwiches and rice dishes), which you can enjoy on the roof-garden terrace providing exhilarating views over Belém and the river. Inexpensive.

Avenida da Liberdade and outer Lisbon

The following are marked on the Lisbon map on pp.80–81.

Bela Ipanema Av da Liberdade 169 ☎213 572 316. Mon–Sat 7am–midnight. Bustling café/bar/restaurant by the São Jorge cinema. The bar attracts a steady stream of locals with its pastries, light lunches, beers and coffees; the small dining area serves very good value food, with outdoor tables facing the avenue. Inexpensive.

O Cantinho do Rato Mercado do Rato, entrance off Rua Alexandre Herculano 64 ☎213 883 160. Tucked up a side alley by Rato's fruit, fish and clothes market and open for lunches only. Geared for market workers, grills are large, satisfying and very good value, from around €5. Closed Sun. Inexpensive.

Centro de Arte Moderna Fundação Calouste Gulbenkian, entrance by Rua Dr N. de Bettencourt; metro São Sebastião. Join the lunchtime queues at the museum restaurant for good-value hot or cold dishes. There are excellent salads for vegetarians; you get a choice of four or six varieties. Closes 5.45pm & Mon. Inexpensive.

Cervejaria Portugália Av Almirante Reis 117 ⓣ218 851 024; metro Arroios. The original beer-hall-restaurant where you can either snack and drink at the bar, or eat fine *mariscos* or steak in the dining room. It's a popular family outing and always busy. Moderate.

Eleven Rua Marquês da Fronteira ⓣ213 862 211 ⓦwww.restauranteleven.com. At the top of Parque Eduardo VII, this Michelin-starred restaurant hits the heights both literally and metaphorically. The interior is both intimate and bright with wonderful city views. Quality here costs about the same as an average London restaurant, with a set menu from around €70. Dishes feature Azorean tuna with sesame, ox consumé with ginger and lobster ravioli or wasabi risotto with prawn crunch, and each course can come with a specially chosen wine. Closed Sun. Very expensive.

Ribadouro Av da Liberdade 155 ⓣ213 549 411; metro Avenida. The Avenida's best *cervejaria*, serving a decent range of grilled meat and fresh shellfish (but no fish). If you don't fancy a full meal, order a beer with a plate of prawns at the bar. Moderate.

Os Tibetanos Rua do Salitre 117 ⓣ213 142 038; metro Avenida. Located in the Buddhist Centre, this stripped-pine restaurant has superb, unusual veggie food, such as tasty vegetarian paella. Closed Sat and Sun. Inexpensive.

Parque das Nações

The following are marked on the Parque das Nações map on p.123.

Sabores a Bacalhau Rua da Pimenta 47 ⓣ218 957 290. Unassuming place with outdoor tables, whose name translates as "tastes of dried cod". It offers around fourteen of the alleged 365 *bacalhau* recipes at good-value prices. Closed Tues. Moderate.

Tartaruga Rua da Pimenta 95 ⓣ218 957 499. Standard Portuguese fare with a few tasty pasta dishes too, with outdoor seats facing the gardens. On Fridays and Saturdays the inside switches to a dance bar after midnight, when the décor seems increasingly lurid. Closed Mon.

Drinking and nightlife

The traditional centre of Lisbon's nightlife is the **Bairro Alto**, with its cramped streets, ageing taverns, designer bars, fado houses and restaurants. The quarter hosts one of Europe's biggest weekly parties, with up to 50,000 people descending on the maze of streets over the weekend, drifting from bar to club before heading out to those around the docks for the small hours. Other downtown areas are not really on the bar and club circuit – you'll be hard pushed to find a bar open late at night in the **Baixa**, though the **Alfama** and **Graça** have a few places catering for the crowds leaving the excellent local restaurants.

Instead, as the night progresses, Lisboetas seek out the classy venues along **Avenida 24 de Julho**, around Santos station, or a little further west at **Alcântara** docks, near Ponte 25 de Abril. To the east, the world-famous club *Lux* typifies the city's most up-and-coming area along the riverfront by **Santa Apolónia** station. The **Parque das Nações** (metro Oriente) also has a lively bar scene. For all these outlying areas, you'll need a taxi or nightbus to get you back to town again. **Gay and lesbian nightlife** focuses on the Bairro Alto and Praça do Príncipe Real, where a generally laid-back group of clubs and bars attracts people of all ages. For more information on the gay and lesbian scene in Lisbon, see "Listings", p.142.

Drinks are uniformly expensive in all fashionable bars and clubs – from €4 for a beer – but the plus-side is that very few charge admission. Instead many places have a "minimum consumption" policy, designed to stop people dancing all night without buying a drink, which many Portuguese would happily do. Mostly, these fees are at the whim of the doorman, who will relax it if it's a quiet night, or whack it up if it's busy or if he doesn't like the look of you. Generally, you can expect to pay anything from €10 to €50 (occasionally up to €150); keep hold of your ticket as drinks will be stamped on it to ensure you consume enough (otherwise you pay on exit).

Friday and Saturday nights tend to be overcrowded and expensive everywhere, while on Sunday, especially in the Bairro Alto, places often close to sleep off the weekend excesses. None of the places listed below open much before 10pm unless otherwise stated; all are open until at least 2am, with most doing business much later than that: 4am is normal, 7am or later not unheard of. Unless stated otherwise, the following are open daily.

Baixa and Santa Apolónia

The following are marked on the Lisbon map on pp.80–81.

A Ginginha Largo de São Domingos 8. Everyone should try *ginginha* – Portuguese cherry brandy – once. There's just about room in this microscopic joint to walk in, down a glassful and stagger outside to see the city in a new light.

Lux Armazéns A, Cais da Pedra a Santa Apolónia ⊕ 218 820 890, ⓦ www.luxfragil.com. This three-storey converted meat warehouse has become one of Europe's most fashionable places to be seen, attracting the likes of Prince and Cameron Diaz. Part-owned by actor John Malkovich, it was the first place to venture into the docks opposite Santa Apolónia station. There's a rooftop terrace with amazing views, a middle floor with various bars, comfy chairs and sofas, amazing projection screens, and music from pop to jazz and dance; while the downstairs dance floor descends into frenzy at times. The club is also increasingly on the circuit for visiting bands. Closed Mon.

Alfama and Graça

The following places are marked on the Alfama and Castelo map on p.99.

Bar das Imagens/Costa do Castelo Calç do Marquês de Tancos 1B ⊕ 218 884 636. Beautifully positioned sunny terrace-café with Baixa views, a long list of cocktails and mid-priced food. There's live (usually Brazilian or jazz) music on Thurs and Fri nights, and poetry readings on others. Closed Mon & Tues.

Esplanada da Graça Largo da Graça ⊕ 217 427 508. Kiosk-bar underneath the Miradouro da Graça, with great views and, as it gets later, pumping music. A good place for a drink at sunset. Closed in poor weather.

Rêsto do Chapitô Costa do Castelo 7 ⊕ 218 867 334. Multi-purpose venue incorporating a theatre and circus school, moderately priced restaurant (closed Mon, weekend lunches only) and a tapas bar attracting Lisbon's bohemian set. The outdoor esplanade commands terrific views over the Alfama.

Cais do Sodré

The following are marked on the Bairro Alto and around map on pp.104–105.

British Bar Rua Bernardino Costa 52 ⊕ 213 422 367. Mon–Sat 8am–midnight. Wonderful Anglo–Portuguese hybrid stuck in a 1930s time warp, featuring ceiling fans, a marble counter and dark wooden shelves stacked with wines and spirits. There's also Guinness on tap and regulars who look as if they've been coming here since the day it opened.

The Pump House Rua da Moeda 1 ⊕ 213 972 059. English-run bar opposite the post office, with British grub and a big-screen TV showing major sporting events.

Bairro Alto

The following are marked on the Bairro Alto bars and clubs map on p.133.

121 Rua do Norte 117–119. Laid-back lounge bar with low, comfy seats, aboriginal art and ambient sounds. Closed Sun & Mon.

Arroz Doce Rua da Atalaia 117–119 ⊕ 213 462 601. A reassuringly normal bar in the middle of the otherwise frenetic nightlife. The owners are friendly and it's a good spot for an early or late beer, or try "Auntie's" sangria. Closed Sun.

Bar Ártis Rua do Diário de Notícias 95 ⊕ 213 424 795. Laid-back jazz bar with arty posters on the wall and marble tabletops. The snacks here are good too (try the chicken toasties). Closed Mon.

Bicaense Rua da Bica Duarte Belo 38–42. Small, fashionable bar on the steep street used by the Elevador da Bica, with jazzy and Latin sounds and a moderately priced list of bar food. Closed Sun.

Clube da Esquina Rua da Barroca 30 ⊕ 213 427 149. Lively corner bar with ancient radios on the wall and DJs spinning discs on a good, old-fashioned turntable. Great for people watching.

Enoteca Rua da Mãe de Água ⊕ 213 422 079. On Bairro Alto and around map pp.104–105. Downhill from Praça do Príncipe Real, this extraordinary wine bar is set in the bowels of a nineteenth-century bathhouse. Serves upmarket wines and other drinks, along with *petiscos* (snacks). Closed Mon.

Frágil Rua da Atalaia 126 ⊕ 213 469 578. An icon of cool for years before the owner opened *Lux* (see opposite). Partly gay, wholly pretentious, this continues to be a fashionable destination – it's best after 1am. Ring the bell to get in. Closed Sun.

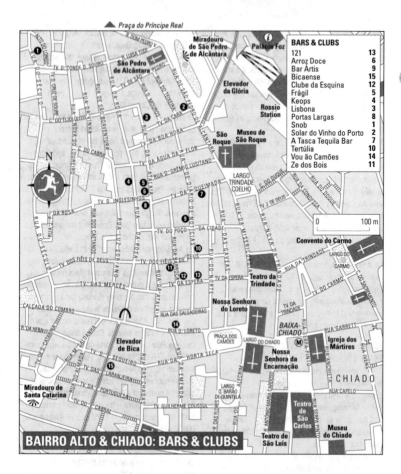

▲ Praça do Príncipe Real

BARS & CLUBS

121	13
Arroz Doce	6
Bar Ártis	9
Bicaense	15
Clube da Esquina	12
Frágil	5
Keops	4
Lisbona	3
Portas Largas	8
Snob	1
Solar do Vinho do Porto	2
A Tasca Tequila Bar	7
Tertúlia	10
Vou ão Camões	14
Ze dos Bois	11

BAIRRO ALTO & CHIADO: BARS & CLUBS

Keops Rua da Rosa 157–159 ☎213 428 773. Friendly music bar with doors open onto the streets, and a candlelit interior, playing the latest sounds most nights. Closed Sun.

Lisbona Rua da Atalaia 196 ☎213 471 412. Earthy, local bar with its share of quirky regulars, but its chequerboard tiles covered in soccer memorabilia, old film posters and graffiti also lure in the Bairro Alto fashionistas. Inexpensive beer, too. Closed Sun.

Pavilhão Chinês Rua Dom Pedro V 89 ☎213 424 729. On Bairro Alto and around map pp.104–105. Once a nineteenth-century tea and coffee merchants' shop, this is now a quirky bar set in a series of comfy rooms, including a pool room. Most are completely lined with mirrored cabinets containing a bizarre range of artefacts from around the world, including a cabinet of model

trams. There is waiter service and the usual drinks are supplemented by a long list of exotic cocktails.

Portas Largas Rua da Atalaia 105 ☎218 466 379. Atmospheric, black-and-white tiled *adega* with cheapish drinks, music from fado to pop, and a varied, partly gay crowd, which spills out onto the street on warm evenings. Often a starting point for clubbers moving on to *Frágil* opposite.

Snob Rua do Século 178 ☎213 463 723. Appropriately named upmarket bar-restaurant towards Principe Real, full of media people. It's a good spot for cocktails or a late-night light meal (the steaks are recommended).

Solar do Vinho do Porto Rua de São Pedro de Alcântara 45 ☎213 475 707. Opened in 1944, the Port Wine Institute's Lisbon base lures in visitors with over 300 types of port, starting at around €2 a glass and rising to €25 for a glass of forty-year-old

133

JW Burmester. Drinks are served at low tables in a comfortable eighteenth-century mansion, and though the waiters are notoriously snooty and the cheaper ports never seem to be in stock, it's still a good place to kick off an evening. Closed Sun.

A Tasca Tequila Bar Trav da Queimada 13–15. Colourful Mexican bar which caters to a good-time crew downing tequilas, margaritas and wicked Brazilian caipirinhas.

Tertúlia Rua do Diário de Notícias 60 ☎213 462 704. Relaxed café-bar with inexpensive drinks, papers to read, background jazz and varied art exhibitions that change fortnightly. If you get the urge to play, there's a piano for customers too. Closed Sun.

Vou ão Camões Rua de Loreto 44. All credit to the owners who have found space for tables on two floors of a bar barely larger than a broom cupboard. Attracts a clientele as quirky as the decor. Closed Mon.

Ze dos Bois Rua da Barroca 59 ☎213 430 205 ⓦ www.zedebois.org. Rambling art venue that hosts various installations, arthouse films and exhibitions along with occasional concerts. At weekends (11pm–2am), local DJs showcase their talents to an alternative crowd.

Santos, Alcântara and the docks

The following are marked on the Alcântara map on p.110 unless otherwise indicated.

Santos, the next stop up on the line from Cais do Sodré, is being promoted as the area of design, and has some up-and-coming clubs to join the established big names on this stretch known for its glitzy clubbing scene.

Armazém F Rua da Cintura, Armazém 65 ☎213 220 160 ⓦ www.armazemf.com. On Lisbon map p.80. Brazilian club/bar on the riverfront at Cais do Gás, though dancing is more the norm than gassing. There's a reasonably relaxed door policy and a mix of live pop bands and resident DJs playing house and samba. Attracts a young, partly Brazilian and lively crowd. Open Thurs–Sun.

Buddha Bar Gare Marítima de Alcântara ☎213 950 555 ⓦ www.buddha.com.pt. Wonderful eastern-influenced bar/club housed in a 1940s maritime station, inspired by the Paris original. There are many chillout areas upstairs, most with an "opium den" feel, with a big dance floor downstairs. Smart dress recommended, and check opening hours in advance as it's sometimes booked for private functions. At other times, there's a mimimum consumption of around €20 (men) and €10 (women).

Doca de Santo Doca de Santo Amaro ☎213 963 535. Large, palm-fringed club, bar and restaurant with a great cocktail bar on the esplanade.

Estado Liquido Largo de Santos 5A ☎213 955 820 ⓦ www.estadoliquido.com. On Lisbon map p.80. Right on Santos' main square, this bar/club has a roomy feel despite the vibrant young crowd and prominent club DJs. Easy-going door policy and efficient service. Minimum consumption around €10. Closed Mon.

Kapital Av 24 de Julho 68 ☎213 955 963. On Lisbon map p.80. Well-established hotspot, with three sleekly designed floors full of *queques* (yuppies) paying high prices for drinks and listening to the latest dance sounds. There's a great rooftop terrace. Open till 6am, until 4am on Sun and Mon.

Kremlin Escadinhas da Praia 5 ☎216 087 768. On Lisbon map p.80. Packed with flash, young, raving Lisboans. Tough door rules, and don't bother showing up before 2am. Open till 7am, and till 9am on Fri and Sat; closed Sun & Mon.

Op Art Doca de Santo Amaro ☎213 956 797 ⓦ www.opartcafe.com. Sat in splendid isolation on the fringes of the Tejo, this small glass pavilion morphs from a simple restaurant serving moderately-priced grills into a groovy evening bar. In summer, you can sprawl on dockside beanbags and gaze over the river. After 1pm, the mood changes again with vibrant dance sounds. Closed Sun.

Queens Rua Cintura do Porto de Lisboa, Armázem H Naves A–B ☎213 955 870. Pedro Luz launched this club as a "high-tech gay disco", but it has always successfully attracted a large following of beautiful people of all sexual persuasions. It's a huge, pulsating place – there's an excellent sound system – which can hold 2500 people – and guest DJs. Closed Sun & Mon.

Parque das Nações

The following are marked on the Parque das Nações map on p.123.

Azul Profundo Sunny esplanade bar overlooking the glittering docks. Offers a good range of snacks, fruit juices and wicked caipirinha cocktails.

Havana Rua da Pimenta. Lively Cuban bar with an airy interior and outdoor seating. After 11pm it turns into more of a club. Closed Tues Oct–April.

República da Cerveja Passeio das Tágides 2–26 ☎218 922 590. In a great position close to the water's edge and facing the Vasco da Gama bridge, this modern bar-restaurant specializes in some fine international beers, though sticking to the local *Superbock* will save a few euros. Steaks and German cuisine are also on offer, and there's live rock Thursday to Saturday.

Gay and lesbian bars and clubs

The following are marked on the Bairro Alto map on p.133.

106 Rua São Marçal 106, Príncipe Real ☎213 427 373. Ring on the bell for admission to this friendly gay bar. Fridays often feature leather nights.

Bric-a-Brac Bar Rua Cecilio de Sousa 82–84, Príncipe Real ☎213 428 971. On a steep road beyond Praça do Prinçipe Real, this cruisy gay club has a large dance floor, "dark room" and various bars. Occasional drag shows. Closed Tues.

Finalmente Rua da Palmeira 38, Príncipe Real. A first-class disco with lashings of kitsch. Weekend drag shows (at 2am) feature skimpily dressed young senhoritas camping it up to high-tech sounds. Opens at midnight.

Max Rua São Marçal 15 ☎213 952 726. Daily 10pm–2am. Cosy gay bar increasingly popular amongst bears, with occasional strip shows.

Purex Rua das Salgadeiras 28, Bairro Alto. Small and friendly dance bar, popular with lesbians but not exclusively so, with upbeat sounds Thurs–Sun nights. Closed Mon.

Sétimo Céu Trav de Espera 54, Bairro Alto ☎213 466 471. Popular with gays and lesbians, this is an obligatory stop for beers and caipirinhas served by the Brazilian owner. The great atmosphere spills out onto the street. Closed Sun.

Trumps Rua da Imprensa Nacional 104B ☎213 971 059. Popular gay club with a reasonably relaxed door policy. Packed from Thurs to Sat, which sees a good lesbian turnout, a bit cruisy midweek. Drag shows on Sun and Wed. Closed Mon.

Live music

Although tourist brochures tend to suggest that live music in Lisbon begins and ends with **fado** – the city's most traditional music – there's no reason to miss out on other forms. Portuguese **jazz** can be good (there's a big annual International Jazz Festival at the Gulbenkian in the summer), and **rock** offers an occasional surprise (look out for emerging bands at the March Super Bock Rock festival and the giant biannual Rock in Rio festival in May). For Lisboans, **African music** from the former colonies of Cabo Verde, Guinea Bissau, Angola and Mozambique is always popular, as is **Brazilian and Latin** music, with major artists touring frequently.

There's often a crossover between musical styles at many of the places listed below; it's always worth checking the listings magazines (see "Arts and culture" p.138) and posters around the city to see what's on. Note, too, that many of the bars listed in the previous section put on live bands on certain nights of the week. There's a charge to get into most music clubs, which usually covers your first drink, and most of them stay open until around 4am, often later. Touring bands and artists also play at a variety of larger venues (listed overleaf).

Fado

Fado is often described as a kind of working-class blues, although musically it would perhaps be more accurate to class it as a kind of light operetta, sung to a viola accompaniment (for more on its roots see pp.637–638). Long popular in Portugal, it has become better known internationally since the success of

---

Tickets for major events

You can usually get advance **tickets** for live music, sports and other major events from the APEB kiosk (☎213 425 360; daily 9am–9.30pm) at the corner of Praça dos Restauradores (near the post office), which also has ticket and programme details for all the city's cinemas and theatres. Tickets can also be purchased from the book-and-music store FNAC (Rua do Nova do Almada 104–110, Chiado) as well as from the venues themselves or online at ⊛www.ticketline.pt.

Lisbon's events calendar

February or March. The **Carnival** has been revived recently with Brazilian-style parades and costumes, mainly at Parque das Nações.

March/April Annual Superbock Superrock festival with local and international bands in various venues (⊕www.superbock.pt).

May sees the five-day biannual Rock in Rio rock festival (⊕www.rockinrio-lisboa.sapo.pt) in Parque Bela Vista to the north of the centre.

June is known for its street-partying to celebrate the saints' days – **António (June 13)**, **João (June 24)** and **Pedro (June 29)**. Celebrations for each begin on the evening before the actual day. The main festival is for **Santo António**, a public holiday when the whole city is decked out in coloured ribbons, with pots of lucky basil on every window sill. There are festivals in each district on the evening of the 12th, with a main parade down Avenida da Liberdade also on the 12th. The best street party is in Alfama, with food and drinks stalls in just about every square. On June 13th, the "Brides of Santo António" sees a collective wedding ceremony at the Igreja de Santo António. In Sintra, the main *festa* is for **São Pedro**, starting on 28 June.

June/July A state-run **handicrafts fair**, with live folk music, is held in Estoril on the Avenida de Portugal, near the Casino. A similar event occurs during the same period at FIL (⊕www.fil.pt), the main exhibition hall at the Parque das Nações, when international and Portuguese regional crafts are displayed and offered for sale.

Also these months see the **Sintra Music Festival** with adventurous performances by international orchestras, musicians and dance groups in parks, gardens and palaces in and around Sintra, Estoril and Cascais. Tickets and programmes for all performances are available from the Gabinete do Sintra-Festival, Praça da República 23, Sintra ⊕219 243 518, ⊕www.cm-sintra.pt. An offshoot of the festival are the "Noites de Bailado" held in the Centro Cultural Olga Cadaval near Sintra train station (⊕219 107 118), a series of ballet, dance and operatic performances, again with top international names.

July sees a **beer festival** in the Castelo do São Jorge, with handicrafts, medieval markets, food stalls and lots of ale (⊕www.centralcervejas.pt).

July/August sees the big annual **Jazz Numa Noite de Verão** (jazz on a summer night) festival at the Gulbenkian's open-air amphitheatre (⊕www.musica.gulbenkian.pt), with a similar event in Cascais.

September sees thousands of runners for the Lisbon marathon which traces a route across Ponte Vasco da Gama with a finish in Parque das Nações (⊕www.maratonclubeportugal.com).

November 11th is celebrated by the traditional tasting of the year's wine downed with hot chestnuts, in memory of Saint Martinho, who shared his cape with a poor man.

The build-up to **Christmas** begins in early December with Europe's tallest Christmas tree filling the centre of Praça da Comércio. Distinctive hooped *bolo-rei* (dried-fruit "king cake") appears in shops and *pastelarias*. Christmas Day itself remains a family affair, with traditional midnight Mass celebrated on December 24, followed by a meal of *bacalhau*.

The best place to head for on **New Year's Eve** is Praça do Comércio, where fireworks light up the riverfront. There are similar events at Cascais and the Parque das Nações.

Mariza, who has won the BBC World Music Awards and frequently tours Europe. Alongside Coimbra (which has its own distinct tradition), Lisbon is still the best place to hear fado, which has its roots in the fado clubs in the Bairro Alto and particularly Alfama – either at a *casa de fado* or in an *adega típica*. There's no real distinction between these places: all are small, all serve food (though you don't always have to eat), and all open around 8pm, get going toward midnight, and stay open until 3 or 4am. Their drawbacks are inflated minimum charges – rarely below €15 – and, in the more touristy places, extreme tackiness. Uniformed bouncers are fast becoming the norm, as are warm-up singers crooning Beatles' songs and photographers snapping your table. We've highlighted some of the more authentic experiences.

Adega Machado Rua do Norte 91, Bairro Alto ☎213 224 640. One of the longest-established Bairro Alto joints, as the photo portraits on the wall testify (heads of state included). The minimum consumption of €16 builds to around €25 a head if you sample the fine Portuguese cooking. Closed Mon.

Adega Mesquita Rua do Diário de Notícias 107, Bairro Alto ☎213 219 280, ⓦwww .adegamesquita.com. Another of the big Bairro Alto names, with better-than-average music and traditional dancing as well as singing. The food is poor though. Minimum consumption €18.

Adega do Ribatejo Rua do Diário de Notícias 23, Bairro Alto ☎213 468 343. Great little *adega*, with one of the lowest minimum charges, enjoyable food and fado that locals describe as "pure emotion". The singers include a couple of professionals, the manager and – best of all – the cooks. Minimum charge around €10. Closed Sun.

Clube do Fado Rua de São João da Praça 92–94, Alfama ☎218 852 704. Intimate place with stone pillars, an old well and a mainly local clientele. Attracts small-time performers, up-and-coming talent and the occasional big names. Minimum charge around €15.

Parreirinha d'Alfama Beco do Espírito Santo 1, Alfama ☎218 868 209. One of the best fado venues, just off Largo do Chafariz de Dentro, often attracting leading stars and a local clientele. Reservations are advised when the big names appear. Minimum charge is around €15, up to around €30 with food.

O Senhor Vinho Rua do Meio à Lapa 18, Lapa ☎213 972 681. Famous club sporting some of the best singers in Portugal, which makes the €20 minimum charge (though rising to around €50 with a meal) pretty reasonable. Reservations are advised. Closed Sun.

A Severa Rua das Gáveas 55, Bairro Alto ☎213 464 006, ⓦwww.asevera.com. A city institution, named after a nineteenth-century gypsy singer. Big fado names and big prices. Minimum consumption around €19. Closed Thurs.

African and Brazilian

B. Leza Largo Conde-Barão 50, Santos ☎213 963 735. Live African music on most nights in this wonderful sixteenth-century building, with a dance floor, Cape Verdean food and table service. Open Wed–Sat.

Chafarica Calç de São Vicente 81, Alfama ☎218 867 449. Tiny, pricey but huge, fun Brazilian bar with live music from 11pm. Closed Sun.

Jazz and blues

Blues Café Rua Cintura do Porto de Lisboa, Doca de Alcântara ☎213 957 085. See Alcântara map on p.110. Converted dockside warehouse serving Cajun food in the restaurant (until 12.30am) in Lisbon's only blues club. Live music on Mon and Thurs, club nights on Fri and Sat from 2.30am. The advertised minimum consumption of €150 is designed to put off the hoi polloi; take it with a pinch of salt. Closed Sun & Mon.

Hot Clube de Portugal Pr de Alegria 39, off Av da Liberdade ☎213 467 369, ⓦwww.hcp.pt; metro Avenida. The city's best jazz venue – a tiny basement club that hosts local and visiting artists. Closed Sun & Mon.

Speakeasy Armazém 115, Cais das Oficinas, Doca de Alcântara ☎213 957 308. See Alcântara map on p.110. Docklands jazz bar and restaurant hosting some big and up-and-coming names, usually on Tues–Thurs after 11pm. Closed Sun.

△ *B. Leza* nightclub

Large venues

Aula Magna Reitoria da Universidade de Lisboa, Alamada da Universidade ☎217 967 624; metro Cidade Universitaria. The student union venue, which feels like a lecture hall; seating only.

Coliseu dos Recreios Rua das Portas de Santo Antão 96, Baixa ☎213 240 580, ⓦwww .coliseulisboa.com; metro Restauradores. Main indoor city-centre rock, pop and classical venue set in a lovely domed building, originally opened in 1890 as a circus.

Freeport Alcochete, around 20km south of Lisbon; reached by bus #431 or #432 from Oriente station; ☎212 343 502, ⓦwww.freeport.pt. Giant designer shopping complex, a twenty-minute bus ride from the Parque das Nações, which has also become a venue for touring bands – Ronan Keating, Sugababes, James Callum and Craig David have all appeared here.

Pavilhão Atlântico Parque das Nações ☎218 918 440, ⓦwww.atlantico-multiusos.pt; metro Oriente. Big-name stars play at Portugal's largest indoor venue, which holds up to 20,000 spectators; hosted the MTV awards in 2005.

Sony Plaza Parque das Nações ☎218 918 440, ⓦwww.pavilhaoatlantico.pt; metro Oriente. The Parque's main outdoor venue holds up to 10,000 people for summer concerts and New Year's Eve extravaganzas.

Arts and culture

Most major cultural events in the city – including just about every **classical music** concert – are sponsored either by the Fundação Calouste Gulbenkian, Culturgest or the Centro Cultural de Belém, all of which have a full annual programme. Tickets range from €5 to €30, though there are also frequent free concerts and recitals at the São Roque church in Bairro Alto, the Sé, the Basílica da Estrela, São Vicente de Fora and the Igreja dos Mártires. For details of **ballet** performances, consult the website of the renowned Lisbon-based Companhia Nacional de Bailado (ⓦwww.cnb.pt).

Classical music aside, there's a fair amount of other entertainment in Lisbon, including several **theatres**, though productions are almost exclusively in Portuguese.

Cinema is a better bet for most tourists, as virtually all cinemas show original-language films with Portuguese subtitles, and ticket prices are low (around €8; cheaper on Mon). For mainstream Hollywood movies you only need to head for any major shopping centre: there are multi-screen complexes at Amoreiras, Edifício Monumental (metro Saldanha), El Corte Inglês (metro São Sebastião), Vasco da Gama in Parque das Nações (metro Oriente) and Colombo Shopping Centre (metro Colégio Militar-Luz). We've picked out a couple of interesting art-house venues below, which often show films for the April Indie Lisboa **film festival**, showcasing independent cinema from around the world (Ⓦwww.indielisboa.com) and the Sept/Oct Gay and Lesbian Film Festival (Ⓦwww.opusgayassociation.com). For the latest happenings in the **Portuguese film scene**, look out for Festroia, a ten-day film festival in Setúbal in June (Ⓦwww.festroia.pt).

To find out **what's on**, pick up a schedule of exhibitions, concerts and events from the reception desks at the Gulbenkian and the Belém Cultural Centre. The best **listings** are in *Agenda Cultural*, a free monthly magazine produced by the town hall, which details current exhibitions and shows (in Portuguese). *Follow Me Lisboa* is a watered-down English-language version produced by the local tourist authorities – both are available from the tourist offices. For other listings and previews of forthcoming events, get hold of *Público*, the *Diário de Notícias* or *O Independente* **newspapers**, or consult the ABEP kiosk at the corner of Restauradores (daily 9am–9.30pm), though remember that the Portuguese titles for films are not always direct translations.

Cinema

Instituto da Cinemateca Portuguesa Rua Barata Salgueiro 39 ⓣ213 596 266, Ⓦwww.cinemateca .pt; metro Avenida. The national film theatre, with twice-daily shows ranging from contemporary Portuguese films to anything from Truffaut to Valentino. It also has its own small cinema museum.

Quarteto Rua das Flores Lima 1, off Av Estados Unidos ⓣ217 971 244; metro Entre Campos. Art-house cinema with four screens.

São Jorge Av da Liberdade 175 ⓣ213 103 400; metro Avenida. Most central cinema for mainstream movies, though sometimes closed for temporary exhibitions and fairs.

Classical music and opera

Centro Cultural de Belém Pr do Império, Belém ⓣ213 612 400, Ⓦwww.ccb.pt. Has both a large and small auditorium for a range of music and dance, from jazz to classical.

Culturgest Av João XXI 63, Campo Pequeno ⓣ217 905 155, Ⓦwww.cgd.pt. Large modern arts complex with two auditoriums for exhibitions, music, dance and theatre.

Fundação Calouste Gulbenkian Av de Berna ⓣ217 823 000, Ⓦwww.gulbenkian.pt. There are three concert halls (including an outdoor amphitheatre) at the Gulbenkian, with performances ranging from jazz to chamber to classical, with prestigious guest soloists.

Teatro Nacional de São Carlos Rua Serpa Pinto 9, Chiado ⓣ213 468 408, Ⓦwww.saocarlos.pt. The opera season runs from September to June and, in addition, there's a regular classical music programme.

Theatre

Lisbon Players Rua da Estrela 10, Lapa ⓣ213 961 946. Check out performances by this amateur but highly rated English-speaking theatrical group consisting largely of expat actors.

Teatro Nacional de Dona Maria Rossio, Baixa ⓣ213 472 246, Ⓦwww.teatro-dmaria.pt. Regular performances of Portuguese and foreign plays.

Sports

Football is the biggest game in Lisbon, and it's usually easy to get match tickets (see overleaf), while summer-season **bullfights** are the other main spectacle. Otherwise, you're going to need to travel out of the capital for sports, either for **golf**, on the upmarket courses around Estoril (consult

Ⓦwww.estorilsintragolf.com.pt), or **watersports**, namely surfing at Caparica (see p.160) and windsurfing at Guincho (p.148) and Ericeira (p.174).

Football

Benfica – Lisbon's most famous football team – have a glorious past (the great Eusébio played for the team in the 1960s), though they have been struggling of late to keep up with city rivals Sporting. The awesome **Estádio da Luz**, Avenida Gen. Norton Matos (Ⓣ217 210 500, Ⓦwww.slbenfica.pt; metro Colégio Militar-Luz), was completely rebuilt in preparation for the 2004 European Championships; it was here that Portugal lost in the final to Greece in front of 65,000 disbelieving spectators.

Sporting Lisbon (officially called Sporting Club de Portugal), Benfica's traditional city rivals, play at the nearby **Estádio José Alvalade**, Rua Professor da Fonseca (Ⓣ217 516 000, Ⓦwww.sporting.pt; metro Campo Grande), also purpose built for Euro 2004 and featuring state-of-the-art stadium-design, with a capacity of 54,000. Top-division action can also be caught at the Estádio do Restelo, Avenida do Restelo, Belém (Ⓣ213 010 461, Ⓦwww.cfbelenenses.pt), home of **Belenenses**, though they last won the title back in 1946.

The **Portuguese Cup Final** is held every May at the Estádio Nacional (National Stadium; Ⓣ214 197 212), Praça da Maratona, Cruz Quebrada (bus #6 from Algés or train to Cruz Quebrada from Cais do Sodré). The stadium holds up to 55,000 but is pretty run-down and soulless – it was not among the eight stadiums selected as venues for the 2004 European Championships.

Daily soccer tabloid *Bola,* available from any newsagent or newspaper kiosk, has fixtures, match reports and news, as does the website Ⓦwww.portuguesesoccer.com. To buy advance **tickets** for big games – which cost between €10 and €40 – go to the kiosks (not the turnstiles) at the grounds.

Bullfights

Bullfights take place most Thursdays (April–Sept) at the principal **Praça de Touros do Campo Pequeno**, just off Avenida da República (see p.121). There are less frequent fights at Cascais in summer, or you can travel out of Lisbon to Vila Franca de Xira (see p.224) and surrounding towns and villages for more traditional events.

Shops and markets

The Bairro Alto and Chiado are the main centres for alternative designer clothes and crafts, while international designer names cluster along Avenida da Liberdade. Antique shops are concentrated along Rua do Alecrim in Chiado, Rua Dom Pedro V in the Bairro Alto, and along Rua de São Bento, between Rato and São Bento. As well as all these areas, don't miss the city's **markets** and major **shopping centres** (listed below) or the Feira da Ladra **flea market** in the Alfama (see p.100). Traditional **shopping hours** are Monday to Friday 9.30am to 7pm or 8pm (some shops close for an hour at lunch), Saturday 9am to 1pm. However, many of the Bairro Alto shops are open afternoons and evenings only, usually 2pm to 9pm or so. Many larger shops, especially in shopping centres, open all day until 11pm or midnight, some even on Sundays. Unless otherwise stated, the shops listed below are closed Saturday afternoon and all day Sunday, though the shopping centres are all open daily.

Other than traditional **ceramics and carpets**, perhaps the most Portuguese of items to take home is a **bottle of port**: check out the vintages at the *Solar do Vinho do Porto* (see p.103), where you can also sample the stuff. Alternatively, you can buy port or the increasingly respected **Portuguese wines** from one of the specialist shops listed below, or from any delicatessen or supermarket.

Antiques, arts and crafts

Branca d' Água Rua da Conceição 28–30. Fine small outlet for beautiful hand-painted ceramics and tiles in contemporary styles, along with a few Portuguese handicrafts.

Casa do Turista Av da Liberdade 159; metro Avenida. Crammed with regional arts, crafts, ceramics, T-shirts and some rather fine toy trams.

Fábrica Sant'anna Rua do Alecrim 95, Chiado. If you're interested in Portuguese tiles – *azulejos* – check out this factory shop, founded in 1741, which sells copies of traditional designs and a great range of pots and ceramics.

Fábrica Viúva Lamego Largo do Intendente 25; metro Intendente. Highly rated *azulejo* factory-shop producing made-to-order designs or reproduction antiques. Closed Sat in July & Aug.

Loja de Artesanato Mercado da Ribeira, Av 24 de Julho; metro Cais do Sodré. Specializing in art and crafts from Lisbon and the Tejo valley, with drinks and preserves too. Open daily.

Santos Ofícios Rua da Madalena 87, near the Sé. Small shop stuffed with a somewhat touristy collection of regional crafts including some attractive ceramics, rugs, embroidery, baskets and toys. Closed Sun.

Solar Albuquerque Rua Dom Pedro V 66–72 ☎213 465 522. A huge treasure trove of antique tiles, plates and ceramics – great for a browse.

Books and music

Casa do Fado e da Guitarra Portuguesa Largo do Chafariz de Dentro 1, Alfama. The museum contains an excellent selection of fado CDs and cassettes, and staff give expert advice.

FNAC Rua Nova do Almada 104–110, Chiado. A good range of English-language books, along with an extensive music department and computer equipment. Also has a desk selling tickets to major events.

Livraria Bertrand Rua Garrett 73, Chiado. Portugal's oldest general bookshop, opened in 1773, once the meeting place of the literary set. Today it has a good range of novels in English, plus a range of foreign magazines. Closed Sun morning.

Livraria Britânica Rua de São Marçal 83, Bairro Alto. Well-stocked English-language bookshop, which caters mainly to the British Council nearby.

Livraria Portugal Rua do Carmo 70–74, Baixa. Excellent Portuguese bookshop that features many of the books reviewed on p.644.

Clothes and accessories

Aba Salazar Rua do Carmo 87, Chiado. One of the country's best-known designer's main Lisbon outlet, with adventurous styles mostly for women.

Espaço Fátima Lopes Rua da Atalaia 36, Bairro Alto. Flagship store for Lisbon's biggest names in fashion; bold, colourful and confident clothes to reflect the mood of Portugal's wanabes.

Freeport Alcochete, around 20km south of Lisbon; reached by bus #431 or #432 from Oriente station; ⊛www.freeport.pt. Giant designer-discount complex, a twenty-minute bus ride from the Parque das Nações, boasting over two hundred shops. International names include Hugo Boss, Zara, Versace, Burberry, Gucci and Pierre Cardin, supported by some forty restaurants, bars and cafés. The complex has also become a venue for touring bands (see p.138).

José Dias Sobral Rua de São Paulo 218, Cais do Sodré. Founded in 1880 and barely changed since, this traditional workshop at the foot of the Elevador da Bica sells quality leather belts, briefcases and shoelaces.

Luvaria Ulisses Rua do Carmo 87a, Chiado. Quality gloves from this superb, ornate shoebox of a shop, with gloves neatly tucked into rows of boxes.

Markets

Mercado 31 de Janeiro Rua Eng. Viera da Silva; metro Picoas or Saldanha. Features everything from fresh fish and flowers to arts and crafts. Mon–Sat 7am–2pm.

Mercado da Carcavelos Carcavelos, on the train line to Cascais. Wonderful rambling Thursday morning market opposite the train station for clothes and ceramics (see p.144).

Mercado da Ribeira Av 24 de Julho, Cais do Sodré. One of Lisbon's most atmospheric covered markets, with a great fish hall (see p.102).

Feira da Ladra Campo de Santa Clara. Lisbon's main Tuesday and Saturday morning flea market (see p.100).

Shopping centres and supermarkets

Most of the shopping centres incorporate super-markets, usually on the lower floors.

Amoreiras Entrance on Av Engenheiro Duarte Pacheco. Bus #11 or #58. Some 250 shops, cinemas, restaurants and a hotel (see p.117)

Armazéns do Chiado Rua do Carmo 2, Chiado Ⓦ www.armazensdochiado.com. This well-designed shopping centre sits on six floors above metro Baixa-Chiado. The top floor has a series of cafés and restaurants, most offering great views over town.

Centro Colombo Av Colégio Militar-Luz Ⓦ www .colombo.pt; metro Colégio Militar-Luz. Iberia's largest shopping complex boasts some four hundred international and national stores, restau-rants, cinemas and play areas.

Centro Comércial Mouraria Largo Martim Moniz, Mouraria.The city's most atmospheric shopping centre, with six levels (three underground) featuring a motley collection of Indian fabrics, Oriental and African foods, and ethnic cafés.

Centro Vasco da Gama Av Dom João II, Parque das Nações Ⓦ www.centrovascodagama.pt; metro Oriente. Three floors of national and international stores under a glass roof permanently washed by running water. Also restaurants, children's areas and disabled access.

El Corte Inglês Av António Augusto de Aguiar Ⓦ www.elcorteingles.pt; metro São Sebastião. Giant Spanish department store spread over nine floors, selling everything from gourmet foods, clothes and sports goods to CDs, books and toys.

Pingo Doce Rua 1 Dezembro 123. Most central branch of the supermarket chain – a good place to stock up on picnic fodder, snacks or inexpensive booze. Open daily until 8.30pm.

Wine and food

Casa Pereira da Conceição Rua Augusta 102–104, Baixa. Art Deco 1930s shop selling aromatic coffee beans and teas.

Manuel Tavares Rua da Betesga 1A, Baixa. On the edge of Rossio, this small, century-old shop has a great selection of chocolate and national cheeses, plus a basement stuffed with vintage wines and ports. Closed Sun and (from Oct–June) Sat afternoon.

Napoleão Rua dos Fanqueiros 70, Baixa, junction with Rua da Conceição Ⓦ www.napoleao.co.pt. Great range of port and wine, with knowledgeable, English-speaking staff. Closed Sun.

Listings

Airlines Air France, Av 5 de Outubro 206 ☏ 808 202 800; Alitalia, Pr Marquês de Pombal 1–5° ☏ 800 307 300; British Airways, Av da Liberdade 36–2° ☏ 213 217 900; Iberia, Rua Barata Salgueiro 286 ☏ 213 110 600; KLM, Campo Grande 220b ☏ 217 955 010; Lufthansa, aeroporto ☏ 214 245 155; TAP, Pr Marquês de Pombal 15 ☏ 707 205 700.

Banks Most main branches are in the Baixa and surrounding streets. Standard banking hours are Mon–Fri 8.30am–3pm. ATMs can be found throughout Lisbon, including at the airport, the main stations and in all the main squares.

Buses The main terminal is at Sete Rios (metro Jardim Zoológico) for international and most domestic departures, including express services to the Algarve and Alentejo. See p.168 for details of other bus terminals and departures. You can buy advance bus tickets from most travel agents.

Car rental Alamo/Nacional, Av Alvares Cabral 45B ☏ 213 703 400, metro Rato; Auto Jardim, Rua Luciano Cordeiro 6, east of Av da Liberdade ☏ 213 549 182 and airport ☏ 218 463 187; Avis, Campo Grande 390 ☏ 217 547 800; Budget, Rua Castilho, west of Av da Liberdade 167B ☏ 213 860 516 and airport ☏ 218 478 803; Europcar, Av António Augusto Aguiar 24c/d ☏ 213 535 115, airport ☏ 218 401 176; Hertz, Rua Castilho 72, west of Av da Liberdade ☏ 213 812 430 and airport ☏ 218 463 154; Nova Rent, Largo Monterroio Mascar-enhas 9, Amoreiras ☏ 213 845 270.

Embassies and consulates Australia, Av da Liberdade 196–2° ☏ 213 101 500 (metro Avenida); Canada, Av da Liberdade 196–200 ☏ 213 164 600; Ireland, Rua da Imprensa à Estrela 1–4° ☏ 213 929 440; UK, Rua de São Bernardo 33 ☏ 213 124 000, Ⓦ www.uk-embassy .pt (metro Rato); USA, Av das Forças Armadas ☏ 217 273 300 (metro Jardim Zoológico).

Gay and lesbian The Centro Comunitário Gay e Lésbico de Lisboa (Rua de São Lázaro 88 interna-tional ☏ 218 873 918, Wed–Thurs 6pm–11pm, Fri & Sat 6pm–1am), Lisbon's main gay and lesbian community centre just north of metro Martim Moniz, is a good place to start, with its own café. The centre organizes events and can help with information. It is run by ILGA whose comprehensive website (Ⓦ www .ilga-portugal.org) is in English and Portuguese.

Hospital The privately run British Hospital, Rua Saraiva de Carvalho 49 (☏ 213 955 067), has

English-speaking staff and doctors on call from 8.30am to 9pm. There are various other public hospitals around the city.

Internet Central options include Ponto Net, above the Lisbon Welcome Centre, Pr do Comércio, Baixa ☎210 312 815 (daily 9am–8pm); Web Café, Rua do Diário de Notícias 16, Bairro Alto ☎213 421 181 (daily 4pm–2am); and Cyberica, Rua Duques de Bragança 7 Chiado ☎213 421 707 (daily 11am–midnight).

Language courses Portuguese language courses are run by the Cambridge School, Av da Liberdade 173 ☎213 124 600, ⓦwww.cambridge.pt; and International House, Rua do Marquês Sa da Bandeira 16, metro São Sebastião, ☎213 151 496.

Laundry The self-service Lava Neve, Rua da Alegria 37, Bairro Alto ☎213 466 195 (Mon 9am–1pm & 3–7pm, Tues–Fri 10am–1pm & 3–7pm) is good value at €5.50 for 5kg of laundry.

Left luggage There are 24hr lockers at the airport (in level 1 of car park 1), and at Rossio, Cais do Sodré and Santa Apolónia stations (around €2–7 a day).

Lost property For anything lost on public transport, call ☎218 535 403 (trains). Major losses should be reported to the police station (see opposite).

Newspapers There are several newsstands around Rossio and Restauradores – such as the one attached to the ABEP ticket kiosk – which sell foreign-language papers, as do the lobbies of many of the larger hotels.

Pharmacies City pharmacies are open Mon–Fri 9am–1pm & 3–7pm, Sat 9am–1pm. Local papers carry information about 24-hour pharmacies and the details are posted on every pharmacy door.

Police The tourist police station is the Foz Cultura building in Palácio Foz, Restauradores ☎213 421 634 (daily 24 hours). You need a report from here in order to make a claim on your travel insurance.

Post office The main post office is at Pr dos Restauradores 58 ☎213 238 700 (Mon–Fri 8am–10pm, Sat & Sun 9am–6pm), from where you can send airmail and *correio azul* (express mail – the fastest service). There's a 24-hour post office at the airport. Stamps can be purchased from some – but not all – newsagents.

Telephones There's a telephone office next to the post office in Pr dos Restauradores (see above). There's a second office on the corner of Rossio (no. 65; 8am–11pm).

Trains See pp.82–83 for details of Lisbon's various stations. Timetables and train information are available from individual stations and on ☎218 884 025, ⓦwww.cp.pt. Always check departure times and stations in advance: many intercity services require a seat reservation (particularly to Coimbra/Porto), which you can do prior to departure.

Travel agencies Marcus & Harting, Rossio 45–50 ☎213 224 550, is a good, central option for bus tickets and general travel information. USIT Tagus, Rua Camilo Castelo Branco 20 ☎213 525 986, specializes in discounted student tickets and sells ISIC cards.

Around Lisbon

The most straightforward way to escape the city is to head for the string of beach resorts west along the coast from Belém, which can be reached by train from Cais do Sodré (see p.83). There are fine beaches at places like **Oeiras** and **Carcavelos**, though water quality is poor and only improves marginally at **Estoril** and **Cascais**. For better sands and a cleaner ocean you'll have to head north to **Guincho**, or cross the Tejo by ferry to reach the **Costa da Caparica**, a 30km stretch of dunes to the south of the capital. Further south still, there are good, clean beaches at **Sesimbra** and in the Parque Natural da Arrábida, a superb unspoilt craggy reserve, while the large town of **Setúbal** is noted for its Igreja de Jesus, the earliest of all Manueline buildings. There's reasonably priced accommodation at all these places, as well as a youth hostel at Oeiras and campsites at Guincho, Costa da Caparica and Arrábida. But, as you might imagine, all the beach resorts in the Lisbon area get very crowded at weekends and throughout August.

Basing yourself in Lisbon, you could also take in a fair part of the provinces of Estremadura (Chapter 2) and Alentejo (Chapter 8) on day trips. Indeed, some of those regions' greatest attractions lie within a 50km or so radius of the capital – such as the palaces of **Queluz** or **Mafra** – and are best seen on a day trip. However, the beautiful town of **Sintra**, the most popular excursion from Lisbon, demands a longer look and reveals a different side if you stay overnight. Bear in mind that most of the Sintra palaces are closed on Mondays, and that at Queluz on Tuesdays.

West to Estoril and Cascais

Stretching for over 30km west of Lisbon, the Estoril coast makes for an enjoyable day out, drifting from beach to bar and strolling along the lively seafront promenades. Sadly, the water itself has suffered badly from pollution and, though steps are being taken to clean it up, most beaches fail to get a blue flag. Nonetheless, the coast retains its attractions, particularly at the main resorts of **Estoril** and **Cascais** – the latter, in particular, makes a pleasant alternative to staying in Lisbon, and is well placed for trips to Sintra or to the wild Guincho beach.

The **Linha de Cascais train** leaves every twenty minutes from Cais do Sodré station (Mon–Thurs & Sun 5.30am–1.30am, Fri & Sat 5.30am–2.30am; €1.50), stopping at the beaches of Oeiras, Carcavelos and stations beyond. If you are staying in Cascais or Estoril, note that there are hourly buses to both resorts to and from Lisbon airport (roughly an hour's journey). By road, the **N6** coastal highway (Avenida Marginal) passes through most of the centres along the seafront; the faster **A5 motorway** (Auto-Estrada da Oeste) is an inexpensive toll road running from Lisbon to Estoril – drive west past Amoreiras and follow the signs.

Oeiras to Estoril

The first suburb of any size after Belém is **OEIRAS** (pronounced *oo-air-esh*), where the Rio Tejo officially turns into the sea. The riverside walkways are being improved and the beach here has recently been cleaned up, though most people still swim in the ocean pool alongside the sands. Unless you're staying at the youth hostel (see p.91), however, the only reason for a stop here would be to see the **Palácio do Marquês de Pombal**, erstwhile home of the rebuilder of Lisbon. The house is now an adult education centre and the park is not technically open to visitors. However, if there's nothing special going on, the guard should be able to show you the attractive formal gardens, or you can peer over the walls at its massive grotto.

The next stop, **CARCAVELOS**, has the most extensive sandy beach on this part of the coast. Swimmers chance the polluted waters in high summer, and at other times it's a lively spot for beach soccer, surfing and blustery winter walks. To reach the beach, it's a ten-minute walk from the station along the broad Avenida Jorge V. There are plenty of beachside cafés and bars; *Perola*, on the promenade at the west end of the beach, offers inexpensive food and great sea views. Try to visit Carcavelos on Thursday morning, when the town hosts a huge **market**; turn right out of the station and follow the signs. Street upon street is taken over by stalls selling cheap goods, clothes (many with brand-name labels) and ceramics.

Along the last stretch of the Linha de Cascais, the beaches improve rapidly and you reach the beginning of an esplanade that stretches virtually uninterrupted to Cascais. **SÃO PEDRO** has a superb beach, just down from the station, and **SÃO JOÃO** is flanked by two lovely stretches of sand. The whole seafront here is pretty animated in the summer months, swarming with young surfers and Portuguese holidaymakers frequenting the numerous cafés and restaurants.

Estoril

ESTORIL gained a postwar reputation as a haunt of exiled royalty and the idle rich, and it continues to maintain its pretensions towards being a "Portuguese Riviera", with grandiose villas and luxury hotels. It is little surprise then that the town's touristic life revolves around its golf courses and **Casino** (Tues–Sat 3pm–3am; free; ☏214 667 700 ⓦwww.casino-estoril.pt). The latter requires some semblance of formal attire, but once inside you'll find roulette, card games, slot machines, restaurants, shops, nightly shows at 11pm and even an art gallery.

The casino sits at the far end of the **Parque do Estoril**, a lovely stretch of fountains and exotic trees, surrounded by Estoril's best-value bars and restaurants. The resort's fine sandy beach, **Praia de Tamariz**, is backed by a seafront promenade that stretches all the way to Cascais, a twenty-minute stroll. From July to mid-September, a free fireworks display takes place above Estoril's beach every Saturday night at midnight.

Practicalities

The **train station** is on Estoril's through-road, with the beach accessible by an underpass. Across the main road from the station, at the bottom of the park, you'll find the very helpful **turismo** (Mon–Sat 9am–8pm, Sun 10am–6pm; ☏214 663 813, ⓦwww.estorilcoast.com), which can provide advice on private rooms and details of the area's various golf clubs.

There's a fair amount of local **accommodation**, with the best budget choice the pleasant rooms at the *Pensão-Residencial Smart*, Rua José Viana 3 (☏214 682 164, ⓔresidencial.smart@netcabo.pt; breakfast included; ❹). It's east of the park – turn right out of the station, turning left when you reach Avenida Bombeiros Voluntarios, which runs up behind the *Hotel Paris*.

Deck Bar, Arcadas do Parque 21 (☏214 680 366; open till 2am; closed Mon), is a nice outdoor **restaurant and café** just behind the tourist office, overlooking the western side of the park. *Jonas Bar*, on the seafront between Cascais and Estoril, is a fun spot day or night, selling cocktails, juices and snacks. However, the best place to eat is the expensive *Cimas* (also known as the *English Bar*) at Avenida Sabóia 9 (☏214 680 413; closed Sun), just off the seafront Avenida Marginal Monte Estoril, between Cascais and Estoril. Originally named after the Englishman who built the mansion in the 1940s, it has a fine wood-panelled interior, sea views and top-quality fish, meat and game.

Cascais

At the end of the train line, **CASCAIS** (*cash-kaysh*) is a major resort, with three fairly good beaches along its esplanade, a flash marina and a fort (closed to the public) that guards the harbour. It is positively bursting at the seams in summer, especially at weekends, but despite the commercialism it's not too large or difficult to get around, and has a much younger, less exclusive, feel than Estoril. It even retains some vestiges of its previous existence as a fishing village.

You'll find the main concentration of bars and nightlife – and consequently most of what makes Cascais tick as a town – around Largo Luís de Camões. The local **fish market** near here is worth a look (Mon–Fri from around 4pm), while for a wander away from the crowds, stroll up beyond Largo 5° de Outubro into the old, and surprisingly pretty, west side of town, at its most delightful in the streets north of the graceful **Igreja da Assunção**.

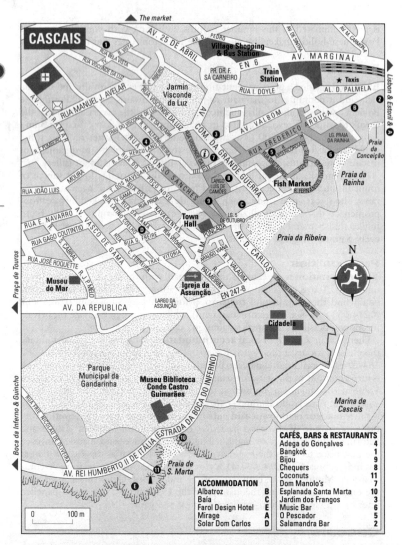

CASCAIS

CAFÉS, BARS & RESTAURANTS
Adega do Gonçalves 4
Bangkok 1
Bijou 9
Chequers 8
Coconuts 11
Dom Manolo's 7
Esplanada Santa Marta 10
Jardim dos Frangos 3
Music Bar 6
O Pescador 5
Salamandra Bar 2

ACCOMMODATION
Albatroz B
Baía C
Farol Design Hotel E
Mirage A
Solar Dom Carlos D

Cascais' other attractions are all to the west of the centre. Beyond the church lies the pleasant **Parque Municipal da Gandarinha**, in whose southern reaches stands the mansion of the counts of Guimarães, preserved complete with its nineteenth-century fittings as the **Museu Biblioteca Conde Castro Guimarães** (Tues–Sun 10am–5pm; €1.65); most days, there's someone around to give you a guided tour of the furniture, paintings and antiques that the count bequeathed to the nation. On the north side of the park, signs point you to the modern **Museu do Mar** (Tues–Sun 10am–5pm; €1.65), an engaging little collection of model boats, sea-related artefacts, old costumes and pictures.

Taking the coastal road, it's about twenty minutes' walk west to the **Boca do Inferno** – the "Mouth of Hell" – where waves crash against caves in the cliff face. The viewpoints above are always packed with tourists (as is the very tacky market on the roadside) but, frankly, the whole affair is rather unimpressive except in stormy weather. It's a pretty walk, however, past the **marina**, backed by rows of modern cafés, shops and restaurants.

Practicalities

From the **train station** it's just a couple of minutes' walk into town; **buses** to Guincho, Cabo da Roca and Sintra leave from the bus station opposite, under Cascais Village Shopping. Walk down Rua Frederico Arouca and cross the main avenue for the **turismo** (Mon–Sat 9am–7pm, Sun 10am–6pm; ☎214 868 204), set in an old mansion on Rua Visconde da Luz, where the staff will usually phone around on your behalf for private rooms. **Accommodation** prices in July and August are very high but most of the places listed below will drop room rates by up to forty percent out of season.

At night, Cascais shows itself off in the smart **pubs, bars and cafés** around Largo Luís de Camões, down the steps on the west side of the main avenue. They nearly all serve food (none of it particularly memorable), but the suntrap square is a pleasant (if expensive) place to sit and drink. On summer nights the bars throw open their doors, turn up the music and, come closing time at 2am, the square is full of bleary-eyed drinkers dancing and shouting the words to tunes they never realized they knew.

There's a lively **market** every Wednesday on Rua do Mercado, off Avenida 25 de Abril, and there are Sunday evening **bullfights** during summer in the Praça de Touros, Avenida Pedro Alvares Cabral, in the west of town some 2km from the centre.

Hotels and pensions

Hotel Albatroz Rua Frederica Arouca 100 ☎214 847 380, ⓦwww.albatrozhotels.com; Built in the nineteenth century as a royal retreat, €240 or so will get you a room in one of Portugal's finest seaside hotels, with glorious views from some rooms (which you pay extra for). There's also a lovely swimming pool on the ocean terrace, and more views from the restaurant. There are also sumptuous rooms in its annexe, *Villa Albatroz*, which has a more homely feel. Parking. ❼

Hotel Baía Av Com. da Grande Guerra ☎214 831 095, ⓦwww.hotelbaia.com. Modern seafront hotel overlooking the harbour. There are over hundred rooms with a/c and satellite TV, many with a sea view (book ahead in summer for these), a great rooftop pool and bar and a rated restaurant. ❻

Hotel Cascais Mirage Av Marginal 8554 ☎210 060 619, ⓦwww.cascaismirage.com. This ultra-modern five-star has won design awards – its stepped, glass-fronted nine floors seem to merge with the slope behind it, while inside the huge lobby and communal areas are bathed in light. Rooms are spacious and all have sea-facing balconies, and there's a pool, restaurant and crisp, friendly service. Parking. ❽

Farol Design Hotel Av Rei Humberto II de Italia ☎214 823 490, ⓦwww.farol.com. Right on the seafront, this designer hotel has a modern wing moulded onto a sixteenth-century villa, and the decor mixes traditional wood and marble with modern steel and glass. Rooms aren't huge but most have sea views and terraces; there's also a fashionable bar, restaurant (serving nouveau Portuguese cuisine) and outdoor pool facing the rocks. Parking. ❼, or ❽ with sea views

Solar Dom Carlos Rua Latina Coelho 8 ☎214 828 115, ⓦwww.solardomcarlos.com. This very attractive sixteenth-century mansion is the best mid-range option in town, so book ahead. It's on a quiet backstreet with cool tiling throughout and a welcoming air. Bright, pretty rooms, garden and even an old royal chapel. Parking. ❸

Restaurants

Adega do Gonçalves Rua Afonso Sanches 54 ☎214 831 519. Little *adega* serving huge portions of good food at moderate prices; the grilled fish is recommended. Also has inexpensive rooms upstairs. Closed Wed. Moderate.

Bangkok Rua da Bela Vista 6 ☎214 847 600. Sublime Thai cooking in a traditional town house, beautifully decorated with inlaid wood and Oriental furnishings. Specials include lobster in curry paste and assorted Thai appetizers; expensive, though moderate with careful choosing.

Bijou Rua Rigimento XIX 55, off Largo Luís de Camões, Cascais. Daily 9am–9pm. Simple café-restaurant in a pretty tiled building with outside seats on the square; one of the cheapest places round here for lunches, snacks, pastries and drinks.

Dom Manolo's Av Com. da Grande Guerra 11 ☏214 831 126. Busy grill-house serving superb chicken and chips; add a salad, local wine and home-made dessert and you'll still pay only around €12. Inexpensive.

Esplanada Santa Marta Praia de Santa Marta. Charcoal-grilled fish served on a tiny terrace overlooking the sea and beach. Closed Mon. Moderate.

Jardim dos Frangos Av Com. da Grande Guerra 66. Permanently buzzing with people and sizzling with the speciality grilled chicken, which is devoured by the plateload at indoor and outdoor tables. Inexpensive.

O Pescador Rua das Flores 10 ☏214 832 054. One of several places close to the fish market, this offers superior fish meals and good service. Closed Sun. Expensive.

Bars and clubs

Chequers Largo Luís de Camões 7 ☏214 830 926. Lively English-style pub, especially once the pumping rock music strengthens its grip; TVs for live soccer too.

Coconuts Av Rei Humberto II de Itália 7 ☏214 844 109 ⓦwww.nuts-club.com. Club on the road to Boca do Inferno with a great little seaside terrace, attracting a mix of fashionable locals and clubbing tourists. Guest DJs on Thursdays. Opens 11pm, closed Mon, Tues & Sun.

Music Bar Largo da Praia da Rainha 121 ☏214 820 848. One of the few bars in town with decent sea views, which you can take in sitting at tables on the patio above the beach. Also serves decent meals. Closed Mon Oct–April.

Salamandra Bar Praia da Duquesa ☏214 820 287. Next to the station with a great view of the seafront, this buzzing bar has something for everyone, from bar games to live TV sports and frequent live music (jazz and rock). Also serves snacks.

Praia do Guincho

Buses from outside Cascais train station (daily 7.15am–7.15pm, every 1–2hr; €2) run the 6km west to **PRAIA DO GUINCHO**, a great sweeping field of beach with body-crashing Atlantic rollers. It's a superb place for surfing and windsurfing – legs of the World Windsurfing Championships are often held here in August – but also a dangerous one. The undertow is notoriously strong and people are drowned almost every year. To add to that, there's absolutely no shade and on breezy days the wind cuts across the sands. Even if you can't feel the sun, you need to be very careful.

The beach is flanked by half a dozen large, moderately priced **terrace-restaurants**, all with standard fish-dominated menus and varying views of the breaking rollers. There's no budget **accommodation** – in fact, quite the opposite. At the deluxe-class *Fortaleza do Guincho* (☏214 870 491, ⓦwww.guinchotel.pt; ⓽) you can stay in a converted fort with a Michelin-starred restaurant. There are 27 tastefully decorated rooms with sea views and others gathered round the internal courtyard; a limousine service takes guests to and from the airport on request. More affordable is *Estalagem O Muchaxo* (☏214 870 221, ⓦwww.muchaxo.com; ⓸), a highly attractive place, with a seawater pool, stone-flagged bar and fine views across the beach from the highly rated restaurant; sea-view rooms here are priced a category higher. The well-equipped Orbitur **campsite** (see p.91) is about 1km back from the main part of the beach; follow the signs from the coast road.

Sintra and around

As the summer residence of the kings of Portugal, and the Moorish lords of Lisbon before them, Sintra's verdant charms have long been celebrated. British travellers of the eighteenth and nineteenth centuries found a new Arcadia in its cool, wooded heights, recording with satisfaction the old Spanish saying: "To see the world and leave out Sintra is to go blind about." Byron stayed here in 1809 and began *Childe Harold*, his great mock-epic travel poem, in which the "horrid crags" of "Cintra's glorious Eden" form a first location. Writing home, in a letter to his mother, he proclaimed the village:

1

... perhaps in every aspect the most delightful in Europe; it contains beauties of every description natural and artificial. Palaces and gardens rising in the midst of rocks, cataracts and precipices, convents on stupendous heights, a distant view of the sea and the Tagus ... it unites in itself all the wildness of the Western Highlands with the verdure of the South of France.

That the young Byron had seen neither of these is irrelevant: his description of Sintra's romantic appeal is exact – and still telling two centuries later. Sintra is home to two of Portugal's most extraordinary palaces, some lavish private estates and a Moorish castle with breathtaking views over Lisbon. Within reach, too, are semi-tropical gardens and small-scale resorts on a craggy coastline boasting Europe's most westerly point. Move mountains and give yourself the best part of two full days here.

The Town

SINTRA loops around a series of green and wooded ravines making it a confusing place in which to get your bearings. Basically, though, it consists of three distinct districts: **Estefânia**, around the train station; the attractive main town of **Sintra-Vila**; and, 2km to the east, the separate village of **São Pedro**

△ Horse and carriage, Sintra

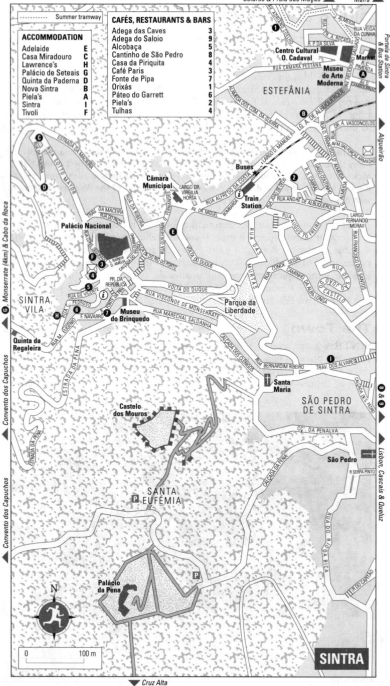

Colares & Praia das Maças

Ericeira & Mafra

Portela de Sintra & Bus Station

Algueirão

ACCOMMODATION

Adelaide	E
Casa Miradouro	C
Lawrence's	H
Palácio de Seteais	G
Quinta da Paderna	D
Nova Sintra	B
Piela's	A
Sintra	I
Tivoli	F

CAFÉS, RESTAURANTS & BARS

Adega das Caves	3
Adega do Saloio	9
Alcobaça	5
Cantinho de São Pedro	8
Casa da Piriquita	4
Café Paris	1
Fonte de Pipa	7
Orixás	
Páteo do Garrett	6
Piela's	2
Tulhas	4

Summer tramway

Centro Cultural O. Cadaval

Market

Museu de Arte Moderna

ESTEFÂNIA

Câmara Municipal

Buses

Train Station

Palácio Nacional

SINTRA VILA

Museu do Brinquedo

Quinta da Regaleira

Parque da Liberdade

Santa Maria

SÃO PEDRO DE SINTRA

Castelo dos Mouros

São Pedro

SANTA EUFÉMIA

Palácio da Pena

Monserrate (4km) & Cabo da Roca

Convento dos Capuchos

Convento dos Capuchos

Lisbon, Cascais & Queluz

N

0   100 m

SINTRA

Cruz Alta

de Sintra. It's Sintra-Vila and its environs that have most of the hotels and restaurants and the main sights, including the extraordinary landmark of the Palácio Nacional. Distinguished by its vast pair of conical chimneys, this dominates the central square around which the old town is gathered.

Palácio Nacional

The **Palácio Nacional** – or Paço Real (Mon, Tues & Thurs–Sun 10am–5.30pm; €4, free Sun morning) – was probably already in existence under the Moors. It takes its present form, however, from the rebuilding and enlargements of Dom João I (1385–1433) and his fortunate successor, Dom Manuel, heir to the wealth engendered by Vasco da Gama's inspired explorations. The palace's style, as you might expect, is an amalgam of Gothic – with impressive roofline battlements – and the latter king's Manueline additions, with their characteristically extravagant twisted and animate forms. Inside, the Gothic–Manueline modes are tempered by a good deal of Moorish influence, adapted over the centuries by a succession of occupants. The last royal to live here, in the 1880s, was Maria Pia, grandmother of the country's final reigning monarch – Manuel II, "The Unfortunate".

Today the palace is a museum (it's best to go early or late in the day to avoid the crowds). Highlights on the lower floor include the Manueline **Sala dos Cisnes**, named for the swans (*cisnes*) painted on its ceiling, and the **Sala das Pegas**, which takes its name from the flock of magpies (*pegas*) painted on the frieze and ceiling. They are holding in their beaks the legend *por bem* (in honour) – reputedly the response of João I, caught by his queen, Philippa (of Lancaster), in the act of kissing a lady-in-waiting. He had the room decorated with as many magpies as there were women at court in order to satirize and put a stop to their gossiping.

Best of the upper floor is the gallery above the palace chapel. In a room alongside, the deranged Afonso VI was confined for six years by his brother Pedro II; he eventually died here in 1683, listening to Mass through a grid, Pedro having seized "his throne, his liberty and his queen". Beyond, a succession of state rooms climaxes in the Sala das Brasões, its domed and coffered ceiling emblazoned with the arms of 72 noble families. Finally, don't miss the kitchens, their roofs tapering into the giant chimneys that are the palace's distinguishing features. The Palace also hosts events for the Sintra Music Festival (see p.136).

Strange happenings in Sintra

Sintra has been a centre for cult worship for centuries: the early Celts named it Mountain of the Moon after one of their gods and the hills are scattered with laylines and mysterious tombs. Locals say batteries drain in the area noticeably faster than elsewhere and light bulbs seem to pop with monotonous regularity. Some claim this is because of the angle of iron in the rocks, others that it is all part of the mystical powers that lurk in Sintra's hills and valleys. There are certainly plenty of geographical and meteorological quirks. In the woods around Capuchos, house-sized boulders litter the landscape as if thrown by giants, while a white cloud – affectionately known as the queen's fart – regularly hovers over Sintra's palaces even on the clearest summer day. Exterior walls seem to merge with the landscape as they are quickly smothered in a thick layer of ferns, lichens and moss. And its castles, palaces, mansions and follies shelter tales of Masonic rites, insanity and eccentricity that are as fantastical as the buildings themselves.

Museu do Brinquedo

Just round the corner from the Palácio Nacional is a fascinating private toy collection housed in a former fire station on Rua Visconde de Monserrate, now the impressive **Museu do Brinquedo** (Tues–Sun 10am–6pm; €3, children €1.50; ⓦwww.museu-do-brinquedo.pt). The huge array of toys over three floors is somewhat confusingly labelled, but look out for the 3000-year-old stone Egyptian toys, as well as the Hornby trains from the 1930s and some of the first ever toy cars, produced in Germany in the early 1900s. Perhaps the most interesting section is that on early Portuguese toys, containing papier-mâché cars, tin-plate animals, wooden trams and trains, as well as a selection of 1930s beach toys, including beautifully painted buckets and the metal fish that appears on the museum brochure.

Sintra Museu de Arte Moderna

Northeast of the train station, in Estefânia, it's worth making the detour to visit the superb **Museu de Arte Moderna** on Avenida Heliodoro Salgado (Tues–Sun 10am–6pm; €3, free on Sun 10am–2pm; ⓦwww.berardomodern.com). Occupying Sintra's former casino, the 1920s building spreads over three floors and houses parts of the collection of tobacco magnate Joe Berardo. Only twenty of the works are shown at any one time; the rest of the space is used for temporary exhibits, which change every two or three months. Depending on when you visit, you can see pieces by Jackson Pollock, David Hockney, Roy Lichtenstein and Andy Warhol. There are plans to display more of the collection at the Centro Cultural de Belém (see p.114).

Practicalities

Trains depart every fifteen minutes from Lisbon's Rossio and Sete Rios stations (45min journey; €1.50 one-way). There's a small turismo desk at **Sintra station** (daily 9am–7pm), while local **buses** depart across the street from the train station, with services to and from Cascais, Colares, Cabo da Roca, the Sintra beaches, Estoril and Mafra. However, Sintra's main **bus station** is at Portela, opposite the train station of the same name, the stop before Sintra. It's a ten- to fifteen-minute walk from Sintra station to Sintra-Vila and around twenty minutes from Sintra-Vila to São Pedro. To see the area, including the coast, consider a **Day-rover** (Turístico Diário) ticket on the local Scotturb buses (ⓦwww.scotturb.com; €8.50, or €12 to include trains to and from Lisbon). Alternatively, **bus #434** takes a circular route from Sintra station or Sintra-Vila to the Pena Palace and the Castelo dos Mouros via São Pedro (every 40min; €3.85) and allows you to get on and off whenever you like on the circuit. Another option is the toy train (departures roughly hourly 10am–5pm, day ticket €5), which shuttles from the Palácio Nacional to Monserrate via Quinta da Regaleira. For the coast, there are the fantastic old trams that shuttle from outside the Museu de Arte Moderna to the coastal resort of Praia das Maças via Colares (see box, p.157). There are also **taxis** outside the train station and in Praça da República, near the Palácio Nacional; check the price first for every journey since the meters aren't always used. It costs roughly €25 return to Pena or Monserrate with an hour's stopover, or around €35 return to the Convento dos Capuchos.

The efficient and helpful **turismo** (daily: June–Sept 9am–8pm; Oct–May 9am–7pm; ⓣ219 231 157, ⓦwww.cm-sintra.pt) lies just off the central Praça da República. You'll also find a **post office** and **bank** on the square.

There's a country **market** – with antiques and crafts, as well as food – in São Pedro's main square on the second and last Sunday of every month. Sintra's annual **festa** in honour of St Peter is held on June 28 and 29, while in July and August the **Sintra Music Festival** puts on classical performances in a number of the town's buildings (see p.136). The end of July also sees the **Feira Grande** in São Pedro, with crafts, antiques and cheeses on sale.

Accommodation

Sintra is a popular resort and you should book ahead or turn up early in the day if you intend to stay, especially if you're here during one of the town's festivals when accommodation will be scarce. At other times it's not a problem as there's a fair range of **accommodation** available including a network of private rooms (best booked through the turismo; ❷–❸). The local youth hostel, located in the hills above São Pedro de Sintra, is closed for extensive renovation.

Pensions, quintas and hotels

Residencial Adelaide Rua Guilherme Gomes Fernandes 11 ☎219 230 873. Very clean if spartan en-suite rooms; the quieter rooms face a patio at the rear. No breakfast. ❷

Casa Miradouro Rua Sotto Mayor 55 ☎219 107 100, ⊛www.casa-miradouro.com. Renovated Swiss-run mansion in terraced gardens, 500m beyond the Palácio Nacional, with terrific views of coast and castle. Six stylishly furnished rooms with bath. Closed Jan. Parking. ❺

Lawrence's Hotel Rua Consigliéri Pedroso 38–40 ☎219 105 500, ⊛www.lawrenceshotel.com. Lays claim to being the oldest hotel in Iberia, first opened in 1764 and restyled as a five-star establishment by Dutch owners in 1999. There are only eleven spacious rooms and five suites, all relatively simply furnished in traditional style, and a highly rated restaurant serving traditional Portuguese cuisine (open to non-residents; expensive; reservations advised). ❼

Pensão Nova Sintra Largo Afonso d'Albuquerque 25, Estefânia ☎219 230 220, ℻219 107 033. Very smart *pensão* in a big mansion above a decent restaurant, which also has a raised café-terrace overlooking the busy street. Modern rooms, all with cable TV, bath and shiny marble floors. ❹

Quinta da Paderna Rua da Paderna 4 ☎219 235 053. Highly attractive accommodation in a small old house reached down a steep cobbled track, just

north of Sintra-Vila. Great views up to Quinta da Regaleira. Rooms with bath cost €15 more. Two nights minimum stay. ❹

Palácio de Seteais 1km west of town ☎219 233 200, ⊛www.tivolihotels.com. The "Seven Sighs Palace", completed in the last years of the eighteenth century and entered through a majestic Neoclassical arch, is now an immensely luxurious hotel – a night here will set you back around €200. The giant rooms have period furniture and comfy beds – it's popular with honeymooners – while the landscaped gardens have their own pool. Parking. ❼

Piela's Av Desiderio Cambournac 1–3, Estefânia ☎219 241 691. Popular budget accommodation in a swish, renovated town house on a busy road above a cybercafé. The welcoming English-speaking proprietor offers rooms of varying sizes, each with TV. Triples also available. No breakfast. ❸

Residencial Sintra Trav dos Alvares, São Pedro ☎219 230 738, Fantastic place with a rambling garden, swimming pool and huge rooms that can easily accommodate extra beds – so it's ideal for families or groups. ❹

Hotel Tivoli Pr da República ☎219 237 200, ⊛www.tivolihotels.com. The only part of the historic centre not part of the UNESCO World Heritage site – not surprisingly, as it's ugly as sin. But it has fine views from the balconies of the comfortable en-suite rooms. There's also an in-house restaurant. Parking. ❹

Eating and drinking

There are some fine **cafés** and **restaurants** scattered about the various quarters of Sintra. With a couple of honourable exceptions the most mundane are in the centre, near the palace or around the train station; the best concentration is at São Pedro, a twenty-minute walk from town. Local specialities include *queijadas da Sintra* – sweet cheese pastry-cakes. If you're out for the day, take a **picnic**: refreshments out of town are exorbitantly priced. You can stock up on supplies at the morning fruit and vegetable **market**, a short walk from the station opposite the Museu de Arte Moderna.

Sintra-Vila

Adega das Caves Rua de Pendoa 2 ☎ 219 239 848. Bustling café-bar beneath *Café Paris*, attracting a predominantly youthful local clientele; good-value pizzas and baguettes. Inexpensive.

Alcobaça Rua das Padarias 7–11 ☎ 219 231 651. The best central choice for a decent, straightforward Portuguese meal. Plain, tiled dining room with friendly service and large servings of grilled chicken, *arroz de marisco*, sardines and pasta for around €15 a head. Moderate.

Casa da Piriquita Rua das Padarias 1 ☎ 219 230 626. On the uphill alley across from the *Café Paris*, this tearoom and bakery is always busy with locals queueing to buy *queijadas da Sintra* and the similarly sticky *travesseiros*. Closed Wed. Its more modern sister branch, up the hill at no. 18 (closed Tues), has a big outdoor terrace. Inexpensive.

Fonte da Pipa Rua Fonte da Pipa 11–13. A laid-back bar (open from 9pm) next to the lovely fountain (*fonte*) that the street is named after.

Café Paris Largo Rainha D. Amélia ☎ 219 232 375. The highest-profile café in town, opposite the Palácio Nacional, which means steep prices for underwhelming food. However, it's a great place to sit and nurse a drink in the sun. Expensive.

Páteo do Garrett Rua Maria Eugénia Reis F. Navarro 7 ☎ 219 243 380. Bar-restaurant with a darkened interior, though the lovely, sunny patio has great views over the village. It serves standard Portuguese meals, or just pop in for a drink. Closed Wed, & lunches only from Jan–April. Moderate.

Tulhas Rua Gil Vicente 4 ☎ 219 232 378. Imaginative cooking in a fine building, converted from old grain silos. The giant mixed grills at €22 for two people will keep carnivores more than happy, while the weekend specials are usually excellent. Closed Wed. Moderate.

Estefânia

Orixás Av Adriano Coelho 7 ☎ 219 241 672. Brazilian bar, restaurant, music venue and art gallery in a lovely building complete with waterfalls and outdoor terrace. The buffet costs around €30, but you'll be here all night and with live Brazilian music thrown in, it's not bad value. Open for lunch and dinner at weekends, dinner only Tues–Fri, closed Mon. Expensive.

Piela's Rua João de Deus 70–72 ☎ 219 241 691. Budget meals and late-night drinks in a friendly café-restaurant, over the tracks from the station. Inexpensive.

São Pedro de Sintra

Adega do Saloio Trav Chão de Meninos ☎ 219 231 422. Around five minutes from São Pedro's main square, close to Rotunda do Ramalha, this fine grill-restaurant has hospitable owners. Also does a good *arroz de marisco*. Closed Wed and Thurs from Sept–April. Moderate.

Cantinho de São Pedro Pr D. Fernando II 18, São Pedro de Sintra ☎ 219 230 267. Large, stone-walled restaurant overlooking an attractive courtyard just off São Pedro's main square. Slightly formal service but excellent food at reasonable prices. Try the daily specials, which are usually good value. On cool evenings, a log fire keeps things cosy. Moderate.

Around Sintra

The **Castelo dos Mouros** and extraordinary **Palácio da Pena**, on the heights above the town, are the most obvious targets for visitors – the circular #434 bus from Sintra station or Sintra-Vila run throughout the day to both places. The nearby estate of **Quinta da Regaleira** is a popular attraction, too, and is a short walk from the town, though other local sights – including the gardens of **Monserrate** and the **Convento dos Capuchos** – will probably require further transport (see "Practicalities", on p.152). West of Sintra, the wine-growing centre of **Colares**, the beach at **Praia Grande** or the westernmost point in Europe, **Cabo da Roca**, can all be seen by public transport.

Castelo dos Mouros

Reached on bus #434, or a steep drive up on the road to Palácio da Pena, the ruined ramparts of the **Castelo dos Mouros** (daily: May–Oct 9am–7pm; Nov–April 9.30am–6pm; €3.50) are truly spectacular. Built in the ninth century, the castle was taken in 1147 by Afonso Henriques, with the aid of Scandinavian Crusaders. The castle walls were allowed to fall into disrepair over subsequent centuries, though they were restored in the mid-nineteenth century under the orders of Ferdinand II. The Moorish castle spans – and is partly built into – two

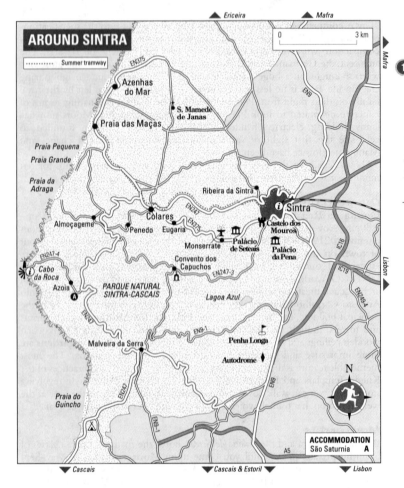

rocky pinnacles, with the remains of a mosque spread midway between the fortifications, and the views from up here are extraordinary: south beyond Lisbon to the Serra da Arrábida, west to Cabo da Roca and north to the Berlenga islands. If you want to walk from Sintra, from Calçada dos Clérigos, near the church of Santa Maria, a stone pathway leads all the way up to the lower slopes, where you can see a Moorish grain silo and a ruined twelfth-century church. To enter the castle itself, you'll need to buy a ticket from the road exit.

Palácio da Pena

The entrance to the castle is on the the the road up to the lower entrance to the **Palácio da Pena** (Tues–Sun: end-June to mid-Sept 10am–7pm, mid Sept–end June 10am–5.30pm; €6, gardens only €3.50). After a short ride on a shuttle bus (€1.50 return) or a twenty-minute walk up through the gardens – a stretch of rambling woodland, with a scattering of lakes and follies – the fabulous palace appears as a wild fantasy of domes, towers, ramparts and walkways, approached through mock-Manueline gateways and a drawbridge that doesn't draw. A compelling riot of kitsch, it was built in the 1840s to the specifications of Ferdinand of Saxe-Coburg-Gotha, husband of Queen Maria II, and it bears comparison with the mock-medieval castles of Ludwig of Bavaria. The architect, the German Baron Eschwege, immortalized himself in the guise of a warrior-knight on a huge statue that guards the palace from a neighbouring crag. Inside, Pena is no less bizarre, preserved exactly as it was left by the royal family on their flight from Portugal in 1910. The result is fascinating: rooms of concrete decorated to look like wood, statues of turbanned Moors nonchalantly holding electric chandeliers. Of an original convent, founded to celebrate the first sight of Vasco da Gama's returning fleet, a chapel and Manueline cloister have been retained.

Above Pena, past the statue of Eschwege, a marked footpath climbs for ten minutes or so to the **Cruz Alta**, highest point of the Serra de Sintra.

Quinta da Regaleira

Quinta da Regaleira (daily: May–Sept 10am–8pm; Oct & Feb–April 10am–6.30pm; Nov–Jan 10am–5.30pm; 90min tours every 30min–1hr; reservations essential ☎219 106 650; €10, unguided visits €5) is just a five-minute walk out of town on the Seteais–Monserrate road. It's one of Sintra's most elaborate estates, laid out at the turn of the twentieth century, and was declared a UNESCO World Heritage site in 1995. The estate was designed by Italian architect and theatrical set designer Luigi Manini for wealthy landowner António Augusto Carvalho Monteiro. The Italian's sense of the dramatic is obvious: the principal building, the mock-Manueline **Palaçio dos Milhões**, sprouts turrets and towers, though the interior is sparse apart from some elaborate Rococo wooden ceilings and impressive Art Nouveau tiles. The surrounding **gardens** are more impressive and shelter fountains, terraces, lakes and grottoes. The most memorable feature is the Initiation Well, inspired by the initiation practices of the Knight Templars and Freemasons. Entering via a Harry Potter-style revolving stone door, you can walk down a moss-covered spiral stairway to the foot of the well and through a tunnel, which eventually resurfaces at the edge of a lake.

Monserrate

Beyond Regaleira and the *Palácio de Seteais* hotel, the road leads past a series of beautiful private *quintas* until you come upon **Monserrate** (daily: May–Sept 9am–7pm; Oct–April 9am–6pm; €3.50.) – about an hour's walk or on the toy train from Sintra (see p.152). The charm of Monserrate, a Victorian folly-like mansion set in a vast botanical park of exotic trees and subtropical shrubs and plants, is immeasurably enhanced by the fact that it's only partially maintained. The name most associated with Monserrate is that of William Beckford, author of the Gothic novel *Vathek* and the wealthiest untitled Englishman of his age, who rented Monserrate from 1793 to 1799, having been forced to flee Britain after he was caught in a compromising position with a 16-year-old boy. Setting about improving the place, he landscaped a waterfall and even imported a flock of sheep from his estate at Fonthill.

Half a century later, a second immensely rich Englishman, Sir Francis Cook, bought the estate. His fantasies were scarcely less ambitious. Cook imported the head gardener from Kew to lay out succulents and water plants, tropical ferns and palms, and just about every known conifer. For a time Monserrate boasted the only lawn in Iberia and it remains one of Europe's most richly stocked gardens, with over a thousand different species of subtropical trees and plants.

Cook's main legacy was the construction of a great Victorian palace inspired by Brighton Pavilion. You can visit sections of the partly restored palace on daily tours (guided tours daily at 10am and 3pm, €7; pre-booking essential on ☎219 237 300), though until renovation is completed, the most impressive part remains the exterior, with its mix of Moorish and Italian decoration – the dome is modelled on the Duomo in Florence.

Convento dos Capuchos

The **Convento dos Capuchos** (45-minute tours daily: May–Oct every 30min 9am–7pm; Nov–Feb roughly hourly 10am–4.30pm; March–April roughly hourly 9.30am–6pm; reservations essential on ☎219 237 300; €3.50) is an extraordinary hermitage with tiny, dwarf-like cells cut from the rock and lined in cork – hence its popular name of the "Cork Convent". Philip II, King of Spain and Portugal, pronounced it the poorest convent of his kingdom, and Byron, visiting a cave where one monk had spent 36 years in seclusion, mocked in *Childe Harold:*

Deep in yon cave Honorius long did dwell,
In hope to merit Heaven by making earth a Hell.

It's hard not to be moved by the simplicity of the place. It was occupied for three hundred years and finally abandoned in 1834 by its seven remaining monks. Some of the **penitents' cells** can only be entered by crawling through 70cm-high doors; here, and on every other ceiling, doorframe and lintel, are attached panels of cork, taken from the surrounding woods. Elsewhere, you'll come across a washroom, kitchen, refectory, tiny chapels, even a bread oven set apart from the main complex.

To get there, the most straightforward approach is by the ridge road from Pena – a distance of 9km. The minor road between Sintra, the convent and Cabo da Roca sports some of the country's most alarming natural rock formations, with boulders as big as houses looming out of the trees.

Colares

About 6km further west of Monserrate is **COLARES**, a hill village famed for its rich red wine made from grapes grown in the local sandy soil. The local producer, Adega Regional de Colares (☎219 288 082), hosts occasional concerts, tastings and exhibitions. In the village, head uphill (signed Penedo) for superb views back towards Sintra. Colares is easily reached on the Sintra–Cascais bus route (#403) or #401 from Sintra. Alternatively you can also take the **tram** (see box, below). The best place to eat in Colares is the smart *Colares Velho*, Largo Dr Carlos Franca 1–4 (☎219 292 406; closed Sun afternoon and all day Mon & Tues).

Praia Grande and the coast

West of Colares, the road winds around through the hills to **PRAIA GRANDE**, the best beach on this section of coast, certainly for surfers. In August the World Bodyboarding Championships are held here, along with games such as volleyball

The Sintra tram route

After a chequered history of closures and temporary openings, it seems Sintra's historic tramway is finally a permanent route to the coast. Opened in 1904, the highly picturesque route now runs from outside the Museu de Arte Moderna in Sintra to the coast at Praia das Maçãs via Colares (Fri–Sun only at 10am, noon, 2pm and 3.30pm; return at 11am, 1pm, 2.55pm and 16.45pm, 45 mins, €2 single).

and beach rugby. Plenty of inexpensive cafés and restaurants spread along the beachside road. Bus #441 from Sintra train station runs here – if you want to stay, head for *Hotel Arribas* (☎219 289 050, Ⓦwww.hotelarribas.com ❺), a modern three-star plonked ungraciously at the north end of the sands. Rooms are enormous while the hotel boasts sea pools, a restaurant and café-terrace with great sea views.

Just north of Praia Grande is the larger resort of **PRAIA DAS MAÇÃS**, a lively little holiday village with plenty of bars and restaurants sprawled round a broad expanse of sand – a good place to spend a day or two. Again, you can get here on bus #441 from Sintra train station or on the tram (see box on p.157). The modern *Oceano*, by the tram terminal on the main Avenida Eugénio Levy 52 (☎219 292 399, Ⓔpensaoooceano@iol.pt; ❹), is much the best place to stay. Of several **bars and restaurants**, *O Loureiro*, Esplanada Vasco da Gama (☎219 292 442; closed Thurs), has great-value seafood and overlooks the beach, or try the *Maças Club* opposite on Rua Pedro Álvaro Cabral 2-12 (☎219 292 024). With an outdoor terrace facing the sands, this is the ideal spot for a cool drink, sandwich or ice cream. The action moves upstairs as the evening progresses, with dance music until 6am. The bus #441 continues another 2km to the north to **AZENHAS DO MAR**, a picture-book cliff-top town with a small beach and sea pool.

Cabo da Roca

CABO DA ROCA, 14km southwest of Colares, is officially the most westerly point in mainland Europe; the tourist office here sells a certificate to prove it; regular buses (#403) from either Sintra or Cascais train stations make the run throughout the year. It's an enjoyable trip, though the cape itself comprises little more than a lighthouse – below which foamy breakers slam the cliffs – a souvenir shop/café and a tourist office (daily: 9am–6.30pm; ☎219 280 892). A cross at the cape carries an inscription by Luís de Camões ("Here … where the land ends, and the sea begins"), whose muse, for once it seems, deserted him. If you want to stay near here, look no further than the ⚓ *São Saturnia* (☎219 283 192, Ⓦwww.saosat.com, ❺). Reached down a steep track – look for the sign on the right just past Azóia on the way back from Cabo da Roca – this former convent dates back to the twelfth-century and sits in a valley where time seems to stand still. The six rooms, three suites and self-catering apartments are all traditionally furnished, while the rambling communal areas are all weathered beams and low ceilings. There's a small outdoor pool, barbecue area, and lots of terraces with stunning views.

Palácio de Queluz

The **Palácio de Queluz** (Mon & Wed–Sun 9.30am–5pm; €4; free Sun 10am–2pm) is one of Portugal's most sumptuous palaces. Commissioned in 1747 and long used as the summer residence for royals, it is the country's finest example of Rococo architecture. Although its low, pink-washed wings and extensive eighteenth-century formal gardens are preserved as a museum, the palace is still pressed into service to accommodate state guests and dignitaries. From May to October (but not August) there's a display of Portuguese horsemanship here every Wednesday at 11am, and the palace also hosts events for the Sintra music festival (see p.136). The palace lies on the Sintra train line, making it easy to see either on the way out (it's just twenty minutes from Lisbon's

Rossio station; €1.10 one-way) or on the way back from Sintra. The station is called Queluz-Belas: turn left out of the station and walk down the main road for fifteen minutes, following the signs through the unremarkable town until you reach a vast cobbled square, Largo do Palácio, with the palace walls reaching out around one side.

The Palace

The palace was built by Dom Pedro III, husband and regent to his niece, **Queen Maria I**, who lived here throughout her 39-year reign (1777–1816), quite mad for the last 27, following the death of her eldest son, José. William Beckford visited when the Queen's wits were dwindling, and ran races in the gardens with the Princess of Brazil's ladies-in-waiting. The palace even once held bullfights in the courtyards.

Visitors first enter the **Throne Room**, lined with mirrors surmounted by paintings and golden flourishes. Beyond is the more restrained **Music Chamber** with its portrait of Queen Maria above the French grand piano. Smaller quarters include bed and sitting rooms, a tiny oratory swathed with red velvet, and a **Sculpture Room**, whose only exhibit is an earthenware bust of Maria. Another wing comprises an elegant suite of public rooms – smoking, coffee and dining rooms – all intimate in scale and tastefully decorated. The **Ambassador's Chamber**, where diplomats and foreign ministers were received during the nineteenth century, echoes the Throne Room in style, with one side lined with porcelain chinoiserie. In the end, though, perhaps the most pleasing room is the simple **Dressing Room** with its geometric inlaid wooden floor and spider's web ceiling of radial gilt bands.

The formal **gardens** are included in the ticket price. Low box hedges and elaborate (if weatherworn) statues spread out from the protection of the palace wings, while small pools and fountains, steps and terracing form a harmonious background to the building.

You can still enjoy a meal in the palace's original kitchen, the **Cozinha Velha** (daily 12.30–3pm & 7.30–10pm; ☎214 356 158), which retains its stone chimney, arches and wooden vaulted ceiling, and sports copper pots, pans and utensils in every niche and alcove. The food – classic French-Portuguese – is not always as impressive as the locale, and you're looking at around €35 a head for a full meal (though there is a cheaper café in the main body of the palace). The kitchens are now part of the *Pousada Dona Maria I* (☎214 356 158, ⓦwww.pousadas.pt; ❼), which gives you the chance to stay in one of 26 plush rooms in an annexe of the palace.

South of the Rio Tejo

As late as the nineteenth century, the southern bank of the Tejo estuary was an underpopulated area used as a quarantine station for foreign visitors; the village of Trafaria was so lawless that the police visited it only when accompanied by members of the army. The huge **Ponte 25 de Abril**, a suspension bridge inaugurated as the "Salazar Bridge" in 1966 and renamed after the 1974 Revolution, finally ended what remained of this separation between "town and country". Since then, Lisbon has spilled over the river in a string of tatty industrial suburbs, the closest being **Cacilhas**, where locals come to eat seafood in a string of good restaurants. To the west, **Caparica** is the main resort on the Costa da Caparica, which stretches for some 20km to the south. On the other side of the peninsula, 50km south of the capital, the industrial city of **Setúbal** sustains one remarkable church and is a pleasant provincial base from which to explore the small town of **Palmela** and its medieval castle, or the River Sado and the **Parque Natural da Arrábida**. The coastal surroundings are particularly attractive, with several beaches within the *parque* and over the Sado estuary at **Tróia**, and one full-blown resort at **Sesimbra**.

Across the river: Cacilhas and the Cristo Rei

The most enjoyable approach to the Setúbal peninsula is to take the ferry from Lisbon's Cais do Sodré (see p.86 for schedules) to **CACILHAS**. The blustery ride grants wonderful views of the city, as well as of the Ponte 25 de Abril, though it's the **seafood restaurants** in the port that are as good a reason as any to make the crossing. Particularly good value is the *Escondidinho de Cacilhas* (closed Thurs), immediately on the right as you leave the ferry. Busier, and with better views, is the moderately priced riverside *Cervejaria Farol* (☎212 765 248; closed Wed), while if you head towards the bridge along the Cais do Ginjal you'll find two other atmospheric riverside restaurants: the pricey Brazilian *Atira-te ao Rio* (☎212 751 380; closed Mon), or the marginally cheaper *Ponto Final* (☎212 760 743; closed Tues), offering Portuguese staples and great views back to Lisbon.

Just past here is the foot of the **Elevador Panorâmico da Boca do Vento** (daily 8am–11.45pm; €1 return), a sleek, modern elevator which whisks you up the cliff face to the old part of **Almada**. From the top there are fantastic views over the river and city, while the surrounding streets are highly atmospheric.

Beyond Almada stands the **Cristo Rei** (daily 9.30am–6pm; €3) – to get here, take bus #101 from Cacilhas. Built in 1959, this relatively modest version of Rio's Christ-statue landmark has a lift that shuttles you up the interior of the statue to a dramatic viewing platform, 80m above the ground. On a good day, Lisbon stretches out like a map below you, with the glistening roof of the Pena palace at Sintra in the distance.

From Cacilhas **bus station**, outside the ferry terminal, there are regular services to Costa da Caparica, Setúbal, Sesimbra and Vila Nogueira de Azeitão.

Caparica

Buses from Cacilhas (Via Rapida buses roughly every 30min, daily 7am–9pm; 30min journey) or from Lisbon's Praça de Espanha (every 30min, daily 7am–12.45am; 40min–1hr) run to the beach resort of **CAPARICA**, at the northern end of the Costa da Caparica. Lisbon's main seaside resort, it was named after the find of a cloak (*capa*) full of golden coins. Today it is high-rise, tacky and packed at weekends in summer, but don't let that put you off. Its family atmosphere, restaurants and beachside cafés full of tanned surfers make it a thoroughly enjoyable day out. From the main Praça da Liberdade (where you'll find the market, supermarkets and banks) the pedestrianized Rua dos Pescadores – lined with cafés, restaurants and inexpensive guesthouses – heads down to the seafront.

The **beach** itself stretches north towards Lisbon and south away into the distance, its initial stretch backed by apartments and cafés. The water is of good quality, though beware the dangerous undertow. A **mini-railway** (May–Sept daily every 30min from 9am–7.30pm; €3.80 return or €2.35 for first nine stops) runs along the 8km or so of dunes to Fonte da Telha – if you're after solitude you need only take it this far and walk. However, each of the nineteen mini-train stops, based around one or two beach-cafés, has a very particular feel. Earlier stops tend to be family-oriented, later ones are on the whole younger and more fashionable, with nudity (though officially illegal) ubiquitons, especially around stop 18–19, which is also something of a gay area.

Practicalities

In summer, **buses** stop at the bus park in town near the beginning of the sands. In winter, they use the station in Praça Padre Manuel Bernades, in which case it is best to get off at the first stop in Caparica, on the edge of the leafy Praça da Liberdade, five minutes back from the beach. From here, walk diagonally across the square, turn right and at Avenida da Liberdade 18 you'll find the **turismo** (Mon–Sat 9am–1pm & 2–5.30pm, closed Sat pm from Oct–April; ☎212 900 071).

There are a growing number of **hotels and pensions** in Caparica, though they are relatively pricey and often full in summer. *Pensão Real*, Rua Mestre Manuel 18 (ⓦwww.hotel-real.com, ☎212 918 870, ❹); is one of the more reasonable central options, with some of the en-suite rooms featuring sea-facing balconies; or try *Residencial Capa-Rica*, Rua dos Pescadores 9 (☎212 900 242, ⒺBenvindo.tours@mail.telepac.pt; breakfast in summer only; ❷), with bright en-suite rooms near the beach. There is also a string of **campsites**, packed out in summer. Your best bet is also the most central, the well-equipped *Orbitur* (☎212 901 366, ⓦwww.orbitur.pt), complete with café and tennis courts – it's one of the few where camping club membership is not required.

Among the dozens of fish and seafood **restaurants**, a couple of recommended, moderately priced, choices include *O Barbas*, Praia da Costa (☎212 900 163; closed Tues evening & all day Wed), at the northern end of the beach, with beachside window seats; and *Primoroso*, Av. 1º de Maio (☎212 903 087; closed Thurs), further along the seafront towards Lisbon, which serves an excellent *cataplana* at outdoor tables.

Setúbal

Some 50km south from Lisbon, **SETÚBAL** is Portugal's third port and a major industrial centre. It was once described by Hans Christian Andersen as a "terrestrial paradise" and, although those days are long gone, its pedestrianized centre and port are enjoyable enough for a short visit. If you're heading south, it's worth stopping at least for a look at the remarkable Igreja de Jesus and to enjoy the views from the Castelo São Filipe.

The Town

Setúbal's greatest monument is the **Igreja de Jesus** (Tues–Sun 9am–noon & 2–5pm, closed public hols; free) designed by Diogo de Boitaca and possibly the first of all Manueline buildings (see box on p.214). Essentially a late-Gothic structure, with a huge, flamboyant doorway, its interior design was transformed by Boitaca, who introduced fantastically twisted pillars to support the vault. The rough granite surfaces of the pillars contrast with the delicacy of the blue and white *azulejos* around the high altar, which were added in the seventeenth century. The adjacent Convento de Jesus now forms the **Museu de Setúbal** (Tues–Sat 9am–noon & 1.30–5.30pm; free) containing treasures from the church and town, though most of these seem to be permanently in storage.

The **Castelo São Felipe**, signposted off the western end of Avenida Luisa Todi, is half an hour's walk from town. Built on the orders of Spanish king

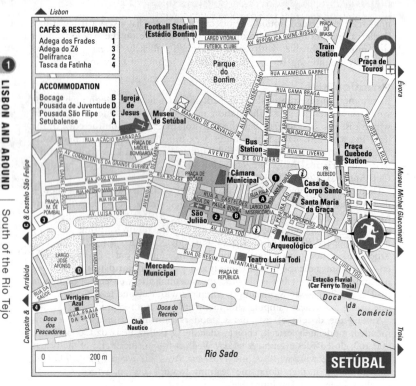

CAFÉS & RESTAURANTS

Adega dos Frades	1
Adega do Zé	3
Delifranca	2
Tasca da Fatinha	4

ACCOMMODATION

Bocage	B
Pousada de Juventude	D
Pousada São Filipe	C
Setubalense	A

Football Stadium (Estádio Bonfim)

Train Station

Praça de Touros

Parque do Bonfim

Igreja de Jesus

Museu de Setúbal

Bus Station

Praça Quebedo Station

Câmara Municipal

Casa do Corpo Santo

São Julião

Santa Maria da Graça

Museu Arqueológico

Teatro Luísa Todi

Mercado Municipal

Estação Fluvial (Car Ferry to Tróia)

Vertigem Azul

Doca do Recreio

Doca dos Pescadores

Club Nautico

Doca da Comércio

Rio Sado

0   200 m

SETÚBAL

N

Felipe II in 1590, it's a grand structure, harbouring an *azulejo*-lined chapel and protected by sheer walls of overpowering height. Legend has it that a series of secret tunnels connect the castle with the coast, but any proof was lost in the Great Earthquake of 1755. Part of the castle is now a *pousada* but the ramparts and bar are open to non-guests and there are superb views over the mouth of the Sado estuary and the Tróia peninsula.

The rest of town has little to detain you, though the pedestrianized shopping streets in the **old town** around Rua A. Castelões are handsome enough. On Largo Corpo Santo, take a peek inside the **Casa do Corpo Santo** (Mon–Sat 9am–12.30pm & 2–5.30pm; free), built in 1714 as part of the Cabedo family's palace and later used as a fisherman's fraternity. The upper floor has a painted ceiling, Baroque chapel and walls decked in superb *azulejos* showing scenes of São Pedro, patron saint of fishermen. In the **Museu Arqueológico**, Avenida Luísa Todi 162 (Tues–Sat 9am–12.30pm & 2–5.30pm; closed Sat in Aug; €1.80), sparse finds from the city's Roman age are displayed along with a few dusty fishing boats and local handicrafts. The regional turismo (see opposite) nearby maintains the foundations of a Roman fish-preserving factory underneath its glass floor. Finally, a ten- to fifteen-minute walk east along Rua Arronches Junqueiro brings you to the **Museu Michel Giacometti** at Largo Defensores da República (Tues–Fri & Sun 9am–noon & 2–6pm; free), a museum of agricultural and trade implements collected by a Corsican ethnologist who was particularly interested in Portuguese culture.

Practicalities

The easiest way to Setúbal is to take the half-hourly Setubalase **bus** from Lisbon's Praça de Espanha, which takes around an hour. There are also buses from Cacilhas (hourly; 50min–1hr). By car, the fast A2 from Ponte 25 de Abril whisks you to Setúbal in around forty minutes; it's about the same from Lisbon airport via Ponte Vasco da Gama. **Trains** from Lisbon's Oriente or Entrecampos stations (roughly every 40 mins; timetable on ☎707 127 127) drop you at Praça do Brasil, north of the town centre; local trains use the more central station at the eastern end of Avenida 5 de Outubro.

There are two **turismos** in Setúbal: the city one across from the local train station in the Casa do Corpo Santo, on Praça do Quebedo (daily 9am–7pm; ☎265 534 402), and the regional one, just off Avenida Luísa Todi at Travessa Frei Gaspar 10 (June–Sept Mon–Sat 9am–12.30pm & 2–7pm, Sun 9am–12.30pm; Oct–May Mon & Sat 9.30am–12.30pm & 2–6pm, Tues–Fri 9.30am–6pm; ☎265 539 120, ⒲www.costa-azul.rts.pt). Both hand out maps and can help with finding rooms. **Accommodation** is rarely a problem as there are plenty of hotels geared to business travellers. Good-value fish and seafood **restaurants** abound at the waterside around the Doca dos Pescadores. There are also plenty of places around the atmospheric **Mercado Municipal**; in midsummer, the market area is considerably expanded with clothes and touristy bric-a-brac. Nightlife in Setúbal revolves around the outdoor café-bars along Avenida Luísa Todi, which bustle with activity all evening. Alternatively, the **Teatro Luísa Todi** stages shows at weekends and often features art-house movies during the week.

The turismos can supply details of a range of privately organized **tours and activity sports** in the area including walking trips, jeep excursions, hot-air balloon flights and off-road driving. The highlight is the year-round **dolphin-watching** tour, organized by ⚓Vertigem Azul May–Sept daily weather permitting at 10am & 3pm; weekends only from Oct–April, minimum six people required; €30 per person; ☎265 238 000, ⒲www.vertigemazul.com), with trips to watch a resident colony of bottle-nosed dolphins, either in the Sado estuary or along the coast. Their offices are on Rua Praia da Saúde 11ᵈ, near the harbour. For information on walking tours round Arrábida (see p.165), contact the **Parque Natural da Arrábida** office on Praça da República (Mon–Fri 9am–12.30pm & 2–5pm; ☎265 524 032).

Hotels, pensions and hostels

The following are marked on the Setúbal map on p.162.

Residencial Bocage Rua de São Cristóvão 14 ☎265 543 080, Ⓔresidencial.bocage@iol.pt. Attractive and well-maintained rooms with private bathrooms and TVs. ❷

Pousada de Juventude de Setúbal Largo José Afonso ☎265 534 431, Ⓔsetubal@movijovem.pt. Futuristic, modern hostel right in the middle of one of Setúbal's main squares, close to the docks. Six four-bedded rooms from €5 per person, four doubles with or without bath. ❶

Pousada São Filipe Castelo São Filipe ☎265 523 844 or 218 442 001, ⒲www.pousadas.pt. Built within the castle, the front rooms command superb views over the estuary, as does the surprisingly good-value restaurant. This is open to non-guests and serves good Portuguese and international cuisine. Parking ❼

Residencial Setubalense Rua Major Afonso Pala 17 ☎265 525 790, ⒲www.hotel-residencial .setubalense.com. Welcoming central *residencial* on a quiet street, with clean, simply furnished rooms, plus a bar for guests. ❸

Cafés and restaurants

Adega do Zé Av. Luísa Todi 588 ☎265 238 970. Unexotic-looking place but very popular thanks to excellent home cooking, including superb *calamari* and *arroz* dishes. Closed Mon. Inexpensive.

Adega dos Frades Rua M. A. Pala 19 ☎265 231 425. Next to the *Residencial Setubalense* on a quiet pedestrianized street, this spacious bar/restaurant serves bargain grills with plenty of locals (and a TV) for company. Inexpensive.

José Mourinho: the special one

Setúbal's most famous son, José Mourinho, is one of Europe's most successful football managers and barely a day goes by without his broodingly handsome face appearing on the sports pages either in Portugal or the UK. Born in Setúbal on 26 January, 1963, Mourinho grew up supporting Vitória Setúbal where his father was goalkeeper. He began his managerial career coaching their junior team after a modest playing career, which included a spell at Sesimbrense of Sesimbra, up the coast. His big break, however, was being former England manager Bobby Robson's translator at Barcelona. Picking up and developing the Englishman's managerial skills, he soon turned round the fortunes of previously useless União Leiria. This alerted Porto to his managerial talents. Under Mourinho, Porto swiftly landed the Portuguese league, Portuguese Cup and UEFA Cup (all in 2003) and they were crowned European Champions in 2004. He moved to Chelsea later that year and promptly won back-to-back league titles with the Londoners (they had not won a league title previously for half a century). No wonder Mourinho calls himself "the special one". To many in the game, his apparent arrogance (and colossal salary) is irksome – witness, "Nobody in this football world is perfect. I am nobody" – though, as a shrewd psychological operator, Mourinho is probably at least as interested in deflecting attention from his team as in showing off.

Despite his wealth and international profile, Mourinho remains loyal to his Portuguese roots. He married his childhood sweetheart (they have two children) and chooses to visit his family in Setúbal or his holiday home near Óbidos when not in London. Not surprisingly he has become a Portuguese national hero – his triumphs and audacity articulate something of the glory and power that the country has long lost. Mourinho has stated his wish to coach the Portuguese national team at some point in the future – and turning one of Europe's smallest football countries into World Cup winners really would be special.

Delifranca Largo Dr Francisco Soveral 20–22. Good for baguettes with interesting fillings – also has outdoor seats on the square. Closed Sun. Inexpensive.

Tasca da Fatinha Rua da Saúde 58 ☎ 265 232 800. Good waterside restaurant, with piles of fresh fish delivered to your table straight from the grill. Closed Mon. Moderate.

Tróia

Setúbal's local beaches, reached by frequent ferries from the town, are on the **Península de Tróia**, a large sand spit that hems in the Sado estuary. The peninsula was settled by the Phoenicians and subsequently by the Romans, whose town of Cetobriga appears to have been overwhelmed by a tidal wave in the fifth century. There are some desultory remains, including tanks for salting fish, on the landward shore. Originally a wilderness of sand and wild flowers, Tróia must once have been magnificent, but it's now a heavily developed resort with its own golf course. Be prepared to walk for twenty minutes or so south along the beach to escape the worst of the development. The **car-ferries** depart daily from Setúbal (every 15min, 7.15am–11pm, hourly overnight; €1 per person, cars from €5); expect long queues for cars in summer. The crossing also provides a useful route into the Alentejo for anyone heading south.

Palmela

The small town of **PALMELA**, 10km north of Setúbal, is worth a quick visit for the views from its medieval **castle**, which on a clear day encompass Lisbon, Setúbal, the Sado estuary and Tróia. This is the centre of a wine-producing area, hence the town's major annual event: the Festa das Vindimas in September, celebrating the first of the year's wine harvest, with processions, fireworks, grape-treading and running of the bulls.

Once the headquarters for the Order of Santiago, the convent in the castle has been restored and extended into a **pousada**, the *Castelo de Palmela* (☎212 351 226/218 442 001, ⓦwww.pousadas.pt; breakfast included; ❽). Recently renovated, it's a fabulous place to stay, incorporating the original cloisters within the design and boasting panoramic views from all points. The castle also incorporates a row of handicraft shops selling *azulejos*, cheese and the highly rated local wines, plus a café and a **museum** (Tues–Fri 10am–12.30pm & 2–5.30pm, Sat & Sun 10am–1pm & 3–5.30pm; free), which houses a small collection of archeological remains dating back to Moorish times. Opposite the museum is Palmela's **turismo** (daily 9.30am–8pm ☎212 332 122), which can provide you with details of other accommodation options in the area.

During the week there are ten **buses** a day to Palmela, four at weekends, from Lisbon's Praça de Espanha; the ride takes forty minutes. There are also buses every twenty minutes on the ten- to fifteen-minute run from Setúbal.

Parque Natural da Arrábida

Between Setúbal and Sesimbra lies the **Parque Natural da Arrábida**, whose main feature is the 500-metre granite ridge known as the Serra da Arrábida, visible for miles around and home to wildcats, badgers, polecats, buzzards and Bonelli eagles. The twisted pillars of Setúbal's Igreja de Jesus were hewn from here. If you want to explore the area on foot, **walking guides** are available from the park's main office in Setúbal (see p.163). Note, too, that from July to August, a one-way system operates on the narrow coastal road through the park, which operates westwards only from 8am–7pm (though the inland N10 and N379-1 roads operate both ways).

Getting round by public transport is tricky. In summer, the coastal road is served by three daily **buses** from Setúbal. Otherwise you can only skirt round the park on year-round buses from Setúbal to Sesimbra that take the main road, well back from the coast. This service passes through the town of **VILA NOGUEIRA DE AZEITÃO**, where the main highlight is the **José Maria da Fonseca wine vaults and museum** on the main Rua José Augusto Coelho (ⓦwww.jmf.pt; Mon–Fri 9.30am–noon & 2.30–4.15pm, Sat & Sun 10am–noon & 2.30–4pm; free). A tour of the vaults, which lasts 45 minutes, includes a free tasting and provides an interesting introduction to the local Setúbal Moscatel. Vila Nogueira de Azeitão can also be reached by **bus** from Lisbon's Praça de Espanha (hourly; 45min). There is a well-equipped **campsite**, *Picheleiros* (☎212 181 322), just outside town, complete with minimarket, café and children's playground.

Drivers should take the N379-1 from Azeitão to the **Convento da Arrábida** (Wed & Sun 3–4pm; reservations needed on ☎212 180 520). Owned by the Fundação Orient, the convent was built by Franciscan monks in the sixteenth century. The convent's white buildings tumble down a steep hillside, offering stunning ocean views.

Around four kilometres south of the convent, the N10 winds down to the coast, reaching the tiny harbour village of **PORTINHO DA ARRÁBIDA**, which has one of the coast's best beaches. The harbour is guarded by a tiny seventeenth-century fort, now housing the **Museu Oceanográfico** (Tues–Fri 10am–4pm, Sat 3–6pm; €2), displaying marine animals from the region either live – in a small aquarium – or stuffed. At weekends, day-trippers head for the *O Galeão* (☎212 180 533; closed Tues) on the seafront, serving a good range of moderately priced fish and seafood. Certified divers can rent equipment from the *Centro de Mergulho* (☎212 183 197) diving school; the waters here are some of the clearest on the entire Portuguese coast.

Some 2km along the coast towards Setúbal you come to **Galapos**, a beautiful stretch of sand with beach cafés. Closer to Setúbal – and correspondingly more crowded – is the wide beach of **Figueirinha**, with the big sea-facing *Restaurante Bar Mar* – and the smaller **Praia de Albarquel**, with its beachside café and disco. Just beyond the beach by the main road, *Outão* (☎265 238 318, ℗265 228 098) is a busy **campsite** set amongst trees.

Sesimbra

If you get up early enough in **SESIMBRA**, you'll still see fishermen mending their nets on the town's beach, but that's about as far as tradition stretches in this old fishing town. It's now a full-blown resort, with apartment buildings and hotels mushrooming in the low, bare hills beyond the narrow streets of the old centre. Sesimbra was an important port during the time of the Portuguese discoveries. Dom Manuel lived here for a while, and the town's fort, **Fortaleza de Santiago**, was built in the seventeenth century as an important part of Portugal's coastal defence. In the eighteenth century, Portuguese monarchs used the fort as a seaside retreat, though today it serves as a police station and prison.

The town is largely a day-trip and second-home destination for Lisbon residents and, although extremely busy in summer, it's still an admirable spot, with excellent swimming from the long beach and an endless row of café-restaurants along the beach road. At high tide the beach splits into two, with a strand either side of the waterfront fort; offshore, jet skis and little ketches zip up and down under a clear blue sky. At night, families crowd the line of restaurants east of the fort, along Avenida 25 de Abril, and round the little Largo dos Bombaldes, with its warren of cobbled alleyways heading uphill.

A Moorish **Castelo** (Mon–Thurs & Sun 7am–7pm, Fri & Sat 7am–8pm; free) sits above Sesimbra, a short drive or a stiff half-hour climb from the centre. Within the walls are a pretty eighteenth-century church, a café and cemetery, while the battlements give amazing panoramas over the surrounding countryside and coastline.

It's also a pleasant walk from the centre along the seafront Avenida dos Náufragos to the original fishing port, **Porto de Abrigo**, with its brightly painted boats, daily fish auctions, and stalls selling a superb variety of shellfish. Various **boat trips** operate out of the port. From June to September, usually daily, the Clube Naval (☎212 233 451, ⓦwww.naval-sesimbra.pt) offers cruises on a traditional sailing boat, the *Santiago*.

Practicalities

There are hourly **buses** to and from Lisbon's Praça de Espanha and Setúbal, and half-hourly services from Cacilhas. Coming from Lisbon in summer, it's usually much quicker to take the ferry across to Cacilhas and pick up a bus there, as the main bridge road is often jammed solid with traffic. In Sesimbra, you're dropped at the **bus station**, halfway up Avenida da Liberdade, a five-minute walk from the seafront. Walk down to the water, turn right past the fort, and the **turismo** (daily: June–Sept 9am–8pm; Oct–May 9am–12.30pm & 2–5.30pm; ☎212 288 540) is on Largo da Marinha 26, a step back from the seafront Avenida dos Náufragos. **Accommodation** can be hard to come by in high season. If you haven't booked in advance, your best bet is to try for private rooms through the turismo (❸).

Mata de Sesimbra

The area north and west of Sesimbra, known as the Mata de Sesimbra, is being developed as the world's first "integrated sustainable building, tourism, nature conservation and reforestation programme". Partly funded by the World Wide Fund for Nature (WWF), all the buildings in the 8000-hectare site will be water and energy efficient and will eventually offer housing for up to 20,000 people, along with golf courses, three hotels and cinemas. Despite the scale of the project, only ten percent of the area will be built on, with much of the land set aside for reforestation, though it will not be completed for at least a decade. Details on ⓦ www.oneplanetliving.org.

Fish **restaurants** line the seafront east of the fort, along Avenida 25 de Abril, and round the little Largo dos Bombaldes. Cheaper places (meals under €15) abound in the back streets on either side of the central spine, Avenida da Nova Fortaleza. West of the fort along the avenue is also where most of the music **bars and cafés** are found, with the sleek *Mareante* at no. 12–13 (closed Wed) and Sereia at no. 22 – with a dartboard and outdoor tables – both popular hangouts. *A Galé*, Rua Capitão Leitão 7 (closed Tues), on a raised terrace overlooking the sea, is a popular student haunt. The best **club** is on Rua Prof. Fernandes Marques, just off the western seafront – the *Bolina* at no. 4, which gets going at midnight (closed Mon; weekends only from Oct–May).

Hotels and pensions

Hotel do Mar Rua Gen. Humberto Delgado 10, ⓣ 212 288 300, ⓦ www.hoteldomar.pt. Enormous, slightly impersonal three-star spreading uphill above the western beach. The older parts are showing their age, but most rooms command superb seaviews as does the top-floor restaurant. There's also a garden with pool. Parking. ⑥

Residencial Náutico Av dos Combatantes 19, ⓣ 212 233 233, ⓔ residencial-nautico@hotmail .com. Steeply uphill above the western end of the beach (and the *Hotel do Mar*), this comfortable place offers spacious rooms, some with sea views. ❹

Sana Park Av 25 de Abril 11 ⓣ 212 289 000, ⓦ www.sanahotels.com. The best upmarket choice, a modern hotel with glass lifts, sauna and pool, restaurant and groovy rooftop bar (open to non-guests). The plush rooms are all en suite, though you'll pay a fair bit more for a sea view. ⑤, sea-view rooms ⑥

Campsite

Forte do Cavalo Porto de Abrigo ⓣ 212 288 508. A well-located site just past the fishing port; closed Nov–April.

Restaurants

Marisqueira Filipe Av 25 de Abril ⓣ 212 231 653. Extremely popular seafood restaurant with fine sea views, and one of the more expensive places in town – €25 and upwards – but it serves great grilled fish, a bumper *arroz de marisco* plus some decent wines. Closed Wed. Expensive.

Modesto Largo dos Bombaldes 4 ⓣ 212 235 165. An apt name for this low-key place round the back of the square (so no sea views). It specializes in octopus dishes, with half a dozen recipes, though other fish and seafood is also good value and tasty. Closed Mon. Inexpensive.

A Sesimbrense Rua Jorge Nunes 19 ⓣ 212 230 148. Friendly family-run local just back from Largo dos Bombaldes (keep going past *Toni Bar*), serving no-nonsense soups, fish and grills with a TV for company. Closed Tues. Inexpensive.

Pedra Alta Largo dos Bombaldes 13 ⓣ 212 231 791. For a quality fish or shellfish meal, this is hard to beat, and though it's in a prime position with outdoor seats on the square, prices are not outrageous. Expensive.

Cabo Espichel and nearby beaches

Twice a day (it's best to take the 1.30pm bus and return at 3.30pm, making a brief day trip feasible), buses make the 11km journey west from Sesimbra t̶ **Cabo Espichel**, an end-of-the-world plateau lined on two sides by rams̶ arcaded eighteenth-century pilgrimage lodgings, with a crumblin̶ perched above the rocks at one end. The whole place has a rather desolate air that has made it a popular location for film directors, including Wim Wenders in *A Lisbon Story*. Beyond, wild and windswept cliffs drop almost vertically several hundred feet into the Atlantic; dinosaur footprints have been found on the nearby Praia dos Lagosteiros.

Four buses a day travel from Sesimbra beyond Cabo Espichel to the southern beaches of the surprisingly verdant and undeveloped Costa da Caparica, though this may change with the Mata de Sesimbra project (see box on p.167). A few kilometres to the north of Cabo Espichel is the village of **ALDEIA DO MECO**, from where a path cuts down to the superb beach of **Praia do Meco**. A large campsite, *Campimeco* (☎212 683 393, ℉212 683 844), complete with tennis courts, restaurant, pool and minimarket, lies northwest of here, just off **Praia das Bicas**. Like the other beaches on this coast, these are both prone to overcrowding in July and August, but can be almost deserted out of season, when the main drawback is the strong surf.

The calmest strip of beach is by the **Lagoa de Albufeira**, a little further south; the lagoon is extremely clean and excellent for windsurfing. There's another somewhat basic campsite, *Parque O Repouso*, 1km back from the lagoon (☎212 684 300; closed Oct–April), while just back from the beach overlooking the lagoon, *O Lagoeiro* (closed Mon) is the best place for grills, drinks or snacks.

Travel details

Trains

Cais do Sodré to: Belém (every 10min; 7min); Cascais (every 20min; 30min); Oeiras (every 10 min; 15 min walk for Youth Hostel); Estoril (every 20min; 25min).
Oriente to: Albufeira (4 daily; 2hr 40min–3hr 25min); Faro (4 daily; 3hr–3hr 45min; change for stations to Vila Real); Lagos (change at Tunes; 4 daily; 3hr 30min–4hr); Setúbal (every 30min; 50min); Tunes (for connections to western Algarve line; 4 daily; 2hr 30min–3 hr).
Rossio/Sete Rios to: Queluz (every 15min; 20min); Sintra (every 15min; 45min).
Santa Apolónia (note some services connect with Oriente trains) to: Abrantes (4 daily; 1hr 40min–2hr 15min); Coimbra (hourly; 2–3hr); Évora (2 daily; 3hr); Porto (hourly; 3hr 30min–4hr); Santarém (hourly; 50min–1hr 5min); Tomar (7 daily; 2hr).

International trains

Santa Apolónia/Oriente to: Biarritz (1 daily via Hendaye; 16hr); Bordeaux (1 daily; 15hr 30min); Caceres (1 night train; 5hr); Madrid (1 night train; 9hr 40min); Paris (1 daily via Hendaye; 21hr); Salamanca (1 daily; 7hr); San Sebastián (1 daily; 13hr 30min).

Buses

The main local services are listed below, but express buses run daily to all main towns throughout the country (see final pages of relevant chapters). Most departures are from Lisbon's main bus terminal at **Sete Rios** (metro Jardim Zoológico) as follows: Évora (hourly; 2hr–2hr 30min); Fátima (7 daily; 1hr 45min); Nazaré (hourly; 1hr 50min); Peniche (9 daily; 1hr 45min); Porto (hourly; 3hr); Tomar (2–4 daily; 1hr 45min); Torres Vedras (12 daily; 2hr).
Go to **Parque das Nações** (metro Oriente) for AVIC services (☎218 940 238) to the northwest coast, and Renex services (☎218 956 836) to the Minho and Algarve.
Other local services depart from the following termini:
From **Praça de Espanha** (metro Praça de Espanha) for Transportes Sul do Tejo (☎217 262 740) and Setubalase (☎265 525 051) services to: Costa da Caparica (every 30min; 40min–1hr); Palmela (Mon–Fri 10 daily, Sat & Sun 4; 40min–1hr); Sesimbra (hourly; 1hr 30min–2hr); Setúbal (every 30min; 1hr); Vila Nogueira de Azeitão (hourly; 45min).
From **Campo Grande 5** (metro Campo Grande) for Mafrense Empresa Barraqueiro (☎217 582 212) services to: Ericeira (10 daily; 1hr 50min); Mafra (hourly; 1hr 30min).

Estremadura and Ribatejo

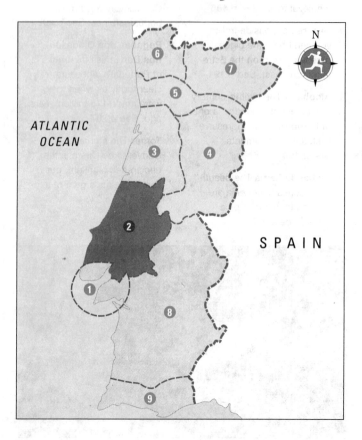

CHAPTER 2 # Highlights

* **Ilha da Berlenga** Take the boat from Peniche to a rocky windswept island bird sanctuary. See p.184

* **Óbidos** After the coach tours have left, enjoy the atmospheric streets of this walled medieval town. See p.185

* **Nazaré** For seaside frolics, you can't beat the biggest, brashest resort on the Estremaduran coast. See p.191

* **Alcobaça** The twelfth-century monastery at Alcobaça is one of Europe's most impressive Cistercian monuments. See p.194

* **Pinhal de Leiria** The beautiful beaches near Leiria are backed by miles of pine forest. See p.200

* **Grutas de Mira de Aire** Visit the most spectacular underground caves in the country. See p.206

* **Fátima** Penitents, pilgrims and kitsch souvenirs – it can only be Fátima, one of the Catholic Church's most popular shrines. See p.207

* **Pegadas dos Dinossáurios** Don't miss the tracks of Portugal's dinosaurs – as clear today as when they were made 175 million years ago. See p.207

* **Tomar** The stunning Convento de Cristo is the undisputed highlight, but Tomar itself is a gem of a town. See p.210

△ Nazaré

Estremadura and Ribatejo

he provinces of **Estremadura** and **Ribatejo** have played a crucial role
in each phase of the nation's history and have the monuments to prove
it. Although they encompass a comparatively small area, the provinces
boast an extraordinary concentration of vivid architecture: the monastery
at **Alcobaça**, the extraordinary abbey at **Batalha** and the headquarters of the
Knights Templar in **Tomar** – some of the most exciting buildings in Portugal
– all lie within a shallow triangle, easily accessible by bus or car. Other attractions are equally compelling, from the completely walled medieval town of
Óbidos to the tremendous castle at elegant **Leiria**, while there's a different
kind of fascination in visiting the almost obscenely ornate palace-monastery of
Mafra. Heads are also turned by the shrine at **Fátima**, the country's (and,
indeed, one of the world's) most important pilgrimage sites.

The Estremaduran coast provides an excellent complement to all this, and if
you're simply seeking sun and sand it's not a bad alternative to the Algarve.
Nazaré and **Ericeira** are justifiably the most popular resorts, but there are
scores of less developed beaches, while ferries sail from **Peniche** to the remote
offshore bird sanctuary of the **Ilha Berlenga**. For isolated beaches, you can also
try the area around **São Martinho do Porto** or the coastline west of Leiria,
backed most of the way by the **Pinhal de Leiria** pine forest. Inland, getting off
the beaten track means delving into the spectacular underground caverns that
can be visited around **Porto de Mós** and viewing the amazing nearby sauropod
tracks, all of which lie within the **Parque Natural das Serras de Aire e
Candeeiros**.

Virtually all of these highlights fall within the boundaries of Estremadura, an
area of fertile rolling hills that is perhaps second in beauty only to the Minho.
Although the flat, bull-breeding lands of Ribatejo (literally "banks-of-the-
Tejo") fade into the dull expanses of northwestern Alentejo, the valley of the
Rio Tejo itself boasts some of Portugal's richest **vineyards**, while many of its
small towns host lively traditional festivals. The wildest and most famous of these
is the Festa do Colete Encarnado of **Vila Franca de Xira**, with Pamplona-
style bull-running through the streets, though it's **Santarém**, the Ribatejo
capital, which has the province's longest history.

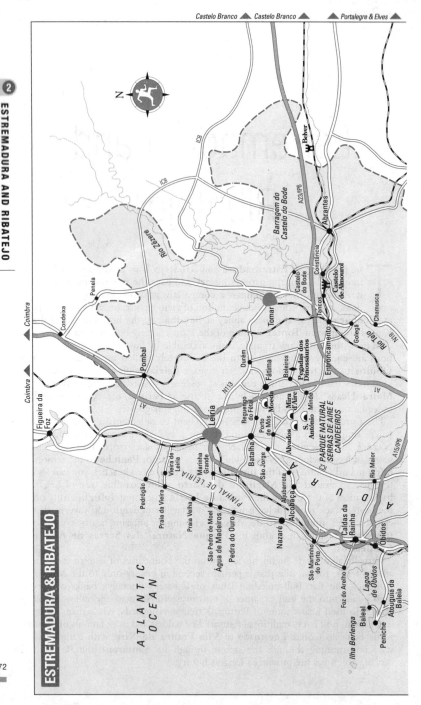

ESTREMADURA & RIBATEJO

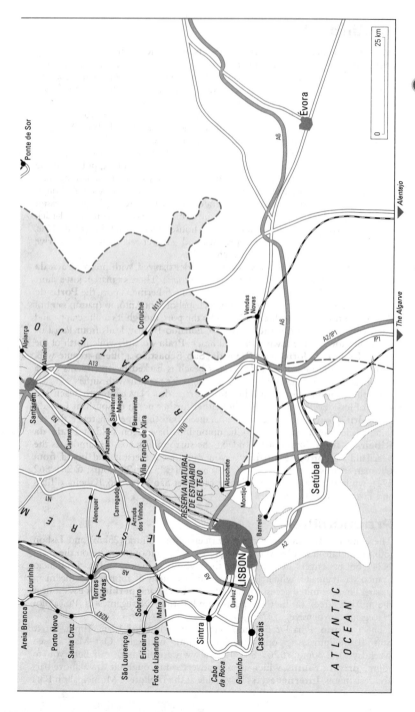

Ericeira

Perched on a rocky ledge thirty metres above a series of fine sandy beaches, **ERICEIRA** offers one of the few natural harbours between Cascais and Peniche. During the nineteenth century the town was a major port, from where boats left to trade with countries as far away as Scotland and Brazil. Later, it was the final refuge of Portugal's last monarch, Dom Manuel II – "The Unfortunate" – who, on October 5, 1910, was woken in his palace at nearby Mafra to be told that an angry Republican mob was advancing from Lisbon. Aware of the fate of his father and elder brother, he fled to the small harbour at Ericeira and sailed into the welcoming arms of the British at Gibraltar to live out the rest of his days in a villa at Twickenham. Baedeker's guidebook, published the same year, described Ericeira as "a fishing village with excellent sea bathing" and development has done little to change the town's original character. Although much built up on the outskirts, and undeniably a busy resort in peak season when people flock here from Lisbon, the centre at least remains a laid-back place of narrow lanes and whitewashed houses picked out in cobalt blue. Ericeira is also renowned for excellent seafood – its very name is said to derive from the words *ouriços do mar* (sea urchin).

Virtually the whole of the town centre is pedestrianized, with pretty **Praça da República** at its hub, ringed with cafés and *pastelarias*. There's a market just a short walk to the north, while below town the working fishermen's port, the **Porto de Pesca**, is overlooked by the whitewashed chapel of Sant António (patron saint of Portuguese fishermen) – there's a beach by the port, though it's a bit scrappy and often crowded. The main street, Rua Dr Eduardo Burnay, leads from Praça da República towards the town's principal beach, **Praia do Sul**, while north of the port is **Praia do Norte**, with **Praia do São Sebastião** a fifteen-minute walk beyond, past the next headland. The last beach is backed by apartments and a shopping centre, and has acres of free parking – it's popular with surfers.

Another option is to take a bus from Praça dos Navegantes to reach the series of less developed local beaches either further north or south: at **Foz de Lizandro** (2km south) the river guarantees safe bathing whatever the sea state, while the World Surfing Championships have been held at **Praia da Ribeira d'Ilhas** (3km north). Indeed, the surrounding coast is famous as the heartland of Portuguese **surfing** – you can rent a wetsuit and board from Ultimar, in town at Rua 5° de Outubro 25 (€25 for 24 hours; ☎261 862 371), while there are surf schools and camps at São Sebastião, Ribeira d'Ilhas and Foz do Lizandro beaches.

Practicalities

There are regular **bus services** to Ericeira from Sintra (25km) and Lisbon (50km), and from nearby Mafra. The bus station is out of town, up on the main N247, but passengers are dropped on the highway at the top of Rua Prudêncio Franco da Trindade, which leads down in a couple of minutes to the main square. There's limited access to the old town by car, and **parking** is easiest near the market (free) or in the underground Parque Navegantes at Praça dos Navegantes (expensive).

The **turismo**, Rua Dr Eduardo Burnay 46 (Mon–Fri 10am–10pm, Sat & Sun 10am–7pm; Aug open weekdays until midnight; Oct–May closed weekdays 1–2.30pm; ☎261 863 122, ⓦwww.ericeira.net), can help you to source **private rooms**, which are also advertised throughout town above bars and restaurants. **Internet** access is available at the Biblioteca Municipal on Rua

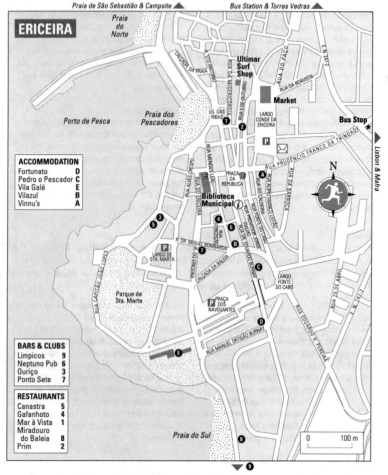

Praia de São Sebastião & Campsite ▲   Bus Station & Torres Vedras ▲

Lisbon & Mafra ▶

ERICEIRA

Praia do Norte

Praia dos Pescadores

Porto de Pesca

Ultimar Surf Shop

Market

Bus Stop ★

Biblioteca Municipal ⓘ

PRAÇA DA REPÚBLICA

LARGO CONDE DA ERICEIRA

PRAÇA DOS NAVEGANTES

LARGO DE STA. MARTA

Parque de Sta. Marta

LARGO FONTE DO CABO

Praia do Sul

N

0   100 m

ACCOMMODATION

Fortunato	D
Pedro o Pescador	C
Vila Galé	E
Vilazul	B
Vinnu's	A

BARS & CLUBS

Limpicos	9
Neptuno Pub	6
Ouriço	3
Ponto Sete	7

RESTAURANTS

Canastra	5
Gafanhoto	4
Mar à Vista	1
Miradouro do Baleia	8
Prim	2

Mendes Leal (Wed–Sat 10am–1pm & 2–7pm) and at Cyber Clube Ericeira, Praça da República (daily 11am–11pm).

Accommodation

Pensões and **hotels** are generally good value, though anywhere in the main part of town can be guaranteed to be noisy in high season. The ones listed below are open all year round (not all are), and most are a good deal cheaper outside July and August (which is what the codes below represent).

Hotels and pensions

Fortunato Rua Dr Eduardo Burnay 7 ☎ 261 862 829, ⓦ www.pensaofortunato.com. A range of simple rooms available, all en suite, though the best are the west-facing ones at the top with good views of Praia do Sul; some have a terrace.

Breakfast included June–Sept. Garage parking included. ❸

Pedro o Pescador Rua Dr Eduardo Burnay 22 ☎ 261 864 302, ⓔ hotelpescador@net.vodafone.pt. Small two-star hotel gathered around a courtyard with a great bar. There's colourful tilework throughout, plenty of plants and a private patio, though it needs a lick of paint here and there. ❸

Vila Galé Pr dos Navegantes ☎800 204 224, ⓦwww.vilagale.pt. Ericeira's ritziest hotel is a large, modern four-star affair on the seafront. The 200 spacious rooms feature dark woods, tasteful fabrics and a wide terrace, while outdoors there are sea-view pools, an alfresco bar-restaurant and manicured gardens. Parking available. ❻

Vilazul Calç da Baleia 10 ☎261 860 000, ⓦwww .hotelvilazul.com. Cheery two-star hotel with blue-shuttered windows and spacious rooms with cane chairs, a/c and plenty of closet space – though bathrooms could do with upgrading. There's a third-floor bar and terrace which offers rooftop and partial sea views, while breakfast is served in the downstairs restaurant. ❹

Vinnu's Rua Prudêncio Franco da Trindade 19 ☎261 863 830. Close to the market and main square (with handy parking opposite), this is the best of the budget options, with nicely kept en-suite rooms – some have small balconies and some of the larger ones have a kitchenette. No credit cards. ❸

Campsite

Ericeira Camping Parque Mil Regos, 800m beyond Praia do São Sebastião ☎261 862 706, ⓦwww.ericeiracamping.com. The large municipal campsite has an outdoor pool, restaurant and shop, and some wooden sea-view bungalows for rent as well – overpriced in July and Aug, but worth considering out of season (from €50).

Eating

Despite its small size, Ericeira has a glut of good **restaurants**, thanks to the holidaymakers from Lisbon who demand a decent dinner. Local seafood specialities are the coastal shellfish or *arroz* (rice), *massada* (pasta) and *feijoada* (beans) *de mariscos* – rich, soupy servings of seafood made for sharing.

A Canastra Rua Capitão João Lopes 8A ☎261 865 367. A little pricey, but a highly recommended seafood restaurant in a harbourfront fisherman's house. Closed Wed. Expensive.

O Gafanhoto Rua da Conceição ☎261 861 514. There's no-frills decor in this backstreet joint, but you get a decent choice of char-grilled meat and fish at budget prices. Closed Tues. Inexpensive.

Mar à Vista Largo das Ribas ☎261 862 928. A superb locals' place above the Praia dos Pescadores, with three basic nooks to dine in and the freshest shellfish on the menu – a great

place for *cataplanas*, *arroz* dishes, or crab and lobster. Closed Wed. Moderate.

O Miradouro do Baleia Praia do Sul ☎261 863 981. The best seafront dining in Ericeira, right before the breakers and with a large menu that includes *arroz*, *massada* and *feijoada* dishes or the catch of the day, served grilled. Expensive.

Prim Rua 5° de Outubro 12 ☎261 865 230. Friendly restaurant serving delicious grilled meat plus a few native dishes of the Brazilian owner, all at around €10 a dish and in belly-busting portions. Moderate.

Nightlife

In Ericeira itself, the bars around the modern Praça dos Navegantes, near Praia do Sul, attract a young crowd, especially at weekends, but most of the "in" places are out of town.

Limpicos Foz do Lizandro. This is one of the best of a group of bars in the small beach resort 2km south of Ericeira – part of the night-time circuit for those with their own transport.

Neptuno Pub Rua Mendes Leal 12. A Portuguese-style pub, with cocktails to complement the *Sagres* beer and fado once a week. Closed Wed in winter.

Ouriço Rua Capitao João Lopes 10. The seafront disco is supposedly Portugal's second oldest (and the music choice can be just as dated). Opens from 11pm.

Ponto Sete Rua Dr Miguel Bombarda 7. A hole-in-the-wall bar decorated with old rock memorabilia, with jazz and blues jam sessions at weekends.

Mafra and around

The small town of **Mafra** is distinguished – and utterly dominated – by just one building: the vast monastery-palace which João V – the wealthiest and most extravagant of all Portuguese monarchs – built in emulation of El Escorial in Madrid. It's only 12km from Ericeira, so makes an easy half-day trip from the coast, or you can see it en route into Estremadura from Lisbon or Sintra. Drivers will also be able to call in at the nearby **Tapada de Mafra** park and at the craft village at **Sobreiro**, on the road between Mafra and Ericeira.

Mosteiro Palácio Nacional de Mafra

Begun in 1717 to honour a vow made on the birth of a royal heir, the **Mosteiro Palácio Nacional de Mafra** (Mon & Wed–Sun 10am–5pm, last entry 4.30pm; €4) was initially intended for just thirteen Franciscan friars. But as wealth poured in from the gold and diamonds of Brazil, João V and his German court architect, Frederico Ludovice, amplified their plans to include a massive basilica, two royal wings and monastic quarters for 300 monks and 150 novices. The result, completed in thirteen years, is quite extraordinary and, on its own bizarre terms, extremely impressive.

In style the building is a fusion of Baroque and Italianate Neoclassicism, but it is the sheer magnitude and logistics that stand out. In the last stages of construction more than 45,000 labourers were employed, while throughout the years of building there was a daily average of nearly 15,000. There are 5200 doorways, 2500 windows and two immense bell towers, each containing over fifty bells. An apocryphal story records the astonishment of the Flemish bell-makers at the size of the order: on their querying it, and asking for payment in advance, Dom João retorted by doubling their price and his original requirement.

Parts of the monastery are used by the military but multilingual guides march you around a sizeable enough portion – the **tours** last 60–75 minutes. The seemingly endless royal apartments are a mix of the tedious and the shocking, the latter most obviously in the **Sala dos Troféus**, with its furniture (even chandeliers) constructed of antlers and upholstered in deerskin. All the rooms are recreations since when João VI fled to Brazil in the face of the French advance he took all the furniture and valuables with him. There is though at least one original piece – the bed in which the last Portuguese monarch, Manuel II, slept the night before he went into exile in England. The undoubted highlight is the magnificent Rococo **library** – brilliantly lit and rivalling Coimbra's in grandeur. Byron, shown the 35,000 volumes by one of the monks, was asked if "the English had any books in their country?" The books are still in place, kept free of insect infestation by a colony of tiny bats that lives in the eaves. The **basilica** itself, which can be seen outside the tour, is no less imposing, with the multicoloured marble designs of its floor mirrored in the ceiling decoration.

Around Mafra

Six kilometres north of Mafra on the Gradil road is the **Tapada de Mafra** (Ⓦ www.tapadademafra.pt), once the palace's extensive hunting grounds, now laid out with walking and mountain-bike trails for the public. Access to the trails is limited to certain hours (9.30–10/11am and 2–2.30pm; €4.40 or €6, depending on the trail, or €20 including bike rental), and it'll take two or three hours to get round – see the website for full details. At weekends, you can tour the park on a road train (Sat, Sun & public hols at 10.45am & 3pm; not Dec & Jan; €10; reservations advised, ☎261 817 050).

En route to Ericeira, the small village of **SOBREIRO**, 5km northwest of Mafra on the N116, is home to the **Aldeia Típica** (daily 10am–6pm), a craft village established by artist José Franco in 1945. As well as Franco's own work, the showroom sells other reasonably priced ceramics from all over the country, while children will enjoy looking round the traditional bakery, smithy, clock-maker, cobbler, schoolroom, distillery, wind- and water-mills and several other small museum-shops, all displaying tools, furniture and artefacts collected over many years. The *adega* is a good stop for lunch, serving local wine, bread and moderately priced meals.

Practicalities

Mafrense **buses** run hourly from Lisbon (1hr 30min) or from Sintra station (30min), stopping near the monastery-palace. There are also hourly buses from Ericeira (20min). A vast car park outside the palace soaks up the day-trip trade. There's a **turismo** in the palace, to the right of the basilica (Mon–Fri 9am–6pm, Sat, Sun & hols 9.30am–1pm & 2.30–6pm; ℡261 817 170, ⓦ www.cm-mafra .pt) and plenty of **cafés and restaurants** in and around the square opposite the palace. None particularly stands out, but as Portuguese visitors are in the majority, prices are reasonable.

Torres Vedras and around

TORRES VEDRAS, 27km to the north and inland from Ericeira, took its name from the Duke of Wellington's famous defence lines (Linhas de Torres) in the **Peninsular War** against Napoleonic France. The "Lines" consisted of a chain of 150 hilltop fortresses, built in a matter of months and – astonishingly – without any apparent reaction from the French. Here, in 1810, Wellington and his forces retired, comfortably supplied by sea and completely unassailable. The French, frustrated by impossibly long lines of communication and by British scorching of the land north of the Lines, eventually retreated back to Spain in despair. Thus from a last line of defence, Wellington completely reversed the progress of the campaign – storming after the disconsolate enemy to effect a series of swift and devastating victories.

In view of this historical glory, modern Torres Vedras is a little disappointing. There are a few ruins of the old fortresses in the vicinity and a couple of imposing sixteenth-century churches but, bar a pleasant pedestrianized kernel of cobbled lanes, the town is swamped by a dull sprawl of apartments and indus-trial estates. It's at its best in the lanes around the central Praça 25 de Abril, where – in the old Convento da Graça – the **Museu Municipal** (Tues–Sun 10am–1pm & 2–6pm; €0.75) features a room devoted to the Peninsular War; an obelisk in the square outside commemorates the battles. Above the old town on a wooded mound sits the **Castelo** (June–Aug Tues–Sun 10am–7pm; Sept–May Tues–Sun 10am–5.45pm; free), which from the thirteenth to the sixteenth century was a popular royal residence. It was here, in 1414, that Dom João I confirmed the decision to take Ceuta – the first overseas venture leading towards the future Portuguese maritime empire. The castle was reduced to rubble by the earthquake of 1755, but the battlements have been restored and in spring the slopes are carpeted with red poppies.

After a drink at one of the cafés on Praça 25 de Abril it's time to move on – and, in truth, unless you're driving (when Torres Vedras makes an interesting coffee break) you're not going to stop at all. The **turismo** at Rua 9 de Abril, in a corner of the square (Mon–Sat 10am–1pm & 2–6pm; ℡261 310 483, ⓦ www.cm-tvedras.pt) might persuade you otherwise, and there is a handful of small hotels. But the local beaches to the west (see below) make the better overnight stop, while Alenquer and the Ribatejo wine country is just a thirty-kilometre drive to the east.

The coast

Thirteen kilometres northwest of Torres Vedras, the resort of **Praia de Santa Cruz** marks the start of a string of local beaches which runs all the way north to Peniche, 40km away. Santa Cruz itself is eminently missable, its admittedly fine, wide beaches backed by a contagious rash of apartments, villas and new estates, and boasting a campsite the size of an independent country. Far better to push on the five kilometres north to the extensive duned sands of **Porto Novo** (follow signs initially for Lourinhã), which has restricted its development to a strip of four simple *residenciais* with restaurants just above the sandy bay at the mouth of the River Maceira. The bay is a quiet place for lunch most of the year, while towering above across the river – and visible for miles around – is the fanciest hotel hereabouts, the three-star *Hotel Golf Mar* (☏261 980 800, ⓦwww.hotelgolfmar.com; ⓪) – there's a pool, a nine-hole golf course and a riding school.

Another 12km north on the Peniche road (or a more direct 21km from Torres Vedras), **Areia Branca** ("White Sand") is the best overnight stop. Little more than a fishing village twenty years ago, it's now been fully developed but it remains a congenial place of low-rise apartments filling a shallow bowl above a sandy beach, with a promenade of café-bars. Surfers and bodyboarders hang out here and, for once, budget travellers have the edge as there's a good **youth hostel** right on the sands (☏261 422 127, ⓦwww.pousadasjuventude.pt; dorms €11, July/Aug €16, rooms ❶, July/Aug ❷). There's also a decent **campsite** at the Parque Municipal (☏261 412 199) – it's signposted from the centre – or you can ask about private rooms at the **turismo** (June–Sept Mon–Sat 10.30am–1.30pm & 2.30–6.30pm; ☏261 422 167), which sits just above the beach and car park. Most prominently, there's the German-owned *Casal dos Patos* (☏261 413 768, ⓦwww.casaldospatos.online.pt; ❸), a hilltop villa with views that's directly above the hostel – there are five double rooms here (closed Nov–Feb) and a cottage (available by the night, open all year) that sleeps up to four. Otherwise, there's the *Residencial Dom Lourenço* on the road out of town (☏261 422 809, ⓦwww.domlourenco.com; ❸), and there are also pensions in the small inland town of **Lourinhã**, but here you're 3km from the beach. Regular daily buses run to Areia Branca from Peniche and from Torres Vedras (via Lourinhã).

Peniche and around

PENICHE, impressively enclosed by ramparts, is one of Portugal's most active fishing ports. As late as the fifteenth century the town was an island but the area has silted up and is now joined to the mainland by a narrow isthmus, with gently sloping beaches on either side. Unsightly development stretches along the coast, but inside the walled town there is a small grid of narrow streets dominated by the fortress, and a busy harbour and marina – Peniche is the embarkation point for the Ilha da Berlenga – while there's an enjoyable regional market held on the last Thursday of the month. Tourism has undoubtedly introduced a tougher edge to the town – determined touts hawk rooms and a glut of seafood restaurants vie for the tourist euro – but, although the balance is changing, Peniche has yet to be seduced entirely from its fishing roots, and gangs of fishermen still repair nets at the harbourside. The first weekend in August sees the festival of **Nossa Senhora da Boa Viagem** (Our Lady of Good Journeys), during which the statue of the Virgin is

△ Baleal beach

brought to the harbour by boat to be greeted by candle-bearing locals. After the village priest has blessed the fleet, there are fireworks, bands and dancing in the street.

Sited above the harbour, the sixteenth-century **Fortaleza** (Tues 2–5.30pm, Wed–Fri 9am–12.30pm & 2–5.30pm, Sat & Sun 10.30am–12.30pm & 2–5.30pm;

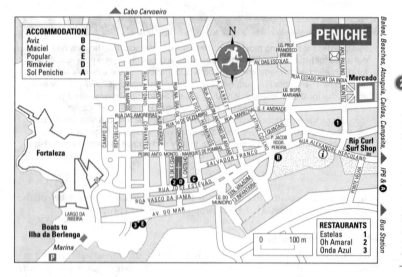

€1.40) was one of the dictator Salazar's most notorious jails. Greatly expanded in the 1950s and 1960s to accommodate the growing crowds of political prisoners, it later served as a temporary refugee camp for *retornados* from the colonies. Despite a fresh coat of paint here and there, it's still a formidable place of bare yards and high walls; the bleak *parlatório* (prisoners' receiving room) by the main entrance presents a small exhibition commemorating those imprisoned here, including some of their poignant letters home. Further within the fort is the municipal museum, with a familiar mix of local archeology, natural history and craft displays, while on the top floor you can see the old cells and solitary confinement pens.

This is it for local sights, and the tight cluster of streets back from the harbour lacks any great charm, certainly compared, say, to Ericeira. Lunch at one of the harbourfront restaurants is the culmination of most visits, since the beaches all lie a good walk or drive out of the centre. Beyond the fortress, to the west, it's 2.5km to the tip of **Cabo Carvoeiro**, a rugged peninsula topped by a lighthouse, where the waves smash against the weathered rock pillars.

South of town (Caldas da Rainha/Lisbon road) and east (Baleal/Ferrel) are the duned surf **beaches**, with periodic beach bars, boardwalks and surf-camps, while **Baleal** – 5km northeast of Peniche – makes a tempting base in its own right. It's an islet-village joined to the mainland by a narrow causeway, with fine sand beaches either side and further long stretches to the north and south. Hourly buses in July and August from Peniche bus station run here in fifteen minutes (around half a dozen a day out of season, though not weekends), and there's a large car park on the mainland side of the causeway – bar-restaurants overlook the sands at both ends.

The other local excursion is the five-kilometre drive east along the N114 (Caldas da Rainha/Lisbon road) to the small village of **Altougia da Baleia**, its name a further reminder of the shifting fortunes of this part of the coastline – *baleia* means "whale", hunted off the shores here when Altougia was a thriving port. The parish church of **São Leonardo** (daily 9am–12.30pm & 2–5.30pm)

Surfing at Peniche

Peniche has the best and most consistent surfing in the country. The turismo hands out a free fold-out **surf-guide** to the local beaches, though anyone here specifically for the surfing will already know all about Supertubos and the other local breaks. You can rent gear from Rip Curl, Rua Alexandre Herculano (℡262 787 206), or from any of the local **surf-camps**, including Baleal Surfcamp (Ⓦwww.balealsurfcamp .com), Bocaxica (Ⓦwww.bocaxicasurf.com) and Peniche Surf Camp (Ⓦwww .penichesurfcamp.com). Lessons cost from €25, while each camp also has accommodation (hostel-style or apartments and private rooms) – one-week inclusive courses for beginners cost around €425 in July and August, cheaper outside high season.

is full of small treasures, like a curious fourteenth-century stone relief of the Nativity and a calcified whalebone propped up in the corner.

Practicalities

The **bus station** is on the isthmus just outside the town walls. It's a ten-minute walk into the centre across the Ponte Velha, which takes you to Rua Alexandre Herculano, where you turn left for the helpful **turismo** (daily: July & Aug 9am–8pm; Sept–June 10am–1pm & 2–5pm; ℡262 789 571, Ⓦwww .cm-peniche.pt) – the **harbour**, for boats to Berlenga, is another five minutes' walk away. There's pay **parking** all over town, including by the gardens outside the turismo and on the harbourfront, though there's some free parking up by the fortress. Nearly all of Peniche's pensions, bars and restaurants are within a few blocks of the harbour, between Avenida do Mar and the parish church.

Peniche is a big **watersports** centre, noted particularly for its surfing (see box, above), but also for diving and deep-sea fishing. **Dive operators** include Haliotis (℡262 781 160, Ⓦwww.haliotis.pt), based in the *Hotel Praia Norte*, 1km north of Peniche centre (behind the *Sol Peniche*) – one-day dive trips in the gin-clear waters off Ilha Berlenga cost around €65, though cheaper coastal dives are also available. Plenty of other sea-charter companies are based at the harbour, most offering sea-fishing trips and **cruises**, either around the local coastline (from €15) or out to Berlenga.

Accommodation

In July and August accommodation can be tricky to find without an advance reservation. You will be approached by people offering **rooms**, but to avoid the hard sell head for the turismo which can also help source private accommodation (from €30). The official town-centre choices are exclusively small pensions – the two larger resort-style three-star **hotels** are both a short way out of town by the Baleal roundabout. A limited number of options in Baleal itself offer a mellow alternative to Peniche, with the advantage of having a beach on the doorstep. All prices ebb and flow with the season – in high summer pension rooms go for €60, though at any other time of the year you're more likely to pay €30.

Hotels and pensions

Aviz Pr Jacob R. Pereira 7 ℡262 782 153. An old-fashioned *residencial* on the main road in, by the tourist office. But it's cared for, rather than decrepit,

and you trade street noise for space, since the rooms are bigger than usual – not all are en suite though. ❸ **Casa do Castelo** Atouguia da Baleia, 5km east on N114 ℡262 750 647, Ⓦwww.casa-do-castelo.net.

Just across the road from the church in Atouguia, this elegant seventeenth-century family home tastefully blends modern style with antiques. It's set in lovely tree-shaded gardens with a swimming pool. No credit cards. ❹

🏃 **Casa das Marés** Praia do Baleal, 5km northeast ☏ 262 769 255/371/200. An impressive property at the far end of Baleal village (over the causeway), by the chapel – actually three conjoined houses, each offering B&B, with views either to the sweeping Baleal sands or back across to Peniche. Breakfast is served on the terrace overlooking the small fisherman's beach where the boats are winched ashore. There's parking in front. ❹

🏃 **Maciel** Rua José Estêvão 38 ☏ 262 784 685, ⊛ www.residencial-maciel.com. The best budget option in town is classier than its neighbours, with a highly polished interior of wooden floors, rugs, plant-pots and co ordinated furniture and decor. ❸

Popular Largo da Ribeira 40 ☏ 262 790 290, ⊛ www.apopular.com. Cosy, bright, modern rooms in a friendly *residencial* by the port – request a harbourside room for views (and to avoid the traffic noise). The attached restaurant is very good for inexpensive grilled fish and seafood. ❸

Rimavier Rua Castilho 6–8 ☏ 262 789 459. Ask in the souvenir shop – shipshape modern rooms with tile floors, matching nautical curtains and bedspreads, and neat little bathrooms. A couple also have balconies overlooking the church. ❷

Sol Peniche Estrada do Baleal ☏ 262 780 400, ⊛ www.solmelia.com. Has the edge over its neighbour, the *Praia Norte*, as it's right across the road from a beach bar, the dunes and miles of sand. It's a bit of a dated three-star hotel but has large tile-floor rooms with wide balconies that make the most of the aspect, and there's an indoor and outdoor pool. On the edge of town, a 25min walk from the harbour restaurants. Off-season discounts drop the price by up to forty percent. ❹

Campsites

Parque Municipal de Campismo Av Monsenhor Bastos ☏ 262 789 529. 2km east of Peniche centre, and relatively handy for the beach.

Peniche Praia Camping Estrada Marginal Norte ☏ 262 783 460, ⊛ www.penichepraia.pt. This is high up on the peninsula, towards Cabo Carvoeiro, 2km from town, and well-equipped with restaurant and pool, and cabins and rooms to rent (from €55 high season). But it's a long way from the beach and not much use to anyone without their own transport.

Eating and drinking

A dozen or so **restaurants** along Avenida do Mar all offer substantially the same thing – grilled fish at pretty reasonable prices (most mains under €10), plus pricier speciality *arroz* and shellfish dishes. The daily catch in town is usually seabass, bream, swordfish, mackerel, sardines, squid and cuttlefish. The snack bars in the **Mercado** (off Rua Arq. Paulino Montez) are just the ticket for breakfast or picnic provisions; visit in the morning and they're often full of fishwives swinging plastic bags of fish and sipping a *bica* as they exchange news. Your best bet for a drink and a view of the world going by is one of the handful of harbourside **bars** amid the restaurants on Avenida do Mar, while Baleal beach has a few bars popular with the surf crowd.

Estelas Rua Arq Paulino Montesa ☏ 262 782 435. Acclaimed as the best restaurant in town (it often represents Peniche at gastronomic competitions), serving super-fresh seafood in a breezy contemporary dining room. Mains are from €15–20. Closed Wed. Expensive.

🏃 **Oh Amaral** Rua Dr Francisco Seia 7 ☏ 262 782 095. A bit more refined than the harbourside restaurants, and a bit pricier (mains €10–15), but it makes for a cosy dinner and you get a mint with your coffee. There's more meat choice than in many places, and the fish is good –

swordfish comes grilled with stewed onions (*cebolada*), while the house specials are *frigideira* (a mix of prawns, clams, squid and cuttlefish) or *arroz de tamboril* (monkfish rice). Closed Thurs & Sun dinner. Expensive.

Onda Azul Largo da Ribeira 38 ☏ 262 787 224. The "Blue Wave" has harbour views from its outdoor terrace, so it's a popular lunch choice. There's the usual grilled-fish menu in three languages, though daily specials are always worth a look, like roast octopus and potatoes in olive oil. Closed Thurs. Moderate.

Ilha da Berlenga

The **Ilha da Berlenga**, 10km offshore and just visible from Cabo Carvoeiro, is a dreamlike place, rather like a Scottish isle transported to warmer climes. Just two-and-a-half square kilometres in extent, it is the largest island of a tiny archipelago, with a jagged coastline of grottoes, miniature fjords and extraordinary rock formations. In summer the sea is calm, crystal clear and perfect for snorkelling and diving – rare in the Atlantic.

The only people permitted to live here are a couple of dozen fishermen because the island has been declared a **natural reserve**, home to thousands upon thousands of sea birds, including gulls, puffins and cormorants, which perch in every conceivable cranny and seem intent on leaving their mark on every possible victim. Makeshift paths on the island are marked out with stones and guardians watch out for visitors straying into the prohibited areas and disturbing the birds.

The island

Human life revolves around the main landing dock, with its small fleet of fishing boats and a tiny **sandy beach** that's a mere golden notch in the cliffs. The only buildings are a cluster of huts and concrete houses above the harbour, a lighthouse on the heights and – across one shoulder of the island, reached by the only track – the highly romantic-looking seventeenth-century Forte de São João Baptista, on a rocky islet reached by a slender arched stone bridge. Despite the daily limit on visitor numbers the harbour area bustles in the summer months, but you can escape by striding out across the marked paths – there's no shade, though, and the ever-present screeching, swooping birds make a restful picnic unlikely. You'll also be able to rent a rowboat or organize a guided **boat tour** for a few euros – don't miss the Furado Grande, a fantastic tunnel 75m long, which culminates in the aptly named Cova do Sonho (Dream Cove) with its precipitous cliffs.

Accommodation is extremely limited and not particularly alluring, being a choice between the half-a-dozen overpriced rooms at the only hotel, the basic *Pavilhão Mar e Sol* (☎262 750 331; mid-May to mid-Sept only; ❹), above the harbour, or dorm beds at the very rudimentary **hostel** (☎262 785 263; June to mid-Sept only; €10) in the fort. It's essential to reserve in advance for either, and for the hostel you'll need to bring your own food, cooking utensils (there is a kitchen) and sleeping stuff. There's also an exposed **campsite** (reservations essential through Peniche tourist office, ☎262 789 571; June to mid-Sept only; from €8 a night), which clings to the rocky slopes above the harbour, and a small **mini-market** (only open in summer when everything else is) – otherwise there's a bar and restaurant at the hotel, but as everything is shipped in prices are high.

Getting there

The **ferry from Peniche** is operated by Viamar (€18 return; ☎262 785 646) and takes around 45 minutes – longer if the sea is rough (it can be a very bouncy ride). The service departs from the harbour below the fort, and operates from mid-May to mid-September, with three ferries a day in July and August (9.30am, 11.30am, & 5.30pm; return at 10.30am, 4.30pm & 6.30pm), and one a day at other times (10am; return at 4.30pm). There's a limit of 300 tickets sold each day from the harbour office (usually open 8.30am–noon & 3–5.30pm). In July and August you need to get there in good time for a ticket, but outside these months it's not usually a problem.

Other companies with offices on the harbour front, such as Turpesca (☎262 789 960 or 963 073 818), Julius (☎262 782 698 or 907 601 114, ⓦwww .julius-berlenga.com) and Noa (☎262 789 997 or 969 134 534), operate **boat trips to Berlenga** all year round except in December. Departures depend on the weather and season, but in summer there are several daily excursions, usually departing in the morning and including a stop on the island and a visit to the caves along the coastline. Ticket prices are pegged to those of Viamar ferry, so you shouldn't pay more than €20 for the trip.

Óbidos

ÓBIDOS is known as the "The Wedding City" and was the traditional bridal gift of the kings of Portugal to their queens, a custom started in 1282 by Dom Dinis and Dona Isabel. It is a very small town, completely enclosed by lofty walls, and although much was rebuilt after the 1755 earthquake, Óbidos retains a medieval feel: cobbled alleys, whitewashed houses framed with bright blue and yellow borders, and steep staircases winding up to the exposed ramparts for distant views. Five hundred years ago, when Peniche was an island, the sea also reached the foot of the ridge on which Óbidos stands and boats were moored below its walls. However, by the fifteenth century the sea had retreated, leaving a fertile green plain and the distant Lagoa de Óbidos with its narrow, shallow entrance to the sea.

The town is touristy, of course, attracting visitors by the coach-load, while the flatter land below the walls has sprouted a small flurry of modern development. However, it's really only the main street and squares that get overly congested: climb the side alleys, or the perimeter walls which girdle the town, and Óbidos seems to retain secrets of its own. The feeling is reinforced if you stay the night, when the town slowly empties of day-trippers and regains its impossibly pictur-esque charm. The annual **summer festival** runs from July to September, with highlights including a ten-day medieval fair, plus opera at the castle, and other concerts and events.

The Town

The main entrance to town is through the **Porta da Vila**, housing a tiled oratory, beyond which stretches the main street, **Rua Direita**, a run of restored houses, gift and craft shops, galleries and cafés. *Ginjinha d'Óbidos*, the local cherry liqueur, is much in evidence, along with the ubiquitous ceramics and lace.

The handsome central square, overlooked by pillory and portico, is flanked on one side by the former town hall, now the **Museu Municipal** (entrance on Rua Direita; Tues–Sun 10am–1pm & 2–6pm; €1.50), notable principally for its work by **Josefa de Óbidos** (1630–1684), one of the finest of all Portu-guese painters, and one of the few women artists afforded any reputation by art historians. Born in Seville, Josefa spent most of her life in a convent at Óbidos. She began her career as an etcher and miniaturist, and a remarkable handling of detail is a feature of her later full-scale religious works. Her portrait of powerful priest Faustino das Neves is the museum's highlight (not always on display), while there's also a *retábulo* attributed to Josefa de Óbidos in the **Igreja de Santa Maria** (daily 9.30am–12.30pm & 2.30–5pm, April–Sept until 7pm), at the back of the main square. The church was the venue of the wedding of the 10-year-old child king, Afonso V, and his 8-year-old cousin,

Isabel, in 1444, and although it dates mainly from the Renaissance period, the interior is lined with blue seventeenth-century *azulejos* in a homely manner typical of Portuguese churches.

Rua Direita climbs eventually to Dom Dinis's massively towered **castle**, whose keep has been converted into a splendid *pousada*. There's access at various points to the **town walls** – at times, a hair-raising walkway with no handrail – while if you drop down through the alleys behind the square you'll find a second town gate, also with an eighteenth-century oratory.

Practicalities

There's a large **car park** just by the tourist office, immediately outside the Porta da Vila; or it's free if you park over the road in the wasteground lot by the aqueduct. **Buses** from Caldas da Rainha (6km to the north) and Peniche (24km west) stop outside the Porta da Vila, where you'll find the **turismo** (May–Sept daily 9.30am–7.30pm; Oct–April Mon–Fri 9.30am–6pm, Sat & Sun 9.30am–12.30pm & 1.30–5.30pm; ☎262 959 231, ⓦwww.cm-obidos.pt). This hands out sketch-plans that mark the restaurants and hotels, and also stocks information on nature walks in the locale. There's a minor **train station** at Óbidos (services from Caldas da Rainha, São Martinho and Leiria), but it's unstaffed and below town, a fair walk from the walls.

Óbidos's appeal to the heart also extends to its **accommodation**, which generally scores high on charm, especially in the town houses or country manors listed below. Most is priced at mid-range – budget travellers are advised to hunt out **private rooms** (❷), advertised in the windows of houses along Rua Direita. **Restaurants** are geared towards day-trippers, so prices tend to be high and menus predictable (and in three languages). To eat with the locals you need to head 1km out of town (Caldas da Rainha road, 15min walk) to the cobbled square by the unfinished rotunda church of **Senhor da Pedra**, where there are half a dozen restaurants serving grills, fish and rice (inexpensive to moderate).

Hotels and pensions

Casa d'Óbidos Quinta de São José, 1km south of town, near Senhor da Pedra church ☎262 950 924, ©obidos@solaresdeportugal.pt. Classy nineteenth-century manor house in lovely gardens, with a swimming pool and tennis court. There are half a dozen rooms in the house (a great breakfast is included), and three cottages in the grounds, and you can walk down to the restaurants by the church. Minimum 2-night stay. ❹

Casa da Relógio Rua da Graça ☎262 959 282. Just outside the walls, through the lower town gate, is this eighteenth-century mansion whose "clock" (*relógio*) is in fact a stone sundial on the facade. Six simply furnished en-suite rooms – those at the front have views, though there's not much space in any and the bathrooms are on the old-fashioned side. ❸

Casa de São Tiago Largo de São Tiago 1 ☎ & ⓕ262 959 587. Beautifully restored family house, dripping with vines and climbing flowers, just below the castle on Rua Direita. It's peaceful and very friendly, and the rooms have wrought-iron bedsteads, tiles and rugs, with views

either over the lemon trees or to the castle walls. Breakfast is served in the walled courtyard. ❹

Casal do Pinhão Bairro Senhora da Luz, 3km north, signposted from town ☎262 959 078. Six en-suite rooms opening on to a verandah, and two small apartments with kitchen, all overlooking pool and gardens on this pretty, rural estate. Children have plenty of space here, and even their own pool. Breakfast not included, but available. ❹

Estalagem Casa das Senhoras Rainhas Rua Padre Nunes Tavares 6 ☎262 955 360, ⓦwww.senhorasrainhas.com. The only serious rival to the *pousada* – an exceptional boutique-style hotel at the bottom of the old town, by the walls. Rooms have been given contemporary furniture, smart marble bathrooms and a soothing colour scheme – some have a private terrace – and there's a lovely courtyard. The restaurant offers a fine-dining experience – say seafood gaspacho and chicken stuffed with prunes – for around €40 a head. ❻

Estalagem do Convento Rua Dr João de Ornelas ☎262 959 216, ⓦwww.estalagemdoconvento.com. A minor convent just outside the walls (lower gate) has been converted into an atmospheric hotel of squeaky tiled floors, granite arches, oak beams and stone staircases. The traditionally furnished rooms overlook internal garden courtyards or the countryside, while there's also patio dining in the restaurant (expensive; closed Sun dinner). You can park outside. ❹

Albergaria Josefa d'Óbidos Rua Dr João de Ornelas ☎ 262 959 228, ⓦ www.josefadobidos .com. You'll find this modern inn on the road up to town, close to Porta da Vila. It's decent enough – rooms are decorated in traditional style but all have TVs and a/c – though some views are compromised by the main road or the high curtain wall of the castle. Parking. ❸

Hospedaria Louro Canastra ☎ 262 955 100. An undistinguished building in a modern neighbourhood, around 500m from the walls – walk away from Porta da Vila, past the car parks. However, the well-kept en-suite rooms are decently priced, parking is easy, and there's a pool. ❸

Pousada do Castelo ☎ 262 955 080, ⓦ www .pousadas.pt. It's only small but this is one of the country's finest *pousadas*, within the castle and approached through an intimate courtyard overlooked by carved windows – the cosy rooms feature four-poster beds and exposed stone walls. Guests tend to eat in the restaurant (mains around €25), where there's a classy take on traditional country food. Advance reservations advised for rooms and restaurant; for parking, follow the *pousada* signs. ❼

Albergaria Rainha Santa Isabel Rua Direita ☎ 262 959 323. The carefully preserved facade hides an up-to-date 20-room hotel with lounge and bar. There's a period feel inside – wooden floors and beams, blue-tiled bathrooms, dried flowers and leather armchairs – while the rooms vary in size and outlook, though the best have rooftop views. ❹

Restaurants

Adega do Ramada Trav Josefa d'Óbidos, off Rua Direita ☎ 262 959 462. Cosy little grill house with summer esplanade seating in the alley. Steaks, lamb chops, pork, seabass and salmon are all prepared on the outdoor charcoal grill. Closed Mon, and closed Sun dinner Oct–April. Moderate.

Alcaide Rua Direita, opposite *Albergaria Rainha Santa Isabel* ☎ 262 959 220. Serves traditional dishes at fairly steep prices (mains €10–16), but it's popular because you can eat on the balcony. Closed Wed. Expensive.

Senhor da Pedra Largo do Santuário do Senhor da Pedra, 1km south, Caldas da Rainha road ☎ 262 959 315. The cheapest meal in Óbidos, bar none – a simple handwritten menu of grills to the accompaniment of a TV broadcasting to Mars. You'll get a full meal for €10 (the price of a main course in town) and while it's hardly a gourmet experience, it's perfectly acceptable. Inexpensive.

Bars

Ibn Errik Rex Rua Direita 100. A garrulous owner presides over this town-house bar which has been in business for half a century. Bottles hang from every available space, and there's a carafe of the local *ginjinha* on every table. Closed Tues.

Lagar da Mouraria Rua da Mouraria, near Santa Maria church. Idiosyncratic bar fashioned from an old wine press – there are seats in the stone chambers and an enormous gnarled wooden beam bisecting the room.

Caldas da Rainha

Six kilometres north of Óbidos, **CALDAS DA RAINHA** ("Queen's Spa") was put on the map by Dona Leonor, queen of Dom João II. Passing in her carriage, en route to meet the king, she was so impressed by the strong sulphurous waters that she founded a hospital here, initiating four centuries of noble and royal patronage. That was in 1484, but the town was to reach the peak of its popularity in the nineteenth century when, throughout Europe, spas became as much social as medical institutions. English Gothic novelist William Beckford (recorded in his *Travels in Spain and Portugal*) found it a lively if depressing place – "every tenth or twelfth person a rheumatic or palsied invalid, with his limbs all atwist, and his mouth all awry, being conveyed to the baths in a chair".

Disappointingly little remains of the royal wealth poured into the spa, although Caldas offers a good break in the journey to Nazaré or Alcobaça. Once through the drab modern outskirts there's a pleasant enough centre focused on the modern spa buildings and the spreading municipal park beyond, which contains two diverting museums. Caldas is also not a bad place for souvenir hunting: its embroidery has a national reputation, though it's best known as a ceramics centre.

The Town

Start at the central **Praça da República**, where there's a large fruit, vegetable and flower market every morning. Monday sees the addition of clothes, shoes and household goods. The lanes running downhill from here lead to Largo da Rainha Dona Leonor and the buildings of the royal **spa complex**, notably the hospital (founded the year after the queen's first visit, in 1485) and the New Baths of 1855. Around the back of the spa is the striking Manueline belfry of **Nossa Senhora do Pópulo**, the hospital church (built 1500), covered in blue-and-yellow *azulejo* tiles and with a *Virgin and Child* by Josefa de Óbidos in the sacristry.

Everything else of interest is in, or just outside, the neighbouring **Parque Dom Carlos I**, an extensive landscaped park centred on a small lake. Principal attraction is the **Museu de José Malhoa** (Tues–Sun 10am–12.30pm & 2–5pm; €2, free Sun morning), largely dedicated to the works of the Caldas-born painter **José Malhoa** (1855–1933), Portugal's leading nineteenth-century exponent of naturalism, a master of costume, genre scenes and country life. There are also works by many of Malhoa's contemporaries on display, particularly those of the so-called "Grupo do Leão" of artists, writers and intellectuals (named after a Lisbon beer-hall), of which Malhoa was a prominent member. In the basement, don't miss the ceramics by **Rafael Bordalo Pinheiro** (1846–1905), notably his masterpiece, the life-sized models representing the Passion.

It's Pinheiro who is most closely associated with the famous Caldas da Rainha pottery. His naturalist tableware (cabbage-leaf bowls, butterfly plates and the like) is still hugely popular, while in the enduring caricature of "Zé Povinho" – a bearded peasant in black hat, with no respect for authority – Pinheiro created a true Portuguese archetype. The ceramics factory Pinheiro founded in 1884, the **Faianças Artisticas Fabrico Bordalo Pinheiro** (Ⓦwww.fabordalopinheiro.pt), lies on the street that bears his name, which runs around the back of the park. The factory shop (Mon–Sat 10am–1pm & 2–7pm) is filled with colourful glazed earthenware, from typical figurines to contemporary dinner services; the adjacent **Casa-Museu San Rafael** (Tues–Fri 9am–1pm only; free) displays a selection of remarkable historical pieces by Pinheiro and his craftsmen. The other place to pursue the subject is the **Museu da Cerâmica** (Tues–Sun 10am–12.30pm & 2–5pm; €2, free Sun morning), a little further up the road. It's set in a delightful rustic stone villa, and contains more of Pinheiro's original work as well as providing an overview of the whole history of Caldas pottery. There are some extraordinary naturalistic pieces here – lobster-garlanded dishes, griffins entwined with snakes, fish-head jars, cabbage-leaf bowls – protected from harm by staff who follow you around the creaking floors at a not-so-discreet distance.

Practicalities

It's a short walk from either the bus or train station to the **turismo** (Mon–Fri 9am–7pm, Sat & Sun 10am–1pm & 3–7pm; ☎262 839 700, Ⓦwww.cm-caldas-rainha.pt), situated at the side of the modern town hall in Praça 25 de Abril. From here, Praça da República is a five-minute walk away: walk down Rua Engheneiro Duarte Pacheo from the turismo, turn right on Rua

Heróis da Grande Guerre, then left down pedestrianized Rua Almirante Cândido dos Reis. There's pay **parking** in Praça 25 de Abril and along Rua de Camões in front of the park, though if you continue around the park heading out of town, the street parking becomes free.

There's a fair amount of **accommodation** in town, although nothing too exciting – in any case, you can be on the coast in less than half an hour.

Hotels and pensions

Caldas Internacional Hotel Rua Dr Figueirôa Rêgo 45 ⊕ 262 830 500. The smartest (four-star) hotel in town, with modern a/c rooms, a swimming pool and its own parking. ❹

Pensão Residencial Central Largo Dr José Barbosa 22 ⊕ 262 831 914. Located in a quiet, restored square between Pr da República and Largo da Rainha Dona Leonor, this has been given a facelift by new owners – rooms have laminate floors and updated bathrooms, and some have French windows you can throw open onto the square. ❷

Residencial Dom Carlos Rua de Camões 39A ⊕ 262 832 551. Traditional old hotel, opposite the park. It's a bit musty, and furnishings and decor have seen better days, but it's a useful standby if you just want a bed for the night. A variety of rooms, with and without bath – those at the front with park views can be noisy. No credit cards. ❷

Cafés and restaurants

Populus Parque Dom Carlos I, at Rua de Camões ⊕ 262 845 840. The park café is by far the most enticing spot for an alfresco lunch – there are salads, snacks, and a few meat and fish dishes. Oct–May closed Mon. Moderate.

Sabores d'Italia Rua Eng Duarte Pacheco 17 ⊕ 262 845 599. It's rare to get proper Italian food in Portugal, though here you'll pay for the experience. It's not just home-made pasta and daily fish and meat specials – there are good pizzas too, which won't break the bank. Closed Mon. Expensive.

Supatra Rua General Amílcar Mota, 1km out of the centre, south on Óbidos road ⊕ 262 842 920. It's worth the walk, since you'll have to go a long way to find another Thai restaurant. Dishes are toned down a bit for local tastes, but it's an attractive place for a meal, decked out in Thai finery. Closed Sun dinner & Mon. Expensive.

Tijuca Rua de Camões 89 ⊕ 262 824 255. The budget choice, a simple basement restaurant opposite the park, with a traditional menu and most dishes costing less than €9. The chicken casserole (*frango na púcara*) is good, served in an earthenware pot. Inexpensive.

North to Nazaré

Heading north from Caldas da Rainha, the trains stay inland, touching the coast only at **São Martinho do Porto**, 13km south of Nazaré. However, with a car you can bear northwest from Caldas along the N360, which takes you past the tranquil **Lagoa de Óbidos**, and then out along the coast via **Foz do Arelho** on a breezy clifftop route – a much better option than taking the busy N8 or the motorway. There are also direct buses out to Foz from Caldas da Rainha several times a day, a twenty-minute ride.

Foz do Arelho

At **FOZ DO ARELHO**, 8km west of Caldas, the small village sits 1km back from a sheltered lagoon beach, which is overlooked by a couple of cafés. The road continues a further 500m or so to another tremendous beach where river meets ocean, and here there's a promenade of fancier bars and restaurants. It's not really overdeveloped – this is more a holiday home place than a resort – and outside July and August you'll have the wide, white sands to yourself. On the lagoon itself, the **Lagoa de Óbidos**, fishermen stand in the shallow waters next to their boats, attending to their nets.

There's limited **accommodation** in Foz village, with the best of two pensions being the *Penedo Furado* (⊕ 262 979 610, ⓦ www.penedo-furado.web.pt; ❸), signposted to the right up a side street as you pass through the village. It's a homely place with spacious modern rooms, distant lagoon views and parking – prices shoot up in August, but are better value the rest of the year. The other good option is *Quinta da Foz* (☎262 979 369; no credit cards; ❺), right in the village (signposted to the left, off the square), a sixteenth-century manor house with five rooms to let and separate apartments. There's also a large forested *Orbitur* **campsite** (☎262 978 683), but it's out on the Caldas road, 2km before the village and thus a fair way from the restaurants and beach.

The presence of some rather fashionable **bars** in the square in Foz village and dotted around the lagoon tell you what kind of place this is in summer, when the city crowds descend from Lisbon. There's a *churrasqueira* and a couple of cafés in the village, but all the action is out at the ocean beach where a line of bars and seafood **restaurants** vie for your attention. *Cabana do Pescador* (☎262 979 451) is an old favourite, though it's the showy *Adamastor* (☎262 978 003), on the road above the beach, that's more typical of the summer clientele – a contemporary warehouse-style restaurant with fabulous views, though distinctly average food. Or for tandoori dishes, kebabs and the like, there's *Monte Horeb* (Fri, Sat & Sun dinner only, though call for confirmation; ☎262 978 000), which is on the hill at Nadadouro above the lagoon – at the roundabout leaving Foz village for the beach, turn left along the lagoon and follow the prolific signs for 2.7km.

São Martinho do Porto

Ten kilometres north of Foz, **SÃO MARTINHO DO PORTO** is the main resort between Peniche and Nazaré, and one of the more developed spots along this stretch of Estremaduran coast. However, it's both low-key and largely low-rise and, compared with Peniche and Nazaré, is an easy-going place favoured by families. Even so, in August you will struggle to find a room – or even a place in the campsite.

The reason for São Martinho's success is its beach, a vast sweep of sand that curls around an almost landlocked bay to form a natural swimming pool, where sardine boats bob before the quay. It's a very pretty aspect, while the shelter of the bay makes it one of the warmest places to swim on the west coast, with the sands sloping down into calm, shallow water. For something more bracing – or less crowded – there's a good northern beach on the open Atlantic coastline beyond the bay, pounded by surf.

The **turismo** (Oct–April Tues–Sun 10am–1pm & 2–6pm; May–Sept Tues–Sun 10am–1pm & 3–7pm; no phone, enquiries go to Leiria turismo ☎244 848 770) might be able to help find you accommodation in private rooms. It's in the heart of the small town centre, on Largo Vitorino Fróis, a square set two blocks from the seafront – the **train station** (services from Caldas da Rainha and Leiria) is a few hundred metres south of here on Largo 28 de Maio, while **buses** stop a bit closer in on Rua Conde de Avelar, with both terminals only a short walk from the seafront.

Avoid July and August if you can, when **accommodation** prices soar – if you can't, book well in advance. The finest address in town is the *Palace do Capitão* (☎262 985 150, ⓦwww.palacecapitao.com; ❺), a beautifully restored mansion overlooking the central seafront promenade (straight down from the turismo). The inlaid parquet floors and handpainted wallpaper set the tone for what is an elegant house with a variety of comfortable rooms – though not all have sea views. The best budget option is the *Pensão Atlântica*, Rua Miguel Bombarda 6 (☎262 989 151; no credit cards; ❸), a jaunty blue-and-white pension nearby, two blocks from the seafront in a pedestrianized square. There's very cheap accommodation most of the year at the *Pensão Americana*, Rua Dr José Saldanha 2 (☏262 989 170; ❶, ❸ in August), just off Rua Conde de Avelar, but it's like a Soviet-era barracks inside and out, with nothing nice about the musty old rooms. The huge, well-equipped **campsite**, *Colina do Sol* (☏262 989 764, ⓦwww.colinadosol.net), 3km to the north, off the Nazaré road (N242), is inconvenient for the town but within walking distance of a beach, the Praia da Gralha. The local youth hostel, 4km inland at Alfeizerão, hasn't been open for some time, but is due to be refurbished.

The **restaurant** at the *Atlântica*, the *Carvalho*, is as good as any of the no-frills eating places in the centre. For more of an experience visit *O Farol* (☏262 989 399), a few hundred metres south down the promenade, overlooking the beach – it's not too pricey despite appearances (daily specials averaging €10) and the views are unsurpassed.

Nazaré

After years of advertising itself as the most picturesque seaside town in Portugal, **NAZARÉ** has more or less destroyed itself. In summer, the crowds are far too heavy for the place to cope with and the enduring characteristics are not so much "gentle traditions" as trinket stalls and high prices with a touch of hard-edged hustle. While elderly local women still don traditional headscarves and embroidered aprons, their immense trays of fish have been replaced by signs touting rooms; the only nets mended on the beach are miniature souvenirs for tourists; and the sardine boats long ago dropped anchor in a new harbour, fifteen minutes' walk from the town. However, as long as you don't expect yesteryear nostalgia or a cosy village, and are steeled for peak-season crowds, Nazaré is highly enjoyable, with all the restaurants, facilities and knockabout cheer of a busy beach resort.

The Town

There's not much old-world charm left in Nazaré, though the sheer sweep of the seafront promenade is impressive. It's backed by a tight warren of narrow alleys and streets filled with houses advertising *quartos* and simple restaurants, with the occasional small square letting in the light. The main **beach** – a grand, tent-studded expanse of clean sand – packs in bathers tightly in summer, with further beaches stretching north beyond the headland. New Year's Eve on Nazaré beach is one of the biggest bashes in Portugal, the music and partying culminating in midnight fireworks over the ocean.

The original settlement was actually at **Sítio**, 110m up the rock face above the north end of the present town. It's a location that was the legacy of pirate raids, which continued well into the nineteenth century. However, legend has a different explanation, telling of a twelfth-century knight, Dom Fuas Roupinho, who, while out hunting, was led up the cliff by a deer. The deer dived into the void and Dom Fuas was saved from following by the timely vision of Nossa Senhora da Nazaré, in whose name a church was subsequently built. You can reach Sítio and the church by taking the **funicular** (daily 7am–midnight, until 2am in Aug; €0.85 one way) from town, which rumbles up to a *miradouro* at the top. The main church square is ringed by souvenir shops and patrolled by formidable *varinhas* (fishwives) touting huge mounds of dried fruit and nuts. The views down to the town and beach are sensational. The church itself hosts a well-attended *romaria* (Sept 8–10) with processions, folk dancing and bullfights, while the Sítio bullring also stages Saturday night *touradas* in summer.

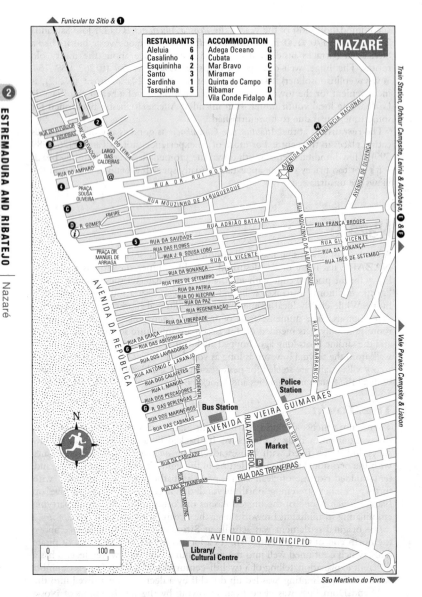

▲ Funicular to Sítio & ❶

NAZARÉ

RESTAURANTS	
Aleluia	6
Casalinho	4
Esquininha	2
Santo	3
Sardinha	1
Tasquinha	5

ACCOMMODATION	
Adega Oceano	G
Cubata	B
Mar Bravo	C
Miramar	E
Quinta do Campo	F
Ribamar	D
Vila Conde Fidalgo	A

Train Station, Orbitur Campsite, Leiria & Alcobaça, ❻ *&* ❼

▶ *Vale Paraíso Campsite & Lisbon*

RUA DO ELEVADOR II FIGUEIRAS
TRAV. DE ELEVADOR
RUA DO LEIRIA
LARGO DAS CALDEIRAS
RUA DO AMPARO
PRAÇA SOUSA OLIVEIRA
RUA DR RUI ROSA
AVENIDA DA INDEPENDÊNCIA NACIONAL
AVENIDA DE OLIVENÇA
FREIRE
R. GOMES
RUA MOUZINHO DE ALBUQUERQUE
RUA ADRIÃO BATALHA
RUA FRANÇA BROGES
RUA GIL VICENTE
RUA DA BONANÇA
RUA TRÊS DE SETEMBRO
RUA MOUZINHO DE ALBUQUERQUE
PRAÇA DR MANUEL DE ARRIAGA
RUA DA SAUDADE
RUA DAS FLORES
RUA J. B. SOUSA LOBO
RUA GIL VICENTE
RUA DA BONANÇA
RUA TRÊS DE SETEMBRO
RUA DA PÁTRIA
RUA DO ALECRIM
RUA DA PAZ
RUA REGENERAÇÃO
RUA DA LIBERDADE
RUA SUB VILA
AVENIDA DA REPÚBLICA
RUA DA GRAÇA
RUA DAS ABEGORIAS
RUA DOS LAVRADORES
RUA ANTÓNIO C. LARANJO
RUA DOS CALAFETES
RUA I. MANUEL
RUA DOS PESCADORES
R. DAS BERLENGAS
RUA DOS MARINEIROS
RUA DAS CABANAS
RUA OCIDENTAL
RUA DOS BARRANCOS
Police Station
Bus Station
AVENIDA VIEIRA GUIMARÃES
RUA ALVES REDOL
RUA SUB VILA
Market
RUA DA CARIDADE
RUA DAS TRAINEIRAS
RUA B. MARTINS
RUA DAS TREINEIRAS
AVENIDA DO MUNICIPIO
Library/ Cultural Centre

N

0   100 m

São Martinho do Porto ▼

Practicalities

Arriving by car, a one-way system filters traffic away from the narrow streets and up and down the flanking thoroughfares. There's pay **parking** in a large car park behind the market, or free spaces along the seafront starting after the cultural centre and library (heading towards port and marina). The **bus station** is centrally located on Avenida Vieira Guimarães, just a minute or two from the seafront. The nearest **train station** is at Valado, 6km inland, on the Alcobaça road; buses run regularly into town. Avenida da República runs the length of the beach, and this is where you'll find most of the hotels and restaurants, as well as the **turismo** (daily 9.30am–1pm & 2.30–6pm, though longer all-day hours in July & Aug; ☎262 561 194, ⓦwww.cm-nazare.pt).

Accommodation

The best of the offical options are reviewed below, but Nazaré is also awash with **private rooms** and you'll be approached by touts at the bus station and throughout town – expect to pay €30–40 in high season. For a laid-back alternative to Nazaré's hustle seek out rooms in the quieter streets of Sítio; notices are displayed in houses and restaurants. In August a local bus runs on a circuit from town out to the two campsites and back, but there's no transport there the rest of the year.

Hotels and pensions

Adega Oceano Av da República 51 ☎262 561 161, ⓦwww.adegaoceano.com. Typical seafront lodgings with restaurant underneath. Rooms are rather plain but all are en suite, and even if yours doesn't have a sea view, there's access to a small terrace at the front. ❸

Cubata Av da República 6 ☎262 561 706. Budget *residencial* on the promenade that's really only worth it if you can get a room at the front, looking out over the ocean and the Sítio cliffs – others, while entirely inoffensive, have no character. ❷

Mar Bravo Pr Sousa Oliveira 71 ☎262 569 160, ⓦwww.marbravo.com. The most upmarket seafront choice has smallish rooms but all have an ocean view and are handsomely styled, with good marble bathrooms, prints on the walls and decent furniture. There's an equally refined restaurant downstairs. ❸

Miramar Rua Abel da Silva, Pederneira ☎262 550 000, ⓦwww.hotelmiramar.pt. Contemporary four-star hotel sited on the eastern heights above Nazaré – it's only 1km above town and beach, in the old village of Pederneira, but access is very steep and you'll really need a car. Views are sensational – from rooms, pool, terrace and breakfast balcony – while there are also some one- and two-bed apartments (good for families) surrounding a small courtyard, across from the hotel. The restaurant (moderate) is a seafood place with views. Avoid Aug, and rates are pretty good – as low as €55 a night in winter. ❺

Quinta do Campo Valado dos Frades, 6km east of town ☎262 577 135. The eight double rooms are traditional but elegant, with heavy wood furniture and immaculate white linen. The building was erected in the fourteenth century as an ecclesiastical agricultural college, and is in extensive grounds that contain a pool and tennis courts. ❻

Ribamar Rua Gomes Freire 9 ☎262 551 58, ⓕ262 562 224. Rooms (above a restaurant) are small, with frilly fabrics and tiny bathrooms tiled with *azulejos*. Some are nicer than others (with the original wooden flooring or plaster cornicing) and others overlook the beach, but you'll pay a bit more for a sea view. ❷

Vila Conde Fidalgo Av da Independência Nacional 21 ☎262 552 361, ⓦhttp://condefidalgo.planetaclix.pt. The best and friendliest budget choice is set back up the hill from the sea (10min walk), with parking outside. It's a secluded complex of simple rooms and apartments on various levels, separated by plant-filled patios and ceramic-tiled walkways. Furnishings are basic but adequate, with a fridge and TV in each room, and kitchenettes in the apartments (which can sleep four). Laundry service available. Prices are variable; good off-season discounts. No credit cards. Rooms ❷, apartments ❸–❹

Campsites

Orbitur 2km east on the N8 road to Valado ☎262 561 111, ⓦwww.orbitur.pt. Well-equipped site shaded by pines; also little A-frame bungalows available (from €45, summer €75). Closed Dec & Jan.

Vale Paraiso 2km north of town on N242 ☎262 561 800, ⓦwww.valeparaiso.com. Nestling in pine woods, and near a long beach. Also has a pool, bike rental, and plenty of self-contained chalets, bungalows and apartments (from €30, summer €55). Closed Dec.

Eating and drinking

The main concentrations of **restaurants**, **cafés** and **bars** are along the seafront Avenida da República, in the squares and alleys behind, and near the lower funicular station. Menus are broadly similar – plenty of grilled fish – and prices at most don't vary by more than a euro or two. Hunt the narrow back streets, or look around the bus station, for the cheapest places.

Aleluia Av da República 38 ☎ 262 561 967. A basic paper-tablecloth place, always busy with locals eating from a menu strong on fish or simply sipping a coffee and chewing the fat. Makes a decent lunch stop – the *caldeirada* is good. Inexpensive.

O Casalinho Pr Sousa Oliveira 7 ☎ 262 551 328. Alfresco dining in the square, or in the contemporary dining room. Service is with a smile, and you can expect good seabass, squid kekabs, sardines, grilled bream and the like for around €8 or €9 – it's not really the place to go if you don't want fish. Moderate.

A Esquininha Rua do Elevador 22 ☎ 262 107 610. Nazaré's first Indian restaurant really deserves more custom. The food's good, and can be spiced for all tastes (even unadventurous Portuguese ones), and they'll rustle you up a *lassi* or a *Cobra* beer if you don't fancy the wine straight from the box. Moderate.

O Santo Trav do Elevador 11, no phone. The cosiest of *adegas*, with a few tables outside and nooks and crannies inside. It's the nearest thing to a pub in town, good for a thimbleful of local wine or a beer and some fresh clams or shrimp. Inexpensive.

A Sardinha Largo de Nossa Senhora de Nazaré 45, Sítio ☎ 262 553 391. Unpretentious seafood restaurant near the church in Sítio whose outdoor barbecue grill turns out what some swear are the finest grilled sardines in the region. Closed Mon. Moderate.

A Tasquinha Rua Adrião Batalha 54 ☎ 262 551 945. Just far enough off the seafront to be a locals' choice, this wooden bench and blue-check-tablecloth joint serves up very reasonably priced tavern-style food. There's always a good list of dishes of the day, meat and fish, with most options costing €6–10. Closed Sun. Inexpensive.

Listings

Hospital The town hospital is up at Sítio on Rua do Alão ☎ 262 550 100.
Internet Access at Espaçao Internet in the Centro Cultural, Av Manuel Remigio (Mon–Fri 9.30am–1pm, 3–7pm & 9pm–midnight). More central terminals are at Online, Centro Commerical, Pr Sousa Oliveira (Mon–Sat 10am–midnight, Sun 2pm–midnight). There is also a terminal in the post office (see below).

Pharmacy Farmácia Silvério and Farmácia dos Pescadores are both at the bottom of Rua Adrião Batalha, just up from the turismo.
Police Headquarters is on Av Vieira Guimarães ☎ 262 551 268.
Post office Av da Independência Nacional 2 (Mon–Fri 9am–12.30pm & 2.30–6pm, Sat 9am–noon).
Taxis You'll find them along Av da República, or call ☎ 262 551 363.

Alcobaça

The Cistercian monastery at **ALCOBAÇA** was founded in 1153 by Dom Afonso Henrique to celebrate his victory over the Moors at Santarém six years earlier. Building started soon after and by the end of the thirteenth century it was the most powerful monastery in the country. Owning vast tracts of farmland, orchards and vineyards, it was immensely rich and held jurisdiction over a dozen towns and three seaports. Its church and cloister are the purest and the most inspired creation of all Portuguese Gothic architecture and, alongside Belém and Batalha, are the most impressive monuments in the country. The church is also the burial place of those romantic figures of Portuguese history, Dom Pedro and Dona Inês de Castro.

A visit to the monastery can comfortably occupy a couple of hours. Alcobaça itself is a small and fairly unremarkable town, though the Rio Baça winds attractively through the few remaining old town streets, and there's a large **market** building (market held Mon) and public gardens. The ruined hilltop **castle** provides the best overall view of the monastery, otherwise the only other point of interest is the **Museu do Vinho** (Mon–Fri 9am–12.30pm & 2–5.30pm; free), fifteen minutes' walk out of town on the Leiria road, which gives a fascinating glimpse into the area's wine-making and agricultural past. Guided tours last about an hour and provide opportunities to purchase local tipples.

Mosteiro de Alcobaça

The **Mosteiro de Alcobaça** (daily: April–Sept 9am–7pm; Oct–March 9am–5pm; last entry 30min before closing; €4.50, free Sun before 2pm, entry to church free), although empty since its dissolution in 1834, still seems to assert power, magnificence and opulence. And it takes little imagination to people it again with monks, said once to have numbered 999. It was their legendary extravagant and aristocratic lifestyle that formed the common ingredients of the awed anecdotes of eighteenth-century travellers. Even English writer William Beckford, no stranger to high living, found their decadence unsettling, growing weary of "perpetual gormandizing . . . the fumes of banquets and incense . . . the fat waddling monks and sleek friars with wanton eyes". Another contemporary observer, Richard Twiss, for his part found "the bottle went as briskly about as ever I saw it do in Scotland" – a tribute indeed. For all the "high romps" and luxuriance, though, it has to be added that the monks enjoyed a reputation for hospitality, generosity and charity, while the surrounding countryside is to this day one of the most productive areas in Portugal, thanks to their agricultural expertise.

The abbey church

The main **abbey church**, modelled on the original Cistercian abbey at Citeaux in France, is the largest in Portugal. External impressions are disappointing, as the Gothic facade has been superseded by unexceptional Baroque additions of the seventeenth and eighteenth centuries. Inside, however, all later adornments have been swept away, restoring the narrow soaring aisles to their original simplicity. The only exception to this Gothic purity is the frothy Manueline doorway to the sacristy, hidden directly behind the high altar and encrusted with intricate, swirling motifs of coral and seaweed.

The church's most precious treasures are the fourteenth-century **tombs of Dom Pedro and Dona Inês de Castro**, each occupying one of the transepts and sculpted with a phenomenal wealth of detail. Animals, heraldic emblems,

---

Dom Pedro and Dona Inês de Castro

Dom Pedro's earthly love for Inês de Castro, cruelly stifled by high politics, forms the great theme of epic Portuguese poetry. Prince **Pedro** (1320–1367), son of Afonso IV and heir to the Portuguese throne, was married to Constance of Castile, but fell in love with her maid, **Inês de Castro** (1320–1355), daughter of a Galician nobleman. The two continued an affair, despite the disapproval of the king, who feared any source of Spanish influence over the Portuguese throne. Following Constance's death in 1345, Afonso IV banished Inês from the court and forbade her marriage to Pedro, but it's possible the ceremony took place nevertheless – secretly at Bragança in remote Trás-os-Montes. The couple also had three children. With Inês's brothers and other Spanish nobles favoured by Pedro, and Afonso in danger of losing control of his court, the king was eventually persuaded to sanction his daughter-in-law's murder, and she was killed in Coimbra in 1355, sparking a revolt by Pedro against his own father. Afonso died two years later and when Pedro succeeded to the throne in 1357 he brought the murderers to justice, personally ripping out their hearts and gorging his love-crazed appetite for blood upon them. More poignantly, he also exhumed and crowned the corpse of his lover, forcing the entire royal circle to acknowledge her as queen by kissing her decomposing hand. Her remains were transferred to Alcobaça, where Pedro had two tombs commissioned, which were placed in the abbey church.

musicians and biblical scenes are all portrayed in an architectural setting of miniature windows, canopies, domes and towers; most graphic of all is a dragon-shaped Hell's mouth at Inês's feet, consuming the damned. The tombs are inscribed with the motto "Até ao Fim do Mundo" (Until the End of the World) and, in accordance with Dom Pedro's orders, were placed foot to foot so that on the Day of Judgement the pair may rise and immediately feast their eyes on one another.

Sala dos Reis

Immediately to the left inside the church is the **Sala dos Reis** (Hall of Kings), inside which is the ticket desk for the monastery. Blue eighteenth-century *azulejos* depict the siege of Santarém, Dom Afonso's vow, and the founding of the monastery, while high up are displayed statues of virtually every king of Portugal up until Dom José, who died in 1777. Also on show here is a piece of war booty which must have warmed the souls of the brothers – the huge metal cauldron in which soup was heated up for the Spanish army before the battle of Aljubarrota in 1385.

The cloisters and monastery quarters

From the Sala dos Reis you enter the **Claustro do Silencio** (Cloister of Silence), notable for its traceried stone windows, built in the reign of Dom Dinis, the "poet-king" who established an enduring literary and artistic tradition at the abbey. An upper storey of twisted columns and Manueline arches was added in the sixteenth century, along with a beautiful hexagonal *lavabo* with Renaissance fountain. This was where the monks washed before entering the **refectory**, itself provided with a stone pulpit so that the scriptures could be read to the brothers as they ate.

The adjacent **kitchen** – with its gargantuan conical chimney, supported by eight trunk-like iron columns – puts Alcobaça's celebrated feasting into perspective. A stream tapped from the River Alcôa still runs straight through the room: it was used not only for cooking and washing but also to provide a constant supply of fresh fish, which plopped out into a stone basin. At the centre of the room, on the vast marble tables, Beckford marvelled at:

... pastry in vast abundance which a numerous tribe of lay brothers and their attendants were rolling out and puffing up into a hundred different shapes, singing all the while as blithely as larks in a cornfield. "There", said the Lord Abbot, "we shall not starve. God's bounties are great, it is fit we should enjoy them".

And enjoy them they did, with a majestic feast of "rarities and delicacies, potted lampreys, strange Brazilian messes, edible birds' nests and sharks' fins dressed after the mode of Macau by a Chinese lay brother". As a practical test for obesity the monks had to file through a narrow door on their way to the refectory; those who failed were forced to fast until they could squeeze through.

After the kitchen, the other side of the cloisters gives access to the monks' hall, a vast dormitory, the *parlatório* (where the monks could break their silence to discuss lay matters) and the chapter house.

Practicalities

There's plenty of **parking** near the market and gardens, while the **bus station** is a couple of blocks away – from either market or bus station it's just a five-minute signposted walk to the monastery, crossing the river en route. The town centre has improved immeasurably since through traffic was diverted away from the monastery, opening up the facing square, **Praça 25 de Abril**, as a ring of cafés and restaurants with grandstand views. The **turismo** (daily: May–Sept 10am–1pm & 3–7pm; Oct–April 10am–1pm & 2–6pm; ☎262 582 377) on the square, opposite the monastery, can supply wholly unnecessary maps of town. Alcobaça has a limited but relatively inexpensive choice of **accommodation**, mostly near Praça 25 de Abril, and there's a small municipal **campsite** (☎262 582 265) right in town, north of the market.

Restaurants and **cafés** are predictably touristy, with little to choose between them – locals favour the restaurant at the Pensão Coracões Unides (see below), though there's no monastery view from the dining room. The middle of November every year sees the **Mostra de Doces Conventuais**, a weekend of feasting on conventual sweets and pastries and fruit liqueurs from convents, monasteries and cake shops in Portugal, Spain and France.

Hotels and pensions

Challet Fonte Nova Palacete Rua da Fonte Nova ☎262 598 300, ⓦwww.challetfontenova .pt. A boutique hotel with luxurious rooms – those on the first floor are classiest, those in an annexe have larger bathrooms – in an aristocratic nineteenth-century villa furnished with antiques. The house is secreted on a back street behind the turismo but signposted from everywhere. Breakfast and free bar included. Parking. ❺

Coracões Unides Rua Frei António Brandão 39 ☎ & ℗262 582 142. Large rooms in a dated but friendly *pensão*, just off the square, some with side views to the monastery. The old-fashioned restaurant downstairs is a reliable place for an inexpensive meal (the *ementa turística* is €10) – *frango na púcara*, a tasty chicken casserole, is the house speciality. ❷

Dona Inês de Castro Rua Costa Veiga 44 ☎262 582 355, ℗262 581 258. Modern three-star hotel, 5min walk from town (follow the Lisbon/Évora signs at the roundabout) and looking out across fields to the back of the monastery. Good off-season discounts. ❹

Santa Maria Rua Dr Francisco Zagalo 20 ☎262 590 160, ℗262 590 161. Tour groups use this straightforward three-star hotel, just up to the right as you face the monastery – front rooms have the sought-after views. It's nothing special, but is reasonably priced and parking is included. ❸

Restaurant

Frei Bernado Rua Dom Pedro V 17 ☎262 582 227. Down the side of the abbey, serving portions in sizes the decadent monks would have approved of. There's an *ementa* for €12, otherwise dishes cost €9–12. Moderate.

Leiria

Thirty-five kilometres north of Alcobaça, a royal castle hangs almost vertically above **LEIRIA**, whose graceful old town is a place of cobbled streets, attractive gardens and fine old squares – cocooned within modern suburbs and a swirling one-way system. If you are travelling around on public transport you will probably want to make it your base for a couple of nights because the three big sights of northern Estremadura – Alcobaça, Batalha and Fátima – are easy day trips by bus. As a student town Leiria also has enough good restaurants and bars to make the evenings go with a swing, while it's also handily poised for the fine beaches of the Pinhal de Leiria to the west.

Leiria was the main residence of Dom Dinis, who gave the town as a wedding gift to his beloved Queen Isabel, along with Óbidos, Abrantes, Porto de Mós and Trancoso. At the heart of the old town is **Praça Rodrigues Lobo**, surrounded by beautiful arcaded buildings and dominated by a splendidly pompous statue of the eponymous seventeenth-century local poet. In fact, Leiria's literary connections go back much further than this – in 1480, the town had one of Portugal's first printing presses, which was run by Jews who printed

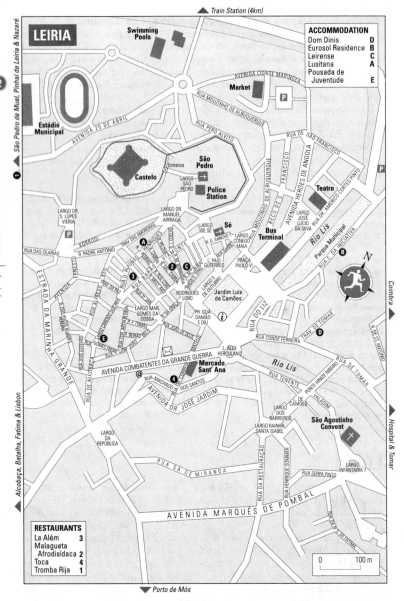

in Hebrew. An antiques and crafts fair is held in the square on the second Saturday of each month.

Leiria's **Castelo** (April–Sept Tues–Sun 10am–6pm; Oct–March Tues–Sun 9am–5pm; €2.25) was once one of the most important strongholds in Moorish Portugal, reconquered by Afonso Henriques as he fought his way south in 1135. The actual building you see today dates mostly from the fourteenth and eighteenth centuries, while the battlements are modern reconstructions. Still, it's an impressive sight, crowning the crags above town, and within its walls stands a royal palace, with a magnificent balcony high above the Rio Lis. Inside the keep is a small museum (closed noon–1pm) containing displays of armour and archeological finds, while the walls also contain the church of **Nossa Senhora da Penha**, erected by João I in about 1400 and now reduced to an eerie, roofless shell.

Outside the walls, on the edge of the old town, stands the sixteenth-century **Sé**, which was built during the reign of Dom João III. Look across the square here to the impressively tiled **pharmacy** opposite – once the meeting place of a literary circle surrounding novelist Eça de Queirós, who lived in Leiria for a year in 1870–71. His novel, *The Sin of Father Amaro* (1876), draws heavily on his experiences in this provincial cathedral city. Finally, have a quick look at the Adam-and-Eve fountain in the square outside the turismo, though it's of no artistic merit – let's just say that Adam is pleased to see you.

Practicalities

The **train station** (services from Figueira da Foz and Lisbon) is 4km north of town – there are frequent buses into the centre or a taxi will cost around €5. The **bus terminal** is right in town on Avenida Heróis de Angola, with the **turismo** (daily: May–Sept 10am–1pm & 3–7pm; Oct–Apr 2–6pm; ☏ 244 814 770, ⊕ www.cm-leiria.pt, ⊕ www.rt-leiriafatima.pt) a five-minute walk away across the Jardim Luís de Camões. Driving into Leiria, following signs for "centro", you end up in a one-way system of some devilment, and though metered street **parking** and pay car parks are widely advertised, parking in the centre can be pricey. There are free car parks on the outskirts (near the market and river), which isn't too long a walk to the centre.

Accommodation

The very cheapest **accommodation** is found in the old-town streets off Praça Rodrigues Lobo – though note that none of these places have parking, and you won't be able to drive to them to unload.

Hotels and pensions

Dom Dinis Trav de Tomar 2 ☏ 244 815 342, ☏ 244 823 552. Across the bridge from the turismo, and up a steep side street – the *residencial* is signposted and there's adjacent parking. Doesn't look much from the outside, but the rooms are more than reasonable, double-glazed against street noise and with satellite TV. ❷

Eurosol Residence Rua Comissão da Iniciativa 13, ☏ 244 860 460, ⊕ www.eurosol.pt. Leiria's central four-star choice provides stylish, modern apartments (studios, or one- and two-bedroom), plus gym, sauna, pool and underground parking – it's signposted from the ring road. The adjacent sister hotels, the *Eurosol Leiria* and *Jardim*, are further out of the centre, but have similar facilities and fine city views. ❹–❺

Leirense Rua Afonso de Albuquerque 6 ☏ 244 823 054, ☏ 244 823 073. A firm favourite for some years, offering cool, quiet *pensão* rooms with parquet floors and handsome wooden furniture. The location is ideal, and it's good value for money. ❸

Lusitana Rua Dom Afonso Henriques 24 ☏ 244 815 698 or 916 042 478, ☏ 244 767 640. A traditional *hospedaria* in the heart of the old town, with plain en-suite rooms with dark wood furniture. No credit cards. ❷

Youth hostel

Pousada de Juventude Largo Cândido dos Reis 9 ☏ 244 831 868, ⊕ www.pousadasjuventude.pt. One of the nicest in the country, fashioned from a grand old house retaining its period features. It's also very close to the old-town bar scene. Dorm beds €9, summer €11.

Eating, drinking and nightlife

There are some good **restaurants** in the old town, with a particular cluster of traditional places on Rua Correia Mateus. September is the ideal time to sample the region's cuisine, when the **Festival de Gastronomia** hits town for nine days, featuring food stalls, restaurant promotions, concerts and crafts. Pretty Praça Rodrigues Lobo has the most popular **cafés** in town, while the **bar scene** is concentrated on Largo Cândido dos Reis and Rua Barão de Viamonte – you'll find all kinds of places tucked away in the alleys off here, from student dives to quite sophisticated lounge bars.

La Além Rua Maria da Fonte, no phone. An Alentejan bar-restaurant with terrace, tucked up a side alley. It's a cheapish place to try *migas*, grilled lamb, steaks and other specialities from Portugal's south. Inexpensive.

Malagueta Afrodisíaca Rua Gago Coutinho 17 ☎244 831 607. Contemporary style that comes as something of a shock in old-town Leiria, and a fun menu – though whether every dish is aphrodisiacal, you'll have to wait until you've eaten to find out. Plenty of fragrant curries – fish and prawn – but also a good chicken *fajita*, Brazilian *vatapá* (fish in palm oil), and a rare vegetarian selection. Dishes mostly €8–11. Dinner only. Moderate.

A Toca Rua Dr Correia Mateus ☎244 832 221. Large portions of traditional, well-cooked food – the *bife a vaca* arrives sizzling in an earthenware dish and the *lulas grelhado* is excellent. It's the best restaurant on the street. Closed Sat. Moderate.

Tromba Rija Rua Professores Portela 22, Marrazes ☎244 852 277. One of Portugal's most famous restaurants, a rustic charmer with an overloaded buffet table of around 100 different dishes, supplemented by roast *bacalhau* and *cabrito*. It's located out of town on the Marrazes road; go west under the N1 and turn left after the Casa da Palmeira. Closed Sun dinner & Mon. Expensive.

Listings

Hospital Hospital Distrital de Santo André, Rua das Olhalvas ☎244 817 000.
Internet Free access at Espaço Internet, at the restored Mercado Sant'Ana, Largo Sant'Ana, Av Combatentes da Grand Guerra (Mon-Fri 9am–7.30pm & 8–11pm, Sat 11am–1.30pm & 2.30–8pm).

Pharmacy Farmácia Batista, Largo 5 de Outubro 33–34 ☎244 832 320.
Police Police headquarters are before the castle on Largo São Pedro ☎244 859 859.
Taxis There's a rank in the main square, or call ☎244 815 900.

Pinhal de Leiria and its beaches

One of the finest stretches of coastline in the country flanks the **Pinhal de Leiria**, a vast 700-year-old pine forest west of Leiria stretching from São Pedro de Moel to Pedrógão. The pines were first planted in the fourteenth century by Dom Dinis, a king renowned for his agrarian reforms, to protect fertile arable land from the menacing inward march of sand dunes. Later, the trees were an essential resource when it came to fitting out ships during the Portuguese "discoveries". The *pinhal* is an area of great natural beauty, with sunlight filtering through endless miles of trees and the air perfumed with the scent of resin. There are bike lanes and tracks throughout the whole area, while beyond the dunes lie vast white-sand beaches soaking up the thundering breakers from the Atlantic. By public transport, the only realistic target is the small resort of São Pedro de Moel, though bikers and drivers will be able to find better, more isolated spots. Expect any of the beaches near São Pedro to be packed in July and August – the straight, fast coastal road north and south has been upgraded to cope with heavy summer traffic. Come any other time and you'll have the sands to yourself.

São Pedro de Moel and around

SÃO PEDRO DE MOEL, 22km west of Leiria, is a largely laid-back resort where old buildings have been renovated and new ones erected with an eye for tradition. Although it's now firmly a holiday-home development, it still resembles in part the fishing village it once was, with many houses boasting wooden balconies, louvred windows and climbing roses. A restored cobbled square sits back from a small central beach, while just to the north, 1km past the lighthouse, **Praia Velha** provides a fantastic sweep of sand. You can walk here – follow signs for "praias" from the roundabout – though the equally fine southern beaches of **Paredes** and **Pedra do Ouro** are a short drive away. North of São Pedro, it's 10km (15min drive) to **Praia da Vieira**, a more developed resort with a long line of beachfront cafés and deckchairs staked out under bamboo parasols. A bike lane runs through the trees all the way here from São Pedro de Moel.

Buses from Leiria sometimes involve a change at Marinha Grande, the congested small town halfway between Leiria and the coast. There are regular daily buses in summer, but the service is less frequent outside the holiday season. The buses stop at the roundabout at the top of São Pedro de Moel, where there's also a seasonal **turismo** (July & Aug Tues–Sun 10am–1pm & 3–7pm; ☎244 599 633). Even in high season you should be able to find accommodation, since most local visitors come for the day or rent (or own) holiday homes here. Still, making an advance reservation in August isn't a bad idea. Several places advertise **rooms** on the road down from the roundabout towards the clifftop; bear left near the church and you'll soon find the square and beach at the bottom of town.

Pensions and hotels

Residencial Água de Madeiros Água de Madeiros, 3km south ☎244 599 324. Sitting in a valley cleft, near often deserted sands (out of season, at least). Twelve nice rooms, plus bar, pool and terrace. ❹

Residencial Dom Fernando I Rua Dom Fernando I 19 ☎244 599 314. Follow the sign from the roundabout, on the way to the lighthouse and Praia Velha – a smallish place on the main road, with its own restaurant. No credit cards. ❸

Mar e Sol Av da Liberdade 1 ☎244 590 000, ⓦwww.hotelmaresol.com. Typical seaside three-star, straight down the hill from the turismo and on the cliffs above the sea. Rooms are hardly at the cutting edge of fashion, but they've all got a balcony and views (sea views cost more), and you can park right outside. Off-season rates are a good deal. ❹

Pensão Miramar Rua dos Serviços Florestais ☎244 599 141. The largest of several places with rooms, just down from the roundabout. It's a family-friendly place – some rooms have bunk-beds, and there's a restaurant downstairs – but despite the balconies it can be a bit dark and poky. Ask to see a couple of rooms. ❸

Campsites

Inatel Av do Farol ☎244 599 289, ⓦwww.inatel .pt. By the lighthouse on the Praia Velha road – it's less shaded than *Orbitur*, and not as well equipped, but it's cheaper. Closed mid-Dec to mid-Jan.

Orbitur Rua Volta dos Sete ☎244 599 168, ⓦwww.orbitur.pt. Closest to town, in the trees just above the turismo (600m from the beach), and packed in high season. It's good though, with a pool with slides, bar and restaurant, and bungalows for rent (from €49).

Restaurants

Brisamar Rua Dr Nicolau Bettencourt 23 ☎244 599 520. Regarded as the best in town, and augmenting its Portuguese menu with things like Greek salad, pasta or tuna steak. But you have to sit inside and there's no sense of being at the seaside. It's a block over from the *Pensão Miramar*. Expensive.

Estrela do Mar Av Marginal ☎244 599 245. Hard to beat for location, tucked into the cliffs above the main beach and with a lot of outdoor seating. The fish choice depends on what's been caught that day. Closed Thurs in winter. Moderate.

🏃 **O Pai dos Frangos** Praia Velha ☎244 599 158. Unmissable beach restaurant, which prepares sensational mixed kebabs (pork and bacon-wrapped prawns), plus grilled chicken, seafood rice and fresh fish. There's no better place for lunch – on the small outdoor terrace, or at tables by the huge picture windows. Closed Tues. Moderate.

Batalha

Eleven kilometres south of Leiria, the Mosteiro de Santa Maria da Vitória, better known as **Batalha** (Battle Abbey), is the supreme achievement of Portuguese architecture – the dazzling richness and originality of its Manueline decoration rivalled only by the Mosteiro dos Jerónimos at Belém, with which it shares UNESCO world monument status. An exuberant symbol of national pride, it was built to commemorate the battle that sealed Portugal's independence after decades of Spanish intrigue.

With the death of Dom Fernando in 1383, the royal house of Burgundy died out, and there followed a period of feverish factional plotting over the Portuguese throne. Fernando's widow, Leonor Teles, had a Spanish lover even during her husband's lifetime and, when Fernando died, she betrothed her daughter, Beatriz, to Juan I of Castile, encouraging his claim to the Portuguese throne. João, Mestre de Aviz, Fernando's illegitimate stepbrother, also claimed the throne. He assassinated Leonor's lover and braced himself for the inevitable invasion from Spain. The two armies clashed on August 14, 1385, at the **Battle of Aljubarrota**, which despite its name was actually fought at São Jorge (see p.205), 10km northeast of Aljubarrota and just 4km south of present-day Batalha. Faced with seemingly impossible odds, João struck a deal with the Virgin Mary, promising to build a magnificent abbey in return for her military assistance. It worked: Nuno Álvares Pereira led the Portuguese forces to a memorable victory and the new king duly summoned the finest architects of the day.

The abbey has spawned a modern village and is rattled by the N1 highway from Lisbon to Coimbra, which runs across an embankment perilously close to the building. Despite years of campaigning, no plans to shift the road have been forthcoming, and the vibrations and fumes are gradually taking their toll. Furthermore, the abbey is showing its age; built largely of limestone, it's increasingly affected by acid rain.

The Abbey

The honey-coloured **Abbey** (daily: April–Sept 9am–6pm; Oct–March 9am–5pm; last entry 30min before closing; main church and Capelas Imperfeitas free, cloisters €4.50, free Sun before 2pm) was transformed by the uniquely Portuguese Manueline additions of the late fifteenth and early sixteenth centuries, but the bulk of the building was actually completed between 1388 and 1434 in a profusely ornate version of French Gothic. Pinnacles, parapets, windows and flying buttresses are all lavishly and intricately sculpted. Within this flamboyant framework there are also strong elements of the English Perpendicular style. Huge pilasters and prominent vertical decorations divide the main facade; the nave, with its narrow soaring dimensions, and the chapterhouse are reminiscent of church architecture in the English cathedral cities of Winchester and York.

Capela do Fundador

Medieval architects were frequently attracted by lucrative foreign commissions, but there is a special explanation for the English influence at Batalha. This is revealed in the **Capela do Fundador** (Founder's Chapel), directly to the right upon entering the church. Beneath the octagonal lantern rests the joint tomb of Dom João I and Philippa of Lancaster, their hands clasped in the ultimate expression of harmonious relations between Portugal and England.

In 1373, Dom Fernando had entered into an alliance with John of Gaunt, Duke of Lancaster, who claimed the Spanish throne by virtue of his marriage to a daughter of Pedro the Cruel, king of Castile. A crack contingent of English longbowmen had played a significant role in the victory at Aljubarrota and in 1386 both countries willingly signed the **Treaty of Windsor**, "an inviolable, eternal, solid, perpetual and true league of friendship". As part of the same political package Dom João married Philippa, John of Gaunt's daughter, and with her came English architects to assist at Batalha. The alliance between the two countries, reconfirmed by the marriage of Charles II to Catherine of Bragança in 1661 and the Methuen Commercial Treaty of 1703, has become the longest-standing international friendship of modern times – it was invoked by the Allies in World War II to establish bases on the Azores and the facilities of those islands were offered to the British Navy during the 1982 Falklands war.

The four younger sons of João and Philippa are buried along the south wall of the Capela do Fundador in a row of recessed arches. Second from the right is the **tomb of Prince Henry the Navigator**, who guided the discovery of Madeira, the Azores and the African coast as far as Sierra Leone. Henry himself never ventured further than Tangiers but it was a measure of his personal importance, drive and expertise that the growth of the empire was temporarily shelved after his death in 1460.

Concerted maritime exploration resumed under João II (1481–95) and accelerated with the accession of Manuel I (1495–1521). Vasco da Gama opened up the trade route to India in 1498, Cabral reached Brazil two years later and Newfoundland was discovered in 1501. The momentous era of burgeoning self-confidence, wealth and widening horizons is reflected in the peculiarly Portuguese style of architecture known (after the king) as Manueline (see feature on p.214). As befitted the great national shrine, Batalha was adapted to incorporate two masterpieces of the new order: the Royal Cloister and the so-called Unfinished Chapels.

Claustro Real and Sala do Capítulo

In the **Claustro Real** (Royal Cloister), stone grilles of ineffable beauty and intricacy were added to the original Gothic windows by Diogo de Boitaca, architect of the cloister at Belém and the prime genius of Manueline art. Crosses of the Order of Christ and armillary spheres – symbols of overseas exploration – are entwined in a network of lotus blossom, briar branches and exotic vegetation.

Off the east side opens the early fifteenth-century **Sala do Capítulo** (chapterhouse), remarkable for the audacious unsupported span of its ceiling – so daring, in fact, that the Church authorities were convinced the whole chamber would come crashing down and employed condemned criminals to build it. The architect, Afonso Domingues, only finally silenced his critics by sleeping in the chamber night after night. Soldiers now stand guard here over Portugal's **Tomb of the Unknown Warriors**, one killed in France during World War I, the other in the country's colonial wars in Africa. The **refectory**, on the opposite side of the cloister, houses a military museum in their honour. From here, a short passage leads into the **Claustro de Dom Afonso V**, built in a conventional Gothic style, which provides a yardstick against which to measure the Manueline flamboyance of the Royal Cloister.

Capelas Imperfeitas

The **Capelas Imperfeitas** (Unfinished Chapels) form a separate structure tacked on to the east end of the church and accessible only from outside the main complex. Dom Duarte, eldest son of João and Philippa, commissioned

△ Capelas Imperfeitas

them in 1437 as a royal mausoleum but, as with the cloister, the original design was transformed beyond all recognition by Dom Manuel's architects. The portal rises to a towering fifteen metres and every centimetre is carved with a honeycomb of mouldings: florid projections, linked chains, clover-shaped arches, strange vegetables and even crawling stone snails. The place is unique among Christian architecture and evocative of the great shrines of Islam and Hinduism: perhaps it was inspired by the tales of Indian monuments that filtered back along the eastern trade routes. It is a perfect illustration of the variety and uninhibited excitement of Portuguese art during the Age of Discovery.

The architect of this masterpiece was Mateus Fernandes (whose memorial slab lies directly inside the main church entrance). Within the chapel portal, a large octagonal space is surrounded by seven hexagonal chapels, two of which contain the sepulchres of Dom Duarte and his queen, Leonor of Aragon. An ambitious upper storey – equal in magnificence to the portal – was designed by Diogo de Boitaca, but the huge buttresses were abandoned a few years later in 1533.

Practicalities

Buses (from Leiria, Fatima and Lisbon) stop on the cobbled square-cum-car park, Largo 14 de Agosto de 1385, at the top end of which the Batalha is visible, on the right, standing alone surrounded by a bare plaza. There's a **turismo** located by the abbey (May–Sept daily 9am–1pm & 3–7pm; Oct–April daily 9am–1pm & 2–6pm; ℡244 765 180), with a sprinkling of tourist shops, bars and restaurants beyond. The large abbey **car park** is the most convenient place to leave your car, though there's plenty of overspill parking in the village beyond.

Most visitors see the abbey and leave, so finding **accommodation** is rarely a problem, should you wish to stay – to be honest, there isn't anything attractive about the village itself (Alcobaça or Leiria are the nicer overnight stops), though it's peaceful once the days' tour buses have left. The **cafés** that flank the abbey plaza are the best places to soak up the views, though none of the **restaurants** stand out – all offer standard menus at moderate prices.

Hotels and pensions

Hotel Residencial Batalha Largo da Igreja ☎ 244 767 500, ⓦ www.hotel-batalha.com. On the through-road that runs around the abbey, this is a comfortable mid-range choice, with decently decorated rooms, some with abbey views. ❸

Casa do Outeiro Largo Carvalho do Outeiro 4 ☎ 244 765 806, ⓦ www.casadoouteiro.com. Signposted 100m up a side road, this small boutique hotel with swimming pool has fifteen bright, a/c rooms, all with terrace (though only some have the abbey view). It's very contemporary – white walls, wooden floors, modern art, stylish furniture and plenty of light. ❸

Residencial Gladius Pr Mousinho de Albuquerque 7 ☎ 244 765 760, ⓕ 244 767 259. The best budget option, right by the abbey – charming en-suite rooms with tasteful fabrics. Has a terrace café below. No credit cards. ❶

Restaurant

Pensão Vitória Largo da Misericórdia ☎ 244 765 678. Don't bother about the rooms – but the *churrasqueira* here is where the locals call in for their takeaway grilled chicken and pork. There's a shaded terrace for diners (and an indoor dining room), and meat fresh from the grill at bargain prices. It's just up from the bus stop (or, from the road, behind *Totta* bank). Inexpensive.

São Jorge: the battle site

The Battle of Aljubarrota was fought on a plain 10km northeast of Aljubarrota itself, at the small hamlet of **São Jorge**, 4km south of Batalha. When the fighting was over a small **chapel** was built and remains at the entrance to the village today. The battle lasted only one hour, but it was a hot day and the commander of the victorious Portuguese forces, Nuno Álvares Pereira, complained loudly of thirst; a jug of fresh water is still placed daily in the porch of the chapel in his memory. Legend has it that Aljubarrota itself was defended by its baker, Brites de Almeida, who fended off the Castilian army with her baking spoon. This fearsome weapon dispensed with seven soldiers, whom Brites promptly baked in her oven.

A short path leads from the chapel to the **Museu Militar** (under restoration in 2006; free), which tackles the battle itself and the contemporary political intrigue. Nearby there's a rather good stone frieze commemorating the battle.

None of this is really enough reason for a special visit, although you can break your journey here on the way to or from Porto de Mós (see below), another 5km to the southeast.

Porto de Mós and around

Eight kilometres south of Batalha lies the small riverside town of **Porto de Mós**, with its distinctive castle. Further south and east extends the **Parque Natural das Serras de Aire e Candeeiros**, a mix of rugged limestone hills, crags and upland farmland divided by ancient stone walls. There are walking trails in both the Aire and Candeeiros ranges, but the *parque natural* is better known for its fabulous **underground caves**, which all lie in a rough triangle between Porto de Mós and Fátima, on the west side of the A1 motorway.

Meanwhile, across the motorway on the east side of the Serra de Aire, Portugal has its own Jurassic Park where you can walk with dinosaurs at the **Pegadas dos Dinossáurios**. You can reach Porto de Mós and the main caves at Mire de Aire by bus, though it can be a time-consuming business involving a change or two – with a car, the caves and dinosaur site are an easy combined day out from Leiria, Nazaré or Tomar.

Porto de Mós

High above **PORTO DE MÓS**, nestled in the folds of the hills, a grandiose thirteenth-century castle stands guard. It was given to Nuno Álvares Pereira in 1385 by the grateful Dom João I, in recognition of his victory at Aljubarrota – significantly, the Portuguese army had rested here on the eve of the battle – and was later turned into a fortified palace reminiscent in scale of that at Leiria. Severely damaged in the earthquake of 1755, the castle has been renovated piecemeal since, and now boasts rather too pristine electric-green tiled towers.

Realistically, you are only going to stop in Porto de Mós if you need transport to the caves of Mira de Aire, 13km to the southeast (see below). The **bus station** (services from Leiria via Batalha, and from Alcobaça) is a short walk from the riverside gardens, where you'll find the **turismo** (May–Sept daily 10am–1pm & 3–7pm; Oct–Apr Mon–Sat 10am–1pm & 3–6pm; ☎244 491 323) – there's plenty of information here on the caves and the dinosaur site. **Accommodation** is available in town at *O Filipe*, Largo do Rossio 41 (☎244 401 455, ⓦwww.ofilipe.com; ❷), a renovated *residencial* by the main roundabout, just down from the turismo. There are also two good **rural tourism** places on the signposted road to the caves (the N243): nearest to town, 1km out, the serene *Quinta do Rio Alcaide* (☎244 402 124, Ⓔrioalcaide@ mail.telepac.pt; ❷; breakfast available) is a converted mill with rooms (including in the windmill), and self-catering studios and larger apartments, plus a swimming pool; while further along at Alvados is *Casa dos Matos* (☎244 440 393, ⓦwww.casadosmatos.com; ❹), a very attractive contemporary country home with plenty of exposed stone and coordinated fabrics, honesty bar, pool and terrace.

Visiting the caves

There are four sets of caves open to the public in the natural park, but unless you are a real fan, a visit to one will probably suffice. As it happens, the largest and most spectacular, at **Mira de Aira**, is the only one directly accessible by bus.

Grutas de Mira de Aire

It's a fabulous thirteen-kilometre drive out into the hills along the N243 from Porto de Mós to the **Grutas de Mira de Aire** (daily from 9.30am – April & May until 6pm, June & Sept 7pm, July & Aug 8.30pm & Oct–March 5.30pm; €4.80; ⓦwww.grutasmiradeaire.com), Portugal's largest show caves, set just outside the drab textile town from which they take their name – there's parking right outside, or it's a signposted one-kilometre walk from the town bus stop. Known locally for decades, but only open to the public since 1974, the caves comprise a fantasy land of spaghetti-like stalactites and stalagmites and bizarre rock formations with names like "Hell's Door", "Jelly Fish" and "Church Organ". The 45-minute guided tour (in English on occasion) culminates in an extravagant fountain display in a natural lake 110m underground; you then take the lift up to emerge beside an aquatic park (summer only; included in the entry fee), a great place to cool off and admire the views. Outside on the road, several cafés and restaurants cater for the crowds.

Porto de Mós turismo has up-to-date local **bus** details, but there are usually two useful daily services (not Sun) to Mira de Aire with Rodoviária do Tejo, currently departing at 12.05 and 2.30pm; it's a half-hour journey. A return service leaves Mira de Aire at around 1.30 and 6.30pm, though there may be other regional services that pass through Mira de Aire and Porto de Mós.

Grutas de Alvados, Santo António and Moeda

There's a combination ticket available to see the **Grutas de Alvados** and neighbouring **Grutas Santo António** (both daily from 9.30am – April & May until 6pm, June & Sept 7pm, July & Aug 8.30pm, and Oct–March 5.30pm; €4.80 each, or €8 for both; ⓦwww.grutasalvados.com, ⓦwww.grutassantoantonio.com) – Santo António has the most impressive stalagmites and stalactites of any of the local caves. The turn-off for these caves is signposted from the N243 before you reach Mira de Aire – you could jump off the Mira de Aire bus, but you're faced with a three-kilometre walk to Alvados and then another 1km to Santo António.

The final series of caves lies further north, off the road between Batalha and Fátima road (N356). The labyrinthine **Grutas da Moeda** at São Mamede (daily: April–June 9am–6pm; July–Sept 9am–7pm; Oct–March 9am–5pm; €4; ⓦwww.grutasmoeda.com) have little that hasn't already been seen, save a chamber that has been converted into a bar with subtle lighting and stalactites nose-diving into your glass of beer.

Pegadas dos Dinossáurios

In a quarry around 10km south of Fátima, paleontologists made an extraordinary discovery in 1994 – namely the oldest and longest set of preserved sauropod tracks found anywhere in the world. The tracks date back 175 million years, and were made as the large herbivores plodded through a shallow lagoon, later preserved as limestone. They are now on display in situ at the excellent **Monumental Natural das Pegadas dos Dinossáurios** (Tues–Sun 10am–12.30pm & 2–7pm; mid-March to mid-Sept until 8pm at weekends; also open Mon in Aug; €2; ⓦwww.pegadasdedinossaurios.org), where a one-and-a-half-kilometre gravel walkway circles the site on high before dropping down to the quarry floor. You can clearly see the footprints (*pegadas*) – hundreds of them, exceptionally well preserved – and follow their route across the stone for around 150 metres; by the spacing, paleontologists reckon that some of the sauropods were up to thirty metres long. There's a video shown at the ticket office, though it's hard to resist the temptation to make straight for the tracks.

The site is signposted from either Fátima or Torres Novas directions, and is just outside the village of Bairro, off the N360 – you'll pick up the signs at Boleiros if you head towards Fátima (via Minde) after seeing the caves. There's only a picnic ground at the site, but 1km back, at Bairro, *O Transmontano* (☎249 521 701; closed Mon) is an inexpensive **restaurant** catering mainly to locals, especially on Sundays when it's packed.

Fátima

FÁTIMA is the fountainhead of religious devotion in Portugal and one of the most important centres of pilgrimage in the Roman Catholic world. Its cult is founded on a series of six supposed apparitions of the Virgin Mary, the first of which, on May 13, 1917, was to three peasant children from the village who were confronted with a flash of lightning and "a lady brighter than the sun" sitting in the branches of a tree.

Since then, Fátima's celebrity has increased exponentially and where once was a simple farming village now stands a vast white basilica fronted by a gigantic esplanade capable of holding more than a million devotees. A multitude of hotels, pilgrims' hostels, car parks, hospices, convents, cafés and restaurants have sprung up in the shadow of the basilica while, seemingly inevitably with each year, the souvenir shops explore new territories of tackiness. Quite what you

Miracles, secrets and pilgrimages

The three Fátima children – Lúcia, Jacinta and Francisco – were tending their parents' sheep when, according to Lúcia's memoirs, the **Virgin Mary appeared** and announced: "I am from Heaven. I have come to ask you to return here six times, at this same hour, on the thirteenth of every month. Then, in October, I will tell you who I am and what I want". News of the miracle was first greeted with scepticism – the Virgin having an uncannily exact grasp of the temporal calendar – and only a few casual onlookers attended the second appearance, but for the third apparition, on July 13, the crowd had swollen to a few thousand. Although only the three children could see the heavenly visitor, Fátima became a *cause célèbre*, with the anticlerical government accusing the Church of fabricating a miracle to revive its flagging influence and Church authorities afraid to acknowledge what they feared was a hoax. The children were arrested and interrogated but refused to change their story. By the date of the final appearance, October 13, 1917, as many as 70,000 people witnessed the so-called **Miracle of the Sun**: a blinding, swirling ball of fire, shooting beams of multicoloured light to earth and, just for good measure, curing lifelong illnesses, and enabling the blind to see again and the dumb to speak.

Only to Lúcia were revealed the three **Secrets of Fátima**. The first a message of peace and a vision of Hell that – during World War I – struck the required populist chord. The second was more prophetic and more useful to the Catholic Church: "If you pay heed to my request", the vision declared, "Russia will be converted and there will be peace" – all this just a few weeks before the Bolshevik takeover in St Petersburg, though not, perhaps, before it could have been predicted. After decades of speculation, the third secret was revealed in May 2000, apparently predicting the attempt on Pope John Paul II's life in 1981. The complete text was released after "appropriate" preparation by the Vatican, whereupon conspiracy theorists pointed out inconsistencies in the commentary and Lúcia's handwriting, and muttered darkly about a forgery.

Lúcia's fellow witnesses both died in the European flu epidemic of 1919–20, while **Lúcia** herself later retreated to the Convent of Santa Teresa near Coimbra. Cocooned from the outside world, crafting rosaries as a Carmelite nun, she was known by all in Portugal as Irmã (Sister) Lúcia. The elderly bespectacled nun made an unlikely pin-up, but her image is as ubiquitous in Fátima as that of the Virgin herself, set poignantly against the fading, black-and-white childhood photographs of Jacinta and Francisco, cast forever in a supporting role by their early deaths.

It's difficult to over-estimate the significance of Fátima to most ordinary Catholic Portuguese, many of whom will make at least part of the **pilgrimage** there at some point. However, unlike Spanish Santiago de Compostela, say, where the pilgrim routes have had centuries to establish themselves along traditional tracks and paths, the routes to Fátima are virtually all along main roads. For a few weeks before May 13 and October 13 each year, it's common to see pilgrims in reflective jackets, marching along the hard shoulders in the blazing heat.

make of it all depends largely on your beliefs – it is, after all, a place built entirely on faith. However, the crowds create an undeniable atmosphere, at its most intense during the great **annual pilgrimages** of May 12–13 and October 12–13. At these times, several hundred thousand people congregate, most arriving on foot from throughout the country, some completing the journey on their knees in penance. The fiftieth anniversary of the apparitions attracted one-and-a-half million worshippers, while more vast crowds greeted John Paul II here in 1982 and 1991. Most recently, the death of the last surviving child witness, Lúcia, in 2005, was marked as a national event – amid blanket media coverage she was buried in the basilica in February 2006, and it's no exaggeration to say that the entire country came to a halt to watch.

The basilica and town

Everything in town is centred on the basilica, completed in 1953, which has little to recommend it but size. Long Neoclassical colonnades enclose part of the huge, sloping **esplanade** in front – twice the size of the piazza of St Peter's in Rome – over which Gregorian chant wafts from flanking speakers. Marble-slab pathways gleam in the sun, polished by the knees of thousands of penitents. The original oak tree in which the Virgin supposedly appeared was long ago consumed by souvenir-hunting pilgrims; the tiny **Capelinha das Aparições** (Chapel of the Apparitions) now stands in its place under a glass hangar, with a new tree a few yards away ringed by a wall. In the **Basílica do Santuário** itself are the tombs of Lúcia, Jacinta and Francisco, while at the top of the esplanade another epic church is under construction. On completion (during 2007) the circular **Igreja de Santíssima Trindade** will be able to hold 9000 faithful pilgrims. There are regular daily masses held in both basilica and chapel – times are posted; some are in English – and a torchlit procession at dusk, largest on the twelfth day of each month.

The esplanade slices the small town in half; on its west side is the main pedestrian street, Rua Jacinta Marto, which becomes Rua Francisco Marto when it reappears on the eastern side. For all but the most devout, a tour around the widely advertised "attractions" is largely an exploration of the grotesque and the kitsch, from the Wax Museum ("29 scenes!, 112 figures!") to the Museum of Apparitions 1917 ("Be present during the Vision of Hell!"), while every shop window displays an endlessly inventive array of *artigos religiosos*. You can get an awful lot of tacky souvenirs for just a few euros – Apparition snowflakes, Virgin Mary keyrings and ballpoint pens, bottled Fátima water, Sister Lúcia desk ornaments – or spend hundreds on a gilded statue of a martyred saint. A **mini-train** (daily 9am–6pm, every 30min; €3.50) trundles around the locality connecting up all the other sights on the Fátima trail, including the original houses of the children, assorted apparition sites and a Sacred Way.

Practicalities

The basilica and town lie just off the A1 motorway, flanked by two large traffic circles (*rotundas*) – Rotunda Norte, nearest the bus station (see below) is the one with the statues of the three shepherd children. Vast **car parks** ring the basilica, while provided you don't coincide with a pilgrimage you'll easily find street parking in the town as well. Otherwise, it's an easy trip by bus from Batalha (18km northwest), Leiria (25km northwest) or Tomar (35km east). Fátima is on the main Lisbon–Porto train line, but the Estação de Fátima is 25km east of town and there's not always an immediate bus connection. The **bus station** is on Avenida Dom José Alves Correia da Silva, which is the main through avenue between the rotundas – turn right along the avenue and walk for 500m to reach the **turismo** (daily: May–Sept 10am–1pm & 3–7pm; Oct–April 10am–1pm & 3–6pm; ☎249 531 139, ⓦwww.rt-leiriafatima.pt), with basilica and town just up to the north of here.

Accommodation abounds and outside the major pilgrimages and weekends there's enough to go round, especially as many of the older boarding houses are built on monastic lines, with scores of rooms and private chapels. The turismo's map of town (also viewable online) lists thirty options alone. During the pilgrimages (when most accommodation is booked up months in advance and prices double) people camp around the back and sides of the basilica. All this said, it's hard to recommend spending the night in Fátima. It really is a very small place, with nothing to do, and while there is also a glut of **cafés and restaurants**, they are all geared towards tourists and pilgrims and none is particularly inspiring.

Ourém

For a better overnight stop altogether than Fátima, aim for **OURÉM**, 12km to the east. From the lower new town, Vila Nova de Ourém, a winding road climbs for 2km up to Ourém castle (Tues 2–6pm, Wed–Sun 10am–1pm & 2–6pm; free), crowning a hill above a cosy nest of medieval lanes, a clutch of old stone houses and a church or two. The town's heyday was in the fifteenth century, when the fourth count of Ourém, Dom Afonso, built several grand monuments and converted the castle into a palace. The castle was virtually destroyed by Napoleon's forces, but is now largely restored. You can walk around its parapet, walls and towers for a marvellous, sweeping panorama, with the basilica of Fátima visible away to the west.

A couple of small places offer rooms, but it's the *Pousada Conde de Ourém* (☎249 540 920, ⓦwww.pousadas.pt; ⓺) that really makes a stay here. It's been fashioned from several fifteenth-century buildings to create a stylish hotel, most of whose rooms have far-reaching views (though only three have balconies). There's a nice terrace-bar and courtyard, while across the street from reception is a fabulous terrace and outdoor pool with more extensive views.

Tomar

The Convento de Cristo at **TOMAR**, 34km east of Fátima, is an artistic *tour de force* which entwines the most outstanding military, religious and imperial strands in the history of Portugal. The Order of the Knights Templar and their successors, the Order of Christ, established their headquarters here and successive Grand Masters employed experts in Romanesque, Manueline and Renaissance architecture to embellish and expand the convent in a manner worthy of their power, prestige and wealth.

In addition, Tomar is a handsome small town in its own right, well worth a couple of days of slow exploration. Built on a simple grid plan, it is split in two by the **Rio Nabão**, with almost everything of interest on the west bank. Here, Tomar's old quarters preserve much of their traditional charm, with whitewashed, terraced cottages lining narrow cobbled streets that frame the convent above.

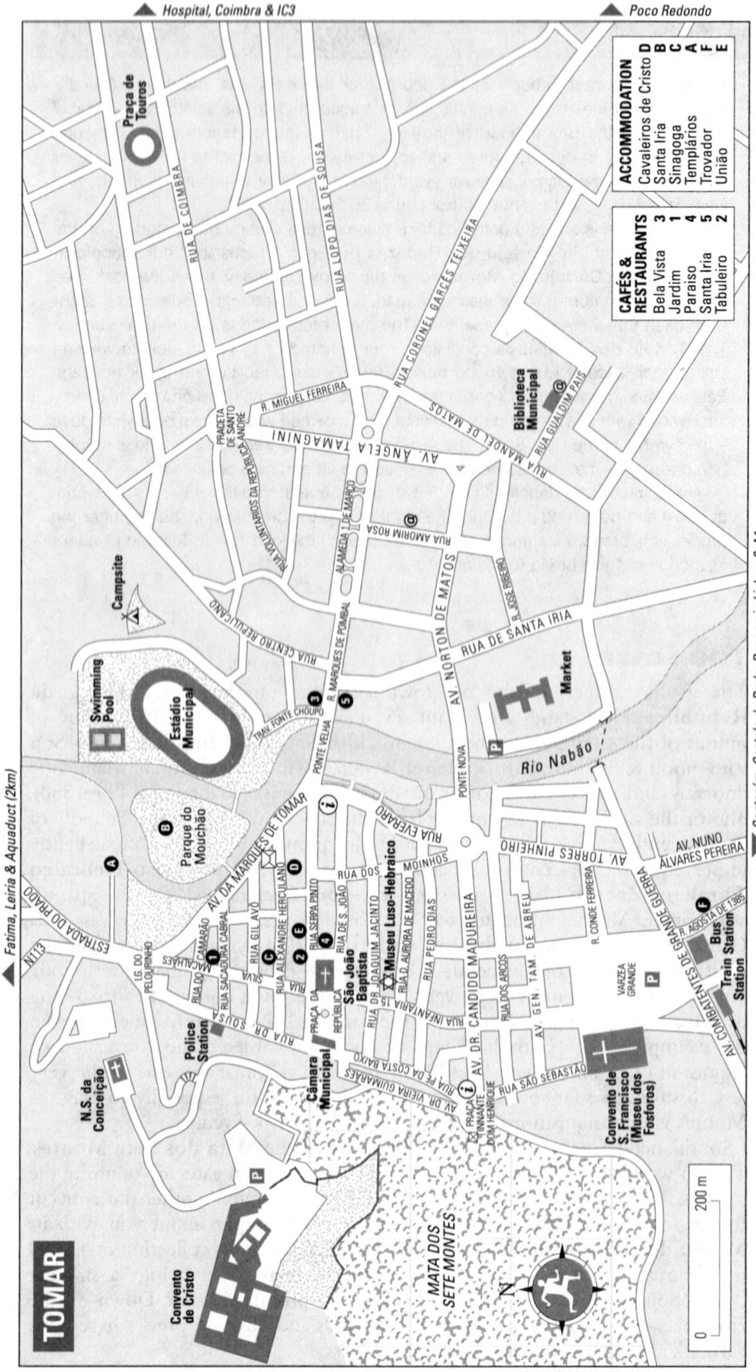

TOMAR
Hospital, Coimbra & IC3
Poco Redondo
Fatima, Leiria & Aquaduct (2km)
Santarém, Castelo do Bode, Reservoir, Lisbon & A1
Torres Novas & N349
CAFÉS & RESTAURANTS
Bela Vista 3
Jardim 1
Paraiso 4
Santa Iria 5
Tabuleiro 2
ACCOMMODATION
Cavaleiros de Cristo D
Santa Iria B
Sinagoga C
Templários A
Trovador F
União E
Praça de Touros
Campsite
Swimming Pool
Estádio Municipal
Parque do Mouchão
Rio Nabão
Market
Biblioteca Municipal
Museu Luso-Hebraico
São João Baptista
Câmara Municipal
Police Station
N.S. da Conceição
Convento de Cristo
Convento de S. Francisco (Museu dos Fosforos)
MATA DOS SETE MONTES
Bus Station
Train Station
VARZEA GRANDE
RUA DE COIMBRA
RUA LOPO DIAS DE SOUSA
RUA CORONEL GARCÊS TEIXEIRA
R. MIGUEL FERREIRA
PRACETA DE SANTO ANDRÉ
AV. ÂNGELA TAMAGNINI
RUA MANUEL DE MATOS
RUA GUALDIM PAIS
RUA VOLUNTÁRIOS DA REPÚBLICA
ALAMEDA 1 DE MARÇO
RUA AMORIM ROSA
AV. NORTON DE MATOS
R. JOSÉ RIBEIRO
RUA DE SANTA IRIA
RUA CENTRO REPUBLICANO
R. MARQUES DE POMBAL
TRAV. FONTE CHOUPO
PONTE VELHA
PONTE NOVA
AV. DA MARQUÊS DE TOMAR
RUA EVERARDO
AV. TORRES PINHEIRO
AV. NUNO ÁLVARES PEREIRA
RUA DOS MOINHOS
RUA SERPA PINTO
RUA DE S. JOÃO
RUA DR. JOAQUIM JACINTO
RUA D. AURORA DE MACEDO
RUA PEDRO DIAS
AV. DR. CANDIDO MADUREIRA
R. CONDE FERREIRA
AV. GEN. TAM. DE ABREU
RUA DOS ARCOS
RUA INFANTARIA 15
RUA ALEXANDRE HERCULANO
RUA GIL AVÔ
RUA SACADURA CABRAL
RUA DO CAMARÃO
MACHADES
SILVA
LG. DO PELOURINHO
ESTRADA DO PRADO
N113
RUA DR. SOUSA
PRAÇA DA REPÚBLICA
RUA PÉ DA COSTA BAIXO
RUA DR. VIEIRA GUIMARÃES
RUA SÃO SEBASTIÃO
PRAÇA INFANTE DOM HENRIQUE
AV. COMBATENTES DE GRANDE GUERRA
R. AGOSTA DE 1385
200 m
N

The Festa dos Tabuleiros

Tomar is renowned throughout the country for its **Festa dos Tabuleiros** (literally, the Festival of the Trays). Its origins can be traced back to the saintly Queen Isabel who founded the Brotherhood of the Holy Spirit in the fourteenth century, though some believe it to derive from an ancient fertility rite dedicated to Ceres. Whatever its origins, it's now a largely secular event, held at four-yearly intervals during the first week in July; the next event runs from June 30 to July 9, 2007.

Various processions and activities take place across several days, starting on the first Sunday with the **Cortejo dos Rapazes** or "Boys' Procession" (for schoolchildren), with the **Cortejo do Mordomo** on the following Friday, when the costumed festival coordinators parade their carriages, carts and cattle (symbols of the sacrificial oxen that were once presented). The main procession is on the final Sunday. The **Cortejo dos Tabuleiros** consists of four hundred or so young women wearing white, each escorted by a young man in a white shirt, red tie and black trousers. Each woman carries on her head a tray with thirty loaves threaded on vertical canes, intertwined with leaves and paper flowers, and crowned with a cross or a white dove – the symbol of the Holy Spirit. The resulting headdress weighs 15kg, and is roughly person-height – hence the need for an escort to lift and help balance it.

There's music and dancing in the flower-filled streets, traditional games, fireworks at dawn and dusk, and a bullfight the night before the procession. The day after the procession, bread, wine and beef are distributed to the local needy, following Isabel's injunction to "give bread to the poor".

The town

The gridded streets of the old town converge on the central **Praça da República**. Here stands an elegant seventeenth-century town hall, a ring of houses of the same period and the church of **São João Baptista** (Tues–Sun 9am–noon & 3–7pm), remarkable for its octagonal belfry, elaborate Manueline doorway and six religious panels attributed to Gregório Lopes (1490–1550), one of the finest artists to emerge from the so-called "Portuguese School" of the sixteenth century. Nearby, at Rua Dr. Joaquim Jacinto 73, is an excellently preserved fifteenth-century synagogue, now the **Museu Luso-Hebraico Abraham Zacuto** (daily 10am–1pm & 2–6pm; free), named after the Spanish astronomer, Abraham Zacuto, who prepared navigational aids for Vasco da Gama. Its stark interior, with plain vaults supported by four slender columns, houses a collection of thirteenth- to fourteenth-century Hebraic inscriptions, but the interest lies more in its very survival in a town dominated for so long by crusading Christian Defenders of the Faith. In 1496 Dom Manuel followed the example of the Catholic Kings of Spain and ordered the conversion or expulsion of all Portuguese Jews. The synagogue at Tomar was one of the very few to survive so far south. Many Jews fled northwards, especially to Trás-os-Montes where Inquisitional supervision was less hawk-eyed.

South and east, below the convent walls, spreads the **Mata dos Sete Montes**, a green wooded area that's excellent for picnics; the main gates are opposite the turismo, facing a fierce statue of Infante Dom Henrique. Another old convent to the south, São Francisco, facing Varzea Grande, might tempt you with its **Museu dos Fosforos** (daily 2–5pm; free), which claims its collection of 40,000 matchboxes is Europe's largest – although its boast of it being "a singular description of universal history and culture" is pushing it a bit. Down on the river, between the bridges, the town's old mills and olive-oil presses have been earmarked by the council for cultural purposes.

Out of town, the highlight is the stunning seventeenth-century **Aqueduto Pegões**, built to supply the convent with water. The best place to see it is 2km from town, signposted (Pegões) off the N113 Leiria road, where a double-storey L-shaped sweep strides across a fertile valley.

Convento de Cristo

The dramatic **Convento de Cristo** (daily: June–Sept 9am–6.30pm; Oct–May 9am–5.30pm; last entrance 30min before closing; closed public holidays; €4.50) is about a quarter of an hour's walk uphill from the centre of town. Founded in 1162 by Gualdim Pais, first and grandest Master of the Knights Templar, it was the headquarters of the Order and, as such, both a religious and a military centre. It's an enormous complex, packed with interest, and though you could whip around the main highlights in an hour, a longer tour could easily take two or three hours. You're given a comprehensive English-language guide and floor-plan on entry, and there's a small café inside with terrace seating.

The Charola of the Knights Templars

One of the main objectives of the **Knights Templars** was to expel the Moors from Spain and Portugal, a reconquest seen always as a crusade – the defence of Christianity against the infidel. Spiritual strength was an integral part of the military effort and, despite magnificent additions, the sacred heart of the whole complex remains the **Charola** (also known as the Rotunda or Templars' Apse), the twelfth-century temple from which the knights drew their moral conviction. It is a strange place, more suggestive of the occult than of Christianity. At the centre of the almost circular sixteen-sided chapel stands the high altar, surrounded by a two-storeyed octagon. Deep alcoves decorated with sixteenth-century paintings are cut into the outside walls. The Templars are said to have attended Mass on horseback. Like almost every circular church, it is ultimately

△ Convento de Cristo

Manueline architecture

With the new-found wealth and confidence engendered by the "Discoveries", came a distinctly Portuguese version of late Gothic architecture. Named after King Manuel I (1495–1521), the **Manueline style** is characterized by a rich and often fantastical use of ornamentation. Doors, windows and arcades are encrusted by elaborately carved stonework, in which the imagery of the sea is freely combined with both symbols of Christianity and of the newly discovered lands.

The style first appeared at the Igreja de Jesus (1494–98), in **Setúbal**, where each of the columns of the nave are made up of three strands of stone seemingly wrapped around each other like rope. This relatively restrained building is the work of Diogo Boitac, who later supervised the initial construction of the great Jéronimos monastery at **Bélem**, a few miles downstream from Lisbon. Commissioned by the king, this is a far more exuberant structure with an elaborately carved south portal opening onto a nave where the vaulting ribs seem to sprout out of the thin, trunk-like columns like leaves from a palm tree. Bélem was the point from which many of the Portuguese navigators set forth, and the new building was largely subsidized by the new, lucrative spice trade.

The Jéronimos monastery is the most unified expression of the new style, but Manuel I also commissioned lavish extensions to existing buildings, like the Convento do Cristo at **Tomar**. This is arguably the most brilliant and original expression of Manueline decoration. In particular, the famous chapterhouse window is a riot of virtuosic stone carving, in which twisted strands of coral, opulent flower heads and intricately knotted ropes are crowned by the royal coat of arms, the cross of the Order of Christ and two armillary spheres.

The armillary sphere – a navigational instrument – became the personal emblem of King Manuel, and frequently appears in Manueline decoration. It can be seen at the great abbey at **Batalha** in the screens set within the top half of the arches of the Claustro Real (Royal Cloister). The intricate tracery of these screens suggest Islamic filigree work and may well have been directly influenced by buildings in India. Beyond the church is a royal mausoleum begun by King Duarte and continued by King Manuel I but never completed. This octagonal building with seven radiating chapels is entered through a vast trefoil-arched portal that is smothered in a profusion of ornament (including snails and artichokes) that seems to defy the material from which it's carved.

Not all Manueline architecture was ecclesiastical: there were also palaces, like that of the Dukes of Bragança at **Vila Viçosa**, and castles, like the one at **Évora Monte** where the whole of the exterior is bound by a single stone rope. Most famous of all secular constructions is Lisbon's **Torre de Bélem**, a fortress built on an island in the Tejo which incorporates Moorish-style balconies, domed lookout posts, battlements in the form of shields, and even a carving of a rhinoceros.

Manueline architecture did not continue much beyond the fourth decade of the sixteenth century. In the reign of Manuel's successor, King João III, a more austere religious atmosphere prevailed in which the decorative excesses of the Manueline style were replaced by the ordered sobriety of Italian classicism.

based on the Church of the Holy Sepulchre in Jerusalem, for whose protection the Order of the Knights Templar was originally founded.

Claustro do Cemitério, Claustro da Lavagem and Chapterhouse

By 1249 the Reconquest in Portugal was completed and the Templars reaped enormous rewards for their service. Tracts of land were turned over to them and they controlled a network of castles throughout the Iberian peninsula. But as the Moorish threat receded, the knights became a powerful political challenge to the stability and authority of European monarchs.

Philippe-le-Bel, King of France, took the lead by confiscating all Templar property in his country and there followed a formal papal suppression of the order in 1314. In Spain this prompted a vicious witch-hunt and many of the knights sought refuge in Portugal, where Dom Dinis coolly reconstituted them in 1320 under a different title: the **Order of Christ**. They inherited all the Portuguese property of the Templars, including the headquarters at Tomar, but their power was now subject to that of the throne.

In the fifteenth and sixteenth centuries, the Order of Christ played a leading role in extending Portugal's overseas empire and was granted spiritual jurisdiction over all conquests. Prince Henry the Navigator was Grand Master from 1417 to 1460 and the remains of his palace in the Convento de Cristo can be seen immediately to the right upon entering the castle walls. Henry ordered two new *azulejo*-lined cloisters, the **Claustro do Cemitério** and the **Claustro da Lavagem**, the latter used for domestic tasks like the washing of monks' robes.

Dom Manuel succeeded to the Grand Mastership in 1492, three years before he became king (1495–1521). Flush with imperial wealth, he decided to expand the convent by adding a rectangular **nave** to the west side of the Charola. This new structure was divided into two storeys: the lower serving as a chapterhouse, the upper as a choir. The **main doorway**, which leads directly into the nave, was built by João de Castilho in 1515, two years before Dom Manuel appointed him Master of Works at Belém. Characteristically unconcerned with structural matters, the architect adorned the doorway with profuse appliqué decoration. There are strong similarities in this respect with contemporary Isabelline and Plateresque architecture in Spain.

The crowning highlight of Tomar, though, is the sculptural ornamentation of the windows on the main facade of the **chapterhouse**. The richness and self-confidence of Manueline art always suggests the Age of Discovery, but here the connection is crystal clear. A wide range of maritime motifs is jumbled up in two tumultuous window frames, as eternal memorials to the sailors who established the Portuguese Empire. Everything is here: anchors, buoys, sails, coral, seaweed and especially ropes, knotted over and over again into an escapologist's nightmare.

The windows can only be fully appreciated from the roof of the **Claustro de Santa Bárbara**, adjacent to the Great Cloisters, which unfortunately almost completely obscure a similar window on the south wall of the chapterhouse.

Conventual buildings and Claustro Príncipal

João III (1521–57) transformed the convent from the general political headquarters of the Order into a monastic community and he endowed it with the necessary **conventual buildings**: monks' cells, dormitories, kitchens, refectory, storerooms, offices and no fewer than four new cloisters (making a grand total of seven). Yet another, much more classical, style was introduced into the architectural melange of Tomar. So meteoric was the rise and fall of Manueline art within the reign of Dom Manuel that, to some extent, it must have reflected his personal tastes. João III on the other hand had an entirely different view of art. He is known to have sent schools of architects and sculptors to study in Italy and his reign finally marked the much-delayed advent of the Renaissance in Portugal.

The two-tiered **Claustro Príncipal** (Great Cloisters), abutting the chapter-house, is one of the purest examples of this new style. Begun in 1557, they present a textbook illustration of the principals of Renaissance Neoclassicism. Greek columns, gentle arches and simple rectangular bays produce a wonderfully restrained rhythm. At the southwest corner a balcony looks out on to the skeletal remains of a second chapterhouse, begun by João III but never completed.

Practicalities

The **train** and **bus stations**, on Avenida Combatentes da Grande Guerra, are within easy walking distance of the centre. Head directly north across the open space of Varzea Grande and you'll soon hit Avenida Dr Cândido Madureira, at the eastern end of which there's the **turismo** (daily: April–Sept Mon–Fri 10am–7pm, Sat & Sun 10am–1pm & 2–6pm; Oct–March daily 10am–1pm & 2–6pm; ☏ 249 329 823, ⓦ www.tomartourism.com). Free **parking** is available on the vast open space of Varzea Grande, in front of the bus station. Anywhere else near the old town is zealously metered or restricted, though that doesn't stop most drivers making at least one loop along the riverfront looking for space – crumbly old Largo do Pelourinho is always worth a look (and it's free here too).

Accommodation

Tomar has a good range of **accommodation** and finding a room should be pretty straightforward. There's a list of recommended places below, or you can ask at the tourist office about the few rural tourism places nearby that offer rooms in the countryside.

Hotels and pensions

Pensão Residencial Cavaleiros de Cristo Rua Alexandre Herculano 7 ☏ 249 321 203, ⓦ www.inncavaleirosdecristo.com. Quiet, sober rooms with white walls, terracotta tiled floors, French windows and little bathrooms. It's a step up from most pensions – there's a/c, satellite TV and a mini-bar in the rooms – but prices are reasonable, and the people welcoming. ❸

Estalagem de Santa Iria Parque do Mouchão ☏ 249 313 326, ⓦ www.estalagemiria.com. At this pretty island retreat by the river, the rooms have spacious balconies onto the park, whose mature trees screen off the traffic. Its restaurant is pretty good value, offering upmarket cooking in quietly elegant surroundings. Private parking right outside – car access is from the riverside avenue across the highly unlikely looking pedestrian bridge. Good discounts available Nov–May. ❹

Residencial Sinagoga Rua Gil Avô 31 ☏ 249 323 083, ⓔ residencial.sinagoga@clix.pt. Standard *residencial* with period (ie 1970s) decor and furnishings. It's hard to get excited about it, but it does the job at a decent price. ❸

Hotel dos Templários Largo Cândido dos Reis 1 ☏ 249 310 100, ⓦ www.hoteldostemplarios.pt. The smartest hotel in the town centre is a large, modern four-star overlooking the river, with a gym, pool and parking for guests. Balconies overlook the riverside lawns. ❺

Residencial Trovador Rua de Agosto de 1385 ☏ 249 322 567, ⓦ www.residencialtrovador .com.sapo.pt. Opposite the bus station, and used by tour groups, this is a bit of a fallback – but the largish rooms are furnished with bright fabrics, and parking outside is easy. ❷

Residencial União Rua Serpa Pinto 94 ☏ 249 323 161. The best of two on this central street, it's deservedly popular, with an air of grandeur, especially in the lovely breakfast room and period piece of a bar. Bathrooms might be on the elderly side, but most rooms are generously sized with decent furniture – you'll need to book in advance in July and August. No credit cards. ❷

Campsite

Parque de Campismo ☏ 249 329 824, ⓕ 249 322 608. Shady spot located behind the football stadium, a 10min walk from the centre.

Eating, drinking and entertainment

The best **cafés** in town are the *Santa Iria* (closed Mon), which has a wide terrace by the old bridge, and the *Paraiso* (closed Tues), which occupies a strategic spot on the main pedestrianized street. Locals are also inordinately fond of the two or three places along the riverfront avenue, though the traffic doesn't help their

Portuguese azulejos

Vibrant blue and white or multicoloured decorative tiles have been used throughout Portugal since the birth of the nation, making up everything from immense religious scenes covering entire walls of churches to tiny, simple geometric patterns on the back of park benches. Less studied than stained glass, less famous than frescoes, many *azulejos* are works of art hand-crafted by trained masters, though even the mass-produced factory items add a touch of flamboyance to otherwise dull buildings. All over Portugal you'll see decorative motifs, geometric patterns, satirical figures, animals and ornate historical scenes, both inside and outside houses, on churches, public buildings, cafés, shops, even motorway bridges and metro stations, reflecting an evolving but enduring craft.

The craft of making decorative tiles was brought over by the **Moors** in the eighth century – the word "azulejo" derives from the Arabic *al-zulecha* meaning "small stone". Originally, tiles were painted using thin ridges of clay to prevent the lead-based colours from running into each other. Early Portuguese tiles – such as the sixteenth-century ones in the Palácio Nacional in Sintra – copied both the technique and typically geometric designs used by the Moors (the Koran prevents the portrayal of living forms). Portuguese *azulejos* developed their own style around the mid-sixteenth century when a new Italian method – introduced to Iberia by Francisco Niculoso – enabled images to be painted directly onto the clay thanks to a tin oxide coating which prevented running.

As any butcher will tell you, ceramic tiles are easy to clean, need little upkeep and are great for keeping a place cool. The churches were already using tiles for these purposes by the seventeenth century, when large *azulejos* panels known as **tapetes** (carpets) – because of their resemblance to large rugs – were used for interior church walls. **Religious imagery** was of course popular – such as the tiles seen in Lisbon's Igreja de São Roque. At the same time, wealthy Portuguese began to commission large *azulejos* panels for their homes or chapels

Speciality shops for tiles

Branca d'Água, Lisbon. p.141.
Contemporary tiles with style.
Centro Regional de Artes Tradicionais, Porto p.352. Riverside crafts centre where you can try your hand at painting *azulejos* – and buy them too.
Fábrica Sant'ana, Lisbon. p.141.
Renowned outlet, with copies of traditional designs.
Fábrica Viúva Lamego, Lisbon p.141.
Made-to-order designs and reproduction antiques.
Porches, Algarve, p.580. Village famed for its ceramics and shops selling tiles in various styles.

▲ Cais do Sodré metro

displaying battles, hunting scenes and fantastic images influenced by Vasco da Gama's voyages to the east. As a result, many of Portugal's key figures and moments in history have been permanently captured on ceramic. By the late seventeenth century, blue and white tiles influenced by Dutch tile-makers were popular with the country's aristocracy, and their favoured images were flowers and fruit – there are examples in Lisbon's Palácio dos Marquêses de Fronteira. Meanwhile, the church used the style to portray the lives of saints, such as in the Capela de São Filipe (Saint Philip) in the Castelo de Sao Filipe near Setúbal. The early eighteenth century saw master artists being highly trained to compete with international rivals, producing elaborately decorated multicoloured ceramic mosaics – such as the *Panel of Christ Teaching in the Temple* in Évora's Misericórdia – culminating in Rococo themes.

By the mid-nineteenth century, British technology was imported to mass-produce *azulejos* which were now used to decorate shops and factories. Seen as good insulation devices, as well as protecting buildings from rain and fire, they began to appear on even humble dwellings. Why paint a restaurant every few years if you have a permanent decoration as in *Cervejaria da Trindade*'s in Lisbon? Why pebbledash or plaster your house if you can coat it in durable tiles, as in Olhão? Why bother with creosoting a bench if you can swathe it in attractive *azulejos*? And why commission a painting when you can have a historical scene tiled to your wall or on your garden steps? By the 1900s Portugal had become the globe's leading producer of decorative tiles and the fashion continues to this day. Some of the best modern tiles were commissioned to embellish Lisbon's expanded underground network in the early 1990s, by leading artists such as Eduardo Nery – whose blue and white tiles light up Campo Grande – and António da Coata, whose *Alice*-inspired white rabbit pokes fun at hassled commuters. The country now boasts over 500 years of tile technology which has been perfected to clad even the most modern of structures. Sporting Lisbon's purpose-built stadium for Euro 2004 is largely tiled, while even motorway bridges and council estates are embellished with patterned tile motifs.

The masters

In the late seventeenth century, a Spaniard, **Gabriel del Barco**, worked in Portugal producing wonderfully ornate tiled scenes. He quickly became known as an artist, even signing his works. His innovations were quickly adopted by Portuguese tile "artists" who produced the so-called golden age of *azulejos* in the eighteenth century. These artists became known as the **Cycle of Masters**. António Bernardes – whose "Foot bath" panel can be seen in Lisbon's Rua das Amoreiras – is still considered the top master for **portraiture**, though his son Policarpo is perhaps the most famous. The father's work can be seen in Évora's Igreja de São João, which dates from 1711. Policarpo's work is more theatrical and colourful, typified by the stunning scenes in the Igreja de São Lourenço in Almancil in the Algarve, showing scenes from the life of Saint Lawrence. The pair also worked together, producing superb *azulejos* scenes such as in the Igreja de Misericórdia in Viana do Castelo.

▲ Igreja de São Lourenço

A night on the tiles

1 **Cervejaria Trindade**, Lisbon p.130. Dine under the gaze of superb tiled scenes depicting the elements and seasons.

2 **Adega do Padrinho**, Viana do Castelo p.410. Titchy local restaurant lovingly embellished in blue and white.

3 **Hotel Bela Vista**, Praia da Rocha, Algarve p.586. The best of early twentieth-century Portuguese decor.

4 **Palace Hotel**, Buçaco p.250. History in ceramic – tiles depicting the Portuguese conquest of Ceuta.

5 **Pensão Bela Vista**, Olhão, Algarve p.558. *Azulejos* give this simple guest house oodles of character.

▲ Cervejaria Trindade

◄ Hotel Bela Vista

ambience. There are plenty of **restaurants** around town, all reasonably priced, while there's a cheap grilled chicken place at the **market** (market day is Fri, 7am–1pm). Tomar has a wide cultural programme, detailed in the monthly *Agenda Cultural*, available from the turismo. Look out for perfomances by the Fatias de Cá **theatre company** (Ⓦ www.fatiasdeca.com), who often stage spectacular events – Shakespeare productions, *The Name of the Rose*, sound-and-light shows – in the Convento do Cristo or the Mata dos Sete Montes.

Restaurants

Bela Vista Trav Fonte Choupo 6 ☎ 249 312 870. Justifiably the town's most renowned restaurant, a rustic place by the river with a delightful covered terrace underneath an old house. Dishes are traditional Portuguese – the roast *cabrito* is highly rated. Closed Mon evening & Tues. Moderate.

Restaurante Jardim Rua Silva Magalhães 39 ☎ 249 312 034. Large portions in a back-street local favourite. There are a few pasta dishes or try the *recheado con farinheira*, pork stuffed with *farinhera* sausage. Closed Sat. Moderate.

🏃 **Restaurante Tabuleiro** Rua Serpa Pinto 148 ☎ 249 312 771. The kind of place that provincial Portugal does so well – a semi-smart family-friendly restaurant serving honest-to-goodness food (roast pork, *bacalhau*, veal, *arroz de peixe*, steak) in coronary-inducing portions. Desserts are all home-made, or there's fresh fruit, and the *padron* summons up menu guidance in half a dozen languages. Inexpensive.

Listings

Hospital Tomar Hospital is north of the centre on the Coimbra road, Av Maria de Lourdes Mello e Castro ☎ 249 320 100.
Internet Free access is available in the Biblioteca Municipal, Rua Gualdim Pais (Mon 2–7pm, Tues–Fri 10am–7pm, Sat 10am–1.30pm), otherwise visit Espaçao Internet on Rua Amorim Rosa (Mon–Sat 10am–10pm).

Pharmacy Farmacia Mísericórdia, Rua Infanteria 159 ☎ 249 313 541.
Police PSP headquarters is on Rua Dr Sousa ☎ 249 313 444.
Post office Av Marquês de Tomar (Mon–Fri 9am–6pm, Sat 9am–noon).
Swimming pool The municipal pool is in the park behind the stadium, on the west bank of the river.

East along the Tejo

Around 20km south of Tomar, the Rio Tejo swings east, past the remarkable castle at **Almourol** and meeting the Rio Zêzere at **Constância**, one of the most attractive towns on the Tejo. By road, an alternative route to Constância is via Castelo do Bode and its dam, the Barragem do Castelo do Bode. From Constância, the Tejo retains its rural hue for the 12km east to **Abrantes**, which has another historic castle. This is the last significant town on the river but there is another stop to be made at **Belver** castle, an extraordinary fortification east of Abrantes, on the north bank of the Tejo. The whole route is an enjoyable approach to the towns of the northern Alentejo or the Beira Baixa, and it's covered by train (the Lisbon–Covilhã service), but drivers are going to have the best of it since you're unlikely to want to stop anywhere for long. However, should you be so inclined, both Constância and Abrantes have tourist offices and accommodation.

Castelo de Almourol

As if conjured up by some medieval-minded magician, the **Castelo de Almourol** stands on a tiny rocky island in the middle of the Tejo. Built by the Knights Templar in 1171, the castle never saw military action – except in sixteenth-century romantic literature – and its double perimeter walls and ten small towers are perfectly preserved. Tancos train station and village lie 2km to the east, and weekend **boats** run to the castle from the river esplanade here, though the more regular service is on the little skiffs that depart from a car park opposite the castle itself (daily: summer 9am–7.30pm; winter 9am–6pm; €1.50 return). You are put ashore to climb up through the trees to the castle, where there's a beautiful rural panorama from the tall central keep. Back above the quayside car park, a bar with a shady terrace serves snacks and sandwiches.

Constância

CONSTÂNCIA, 3km upstream from Almourol, is a sleepy, picturesque white-washed town arranged like an amphitheatre around the Tejo and the mouth of the Rio Zêzere. It is best known in Portugal for its association with **Luís de Camões**, Portugal's national poet. In fact, Camões was here for only three years (1547–50), taking refuge from the court of Dom João III, whom he had managed to offend by the injudicious dedication of a love sonnet to a woman on whom the king himself had designs. However, Constância is said to have remained dear to the poet's heart until the end of his life, and the riverside Camões gardens are based on those described in Camões's epic poem *Os Lusíadas*. In more troubled times the town served the Duke of Wellington: he amassed his forces here in 1809 and prepared for the Battle of Talavera in Spain. Nowadays, Constância is at its liveliest during the **Festa dos Barqueiros**, on Easter Monday, with parades and traditional boats on the Tejo. If you're travelling by train, you need to get get off at Praia do Ribatejo-Constância, the stop after Almourol.

Abrantes

ABRANTES is perched strategically above the Rio Tejo, 12km upstream of Constância. Hidden at the centre of a dreary modern town is a historic kernel of pretty narrow alleys and squares lined with crumbling houses. It looks its best in spring and summer when flowers on Rua da Barca and in the Jardim da República are in bloom; the views are also impressive. The high point – in all respects – is the town's much-restored castle, constructed in the early fourteenth century. As at Santarém, Romans and Moors established strongholds here and the citadel was again sharply contested during the Peninsular War. From the battlements there are terrific views of the countryside and rooftops of Abrantes, and the gardens around its old town walls.

Castelo de Belver

The **Castelo de Belver** is one of the most famous in the country, its fanciful position, name and tiny size having ensured it a place in dozens of Portuguese legends. The name comes from *belo ver* (beautiful to see), the supposed exclamation of a medieval princess, waking up to look out from its keep at the river valley below. It dates from the twelfth century, when the Portuguese frontier stood at the Tejo, the Moors having reclaimed most of the territories to the south. Its founder was Dom Sancho I, who entrusted its construction and care to the knight-monks of the Order of St John.

The walls form an irregular pentagon, tracing the crown of the hill, with a narrow access path to force attackers into single file. Inside the castle chapel is a formidable fifteenth-century reliquary. All the pieces of bone were stolen during the French invasions in the nineteenth century, but fortunately for the villagers there was a casket of "spares" hidden away by the priest, and these substitutes are today paraded at the **Festa de Santa Reliquária**, held around August 18.

Although technically in the Alentejo, Belver is best approached from Abrantes, by public transport at least. Buses stop in the village square, while the train station is directly below the village beside the river. If you take the train north along the valley towards Castelo Branco, look out for the striking rock faces before Vila Velha de Ródão, known as the **Portas do Ródão** (Gates of Ródão).

Golegã and around

GOLEGÃ, on the west bank of the Tejo, midway between Tomar and Santarém, is a pleasant riverside town which touts itself as "Capital of the Horse", a claim it backs up with black-horse silhouettes hanging outside virtually every business. It is best known for its **Feira Nacional do Cavalo** (National Horse Fair), held during the first two weeks in November. The fair incorporates celebrations for St Martin's Day on November 11, when there's a running of the bulls and a grand parade in which red-waistcoated grooms mingle with gypsies. Roasted chestnuts and barbecued chickens are washed down with liberal quantities of *água-pé* (literally "foot water"), a light wine made by adding water to the crushed grape husks left after initial wine production. During the evening, people crowd into *Restaurante Central* on the main square to mingle with the haughty *cavaleiros* who have survived the bullfighting.

The town is centred on the sixteenth-century **Igreja Matriz**, with its fine Manueline door. This flanks the main square, opposite the *Restaurante Central*, while just up the road from here (signposted), opposite the modern Câmara Municipal, is the **Casa-Museu de Fotografia Carlos Relvas** (under restoration at the time of writing). This was the home of Carlos Relvas – father of José Relvas, who proclaimed the Portuguese Republic in Lisbon in 1910. Relvas senior had an interest in the newly discovered art of photography, early examples of which are displayed, while the house itself is a whimsical pavilion of wrought-iron and glass set in landscaped gardens.

A couple of **cafés** put out tables on the tree-shaded square outside the church, while the old market has been turned into a small shopping complex. There's also a lovely riverside **campsite** in town (☎249 976 222), not far from the Igreja Matriz.

Golegã is one of the main crossing points to the **east bank of the Rio Tejo** – a bull-breeding and vine-growing territory of rich plains and riverside marshes. The N118 marks the most attractive route along the river, taking in several small towns and *quintas* en route to Santarém, 45km away. There's nothing much to stop for in Chamusca, Alpiarça or Almeirim – the latter once the site of a royal summer palace – but local wine producers line the road at intervals, open for sales to the public; look for signs saying "vinho do produtor".

Santarém

SANTARÉM, capital of the Ribatejo, rears high above the Rio Tejo, commanding a tremendous view over the rich pasturelands to the south and east. It ranks among the most historic cities in Portugal: under Julius Caesar it became an important administrative centre for the Roman province of Lusitania; Moorish Santarém was regarded as impregnable (until Afonso Henriques captured it by enlisting the aid of foreign Crusaders in 1147); and it was here that the royal *Cortes* (parliament) was convened throughout the

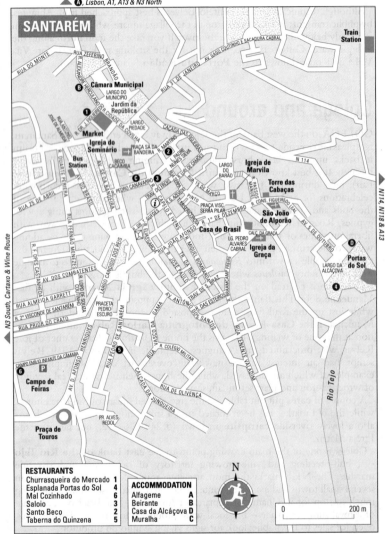

SANTARÉM

B Câmara Municipal
LARGO DO MUNICIPIO
Jardim da República
1
LARGO PIEDADE
Market
Igreja do Seminário
Bus Station
BECO CACAIMBA
2
PRAÇA SÁ DA BANDEIRA
Igreja de Marvila
3
Torre das Cabaças
i
PRAÇA VISC. SERRA PILAR
São João de Alporão
Casa do Brasil
LG. PEDRO ALVARES CABRAL
Igreja da Graça
LARGO DA ALCÁÇOVA
D Portas do Sol
4

PRACETA PEDRO ESCURO
P
6 Campo de Feiras
5
Praça de Touros
PR. ALVES REDOL

Rio Tejo

Train Station

N 114

▶ *N114, N118 & A13*

◀ *N3 South, Cartaxo & Wine Route*

N

0 ——— 200 m

RESTAURANTS	
Churrasqueira do Mercado	**1**
Esplanada Portas do Sol	**4**
Mal Cozinhado	**6**
Saloio	**3**
Santo Beco	**2**
Taberna do Quinzena	**5**

ACCOMMODATION	
Alfageme	**A**
Beirante	**B**
Casa da Alcáçova	**D**
Muralha	**C**

fourteenth and fifteenth centuries. All evidence of Roman and Moorish occupation has vanished but, with its two exquisite churches and surviving old-town alleys and squares, modern Santarém remains a pleasant enough place to visit – not least for the famous view from the *miradouro* known as the Portas do Sol.

The thinly populated agricultural plain above which Santarém stands is the home of Portuguese **bullfighting**: here, the very best horses and bulls graze in lush fields under the watchful eyes of *campinos*, mounted guardians. Agricultural traditions, folk dancing (especially the fandango) and bullfighting come together in the great annual **Feira Nacional da Agricultura**, held at Santarém for two weeks starting on the first Friday in June, while dishes from every region in Portugal are sampled at the **Festival de Gastronomia** (third and forth week of October). In addition, a large **market** sprawls around the bullring on the second and fourth Sunday of every month.

The town

The market and municipal gardens mark the northern edge of the town, with the spacious **Praça Sá da Bandeira** just beyond. This is named for the Marquês de Sá da Bandeira (1795–1876), Portuguese prime minister in the 1830s and the town's most famous son, whose statue is overlooked by the fussy Baroque facade of the Jesuit **Igreja do Seminário** (1676). The largely pedestrianized old town lies beyond, with Rua Serpa Pinto or Rua Capelo e Ivens threading towards the signposted Portas do Sol, about fifteen minutes' walk away, with the best of the churches conveniently en route.

First of these is the Manueline **Igreja de Marvila** (Wed–Sun 9am–12.30pm & 2–5.30pm) at the end of Rua Serpa Pinto, with brilliant seventeenth-century *azulejos* covering every inch of the nave and an unusual stone pulpit comprising eleven miniature Corinthian columns. From here, it's a short walk across Rua 1º de Dezembro and down Rua Vila Belmonte to the architectural highlight of Santarém, the early fifteenth-century **Igreja da Graça** (Wed–Sun 9.30am–12.30pm & 2–5.30pm). A spectacular rose window dominates the church and overlapping blind arcades above the portal are heavily influenced by the decorations on the main facade at Batalha. Inside, it's the elaborately carved sarcophagus of Pedro de Meneses, the first Governor of Ceuta (died 1347), which draws the eye, though Portuguese know the church as the burial place of **Pedro Álvares Cabral**, discoverer of Brazil in 1500. A simple tombstone set in the floor near the Meneses sarcophagus marks the spot, with Cabral "the discoverer" honoured more prominently outside the church by a heroic statue – cross in one hand, sword in the other. The Cabral family lived in Santarém, and a house by the church thought to be theirs (though with no real evidence) is now the **Casa do Brasil**, a cultural centre with art and other exhibitions.

Back on the main route towards the *miradouro*, opposite the fifteenth-century clocktower of the **Torre das Cabaças**, is the city's archeological and medieval art museum, housed in the twelfth-century church of **São João de Alporão** (Wed–Sun 9.30am–12.30pm & 2–5.30pm; €2). Take a look at the flamboyant Gothic tomb of Duarte de Meneses who met his gruesome fate in 1464 – so comprehensively was he butchered by the Moors in North Africa that only a single tooth was recovered for burial.

Avenida 5º de Outubro runs out along the promontory and finishes at the **Portas do Sol** (Gates of the Sun; summer 9am–10pm, winter 9am–6.30pm), a large shady garden occupying the site of the Moorish citadel. A swashbuckling statue of Afonso Henriques celebrates his pivotal capture of the town – so elated was he that he founded Alcobaça abbey in thanks. The gardens are a pretty spot, with a kiosk-café and terrace-restaurant, while modern battlements look down on a long stretch of the Tejo, with its fertile sandbanks. Beyond, a vast swathe of the Ribatejo disappears green and flat into the distance.

Practicalities

The **train station** is 2km below the town. There are half-hourly buses into the centre, or a taxi will cost €5. The **bus station** is more central, on Avenida do

Brasil, and Rua Pedro Canavarro, across the gardens opposite, leads into Rua Capelo e Ivens, the main pedestrian street of the old town. **Parking** in the old town is impossible, though there are pay-parking spaces (free at weekends) around the market and down Avenida Sá da Bandeira, near the bus station. A good free map is available from the **turismo** at Rua Capelo e Ivens 63 (Mon–Fri 9am–7pm, though sometimes closed for lunch; Sat & Sun 10am–12.30pm & 2.30–5.30pm; ☎243 304 437, Ⓦwww.cm-santarem.pt).

City-centre **accommodation** is fairly limited, and establishments at the budget end of the scale are a bit long in the tooth. The turismo might be able to help source a private room. The choice of **restaurants** is better, though be aware that hardly any are open on Sundays. Rua Dr. Jaime Figueiredo, the street behind the market, is the place to look for an inexpensive meal. Among local specialities there's *fataça na telha* (mullet cooked on a hot tile), which has its origins in the fishing village of Caneiras, 5km south of town. For an evening **drink** the best places are the outdoor cafés in Praça Sá da Bandeira or the *esplanada* bar that's attached to the restaurant in the Portas do Sol gardens.

Hotels and pensions

Hotel Alfageme Av Bernardo Santareno 38 ☎243 370 870, Ⓦwww.hotelalfageme.com. The selling-point of this typical three-star hotel is the easy parking, right outside. Otherwise, although the rooms are relatively spacious and a/c, there's little character here and your only views are of the surrounding residential-retail suburb. Plus you're a stiff 500m walk from the centre. ❹

Residencial Beirante Rua Alexandre Herculano 5 ☎243 322 547, ℻243 333 845. Looks pretty grim from the outside but improves once you're through the door. Even so, the rooms are plain, the beds on the lumpy side and the bathrooms dated, but there's enough space, rooftop views from the third-floor rooms and plenty of hot water – and the price is right. Parking is just a short walk away by the market. No credit cards. ❸

🏃 **Casa da Alcáçova** Largo da Alcáçova 3 ☎243 304 030, Ⓦwww.alcacova.com. The premier choice in town, this aristocratic manor house at the shoulder of the Portas do Sol has jaw-dropping river views. Antiques, original fireplaces and magnificent beds (including some four-posters) furnish the eight rooms – dressing gowns and slippers are supplied. Drinks are served in the elegant lounge, and there's a lovely pool and outdoor eating area. Parking available. ❻

Residencial Muralha Rua Pedro Canavarro 12 ☎243 322 399, ℻243 329 477. Simple budget rooms in a bright, airy family-run place adjacent to a surviving chunk of the city walls. A couple have balconies over the street. No credit cards. ❷

Quinta de Vale de Lobos Azóia de Baixo, 6km north on N3 ☎243 429 264, Ⓦwww.valedelobos .com. Four double/twin rooms and guest lounge in a nineteenth-century farmhouse where the historian Alexandre Herculano spent his final years. Surrounded by cedar and oak woods, it's set in lovely gardens with a swimming pool. Also has two cottages available, suitable for families. ❹

Restaurants

Churrasqueira do Mercado Rua Dr Jaime Figueiredo 24 ☎968 089 364. A basic grill house behind the market, one of the few places open on a Sun night – when you'll be watching the football with the locals (you should be supporting Sporting). There's only a short menu, all meat, but the grilled chicken is really good – the thermonuclear *piri-piri* sauce is optional. Closed Thurs. Inexpensive.

Esplanada Portas do Sol Jardim das Portas do Sol ☎243 321 220. The location is all, with a terrace with views over the Portas do Sol gardens and walls to the plains below. The menu is the usual grills (meat and fish), but it's pretty nicely done and not too pricey – most mains are €8–11. Closed Mon. Moderate.

O Mal Cozinhado Campo de Feiras ☎243 323 584. Small, rustic place where you may need to reserve a table, particularly on Fri, which is fado night. Some of the meat comes from bulls recently on duty in the nearby bullring, and, despite the name ("badly cooked"), meals are delicious. Closed Sun & Mon. Moderate.

O Saloio Trav. do Montalvo 11, off Rua Capelo e Ivens ☎243 327 656. Popular with local families, and with a little outdoor patio, this *casa de pasto* is good value for money. Closes at 9.30pm; closed Sat after 4pm & Sun. Inexpensive.

Santo Beco Beco do Feleijo 13 ☎916 510 667. Down a dead-end alley in a hidden square off Rua Serpo Pinto, this shows a more inventive approach than most – starters include a fresh tomato soup with quail's egg, while mains range from prawn stroganoff and seafood pasta to steaks from the fertile grazing grounds below town. Lunch dishes are from €5, otherwise mains €10–15. Closed Sun. Expensive.

Taberna do Quinzena Rua Pedro de Santarém ☎ 243 322 804. Simple grills in a no-nonense *tasca* with a bullfighting obsession. Closed Sun. Inexpensive.

The Ribatejo wine route

Few of the local **wine towns** south of Santarém stand up to a visit in their own right but if you're not in a hurry the drive down the N3 towards Vila Franca and Lisbon isn't a bad one. Many vineyards offer tours and tastings – they are all signposted from the road – and the route below can occupy half a day, with lunch taken in either of the two prettiest towns, Alenquer or Arruda dos Vinhos.

Wine has been produced on the banks of the Tejo for around 2000 years and, while it's long had a reputation for quantity rather than quality, the offerings of some new producers have recently begun to acquire an international profile. There are five denominations in the Ribatejo region – Almeirim, Cartaxo, Chamusca, Coruche and Santarém. Ribatejan whites are typically from the Fernão Pires or Trincadeira-das-Pratas grapes, which give rise to a dry, lemon-coloured and fruity wine. Reds tend to be from the Periquita, Tincadeira Preta and Castelão Nacional grapes, though Cabernet Sauvignon produces some of the best wines.

At **CARTAXO**, the self-declared "capital do vinho" 14km south of Santarém, the **Museu Rural e do Vinho** (Tues–Fri 10.30am–12.30pm & 3–5.30pm, Sat & Sun 9.30am–12.30pm & 3–5.30pm; €0.85) is the single best place to investigate the subject. It's housed in the signposted Quinta das Pratas, a municipal park and sports complex on the town outskirts, and as well as the exhibits you can taste and buy the local, full-bodied, fruity wines.

AZAMBUJA, 13km to the southwest, is known for its reds made from the Periquita grape, though the town itself isn't worth a stop. However, for a true off-the-beaten-track sight, follow the signs from the main through road to the **Vala de Azambuja**, a 26-kilometre-long canal built parallel to the river by the Marquês de Pombal, designed to drain the land when the Tejo was in flood. Three kilometres up a dirt road (fine for cars; signposted "Palácio") stand the forlorn ruins of the **Palácio das Obras Novas**, used as a staging post for the steamers plying from Lisbon north to Constância in the nineteenth century.

At Carregado, the N3 meets the N1, and offers a choice of routes further into the rolling hills. Five kilometres north, and perched on a hill above the Alenquer river, **ALENQUER** mainly produces lemony flavoured white wines. Traffic chokes the main road alongside the river, but it's an enjoyable climb up to the attractive upper town, where you can visit the Manueline cloisters of the church and convent of São Francisco, the oldest Franciscan house in Portugal, built during the lifetime of St Francis of Assisi.

However, it is in the valleys around **ARRUDA DOS VINHOS**, 13km west of Carregado, that the region's vineyards are at their most attractive. It's a pretty town, too, with an enormous eighteenth-century public fountain and handsome Manueline church, top-heavy with restaurants and real estate agents, both the consequence of the weekend influx of Lisboans. The traditional lunch spot is O Fuso (☎263 975 121), on the main street, a rustic barn of a restaurant where vast slabs of meat and *bacalhau* are grilled over open fires. It's not cheap (meals from around €20) but it is excellent, and you can drink the fresh, beaujolais-style Arruda (also known as Arruta) red wines.

Vila Franca de Xira

The west bank city of **VILA FRANCA DE XIRA**, 45km downriver from Santarém, makes a rival (but unsubstantiated) claim to be the capital of the Ribatejo. English Crusaders favoured its riverside location, naming it Cornogoa after Cornwall, but today it's a largely drab industrial city; a poor second to Santarém in cultural attractions and only worth the effort of a visit for aficionados of the Portuguese bullfight. The rearing of bulls and horses dominates the local economy and the town celebrates its obsession in café names and statues, while posters everywhere announce forthcoming fights. The two great annual events are the **Festa do Colete Encarnado** ("Red Waistcoat Festival", a reference to the costume of the *campinos*) held over several days in the first two weeks of July; and the **Feira de Outubro** (October Fair), in the first two weeks of the month. On both occasions there are bullfights and a Pamplona-style running of the bulls through the streets – leading to the usual casualties among the bold (and drunk).

Travel details

Trains

You can check train timetables online at ⓦ www .cp.pt.

Caldas da Rainha to: Leiria (6 daily; 1hr); Lisbon (up to 11 daily; 1hr 15min–2hr); São Martinho do Porto (6 daily; 10–15min).

Leiria to: Caldas da Rainha (6 daily; 1hr); Figueira da Foz (6 daily; 45min–1hr 20min); Lisbon (4 daily; 2–3hr 20min); São Martinho do Porto (6 daily; 35–50min).

Lisbon to: Caldas da Rainha (9 daily; 1hr 15min–2hr); Leiria (5 daily; 2hr–3hr); Santarém (every 30–60min; 1hr–1hr 30min); Torres Vedras (9 daily; 45min–1hr 15min); Vila Franca de Xira (hourly; 30min).

Santarém to: Castelo Branco (6 daily; 2hr–2hr 35min); Covilhã (5 daily; 3hr 5min–4hr 5min); Lisbon (every 30–60min; 1hr–1hr 30min); Tomar (roughly hourly; 45min–1hr); Vila Franca de Xira (every 30–60min; 30–40min).

Tomar to: Lisbon (roughly hourly; 1hr 50min–2hr 40hr); Santarém (roughly hourly; 45min–1hr).

Buses

Alcobaça to: Batalha (8 daily; 30min); Leiria (4 daily; 45min); Lisbon (3 daily; 2hr); Nazaré (up to 9 daily; 20min).

Batalha to: Fátima (4 daily; 25min); Leiria (5 daily; 15min); Lisbon (5 daily; 2hr).

Caldas da Rainha to: Foz do Arelho (3–8 daily, though hourly at weekends in July/Aug; 20min); Leiria (2–4 daily; 1hr 20min); Lisbon (hourly; express service 1hr 10min, otherwise 1hr 30min); Nazaré (3–10 daily; 45min); Óbidos (every 30–60min; 15min).

Ericeira to: Lisbon (7 daily; 1hr 20min); Mafra (hourly; 20min); Sintra (hourly; 45min).

Leiria to: Alcobaça (4 daily; 45min); Batalha (5 daily; 15min); Coimbra (10 daily; 50min); Fátima (Mon–Sat 7 daily, Sun 2; 35min–1hr); Lisbon (9 daily; 1hr 10min); Porto de Mós (3 daily; 35min); São Pedro de Moel (July/Aug up to 10 daily, rest of the year 2–3 daily; 30min); Tomar (4 daily; 1hr).

Nazaré to: Alcobaça (up to 9 daily; 20min); Caldas da Rainha (3–10 daily; 45min); Leiria (10 daily; 1hr 10min); Lisbon (6 daily; 2hr); Óbidos (3 daily; 1hr); São Martinho do Porto (3 daily; 20min).

Óbidos to: Caldas da Rainha (every 30–60min; 15min); Nazaré (7 daily; 1hr); Peniche (3–7 daily; 30min).

Peniche to: Areia Branca (6 daily; 30min); Caldas da Rainha (3–7 daily; 45min); Lisbon (9 daily; 1hr 45min); Óbidos (3–7 daily; 30min); São Martinho do Porto (3 daily; 1hr); Torres Vedras (8 daily; 50min).

Santarém to: Abrantes (6 daily; 1hr 25min); Fátima (9 daily, 1hr); Lisbon (12 daily; 1hr 15min); Ourem (1 daily; 1hr 10min); Tomar (2–6 daily; 1hr).

Tomar to: Fátima (2–4 daily; 45min); Leiria (4 daily; 1hr); Lisbon (2–4 daily; 1hr 15min–2hr); Santarém (2–4 daily; 1hr 5min).

Coimbra and the Beira Litoral

CHAPTER 3

Highlights

✳ **Velha Universidade, Coimbra** Wind your way up to the splendidly sited university, with its striking Baroque library. See p.235

✳ **Coimbra fado** Best listened to in a smoky bar, drink in hand, or with the atmospheric backdrop of an old-town alleyway. See p.239

✳ **Roman ruins at Conímbriga** Mosaics, baths, forum, aqueduct and a mighty defensive wall survive at Portugal's finest Roman site. See p.240

✳ **Kayaking down the Mondego** Paddle between Penacova and Coimbra down the meandering Rio Mondego. See p.243

✳ **Serra do Açor** A little-visited mountain range full of serendipitous delights – schist villages, river beaches, mountain walks and elegant old bridges. See p.246

✳ **Mata Nacional do Buçaco** Spend the day in the shaded Buçaco forest, and then drop down into the neighbouring spa town of Luso for afternoon tea. See p.249

✳ **Caramulo** A hiking base in the midst of a stunning mountain range, with an excellent museum of art and automobiles. See p.254

✳ **Figueira da Foz** Central Portugal's finest resort, with some great beaches and local walks. See p.257

✳ **Aveiro** Cruise on a traditional boat through the canals of Aveiro. See p.263

△ Coimbra old town

Coimbra and the Beira Litoral

The province of Beira Litoral is dominated by the city of **Coimbra**, which, with Guimarães, Lisbon and Porto, forms the quartet of Portugal's historic capitals. Situated on a hill above the Rio Mondego, it's a wonderfully moody place, full of ancient alleys and lanes, spreading around the country's oldest university. As a base for exploring the region, the city can't be beaten, with Portugal's most extensive Roman site, **Conímbriga**, 16km to the southwest, the castle at **Montemor-o-Velho**, 32km west, and the delightful spa town of **Luso** and ancient forest of **Buçaco** under an hour's journey to the north.

Beira's endlessly sandy coastline, from Figueira da Foz north as far as Porto, has been dubbed the **Costa de Prata** ("Silver Coast"). Although slowly succumbing to development, most noticeably around the pretty lagoon town of **Praia de Mira**, it remains one of the least spoiled coasts in Portugal, backed by rolling dunes and pine forests. The only resort of any real size is **Figueira da Foz** and even this remains thoroughly local in character. Inland, the villages and towns of the fertile plain have long been conditioned by the twin threats of floodwaters from Portugal's highest mountains, and silting caused by the restless Atlantic. Drainage channels were cut to make cultivation possible and houses everywhere are built on high ground. At **Aveiro**, positioned on a complex estuary site, a whole network of canals was developed to cope with the currents, and to facilitate salt production and the harvesting of seaweed.

The Beira region also hints at the river valley and mountain splendour to come, in the Douro and Minho, further north. Following the delightful **Rio Mondego** upstream from Coimbra, you'll come to see why it has been celebrated so often in Portuguese poetry as the "Rio das Musas" – River of the Muses. A tributary of the Mondego, the **Dão**, is the source of some the country's finest wines, while there's an equally beautiful route along the **Rio Vouga** up to the pretty little town of **Vouzela**. To the north is the impressive convent at **Arouca**, and the *serras* of Freita and Arada, both peppered with remote hamlets and offering more scenic routes for drivers. To the south lies the **Serra do Caramulo**, where the village of **Caramulo** makes a good base for mountain pursuits. East of Coimbra, as the land slowly rises towards the mountain Beiras region and the Serra da Estrela, the first foothills are encountered in the **Serra da Lousã** and the **Serra do Açor**, rustic regions containing

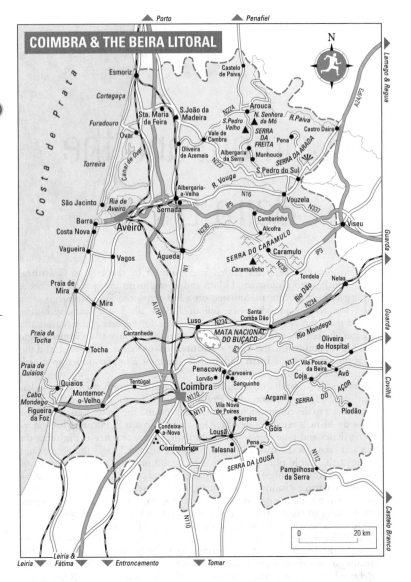

COIMBRA & THE BEIRA LITORAL

a range of pretty settlements like riverside **Góis** and the incredibly sited schist village of **Píodão**.

Coimbra

COIMBRA (pronounced *queem-bra*) was Portugal's capital for over a century (1143–1255) and its famous university – founded in 1290 and permanently established here in 1537 after a series of moves back and forth to Lisbon – was the only one in Portugal until the beginning of the last century. It remains highly prestigious and provides the greatest of Coimbra's monuments and buildings, most notably the renowned Baroque library. In addition, there are a remarkable number of other riches: two cathedrals, dozens of lesser churches, and scores of ancient mansions.

This roll-call of splendours is promoted zealously by the inhabitants of what – when all is said and done – is little more than a large, provincial town, with a population of 140,000. There's an air of self-importance that whistles through both city and citizens, bolstered by Coimbra's long academic tradition and fed by a wide array of shops, galleries, cafés, bars and taverns, at their busiest when the students are in town. The liveliest time to be here is in May, when the end of the academic year is celebrated in the **Queima das Fitas**, with late-night concerts, parades and graduates ceremoniously tearing or burning their gowns and faculty ribbons. Although the student's alcohol-fuelled antics can get rather excessive, this is when you're most likely to hear the genuine **Coimbra fado**, distinguished from the Lisbon version by its mournful pace and romantic or intellectual lyrics.

Arrival, information and city transport

There are three **train stations** – Coimbra A, Coimbra B and Coimbra Parque. Riverside **Coimbra A** (often just "Coimbra" on timetables) is right at the heart of things; all long-distance and express trains call only at **Coimbra B**, 2km to the north, from where you pick up a local train into Coimbra A – just follow everyone else across the platform (you don't need another ticket). **Coimbra Parque**, a short walk southeast of the centre, is for services to and from Lousã, to the south.

The main **bus station** on Avenida Fernão de Magalhães (15min walk northwest of the centre) is for long-distance Rede Expressos and RBL regional services, and any international services that stop in Coimbra. Joalto Mondego services to and from Condeixa-a-Nova and Conímbriga use a stop further down the avenue (towards the city centre) – for all departure details, see "Listings", pp.239–240.

Most of the upper old town is closed to traffic, and finding on-street parking anywhere is difficult. It's best to use one of the signposted **car parks** and then walk into the centre – there's a small pay car park by the Santa Clara bridge, a very large one further down opposite Coimbra Parque station, or free on-street parking all the way down the other side of the river (Avenida de Conimbriga) used by commuters. Incidentally, don't be misled by signs directing you to the Universidade Polo II (which is on the outskirts of town) – instead, follow signs to the city centre, before taking those to the main university.

Information and transport

There's a **regional turismo** on Avenida Emídio Navarro, by Largo da Portagem and facing the Ponte Santa Clara (Easter–Sept Mon–Fri 9am–7pm, Sat, Sun & hols 10am–1pm & 2.30–5.30pm; Oct–Easter Mon–Fri 9.30am–12.30pm & 2–5.30pm, Sat, Sun & hols 10am–1pm; ☏239 488 120, ⓦwww.turismo-centro.pt). There are also **municipal turismos** (ⓦwww.cm-coimbra.pt) on Largo Dom Dinis (Mon–Fri 10am–6pm, Sat & Sun 9am–12.30pm & 2–5.30pm; ☏239 832 591), on Praça da República (Mon–Fri 10am–6.30pm; ☏239 833 202) and next to the main market (Mon–Fri 9am–6pm; ☏239 834 038). All have helpful English-speakers and you'll be

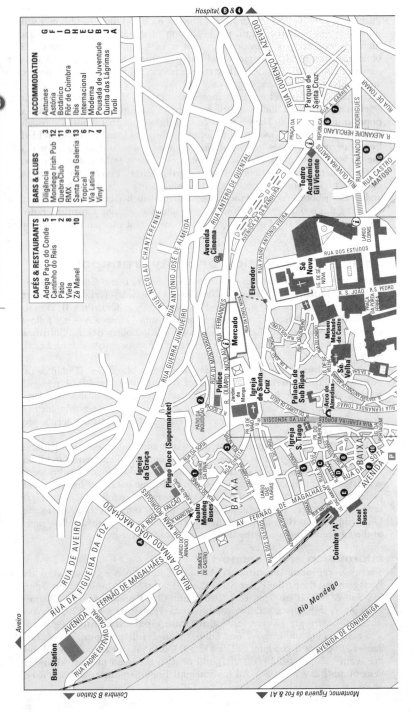

Hospital, **B** & **C** ▲

ACCOMMODATION

Antunes	G
Astória	F
Botânico	I
Flôr de Coimbra	D
Ibis	H
Internacional	E
Moderna	C
Pousada de Juventude	B
Quinta das Lágrimas	J
Tivoli	A

BARS & CLUBS

Diligência	3
Mondego Irish Pub	12
QuebraClub	11
RMX	9
Santa Clara Galeria	13
Tropical	6
Via Latina	7
Vinyl	10

CAFÉS & RESTAURANTS

Adega Paço do Conde	5
Cantinho do Reis	1
Pátio	2
Viela	8
Zé Manel	10

Igreja da Graça

Pingo Doce (Supermarket)

João Mondego Buses

BAIXA

Mercado

Police

Igreja de Santa Cruz

Jardim da Manga

Igreja S. Tiago

Palácio de Sub Ripas

Arco de Almedina

Sé Velha

Museu Machado de Castro

Sé Nova

Teatro Académico Gil Vicente

Parque de Santa Cruz

Avenida Cinema

Elevador

Coimbra 'A'

Local Buses

Bus Station

Rio Mondego

◀ Aveiro

◀ Coimbra B Station

◀ Montemor, Figueira da Foz & A1

▲ Montemor, Figueira da Foz & A1

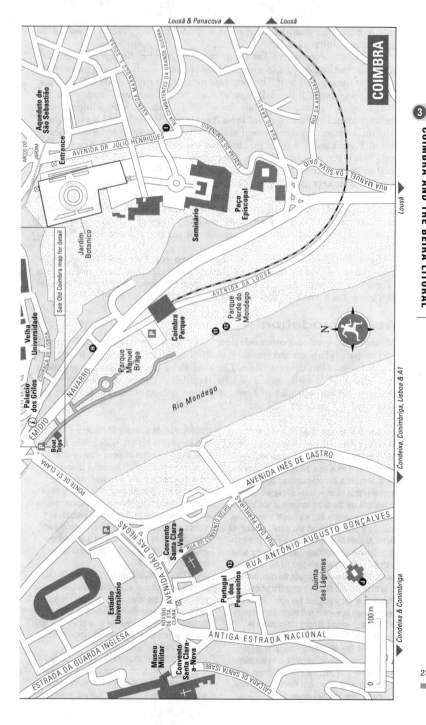

Lousã & Penacova

Lousã

Aqueduto de São Sebastião

Entrance

AVENIDA DR. JÚLIO HENRIQUES

AVENIDA MARQUÊS D'ANGEJA E SOUSA

RUA COMBATENTES DA GRANDE GUERRA

RUA DA ARREGAÇA

RUA DO BRASIL

ABOBADA DO SEMINÁRIO

Seminário

Paço Episcopal

Jardim Botânico

See Old Coimbra map for detail

RUA MANUEL DA SILVA GAIO

Lousã

AVENIDA DA LOUSÃ

Velha Universidade

Coimbra Parque

Parque Verde do Mondego

COURAÇA DE LISBOA

Palácio dos Grilos

NAVARRO

Parque Manuel Braga

Rio Mondego

N

Condeixa, Conimbriga, Lisboa & A1

EMÍDIO

Boat Trips

PONTE DE ST CLARA

AVENIDA INÊS DE CASTRO

RUA DAS FERREIRAS

ARCOS DO JARDIM

RUA DO CONVENTO VELHO

Estádio Universitário

AVENIDA JOÃO DAS REGAS

ROSSIO DE STA CLARA

Convento Santa Clara-a-Velha

Portugal dos Pequenitos

RUA ANTÓNIO AUGUSTO GONÇALVES

Quinta das Lágrimas

ESTRADA DA GUARDA INGLESA

Museu Militar

Convento Santa Clara-a-Nova

ANTIGA ESTRADA NACIONAL

CALÇADA DE SANTA ISABEL

Condeixa & Conimbriga

100 m

0

able to pick up a good fold-out street map and the very useful *Coimbra Viva* guide and cultural agenda.

You can walk everywhere you'll want to go in Coimbra, though the university is right at the highest part of town, and the stepped streets and alleys take it out of you in the summer heat. The local **bus network** is run by SMTUC (ⓦwww .smtuc.pt) – bus #1 (weekdays only) runs from Coimbra A station via the market up to the university, while the #3 (daily) runs the same route to Praça da República. The little electric **Linha Azul** buses (Mon–Fri and Sat mornings) run on a circular route through the otherwise pedestrianized Baixa (lower town). There's also a very useful **elevador** (Mon–Sat 7.30am–11.30pm, Sun & hols 10am–10pm), which rises from by the market on Avenida Sá da Bandeira to Rua Padre António Vieira, a short walk from the Sé Nova in the upper town. Integrated **tickets** for all forms of city transport are sold onboard buses (€1.50), though it's much better value to pre-buy tickets (3 journeys €1.70, 11 journeys €5.70, 1-day pass €2.50) from kiosks and automatic machines dotted around town or from SMTUC **transport shops** (Mon–Fri 7.30am–7.30pm, Sat 8am–1pm) – there's one by the *elevador* by the market, and another in Praça da República.

Alternatively, hop-on-hop-off, one-hour **open-top bus** tours visiting all the major sights are run by fun(tastic) Coimbra and leave from Largo da Portagem (Tues–Sun 10am–noon & 3–6pm on the hour; €8; ☎800 203 280). The ticket also gives you a free boat trip with Basófias (see "Listings" p.239).

Accommodation

Much of the city's **accommodation** is within a short walk of Coimbra A station, particularly on and around Rua da Sota, where the range is from rock-bottom *pensões* to three-star hotels. There are also a few good budget options at the other end of town, near Praça da República. The nearest campsite is in Penacova, 22km northeast of town, while the nearest *pousada* is 16km to the southwest at Condeixa-a-Nova.

Hotels and pensions

Pensão Residencial Antunes Rua Castro Matoso 8 ☎239 854 720, ⓦwww.residencialantunes .pt vu. A short walk from the bars and clubs around Pr. da República, this old-fashioned place has squeaky clean wooden floors and high ceilings – downsides are the dated furnishings and furniture, and bare bathrooms that are a tight squeeze, but rooms are decently priced and there's parking. ❷
Hotel Astória Av. Emídio Navarro 21 ☎239 853 020, ⓦwww.almeidahotels.com. Three-star hotel with an Art Deco interior – look for the landmark dome. The best rooms overlook the river, and they're all a/c and double-glazed, if a bit tired. Rooms only just shade into this price category – and between November and March rates drop by €20. There's secure parking 200m away. ❺
Residencial Botânico Bairro de São José 15 ☎239 714 824, ☎239 722 010. Up near the botanical gardens – although sited on the main road the en-suite rooms are double-glazed and quiet, with polished wooden floors and thin rugs. Limited private parking outside. ❸

Pensão Flôr de Coimbra Rua do Poço 5 ☎239 823 856, ☎239 821 545. Well-cared-for *pensão* with a large selection of rooms – the en-suite ones on the first floor are the better choice, decently sized and with old carved beds; those above are simple to the point of brutality at times (floor-to-ceiling tiling, shower cubicle in corner), so it pays to look around. Breakfast is available and there's also a good restaurant (moderate; dinner only, closed Sun) that has at least one vegetarian special daily, plus a menu of Portuguese favourites. ❶, en suite ❷
Hotel Ibis Av Emídio Navarro 70 ☎239 852 130, ⓦwww.ibishotel.com. Good-value motel-style en-suite rooms in the heart of the city, with wifi access and garage parking. Prices go up a few euros at weekends and in summer, but most of the year you can sleep here for under €50 – the price is room-only, but breakfast is available. ❸
Residencial Internacional Av Emídio Navarro 4 ☎239 825 503, ✉international.coimbra@yahoo .com. Facing the river by the station, this once-grand, good-value *residencial* has a/c rooms with

high ceilings and reasonable bathrooms – some are smaller and without a river view, while other cheaper ones are tucked into the attic. It's a decent budget stand-by. No credit cards. **②**

Quinta das Lágrimas Off Rua António Augusto Gonçalves ⌕ 239 802 380, ⌾ www .quintadaslagrimas.pt. Situated across the river, this is Coimbra's grandest choice – a plush stately house set in beautiful gardens and offering regally decorated palace and garden rooms, as well as more contemporary spa rooms. The Garden Spa has various treatments, plus pool, sauna and Turkish bath, and there are two restaurants – the more formal *Arcadas da Capela* boasts a rare (for Portugal) Michelin star. **⑥**

Pensão Moderna Rua Adelino Veiga 49 ⌕ 239 825 413, ⌔ r.moderna@mail.pt. The entrance is upstairs, through a shopping gallery, and the tiled reception full of knick-knacks lowers expectations further, but the rooms are a distinct improvement – simply furnished but perfectly fine for the price, with a/c and small en-suite bathrooms. Some rooms have a small terrace overlooking the busy pedestrian street below. No credit cards. **②**

🛴 **Casa Pombal** Rua dos Flores 18 ⌕ 239 835 175, ⌾ www.casapombal.com. The only choice up in the old town is a very friendly Dutch-run

town house near the university with lashings of atmosphere. Rooms are small but pretty, with wooden floors, rugs and throws, some peering down over the rooftops to the river – rooms 6 and 10 have the best outlook, and from room 8 the view is from the bath! A splendid breakfast is served in the tiled dining room and there's a small patio-garden – it's a real home-from-home. **②**, en-suite **③**

Hotel Tivoli Rua João Machado 4 ⌕ 239 858 300, ⌾ www.tivolihotels.com. The city's most central four-star hotel doesn't have much of a location (out near the bus station), though it's less than ten minutes' walk to the historic centre. Rooms are reliable and modern, and there's an indoor pool and garage parking. **⑥**

Youth hostel

Pousada de Juventude Rua Henrique Seco 14 ⌕ 239 822 955, ⌾ www.pousadasjuventude.pt. Above Parque Santa Cruz, and close to the bars and clubs around Pr da República, this is a decent modern hostel with nice 4–8-bed dorms and private en-suite twin rooms, plus patio, kitchen and TV room. There's 24hr reception, but check in is only from 6pm–midnight. Buses #7 and #29 Coimbra A run to the hostel. Dorm beds €11, rooms **①**

The city

Coimbra straddles a hilly site on the north bank of the Rio Mondego, with the faculty buildings of the **Velha Universidade** (Old University) crowning its summit. The slopes below are a convoluted mass of ancient alleys, centred on the medieval cathedral, the **Sé Velha**, while at the foot of the hill is the largely pedestrianized **Baixa**, or lower town, which is the principal shopping area. The western side of the old town is bounded by Rua Ferreira Borges and its continuation, Rua Visconde da Luz, which runs north from the café-filled **Largo da Portagem** to the **Igreja de Santa Cruz**. Off to the west, behind the large square of **Praça do Comércio**, the narrow rat-runs and alleys that cut down to Coimbra A train station are riddled with mini-markets, budget restaurants, traditional grocery shops, discount clothing stores and smarter boutiques and shoe shops.

On foot, the best approach to the upper old town is from halfway along the Baixa's main street, up through the **Arco de Almedina**, an arch cut through the medieval city wall. Stepped streets climb beyond into the heart of old Coimbra – the name of one, Rua de Quebra Costas (Back-breaker Street) lets you know what you're in for – with alleys off to either side revealing hidden courtyards, flower-decked balconies, cobbled dead-ends and glimpses of sky. Chances are you'll get lost as soon as you start to climb, but that's half the fun.

Igreja de Santa Cruz

Restraint and simplicity are simply not the words that spring to mind when considering the **Igreja de Santa Cruz** (Mon–Sat 9am–noon & 2–5.45pm, Sun 4–6pm; church free, sacristy, chapter house and cloister €2.50), at the

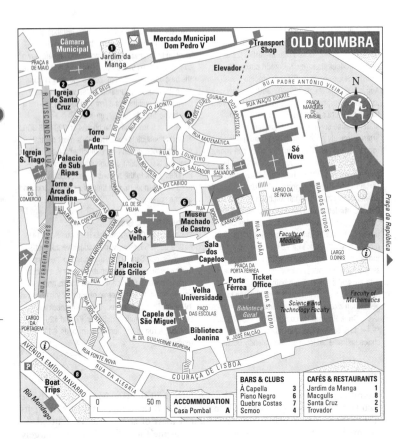

OLD COIMBRA

Map labels: Câmara Municipal, Jardim da Manga, Mercado Municipal Dom Pedro V, Transport Shop, PRAÇA 8 DE MAIO, Elevador, RUA PADRE ANTÓNIO VIEIRA, RUA VISCONDE DA LUZ, Igreja de Santa Cruz, RUA DO CORPO DE DEUS, COURAÇA DOS APÓSTOLOS, RUA INIAÇO DUARTE, PRAÇA MARQUÊS DE POMBAL, RUA DOS ESTORES, RUA DO COLÉGIO NOVO, RUA DO JOÃO JACINTO, A, RUA MATEMÁTICA, Torre de Anto, RUA DAS COUTINHAS, RUA DA VISTA, RUA DO LOUREIRO, LG. S. SALVADOR, RUA DES. SALVADOR, Sé Nova, Igreja S. Tiago, Palacio de Sub Ripas, Torre e Arca de Almedina, RUA SUB RIPAS, RUA DO CABIDO, LARGO DA SÉ NOVA, RUA DOS ESTUDOS, PR DO COMERCIO, RUA FERREIRA BORGES, RUA JOAQUIM ANTÓNIO DE AGUIAR, LG. DE SÉ VELHA, Sé Velha, Museu Machado de Castro, RUA BORGES CARNEIRO, RUA S. JOÃO, Faculty of Medicine, Praça da República, Sala dos Capelos, Palacio dos Grilos, R. CRISTOVÃO, RUA DA ILHA, PRAÇA DA PORTA FÉRREA, Porta Férrea, Ticket Office, LARGO D. DINIS, RUA FERNANDES TOMAZ, RUA DOS ESTEIROS, Velha Universidade, PAÇO DAS ESCOLAS, Biblioteca Geral, RUA S. PEDRO, Science and Technology Faculty, Faculty of Mathematics, Capela de São Miguel, R. DR. GUILHERME MOREIRA, Biblioteca Joanina, R. JOSÉ FALCÃO, LARGO DA PORTAGEM, AVENIDA EMÍDIO NAVARRO, RUA FONTE NOVA, RUA DA ALEGRIA, COURAÇA DE LISBOA, Boat Trips, Rio Mondego, Casa Pombal A

0 — 50 m

BARS & CLUBS		CAFÉS & RESTAURANTS	
À Capella	3	Jardim da Manga	1
Piano Negro	6	Macgulls	8
Quebra Costas	7	Santa Cruz	2
Scmoo	4	Trovador	5

ACCOMMODATION	
Casa Pombal	A

northern end of Rua Visconde da Luz, overlooking Praça 8 de Maio. Originally a monastery church, founded as early as 1131, nothing remains of the original design that was not substantially remodelled during two periods of a huge influx of wealth into Portugal. The exuberant facade and rich interior *azulejos* are from the eighteenth century, though it's the sixteenth-century Manueline additions that first transformed Santa Cruz. Coimbra was the base of a major sculptural school that included the French artists Nicolas Chanterene and Jean de Rouen (João de Ruão), as well as the two Manueline masters João de Castilho and Diogo de Boitaca, all of whom had a hand in rebuilding the church. These artists designed a variety of projects, viewed via the sacristy: tombs to house Portugal's first kings, Afonso Henriques and Sancho I; the elaborate Sala do Capitulo (chapter house); and, most famously, the Cloister of Silence. It is here that the Manueline theme is at its clearest, with a series of airy arches decorated with bas-relief scenes from the life of Christ.

Around the back of the church, the small **Jardim da Manga** is all that remains of the Manga fountain, once attached to Santa Cruz. The monastery was always a royal favourite and a fixture on the pilgrim route to Santiago de Compostela in Spain. It's claimed that it was here that Dom Pedro's royal mistress, Inês de Castro, was captured before being murdered later in Coimbra by assassins (see "Quinta da Lágrimas", p.236).

Sé Velha

The **Sé Velha** (Mon–Thurs & Sat 10am–6pm, Fri 10am–1pm; free), an unmistakable fortress-like bulk, squats about halfway up the hill in its own steeply shelving square. Begun in 1162, it's one of the most important Romanesque buildings in Portugal, little altered and seemingly unbowed by the weight of the years. The one significant later addition – the Renaissance Porta Especiosa in the north wall – has, in contrast to the main structure, almost entirely crumbled away. Solid and square on the outside, the cathedral is also stolid and simple within, the decoration confined to a few giant conch shells holding holy water and some unobtrusive *azulejos* from Seville around the walls. The Gothic tombs of early bishops and the low-arched **cloister** (€1) are equally restrained.

Museu Machado de Castro and Sé Nova

Coimbra's most important art and applied art museum, the **Museu Nacional de Machado de Castro**, remains closed for "works", and is not expected to re-open until 2010. The building, named after an eighteenth-century sculptor, is housed in the former archbishop's palace, under which lies the Roman **Cryptoportico** (no public access), a series of subterranean galleries probably used by the Romans as a granary and subsequently pressed into service for the foundations of the palace.

Across the way stands the unprepossessing **Sé Nova**, or New Cathedral (Tues–Fri 9am–noon & 2–5.30pm; free), a seventeenth-century Jesuit foundation which replaced the Sé Velha as cathedral in 1772.

Velha Universidade

From the Sé Nova, head up Rua de São João and turn right into the Praça da Porta Férrea, which stands at the heart of the university enclave. The elaborate seventeenth-century **Porta Férrea** itself – named for the "iron gate" that once guarded the entrance – provides access to the main part of the **Velha Universidade** (daily: April–Oct 9am–7.30pm; Nov–March 9.30am–5.30pm; €6 for university, library and Sala dos Capelos, €3.50 library or Sala dos Capelos only), though first you have to buy tickets from the Loja da Universidade, inside the Biblioteca Geral in Praça da Porta Férrea.

Dating from the sixteenth century, when João III declared its establishment at Coimbra permanent, the buildings are set around an open courtyard dominated by the Baroque **clock tower** nicknamed *A Cabra* – "the goat" – and a statue of the portly João III. You don't need to buy a ticket to come into the courtyard, and from the terrace in front of the statue there are some sweeping city and river views.

The elaborate stairway to the right of the main court leads into the administrative quarters and the **Sala dos Capelos**, hung with portraits of Portugal's kings and used for conferring degrees. It has a fine wood-panelled ceiling with gilded decoration in the Manueline style. The highlight of this part of the building, though, is the narrow catwalk around the outside walls.

The central door off the courtyard leads past the **Capela de São Miguel**, covered with *azulejos* and intricate decoration including twisted, rope-like pillars, a frescoed ceiling, and a gaudy Baroque organ. To the left is the famous library, the **Biblioteca Joanina**, a Baroque fantasy presented to the faculty by João V in the early eighteenth century. Its rooms telescope into each other, focusing on the founder's portrait in a disconcertingly effective use of *trompe l'oeil*. The richness of it all is impressive, such as the expanse of cleverly marbled wood, gold leaf, tables inlaid with ebony, rosewood and jacaranda, Chinese-style lacquer work and carefully calculated frescoed ceilings. The most prized valuables, the rare and ancient books, are locked away out of sight and, despite their impressive multilingual titles, the volumes on the shelves seem largely chosen for their aesthetic value; no one seems likely to disturb the careful arrangement by actually reading anything.

Their lofty position notwithstanding, the other surrounding university faculty buildings have little to recommend them. Most are foursquare marble and concrete excrescences of the Estado Novo period (1940s and 1950s), part of a controversial modernization programme under Salazar. The wide spaces in between are tempered by heroic statues and *calçada* paving, and only the lure of the student-frequented pavement cafés and bars on **Praça da República** – down the monumental steps from Largo Dom Dinis – merit the diversion.

Jardim Botânico

Just down the hill from Largo Dom Dinis, five minutes or so to the south, the **Jardim Botânico** (daily: April–Sept 9am–8pm; Oct–May 9am–5.30pm; free) provides a shaded respite from the city heat and noise. Founded in the eighteenth century, the gardens once enjoyed a worldwide reputation, though that's hard to believe nowadays. Still, the watered lawns, sunken gardens, plant beds and soaring palms make for a pleasant stroll and for €2 you can visit the **estufas** (greenhouses) and nearby **Museu Botânico** (both Mon-Fri 9am–noon & 2–5pm). As you walk back uphill towards the university you follow the line of the impressive sixteenth-century **Aqueduto de São Sebastião**.

The Santa Clara convents

A ten-minute walk from Largo da Portagem, across the Ponte de Santa Clara, leads to the **Convento de Santa Clara-a-Velha**, original burial place of Coimbra's patron, saint-queen Isabel, wife of Dom Dinis. The convent suffered continually from floods from the fourteenth century onwards, but by 1677 the nuns conceded defeat and moved up the hill to the Convento de Santa Clara-a-Nova, taking Isabel with them. Remarkably, the convent remained immersed in water and silt for more than three hundred years, with only the highest part visible. Between 1995 and 1999 the site was drained and the well-preserved convent can now be seen on **guided tours** in Portuguese and English (Tues–Sun at 10am, 11am, 3pm & 4pm, plus 5pm & 6pm from April-Sept; €3; Ⓦhttp://sta-clara-a-velha.ccg.pt). A museum containing the many artefacts found during the restoration is planned at the site.

The **Convento de Santa Clara-a-Nova** (daily 9am–noon & 2–5pm; cloister €1.50), higher up the hill and safe from the shifting river, was built in 1650; it doesn't have much of the charm of the old and the fact that the nuns' quarters now house a Portuguese army barracks doesn't help. Indeed, this must be the only convent outside a war zone with a tank and gun carriages surveying the entrance. Its two saving graces are **Isabel's tomb** – made of solid silver collected by the citizens of Coimbra – and the vast **cloister**, heady with honeysuckle, which was financed by João V, a king whose devotion to nuns went beyond the normal bounds of spiritual comfort. The army's presence exerts itself in a small **Museu Militar** (daily 10am–noon & 2–5pm; €1.50), but you're better off saving your money and simply taking in the city and river views from the wide terrace outside.

Portugal dos Pequenitos and Quinta das Lágrimas

Between the two convents extends the parkland site of **Portugal dos Pequenitos** (daily: June to mid-Sept 9am–8pm; mid-Sept to Feb 10am–5pm; March–May

△ Convento de Santa Clara-a-Velha

10am–7pm; Easter week and summer €6, otherwise €5, under 5s free; @www
.fbb.pt), a theme park built in the 1940s where scale models of many of the
country's great buildings are interspersed with "typical" farmhouses and sections
on the overseas territories, heavy with the White Man's Burden. Historically and
architecturally accurate it's not, but the place is great fun for children who can
clamber in and out of the miniature houses. There's a good playground too.

A short distance beyond lies the **Quinta das Lágrimas** (Estate of Tears), now a luxury hotel, but once an estate hideaway for medieval Portugal's star-crossed lovers Dom Pedro and Inês de Castro. In the gardens (open to the public Tues-Fri 10am–1pm & 2-4.30/6pm; €3), so legend has it, Inês was brutally murdered on the orders of King Afonso IV – her tears (*lágrimas*) as she died lent the estate its name. Her lover, meanwhile, the crown prince Pedro, rose in open revolt against his own father and later extracted horrible revenge upon the murderers (see box on p.195 for all the gory details).

Eating

Most of the city's traditional **cafés** and **coffee houses** (open all day from 8am or so) are found in the Baixa, principally in Largo da Portagem, along Rua Ferreira Borges and Rua Visconde da Luz, and in traffic-free Praça do Comércio. The cheapest meals are to be found in the dives along Rua Direita in the Baixa, where if you're not too bothered about your surroundings – basement saloons and rough tables – you can eat for €5. For a tad more sophistication, search out the atmospheric little **restaurants** tucked into the tiny alleys between Largo da Portagem, Rua da Sota and Praça do Comércio – Rua das Azeiteiras, in partic-ular, has several good possibilities. Local specialities include *chanfana* – kid goat braised in wine – and *pasteis de Santa Clara* (cream-filled pastries traditionally made at the Santa Clara convent).

Adega Paço do Conde Rua Paço do Conde 1 ☎239 825 605. Great, locally renowned *churrasqueira*, with a dining room either side of a shady covered terrace. Chicken, meat and fish comes straight off the outdoor grill – meals come to around €10 including salad, wine and coffee. Closed Sun. Inexpensive.

Cantinho do Reis Terreiro da Erva 16 ☎239 824 116. The sun-trap terrace is the big attraction here, on the edge of an off-the-beaten-track square where the neighbourhood is slowly being demol-ished around it. But the food attracts a steady stream of regulars, and lunch is a particularly good deal – it's a fish and grills place, with reliable *bacalhau* dishes and a tasty house steak. Closed Sun. Moderate.

Jardim da Manga Rua Olímpio Nicolau Rui Fernandes ☎239 829 156. A self-service restaurant with Portuguese standards on offer – the best thing about it is the location, with outdoor seating on the terrace behind Santa Cruz church, overlooking the Manga fountain. Closed Sat. Inexpensive.

Macgulls Av Emídio Navarro 37 ☎239 405 800. Enjoy delicately spiced, aromatic Indian and Pakistani dishes in this rather formal but friendly restaurant near the riverside gardens. There's an English-language menu, but the Portuguese one has a more extensive list of Pakistani specialities. You can even get a *Cobra* beer. Expensive.

O Pátio Pátio da Inquisição 26 ☎239 828 596. Good for lunch on a sunny day, this small restaurant sits on a little terrace above a tastefully

renovated square. The *pratos da dia* are the best value, but nothing is too expensive and nobody is in much of a hurry. Moderate.

Café Santa Cruz Pr 8 de Maio. Coimbra's most appealing café, set in part of the monastery buildings. There are tables in the vaulted stone interior, but it's even nicer on the terrace above the square where you can watch the world go by. There's a big list of sandwiches, otherwise it's a cake and pastries place. Inexpensive.

Trovador Largo da Sé Velha 17 ☎239 825 475. The location – next to the old cathedral – pushes the price up here (meals around €20), but it's a cosy, traditional choice, replete with wood panelling and *azulejos*. Dishes are of the *cabrito, bacalhau, chanfana* variety and it's the kind of place that sees Coimbra fado sessions at weekends. Closed Sun. Moderate.

Viela Rua das Azeiteiras 33 ☎239 832 625. The street's best bargain – the daily €5 lunch runs from soup to dessert, wine included. There's a longer *a la carte* menu too, all very reasonably priced, and though it's only a simple pack-em-in place, there are outdoor tables around the corner in a quiet square. Inexpensive.

Zé Manel Beco do Forno 12 ☎239 823 790. Atmospheric little place, tucked away in a quiet street behind *Hotel Astória*. The walls are adorned with cartoons and poems, the service is brisk and friendly, and the regional food excellent. If you don't want to queue, turn up by 1 or 7pm. Closed Sat eve & Sun. Moderate.

Drinking, nightlife and entertainment

Praça da República, across town beyond the university, is where the student **bars** congregate, while there's a line of fashionable esplanade bars down along the riverside Parque Verde do Mondego (close to Coimbra Parque station). Unless otherwise stated below, bars tend to open around 9 or 10pm and stay open until 2am or later at weekends. In Coimbra's **clubs** you can expect the music to start at around midnight and keep going until 6am. As a rule, you'll pay a minimum entrance fee of €2.50–5 in the clubs, and in bars where there's a DJ or live music.

There's **fado** and other **live music** performances held all year, though you'll catch open-air gigs during the student celebrations in May and in the old town in summer (July to Sept). For other concerts and events, watch for fly posters stuck up all over university buildings or check what's on at the university theatre, the **Teatro Académico de Gil Vicente** in Praça da República (Ⓦwww .uc.pt/tagv), which has a full calendar of theatre, art-house movies and music.

Bars and live music

À Capella Rua do Corpo de Deus, Largo da Vitória Ⓦwww.acapella.com.pt. Housed in a former chapel, this stylish venue hosts late-night fado and other music performances – usually separate shows at 9.30, 10.30 and 11.30pm.

Diligência Rua Nova 30. Atmospheric candle-lit fado joint, though the feelings of *saudade* (loss and longing) from which the music draws its spirit will also be felt in your wallet. Open 6pm–2am.

Mondego Irish Pub Parque Verde de Mondego, Av da Lousã. Open from noon daily, so a great place for an afternoon riverside beer or late-night drinks and Irish music.

Piano Negro Rua Borges Carneiro 19. Small and smoky, this unpretentious bar attracts a good-humoured international student crowd, listening to jazz and chilled-out tunes.

Quebra Costas Rua de Quebra Costas 45-49 Ⓦwww.quebracostas.com. Laid-back music bar (open from 4pm) tucked away on the steps leading down from the Sé Velha. It's a jazzy, arty place, with an offshoot, *QuebraClub* (live Latin and jazz, DJs, exhibitions and events), down on the riverbank at Parque Verde do Mondego. The website has up-to-date event schedules.

Santa Clara Galeria Rua António Augusto Gonçalves 67 Ⓦwww.galeriasantaclara.com. Gallery café-bar with a large terrace overlooking Santa-Clara-a-Velha. A relaxed place for a coffee or a late drink (open 2pm–2am, Fri & Sat until 3am), and with exhibitions, music nights and other events.

Schmoo Rua do Corpo de Deus 68. Tiny, funky bar tucked away up an old back street, often with good DJs. Closed Sun.

Tropical Pr da República 35, corner of Rua Alexandre Herculano. The pick of the República bars is this studenty joint which heaves at the weekends. The pavement tables soon get swamped, while the barman roves around with trays of ice-cold Super Bocks. Closed Sun.

Clubs

RMX Rua Venâncio Rodrigues 11 & 19. A young crowd hangs out at this popular, down-to-earth club where everyone is up for a good time. Music tends towards chart hits and commercial dance (as in the name, ie "Re-mix").

Via Latina Rua Almeida Garrett 1. Relaxed space near Pr da República, on two floors. Music changes nightly but includes house, hip-hop, drum 'n' bass and R&B. Closed Sun.

Vinyl Av Afonso Henriques 43. Fashionable club favoured by the well-heeled glamour crowd. Usually showcases home-grown DJs as well as international names, such as Fatboy Slim. Closed Sun & Mon.

Listings

Boat trips Basófias runs 1hr cruises on the Rio Mondego, departing from beside Parque Dr. Manuel Braga (Ⓣ969 830 664, Ⓦwww.basofias.com; €8). Trips depart Tues–Sun at 3, 4, 5 & 6pm, though services may be restricted between October and April. O Pioneiro do Mondego arranges downriver kayak trips from the nearby town of Penacova to Coimbra (see p.243).

Buses Rede Expressos (intercity services; Ⓣ239 827 081, Ⓦwww.rede-expressos.pt) and

Rodoviária Beira Litoral (to Figueira da Foz, Leiria, Lousã, Luso, Penacova, Porto, Tondela and Viseu; ⊤ 239 855 270) operate from the main bus station on Av Fernão de Magalhães. Joalto Mondego (⊤ 239 823 769) runs to the Costa de Prata resorts, Figueira da Foz, Aveiro, Condeixa-a-Nova and Conímbriga – there's an office on Rua Simões de Castro at Rua João de Ruão (next door to the Mondego travel agency). Moisés Correia de Oliveira, Rua Rosa Falcão 10 (⊤ 239 828 263), runs to Montemor-o-Velho and Figueira da Foz. Rodonorte, at Bufete Teresinha, Av Emídio Navarro (⊤ 239 825 190, ⊛ www.rodonorte.pt) is for services to the mountain Beiras and the north.
Car rental Avis, Coimbra A station ⊤ 239 834 786, ⊛ www.avis.com; Hertz, Rua Padre Estêvão Cabral ⊤ 239 834 750, ⊛ www.hertz.com; Salitur/Europcar, Rua Padre Estêvão Cabral ⊤ 239 820 594.
Hospitals Hospital da Universidade de Coimbra, Largo Prof Mota Pinto ⊤ 239 400 400.
Internet You can get 30min free access at Espaço Internet, Pr 8 de Maio (Mon-Fri 10am–8pm, Sat 10am–10pm). Otherwise there are plenty of places around town, including Central Modem, Escadas do Quebra Costas (Mon-Fri 11am–4pm, Sat & Sun 3pm–4pm); and CiberEspaço, Galerias Avenida, Av Sá da Bandeira (Mon–Sat 10am–midnight, Sun 1pm–midnight).

Newspapers Foreign press available from Tabacaria Espírito Santo, Rua Martins de Carvalho, by Pr 8 de Maio.
Police Main PSP HQ is at Rua Olímpio Nicolau Rui Fernandes ⊤ 239 851 300, across from the post office.
Post office The main post office is at Av Fernão de Magalhães 223, near Largo do Arnado (Mon–Fri 8.30am–6.30pm, Sat 9am–12.30pm); other central offices are on Rua Olímpio Nicolau Rui Fernandes, just below the market, and on Pr da República (both same hours as main post office).
Shopping The Mercado Municipal Dom Pedro V (Mon–Sat), Rua Olímpio Nicolau Rui Fernandes, close to the post office, is the biggest market in the region, well worth a look. There are souvenirs (rugs, lace, ceramics, cockerel tea towels, postcards) up Rua de Quebra Costas and around Pr 8 de Maio. Big out-of-town shopping malls with cinemas and hypermarkets include Dolce Vita (near the city stadium) and Coimbra Shopping (near the modern bridge) and, over the river, Forum Coimbra – all signposted from every approach road.
Taxis There are taxi ranks outside Coimbra A and B train stations, by the police headquarters near Pr 8 de Maio, and in Pr da República. To call a cab, ring Politaxis ⊤ 239 499 090.

Around Coimbra

There are several sights within easy reach of Coimbra that are worth a day trip. The one unmissable visit is to the Roman city of **Conímbriga** and its fine mosaics, while west towards the coast stand the impressive ruins of the castle at **Montemor-o-Velho**. To the northeast of the city the kayaking possibilities on the **Rio Mondego** and the attractive scenery around the hilltop town of **Penacova** are similarly enticing and, if you were looking for an overnight stop in the Coimbra countryside, this would be the best choice. All the destinations can be reached easily by public transport.

Conímbriga

The ancient city of **Conímbriga** (daily: June–Sept 9am–8pm; Oct–May 10am–6pm; €3, free Sun; ⊛ www.conimbriga.pt), 16km southwest of Coimbra, is by far the most important Roman site in Portugal. It was almost certainly preceded by a substantial Celto-Iberian settlement, dating back to the Iron Age, but the excavated buildings nearly all belong to the latter days of the Roman Empire, from the second to the fifth century AD. Throughout this period Conímbriga was a major stopping point on the road from Olisipo (Lisbon) to Bracara Augusta (Braga). Although by no means the largest town in Roman Portugal, it has survived better than any other – principally because when attacked its inhabitants abandoned Conímbriga and never resettled it. That the city came to a violent end is clear from the powerful wall thrown up right through its heart, a wall erected so hurriedly and determinedly that it even cut houses in two.

There are some explanatory notes in English posted across the site, and you get a site plan on entry, but in summer especially you may find students and archeologists on site to explain the finer points. Allow a good couple of hours for the whole site, as there's an interesting museum too – you can refuel at the **café-restaurant**, which has a terrace overlooking part of the site.

The site

It is the **wall**, with the Roman road leading up to and through it, that first strikes you. In the urgency of its construction anything that came to hand was used and a close inspection reveals pillars, inscribed plaques and bricks thrown in among the rough stonework. Most of what has been excavated is in the immediate environs of the wall, notably a series of houses with exceptional **mosaic floors**, some covered to protect them from the elements. In the "House of Fountains" there are vivid hunting scenes showing animals in flight, while the villa's original fountains and water-ducts have been restored to working order (drop a coin into the machine to watch them play). Elsewhere, a complex series of **baths** reveals their elaborate under-floor heating system – the city was supplied with water by an impressive **aqueduct**, large parts of which still stand.

Beyond the wall recent work has been undertaken to recreate something of the spirit and scale of the city's public areas. There's the **forum**, built at the end of the first century AD, with its market place, shop entrances and nearby **temple**, while at the edge of the site, on a bluff above the steep valley – for many years Conímbriga's main defence – a series of **public baths** enjoy a stupendous view.

The museum

The excellent **Museu Monográfico de Conímbriga** (same hours as site but closed Mon), opposite the site entrance, displays fascinating finds from the dig, presented thematically. Cabinets detail the minutiae of various trades (glass-making, ironmongery, weaving, even house-building) and aspects of daily life; the section on health and hygiene contains scalpels, needles and some quite alarming "probing spoons". On the other side of the museum are displayed the larger spoils – statues of torsos, carved lintels, gargoyles from temples, monochromatic mosaics, remarkably bright mural fragments, and inscribed slabs, pillars and tombstones from the necropolis.

Practicalities: Condeixa-a-Nova

Only a very limited Joalto Mondego **bus** service runs directly from Coimbra to Conímbriga, currently at 9.05am (Mon–Fri only) and 9.35am, returning from the site at 1pm (Mon–Sat only) and 6pm. The bus leaves Coimbra from a stop by the traffic lights on the main Avenida Fernão de Magalhães, just up from the Joalto Mondego bus office (see Coimbra "Listings") – it's a half-hour journey. There are far more regular Joalto services (roughly every 30–60min) to and from **CONDEIXA-A-NOVA**, though it's a two-kilometre walk from there to the site – follow the signposts – and you have to cross the main highway. There's a big car park at the site.

Condeixa itself is a pleasant little market town, known for its hand-painted ceramics that are sold at various outlets around town. The *Pousada de Santa Cristina* (☎239 944 025, ⊛www.pousadas.pt; ◑), north of the main square, is a modern one, but it's an elegant place in peaceful grounds with a swimming pool and restaurant tables set on the lawn in summer. Just down the road from here (back towards the centre, in front of the Sotto Mayor palace) is *O Cabritino*, Rua Francisco de Lemos 9 (☎239 944 111; closed Tues), a handsome fine-dining restaurant (mains €11–16) with a summer terrace and garden; or you can eat at the cheaper cafés and bars around the main square, Praça da República. *O Regional do Cabrito* (☎239 944 933), for example, does decent meals at reasonable prices. The local speciality – as perhaps you're beginning to realize from the restaurant names – is *cabrito* (roast kid), usually slow-roasted and served with roast potatoes and greens.

Montemor-o-Velho

Thirty-two kilometres west of Coimbra, the keep and crenellated silhouette of the castle at **MONTEMOR-O-VELHO** brood over the flood plain of the Mondego. First the Romans, then the Moors, fortified this conspicuous rocky bluff; finally taken from the Moors at the end of the eleventh century, it became a favoured royal residence. It was here in 1355 that Dom Afonso IV met with his council to decide on the fate of Inês de Castro, and here, thirty years later, that João of Avis received the homage of the townspeople on his way to Coimbra to be acclaimed Dom João I. Despite this royal attention, the town itself never really prospered, and there's little enough to see inside the **castle** (Tues–Sun: June–Sept 10am–8pm, Oct–May 10am–12.30pm & 2–5pm; free), though the views from the walkways are stunning. The main attraction within the walls is the Manueline Igreja de Santa Maria de Alcáçova, said to have been designed by Diogo de Boitaca of Belém fame; it has a beautiful wooden ceiling, fine twisted columns and Moorish-style *azulejo* decoration. Otherwise, the lawns are a good place to let children run free and there's a nice terrace-café.

On the second or fourth Wednesday of the month, Montemor's vast morning **market** spills across the plain in the lee of the castle. Families swarm in from the surrounding countryside, soon clogging up the congested central streets. The **train station** is a one-kilometre walk from town and castle; **buses** from Coimbra drop you much more centrally. Best place for **lunch** is *A Grelha* (☎239 689 372; closed Sat), a *churrasqueira* in town below the castle on the main avenue, where a *meia dose* of grilled fish or meat goes for around €7.

Drivers can follow the signs from the roundabout at the edge of town to "Torre" and "Parque Zoológico", which lead for 2km up the hill to **Europaradise** (Tues–Sun 10am–6pm, open Mon in Aug; €5, children €2.50) – if it looks closed, ring the number posted on the gate and someone will come and let you in. Zoos in Portugal don't have much of a reputation but this family concern is rather sweet, with nothing too inappropriate (a fair few monkeys and a single zebra, but otherwise mainly ducks, goats, deer and peacocks). There's a shady circuit around the various enclosures, fine for pushchairs.

Penacova, Lorvão and the Rio Mondego

Northeast of Coimbra, the hilly, wooded valley of the **Rio Mondego** is a delight. The river is trailed by the minor N110 road, affording the occasional sweeping view of glistening water and improbably perched hamlets. Regular weekday buses make the trip from Coimbra, while during the summer it's possible to kayak downriver from **Penacova** back to Coimbra (see below). The town is also just off the fast IP3, so drivers can always see Penacova en route to Buçaco and Luso (via the N235) or the Dão valley and Viseu.

PENACOVA itself, 22km northeast of Coimbra, is a small town of some antiquity set high above the river, with stunning views of the valley. There is little enough to the place itself – a pint-sized square with a town hall, a modest cobbled historic quarter along the ridge and a couple of cafés and restaurants. For sweeping views of river and valley make a beeline for the terrace of the *Café Turismo*, by the side of the town hall. With a car you can then follow the signs the few kilometres up into the wooded hills above Penacova to the **Mosteiro de Lorvão**, an ancient monastic foundation that traces its history back to the sixth century AD, though what you see today dates from sweeping alterations made in the seventeenth and eighteenth centuries. With the monastery the overwhelmingly dominant building, Lorvão is still in effect a monastic village. If you're here on the last Sunday of the month, you'll coincide with the huge open-air **market**, and can eat barbecued chicken straight from the grill – or duck into one of the cafés for a traditional *pastel de Lorvão*. Penacova's equivalent market is on the second Thursday of the month – at either, look out for the highly elaborate toothpicks that are a local speciality, hand-carved from willow, the more delicate ones resembling feathered darts.

Practicalities

The **bus** from Coimbra drops you in the main square, where you'll find the helpful **turismo** (Mon–Fri 9am–5pm, Sat & Sun 10am–1pm & 2–5pm; ☏239 470 300, Ⓦwww.cm-penacova.pt), located in the town hall. There's also a weekday bus service from Penacova on to Tondela and Viseu that leaves in the late afternoon.

Plushest **accommodation** is the four-star ⅍ *Palacete do Mondego* (☏239 470 700, Ⓦwww.palacete-penacova.net; ❸, Easter–Sept ❹), set on the ridge high above the river (follow the signs). This grafts an Art Deco facade on to a former fort and chapel and provides 38 tastefully decorated rooms, plus fantastic views from terrace, pool and restaurant. Otherwise, the budget choice is the friendly, traditional *Pensão Avenida*, Avenida Abel Rodrigues da Costa (☏ & Ⓕ239 477 142; no credit cards; ❷), just down the hill from the main square, with a polished wood interior, sun-terrace and inexpensive restaurant – the large, slightly musty rooms all come with shower. There's a municipal **campsite** (☏239 477 664; closed mid-Dec to mid-Jan), on the opposite bank of the Mondego, 2km below town (Vila Nova de Poiares road); turn right after crossing the bridge. There's a restaurant and river beach here too.

Penacova specialities include *lampreias* (lampreys) and other river fish, while *chanfana* (goat stew) is on every **restaurant** menu too. A good place for these is *A Cota*, Azenha do Rio (☏239 474 841), though it's way below town by the bridge (Vila Nova de Poiares road). Actually in Penacova, the people's choice is the *Marisqueira Piscinas* (☏239 476 306); of all places, it's located in the swimming pool. Or there's the more formal, more expensive *O Panorâmico* (☏239 477 333) – next to the town hall and turismo – which has a glorious view down the valley.

On the river

Kayaking down the **Mondego river** has become pretty popular in recent years, and several local operators offer trips, most notably *O Pioneiro do Mondego* (☏239 478 385, Ⓦwww.opioneirodomondego.com), which arranges downriver trips from Penacova to Coimbra daily from June to September. Departure is usually at 11am and the 25-kilometre trip all the way to Coimbra can take the rest of the day (bring a picnic); it's largely a float trip though the last few kilometres require a bit more effort due to lack of current and the wind, so you can arrange to bail out after 18km. You'll need to book in advance – the day before is usually fine – and it costs €20 per person, or €18 for the shorter trip. Morning pick-ups from Coimbra are included, or you can arrange to be taken back to Penacova afterwards.

Serra da Lousã

The rugged hills of the **Serra da Lousã,** only 25km southeast of Coimbra, make another fine day trip from the city, though you'll really need to stay the night if you plan on doing any serious exploration or hiking. The handsome town of **Lousã** is the main base (easily accessible by train from Coimbra), providing access to a series of *aldeais serranas*, or **mountain schist villages**, that were largely depopulated in the 1960s but are now gradually being revived by the increasing interest in adventure and rural tourism.

Lousã and around

Although no longer the diminutive village it once was, **LOUSÃ** retains an attractive old kernel within the wider modern town, with the forested green slopes of the *serra* rising behind. A few intricately decorated chapels and *casas brasonadas* (heraldic mansions) survive in the older streets, while the grand town hall on the main square speaks loudly of more important times.

Best days to visit are Tuesdays and especially Saturdays, when the covered **market** is in full swing and the stallholders come in from the outlying villages to hawk their seasonal produce. Otherwise, Lousã's only real attraction is its miniature **castle**, though if you're not driving you're faced with a forty-minute uphill walk to reach it – it's signposted from the square near the town hall, and when you reach the main road above town turn right and continue for roughly 1.5km. Here, a tributary of the Mondego curls around a splendid narrow gorge between two wooded hills: on one sits the castle, whose stone keep provides views across the valley; on the other is a small hermitage dedicated to Nossa Senhora da Piedade. In July and August, bathers crowd the river beach and pool between the two, above which sits the *Burgo* restaurant (see below), while stepped paths climb up the hillside beyond past a succession of small caves, terraces and viewpoints.

Drivers can also visit other popular river beaches (signposted *praia fluvial*) in the area, notably at attractive **Casal de Ermio**, 6km north of Lousã (en route to Serpins), where a terrace-bar is erected over the water (June–Aug) – this place heaves in hot weather at weekends. There's not much to **Serpins** itself, 2km further on, though it has a small Sunday morning market, while on the last Sunday of each month at **Foz de Arouce** (10km north, Coimbra road) the "Mercadilho" is an outdoor organic farmers' and craft market that attracts an eclectic crowd.

Practicalities

Trains run from Coimbra Parque station, roughly an hourly service that continues on from Lousã to Serpins, the end of the line, ten minutes further on. There are two train stations at Lousã: get off at the second, Lousã (not Lousã-A), and walk up Avenida do Brasil (at right angles to the rail line) to the centre. **Buses** from Coimbra stop by the *Café Avenida* on Avenida do Brasil; there are also early morning weekday services to Arganil (7.10am) and Góis (8am) in the Serra do Açor. The **turismo** (Mon–Fri 9am–12.30pm & 2–5.30pm, Sat & Sun 10am–12.30pm & 2.30–4pm; ☎239 990 040, ⓦwww.cm-lousa.pt) is rather inconveniently sited, in the Museu Etnográfico, on Rua João Luso, actually easiest to find from the train station – turn right (instead of straight ahead down the avenue) and it's a few hundred metres along, where the train track crosses the Coimbra road.

There's not much **accommodation**, but what there is is pretty good, and the town makes a peaceful overnight stop. There's also rural accommodation and a **campsite** (T 239 971 141) 8km away in Serpins, at the end of the train line from Lousã. **Restaurants** are plentiful, while **cafés** put out tables around the modern Praça Sá Carneiro (behind the school that stands in front of the market). Incidentally, it was a pharmacist from Lousã who originally came up with the secret recipe for **Licor Beirão**, a herb-flavoured, sickly sweet sort of cognac, drunk all over Portugal.

Hotels, pensions and B&B

Quintal de Além do Ribeiro Ceira dos Vales, 4km northeast of Lousã T 239 996 480, W www .quintal-turismorural.web.pt. A well-run, homely collection of rustic rooms, some with kitchenettes and all with antique radios, peacefully set around a thoughtfully restored farmhouse, complete with simple bar, pretty garden and pool. Plentiful and delicious buffet breakfast. No credit cards. ❸, weekends, & July–Sept ❹

Jardim da Tia Terra da Gaga, Serpins, 8km north of Lousã T 919 958 044, E info@jardimdatia. com, W www.jardimdatia.com. Charming self-catering two-bedroom cottage (available by the night or week, for exclusive use), nestling in the foothills of the Serra da Lousã – there are panoramic views from the terrace and a separate sun terrace-barbecue area. The friendly English/French owners live opposite and provide a huge, delicious breakfast. Email for driving directions or take the train to Serpins from Coimbra/Lousã (possible station pick-up available). No credit cards. ❸

Residencial Martinho Rua Forças Armadas T 239 991 397, F 239 994 335. A dozen simple, sunny en-suite rooms in an extension to the family house, with distant hill views and a log fire downstairs in winter. It's up the hill from the town hall square, and turn left. ❷

Mélia Palácio da Lousã Largo Viscondessa do Espinhal T 239 990 800, W www.solmelia.com. In the old town below the town hall, this boutique hotel occupies an impressive eighteenth-century mansion. It's a very handsome conversion, with rooms in contemporary style, plus a nice pool. ❹

Restaurants

Borges Rua Dr João Santos 2 T 239 993 489. Basic check-tablecloth grill-restaurant, serving up veal chops, chicken and steaks (though some fish too), with quaffable local wine by the jug and home-made desserts. Closed Mon. Moderate.

Burgo Ermida da Senhora da Piedade T 239 991 162. Up by the castle, *Burgo* enjoys a lovely setting and specializes in excellent regional cuisine and wine, served in a dining room overlooking the river. A veritable smorgasbord of appetizers appears as you sit down – you'll be charged for it, so if you don't want it say so. Closed Mon. Expensive.

Casa Velha Pr Sá Carneiro 14 T 239 991 555. Set in the modern plaza beyond the market, *Casa Velha* is the favoured family choice in town. There's a long menu of Portuguese standards and mountain cuisine, including a terrific *porco à alentejana*, and portions are vast. Closed Tues eve, all Wed & last two weeks of July. Moderate.

Gato Rua Dr João Santos 6 T 239 994 640. Popular local dining room at the rear of a rustic bar, serving up great grills and fries as well as inexpensive daily specials. Closed Tues. Moderate.

Serra da Lousã

The schist villages in the hills of the **Serra da Lousã** were largely deserted in the 1960s as a result of rural emigration. Having lain abandoned for forty years, some of the *aldeais serranas* are now being renovated and repopulated, boosted by an influx of get-away-from-it-all foreigners (attracted by cheap property prices) and by an increasing awareness of the possibilities of rural tourism. Lousã turismo has a sketch map of the villages and, while it's not brilliant, it does at least point you in the right direction – note that not all the roads are surfaced, though unless otherwise indicated they are usually fine for normal cars. Or you can ask about local operators who run **4WD tours** into the hills – Transserrano

A hike into the Serra da Lousã

This three-hour, six-kilometre circular hike in the **Serra da Lousã** provides marvellous views and a fascinating glimpse of mountain village life.

From the *Burgo* restaurant near Lousã's castle, walk up the stone steps to the end of the picnic area, and follow the sign to Casal Novo and Talasnal. The steep rocky path climbs for 1km until it reaches a junction; follow the right-hand fork and after 700m or so you will emerge onto a wider track, which you should follow uphill until it joins a second similar track – turn left and continue the ascent. As the path comes clear of the trees your toil is rewarded by stunning views of the valley below. At the top of this path turn left and continue upwards where you'll meet an unsurfaced road; Talasnal is visible to your left – or you can head right to sleepy **Casal Novo**, which spills down the hillside.

Retrace your steps, ignoring the track you came up and continue in the direction of **Talasnal**, probably the most beautiful of the range's villages with a harmonious mix of ruined and restored cottages amidst stunning mountain views. Once you've wound round the side of the mountain you descend to the entrance of the village, whose narrow, higgledy-piggledy passageways are worth a wander.

To exit the village, follow the stream downhill, passing numerous small dwellings in various states of repair to your left and right. Continue downwards on a path mostly marked by dry stone walls on both sides. When the trail meets a T-junction turn left downhill and cross the river via an old stone bridge. Follow the good, easily navigable path all the way back to the river pools, keeping an eye out for occasional fallen logs blocking the path and the dizzy drop to your right. A well-earned dip in the pools below the castle makes a refreshing end to the walk.

(Ⓦ www.transserrano.com) in Góis (see below) is the most reliable. A number of people also offer private rooms and other **accommodation** in tiny villages like Casal Novo, Talasnal and Cerdeira (details from Lousã turismo or on their website). A circular walk from Lousã castle (see below) leads to both Casal Novo and **Talasnal**, the latter with the bonus of the beautifully sited restaurant *Ti'Lena* (Ⓣ 933 832 624 or 917 045 608) in a restored schist house. It's open all year for dinner (plus lunch at weekends), but you have to call ahead to let them know you're coming and the menu is fairly limited (*cabrito, chanfana, bacalhau*).

Serra do Açor

East of Lousã stretches the **Serra do Açor**, a mountain range that borders the Serra da Estrela at its southwestern edge. It's a very attractive region, a mix of bucolic river valleys, pine and eucalyptus forest and the higher traditional schist villages of the mountains proper. **Góis**, 20km northeast of Lousã, is the gateway, prettily set in a river valley, with the small market town of **Arganil** another 13km to the north. You can reach both by bus from Coimbra/Lousã, though you'll have far more flexibility with your own transport – essential if you're to visit any of the secluded picnic spots and river beaches that make this area so beguiling, or specifically to visit the marvellous schist village of **Piódão**, high in the peaks.

Góis

GÓIS is beautifully set on the Rio Ceira, crossed by an arched sixteenth-century bridge which leads up to a sloping cobbled square backed by a couple of old-town streets. There's not a lot to occupy you here – as a town, it makes a great village – but it comes into its own in summer (June to mid-Sept) when boardwalks are erected and white sand imported to construct a fantastic river beach. A beach bar opens by the bridge and main beach – there's another seasonal sand beach, bathing area and garden bar a few hundred metres downstream by the municipal park. Transerrano (☎235 778 938, Ⓦwww.transserrano.com; English spoken) – back from the bridge on the Lousã road – operates **outdoor activities** year-round, including kayaking, jeep safaris, canyoning, mountain biking and mountain walking. These are aimed at groups (with a minimum number of participants), but

△ Góis

you can check the website or call to see if you might coincide with anything interesting – or they'll rent you a kayak or a bike (€10) for a day's gentle unescorted river paddling or touring.

Buses drop you at the top of town in front of the fire station. Head down the cobbled road to the central square, on which you'll find the **turismo** (variable hours, most consistently open June–Sept daily 9am–7pm; ☎235 772 090, ⓦwww .cm-gois.pt) and, just off it, the simple, unsigned *Casa Santo António*, Rua de Santo Antonio 18 (☎235 770 120; ❷), which has the only official **accommodation** in town. The same people also operate the town **campsite** (☎235 778 585), sited in a lovely position up the hill from the west bank of the river. For B&B in peaceful surroundings call Kate and Jules (☎235 778 094 or 918 156 181), an English couple with a house in a rustic hamlet 2km above Góis. Dinner is by arrangement, while Jules can organize local self-guided walking tours or take guests on trips to Conímbriga and other Roman sites. There are half a dozen straightforward **cafés and restaurants** in town, the best being the *Encosta da Seara* (☎235 778 6098; closed Thurs), which is on the road out of town past the fire station (Arganil direction), and opposite the school. It's a pizza place, with a proper wood-fired oven, but also serves pasta and Portuguese grills.

Góis is pretty quiet for most of the year, though it perks up in the holiday month of August, no more so than for the huge **motorbike rally** (Concentração de Góis) organized by the Góis Moto Clube (ⓦwww.goismotoclube .net). This attracts up to 40,000 bikers for a good-natured four-day festival of bike shows, radical sports, live bands and DJs – a tent city lines the river just outside town, and the roads are packed with preening speedsters.

Arganil

The bumpy N342 winds through the trees for 13km from Góis, finally descending to the small town of **ARGANIL**. It's quite the largest settlement hereabouts, which isn't saying much, and makes for a useful break in the journey – to which end, the nicest terrace café is the one by the roundabout at the top of town, attached to the theatre building. There's a pedestrianized main street full of traditional shops, and another couple of cafés by the square. That said, by far the best day to visit is a Thursday when Arganil's huge regional weekly **market** takes place on the open-air space above town, from early morning onwards. Part market, part bazaar, you can buy anything from a garden spade to a dining-room suite, and it's particularly good for cheap clothes, shoes, local basketware and agricultural hardware and supplies. Smallholders come in with produce from their plots and allotments, while the eco-folk and foreign hippies come down from the hills for a bit of a chat and some hair-braiding or to sell organic produce and plants. Inside the market building on the edge of the grounds there's a simple first-floor *churrasqueira* where everyone goes to eat grilled chicken or *leitão* for lunch – you'll get the works for just a few euros.

Piódão

From Arganil, it's around an hour's beautiful drive via Coja to **PIÓDÃO**, a fascinating traditional schist village, set on a steeply terraced mountainside. It's 25km from Coja (signposted off the N342), yet was unconnected by road or to an electricity supply until the 1970s, so Piódão has changed somewhat over the intervening years with the advent of tourism. If you can get over the slight theme-park atmosphere, however, its narrow streets are great to explore, and the whole village affords superb valley views. The **turismo**, based in the small museum (June–Sept daily 10am–noon & 1–6pm; Oct–May

Wed–Sun 9am–noon & 1–5pm; ☎235 732 787) on the main square at the bottom of the village, hands out an excellent "urban circuit" in English, to help you locate the main points of interest and navigate the confusing layout. The museum itself provides an insight into traditional village life with displays that cover emigration and economy, as well as daily toil. It's also possible to follow a couple of short walks from Piódão into the countryside – these are well signposted from the village.

For **accommodation**, the mainstay is the imposing *Inatel Piódão*, on the road into the village (☎235 730 100, ⓦwww.inatel.pt; ❸); it looks rather like a prison but the interior is comfortable enough, and there are good views from the restaurant. There are also plenty of rural tourism options in restored village houses, including *Casa da Padaria* (☎235 732 773; no credit cards; ❷) – the turismo can provide details of others. The village's only **restaurant** *O Fontinha* (☎235 731 151), is basic and inexpensive, one road up from the main square, where there are also a couple of **cafés**.

The Mata Nacional do Buçaco and Luso

Around 30km northeast of Coimbra, the Buçaco forest – properly the **Mata Nacional do Buçaco** – is something of a Portuguese icon. The country's most famous and most revered woods were a monastic domain throughout the Middle Ages, and the site in the Peninsular War of a battle that saw Napoleon's first significant defeat. Today, they are a little overvisited, but remain an enjoyable spot for rambling. It's easy enough to visit the forest from Coimbra for the day, or stop en route to Viseu or the Serra do Caramulo, though there's also plentiful overnight accommodation at the old spa town of **Luso**, just 3km by road from the forest.

The forest

Benedictine monks established a hermitage in the midst of Buçaco forest as early as the sixth century, and the area remained in religious hands right up to the dissolution of the monasteries in 1834. The forest's great fame and beauty, though, came with the **Carmelite monks** who settled here in the seventeenth century, building the walls that still mark its boundary. In 1643 Pope Urban VIII issued a papal bull threatening anyone who damaged the trees with excommunication; an earlier decree had already protected the monks' virtue by banning women from entering. The monks, meanwhile, were propagating the forest, introducing varieties new to Portugal from all over the world. Nowadays there are estimated to be more than seven hundred different types of tree, but the most impressive remain some of the earliest – particularly the mighty Mexican cedars.

Walls enclose the entire forest and **access** is via a number of gates (May–Oct cars €2.50, Nov–April free). All non-express **buses** from Coimbra to Viseu take a short detour through the forest from Luso, stopping at the old royal forest lodge, now the swanky *Palácio do Buçaco*, and again by the Portas da Rainha (for the military museum). You can also easily walk in to the forest from Luso – it only takes twenty minutes or so to get from town right in among the trees.

The Palácio do Buçaco and the Convento dos Carmelítas

Built on the site of the old Carmelite monastery as a summer retreat for the Portuguese monarchy, the royal lodge was only completed in 1907, three years

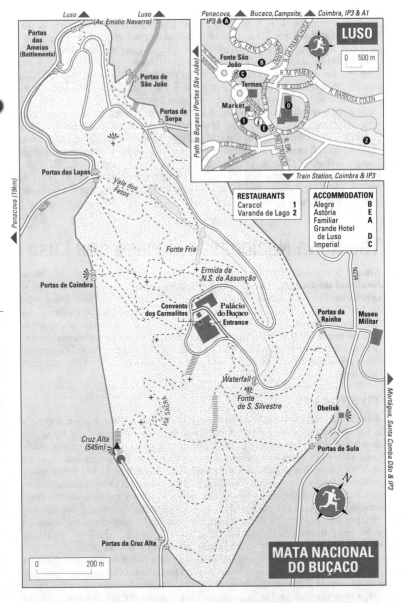

Luso ▲   Luso ▲
(Av. Emidio Navarro)

Portas das
Ameias
(Battlements)

Portas de
São João

Portas da
Serpa

Portas das Lapas

Vale dos
Fetos

Penacova (19km) ▲

NZ35

Portas de Coimbra

Fonte Fria

Ermida de
N.S. da Assunção

Convento
dos Carmelitos

Palácio
do Buçaco
Entrance

Portas da
Rainha

Museu
Militar

NZ34

Waterfall

Fonte
de S. Silvestre

VIA SACRA

Obelisk

Mortágua, Santa Comba Dão & IP3 ▶

Cruz Alta
(545m)

Portas de Sula

Portas da Cruz Alta

0   200 m

N

**MATA NACIONAL
DO BUÇACO**

LUSO (inset)

Penacova,   Bucaco, Campsite, ▲   Coimbra, IP3 & A1
IP3 & Ⓐ

R. AVG. ERNESTO NAVARRO

R. DA PAMPLHOSA

Fonte São
João   Ⓑ

R. M. PIMENTA

Ⓒ

R. DE ASSISTÊNCIA

R. BARBOSA COLEN

Termas

R. NAVARRO

R. DE ASSISTÊNCIA

Market

Ⓓ

Ⓘ
Ⓔ

R. EMIDIO NAVARRO

R. ANTÓNIO GRANJO

R. DR. LÚCIO PEREIRA

Ⓒ

R. DR. C. SIMÕES

R. CARLOS DINIZ

R. DR.
FRANCISCO BRANCO

0   500 m

N

Path to Buçaco (Portas São João) ▶

▼ Train Station, Coimbra & IP3

RESTAURANTS
Caracol   1
Varanda de Lago   2

ACCOMMODATION
Alegre   B
Astória   E
Familiar   A
Grande Hotel
de Luso   D
Imperial   C

---

before the declaration of the Republic, so saw little official use. It's an enormous imitation Manueline construction, now a five-star hotel, the **Palácio do Buçaco** (☎231 937 970, ⓦwww.almeidahotels.com; ⑤, April-Oct ⑥). It's surrounded by formal gardens (free to look around) while the interior makes full use of the grand space, particularly the impressive restaurant and bar – it's also not as forbiddingly posh as you might imagine since it sees a lot of tour-group traffic. You can view what remains of the **Carmelite convent**, namely its church (Tues–Sat 10am–12.30pm & 2–5.30pm; €0.60) found in the hotel grounds, and admire the sequence of *azulejos* depicting the Portuguese conquest of Ceuta and the Battle of Buçaco.

The Battle of Buçaco and the Museu Militar

The **Battle of Buçaco** (1810) was fought largely on the ridge just above the forest, and it marked the first serious reverse suffered by Napoleon in his campaigns on the peninsula. The French under Massena launched a frontal assault up the hill on virtually impregnable Anglo-Portuguese positions, sustaining massive losses in what for the Duke of Wellington amounted to little more than a delaying tactic, which he exploited in order to give himself time to retreat to his lines at Torres Vedras. A small **Museu Militar** (Tues–Sun 10am–5pm; €1), outside the forest near the Portas da Rainha, contains maps, uniforms and weapons from the campaign. Just above it, a narrow road climbs to the **obelisk** raised as a memorial to the battle, with vistas inland right across to the distant Serra da Estrela.

Walks around the forest

Buçaco is a lovely place to wander around, if not always the haven of peace the monks strove to create – at weekends and holidays the paths through the woods are packed with picnicking Portuguese. There's parking at various designated spots, including by the hotel, and walks (most of 1–2hr) are laid out everywhere: along the delightful **Vale dos Fetos** (Valley of Ferns) to the lake and cascading **Fonte Fria**, for example, or up to the **Portas de Coimbra**. But you can wander freely anywhere in the forest, and in many ways it's at its most attractive where it's wildest, away from the formal pathways and tour groups.

The **Via Sacra**, lined with seventeenth-century chapels in which terracotta figures depict the stages of Christ's journey carrying the cross to Calvary, leads steeply up from the *Palácio do Buçaco* to the **Cruz Alta**, a giant cross at the summit of the hill. From here, as from the Portas de Coimbra, there are magnificent panoramas of the surrounding country.

Luso

LUSO lies downhill from the forest, 3km by winding road into the centre or a far more direct walk on shady paths. A spa town for the past hundred years or so, it still draws crowds of Portuguese, taking the waters as a cure for rheumatism and other complaints. As such places go, its dated charm makes it worth a brief stop, and visitors are welcome to try the various treatments at the **Termas de Luso** (May–Oct; ⓦ www.termasdoluso.com), by the twin roundabouts on the main thoroughfare, Rua Emídio Navarro. Otherwise, a turn around the small town centre (population 3000) and municipal park won't occupy more than an hour. Locals take the opportunity to fill bottles and plastic containers for free with spa water from the **Fonte São João** spring – Luso water is sold all over the country – next to which there's an old-fashioned Art Deco *casa do chá* (tea room) with a terrace overlooking the central gardens and spa buildings.

Practicalities

The only two useful **train** services are the daily 7.44am and 11.45am from Coimbra A, which take 35 minutes to Luso-Buçaco station (return at 12.42pm or 6.08pm); it's a fifteen-minute walk into town from the station – take the road on the left. More convenient are the **buses**, running Monday to Saturday from

Coimbra bus station, that stop first at Luso (right in the centre, on the avenue near the spa) and then at Buçaco.

The **turismo** (June–Aug Mon–Fri 9am–7pm, Sat & Sun 10am–1pm & 3–5pm; Sept–May Mon–Fri 9.30am–12.30pm & 2–6pm, Sat & Sun 10am–1pm & 3–5pm; ☎231 939 133, ☯www.jtluso-bucaco.pt) is opposite the *Grande Hotel*, near the post office on the main Rua Emídio Navarro. They have a fold-out map of town and forest to give away, as well as accommodation lists, including details of private rooms (❷) in the town centre. There's a little daily fruit-and-veg **market** just down from the turismo, while a souvenir market (lace, basketware, footy shirts and regional cakes) sets its stalls out between the roundabouts in town.

Hotels and pensions

Pensão Alegre Rua Emídio Navarro 2 ☎231 930 256, ☯www.alegrehotels.com. Just 100m up the road to the forest, this impressive building, once home to a count, is full of nineteenth-century style. Some of the rooms have balconies and great views, and there's also a swimming pool in the pretty garden and parking. In the *Alto do Maia* restaurant (mains €8–10, open to the public), the chef runs to pasta and shrimp curry as well as Portuguese standards and you can take your drinks out onto the terrace. ❸

Pensão Astória Rua Emídio Navarro 144 ☎231 939 182. A stone's throw from the turismo, the *Astória* has a certain faded charm as long as you're not expecting up-to-the-minute comforts and facilities. There's a budget restaurant here too. Parking available. ❷

Grande Hotel de Luso Rua Dr Cid de Oliveira 86 ☎231 937 937, ☯www.hoteluso.com. You can't fail to miss the yellow, turreted *Grande Hotel* – a four-star Art Deco-era beauty with tastefully designed rooms, most with balconies. There's a huge Olympic-sized outdoor pool, as well as indoor pool and Jacuzzi, kids' club and parking. ❺

Casa de Hospedes Familiar Rua Ernesto Navarro 34 ☎231 939 612. Just up the forest road from town – a charming old house with a variety of rooms, a few with small balconies and some sleeping up to four people. No credit cards. Parking. ❷

Residencial Imperial Rua Emídio Navarro 25 ☎231 937 570, ☯www.residencialimperial.com. Just above the *casa do chá* and *fonte*, this modern building provides very comfortable rooms furnished with sturdy new furniture – all have bathrooms and TV, while some rooms sleep four, and there's a restaurant downstairs. ❷

Campsite

Parque de Campismo ☎231 930 916, ☯www .orbitur.pt. Luso's campsite also has family bungalows (❷) and a swimming pool. It's about 1.5km out of town on the way to the football ground.

Restaurants

O Caracol Rua Dr Francisco Diniz ☎231 939 405. Reliable grill house up a back street behind the turismo – there's usually barbecued chicken on the menu, plus the usual grilled meat and fish, and prices are very fair (€5–8). Inexpensive.

Varanda do Lago Parque do Lago ☎231 930 888. Round past the *Grande Hotel* and down into the park, you can eat in the glass-walled dining room here, or on the terrace overlooking the picturesque lake. There are café snacks as well as full meals. Closed Mon. Moderate.

The Dão valley wine route

The route northeast from Coimbra along the IP3 sweeps through the **valley of the Rio Dão**, a name synonymous in Portugal with wine. The Dão is a tributary of the Mondego and flows through the heart of the demarcated region where Dão wines are produced, principally some of the country's finest and richest reds (the lighter whites aren't nearly as successful). It's a granite, hilly region, cold and rainy in the winter, hot and dry in the summer – where they are not covered with terraced vineyards, the slopes are thickly wooded with pine and eucalyptus, subject (as in much of central Portugal) to occasional ravaging forest fires during the sweltering summers.

The small market town of **Santa Comba Dão**, a little over 50km from Coimbra, marks the start of the wine region. There's not much to it, save a very small historic centre and some grandstand views of tumbling river and the *barragem* (reservoir) outside town. If it's known at all in Portugal, it's as the home town of **António de Oliveira Salazar** (1889–1970). The Portuguese dictator, leader of an authoritarian regime that lasted forty years, was born (and is buried) in the nearby village of Vimeiro.

Many of the estates and wineries fall within a triangle formed by Santa Comba Dão and the divergent IP3 (to Viseu) and IC12/N234 (to Mangualde), while the Dão wine region also stretches beyond Viseu into the Beira Alta. Although there are no overwhelming points of interest, you can spend a happy day pottering through small country towns, following winery signs on the **Rota**

Forest fires and the Bombeiros Voluntários

Portugal's famed green countryside is ravaged each year by **forest fires**, and the problem has worsened markedly in recent years. In 2005, a particularly bad year, exacerbated by a widespread and longstanding drought, almost four percent of the country's forests went up in flames – over 300,000 hectares destroyed. The reasons for the fires are numerous, though it's estimated that ninety percent are caused by human activity, whether it's arson or carelessness with cigarettes, bonfires and barbecues. Matters aren't helped by the country's important **timber industry**, which has replaced native tree species with the highly flammable eucalyptus and pine. Moreover, in rural areas the land often lies unmaintained – householders are obliged to clear brush and undergrowth for up to fifty metres from their properties, but often in depopulated areas with ageing populations there's no one left to do the work.

Peak **fire season** is mid-summer, but in drought years forest fires break out as early as January and as late as November. You don't need to drive through the forests and plantations of central and northern Portugal for long before seeing the evidence of past fires – hillsides burned black and trees torched like candles – or the telltale plumes of thick smoke from the latest conflagration. On the worst days, ash falls to the streets in distant towns and cities, and major train lines and motorways are closed.

Extraordinarily, the firefighting service that has the unenviable task of dealing with the problem is almost entirely voluntary. The country's 20,000 or so **Bombeiros Voluntários** make up over ninety percent of Portugal's firefighting forces, with the few (and far better equipped) professional corps (Bombeiros Sapadores) based in the cities or working privately for the country's timber and paper-pulp concerns. You'll see ageing Bombeiros Voluntários vehicles in every region – helping out with ambulance duties too as part of their remit – and the volunteers are usually the first and only firefighters on the scene when a blaze breaks out. Equipment and vehicles are often wholly inadequate; in the past, urgent appeals to the EU have led to specialist aircraft and foreign crews arriving to help.

It is, of course, horribly dangerous work and in 2005 fourteen firefighters lost their lives, the worst year's total on record. For this reason – and for their astonishing success rate in saving local homes and properties – the Bombeiros Voluntários have an almost heroic status in Portugal. Rare is the town without a street or avenue named after them, while proud **municipal statues and memorials** to their deeds proliferate.

The government has belatedly accepted the need for a professional core of firefighters within the wider service – most Bombeiros Voluntários outfits already have at least one paid, full-time officer. The recent devastation has focused minds, and more money has been pledged, but whatever changes occur in future are unlikely to dislodge the high regard in which the volunteer locals are held.

. Details of all the estates open to the public for tours and tastings are given on the website ⓦwww.cvrdao.pt, and there's more information (in English) on the regional tourism site ⓦwww.rtdaolafoes.com.

Serra do Caramulo

Beyond Santa Comba Dão, the IP3 bears away from the Dão valley and the views are soon of the **Serra do Caramulo**, breaking to the northwest. The eastern turn-off point for the mountains is the small, unassuming town of Tondela, 20km from Santa Comba Dão, from where the minor N230 winds through a succession of tiny villages at the heart of the mountain range, including **Caramulo**, a twisting 19km from Tondela. This has an amazing museum, and makes a good hiking base; most of the other *serra* villages are little more than hamlets, surrounded by rhododendrons, brightly coloured azaleas and thick green shrubs growing wild on the hillside. After Caramulo, the N230 descends to Águeda, western access point to the mountains, 37km from Caramulo, which is close to both the N1 and A1 north-south routes between Coimbra and Aveiro/Porto.

With a car, you could describe the circle from Coimbra or Aveiro, seeing Luso and Buçaco forest on the way. Coming from Luso (N234), there's a minor route north instead along the N228 which winds up to join the mountain road between Tondela and Caramulo. It is possible to make the same circuit by bus, though to reach Caramulo – the only worthwhile overnight stop – from Coimbra, you'll need to take the Viseu bus, change at Tondela and hope for a reasonable connection. On from Caramulo, weekday buses run to Águeda where, again, you'll have to change for Coimbra or Aveiro. All in all, it's far easier by car – note that Vouzela and the Rio Vouga to the north is the obvious next destination after Caramulo, up the N228.

Caramulo

Tucked beneath the granite outcrops and wind turbines of the high Beiras *serra*, the straggling village of **CARAMULO** glories in some staggering views. It's a somnolent place, with a belvedere garden and vast, shady chestnut trees at its heart, and makes a great walking base – several footpaths radiate from the village through neighbouring hamlets and up to the local peaks. The summit of the loftiest, **Caramulinho** (1075m), is a five-kilometre drive from the village – a five-and-a-half-kilometre (2hr 30min) circular walk rounds the peak – while at **Cabeço da Neve** (same initial direction, 4km) there's another sweeping viewpoint. Outdoor **activities** such as canyoning, rafting and kayaking, or mountain-bike rental, can be arranged through Desafios Caramulo (☎232 868 017, ⓦwww.desafios-caramulo.pt), based at the *Hotel do Caramulo* (see below). You'll need to call in advance as minimum participatory numbers are required.

Caramulo itself also boasts the extraordinary **Museu do Caramulo** (daily 10am–1pm & 2–6pm; closes at 5pm in winter; €6; ⓦwww.museu-caramulo .net), signposted a couple of hundred metres down the avenue from the village centre. Based on the collection of one Abel Lacerda, it promises "art and automobiles" and doesn't disappoint, with everything from primitive religious sculpture to souped-up Harley Davidsons. Having browsed sketches by the greatest modern masters – minor works by Picasso and Dalí among them – you can examine sixteenth-century Tournai tapestries depicting the earliest Portuguese explorers in India, full of weird animals and natives based on obviously very garbled reports. Then it's on to the superb collection of vintage cars and motorcycles, including some of the earliest Benz, Buggatti and Fiat models, and an elegant series of Rolls-Royces. These are all in working order and given a run-out once a year, many appearing in the **Caramulo Motorfestival** (Sept; Ⓦ www.caramulo-motorfestival.com) of classic and sports cars.

Practicalities

The **turismo** (Mon–Fri 9am–12.30pm & 2–5.30pm, Sat & Sun 10am–12.30pm & 3–5.30pm; Ⓣ232 861 437) is a little way down the Tondela road from the village roundabout, on the left-hand side – you might be able to pick up some walk brochures here, but don't expect any first-hand advice.

Accommodation options are limited, though you might get a private room by asking at the *Mercado Serrano* – walk up the main road past *Restaurante Marte* and take the left fork opposite the petrol station; the *mercado* is past the chemist on the left. Otherwise, the choice is between two four-star hotels, best the excellent *Hotel do Caramulo*, on Avenida Dr Abel Lacerda, opposite the museum (Ⓣ232 860 100, Ⓦ www.hoteldocaramulo.pt; ⓺), with contemporary rooms, fitness centre, indoor and outdoor pools, Jacuzzi and hydrotherapy facilities, and unbeatable views towards the Serra da Estrela. The older, smaller, less inspiring *Estalagem do Caramulo* (Ⓣ232 861 291; ⓺), a kilometre down the Tondela road, also has a swimming pool and great views.

The best **restaurant** is the moderately priced *Casa do Monte* (Ⓣ232 861 558; closed Tues) on Rua do Clube, at the top of the village – head up the main road past the garage and after about 200m look for the signpost pointing to the left. The restaurant has views over the surrounding mountains, as well as a pretty garden bar, and serves delicious trout. Otherwise, the *Café-Restaurante Marte* (Ⓣ232 861 253) on the main road opposite the garage is a reliable lunch stop, with mains for €7 or €8.

Vouzela and the Rio Vouga

North of Caramulo, and just beyond the fast Aveiro-Viseu road (IP5), **Vouzela** is one of the most immediately attractive of Beira towns, a small place with a palpable sense of civic pride. It's set on the beautiful **Rio Vouga** and makes a fine destination if you feel like taking in a little of backwater Portugal. Bus services run from Coimbra or Aveiro and, on reaching the Vouga, follow the route of the old train line along the river on the N16. For drivers, there are equally bucolic approaches from Caramulo from the south (N228) or from Viseu and the IP5 to the east, from where the minor N337 makes a particularly memorable approach. Beyond town lies the spa resort of **São Pedro do Sul**, the "Sul" in question being the Rio Sul which flows down from the lovely **Serra da Arada** that flanks Vouzela to the north.

Vouzela

The river is at the heart of all that's attractive about **VOUZELA**, though the locals also boast of the town's *pasteis de Vouzela* (only for the most sweet-toothed), its richly flavoured traditional dishes such as *vitela de Lafões*, and the heady local *vinho Lafões* (similar to *vinho verde*). There's a *feira* on May 14 when flowers are strewn in the streets in honour of **São Frei Gil**, and everyone drives up into the hills to witness the blossoming of the rare *loendros*, a type of rhododendron peculiar to this area which is now protected by law. Otherwise, a good time to be in town is the first Wednesday of the month when there's a morning street **market**.

The old centre is built around the sluggish river, crossed by a low **Romanesque bridge**, overhung by willow and bordered by small-town manor houses with granite steps and whitewashed plasterwork. Beyond are the riverside gardens, manicured lawns and municipal pool, towering over which is the **viaduct** of the former railway which stretches across a narrow terraced gorge. It's a handsome scene and you can get more rewarding views (and cross both bridge and viaduct) on an eight-kilometre circular walk – a board at the top of the gardens by the viaduct shows the route.

From the river, narrow Rua São Frei Gil climbs up past manor houses to a small square where you'll find the **Museu Municipal** (Tues–Sun 10am– 12.30pm & 2–5pm; free), housed in a former prison and containing a varied collection of religious artefacts, Romanesque stone fragments and local weaving and craftwork. Around the corner, the main road through town climbs up to Praça da República and its striking *azulejo*-clad thirteenth-century church.

A summer **Comboio Turístico** (tourist train: June–Sept Wed–Sun; €1) runs from near the viaduct on a loop around the surroundings, including to the campsite and **Senhora do Castelo**, a low hill that is the location for much merrymaking and picnicking on the first Sunday after August 5.

Practicalities

From the **bus station** at the top of town (services from Aveiro, Porto and Lisbon/Coimbra), head downhill and turn right down Avenida João de Melo where you'll find the **turismo** at no. 23 (Mon–Sat 10am–1pm & 2–7pm, Sun 2–7pm; reduced hours in winter; ☎232 771 515, ⊛www.rtdaolafoes.com). Continuing down this street brings you to Praça da República, where you turn left for the old town and river.

Cheapest **accommodation** is at *Residencial Ferreira*, Rua Barão da Costeiro 3 (☎ & ⓕ232 771 650; no credit cards; ❷), 50m down the hill from Praça da República, which has adequate en-suite rooms. Far more in keeping with the town is *Casa das Ameias*, Rua São Frei Gil 43 (☎232 772 625, ⊛www .ameias-viaromana.com; book ahead; ❹), next to the museum, which is elegantly decorated and has a pretty terrace at the rear. Best of all, however, is *Casa de Fataunços* (☎232 772 697, ⓔcasa.fatauncos@oninet.pt; ❹), 3km northeast of Vouzela in the village of the same name. It's a beautifully restored manor house with lovely rooms, gardens, a pool, tennis court and a small art gallery. There is also a municipal **campsite** with fine views (☎232 740 020), 4km up the road towards Mortágua and Senhora do Castelo.

The nicest **café** is *Café Rocha* in the pint-sized square outside the museum, while the town also has a handful of decent **restaurants**, including *O Meu Menino*, Avenida Sidónio Pais 6 (☎232 771 335), just down from the bus station and a good option for lunch. Or there's the simple, rustic and very friendly *Forno do Rei*, Rua Escolar 19 (☎232 772 722), in a cobbled back street behind *Residencial Ferreira*, providing inexpensive local dishes.

Termas de São Pedro do Sul

Four kilometres northeast of Vouzela is the thermal resort area of **TERMAS DE SÃO PEDRO DO SUL**, possibly the oldest spa in Portugal. It was a great favourite with the Romans, a popular haunt of Portuguese royalty – Dom Afonso Henriques is said to have bathed his wounded leg here after the battle at Badajoz – and remains among the most attractive in the country. Its position beside the Vouga, with pine trees all around, certainly lends it charm and the resort makes for a pleasant side trip from Vouzela. Buses run up here once or twice daily, a ten-minute ride, and if you fancied overnighting here instead of Vouzela you could try your luck at one of the many pensions and hotels stacked up above the river. The turismo might be able to help, just across the bridge from the spa. Note that the unremarkable town of São Pedro do Sul itself is another 3km to the northeast, where you can pick up buses to Viseu or Lamego.

Serra da Arada

With a car it's easy to see some of the beautiful **Serra da Arada**. Head northeast for São Pedro do Sul and having passed through it and crossed a narrow bridge, take a left towards Castro Daire. On reaching the small village of São Felix follow signs to Sul and then Pena. From here the road begins to rise into the mountains and emerges on the heather-spotted mountain top with staggering views to the valley below. At the next junction take a left, then right, for **Pena**, 20km all told from Vouzela. The road winds precariously downhill, hugging the mountainside before reaching the tiny schist village (population eight), where you can snack at the *Adega Tipica Pena* (no phone) and buy local honey and *aguardente*. After backtracking to the junction you can continue another 1km to the tiny mountain-top **São Macario** chapel, from where views unfold down the valley.

Another spectacular mountain route from Vouzela takes you over the **Serra da Freita** to Arouca, a 43-kilometre drive (see p.270 for route in reverse).

Figueira da Foz

FIGUEIRA DA FOZ is one of the liveliest towns on the west coast, a major resort and deep-sea fishing port (population 60,000) sited at the mouth of the Rio Mondego. Roughly equidistant from Lisbon and Porto, and 42km (just over an hour by train) from Coimbra, it attracts people from all over the country to its superb beaches and surf. That said, it's not the most initially alluring of beach resorts: there's a somewhat industrial approach from the south, and the town itself is resolutely modern, its long promenade backed by a line of anonymous apartment buildings. But most of the action, in fact, takes place away from the sands in the atmospheric back streets, where a bubbling good humour prevails, even when the town is packed to the gills.

Arrival and information

Parking can be tricky in August but there's plenty of space during the rest of the year, either in the huge free car park near the clocktower or anywhere along the long promenade in the direction of Buarcos. The adjacent **train and bus stations** are a twenty-minute walk from the centre and beach. Keep parallel to the river until you see the ocean and then cut into the town – a useful beach-front landmark is the concrete clock tower. **Buses to Buarcos** – the fishing village at the northern end of the bay, 2km from town – run directly from the stations (Mon–Fri every 30min, hourly at weekends), also making stops in town outside the Mercado Municipal and on Rua da Liberdade. There are also regular buses to **Praia do Cabadelo** and the campsites – destination "Cova Gala" – from outside the Mercado Municipal (Mon–Fri every 30min, Sat hourly, Sun every 2hr), which also stop by the stations on their way out of town.

△ Figueira da Foz

The **turismo** (July & Aug daily 9am–midnight; Sept–June Mon–Fri 9am–12.30pm & 2–5.30pm, Sat & Sun 10am–12.30pm & 2.30–6.30pm; ☎233 422 610, ⊛www.figueiraturismo.com) is on Avenida 25 de Abril, in the parade of cafés near the clocktower. There's another in Buarcos at the museum, just back from the seafront at Rua Governador Soares Nogueira 32 (July & Aug daily 9am–8pm; Sept–June Mon–Fri 9.30am–1pm & 2–5pm; ☎233 433 019). Look out for the series of pamphlets on **local walks**, which offer something a bit different from sea and sand.

Accommodation

In high season you might well be met at the train station by people offering **private rooms** (❷), either in town or in Buarcos, which – provided they're handy for the beach – will be the best bargains available. Otherwise, there are a couple of cheap *pensões* just in front of the train station on Rua Fernandes Tomás and Rua da República, but these are a long way from the beach. It's much better to head for the centre, where both Rua Bernardo Lopes and Rua da Liberdade have several possibilities. Prices – already comparatively high in Figueira – tend to shoot through the roof in July and August.

Hotels and pensions

🏃 **Residencial Aviz** Rua Dr Lopes Guimarães 16 ☎233 422 635, ⊛www.residencialaviz.pt.to. The best budget choice in town is this well-cared-for place with a friendly owner who spent almost thirty years in Germany. Rooms are on the small and chintzy side, but are good quality with polished wooden floors, carved furniture, double-glazing and cable TV. It's on a quiet side street, not far from the seafront avenue, and you can park outside. ❷, Aug ❸

Pensão Bela Figueira Rua Miguel Bombarda 13 ☎233 422 728, ℻233 429 960. Some rooms are nicer and lighter than others, and some a bit close to the noisy street, so see a selection if you can. But all have had a recent lick of paint, and boast laminate floors and pretty bedspreads, and there's a streetside terrace for drinks. ❷

Pensão Central Rua Bernardo Lopes 36 ☎233 422 308, ⊛www.pensaocentral.nafigueira.com. Big rooms with high ceilings in a large town house approached up a flight of side-steps. A couple of rooms share a grand street-facing balcony, though these are noisy. But it's a struggle to keep up the maintenance in places like this, and beds, carpets and bathrooms are all old and tired. No credit cards. ❷, July/Aug ❸

Orbitur & Foz do Mondego campsites (via bridge), Coimbra, Aveiro, Leira & ▲ ① ▲ Train & Bus Station

FIGUEIRA DA FOZ

RUA VASCO DA GAMA

RUA 28 DE INFANTARIA

RUA 10 DE AGOSTO

RUA DA REPÚBLICA

AV DE SARAIVA DE CARVALHO

RUA HERÓIS DO ULTRAMAR

RUA DO HOSPITAL

R. D RESTAURAÇÃO

R. D. COMBATENTES DA GRANDE GUERRA

RUA DR SANTOS ROCHA

RUA DAS ROSAS

AV DA LIBERDADE

PRAÇA 8 DE MAIO

LARGO LUÍS DE CAMÕES

A. 5 DE OUTUBRO

Centro de Artes e Espectáculos

Museu Municipal Dr. Santos Rocha

Parque Municipal de Campismo ▲

Police ▲

RUA DOS BOMBEIROS VOLUNTÁRIOS

RUA DR JOSE DE SILVA FONSECA

RUA MAURÍCIO PINTO

PRAÇA DEL FREIRE DE ANDRADE

S. Julião

Casa do Paço

Jardim Municipal

Bus to Cova Gala

Marina

Rio Mondego

Parque das Abadias

PAS. INFANTE D.HENRIQUE

AVENIDA DO DR. MANUEL GASPAR DE LEMOS

RUA DA FONTE

Casino

Laundry

Mercado Municipal

RUA CÂNDIDO DOS REIS

RUA DR FRANCISCO A DINIS

RUA FRANCISCO A DINIS

See inset for detail

RUA DA LIBERDADE

LARGO ANTUNES MARTINS

RUA SÃO LOURENÇO

RUA JOAQUIM SOTTO MAYOR

COSTA DE SOUSA

RUA M. FRED

RUA DR LUIS CARRIÇO

LARGO DO COLISEU

Coliseu (bullring)

Piscina de Mar

R.S. CATARINA

RUA MIGUEL BOMBARDA

AVENIDA 25 DE ABRIL

Clocktower

AVENIDA DE ESPANHA

Foz do Mondego Campsite ⋏

CABEDELO

Praia do Cabedelo (beach)

Rio Mondego

N

100 m
0

① ② ③ & Buarcos ▲

Inset map:

Press Center

Bus to Buarcos ★

Casino

RUA DE CALADO

RUA DA LIBERDADE

RUA CÂNDIDO DOS REIS

A CÂNDIDO DINIS

B LOPES

RUA DR FRANCISCO A DINIS

BARS & CLUBS

Discoteca Bergantim 4
Dona Bárbara 8
Flashen 3
Perfumaria Pub 10
Três Chamines 9

RESTAURANTS

Caçarola I 5
Challet das Cabanas 7
Cristal 11
Escondidinho 6
Ferreiro 1
Plataforma 2

ACCOMMODATION

Aviz B
Bela Figueira D
Central G
Mercure C
Sãozinha E
Sottomayor A
Wellington F

Hotel Mercure Av 25 de Abril 22 ☏ 233 403 900, ⓦwww.mercure.com. On the seafront, this four-star chain hotel has a bit of class and comfortable rooms that are not bad value. You pay more in August, and for a balcony and sea view, but for most of the year you can get a room for well under €100 – check the website for special offers. ❹, Aug ❺

Hospedaria Sãozinha Ladeira do Monte 43 ☏ 233 425 243, ⓦwww.pensaozinha.com. Offers quiet, spotlessly clean en-suite rooms with tile floors, rugs and dark-wood furniture, some with streetside balconies. It's a cool oasis, with parking outside, a 15min walk from the beach (it's signposted off Pr 8 de Maio). No breakfast available, but there's a café-*pastelaria* in the square. ❷, Aug ❸

Hotel Wellington Rua Dr Calado 23–27 ☏ 233 426 767, ⓦwww.sabirhoteis.pt. Three blocks from the beach, the three-star *Wellington* offers tasteful rooms with modern wooden furniture, bathrooms and cable TV. There's a basement restaurant, the *Scala*, offering an unusual mix of Indian and Italian dishes which, while not fantastic, is different for Figueira. The same hotel group also operates the *Sottomayor* apartment-hotel (halfway between Figueira and Buarcos), where all the rooms have kitchenette and there's a big swimming pool – details on the website. ❹

Campsites

Foz do Mondego Cabadelo ☏ 233 402 740. Across the river mouth and next to Cabadelo beach, this is by far the cheapest in the area, but it's an exposed site with no shade, overwhelmed in season by motorhomes and caravans. Closed mid-Nov to mid-Jan. Bus to Cova Gala.

Orbitur Mata de Lavos, Gala, 4km to the south, across the river ☏ 233 431 492, ⓦwww.orbitur .com. A wooded site, 400m from Praia da Cova beach, with pool, restaurant and childrens' playground – it's the best choice in the region, though also the most expensive. Camping cabins available from €50–60 (sleeps 4). Bus to Cova Gala.

Parque Municipal de Campismo Estrada de Tavarede, 2km northeast of town ☏ 233 402 810, ⓦwww.figueiracamping.com. Nowhere near the beach, but the inland municipal site is large and well equipped, with a swimming pool (you have to pay), tennis courts, mini-market and restaurant. It's signposted from town, or there's a bus from stations and market, or a taxi there isn't expensive.

The town and local beaches

Figueira's **town beach** is enormous, 2km long and very wide, a good five-minute walk across the sand to the sea – unless you wear shoes or stay on the wooden walkways, the soles of your feet will have been burned long before you get there. There's a saltwater pool raised above the main beachfront Avenida 25 de Abril (see "Listings"), with the road and promenade lined with apartment buildings and cafés as far as **Buarcos** at the far northern end, a 25-minute walk away. This is the nicest part of Figueira, with a row of candy-striped fish restaurants sitting right on the beach and a huddle of pastel-coloured fishermen's houses lurking behind what remains of the old defensive wall. The old sea-faring life is covered in the signposted **Núcleo Museológico do Mar** (Tues–Fri 9.30am–12.30pm & 2–5pm, July–Sept also Sat 2–7pm; free), which also houses Buarcos turismo.

Back in town, Figueira's central streets form a tight little grid set back from the eastern end of the beach. It's largely pedestrianized, brimming with shops and pavement cafés, while down towards the river is the **Mercado Municipal** (Mon–Sat 6am–3pm), good for fresh produce, as well as beachwear, childrens' clothes, lace, embroidery and other crafts and souvenirs. On the edge of the town park, Parque das Abadias, the **Museu Municipal Dr Santos Rocha** (June to mid-Sept Tues–Sun 9.30am–5.15pm; mid-Sept to May Tues–Fri 9.30am–5.15pm, Sat & Sun 2.15–5.15pm; €1.30), is the only other sight of note, with an impressive archeological section.

Popular out-of-town beaches include **Praia do Cabadelo**, behind the mole on the south bank of the Mondego's river mouth (the bus drops you at the hospital, a ten-minute walk away). Although there's a surf school and bar here (see "Listings" p.262) it's not at all attractive – though locals like it – and the better beach is a little way further south at **Praia da Cova**, below a large car park. There are a few restaurants in the street behind the beach, good places to come and eat fish. North of Buarcos and the **Cabo Mondego** headland you'll find another good beach and campsite at **Praia de Quiaios**, 10km from Figueira. There are buses here in summer, but it's far more convenient as a day trip for drivers, who can wind there through the **Serra de Boa Viagem** – follow the signpost from the coastal road at the end of Buarcos. The *serra* is a hilly, wooded reserve inland of the cape and though parts have been affected by forest fires there are still plenty of lovely shaded picnic areas and woodland walks, including one detailed on a turismo pamphlet (*Rota da Boa Viagem*).

Eating, drinking and nightlife

The centre of town is packed with snack bars, **cafés** and seafood **restaurants** – the best place to eat on the beach is up at Buarcos. Menus are strong on sole, skate and sea bass, while eels from the estuary waters are also a local delicacy; a common restaurant dish is a *massada de peixe* (a kind of soupy pasta with fish). For a lunch of takeaway chicken and chips visit the *churrasqueira* in the town market.

The town's numerous **bars and clubs** (open from around 11pm until 4am or later in summer) blow hot and cold depending on the season, but there's usually something happening somewhere. Bars on Rua Académico Zagalo and Rua São Lourenço have summer terraces; otherwise, head up to Buarcos for a beachside sundowner. Otherwise, nightlife centres on the **casino**, which hosts a variety of shows – from Portuguese crooners to stage spectaculars – throughout the summer. Other concerts, plus theatre, art-house movies, events and exhibitions are staged at the **Centro de Artes e Espectáculos** (☎233 407 200, ⓦwww .cae.pt), up near the municipal museum. Best of the year's parties is **St John's Eve** (São João; June 23 & 24) with bonfires on the beach and a "Holy Bathe" in the sea at dawn. During June in the run-up to São João, the **Festas da Cidade** promote all sorts of concerts and events, including a "Festa da Sardinha" where grilled sardines are sold at budget prices at restaurants across town.

Restaurants

Caçarola I Rua Cândido dos Reis 65 ☎233 424 861. Shellfish bar-and-restaurant with daily specials of crab, lobster, clams and the like. There's a street-side deck, or you can eat inside at the bar or tables, and while prices can rocket for the decent stuff it's a longstanding, reliable choice. Expensive.

Challet das Cabanas Rua Dr Francisco António Dinis 34 ☎233 423 449. The town's best *churrasqueira*, in business for over thirty years – a budget place to eat grilled chicken or meat and fish prepared over charcoal. Inexpensive.

Cristal Rua Académico Zagalo 28 ☎233 422 439. Great little restaurant with outdoor terrace specializing in *cataplanas* (around €30 for two), but also does a rich fish soup served in an iron pot, a good *massada* and other regional specialities. Expensive.

🎿 **O Escondidinho** Rua Dr Francisco António Dinis 62 ☎233 422 494. A courtly owner oversees this simple Goan dining room that's a real Rough Guide favourite, recommended since the very

first edition. Let yourself be guided through the short menu ("the first is better than the second" – "don't mix the dishes"), perhaps starting with prawn *balchão* (a spicy paste to spread on a pappadum), followed by a chicken, beef, veg (all €7) or prawn (€14) curry, with a sweet chickpea cake to finish. The entrance is through a doorway opposite *Hotel Hispânia*; it's only open Thurs–Sat plus Sun lunch, and closes at 9/9.30pm. Inexpensive.

O Ferreiro Rua Capitão Guerra 4, Buarcos ☎233 421 403. A simple restaurant, just back from the Buarcos roundabout, where the meat and fish is very reasonably priced (€7–9) – what's more, there's a rare vegetarian menu. Moderate.

Plataforma Praia de Buarcos ☎233 413 500. Not much more than an extended beach shack (at the Buarcos end, by the car park), but great for fish and shellfish with a sea view. It's not cheap – even half a dozen sardines are €10 – but the fish is straight from the boat, and the daily specials are chalked on a board, barnacles to lobster. Expensive.

Bars and clubs

Discoteca Bergantim Rua Dr Lopes Guimarães 28. A long-standing favourite, right in the centre of town.

Dona Bárbara Rua Académico Zagalo 7. Established bar playing classic rock and pop.

Flashen Praia de Quiaios, 10km north. The big dance club scene is way out of town at Quiaios beach, but it doesn't stop the local preening youth rocking up and partying (Fri & Sat nights until 4am).

Perfumaria Pub Rua Dr Calado 37. Small, atmospheric and friendly bar on two levels, with a pool table and a good cocktail list.

Três Chaminés Carritos, 4km east, N111 Coimbra road ☎ www.3chamines.com. At the "Three Chimneys" there's a bowling alley, restaurant and cocktail bar, plus club and Latin sounds. Fri, Sat & Sun from 10pm.

Casino

Casino Figueira Rua Bernardo Lopes 1 ☎ www .casinofigueira.com. One of the north's glam nights out, though in the end it's not that exclusive. There's a fancy bar, all the usual games and slots, and a nightly roster of concerts and shows – you'll need to dress up a bit. Open daily 3pm–3am.

Listings

Boat trips Charter outfit Cruzeiros Atlântico (☎ 965 316 162) offer full-day bay and river cruises (from €60). Minimum numbers are required, but you can check on possible departures at the travel agency Rotasmundo, Rua Miguel Bombarda 25 ☎ 233 411 635.

Car rental A. A. Castanheira, Rua Maestro David Sousa 103 ☎ 233 425 113; Auto Jardim, Av 25 de Abril 27 ☎ 233 427 163, ☎ www.auto-jardim .com.

Hospital Across the river: Hospital Distrital da Figueira da Foz, Gala, São Pedro ☎ 233 402 097.

Internet At the library, by the Museu Municipal Dr Santos Rocha (Tues–Fri 9.30am–5.15pm, Sat & Sun 2.15pm–5.15pm; free for 30min). Also WebGest, Pr Comendador Aug. Silva, off Av 25 de Abril (daily 10.30am–11pm).

Laundry Lavanderia, Rua Candido dos Reis 15; closed Sat afternoon and Sun.

Newspapers Foreign press available from Press Center, Rua Bernado Lopes 113.

Police PSP, Rua de Mortágua ☎ 233 407 560.

Post office Passeio Infante Dom Henrique (Mon–Fri 9am–1pm & 2–6.30pm).

Swimming pool Piscina de Mar, Av 25 de Abril (June–Sept 9am–6pm; €6.50) is a popular outdoor saltwater swimming pool, terrace and bar.

Surfing At Praia do Cabadelo, Escola de Surf da Figueira (☎ 233 412 413, ☎ www.surfingfigueira .com), located opposite the campsite, offers lessons and they also rent out the gear.

Taxis Available outside the train station ☎ 233 423 218 or in Pr 8 de Maio ☎ 233 423 500; or call Radio Taxis ☎ 233 420 880.

An estuary walk near Figueira da Foz

Figueira da Foz turismo has details of several waymarked walks in the area, including the four-kilometre **Rota das Salinas**, an interesting estuary route around the salt pans that you glimpse from the bridge on the way into town. The start of the walk is 7km from Figueira at Armazens de Lavas: from the Cabadelo and Gala roundabout, just over the bridge, take the minor Leiria road (there's a signpost for "Ecomuseu do Sal"); 3.4km along here, look for a left turn at a GALP station and *O Grazina* (*Casa das Enguias*) restaurant; 600m down the track there's a noticeboard, map and *Rota das Salinas* signpost at a group of wooden buildings by the canal, where you can leave your car.

Despite the sporadic Ecomuseu signs, there's not yet a museum, though an interpretation centre is being built – salt has been produced in the Mondego estuary for almost a thousand years, and around fifty *salinas* still operate that are worked between May and September each year. A boardwalk leads out across the salt pans, past weatherbeaten plank huts with salt bags piled outside. The well-signposted circular route takes about an hour (at a brisk stroll), through a pretty estuarine habitat of hedgerow flowers, rustling stands of bamboo and salt-resistant shrubs. Black-winged stilts and other estuarine birds are a common sight, while the return leg of the path runs along the muddy banks of the Mondego, where a few fishermen still eke out a living from their painted wooden boats.

Praia de Mira

The coastline immediately north of Figueira da Foz consists of a virtually deserted thirty five-kilometre stretch of low-lying dunes, with little protection against the Atlantic winds. The sands are easily accessible only at a couple of points – Praia de Quiaios and Praia de Tocha – before reaching the one developed resort between Figueira and Aveiro. **PRAIA DE MIRA** is set on a small lagoon known as a *barrinha* – the southernmost point of Aveiro's waterways and canals – and has a cobbled quayside planted with palms, with ducks and brightly coloured pedalboats bobbing around in the water. Its one extremely long main street spears past the lagoon towards the sea, where a seemingly endless duned beach stretches to either side – ideal if your aims extend no further than beach-lounging and lazy walks.

There are infrequent direct **buses** from Aveiro, Figueira da Foz and Coimbra but you'll usually have to change in Mira, the inland town 7km to the west. The Mira road is the main road into town and runs right to the beach – the sea is separated from the lagoon by two blocks of shops, apartments and restaurants, while there's a **turismo**, in the boathouse-like building up the side road beside the lagoon (erratic hours, but officially July & Aug daily 9.30am–12.30pm & 2–6pm; Sept–June Mon-Fri 9.30am–12.30pm & 2–5.30pm, Sat & Sun 2-6pm; ⑦231 472 566, ⓦwww.cm-mira.pt). The building itself is a restored *palheiro* (hayloft), built on stilts by the water and once typical of the region – it now doubles as a small museum dedicated to Mira's traditions and trades.

You can look out for notices advertising **rooms** or try one of the few official pensions and hotels. *Residencial Senhora da Conceição* (⑦231 471 645; ❷, Aug ❸), on the main avenue by the lagoon and GALP station, is unmemorable but fine for the money (though not in Aug) – get a room at the back for lagoon views over the rooftops. Much nicer is the mustard-yellow, chalet-style *Residencial Maçarico* (⑦231 471 114, ⓦwww.residencial-macarico.com; ❸) – turn left at the end of the main street – which is hemmed in by the other seafront buildings but retains some charm with its terracotta-tiled floors and wood-framed balconies.

There are two **campsites** a short way from the village and near the sands – for either, just keep following the road around past the turismo, along the lagoon. The municipal *Parque de Campismo* (⑦231 472 173; closed Oct–April) is closer and considerably cheaper, though less well equipped, than the *Orbitur* site (⑦231 471 234, ⓦwww.orbitur.com; closed Dec & Jan). The latter also has four-person A-frame cabins to rent (from €65 July & Aug, much cheaper the rest of the year). There's also a seasonal **youth hostel** (⑦231 471 199, ⓦwww.pousadasjuventude .pt; dorm beds €10, rooms ❶, camping also available; open June–Aug only) at a youth accommodation centre, signposted from the road by the *Orbitur* site – advance bookings are essential, as it's usually busy with groups.

There are **restaurants and bars** on the seafront and in the small grid of streets between ocean and lagoon. There's also a line of places facing the lagoon itself, the most appealing of which is *A Cozinha*, where you can sit outside and eat grilled fish for €10 or €11, meat for a little less. Summer sees the late-night bars around the lagoon come into their own.

Aveiro and around

The small, vibrant town of **AVEIRO** is best known for its local beaches, though it's a place of some antiquity and interest. It was a thriving port on the Rio

Vouga up until the 1570s, when the mouth of the river silted up, closing its harbour and creating vast, fever-ridden marshes. Recovery began only in 1808 when a canal was cut through to the sea, reopening the port and draining much of the water; only the shallow lagoons you see today were left. These were put to use as vast saltpans, and although salt is still produced in this way it is no longer the mainstay of the economy it once was. Instead, tourism is increasingly important, boosted by a terrific series of **beaches** north and south of town, and the varied attractions of the **São Jacinto** nature reserve and the famous **Vista Alegre** porcelain manufactory.

Aveiro itself has a compact, restored centre of handsome buildings, open squares, canals, footbridges and cruise boats. For once, the local authorities have restrained themselves – there are no ludicrous claims to be the "Venice of the West" – and Aveiro grows upon visitors, rather than being thrust upon them: it lends itself rather easily to a couple of days doing not very much, and with no fixed plans you might well end up staying an extra night or two. In this you're ably supported by an excellent range of restaurants and some lively bars, courtesy of the large student population at the Universidade de Aveiro.

The town's big annual event is the **Festa da Ria** (last two weeks of Aug), celebrated with boat races, folk dances, and competitions for the best decorated *barcos moliceiros*, the lagoon boats used to collect seaweed. The other major celebration is the **Festa de São Gonçalinho** (second week of Jan), held in honour of the patron saint of fishermen and single women. Those who have made vows during the year, either for the safe return of a fisherman or for the finding of a husband, climb to the top of the São Gonçalinho chapel and throw down loaves of bread to the crowd below; the aim is to catch as much as possible.

Arrival, information and tours

Aveiro is easily accessible by train from Porto (hourly "Urbano" services from São Bento and Campanhã) or Coimbra B, with the **train station** at the north-eastern end of town, a fifteen-minute walk from the centre. There's no bus station, but **buses** will either drop you centrally or run on to a number of stops in streets adjacent to the train station; see "Listings" for bus departure details. Driving into the small centre isn't difficult but **parking** can be. Metered on-street parking costs €0.60 per hour (usually 2hr maximum; free Sat afternoon & Sun) – try Largo do Rossio by the canal or there are plenty of places along the avenue up near the train station. For long-term parking you're best in a covered **car park**, with the one under Praça Marquês de Pombal the most central (and signposted from everywhere).

The **turismo** is just along the canal from the bridge in the town centre, at Rua João Mendonça 8 (June–Sept daily 9am–8pm; Oct–May Mon–Sat 9am–7pm; ☎234 420 760, ⓦwww.rotadaluz.pt). It supplies a good free map of town, and is pretty helpful, particularly when it comes to booking you on local **tours** – there's a circular city tour-bus route, plus specific minibus tours out to places like the Vista Alegre porcelain factory (see below). You also buy tickets here for the one-hour **boat trips** (June–Sept hourly 10am–7pm; Oct–May by arrangement; ☎967 088 183; €7) by traditional boat around the lagoon, which leave from right in front of the turismo. In July and August, there are also daily two-hour lunch cruises (€20).

Bicycles are available free from the green-trimmed "Loja BUGA" kiosk (daily 10am–7pm, closed 1–2pm at weekends), which is located at the back of the Forum Aveiro shopping mall, just across the footbridge (in front of the old market). You need to show ID to get a bike, but are then free to use it around the town for the whole day.

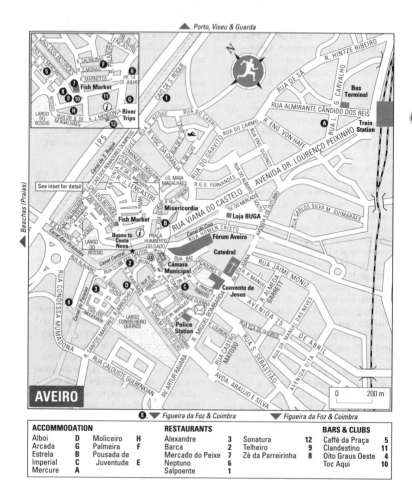

ACCOMMODATION		RESTAURANTS				BARS & CLUBS	
Alboi	**D**	Alexandre	**3**	Sonatura	**12**	Caffé da Praça	**5**
Arcada	**G**	Moliceiro	**H**	Barca	**2**	Telheiro	**9**	Clandestino	**11**
Estrela	**B**	Palmeira	**F**	Mercado do Peixe	**7**	Zé da Parreirinha	**8**	Oito Graus Oeste	**4**
Imperial	**C**	Pousada de		Neptuno	**6**			Toc Aqui	**10**
Mercure	**A**	Juventude	**E**	Salpoente	**1**				

Accommodation

You shouldn't have much trouble finding a **room** in Aveiro, except perhaps during the Festa da Ria in August, when you'd be wise to book ahead. There are several places near the train station, but they're a little far from things; in the centre, try the back streets around the fish market for inexpensive *dormidas* or the pensions along Rua José Estevão, just by the main bridge. The beachside **campsites** are way out of town, at São Jacinto to the north, or to the south at Praia da Barra and Costa Nova, but there's a regular bus service to each of them.

Hotels and pensions

Residencial do Alboi Rua da Arrochela 6
☎ 234 380 390, ⓦ www.residencial-alboi
.com. This characterful place is a cut above most pensions – more like a hotel – and offers cool doubles and triples with shower, overlooking a

quiet street or a pretty patio at the back. There are Aveiro photos on the walls, tea and coffee in the rooms, courteous staff and on-street parking nearby. Also some rooms with kitchenette available around the corner. ❸

Hotel Arcada Rua de Viana do Castelo 4 ☎234 423 001, ⓦ www.hotelarcada.com. A grand building by the station and canal – rooms and bathrooms require upgrading, and it's hard to believe the 70s decor and furniture were ever fashionable, but you get reasonable two-star rooms and nice canal views for the money. Some cheaper rooms available with just shower (not bath). ❹

Pensão Residencial Estrela Rua José Estevão 4 ☎234 423 818. There's a varied choice of rooms in this old, converted house with a plant-filled staircase and polished wooden corridors. Some are en suite, all are old-fashioned, but are cheap and cheerful. Friendly owners offer big discounts out of season. No credit cards. Breakfast not included but available. ❷

Hotel Imperial Rua Dr Nascimento Leitão ☎234 380 150, ⓦ www.hotelimperial.pt. Best Western have this box of a building with dowdy decor, a three-star place, but it's right in the pedestrianized centre and there are fine views of the lagoon from the top-floor "solarium" terrace. Parking. ❸

Hotel Mercure Aveiro Rua Luís Gomes de Carvalho 23 ☎234 404 400, ⓦ www.mercure.com. Three-star hotel with very comfortable en-suite rooms (with a/c and satellite TV) in a gracious, quiet 1930s town house. It's near the station, and so a bit of a walk from things, but has its own parking. Breakfast not included but available. ❹

Hotel Moliceiro Rua Barbosa de Magalhães 15–17, Largo do Rossio ☎234 377 400, ⓦ www.hotelmoliceiro.com. The top choice in town, the four-star *Moliceiro* is pretty affordable even so – the regular room rate usually hovers around €100, though suites and superior rooms are more expensive. It's a contemporary design – rooms in earth tones with flat-screen TVs, dark-wood furniture and marble bathrooms – and you overlook the canal or rear street, with effective double-glazing keeping the noise at bay. There's a good buffet breakfast, chamomile tea delivered to your room each evening, and limited parking out the front. ❺

Palmeira Rua da Palmeira 7–11 ☎234 422 521, ⓔ r.palmeira@netcabo.pt. Modern, tiled town house with attached dining room, in the old quarter between the fish market and the Canal de São Roque. Bright rooms, some with shower or bath, and most with TV. ❷

Youth hostel

Pousada de Juventude Rua das Pombas, Edifício do IPJ ☎234 420 536, ⓦ www.pousadasjuventude .pt. Aveiro's hostel is situated inside a town centre and is small, far from the action and has no self-catering facilities. Eight double rooms available (two of them en suite). Bus #5 or #7 from the train station. Dorm beds €10, rooms ❶

Campsites

Camping Costa Nova Quinta dos Patos, Costa Nova ☎234 393 220, ⓦ www.campingcostanova .com. Huge, well-equipped campsite, with direct access to beach and river, complete with laundry, supermarket, restaurant and bar (live music on summer weekends), and also offering rooms (❷) and bungalows (❹). It's 600m south of Costa Nova bus stop (Vagueira direction) – see "Barra and Costa Nova beaches", p.268, for bus details.

Camping Praia da Barra Rua Diogo Cão 125, Praia da Barra ☎234 369 425, ⓦ www.campingbarra .com. Five minutes from Barra beach, with laundry, mini-market and restaurant. Also apartments here, but they're three-bedroom (sleeping up to 8) and pricey in summer. See "Barra and Costa Nova beaches", p.268, for bus details.

The town

Stand on the bridge over the **main canal** and most of central Aveiro is within a couple of minutes' walk. The traditional industries here are recalled by imposing statues of local workers on the bridge, notably the *salineira* with her salt tray. Handsome, pastel-coloured houses line Rua João Mendonça on the north side, with the old town streets and **Mercado do Peixe** (fish market) just behind. Other arms of the canal branch off at intervals, with tiled houses facing each other across the water. Locals tie up their motor boats and cruisers in front of the fish market, while on the main canal the traffic is largely of *barcos moliceiros*, the traditional flat-bottomed lagoon boats with raised prows. Once used to collect seaweed (used as a fertilizer), they are now almost exclusively in service as tourist cruise boats.

Aveiro has a preponderance of **Art Nouveau buildings** – the turismo is housed in a particularly fine example – the legacy of returning wealthy emigrants in the early years of the twentieth century. However, these aside, there's very little in the way of sights in the city centre, though the canal promenades and old-town streets are very attractive. On the south side of the bridge, by the canal, the huge **Forum Aveiro** shopping mall is at least a largely sympathetic addition, while up the pedestrianized Rua Coimbra you come to Praça da República, flanked by the blue snowflake-design tiled façade of the seventeenth-century **Igreja da Misericórdia** and the **Câmara Municipal**, a century older. Both buildings face a declamatory statue of Aveiro's famous son, the nineteenth-century politician José Estêvão Coelho de Magalhães.

Otherwise, there's only one sight of real note, the fifteenth-century **Convento de Jesus**, a few minutes' walk away on Avenida Santa Joana, which now houses the town museum (Tues–Sun 10am–5.30pm; €2, free Sun and public hols until 2pm), whose finest exhibits all relate to Santa Joana, a daughter of Afonso V who lived in the convent from 1475 until her death in 1489. Barred from becoming a nun because of her royal station and her father's opposition, she was later beatified for her determination to escape from the material world (or perhaps simply from an unwelcome arranged marriage). Her tomb and chapel are strikingly beautiful, as is the convent itself, and there's a fine collection of art and sculpture – notably a series of naive seventeenth-century paintings depicting the saint's life.

Eating, drinking and nightlife

Aveiro has some excellent **restaurants**, ranging from the little *casas de pasto* in the old town streets around the fish market to full-blown seafood and fish specialists. **Local specialities** include eels and shellfish from the lagoons (served fried, or with rice, *arroz*, or as a stew, *ensopado*) and powerful Bairrada wine, and you shouldn't pass up the opportunity to try the celebrated Aveiros *ovos moles*, which are very sweet candied egg yolks. The liveliest **bar** area is immediately around the fish market, where tables are scattered across the cobbles. A ten-minute walk from the fish market, there's another line of late-opening canal-side bars up along Cais de São Roque, some set in renovated salt storage barns.

Restaurants

Alexandre Cais do Alboi 14 ☎ 234 420 494. A short walk south along the Canal do Paraiso, this is a well-regarded snack bar and adjacent restaurant with a local clientele. It's a *churrasqueira*, with grilled meats – quail to steaks – a speciality. Closed Thurs & mid-July to mid-Aug. Moderate.

A Barca Rua José Rabumba 5 ☎ 234 426 024. Intimate, long-running restaurant where diners can see the top-quality fresh fish and seafood being prepared in the kitchen at the back. Try the sea bass or sole. Closed Sat eve & Sun. Moderate.

Mercado do Peixe Largo da Praça do Peixe ☎ 234 383 511. In the rafters of the fish market, with crisp decor, attentive service and exceedingly fresh fish and seafood. Come here for *caldeirada de enguias* (eel stew; €25 between 2), *ensopadas* and *cataplanas* – there's also a good-value weekday lunch deal, and great views out to the Ria or to the square below from the tiny terrace. Closed Sun eve & Mon. Expensive.

Neptuno Rua Mendes Leite 1 ☎ 234 424 566. Functional but decent little grill house serving large portions of chicken, sausage, chops, sardines or fish. Around €5 for a plateful, €10 for a *dose* to feed two. Closed Sun. Inexpensive.

Salpoente Cais de São Roque 83 ☎ 234 382 674. Ten minutes' walk north along the Canal de São Roque, this superior fish restaurant is set inside a renovated wooden salt barn. There are clams, crabs, fish and eels on the menu, as well as plenty of meat, while the restaurant has an enjoyable bar which opens at 11.30pm and has live music on Fri and Sat until 2.30am. Closed Sun & Mon lunch. Expensive.

Sonatura Rua Clube dos Galitos 6 ☎ 234 424 474. A lunch-only self-service veggie-wholefood place, by the bridge, that shares premises with a natural remedy/diet/healthfood store. Meals are priced between €5 and 8, depending on what you have. Closed Sat & Sun. Inexpensive.

O Telheiro Largo da Praça do Peixe 20–21 ☎ 234 429 473. A great place for grilled meat and fish, this buzzy *adega* sits you at the bar, or at rustic wooden benches and tiled tables. There's a good range of tapas-style starters (all €3–4), tender beef (try the *bife á caçarola*), *enguias fritas* (fried eels) and a terrific *lulas grelhados* (grilled squid) – mains range from around €9–14. Closed Sat. Moderate.

Zé da Parreirinha Trav do Lavadouro 10 ⊕234 426 137. Rough-and-ready *casa de pasto* with full meals for under €10. Just off Praça da Peixe. Closed Wed. Inexpensive.

Bars and clubs

Caffé da Praça Rua Antonio Santos Lé 18. Round the corner from the action on Praça do Peixe and up a set of stairs, this fashionable bar has very friendly staff and table service. Large windows overlook the canal.

Clandestino Rua do Tenente Resende 35. There's no sign but it's recognizable by its dark-red exterior and location bang next to the Evangelical church. Friendly and warm atmosphere, with more tables upstairs and a DJ playing jazzy, mellow tunes.

Oito Graus Oeste Cais do Paraíso. Dance club with its own bar and terrace overlooking the Ria. Weekends only, from late.

Toc Aqui Pr do Peixe. One of a number of fashionable bars around the fish market, whose name (which isn't signed – it's the one with the blue facade) means "play here", and on more raucous nights, that's exactly what you can do with the instruments hung on the back wall.

Listings

Buses Buy tickets for Rede Expressos (express) services to Lisbon, Coimbra and Porto from Loja das Revistas, a newsagents in Pr Humberto Delgado, by the bridge on the south side; you can catch the bus around the corner up Rua Batalhão de Caçadores (opposite Forum), though they also depart from an office near the train station on Rua Almirante Cândido dos Reis. All other bus companies use stops around the train station.

Hospital Hospital Distrital, Av Dr Artur Ravara ⊕234 378 300.

Internet Espaçao Internet, Pr da República (9am–8pm), offers free access for 30min.

Newspapers Foreign press available from Galeria Rossio, down the canal from the turismo on Rua João Mendonça.

Police Pr Marquês de Pombal ⊕234 302 510.

Post office Pr Marquês de Pombal ⊕234 380 840 (Mon–Fri 8.30am–6.30pm).

Supermarket There's a large Pingo Doce at the Forum Aveiro shopping mall.

Taxis Available in front of the train station, or at the bottom of Rua Viana do Castelo, near the bridge.

Barra and Costa Nova beaches

There's no beach in Aveiro itself but the coast to the west is a more or less continuous line of sand, cut off from the mainland for much of the way by the meandering lagoon. Developers have long caught on and the beaches closest to town – at Barra and Costa Nova – are built up and packed in summer, but still good fun. The vagaries of Aveiro's estuarine climate mean there's often a stiff breeze, even in the dog days of August; out of season, you'll have the vast strands to yourself. There are rooms and pensions at both resorts, but Aveiro itself is a far nicer place to stay and bus connections are very regular. The popular campsites are listed under Aveiro "Accommodation", p.266.

Auto Viação Aveirense **buses** (roughly hourly 7.05am–12.40am) depart from outside Aveiro train station, and then stop in town on Rua Clube dos Galitos, across the bridge from the turismo and about 150m down the canal on the right (opposite the Royal School of Languages). Drivers should follow the signs from the town centre for "praias".

The buses call first at **Praia da Barra**, 9km west of Aveiro, a large, developed stretch of sand overlooked by the Iberian Peninsula's tallest lighthouse. There's more of the same at **Costa Nova**, 3km south of Barra, though the development here is ameliorated by the very attractive line of candy-striped wooden buildings facing the lagoon (ie inland). The bus stops on the lagoon road, next to a wave-shaped turismo, with the excellent beach a couple of blocks back. Cafés and seafood restaurants line the lagoon road. Drivers can always push on for the day further down the minor lagoon road to the beach at Praia da Vagueira (7km) and, eventually, Praia de Mira (around 20km from Costa Nova).

Vista Alegre

Portugal's celebrated **Vista Alegre** (Ⓦ www.vistaalegre.pt) porcelain works was established in 1824 at Ílhavo, around 5km west of Aveiro – you'll pass the signs en route to the beaches from town. It soon acquired royal patronage and expanded from a simple porcelain and glass manufactory to an estate with its own workers' village, along the lines of the model villages built by enlightened British entrepreneurs of the period. Today on the site there's a **museum** and tiled and frescoed seventeenth-century **chapel** to visit (Tues–Fri 9am–6pm, Sat & Sun 9am–12.30pm & 2–5pm; €1.50), and both a Vista Alegre **shop** (porcelain, crystal, silverware) and factory shop for seconds (both shops Mon–Sat 9.30am–6.30pm). You can also tour the **factory** (Mon–Fri only; reservations required, ℡ 234 320 600; €10), in which case you also get shown around the museum, chapel and shops. There's a **Vista Alegre Tour** available from Aveiro turismo (currently Wed & Fri; €12), which runs you there and back in a minibus and includes all arrangements and entrance fees.

São Jacinto

The other escape from Aveiro is to the beach and nature reserve of **SÃO JACINTO**, located on the north side of the lagoon. It involves a bit more effort than other local trips, but is worth it. Catch the bus from the Rua Clube dos Galitos stop in Aveiro to the end of the line at Forte da Barra (roughly hourly, journey time 15min – exact timetables available from Aveiro turismo). Once at the port, a connecting boat runs you across the water to São Jacinto (you can pay for the full journey on the bus, currently €2.60). There's no great benefit in driving from Aveiro, incidentally, as the circuitous trip by road to São Jacinto is 50km.

Unlike its neighbours along the coast, São Jacinto isn't a resort but rather a thriving little port with a handful of dockside cafés and restaurants. With a military base at one end and a forest of cranes cluttering the skyline, it's not beautiful, but there is an enormous, undeveloped dune-fringed **beach** twenty minutes' walk away. Parts of the beach, plus the encroaching pine forest and coastal scrub, have been preserved within the **Reserva Natural das Dunas de São Jacinto**, where boardwalks and paths are laid out though the marram grass and past willow-shrouded ponds. More than a hundred bird species have been spotted here, including goshawk, teal and wigeon. To visit you need to call the **interpretation centre** at least a day in advance (park & centre closed Sun & Thurs; ℡ 234 331 282 or 234 831 063, Ⓦ http://camarinha.aveiro-digital.net) as numbers are limited. You're only allowed in between 9 & 9.30am, or 2 & 2.30pm – you're then given a map for a self-guided seven-kilometre walk through the reserve, which takes around two and half hours. The reserve entrance is a ten-minute walk from the boat, out of town along the road to Torreira.

Boats cross back regularly (every hour or so) to Forte da Barra for the connecting bus to Aveiro. North of São Jacinto the minor N327 (and summer bus service) runs all the way up the lagoon, past a couple of campsites en route to the beach at **Torreira**. There's another popular small resort at **Furadouro**, 26km from São Jacinto, where a long stretch of pine-fringed dunes marks the point at which the distinctive Ria countryside finally comes to an end.

Santa Maria da Feira

North of Aveiro, away from the lagoon, the highways and train line all sweep towards Espinho and Porto. There's no great reason to delay the journey, though **SANTA MARIA DA FEIRA** (or, more simply, Feira), halfway to Porto, does sport one of the most spectacular castles in Portugal. Feira itself is filling up fast with commuters, but there's a small historic kernel at the bottom of town, with shady woods and picnic grounds laid out up the hill as far as the resplendent **Castelo da Feira** (Tues–Fri 9.30am–12.30 & 1.30pm–6pm, Sat & Sun 10am–12.30pm & 1.30–6.30pm; closes at 5pm in winter; €3) – follow "castelo" signs and park right outside, or walk up from the bus stop at the bottom in ten minutes. The castle has been zealously restored and is a magnificent example of defensive engineering, with high walls, squat towers, battlements and witches' hat turrets. Its various sections are linked by tunnels and hidden entrances in such a way that no direct access can ever have been offered to intruders – arrow slits, keyhole windows and an underground cistern emphasize the point that this castle would not fall easily.

Buses stop at the bottom of the hill up to the castle – from Aveiro, Porto-bound express services sometimes stop here, but Feira is actually far easier to reach directly from Porto, only a twenty-minute ride away. A few simple restaurants line the road here, while around the corner and up in the old town are a couple of squares with outdoor **cafés**. Drivers could easily see Feira's castle en route to Arouca, to the east – the route there is back down the N1 to São João de Madeira and Vale de Cambra.

Arouca and the Serra da Freita

Picking up the N224 from Vale de Cambra, it's a splendid drive to **Arouca**, 20km to the east, a winding route through forested hills and small terraced slopes of tumbling vineyards, the air heady with the scent of pine resin and eucalyptus. There are regular buses from Santa Maria da Feira (change at São João de Madeira), and although there are no public transport links south from Arouca, through the magnificent **Serra da Freita**, buses do run on north to Porto (via São João de Madeira).

Arouca

The small town of **AROUCA** is entirely overshadowed by the vast **Convento da Arouca** (accompanied visits, sometimes in English; Tues–Sun 9.30am–noon & 2–5.30pm; €2.50), whose imposing walls loom over the main road that cuts through town. It was founded as early as 1091, though most surviving parts are from rather later medieval times. In the kitchen there are huge fireplaces along Alcobaça lines. The Baroque church (which you can see without buying a ticket; enter from the main road) holds richly carved choir stalls and a great organ with 1352 notes, played on rare occasions by one of the country's few experts, while off the central cloisters the airy Sala Capítula, lined with *azulejos*, is where the abbesses once held court.

The convent peaked in importance when Dona Mafalda, of whose dowry it had formed a part, found her marriage to Dom Henriques I of Castile annulled and retired here to a life of religious contemplation. In the extensive **museum** upstairs, you can see some of Queen Mafalda's most prized treasures, including an exquisite thirteenth-century silver diptych. In 1792, four centuries after Mafalda's death, villagers claimed to have witnessed her saving the convent from the ravages of a terrible fire. She was promptly exhumed and beatified.

The rest of town struggles to make a mark in the face of its prize exhibit, but it's a handsome little place with a certain sleepy appeal. The central square holds a couple of cafés with pavement seats, while in the medieval back streets there are some beautiful old houses decked with wisteria. Local heart rates increase

△ Castelo da Feira

slightly during the annual **Festa de Nossa Senhora da Mó** (Sept 7–8), when the whole town turns out for a picnic on the crown of a hill 8km to the east. **Holy Week** processions are a big deal here, too, starting on the Wednesday and culminating on the Saturday night, when most of the inhabitants parade behind the local saints' statues to the Misericórdia church, with candles lit in all the town's windows.

Practicalities

From the **bus station**, head down to the main square, Praça Brandão de Vasconcelas, opposite the convent. There's a **turismo** (daily 9.30am–12.30pm & 2–5.30pm; mid-Sept to June closed Sat afternoon & Sun; ☏256 943 575, ⓦwww.cm-arouca.pt) in the street at the back of the square (just behind the small church), where they'll give you a map of town. If you fancy a night in what are undeniably quiet surroundings, check out the **accommodation** at *Residencial São Pedro*, Avenida Reinaldo de Noronha (☏256 944 580, ⓦwww. aroucanet.com/rspedro; ❷), a five-minute walk up the main road from the square (take the left fork, to Castro Daire, at the top). It's not fantastic, but most rooms have views over town and there's a decent restaurant (closed Mon). A more rustic choice is the *Quinta do Bóco* (☏256 944 169; no credit cards; ❸), in a lovely farmhouse dating from the sixteenth century, which also has views, gardens and a pool; continue up from the *São Pedro* and it's on the left. The turismo has details of other rural tourism places in the vicinity.

For an inexpensive **meal** locals like *O Tranca*, Rua Alexandre Herculano 13 (☏256 941 777), 20m up the main road from the square and on the right – it serves good regional food, and lunch is a mere €5. Otherwise, several other traditional restaurants in town specialize in the local *arouquêsa* beef.

Serra da Freita

South of Arouca lies the beautiful, terraced countryside of the **Serra da Freita**, rising to over 1000m and littered with dolmens, crumbling villages and waterfalls with ancient bridges. A regional map available from Arouca turismo shows all the local sights and attractions, and you could easily spend a day or two touring and walking in the hills. Vines grow on precipitous terraces, while the roads snake through pine forest and then high across the heather-dotted moorland. Heading south, there's a twisting 43-kilometre route over the peaks to Vouzela, climbing first to the radio mast on the heights of **São Pedro Velho** (1100m), from where views of the valley are tremendous. At the medieval hamlet of **Albergaria da Serra** the road disappears altogether for an instant and degenerates into cart-rutted cobbles worn by centuries of use. There's a good river beach here and at nearby Mizarela a spectacular waterfall with a 60-metre drop. After leaving Albergaria take the next available left and follow signs to **Manhouce**, a slightly larger village amid the pine forests and rocky uplands, beyond which there's another 12km of incredible bends and views before you emerge onto the N227 for São Pedro do Sul and Vouzela. It's a spectacular drive but be prepared to take evasive action along the whole route, against other drivers or, occasionally, wandering cattle.

Travel details

Trains

You can check train timetables online at ⓦ www .cp.pt.

Aveiro to: Coimbra (hourly; 45min–1hr); Espinho (hourly; 35–50min); Lisbon (hourly; 2hr 30min–4hr 50min); Porto (hourly; 1hr–1hr 15min).

Coimbra to: Aveiro (hourly; 45min–1hr); Braga (2–3 daily; 2hr); Figueira da Foz (hourly; 1hr–1hr 20min); Guarda (4–7 daily; 3hr–3hr 20min); Lisbon (hourly; 1hr 50min); Lousã (hourly; 50min); Luso-Buçaco (4 daily; 35min); Porto (hourly; 1hr 20min–2hr).

Figueira da Foz to: Caldas da Rainha (2–4 daily; 2hr–2hr 25min); Coimbra (hourly; 1hr–1hr 20min); Leiria (2–4 daily; 1hr–1hr 15min).

Buses

Arouca to: Porto (via São João de Madeira, Mon– Fri every 1–2hr, Sat & Sun 2 daily; 2hr); Santa Maria da Feira (via São João de Madeira, Mon–Fri every 1–2hr, Sat & Sun 1 daily; 1hr 20min).

Aveiro to: Figueira da Foz (up to 5 daily; 1hr 15min); Lisbon (1–2 daily; 3hr 15min); Porto (roughly hourly; 2hr 45min); Praia de Mira (Mon–Fri 3 daily; 1hr); Vouzela (1–2 daily; 1hr–1hr 30min).

Coimbra to: Covilhã/Guarda (1–2 daily; 3hr/4hr); Fátima (roughly hourly; 1hr); Figueira da Foz (up to 12 daily; 1hr 15min); Góis/Arganil (Mon–Fri 1–2 daily; 1hr 25min/2hr); Leiria (12–16 daily; 50min); Lisbon (at least hourly; 2hr 30min); Luso via Buçaco (Mon–Sat 2–5 daily; 40min); Montemor-o-Velho (6–19 daily; 40min); Penacova (Mon–Fri up to 16 daily; 45min–1hr); Porto (at least hourly; 1hr 30min); Vila Real (2 daily; 3hr); Viseu (via Santa Comba Dão and Tondela, up to 17 daily; 1hr 15min–1hr 25min); Vouzela (1–2 daily; 1hr 45min).

Figueira da Foz to: Aveiro (up to 5 daily; 1hr 15min); Coimbra (up to 12 daily; 1hr 15min); Leiria (9–11 daily; 1hr–1hr 25min); Lisbon (4 daily; 2hr 45min–3hr); Mira (2–5 daily; 1hr); Montemor-o-Velho (Mon–Fri roughly every 30min, Sat & Sun 4–8 daily; 30min).

Góis to: Arganil (Mon–Fri 1 daily; 30min); Coimbra (Mon–Fri 1–2 daily; 1hr 25min); Lousã (Mon–Fri 1 daily; 1hr).

Lousã to: Góis (1 Mon–Fri; 1hr).

Luso to: Coimbra (Mon–Sat 2–5 daily; 40min); Viseu via Buçaco (5–7 daily; 1hr 45min).

Mira to: Aveiro (9–12 daily; 50min); Coimbra (1–2 daily; 1hr); Figueira da Foz (2–5 daily; 1hr).

Penacova to: Coimbra (Mon–Fri up to 16 daily; 45min–1hr); Tondela (Mon–Fri 1 daily; 25min); Viseu (Mon–Fri 1 daily; 1hr).

Praia de Mira to: Aveiro (1 daily; 1hr); Coimbra (1–2 daily; 1hr 15min).

Vouzela to: Aveiro (1–2 daily; 1hr–1hr 30min); Lisbon, via Coimbra (1–2 daily; 4hr 30min); Porto (1–2 daily; 2hr).

Mountain Beiras

CHAPTER 4

Highlights

✳ **Museu Grão Vasco, Viseu**
Explore the works of one of
Portugal's greatest artists in
Viseu's fine museum. See
p.279

✳ **Trancoso** This beautifully
preserved walled town is the
best overnight stop in the
Beira Alta tableland. See p.289

✳ **Fortified walls of Almeida**
The extraordinary
fortifications here are built in
the form of a twelve-pointed
star. See p.294

✳ **Linhares** The western flank of
the Serra da Estrela provides
a gentle introduction to the
mountains, with Linhares its
most eye-catching village.
See p.298

✳ **Hiking in the Parque
Natural de Serra da Estrela**
The mountain town of Manteigas is the best base for *serra*
walks and tours, including the
half-day circuit to the Poço do
Inferno waterfall. See p.303

✳ **Belmonte** An unsung treasure
of a town, from the picturesque castle to its restored
Jewish quarter. See p.309

✳ **Village stay, Sortelha**
Stay the night in one of the
restored houses in this eerie
walled village in the Beira
Baixa. See p.311

✳ **Monsanto** Houses hewn out
of granite cling to a boulder-
strewn hillside below a
formidable castle. See p.314

△ Fortified walls, Almeida

Mountain Beiras

Composed of two historic provinces, the Beira Alta (Upper) and Beira Baixa (Lower), the **mountain Beiras** region features some of the most spectacular but least explored country in the Iberian peninsula: the enormous boulders which lie strewn across much of the land limit agriculture and have instead favoured a pastoral culture of grazing animals, rugged hamlets and isolated country towns. It's also arguably the most quintessentially Portuguese part of the country, little touched by outside influence. The Beiras form the historic heart of ancient Lusitânia, where Viriatus the Iberian rebel (a symbol of the spirit of independence in Neoclassical literature) made his last stand against the Romans. Later, as Portugal strived for nationhood, many of the towns near the disputed border with Spain acquired mighty castles, which are still a characteristic feature of the region today. Age-old traditions linger on, whether it's the chestnut blessings of Beira Alta or the burning logs kept alight outside Beira Baixa churches at Christmas.

Sitting at the junction of routes from Coimbra, Porto and Vila Real, the ancient town of **Viseu** is the gateway to the mountains: it's also the capital of Beira Alta province, and the only place of any real size in the whole region. The fast east-west IP5 highway links Viseu to the mountain-top town of **Guarda** – with Spain another 40km to the east – while to the north, between the highway and the Douro river, are the high-sited castle-towns of the **Beira Alta planalto** (or tableland). Some, like medieval, walled **Trancoso**, or the star-shaped fortress town of **Almeida**, are worth a day of anyone's time; half a dozen others have lesser charms but are easily seen en route to or from the Douro.

South of the IP5 rises the austere **Serra da Estrela** mountain range, the undisputed regional highlight. The landscape is protected under the auspices of the **Parque Natural da Serra da Estrela**, whose mountain villages, tumbling rivers, high peaks and glacial valleys are linked by an extensive series of hiking trails, though there's also road access to the major settlements, notably the enjoyable small mountain town of **Manteigas**. The park's southeastern boundary is flanked by the pleasant university town of **Covilhã**, handy for the winter ski fields and the ascent of Portugal's highest mountain, Torre.

South and east of Covilhã lies the sombre plain of the lower province, **Beira Baixa**, whose monotonous, parched landscape has its own mysterious beauty, dotted with cork, carob and olive trees and the occasional orchard. **Castelo Branco** in the south is the provincial capital, but most tourist attention is centred on the ancient hilltop villages rising dramatically from the surrounding plains, notably **Sortelha** and **Monsanto**. There's historic

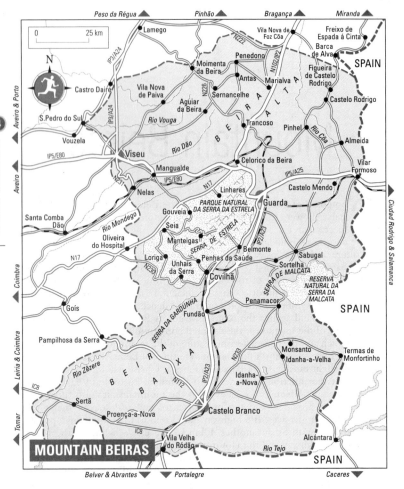

interest, too, in pretty **Belmonte**, halfway between Covilhã and Guarda – surely a candidate for most appealing small town in Portugal – and in the extensive Roman remains at isolated **Idana-a-Velha**. Meanwhile, in the border hills and reservoirs of the **Serra da Malcata**, there are hiking, biking and wildlife-spotting opportunities – though the famed Iberian lynx is no more to be seen.

You can visit the main settlements of the mountain Beiras – Viseu, Guarda, Belmonte, Covilhã and Castelo Branco – easily enough by **public transport**, and reach the flanks of the Parque Natural da Serra da Estrela, too. But this is one region where it really pays to have a car, as buses to the Beira byways and backwaters are few and far between. Budget **accommodation** is patchily available too: many of the most interesting restored mountain villages are pinning their hopes on mid-range and upmarket rural tourism, so prices are often higher than you might expect.

Viseu

From its high plateau, the dignified city of **VISEU** surveys the surrounding countryside with the air of a feudal overlord. It's a place of great antiquity. There was a Roman town here, and on the northern outskirts you can still make out the remains of an encampment claimed to be the site where Viriatus (Viriato in Portuguese) fought his final battle – it's marked by a monument to the Iberian warrior. The heart of the medieval city around the cathedral has changed little, though it's now approached through the broad avenues of a prosperous provincial centre. There's more going on in Viseu than in any other place in the mountain Beiras – the large student population helps – but even so, you'll probably find that one night will suffice. It's a good place to look for handicrafts and souvenirs, while the local Dão wines are justly celebrated. The main annual event is the **Feira de São Mateus** which takes place from mid-August until its climax on September 21 (Dia do São Mateus) – it's largely an agricultural show, but is enlivened by bullfights, fireworks, fun-fair and folk-dancing.

The city

Only a few sections of the old city wall survive, breached by two gateways, but the medieval quarter is clearly defined on its hill around the cathedral. The lower town centres on the large square outside the town hall, known as the **Rossio**, from where you can climb up along Rua Soar de Cima to the granite **Porta do Soar**, the plain, fortified gateway to the jumble of alleys immediately behind the cathedral. To the east, off Rua Formosa, narrow **Rua Direita** offers a second approach, a winding medieval street mixing boutiques, shoe and gift shops with more prosaic trades – printers, key-cutters, florists, undertakers and grocers. Here, and in the side streets, sixteenth-century stone mansions proudly display their Manueline windows and coats of arms, while at the northern end of Rua Direita – just beyond the theatre, on the main avenue – stands the other surviving town gate, the **Porta dos Cavaleiros**. Beyond here, on the outskirts, lies the **Parque do Fontelo**, a municipal park laid out across the woods and gardens of the old bishop's palace.

Around the cathedral

The wide cathedral square, Praça da Sé, is lined with noble stone buildings, most striking of which is the **Igreja da Misericórdia** with its white Baroque facade. Silhouetted against a deep blue sky it looks like a film set without substance – you expect to walk around the back and find wooden props holding it up.

There's nothing two-dimensional, however, about the **Sé** (daily 9.30am–noon & 2–5.30pm; free), a weighty, twin-towered Romanesque base on which a succession of later generations have made their mark. The granite frontage, remodelled in the seventeenth century, is stern and makes the church look smaller than it actually is – inside it opens out into a great hall with intricate vaulting, twisted and knotted to represent ropes. The cathedral's Renaissance **cloister**, of which you get no intimation from outside, is one of the most graceful in the country. The lower level is decorated with *azulejos* and while it's interesting to climb to the upper level, and look down upon town and square, you have to pay to do so (€2.50; closed Mon) since its rooms house the cathedral's religious art and sculpture collection.

Museu de Grão Vasco

The greatest treasure of Viseu is the **Museu Grão Vasco** (Tues 2–6pm, Wed–Sun 10am–6pm; €3, free Sun until 2pm) in the Paço dos Três Escalões – once

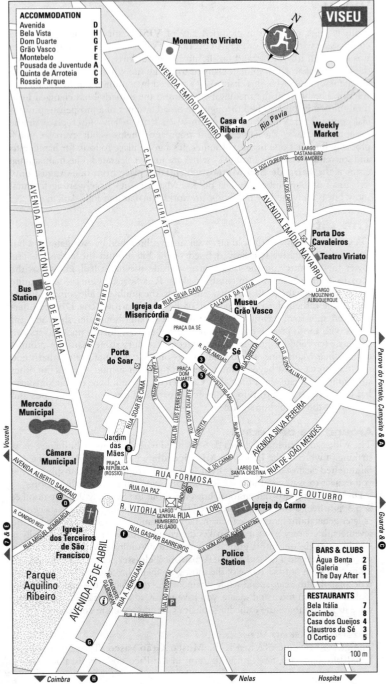

①, Aveiro, Lamego, Chaves & Vila Real

VISEU

N

ACCOMMODATION
Avenida	D
Bela Vista	H
Dom Duarte	G
Grão Vasco	F
Montebelo	E
Pousada de Juventude	A
Quinta de Arroteia	C
Rossio Parque	B

Monument to Viriato

AVENIDA EMIDIO NAVARRO

Casa da Ribeira

Rio Pavia

Weekly Market

LARGO CASTANHEIRO DOS AMORES

R. DOS LOUREIROS

AV. DOS CAPITES

CALÇADA DE VIRIATO

AVENIDA EMIDIO NAVARRO

Porta Dos Cavaleiros

Teatro Viriato

AVENIDA DR. ANTÓNIO JOSÉ DE ALMEIDA

Bus Station

RUA SERPA PINTO

RUA SILVA GAIO

CALÇADA DA VIGIA

LARGO MOUZINHO ALBUQUERQUE

Igreja da Misericórdia

Museu Grão Vasco

PRAÇA DA SÉ

②

Sé

R. DAS AMEIAS

RUA DO GONÇALINHO

Parova do Fontelo, Campsite & ⓐ

Porta do Soar

RUA SOAR DE CIMA

③

PRAÇA DOM DUARTE ⑥

⑤

RUA AUGUSTO HILÁRIO

④

RUA DIREITA

Mercado Municipal

RUA DR. LUÍS FERREIRA

RUA DOM DUARTE

RUA ÁRVORE

AVENIDA SILVA PEREIRA

RUA DE JOÃO MENDES

Vouzela

Câmara Municipal

Jardim das Mães

Ⓑ

PRAÇA DA REPÚBLICA (ROSSIO)

R. DO CARMO

LARGO DA SANTA CRISTINA

RUA FORMOSA

RUA 5 DE OUTUBRO

Guarda & ⓒ

RUA DA PAZ

R. ANDRADES

R. VITORIA

LARGO GENERAL HUMBERTO DELGADO

RUA A. LOBO

Igreja do Carmo

AVENIDA ALBERTO SAMPAIO

Ⓓ

R. CANDIDO REIS

② & ⓔ

Igreja dos Terceiros de São Francisco

Ⓕ

RUA GASPAR BARREIROS

RUA DOM AFONSO ALVES MARTINS

Police Station

Parque Aquilino Ribeiro

AVENIDA 25 DE ABRIL

AV. GULBENKIAN

RUA A. HERCULANO

ⓘ

⑧

RUA J. BARROS

RUA DO HOSPITAL

Ⓟ

Ⓖ

BARS & CLUBS
Água Benta	2
Galeria	6
The Day After	1

RESTAURANTS
Bela Itália	7
Cacimbo	8
Casa dos Queijos	4
Claustros da Sé	3
O Cortiço	5

0 — 100 m

▼ Coimbra ▼ Ⓗ   ▼ Nelas   Hospital ▼

the Bishop's palace – which adjoins the cathedral; the entrance is on Praça da Sé. The museum celebrates the work of Vasco Fernandes (known always as Grão Vasco, The Great Vasco; see box), who became the key figure in a school of painting that flourished here in the first half of the sixteenth century. His earliest work was on the fourteen panels tracing the *Life of Christ* (1501–1506), commissioned from Flemish artist Francisco Henriques for the altarpiece of Viseu

△ *St Peter on His Throne*, Museu Grão Vasco

Desperately little is known about Vasco Fernandes, universally known as **Grão Vasco**; it can only be said that he was born in or near the city of Viseu, probably in 1475, and that he died in 1542 or 1543, leaving a widow and two daughters. There was no major artist living in Viseu at the time to take the young Vasco Fernandes under his wing, so it's supposed that he trained in Lisbon or even abroad. Even more problematic for art historians is that virtually all the works associated with him – up to 100 by some counts – have had to be identified by comparisons with the only two that he definitely signed, and with his known work on the surviving altar panels for Lamego and Viseu cathedrals. In many cases, his attributed works are collaborations, particularly with his Viseu contemporary **Gaspar Vaz** (1490–1569). Either way, the two have a fair claim to being among the greatest artists Portugal has produced. The style of these "Portuguese primitives" was influenced heavily by Flemish masters and in particular by van Eyck, but certain aspects – the realism of portraiture and richness of colour – are distinctively their own.

cathedral – note the vividly imagined *Adoration of the Magi* which topically presents Balthasar as a Brazil-inspired Indian with feathered head-dress (Cabral had discovered Brazil in 1500). Centrepiece of the collection is Grão Vasco's masterly *St Peter on His Throne* (1530–1535), painted for a chapel altar in Viseu cathedral – its Flemish roots are evident, particularly in the intricately detailed background, while the painting has been mounted free-standing so that you can see how the original frame and canvas were assembled. Several other large-scale collaborations with his contemporary and rival **Gaspar Vaz** are also displayed, though it's Vaz's much smaller, intense studies of saints Peter and Paul that make their mark.

There is more in the museum – nineteenth-century Portuguese art to Oriental porcelain and textiles – but the sixteenth-century artworks are the undisputed highlight. You can take a break in the pleasant courtyard **café**.

Shopping: the markets and Casa da Ribeira

The weekday **Mercado Municipal**, just west of Rossio, is worth a look, while there's a bigger **weekly market** held every Tuesday, on the ring road by Largo Castanheiro dos Amores. For crafts and souvenirs, browse in the shops along **Rua Direita** in the old town, though you might not want to buy until you've had a good look in the excellent **Casa da Ribeira** (Tues–Sat 9am–12.30pm & 2–5.30pm), a short walk from the centre, just across the river. Based in an old manor house, this is the local handicrafts centre, with someone usually on hand to show you the working loom and potters' wheel. There's plenty of traditional work here, from the typical black Tondela earthenware to Viseu stained glass and decorative ironwork. But there's also studio space for contemporary sculptors, basket-weavers and wood restorers, with plenty to catch your attention.

Practicalities

The **bus station** is down Avenida Dr António Jose de Almeida, a five-minute walk from the Rossio. There's metered **parking** all over the centre (free after 8pm, 2pm on Sat, and all Sun), though there's a four-hour limit – it's more convenient to use the large open-air car park on Rua do Hospital, where there's no time limit and you pay at the machine when you leave. The informative **turismo** (mid-June to mid-Sept Mon–Fri 9am–12.30pm & 1–7pm, Sat 10am–1pm & 2–6pm, Sun 10am–1pm; rest of the year Mon–Fri 9am–12.30pm & 2.30–6pm, Sat 10am–1pm

& 2–6pm, Sun 10am–1pm; ☏232 420 950, ⓦwww.rtdaolafoes.com) is just south off the Rossio on Avenida Calouste Gulbenkian, and has information about the whole region, including a booklet detailing all the local archeological sites.

Accommodation

Viseu has a youth hostel and campsite, but it's short on reasonable budget *pensão* accommodation. For the nicest lodgings you need to head out of town to one of the rural tourism manor houses.

In town

Hotel Avenida Av Alberto Sampaio 1 ☏232 423 432, ⓦwww.hotelavenida.com.pt. The location is excellent, and it exudes a stately air – granite balconies, deep green and red colours, uniformed staff – but in the end the rooms don't quite match up. There's some scuffed paintwork, elderly bathrooms, and street noise at the front – prices are pretty good though. ❸

Residencial Bela Vista Rua Alexandre Herculano 510 ☏232 422 026. A barebones choice in a character-free residential building, 10min walk from the Rossio. However, it's as cheap as you'll find in town, and there's private parking at the back. No credit cards. ❷

Residencial Dom Duarte Rua Alexandre Herculano 214 ☏232 421 980. Ask to see a couple of rooms here if you're not satisfied – some have worn carpets and dark, heavy furniture, others are a bit slicker with more modern fixtures and fittings. All are somewhat overpriced. Pay parking immediately outside. ❸

Hotel Grão Vasco Rua Gaspar Barreiros ☏232 423 511, ⓦwww.hotelgraovasco.pt. The town centre's top (four-star) hotel, with calm, subdued rooms giving onto a neatly manicured lawn and – rare for these parts – a swimming pool. It's in a very convenient location, with parking. ❹

Pensão Rossio Parque Pr da República 55 ☏232 422 085. The best budget choice, now it's been renovated – space is a bit tight in some rooms, but they all have laminate flooring, a/c and new bathrooms, and the front ones overlook the Rossio. No credit cards. ❷

Outside town

Quinta de Arroteia Póvoa de Sobrinhos, 3km east of town, N16 (Mangualde road) ☏232 478 450, ⓦwww.quintadarroteia.com. Exposed stone walls, inviting white bed linen, a full-sized snooker table, an open fire in winter and a large pool in summer – perfect for a relaxing few days away from it all. No credit cards. ❸

Hotel Montebelo Urbanização Quinta do Bosque, 2km from town ☏232 420 000, ⓦwww .hotelmontebelo.pt. Five-star high-rise hotel in Viseu's suburbs. The well-appointed rooms have full-length windows allowing views to the green lawns and the hills beyond. The outdoor pool is huge, and there's an indoor pool too, with sauna and health club, while golf and horse-riding are available. ❻

Youth hostel and campsite

Orbitur Av Jose Relvas, Fontelo ☏232 436 146, ⓦwww.orbitur.pt. Fair-sized campsite with good facilities and adequate shade. It's adjacent to the municipal stadium, a 15min walk northeast of Rossio. Closed Oct–March.

Pousada de Juventude Rua Aristides Sousa Mendes, Portal do Fontelo ☏232 435 445, ⓦwww.pousadasjuventude.pt. Modern hostel a 10min walk northeast of Rossio, with half a dozen en-suite rooms and fifteen mini-dorms with either four or five beds. Reception open 8am–noon & 6pm–midnight. Dorm beds €10, rooms ❶

Eating, drinking and nightlife

The locally produced **Dão wines**, especially the mature reds, are some of the best in the country (see p.49 for more). The administration of the wine region is overseen from the *Solar do Dao* in the Parque do Fontelo, though plans to open a wine museum and tasting room here have still not been fulfilled. **Cafés** and **restaurants** are plentiful – for the cheapest eating look along Rua Direita where several old-fashioned *tascas* and *casas de pasto* turn out full meals at lunch for around €5. The presence of students means there's a lively nightlife scene, with most of Viseu's late-night **bars** found in the old town around Rua Augusto Hilário, Rua Dom Duarte and near the Sé and Misericórdia churches.

Restaurants

Bella Itália Rua Migel Bombarda 3 ☏ 232 982 189. A genuine Italian-owned pizza and pasta place. Closed Mon. No credit cards. Moderate.

Cacimbo Rua A. Herculano 95 ☏ 232 642 264. Bustling, down-to-earth joint, regularly crammed with locals who come for the good-value Portuguese food – mainly grills and omelettes – and friendly service. No credit cards. Inexpensive.

Claustros da Sé Rua Augusto Hilário 60–62 ☏ 232 426 452. Stylish, compact bar-restaurant run by an enthusiastic young Portuguese couple. The Brazilian cook can rustle you up a *picanha* (rice, black beans and pork) or try the excellent *bife a cervejeiro* (steak in beer – Super Bock, apparently – and mushroom sauce). Closed Sun dinner & Mon. No credit cards. Moderate.

O Cortiço Rua Augusto Hilário 45 ☏ 232 423 853. This snug little restaurant boasts walls filled with messages of praise from customers heartily satisfied with the strictly traditional but creatively prepared food, named after figures who have passed into local folklore. Moderate.

Casa dos Queijos Trav Escadinha da Sé 9 ☏ 232 422 643. Located in the heart of the old town, the "House of Cheese" lives up to its name with a shop full of tempting mountain cheeses and – up a narrow, creaky staircase – a traditional restaurant with delicious meat and fish choices. Closed Sun. No credit cards. Moderate.

Bars and clubs

Água Benta Largo da Misericórdia. Fashionable lounge bar where young professionals go to soak up the mellow atmosphere, with the occasional guest DJ playing new jazz and trance – there's a great outdoor terrace.

The Day After 1.5km north of town, N16. A huge entertainment/disco complex, featuring four dance floors and twelve bars, with DJs spinning everything from salsa to techno. Closed Mon.

Galeria Bar Pr Dom Duarte 37–39. This stylish bar attracts a decent mix of people, with occasional live jazz alongside the DJs and theme nights. Open until 4am; closed Mon.

Listings

Hospital Hospital Distrital de Viseu, Av Rei Dom Duarte ☏ 232 420 500.

Internet Free access at Espaço Internet on Rua dos Andrades (Mon–Fri 10am–7pm, Sat 10am–1pm & 2–7pm, Sun 2–7pm). Otherwise at *A Nortenha* arcade/pool room next door to *Hotel Avenida* on Av Alberto Sampaio (Mon–Fri 8am–midnight, Sun 9am–midnight).

Pharmacy *Farmácia Confiança*, Rua Formosa 10 ☏ 232 480 340.

Police Rua Dom António Alves Martins ☏ 232 480 380.

Post office Largo General Humberto Delgado (Mon–Fri 8.30am–6.30pm, Sat 9am–12.30pm).

Taxis There's a rank in the Rossio ☏ 232 425 444.

Guarda

GUARDA – 70km east of Viseu, and at an altitude of over 1000m – is claimed by its inhabitants to be the highest city in Europe, an assertion to be taken with a pinch of salt. However, it's certainly the highest in Portugal, lofty enough to be chilly and windswept for large parts of the year and to offer endless views, especially to the east into Spain. Guarda was founded in 1197 by Dom Sancho I, to guard (as the name implies) the borders against both Moors and Spaniards. Both castle and walls have all but disappeared, or been subsumed into other structures, but an impressive cathedral survives to dominate the picturesque centre of Guarda, with its arcaded streets and little squares. You could see everything in half a day, though it's worth a night, if only to consider whether the city's traditional description as *Fria, Farta, Forte e Feia* – cold, rich, strong and ugly – is at all fair. Ask any local, however, and they'll swear that it's been "five Fs" – *Feia* being replaced with *Fiel* (loyal) and *Formosa* (beautiful) – for as long as they can remember.

The biggest annual events are the great **feiras** (June 24 & Oct 4), which are basically extended markets full of life and character. The **Festas da Cidade**

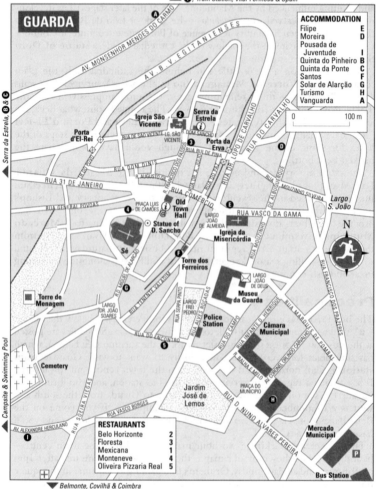

GUARDA

ACCOMMODATION	
Filipe	E
Moreira	D
Pousada de Juventude	I
Quinta do Pinheiro	B
Quinta da Ponte	C
Santos	F
Solar de Alarção	G
Turismo	H
Vanguarda	A

0   100 m

RESTAURANTS	
Belo Horizonte	2
Floresta	3
Mexicana	1
Monteneve	4
Oliveira Pizzaria Real	5

▼ Belmonte, Covilhã & Coimbra

(July & Aug) are annual cultural celebrations with exhibitions, concerts and folk events of all kinds.

The town

At the heart of it all, dominating Praça Luís de Camões (also known as Praça Velha), is the imposing bulk of the **Sé** (Tues–Sun 9am–noon & 2–5pm; free), one of those buildings which took so long to complete (1390–1540) that several architectural styles came and went during its construction. The castellated main facade, with its two heavy octagonal towers, looks like the gateway of a particularly forbidding castle, but around the sides the design is lightened by flying buttresses, fantastic pinnacles and grimacing gargoyles – the ones facing Spain are particularly mean-looking. Restoration has slightly softened the dour granite exterior while inside it's surprisingly long and lofty, with twisted pillars and vaulting influenced by the Manueline style of the later stages of its development. The huge carved stone *retábulo* is the work of João de Ruão, a leading figure in the sixteenth-century resurgence of Portuguese sculpture at Coimbra. Outside in the square, in the shadow of the cathedral facade, a **statue of Dom Sancho** looks across to the arcade cafés.

Of the castle, on a bleak little hill behind the cathedral, only the plain square keep, the **Torre de Menagem** (no public access), survives. The walls are recalled by just three remaining gates, the most impressive being the **Torre dos Ferreiros** (Blacksmiths' Tower). The tangled, somewhat decaying area between the other two gates – the **Porta da Erva** and **Porta d'El-Rei** – can have changed little in the past 400 years. You can climb the steps of the latter for some distant *serra* views, although you'll have to negotiate the broken beer bottles.

The city's history, art and culture is explored in the **Museu da Guarda**, Rua Alves Roçadas 30 (Tues–Sun 10am–12.30pm & 2–5.30pm; €2, free Sun morning), housed in the seventeenth-century former seminary and Bishop's palace. In the end, though, it's the cobbled streets of the old town that provide the best diversion, along with a visit to Guarda's **Mercado Municipal**, five minutes' walk down Rua Dom Nuno Álvares Pereira from the centre. It's a fair-sized regional market, busiest on Saturdays, with rural smallholders selling seasonal vegetables, fruit and flowers alongside brimming meat and fish counters.

Practicalities

The **bus terminal** is on Rua Dom Nuno Álvares Pereira, just below the market – it's a fifteen-minute (uphill) walk to the cathedral square. Schedules are posted at the bus station, but it's much easier to ask at the turismo (see below), which has timetables for everywhere you're likely to want to visit. Guarda's **train station** is 5km northeast and downhill from the town centre, out towards the IP5 – there's a regular bus service up to the bus station, and you'll find taxis outside the station. The most direct train route to Guarda from the south and west is via Coimbra; from Porto change at Pampilhosa. If you come on the Beira Baixa route via Santarém and Castelo Branco it will take longer and you'll have to change at Covilhã.

There's metered **parking** (two-hour maximum) all over the town centre – basically, the area shown by our map – though these spaces are free after 1pm on Saturday and all day Sunday. Or there's free parking at any time in the square outside the market or along Avenida dos Bombeiros Voluntarios Egitanienses.

The well-informed **turismo** is in the arcaded old town hall building, just across from the Sé on the main square (daily 9am–12.30pm & 2–5.30pm; ☏271 205 530, ⓦwww.mun-guarda.pt). There's plenty of printed information available here, including some on the Serra da Estrela, useful if you arrive at the weekend when the **Serra da Estrela information office**, Rua Dom Sancho I (Mon–Fri 9am–12.30pm & 2–5.30pm; ☏271 225 454), is closed. This, however, has a larger range of guide books and a mounted wall map.

Accommodation

You should have no trouble getting a room at one of the places detailed below, though you might want to book ahead at weekends, summer and winter. Guarda's **campsite** (☏271 221 200) is located in the municipal park, a short way from the youth hostel; it's open all year round, but beware that even in spring and autumn the nights can get extremely cold.

In town

Residencial Filipe Rua Vasco da Gama 9 ⊕271 223 658, ⊕271 221 402. Van Gogh prints and marble in the public areas give way to more traditional rooms with parquet floors and heavy wood furniture, not to mention some rather garishly tiled bathrooms. Rooms 103, 104 and 108 have the best views of the church. ❷

Residencial Moreira Rua Mouzinho de Albuquerque 47 ⊕271 214 131. Quiet, unassuming place with friendly staff and peaceful en-suite rooms with spotless white bed linen. No breakfast. No credit cards. ❶

Residencial Santos Rua Tenente Valadim 14 ⊕271 205 400, ⓦwww.residencialsantos .com. By far the best mid-range choice, the stylish *Santos* incorporates part of the original city walls into its design – a glass lift rises past suspended internal terraces and exposed stonework to modern rooms that frame views of the cathedral or countryside within granite sills. The beds are comfortable, bathrooms superior, and a nice buffet breakfast is included. There's street parking almost outside (provided you can find your way there). ❷

Solar de Alarcão Rua Dom Miguel de Alarcão 25–27 ⊕271 214 392. Magnificent granite manor house dating back to the seventeenth century. The atmospheric rooms come with huge antique mirrors, chandeliers, carved wooden ceilings and vintage shutters, while secure parking is available in the courtyard. No credit cards. ❹

Hotel de Turismo Pr do Município ⊕271 223 366, ⓦwww.hturismoguarda.com. Formerly Guarda's grandest hotel, the three-star *Turismo* now faces stiff competition from its more modern peers. It's still comfortable enough for a night, with a good central location across from the gardens and with the bonus of garage parking and a pool. ❸

Hotel Vanguarda Av Monsenhor Mendes do Carmo ⊕271 208 390, ⓦwww.hotelvanguarda .com. The up-to-date rooms in Guarda's most contemporary hotel feature plush carpets, gleaming bathrooms and sweeping views. Buffet breakfast included, plus bar and restaurant with more panoramic views. It's out on a limb at the edge of town (15min walk), though drivers will pass it on the way up from the IP5 – you can't miss the wave-style roof. ❸

Outside town

Quinta do Pinheiro Cavadoude, N16, 15km northwest of Guarda ⊕271 926 162, ⓦwww.quintadopinheiro.com. A pastoral idyll dating from the fifteenth century and located near the Rio Mondego. Rooms come with fearsomely Gothic four-poster beds and good views, while the sprawling grounds allow ample space for hammock-lounging, walking and swimming. ❹

Quinta da Ponte Faia, 12km northwest of Guarda ⊕271 926 126, ⓦwww.quintadaponte.com. Attractively situated near a Roman bridge in the Mondego valley, this impressive seventeenth-century manor house features lots of exposed granite, and even a private chapel. The accommodation – two twin rooms and five two-person apartments – is traditionally furnished and there are lovely gardens and a swimming pool. ❹

Youth hostel

Pousada de Juventude Av Alexandre Herculano ⊕271 224 482, ⓦwww.pousadasjuventude.pt. Beds in small four-bedded dorms, as well as four double en-suite rooms available. Reception daily 8am–noon & 6pm–midnight. Dorm beds €10, rooms ❶

Eating and drinking

Most of the town's **restaurants** are to be found in the area between the Sé and the Igreja de São Vicente, with half a dozen alone squeezed into the narrow Rua Francisco dos Passos. There really isn't too much variety on offer, although regional *serrano* specialities – *chouriçada* (spiced sausage), *morcela* (black pudding), *cabrito* (kid), *javali* (wild boar) and trout from Manteigas – are all widely available. A few late-night **bars** have been carved from the granite buildings of the old town: *Pecado do Rei*, Rua Dom Dinis 9, and *Catedral Café*, Rua General Póvoas 9, are typical.

Belo Horizonte Largo de São Vincente 1–2 ⊕271 211 454. A Guarda institution for over sixty years. A kindly old chef and matronly waitresses keep locals supplied from a menu strong on regional specialities. Closed Sat. Moderate.

A Floresta Rua Franciso dos Passos 40 ⊕271 223 746. Rustic decor and local

cuisine provide an atmospheric old-town eating experience. The three-course *ementa turística* is a bargain at €10, though there's also a long menu of regional favourites, with most dishes priced between €5 and €8. Moderate.

A Mexicana Av Monsenhor Mendes do Carmo 7 ⊕271 211 512. Nothing to do with Mexico, but instead one of Guarda's best, presenting creatively prepared and presented food – both regional and national Portuguese fare with a twist. Their strawberry mousse is unforgettable. Closed Wed. Expensive.

O Monteneve Pr Luís de Camões 24 ℗ 271 212 799. One half bar, one half brick-walled restaurant, up a flight of steps in the main square – it's a bit pricier than many in town, reflecting the view of the Sé from the dining room. Closed Mon. Moderate.

Oliveira Pizzeria Real Rua do Encontro 1 ℗ 271 214 446. About the only place in the upper town where you can get something non-Portuguese. There are a few Italian pasta and meat dishes alongside the pizzas, but nothing is particularly memorable. Moderate.

Listings

Hospital Hospital Distrital, Av Rainha Dona Amélia ℗ 271 200 200.
Internet Free access at the Mediateca VIII Centenário (Mon–Fri 9am–12.30pm & 2–5.30pm), next to the turismo on Pr Luís de Camões – the turismo itself has a solitary computer, useful at weekends when the Meditaeca is closed.

Pharmacy Farmácia Central, Largo Dr João Almeida ℗ 271 211 972.
Police Rua Alves Roçadas ℗ 271 222 022.
Post office Largo João de Deus 24 ℗ 271 200 010 (Mon–Fri 8.30am–6.30pm, Sat 9am–12.30pm).
Taxis Largo Dr João Almeida.

The Beira Alta planalto

North and east of Guarda stretches a rough and barren-looking territory known as the **planalto** – tableland – of the Beira Alta. Villages are spread far apart, with much of the boulder-strewn land between untamed by agriculture. Even potatoes found it hard to take root – in bygone days, roast or dried chestnuts were used as a substitute, plucked from the vast, shady trees lining the approaches to most villages. Winters can be harsh – hence the proverb "*O frio almoça em Penedono, merenda em Trancoso e ceia na Guarda*" (the cold lunches in Penedono, takes tea in Trancoso and dines in Guarda). The frost has an extraordinary effect on the *planalto*, with trees linked by boughs of crystal and metre-long icicles hanging from every house.

Travel here sounds an unrewarding prospect, but in medieval times the region's many Jewish settlements prospered, though their merchant trade went into decline from the Age of Discovery onwards as business moved to the coast. The restored town of **Trancoso**, especially, is still full of interest, while the region's erstwhile wealth is clearly evident in the harmonious squares and mansions of now somnolent **Sernancelhe**. In successive centuries, the *planalto* towns became closely associated with Portuguese independence from Spain, and in particular with Afonso Henriques's march south down the length of the country. Today, their castles are the highlight of the region, most notably the spectacular star-shaped border fortress at **Almeida**, the site of the penultimate battle in the Peninsular Wars against Napoleon. Other castles and fortified settlements are scattered across the *planalto*, with particular interest in those at **Castelo Rodrigo**, to the north of Almeida, and **Penedono** and **Marialva** far to the west. Anyone with a car and a passion for castles would also want to tick off the lesser examples at Pinhel (southwest of Castelo Rodrigo) and Castelo Mendo (southwest of Almeida).

Trancoso is the easiest place to reach by **bus** from Guarda, and it's also the best choice if you only have time to visit one destination; there are also bus services to Almeida and Castelo Rodrigo, but you'd have to spend the night in either place (and there's no service at weekends). With a car, you could see the whole region in a couple of days, with the best **overnight stops** at Trancoso, Almeida or the upmarket holiday village accommodation at Marialva.

Trancoso

Forty-four kilometres north of Guarda, just off the N102, **TRANCOSO** is still largely contained within a circuit of medieval walls. It's an uncommonly atmospheric little town, full of cobbled alleyways, well-kept gardens, shady squares, and restored pillories and churches, all of which represent a tangible civic pride. It was here that Dom Dinis married the 12-year-old Isabel of Aragon in 1282, and later gave her the entire town as a gift; the wedding was solemnized in the small **Capela de São Bartolomeu,** by the side of the dusty avenue leading up to the town's surviving main gate, the **Portas d'el Rei,** surmounted by the Trancoso coat-of-arms.

Within the walls, on the north side of town, is the **castle** (Mon–Fri 9am–noon & 2–5pm; currently closed weekends for archeological work; free) with its squat tower a distinctive silhouette visible from many miles away. The Moorish design is a reminder of the Saracen domination of the town in the tenth century, though the following two centuries saw frequent siege and battle, with the fortress taken by Fernando Magno in 1033, and finally by Afonso Henriques and Egas Moniz in 1139. Trancoso's later military history includes

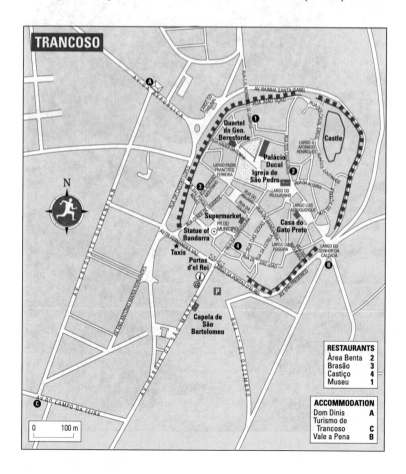

RESTAURANTS

Àrea Benta	2
Brasão	3
Castiço	4
Museu	1

ACCOMMODATION

Dom Dinis	A
Turismo de Trancoso	C
Vale a Pena	B

the usual invasions and billeting during fourteenth-century Castillian trouble-making and the nineteenth-century Peninsular War – on the central Largo Dr Eduardo Cabral, look out for the charming corner house with an open stone stairway, tellingly known as the **Quartel do General Beresforde** (and used as Beresford's HQ).

The presence of a large **Jewish community** during the Middle Ages is apparent from the facades of the town's more ancient houses. Each has two doorways – a broad one for trade and a narrow one (leading to the first floor)

△ Trancoso

Bandarra, the cobbler-prophet

Trancoso takes its place in Portuguese history through the legend of one **Gonçalo Bandarra**, a cobbler-prophet who lived in the town in the sixteenth century. He was known for his four-line rhyming poems or *trovas* which, among other things, supposedly foretold the end of the Portuguese kingdom. In an age of religious dilemma and disillusionment with monarchical rule his obscure prophecies struck a chord, and attracted the attention of the Inquisition. Their circulation was banned and Bandarra condemned to death – a sentence commuted, after popular outcry, to a punishment of walking barefoot around town carrying a massive candle until it burned to the wick.

There the matter might have rested, but twenty years after Bandarra's death in 1556, Dom Sebastião did indeed die (along with most of the Portuguese nobility) in the battle of Alcáçer-Quibir in Morocco (1578), leaving no heir to the throne. Portugal subsequently lost independence to Spain, and Bandarra was pronounced the Nostradamus of his time. He's now remembered by a statue in Trancoso's Praça do Municipio (with cobbler's last and shoe, and rolled prophecy in hand), while his tomb is found in the town's Igreja de São Pedro.

---

for the family – and, above the carefully crafted stonework, some have clumsy crosses, inscribed by the Inquisition to indicate the family's conversion to Christianity. The most striking is the former rabbi's house - known as the **Casa do Gato Preto** – which is decorated with the Lion of Judea; it's on Largo Luis Albuquerque next to the restaurant *São Marcos*.

Practicalities

There's a direct **bus** from Guarda on Monday morning, and two on Friday afternoon, or you can take the hourly bus from Guarda to Celorico da Beira, from where there are three daily buses on to Trancoso (currently 10.40am, 4.50pm & 7.30pm). There's also a daily weekday service from Lamego, and a daily service from Viseu, while you can pick up express services to and from Bragança, Coimbra and Lisbon. All buses stop in the square in front of the main gate, with tickets and schedules available from the café next to the **turismo** (Mon–Fri 9am–12.30pm & 2–5.30pm, Sat & Sun 10am–12.30pm & 2pm–5.30pm; ☎271 811 147, ⓦwww.cm-trancoso.pt). There's **Internet access** next door at Espaçao Internet (Mon–Fri 3–7pm & 8–10.30pm, Sat 3–7pm). Markets are held on Fridays, with the big annual bash, the **Feira de São Bartolomeu**, on August 8–14, followed by the **Festa de Nossa Senhora da Fresta** on August 15.

Trancoso makes an excellent night's stop, and though regular **accommodation** is limited the turismo can point you in the direction of private rooms.

Hotels and Pensions

Residencial Dom Dinis Av da República 10 ☎271 811 525, ⓦwww.domdinis.net. Unpromisingly sited above the post office (follow signs for "Correios" to find it), this picks up markedly inside where modern rooms have laminate floors, good bathrooms with proper showers, central heating, and wall-mounted fans. Not much of a view, it's true, though some rooms have a glimpse of the walls and Portas do Prado, but it's good value for money and puts on a great spread for breakfast – cornflakes, fresh orange juice, *presunto*, cake and home-made pumpkin jam. Private parking out the back. ❷

Hotel Turismo de Trancoso Rua Prof Irene Avillez ☎271 829 200, ⓦwww.hotel-trancoso.com. The swish, contemporary four-star on the edge of town (10min walk) seems out of place in homely Trancoso, and when guests are thin on the ground you'll rattle around the spacious sculpture-dotted lobby, terrace and fancy restaurant. Rooms are good, though, and prices still reasonable, at least during the week (and in winter, when rates drop 20 percent). ❺

Pensão Vale a Pena Largo Senhora da Calçada ☎271 811 219, ⊕271 828 027. Second-best to the *Dom Dinis* – genial enough, with sweeping plains views from the back, and garage parking, but the en-suite rooms are old-fashioned and a bit musty. Although there's a sign on the side nearest to the town walls, next to the tyres place (*Auto Pneus*) of the same name, the entrance is around the back. No credit cards. ❷

Restaurants and taverns

Área Benta Rua dos Cavaleiros 30 ☎271 817 180. The town's best choice, offering handsomely prepared meals – say, grilled squid with coriander vinaigrette, *cabrito* with chestnuts or black-pepper steak – in an arty setting. Closed Sun dinner & Mon. Moderate.

O Brasão Rua Adriano Moutinho 3 ☎271 811 767. A simple, traditionally tiled place for steaks, grills, chops and sausages. Closed Sat. Moderate.

O Castiço Rua de São João, no phone. Stone-walled tavern with a parodically rustic interior – don't trip over a pumpkin or knock a scythe off the wall. The tap beer's a dark *Boemia*, while *petiscos* are of the cod-cake, sausage, octopus and boiled egg variety. Inexpensive.

O Museu Largo de Santa Maria de Guimarães ☎271 811 810. The dishes of the day in this rustic charmer are good value at around €6; otherwise €9–11 for grilled meat and fresh fish (including trout and salmon), with advance orders required for the speciality fondues and raclettes. Closed Mon. Moderate.

Sernancelhe

Sited 30km northwest of Trancoso, four kilometres off the Lamego road (N226), quiet **SERNANCELHE** offers further reminders of the area's Jewish past in an old quarter of canted lintels, pairs of granite doorways of unequal size, and the occasional cross for the converted. This part of town, though restored, is now sparsely populated and comes alive only for the weekly Thursday market and the annual **Festa de Nossa Senhora de Ao Pé da Cruz** (May 1), when you'll witness a curious mixture of religious devotion, springtime merrymaking and folkloric superstition. In particular, there's a dance of the chestnuts, a blessing of the ubiquitous trees (producing, it's said, the *planalto*'s finest chestnuts) and the exchange of handfuls of blossom by local lovers. In the main square the Romanesque **Igreja Matriz** has a curious facade. Fixed into twin niches on either side of the main doorway are six weathered apostles – said to be the only free-standing sculptures of the period in the whole of Portugal. Equally notice-able are a number of large town houses dating from the sixteenth and seven-teenth centuries – one is the supposed birthplace of the Marquês de Pombal, who has a square named after him.

Sernancelhe is only a realistic visit for drivers, who can call in on the increas-ingly attractive N226 route to Lamego, another 45km northwest. There's also a back-country road (N229) to Penedono, 15km northeast. Good **accommoda-tion** is available at *Casa da Comenda de Malta* (☎254 559 166; ❹), a grand granite house in the middle of the old town – opposite the *pelourinho* – with comfortable rooms and an outdoor pool. Even more impressive is the *Hotel Rural Convento Nossa Senhora do Carmo* (☎254 594 080, ⓦwww.hoteldocarmo .com; ❹) in the nearby village of Freixinho. It's a restored sixteenth-century convent whose most alluring feature is the dining room, situated in the convent's former chapel and retaining some of the original frescoes.

Penedono and around

Isolated **PENEDONO** has a simply fantastic castle, the lichen-encrusted **Castelo Roqueiro** (Mon–Fri 9am–5pm, Sat 10am–12.30pm & 3.30–5pm, Sun 2.30–5pm; June–Aug until 6pm, weekends till 7pm; free), visible from miles around. The *roqueiro* ("rock") part of the name is due to the castle's emergence from its granite base, as if the rock and the walls were one and the same. From the top there are grand views, although the Rapunzel-style turrets and sparsely railed walkways are not for the faint hearted. There's a café at the foot of the castle, with the mock-baronial *Estalagem de Penedono* (☎254 509 050, ⓦwww .estalagempenedono.com; ❹), directly opposite, providing a comfortable night – in their restaurant (expensive) try the trout stuffed with ham or their delicious spin on *bacalhau*, roasted in the oven with local chestnuts.

Penedono's castle was supposed to have been home to Álvaro Gonçalves Coutinho, the legendary king **Magriço** ("Lean One"), sung of in Camões's *Os Lusíadas*. It's a claim fought over fiercely with the inhabitants of Trancoso, who likewise are prepared to swear he is their man. According to Camões, the Magriço led eleven men to England to champion the cause of twelve noble English ladies, who found themselves without knights, and fought a joust on their behalf. Such tales of chivalry made them the subjects of numerous allegorical murals and panels of *azulejos* around the country.

Antas

Six kilometres south of Penedono (Trancoso road) lies the small village of **ANTAS** – an *anta* is a megalithic tomb, and a modern recreation of one sits in the traffic roundabout on the main road. Follow the sign from here, through the village, east for 3.5km up a country road, and then park by the roadside sign for "Necrópole Megalítica da Lameia da Cima". It's a one-and-a-half-kilometre walk from here up a dusty track to two megalithic **burial chambers**, 5000 years old, formed by overlapping stones. The cap stones are missing, but it's a scene of some mystery, with sweeping views down across the distant plain. If you're not travelling to the Alentejo, where more dramatic examples await, it's probably worth the hour's walk there and back. Typically, the crucial last turn isn't marked – there's a signposted right turn 1km up the track, and then 300m after that, at a general meeting of the ways, you should turn right again down a low-walled lane and walk up to the little tree-ringed burial plateau.

Marialva

The tiny village of **MARIALVA** is also dominated by its castle, but it offers an entirely different experience to that of Penedono. Here, within a complete circuit of walls, originally built by Dom Sancho I in 1200, lies a deserted village, centuries old, where town hall, prison, watch-towers, houses and streets stand in ruins, overgrown with olive trees and overrun by geckos. Depopulated for obscure reasons, the only buildings restored in modern times are the sixteenth-century Igreja Matriz, the stone keep and a lone belltower, with a geometrically cobbled square and *pelourinho* below. A rather rigid timetable of hourly visits is posted (daily 10am–6pm; €1.50), but in practice you can apply for entrance at the concrete-box **turismo** (daily 10am–1.30pm & 3–6.30pm) just below the castle gate – you'll be let in, free to wander through the roofless buildings, haphazard streets and doorways leading nowhere.

By way of contrast, the small village outside the castle walls – similarly ancient – has been well restored, its crosses, chapels, fountains, squares and cisterns all labelled on a map found at the car park by the only café. There's **accommodation** here in the well-signposted *Casas do Côro* (☎917 552 020, ⓦwww.assec .pt/casa-do-coro; rooms ❺, whole house ❻, weekday rates slightly cheaper), a mini-village-within-the-village of traditional granite houses, restored with painstaking attention to detail and design. Minimalist chic vies successfully with four-poster beds and stone walls, while the outdoor pool is set amidst manicured lawns and olive trees. Both rooms and independent houses with kitchenette are available; breakfast is included; other meals are available with advance booking.

Marialva is 23km north of Trancoso, just off the N102, and it's a quick drive on a good road; there's also a winding, 28-kilometre back-road route from Penedono via Mêda.

Almeida

The most impressive of all the fortified border towns is **ALMEIDA**, 45km northeast of Guarda and within cannon-shot of Spain. It's a beautifully preserved eighteenth-century stronghold, with walls in the form of a twelve-pointed star – a Dutch design, influenced by the French military architect Vauban. A three-kilometre walk around the walls – now overgrown with grass, and grazed by horses – takes in all the peaks and troughs, though you can only really appreciate the shape by looking at the aerial shot postcards sold around town. Although recognized as officially Portuguese since 1297, Almeida and the border lands were occasionally reoccupied by Spain, the last time being in 1762, after which the present stronghold was completed. Almeida later played a key role in the **Peninsular War**, the Luso-Britannic forces here besieged in 1810 by the Napoleonic army. They held out for seventeen days until, on July 26, a leaky barrel of gunpowder ignited and began a fire that killed hundreds. The survivors gave themselves up, but Wellington, on his victorious return from Torres Vedras, subsequently took the fortress with no bloodshed as the French army scuttled away during the night.

The main entrance is still through the original two consecutive gates of the **Portas de São Francisco** – long, shell-proof tunnels with emblazoned entrances, separating a wide, dry moat between inner and outer walls. Immediately inside the gates, to the left, are the long infantry barracks, while a right turn, past the gardens and along the walls, leads to the **Casamatas** (Mon–Fri 9am–12.30pm & 2–5.30pm, Sat & Sun 10am–12.30pm & 2–5.30pm; free), an underground storage area with a capacity for five thousand men and their supplies (there's no signpost – it's opposite the fire station). The layout of interconnected, reinforced rooms explains how Almeida withstood lengthy sieges, with water supply, rubbish chute, breathing holes, hidden escape routes, munitions chamber and dormitory space.

Elsewhere, the town walls enclose an atmospheric warren of cobbled lanes and whitewashed houses, punctuated by airy squares. You'll find your way up to what's left of the **castle** at some point, blown up in 1810, the foundations now exposed under a modern walkway. Behind here, in one of the star-points, is the **picadeiro**, the restored cavalry barracks and horse-training area.

Practicalities

It only takes a couple of hours to do Almeida justice, though there's something irresistible about staying the night and watching the lights come on in a hundred tiny villages across the plateau. You'll have no choice if you come by **bus**, as there's currently just one service a day from Guarda, at 4.30pm in the afternoon, and even that only on weekdays. It stops outside the main gate in Largo 25 de Abril, which is also where drivers should park. The **turismo** is just inside the inner gate, within a former guardroom (Mon–Fri 9am–12.30pm & 2–5.30pm, Sat & Sun 10am–12.30pm & 2–5.30pm; ☎271 574 204), while in the walled town itself is a post office, bank with ATM, bakery, grocery, mini-market and a few cafés. Twice-monthly **feiras** (on the eighth day and last Sat) add a bit more focus to a visit.

There's pricey **accommodation** within the walls – notably at the *pousada* – and cheaper rooms at two places without, by the GALP station, just down from the main gate, though the main road location does neither of these any favours; ask for a room at the back.

Hotels and pensions

Casa do Cantinho Rua Afonso de Albuquerque, ☏271 574 162. Endearingly hospitable *turismo rural* offering two snug en-suite rooms in a family home inside the walls. There's no obvious sign, but come through the main gate, cross the little square, and it's opposite *Casa da Amelinha* bar. No credit cards. ❹

Morgado Adjacent to the GALP station ☏271 574 412. A more frayed *residencial* than its counterpart across the road, where the prevailing colours are brown (bathroom tiles and furniture) and yellow (bedspreads). That said, it has the nicer restaurant, *A Tertúlia* (closed Tues), a moderately priced place with fresh fish on the menu most days. ❶

A Muralha Opposite the GALP station ☏271 574 357. The decent en-suite rooms have French windows opening on to balconies. There's an unpretentious restaurant where hearty portions of meat and fish cost €6–8. ❷

🏃 **Casa Pátio da Figueria** Rua Direita 48 ☏271 571 133 or 963 367 237. Four refined rooms nestled in a back street around the corner from the *pousada*. It's very pretty inside,

with exposed stone walls and tiled floors, and there are charming gardens and a secluded swimming pool. No credit cards. ❹

Pousada Senhora das Neves Rua das Muralhas ☏271 574 283, ⊛www.pousadas.pt. Well signposted near the upper walls, this slightly dated *pousada* boasts comfortable rooms with four-poster beds and glorious views to Spain. There's also a pricey restaurant and a terrace although the latter's preponderance of concrete renders it somewhat claustrophobic. ❻

Restaurants

Granitus Largo 25 de Abril ☏271 574 834. A down-to-earth place, just outside the main gates, with cheap dishes of the day served on paper tablecloths, and a few café tables outside with a view of the ramparts. Inexpensive.

O Picadeiro d'El Rey ☏271 346 974. Slick equine-themed bar-restaurant that allows you to dine on carefully prepared regional specialities such as wild boar, while gazing down at glossy horses ambling around their stables. No credit cards. Closed Tues. Expensive.

Castelo Rodrigo

The obvious route north of Almeida is up the N332 towards the Douro. After 20km – and 3km before the town of Figueira de Castelo Rodrigo – look for the signs to **CASTELO RODRIGO**, a fortified medieval settlement cresting an isolated hill with splendid views over into Spain. Its original roots probably go back as far as 500 BC, when the mysterious Túrdulos people established a *castro* (hilltop settlement) here. In the last few years, its huddled houses and cobbled alleys – once largely abandoned – have been fully restored by Portugal's *Aldeias Históricas* ("Historic Villages") scheme for particularly important or picturesque villages. Inevitably, there are *artesanato* gift shops and a slightly unreal, too-tidy air, but it's a great place to spend a couple of hours, with terrific views from all sides.

The village is surrounded by a new road, punctuated by three surviving thirteenth-century gates – don't venture in with your car, but park outside. Near the southeastern **Porta do Nascente** – facing the town of Figueira below – an inscription above the white-walled cemetery warns: "Consider with attention this place of terror, the end of this duplicitous world's vanities", a possible allusion to the castle's long and often violent history. Suitably chastened, enter the village, where the gatehouse now contains the *Sabores do Castelo* shop, selling cheese, smoked meats, local wines and liqueurs, plus age-old delicacies like honey vinegar and honeycombs. It also has a small terrace and bar. The **castle** itself – pay the €1 fee at the adjacent **turismo** (daily 9am–6pm; ☏271 311 277) – is built on a rocky outcrop, and remains impressive despite having been torched and sacked by locals in 1640, furious at the oppressive rule of the Spanish-leaning Count, Manuel de Moura y Corte Real. Indeed, the defensive nature of the palace – evidently intended to defend against locals rather than Spain – is evident from the arrow slits that open out over the village.

To or from the village, you might as well divert up to the **Serra de Marofa** viewpoint – it's signposted at the Pinhel junction on the Almeida road. A rough but paved road runs 3km up through the pines to the antennae-festooned summit, where there's a Rio-like Christ in Benediction, looking out over the brown walls and red roofs of Castelo Rodrigo, with Spain beyond.

Practicalities

You'll inevitably pass through the bigger town of **Figueira de Castelo Rodrigo**, below the village, and it's an attractive enough place with a broad central square with fountains and a large Romanesque church topped by a stork's nest. It provides a minor route to Barca d'Alva (the last settlement on the Douro river), a slow 20km to the north, or it's 35km from Figueira to Vila Nova de Foz Côa and its rock carvings. Without your own car, Castelo Rodrigo is an unlikely visit – there is a daily bus (not Sun) from Guarda, but only to Figueira (ie not the restored village) and on to Foz Côa.

There's a reasonable amount of **accommodation**, rather surprisingly perhaps, though Figueira gets a few Spanish trippers while Castelo Rodrigo is slowly gearing itself up for *turismo rural*-type accommodation. Street names and directions up at the castle, incidentally, are a bit pointless – you'll find everything within two minutes of everything else.

Accommodation

Casa da Cisterna Rua da Cadeia 7, Castelo Rodrigo ☎271 313 515 or 917 618 122. Currently the only rooms up at the castle are the four here, in a lovingly restored house in the centre of the village. ❸

Estalagem Falcão de Mendonça Rua Álvaro Castelões 20, Figueira ☎271 319 200, ⓦwww .falcaodemendonca.com. Just off the town square, near the turismo, hides a splendidly refurbished 1820 mansion with lots of stonework and modern glass separations. There's a small covered swimming pool and sundeck, courtyard bar and a silver-service atmosphere at the hotel's moderately priced restaurant, a formality ruined by the "Greatest Hits" radio piped in the background – the speciality is a seafood *cataplana*. ❹

Residencial Transmontano Av 25 de Abril 66, Figueira, at the top end of the square ☎271 319 020. The cheap choice in town with scuffed en-suite rooms on three floors, lacksadaisical service and an inexpensive restaurant. That said, you'd go a long way before you saw another buffet breakfast table with a Tardis-style elevating glass lid. ❷

Restaurant

🏃 **Cantinho dos Avôs** Rua da Sinagoga 1, Castelo Rodrigo ☎271 312 643. A delightful café-restaurant with great views of the Serra da Marofa from its shady terrace. The food is good – quality olive oil on the table, local cheeses to start – and extremely reasonably priced (mains are all €5–8). If you're not familiar with the various parts of a pig (grilled, smoked or cured) before you sit down, you soon will be. Inexpensive.

The Serra da Estrela

The peaks of the **Serra da Estrela** – the highest mountains in Portugal – rise to the southwest of Guarda. The range is basically a high alpine plateau cut by valleys, from within which emanate two of the country's greatest rivers, the Rio Mondego and the Rio Zêzere – the only rivers to begin and end in Portugal rather than crossing the border from Spain. The mountains – snow-capped in winter – soon impose themselves upon any approach from Beira Alta or Beira Baixa, while the lower flanks on either side of the range reveal a patchwork of small villages and hamlets that retain much charm. Some Portuguese come to

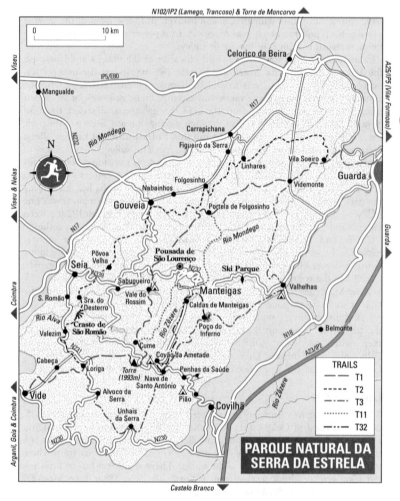

the *serra* to ski in winter; many more clog the narrow roads in summer looking for picnic space, or wind in convoy up the mountain highway between Seia and Covilhã to park right on top of Torre, at 1993m, the country's highest peak. A network of hiking trails covers the peaks and valleys, though relatively few people take to the paths to explore the region.

Over the last few decades life in the mountains has changed markedly, as roads and communications have improved. Where farmers once lived in stone houses with straw roofs, dotted across the peaks and valleys, they have now largely moved to more modern dwellings on the valley floor – thus, what appear to outsiders as unsightly concrete houses and apartments ringing otherwise pictur-esque villages represent progress for the inhabitants. Moreover, many of the former intensively cultivated Zêzere valley terraces have been abandoned in favour of spreading pine plantations, while local village production is often now directed towards the increasing tourist traffic – widely available are *queijo da serra*, an unctuous mountain cheese, and blankets from the wool of the grazing upland sheep, and rye bread (*pão de centeio*), fruit preserves and honey from the fields, orchards and hives of the fertile valleys.

In an attempt to preserve the essential character of the villages and landscape, the **Parque Natural da Serra da Estrela** (Ⓦwww.rt-serradaestrela.pt) was established in 1976. This covers around 1000 square kilometres, and stretches for around 55km from north to south and around 25km east–west at its widest point. From the west, access is from the N17, through the small service towns of **Seia** or **Gouveia** and then on over the high mountain roads, deep into the park; the smaller western-flank villages of **Linhares**, **Folgosinho** and **Loriga** offer a prettier introduction to the mountain landscape. The valley town and spa of **Manteigas**, pretty much in the centre of the park, is the single best base for hiking and touring, while the ski industry – such as it is – centres on the road between Torre peak and **Covilhã**, south of Manteigas. Covilhã lies just outside the park proper, and is the only town of any size or life in the region – it's one of several points of access from the east, reached via the N18 or fast IP2 (between Guarda and Castelo Branco); historic Belmonte in the Beira Baixa is another.

Covilhã and Guarda can be reached by **train** or **bus**, and there are bus services to Seia and Gouveia but none across the park itself or to any of the more interesting villages. However, **taxis** are not as expensive as you might expect; Covilhã to the youth hostel and ski fields of Penhas da Saúde costs around €15, Seia to Manteigas around €30. Day-hikers will almost certainly have to use taxis at some point, since short circular walking routes are rare. **Drivers** could see all the sights in a couple of days – a good route starts from Seia, climbs to the heights of Torre, cuts down the majestic glacial valley road to Manteigas, then switchbacks west again to Gouveia and north to the pretty villages of Folgosinho and Linhares. There are park **information offices** in Manteigas, Guarda, Gouveia and Seia; contact details are given in the relevant sections.

Linhares

The most historic village on the western flank of the *serra* is **LINHARES**, 20km southwest of Celorico da Beira and the IP5, and 810m up, perching on a slope overlooking the Rio Mondego valley. It's easily accessible by car, though the Guarda–Gouveia buses only stop on the N17 at Carrapichana, from where it's a six-kilometre walk uphill to the village. There is a direct bus to Linhares, but it's a return school service from Celorica da Beira (Sept–June Mon–Fri afternoon), which itself can be reached by hourly bus from Guarda.

The twin towers of the **Castelo** (Mon–Fri 10am–1pm & 2–6pm; free) are visible on the approach, and date from 1169 when Linhares was claimed for Portugal. In the castle walls are traces of the *cisternas* that gave the village a constant supply of water during times of siege. You can still see the course of the spring, which now runs along the gully beneath the great slabs of rock on which the castle was constructed. Soak up the views from the walls before wandering down through the restored cobbled alleys with their thick-walled stone houses, some sporting Manueline doorways. It's cool and somewhat gloomy amid the buildings even in high summer; in winter, the village buttons itself up against the harsh *serra* winds. Near the parish church a path branches off towards Figueiró da Serra to the west (part of the T2 hiking trail), forming a section of an old **Roman road**, with heavy slabs of rock for paving stones looking like something out of an Asterix cartoon. The walk is a beauty, the hedgerows lined with flowers in the spring and blackberries in the autumn – the next stop, Folgosinho (see below) is around three hours away.

Hiking in the Parque Natural

Three major **hiking trails** cut across the Parque Natural da Serra da Estrela from north to south. **T1** (87km), runs from Guarda to Vide and takes in Torre, the highest mountain in Portugal; **T2** (83km) and **T3** (85km) trace the western and eastern flanks of the range respectively. In addition, half a dozen shorter trails link at various points with the main trails, allowing detours and connections to other settlements and points of interest. The paths are waymarked, with campsites and accommodation en route, meaning you can walk an entire trail in three to four days, or break them down into day- or half-day segments. The routes are all described in an English-language hiking guide, *Discovering the Region of the Serra da Estrela* (€4.25), and marked on the 1:50,000-scale *Carta Turística Serra da Estrela* map (€6.60), while there are also four dedicated park information offices.

That's the theory. In practice, it's much harder to walk in the *serras* than it should be. The **park information offices** tend not to have English-speaking staff, and it's rare for the personnel to have any first-hand experience of the trails – often, you'll simply be pointed to the mounted wall map and the array of (mostly Portuguese) guide books on offer. Both **map** and English-language **guide** were published in 1992 (and have not been updated since); moreover, the map was largely unavailable for sale at the time of writing. In any case, its scale (1:50,000) makes it unsuitable for route-finding, though there's nothing better on the market.

All this wouldn't be too bad if the **waymarking** was reliable, but it isn't. Red and yellow paint markings on trees, stones and walls should point the way on all major and minor routes, but the harsh summer sun and winter snows have taken their toll and maintenance doesn't appear to be a priority. Plantation clearance and forest fires have destroyed or removed other paint marks; and signposting at village trailheads is woeful or non-existent.

None of this should put off keen, experienced, well-prepared walkers who, with a bit of patience and a decent sense of direction, will eventually find their way. You'll need to be self-sufficient, and be prepared to camp, if you want to complete the longer trails. You must use the official campsites, and don't light any fires. The best time to walk the trails is from May to October.

For the **day-hiker**, who just wants a taste of the mountains, the best advice is to try the easy circular route from Manteigas to the Poço do Inferno waterfall (see box on p.305). You could also tackle a short stretch of the lower-level T2 – Linhares to Gouveia, via Folgosinho, is a good full day's walk, with facilities in each place – though unless you have access to two cars, parked either end, you'll need to take a taxi back to your starting point (easily done).

There's not much to Linhares, though there is a **café** in the church square by the castle and, just downhill on the only street, the *Taberna do Alcaide* (☎271 776 578; open Thurs–Sun only; ❷; no credit cards), a country tavern serving snacks and pricier meals of local lamb, goat stew, mountain sausage and the like; there are also three pretty rooms available, two of them en suite. Otherwise, for **accommodation** you have to head 1.5km down from the village (towards the N17, the Carrapichana road) to the motel-style *Tasquinha Serrana* (☎271 776 671; no credit cards; ❷; no breakfast Mon), whose simple rooms come complete with pine shutters and a modest patio with lovely views. There's also a rather scruffy pool and a reasonably priced restaurant (closed Sun dinner & Mon). Far fancier is the *Quinta do Adamastor*, at Figueiró da Serra, halfway to Folgosinho (☎271 770 010, ❺www.quintadoadamastor.com; ❹), with lovely gardens and a very impressive pool. Rates are highest from mid-June to mid-September and at weekends, though they drop €30 or so at other times, while the restaurant (closed Tues dinner & Wed) is pretty reasonable too.

Folgosinho

FOLGOSINHO, 14km southwest of Linhares along a bumpy country lane (head back towards Carrapichana and turn left before the N17), is altogether more welcoming and less inward-looking. It's a hundred metres higher than Linhares, with a mountain tang to the air, and is topped by not so much a castle as a perky turreted clocktower clinging to the crags. There's a cute, tree-shaded village square, and a central kernel of granite houses, a few of which tout the local produce – mainly cheese, honey, hams and woolly jumpers (though it's shepherds' cloaks that are the more traditional habit).

O Albertino on the square (☎238 745 266; ❷; restaurant closed Mon; whole place closed 1 week April & 2 weeks Sept; no credit cards) has some simple, country-style **rooms** available in a traditional granite house; the restaurant is an earthy meat-and-game place (suckling pig, wild boar, goat and veal) with every dish accompanied by *arroz de cabidela* (rice cooked with blood). The cheerier place to eat is *O Mocas* (☎238 748 999; closed Tues & Sept), around the corner and up the road, which has a downstairs café and upstairs **restaurant**, with a shorter, cheaper menu of half a dozen daily dishes (often including a fish choice). The unusual name ("stubs") is explained (in English) on the plaque outside, but it might have been better if they had kept it to themselves, since it's a reference to a particularly nasty kitchen accident that befell the present owner's grandfather.

It's 11km by road to Gouveia from Folgosinho, or around three hours' walking on the T2 trail, whose paint marks you can pick up in the village. There's a taxi stand and posted telephone numbers in Folgosinho's square, handy for day-walkers who want to arrange a pick-up or drop-off in Linhares or Gouveia.

Gouveia

GOUVEIA might have lost the rural *serra* feel that once constituted its principal charm, but it's developed into a small provincial town of well-kept gardens and terrace-cafés. There's a bustling Thursday market as well as the striking Baroque Igreja de São Pedro in the centre of town, which has a colourful *azulejo*-lined exterior. Around the corner from here (signposted), the **Museu de Abel Manta** (Tues–Sun 9.30am–12.30pm & 2–6pm; free), Rua Direita 45, shows a selection of contemporary Portuguese art donated by Gouveia-born artist Abel Manta (1888–1982).

Still, you're not here for art but are rather en route to the mountains. Gouveia itself is easily reached by **bus**, with services from Coimbra (up the N17), and also from Guarda via Celorico da Beira; and there are daily weekday buses along the flank of the range to Seia. But Manteigas and the mountains proper are a further winding 37km southeast – there's no bus, but you can take a taxi for around €30. There's a **turismo**, to the side of the huge town hall on the avenue, near the church (Mon–Sat 9.30am–12.30pm & 2–6pm, Sun 10am–12.30pm & 2–4pm; ☎238 490 243, ⓦwww.cm-gouveia.pt), while down past the church and around the corner is the **park information office**, Avenida dos Bombeiros Voluntários 8 (Mon–Fri 9am–12.30pm & 2–5.30pm; ☎238 492 411) – it's the building by the *pelourinho*. A hundred metres up the road from here, at the end of the new gardens, *O Mundo Rural* is the place to browse for mountain produce and local crafts.

Gouveia has all the services you might need, including a supermarket, a handful of decent **accommodation** possibilities, and plenty of cafés and restaurants – it's not that interesting or convenient a base for the high mountains, but it is a perfectly decent night's stop. The local **campsite** (☎238 491 008;

closed Dec–Feb) is at Curral do Negro, 3km east on the Folgosinho road (the T2 path passes by), or you can camp 3km further on at the better-equipped *Quinta das Cegonhas* (see "Accommodation").

Accommodation

Quinta das Cegonhas Nabainhos, 6km east of Gouveia, Folgosinho road ☎238 745 886, ⊛www .cegonhas.com. There are two rooms and two apartments to rent at this pretty, restored manor house, which revels in its country location and sweeping views. Also a shady campsite (open all year), swimming pool, bar and restaurant (open to non-guests, best to call ahead) – meals are served daily in summer, a couple of days a week in spring and autumn, and by request in winter. Rooms ❷, apartments ❸

Hotel de Gouveia Av 1º de Maio ☎238 491 010, ⊛www.hoteldegouveia.com. The splash of flamingo-pink below the turismo fails to impress in terms of price or taste, although the travel-lodge style rooms are comfortable enough and there's also a pool, traditional restaurant and parking. ❸

Casas da Mata da Cerca Cerca ☎238 492 315, ⊛www.casasdamatadacerca.com. On the north-eastern outskirts of Gouveia – close enough to town to make it feasible without a car, but secluded enough to feel like you're in the middle of nowhere – this consists of two lovely houses surrounded by acres of mature woodland. The restored granite building with the balcony offers the best value. ❹

Residencial Monteneve Av Bombeiros Voluntários 12 ☎238 490 370 or 964 755 064, ⊛www .monteneveresidencial.com. This chic, restored house is the best choice in town, with inviting en-suite rooms and a bar that's perfect for lounging. It's just behind the church, next to the park information office. The restaurant here is stylish but moderately priced, offering a mix of continental and Portuguese dishes. ❸

Restaurant

O Júlio Rua do Loureiro 11A ☎238 498 016. Other than the *residencial*, this is the most reliable place to eat in town – strictly traditional, offering dishes like wild boar with onions, rabbit stew, or local kid and game. If the prices seem a bit high, head for the much cheaper places just down the alley. Closed Tues. Moderate.

Seia and around

The largest town on the western side of the *serra* is **SEIA**, 16km southwest of Gouveia and rather better located as a base for mountain trips – though there's still no onward public transport. The historic centre is small indeed, and not particularly historic, with only an indifferent eighteenth-century church topping a hillock above a handful of streets. Where Seia scores is in its proximity to smaller, higher villages (see below) and for the direct road route up to Torre peak, 30km to the southeast. There's also some diversion in the local **Museu do Pão** (Tues–Sun 10am–6pm; €2.50; ⊛www.museudopao.pt), a steep 1km above the centre (Sabugeiro road), which concentrates on the very stuff of life. Along with rustic reconstructions of bread-making equipment and a traditional mill, there are displays on the religious and political significance of bread – if nothing else, you could emerge knowing the word for bread in 125 languages. The terrace café has excellent views and there's also a restaurant (closed Sun dinner & Mon) and *mercearia* (grocers) where you can buy large loaves of tasty home-made bread, *broa* (corn), *senteio* (rye) or *mistura* (mixed).

Buses run to Seia directly from Lisbon and Coimbra, and Covilhã and Guarda, and there are three weekday services to Gouveia; the bus station is on the ring-road at the bottom of town, a few hundred metres from the centre. There's both a **turismo**, opposite the market on Rua Pintor Lucas Marrão (Mon–Sat 9am–12.30pm & 2–5.30pm; ☎238 317 762, ⊛www.cm-seia.pt), and a nearby **park information office** at Praça da República 28 (Mon–Sat 9am–12.30pm & 2–5.30pm; ☎238 310 440) – this is actually a road (not a square), immediately below the church hill, that runs between the Biblioteca Municipal and the Casa Municipal das Artes. The **market** building opposite the turismo is open every morning (not Sun), though best day to visit is Wednesday when a large **open-air market** takes place in the open space below Avenida 1º de Maio, past the *Hotel Camelo*.

Accommodation

Hotel Camelo Av 1º de Maio 16 ☏ 238 310 100, ⓦ www.eurosol.pt. Agreeable three-star hotel with good-value tartan-trimmed rooms, manicured grounds with swimming pool and play area, and well-regarded regional restaurant (closed Mon). Just follow the road through town (São Romão direction) to find it. ❸

Residencial Jardim Av Luís Vaz de Camões ☏ 966 221 357. The only budget place to stay is opposite the Casa Municipal da Cultura at the bottom of town – follow the signs for Coimbra/Guarda. It's in the middle of the shopping arcade, by the health/nutrition shop (*not* at the restaurant of the same name at the end) – rooms are clean but fairly spartan. No credit cards. ❶

🚶 **Casas da Ribeira** Pôvoa Velha, 5km east, signposted off the Sabugueiro road ☏ 238 311 221, ⓦ www.casasdaribeira.com. Eight rustically restored stone houses to rent in an ancient village, some dating back more than six hundred years. They range from studios to three-bed cottages, all handsomely furnished, and equipped with kitchens, central heating and wood-burning stoves and fireplaces. There's a pool on site, while a breakfast of fresh bread, ham, cheese and preserves is delivered to your door in the morning. Outdoor activities can be arranged. Prices are variable, but start at €120 per cottage for a 2-night stay. No credit cards.

Estalagem de Seia Av Dr Afonso Costa ☏ 238 315 866, ⓕ 238 315 538. Eighteenth-century town house with a granite staircase and a pleasant garden pool. Features and furnishings are a bit long in the tooth, and the relatively low price reflects this. It's just off the roundabout by the post office. No credit cards. ❸

Restaurant

Restaurante Regional da Serra Av dos Combatentes da Grande Guerra 12–14 ☏ 238 312 717. Just off the top of Pr da República, serving *serra* specialities – river trout, *cabrito*, sausages and so on. Stick with the dishes of the day and mains average around €7, and though it's pricier *a la carte* you'll not break the bank. About 50m downhill from here, *Tertulia* is a nice little bar for a sundowner. Moderate.

Sabugueiro

SABUGEIRO, 10km east of Seia, is said to be Portugal's highest village (1050m), a cachet that has led to some rampant overdevelopment, certainly along the main road, which is now nothing more than a drive-through shopping experience. Mountain cheese, ham, rye bread, honey, leather coats, woolly slippers and fluffy mountain dogs are piled high in the rash of souvenir shops – real mountain-dog pups (*cães*) are sold as a sideline, yelping piteously in tiny roadside cages. The surviving old village is at the bottom of the hill, near the Rio Alva. The slate-roofed stone cottages are in varying states of repair, although many have been restored and can be rented for a night's stay. There are also plenty of identikit rooms above the souvenir shops and cafés, but you'd do far better to press on to Manteigas, 25km to the east.

Loriga

The minor N231 road south of Seia (signposted initially to São Romão) winds for 18km to **LORIGA**, a prettily sited village sitting at 770m above agricultural terraces that slope steeply down to the Loriga river. The fast-flowing water once powered woollen mills here, and still irrigates the fields, while the settlement itself dates back at least to Roman times – there are traces of the Roman road signposted near Loriga and at Valezim just to the north. For *serra* hikers, Loriga is something of a destination, despite its small size – both T2 and T3 trails end here, while the T1 (having descended steeply from Torre, Portugal's highest peak) only has one section to go, south down the valley to Vide.

A couple of houses in the village advertise **rooms**, or there's *Residencial O Vicente* (☏ 238 953 127, ⓦ www.ovicente.com; ❷) out on the N231, which has a restaurant. *Churrasqueira Serrana* (☎238 954 295) at the top of the village is a good little chicken-and-chips place. A bus from Seia calls here once a day in the morning from June to September, just on Sundays and holidays during the rest of the year; a taxi from Seia costs €15. By car, you can continue south to the very picturesque N230 and then east for an alternative approach to Covilhã.

Manteigas

If there's one town in the *serra* with a true mountain air it's **MANTEIGAS**, 700m up, whose whitewashed houses and red roofs run along the contour above the Rio Zêzere. The approach from any direction is dramatic: from Seia, Sabugeiro and the west, the road winds down in convoluted switchbacks; from Belmonte and the east, the river scenery is at its most bucolic; while from the south is the breathtaking descent down the glacial valley of the Rio Zêzere. The latter route brings you into town past the therapeutic spa of **Caldas de Manteigas** and to the fertile valley bottom of the Zêzere, with Manteigas itself spreading across the steep slope opposite. The roofless ruins of old textile mills can be seen further down the valley, though Manteigas these days is an out-and-out tourist destination, especially in winter. It's of no great attraction in itself, but it does make a good base for exploring the *serra*, while its café terraces and hotel windows offer sweeping pine-carpeted mountain views.

There's no public transport further into the park from town, but with a car you can use Manteigas as a base to visit Torre, the glacial valley and ski fields, and the nearby hamlets and villages. The town is on two of the official **walking trails**, but local routes are on the tough side since – south and west at least – you have to climb steep and far to get anywhere. There's one good, easy circular walk to the Poço do Inferno; all the details are given in the box on p.305. Most other routes require you come back the same way, notably the shadeless four-hour Vale do Zêzere track to the Covão d'Ametade summer campsite – indeed, this particular hike can no longer be recommended since forest fires in 2005 destroyed the broom, oak and pine that gave the eastern valley side its character.

That leaves **Ski Parque** (☎275 982 870, ⓦwww.skiparque.pt) as the only other local diversion, an artificial winter-sports slope and adventure park 8km east of Manteigas down the N232 Belmonte road. It's open all year round for dry-slope skiing and snowboarding, plus everything else from mountain-biking to paint-ball manouevres, hang-gliding to horse-riding. Half-day activities and ski lessons start at around €30, or you can rent a bike for €10. If you're intent on some outdoor action it pays to call ahead since it's either heaving (winter and weekends) or deserted, but there's a river beach, campsite, restaurant and bar here in any case.

Practicalities

Bus services to Manteigas are limited to weekdays (though not public holidays) and are liable to change. Manteigas turismo (see below) can confirm times, but current weekday services are from Guarda at around 11am and 5pm, and from Covilhã via Belmonte at 5pm (you might have to change buses); there's also a bus from Belmonte at around 9am. Return services leave Manteigas for Guarda at around 7am and 1pm, and for Belmonte/Covilhã at 7am and noon with an extra 4.30pm service on Monday and Friday.

The centre of town, such as it is, focuses on the GALP service station and a very small green area with outdoor café. Buses stop here, near the large **park information office** (Mon–Fri 9am–12.30pm & 2–5pm; ☎275 980 060) on the main street, Rua 1° de Maio – this curves around to the left through town and contains a small supermarket, ATM, Internet place and a few other shops. The helpful English-speaking **turismo** (Tues–Fri 9.30am–noon & 2–6pm, Sat 9.30am–noon & 3–7pm; ☏275 981 129, ⓦwww.cm-manteigas.pt) is below GALP, opposite the café, and though it's not strictly their job, it's a far better place than the park office to ask about local walks. Indeed, they may try to give you a photocopied page of walks taken from a guidebook – if it's not this one, you'd be unwise to rely on it.

△ Manteigas

A circular walk from Manteigas to the Poço de Inferno

The best circular walk **from Manteigas** is to the Poço de Inferno waterfall and back, which takes around four hours. Most of the paint-mark trail signs are missing or faded, but it's a straightforward route with plenty of shade and some gorgeous views. The walk starts in the Zêzere valley bottom, from the small bridge and picnic area reached down the steep road behind the turismo. There are a few parking spaces by the picnic tables.

Cross the bridge, turn left (signposted "Leandres") and walk for 500m along the road, past the recycling plant, before turning right onto a clear forestry track. Keep straight on along this main path, ever upwards through the woods – the first yellow paint sign is on a tree on the righthand side (6min) and there isn't another until you reach a ruined white house in a clearing (45min) marked with the words "Matas Nacionais".

Five minutes after the house is the only turn off the main path – to the left (with paint marks before and after the turn). In another 15min, having crossed a small bridge over a tumbling stream, the path ends at a bend in a tarmacked road. Walk uphill (there's a yellow paint mark almost immediately) and it's 20min further up the road to the **Poço do Inferno**, "hell's well", where the water of the Leandres river pours down the narrow gorge into clear pools shrouded by trees and overlooked by viewing platforms. It's a great spot for a picnic.

To return, follow the minor road around past the falls, heading back towards Manteigas. This road actually runs all the way, steadily down, to Caldas de Manteigas, though this would be a long (8km) and unnecessary return to Manteigas itself. Instead, after an hour, at a large water tank by the righthand side of the road (there's also a white house, just before a small bridge), turn right down an ancient track – walled in parts – which drops in zigzags through the trees. Ultimately, there are several divergent paths, but as long as you keep going downhill you'll end up in the group of houses by the *Albergaria Berne* (another 30min) – from where it's a steep 15min climb into Manteigas proper.

There's plenty of local **accommodation**, though not too much at the budget end of the market – note that high season here is January to April. The most convenient **campsite** is the year-round *Relva da Reboleira* at Ski Parque (☏275 982 870), 8km west of Manteigas, though there's a far nicer summer site further down the N232, by the river at **Valhelhas** (☏275 487 160; closed Oct–April), a small village 17km from Manteigas – the Covilhã/Belmonte bus passes by both. Other locally used summer sites are on stiff hiking routes out of Manteigas, at Covão da Ametade (4hr) and Vale do Rossim (3hr).

Hotels and pensions

Albergaria Berne Quinta de Santo António ☏275 981 351, ⊕www .albergariaberne.com. A friendly family takes good care of you in this pine-furnished inn, with simple but decent-sized rooms – there's a/c and central heating, and the bathrooms have baths which walkers will appreciate. Views from the room terraces are up to Manteigas or over the swimming pool, and there's a good restaurant (moderate) where you'll eat heartily. It's down at the foot of town, by the river – a very steep 15min on foot, or 3km by road (Caldas/Torre road and look for the signs). ❷

Quinta dos Fragas N232, Belmonte road, 2km east of town ☏275 982 420, ⊕www .quintadosfragas.com. Comfortable, attractively furnished rooms in a restored granite mountain house, just below town. The best bit's the pool and barbecue area outside. ❸

Casa das Obras Rua Teles de Vasconcelos ☏275 981 155, ⊕www.casadasobras.pt. Follow the blue signs in town to find this restored eighteenth-century mansion. The faded dining room murals, giddy, uneven floorboards, and the tiny cellar-like bar are delightful, and there's an enchanting garden with fruit trees, great views, a big, soppy mountain dog and a secluded swimming pool. No credit cards. ❹

Pousada de São Lourenço N232, 12km west of Manteigas; follow the signs from town ⊤ 275 980 050, ⊛ www.pousadas.pt. Reached by a series of careering switchbacks and perched at a height of 1290m, this marvellous *pousada* is best enjoyed in winter when log fires are roaring in the wood-panelled bar and the tartan curtains are drawn against howling mountain winds. That said, you can negotiate some serious discounts and last-minute deals in summer, when the views are superlative. The expensive restaurant has an innovative menu (try fried blood sausage with orange), including a surprising range of vegetarian options. ⑥

Dormidas Santa Luzia Rua Dr Esteves de Carvalho ⊤ 275 981 283. Tattered, slightly peeling rooms below an inexpensive restaurant, next to the turismo – but they are clean, afford good views and are the cheapest in town. No credit cards. ①

Casa de São Roque Rua de St António 51 ⊤ 275 981 125. An old town house with characterful rooms – oak-panelled room 8 has the most atmosphere – and a grand old dining room on the top floor. It's off Rua 1° de Maio, on the left, 150m after the *Serradalto*. No credit cards. ②

Residencial Serradalto Rua 1° de Maio ⊤ & ⊕ 275 981 151. Stylish, spotless rooms with wooden ceilings and wonderful views. The guests' terrace is one of the best spots in Manteigas for a

sunset beer, while full-length windows in the restaurant give on to the valley below. The most popular dish is steak cooked on a hot stone on your table. Restaurant and hotel closed Tues, though in summer if you drop by after around 7pm you may be allowed a room. ②

Restaurants

Cascata Rua 1° de Maio ⊤ 275 982 511. A terrace with expansive views is the main selling point, although the food is pretty good too – the likes of grilled trout, mountain sausage or roast pork make it a reliable lunchtime stop. No credit cards. Moderate.

Dom Pastor Rua Sá da Bandeira ⊤ 275 982 920. Tucked away in an idyllic little lane by the river, this fashionable restaurant has a creative take on traditional cuisine. Dishes such as fillet of perch with shrimp sauce or *farinheira frita* (a local type of curled sausage) are eaten in a modern interior constructed using local materials. Closed Tues. No credit cards. Expensive.

LusoPizza Rua Teles de Vasconcelos 15–17 ⊤ 275 982 928. The pizza – a rarity itself in the Beiras – at this tiny restaurant/takeaway (just behind the park office) is the genuine article, as is the humorous banter of the owner, a former professional footballer. No credit cards. Inexpensive.

Torre and around

The trans-mountain N339 between Seia and Covilhã climbs right across the bleak, scoured landscape of Portugal's highest mountains. The peak is known as **Torre** (1993m) after the stone *torre* (tower) added on the orders of Dom João VI in 1817 to raise the height to a more impressive 2000m. There's something typically Portuguese about that gesture, as there is about the summit shopping centre, with nineteen shops all selling smelly cheese and woolly slippers. As you're probably beginning to discern, any sense of natural beauty and grandeur at the top of Portugal's highest mountain has been severely disfigured by the coach parking, radar domes, concrete buildings, swirling litter and broken glass. There's a café and self-service restaurant, while ski-lifts march across the tundra-like wastes just below the summit.

It goes without saying that the route there is the best thing about Torre, and there's no better approach than the 15km from Manteigas up the dramatic glacial **Zêzere valley**. A viewpoint offers some stunning valley views, while the **Cântaros crags** above conceal the source of the Rio Zêzere. The valley road joins the N339 at the Nave de Santo António plateau, where you turn right for Torre (7km). En route to the peak you will pass the vast statue of **Nossa Senhora da Boa Estrela**, carved into a niche in the rock, to which there's a massive procession from Covilhã on the second Sunday in August.

Turn left at the junction instead (towards Covilhã) and it's 10km to the mountain outpost and rudimentary ski station of **Penhas da Saúde** (1900m). It's a rather desolate-looking place, not really a village and with few facilities save a sprinkling of accommodation (including the *serra*'s only youth hostel; see Covilhã below) and some cafés.

Covilhã

Just outside the eastern park boundary, and 44km south of Guarda, the cheery, prosperous town of **COVILHÃ** lies immediately below the highest peaks. It's busiest at winter weekends, when it's used increasingly as a base for trips to the ski slopes, but it has a life independent of the mountains which makes it an agreeable place to visit at any time. It's steeply terraced, with every thoroughfare looking out across the plain below or up to the mountain, crags – the café in the pretty **Jardim Público** has the best view in town.

A market town since the Middle Ages, Covilhã developed a textile industry in the seventeenth century using wool from the local sheep, which also provide the milk for the renowned local *queijo da Serra*. After industrialization, the woollen industry began to harness water power from the mountain streams; factories today, down on the plain below town, are powered by hydroelectricity.

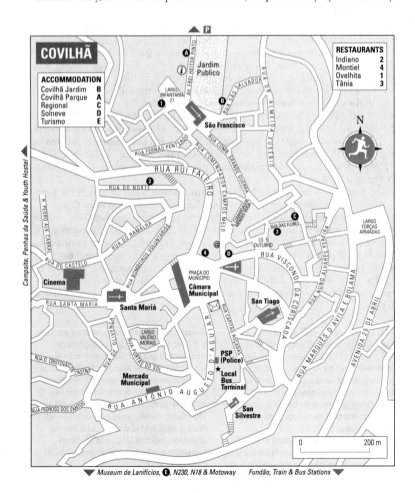

You can view the enormous vats used in the traditional wool-dyeing processes in the **Museo de Lanifícios** (Tues–Sun 9.30am–noon & 2.30–6pm; €2; ⓦ www.ubi.pt/museu) on Rua Marquês d'Avila e Bolama, a short walk downhill from the centre. The vats were unearthed in the mid-1970s when Covilhã's university was renovating the old *Real Fábrica de Panos*, a woollen mill originally opened by the Marquês de Pombal in 1764.

Covilhã's favourite son is **Pêro de Covilhã**, who set out in 1487 on behalf of Dom João II, to search for Prester John (legendary Christian priest and king) in what is now Ethiopia. However, having reached Cairo, de Covilhã sailed instead to India before returning to Cairo and then heading south on his original errand. He never found Prester John and never returned to Portugal, though Vasco da Gama found his report about India useful when he made his own celebrated voyage there, around the Cape of Good Hope, in 1498. In front of the town hall on **Praça do Municipio** there's a huge, polished granite slab depicting Pêro de Covilhã's voyages and a decidedly queasy-looking statue of the man himself.

Practicalities

Parking in the centre of town is metered (4hr maximum; free after 8pm and on Sun); for full-day or overnight stays, best bet is the large public parking area below the fire station (*Bombeiros*) – from the public gardens, head up past the *Covilhã Parque* hotel and *Telepizza*, turn sharp left at the garage (*Pneus*) and there's a blue parking sign immediately on the left. Both **train and bus stations** are 2km below the town, but a bus runs up the hill every ten minutes and drops you at the **local bus terminal** outside the PSP (police station); or take a taxi (€4). The **turismo**, Avenida Frei Heitor Pinto (Mon–Fri 9am–5.30pm, Sat 9am–12.30pm & 2–5.30pm; ☎ 275 319 560; ⓦ www.cm-covilha .pt) is in the pink building opposite the Jardim Público. **Internet access** is available at Postweb at Rua Comendador Campos Melo 27 (Mon–Sat 9am–7pm). Covilhã has a daily **market** (mornings only, not Sun) on Rua António Augusto d'Aguiar.

The town has a decent range of **accommodation**, most of which has great views to the surrounding mountains and plain. Prices shoot up from Christmas to April, but there are some real bargains to be had in summer. The nearest **campsite** to town, *Parque de Campismo do Pião* (☎ 275 314 312; open all year), lies 4km out on the N339 road up to Penhas da Saúde, while at **Penhas da Saúde** itself (11km from Covilhã) there are a couple more hotels and the local youth hostel. The only public transport up here is the summer-season bus to Penhas (July–Sept only, daily at 8.50am, plus 2pm in Aug), either from Covilhã's bus terminal or ten minutes later from the local bus terminal in town – current schedules from the green kiosk by the PSP.

Hotels and pensions

Covilhã Jardim Rua São Salvador 40 ☎ 275 322 140. Fifteen smart en-suite rooms with either public garden or distant views, some with French windows opening on to a terrace. It's been newly renovated (2006), and is a genial family concern, which makes the prices something of a steal. There's pay parking right outside. No credit cards. ❷

Hotel Covilhã Parque Av Frei Heitor Pinto ☎ 275 327 518, ⓦ www.imb-hotels.com. This place is ten floors high and thus offers the best views in town,

at least from the front – change rooms if you have to. It's two-star, and not quite as swish as the reception area suggests, with slightly worn decor and bathrooms on the basic side. But the location and the summer rates are excellent – and there's direct access from the fire-station parking area. ❷

Pensão Regional Rua das Flores 4–6 ☎ 275 322 596. Friendly *pensão* tucked away on a quiet side street. A steep flight of stairs leads up from the downstairs restaurant to peaceful rooms with heavy, dark wooden beds and amazing views. No credit cards. ❶

Residencial Solneve Rua Visconde da Coriscada 126 ☎275 323 001, ⓦwww.solneve.pt. Overlooking the main square, the businesslike rooms come with ochre-tiled bathrooms, Internet access, DVD and cable TV, although there's a small charge for the car park. Guests tend to forego the cavernous downstairs restaurant, but they're missing some of Covilhã's best-value food. Grilled or steamed fish will set you back a mere €7, while the menu also extends to lasagne and stroganoff. ❸

Hotel Turismo Acesso à Variante ☎808 200 307, ⓦwww.imb-hotels.com. The *Colvilhã Parque's* three-star sister hotel is one of the flashiest in town, with a glass elevator, outdoor pool, health spa, Jacuzzi and car park. ❸

Youth hostel

Pousada de Juventude Penhas da Saude, 11km northwest of town ☎275 335 375, ⓦwww .pousadasjuventude.pt. The huge 108-bed youth hostel is at the crest of a rise as you enter Penhas on the Covilhã road. It has superb views and pretty good facilities, including self-catering kitchen and bar. Some private rooms available, with/without bathroom. Unfortunately, the bus up here only runs from July to Sept. Reception open daily 8am to midnight. Dorm beds €9, winter €16, rooms ❶, winter ❷

Restaurants

Indiano Rua do Norte 8 ☎913 039 234. Covilhã's – heck, the *serra's* – first Indian restaurant throws a surprise in this meat-and-potatoes town. An English-language menu offers a Goan fish curry, lamb *jalfrezi* and a good vegetarian choice, and it's all very reasonably priced. Closed Mon. Moderate.

Montiel Pr do Município 33–37 ☎275 322 086. Café and *pastelaria* downstairs, slightly genteel restaurant upstairs, filled to bursting with families at Sun lunchtime. The menu concentrates on regional specialities, trout to *cabrito*, and although some dishes are pricey the *pratos do dia* cost around €6 for a *meia dose*. No credit cards. Moderate.

Ovelhita Largo Infantaria XXI 19 ☎275 088 554. On summer nights sit outside on the cobbles at the "Little Sheep" as students play classical guitar music. There's a short menu of *típico* dishes, but the three-course lunch and dinner buffet is excellent value – the price varies, according to day of the week and number of dishes taken, but averages €9. Moderate.

Tânia Rua das Flores 23 ☎275 336 744. Low-ceilinged, atmospheric little backstreet *tasca* serving up plain portions of meat and fish. Try the grilled squid, or the good-value three-course *ementa turística*. Closed Sun night. No credit cards. Inexpensive.

Beira Baixa

The area east of Covilhã and the IP2 motorway forms the upper boundary of the **Beira Baixa**, a landscape of undulating, heather-clad hills that extends to the Spanish border. The sun-bleached fields, grazing livestock and extensive olive groves provide a distinct contrast to the *serra* scenery, with visits concentrating on a series of fortified towns and fascinating villages the equal of any in the upper Beira province. With a car you can see the whole region in a couple of days, with the best overnight stops either at the underrated town of **Belmonte** or in one of the atmospheric restored houses of medieval **Sortelha**. On the other hand, travel by public transport is particularly difficult and slow. Only Belmonte and **Sabugal** can be reached easily by bus, though if you're determined you'll also get to Sortelha, while the provincial capital of **Castelo Branco** (on the Lisbon–Guarda train route) has services to **Monsanto**. But isolated destinations like **Idana-a-Velha** and the **Serra da Malcata** nature reserve are impossible to see by public transport.

Belmonte

The delightful small town of **BELMONTE** springs one of the best surprises in the Beiras. It's often overlooked, despite its proximity to Guarda, Covilhã and even Manteigas in the Serra da Estrela, but it's a charming place – still hardly more than a large village – of sun-dappled squares, stone houses dripping with window boxes and lazy dogs basking on the cobbles. Although it has belatedly embraced its Jewish heritage (see below), for the Portuguese it's better known as being the birthplace of **Pedro Álvares Cabral** (1467–1520), the "discoverer" of Brazil, who was born in the thirteenth-century **castle** (Tues–Sun 10am–1.30pm & 3–6.30pm; free) overlooking town. Cabral's father had received the castle from Dom Afonso V, and adapted it as the family residence, though it later fell into disrepair. It's been tidily restored, and equipped with a modern amphitheatre for summer concerts. The **Igreja de São Tiago** (Tues–Sun 9.30am–12.30pm & 2–6pm; €1), in the *plaça* just outside the walls, contains the Cabral family pantheon (though not the tomb of Pedro Álvares, which is in Santarém), while one of two tiny stone chapels on a hillock opposite is inscribed with the Cabral family coat-of-arms – two goats within a shield. The Cabral trail also extends to the main through-road named in his honour where there's a statue of the explorer clutching a large cross; while inside the modern **Igreja Matriz** in the centre of town there's an ancient image of Nossa Senhora da Esperança, said to have accompanied Cabral on his first visit to Brazil.

Belmonte's restored **Jewish quarter** is tucked below the southern wall of the castle. Belmonte once maintained one of Portugal's largest Jewish communities and records show that there was a synagogue here as early as 1297, but this fell into ruins after the Inquisition, when many Jews fled the country or were forced to convert to being "New Christians". However, the faith endured for centuries in secret, and not till after the 1974 Revolution did local Jewish families feel secure enough to worship again publicly. The modern **Sinagoga** (Tues–Sun 9.30am–12.30pm & 2–6pm; €2) built in the Jewish quarter is now open for visits, while behind Largo do Pelourinho in the old town the **Museu Judaico**, Rua da Portela (Tues–Sun 9.30am–12.30pm & 2–6pm; €2.50; price includes entry to all town museums, which have the same hours), explores the history and culture of Portuguese Judaism.

The rest of the old town is a delight to wander, with every sight marked on carved wooden signs. There's an outdoor café in pretty **Largo do Pelourinho** – the unusual pillory itself is in the shape of an olive press – while along the main Rua Pedro Álvares Cabral you'll find the second of the town museums, the **Ecomuseu do Zêzere**, housed in a barn-like granite building, formerly a granary owned by the Cabral family. This provides the background on the Zêzere river, whose valley Belmonte overlooks, while for an investigation of the local olive oil industry, follow the signs around the corner to the **Lagar Municipal**.

Torre Centum Cellas

There's an extraordinary sight a couple of kilometres north of Belmonte, just off the N18 – drive 600m along the road from the Belmonte junction towards Guarda and then 400m up a side road to the right. The **Torre Centum Cellas** presents a very odd picture – rather like a child's brick building – with the further curiosity that no one quite knows what it was. The stone tower measures around ten by eight metres and stands three storeys high, and there are no fewer than forty intact window and door frames. Possibly it formed part of a Roman villa, and survived due to later use as a watchtower.

Practicalities

There are daily **bus** services from Guarda (26km) and Covilhã (20km), which drop you at the end of Rua Pedro Álvares Cabral, a 500m walk from the centre; long-distance buses to Lisbon, Viseu and Coimbra stop at Gingal junction on the N18, 2km below town. Belmonte is also well sited for the Serra da Estrela, with Manteigas just 27km to the west – the twice-daily weekday Manteigas bus currently leaves at 8.50am and 5.10pm. The **turismo** at the castle (Tues–Sun 10am–1.30pm & 3–6.30pm; ☎275 911 488, ⓦwww.cm-belmonte.pt) can give you a map of town.

Belmonte makes an appealing night's stopover, though the only budget **accommodation**, the *Pensão Altitude* (☎275 911 170), down Rua Pedro Álvares Cabral near the bus stop, was closed at the time of writing. That leaves two rather finer choices, notably the town's stunning *Pousada Convento de Belmonte* (☎275 910 300, ⓦwww.pousadas.pt; breakfast included; ❼), 1km or so out of the centre; follow the signs. A residual sense of spirituality lingers in the granite cloister, while the sumptuous rooms in the restored convent combine natural textures, light and space. There's a plunge-pool and terrace, and an excellent restaurant. Otherwise, the apartment-style *Hotel Belsol* (☎275 912 206, ⓦwww.hotelbelsol.com; ❹) has a larger pool, tennis court and well-kept gardens – this is about 3km from town, on the main N18 road between the Belmonte junction and the turn-off for Valhelhas and Manteigas (N232).

Sortelha

Twenty kilometres east of Belmonte, the amazing circuit of walls around **SORTELHA** rises amid an unearthly, undulating highland plateau strewn with giant glacial boulders. When the mist drifts down from the *serra*, its mystery is complete – stories are spun around the figure of an old lady (*a velha*) whose profile you can see on rocks from outside the top gates of the castle. It's an ancient place, with Hispano-Arabic origins, and for most of its existence has gone about its business quietly, though the rock-built fortress suggests some frontier excitement in times past. Today it presents itself almost as a museum-piece – with some beautifully restored lodgings available – though the number of permanent residents in the old town still barely struggles into double figures.

From the modern quarters on the Sabugal road it's a five-minute walk uphill (follow "Castelo" signposts) to the walled **old town** – or you can drive up and park outside the main gate. The walls follow the contours of the moss-covered boulders, with defensive gates and towers placed at strategic intervals. Within, a tight web of cobbled lanes wends between squat stone houses with red tiled roofs, while rough carved steps in the castle keep offer a beautiful view over the valley below and the rock-speckled hillsides beyond. The Igreja Matriz has a fine ceiling, executed by medieval Moors, while Arabic script can be seen on several house lintels near the top of town.

Sortelha's major event is a **bullfight**, which takes place on August 15, once every two or three years, when the local council has the money to stage it. It retains the ancient custom of the *forca* – a rudimentary defence against the bull, using branches – which has been handed down from generation to generation. In non-bullfight years there's still a *festa* on August 15, and a *romaria* in honour of Santo António takes place on June 13.

Practicalities

You *can* reach Sortelha by **bus**, but only from nearby Sabugal, 13km to the east (see below) and only with any regularity during school term time (Sept–June, every weekday afternoon at 5.25pm); there's also a 1.30pm bus on Tuesdays and Thursdays; you'll have to stay the night, as the schoolday return service isn't until 7.50am the next morning. Otherwise, a taxi from Sabugal should cost around €15.

Sortelha is blessed with a surplus of enticing *turismo rural* **accommodation**, some places up in the walled town, others down on the main road – advance reservations are recommended. Note that there are no credit card or banking facilities in Sortelha. Three places – *Casa da Cerca*, *Casa da Villa* and *Casa do Páteo* – are owned by a vivacious Viscountess, originally from Seville in Spain, who presides over her mini-empire from the *Ferrolho* **antique shop**, next door to *Casa do Páteo*, just off the main road. This is worth a browse, if only to chew the fat in broken English with the Viscountess, who has certainly brought some life to the place – the shop also sells the handsome rugs woven by local women in their own homes.

Rooms

Casas do Campanário ☎277 388 198. Enquire at the adjacent *Bar Campanário* at the top of the old town – follow the signs from the top gate. The bar has a spectacularly sited boulder-terrace, while in the cosy, antique-stuffed rooms you'll have to mind your head on the sloping ceilings. ❸

Casa da Cerca ☎271 388 113, ⓔcasadacerca@clix.pt. By the main road, opposite *Casa do Páteo* and the antique shop, this rambling, restored house has six atmospheric, en-suite bedrooms; the granite seats carved into the window sills are a nice touch, and there's a pretty garden where breakfast is served in the summer. ❸

Casa do Páteo ☎271 388 113, ⓔcasadacerca@clix.pt. Forming part of the granite outbuildings of the Viscountess' own Solar de Nossa Senhora da Conceição, this is a charming place to bed down, with wooden furniture, hot baths, a patio with logpile, ancient TV and cobwebs – all in all, a splendid mix of modern comforts and medieval surroundings. ❸

Casa da Villa ☎271 388 113, ⓔcasadacerca@clix.pt. On the main street in the old town, just up from the castle. The air is permeated by the smell of reclaimed wood (old railway sleepers, inventively refashioned) while the patio and first-floor rooms afford some breathtaking views. ❷, rooms with a view ❸

Cafés and restaurants

Restaurante O Celta ☎271 388 291. A functional and surprisingly pricey rendezvous for bus parties and day-trippers, though the *pratos do dia* and an *ementa turística* soften the blow. It's halfway along the main road below town. Closed Tues. Expensive.

Restaurante Dom Sancho I ☎271 388 267. The only proper restaurant in the old town, just inside the main gate, with a rustic stone-walled interior. It's the perfect place to sample grills and game from a strictly traditional menu. Expensive.

Bar Forno Esplanada ☎271 388 034. The best place for an inexpensive lunch is this friendly café with a stone-flagged terrace, right under the castle walls. There are sausage and cheese *petiscos* and other snacks, or they will rustle you up a *febras* or steak and chips for €6.50. Stays open until 9pm. Closed 2 weeks Sept. Inexpensive.

Sabugal

SABUGAL is a perfectly pleasant place with a riverside setting on the Côa, attractive gardens and a small restored old-town area. The hill is topped by a neatly restored castle with high walls, but the setting isn't a patch on that at Sortelha. Most visitors will just drive on by, though Sabugal does make a good base for visiting the Serra da Malcata reserve (see below), as accommodation and restaurants are better here than at the other town near the reserve, Penamacor, 35km to the south. Anyone bound for Sortelha by bus will also have to come here first.

There are weekday **bus** services to and from Guarda, Belmonte, Penamacor and Castelo Branco, and a limited service to Sortelha. There's a **turismo** (daily 9.30am–12.30pm & 2–5.30pm; ☎271 751 046, ⓦwww.cm-sabugal.pt) up near the castle in the Câmara Municipal on Praça da Republica. The bus station is at the bottom of town, by the market, with the best place to eat in Sabugal just over the road, in the yellow building – *Restaurante Robalo* (☎271 753 566; closed Sun except in Aug) serves grilled trout from the Rio Côa and has a reputation for its *cabrito* and *borrego*. Across the road from here – there's an H on top of the tall

building – the *Albergaria Santa Isabel*, Largo do Cinema 9 (☎271 750 100, ⓦwww
.raihotel.pt; ❸), provides decent **accommodation** – its restaurant is pretty good
too. There are cheaper rooms down by the river bridge on the way into town at
Residencial Sol Rio (☎271 753 197, ⓕ271 752 070; ❶), where French windows and
balconies overlook the water. There's also an inexpensive restaurant here.

Reserva Natural da Serra da Malcata

Between Sabugal and Penamacor, and reaching east from two local reservoirs to
the Spanish border, spreads the **Reserva Natural da Serra da Malcata**. It's
one of the least-visited Portuguese nature reserves – access isn't easy, and you
really need to bike or hike to get much out of it – but it rewards the effort,
certainly if you have any interest in wildlife. If you're fortunate, you might just
see a wild boar disappearing into the forests of black oak, or catch a glimpse of
the magnificent golden eagle or black vulture. Foxes, badgers, weasels, otters,
frogs and salamanders are common. What you won't see – despite the emblem
on all the promotional material – is the **Iberian lynx**, which is under serious
threat of extinction: at the time of writing, it was the most endangered carnivo-
rous species in Europe and the most endangered feline in the world. The last
lynx was caught in the park in 1992, and there's been no sign of one now for
over a decade – though they are still present on the Spanish side of the border.
A joint project aims to reintroduce the creature from Spain, but it's a long-term
plan with no guarantee of success.

The reserve covers 16,000 hectares of undulating, heather-clad hills and oak
woodland, with the reserve headquarters found in Penamacor (see below for
contact details). They can usually rustle up an English-speaking member of staff
to advise about where best to go at different times of the year; and the office
also sells a map and separate walking booklet in English. Note that not all the
hiking trails are currently signposted, forest fires and vandalism having taken
their toll – ask before you set off.

From Sabugal it's easy to drive to the small village of **Malcata** (where there's
a café) near the **Barragem do Sabugal**. This lies on a waymarked 44-kilometre
trail called the "Grande Rota do Vale da Ursa", which loops through the
northern sector of the reserve – mountain-bikers can complete the circuit in a
long day out. Or you can drive down the minor 538 road from Sabugal past
Quadrazais towards Vale de Espinho (15km), where the *Trutal Côa* **restaurant**
(open all year, lunch and dinner; ☎271 606 227) serves grilled trout fresh from
its trout farm. A couple of short, five-kilometre (2hr) nature trails, covered in
the walking booklet, can be accessed nearby. Approaching from Penamacor, the
first signposted turn-off to the reserve is 6km north along the N233. More
hiking trails then fan out from the **Barragem da Ribeira da Meimoa**, which
has good swimming spots, though you should check how far you can take your
car as much of the reserve is 4WD access only. **Meimoa** itself, 13km from
Penamacor and just west of the reserve, has a couple of simple restaurants.

Penamacor

PENAMACOR has another medieval castle, not as impressive as those in
Sabugal and Sortelha but still offering great views over the Serra da Malcata
towards Spain. It's reached by a short but punishing climb up from the newer
part of town, and the restored walls enclose a dilapidated village that's just
beginning to get a facelift. Back down the hill, the public gardens have more
sweeping views over the southern plains of the Beira Baixa – there's an outdoor
café here – while on a terrace above the gardens sits the **Museu Municipal**

(daily 9am–12.30pm & 2–5.30pm; free). This is probably the only place you're going to get to see a lynx, sadly stuffed.

There are a couple of turismos in town, including one in the castle gatehouse, both fairly hopeless. The **Reserva Natural da Serra da Malcata headquarters**, Rua António Ribeiro Sanches 60 (Mon–Fri 9am–12.30pm & 2–5.30pm; ☎277 394 467, ⓦwww.icn.pt), on the other hand, is knowledgeable and informative – follow the main street uphill from the gardens and around to the left towards the church. There's limited **accommodation**, with the only really appealing place being the *Estalagem Vila Rica* (☎277 394 311, ⓕ277 394 901; ❸), 500m from the centre, down the main road; the views from this ivy-cloaked eighteenth-century *solar* are marvellous and the rooms comfortable. **Campers** and tourers looking for isolation should head 11km east down the Spain road (N569) to the beautiful surroundings of the *Parque de Campismo do Freixal* (☎277 394 106; closed Nov–March), where you can swim in their pool or in the babbling river.

Monsanto

MONSANTO claims to be the most ancient settlement in Portugal, while it also jealously guards its title of the "most Portuguese" village in the country, an award originally bestowed in 1948. Sited high on a hill above the plain, beneath the protection of a castle, its houses huddle between giant granite outcrops, their walls carved from and moulded around enormous grey boulders – in the case of the **Casa de Uma Só Telha** ("the house with only one tile"), the entire roof is formed from a single rock. Everywhere, flowers tumble from windows and vines and ivy clings to the walls, while the streets, barely wide enough for a mule, are cut out of and around the mountain rock. The local women perch on their steps, touting *marafonas*, rag dolls fashioned from a wooden cross and originally used as a defense against sorcery. A few houses lie abandoned, but on the whole Monsanto seems to be doing well from Spanish day-trippers and from tourists still searching for the "real" Portugal.

Specific sights are few, though a leaflet available from the turismo (see below) dutifully leads you through the alleys, past churches, chapels, crosses, decayed mansions and restored fountains. The main cobbled path heads up between the giant boulders to the walls of the **castle**, overseeing a windswept rockscape at a height of more than 700 metres. Monsanto dates back at least to paleolithic times, and there were Roman, Visigothic and Arab settlements here; it was taken from the Moors by Afonso Henriques in the twelfth century, later fortified by Gualdim Pais, Grand Master of the Knights Templar, and rebuilt many times subsequently before it finally became the victim of cross-border warfare in 1810. The restored walls offer remarkable views across the parched plains to the distant mountains, while in the castle grounds stand a simple stone chapel and an unusual central well, crisscrossed by stone arches which originally numbered seven – only two remain. Legend has it that a villager once tried to renovate the cistern but was buried alive by rocks after witnessing an apparition of a beautiful Moorish woman. A big celebration takes place every May 3 (or the following Sun), when the village girls throw baskets of flowers off the ramparts. The rite commemorates an ancient siege when, in desperation and close to starvation, the defenders threw their last calf over the walls: their attackers, so disheartened at this evidence of plenty within, gave up and went home.

Practicalities

Monsanto is 48km northeast of Castelo Branco, and around 25km south of Penamacor. There's a newer settlement right at the bottom of the hill and, further up, a small **parking** area immediately outside the old village – don't drive any further in. **Buses** from Castelo Branco (not Sat) stop at the parking area; the return service is at the unearthly hour of 6.15am (though Sun at 2.30pm). There's only really one street, and everything is signposted: walk up from the parking area to the church and turn right for the small **turismo** (daily 10am–1pm & 2–6pm; ☎277 314 642) and – eventually – the castle.

There is a handful of souvenir shops and just two **places to stay**, notably the small *Estalagem de Monsanto* (☎277 314 471, ⓦ www.estalagemdemonsanto.pt; ❸, weekends ❹), a rather incongruous edifice amid the village's medieval charms, but attractive enough inside, and with its own restaurant and bar. This is just up from the parking area, opposite the church, while to the left along the main street is the *Adega Tipica O Cruzeiro* (☎277 314 528; no credit cards; ❷), a rustically refurbished place that has a couple of upstairs rooms with stunning views. Lunch is available at *O Cruzeiro*, which chalks its inexpensive *pratos do dia* up outside, or there's the moderately priced *Restaurant Jovem* (☎277 314 590; no credit cards), right by the parking area, with a menu centred on Portuguese standards and a few typical mountain dishes like *cabrito* and *feijoada*.

Idanha-a-Velha

The tiny backwater of **IDANHA-A-VELHA** is 15km from Monsanto by road and if you're driving to one, you should certainly make the effort to see the other. Known as "Igaeditânia", it was once a major Roman city of the first century BC and, subsequently, under Visigothic rule, "Egitânia" was the seat of a bishopric – which endured even Moorish occupation. Wamba (620–680 AD), the legendary King of the Goths, is said to have been born here. During the reign of Dom Manuel, however, early in the fifteenth century, it is said that a plague of rats forced the occupants to move to Monsanto or nearby Idanha-a-Nova.

The village looks much as it must have done when the rats moved in, and perhaps not very different from when the Romans left, either. Beautifully set amid burned plains and olive groves, it's still partly girded by a massive **Roman wall**, with a modern walkway built on top of it. Down by the languid river the **Roman bridge** is still in use, while roses and vines are trained up the weathered walls of the houses, many built from plundered Roman stone. A stork's nest tops the very ancient **basilica** – signposted as the Sé – which is at least part Visigothic, while outside here stand the ruins of the **bishop's palace** and an even earlier Roman house. Perhaps the most fascinating restoration is the old oil press or **lagar de varas**, with an ingenious pressing system utilizing two huge tree trunks, with roots intact. This stands across from the basilica, and a modern shelter in its rear yard houses various inscribed Roman stones found in the village.

People do live in Idana-a-Velha – grazing sheep on the plains and tending allotments down by the river – but it often seems almost deserted. You'll generally find someone at least in the **turismo** (daily 10am–1pm & 2–6pm; ☎277 914 280) – near the square with the *pelourinho*, on the way to the basilica. This too is built atop a Roman dwelling, whose foundations you can see through glass panels in the floor. The basilica and the olive-oil-press building should be open during turismo office hours, but if not, just ask. There's a solitary, authentically local **café** by the *pelourinho* – you'll have no trouble ordering a drink or a snack because it's the kind of place where everyone stops talking when you enter.

There's no public transport to the village, although there is a **footpath from Monsanto** (7km). This forms part of the signposted GR12 route (total 80km) that connects Termas de Monfortinho on the Spanish border with the town of **Idanha-a-Nova**, around 15km to the southwest of Idana-a-Velha (by road, longer by footpath), where there's accommodation in and around town and a campsite by the local reservoir. You can download walking route details from the Idanha-a-Nova municipal website (🆆www.cm-idanhanova.pt).

Castelo Branco

As capital of the Beira Baixa region, **CASTELO BRANCO** has an air of prosperity and activity in contrast with many of the nearby villages. Unfortunately, that is about all it has – for the visitor at least – since little of interest survived the successive wars of this frontier area. The sixteenth-century former town hall and a few later handsome mansions withstood the various battles, while narrow cobbled alleyways and stepped side streets lead up to the castle ruins, where a garden *miradouro* has been laid out. Otherwise, it's a predominantly modern town of sweeping boulevards, squares and parks – pleasant enough, but hardly a major draw.

There are just two sights of note. Flanking one side of the remaining old town is the **Jardim do Paço Episcopal** (daily 9am–7pm, closes 5pm in winter; €2), the formal, eighteenth-century garden of the old bishop's palace. This presents a sequence of box hedges, fountains, flowerbeds, *azulejos* and orange trees, while the balustrades of the two grand staircases are peopled with statues – on one, the Apostles; on the other, the kings of Portugal. Three of the latter are much smaller than the rest: the hated Spanish rulers, Felipe I, II and III, the so-called "intruder kings".

The palace itself now houses the **Museu Tavares Proença Júnior** (Tues–Sun 10am–12.30pm & 2–5.30pm; €2, free Sun morning), whose collections roam through the usual local miscellany, save for a large display of finely embroidered bedspreads, or *colchas*, a craft for which the town is known throughout Portugal. These lavish status symbols were originally produced in India and China where wealthy Portuguese commissioned them from local artisans. The craftspeople duly incorporated motifs from their own myths and culture – typically animals, flowers and mythical figures – which subsequently influenced Portuguese manufacturers in Castelo Branco's newly created domestic *colcha* industry. The museum has a room where you can still see women beavering away on these intricate works of art. You can even commission one yourself although you'd better have a fat wallet handy – a typical *colcha* costs thousands of euros.

Practicalities

It's difficult to summon up much enthusiasm for a night in Castelo Branco – and the town is conspicuously lacking in budget accommodation of a decent standard – but as a regional transport hub, you might end up staying. From the **bus station** turn right and it's a short walk up to the Alameda da Liberdade, the main avenue through town. The **train station** is 500m from the *alameda*, down the broad Avenida de Nuno Álvares. Driving in can be tortuous, thanks to the one-way system – grab a **parking** space where you can along the two main avenues approaching the *alameda* (Avenida 1° de Maio and Avenida de Nuno Álvares), or try Largo de São João near the Paço Episcopal gardens. If you're stopping overnight, you'd be better off following the hotel signs from the ring-road roundabouts – direct to the *Tryp Colina* or *Rainha Dona Amelia* (with the *Arraiana* very near the latter).

Now the traffic has been tunnelled under the Alameda da Liberdade, the central avenue has been opened up for pedestrians. Three or four café-bars line the concrete piazza below, while there's a **turismo** here in Praça do Municipio (Mon–Fri 9.30am–7.30pm, Sat & Sun 9.30am–1pm & 2.30–6pm; ☎272 330 339 ⓦwww.cm-castelobranco.pt). The daily **Mercado Municipal** is nearby, down Avenida 1° de Maio. The municipality puts on a wide variety of annual events, including a noted classical music spring festival every May and June (ⓦwww.primaveramusical.org).

Hotels and pensions

Residencial Arraiana Av 1 de Maio 18 ☎272 341 634, ℻272 331 884. White woodchip, brazenly blue-tiled bathrooms and cork floors lend this somewhat overpriced *residencial* a frumpish 1970s feel. ❷

Residencial Império Rua dos Prazeres 20 ☎272 341 720. Behind the post office, in a quiet street close to the cathedral – follow the *alameda* around towards the gardens and museum. A modern place with a/c rooms with gleaming bathrooms, and a compact dining room where breakfast is served. The downstairs rooms are gloomier but wonderfully cool in summer. No credit cards. ❷

Hotel Rainha Dona Amélia Rua Santiago 15 ☎272 348 800, ⓦwww.rainhadamelia.pt. Good, reasonably spacious, a/c rooms in warm tones make this the best mid-range choice. The hotel itself – a *Best Western* – is a bit traditional (restaurant no one uses, souvenirs no one buys), but there's a buffet breakfast, garage parking and negotiable rates towards the end of the day. It's off the bottom of Av 1° de Maio, around the corner from the *Arraiana*. ❹

Hotel Tryp Colina do Castelo Rua da Piscina ☎272 349 280, ⓦwww.solmelia.com. The fanciest place in town has a lofty location by the castle, rooms with soft-focus interiors and breathtaking views from the balconies, bar and reception area. There's also parking, a health club with sauna, Turkish baths and squash courts. You'll usually beat the posted rates, while Internet deals can be as low as €50. ❻

Restaurants

O Jardim do Paço Largo de São João ☎272 321 481. A cheap choice around the corner from the Paço gardens – unfussy plates of pork, steak, fish and squid. An enormous TV drowns out any conversation, so not one for a romantic night out. Inexpensive.

Kalifa Rua Cadetes de Toledo 10 ☎272 344 246. Contemporary restaurant with a lengthy, imaginative menu – an appetizer of sheep's cheese with banana, say, followed by chicken curry. There's also half a dozen daily fresh fish choices, plus a tree-shaded summer terrace at the back. Moderate.

Praça Velha Largo Luís de Camões 17 ☎272 328 640. Once the granary of Castelo Branco's Knights Templar, this fashionable old-town restaurant now feeds the well-heeled townsfolk. There are a few twists – stuffed tomato with prawns, or *tourndeos* with sheep's cheese – but otherwise this is a fairly traditional menu. Closed Sun lunch & Mon. Expensive.

Travel details

Trains

You can check train timetables online at ⓦwww.cp.pt.

Castelo Branco to: Covilhã (6 daily; 1hr–1hr 20min); Lisbon (5 daily; 3hr 10min–3hr 45min).

Covilhã to: Castelo Branco (6 daily; 1hr–1hr 20min); Guarda (3 daily; 1hr 15min); Lisbon (5 daily; 4hr 15min–5hr 15min).

Guarda to: Coimbra (7 daily; 2hr 10min–2hr 40min); Covilhã (3 daily; 1hr 15min); Lisbon (7 daily; 4hr 30min–5hr 45min); Vilar Formoso, Spanish border (6 daily; 45min).

Buses

Almeida to: Guarda (Mon–Fri 1 daily; 1hr 10min).

Belmonte to: Covilhã (3 daily; 30min); Guarda (3 daily; 45min); Manteigas (Mon–Fri 2 daily: 45min); Sabugal (1 daily; 1hr 30min).

Castelo Branco to: Covilhã (1–5 daily; 1hr); Guarda (1–5 daily; 1hr 40min); Lisbon (7 daily; 2hr 30min); Monsanto (Mon–Fri 2 daily, Sun 1; 1hr 30min); Penamacor (1–2 daily, not Sat; 1hr 20min); Sabugal (1 daily, not Sat; 2hr); Viseu (1–5 daily; 3hr 10min).

Covilhã to: Castelo Branco (1–5 daily; 1hr); Guarda (3–7 daily; 45min); Lisbon (4–9 daily; 3hr

35min–6hr); Manteigas (Mon–Fri 1 daily; 1hr 30min); Penhas da Saúde (July–Sept only: 1 daily; 2 daily during Aug; 35min); Seia (Mon–Fri & Sun 1 daily; 2hr); Viseu (2–6 daily; 2hr).

Gouveia to: Coimbra (3 daily; 2hr); Seia (Mon–Fri 3 daily; 30min).

Guarda to: Almeida (Mon–Fri 1 daily; 1hr 10min); Belmonte (Mon–Fri 3 daily; 45min); Braga (2–7 daily; 4hr 15min); Castelo Branco (1–5 daily; 1hr 40min); Celerico da Beira (hourly; 30min); Coimbra (2–6 daily; 2hr 45min); Covilhã (3–9 daily; 45min); Gouveia (1–3 daily; 45min); Figueira de Castelo Rodrigo (Mon–Fri 2 daily, Sat 1; 1hr); Lisbon (4 daily; 4hr); Manteigas (Mon–Fri 2 daily; 1hr 20min); Sabugal (Mon–Fri every 2hr, Sat 1daily; 45min); Seia (1–3 daily; 1hr 15min); Trancoso (1daily on Mon, 2daily on Fri; 1hr 30min; otherwise, change at Celerico da Beira); Vila Nova de Foz Côa (Mon–Fri 1 daily; 1hr 30min); Viseu (2–6 daily; 1hr 15min).

Manteigas to: Belmonte (Mon–Fri 2 daily; 45min); Covilhã (Mon–Fri 2–3 daily; 1hr 30min); Guarda (Mon–Fri 2 daily; 1hr 20min).

Sabugal to: Belmonte (1 daily; 1hr 30min); Castelo Branco (1 daily, not Sat; 2hr); Guarda (Mon–Fri every 2hr, Sat 1 daily; 45min); Penamacor (1–2 daily, not Sat; 1hr); Sortelha (2 weekly on Tues & Thurs, plus Sept–June Mon–Fri 1 daily; 30min).

Seia to: Coimbra (1–3 daily; 1hr 45min); Covilhã (Mon–Fri & Sun 1 daily; 2hr); Gouveia (Mon–Fri 3 daily; 30min); Guarda (Mon–Fri 3 daily, Sun; 1hr 15min–2hr).

Trancoso to: Bragança (2 daily; 3hr); Celorico da Beira (2 daily; 25min); Guarda (1 on Mon, 2 on Fri; 1hr 30min); Lamego (Mon–Fri 1 daily; 1hr 30min); Lisbon (2 daily; 5hr); Viseu (2 daily; 1hr 10min).

Viseu to: Castelo Branco (1–5 daily; 3hr 10min); Celorico da Beira (8 daily; 45min); Coimbra (hourly; 1hr 25min); Covilhã (2–6 daily; 2hr); Guarda (2–6 daily; 1hr 15min); Lisbon (hourly; 3hr 30min–4hr); Porto (hourly; 1hr 50min); Trancoso (2 daily; 1hr 10min).

5

Porto and the Douro

ATLANTIC
OCEAN

SPAIN

N

CHAPTER 5 # Highlights

* **Douro river cruise** Pass under the city bridges, or let the vineyards drift by, on a trip along the "River of Gold". See p.330

* **Festa de São João** Porto's wildest annual festival, St John's Eve (June 23–24), sees riotous behaviour on an epic scale. See p.338

* **Fundação Serralves, Porto** Don't miss the contemporary art gallery, housed in an amazing building by Portugal's leading architect and surrounded by the city's most enjoyable park. See p.341

* **Touring the port-wine lodges, Vila Nova de Gaia** Wine tastings and tours galore are offered by the

country's leading port wine producers. See p.344

* **Amarante** A dreamy riverside town that you can reach by narrow-gauge railway. See p.357

* **Manor house stay, Lamego** This pretty town is known for its *quintas* and *solares* – manor houses that offer a restful night in peaceful surroundings. See p.363

* **Pinhão Road and river hug the Rio Douro** as far as this beautifully sited port-producing town. See p.370

* **Rock art at Foz Côa** Some of the world's oldest works of art, dating back over 20,000 years. See p.372

△ Port wine lodge

Porto and the Douro

P ortugal's second-largest city, **Porto**, is dramatically situated at the mouth of the Rio Douro, its old quarters scrambling up the rocky north bank in tangled tiers. As the de facto capital of the north, it's the hub of the region's road and railway system, and while you can't quite avoid it on any trip to the north of the country, nor would you want to. It's a massively atmospheric place, almost Dickensian in parts, well worth a couple of days of your time – more if you plan to make a serious attempt at touring the port-wine lodges of **Vila Nova de Gaia**, across the river. The coast north and south of Porto is an acquired taste, more for locals than tourists, but the pretty town of **Vila do Conde**, 45 minutes to the north, offers a taste of what's to come as you head into the Minho.

Inevitably, it's the **Rio Douro** ("River of Gold") that dominates almost every aspect of this region, winding for over 200km from the Spanish border to the sea, with port wine lodges and tiny villages dotted above the intricately terraced hillsides. It was once a wild and unpredictable river, though after the port-producing area was first demarcated in the eighteenth century, engineering works soon tamed the worst of the rapids and opened up the Douro for trade. The railway reached the Spanish border by the end of the nineteenth century, with the three narrow-gauge branch lines up the river's tributaries completed by 1910, while the building of hydroelectric dams and locks along the river's length in the 1970s and 1980s turned the Douro into a series of navigable ribbon lakes – it's now possible to cruise all the way from Porto to Barca d'Alva on the Spanish border.

The finest sections of the river are well to the east of Porto and the main route out of the city instead follows the N15 or much faster A4 motorway to the *vinho verde*-producing towns of **Penafiel** and **Amarante**. The latter is perhaps the single most attractive town in the region, set on the lazy tributary of the Rio Tâmega – the first of the Douro's splendid branch train lines runs up the valley here from the main-line station at Livração, about 60km from Porto. The **Douro train line** itself shadows the motorway from Porto and passes close to Penafiel, but shortly after Livração the line finally turns south to reach the Rio Douro and then heads upstream. The rough halfway point is marked by the commercial port wine town and cruise centre of **Peso da Régua**, the capital of Alto Douro ("Upper Douro") province – it's also the starting point of the Corgo branch train line to Vila Real in Trás-os-Montes (see Chapter 7). Just to the south of Régua, a slight detour can take in the delightful Baroque pilgrimage town of **Lamego**, home of Portugal's champagne-like wine, *Raposeira*, and the fascinating churches and historic buildings of its little-explored surroundings.

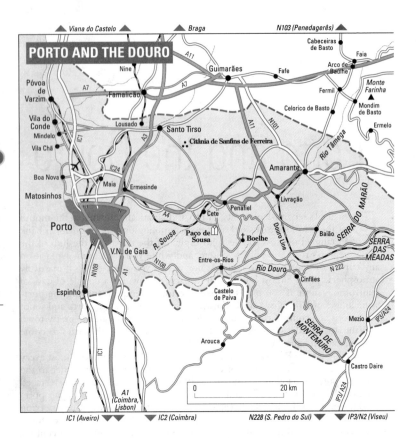

Beyond Régua starts the *Terra Quente* (hot lands) where the landscape becomes more noticeably Mediterranean, and where you begin increasingly to see the characteristic terraced Douro **vineyards**. They're seen at their best in August, with the grapes ripening, and in September, when the harvest has begun and leaves take on beautiful shades of gold and red. Régua also marks the point at which the Douro train line turns from a good route into a great one, sticking closely to the river from then on, cutting into the rock face and criss-crossing the water on a series of rickety bridges. It's one of those journeys that requires no other justification, though the idyllically set port wine town of **Pinhão** makes a tempting overnight stop, while from the rail junction of **Tua**, a little further east, carriages toil up the scenic Tua valley branch line to Mirandela in Trás-os-Montes (see Chapter 7). The main line hugs the river as far as its terminus at **Pocinho**, though the Douro river still has a way to go in Portugal, winding on to the border at **Barca d'Alva**. However, following the uppermost reaches of the Portuguese Douro is impossible by road beyond Pinhão, with the N222 finally veering well south of the river to reach the extraordinary collection of outdoor palaeolithic rock engravings near the otherwise unremarkable town of **Vila Nova de Foz Côa**.

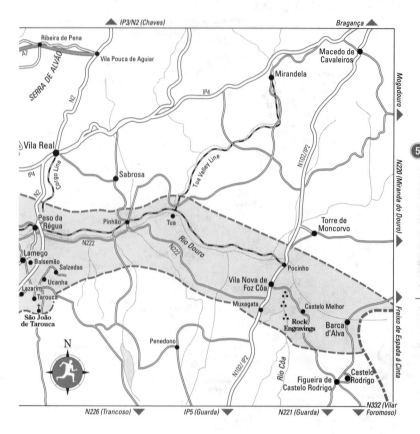

Map labels: IP3/N2 (Chaves), Bragança, Ribeira de Pena, Macedo de Cavaleiros, Vila Pouca de Aguiar, Mirandela, SERRA DE ALVÃO, A7, N2, IP4, Mogadouro, Vila Real, N102/IP2, N220 (Miranda do Douro), Sabrosa, Tua Valley Line, Corgo Line, IP4, N2, Peso da Régua, Pinhão, Tua, Torre de Moncorvo, Lamego, N222, Rio Douro, N222, Pocinho, Balsemão, Salzedas, Ucanha, Vila Nova de Foz Côa, Freixo de Espada à Cinta, Lazarim, Tarouca, Muxagata, Castelo Melhor, São João de Tarouca, Rock Engravings, Barca d'Alva, N, Penedono, Rio Côa, Castelo Rodrigo, N102/IP2, Figueira de Castelo Rodrigo, N332 (Vilar Foromoso), N226 (Trancoso), IP5 (Guarda), N221 (Guarda)

Porto

As with Lisbon, it's hard not to like **PORTO**. A large city, maybe, but it's also a beguiling one, with a lengthy history – it was known in Roman times as *Portus Cale* (the "sheltered port"). However, there the comparison with the capital ends: as the saying goes: "Coimbra studies, Braga prays, Lisbon shows off and Porto works". Rather than a prettified tourist destination, it's a busy commercial city whose fascination lies more in its riverside setting and day-to-day life.

The prosperous business core – surrounded by well-to-do suburbs as well as depressed housing estates – is tempered by a kernel of cramped streets, ancient alleys and antiquated shops largely untouched by planners. But since 2001, when Porto was declared European City of Culture, the city's streets and squares have been turned upside-down in a flurry of construction work, including the provision of a new metro system. Many historic buildings have been restored, particularly in the riverside *bairro* of **Ribeira** – now a UNESCO World Heritage Site – where the waterfront cafés and restaurants are an obvious attraction. This apart, there is only a handful of true tourist sights in the **city centre**, including the landmark Clérigos tower, the cathedral, and a couple of good museums. The one must-see attraction, the contemporary art gallery and park at the **Fundação de Serralves**, is a short way out of the centre, and most

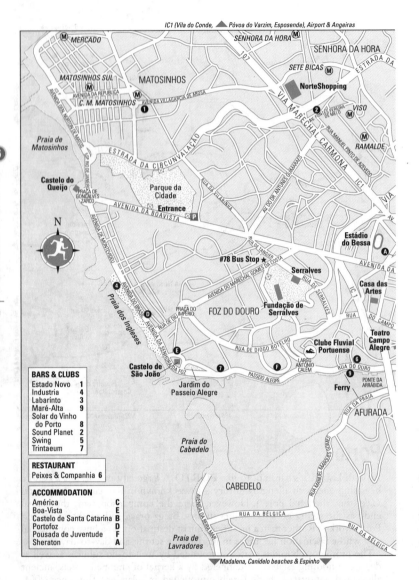

BARS & CLUBS

Estado Novo	1
Industria	4
Labarínto	3
Maré-Alta	9
Solar do Vinho do Porto	8
Sound Planet	2
Swing	5
Trintaeum	7

RESTAURANT

Peixes & Companhia	6

ACCOMMODATION

América	C
Boa-Vista	E
Castelo de Santa Catarina	B
Portofoz	D
Pousada de Juventude	F
Sheraton	A

▼Madalena, Canidelo beaches & Espinho ▼

visitors also choose to take the antique tram out to the local beach at **Foz do Douro**, at the mouth of the River Douro. For many, though, it is the port wine trade that defines the city, with its centre of operations at **Vila Nova de Gaia** (just Gaia to locals), on the south bank of the river, the home of the famous port wine lodges.

Arrival

The **airport** (information on ☎229 432 400, ⓦwww.ana.pt) is 13km north of the city in Maia, where there's a bank, ATMs, 24-hour exchange bureau, car

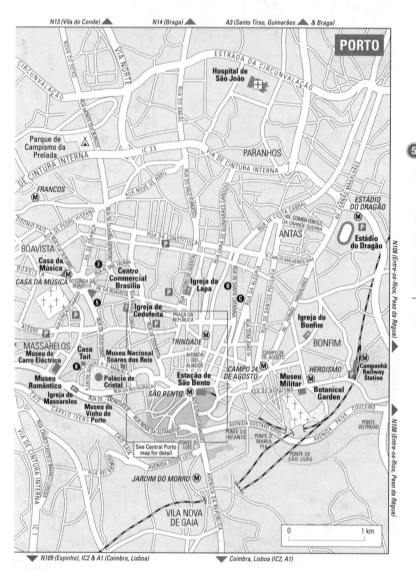

rental companies, and a turismo counter (daily 8am–11.30pm; ☎229 412 534). The **metro** (one-way travel ticket €1.35; see "City transport – Andante card" p.329) runs you directly into the centre in around half an hour – change at Estádio do Dragão for Casa da Música (for Boavista hotels), Trindade, Aliados or Bolhão (for city-centre hotels), or São Bento or Campanhã (for onward train services). **Taxis** from the airport into the centre cost around €20. Make sure you get a taxi from the authorized rank outside arrivals and not one touting his services – some of these drivers might as well wear an eye-patch and carry a cutlass.

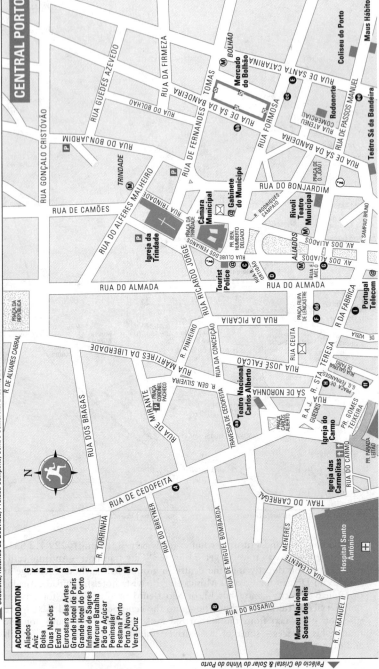

▲ Cedofeita, Rotunda da Boavista, Prelada Campsite, Centro Comercial Brasília, Boavista Stadium & Serralves

▲ Antas & Bonfirm

▲ Palácio de Cristal & Solar do Vinho do Porto

CENTRAL PORTO

ACCOMMODATION

Aliados	G
Aviz	K
Bolsa	N
Duas Nações	H
Estoril	A
Eurostars das Artes	B
Grande Hotel de Paris	I
Grande Hotel do Porto	E
Infante de Sagres	F
Mercure Batalha	L
Pão de Açúcar	D
Peninsular	J
Pestana Porto	O
Porto Novo	M
Vera Cruz	C

RUA GONÇALO CRISTÓVÃO

RUA DE ÁLVARES CABRAL

RUA GUEDES AZEVEDO

RUA DA FIRMEZA

RUA DO BOLHÃO

RUA DE SÁ DA BANDEIRA

RUA DE FERNANDES TOMAS

BOLHÃO

Mercado do Bolhão

RUA DE SANTA CATARINA

Maus Hábitos

Coliseu do Porto

RUA FORMOSA

Rodonorte

Teatro Sá da Bandeira

RUA DE PASSOS MANUEL

RUA ATENEU COMERCIAL

RUA DO BONJARDIM

RUA DE CAMÕES

TRINDADE

RUA DO ALFERES MALHEIRO

RUA TRINDADE

Igreja da Trindade

PRAÇA DA TRINDADE

Câmara Municipal

Gabinete do Municipé

PR. BENJ. HUMBERTO DELGADO

R. RODRIGUES SAMPAIO

Rivoli Teatro Municipal

R. SAMPAIO BRUNO

RUA DO ALMADA

RUA RICARDO JORGE

Tourist Police

RUA R. ORTIGÃO

RUA CLUBE FENIANOS

ALIADOS

AV. DOS ALIADOS

IRIA E J. DE MELO

RUA DO ALMADA

R DA FABRICA

Portugal Telecom

PRAÇA FILIPA DE LENCASTRE

RUA DA PICARIA

R. PINHEIRO

RUA DA CONCEIÇÃO

RUA CEUTA

DE VIZELA

RUA MÁRTIRES DA LIBERDADE

RUA DOS BRAGAS

RUA DE MIRANTE

PRAÇA CORONEL PACHECO

RUA JOSÉ FALCÃO

R. GEN. SILVEIRA

TRAVESSA DE CEDOFEITA

SÁ DE NORONHA

RUA STA TERESA

RUA GALERIA DE PARIS

G.G. FERNANDES

Teatro Nacional Carlos Alberto

PRAÇA CARLOS ALBERTO

PRAÇA DE PARIS

R.A.J. GUEDES

Igreja do Carmo

Igreja das Carmelitas

RUA DO CARMO

PR. PARADA LEITÃO

PR. GOMES TEIXEIRA

RUA DE CEDOFEITA

R. TORRINHA

RUA DO BREYNER

RUA DE MIGUEL BOMBARDA

RUA DO ROSARIO

R. D. MANUEL II

Museu Nacional Soares dos Reis

TRAV. DO CARREGAL

MENERES

RUA CLEMENTE

Hospital Santo António

N

SHOPS	
Casa Chinesa	bb
Casa Margaridense	aa
Chaminé da Mota	gg
CRAT	jj
FNAC	ee
Galo	hh
Garrafeira do Infante	ff
Lello & Irmão	ii
Pérola do Bolhão	cc
Porta Editora	dd

Igreja de S. Ildefonso

Garagem Atlântico

Batalha Cinema

Teatro Nacional São João

Police

City Wall

Casa-Museu Guerra Junqueiro

Funicular dos Guindais

Ponte Dom Luís I

RUA DO DUQUE DE LOULE

PASSEIO DAS FONTAINHAS

AVENIDA G. EIFFEL

RUA MIRADOURO

RUA DE S. LUÍS

RUA DO SOL

ROSA

RUA AUGUSTO

RUA CIMO DA VILA

PRAÇA DA BATALHA

RUA 31 DE JANEIRO

RUA DA MADEIRA

R. DO CATIVO

R. DO LOUREIRO

RUA CHÃ

EST. S. BENTO

Estação de São Bento

PRAÇA ALMEIDA GARRETT

STCP

PRAÇA DA LIBERDADE

AV. D. AFONSO HENRIQUES

SÃO BENTO

Paço Episcopal

Sé

City Wall

AV. DE VIMARA PERES

Tunnel

BARREDO

RIBEIRA

CAIS DA RIBEIRA

Vila Nova de Gaia

5

PORTO AND THE DOURO

R. DOS CLÉRIGOS

RUA DO CONDE

R. DAS CARMELITAS

PRAÇA DE LISBOA

Igreja & Torre dos Clérigos

RUA DAS FLORES

RUA MOUZINHO DA SILVEIRA

Torre Medieval

Igreja dos Grilos

RUA DOS MERCADORES

RUA DE SÃO JOÃO NOVO

Mercado Ferreira Borges

Casa do Infante

Igreja da Misericórdia

RUA FERREIRA BORGES

R. DR. SOUSA VITERBO

Police

Teatro de Marionetas

Palácio da Bolsa

Igreja de S. Francisco

Medieval Tower

RUA DA ALFÂNDEGA

RUA S. NICOLAU

R. REBOLEIRA

Universidade

Palácio da Justiça

Jardim da Cordoaria

Cadeia da Relação

Mosteiro de São Bento da Vitória

Palácio de S. João Novo

Ig. de S. João Novo

RUA AFONSO ALBUQUERQUE

RUA DA RESTAURAÇÃO

RUA NOVA DE ALFÂNDEGA

Ig. de S. Pedro de Miragaia

Alfândega (Museu dos Transportes e Communicações)

Rio Douro

0 — 200 m

Long-distance (international, intercity and ALFA Pendular) trains call at **Estação de Campanhã**, 2km east of the city centre. With a ticket to Porto you can simply change on to any local train for São Bento station, a five-minute ride away – the next departures are shown on the monitors in the ticket office. Campanhã is also on the metro, or it's a €5 taxi ride into the centre.

Estação de São Bento is the city-centre station (for suburban and regional services), facing Praça Almeida Garrett. There's a metro station here, taxis outside and the STCP transport office opposite (see "City transport"), while buses can be caught from the station and in nearby Praça da Liberdade. Note that São Bento can be a bit of a zoo, with hawkers and touts much in evidence, while ongoing construction work outside the station adds to the initial confusion.

Buses to Porto arrive at stops and garages all over the city, though most are fairly central. The Garagem Atlântico on Rua Alexandre Herculano, near Praça da Batalha, is a hub for several companies including the national operator Rede Expressos; Rodonorte stops on Rua Ateneu Comercial, near Bolhão market; Minho services tend to stop near Praça da República, north of the centre (near Trindade metro); while Eurolines (international services) and several others use Campo 24 de Agosto, 1km east of the centre (on the metro).

Driving into Porto is to be avoided, if at all possible – the city centre is congested and the one-way system confusing. You don't need a car to see the city, so best advice is to park where you can and use public transport. The major suburban metro stations have lots of parking – particularly at the football stadium, Estádio do Dragão – or use one of the many signposted city-centre car parks or garages; following signs for "Centro" or "Aliados" will send you into the maelstrom. Garage **parking** is expensive – around €1 an hour between 8am and 8pm, slightly cheaper overnight – but you'll have little choice if your hotel doesn't have parking, as on-street **metered parking** (€0.60/hour in the centre) is limited to two hours (though it's free after 8pm and at weekends).

See "Listings", p.252, for all airport, bus and train departure and contact details.

Information

There are three **city turismos** (and an office at the airport) where you can pick up a free map, and get information about accommodation, restaurants and current events – the main office is the one by the town hall at the top of Avenida dos Aliados. The same practical information is on the city council's excellent **website**, ⓦwww.portoturismo.pt (also in English). The city turismos sell guidebooks, walking itineraries and the **Passe Porto** (€7.50 one day, €15.50 three days), which gives unlimited bus and tram travel plus discounts for or free entry to many museums and monuments, theatre tickets, tours and shops. The main turismo also has a useful transport enquiries desk (Loja da Mobilidade; see "City transport" below).

The **ICEP office** is an arm of the national tourist authority and isn't really for city information but more for general enquiries about the rest of northern Portugal. There's also a turismo on the riverfront in **Vila Nova de Gaia**, geared almost exclusively to pointing you towards the various port wine lodges – they have a useful map showing lodge locations and opening hours.

Posto de Turismo Central Rua Clube dos Fenianos 25, top of Av dos Aliados ☎ 223 393 470. Mid-June to mid-Sept Mon–Fri 9am–7pm, Sat, Sun & hols 9.30am–6.30pm; mid-Sept to mid-June Mon–Fri 9am–5.30pm, Sat, Sun & hols 9.30am–4.30pm.

Posto de Turismo Zona Histórica Rua Infante Dom Henrique 63 ☎ 222 060 412. Mid-June to mid-Sept Mon–Fri 9am–7pm, Sat, Sun & hols 9.30am–6.30pm; mid-Sept to mid-June Mon–Fri 9am–5.30pm, Sat, Sun & hols 9.30am–4.30pm.

Tourist Welcome Centre Casa da Câmara, Terreiro
da Sé, opposite the cathedral ☎223 325 174. Mid-
June to mid-Sept Mon–Fri 9am–7pm, Sat, Sun &
hols 9.30am–6.30pm; mid-Sept to mid-June Mon–
Fri 9am–5.30pm, Sat, Sun & hols 9.30am–4.30pm.
ICEP Pr Dom João I 43, one block east of Aliados
☎222 057 514, ⓦwww.visitportoandnorth.com.

Mid-June to mid-Sept Mon–Fri 9am–7.30pm, Sat,
Sun & hols 9.30am–3.30pm; mid-Sept to mid-
June Mon–Fri 9am–7pm, Sat, Sun & hols
9.30am–3pm.
Posto de Turismo, Vila Nova de Gaia Av Diogo
Leite 242, next to Sandeman ☎223 703 735,
ⓦwww.cm-gaia.pt. Mon–Sat 10am–6pm.

City transport

Although Porto sprawls for eleven kilometres from the coast inland, most sights
lie within the compact and very hilly centre. You'll be able to walk – or perhaps
more accurately, climb – between all the city-centre attractions, but you'll have to
use the public transport system to get out to the Serralves art museum, the coast
and the airport. There's an extensive bus network, and a brand new metro system
and funicular railway, while a couple of old tram lines still remain in service.

The local transport authority, **STCP** (☎808 200 166, ⓦwww.stcp.pt), has a
useful website (English version available) and telephone information service, or
you can call into the **STCP office** (Mon–Fri 8am–7.30pm, Sat 8am–1pm),
opposite São Bento station, where you can pick up a route map and information and buy passes and tickets. At the **Loja da Mobilidade** in the main city
turismo (July–Sept daily 9am–7pm; Sept–June Mon–Fri 9am–5.30pm, Sat, Sun
& hols 9.30am–4.30pm; ☎800 220 905) you can find out all the same information, and pick up a transport guide (in English) detailing city ticket and taxi
prices, car park locations and other useful stuff.

To use the metro, trams, funicular, suburban trains and some of the buses you
need an **Andante** card (€0.50; ⓦwww.linhandante.com), available from station
ticket machines, the STCP office, Loja da Mobilidade and other marked
Andante shops and kiosks (Lojas Andante). You then credit the card with one,
two or ten trips, which are priced according to your destination – the whole
region is divided into concentric colour-coded zones, though everywhere
you're going to want to go in Porto all falls within the same (Z2) central zone.
Current price for a single trip in the central zone is €0.85. You hold the ticket
in front of the validation machine on the bus or tram, or at the platform – you
can change transport for free within the hour. When you've used up your one,
two or ten credits, simply re-charge the card with more at a machine. It sounds
complicated, but in practice it isn't, and there are instructions in English on
every machine and at every station. The only caveat is that the Andante system
doesn't yet extend to all the city's buses (see below) so check you're likely to get
the use out of it before you charge the card up with more than one or two trips.
Alternatively, you can buy a **24hr Andante card** (€3), or there are so-called
"Euro fare" **passes** valid for one day (€4) or three days' (€9) travel on everything in the Andante system.

Buses

Major **city bus stops** include Praça Almeida Garrett opposite São Bento
station, Praça da Liberdade at the bottom of Avenida dos Aliados, Jardim da
Cordoaria, and the interchange at Casa da Música metro station. Each major bus
stop displays a route map and timetable – note that ongoing roadworks often
shift the site of some stops, or even alter routes. Normal **hours of operation**
are 5am to around 9pm, followed by an extensive **nightbus** service running
approximately hourly until 5am. Parts of the very hilly historic zone are covered
by minibuses on the ZH line (daily 8am–7pm) – you'll see the stops as you

PORTO AND THE DOURO | Porto

329

trudge around but as departures are only every 45min or so, it's usually not worth waiting for one.

The Andante system doesn't cover all the city bus routes – for example, currently not the useful #78 to Serralves art museum and Foz do Douro, or the #32, #57 or #91 buses across the bridge to Vila Nova de Gaia. In this case, you'll have to buy a specific bus **ticket** – either €1.30 for a single journey from the driver, or much cheaper in advance from newsagents or kiosks at the main bus stops (ask for a T1 for 2 journeys €1.55, or 10 journeys €6.65).

The metro

The **metro system** (Ⓦ www.metrodoporto.pt) runs on five lines, A to E, underground in the city centre and then overground to the airport and to suburban destinations. Hours of operation are daily from 6am to 1am (departures every 10–30min), and you need an Andante card to use the system. Other than for the ride in from the airport, or for the trip up the coast to Vila do Conde, the metro isn't particularly useful for sightseeing, though there are handy city-centre stops at Trindade, Aliados, Bolhão and São Bento, and you can also use it to go to the Casa da Música at the Rotunda da Boavista and FC Porto's stadium, Estádio do Dragão, in the northeast of the city. A spectacular ride to know about is Line D (from Trindade, Aliados or São Bento), which crosses the river to Vila Nova de Gaia along the top tier of Ponte Dom Luís I – after enjoying the view you can get off at Jardim do Morro and walk down to the Gaia riverside.

Trams, funicular and taxis

Porto's **trams** (*eléctricos*) currently run on three interconnected lines, basically the 5km from the Ribeira along the river to Foz do Douro, with a branch from the Igreja do Carmo at Cordoaria in the city centre; to go all the way to the coast at Foz do Douro (25min), you have to change halfway at Massarelos (where the tram museum is). The service operates daily (9.15am–6.45pm, departures every 15–30min), and you use your Andante card or other pass.

The quickest way from the eastern end of the city centre down to the Ponte Dom Luís I (for Vila Nova de Gaia) and Ribeira is to take the **Funicular dos Guindais** (every 10min: June–Sept Sun–Wed 8am–10pm, Thurs–Sat 8am–midnight; Oct–May Sun–Thurs 8am–8pm, Fri & Sat 8am–10pm; use Andante card); the upper entrance is below Praça da Batalha, down Rua Augusto Rosa; the lower is right by the bottom tier of the bridge. After a ninety-metre crawl through a tunnel, the carriage drops rather thrillingly down a painfully steep 1-in-3 gradient beside the medieval city wall.

Otherwise, **taxis** are pretty reasonable – a typical cross-town ride costs €5–7 – and most squares have taxi ranks (or see "Listings", p.253, for cab companies).

Tours and cruises

You can book all tours and cruises at **Porto Tours** (Mon–Fri 9am–5.30pm, Sat 9.30am–1pm & 2–6.30pm, Sun & hols 9.30am–3pm; ☏222 000 073 or 222 000 045, Ⓦ www.portotours.com), a general information centre at the Torre Medieval, close to the Sé. The venture is a partnership between the authorities and tour and cruise operators, so it saves a lot of footwork; trips can also be booked at the main city turismo.

Porto's stock-in-trade is the **river cruise** along the Douro, with boats leaving from either the Ribeira or Vila Nova de Gaia riverside. Services are daily and frequent in the summer, much reduced or non-existent between November and February. The basic cruise is the fifty-minute **bridges cruise** (€7.50–10), though there are also evening and dinner cruises, and full-day or weekend cruises all the way up the Douro, with prices ranging from €45 to 200. The full-day and longer cruises all operate via the port wine town of Peso da Régua, halfway along the Douro, where – depending on your choice – you're shuttled around a port wine lodge or take a trip on a steam train.

There's also a hop-on-hop-off open-top **tour bus** (hourly departures from 10am; €10, under 12s €5, tickets available on board), which takes around 90 minutes to loop around the entire city; the start-point is Rua Dom Infante Henrique, just above Ribeira, though it also calls at Aliados and runs out to Serralves and Foz do Douro, then back in along the river and across the bridge to Gaia. Other options include the **road-train** from outside the cathedral (April–Sept; total loop 1hr 45min; departures daily at 10am, 11am, noon, 3pm, 4pm & 5pm; €6), or such diverse possibilities as themed **walking tours** (June–Oct; 3hr; €10) or **helicopter flights** over the city (€50–70).

Accommodation

Porto has a wide range of accommodation to suit all tastes and pockets, though it's best to book ahead, especially between June and September. Rooms start at €25, though many of the older **pensions** are dog-eared, noisy or dodgy, or all three – budget on €40 for something tolerable and en-suite. Nearly all the cheapest accommodation is in the city centre, rather than in the medieval streets nearer the river or by the river itself – as well as the places reviewed below, there are concentrations along Rua de Cedofeita, Rua do Alamada, around Avenida dos Aliados, and near Praça da Batalha.

The upmarket suburbs of Boavista and Serralves, a fair distance west of the centre, contain most of the city's four- and five-star **hotels**, but the suburban location is a drawback, meaning plenty of travelling to and fro. Only a few hotels have their own **parking**, but a handful have negotiated deals with nearby car parks for their guests. The **youth hostel** and municipal **campsite** are both also out of the centre, though easily reachable by bus – there are better-sited coastal campsites south across the river, at or near the Vila Nova de Gaia beaches of Madalena and Salgueiros, but these are a good 10km from the city.

The city centre and Ribeira hotels are all marked on the Central Porto map, p.326; all others, plus youth hostel and campsite, are shown on the Porto map, p.324.

City centre

Residencial dos Aliados Av dos Aliados, entrance at Rua Elísio de Melo 27-2º ☏ 222 004 853, ⓦ www .residencialaliados.com. Occupying a monumental late nineteenth-century building, the 38 rooms fill quickly in summer. Front rooms give dizzying views over the avenue, though ones at the back are quieter – you can save yourself around €10 if you don't want a/c. There's also a bar and coin-op Internet access, and public parking nearby. ❹

Pensão Aviz Av Rodrigues de Freitas 451 ☏ 222 008 937, ⓔ residencialaviz@sapo.pt. Just around the back of Batalha – decently priced en-suite rooms with cable TV. It's a friendly place, used to foreign tourists. ❷

Pensão Duas Nações Pr Guilherme Gomes Fernandes 59 ☏ 222 081 616, ⓦ www .duasnacoes.com.pt. A real budget gem, with updated rooms with satellite TV, fan and central heating, and double-glazed against the street noise. It's popular with backpackers, as some bunk-style rooms sleep four. Best to book ahead if you want a private bathroom. Also friendly English-speaking staff and Internet access. Breakfast not included. No credit cards. ❶

Pensão Estoril Rua de Cedofeita 193-1º ☏ 222 002 751, ⓦ www.pensaoestoril.com. You might need to look at a couple of rooms before settling on one – some have retained their original proportions, though others have been squeezed in (as have many of the elderly bathrooms). A few, however, have balconies overlooking a garden at the back, and it's generally cool and quiet. You can usually shave a few euros off by forgoing breakfast. ❷

🏃 **Hotel Eurostars das Artes** Rua do Rosarió 160–164 ☎ 222 071 250, ⓦ www .eurostarshotels.com. Porto's best boutique hotel (four-star) occupies an impressively restored town house in a residential and shopping district near Soares dos Reis museum. There's a garden and roof-deck, and plenty of space in the rooms which come with hardwood floors, six-foot-wide beds, flat-screen TVs, specially commissioned Porto photography and classy marble bathrooms. Special offers and advance bookings from €69. ❻

🏃 **Grande Hotel de Paris** Rua da Fábrica 27–29 ☎ 222 073 140, ⓦ www.ghparis.pt. Consistently recommended by readers, the "Grande Hotel" is actually more pension in price and feel. The building retains many of its original fittings, with period furniture and high ceilings, while nice touches proliferate – thick bathroom towels, a small garden, and a good breakfast served in a splendid drawing room. Rear rooms (more expensive) have balconies and old-town views. No parking, but airport shuttle available. ❸

Grande Hotel do Porto Rua de Santa Catarina 197 ☎ 222 076 690, ⓦ www.grandehotelporto .com. Porto's oldest hotel is steeped in nineteenth-century mercantile style, with tons of polished marble and crystal chandeliers, and an echoing gilt-tinged restaurant where the buffet breakfast is served. It's also in a very handy location, on the main pedestrianized shopping street. Rooms are on the dowdy side, but have all mod cons, and the fact it's only three stars means prices are pretty good – down to €55 a night during special summer promotions (check the website). Limited parking available. ❺

Hotel Infante de Sagres Pr Dona Filipa de Lencastre 62 ☎ 223 398 500, ⓦ www .hotelinfantesagres.pt. Old-school five-star hotel on six floors, its public areas, restaurant and bar lavishly furnished with Persian carpets, crystal chandeliers, Chinese porcelain and stained-glass windows. Rooms are elegant rather than luxurious, and have gleaming marble bathrooms. There's also an open-air patio for light meals, and a classy cocktail bar and restaurant. There's public parking nearby. ❼

Hotel Mercure Batalha Pr da Batalha 116 ☎ 222 043 300, ⓦ www.mercure.com. A large chain hotel, favoured by tour groups. Smart rooms in warm tones have matching bedspreads and curtains, and the bathrooms are pretty. Prices vary – there are some good deals – and breakfast isn't always included. Parking available for €7 a day. ❹

Residencial Pão de Açúcar Rua do Almada 262 ☎ 222 002 425, ⓦ www.residencialpaodeacucar .com. Well-kept, 1930s-era building with fifty reasonably large and quiet en-suite rooms with parquet floors – it's very popular. The best are indisputably the half-dozen at the top which open out onto a private terrace overlooking the town hall. Parking nearby costs €5 a night. ❹

Hotel Peninsular Rua Sá da Bandeira 21 ☎ 222 003 012, ⓔ hotel.peninsular@clix.pt. Comfortable family-run place with a range of rooms, all with private bath and TV, though you'll pay more for a/c, better bathrooms or a front view. The *azulejos* in the entrance reveal it to have been an outbuilding of the nearby church. ❶–❷, better rooms ❹

Residencial Porto Novo Rua Alexandre Herculano 185 ☎ 222 055 739, ⓦ www.residencialportonovo .com. Some along this street are grotty, short-time places, but this is a reliable budget choice for clean if old-fashioned en-suite rooms. Insist on the top floor where the rooms have magnificent river views from their terraces. ❶

Residencial Vera Cruz Rua Ramalho Ortigão 14 ☎ 223 323 396, ⓦ www.residencialveracruz.com. An elegant charmer disguised as a modern apartment block. There's almost a feeling of being in someone's very tidy house, and the pleasant rooms are painted in soothing colours and have decent bathrooms. Service is efficient and friendly. ❷

Ribeira

Hotel da Bolsa Rua Ferreira Borges 101 ☎ 222 026 768, ⓦ www.hoteldabolsa.com. A modernized, well-placed three-star hotel with a classical facade – it's just a 5min walk downhill to the river. Rooms are on the fussy side, with chintzy fabrics and repro furniture, but the staff are friendly and there's underground parking 200m away. Also airport pick-ups. ❹

Pestana Porto Pr da Ribeira 1 ☎ 223 402 300, ⓦ www.pestana.com. Enjoying the city's best location, atop the medieval wall next to the river, there's been little expense spared on the restoration of this cluster of sixteenth- to eighteenth-century buildings into a boutique-style four-star hotel. Most rooms face the Douro, and corner rooms also overlook the bridge. Also a nice contemporary restaurant, *Vintage* (expensive), which occupies a raised terrace above the river, where a few outdoor tables are lit by candles on the walls. Breakfast not usually included. ❻

North of the centre

Hotel América Rua de Santa Catarina 1018 ☎ 223 392 930, ⓦ www.hotel-america.net; 15min walk from the centre or bus #701/702/703 from

Mercado do Bolhão. Well-regarded mid-range choice with bright and relatively spacious a/c rooms, plus 24hr reception and private underground parking. There's also a bar and what the hotel optimistically calls a "winter garden" and we call a plexiglass conservatory with plants. ❸

🏃 **Castelo de Santa Catarina** Rua de Santa Catarina 1347 ☎ 225 095 599, ⓦwww .castelosantacatarina.com.pt; 15min walk from the centre or bus #701/702/703 from Mercado do Bolhão. A turreted folly of the most romantic kind makes a superb in-the-city retreat. Rooms aren't grand or expensive, but are furnished in period style and are perfectly comfortable, while breakfast is eaten in the lush *azulejo*-tiled gardens. There's parking too, and good off-season discounts. ❹

Boavista

Sheraton Hotel & Spa Rua de Tenente Valadim 146 ☎ 220 404 000, ⓦwww.sheratonporto.com; Casa da Música metro and taxi. The *Sheraton* has the five-star designer market wrapped up – a flash place of marble, steel and glass with elegant rooms featuring deep colours, hardwood furniture and massive beds. A "club" level offers a superior set of services, including flat-screen TV/DVDs and use of the Club Lounge; there's a cool bar and juice bar, plus impressive spa facilities and parking. Check the website for good deals. Breakfast not usually included. ❻

Foz do Douro

Hotel Boa-Vista Esplanada do Castelo 58 ☎ 225 320 020, ⓦwww.hotelboavista.com; bus #500 from São Bento. Ocean and river views are the

thing at this classy villa, set over the road from the fort at Foz – it's worth paying the extra (and booking in advance) to be able to see the water. It's only a three-star, so the rooms are comfortable if unexceptional, but there's a fine rooftop pool and sun terrace, plus bar, restaurant and parking. ❹

Residencial Portofoz Rua do Farol 155 ☎ 226 172 357, ⓦwww.portofoz.com; bus #78 from Bolhão metro. Head up to the third-floor reception in this apartment block for surprisingly characterful rooms featuring old fireplaces, wind-up blinds, carved beds and rugs; larger "suites" have armchairs and a terrace, while many rooms have partial sea views. It's nicely old-fashioned and quiet, but just two blocks from the beach. ❸, suite ❹

Youth hostel

Pousada de Juventude Rua Paulo da Gama 551, Pasteleira, 4km west of the centre ☎ 226 177 257, ⓦwww.pousadasjuventude.pt; bus #36 from Casa da Música metro interchange. Over 140 beds in four-bed dorms, plus around 30 self-contained twin rooms, with/without private bathroom. Facilities include a kitchen (meals available), bar, and arrangements for disabled guests. Reception open 9–10am & 6pm–midnight; it's essential to book ahead in summer. Dorm beds €14, high season €16, rooms ❷

Campsite

Parque de Campismo da Prelada Rua Monte dos Burgos, 3km northwest of the centre ☎ 228 312 616; bus #50 from Cordoaria. The closest campsite to the city centre – well-equipped, but with 650 pitches it's not exactly intimate. Open all year.

The city

The city centre is focused on the sloping boulevard of **Avenida dos Aliados**, with Praça da Liberdade at its southern end and **São Bento** train station just around the corner. The streets leading off the avenue form the main commercial area, notably along Rua Formosa and around the principal market, **Mercado do Bolhão**. South of the landmark **Torre dos Clérigos**, a labyrinth of medieval streets and alleyways tumbles below the **Sé** (cathedral) down to the waterfront **Ribeira** district, which is lined with restaurants, bars, clubs and cafés. Across the elegant two-tier **Ponte Dom Luís I**, on the south bank of the Douro, lies **Vila Nova de Gaia** and its port wine lodges; while trams and buses travel west along the north bank of the river from Ribeira to the beach suburb of **Foz do Douro**.

Throughout the city small town-house museums and elaborately decorated churches proliferate, but the only two essential cultural attractions are the applied art collections of the **Museu Nacional Soares dos Reis** and the world-class **Fundação Serralves** museum of contemporary art. Otherwise, tourism in Porto consists of lounging at a riverside café or lazing in the city's gardens, notably those of the **Palácio de Cristal** which hang high above the

An English-language pamphlet available from the main city turismo details four **architectural city walks**, each focusing on a particular style or theme. All major sights are included, but there's a lot of uphill legwork involved.

The city's oldest secular building is the **medieval** Alfândega Velha (or Casa do Infante), built in 1325, while from the same period date parts of the city wall flanking the Cais da Ribeira, completed in the reign of Dom Fernando. Unfortunately, most medieval churches and chapels were greatly altered in the eighteenth century, but the simple **Romanesque and Gothic** aesthetic remains apparent in the outward appearance of the Sé and the old church of Cedofeita – arguably Iberia's oldest Christian temple.

Porto's eighteenth-century churches provide one of the country's richest concentrations of **Baroque** architecture. The style was brought to Portugal by Italian painter and architect **Nicolau Nasoni** (1691–1773), who arrived in Porto at the age of 34, and remained here all his life. Together with local stonemason António Pereira, Nasoni bequeathed the city a marvellous legacy, characterized by his masterful conception of space, clever use of local granite and theatrical facades. The church and tower of Clérigos is perhaps his greatest work; others include the interior of the Sé, the adjacent Paço Episcopal, the facade of the Igreja da Misericórdia, and the churches of Carmo, Santo Ildefonso and São Francisco. All are remarkable for their decorative exuberance – notably cascading masses of intricate carvings, and lots of gold leaf – which reflects the wealth derived from Portugal's colonies.

In the second half of the eighteenth century, out went the luxuriant complexity of Baroque and in came the studied lines, pillars and capitals of ancient Rome and Greece. This **Neoclassical** period coincided with the booming port wine trade, which provided the necessary finance for the first concerted attempts at treating whole districts as architectural entities: broad avenues were opened, and much of the city's medieval wall gave way to riverside esplanades. Neoclassicism also incorporated hints of Gothic and Baroque art, but most of all, Islamic, which reached its apotheosis in the Salão Árabe of the Palácio da Bolsa.

By the turn of the twentieth century Porto's Neoclassicism had acquired a distinctly French Renaissance touch, thanks largely to the architect **José Marques da Silva** (1869–1947), who studied in Paris. His most notable works were São Bento railway station, the exuberant Teatro Nacional São João and the distinctly less elegant monument to the Peninsular War that dominates the Rotunda da Boavista. **Art Nouveau** saw little monumental expression in Porto, although several shops in this style survive, while the 1920s coincided with the establishment of the fascist **Estado Novo**, whose morose buildings reflected its overbearing character. The Palácio da Justiça facing the Cordoaria is a prime example, its blank facade bearing angular "heroic" sculptures (resembling those of contemporary Soviet socialist-realism).

Not until the 1950s did Porto see the emergence of a style of architecture that it could call its own, with the beginning of the so-called **Porto School**, centred on the city's School of Fine Arts. This proved fertile ground for many of Porto's contemporary architects, including Eduardo Souto Moura (Casa das Artes, and the conversion of the Alfândega), Alcino Soutinho (the conversion of the Casa-Museu Guerra Junqueiro; and Amarante's Museu Amadeo Sousa Cardoso), and – most famously – **Álvaro Siza Vieira**, best known for his redesign of Lisbon's fire-gutted Chiado district. In Porto, his masterpiece is the contemporary art museum at the Fundação Serralves (1999), but there are earlier works of his in Leça da Palmeira, north of the city: the imaginative Casa de Chá da Boa Nova (1963), a café-restaurant built into the rocks and with a grand ocean view, and the Piscina de Mar swimming pool (1966), similarly hidden in the rocks by the shore.

river. Getting out on the water itself is a must, and the various Douro cruises (see p.331) are the best way to see the city's famous **bridges** – there are five more besides the Ponte Dom Luís I, notably the Ponte do Infante, whose central 280-metre reinforced concrete arch is the world's longest, and further east upriver, Gustave Eiffel's iron railway bridge, Ponte Dona Maria Pia.

City centre

Not quite all roads lead to the central **Avenida dos Aliados** (just "Aliados" to locals) but most do. At the foot of the avenue – in the area known as Praça da Liberdade – are a couple of pavement cafés and an equestrian statue of Dom

△ Torre dos Clérigos

Pedro IV; at the head stands the statue of celebrated local boy Almeida Garrett (1799–1854), poet, novelist, dramatist and Liberal politician. Behind the statue at the top of the avenue, Porto's city hall, the **Câmara Municipal** (1920–56), was designed to look a good deal older than it is in order to fit in with the avenue's otherwise largely Neoclassical design. Off the bottom, southeastern, side of the avenue, the **Estação de São Bento** (1903) might be a mere train station but it's one of the city's grandest buildings, with an entrance hall containing 20,000 magnificent *azulejos*. These – somewhat arbitrarily – take on two great themes: the history of transport, and the history of Portugal, including the battle of Aljubarrota and the taking of Ceuta.

North of the station lies one of the busiest commercial areas, centred on **Rua Formosa**. Here you'll find a few surviving antiquated groceries, stocking *bacalhau*, bottles of port, cheese and smoked sausage, while the gates of the **Mercado do Bolhão** (Mon–Fri 8am–5pm, Sat 8am–1pm) loom large. This is an impressive wrought-iron construction on two levels, packed with stalls selling meat, fish, fruit and veg, though it also deals in handicrafts. It's particularly good for bread (sold from little cabins in the middle) and flowers – fresh and dried – as well as dried mountain herbs and teas, while one stall sells nothing but enormous mounds of garlic.

Just 300m west of Aliados the centre's main landmark is the Baroque **Torre dos Clérigos** (entrance on Rua São Filipe Nery; April–Oct daily 9.30am–1pm & 2.30–7pm; Nov–March 10am–noon & 2–5pm; €2), which towers 75m above the streets – it was the tallest structure in Portugal when completed in 1763 and, having puffed up the two-hundred-odd stairs, you can enjoy the sweeping views. Like the curious oval **Igreja dos Clérigos** beneath it (Mon–Sat 8.45am–12.30pm & 3.30–7pm, Sun 10am–1pm & 9–10.30pm), the tower was designed by the Italian architect Nicolau Nasoni (see feature on Porto's architecture), who was buried in the church at his own request.

West of the tower is the large block containing the science and other faculties of the **Universidade do Porto**. Students hang out in the pavement cafés flanking the western side, down Praça de Parada Leitão, while below the university building spreads the shaded **Jardim da Cordoaria**, sheltering impromptu card and chess schools beneath some gigantic plane trees. The imposing Neoclassical building to the south of the gardens – distinguished by 103, mostly barred, windows – was the city's former prison, the **Cadeia da Relação** (Tues–Fri 3–6pm, Sat & Sun 3–7pm; free). It was restored in the 1990s and the cells and a small exhibition can now be visited, while the ground floor houses the **Centro Português de Fotografia**. The collection includes the work of Scotsman Frederick William Flower (1815–1889), who spent much of his life in Porto and is considered a pioneer of Portuguese photography.

A steep drop down Travessa do Ferraz and Rua do Ferraz leads to the **Igreja da Misericórdia**, whose museum (Mon–Fri 9.30am–noon & 2–5.30pm; €1.50) contains a remarkable *fons vitae*, depicting Dom Manuel I with his wife Leonor and eight children, richly clothed, kneeling before the crucified Christ. Academics still dispute the nationality of the unknown artist, but no matter: it's an exceptional example of Flemish-style realism in the manner of Van Eyck and the School of Brussels.

On the north side of Cordoaria, above the university, the eighteenth-century **Igreja do Carmo** (Mon–Fri 8am–noon & 2–5pm, Sat 8am–noon, Sun 7.30am–1pm) is instantly recognizable by virtue of its deliriously over-the-top exterior *azulejos*, the work of Silvestre Silvestri (1910–12). Inside, the elegant gilt carvings – including all seven altars – are among the finest examples of Portuguese Rococo. The older and rather more sober **Igreja das Carmelitas** is almost adjacent, but not quite, as a law stipulated that no two churches were to share the same wall (in this case perhaps to hinder amorous liaisons between the nuns of Carmelitas and the monks of Carmo). As a result, what is probably the **narrowest house in Portugal** – barely a metre wide, and with its own letterbox – was built between them and, though now empty, remained inhabited until the 1980s.

The Sé and around

Set on a rocky outcrop, a couple of hundred metres from São Bento station, the **Sé** (April–Oct daily 8.45am–12.30pm & 2.30–7pm; Nov–March closes 6pm; free) commands a wide terrace with fine views over the rooftops of old Porto. Despite wholesale remodelling of its interior in the eighteenth century, the cathedral retains the austere, fortress-like lines of its twelfth-century origins. On the north tower (the one with the bell), look for the worn bas-relief depicting a fourteenth-century ship – a reminder of the earliest days of Portugal's maritime epic, when sailors were still inching tentatively down the west Saharan coastline in fear of monsters. Inside, the blend of Baroque, original Romanesque and Gothic architecture is a strange marriage, not much aided by the prevailing gloom. However, you can escape into the **cloisters** (April–Oct Mon–Sat 9am–12.15pm & 2.30–6pm, Sun & hols 2.30–6pm; Nov–March closes 5.15pm; €2), with their magnificent Baroque *azulejos*, from where a grand staircase climbs to the dazzling chapterhouse for sweeping views from the casement windows.

The shaper of much of eighteenth-century Porto, Nicolau Nasoni, left his mark both on the Sé – he designed the cloister staircase, the silver altarpiece and much more – and on the surrounding buildings. On the south side of the Sé stretches the grandiose facade of the **Paço Episcopal** (not open to the public), the medieval archbishop's palace that was completely rebuilt by Nasoni in 1737. He's also thought to have designed the house behind and below the cathedral, at Rua de Dom Hugo 32, that's now the **Casa-Museu Guerra Junqueiro** (Tues–Sat 10am–12.30pm & 2–5.30pm, Sun 2–5.30pm; €2, free at weekends), later the home of the poet Guerra Junqueiro (1850–1923), who spent a lifetime collecting Iberian and Islamic art. Seljuk pottery, glassware, paintings and glazed earthenware are exhibited here in rooms recapturing the atmosphere of the poet's last home.

Rua de Dom Hugo curls around the south side of the cathedral to merge with crumbling stairways and alleys that plunge down to the riverside. It's a medieval maze that would have been demolished in most other European cities – the rickety houses have grown upwards into every available space, while children try their best to play ball games on the steep staircases.

Ponte Dom Luís I and the Ribeira

Porto's iconic double-decker bridge, **Ponte Dom Luís I**, provides one of the city's favourite photo opportunities – enchanting if you can catch it on mornings when the overnight mist is clearing. The bridge was inaugurated in 1886 to replace the short-lived Ponte Pênsil, part of whose obelisk-shaped pillars stand rather pointlessly beside it. You can walk across either level to the port wine lodges, bars and restaurants of Vila Nova de Gaia – there's traffic on the bottom level, the metro across the top – and the upper level crossing especially (a nerve-jangling 60m above the water) is worth doing at least once.

West of the bridge on the Porto side stretches the **Ribeira** – Porto's water-front – which has changed dramatically in recent years, from a rough dockside cargo zone to one of the city's major tourist attractions. The arcaded quayside, the **Cais da Ribeira**, is one long run of restaurants and cafés, with hundreds of outdoor tables looking across the river to the port wine lodges on the other side. At the western end of the quayside is the sloping **Praça da Ribeira**, with more outdoor cafés, a floating cube fountain in the middle and a more traditional one at the rear bearing the Portuguese coat-of-arms.

It's hard these days to look beyond the tourist cafés and souvenir stalls, but come down in the morning – before the parasols and blackboard menus have been put out – and the Ribeira still ticks along in local fashion. Between the postcards and touristy ceramics you'll find grocery stores, a butcher's, and a warehouse or two, piled high with bags of potatoes. Sections of the city's medieval wall survive along the quayside, while behind the arcades and heading up towards the cathedral is a mazelike warren of stepped alleys that cock a snook yet at the riverside gentrification.

Ribeira is now a major nightlife destination, much of it centred on Praça da Ribeira and the surrounding alleys, like the delightfully poky Rua da Fonte Taurina and Rua da Reboleira – along the latter, at no. 59, is a **medieval tower-house**, lived in since the fourteenth century. Turn north instead up Rua da Alfândega for the **Casa do Infante**, where Prince Henry the Navigator is said to have been born in 1394. It's an impressive mansion, constructed in 1325, which for over five centuries served as the Crown's customs house. Miraculously, the building's original fabric has remained largely intact and now contains the city **archives** (Mon–Fri 8.30am–5pm; temporary exhibitions here are free) and a **museum** (Tues–Sat 10am–12.30pm & 2–5.30pm, Sun 2–5.30pm; €2) displaying finds from *in situ* excavations that revealed the remains of a large Roman palace.

Over on Rua Infante Dom Henrique stands the **Igreja de São Francisco** (daily: July & Aug 9am–8pm; June, Sept & Oct 9am–7pm; Feb–May 9am–6pm; Nov–Jan 9am–5.30pm; €3), perhaps the most extraordinary church in Porto (now deconsecrated). It's the city's only truly Gothic survivor, dating from the fourteenth century, but the interior was completely transformed in the eighteenth century by a fabulously opulent refurbishment. Altar, pillars, even the ceiling, drip with gilded Rococo carvings, reaching their ultimate expression in an interpretation of the Tree of Jesse on the north wall. The church's small museum is housed in the catacombs below, and here, beneath the flags of the cellar, is an *ossário* – thousands of human bones, cleaned up and stored to await Judgement Day. Until 1839, public cemeteries didn't exist in Porto and the dead were buried in and around churches in an effort to bring them closer to God.

Adjoining the church, but facing the square, Porto's stock exchange – the **Palácio da Bolsa** – is a pompous nineteenth-century edifice with a vast Neoclassical facade, whose keepers are inordinately proud of it. During the half-hour **guided tours** (daily: April–Oct 9am–7pm; Nov–March 9am–1pm & 2–6pm, Ⓦwww.palaciodabolsa.pt; €5) they dwell, with evident glee, on the enormous cost of every item, the exact weight of every piece of precious metal, and the intimate details of anyone with any claim to fame ever to have passed through the doors. The highlight is the Salão Árabe, an oval chamber modelled on designs from Granada's transcendent Alhambra Palace; here the guide's superlatives achieve apotheosis. However, you don't need to buy a ticket to see the elegant iron-and-glass-covered courtyard, whose side rooms contain a craft/jewellery store, wine bar and shop, and *O Comercial* restaurant – a rather grand space that is open to the public for a good-value lunch.

Along the river

It's around 2km from the Ribeira along the riverfront pavement and quayside to the Ponte da Arrábida (heading west towards Foz do Douro). This is a good half hour's walk, which is enough for most people to get a flavour of the Douro; there are several attractions en route, and you can then jump on the tram or the #500 bus back to the city centre or on to Foz and the beach.

First stop is the imposing Neoclassical Alfândega, or customs house, constructed on the riverbank just west of Ribeira between 1860 and 1880. It's a vast building, originally designed to store the cargo of up to forty ships, which has been renovated as the **Museu das Alfândegas** (Tues–Fri 10am–6pm, Sat, Sun & hols 3–7pm; €3; Ⓦwww.amtc.pt). Its mighty rooms and storage areas, supported by cast-iron columns, are the backdrop for a variety of exhibitions using computers and other trickery to recount the history of Porto, its trades and industries. The building also encompasses the Museum of Transport and Communications, which has always had a place here – the "car through time and space" exhibition entertainingly relates the development of the motor car to social and economic advances.

A few hundred metres west of here, at Rua de Monchique 45–52, the **Museu do Vinho do Porto** (Tues–Sun 11am–7pm; €1) occupies an eighteenth-century former wine warehouse. It traces the history of the port wine trade, a dry subject in many ways though tackled here with vim – there are plenty of activities for children. Further downriver, the *azulejo*-fronted **Igreja do Corpo Santo de Massarelos** is unlikely to be open, but it has an interesting lineage. Founded first in 1394, and rebuilt in 1776, it's dedicated to São Pedro Gonçalves Telmo (St Elmo), patron saint of sailors. Prince Henry the Navigator was a member of the Almas do Corpo Santo brotherhood, founded in Porto by mariners who survived a storm when returning from England. The brotherhood kept a number of fighting ships, seeing action fending off north African pirates.

The trams make a fitting halt 200m further along, outside the **Museu do Carro Eléctrico**, the city's tram museum (Tues–Fri 9.30am–12.30pm & 2.30–6pm, Sat, Sun & hols 3–7pm; Ⓦhttp://museu-carro-electrico.stcp.pt; €3.50), where you can see Iberia's oldest streetcar (1872) alongside other gleaming vintage specimens.

The **Ponte da Arrábida** looms just beyond, and though it may be the least attractive of the city's six bridges, it represents a mean feat of engineering. Spanning 270 metres, and supported by a single arch, the collapse of similar bridges previously had stirred something of a media frenzy and, when the final section was winched into place, everyone expected it to tumble away.

It didn't, and its designer, Porto's Edgar Cardoso, went on to receive worldwide acclaim.

A few hundred metres west of the bridge, anglers try their luck in the murky water from a small quayside on Rua do Ouro (the stop is "Fluvial"), by the floating pontoon bars. Small **ferries** (every 15min or so, 6am–11pm; €1 each way) cut across the river from here to **Afurada** on the south bank. This used to be the centre of Portugal's *bacalhau* industry, with cod once strung out to dry along the shore all the way to the river's mouth. Afurada still contains a lively fish market (Tues–Sat mornings) and a number of cheap and cheerful restaurants; or back on the Porto side there's a run of dirt-cheap *tascas* on the raised section of **Rua do Ouro** just beyond the ferry dock.

Museu Nacional Soares dos Reis

A five-minute walk from the Cordoaria, behind the hospital, stands the **Museu Nacional Soares dos Reis**, at Rua Dom Manuel II 44 (Tues 2–6pm, Wed–Sun 10am–6pm; €3, free Sun & hols 10am–2pm; Ⓦ www.mnsr-ipmuseus.pt). Serralves aside, it's the best museum in Porto and in fact was Portugal's first designated art museum, founded in 1833 to preserve works confiscated from dissolved monasteries and convents. The present building, into which the collection moved in the 1940s, was once a royal residence that served as French headquarters in the Peninsular War.

The museum takes its name from sculptor António Soares dos Reis (1847–89), whose best-known work is here – *O Desterrado* (The Exile) – along with other pieces by his pupil, Teixeira Lopes (born across the river in Vila Nova de Gaia), as well as a formidable display of Portuguese art from the sixteenth to twentieth centuries. But it's the **applied** and **decorative art** that's perhaps most accessible to the general visitor, especially since remodelling and expansion have improved much of the presentation – the museum contains excellent collections of gold jewellery, religious silverwork, Portuguese glassware, earthenware and textiles, delicate Chinese ceramics, noble French furniture and painted screens and laquered cabinets from the Far East. Special exhibitions concentrate on particular periods, artists or themes, and you could spend hours here just browsing; there's a garden and a good **café**, serving a daily lunch.

Jardim do Palácio de Cristal

Follow Rua Dom Manuel II for 100m or so past the Soares dos Reis museum and you reach the **Jardim do Palácio de Cristal** (daily: April–Sept 8am–9pm, Oct–March 8am–7pm; free), Porto's finest central park, dominated by a huge domed pavilion built in 1956 to replace the original 1860s iron-and-glass "Crystal Palace". The pavilion hosts all sorts of concerts and events, and there's a popular open-air self-service café by the lake, but it's the surrounding **gardens** that are the real draw – partly formal, partly wooded, with an avenue of lime trees and lovely river views from high vantage points on the south side. The municipal library is sited near the main entrance, while other buildings, galleries and pavilions host exhibitions, workshops, summer concerts and children's activities.

The west side of the gardens adjoin the grounds of two neighbouring *quintas* – there's also access from the cobbled Rua de Entre Quintas, which is a left turn off Rua Dom Manuel II, past the park entrance. There are attractive shaded botanical gardens at **Casa Tait**, Rua de Entre Quintas 219 (Tues–Fri 10am–12.30pm & 2–5.30pm, Sat & Sun 2.30–6pm; free), while the house itself contains the city's numismatic museum. More often visited is the adjacent **Quinta da Macieirinha**, a stately nineteenth-century house that contains both the **Museu Romântico** (Tues–Sat 10am–12.30pm & 2–5.30pm, Sun 2–5.30pm; €2) – dedicated to Carlos Alberto, exiled King of Piedmont and Sardinia, who died here in 1849 – and the famed **Solar do Vinho do Porto** (Mon–Sat 2pm–midnight; ⓦwww.ivp.pt). The headquarters of the Port Wine Institute provide elegant surroundings in which to sample port wine – there are scores available by the glass – and on a sunny day there's no nicer place to call a halt than the terrace overlooking Gaia and the river.

Rotunda da Boavista

The northwestern edge of the city centre – around 2km from downtown Aliados – is marked by the large park-cum-roundabout popularly known as the **Rotunda da Boavista**. It's overlooked by a huge column bearing a lion astride a French eagle, celebrating the victory of the Portuguese and British in the Peninsular War.

There's no call to come up here save to see Rem Koolhaas' **Casa da Música** (take the metro to the station of the same name) on the northwestern side of the roundabout. Porto's contemporary concert hall – a vast white wedge on a bare esplanade – looks as if the Mother Ship has landed, an impression reinforced by the steel staircase leading up into the black maw of the entrance. There are guided visits in English daily at 11.30am and 4pm (€2); all the concert and contact details are on p.351.

By way of extreme contrast, a few blocks to the east, down Avenida da Boavista and then right along Rua Aníbal Cunha, is the very simple **Igreja Românica de Cedofeita**, whose name means "built quickly". Reputed to be the oldest Christian building in the Iberian peninsula, it was supposedly built by the Suevian king Theodomir in 556 AD. However, the existing Romanesque building is a thirteenth-century refashioning of a church whose existence can only be dated certainly to 1118. Cedofeita is unique, however, in being Portugal's only Romanesque church to have kept its original dome, supported by bulky exterior buttresses.

Fundação Serralves

If there's a must-see cultural attraction in Porto it's the contemporary art museum and park at the **Fundação Serralves** (April–Sept Tues–Fri 10am–7pm, Sat, Sun & hols 10am–8pm, museum hours sometimes extended to 10pm; Oct–March Tues–Sun 10am–7pm; €5, park only €2.50, both free Sun 10am–2pm; ⓦwww.serralves.pt), 4km west of the centre; bus #78 runs there directly from Rua Fernando Tomas (opposite Bolhão metro), stopping on Avenida Marechal Gomes da Costa, just around the corner from the main entrance.

The **Museu de Arte Contemporânea** (1999) is the work of Porto architect Álvaro Siza Vieira, and is a minimalist triumph of white facades and terraces strikingly set in an overwhelmingly green park. There's no permanent collection, but instead several changing exhibitions a year draw on the works of Portuguese and international artists, mainly from the 1960s to the present day. Other exhibitions are held in the separate, pink Art Deco **Casa de Serralves** in the grounds. Details of all exhibitions and forthcoming events are posted on the website, or there's an information desk inside the museum.

You can get a flavour of the building from the outside, and from the terrace café, more formal restaurant and museum shop (all free to enter), which means if the exhibitions aren't to your taste, you miss nothing by just visiting the **park**. Indeed, many people prefer this to the museum itself and it's easy to spend a lazy afternoon here, winding along the swept gravel paths and clipped lawns of the formal gardens before descending wooded tracks to the herb gardens and farmland beyond, grazed by goats and cattle. There are some art installations dotted around – notably a huge Pop Art trowel (Claes Oldenburg) near the main entrance – and a tea house in a glade with a vine colonnade. July and August see a sequence of "Jazz no Parque" (jazz in the park) **concerts** held in the gardens.

Foz do Douro

Foz do Douro, formerly a fishermen's quarter but a distinctly more upmarket beach suburb these days, is literally the "end of the Douro", around 5km from the city centre. It's on several bus routes, including the #500 from São Bento (and the #78, on from the Serralves museum and park), but it's a nice idea to take the **tram** along the river at least one way – catch #1 (from Ribeira) or #18 (Igrjeja do Carmo) down to the terminus at Massarelos and change there on to the #1 which stops by the riverside gardens in Foz. The confluence of river and ocean is dominated by the squat **Forte São João Baptista**, still a military base, beyond which stretch several kilometres of coves and beaches, backed by the cafés and bars of Avenida do Brasil, which becomes the hub of Porto's summer nightlife. At the northern end stands the **Castelo do Queijo**, so-named (Cheese Castle) because it was built upon boulders that apparently looked like cheese. From here, Avenida da Boavista (and the #502 bus) runs straight back into the city. The water at Foz isn't the cleanest – being downstream from Matosinhos port and its refinery – but the beaches are fine, sheltered bathing areas are marked out and children can paddle in the rock pools.

Vila Nova de Gaia and the port wine lodges

Cross to the south side of the Douro river, over the Ponte Dom Luís I, and you leave the city of Porto for the separate town of **Vila Nova de Gaia** (or just Gaia), though the distinction is irrelevant to visitors. The riverfront here – facing Porto's Ribeira – has been similarly developed in recent years with a long line of cafés, bars and restaurants; cruise boats dock along the esplanade, while the wooden craft with sails are known as *barcos rabelos*, the traditional boats once used to transport wine casks downriver from the Douro port estates. The views are, if anything, better from Gaia than from

---

A day by the sea

The local coast, north and south of the city, is much loved by Porto's inhabitants, but visitors tend to be more impressed by the beaches of the Minho further north or the Beira Litoral to the south. The chilly Atlantic near Porto has had pollution problems in the past, both from oil refinery discharges and from untreated effluent from Porto and the Douro. Things are improving as water treatment plants are opened, though bathers are still advised only to swim in marked areas.

The easiest beach escape is to **Foz do Douro** (tram or bus #500) – really, if all you want is a lie on the sand and a beachside beer, there's no need to go anywhere else. **Matosinhos** (metro Line A), further north, is where the locals go to eat seafood and for a night's clubbing, while the **Vila Nova de Gaia** beaches (bus #57), across the Douro to the south, have extensive sands and big campsites. Further south still is the resort of **Espinho**, 18km from Porto (very frequent local trains from São Bento, 35min), once the darling of northern Portugal's monied classes, though largely ruined by unchecked construction since the 1970s. The better day out is by metro (Line B) to the north of the city: the old seafaring town of **Vila do Conde** (p.353) is easily the best target, though the brash resort of **Póvoa do Varzim** just beyond (end of the line, 1hr from Porto) might tempt you with its 8km of sands.

VILA NOVA DE GAIA

BARS & CLUBS

Boganicafe	3
Hard Club	1

RESTAURANTS

Adega e Presuntaria Transmontana	2
Barão de Fladgate	6
Casa Adão	5
Real Indiana	4

▷ *Real Companhia Velha*

♀ Port Wine Company

the Porto side, looking back across to a largely eighteenth-century cityscape, with few modern buildings intruding in the panoramic sweep from Palácio de Cristal gardens to cathedral towers. The quickest way here from Porto's upper town is to take the funicular down from near Praça da Batalha and

△ Sandeman lodge, Vila Nova de Gaia

walk across the bridge; or buses #57 and #91 run from São Bento across the bridge and along the Gaia riverfront.

Gaia, of course, is completely dominated by the **port wine** trade, whose company lodges and warehouses spell out their names in huge letters across the roofs. The lodges are lined along the riverfront and tucked away up the steep eighteenth-century back streets, and though most have long since been bought by multinationals – including famous brands like Cockburn – they still try hard to push a family image. Almost without exception, they offer **tastings and tours**, conducted in English, with a view to enticing you to buy their product. Most lodges are open daily between May and October; some close at weekends in winter, or are only open then by appointment; where there's an entrance fee, usually just a couple of euros, the amount is deducted from anything you buy. Tours of the smaller, lesser known companies (like Barros, Almeida or Cálem) tend to be more personal than those of larger producers, but they are all pretty informative and you'll soon know the difference between a tawny and a ruby, and which vintages are best. For much more on port and its history, including the best lodges to visit, turn to the colour section.

Eating: cafés and restaurants

There are hundreds of places to eat in Porto, from little old-town *tascas* and Art Nouveau **cafés** to riverfront designer **restaurants**. However, on any lengthy stay you might struggle for variation, despite the size of the city and number of establishments. Menus are broadly similar, with grilled fish, seafood and *bacalhau* as staples. The local **speciality** is *tripas* (tripe) – the story goes that the inhabitants selflessly gave away all their meat for Infante Dom Henrique's expeditions to North Africa, leaving themselves only the tripe, and it's been on the menu ever since, cooked *à moda do Porto* (stewed with *chouriço* and white beans). Also typically *portuense* are *caldo verde* (a thick vegetable soup) and grilled sardines, whilst courtesy of returning emigrants is the *francesinha* ("little French thing") – a doorstep of steak, sausage and ham between toasted bread, covered with melted cheese and a peppery tomato-and-beer sauce.

Both sides of the Douro have become the default places to spend the evening. Along Porto's **Cais da Ribeira** a dozen largely touristy fish restaurants are installed under the arches, with more simple places hidden along Rua da Fonte Taurina and other back streets. Over the bridge in **Vila Nova de Gaia**, there's a mix of traditional fish places and international restaurants and bars – Spanish tapas, Indian and Italian restaurants, Brazilian grill house and Irish pub are all present. However, the cheapest meals tend to be found in the **city centre** – there are lots of budget places around the university (facing the Jardim da Cordoaria), up Rua do Bonjardim, south of the Clérigos church (on streets like Rua dos Caldeireiros) and near Praça da Batalha. In the main market, the Mercado do Bolhão, you can also eat a very cheap lunch of grilled sardines and the like at a couple of little cafés amid the flower stalls.

For an explanation of **restaurant price categories** (inexpensive, moderate, etc) see p.47. Most of the following cafés and restaurants are marked on the map on pp.346–347 – exceptions are noted.

City centre

Abadia Rua do Ateneu Comercial 22–24 ☎222 008 757. A big, busy and unpretentious tiled restaurant dishing out a daily changing menu geared towards lunching locals. There's *bacalhau* and *tripas*, naturally, but also things like tuna salad with black-eyed beans, roast pork with pineapple or *rojões* (cubes of pork) with chestnuts. A *meia dose* (half portion) of most things, more than enough for one, costs €7–8. Moderate.

Antunes Rua do Bonjardim 525 ☎222 052 406. Rustic eating house that famously uses only wood-fired ovens, in which are prepared the daily house specials – notably melt-in-the-mouth roast pork, served with gravy and sticky roast potatoes. Add a baked apple for dessert, and a carafe of house *rosado*, and you'll eat for €10. Closed Sun and 4 weeks Aug–Sept. Inexpensive.

Confeitaria do Bolhão Rua Formosa 339 ☎222 009 291. Busy, traditional cake and coffee shop opposite the market, repainted in Art Nouveau style. They do good value *pratos do dia* in the restaurant above, and there's an associated old-style grocery store up the street. Inexpensive.

O Escondidinho Rua de Passos Manuel 144 ☎222 001 079. "The little hidden place" – it isn't, particularly – has a country-house interior (plus TV, unfortunately) that's the backdrop for French-influenced cuisine. Steaks, hake and sole are menu mainstays, costing €12–15, though a daily all-in lunch menu for a similar price is a good buy. Closed Sun. Expensive.

Café Majestic Rua de Santa Catarina 112 ☎222 003 887. Best known of the Belle Epoque cafés, with outdoor tables at the foot of the pedestrianized shopping street, perfectly preserved decor (celestial cherubs, bevelled mirrors, carved chairs and wood panelling) from 1921, and braided waiters flitting about to the strains of the *Blue Danube*. You have to come once for coffee or afternoon tea – or maybe have a Caesar salad, club sandwich or *francesinha* for lunch (mains around €10). Moderate.

Mariazinha Rua Belomonte 2 ☎222 009 137. The city's most idiosyncratic gourmet dining experience hides itself away behind a battered town-house facade. There's no real menu, just a presentation of that day's dishes, according to the whim of the chef, accompanied by wines (lots of wines) to suit. Dinner only; reservations advised. Closed Wed. Very expensive.

Café Progresso Rua Actor João Guedes 5, off Pr Carlos Alberto ☎222 322 647. Founded by academics from the nearby university in 1899, it's still popular with students though it's been given a contemporary facelift – hardwood furniture and contemporary art prevail, while food tends towards croissants, snacks and sandwiches. Closed Sun. Inexpensive.

Tripeiro Rua de Passos Manuel 195 ☎222 005 886. A consistently good bet for generous portions of filling northern nosh – mains cost €13–14. It's much loved for its tripe, but the menu also runs to half a dozen daily soups, salt-cod served various ways, plenty of grilled meat and a selection of creamy desserts. Closed Sun. Expensive.

Ribeira

Casa Cardoso Rua da Fonte Taurina 58 ☎222 058 644. A simple stone backstreet *tasca* that's hard to beat on price for grilled fish. There's no outdoor seating, and not much atmosphere, but the owners are friendly and it's cool in the heat of the day. Closed Sun. Inexpensive.

Dom Tonho Cais da Ribeira 13–15 ☎222 004 307. Contemporary bar and restaurant overlooking the river, where anyone who's anyone comes when in town – weekend reservations advised. It combines chrome, pine and glass with the original granite walls, and the menu has been given a twist as well, with a modern take on traditional dishes – seabass in a salt crust is a house special and there's an enormous wine list. There's a snackier bar-and-grill offshoot over the river on the Gaia esplanade, near the bridge. Expensive.

Filha da Mãe Preta Cais da Ribeira 40 ☎222 055 515. Built into the arches, the *azulejo*-decorated upper floor provides a river view, or you can sit outside. It's resolutely local fare – *arroz de marisco*, stuffed squid, *tripas* and grilled fish – but is well-regarded. The unusual name ("daughter of the black mother") comes from an original establishment, "Mãe Preta", once popular with charcoal makers from upriver. Closed Sun. Moderate.

O Muro Muro dos Bacalhoeiros 87 ☎222 083 426. A reliable dinner-only place (from 4pm) on the raised wall above the quayside – sardines and other fresh fish (€7–9) are grilled outside over charcoal, and you can drink until late or just come to snack. Moderate.

Massarelos

The following is marked on the Porto map, p.324.

Peixes & Companhia Rua do Ouro 133, on the riverbank west of Arrábida bridge ☎226 185 655; tram to Foz or bus #500 from São Bento/Ribeira, get off at "Fluvial". A cosy renovated town house with river views from its upper-floor dining room. The elegance is rather diffused by the MOR music, but it's a popular business lunch place – the menu is chalked on little slate menus, and it's all grilled fish, depending on the day's catch, preceded by *petiscos* of *presunto*, pickled veg, olives and the like. Closed Sun. Expensive.

Leça da Palmeira

The following is marked on the Porto map, p.324.

Casa de Chá da Boa Nova Leça da Palmeira, 3km north of Matosinhos ☎229 951 785; bus #45 or #76 from Casa da Música interchange. This sophisticated seaside café and restaurant was Porto architect Álvaro Siza Vieira's first work, tucked dramatically into the boulders on the

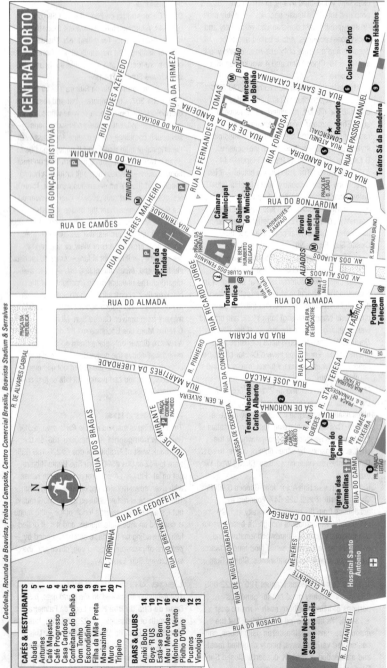

▲ Antas & Bonfirm

◀ Cedofeita, Rotunda da Boavista, Prelada Campsite, Centro Comercial Brasília, Boavista Stadium & Serralves

▲ Palácio de Cristal & Solar do Vinho do Porto

CAFÉS & RESTAURANTS

Abadia	5
Antunes	1
Café Majestic	6
Café Progresso	4
Casa Cardoso	15
Confeitaria do Bolhão	3
Dom Tonho	18
Escondidinho	9
Filha da Mãe Preta	19
Mariazinha	11
Muro	20
Tripeiro	7

BARS & CLUBS

Aniki Bobo	14
Boys 'R US	10
Está-se Bem	17
Meu Mercedes	16
Moinho de Vento	2
Piolho D'Ouro	8
Pucaros	12
Vinologia	13

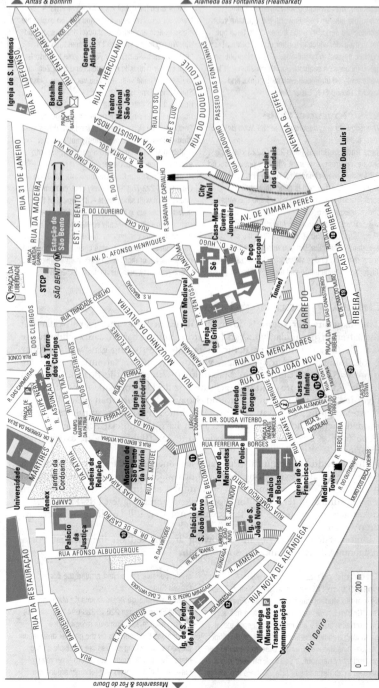

▶ Vila Nova de Gaia

5

PORTO AND THE DOURO

Rio Douro

200 m

0

▼ Masserelos & Foz do Douro

seashore, with sweeping views from the dining room. The hike up here is worth it if you take your architecture seriously – the buses go to Leca but not to the café, which is further up the seafront avenue, beyond the lighthouse. The restaurant menu focuses on seafood, but it's possible just to while away an afternoon with café drinks and snacks. Closed Sun. Expensive.

Vila Nova de Gaia
The following are marked on the Vila Nova de Gaia map, p.343.

Casa Adão Av Ramos Pinto 252 ☎ 223 750 492. Simple riverfront restaurant with low prices (around €7 for fish, even cheaper for meat). It's well used to tourists, but the food is good (though it sometimes takes an age to come) and the wine cheap. Inexpensive.

🏃 **Barão de Fladgate** *Taylor's*, Rua do Choupelo 250 ☎ 223 742 800. It's a punishing uphill hike, but you're rewarded by the finest river and bridge views from the terrace of *Taylor's* port wine lodge restaurant. A fleet of smart waiters is on hand, but it's not really formal – lovely for an *alfresco* lunch – and not too expensive either (mains around €10, though drinks soon add up). What's more, you don't see vegetarian and "light" dishes like these anywhere else in Porto – soya burger with wild rice, pasta and New Zealand mussels, or hake with steamed vegetables. Closed Sun dinner. Expensive.

Real Indiana Cais de Gaia ☎ 223 744 422. Upscale Indian dining – it makes a change for Porto, and the rich curries and tandoori dishes are pretty authentic (or at least pretty authentically British in style). There's also a great terrace with excellent views. Expensive.

Adega e Presuntaria Transmontana Av Diogo Leite 80 ☎ 223 758 380. Lovely cool, contemporary dining room with stone walls – it's typical of the newer places along here though its USP is meat rather then fish, specifically specialities from Trás-os-Montes. You can choose to eat tapas-style, from smoked meat platters, a large cheese selection and other snacks, or more substantial meals (grilled veal is one speciality, octopus another). Expensive.

Drinking and nightlife

The main city **bar scene** is down at Ribeira or across the river in Gaia – at the latter, in particular, you can hop from lounge bar to dance club in the Cais de Gaia development at the far end, where soaring glass walls, infinity pools, fountains and roof terraces vie for the punters' attention. There are more bars out to the west in Massarelos (particularly the floating pontoon bars of Rua do Ouro) and in beachside Foz do Douro, while most of Porto's favoured **clubs** tend to be around Boavista, in suburban Ramalde near NorteShopping, and way out in Matosinhos. For **port wine tasting** in refined surroundings there are two main bars, the official *Solar do Vinho do Porto* (city centre) and the *Vinologia* wine bar (Ribeira), both excellent in their own way.

Most bars don't open until 10pm and stay open until 2am, later at weekends (often until 4am); exceptions are noted below. **Clubs** open (or really only get going) at midnight, and most stay open until 4 or 5am or later, with a standard €5–15 admission fee, more for special events and top guest DJs. The entrance ticket acts as a voucher for free drinks, not that it'll last long as prices are pretty high.

Unless stated otherwise, the following are marked on the Central Porto: restaurants, cafés, bars and clubs map, p.346.

City centre
Piolho D'Ouro Pr Parada Leitão no phone. The best of the student cafés facing the university, the "Golden Louse" is open all day and has a nice terrace, but it's a good drinking spot too. It's got a long tradition behind it – class graduation plaques line the walls, and it used to be quite the revolutionary hangout. If you kick off your night here you can get a cheap bite, or there are plenty of inexpensive *tascas* just around the corner. Closed Sun.

Solar do Vinho do Porto Quinta da Macieirinha, Rua de Entre Quintas 220 ☎ 226 094 749; see the "Porto" map, p.324. Patrician manor house overlooking the Douro that's the genteel destination for port wine tasting. Scores are available by the glass – from little more than a euro – served by old-school waiters who pad forlornly around the granite bar and terrace. Mon–Sat 2pm–midnight; closed Mon when a public holiday.

Ribeira

Aniki Bóbó Rua da Fonte Taurina 36–38 ☎ 223 324 619. Named after a cult 1930s film about Ribeira's kids, this cool DJ bar is popular with fashionable darlings, artists and musicians, and there's usually a strong gay crowd too. Closed Sun & Mon.

Está-se Bem Rua da Fonte Taurina 70–72 ☎ 222 002 249. A nice little *tasca* where a pre-club crowd hangs out, probably because it's cheap and there's no cover charge. Opens 8pm; closed Sun.

O meu Mercedes é maior que o teu Rua da Lada 30 ☎ 222 082 151, ⓦ www.omeumercedes .com. Hands-down winner of the world's silliest bar name contest ("My Mercedes is bigger than yours") – although there's no name on the door – but inside it's a friendly joint which attracts regulars. Closed Sun & Mon.

Púcaros Bar Rua de Miragaia 55 ☎ 222 087 051. A relaxed, cellar-like pub with medieval stone arches and bare walls bearing temporary art and photography exhibitions. Closed Sun.

Vinologia Rua de São João 46 ☎ 936 057 340, ⓦ www.vinologia.eu.com. A short way up the hill from the river, this French-owned wine bar-cum-tasting shop is a cosy place to get acquainted with Porto's top tipples. The enthusiastic English-speaking staff really know their stuff, and can recommend all sorts of ports from mainly small producers – from €1.50 a glass or tasting sessions from €6–20. Daily 2pm–midnight.

Vila Nova de Gaia

The following are marked on the Vila Nova de Gaia map, p.343.

Boganicafé Cais de Gaia ☎ 223 747 070. A lounge bar minus the lounge – instead, drape yourself across a moulded plastic seat on the elevated terrace for some of Porto's best views. Daily 10am–midnight, Fri & Sat until 1am.

Hard Club Cais de Gaia 1158 ☎ 223 753 819, ⓦ www.hard-club.com. A pretty dramatic conversion of a Gaia warehouse is one of the city's best venues for Portuguese and international DJs, live bands and guest appearances. Days and styles vary, but you get anything from free jazz to drum and bass here; check the website for the current schedule.

Boavista

Labirinto Rua Nossa Senhora de Fátima 334 ☎ 226 063 665, Casa da Música metro; see "Porto" map, p.324. Just a couple of minutes off

the Rotunda, this is a great bar in a converted house, with a shaded back garden, gallery space and occasional live music and other events. You get a really mixed crowd here.

Swing Pr Eng Amaro da Costa 766, off Rua Júlio Dinis ☎ 226 090 019, Casa da Música metro; see "Porto" map, p.324. The longstanding disco-goers' number one, with five bars, a lively straight/gay clientele and a daily changing music policy, though it's all fairly mainstream.

Ramalde

Chic Rua Manuel Pinto de Azevedo 2 ☎ 226 163 220, Ramalde metro; see "Porto" map, p.324. Glitzy house and techno temple. Fri & Sat only.

Sound Planet Av Fontes Pereira de Melo 449 ☎ 226 107 262, Viso metro; see "Porto" map, p.324. Popular club for international house sounds. Thurs–Sat only.

Massarelos

Maré Alta Rua do Ouro, west of Ponte da Arrábida ☎ 226 162 540; bus #500; see "Porto" map, p.324. Bar-restaurant under twin teepees on a moored pontoon – you can't miss it. It's open for lunch, but it's more of a late-night place for trendy young things. Closed Mon.

Foz do Douro

Indústria Centro Comercial do Foz, Av do Brasil 843 ☎ 226 176 806; bus #500; see "Porto" map, p.324. A sophisticated dance club that gets packed in summer – it's no longer the bee's knees in Porto, though a thoroughly good time is still had by a cosmopolitan crowd. Thurs–Sat only.

Trintaeum Rua Passeio Alegre 564 ☎ 226 107 567, ⓦ www.tritaeum.com; bus #500; see "Porto" map, p.324. "31" is a hip bar on Foz's riverfront avenue – sounds are very varied, courtesy of a full roster of resident and guest DJs. Closed Sun.

Matosinhos

Estado Novo Rua Sousa Arosa 722 ☎ 229 385 989. Converted sardine factory that's a current favourite for serious dancing and drinking. Thurs–Sat only.

Gay and lesbian

Boys 'R US Rua Dr Barbosa de Castro 63 ☎ 917 549 988. The number-one port of call – a decent bar, lashings of fashionable tunes and drag acts for discerning punters of all ages. Wed & Fri–Sun only.

Moinho de Vento Rua Sá Noronha 78. Well-known gay and lesbian bar, best and busiest at the weekends, when the dance floor heaves. Wed–Sun only.

Arts, music and culture

The city has a full cultural programme and there will be something worth catching almost any night of the year. The big new concert hall, the **Casa da Música**, has a wide musical remit, but it's also home of the **Orquestra Nacional do Porto** (Ⓦwww.onp.pt), one of the country's leading symphony orchestras. Otherwise, concerts of all kinds are held at a variety of venues, notably the Casa das Artes and the central Coliseu do Porto. In summer, too, there's always a series of **outdoor concerts** in places like the Jardins do Palácio de Cristal and at the Serralves park. Local **theatre** is almost always in Portuguese, though there's a strong tradition of contemporary dance and other visual and experimental genres. On the whole, though, visitors are more likely to go to the **cinema**, as films in Portugal are shown in their original language. You can check film listings in the paper (see below), or

Porto's festival calendar

You can check exact festival and event dates on Porto's tourism website Ⓦwww.portoturismo.pt/en/eventos. The following are the annual highlights.

February *Fantasporto* (Ⓦwww.fantasporto.online.pt), the respected international fantasy, sci-fi and thriller film festival, is held during the last two weeks at the Teatro Municipal Rivoli.

March–April *Festival Intercéltico do Porto* – Celtic sounds from Portugal, Galicia, Brittany, Wales, Ireland and Scotland.

May *Fazer a Festa* (Ⓦwww.teatroartimagem.org) – international theatre festival held in a "theatre village" in the gardens of the Palácio de Cristal. Also at the Palácio de Cristal, at the Biblioteca Almeida Garrett, is *Corta!* (Ⓦwww.corta.com.pt), the international short film fest.

June *Santo António* (closest Sat to June 13) sees services in the churches of Massarelos and Bonfim districts, in honour of the protector of brides and newly-weds. For the city's biggest popular festival, *São João* (June 23–24), see the feature on p.338. June 29 is *São Pedro*, with more street decorations, music and dancing. The month also marks the start of the respected PortoCartoon World Festival (at the Museu da Imprensa, until Sept), one of the three biggest festivals of caricature in the world.

July International Folklore Festival held during the last week. The annual *Festa da Cerveja* (beer fest) begins in Foz do Douro and runs through to August. Also the annual GLBT Porto Pride march and celebration.

August *São Bartolomeu* (Sun after Aug 24) – a procession in Foz do Douro culminating in a health-giving bath (*banho santo*) in the sea. On the last weekend there's the *Noites Ritual*, an exclusively Portuguese rock (plus hip hop, reggae and pop) festival at the Palácio de Cristal.

September Market stalls, folk music and dancing near Campanhã train station for the festival of *Nossa Senhora de Campanhã* (closest Sun to Sept 8). The *Porto Jazz Festival* is held during the month, and the *Concurso Internacional de Música* begins (international music competition, held at the Rivoli Teatro Municipal). The *Festival Internacional de Marionetas do Porto* (FIMP) is a 10-day festival of dance, circus, puppetry and theatre.

December Children wait for the arrival of *São Nicolau* (Dec 6) by boat at the Ribeira, to escort him along Rua da Alfândega to the Igreja de São Francisco. December 8 is a national holiday, with a feast held in Foz do Douro in honour of Nossa Senhora da Conceição, followed by a night procession though Foz's streets. Also the *Feira de Artesanato* (handicraft fair), a two-week bash at the Palácio de Cristal.

head out to one of the multiplexes in the suburban shopping malls, like NorteShopping.

Listings for all cultural events are given in the quarterly *Agenda do Porto* (in Portuguese and English; Ⓦ www.agendadoporto.pt), available at the turismos. Porto's daily newspaper, the *Jornal de Notícias* (Ⓦ www.jnoticias.pt), is also a useful source of information. **Tickets** for most shows (usually in the range €10–40) can be bought in advance from the FNAC books and music stores (see "Shopping", below), which also promote gigs, events and talks.

Concert halls

Casa da Música Av da Boavista 604 ℡ 220 120 220, Ⓦ www.casadamusica.com; Casa da Música metro. Porto's major concert hall is a striking building with an international music programme, not just classical concerts and recitals but early and contemporary music, fado, world and folk. Tickets cost as little as €2, though most concerts are €5–20.

Coliseu do Porto Rua de Passos Manuel 137 ℡ 223 394 940, Ⓦ www.coliseudoporto.pt. City-centre venue for international acts, from rock, indie and pop to ballet, classical and big-stage musicals.

Arts centres

Casa das Artes Rua de Ruben A 210, off Rua do Campo Alegre ℡ 226 006 153; bus #78 from Bolhão. Hub of the city's alternative arts scene, with daily art-house movies in addition to theatre, classical recitals and concerts.

Maus Hábitos Rua Passos Manuel 178-4° ℡ 222 087 268, Ⓦ www.maushabitos.com. "Bad Habits" is an in-crowd venue for alternative music and arts, including dance productions, jazz, funk, indie and world music gigs, and art exhibitions.

Theatres

Rivoli Teatro Municipal Pr Dom João I ℡ 223 392 200, Ⓦ www.rivoli.culturporto.pt. Home of the tireless Culturporto arts organization, and a reliable venue for theatre, contemporary dance and music. Some foreign productions are in their original language (subtitled in Portuguese).

Teatro do Campo Alegre Rua das Estrelas 57 ℡ 226 063 017; bus #31 from Casa da Música interchange. A superb auditorium worth checking out for performances from the Porto.Bando theatre company (an exuberant blend of music, theatre, burlesque and all-round weirdness).

Teatro de Marionetas do Porto Teatro de Belomonte, Rua de Belomonte 57 ℡ 222 083 341, Ⓦ www.marionetasdoporto.pt. Portugal's best puppet theatre, run by real fans of the genre, and presenting children's productions in addition to thought-provoking commentaries on contemporary themes.

Teatro Nacional São João Pr da Batalha ℡ 223 401 900, Ⓦ www.tnsj.pt. The city's major theatre and opera venue, for Portuguese and international productions – it's a gorgeously over-the-top building (1909), inspired by Charles Garnier's Paris Opera.

Shopping

One of the city's abiding pleasures is its surviving **traditional shops**, often in beautiful Art Nouveau or Art Deco premises, in which you'll find anything from *bacalhau* and dusty bottles of vintage port to filigree gold jewellery and antiques. Even right in the city centre, people still do much of their day-to-day shopping at small, independent shops – in the line of shops below the Clérigos tower, for example, you could, if you so wished, buy an apple, a pair of shoes, a pig's tongue or a bucket. The main **market**, Mercado do Bolhão still sees brisk business too, though most of the other neighbourhood markets have been eclipsed by the city's modern **shopping centres** – the biggest is NorteShopping, in the northwest at Senhora da Hora (on the metro).

Porto's two main pedestrianized **shopping streets** are Rua de Cedofeita and the more upmarket Rua de Santa Catarina – these are where you'll find high-street fashion chains (Zara, H&M, etc), designer boutiques, jewellers, shoe shops, electrical and phone stores, and small malls. Rua de Santa Catarina also has a few stalls selling beads, cheap jewellery and accessories. Bookshops are concentrated along Rua de Ceuta and Rua da Fábrica, west of Avenida dos Aliados.

Shopping hours are Monday to Friday 9am to 6/7pm (some shops close for an hour at lunch), Saturday 9am to 1am. Some of the larger shops open all day until 8pm, even on Sundays, whilst the shopping centres are open daily 10am to 10pm (restaurants until midnight). Unless otherwise stated, the shops listed below are closed Saturday afternoon and all day Sunday.

Arts and crafts

Centro Regional de Artes Tradicionais (CRAT) Rua da Reboleira 37. Regional craft outlet, housed in a seventeenth-century riverside building. There's not actually too much choice – though it's not bad for ceramics, linen and lace – but it also stages temporary exhibitions and runs craft workshops (ask at the desk). Closed Sat & Sun.

O Galo Rua Mouzinho da Silveira 68. Decorative ceramics, including ubiquitous Barcelos cockerels, but also works by celebrated regional ceramicists, plus wooden toys and miniature models, and unusual granite sculpture from Porto.

Books and music

Chaminé da Mota Rua das Flores 28. Gorgeous secondhand bookshop (*alfarrabista*) complete with antique decorations, including giant music boxes that play punched metal discs.

FNAC Rua de Santa Catarina 73; also at Norte-Shopping; ⓦ www.fnac.pt. The city's biggest selection of music CDs, books and computer games.

Lello & Irmão Rua das Carmelitas 144. Galleried Art Nouveau bookshop (1906), with its staircase just begging for a grand entrance, is a delight beyond words. Sells both new and secondhand books, plus CDs, and has a small café on the first floor. Closed Sun.

Porto Editora Pr Dona Filipa de Lencastre 42. Up-to-date road maps and guides; also the only place

you can buy the 1:25,000 Carta Militar de Portugal maps, essential for serious hiking.

Food and drink

Casa Chinesa Rua Sá da Bandeira 343. One of Porto's best-known traditional groceries, now concentrating on health food and remedies, and otherwise hard-to-find Portuguese produce.

Casa Margaridense Trav de Cedofeita 20A. One of the oldest bakeries in the country, best known as purveyors of Porto's finest *pão de ló* – large sponge cakes containing precisely 24 egg yolks each.

Garrafeira do Infante Rua Infante Dom Henrique 83–85. A huge selection of vintage ports and wines in this bottle shop, housed in a lovely sixteenth-century building.

A Pérola do Bolhão Rua Formosa 279. A great little grocery, founded in 1917, loved as much for its Art Nouveau facade as for its cluttered stock of *bacalhau*, port wine, cheese and smoked hams.

Markets

Feira das Flores Pr da Liberdade. An all-day Sunday flower fest between April and Oct.

Feira dos Passarinhos Campo dos Mártires da Pátria. Birds, cages, and birds in cages on Sun mornings.

Feira de Vandôma Rua das Fontaínhas down to Alameda das Fontaínhas. A long-established Sat-morning flea market. Most stalls have a splendid spread of unremitting if fascinating junk.

Listings

Airport The metro Line E runs to the airport from Estádio do Dragão station (every 20–30min, daily 7am–1am), journey time 28min.

Buses Asa Douro (services to the Douro; ☎ 225 376 737), Eurolines (international; ☎ 225 189 299, ⓦ www.eurolinesportugal.com) and Santos (Beiras, Trás-os-Montes, Lisbon; ☎ 225 104 915, ⓦ www .santosviagensturismo.pt) depart from Campo 24 de Agosto; Auto Viação do Minho (Minho coast; ☎ 222 006 121) from Pr da República; Auto Viação do Tâmega (Trás-os-Montes, Coimbra, Lisbon; ☎ 222 083 019, ⓦ www.avtamega.pt) from Rua Alexandre Herculano 68; Marques (mountain Beiras; ☎ 222 039 889) from Rua da Restauração; Rede Expressos (national express services;

☎ 222 052 459, ⓦ www.rede–expressos.pt) and Caima (Beiras; ☎ 222 002 660) from Garagem Atlântico, Rua Alexandre Herculano; REDM (Braga; ☎ 222 003 152) from Rua Dr Alfredo Magalhães 94; Renex (Estremadura, Ribatejo, Lisbon, Algarve and Minho; ☎ 222 285 134) from Campo dos Mártires da Pátria 37, next to Palácio da Justiça; Rodonorte (Estremadura, Ribatejo, Minho, Trás-os-Montes; ☎ 222 005 637, ⓦ www.rodonorte.pt) from Rua Ateneu Comercial 19.

Car rental Most companies have both downtown and airport offices; it's far easier to pick up your car the day you leave Porto. Auto-Jardim ☎ 226 053 197, ⓦ www.auto-jardim.com; Avis ☎ 222 055 947 or airport ☎ 229 449 525; Budget/A.A.

Coastal Portugal

"The coast of Portugal,
birthplace of countless
mariners whose bones have
merged with so many seas,
survives human assault with
grace and forbearance."
Marion Kaplan,
The Portuguese

With 1,793 kilometres of Atlantic coastline (including its islands), Portugal's history, climate and economy is inexorably linked with the ocean. With a hostile Spain to the east, Portugal has long befriended the ocean, opening up routes to Africa, South America and the Orient and transforming itself into a significant mercantile power. Though the maritime empire based on slavery, spices and gold has long since foundered, the Atlantic still helps to generate much of Portugal's income thanks to the lure of miles of golden beaches.

Beaches and resorts

Portugal has some of the best **beaches** in Europe. Whole package companies have spawned on the most established of these, especially in the Algarve where soft sands backed by eroded cliffs and dramatic rock pillars have made resorts like Albufeira and Praia da Rocha internationally famous. For a beach holiday, the Algarve is still hard to beat, whether at the glitzy modern Vilamoura and Vale de Lobo or the more authentic towns of Tavira, Lagos or Olhão: each one offers access to a superb swathe of safe Atlantic sand.

But the country offers a whole host of other beach possibilities. Around Lisbon you can combine a city break with the superb dune-backed sands of Caparica or the sophisticated beach suburbs of Cascais and Estoril. **Families** should consider the tranquil waters of the Arrábida coastline and Sesimbra near Lisbon, the cliff-backed beach at Nazaré or the sheltered bay of São Martinho do Porto in Estremadura. There are some great places for **backpackers**, too, from the relatively undiscovered coastal villages of Fuzeta, Salema or

Odeceixe in the Algarve to the remoter resorts of the Alentejo such as Vila Nova de Milfontes and Zambujeira.

The west coast faces the full brunt of the Atlantic, making many of the beaches ideal for **surfers** and water-sports enthusiasts. From Sagres, the most southwesterly town in mainland Europe to Figueira da Foz near Coimbra, surf, windsurf and body-board competitions attract professionals, though plenty of amateurs enjoy the crashing waves at Praia Grande, Guincho, Ericeira and Peniche. And there are many other fine resorts that are rarely visited by non-Portuguese, such as the little bays of Porto Covo, the pine-fringed beaches of São Pedro de Muel or the candy-striped settlements of the Aveiro coast in the north.

Though all these places attract crowds in high summer, visit out of season and you'll find many of the beaches deserted apart from a few fishermen and dog walkers. And even in August you can still find solitude on the Costa Verde (Green Coast) in the cooler north, and in pockets of the Parque Natural do Sudoeste Alentejano e Costa Vicentina in the far southwest of the country.

◄ Praia de Dona Ana, Algarve

Portugal's top ten beaches

1 **Ilha de Tavira**, Algarve. Miles of sand without a hotel in sight. See p.564.
2 **Praia da Marinha**, Algarve. Classic cliff-backed cove beach. See p.581.
3 **Praia da Bordeira**, Algarve. A wild and wonderful stretch of sand in a remote corner of the Algarve. See p.609.
4 **Lagoa de Santo André**, Alentejo. This lagoon is sheltered even when the Atlantic pounds the nearby beaches. See p.536.
5 **Galapos**, Parque Natural da Arrábida. Beautifully positioned beach in one of Portugal's loveliest natural parks. See p.166.
6 **Caparica**. A favourite for surfers and day-trippers from Lisbon. See p.160.
7 **Baleal**, Peniche, Estremadura. Soft sands and great for beach combing. See p.181.
8 **São Martinho do Porto**, Estremadura. A perfect crescent bay, ideal for families. See p.190.
9 **Praia Velha**, São Pedro de Muel, Estremadura. A fine beach by one of the west coast's prettiest towns. See p.201.
10 **Praia do Cabedelo**, Viana do Castelo. The pride of the north and rarely packed even in high summer. See p.410.

▼ Praia do Cabedelo

Departure points

When you stand on the beach of Belixe in the Algarve there is no sign of the events that took place over five hundred years ago. But in the mid fifteenth century, the earliest **caravels** were launched off these sands for pioneering journeys down the coast of Africa. The beach is close to **Henry the Navigator's** School of Navigation in Sagres (p.604), where the king had gathered the greatest cartographers and sailors of his age to help charter the unknown world. Over the next century, sailors would return to Sagres with tales of exotic lands: Porto Santo and Madeira (discovered in 1419), the Azores (in 1427), Cape Verde (in 1460) and Brazil (in 1500). Portugal – with Spain – soon had the run of the world's leading trading posts, which it either colonized or traded freely with. Later, Belém (now

▲ Belém, Lisbon

a suburb of Lisbon) took over as the main port for overseas explorations, and it was here that the fabulous **Mosteiro dos Jerónimos** was built as a suitably impressive monument to Vasco da Gama's opening up of a sea route to India in 1498.

Aside from **Vasco da Gama**, who was born in the port town of Sines, most of the great navigators came from small inland towns – these were humble men who made it big. Head to the unassuming town of Sabrosa, near the Douro, and you can seek out a small plaque marking the birthplace of Fernão de Magalhães (aka **Magellan**) – a modest memorial to the first man to circumnavigate the globe. The same applies to the tiny Beira Baixa town of Belmonte (p.000), birthplace of Pedro Álvares Cabral, who discovered Brazil, and to Covilhã (p.000) in the Serra da Estrela, where a statue commemorates Pêro de Covilhã, who set Vasco da Gama on his way to India after visiting it in 1487.

The Portuguese have left place names around the world – Natal (Christmas) in South Africa, Lagos (lakes) in Nigeria, Rio de Janeiro (River of January) in Brazil, and Labrador in Canada, named after the humble farmers who went there in search of cod. These are the strongest reminders of the lengths Portuguese navigators went to in their quest for trade.

Top ten coastal beauty spots

- **Benagil**, Algarve. Start of a superb clifftop path past an awesome sea cave. See p.581.
- **Cabo de São Vicente**, Algarve. The ancients believed this was the end of the world – it remains a great spot for sunsets. See p.607.
- **Serra da Arrábida**. These scenic hills offer spectacular views over the Bay of Setúbal. See p.165.
- **Cabo da Roca**, near Sintra. A wild headland, the most westerly point in mainland Europe. See p.158.
- **Ilha da Berlenga**. The only island off western Portugal is a remote bird sanctuary, buffeted by the Atlantic. See p.184.
- **Casa de Chá da Boa Nova**, Leça de Palmeira, near Porto. Sublime seaside café by leading architect Álvaro Siza Viera. See p.345.
- **Monte de Santa Luzia**, Minho. Hilltop with a sea view that National Geographic magazine calls "the most beautiful in the world." See p.409.
- **Almograve**, Alentejo. The full force of the Atlantic crashes on to the rocks and dunes at this small resort. See p.540.
- **Praia de Odeceixe**, Algarve. Follow the river valley to a superb bay with sheltered river swimming and a wide sandy beach. See p.610.

▼ A beach off Serra da Arrábida

Castanheira ☏226 076 970 or airport ☏229 443 914; Europcar ☏222 057 737 or airport ☏229 482 452; Guerin/National ☏222 002 363 or airport ☏229 484 250, ⓦ www.guerin.pt; Hertz ☏800 238 238.

Consulates All serious matters are better directed towards the embassies in Lisbon. Consulates include: South Africa, Rua Antónia José da Costa 78 ☏226 076 010 (Mon–Fri 9am–noon); UK, Trav Barão de Forrester 86, Vila Nova de Gaia ☏226 184 789, ⓦ www.uk-embassy.pt (Mon, Wed & Thurs 9.30am–12.30pm & 2.30–6pm, Tues & Fri 9.30am–12.30pm); USA, Av da Boavista 3523 ☏226 186 607 (Mon–Fri 8am–noon & 1–5pm).

Football Futebol Clube do Porto, European champions in 2004, play at the Estádio do Dragão in Antas, off Av Fernão Magalhães ☏707 200 384, ⓦ www.fcporto.pt (metro Estádio do Dragão). Boavista FC play at Estádio do Bessa, Rua 1 de Janeiro, off Av da Boavista ☏226 071 000. Tickets cost €10–40 depending on the match and the seat location.

Hospital The most central hospital is Hospital Geral de Santo António, Largo Prof Abel Salazar ☏222 077 500. In an emergency, call ☏112.

Internet There's wireless access at hot spots all over Porto now, including many hotels and public buildings. You can get online for free at the Almeida Garrett library (see below) and at Espaço Internet in the Gabinete do Municipé, Av dos Aliados (town hall building, opposite the main turismo, go up to 1st floor; Mon–Fri 9am–5pm, Wed until 8pm) – expect to have to wait or book a slot at either. Otherwise, there are Internet points and cafés all over the city: central ones include FNAC, Rua de Santa Catarina 73 (Mon–Fri 10am–10pm, Sat 9am–10pm, Sun 11am–8pm); Portoweb, Pr General Humberto Delgado 291 (Mon–Sat 10am–2am, Sun 3pm–2am); and Portugal Telecom (PT), Pr da Liberdade 62 (Mon–Sat 8am–8pm, Sun 10am–8pm).

Left luggage There are coin-operated lockers at Campanhã and São Bento train stations.

Libraries Biblioteca Municipal Almeida Garrett, Palácio de Cristal, Rua de Entre Quintas 328 (Mon 2–6pm, Tues–Sat 10am–6pm; ☏226 081 000); or Biblioteca Municipal do Porto, Rua Dom João VI (Mon–Fri 9am–8pm, Sat 10am–6pm; ☏225 193 480). There's an English-language library (Mon–Fri 2–5.30pm) and other services at the British Council, Rua do Breiner 155 ☏222 073 060, ⓦ www.britishcouncil.org/portugal.

Newspapers Only a few newsagents regularly carry foreign newspapers and magazines. One reliable place is Lotarias Atlânticos, Rua Sampaio Bruno, off Av dos Aliados.

Pharmacies Late-night and 24hr pharmacies (*farmácias de serviço*) operate on a rota basis; details posted in the windows and given in the daily *Jornal de Notícias*.

Police For English-speaking assistance go to the Tourist Police (Polícia de Turismo, a branch of the PSP), Rua Clube dos Fenianos, next to the main turismo (daily 8am–2am; ☏222 081 833).

Post office The main post office faces the east side of the town hall on Pr General Humberto Delgado (Mon–Fri 8am–9pm, Sat 9am–6pm); also an office in Pr da Batalha (Mon–Fri 8.30am–6pm).

Taxis Radio Táxis ☏225 073 900, Taxis Invicta ☏225 076 400, Taxis Unidos ☏225 029 898.

Telephones There are phone booths at the main post office (see above) and at Portugal Telecom, Pr da Liberdade 62 (Mon–Sat 8am–8pm, Sun 10am–8pm).

Trains For trains to Aveiro, Braga and Guimarães, use the cheap suburban (*urbanos*) services from São Bento station – they also all call at Campanhã station 5min later. Long-distance and inter-city services (including along the Douro to Peso da Régu/Pocinho) all start from Campanhã, but you can buy tickets for these at São Bento (and jump on any local connection to Campanhã for free). Many intercity and ALFA Pendular services require a seat reservation, which you can do prior to departure, though allow plenty of time. There are information offices at both stations or consult CP's website (ⓦ www.cp.pt) or call ☏808 208 208.

Vila do Conde

VILA DO CONDE, 27km north of Porto, has become quite a significant resort over recent years, but has lost refreshingly little of its original character in the process. In part, it's because the villas and apartments overlooking the beach are set away from the rest of town; the old centre, 1km inland on the north bank of the Rio Ave, retains an active fishing port and an atmospheric medieval quarter, while the more modern town is a handsome place of boulevards, gardens and cafés. If you want more than just a beach then it's the best day out

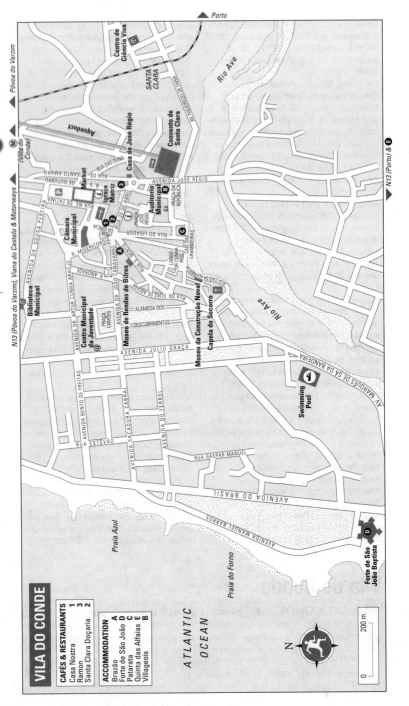

VILA DO CONDE

CAFÉS & RESTAURANTS
Casa Nostra — 1
Ramon — 3
Santa Clara Doçaria — 2

ACCOMMODATION
Brazão — A
Forte de São João — D
Patarata — C
Quinta das Alfaias — E
Villageois — B

ATLANTIC OCEAN

Praia Azul

Praia do Forno

N

0 — 200 m

Porto

Póvoa do Varzim

N13 (Póvoa do Varzim), Viana do Castelo & Motorways

N13 (Porto) & E

Centro de Ciência Viva

Rio Ave

SANTA CLARA

Convento de Santa Clara

Aqueduct

Vila do Conde

AVENIDA JOSÉ RÉGIO

Casa de José Régio

Auditório Municipal

Câmara Municipal

Market

Igreja Matriz

Biblioteca Municipal

Centro Municipal da Juventude

Museu de Rendas de Bilros

Museu da Construção Naval

Capela do Socorro

Swimming Pool

AVENIDA JÚLIO GRAÇA

AVENIDA BENTO DE FREITAS

RUA ESTÊVÃO

AVENIDA SACADURA CABRAL

AVENIDA DO FERROL

RUA GASPAR MANUEL

AVENIDA DO BRASIL

AVENIDA MANUEL BARROS

AV MARQUES DE SÁ DA BANDEIRA

Forte de São João Baptista

Rio Ave

from Porto, especially as you can zip up and down easily on the metro. The more developed sands of Póvoa do Varzim are just a few minutes' beyond, at the end of the line.

The town

The enormous hulk of the eighteenth-century **Convento de Santa Clara** dominates the town. It sits high above the old bridge and, while it's not open to the public, it is worth climbing up to the *miradouro* for sweeping views of town and river. Running into the north side of the convent is a well-preserved early eighteenth-century **aqueduct** which once carried water over a reputed 999 arches from Terroso, 5km north of town – the metro line to Póvoa do Varzim now cuts right through part of the remaining course.

The town's central **market** is at its busiest on Friday, when you'll find everything from farm produce and shoes to traditional children's toys and articulated puppets. The nearby **Igreja Matriz** is a Manueline beauty with a soaring, airy interior and – thanks to the Basque workmen who helped with its construction – an unusual but very effective mix of Spanish and Portuguese styles, including a distinctly Moorish dome.

South of the church, the cobbled alleys and whitewashed buildings of the remaining **old town** have been largely cleared of traffic – on local saints' days, the little street-corner votive chapels are illuminated by candles, while the *Festa de São João* (June 23/24) sees a procession through the streets. Vila do Conde is known for its traditional lacework and embroidery (*rendas de bilros*), and there are displays (and sales) at the **Museu de Rendas de Bilros**, within an attractive eighteenth-century town house at Rua de São Bento 70 (Mon–Fri 9am–noon & 2–6pm, Sat & Sun 2–5pm; Ⓦwww.mrbvc.net; free). Further down, on the river, there are cafés in the elegant **Praça da República**, by the bridge, while walking west takes you through the old **fishing quarter**, with the shipyards on the other side of the river. Vila do Conde's shipbuilding industry is amongst the oldest in Europe, and fishing boats reminiscent of fifteenth-century caravels are still constructed here, albeit in metal rather than in wood. The old skills survive, though – it was here that a replica of Bartolomeu Dias's caravel was constructed in 1987 as part of the 500th anniversary celebrations of his epic voyage around the Cape of Good Hope. You can trace this heritage (and see another replica vessel) in the excellent **Museu da Construção Naval,** Rua do Cais da Alfândega (Tues–Sun 10am–6pm; free), which displays material relating to shipbuilding, cartography, navigation, and life at sea. It's housed in the impressive former royal customs house (1487), while further along the riverside you can't miss the conspicuously Moorish white dome of the **Capela do Socorro** (1603), which bears witness to the conversion of Moorish craftsmen during the Inquisition. Inside, the *azulejos* depicting the Adoration of the Magi provide further proof of Moorish pragmatism, as several of the figures are wearing turbans.

The **beach** is a good fifteen-minute walk west of the town centre, and boasts long stretches of coarse sand that have been steadily developed right up the coast as far as Póvoa do Varzim. There are rock pools, and a few beach cafés, while to the south the sands come to an end at the mouth of the Rio Ave, marked by the stumpy **Forte de São João Baptista**, now a hotel.

Practicalities

The **metro** Line B runs from Porto (Estádio do Dragão) every 20 minutes and takes around an hour – you need a Z6 Andante card to travel this far (total, with card, €1.85 each way). There are two stations: get off at Santa Clara, 300m east of the convent, though quicker express services (50min) call at Vila do Conde station, still only five minutes walk from the centre. Except on Friday mornings, when the weekly market is held, you'll always find shaded **parking** space in the enclosure just to the north of the market on Rua 5 de Outubro; and there's plenty of parking space out by the beach. The **main turismo**, an attractive ivy-clad house, is at Rua 25 de Abril 103 (Mon–Fri 9am–6pm, Sat & Sun 10am–1pm & 2.30–5.30pm; ℡252 248 473, ⓦwww.cm-viladoconde.pt). There's another office by the market, which also displays and sells handicrafts, but opening hours aren't reliable.

There's no pressing reason to stay, though it is a pretty town and makes a nice respite from the city. The turismo can help with private **rooms** (❶) – prices at the places reviewed below can drop by a third outside July and August. A good time to be here is for the nine-day **Feira de Gastronomia** (food fair; end of Aug), and there's also a renowned **Feira Nacional de Artesanato** (crafts fair; last week July to first week Aug). People also come from far and wide for **Curtas** (ⓦwww.curtasmetragens.pt), the European short-film festival held here for a week every July. A few fashionable **bars** can be found on Praça da República, by the **Auditório Municipal**, which has temporary exhibitions and hosts theatre, dance and live music.

Accommodation

Quinta das Alfaias 2km inland of Mindelo, 10km south of town ℡252 662 146 or 919 900 509, ⓦwww.quintadasalfaias .com. A wonderfully elegant country house set in extensive gardens and orchards, and with a comfortable verandah, large swimming pool and tennis court. It has four en-suite rooms, plus one suite and a self-catering apartment with two double rooms, verandah and views – decor throughout is simple, with plenty of bare granite. Meals on request. There are directions on the website. ❹

Estalagem do Brazão Av Dr João Canavarro 14 ℡252 642 016, ⓔestalagembrazao@mail .telepac.pt. Four-star inn set in a partially modernized seventeenth-century mansion, and decked out in a strange mixture of period furnishings and 1960 and 1970s decor. There's a bar and reasonable restaurant. Parking. ❹

Forte de São João Av do Brasil ℡222 240 600, ⓦwww.hotelfortesjoao.com. This airy conversion of the town's seventeenth-century pentagonal fortress is very well done, in a contemporary, minimalist style. The best rooms have ocean or river views – and the hotel's seven suites feature aquariums –

there's also a library, wine bar and chic restaurant (expensive; reservations advised). Parking. ❻

Pensão Patarata Cais das Lavandeiras 18 ℡252 631 894. A simple *pensão* over a local restaurant and bar. There's a mixed bag of rooms, the better ones being big, airy and overlooking the waterfront. Breakfast not included. ❷

Le Villageois Pr da República 94 ℡252 631 119. This is the best budget option in town, with well-furnished en-suite rooms, though some lack windows and there are no river views, despite its position. The pretty restaurant below (moderate; closed Mon) is the nicest place to sit outside in town. ❷

Cafés and restaurants

Casa Nostra Rua da Igreja ℡252 631 730. A classy *restaurante típico* by the church, specializing in *petiscos* and fish. Closed Sun. Moderate.

Ramon Rua 5 de Outubro 176 ℡252 631 334. The place for fish and shellfish – there's a good-value set lunch and outdoor seating in the alley. Closed Tues. Moderate.

Santa Clara Doçaria Conventual Rua 25 de Abril ℡252 647 892. A tea room with the best pastries and cakes in town, using recipes originally concocted in the convent. Inexpensive.

Penafiel and around

At **PENAFIEL**, 35km east of Porto, you enter *vinho verde* country. The wine's origins lie with the Benedictine monks, who were famed in this region for their laborious terracing of the valley slopes. The Benedictine legacy also extends to a handful of fine Romanesque churches, hidden away in folds of the rolling hills hereabouts. However, despite the promise, Penafiel itself comes as something of a disappointment, though that's much to do with the main road traffic that splits the town and jars the ears. The few old streets of granite mansions behind the handsome Renaissance Igreja da Misericórdia are barely reason enough to stop – certainly not if you're reliant on public transport (and the train station is 3km from the centre in any case). Drivers should instead divert to the charming, ivy-festooned **Quinta da Aveleda** (Mon–Fri 9am–noon & 2–5pm; ☎255 718 200, ⓦ www.aveleda.pt; reservations advised; €4), where the local *vinho verde* is made – coming from Porto, leave the A4 at the "Penafiel Sul/Entre-os-Rios" exit and follow the signs towards Paredes. The guided tours include wine and cheese tasting, but it's really the gorgeously unkempt, wooded gardens that make the visit.

Penafiel's local boy made good is one **Egas Moniz**, a great figure of loyalty in Portuguese history, whose statue stands by the public gardens on the main avenue. He's buried in the abbey church of **Paço de Sousa**, 10km south of Penafiel (signposted off the N106), which was the former headquarters of the Benedictines in Portugal. The dark and dank Romanesque church was founded in 962, and the panels on the tomb of Moniz – tutor and adviser to the first king of Portugal, Afonso Henriques – tell his story. In 1127, shortly after Afonso Henriques had broken away from his grandfather, the King of León, Egas was sent to negotiate a settlement, thus enabling Afonso to concentrate his efforts on defeating the Moors in the south. Within three years, the King of León considered the treaty to be broken on the Portuguese side and threatened all-out war. Egas made his way to León, presented himself and his family and offered to receive the punishment due to his master. Impressed by his loyalty, mercy was granted and the king sent the minister home unscathed. The church is set in a shaded dell beside the Rio Sousa – a popular picnic spot – and there are a couple of cafés in the village below.

Apart from Paço de Sousa, the easiest local Romanesque church to locate is at **Boelhe**, 10km further southeast, signposted off the N106 road to Entre-os-Rios. Tucked up a minor country road, São Gens is reputedly the smallest Romanesque church in the country, and gains its power from a stunning position on the brow of a hill overlooking the Tâmega valley. The N106 continues south to **Entre-os-Rios** ("between the rivers"), the point at which the Douro and Tâmega rivers meet – cross the bridge to the south bank of the Douro and you're in for a treat of a drive east along the increasingly picturesque N222 (see p.363) towards Lamego and Peso da Régua.

Amarante

The A4 motorway has made it a quick sixty-kilometre drive from Porto to the beautiful riverside town of **AMARANTE**, but train travellers have the best of it. The twelve-kilometre Tâmega branch line leaves the Douro main line at Livração and from the very start it's a scenic ride, hugging the ravine of the Rio Tâmega, with pine woods and vines clinging to steep slopes, and goats scrambling across the terrace walls to nibble at haystacks. Amarante itself is immaculately set in a gorge of the Rio Tâmega, with the wooden balconies of its old houses leaning over the water. Much of the town's history revolves around the thirteenth-century hermit Gonçalo, later **São Gonçalo**, who is credited with just about everything positive about Amarante – most of the attractions bear his name or have some link to him. The town has been "discovered" in recent years

△ Amarante

by weekenders from Porto and foreign visitors, and there's a definite air of prosperity about its old-town restaurants, bars, *pastelarias*, boutiques and jewellery shops. It's certainly a fine place to spend the night, with a wide choice of accommodation, much of it still reasonably priced.

The town

The **Igreja de São Gonçalo** (daily 8am–7pm), fronting a wide square beside the elegant town bridge, is Amarante's most prominent monument. Legend has it that the church marks the spot where Gonçalo's hermitage once stood, although the site is almost certainly much older. It formed the heart of an ancient fertility cult, probably with pagan origins, which still persists here at the saint's annual festival – now known as the *Festas do Junho* – celebrated over the first weekend in June. The large Sunday procession is the religious highlight, though for a hangover from pagan times you need look no further than the traditional exchange of phallic-shaped cakes by unmarried couples as tokens of their love. Moreover, in the church, the saint's tomb (in a small chapel, just to the left of the altar) is said to guarantee a quick marriage to anyone who touches it – his face, hands and feet have been almost worn away by hopeful suitors.

The church and associated monastery were built between 1540 and 1620. The remodelled Renaissance cloisters around the side now contain the **Museu Amadeo de Souza-Cardoso** (Tues–Sun 10am–12.30pm & 2–5.30pm; €1), largely based around the Cubist and avant-garde works of local boy Souza-Cardoso (1887–1918), who spent his formative years as an artist in Paris but died young in the influenza pandemic of 1918. He's still relatively little known outside Portugal but the absorbing collection is well worth a look. There are also works by other Portuguese artists, as well as temporary exhibitions and a monthly cinema club.

A steep granite stairway climbs from the square, past the **Igreja de São Domingos**, whose belltower marks the hours. Take a quick look inside the

Map labels:

N15 (Penafiel & Guimarães) ▲ ▲ N15 (Penafiel & Guimarães) ▲ N210 ▲ (Celorico de Basto & Mondim de Basto) ▲ Campsite

Train Station

Cinema

AMARANTE

0   100 m

RUA PAULINO CABRAL
RUA JOÃO PINHEIRO
RUA M. MONTEROSO
RUA CÂNDIDO DOS REIS

AVENIDA 1 DE MAIO

Museu Amadeo de Souza-Cardoso

Igreja de S. Pedro

RUA CAPITÃO AUGUSTO CASIMIRO

Mercado

Rio Tâmega

AVENIDA ALEXANDRE HERCULANO

N

S. Domingos

R. S. PEDRO

i

Igreja de São Gonçalo

PR. DA REPÚBLICA

PONTE DE SÃO GONÇALO

RUA 31 DE JANEIRO

CAMINHO DE SANTO ANTÓNIO

Bus Station

LARGO C. ANTÓNIO CÂNDIDO

RUA ANTÓNIO CARNEIRO

AVENIDA 1 DE MAIO

Rio Tâmega

AV. GENERAL SILVEIRA

Parque Florestal

Swimming Pools

Supermarket

ACCOMMODATION
Casa de Calçada **D**
Dona Margaritta **C**
Estoril **A**
Navarras **F**
Príncipe **E**
Zé de Calcada **B**

CAFÉS, RESTAURANTS & BARS
Confeitara da Ponte **3**
Quelha **5**
São Gonçalo **2**
Spark Bar **4**
Triunfante **1**

▼ IP4 (Porto & Vila Real)

Livração

---

intimate chapel – by the door is an extraordinary carved wooden tablet showing Christ suspended upside down on the Cross, hoisted by three men operating a rope and pulley. The narrow street continues around the back of the church and up to Largo Santa Clara, where there are the scant ruins of the former **Santa Clara** convent – whose nuns once made the town's famous sweets – and views down into the São Gonçalo church cloisters.

That's it for sightseeing, other than the photogenic bridge (see box below) and the main riverside street, Rua 31 de Janeiro, whose granite buildings bear small plaques showing the level of flood water over the last century or so (over head height in 2001). Sadly, the polluted river is not recommended for swimming – though in summer you'll see some brave souls risking it – but pedal boats and rowing boats can be hired for an hour or two and there's a swimming pool complex on the south bank. Just past the complex is the peaceful, forested **Parque Florestal** which makes a good spot for a picnic.

Practicalities

The **train station** is a ten-minute walk northwest of the river, in the newer part of town – it's a bit ramshackle and although timetables are posted in the window you buy tickets on the train. The **bus station** is right in the centre, on the south side of the river on Largo Conselheiro António Cândido. Driving from Porto takes less than an hour if you take the fast A4 – traffic runs one-way only in town, around the two bridges. **Parking** is free along the river beside the market, along the road under the new bridge, and in a wasteground lot beyond *Hotel Navarras*; everywhere else, you'll need to feed the parking meters (2hr maximum). You can pick up a town map from the **turismo** (July–Sept daily

Bridge over troubled water

The north and south parts of town are linked by the **Ponte de São Gonçalo**, scene of a heroic stand-off in spring 1809 between the Portuguese, under General Francisco da Silveira, and the retreating French, under Marshall Sault. Fleeing Porto, having lost their brief tenure of Portugal, the French were ransacking villages along the way but when they reached Amarante they met with unexpected resistance. The bravery of the Portuguese army held up the French at the bridge, temporarily halting their rampage and allowing the people of the town to escape to safety. For two weeks there was a stalemate but on the night of May 2, under cover of darkness, the French planted explosives close to the Portuguese lines. The resulting explosions eventually caused enough panic to allow the French to cross the bridge and continue their plundering, but by then the people were safe. Today, canvases hanging inside the church of São Gonçalo still bear French bayonet marks from soldiers searching for treasure that may have been hidden behind.

9am–6pm, rest of the year daily 9am–12.30pm & 2–5.30pm; ☏255 420 246, ⓦwww.cm-amarante.pt), to the side of the main church next to the museum. **Market days** are Tuesdays and Saturdays – it's all over by 3pm. There's a small **supermarket**, and a newsagent selling foreign newspapers, in the shopping arcade under the *Hotel Navarras*; otherwise, the main shopping streets are all on the way up to the train station

Accommodation

There's a fair range of accommodation in town, as well as some lovely *turismo rural* places in the area – even so, it's a good idea to book ahead in summer if you want to stay at a particular place (and especially if you want to visit during the June festival). The municipal **Parque de Campismo** (☏255 437 630) is on the river, 1.5km upstream at Peneda da Rainha.

In town

Casa da Calçada Largo do Paço 6 ☏255 410 830, ⓦwww.casadacalcada.com. The restored palace of the Counts of Redondo is set in magnificent gardens and stuffed with *objets d'art*. The thirty rooms and suites vary in size, decor and outlook – with some classed deluxe – but all are extremely comfortable. Facilities include a swimming pool and tennis court, while there's a fine restaurant (open to non-guests; very expensive; reservations advised) with a contemporary twist to its regional menu. Excellent buffet breakfast included. ❻, deluxe ❼

Albergaria Dona Margaritta Rua Cândido dos Reis 53 ☏255 432 110, ⓦwww.albergariadon-amargaritta.pa-net.pt. A traditional place on the north side of the river, with reasonable en-suite rooms – not too elderly, not too pricey, though some are a bit close to the road outside. There's a shady breakfast terrace at the back. No credit cards. ❸

Residencial Estoril Rua 31 de Janeiro 49 ☏255 431 291. A friendly budget choice near the old bridge, with river views from some of the simple rooms, a couple of which also have balconies. The attached restaurant is a firm favourite for inexpensive riverside terrace dining – no need to go anywhere else if you're staying. ❷

Hotel Navarras Rua António Carneiro ☏255 431 036. The central three-star choice doesn't throw any great surprises in the rooms – they're shipshape, businesslike and a/c – but many have a large terrace (though no views to speak of), and there's a proper bath in the bathroom. Also a restaurant, bar and private parking, and you can eat breakfast on the terrace, though the main road traffic intrudes. Prices drop €20 between Oct and May. ❹

Residencial Príncipe Largo Conselheiro António Cândido 53 ☏255 432 956. On the square across from the bus station – the front rooms have balconies, though the views aren't up to much, and the decor is a bit weary. It's cheap, though, and there's a restaurant and café downstairs. No credit cards. ❶

Zé da Calcada Rua 31 de Janeiro 83 ☏255 426 814, ⓕ255 426 844. Seven comfortable and good-value en-suite rooms, most with river views. The restaurant is the real draw, with a river terrace, renowned regional food and a good wine list – it's pricier than many in town (dishes cost from around €9.50) but better too. Breakfast not included. **②**

Outside town

Casal Aboadela Aboadela, 9km east of town, off the IP4 ⓣ 255 441 141. A rustic farmhouse with log fires, pool, playground, bicycles and farm

activities for kids. There are four en-suite rooms, plus a self-catering apartment. Two-night minimum stay. No credit cards. Room **②**, apartment **③**

Pousada de São Gonçalo Serra do Marão, 20km east of town, along the IP4 (Vila Real) ⓣ 255 460 030, ⓦ www.pousadas.pt. The views from this small (15-room) clifftop *pousada* are unbeatable. There's an excellent (if expensive) restaurant, featuring regional highlights like pork with chestnuts or trout stuffed with *presunto*. **⑥**

Eating and drinking

The cakes and sweets once made by nuns – known as *doces conventuais* – are available at **cafés** and *pastelarias* all over town. Many of the places to stay (see above) have **restaurants** attached – some simple, some rather grand – though the locals tend to eat in the cheaper places found near the bus station or up in the new town. The local hooch is *Gatão*, a fruity *vinho verde*. As the money has moved in, so the nightlife scene has moved up a notch or two, with a few late-opening esplanade **bars** found on the south side of the river near either bridge – the contemporary *Spark Bar* by the new bridge is typical.

Confeitara da Ponte Rua 31 de Janeiro no phone. The best place for cakes and sweets is right by the bridge, with an attractive ivy-festooned riverside terrace. *Pão de ló* (sponge cake) is made on the premises, and they box up the local *doces* to take away. Inexpensive.

A Quelha Rua de Olivença ⓣ 255 425 786. This *adega*'s well-spiced dishes are a meat-eater's dream, especially when washed down with jugs of the rich local wine. There's also some fish. Moderate.

Café-Bar São Gonçalo Pr da República ⓣ 255 432 707. Occupies prime position on the square

outside the church – the meals are pricey (mains around €14), but it's still extremely reasonable for a drink at an outdoor table, and it's a good breakfast choice since there are fresh bread and pastries daily. Expensive.

Triunfante Rua Teixeira de Vasconcelos ⓣ 255 437 978. The daily lunch dish for €4 brings in the locals to this cheery granite-walled *adega*, but there's not much that costs over €5 in any case – rabbit stew, steak, chicken, pork and *bacalhau* are generally on the menu. Closed Sun dinner. Inexpensive.

Peso da Régua

PESO DA RÉGUA (usually just Régua) is an expanding provincial town that was known for over two centuries as the "Capital of the Upper Douro" because of its role as the first capital of Pombal's demarcated port-producing region. In fact, the centre for quality port wines has shifted to Pinhão, half an hour further east; Régua is simply the depot through which all the wine must pass on its way to Porto. It's not a particularly pretty place, dominated by a vertiginous motorway bridge, though the ornamental *barcos rabelos* anchored on the wide river and the trademark Sandeman port wine company cutout on the terraced hills beyond provide some attraction. More to the point, Régua is the hub of the Douro river cruise trade, with the boats disgorging hundreds of passengers for lunch stops, train trips and wine-lodge visits, so for most of the year there's an agreeable hubbub along the riverside promenade.

There are only two streets of note – the riverfront avenue with the boat quay and the long town main street which runs parallel, one block inland. It's along the latter that you'll find the **Solar do Vinho do Porto** (Mon–Sat 11am–8pm; ⓦ www.ivp.pt), housed in a converted warehouse, which offers a large choice of wines for tasting and features temporary thematic exhibitions and events about port wine and the Douro. A little way down the street is the imposing granite **Casa do Douro**, the headquarters of the port wine growers' organization – duck inside the entrance hall to see the enormous medieval-style stained-glass window depicting the port trade.

Between March and November, a huge variety of **river cruises** with various companies departs from, or passes through, Régua. Kiosks by the quayside sell tickets, or you can consult Porto Tours in Porto (see p.330) or Régua turismo (see below) for full schedules. Short, hour-long cruises cost around €10, while typical tours run up to Pinhão and back (around €60, including lunch), or combine a cruise with a trip on a steam train and a wine lodge visit (around €100). One of the operators, Douro Verde (ⓦwww.douroverde.com), also has a tourist **road-train service** from the quayside (€6) that whisks you up to a viewpoint and throws in a lodge visit and tasting.

There's a concentration of **port wine quintas** – or vineyard estates – huddled around Peso da Régua. The turismo has plenty of information on these, including a *Rota do Vinho do Porto* map of wine-related sites along the Douro (also available online at ⓦwww.rvp.pt). Many offer vineyard tours and tastings, though you might want to give the larger concerns a miss in favour of a smaller family-owned *quinta* like **Quinta de Marrocos** (ⓣ254 313 012, ⓦwww .quintademarrocos.com), 2km from town along the N222 towards Pinhão, on the Douro's south bank. The owners also operate the delightfully nonconformist *quinta* at *Vale de Sapos* (Valley of Toads), with assorted vines growing all over the place, rather than in the regimented rows common elsewhere; it's along the Rio Varosa, south of Régua, close to Cambres.

Practicalities

From the quayside, the **turismo** (July–Sept daily 9am–12.30pm & 2–5.30pm; Oct–June Mon–Fri 9am–12.30pm & 2–5.30pm; ⓣ254 312 846, ⓦwww .cm-peso-regua.pt) is a five-minute walk away to the left (Porto direction), near the large car park, at one end of the town's main street. The **train station** is right at the other end of town (towards the bridges), about 1km away down the waterfront avenue – there are daily services to Pinhão, Tua, Pocinho and Vila Real, while **steam train services** to Pinhão and Tua usually depart on Saturday afternoons between May and October (€38 return, reservations advised through Portuguese Railways, CP, ⓣ211 021 129 or 211 021 187, ⓦwww.cp.pt). **Buses** stop outside the station, with regular daily services to and from Lamego and Vila Real. For a **driving** route to Régua, see below.

Bars and restaurants line the riverfront avenue, or try the popular *O Maleiro*, Rua dos Camilos 108 (ⓣ254 313 684), opposite the post office on the town's main street (it's also signposted up from the waterfront). It's a friendly, bustling place with a vine-draped inner courtyard, serving huge portions of typical Portuguese food – dishes big enough to feed two cost €9–10.

It's difficult to see anyone making the choice to stay in Régua, with prettier destinations like Pinhão and Lamego so close. In any case, **accommodation** here is distinctly underwhelming, typified by the two high-rise eyesores close to the train station, the mid-market *Residencial Império* (ⓣ254 320 120; ❷) and the four-star *Hotel Régua Douro* (ⓣ254 320 700, ⓦwww.hotelreguadouro.pt; ❹, weekend ❾) – the latter at least improves substantially inside, with a pool on a river-view terrace and top-floor panoramic restaurant. If you did want to stay near town, you'd be far better off reserving one of the four rooms at the guest house at *Quinta de Marrocos* (see town account above for contact details; ❸; meals also available for €20).

The N222: along the south bank of the Douro

The **N222 road** along the south bank of the Douro is one of those "best in Portugal" routes; you can pick it up south of Penafiel at Castelo de Pavia, though the most compelling section is the 40km or so between Cinfães and Peso da Régua, where the road hugs the terraced hills high above the glinting river. It's a glorious route, lined with cherry and olive trees, plus the occasional panoramic café, and with iron gates at intervals announcing venerable *quintas* tucked into the hillside folds. At the sleepy spa town of **Caldas de Aregos**, where the Douro has been dammed, there's a whiff of sulphur in the air, a quayside marina and an outdoor café; the modern spa buildings sit next to a sixteenth-century chapel with flood markings traced up its facade.

The settlements beyond nearly all boast a Romanesque church or chapel, the most significant being **Santa Maria de Carquere**, a twisting 5km above the small town of Resende. Part of a convent dating back as early as 1099, this is now set amidst family vineyards, with extensive views across the rolling hills beyond. Past Resende, another signpost points you 1km off the N222 to **São Martinho de Mouros**, a squat fortified church with mere arrow slits for windows. The N222 winds on past **Barrô** (with another Romanesque chapel) and eventually descends to Peso da Régua, though you can also cut south over the hills on the N226 to reach Lamego.

Lamego and around

Although technically in the Beira Alta region, the attractive town of **Lamego**, 11km south of Régua, is much more accessible from the Douro, with which it shares a passion for wine. Indeed, port wine may have its origins in the vineyards that drape the length of the Balsemão valley, from below town to the Douro. Although the demarcated wine region now excludes Lamego, it makes up for lost pride in the form of *Raposeira* – Portugal's answer to champagne – and produces celebrated smoked hams and sausages. But the region around Lamego is perhaps best known for its **churches** and **monasteries**, a legacy of the twelfth-century Reconquista, which attracted a number of religious orders to these lands. Lamego was among the first towns to be retaken from the Moors, and the surrounding verdant valleys are full of ancient places of worship in varying states of preservation.

Lamego

Although small (with a population of under 10,000) **LAMEGO** has always been a well-to-do place. Once through the fairly charmless modern outskirts, the overriding impression is one of graceful white villas on the hillsides, and the luxuriant architecture of its many manor houses and churches. Much of the wealth derived from the geographical position astride a valuable trade route from the Beiras to the Douro, but the town's real importance stems from its history: in 1143, less than a century after its Reconquest from the Moors by Fernando Magno and Rodrigo de Vivar (the famous "El Cid"), Lamego hosted Portugal's first parliament, when a group of clergy and noblemen assembled to

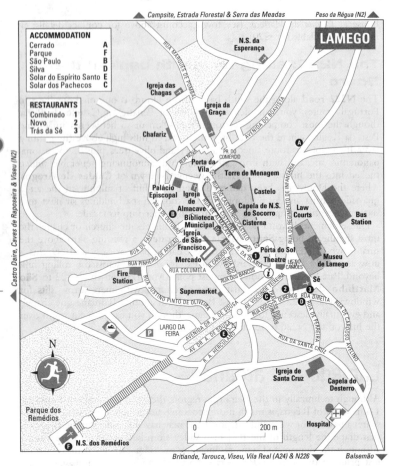

LAMEGO

ACCOMMODATION
Cerrado	A
Parque	F
São Paulo	B
Silva	D
Solar do Espírito Santo	E
Solar dos Pachecos	C

RESTAURANTS
Combinado	1
Novo	2
Trás da Sé	3

N.S. da Esperança

Igreja das Chagas

Igreja da Graça

Chafariz

PR. DO COMERCIO

Porta da Vila

Torre de Menagem

Castelo

Palácio Episcopal

Igreja de Almacave

Capela de N.S. do Socorro

Biblioteca Municipal

Cisterna

Law Courts

Bus Station

Igreja de São Francisco

Mercado

Porta do Sol

Theatre

Museu de Lamego

Fire Station

Supermarket

Sé

RUA COLUMELA

RUA DOS BANCOS

LARGO DA FEIRA

Igreja de Santa Cruz

Capela do Desterro

N

Parque dos Remédios

N.S. dos Remédios

0 — 200 m

Hospital

Britiande, Tarouca, Viseu, Vila Real (A24) & N226 ▼ — Balsemão ▼

recognize Afonso Henriques as the nation's first king. As such, Lamego lays claim to being the birthplace of both country and crown, something hotly disputed by Afonso Henriques' birthplace, Guimarães. The town also has one of the very greatest Baroque structures in Europe – the dominant shrine of **Nossa Senhora dos Remédios** – which plays host to an annual pilgrimage from late August to early September. Other notable *festas* and events include *Santa Cruz* (May 3), with its displays of horsemanship and cattle, and Easter, for magnificent religious processions and a curious ceremony where an effigy of Judas goes up in smoke amid a blaze of fireworks. The weekly **market** is on Thursdays, a colourful combination of local farm produce, trailers with grilled chicken, and gypsies selling clothes and shoes.

Arrival, information and accommodation

Coming from the Douro by **train**, alight at Peso da Régua and take one of the hourly buses from outside the station, a thirty-minute ride. Lamego's **bus station** is a stone's throw from the main sights; **taxis** wait outside and also line up along the main avenue, which splits into two distinct halves (with separate names) either side of a central roundabout marked by a war-memorial statue of a soldier. There's metered **parking** along the bottom half of the avenue (nearest the cathedral) and free parking along the top half (including on the large Largo da Feira market place, though not here on market day, Thursday). The town's **road train** (weekends all year, otherwise daily mid-May to mid-Sept, departures roughly hourly 2–7pm; €3) is perfect for seeing the sights without the legwork. It covers pretty much everything except the castle (too steep), and starts at the roundabout in the middle of the avenue. The **Biblioteca Municipal** on Rua de Almacave has Internet access (Mon–Fri 9.30am–12.30pm & 2.30–6pm).

The **turismo** is at the bottom end of Avenida Visconde Guedes Teixeira (July–Sept Mon–Fri 10am–12.30pm & 2–6pm, Sat & Sun closes at 5pm; Oct–June Mon–Fri 9.30am–12.30pm & 2–5.30pm, Sat 9.30am–12.30pm; ☎254 612 005, ⓦwww.cm-lamego.pt), across from the cathedral – the hours sometimes vary from those given depending on staffing. **Accommodation** in town is reasonable, if unexciting – Lamego has much more atmospheric rural accommodation in local manor houses and *quintas*, the pick of which are reviewd below. The closest **campsite** (☎ & ⓕ254 613 918; closed mid–Sept to May) is at the *Complexo Turístico Turissera*, 5km northwest of town towards Avões in the Serra das Meadas (see "Out of town" accommodation, below).

In town

Albergaria do Cerrado Lugar do Cerrado ☎254 613 164. Reliable but characterless – a business-class guest-house, 200m out of town, with private parking and a/c; the best also have bathtubs and balconies, though the view is of the suburbs and bus station. You can usually do better than the posted rates by simply asking. ④

Residencial São Paulo Av 5 de Outubro 22 ☎254 613 114, ⓕ254 612 304. Charm is in short supply in this tiled 1970s residential building above a parade of shops, but the plain rooms are massive and those at the back look up to the old town and the Igreja de Almacave. Lift access; parking for guests. No credit cards. ②

Pensão Silva Rua Trás da Sé 26 ☎254 612 929. A friendly place up a long flight of stairs next to the cathedral; the bells might disturb, but are not as loud as you might expect. Rooms, sharing bathrooms, are antiquated, but it's cheap. No credit cards. ①

Residencial Solar do Espírito Santo Rua Alexandre Herculano, entrance also on Av Dr Alfredo de Sousa ☎ & ⓕ254 655 060. Comfortable if smallish en-suite rooms in the "Holy Ghost" house come with cool parquet floors and a/c. Those at the front with balconies have avenue and shrine views, though you also get some traffic noise. Lift access and private parking a bonus, and there's a *pastelaria* below, from which come your breakfast rolls and croissant. ③

Albergaria Solar dos Pachecos Av Visconde Guedes Teixeira ☎254 600 300, ⓦwww.solar-pachecos.com. The smartest town-centre choice is this grandiose granite-walled *solar* renovated in modern, if minimalist style. The rooms, with baths or showers, have cable TV and a/c, and many have avenue views. Prices drop markedly out of summer. No credit cards. ④

Out of town

Villa Hostilina Ortigosa, 2km north, off the N2 to Régua ☎254 612 394, ⓦwww.villahostilina.com. Set amidst vineyards and orchards, the grand nineteenth-century house – with its formal gardens and period trappings – contrasts rather oddly with its ultra-modern "Instituto Kosmos" health club, tennis courts and pool. Meals by arrangement. ④

Hotel Parque Parque dos Remédios ☎254 609 140, ⓦwww.hotel-parque.com. A three-star hotel in an unbeatable location next to the shrine, set in its own gardens, with rather nice, traditionally furnished en-suite rooms, plus a bar and restaurant, and parking right outside. It's a 3km drive from town – or walk straight up the steps from the end of the main avenue. ③

Casa de Santo António de Britiande Britiande, 5km southeast, along the N226 ☎254 699 346, ⓔbritiande@solaresdeportugal.pt. A sixteenth-century antique-filled manor house with *azulejo*-lined chapel and four guest rooms, plus swimming pool, tennis court, bicycles, and meals on request. It's in a handy location for touring the nearby Romanesque churches. Closed 2 weeks in Aug. ⑤

Quinta do Terreiro Lalim, 7km south of Lamego, off N226 ☎254 697 040, ⓦwww.geocities.com /quintadoterreiro. An impressive eighteenth-century manor house with ten atmospheric granite-walled rooms, some with fireplaces. A lovely period dining room and cosy cellar-bar complete the picture, and there's a swimming pool, tennis court, and trips to the Serra de Santa Helena on offer. ❹

Complexo Turístico Turissera 5km northwest along the Estrada Florestal towards Avões ☎254 609 100, ℻254 656 152. A large motel, campsite and restaurant rolled into one, occupying a lofty position in the Serra das Meadas. Rooms are reasonable for the price, and there's a tennis court and mini-golf. ❸

Casa dos Varais Cambres, 9km northwest along the Estrada Florestal ☎254 313 251, ✉varais@ solaresdeportugal.pt. This eighteenth-century mansion, perched on the northern flank of the

Serra das Meadas, overlooking Régua and the Douro, has three guestrooms decked out in Victorian style, complete with old wallpaper. Meals on request. Closed Nov–March. ❹

Casa dos Viscondes da Várzea Várzea de Abrunhais, 10km southeast, signposted off the N226 at Britiande ☎254 690 020, ⊛www .hotelruralviscondesvarzea.com. A palatial nineteenth-century *quinta* with shady verandahs overlooking 180 acres of gardens, orchards and farmland. It's elegantly decorated throughout, the comfortable bedrooms featuring attractive wooden furniture and traditionally tiled bathrooms. Meals, taken in a romantic *azulejo*-lined dining room, are a treat, and there's a pool. Good weekday discounts Nov–April. ❻

The town

Lamego's cathedral – the **Sé** – dominates the centre of town (daily 8am–1pm & 3–7pm), basically a Renaissance structure, though a thirteenth-century tower survives from its earlier Romanesque incarnation. The sculpted Gothic front is still impressive and the rose-planted cloister is a beauty. Facing the Sé, occupying the eighteenth-century Episcopal Palace, is the excellent **Museu de Lamego** (Tues–Sat 10am–12.30pm & 2–5pm, Sun 10am–12.30pm; €2, free Sun), whose exhibits include five of the remaining panels of a polyptych commissioned from Grão Vasco by the Bishop of Lamego in 1506. Also on show are a series of huge sixteenth-century Flemish tapestries, some curious statues of a conspicuously pregnant Virgin Mary (a genre peculiar to this region), a fine assembly of *azulejos*, and piles of other ecclesiastical treasures.

Across the square, the steep **Rua da Olaria** leads up from beside the turismo to the castle, passing an array of antiquated shops, grocers and *casas de pasto* selling the regional bread, cheese, hams and smoked sausages. A right turn at the top takes you to the castle's Porta do Sol (see below), whilst straight ahead along Rua de Almacave is the **Igreja de Almacave**, a simple Romanesque church thought once to have been a mosque. At the top of Rua de Almacave an alley on the right heads up along the town's massive thirteenth-century walls to the castle's north gate, the **Porta da Vila**, straddled by a sorry-looking wooden oratory constructed in the 1700s. This gives access to the **Castelo** – a cluster of stone houses huddled around the twelfth-century **Torre de Menagem** (mid-June to Sept Tues–Sun 10am–noon & 3–6pm; Oct to mid-June Sun 10am–noon only; free). The castle has been inhabited since at least the fifth century BC, while a number of Roman engraved stones and stelae can be seen inside and just outside the walls. If the tower's open, it's worth clambering up the rickety stairs onto the roof for the views.

Past the tower, along Rua do Castelo, the small **Capela da Nossa Senhora do Socorro** was built – according to the inscription – on the site of Lamego's first cathedral, founded by the Suevian Idácio, who crowned himself Bishop of Lamego in 435. Further down the narrow street is a small circular *praça*, to the right of which, behind the wall, lies a thirteenth-century subterranean **cisterna** (water cistern) – apparently one of the most beautiful in the country, with a vaulted Romanesque interior, but unfortunately closed to visitors. The enclosing wall itself is remarkable in that virtually every stone contains a different stonemason's mark. Beyond lies the castle's southern gate – the **Porta do Sol** – and the route back down to the avenue.

△ Nossa Senhora dos Remédios

Nossa Senhora dos Remédios

The celebrated shrine of **Nossa Senhora dos Remédios** (daily: May–Sept 7.30am–8pm; Oct–Apr 7.30am–6pm) is a major point of pilgrimage in late August and early September, when a reputation for healing miracles draws devotees from all over the country. Standing on a hill overlooking the city, at the end of a wide avenue of shady chestnut trees, it's approached by a magnificently elaborate eighteenth-century stairway, modelled on the one at Bom Jesus near Braga. Its 611 steps – which the most committed ascend on their knees – are punctuated by a *via santa* of *azulejo*-lined devotional chapels and allegorical fountains and statues. The church itself is surprisingly bright and airy, more colourful than many in the region and a pleasant assembly hall for the ever-present faithful. To escape the crowds, stroll back down the forested tracks of the **Parque dos Remédios** on either side of the steps; early in the morning the air is filled with cuckoo calls and warbling birdsong, although the arrival of picnicking families later in the day can make the park almost as crowded as the steps themselves.

The **Festas de Nossa Senhora dos Remédios** (nicknamed *Romaria de Portugal*) kick off on the last Thursday of August, and continue until 8 September. The opening day sees a popular fair, whilst the pilgrimage itself climaxes over the last three days, when the image of Our Lady leaves Remédios in procession to the Igreja das Chagas in town, where it stays in adoration for two days. The main procession takes place on the last day, with cavalcades of young children in white, and bulls pulling the carriage that transports Our Lady between the Igreja das Chagas and Igreja de Santa Cruz. In addition to the pilgrimage, there's a traditional "Battle of Flowers", torchlit parades, dances, concerts, car races, and a fair on the Recinto da Feira, below the sanctuary.

Eating and drinking

Lamego has plenty of **restaurants**, including several characterful *adegas* and *casas de pasto* tucked away from the main avenues – for simple places serving inexpensive regional food look up Rua da Olaria, or at the back of the cathedral along Rua Trás de Sé ("Back-of-the-cathedral street", no less) and Rua Direita. Specialities include *fumeiros* (smoked meats), particularly *presunto* (ham) – often stuffed into grilled trout – and *salpicão* sausages, which even find their way into unleavened *bôla* cakes. The town's food **market** (closed Sat afternoon & Sun) is along Avenida 5 de Outubro. The esplanade **bars and cafés** in the middle of the avenue are the hub for summertime evening drinkers (and ice cream addicts), and the trees here provide ample shade for a midday rest.

The local **Caves da Raposeira** is no longer open for public visits, though every restaurant serves its sparkling *espumante* wine. The only possible vineyard visit is to the *Caves da Murganheira* between Ucanha and Salzedas (see "Around Lamego", below).

O Combinado Rua da Olaria 84 ☎254 612 902. A typical local *tasca* where you can eat well for around €6. Apart from staples like grilled pork chops and trout, a speciality is *arroz de cabidela* – rice with blood and seasoning. Closed Sun in winter. Inexpensive.

O Novo Largo da Sé 9 ☎254 613 166. Inside, it's a mix of old *azulejos* and modern design, though the big draw is dining at an outdoor table in front of the cathedral. It's a bit pricier than usual (dishes €7–9) and the menu ranges from local *salpicão* sausages and rice to grilled fish. Closed Sat in winter. Moderate.

Trás da Sé Rua Trás da Sé 12 ☎254 614 075. The paint-daubed walls are lined with notepaper messages of congratulation, and the food and local wine is reliably good. There's a short menu, with a handwritten list of daily specials, including grilled trout stuffed with *presunto* – most dishes cost €5–8. Closed Wed evening. Inexpensive.

Around Lamego

The country **around Lamego** is characterized by a series of sparsely inhabited mountain ranges whose fertile valleys are strung with picturesque villages and vineyards. All sport long traditions of local handicraft industries, and there's still a thriving cultural life, but the tourist infrastructure is minimal, save for a smattering of rural tourism manor houses. These lands were among the earliest to be relinquished by the Moors in the face of the Christian Reconquista, and the resultant chapels and monasteries are their glory. Needless to say, public transport is patchy, and tends to follow school timetables (ie, no service at weekends): Balsemão aside (which you can walk to), you *could* reach all the places mentioned below by bus from Lamego bus station, but you would be hanging around for ages at sights that – though worth seeing – are more realistically done as half-day car trips from town. Incidentally, the N226, off which several of the churches lie, makes a useful approach to the Beira Alta region (see p.289), with Trancoso a pretty 75-kilometre drive away.

Balsemão

The ancient **Capela de São Pedro de Balsemão** (Tues 2–6pm, Wed–Sun 10am–12.30pm & 2–6pm, closed on the third weekend of the month) sits in a small square of granite cobbles in the tranquil hamlet of Balsemão. It's a pleasant three-kilometre walk from Lamego, with the turns all signposted: left at the Capela do Desterro, down into the old quarters of town and across a bridge; another left at a fork on to the hillside road; the third left a little later, taking you down into the valley and above a rushing river. Believed to have been founded in the seventh century by the Suevi, the present foundations were actually laid in the tenth century during the Reconquista. The undistinguished granite facade and dark interior give it the air of a family vault, an impression strengthened by the imposing fourteenth-century sarcophagus of the Bishop of Porto, Dom Afonso Pires, who was born in Balsemão. The florid capitals encircling the tomb

A left turn off the N2 Lamego–Castro Daire road leads to the small and normally unre-markable village of **Lazarim**, which plays host to one of the oddest rituals to survive in Portugal. The **Entrudo dos Compadres** is a carnival that has taken place every Shrove Tuesday since the Middle Ages. Revellers celebrate the end of winter and the beginning of spring by taking to the streets wearing beautifully carved wooden masks, symbolic of the event's licentiousness. Despite the lewd masquerades, Entrudo dos Compadres is also a time of castigation for the year passed: from a balcony on Largo do Padrão, two colourful dolls loaded with fireworks are presented to the crowd – the *compadre*, carried by two young women, and *comadre*, toted by two young men. The couples proceed to recite insulting rhymes centring on sexual behaviour, which, in the manner of Punch and Judy, are often maliciously aimed at certain unnamed people in the crowd below. After the recital, the fireworks are lit and the dolls disintegrate in an explosive fury of smoke and flame, marking the end of the festival and the old year and the beginning of the new.

make the few remaining Suevi curls on the archway into the choir seem subdued by comparison. Look out for the profoundly pregnant statue of Nossa Senhora do Ó (that's Ó as in the shape of her belly, though others ascribe it to the excla-mation uttered when seeing it: *Ó! Nossa Senhora, Mãe de Deus...*).

Ucanha and Salzedas

Twelve kilometres from Lamego, down the N226 Moimenta da Beira road and just past Tarouca, there's a signposted left-turn for **UCANHA**, another 3km beyond. The old village sits below the road, where a majestic fortified stone tollgate and single–arched bridge (signposted "Torre Fortificada") straddle the lazy river. They date from the 1160s, when the diocese was awarded to Teresa Afonso, erstwhile nursemaid to Afonso Henriques' five sons and heirs and widow of Egas Moniz, the first king's tutor and closest adviser. Besides marking and protecting the border of her domain, these structures were also, of course, an ostentatious mark of manorial power. Today, clothes are hung out to dry under the arches, though the adjacent open-air washing pools are no longer used. It's a pretty scene, with a little bar at either end of the cobbled bridge, and a riverside path that runs up through the woods to a local river beach.

SALZEDAS lies another 3km along the road beyond Uncanha, its Augus-tinian – later Cistercian – **monastery** (daily 10am–12.30pm & 2–6pm) dating from 1168. The mildewed main facade presides over the small square of the diminutive village, where there are a couple of simple cafés. Inside, the musty smell is kept at bay by a team of volunteers, scrubbing the stone and swabbing the floors, while out through a side door a succession of abandoned courtyards and cloisters bear the scars of a period of extensive pillage and decay, which began in 1834 with the dissolution of the monasteries.

On the road between Uncanha and Salzedas lie the **Caves da Murganheira** (visits usually at 10am, 11am, 3pm & 4pm), producers of a renowned *espumante* wine – if you're going to make a special trip out here, get Lamego turismo to check current visiting hours first.

São João de Tarouca

The small village of **SÃO JOÃO DE TAROUCA**, off the N226, 17km southeast of Lamego, was the site of the first Cistercian monastery to be founded on the Iberian peninsula, the earliest known reference to it dating from 1139. It's associated with Afonso Henriques, the first king of Portugal, who, it is said, laid the founding stone after his victories at Trancoso and Sernancelhe in Beira Alta. Rebuilt in the seventeenth century, it was thoroughly trashed after the 1834 dissolution, leaving only a vast ruined shell of roofless monastic buildings, scattered tombstones and a lone belltower. The scale is impressive, if nothing else, while the adjacent Romanesque **church** (May–Sept Tues 2.30–6pm, Wed–Sun 10am–12.30pm & 2–6pm; Oct–April Tues 2–5.30pm, Wed–Sun 9.30–12.30pm & 2–5.30pm) – consecrated in 1169 – remains intact. Note the fine carved choir and the Baroque organ (1766) whose central figure marks time with his arm during Mass. *Azulejos* in the transepts depict the life of Saint Bernard, including one of him standing in a wine barrel (a pre-Christian symbol of abundance).

Entry to the church is free, though if the guide accompanies you, pointing things out, you should tip him. There's a local café-bar nearby, and five minutes' walk downhill is a lovely Roman bridge over the Rio Varosa – a pleasant spot for a picnic. The church is signposted off to the right, past Mondim da Beira, 1.5km after the Uncanha junction on the N226, and it's another 3.5km from the turn.

Pinhão

East of Peso da Régua the country continues craggy and beautiful, with the softer hills of the interior fading dark green into the distance. The minor N222 hugs the south side of the Douro river, the train the north side, until the small town of **PINHÃO**, 25km to the east, the main centre for quality ports. It's a wonderful route and there's a real sense of arrival at Pinhão, where the river broadens and the terraced hills close in. Cruise boats tie up along a broad riverside esplanade, where a couple of bars look out over a fjord-like vista and there's a welcome breeze in the evening air.

Trains pull in at the *azulejo*-clad station in town, just above the river – timetables are posted on the station walls, including (rather optimistically, in this backwater) connections from Lisbon for services to Paris. There are five daily trains on to Tua (15min) and the end of the Douro line at Pocinho (1hr); change at Tua for the branch line service to Mirandela (two connections a day).

Pinhão is only a one-street place, but warrants a night if you book your **accommodation** ahead. It's also an early-to-bed place, with most of its efforts put into catering for day-trippers. **Restaurant** choices are a bit disappointing, with both the *Veladouro* on the quayside and the *Cais da Foz*, across the pedestrian bridge, admirably sited with river views but sporting lacklustre, though inexpensive menus. *Vintage House* has a good, formal and expensive restaurant; otherwise, best choice is the restaurant at the *Residencial Douro* – it charges more than it should (dishes €8–10), but there are a few fish choices alongside the standard meat menu and the house wine is excellent.

Residencial Douro ☎ & ℱ 254 732 404. The best of the two similarly priced, adjacent places opposite the station, with a vine-covered terrace and simple en-suite rooms with balconies that overlook the water. It's hard to say what's more disconcerting – the cruise ships or the weekend steam trains, both disgorging their passengers below your window. ❸

Pousada de Alijó 15km northeast of Pinhão ☎ 259 959 467, ⓦ www.pousadas.pt. The nearest *pousada* is in a small village north of the Douro river – it's a handsome country house with many of the 21 rooms having a terrace overlooking the pool. There's a bar and restaurant. ❻

Quinta de la Rosa 1.5km west of Pinhão, on the north bank of the river ☎ 254 732 254, ⓦ www.quintadelarosa.com. Stay on a working wine estate for the chance to see at first hand the early processes of port wine making. The five rooms are split between main house and annex, and there are also two larger suites and a swimming pool. Discounts for stays longer than one night, ④, river view suite ⑤ **Vintage House** ☎254 730 230, ⓦwww .hotelvintagehouse.com. Top-of-the-range is this sumptuously decorated former warehouse on the riverfront, whose 37 rooms and six suites all have a water-view balcony or terrace. It's extremely agreeable, with lovely grounds, a pool, and a shop selling some of the region's rarest tipples. *Quinta* visits, wine tastings and courses, and train tours can be arranged from the hotel. ⑥, Nov–March ⑤

Vila Nova de Foz Côa

Sitting high above the Côa valley, 60km southeast of Pinhão, the small town of **VILA NOVA DE FOZ CÔA** would attract no interest at all had it not been for the discovery in 1992 of the most extensive array of outdoor **Palaeolithic art** in Europe. The engravings – found along 17km of the river's rocky schist valley – are of a similar style to those found in caves across Europe, but their uniqueness lies in the fact that they are outside on exposed rock faces. With the oldest dated at around 23,000 years, their survival is remarkable, even more so since the proposed building of a controversial dam threatened to submerse the site and the engravings completely. However, after a vociferous campaign the sites were declared a National Monument in 1997 and a UNESCO World Heritage site a year later. The bulk of the rock art is now protected by the park, which covers much of the area east and south of the town.

There are three rock art sites to visit (see below), though the restrictions on numbers and visiting hours mean you're unlikely to see more than two in any one day. Depending on how keen you are, this might mean an overnight stop in Foz Côa, though there is no earthly reason otherwise to stay. A tiny old town area preserves an **Igreja Matriz** with an impressive Manueline doorway and sixteenth-century pillory in the square outside, but that's it. Although the blistering midsummer heat and winter cold makes it hard to believe, the town benefits from a Mediterranean microclimate, proof of which is provided by the locally produced almonds, fruit, cheese, wine and – especially – olive oil, among the country's finest. You can stock up at the **Adega Cooperativa** (daily 9am–12.30am & 2–6pm), 200m down the Pocinho road from the bus station. The big annual shindig is the Festa de São Martinho on November 11, with parades, music and a couple of oxen pulling a 200-litre barrel of wine whose contents become lighter as the day wears on. The **monthly market** is on the first Tuesday of the month next to the football field, and the blossoming of **almond trees** draws the crowds in late February and early March.

Practicalities

Foz Côa is an hour's drive from Pinhão along the highly scenic N222, which veers south over the hills away from the Douro river. The train meanwhile sticks with the Douro as far as its terminus at **Pocinho**, which is little more than its railway station, a hydroelectric dam and a couple of restaurants. Vila Nova de Foz Côa is 8km south of Pocinho and if there's no connecting bus into town you'll be able to take a taxi for around €6.

In Foz Côa the **bus station** is along the road in from Pocinho – there are daily services back to Pocinho, and on to destinations in Trás-os-Montes, as well as south to the Beiras and beyond. From the bus station, walk 200m up the road to the red mansion at the junction with the main avenue, Avenida Gago Coutinho. The three places to stay are right opposite, on the avenue;

△ Vila Nova de Foz Côa

turn left for the park office (150m down the avenue) and old town beyond; turn right for the **turismo** (daily 9am–12.30pm & 2–5.30pm; ☎279 760 329, ⊕www.cm-fozcoa.pt), in the same complex as the library, theatre, cinema, and **municipal museum** (same hours; free), with all sorts of temporary exhibitions. There's a **taxi** rank on Avenida Gago Coutinho, facing the park office, while for **tours and outdoor activities** in the area – including night visits to the rock art sites – contact Impactus (☎962 838 261, ⊕www.impactus.pt), based in nearby Castelo Melhor.

Finding **accommodation** isn't difficult, though the two cheaper places on the avenue, the adjacent residencials *Avenida* and *Marina*, leave something to be desired – not least the immediate proximity of the main road and the late-night *Gaiteiro Bar* with outdoor terrace.

Accommodation

Quinta do Chão d'Ordem 5km south, just south of Muxagata, off the N102 ☎279 762 427, ⊕www.chaodordem.com. Eight bedrooms available on a working farm, with a cosy lounge and bar, library, tennis court and pool, and wine cellar in a converted dovecote. It's an artistically minded place with tasteful decor, and much of the produce, from the wine to the home-cured sausages, is grown and made on the farm. ❸

Pousada de Juventude 1.5km northwest of town off the Pocinho road ☎279 768 190, ⊕www.pousadasjuventude.pt. Not a great location if you don't have transport, but redeemed by good facilities and windswept views. Private rooms available, with and without toilet, and also four-person apartments with kitchenette. Dorm beds €11, rooms ❶, apartments ❸

Albergaria Vale do Côa Av Cidade Nova 1A, facing the turismo ☎279 760 010, ⊕www.albergariavaledocoa.net. The best place in town has spacious a/c rooms with satellite TV and polished wooden floors, most with balconies, plus double glazing and spotless bathrooms with bathtubs. There's also a good restaurant attached, the *Rota das Gravuras* (moderate; closed Mon), serving regional specialities and wine from their own *quinta*. No credit cards. ❸

Restaurant

A Marisqueira Rua de São Miguel 35 ☎279 762 187. Just 2min from the park office, down the pedestrianized continuation of the avenue, this is a reliable stop for lunch or dinner. There is seafood, as the name suggests, including *arroz de marisco*, but in the end it's just as much a meat-and-potatoes place as anywhere else. For snacks and bread, visit *A Terrinca* bakery- tea room next door. Moderate.

Parque Arqueológico do Vale do Côa (PAVC)

Visits to the rock art sites have to be booked through the **PAVC headquarters** in Foz Côa, signposted throughout town as "Sede do PAVC", Avenida Gago Coutinho 19A (Tues–Sun 9am–12.30pm & 2–5.30pm; ☎279 768 260,

@ www.ipa.min-cultura.pt/pavc). Bookings can also be made by telephone; in summer, reserving two or three days in advance is recommended – there are **no tours on Mondays**. The €5 per-site fee includes a guide and 4WD transport from the appropriate visitor centre (see below); each trip has a maximum of eight visitors, and children under 3 are not allowed. There is some walking involved, so it's a good idea to bring a hat and a bottle of water.

The park contains thousands of engravings on several hundred rocks, a good number of which are clustered around the three major sites. The engravings are of horses, deer, goats and other animals, as well as later, Neolithic, images of people – many are quite hard to make out, as unlike cave art they are not painted but were scratched or chipped with stones. If you only have time to visit one site, Penascosa is considered the most interesting, while Canada do Inferno is the easiest option without your own transport as you're taken directly from the park office in Foz Côa.

The sites

A short drive from the park office, **Canada do Inferno** (Tues–Sun: May–Sept 9.15am–10.30am; Oct–April 10am–2.30pm; tour lasts 1hr 30min) – close to the abandoned Côa dam – was the first site to be identified. It contains a wide variety of engravings, from bisons to horses, some very close to the current water line and many more underwater since the construction of the Pocinho dam upstream raised the level.

For the other two sites, you have to make your own way to the respective visitor centres. Trips to **Ribeira de Piscos** (Tues–Sun, May–Sept 9.30am–3pm; Oct–April 10am–2.30pm; 2hr 30min) head out from Muxagata, 1km off the N102 to Guarda, which has a bar beside the visitor centre. The engravings are spread out along the eponymous *ribeira* down to its confluence with the Côa – a beautiful place, but there's a lot of walking involved. The highlights are a tender engraving of two horses "kissing", some fine engravings of auroch bisons (now extinct) and an exceptionally rare Palaeolithic engraving of a man.

The least strenuous visit is to **Penascosa** (Tues–Sun, May–Sept 2–5.30pm; Oct–April 1–3.30pm; 1hr 30min), as the jeeps park right next to it. The starting-point is the visitor centre in Castelo Melhor, just off the N322 to Figueira de Castelo Rodrigo. Penascosa's highlights include an engraving of a fish (one of very few such depictions worldwide), and a rock containing over a dozen superimposed animals, the meaning of which archeologists are at a loss to understand. The village itself has a gorgeous ruined castle, and a couple of café-restaurants, one opposite the visitor centre.

There's also a private site at **Quinta da Ervamoira** (closed Mon; visits by appointment: ☏ 279 759 229), a secluded vineyard on the west bank of the Côa between Ribeira de Piscos and Penascosa, accessed from Muxagata. It's owned by the Ramos Pinto port wine company, whose granite estate house is now a museum housing finds from Roman and medieval times and other displays – the park office can add this as an option to the Ribeira de Piscos tour, if you tell them in advance.

Barca d'Alva

The last Portuguese village along the Douro, **BARCA D'ALVA** is less than 2km from the Spanish border. Overlooked by mountains on all sides, and with a row of whitewashed cottages facing the river, it is the final destination of some of the river cruises from Porto, but it's looking a little neglected since the railway line across the border was discontinued in the 1980s. There really is no need to visit, though it's set in attractive enough surroundings – agricultural land dotted with boulders, storks' nests and conical, stone-roofed houses, with the terraced vineyards still providing grapes for the port companies in Porto. Unless you arrive on a cruise, access is a problem, in so much as there is no road along the Douro river in its latter stages after Pocinho. From Foz Côa, it's a 35-kilometre drive south along the N332 to Figueira de Castelo Rodrigo in Beira Alta (see p.296), and then another 20km north along the N221 to the village and border – a bit of a schlep for a one-horse village where there's nothing to do when it's not your turn with the horse. Still, it's a roundabout back-country route into Trás-os-Montes, were you so inclined, with similarly isolated Freixo de Espada à Cinta another 22km beyond, and further long hauls in prospect on to Mogadouro and Miranda do Douro.

Travel details

Trains

Amarante to: Livração (6–8 daily; 26min); Porto (6–8 daily; 1hr 30min).
Livração to: Amarante (6–8 daily; 26min).
(Peso da) Régua to: Pinhão (5 daily; 26min); Pocinho (5 daily; 1hr 25min); Porto (12 daily; 1hr 45min–2hr 20min); Tua (5 daily; 42min); Vila Real (5 daily; 55min).
Pinhão to: Pocinho (5 daily; 1hr); Régua (5 daily; 26min); Tua (5 daily; 15min).
Pocinho to: Pinhão (5 daily; 1hr); Régua (5 daily; 1hr 25min); Tua (5 daily; 40min).
Porto to: Aveiro (every 10–30min; 40–55min); Barcelos (14 daily; 1hr); Braga (every 30–60min; 1hr); Coimbra (hourly; 1hr 15min–1hr 50min); Espinho (every 10–30min; 15–55min); Guimarães (12 daily; 1hr 5min); Lisbon (hourly; 3hr 20min–4hr); Régua (12 daily; 1hr 45min–2hr 20min); Valença (9 daily; 2–3hr); Viana do Castelo (every 1–2hr; 1hr 30min–2hr).
Tua to: Mirandela (2 daily; 1hr 35min); Pinhão (5 daily; 15min); Régua (5 daily; 42min); Pocinho (5 daily; 40min).

Buses

Amarante to: Braga (5–8 daily; 1hr 20min); Guimarães (5–8 daily; 50min); Porto (up to 10 daily; 1hr); Vila Real (hourly; 1hr 40min).

Lamego to: Braga (daily; 2hr 50min); Lisbon (2–4 daily; 6hr); Penafiel (3–5 daily; 1hr 40min); Peso da Régua (hourly; 30min); Porto (3–5 daily; 3hr); Trancoso (1–2 daily; 2hr); Viseu (5–7 daily; 1hr 20min).
Peso da Régua to: Coimbra (1–2 daily; 3hr 40min); Guarda (daily; 2hr 30min); Lamego (hourly; 30min); Vila Real (hourly; 40min); Viseu (6 daily; 1hr 30min).
Porto to: Amarante (up to 10 daily; 1hr); Barcelos (7 daily; 1hr 45min); Braga (17 daily; 1hr 15min); Bragança (6 daily; 3hr 30min); Chaves (6–12 daily; 3hr 30min); Coimbra (8–10 daily; 1hr 30min); Guimarães (12 daily; 1hr); Lamego/Peso da Régua (3–5 daily; 3hr); Lisbon (hourly; 3hr–3hr 30min); Viana do Castelo (hourly; 1hr 15min); Vila Real (9 daily; 2hr).
Vila do Conde to: Viana do Castelo (hourly; 1hr 20min).
Vila Nova de Foz Côa to: Bragança (2 daily; 2hr); Coimbra (1 daily; 4hr); Guarda (Mon–Fri 1 daily; 1hr 30min); Miranda do Douro (4–5 daily; 2hr 10min); Trancoso (4 daily; 40min); Viseu (4 daily; 2hr).

The Minho

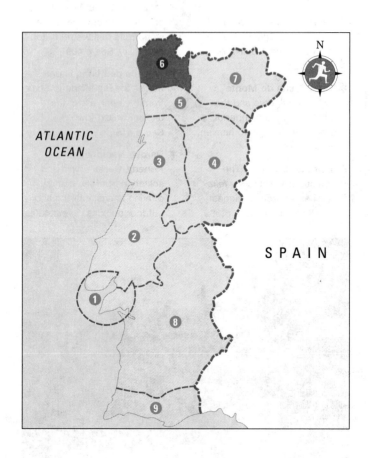

CHAPTER 6 Highlights

* **Guimarães** The country's first capital is an attractive maze of cobbled streets, medieval monuments and hidden squares. **See p.379**

* **Citânia de Briteiros** Step back to pre-Roman times at the magnificent Celtic hill fort. **See p.386**

* **Bom Jesus do Monte** Join the pilgrims and the penitents on a wonderful Baroque stairway to heaven. **See p.396**

* **Feira de Barcelos** The spectacular Thursday *feira* is one of Europe's biggest weekly markets. **See p.399**

* **Costa Verde beaches** There's always space to lay your towel on the golden sands of the rugged Atlantic coast. **See p.403**

* **Monte de Santa Luzia** Enjoy one of the best views in the world from this breezy hilltop sanctuary. **See p.409**

* **Valença do Minho** Gaze across the Rio Minho to Spain from the ramparts of the ancient walled town. **See p.415**

* **Parque Nacional da Peneda-Gerês** A wild and solitary part of the country offering fantastic hiking and outdoor pursuits. **See p.430**

△ Castle, Guimarães

6

The Minho

Many Portuguese consider the **Minho** – the province north of Porto – to be the most beautiful part of their country. A rolling province of lush river valleys, forested hillsides, trailing vines and long, sandy beaches, it is certainly pleasing to the eye, especially in the mountainous east, where you can still see wooden-wheeled ox-carts creak down cobbled lanes. Age-old customs are also maintained throughout the region at dozens of huge country markets, *festas* and *romarias*. In summer, especially, you're likely to happen upon these fairs and festivals and it's worth trying to plan a trip around the larger events if you're keen to experience Minho life at its most exuberant.

In the late 1950s, Minho, more than any other area of Portugal, suffered severe depopulation as thousands migrated to France, Switzerland, Germany and the United States in search of more lucrative work. In the last decade or so, however, European Union money has helped fund an efficient and growing network of fast new roads. With Porto and Galicia in Spain just a short drive away, Minho has become a relatively prosperous region. Many emigrants have returned, and a wave of building on the back of their new-found prosperity has all but engulfed many of the smaller towns.

But the historical centres are as appealing as ever, none more so than **Guimarães**, first capital of Portugal with UNESCO World Heritage status. Equally spruce and historic is neighbouring **Braga**, the country's ecclesiastical centre. Between them lie the extensive Celtic ruins of the **Citânia de Briteiros**, one of the most impressive archeological sites in Portugal, while from Braga it's also easy to visit **Barcelos**, site of the best known and biggest of the region's weekly markets. It takes place on Thursdays, although for the full experience reserve a room in advance and arrive on Wednesday evening.

At Barcelos, you're only 20km from the **Costa Verde**, the Minho coast, which runs north all the way to the Spanish border. Although this boasts some wonderful beaches along the way, the weather is as unpredictable as the sea, with cool temperatures possible even in midsummer. The principal resort is **Viana do Castelo**, a lively town with an elegant historic core and, if you're seeking isolation, beaches to the north and south that scarcely see visitors. The coast ends at **Caminha**, beyond which the **Rio Minho** runs inland, forming the border with Spanish Galicia. This is a delightful region, featuring a string of compact fortified towns flanking the river on the Portuguese side. Their fortresses, in various stages of disrepair, stare across at Spain, with the most compelling stop at the bustling old town of **Valença do Minho**.

Inland from Viana, the Minho's other major river, the beautiful **Rio Lima**, idles east through a succession of gorgeous small towns where there's little to do but soak up the somnolent scenery. Indeed, it's in the Lima valley, particularly around the town of **Ponte de Lima**, that you'll find the pick of the region's famous rural-tourism and manor-house accommodation. Further east, the gentle Minho scenery eventually gives way to the mountains, waterfalls, river gorges, reservoirs and forests of the protected **Parque Nacional da Peneda-Gerês**, Portugal's only national (as opposed to natural) park. This is superb camping and hiking territory, stretching from the main town and spa of **Caldas do Gerês** north as far as the Rio Minho and the Spanish border and east into Trás-os-Montes. It's possible to dip into the park from nearby towns, but you really need to devote several days if you're going to see the more isolated regions as bus services are limited. Even by car the going's slow and on foot you could spend weeks exploring the trails.

Southern Minho

The southern Minho's two chief towns, **Guimarães** and **Braga**, are both small enough to walk around in a busy day's sightseeing, although a night's stay brings greater rewards. This is especially true if you want to explore the series of religious attractions around Braga, none more extraordinary than the pilgrimage sites of **Bom Jesus do Monte** and **Tibães**, while you'll need to set aside another half-day at least to see the Celtic remains of **Citânia de Briteiros**. For shoppers, the best overnight stop is undoubtedly at **Barcelos**, provided you can find a room on a Wednesday night before the weekly market.

You can easily reach any of these places within an hour's drive of Porto. Braga is on a branch of the main train line from Porto to Viana do Castelo; for non-direct **trains** you need to change at Nine. Direct but dawdling trains travel to Guimarães from Porto on a separate branch line. Regardless of this, it is far quicker to use the direct **bus** between Braga and Guimarães rather than fiddle about with connections between train lines.

Guimarães and around

GUIMARÃES never misses an opportunity to remind you of its place in Portuguese history. Birthplace of the first king, Afonso Henriques, in 1110 and first capital of the fledging kingdom of "Portucale", it has every right to be proud of its role in the formation of the nation. It was from here that the reconquest from the Moors began, leading to the subsequent creation of a united kingdom that, within a century of Afonso's death, was to stretch to its present borders. Although Guimarães subsequently lost its pre-eminent status to Coimbra (elevated to Portuguese capital in 1143), it has never relinquished its sense of self-importance, something that's evident from the careful preservation of an array of impressive medieval monuments and the omnipresent reminder "*Portugal nasceu aqui*" (Portugal was born here). Today, despite its industrial outskirts, the centre of Guimarães retains both a grandeur and a tangible sense of history in a labyrinth of attractive, narrow streets that have earned it UNESCO World Heritage status. But it's far from a museum piece – the local university gives it a youthful exuberance and lively nightlife, at its best during the end of May student week festivities.

The major event, however, is the **Festas Gualterianas** (for São Gualter, or St Walter), which has taken place on the first weekend in August every year since 1452. If you miss this you can catch most of the same stallholders and something of the atmosphere on the following weekend in Caldas de Vizela, a spa town 10km south of Guimarães. Next in importance is the long-established *romaria* to **São Torcato**, 6km northeast of town, on the first weekend in July, while a well-timed visit in winter will enable you to see one or more of the festivals of **Nicolinas** (Nov 29 to Dec 7), **Nossa Senhora da Conceição** (Dec 8) and **Santa Luzia** (Dec 13).

Guimarães is also just 15km from **Citânia de Briteiros**, one of Portugal's most impressive and atmospheric archeological sites.

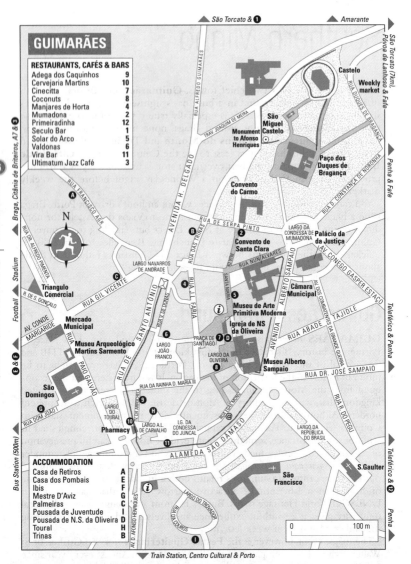

GUIMARÃES

RESTAURANTS, CAFÉS & BARS

Adega dos Caquinhos	9
Cervejaria Martins	10
Cinecitta	7
Coconuts	8
Manjares de Horta	4
Mumadona	2
Primeiradinha	12
Seculo Bar	1
Solar do Arco	5
Valdonas	6
Vira Bar	11
Ultimatum Jazz Café	3

ACCOMMODATION

Casa de Retiros	A
Casa dos Pombais	E
Ibis	F
Mestre D'Aviz	G
Palmeiras	C
Pousada de Juventude	I
Pousada de N.S. da Oliveira	D
Toural	H
Trinas	B

0   100 m

▼ Train Station, Centro Cultural & Porto

Arrival and information

Guimarães's historic centre is pedestrianized, although metered **parking** is available in the streets around the old town walls. Free parking can be had at the big Largo das Hortas car park (follow signs to the Teleférico); there are also usually spaces on the far side of the Castelo (though not on Fri when it hosts a market). The **bus station** is fifteen-minute walk southwest of the town centre at the bottom of Avenida Conde Margaride. It's part of the Guimarães shopping complex, unmarked but identifiable by the Continente supermarket or

McDonald's sign above the entrance. There are express bus services from Porto and Lisbon, and regular weekday connections with Braga, Amarante, Cabeceiras and Mondim de Basto, and Póvoa do Lanhoso. Guimarães train station is ten minutes' walk south of the centre; to get into town, bear left from the station and take the first right down Avenida Dom Afonso Henriques, which takes you to the leafy boulevard of Alameda São Damaso.

The **main turismo** is at Alameda São Damaso 83 (Mon–Fri 9.30am–12.30pm & 2–6.30pm; ☎253 412 450, ⓦwww.cm-guimaraes.pt). There's also a **branch turismo** in the old town at Praça de Santiago 37 (Mon–Fri 9.30am–6.30pm, Sat 10am–6pm, Sun 10am–1pm; ☎253 518 790).

Accommodation

Apart from during the major festivals, **accommodation** is rarely a problem, though it's best to book ahead, especially if you're planning to stay in the *pousadas* or in one of a number of superb manor houses in the vicinity. The turismo has details of these (ask for *turismo rural*), but we've highlighted a couple of the best below. The town also has one of the country's top **youth hostels**.

In Guimarães

Hotel Ibis Av Conde Margaride 4810 ☎253 424 900, ⓦwww.ibishotel.com. The rooms are bland and small but adequate in this modern chain hotel, next to the bus terminal. Very good low season rates. ❷

Residencial Mestre D'Aviz Rua Dom João I 40 ☎253 422 770, ⓕ253 422 771. On a quiet street just outside the old town, this is the best value place in town, with very pleasant rooms in a lovely converted town house. Best rooms have balconies, though those in the attic are also atmospheric. It even has its own neat living room and bar. ❷

Albergaria das Palmeiras Centro Comercial das Palmeiras 4°, Rua Gil Vicente ☎253 410 324, ⓕ253 417 261. Reached by a lift on the fourth storey of a commercial mall, which can make access hard when the mall closes at midnight (ring for entry). Once in, rooms are modern and roomy and some have a balcony – there's also a roof terrace. ❸

Casa dos Pombais Av de Londres ☎253 412 917, ⓦwww.solaresdeportugal.pt. Opposite the bus station and marooned by a busy road, this eighteenth-century manor house is an oasis with attractive gardens. There are only two guest rooms, with grand furniture but homely touches, though they have received mixed reports from readers. There's no reception, so phone ahead to ensure owners are in. ❸

Pousada de Juventude Largo da Cidade ☎253 421 380, ⓦwww.pousadasjuventude .pt. One of Portugal's newest and nicest hostels, partly built into a renovated mansion (and partly in a new wing). On a quiet side street, it boasts its own gardens, café, courtyard, shared kitchens and parking. Recommended. Dorms €13, double rooms ❷.

Pousada de Nossa Senora da Oliveira Rua de Santa Maria ☎253 514 157, ⓦwww.pousadas.pt. Converted from a row of sixteenth-century houses, right in the medieval centre, this sixteen-room *pousada* is beautifully furnished with antiques and exudes a sense of history. Overlooking narrow alleys, the rooms are slightly dark but extremely comfortable. The restaurant (reservations required; expensive) is the finest in town, with traditional Minho dishes served in a wonderful antique dining room or at outside tables in summer. ❻

Casa de Retiros Rua Francisco Agra 163 ☎253 511 515, ⓕ253 511 517. A pilgrims' hostel and as a result one of the cheaper places in town. Be prepared for a simple existence: spartan surroundings, bland breakfasts, lots of house rules and a strict 11.30pm curfew. Single rooms offer good value. No credit cards. ❷

Hotel Toural Largo do Toural, entrance in Largo A. L. de Carvalho at the back ☎253 517 184, ⓦwww .hoteltoural.com. Elegant town house renovated into a modern four-star establishment next to the music academy – so expect delightful sounds to waft through the window. Rooms are spacious and plush, there's a pleasant bar overlooking a central courtyard and it has parking. ❹

Residencial das Trinas Rua das Trinas 29 ☎253 517 358, ⓦwww.residencialtrinas.com. In a fine town house in a great position right in the old-town, this good value *residencial* has eleven modest but comfortable rooms. Rooms overlooking the street have the atmosphere – rear rooms are noisier, although are double-glazed – and all have private bathrooms and satellite TV. ❷

Outside Guimarães

Casa de Sezim Nespereira, 4km south of Guimarães off the Santo Tirso road – turn right at Covas ℡ 253 523 000, ⓦ www.sezim.pt. Ten rooms in a delightful aristocratic country estate owned by the same *vinho verde*-producing family for over six centuries – the current incumbent is charming. Eight rooms in the main powder-pink eighteenth-century *solar* (manor) are furnished with Murano chandeliers and *objets d'art*, with four-posters in many. There's also a swimming pool, tennis court and walking and horse-riding trips can be arranged. ⑥

Paço de São Cipriano Tabuadelo, 6km south of Guimarães off the Santo Tirso road – turn left at Covas ℡ 253 565 337, ⓦ www.solaresdeportugal .pt. The owners of this stunning partly fifteenth-century country house have traditionally received pilgrims en route to Santiago de Compostela, and the property comes complete with chapel and medieval tower. There are seven guest rooms, plus orchards, vineyards and a swimming pool. Closed Nov–March. ⑤

Pousada de Santa Marinha da Costa 2km southeast of Guimarães along Rua Dr José Sampaio ℡ 253 511 249, ⓦ www.pousadas.pt. Occupying a convent at the foot of Monte Penha, parts of which date from the ninth century, this is reckoned to be one of the top *pousadas* in the country. Elegant, comfortable rooms gather around a serene courtyard; the original rooms have more character than the new additions. There's also an outdoor pool with splendid views and an excellent restaurant. ⑦

Campsites

Caldas das Taipas 7km northwest of Guimarães ℡ 253 576 274. By the banks of the Rio Ave, off the N101. Pricey but attractive, with a swimming pool and a thermal spa nearby. Closed Oct–May.

Parque de Campismo da Penha 2km southeast of Guimarães ℡ 253 515 912, ℻ 253 515 085. The nearest site to town is a pleasant place on the slopes of Penha and accessible by the cable car at the end of Rua Dr José Sampaio. There's a small swimming pool and some bungalows for rent (③). Officially open April–Oct, though worth ringing ahead at other times.

The town

The **old centre** of Guimarães is an elongated kernel of small, enclosed squares and cobbled streets dominated by warm, honey-coloured balconied houses. Bounded at its southern end by the town gardens and overlooked from the north by the imposing castle, it is an enduring symbol of the emergent Portuguese nation. In between lie a series of medieval churches, convents and buildings that lend an air of dignity to the streets – two of the convents provide an impressive backdrop to a couple of the country's more illuminating museums. The presence of the University of the Minho gives local cafés and bars a lively, student-orientated feel, particularly in the old town.

Around the Castelo

Partly built into huge granite outcrops, the imposing **Castelo** (Mon–Wed 9.30am–5.30pm, Thurs–Sun 9.30am–6.30pm; free) was originally built in the tenth century by the Countess of Mumadona to protect the people of Guimarães from attack by Moors and Normans. It was extended by Afonso Henriques, who established the first Portuguese court here in the twelfth century. After falling into disrepair, and being used as a debtor's prison in the nineteenth century, the castle was rebuilt in the 1940s. You can wander the ramparts and check out the fine views of town. Afonso is reputed to have been born in the great square **keep** (hours as castle, but closes 12.30–2pm Mon–Wed; €1.50), which is surrounded by seven fortified towers. Reached from the walls over a high walkway, you can climb the 77 steps to the top, which opens out onto a narrow tower. Take care because stonework is uneven and narrow in places. The castle is juxtaposed with the diminutive Romanesque chapel of **São Miguel do Castelo** (Mon–Wed 9.30am–5.30pm; Thurs–Sun 9.30am–6.30pm; free) on the grassy slope below, in whose font Afonso is said to have been baptized.

Paço dos Duques de Bragança

Just across from the chapel is the Paço dos Duques de Bragança (July & Aug daily 9.30am–12.30pm & 2–6.30pm; Sept–June daily 9.30am–12.30pm & 2–5.30pm; €3, free Sun mornings). Built in the fifteenth century by the illegitimate son of Dom João I, Dom Afonso, it was constructed along Burgundian lines by a French architect, reflecting Afonso's cosmopolitan tastes. It served as the medieval palace of the all-powerful Bragançan duchy until it fell into decline at the end of the sixteenth century. Under the Salazar dictatorship, its ruins were "restored" as an official residence for the president (the second floor is still reserved for this function), but today it looks faintly ludicrous, like a mock-Gothic Victorian folly. Inside is an extensive collection of portraits (including a room of colourful paintings and sculptures by modern artist José de Guimarães), tapestries, furniture, weapons and porcelain. Free concerts are occasionally held here on summer weekends as part of the annual "Encontros da Primavera" season of concerts; enquire at the turismo for details.

Along Rua de Santa Maria

From the castle, Rua de Santa Maria leads down into the heart of the old town, a beautiful thoroughfare flanked by iron grilles and granite arches. Many of the town's historic buildings have been superbly restored and as you descend to the centre you'll pass one of the loveliest, the sixteenth-century convent of Santa Clara, with its Baroque facade. Today, this serves as the Câmara Municipal. Many of the convent's furnishings were removed after the dissolution of the monasteries and are now displayed in the Museu Alberto Sampaio (see below).

On a much more intimate scale are the buildings ranged around the delightful central squares at the end of the street, **Praça de Santiago** and **Largo da Oliveira**. The latter is dominated by the **Igreja de Nossa Senhora da Oliveira** (daily 7.15am–noon & 3.30–7.30pm; free), a convent-church built (like the great monastery at Batalha) to honour a vow made to the Virgin Mary by João I prior to his decisive victory over Castile at Aljubarrota. Its unusual dedication to "Our Lady of the Olive Tree" dates from the fourteenth century, when an olive tree from the shrine of São Torcato was replanted in the monastery to provide oil for the lamps of the church. The tree died and remained lifeless until September 8, 1342, when a cross, hung from one of its branches, made it grow again. Before it stands a curious Gothic **canopy-shrine**, erected in 1340 to commemorate the Battle of Salado, another one of many disagreements with the Castilians. It also marks the legendary spot where Wamba, unwilling king of the Visigoths, drove a pole into the ground swearing he would not reign until it blossomed. Naturally, it sprouted immediately, in keeping with remarkable growth rates hereabouts. João I, interpreting this as indication of divine favour, rode out to meet the Castilian forces from this very point.

Next door is the convent's simple Romanesque cloister with varied, naively carved capitals. This, and the rooms off it, house the **Museu Alberto Sampaio** (Tues–Sun 10am–6pm, July & Aug open until midnight as Museu à Noite; €2, free Sun mornings), essentially the treasury of the collegiate church and convent but here outstandingly exhibited and containing pieces of real beauty. The highlight is a brilliantly composed silver-gilt *Triptych of the Nativity*, said to have been found in the King of Castile's tent after the Portuguese victory at Aljubarrota in 1385, although it was more probably made from melting down the king's silver measuring weights. Close by is the tunic worn by João I in the battle and beginning to show its age.

Opposite the museum, and housed in a heavy arched structure that was formerly the council chambers, the **Museu de Arte Primitiva Moderna**

(Mon–Fri 9am–12.30pm & 2–5.30pm; free) contains over 300 works by self-taught artists. This provides a fascinating excursion through daily, secular and ritual life and ranges from pure kitsch to the odd gem.

Museu Martins Sarmento

Across to the west, over the main Largo do Toural, the Museu Arqueológico Martins Sarmento (Tues–Sun 9.30am–noon & 2–5pm; €1.50) is another superb collection, named after Martins Sarmento, an archeologist, born in the town, who discovered the Celtic Citânia de Briteiros. Finds from the site and elsewhere in the region are well-displayed in wooden cases in upstairs rooms to show the development of tools and utensils from Paleolithic to Iron Age man. Downstairs, the fourteenth-century Gothic cloister of the Igreja de São Domingos displays a remarkable series of bronze votive offerings (among them, a "coach", pulled at each end by men and oxen) and ornately patterned stone lintels and door-jambs from the huts at Citânia de Briteiros. Most spectacular of all are the Pedras Formosas ("beautiful stones"). Once assumed to be sacrificial altars or portals to funerary monuments, it's now agreed that these were more likely to have been taken from the interiors of bathhouses.

The **Colossus of Pedralva**, a vast granite hulk of a figure with arm raised aloft and an oversized phallus, once the museum's prize exhibit, now stands guard at the pedestrian precinct outside the bus station. More enigmatic and considerably more ancient than the Pedras Formosas, it shares the bold, powerfully hewn appearance of the stone pigs found in Trás-os-Montes and, like them, may date from pre-Celtic fertility cults of around 1500 to 1000 BC.

Santa Marinha da Costa

Two kilometres southeast of Guimarães on the slopes of Penha stands the region's best-preserved medieval building, the former monastery – and now *pousada* – of Santa Marinha da Costa. It can be reached by taking the São Roque bus (Mon–Sat 6am–10pm, Sun 6am–8pm; every 30min) from the main turismo; alight at "Costa" and follow the signs.

The monastery was founded in 1154 by order of Dona Mafalda, the wife of Afonso Henriques, in honour of a vow to Santa Marinha, patron saint of pregnant women. Originally Augustinian, the foundation passed into the hands of the Order of St Jerome in the sixteenth century. In the **chapel** (official hours July–Sept 9am–1pm & 2–7pm, but often closed), Jerome's twin emblems of the skull and the lion are recurring motifs. They are surrounded by an oddly harmonious mixture of styles – tenth-century doorways on the south wall, sixteenth-century panels in the sacristy (including one depicting Jerome beating his breast with a stone against the temptation of women) and an eighteenth-century organ and stone roof in the choir. A catastrophic fire ravaged the monastery in 1951, but careful restoration and its transformation into a *pousada* have returned it to some semblance of its former glory. Strictly speaking, the rest of the monastic buildings are off limits except to guests of the *pousada*, but you can peek into the magnificent **cloister**, with a Mozarabic doorway, while the beautiful **gardens** are open to the public.

Penha

The peak of **Penha** (617m) is crowned by a dull grey church but offers spectacular views over Guimarães. Its surrounding woods are the locals' favourite spot for a Sunday picnic, off paths that skirt round and sometimes under enormous moss-covered boulders. By far the most fun way to reach Penha is to take the ingenious **Teleférico da Penha**, a cable car whose hi-tech bubbles leave from just off Rua Dr José Sampaio (Mon–Fri 10am–7pm, Sat & Sun 10am–8pm; €3.50 return), a five-minute walk from Largo da República do Brasil. If you don't fancy the final five-minute walk to the top from the cable-car station, a little **road train** rumbles up via a cluster of cafés (roughly hourly, €1.50), past one colossal boulder carved with the shape of an eagle.

Eating, drinking and entertainment

Guimarães has no shortage of **cafés** and **restaurants**. Local specialities to look out for – or avoid – include *chispalhada de feijão* (beans, sausage and pig's trotters), *papas de sarabulho* (a blood and bread stew) and *rojões de porco* (roast pork, blood-sausage and potatoes). Desserts include *melindres* (honey cakes), *aletria* (like vermicelli) and *toucinho do céu* ("heavenly bacon"), actually a super-sweet concoction of sugar, almonds, eggs and lemon.

Outside festival time, at the beginning of July and August, the only time the town erupts into spontaneous celebration is when the local football team, **Vitória Guimarães**, wins at home. The stadium – one of the venues for the Euro 2004 Championships – is located to the northwest of the centre, along Rua de São Gonçalo; tickets may be available depending on the status of opponents – consult the turismo or the monthly *Agenda Cultural* listings magazine, which also includes cinema and events at the Centro Cultural de Vila Flôr, near the train station.

Restaurants and cafés

Adega dos Caquinhos Trav da Arrochela ☎253 516 917. Good, reasonably priced food – around €15 for a full meal and drinks – in a rough and ready *adega* whose name reflects its decor; walls are covered in broken crockery (*caquinhos*). Moderate.

Cervejaria Martins Largo do Toural 32–34 ☎253 416 330. Small bar-restaurant liberally swathed in soccer scarves. Grab a seat at the bar and tuck into the speciality prawns or other tasty meals. A great lunch spot. Closed Mon. Inexpensive.

Cinecitta Praça de Santiago 26 ☎963 796 910. This arty place specializes in a big range of salads, pastas and sandwiches. There's a film-themed decor, though most people grab an outdoor seat on the square. Try the smoked ham salad, which is superb. Closed Mon. Inexpensive.

Coconuts Largo da Oliveira 1 (no phone). Small café-bar with its own *azulejos* on one wall. Popular with students, especially the outdoor tables that sprawl out onto the lovely square.

Manjares da Horta Rua João Lopes Faria ☎253 413 277. Bright, modern vegetarian restaurant in an upstairs dining room, above a small deli. Good value and tasty dishes include veggie spaghetti bolognaise, quiche, lasagne and crepes, which you can down with freshly squeezed juices. Closed Sun evening. Inexpensive.

Mumadona Corner of Rua Serpa Pinto and Rua Santa Maria ☎253 416 111. Reliable, friendly and unpretentious, serving all the usual dishes to a largely local clientele. Closed Sun. Inexpensive.

Solar do Arco Rua de Santa Maria 48–50 ☎253 513 072. The daily specials here are always worth sampling – try the *feijoada de camarões* (bean stew with shrimps) if it's on – as are the home-made desserts. It's in a central position, and priced accordingly, at around €12–14 for main dishes. Closed Sun eve. Moderate.

Valdones Rua de Donas 4 ☎253 511 411. This bijou restaurant sits in a whitewashed rustic-style building, with minimalist design and tables in a superb courtyard. Food is equally classy, from moderately priced dishes such as *arroz de tamboril* (monkfish rice) to pricey creations such as barbecued ox. Expensive.

Vira Bar Largo da Condessa do Juncal 27 ☎253 518 427. Smart, split-level restaurant in a fine old town house. Tasty rice dishes and a good-value tourist menu, though the best dishes – such as stuffed crabs or lobster – are decidedly pricey. Closed Sun. Expensive.

Bars and clubs

Most evenings kick off in the **bars** around Praça de Santiago. *O Tunel* at no. 29 and *Rocks Bar* at no. 33 try to outdo each other with the loudest music and stay open till midnight, with most customers sitting outside before moving on to one of the places listed below. Many **clubs** make mayfly-like appearances in summer, only to disappear without trace in winter – ask at the turismo for details or (more reliably) collar a student at a Largo da Oliveira bar.

Primeiradinha At foot of the *Teleférico da Penha*. The closest club to the town centre plays Euro-pop, Latin and house. Fri & Sat 10pm–4am.
Seculo Off Av da Universidade, a continuation of Rua Alfredo Guimarães. House sounds, beefed up by techno and spiced with Latin tunes, in a stylish garden club. Wed–Sun 10pm–4am.

Ultimatum Jazz Café Rua Francisco Agra, off Rua Dr Alfredo Pimenta. An atmospheric café-cum-restaurant, occasionally with live music, that metamorphoses into a disco after-hours.

Listings

Banks Banks and ATMs line Rua Gil Vicente and Largo do Toural.
Hospital Accident and emergency services are available in the hospital opposite the bus station ℡253 512 612.
Internet Free municipal terminals are at Rua Egas Moniz 31 (Mon–Fri 9.30am–1pm & 2–10pm, Sat 9.30am–2pm).
Market The lively weekly gypsy market is held round the back of the castle every Fri morning, along Rua Duque de Bragança.

Pharmacy Barbosa, Largo de Toural 36 ℡253 516 184.
Police PSP headquarters is 500m northeast of the market on Rua Dr Alfredo Pimenta ℡253 513 334.
Post office On the corner of Largo Navarros de Andrade, at the top of Rua de Santo Antonio (Mon–Fri 8.30am–6.30pm, Sat 9am–12.30pm).
Taxis On Largo do Toural and Alamdea São Dâmaso, or call ℡253 522 522 or 253 515 515.

Citânia de Briteiros

Midway between Guimarães and Braga is one of the most impressive and exciting archeological sites in the country, the **Citânia de Briteiros**. Citânias – Celtic hill settlements – lie scattered throughout the Minho: remains of 27 have been identified along the coast, plus sixteen more in the region between Braga and Guimarães alone. Most date from the arrival of northern European Celts in the Iron Age (c.600–500 BC), though some are far older, their inhabitants having merged with an existing local culture established since Neolithic times (c.2000 BC). The hilltop site at Briteiros, straddling the boulder-strewn hill of São Romão, was probably the last stronghold of the Celt-Iberians against the invading Romans, finally being taken around 20 BC and eventually abandoned in 300 AD.

The Roman historian Strabo gave a vivid description of the northern Portuguese tribes, who must have occupied these *citânias*, in his *Geographia* (c.20 BC). They organized mass sacrifices, he recorded, and inspected prisoners' entrails without removing them. Otherwise, they liked to:

…live simply, drink water and sleep on the bare earth … two-thirds of the year they live on acorns, which they roast and grind to make bread. They also have beer. They lack wine but when they have it they drink it up, gathering for a family feast. At banquets they sit on a bench against the wall according to age and rank … When they assemble to drink they perform round dances to the flute or the horn, leaping in the air and crouching as they fall.

Entrails aside – and they may have been literary licence – none of this seems far removed from the Minho and Trás-os-Montes of recent memory.

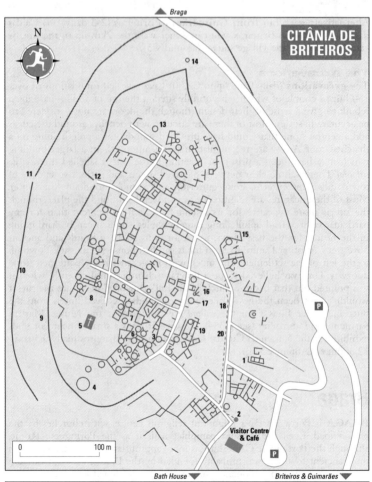

CITÂNIA DE BRITEIROS

N

▲ Braga

○ 14

○ 13

11 12

15

10

8
16
17 18

9
5 7 6 3 19 20 1
4

2

Visitor Centre & Café

0   100 m

Bath House ▼   Briteiros & Guimarães ▼

1 Area reserved for cattle	11 Gateway
2 Early fountain	12 Gateway
3 Cross and Christian cemetery	13 Well for water provision
4 Circular house belonging to community	14 Single, isolated house outside inner walls
5 Chapel of S.Romão	15 Water source (now defunct)
6 House with helix	16 Houses with stone benches
7 Houses reconstructed by Martins Sarmento	17 Law courts (?), prisons (?)
8 Small paved area	18 Ingenious method of transporting water
9 Inside wall	19 House with various rooms
10 Second (of four) walls	20 Cistern

Getting there

Coming from Guimarães, it's 7km to Caldas das Taipas, from which a small road winds 5km to the small town of Briteiros – here, signs direct you to the *citânia* on the hill above town. There is limited parking on the road before the site and by the entrance.

Getting there by bus is far harder. Infrequent buses between Guimarães and Braga stop in Caldas das Taipas, where you can take a taxi (around €10).

Alternatively, get a bus **from Guimarães** to Briteiros (2-3 daily), via Caldas das Taipas. Once in Briteiros, you can either walk the 2km up to the site, or catch a taxi from the village square (around €5).

The excavations

The **excavations** (daily 9am–6pm; €2.50) have revealed foundations of over 150 huts, a couple of which – beautifully sited at the top of a hill – have been rebuilt to give a sense of their design (though the doors are not considered to be accurate in scale). Most of them are circular, with benches around the edges and a central stone that would have provided support for a pole holding up a thatched roof. A few are rectangular in shape, among them a larger building which may have been a prison or meeting house – it is labelled the *casa do tribunal*. There's also a clear network of paved streets and paths, two circuits of town walls, plus cisterns, stone guttering and a public fountain (the fonte). Most of these features are identifiable as you wander around the place, though the site is more evocative for its splendid location and extent than for any particular sights. Head uphill along rough cobbles – which can be hard going in the heat – for the best views, past enormous rubbery lizards and ancient olive trees. Another feature to head for is the bathhouse (a fair walk downhill to the left of the settlement entrance), with its geometrically patterned stone doorway. This was believed to be a funerary chamber until recently, when it was pointed out that because much of the hill's run-off flowed into the site, it wouldn't have been the best place to lay out bodies. Carved lintels from the huts and other finds from the *citânia* are displayed at the Museu Martins Sarmento in Guimarães (see p.384). However, there's a smaller hoard of finds exhibited in the Museu da Cultura Castreja in nearby Briteiros (daily 9.30am–12.30pm & 2–6pm; €3.50).

Braga

BRAGA is Portugal's most important religious centre, with churches by the bucket load. Even the turismo pamphlet hails it as the Portuguese Rome, although the Portuguese Canterbury is more appropriate. One of the country's most ancient towns, it was probably founded by the Bracari Celts (hence the name), later falling into Roman hands and being christened Bracara, capital of Roman Gallaecia. Its history is then one of conquest and reconquest, being occupied at various times by the Suevi, Visigoths and eventually the Moors. Braga was an important Visigothic bishopric and by the end of the eleventh century its archbishops were pressing for recognition as "Primate of the Spains", a title they disputed bitterly with archbishops of Toledo and Tarragona over the next six centuries.

The city is still Portugal's religious capital. Look around and you soon become aware of the weight of ecclesiastical power, embodied by an archbishop's palace built on a truly presidential scale. The city's outlying districts also boast a selection of important religious buildings and sanctuaries, notably Tibães and **Bom Jesus** (see next section), the latter one of the country's most extravagant Baroque creations.

Not surprisingly, perhaps, Braga retains a reputation as a bastion of reactionary politics. It was here, in 1926, that General Gomes da Costa appealed to "all citizens of dignity and honour" to overthrow the democratic regime, kickstarting the process that eventually led to Salazar's dictatorship,

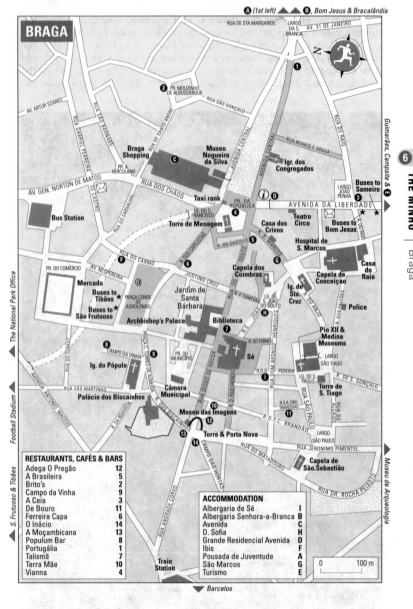

The National Park Office ▲ Football Stadium ▲ S. Frutuoso & Tibães ▲

▲ (1st left) ▲▲ ▲ ⑧, Bom Jesus & Bracalândia

Guimarães, Campsite & ⑧ ▶

Museu de Arqueologia ▶

RESTAURANTS, CAFÉS & BARS

Adega O Pregão	12
A Brasileira	5
Brito's	2
Campo da Vinha	9
A Ceia	3
De Bouro	11
Ferreira Capa	6
O Inácio	14
A Moçambicana	13
Populum Bar	8
Portugália	1
Talismã	7
Terra Mãe	10
Vianna	4

ACCOMMODATION

Albergaria de Sé	I
Albergaria Senhora-a-Branca	B
Avenida	C
D. Sofia	H
Grande Residencial Avenida	D
Ibis	F
Pousada de Juventude	A
São Marcos	G
Turismo	E

0   100 m

▼ Barcelos

while in the more recent past, after the 1974 Revolution, the Archbishop of Braga personally incited a mob to attack local Communist offices. Desperate to escape its traditionally conservative image, Braga is keen to acquire a new energy that reflects less of the Church and more of its status as a fast-growing commercial centre. This is most clearly evident in the scores of fashion boutiques scattered liberally among the churches and stores peddling religious paraphernalia. However, the network of fast roads, underpasses and big, modern tower blocks in and around the ancient town has angered many residents who feel that the old centre of Braga (the phrase "as old as the cathedral of Braga" is the Portuguese equivalent of "as old as the hills") should have been better preserved. They point, in particular, to the digging up of the gardens around Praça da República and Avenida Central to make an

△ Braga, Vianna

Braga's festivals

At **Easter**, Braga is the scene of spectacular celebrations which climax in the three days before Easter Sunday, when the priest blesses each house with a crucifix and holy water, while torchlit processions of hooded penitents known as *farricocos* parade spinning large rattles. In addition to the costumed parades of the **Semana Santa** (Holy Week) celebrations, the city is illuminated for the **Festas de São João** (June 23–24), which provides the excuse for ancient folk dances, a fairground and general partying. There's also a festival of *gigantones* (giant carnival figures; June 18–20). The main **pilgrimage to Bom Jesus** takes place over Whitsun (six weeks after Easter).

underground car park. The excavations uncovered, and promptly destroyed, a number of Roman houses.

Arrival and information

Modern Braga is a fair-sized city and even boasts its own ring road, although the old town – an oval of streets radiating out from the Sé – is easy to see on foot. The uneasy alliance of old and new is never more apparent than when **driving** – a confusing one-way system does its best to keep you out if you're trying to enter and keep you in when you're trying to leave. If you don't want to pay for the underground car park on Praça Conde de Agrolongo, the side streets around Praça Mouzinho de Albuquerque are your best hope for free parking.

From the **train station** (☎808 208 208), west of the centre, it's a fifteen- to twenty-minute walk to the old town, reached down Rua Andrade Corvo. The main **bus station** is a bit closer in, under ten minutes' walk from the central Praça da República. Here, on the corner of Avenida da Liberdade, you'll find the **turismo** (June–Sept Mon–Fri 9am–8pm, Sat & Sun 9am–12.30pm & 2–7pm; Oct–May Mon–Fri 9am–12.30pm & 2–6.30pm, Sat & Sun 9am–12.30pm & 2–5pm; ☎253 262 550, ⓦwww.cm-braga.pt), which offers an impressive large-scale map of the city and displays bus and train timetables.

If you're heading for the Peneda-Gerês national park, it's worth calling at the **national park headquarters** (Mon–Fri 9am–12.30pm & 2–5.30pm; ☎253 203 480, ⓕ253 613 169), a large, white house on Avenida António Macedo in the Quinta das Parretas suburb, a twenty-minute walk from the centre, where you can buy a useful map and booklet, and pick up information on walking trails.

Accommodation

Braga has plenty of hotels and **pensões**, and a good central **youth hostel**, though it's unwise to turn up without a reservation during religious events and local festivals. If none of the options in town appeals, you can always stay out at the hilltop pilgrimage site of Bom Jesus (see p.396), 5km from the centre, which makes a peaceful and attractive place to spend the night.

Albergaria da Sé Rua D Gonçalo Pereira 39–51 ☎253 214 502, ⓕ253 214 501. This is a good first place to head for, in a great position on a pedestrianized street a stone's throw from the cathedral. Sparkling modern rooms, its own smart restaurant and friendly service.❸
Albergaria Senhora-a-Branca Largo da Senhora-a-Branca 58 ☎253 269 938,

ⓦwww.albergariasrabranca.pt. Facing a leafy square and attractively furnished, this is inconveniently sited but does offer parking for guests and smart rooms. It's about a kilometre from the centre; keep going out of town down Av Central. ❸
Residencial Avenida Braga Shopping, Av Central 27–37 ☎253 616 363, ⓦwww.hotel-recavenida .com. On the second floor of the Braga shopping

complex, which is open late for easy access. Big, comfortable rooms (including some that sleep 3–4) with TVs and baths, although some at the back lack windows and can be a bit dingy. **❷**

Hotel Donna Sofia Largo São João do Souto 131 ☎ 253 263 160, ⓦ www.hoteldomsofia.com. Swish rooms in a smart central hotel on a lovely square – all come with satellite TV and fridges. There's a small bar downstairs too. Good value. **❸**.

Grande Residencial Avenida Av da Liberdade 738–2° ☎ 253 609 020, ⓦ www.residencialavenida .net. Far from grand nowadays, but a fine old *pensão* nevertheless and in a great location. Rooms are spacious and high-ceilinged, and those at the rear are quieter than the front rooms, which overlook the underpass and the avenue. Reservations advisable in summer. No credit cards. **❷**

Hotel Ibis Rua do Carmo 38 ☎ 253 204 800, ⓦ www.ibishotel.com. Bland but clean and modern chain hotel in a tall modern block; upper rooms have good views. Good low season rates; €4 charge for parking. **❷**

Residencial São Marcos Rua de São Marcos 80 ☎ 253 277 187, ⓕ 253 277 177. Big, airy rooms, each with its own bath. TV and a/c, in a welcoming place on a quiet side street. Breakfast is served in a grand dining room. **❸**

Hotel Turismo Praceta João XXI ☎ 253 206 000, ⓦ www.hotelturismobraga.com. The big attraction here is a fine top-floor swimming pool. Otherwise this ageing four star offers standard international comforts, including a restaurant, bar and garage parking (€5 a day). **❹**

Youth hostel

Pousada de Juventude Rua de Santa Margarida 6 ☎ 253 616 163, ⓦ www.pousadasjuventude.pt. Braga's excellent youth hostel, very popular in summer with hikers, has some double rooms, as well as a good noticeboard, lockers for valuables, a kitchen, and a common room with satellite TV and a pool table. Reception open 9am–noon & 6pm–midnight. Dorm beds €7, rooms **❶**

Campsite

Camping Parque da Ponte 2km south of the centre, next to the municipal swimming pool ☎ 253 273 355. Passable, but far from inspiring, city-based site – officially, you need an international camping carnet to stay here. Closed Nov–March.

The city

The obvious point from which to start exploring Braga is **Praça da República**, a busy arcaded square at the head of the old town, marked by an impressive trio of fountains. It's backed by the former town keep, the fourteenth-century Torre de Menagem, while in the arcade itself you'll find two fine coffee houses which look out down the length of the long central square. From here, the main attractions and attractive pedestrianized old town is reached down and off Rua do Souto. This is also Braga's principal shopping street, though few commercial centres are like this one, where shops selling phallic-shaped bottles rub shoulders with those selling candles and religious icons.

The Sé

The old centre is dominated by the **Sé** (cathedral; May–Sept daily 8am–7pm; Oct–April 8am–6.30pm; free) a rambling structure founded on the site of a Moorish mosque in 1070 after the Christian Reconquest. The original Romanesque building encompasses Gothic, Renaissance and Baroque additions, though the cathedral's south doorway is a survival from the building's earliest incarnation, carved with rustic scenes from the legend of Reynard the Fox. However, the most striking element of the cathedral is the intricate ornamentation of the roofline, commissioned by Braga's great Renaissance patron, Archbishop Diogo de Sousa, and executed by João de Castilho, later to become one of the architects of Lisbon's Mosteiro dos Jerónimos, the greatest of all Manueline buildings. Inside, the cathedral complex is disorientating and, with the exception of the Baroque organs, somewhat disappointing.

You enter through a courtyard fronting three Gothic chapels, a cloister and, most prominently, a ticket desk, where you can gain access to the **Tesouro da Catedral** and Capela dos Reis (daily 9am–noon & 2–6pm; €2). The cathedral's treasury is one of the richest in Portugal, containing representative pieces from the tenth to the eighteenth centuries, but visits are accompanied by a guide, who locks every room behind you and offers a rather cursory commentary on the age and value of each piece. After several rooms of very similar, unlabelled displays, light relief comes with the shoes of the diminutive Archbishop Dom Rodrigo de Maura-Teles. Measuring just 1m 20cm high, he commissioned 22 monuments during his term of office at the beginning of the eighteenth century, among them the fabulous shrine at Bom Jesus. Eventually you emerge alongside the magnificent twin Baroque organs in the **Coro Alto**, supported by life-sized figures of satyrs, mermen and monstrous fish.

Of the three outer chapels, the fourteenth-century **Capela dos Reis** (King's Chapel) is the most significant, built to house the tombs of the cathedral's founders, Henry of Burgundy, first Count of Portucale, and his wife Teresa – the parents of Afonso Henriques. Exposed beside them is the mummified body of Archbishop Lourenço, found "uncorrupt" when his tomb was opened in the seventeenth century. He had fought in the great victory over the Castilians at Aljubarrota in 1385, riding around bestowing indulgences on the ranks, and there sustained a scar on his cheek, which he himself is said to have carved proudly on his effigy.

Palácio dos Biscaínhos

To get an idea of how the wealthy lived in the seventeenth and eighteenth centuries, visit the splendid **Palácio dos Biscaínhos** on Rua dos Biscainhos (Tues–Sun 10am–12.15pm & 2–5.30pm; €2) whose flagstoned ground floor was designed to allow carriages through to the stables. Made up of seventeenth-century mansions for the nobility, the complex houses a small museum of decorative arts, paintings and sculpture from the seventeenth to nineteenth centuries, mostly Rococo and Baroque. This, together with exquisite tiles and wooden ceilings, demonstrates some of the best of Portuguese interior decor. The pretty landscaped **gardens** behind, complete with a 200-year-old Virginian magnolia tree, were designed by André Soares da Silva, the archbishop's architect.

The Archbishop's Palace

Opposite the cathedral, across Rua do Souto, is the old **Archbishop's Palace**, a great fortress-like building, most of it dating from the sixteenth to eighteenth centuries and embracing a variety of architectural styles from Gothic to Baroque. In medieval times the palace covered a tenth of the city. Since it was devastated by fire in 1866 it has been used for a variety of purposes and today it easily accommodates the impressive **Biblioteca** (Mon–Fri 9am–noon & 2–8pm; free), or municipal library, and various faculties of the university. Inside you can inspect the ornate ceilings of the medieval reading room and the Sala do Doctor Manuel Monteiro.

The rest of the old town

Unless you have an academic interest, you're unlikely to find Braga's other 35-odd churches particularly inspiring: most, like the cathedral, were stripped and modernized in the late-seventeenth and eighteenth centuries. The most authentic is the **Capela de Conceição** on Largo São João de Souto, with a crenellated tower. Located just east of the Sé and built in 1625, it houses magnificent statues of St Anthony and St Paul, as well as *azulejos* which depict the story of Adam and Eve.

On the whole, more appealing are the numerous mansions from earlier ages, with their extravagant Baroque and Rococo facades. Both the **Câmara**

Municipal and **Casa do Raio** are by André Soares da Silva; look out, too, for the apostle-clad roofline of the **Hospital de São Marcos**, adjacent to the Casa do Raio, and the distinctive medieval facade of the **Casa dos Crivos** on Rua São Marcos.

Also worth seeking out is the small **Museu das Imagens** (Tues–Fri 11am–7pm, Sat & Sun 2.30–6.30pm, free), on Campo das Hortas 35–37 by the old town gates, the Porta Nova. This has a monthly changing programme of photographic exhibitions, usually related to the local area.

Further archeological exhibits, from Palaeolithic stone tools to Roman and medieval items, are displayed in the **Museu de Arqueologia Dom Diogo de Sousa** (Mon–Fri 9am–noon & 2–6pm; €1.50). It's a fifteen-minute walk from the centre, beside some Roman excavations on Rua dos Bombeiros Voluntários, the southern continuation of Rua Jeronimo Pimentel (or take bus #7).

Museu Medina e Pio XII

On the southern side of town, in Campo São Tiago, a former seminary houses the **Museu Medina** and the **Museu Pio XII** (Tues–Sun 9am–12.30pm & 2.30–6pm; €2 per museum or €4 for both, includes entry to Torre de São Tiago), which consists of two distinct collections: the Pio XII, housing dusty religious regalia from the eleventh to seventeenth centuries, and the Medina, named after the Portuguese painter Henrique Medina (born Porto, 1901), whose oils and sketches were donated on the understanding that they would be housed separately from any other exhibits. Save your energy for the collection of fonts and capitals gathered in a courtyard like standing stones, or for the small excavation of a first-century Roman water tank. There's also a small collection of Stone and Bronze Age tools. In the **Torre de Sao Tiago** bell-tower, opposite, a further wing of the museum (same hours and price) narrates Braga's history.

Estádio Municipal

Around 2km north of the centre, and easily walkable thanks to a well-marked route, Braga's spectacular **Estádio Municipal** (Municipal Stadium) was built for the Euro 2004 football championships and has become something of an icon for the city. Designed by eminent architect Eduardo Souta Moura, the stadium merges into the Monte Castro hillside, with parts of an old quarry forming a natural rock amphitheatre. The stadium is home to Sporting Braga, one of Portugal's better top-league sides, and also hosts occasional international matches. If you want to see the stadium when there's not a match on, there are weekly **tours** (Tues, Thurs and Sat at 10.30am & 3.30pm, €5), though these must be booked in advance on ☎253 206 860.

São Frutuoso

Three kilometres northwest of Braga, and a short distance from the football stadium, the church of **São Frutuoso** (April–Sept daily 9.30am–12.30pm & 2–5.30pm; otherwise keys are kept in a nearby house; tours available on request, €1) was built by the Visigoths in the seventh century, adapted by the Moors, then restored to Christian worship after the reconquest. It's a gem of a church, flanked by an eighteenth-century chapel but its previously tranquil setting has now been engulfed by Braga's ever-expanding suburbs. Buses for São Frutuoso leave every thirty minutes from Praça Conde de Agrolongo (they are marked "Sarrido"); get off at the hamlet of São Jerónimo Real, from where it's a five-minute walk.

Eating, drinking and entertainment

The city's most characterful locales are its nineteenth-century **cafés**, busy throughout the day and into the evening, though Braga is also well endowed with tempting **restaurants**. Local specialities include *caldo de castanhas* (chestnut soup), *charutos de chila* (cigar-shaped squash pastries) and *rabanadas* (fried slices of milk-soaked bread with a sweet cinnamon sauce) for dessert. Braga also has a daily produce market in town and a **Tuesday market** (produce and general goods) held at the exhibition park in Avenida Pires Gonçalves, at the end of Avenida da Liberdade.

For details of local **cultural events**, including shows at the Teatro Circo, get hold of a copy of the monthly what's-on booklet *Braga Cultural*; the turismo usually stocks display copies and is happy to offer advice. During summer, there's popular entertainment in the **Bracalândia** theme park (daily 10am–midnight; €14, €11 after 8pm; ⓦ www.bracalandia.com), 1km out of town on the Bom Jesus road – any bus to Bom Jesus stops at its assortment of low-tech fairground rides, including a ferris wheel and helter-skelter.

Cafés

A Brasileira Largo Barão de São Marinha ☎253 262 104. Lovely old café with glass-topped tables and faded mirrors. The outside seats are fine for watching the world go by. Closed Sun.

Pastelaria Ferreira Capa Rua dos Capelistas 38–50 ☎253 262 064. Tasty pastries and coffee away from the Praça da República masses, with outdoor tables and some good vegetarian lunches too.

Vianna Pr da República, ☎253 262 336. A marvellous Art Nouveau establishment whose location, by Braga's showpiece fountains, make its outside tables a mite cooler than those of the adjacent *Astória*. As well as a wide snack menu – steak sandwiches (*pregos*) are wonderful – lunches are good value.

Restaurants

De Bouro Rua Santo António das Travessas 30–32, ☎253 261 609. Tucked away in the old centre, this Cistercian monastic lodging house has been buffed up into an haute cuisine establishment with streamlined modern decor. Traditional – big spenders can try the €18 *arroz de marisco* – and Minho specialities are bolstered by French dishes such as duck with *foie gras*. Closed Sun and all Dec–Jan. Expensive.

Brito's Pr Mouzinho de Albuquerque 49 ☎253 617 576. An ornate, dark-panelled restaurant with traditional dishes prepared from old recipes, like the house-special *bacalhau* and salmon in shellfish sauce. Home-made desserts and a good wine list complete the experience. Closed Wed. Moderate.

Campo da Vinha Pr Torres de Almeida 5–6 ☎253 214 359. A popular place in an upstairs dining room, with a home-recipe beef dish and tasty chicken. Mains from €9. Moderate.

A Ceia Rua do Raio 331 ☎253 263 932. An excellent restaurant, always crowded with locals – arrive early, especially at weekends, or you'll have to eat at the bar. Spit-roast chickens and steaks are served in enormous portions at moderate prices and there's a fine wine list. Closed Mon. Inexpensive.

O Inácio Campo das Hortas 4 ☎253 613 235. Rather pricey, but this offers atmospheric dining in a rustic old stone house, beneath log beams. The menu encompasses both Portuguese and Spanish dishes. Closed Tues. Expensive.

A Moçambicana Rua Andrade Corvo 8 ☎253 262 260. As the name suggests, *bacalhau*, veal and beef here have African accents. A three-course *menu turística* (€15) is good value despite the rather rough house wine. Moderate.

Portugália Largo da Senhora-a-Branca 144 ☎253 214 394. Take a seat at the central bar, as long as a tennis court, and tuck into superb prawns and shellfish. Other dishes are also good value, and if you want a table, there are bench-like rows by the separate entrance on Av Central 170. Closed Sun. Moderate.

Adega O Pregão Praça Velha 18–19, ☎253 277 249. On a quiet side road, this imaginative *adega* with outdoor tables has an intimate, arty interior. It serves unusual dishes such as wild boar and *picanha* (garlicky Brazilian beef). Even the Portuguese staples have a twist, such as pork with chestnuts. Moderate.

Talismã Largo do Paço ☎253 611 947. Despite its position on the main drag, this is very much a local diner serving excellent-value lunches. Fish, meat, omelettes and salads from €5; in summer, tables spill out onto the square. Closed Sun. Inexpensive.

Bars and clubs

There's a fair **bar** and **club** scene in Braga, with most of the action on and around Rua Nova de Santa Cruz, below Bom Jesus, where the students from the Universidade do Minho have a good time. Things are somewhat quieter in the university holidays.

Populum Bar Campo da Vinha ⊕965 619 233. Large central club, with two dance floors. Dance nights, Latin sounds and Thurs "Ladies" night. Open from 10pm Wed–Sun.
Sabão Rosa Rua Quinta Armada, Pavilhão 5 ⊕253 258 970. Out near the university, this is the "in" place for late-night action: it doesn't get going until

1am or so. A taxi here will cost around €5.
Terra Mãe Rua D Frei Caetano Brandão 120–122 ⊕253 265 475. A tiny wine bar attached to a quality deli selling alcohol and local produce. You can try wine by the glass, or have a coffee, at its attractive outdoor patio. Evenings only except Sat; closed Sun.

Listings

Ambulance Call ⊕253 264 077 or 253 200 430.
Banks and exchange Banks with ATMs are located on pedestrianized Rua dos Capelistas.
Books and newspapers English-language books from Livraria Cruz, Rua Dom Diogo da Sousa 129. International newspapers are available from the tobacconists at Rua Dr Justina Cruz 149.
Hospital São Marcos, Largo Carlos Amarante ⊕253 209 000.
Internet Free at Espaçao oInternet, Pr Conde de Agrolongo 177 (Mon–Fri 9am–7.30pm, Sat 9am–1pm).
Pharmacy Farmacia Central, Rua dos Capelistas 34, ⊕253 262 755.
Police The PSP headquarters is at Campo Santiago 6 ⊕253 200 420.
Post office Avenida da Liberade (Mon–Fri 9am–6pm, Sat 9am–12.30pm).

Swimming pools Both are 2km from the centre: the Complexo Desportivo da Rodovia ⊕253 616 773, at the junction of the main ring road and Av João Paulo II, before Bracalândia (most easily reached down Av Central, turning right onto Av Padre Julio Fragata); and the municipal Piscina da Ponte ⊕253 264 424, open July only, at the far end of Av da Liberdade by the campsite.
Taxis Central Rádio Táxi ⊕253 683 228.
Tours One-day canoeing and hiking tours (from €25) are offered by Gota Verde, at the Instituto da Juventude, Rua de Santa Margarida 215 ⊕253 616 836, ℗253 616 835, by the youth hostel.
Travel agents Abreu, Av Central 171 ⊕253 200 540; Atlas, Pr Conde de Agrolongo 129 ⊕253 613 731.

Around Braga

Having soaked up the religious atmosphere in Braga itself, a number of fascinating sites are within easy reach, most of which can be visited by public transport. The Baroque stairway and pilgrim church of **Bom Jesus do Monte**, 5km east of Braga, is a good enough reason to come to the city in the first place and is within striking distance of the massive (if distinctly oppressive) **Santuário do Sameiro**.

Of more peripheral interest – though revered in Portugal – is the shrine of **Nossa Senhora da Abadia**, to the north of the Braga–Gerês road, turning off at Santa Maria do Bouro, close to one of Portugal's swishest *pousadas*. You'll need your own transport to visit this. To the northwest, the fabulous monastery at **Tibães** was once the grandest Benedictine establishment in the land and you could easily spend a day enjoying its interior and extensive gardens.

Bom Jesus do Monte

Bom Jesus do Monte is one of Portugal's best-known images. Set in the woods high above the city, the glorious ornamental stairway of granite and

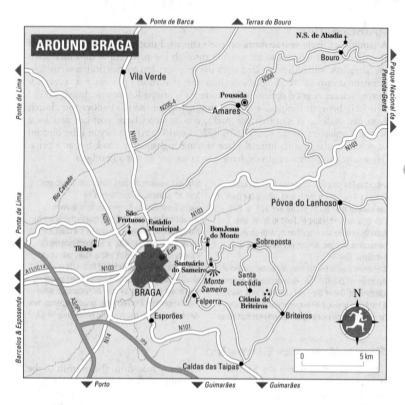

AROUND BRAGA

Ponte de Barca   Terras do Bouro

N.S. de Abadia

Bouro

Vila Verde

Pousada
Amares

Póvoa do Lanhoso

São
Frutuoso   Estádio
Municipal
BomJesus
do Monte
Sobreposta

Tibães

Santuário
do Sameiro
Santa
Leocádia
Monte
Sameiro

BRAGA
Falperra
Citânia de
Briteiros

Esporões
Briteiros

N101

Caldas das Taipas

0   5 km

Porto   Guimarães   Guimarães

white plaster is a monumental homage, commissioned by Braga's vertically challenged archbishop Maura-Teles in 1723 but which took sixty years to complete. There is no particular reason for its presence – no miracle or vision – yet it remains the object of devoted pilgrimage, with many penitents climbing up on their knees. It is a very pleasant place to spend an afternoon or, best of all, early evening. There are wooded gardens, grottoes and miniature boating pools behind the church and, at the far end, just outside the park up the hill, horse rides are available at negotiable rates.

Buses (#2, at 10min and 40min past the hour) run the 5km to the foot of the stairway at Bom Jesus from Avenida da Liberdade, close to the post office. At weekends they are packed, as seemingly half the city piles up to picnic in the woods. Most of the local families, armed with immense baskets of food, ride straight to the top in a hydraulic **funicular** (daily 8am–8pm; every 30min and usually timed to coincide with buses; €1 single), inaugurated in 1882 and still going strong. If you resist the temptation to ride the funicular and make the climb up the stairway, Bom Jesus's simple allegory unfolds. Each of the **stairway** landings has a fountain: the first symbolizes the wounds of Christ, the next five the Senses, and the final three represent the Virtues. At each corner, too, are chapels with larger-than-life wooden tableaux of the Life of Christ, arranged chronologically, leading to the Crucifixion at the altar of the church at the top of the steps. As a design it's a triumph – one of the greatest of all Baroque architectural creations – and was later copied at Lamego.

Practicalities

A handful of lively **restaurants** on the main road that skirts round the back of Bom Jesus (and which can be reached through the park) come into their own on Saturdays, when they're filled with day-trippers and parties from a seemingly constant stream of weddings. Note, however, that most open only at weekends during winter. A good option is the moderately priced *Restaurante Águeda* (T 253 676 521) beneath the *pensão* of the same name, on the road above the church (you can walk to it through the park), which serves large portions and local wines. *Restaurante Portico* (T 253 676 672; closed Thurs) just beyond the bottom of the funicular, is a traditional place serving high-quality food, but at a price. There are also plenty of atmospheric places to stay to suit all budgets.

Hotels and guest houses

Pensão Águeda On main road behind the park at the back of the church T 253 676 521, F 253 281 220. At the budget end of the scale, this friendly *pensão* has basic rooms with shared bathrooms, but the downstairs restaurant is excellent. **②**

Casa dos Lagos On the road just below the top of the steps T 253 676 738, E casadoslagosbomjesus @ominet.pt. One of the most charming local places – a lovely old house, with two spacious traditionally furnished rooms, four modern apartments that sleep four, and a swimming pool. Views are sensational from all quarters. **④**, apartments **⑤**

Hotel Elevador/do Parque/Templo W www .hoteisbomjesus.web.pt. Three quality hotels run by the same management, all right by the church. *Hotel Elevador* (T 253 603 400) is a superb nineteenth-century hotel furnished in 1920s style, with huge rooms; *Hotel do Parque* (T 253 603 470) is of similar standard but its best rooms boast sweeping views over the valley, as does its restaurant; while *Hotel Templo* (T 253 603 610), recently opened, has 42 plush rooms, a bar, pool and health club. All **④**.

Santuário do Sameiro

The domed **Santuário do Sameiro** – 1.5km by road from the bottom of the staircase to Bom Jesus or reached by a 20-minute walk uphill beyond the pine woods at the top – is impressive for its size and its grimly monolithic monumental stairway, which affords fantastic views across the city. Although built in 1837, it bears the heavy marks of interference during Salazar's regime in its swathes of concrete and enormous statues. Like it or loathe it, it's a powerful monument to the might and authority of the Roman Catholic Church in Portugal and the church is the second most venerated shrine in the country after Fátima. There's a very good, if somewhat pricey, restaurant here, too, the *Restaurante Maia Sameiro* (T 253 675 114; closed Mon).

Nossa Senhora da Abadia

Drivers can follow an alternative route into Gerês from Braga, along the minor N205-4 via Amares, after which the road becomes the N308. Some 13km along you come to **Santa Maria do Bouro** (Bouro to the locals) – which has a shell of a monastery and a large Baroque church. Turning off from here, you arrive at the shrine of **Nossa Senhora da Abadia**. This is said to be the oldest sanctuary in Portugal and, like Bom Jesus, is a centre of pilgrimage: the main festival is on August 15. The focus of devotions is a twelfth-century wooden statue of the Virgin and Child and, while the church itself was largely rebuilt in the eighteenth century, outside are two earlier, elegant wings of monks' cells and, usually, some market stalls.

If you want to stay in the area, look no further than the *Pousada de Santa Maria do Bouro* in Amares (T 253 371 971, W www.pousadasofportugal.com; **⑦**). This twelfth-century Cistercian monastery has been stylishly renovated under eminent architect Eduardo Souto Moura and combines monastic simplicity with daring modern flare. It also boasts tennis courts, a swimming pool and a top-notch restaurant.

Tibães

Around 5km northwest of Braga, signed from the village of Mire de Tibães, stands the ancient bulk of **Tibães** (tours Tues–Sun 10am–6.30pm; €4, free Sun 10am–2pm, gardens only €1.50), a stunning former monastery that partly dates back to the eleventh century, thus predating the modern Portuguese state. Fabulously wealthy in the seventeenth century, it was for a time one of the county's main schools for master stone masons and artists. It was finally dissolved by the state in 1833.

The vast complex of medieval buildings, cloisters and rambling gardens open to the public, though renovation is ongoing. From the grand cobbled entrance – heavily grooved from hundreds of carts passing through – tours (usually in Portuguese) take you round the old stables, through beautiful **cloisters** lined with eighteenth-century *azulejos* showing the life of St Benedict. It is interesting to compare the ornate grand hall, where bishops were elected, with the spartan cells where monks – and guests – were put up, though perhaps most impressive is the huge church, a mishmash of Baroque, Rococo and Neoclassical styles.

Leave time to explore the 40-hectare monastic **gardens**, dotted with chapels, hermits' hideaways and little lakes. It's a delightful place for a wander and is far quieter than Bom Jesus, despite boasting a similar set of stairs up to a hilltop shrine. There are also two marked trails, a 45-minute one round the cultivated lower slopes, or a 90-minute one which climbs into the surrounding woodlands.

There are daily direct **buses** to the monastery from Braga's Praça Conde de Agrolongo at 8.40am, 9.40am, 12.40pm and 13.40pm, with the last return being 2.10pm. Alternatively, ten buses daily for Mire de Tibães, marked "Padim da Graça", leave from Braga's Praça Conde de Agrolongo, though these involve a steep ten-minute walk up a cobbled slope to the monastery.

Barcelos

It's worth making plans to arrive in **BARCELOS**, 20km west of Braga, for the Thursday market, the **Feira de Barcelos**. The great weekly event of southern Minho, it takes place from around dawn until late afternoon on the Campo da República – known colloquially as the Campo da Feira – a vast open square in the centre of town. At other times, Barcelos idles along at a small-town pace and, with a few historical sights and an attractive riverside location, it's an enjoyable enough place to spend half a day wandering around. There are traditional events throughout the year, too: the Festa das Cruzes (Festival of the Crosses) on May 3 and, on the last Saturday of July, a renowned folklore festival in Barcelinhos, on the opposite bank of the river, with live music and fireworks.

Feira de Barcelos

The Minho's markets are always interesting and the **Feira de Barcelos**, one of the largest in Europe, is the pick of the bunch. As a spectacle and crash course in the region's economics, it is hard to beat and even the most conservative budget shoppers are sure to find something that arouses their interest. In addition to row upon row of village women squatting behind baskets of their own produce, there are stalls selling a mind-boggling array of goods – sausage skins, fresh bread plus less traditional lines in counterfeit sportswear and CDs. The Minho is made up of hundreds of tiny, walled smallholdings, rarely more than allotments, and many people here are just selling a few vegetables, some fruit, eggs, and maybe even cheese from the family cow. It all looks refreshingly wholesome.

Apart from produce, clothes and kitchen equipment, the *feira*'s big feature is local **pottery and handicrafts**, for Barcelos is at the centre of Portugal's most active *artesanato* region. The pottery ware – *louça de Barcelos* – is characteristically brown with distinctive yellow dots and has been highly acclaimed

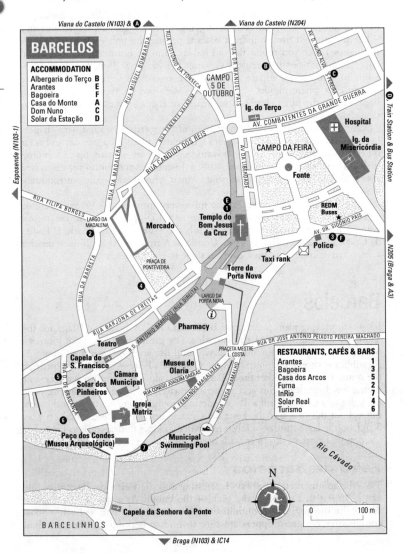

Viana do Castelo (N103) & Ⓐ ▲▲   ▲ Viana do Castelo (N204)

BARCELOS

ACCOMMODATION
Albergaria do Terço   B
Arantes   E
Bagoeira   F
Casa do Monte   A
Dom Nuno   C
Solar da Estação   D

Esposende (N103-1)

RUA MIGUEL BOMBARDA
RUA TEOTÓNIO DA FONSECA
RUA DE MANUEL PAIS
RUA DR NUNO ÁLVA
AV. D NUNO ÁLVA
S PEREIRA

CAMPO 5 DE OUTUBRO
Ⓑ
Ⓒ
Ⓓ Train Station & Bus Station

Ig. do Terço

RUA TENENTE VALADIM
RUA CÂNDIDO DOS REIS
AV. COMBATENTES DA GRANDE GUERRA

RUA DA MADALENA
AV. DA LIBERDADE
CAMPO DA FEIRA
Hospital
Ig. da Misericórdia

RUA FILIPA BORGES
Fonte

LARGO DA MADALENA
Ⓐ
Mercado
Ⓔ
Ⓘ
Templo do Bom Jesus da Cruz
REDM Buses
AV. DR. SIDÓNIO PAIS

RUA DA BARRETA
PRAÇA DE PONTEVEDRA
Ⓒ Ⓕ
Police

Taxi rank

RUA BARJONA DE FREITAS
Torre da Porta Nova

R.O ANTÓNIO BARROSO (RUA DIREITA)
LARGO DA PORTA NOVA
ⓘ

Pharmacy
RUA DR DE JOSÉ ANTÓNIO PEIXOTO PEREIRA MACHADO

Teatro
PRAÇETA MESTRE L. COSTA

RESTAURANTS, CAFÉS & BARS
Arantes   1
Bagoeira   3
Casa dos Arcos 5
Furna   2
InRio   7
Solar Real   4
Turismo   6

Capela de S. Francisco
Câmara Municipal
Museu de Olaria
RUA D DE BRAGANÇA
Solar dos Pinheiros
Ⓔ

RUA CÓNEGO JOAQUIM GAIOLAS
RUA FERNANDO MAGALHÃES
RUA ROSA RAMALHO

Igreja Matriz
Ⓕ
Paço dos Condes (Museu Arqueológico)
Ⓖ
Municipal Swimming Pool

Rio Cávado

N205 (Braga & A3)

0   100 m

N

Capela da Senhora da Ponte

BARCELINHOS

▼ Braga (N103) & IC14

since the 1950s when the imaginative earthenware figurines of Rosa Ramalho (marked RR) began to be collected throughout Europe. In comparison, most of today's pieces look as if they fell off a production line (indeed, some are Far Eastern imports), but there are some good items to be found, sold at around half the price of outlets elsewhere. Look out for the work of Rosa's granddaughter, Júlia Ramalho, marked JR. Other crafts, too, are impressive, especially the basketwork, traditionally carved yokes (*cangas*) and wooden toys.

The town

Prominent on the southwest side of the Campo da Feira, the fifteenth-century **Torre de Porta Nova** (Mon–Fri 9.30am–6pm, Sat 10am–12.30pm & 2.30–5.30pm, Sun 2.30–5.30pm; free) was once part of the city walls, and was used as a prison until 1932. Now the tower features a permanent display and sale of Barcelos handicrafts. At the southwest corner of the Campo da Feira is the town's most striking church, the **Templo do Bom Jesus da Cruz**, fronted by a Baroque garden of obelisks and highly pruned box-hedges. Built in 1704, its distinctive exterior, created by a simple contrast of dark granite and white plasterwork, was to be influential in the design of churches throughout the region. It's an odd addition to the old part of town, though, which is essentially medieval in character – a small, hillside web of streets spun above the Rio Cávado. Heading south from the Campo, you'll soon end up at the river, as beautiful a stretch as any in the Minho, overhung by willows, fronted by gardens with Gothic pillories (*pelourinhos*), and spanned by a fourteenth-century bridge. Just above the bridge loom the ruins of the **Paço dos Condes**, the former fifteenth-century Palace of the Counts of Barcelos, wrecked by the Great Earthquake of 1755 and, since 1920, providing a shell for the outdoor **Museu Arqueológico** (daily: May–Sept 9am–7pm; Oct–April 9am–6pm; free). This is a miscellaneous assembly of gravestones, gargoyles and cornerstones, notable for a sixteenth-century crucifix locally famed for its connection with the legend of Senhor do Galo – the Gentleman of the Cock (see box above). Note also the religious tombstone emblems of the various peoples to have lived in Barcelos: both Celtic and Catholic crosses, six-point Jewish Stars of David, and five-point Islamic pentagrams. Finally, if you wanted to pursue an interest in the local ceramic wares, you could visit the **Museu de Olaria** (Tues–Fri 10am–5.30pm, Sat & Sun 10am–12.30pm & 2–5.30pm; €1.45, free Sun), in the Casa dos Mendanhas on Rua Conégo Joaquim Gaiolas, 300m from the archeological museum. Started in 1963 as a private collection, it has since become a national display of some 7000 pieces including fine ceramic figurines and urns.

Practicalities

The **bus station** is at the drab eastern edge of town, with the **train station** virtually next door. Follow Avenida Alcaides de Faria straight ahead for fifteen minutes until it becomes Avenida Combatentes da Grande Guerra and you'll emerge on the Campo da Feira. Note that some buses to and from Porto, Braga and Viana do Castelo also pull up opposite the Hotel Bagoeira on the Campo da Feira.

The **turismo** (mid-March to mid-Sept Mon–Fri 9.30am–6pm, Sat 10am–1pm & 2–5pm, Sun 10am–1pm & 2–4pm; mid-Sept to mid-March Mon–Fri 9.30am–5.50pm; ☎253 811 882) is housed in Largo da Porta Nova, opposite the Torre da Porta Nova, just off the Campo. The river is too polluted for **swimming** but there are two municipal pools under one roof, on Rua Rosa Ramalho, just upstream from the bridge.

Accommodation

There's a fairly limited choice of cheap **accommodation** in Barcelos, and you will definitely need to book ahead if coinciding with the market (Wed & Thurs nights), as rooms fill up quickly.

Residencial Arantes Av da Liberdade 35-1° ☎253 811 326, ℱ253 821 360. Very characterful old place full of *azulejos* and potted plants. The best rooms overlook the Campo and all come with TV and bath. There's also a sunny breakfast room with its own balcony. Avoid the cell-like rooms overlooking a central well. ❷

Hotel Bagoeira Av Dr Sidónio Pais 495 ☎253 809 500, ⓦ www.bagoeira.com. A former market inn facing the Campo, this has been thoroughly modernized to provide all mod-cons, though offers little in way of character. Bland rooms come with satellite TV and a/c, there's a top-floor bar and garage parking. ❻

Residencial Dom Nuno Av Dom Nuno Álvares Pereira 76 ☎253 812 810, ⒺＬresidencial-dnuno @sapo.pt. Not a first choice, but if there's no space elsewhere this offers comfortable if unspectacular rooms in the new town with bath, telephone and TV in a modern *residencial* with its own bar. Visa only. ❷

Casa do Monte Abade de Neiva, 3km west of Barcelos on the N103 (Viana do Castelo road)

☎253 811 519, ⓦ www.solaresdeportugal.pt. Delightful country manor house with three double and three twin rooms dressed with charming Alentejo furniture painted with floral designs. Large gardens and a verandah give wonderful panoramic views and there's a swimming pool and tennis court – advance reservations recommended. ❸

Albergaria do Terço Rua de São Bento ☎253 808 380, ⓦ www.arterco.com. If you don't mind being out of the centre, this is a great first choice. Potted bamboos and wood paneling set the tone for a bijou inn reached by a lift next to a shopping centre. Rooms are small but well furnished, with large balconies. There's also a top-floor bar. ❸

Residencial Solar da Estação Largo Marechal Gomes da Costa 1 ☎253 811 741. Friendly budget option bang opposite the train station – so great for train spotters or those with early departures. Rooms are bright and come with TVs and own bath, while breakfast (€5 extra) is served in the lively café-bar downstairs. ❶

Eating and drinking

There are places to suit all budgets round town; the best local **cafés** and **restaurants** are highlighted below. The finest place for a beer while catching the last of the day's sun is *Turismo*, a **bar** at the bottom of Rua Duques de Bragança, with a terrace overlooking the river; it turns into more of a disco after dark. *InRio*, at the foot of Rua Fernando Megalhães, also has a fine riverside terrace. Other lively bars can be found on the unnamed alley opposite the Templo; *Paulista* at no. 44 has some local character, while *Porta Nova* at no. 22 combines loud music with inexpensive meals.

The miracle of Moure

If you want to witness a miracle, head for the **Igreja de Moure**, 7km southwest of Barcelos off the road to Vila Nova de Famalicão and reachable on REDM buses from Barcelos. The church has become a minor centre of pilgrimage since May 18, 1996, when a ghostly "shadow of the top half of Christ" first appeared. The miracle has since returned every year on May 18, and during its 1998 appearance the congregation entered "total delirium and nervosity" according to a newspaper report: some circled the image, others clapped, while others begged forgiveness for their sins. The archbishop of Braga pooh-poohed the miracle, declaring to the press, "it is a singular event generated from sentiments of faith and piety but explainable by the laws of optical physics". Further tests concluded that the miracle was indeed caused by a mere trick of the light. However, science has not dissuaded the faithful, who still flock here every May to witness what the *Diário de Notícias* calls the "marvellous half-bodied manifestation of Moure".

Arantes Av da Liberdade 33 ☎253 811 645. Take a seat under the cured hams that hang from the ceiling in this characterful place with very good-value dishes (mains from €6). As you'd expect, the ham's good too. Closed Tues. Inexpensive.

Casa dos Arcos Rua Duques de Bragança 185 ☎253 811 975. The traditional old stone house is a local favourite for Sunday lunch. Regional specialities include suckling pig, while the house-special steak and *bacalhau* are always popular. Closed Mon. Moderate.

Bagoeira Av Dr Sidónio Pais 495 ☎253 811 236. Showpiece restaurant on the square, with stone walls and black-and-white photos of the town. Fine traditional Portuguese dishes and waiter service. Moderate.

🏃 **Furna** Largo da Madalena 105 ☎253 861 879. The queues for the takeaway charcoal-grilled chicken stretch out of the door, which gives a good clue as to the best dish here. There's an upstairs dining room, or take a stool at the downstairs bar. The bargain tourist menu is €7. Closed Mon. Inexpensive.

Solar Real Praça de Pontevedra 15 ☎253 813 439. Ornate dining in a lavish upstairs room of a historic town house. A good place to try Minho specials, such as *posta de vitela* (veal steaks). Closed Mon. Expensive.

The Costa Verde

The Minho's long sandy coastline is promoted as the **Costa Verde**, but despite the enticing promises of "unpolluted beaches with a high iodine content … health for the whole year", Costa Verde is green for a reason. It can be drizzly and overcast even in summer and the Atlantic here is never too warm. That said, pick almost any road, any village, and you'll find a great beach virtually to yourself. The coast between Póvoa de Varzim, north of Porto, and Caminha, at the mouth of the Rio Minho, is virtually one long beach, with the road running, for the most part, 1km or so inland. Much of the coast is protected from development by law, including the 18km from Apúlia to the mouth of the River Neiva, which has been designated the Área de Paisagem Protegida do Litoral de Esposende (Esposende Protected Coastal Area).

The attractive resort of **Viana do Castelo** is very much the main event on the coast, with frequent daily buses chugging north from Porto to Viana, many via the resort of **Esposende** and the small fishing village of **São Bartolomeu do Mar**. Note that trains north from Porto run inland via Barcelos and do not reach the coast until Viana. **North of Viana**, though, the train line follows the coast all the way to Caminha, with trains stopping at all the villages en route – notably at Carreço, Afife, Gelfa, Vila Praia de Âncora and Moledo do Minho – offering easy access to a sequence of largely deserted beaches, with Vila Praia de Âncora being the only out and out resort on this stretch. Buses cover the same route, while it is even possible to **walk** along the northern coast from Viana's Praia do Cabadelo, covering the whole stretch in a couple of days, stopping overnight in one of the small villages.

Esposende and around

ESPOSENDE, on the estuary of the Rio Cávado, 20km north of Póvoa, is not the coast's handsomest resort, but does lie within reach of a fine beach and attracts a largely local crowd. Passing the rather drab sprawl of buildings on the town's outskirts, things brighten up in the compact centre, which has some lovely old buildings and squares, including a small **museum** in a former theatre on Largo Dr Fonseca Lima (Tues–Fri 10am–6pm, Sat & Sun 3–6pm; free), which contains displays of local ethnography, items from nearby *antas* (megalithic Bronze Age tombs), and ceramics and tools from the 2000-year-old *castro* of São Lourenço, a local Bronze Age settlement. If you'd like to explore the sites themselves, ask at the turismo (see below) for the leaflets containing directions to the *antas* and to the *castro*.

The town's **beach** is a two-kilometre walk to the north, accessed via the lighthouse that protrudes from the late-seventeenth-century Forte de São João Baptista. Continuing north another 3km, you probably won't see another tourist all the way to the little fishing village of **São Bartoloeu do Mar** (aka Mar), which is on the N13, 1km back from one of the best stretches of the Costa Verde. There is refreshingly little to the place: just a lovely church, shop and café (with a few rooms to let), and unofficial camping amid the pines. If you're here on August 24, you'll catch the *romaria* that takes place at the end of the **Festas de São Bartolomeu**. The festivities draw thousands of people from the area, many of them families with sick children who come in the hope that they will be cured by taking the traditional Banho Santo – a bizarre ritual in which the child circles the church three times with a black cockerel tied to his or her head before being thrown into the ocean three times by an attendant. The **menhir** (standing stone), in the field immediately behind the church, is believed by many archeologists to be a fertility symbol and could well have something to do with the roots of the ritual, as many Portuguese parish churches tended to be built adjacent to pre-Christian ritual sites, or else were constructed on top of them.

Practicalities

Buses drop you at Esposende's Largo do Mercado, on the riverfront beside the market – come on a Monday and the stalls spread right up the riverfront. Two hundred metres south along the river is the **turismo** (Mon–Sat 9.30am–12.30pm & 2.30–6pm; ☎253 961 354), which gives out a good local map. There's a **swimming pool** complex on the riverbank opposite the turismo (daily 10am–10pm; €8), with waves in its indoor pool and great views over the Rio Cávado from the outdoor one.

Accommodation

There's a decent **campsite** (open all year; ☎253 981 777, ℱ253 817 786) at Fão, and a **youth hostel** at Foz do Cávado, Fão, 3km south of Esposende

(☎253 981 790, ⓦwww.pousadasjuventude.pt). The latter has a swimming pool, kitchen, bar and bicycles for rent, and can arrange canoeing trips. Dorm beds €11, rooms ❶. Otherwise, the turismo may be able to help you find rooms in private houses if you have no luck with those below.

Residencial Acrópole Pr Dom Sebastião, near the turismo ☎253 961 941, ⓦwww.residencialacropole .com. A smartish option close to the action – the 30 modern rooms are comfortable, all en suite and with TVs, telephones and a/c. Breakfast is excellent. ❸

Hotel Nélia Av Valentim Ribeiro ☎253 965 528, ⓕ253 964 820 Three blocks behind the turismo this central three-star is in a large 1960s block facing a pedestrianized street. Large rooms – some with balconies – are functional and pleasant, and there's a decent restaurant downstairs. ❷

Quinta do Monteverde Sendim de Cima, Castelo do Neiva, ☎258 871 134 ⓦwww .soalresdeportugal.pt. Lying 12km north of Esposende and around 3km north of Mar, this beautifully restored seventeenth-century manor house is cocooned from modernity behind walls and located just 2km from a lovely sand beach. It also has a pool. Period rooms – two doubles and a twin – are spacious and elegant and there are three two-person apartments available for the same price. ❺

Eating, drinking and nightlife

Esposende's **speciality** is *arroz de lampreia* (lamprey cooked with rice, *chouriço*, wine, onion, pepper and cloves). For dessert, try *clarinhas de Fão*, pastries filled with sweet marrow (*chila*) vermicelli.

Adega Regional O Barrote Largo Dr Fonseca Lima, facing the museum ☎253 963 884. With outside tables on the square, this is the best option, a charming place with dried vines strung over the bar. *Bacalhau* and *rojões* are reliable standbys, although the daily specials are always worth exploring. Inexpensive.

Dom Sebastião Rua 19 de Augusto ☎253 961 414. A simple restaurant behind the *turismo*. The

adventurous can try stewed rabbit or stewed bull's tongue. Inexpensive.

Foz do Cavado Av Eng Eduardo Abrantes de Oliveira 56 ☎253 966 755. 100m east of the turismo and with a terrace overlooking the river. Seafood is highly rated: if you want to splash out go for the grilled tiger shrimps. Closed Mon. Moderate.

Viana do Castelo

VIANA DO CASTELO is the Minho's principal resort town and a highly appealing one it is, too, with a historic old centre, above-average restaurants and, some distance from the town itself, one of the best beaches in the north. As a prosperous seafaring town, Viana produced some of the greatest colonists of the "discoveries" under Dom Manuel, and was later a departure point for fishing expeditions to Newfoundland's Great Banks. In the eighteenth century, the

Dune agriculture

All along the Costa Verde, local people have perfected the art of **dune agriculture**. Small "fields" are created by digging out depressions in the sand dunes, which trap moisture from the Atlantic mists and protect crops from wind. In late summer, families harvest **seaweed** from the beaches using huge shrimping nets, which are then hauled across the sands by tractors (the traditional ox carts having now been usurped). The seaweed is then stacked at the edge of the village to dry before being spread as fertilizer on the coastal fields, which over the centuries has created a soil so fertile that many believe these dune fruits and vegetables to be the best in the country.

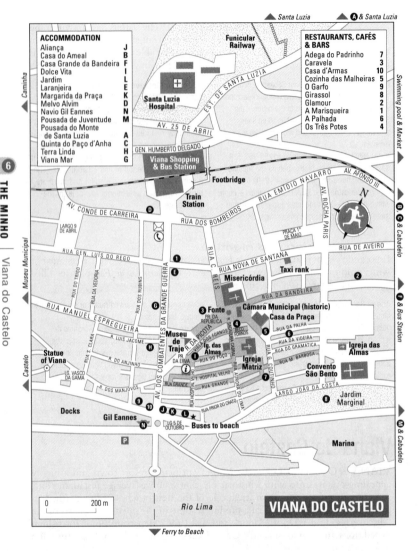

ACCOMMODATION

Aliança	J
Casa do Ameal	B
Casa Grande da Bandeira	F
Dolce Vita	I
Jardim	L
Laranjeira	E
Margarida da Praça	K
Melvo Alvim	D
Navio Gil Eannes	N
Pousada de Juventude	M
Pousada do Monte de Santa Luzia	A
Quinta do Paço d'Anha	C
Terra Linda	H
Viana Mar	G

RESTAURANTS, CAFÉS & BARS

Adega do Padrinho	7
Caravela	3
Casa d'Armas	10
Cozinha das Malheiras	5
O Garfo	9
Girassol	8
Glamour	2
A Marisqueira	1
A Palhada	6
Os Três Potes	4

VIANA DO CASTELO

town was the first centre for the shipment of port wine to England. The most interesting buildings are a throwback to these times where, unusually for the north, you'll notice Manueline mouldings around the doors and windows of the local mansions. The town is also beautifully positioned, spread along the north bank of the Lima estuary and shaped by the thick wooded hill of Monte de Santa Luzia, which is strewn with Celtic remains and crowned by an imposing basilica. If this wasn't enough of an incentive to come, Viana's romaria at the end of August (see box on p.408) is the biggest and most exciting festival in the Minho, while the weekly Friday market is another mass of Minho produce and artefacts.

Arrival and information

The **train station** is at the north end of the main Avenida dos Combatentes da Grande Guerra, which runs right through the town and down to the river at Largo 5 de Outubro. The **bus station** is right behind it under the Estação Viana shopping complex.

The **turismo** is in the centre on Rua do Hospital Velho, off Praça da Erva (Mon–Fri 9am–12.30pm & 2.30–6pm, Sat 9.30am–1pm & 2.30–6pm, Sun 9.30am–1pm; ☎258 822 620, ⓦwww.cm-viana-castelo.pt); walk down the main avenue and look for the sign pointing to the left. The building dates from 1468 and was first used as a hospital for pilgrims travelling to Santiago de Compostela in Spain. Today's helpful staff hand out a good map-booklet and pamphlets detailing walks in the city and trips in the surrounding countryside.

Accommodation

Hotels and **pensions** – mostly ranged down and off the main avenue – are easy enough to find, although in summer private rooms (❷) offer the best deals. They are generally of good quality and the chances are that you'll be offered one on arrival – otherwise look for signs in house windows or try the turismo. You can also ask the turismo about accommodation at farms and manor houses in the surrounding villages – an ideal way to get to know the countryside, provided you have transport; some are listed below.

In Viana

Hotel Aliança Av dos Combatentes da Grande Guerra ☎258 829 498, ⓕ258 825 299. An atmospheric eighteenth-century building, all dark polished wood, with pleasant, comfortable rooms; those on the top floor boast balconies and views. ❸

Casa Grande da Bandeira Largo das Carmelitas 488, Rua da Bendeira ☎258 823 169, ⓦwww.solaresdeportugal.pt. This charming seventeenth-century house has a small enclosed garden containing camellias and Chinese black bamboos. Only three rooms with traditional furnishings, so book ahead. ❹

Residencial Dolce Vita Rua do Poço 44 ☎258 824 860, ⓔpizzeriadolcevita@iol.pt. Bright, modern, spotless rooms, all en suite and a/c, and well located in a quiet square above a great, inexpensive restaurant (opens at 7pm, busy by 8pm), serving excellent freshly baked pizzas, and good pasta and wine. ❷

Residencial Jardim Largo 5 de Outubro 68 ☎258 828 915, ⓦwww.residencialjardim.com.sapo.pt. Overlooking the river, at the bottom of town, with nicely furnished rooms with bath and TV. Front rooms with a balcony have good views but can be noisy in summer. Excellent value, especially considering the huge breakfasts. ❸

Albergaria Margarida da Praça Largo 5 de Outubro 58 ☎258 809 630, ⓦwww.margaridadapraca.com. A simple and stylish hotel above a good restaurant, hewn from an eighteenth-

century building, whose rooms sport pale-wood floors and modern fabrics. Good value. ❸

Melo Alvim Av Conde da Carreira 28 ☎258 808 200, ⓦwww.meloalvimhouse.com. A sixteenth-century *solar* superbly renovated to provide twenty elegant but individually furnished rooms. Service is faultless, there's a leafy garden, while a good restaurant serves a polyglot of international flavours. Parking. ❻

Residencial Terra Linda Rua Luís Jácome 13–15 ☎258 828 981. Probably the cheapest rooms in Viana, with and without private facilities – all fairly dowdy but adequate, and the owner tries hard to please. No credit cards or breakfast. ❶

Pensão Viana Mar Av dos Combatentes da Grande Guerra 215 ☎ & ⓕ258 828 962. High-ceilinged *pensão* rooms create a feeling of spaciousness, though as it's on the main drag, front rooms contend with street noise. ❸

Outside Viana

Casa do Ameal Rua do Ameal 119, Meadela, 2km east off N202 (Ponte de Lima road) ☎258 822 403 ⓦwww.solaresdeportugal.pt. Sixteenth-century stone-walled noble mansion whose rooms are furnished with dark-wood Minho furniture. There's a pool, plus separate apartments sleeping two or four. Rooms ❹, apartments ❺.

Quinta do Paço d'Anha Vila Nova de Anha, 3km south off N13 ☎258 322 459, ⓦwww.solaresdeportugal.pt. Once a hiding place for

Dom António from the invading Spanish in 1580, this sixteenth-century manor house on a peaceful wine-producing estate maintains six comfortable apartments in the outbuildings (one sleeps 2, others 3 or 4), lifted by cheerful fabrics and equipped with kitchenettes. There are also tennis courts. ❻

🏃 **Pousada do Monte de Santa Luzia** Monte de Santa Luzia ☎258 800 370, ⓦwww .pousadas.pt. Built in 1918 and refurbished in elegant but relaxed style, this *pousada* is all chandeliers, comfy sofas and squeaky floor boards. Beg for a room at front (ideally with a balcony) to enjoy the best views in Viana, right over the Basilica and the coast. The restaurant shares the same views and serves excellent if pricey local cuisine, and there's also parking and a (somewhat chilly) outside pool. ❼

Youth hostels

Navio Gil Eannes Doca Comercial ☎258 821 582, ⓦwww.pousadasjuventude.pt. Part of a former hospital ship has been turned into use as a youth hostel, with dorm beds, and single and double cabins. Facilities are pretty basic – there's only a common room-cum-bar – but it's hugely atmospheric. Dorms beds €8, cabins ❶.

Pousada de Juventude Rua da Argaçosa ☎258 800 260, ⓦwww.pousadasjuventude.pt. Viana's other hostel is a modern affair with dorm beds, nine en-suite double rooms, plus kitchen, bar and Internet access. Rent its bicycles if you can't face the 15min walk back into town. Dorm beds €13, rooms ❶, ensuite ❷.

Campsite

Orbitur Praia do Cabedelo ☎258 322 167, ⓦwww.orbitur.com. Overcrowded in summer (there's a minimum stay of 1 week in July and Aug and 2 days at other times) and overpriced for what you get. However, it does at least have the advantage of an attractive, pine-shaded beach location and has also some six-bed bungalows for rent (❷). The bus to the beach passes the site or, if the Viana ferry runs again, cross the river and walk from there. Closed Dec to mid-Jan.

Praça da República

At the heart of Viana's pedestrianized old town is the distinctive **Praça da República**, enclosed by an elegant ensemble of buildings. You'll see copies of its showpiece Renaissance fountain in towns throughout the Minho, but few structures as curious as the old **Misericórdia** (almshouse) that lines one side of the square. Built in 1589, this is one of the most original and successful buildings of the Portuguese Renaissance, its upper storeys supported by deliberately archaic caryatids. The almshouses are part of the adjoining **Igreja de Misericórdia**, a fine eighteenth-century structure lined with superb *azulejos* by master craftsman António de Oliveira Bernardes and his son Policarpo (see

---

The Viana romaria

Viana's main *romaria*, dedicated to **Nossa Senhora da Agonía** – Our Lady of Sorrows – takes place for three days around the weekend nearest to August 20. A combination of carnival and fair, and fulfilling an important business function for the local communities, it's a great time to be in town.

Events kick off with an impressive **religious parade** on the Friday. But the best day is **Saturday**, when there's a massive parade of floats with every village in the region providing an example of a local craft or pursuit: a marvellous display of incongruities, with threshers pounding away in traditional dress while being pulled by a new Lamborghini tractor. If you want a seat in the stands, get a ticket through the turismo well in advance.

On each of the three days there are lunchtime **processions** with *gigantones* (carnival giants), folk dancing, loud drum bands, pipe bands and, needless to say, concerted drinking. The blessing of the fishing boats on Monday morning is rather moving – women in the fishing quarter, east of the centre and behind the docks, decorate their streets with pictures in coloured sawdust on religious and quotidian themes, and there are spectacular nightly **firework displays** too.

Portuguese azulejos colour section). The adjacent sixteenth-century former **Câmara Municipal** stands foursquare above a medieval arcade, while just off the square is the **Igreja Matriz**, Viana's parish church, which retains a Gothic door of some interest as well as some unusual sculpturework on the towers.

On the southwest edge of the square, an imposing former bank – built under the Salazar regime in Estado Novo style – now hosts the **Museu do Traje** (Tues–Sun 10am–1pm & 3–7pm; closes at 6pm from Oct–May; €2 includes entry to Museu Municipal). This costume museum on two floors displays a fine array of traditional clothing including wedding outfits, colourful costumes worn for festivals and the extraordinary *croça*, a rain cape completely made from straw.

The rest of the old town

The **Museu Municipal** (June–Sept Tues–Sun 9am–1pm & 3–7pm; Oct–May 10am–1pm & 3–6pm; €2 includes entry to Museu do Traje) adds further to these impressions of Viana's sixteenth- to nineteenth-century opulence. It's at the far end of Rua Manuel Espregueira, ten minutes' walk east from the square, housed in an eighteenth-century palace. The interior has been maintained close to the original and displays beautifully a large collection of ceramics, *azulejos* and furniture, alongside more modern temporary exhibitions and some simple paintings of nineteenth-century Viana.

If you continue past the museum, you'll eventually reach the **Castelo de Santiago da Barra**, commissioned by Philip II of Spain for the defence of the port. Outside the walls, in the area known as Campo do Castelo, Viana's **Friday market** takes place. It's much smaller than the famous one at Barcelos but attracts many of the same stallholders and always turns up a few surprises.

On the scrappy waterfront, moored in the dock off Largo 5 de Outubro, is the **Gil Eannes**, Portugal's first hospital ship, returned to its home port after mouldering as scrap in Lisbon. It's a floating museum dedicated to the ship's history as a hospital and supply ship for cod fishermen on the Newfoundland and Greenland seas from 1955 to 1973 (daily 9am–7pm; €1.50). Part is now also in service as a youth hostel (see "Accommodation").

Monte de Santa Luzia

Wherever you stand in Viana, the twentieth-century basilica atop **Monte de Santa Luzia** makes its presence felt. There are plans to reopen the funicular railway to the top; otherwise it's a lengthy (4km) but pleasant walk to reach it along the Estrada Santa Luzia, up through the pines and eucalyptus trees. Shorter and far more rewarding are the stairs. These start just past the hospital – though take note of the inscription at the bottom which translates as "My God help me get up". However, the effort is worth it because from the top are fantastic views of the coast and Rio Lima. A taxi up will cost around €6.

At the summit there's a café, restaurant and plenty of picnic tables amongst the trees. While the **basilica** itself is of little interest, look for the small Núcleo Museológico at the side, showing a few religious icons. Here is the entrance (marked *Zimbório*; April–Sept daily 8am–7pm; Oct–March daily 8am–5pm; €0.80) to a narrow winding staircase that climbs right through the building, past traffic lights laid on during summer to keep tourist hordes in check, and out on top of the dome itself. It's very narrow, very steep and – at the top – pretty hair-raising when the wind picks up, but the magnificent views were once acclaimed by National Geographic Magazine as "the most beautiful in the world".

Behind the *pousada*, at the crown of the hill (see "Accommodation"), lie the ruins of a Celto-Iberian **citânia** (Tues–Sun 9am–noon & 2–5pm; €1). The ruins are viewed from a raised walkway and include the foundations of dozens of small, circular stone huts, a thick village wall and partly paved streets. Occupied from around 500 BC, the settlement was only abandoned with the Roman pacification of the north under Emperor Augustus (c.26 BC) and is worth a look, particularly if you can't get to any of the larger *citânias* in the region.

Praia do Cabedelo

Viana's town beach, **Praia do Cabedelo**, lies across the river. A ferry crosses from the harbourside near the Gil Eannes boat roughly hourly (9am–dusk; check with the boatman for the last return, €1 single). Alternatively, buses leave roughly three times daily from Largo 5 de Outubro.

Given sun, the beach is more or less perfect – a low, curving bay with good (but not wild) breakers and a real horizon-stretching expanse of sand. Praia do Cabedelo is ideal for **watersports** – several companies rent out equipment and offer lessons (see "Listings", p.411) and there are a few cafés close to the ferry dock. From Viana, the beach extends northwards, virtually unbroken, to the Spanish border at Caminha and south to Póvoa de Varzim.

Eating, drinking and nightlife

There's a wide choice of **cafés** and **restaurants** in town, as you might expect from a busy resort. The most appealing cafés with outdoor tables face the fountain on Praça da República. This is where **nightlife** starts, too, before moving into the bars along Rua da Bandeira.

For **cultural** events, consult the *Agenda Cultural*, a monthly diary issued by the Câmara Municipal; the turismo holds copies and can provide information on regional festivities.

Cafés and bars

Caravela Praça da República 62–68 ☎258 822 553. The outdoor tables on the square are hard to resist, but don't miss the interior. Hollowed out behind the historic facade is a swish, stylish café with mezzanine seating and counters groaning under the weight of delicious cakes and pastries.

Girassol Café Jardim Marginal. A lovely spot for a *bica*, among the trees of this small park. Shame it closes at 7pm.

Glamour Rua da Bandeira 177 ☎258 822 963. Glamour, indeed, for small-town Viana – a stylish metropolitan-style bar, also serving food, which morphs into a nightclub (10pm–4am) with live jazz, blues and salsa during the week and house tunes at weekends.

Restaurants

Casa d'Armas Largo 5 de Outubro 30 ☎258 824 999. A quality restaurant in a lovely building, but high prices as a result. It's strong on seafood – choose your lobster from the tank – but carnivores are well catered for too, with a fine *picanha* (a Brazilian beef dish). Closed Wed. Expensive.

O Garfo Largo 5 de Outubro ☎258 829 415. Friendly, small place, as popular with locals for an afternoon gossip over brandy and a *bica* as with tourists dining on seafood at tables facing the waterfront. Closed Mon. Moderate.

Cozinha das Malheiras Rua Gago Coutinho 19 ☎258 823 680. A well-priced place – main courses are €8–12 – with ornate, high ceilings. Try the *arroz de tamboril* (monkfish rice) or *feijoada de marisco* (bean and seafood stew). Closed Tues. Moderate.

A Marisqueira Rua General Luís do Rego 36 ☎258 823 225. Generous portions – try a house special *rojões* – go some way towards making up for the brusque service. The €8 *ementa turística* is a bargain. Closed Sun. Inexpensive.

Adega do Padrinho Rua Gago Coutinho 162–164 ☎258 826 954. There are tables outside on a quiet street, though you'll be tempted by the lovely interior with its *azulejos*, ceramics and low chandeliers. For all that, the food and prices are down to earth, with a long list of well-prepared fish and meat. Closed Tues. Moderate.

A Palhada Rua da Palha 8 ☎ 258 821 841. One of the least expensive places in the old town. A long list of starters and desserts is complemented by tasty mains from under €5. Closed Sun. Inexpensive.

 Os Três Potes Beco dos Fornos 7 ☎ 258 829 928. An undeniably touristy but also thoroughly charming sixteenth-century former bakery, now tastefully furnished in rustic style. Live folk music and dance on Saturdays attracts a packed house (book ahead), while at other times the folky ambience is maintained. Good traditional food – try the chargrilled *polvo* (octopus) and less local fondues. Closed Mon. Expensive.

Listings

Banks Banks are on Pr da República and along the main avenue.

Boat trips *Irmãos Portela* (☎ 258 842 290) offer 45min boat trips from the pier at the bottom of the avenue for trips up the Rio Lima for around €5 per person.

Car rental Avis, Rua do Gontim ☎ 258 817 540; Hertz, Estrada da Papanata 16 ☎ 258 822 250.

Hospital Hospital Santa Luzia, Estrada Santa Luzia ☎ 258 829 081.

Internet Esp@ço.net at Rua General Luís do Rego 23 (Mon–Sat 9am–8pm).

Pharmacy Nelsina, Pr da República ☎ 258 822 235; Central, Rua Manuel Espregueira ☎ 258 822 527. The turismo has details of late-night openings.

Police Headquarters at Rua de Aveiro ☎ 258 822 022.

Post office Av dos Combatentes da Grande Guerra 66 (Mon–Fri 8.30am–6pm, Sat 9am–12.30pm); you can make phone calls from the Portugal Telecom office next door.

Swimming pool The municipal pool is on Av Capitão Gaspar de Castro, 700m along the eastern continuation of Rua Emídio Navarro. The Foz Health Club, Cabedelo ☎ 258 331 274, also has a pool.

Taxis Available from Rua Nova de Santana or outside the station. To call Taxi Vianeses try one of three numbers: ☎ 258 826 641, 258 822 322 or 258 822 061.

Watersports Several companies at Praia do Cabedelo rent windsurfing gear for around €30 per day with wetsuit, including the Associação de Windsurf do Norte ☎ 919 048 379, and the Escola Zurf School ☎ 966 221 092, ⓦ www.surfingviana .nortenet.pt, which also features kitesurfing lessons for €50 for three hours (June to mid-Sept only) and surf lessons for €30 an hour. Dive trips – €35 one dive, €160 for five – are available through Cavaleiros do Mar, Edifício do Parque, Estrada da Papanata 204 (15min walk beyond the marina) ☎ 258 824 455 or 964 397 293, ⓦ www .cavaleirosdomar.com.

Carreço, Afife and Gelfa

The small village of **CARREÇO**, 5km north of Viana, is set back a couple of kilometres east of its beach, where there's a café-bar, toilets and showers. Accessible by train, **AFIFE**, another 2km further north, sprawls along a road either side of the station but is not a bad goal with a fort and several cafés, though it is 1km inland from its fine beach. The modern *Residencial Compostela* (☎ 258 981 590, ⓕ 258 981 244; includes breakfast; no credit cards ❸) is on the main road just north of the turning to the beach; it also has a restaurant, although the two on the beach are preferable. If you're looking for a more dramatic place to stay, *Casa do Penedo* (☎ 258 980 000, ⓕ 258 980 009; includes breakfast; no credit cards; closed Nov–March ❸) is a typically attractive stone Minho home with a garden, 1km south of the station, up a hillside with sea views.

At the village of **GELFA**, between Afife and Vila Praia de Âncora, there's the huge Sereia da Gelfa **campsite** in the pinewoods (☎ 258 911 537; mid-March to mid-Oct daily; rest of year weekends only), with good facilities. However it is right on the main road on the inland side of the train station, around 2km from the beach.

Vila Praia de Âncora and around

Six kilometres up the coast from Afife, the next major stop on the train line is **VILA PRAIA DE ÂNCORA**, a flourishing, built-up resort popular with locals at weekends and Portuguese tourists in summer. Sitting on the basin of the River Âncora, there is a superb beach right alongside the train line, sheltered by the surrounding hills and drifting back into the river's estuary. Here you can swim enjoyably even when the Atlantic breezes are blowing towels around the sands. For good measure there are two **forts** guarding the bay: the Fortim de Cão, south of the estuary, and the better-preserved Forte de Lagarteira, to the north by a bustling fishing harbour. Legend has it that the river, and indeed the town, owes its name to a punishment doled out to the adulterous Queen Urraca of Navarre, drowned in the river by her jealous husband King Ramiro II of Asturias, Galicia and Leon with an anchor (*âncora*) around her neck.

Four kilometres north of Vila Praia de Âncora, **Moledo do Minho** is the train traveller's last chance to swim in the sea. Very much in the same mould as Vila Praia, it too has a fort – this time half-ruined, guarding the river from a long, sandy spit. If you're heading for Caminha, Valença, or even Spain, you could easily stop off here or at Vila Praia, wander down to the beach and catch the next train.

The **train station** for Vila Praia is Âncora-Praia, and is the only station between Viana do Castelo and Caminha at which express trains stop. Just down the road on Rua 31 de Janeiro, is the well-signposted **bus station**. The **turismo** (Mon–Sat 9.30am–12.30pm & 2–5.30pm, Sun 9.30am–1pm; ☏258 911 384) is right on the seafront Avenida Dr Ramos Pereira – a path behind it leads to the beach.

Finding accommodation is straightforward, except during the Day of the Fishermen (27–28 May) when people flock in to see the festivities and fishermen's processions. The turismo has a list of **private rooms** (❷), while **hotel** choices include the popular, mid-range *Hotel Meira*, Rua 5 de Outubro 56 (☏258 911 911, ✉hotel.meira@mail.telepac.pt; ❹) with parking and an outdoor pool, and the more reasonably priced *Albergaria Quim Barreiros*, on the seafront behind the train station (☏258 959 100, ⓦwww.albergariaquimbarreiros.com; ❸) with pleasant, modern rooms, the priciest with balconies. The *Parque de Campismo do Paço* (☏258 912 697, Ⓕ258 951 228; closed mid-Oct to mid-March) is 1.5km from town on the south bank of the Rio Âncora, which also offers canoes and rafting.

Restaurants are plentiful, as is fresh fish. *Tasquinha*, near the fishermen's harbour on Rua dos Pescadores (☏258 911 689; closed Tues), is a good first point of call, with seafood in bubbling tanks in a fine stone building with moderately priced fish. Round the corner, *Atlântico* on the seafront Rua Laureano Brito (☏258 951 983) is an unglamorous but reliable place for inexpensive *petiscos* and grilled chicken, with a small terrace facing the sands.

Along the Rio Minho

At Moledo do Minho, the train line moves inland along the south bank of the broad **Rio Minho**, which forms the country's border with Spain. **Caminha** is the first river town, a pleasant stopover with a little ferry service over the border. Beyond here the river valley narrows and deepens, with several small fortified towns guarding the Portuguese side of the river. The Minho train line terminates in the best of the lot, the spectacular walled town of **Valença do Minho**. This is a major crossing-point into Spain and also the site of a splendid weekly market. East of here regular buses serve the little spa town of **Monção**, which sits high above the river, and **Melgaço**, which offers easy access to the northern stretches of the Parque Natural de Peneda–Gerês. Food is a highpoint along the Minho, especially the local eels (*enguias*), shad (*savel*) and the rich, eel-like lamprey (*lampreia*), in season between January and March; Minho trout and salmon are always tremendous, too.

Caminha

At the broad estuary of the Rio Minho, and straddling the Rio Coura, **CAMINHA** was a thriving port in the seventeenth century, but is now a sleepy provincial town that is certainly worth a few hours' exploration. Reminders of more prosperous days remain, principally in and around the main square, Praça Conselheiro Silva Torres, known locally as Largo Terreiro. Here a battlemented town hall, Renaissance clock tower and large fountain vie for your attention. However, Caminha's most distinguished building is the magnificently restored **Igreja Matriz**, a couple of minutes' walk from the square towards the river; take the street through the arch by the clock tower, past the turismo (see below). The church was built towards the end of the fifteenth century, when the town was reputed to rival Porto in trade, and it still stands within part of the old city walls. Inside there's a superb inlaid ceiling, intricate *azulejos* and a carved granite pulpit. Note also the figures carved on the two Renaissance doorways, one on the north side giving the finger to Spain across the river. Nearby, a small **museum** (daily 9.30am–2.30pm & 2–6pm; free) in the library opposite the turismo houses a collection of items plundered from local archeological sites.

△ Caminha

Caminha also has a **ferry** link to La Guardia in Spain, a pleasant ride over the river which leaves from beside the bridge over the Rio Coura. There are daily services throughout the year (Mon–Sat 8am–7pm, till 8pm May–July, Sun same hours from 10am; €0.70, cars €2.50).

Practicalities

The bus terminal is out of town at Vilharelho, 2km northeast of the centre, but all buses stop on the central artery of Avenida Manuel Xavier. This runs to the train station on Avenida Saraiva Carvaero, about 800m north of the centre. The **turismo** (Mon–Sat 9.30am–12.30pm & 2–5.30pm; ☎258 921 952, ⓦwww .caminha.pt), on Rua Ricardo Joaquim Sousa, reached via the clock tower, provides good town maps.

A few hotels and pensions provide **accommodation**, or consult the turismo to locate **private rooms** in town. The best **bars** gather along Rua Ricardo Joaquim de Sousa, which threads from the main square beneath the clock tower and down towards the Igreja Matriz.

Hotels and pensions

Casa de Esteiró Rua Benemérito Joaquim Rosas ☎258 721 333, ⓦwww.manorhouses.com. Originally an eighteenth-century hunting lodge, this charming house – crammed with family mementoes – is set in lovely gardens with its own pool behind the *Hotel Porta do Sol*. There are two homely doubles and a single room, all en suite, plus two self-catering apartments. Two nights' minimum stay for most of the year. ❹

Residencial Galo d'Ouro Rua da Corredoura 15 ☎ & ⓕ258 921 160. Just off the main square with a fine *azulejo*-lined entry hall, this is friendly and full of character. Some rooms in the eight-eenth-century building have stucco ceilings or chunks of original stone wall, though comforts are far more simple. No credit cards or breakfast. ❷

Quinta da Graça Vilarelho, 2km northeast of town ☎258 921 467, ⓦwww.quintadagraca .com. Grandstand views over the river – breakfast (included) is served on the balcony – and four cosy rooms of heavy Minho furniture in a seventeenth-century *quinta* snug against the town walls. ❹

Hotel Porta do Sol Av Marginal ☎258 740 360, ⓦwww.hotel-portadosol.com. Spacious modern rooms, some with river views, in Caminha's most modern hotel, a four-star which boasts a pool, sauna and gym. It's located off the main road to Viana. Prices drop by a third outside July–Sept. ❺

Campsites

Parque de Campismo Natural Vilar de Mouros, 4km west ☎258 727 472, ⓔpnvm.anta@cartao postal.com. A little way inland and nicely positioned by a small river gorge. It has a swimming pool, tennis court and some bungalows for rent (❷); two buses daily (Mon–Fri) travel to the site from outside the café 200m left of the train station.

Orbitur Mato do Camarido, 2km south of town at Foz do Minho ☎258 921 295, ⓦwww.orbitur.com. At the river mouth opposite the Fortaleza da Ínsua and 200m from the beach; buses (Mon–Fri 3 daily) from the town hall stop close by. Tends to be crowded in summer. Closed Dec to mid-Jan.

Cafés and restaurants

Adega do Chico Rua Visconde de Sousa Rego 30, off the main square ☎258 921 781. Specializes in river fish: choose the catch of the day or, for a real blow-out, the chef-special *arroz do marisco*. Moderate.

Amandio Rua Direita 129 ☎258 921 979. At the end of the road with the turismo, and marked by a window full of books, this characterful place offers "authentic travel through wine and gastronomy" – not an unreasonable claim for its fine local produce. Moderate.

Colmeia Pr Conselheiro Silva Torres 33 ☎258 722 456. Aromatic café with a splendid array of pastries including a divine straw-berry tart. There's also a little bar area where you can sample wines that are also for sale, and alluring outdoor tables on the square.

Duque de Caminha Rua Ricardo Joaquim de Sousa 111–113 ☎258 722 046. Top-notch cuisine, which gives a nod to its Spanish neighbours, and an excellent wine list in a classy, rustic-styled restaurant by the Igreja Matriz. Closed all Sun & Mon evening. Expensive.

Pêro de Caminha Pr. Conselheiro Silva Torres 23–25, no phone. All the usual *bacalhau* and

frango standards, plus decent pizzas and pastas for around €5. Lunches only except on Fri & Sat, closed Tues. Inexpensive.
Petisqueria Rua Ricardo Joaquim de Sousa 32, no phone. Snug locals' choice for a weekday set-menu

lunch, a bargain at €6. Or try the *porco á alentejana* from the weekend menu. Closed Sat evening and all day Sun. Inexpensive.

Vila Nova de Cerveira

The small town of **VILA NOVA DE CERVEIRA**, 11km northeast of Caminha, huddles behind the walls of a castle that peers across the Rio Minho to Spain, a short ride away over a road bridge. The town is home to an art school, which has spawned a surprising prevalence of modern works around town. It is this that has spawned a biennale **arts festival**, held here in August on alternate (odd) years, much the best time to visit.

Vila Nova's most impressive building is the **Solar dos Castros** on Praça da Liberdade, once a manor house and now a library and cultural centre. Behind, facing a beautifully manicured garden, is the **Câmara Municipal**, alongside which, in a small garden, is a striking sculpture of a tripod holding aloft a rock, the symbol of the arts festival.

Practicalities

The train station is at the far western end of Vila Nova de Cerveira, a fifteen-minute walk from central Praça da Galicia. Adjacent to the Câmara Municipal is the **turismo** (Mon–Sat 9.30am–12.30pm & 2.30–6pm, Sun 10am–12.30pm; ☎251 708 023, ⓦwww.cm-vncerveira.pt), which has free Internet access.

Although there is little in the way of **accommodation**, there is something to fit every budget. The cheapest option is the pleasant **youth hostel** at Largo 16 de Fevereiro 21 (☎251 796 113, ⓦwww.pousadasjuventude.pt; dorms €17, rooms ❶), which boasts its own kitchen and a terrace. Anyone with a fat wallet can do no better than stay in the excellent *Pousada de Dom Diniz* (☎251 795 601, ⓦwww.pousadas.pt; breakfast included; ❻), built hard against the sixteenth-century fortress walls and ramparts. Although not a historic building itself, it has been charmingly modernized and would provide a memorable first or last night in Portugal; not surprisingly, it also has the best restaurant in town featuring Minho specialities. In between these two extremes, rather dated but comfortable rooms are available at the *Residencial Rainha de Gusmão*, Avenida Heróis do Ultramar (☎& ⒻⒻ 251 796 227; Visa only; ❷), some of which have river views.

For **food**, the upstairs dining room of *Café Central* (☎251 794 898; closed Wed) in the main square is a good choice for light lunches, while *Adega Real* on Largo do Terreiro (☎251 795 366; closed Tues), adjacent to the pousada, has fine *petiscos* and a range of mid-priced dishes such as *arroz de marisco* in an attractive tiled building.

Valença do Minho and around

The undoubted must-see town along the Minho is **VALENÇA DO MINHO** (or just Valença), 17km northeast of Vila Nova de Cerveira, an absurdly quaint old town clumped amid perfectly preserved seventeenth-century double ramparts on a hillock above the river. The fortress has repelled innumerable Spanish and French invasions over the centuries, and it stands as the backdrop

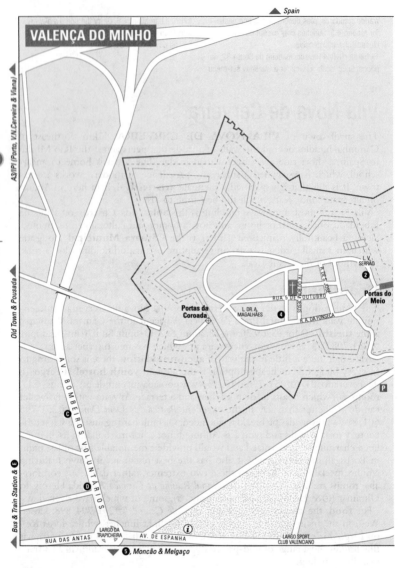

VALENÇA DO MINHO

Spain

A3/IP1 (Porto, V.N.Cerveira & Viana)

Old Town & Pousada

Bus & Train Station & E

L. V. SERRÃO

Portas do Meio

Portas da Coroada

L. DR. A. MAGALHÃES

RUA 5 DE OUTUBRO

TV. DE JESUS

R. A. DA FONSECA

TV. D. S. JOSÉ

P

AV. BOMBEIROS VOLUNTÁRIOS

C

D

LARGO DA TRAPICHEIRA

RUA DAS ANTAS

AV. DE ESPANHA

LARGO SPORT CLUB VALENCIANO

Moncão & Melgaço

to some lovely local walks, down by the river and along the ramparts (watch out for hidden stairwells), the impressive design of which was influenced by the work of the seventeenth-century French military architect, Vauban. Reached through two lots of narrow town gates, the town's undoubted charms are exploited by a myriad of souvenir shops that cater for Spanish day-trippers picking up inexpensive baby clothes, bed linen, towels and ceramics. Increasingly, the extent of this commercialism is reducing the appeal of the town and even the regional tourist office describes Valença as a "shopping fortress". But by late afternoon the crowds have gone and by evening you have old Valença to

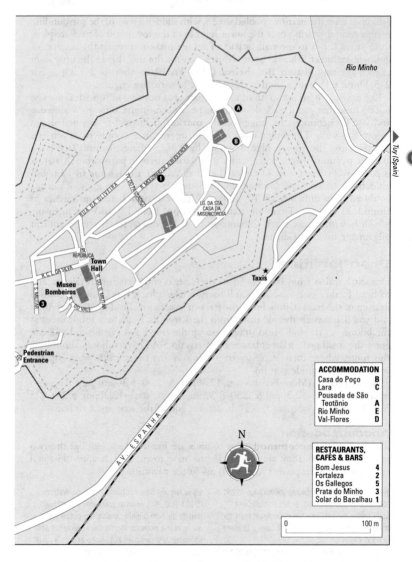

Rio Minho

ACCOMMODATION

Casa do Poço	B
Lara	C
Pousada de São Teotónio	A
Rio Minho	E
Val-Flores	D

RESTAURANTS, CAFÉS & BARS

Bom Jesus	4
Fortaleza	2
Os Gallegos	5
Prata do Minho	3
Solar do Bacalhau	1

N

0   100 m

yourself, and can lazily explore what is almost a ghost town – the only disadvantage being that many of the cafés and restaurants also shut up shop.

The town

You access the old town first through the narrow **Portas da Coroada**, where there is a small outer town. Another set of gates, the **Portas do Meio**, takes you into the main town. This can also be accessed by a small pedestrianized gate, Portas do Sol. Throughout the area around Praça República, a rich diversity of buildings lines the narrow, cobbled streets, with sudden views of the surrounding countryside appearing over the lower reaches of the town walls. There are plans to improve access to the walls as part of a town makeover under the auspices of eminent architect Eduardo Souto Moura, but for the time being the only sight as such is a tiny **Museu Bombeiros** (Mon–Fri 10am–noon & 2–5.30pm, Sat 2–5.30pm; €1), with a motley collection of historic fire engines.

The new town, to the south of the ramparts, has nothing of historical interest but it's here that you'll track down all the basic necessities. Come on Wednesday and you'll encounter the huge weekly **market**, held on the wooded slopes below the walls. The other local point of interest is a couple of kilometres north, across the iron bridge designed by Eiffel, where Spanish **Tuy** is an ancient, pyramid-shaped town with a grand battlemented parish church. It, too, is partly walled and it looks far sturdier than Valença, though the first English guidebook to Portugal (*Murray's* in 1855) reported that "the guns of Valença could without difficulty lay Tuy in ruins". You can walk here from Valença in around 30 minutes. There are train connections from Tuy to Vigo in Spain, which is within easy reach of Santiago de Compostela, the beautiful ancient pilgrimage town of Galicia.

Practicalities

Domestic **trains** from Porto or Viana do Castelo end their run in Valença, and to head further east or south you'll have to take a local **bus** – the terminus is in front of the train station. From the train or bus station, head up Rua das Antas and you'll approach the old town from the Largo da Trapichera roundabout at the bottom of the hill. Head straight on up the tree-lined avenue and you can enter the small pedestrian entrance by Portas do Sol. Drivers should also follow this route, where there is plenty of parking by the outer castle walls (tip the attendants who guide you in).

The **turismo** (Mon–Fri 9.30am–12.30pm & 2.30–5.30pm, July–Aug also open Sat 9.30am–12.30pm & 2.30–5.30pm, Sun 9.30am–12.30pm; ☏251 823 329, Ⓦ www.cm-valenca.pt) is at the station end of the tree-lined avenue.

Accommodation

The best of the **accommodation** options are listed below and, bar the two upmarket choices, they are located in the new town. For cheaper old-town accommodation in private rooms (❷) ask at the turismo.

Hotel Lara Av dos Bombeiros Voluntários ☏251 824 348, Ⓕ251 824 358. Smart and efficient hotel facing the walls on the main Spain road. Its thirty modern, spacious rooms all have a balcony and TV. ❸

Casa do Poço Trav da Gaviarra 4 ☏251 825 235, Ⓦ www.casadopoco.com. The connoisseur's choice is this sixteenth-century former doctor's home in the old town, near the *pousada*, which it surpasses in atmosphere and antique furnishings. There are only six rooms so book ahead. American Express only. Closed Jan. ❻

Residencial Rio Minho Largo da Estação ☏251 809 240, Ⓕ251 809 248. Opposite the train station and one of the cheapest options in town, with basic but high-ceilinged en-suite rooms and a budget restaurant. No breakfast. Visa only. ❷

Pousada de São Teotónio Inside the fortress ☏251 800 260, Ⓦ www.pousadas.pt. Although a largely modern building within the castle walls, many of the *pousada* rooms have balconies and sensational views over the Minho and as a result this is one of the most popular *pousadas* in Portugal – book ahead to be sure of a room. If you don't stay, at least have a drink in the bar or dine in the excellent restaurant (around €25–30 a head). Parking available; follow the signs into the "Fortaleza" and drive right round the old town. ❻

Residencial Val-Flores Av dos Bombeiros Voluntários ☏251 824 106, Ⓕ251 824 129. A friendly, modern high-rise with spotless rooms, which all have bath and satellite TV. ❸

Eating and drinking

The most atmospheric dining is in the old town, especially round **Praça República**, though many places close in the evening. There are also plenty of less expensive options in the new town, near the station or along Av dos Bombeiros Voluntários. Local **specialities** include *cabrito à Sanfins* (a goat dish prepared at Easter) and *sável frito* (fried shad). The best place to stock up on wine, port, cheese and chocolate is Garrafeira Vasco da Gama, on Largo da Esplanada in the new town.

Bom Jesus Largo do Bom Jesus 3 ☎ 251 822 088. Outdoor tables on a square make this café-restaurant an appealing venue for a drink or a meal from its long menu. Many dishes have a Spanish twist, and include fish, seafood, grills and tapas. The octopus stew is recommended. Moderate.

Fortaleza Rua Apolinário da Fonseca 5 ☎ 251 823 146. Just outside the Portas do Meio and not as pricey as it looks. House special is roast goat, although the chef also prepares an excellent *arroz de marisco*, best enjoyed at the outdoor tables. Moderate.

Os Gallegos Av Dr Tito Fontes Valença ☎ 251 824 152. A snack-bar located just off Av de Espanha, south of the tourist office, that's popular with

day-trippers from across the border because of a Spanish-orientated menu. Moderate.

Prata do Minho Trav da Secretaria Militar ☎ 251 824 212. The food and service is nothing special but this does have some of the lowest prices in the old town, with outdoor seating. Go for grilled chicken and salad and you can't go wrong. Inexpensive.

Solar do Bacalhau Rua Mouzinho de Albuquerque 99–103 ☎ 251 822 161. As you'd expect, *bacalhau* is the speciality in this stylish old-town restaurant, with a good range of moderately priced dishes (*bacalhau a brás* is always good). Also serves a range of other well-prepared dishes Closed Mon. Moderate.

Monção

MONÇÃO, 16km east of Valença still boasts a high defensive walkway that runs along the northern, river-facing, side of town, offering superb views across the deep Minho valley into Spain. It's a pleasant enough place to pause, with a mosaic-cobbled square, Praça Deu-la-Deu, a grid of narrow streets round the Igreja Matriz and a riverside spa popular with elderly Portuguese visitors. The liveliest day to visit is Thursday, market day, though best of all is to coincide with the local festivals of Corpo de Deus (Corpus Christi, usually second week in June) and Nossa Senhora das Dores (August), though you are unlikely to be able to find any accommodation then. In the former, the procession is followed by a hilarious mock battle between an unconvincing St George and an elaborately painted wooden dragon (the "coca") manoeuvred by several locals.

For all the town's history (see box), only a couple of sites reward a visit. The seventeenth-century **Igreja da Misericórdia** on Praça Deu-la-Deu contains some magnificent *azulejos*, as does the sixteenth-century Romanesque **Igreja da Matriz** which houses various tombs, including that of Deu-la-Deu herself.

Practicalities

The road to Spain crosses the bridge to Salvatierra, outside town and to the west. The local **bus station**, for services to Melgaço, Valença and Viana do Castelo, is at the western outskirts of town at Veiga Velha. Other stops are dotted around town. The **turismo** (Mon–Sat 9.30am–12.30pm & 2–6pm; ☎ 251 652 757, Ⓦ www.cm-moncao.pt) is in a small handicrafts and cultural centre, the Casa do Curro on Praça Deu-la-Deu, further on from Praça da República.

Apart from the **accommodation** choices reviewed below, the turismo lists some reasonably priced private rooms (❷). **Restaurants** are pretty good here.

Two local women played a prominent part in the Monção's history, which provides a colourful backdrop to the surviving fortifications and buildings. The principal figure is **Deu-la-Deu Martins** (the name means "God gave her"), a mayor's wife, commemorated by a statue and fountain in Largo da Lorento. Her tale, similar to a number of other accounts across Portugal and Spain, recalls a crucial moment in the fourteenth century when the Spanish troops had besieged the townspeople to the point of starvation. With their food store almost exhausted, surrender seemed the only option, but the Spanish had not accounted for the resilience of Deu-la-Deu. With the town's remaining flour stocks mustered together, she baked some cakes and had them presented to the Spanish camp with an offer to "make more if they needed them". Fortunately for the town, the Spanish had eaten all the bread they could handle and the psychological effect of the bluff was so great they promptly gave up and went away. Local *pãozinhos* (little bread cakes) are still baked in her honour.

A second Spanish siege, in the seventeenth-century Wars of Restoration, was relieved in 1659 when the **Countess of Castelo Melhor**, perhaps inspired by earlier example, also resorted to psychological warfare. Aware that the Spanish were unlikely to fall for the bread trick again, she negotiated a ceasefire on condition that full military honours be given to her men. When the countess relinquished her 236 surviving fighters to the Spanish army, the enemy, oblivious of the town's two thousand fatalities, assumed they had been kept at bay by this paltry platoon and duly retreated in shame.

Praça Deu-la-Deu is the best place for cafés with outdoor tables, many alongside the superb *miradouro* with views over to Spain.

Hotels, pensions and rooms

Café Croissanteria Raiano Pr Deu-la-Deu 34 ☎251 653 534. Modern, good-value rooms (some en suite) above a café (closed Wed); the best ones look out over the square to Spain. **❷**

Residencial Deu-la-Deu Rua 1 Dezembro ☎251 651 996. Friendly and good-value *residencial*, with clean rooms in a peaceful nest of back streets. **❷**

Residencial Esteves Rua General Pimenta de Castro ☎251 652 386. Near the old train station, with simple en-suite rooms with TVs. The entrance is on Rua de Santo António. No breakfast. **❶**

Solar de Serrade 3km south of Monção on the Sago road, off N101 to Arcos de Valdevez ☎251 654 008, ⓦwww.solardeserrade.pt. Aristocratic rooms, some with chandelier and four-poster bed, in the seventeenth-century manor house of an excellent *vinho verde* wine estate. Highly recommended. **❹**

Hotel Termas de Monção Av das Caldas, ☎251 640 110, ⓦwww.hotelmoncao.com. Down by the spa building, this modern place offers fairly bland four-star comforts, but it does boast an alluring outdoor pool, a restaurant and can arrange local adventure sports. Parking. **❺**

Cafés and restaurants

Cabral Rua 1 de Dezembro ☎251 651 775. The best place to head for, with unpretentious, ever-reliable cuisine in an atmospheric stone dining room. Moderate.

Firmino's Pr Deu-la-Deu ☎251 652 491. Highly rated dining and a keenly priced menu on the town's showpiece square – try the hearty pork-and-potatoes special *rojões à Minho*. Moderate.

Mira Espanha Largo da Lorento ☎251 652 152. On the square abutting Praça Deu-la-Deu is this pleasant café overlooking the river. Inexpensive.

Melgaço and around

MELGAÇO – the country's northernmost outpost – is a small border town sitting high above the Rio Minho, 23km from Monçao (served by four weekday buses, two at weekends). Although the town's rural origins are somewhat obscured by modern development, it's still defiantly traditional at heart. It is also known for its **local wine,** the area around it producing the finest *vinho verde* in the country. It's made from the Alvarinho grape, which produces a full-bodied wine with a much higher alcoholic content (around 12.5 percent) than other *vinhos verdes*, and consequently has the ability to age. You can try this and other types in the **Solar do Alvarinho** (℡251 410 115; closed Mon) on Rua Direita, which also doubles as a handicrafts shop in a sixteenth-century former prison.

Try to arrive for the **Friday market** when sticky buns, furniture, pottery, cabbages and corsets cover the stretch of road around the old walls. Otherwise, the major event is the three-day **Festa da Cultura**, starting on the second Friday of August, when – among other dizzy highlights – there's an array of the town's long-reputed smoked hams and a performance from the school banjo band.

At other times, the only likely reason for visiting Melgaço is that it provides easy access to the remote northern part of the Parque Nacional da Peneda-Gerês (see p.440). Its one historic feature is the ruined tenth-century **fortress**, much fought over during the Wars of Restoration but now little more than a tower and a few walls handy for hanging out washing. However, there are attractions in the vicinity, including a couple of Romanesque churches and the local spa resort (see below), while the **Spanish border** is only 11km to the east.

Practicalities

All **buses** leave from Largo da Calçada – 300m east of the central Praça da Republica. Auto Viação Melgaço buses to Lamas de Mouro and Castro Laboreiro (for the Peneda-Gerês park, see p.441) leave on weekdays only. There are also services to São Gregório, for the Spanish border where you'll get connections to Orense.

The town's helpful **turismo** (Mon–Fri 9.30am–12.30pm & 2.30–5.30pm; ℡251 402 440, 🌐www.cm-melgaco.pt) is just out of town in the stone Casa Castreja, on the road to Monção near the Parque Nacional da Peneda-Gerês turning. It has details on the local *vinho verde quintas* (estates) that welcome visitors, and can provide details of local adventure sports operators. There's inexpensive **accommodation** at *Miguel Pereira*, Rua Dr José Candido Gomes de Abreu 16, near the cinema (℡251 402 212; no credit cards or breakfast; ❷). The most charming property, however, is the seventeenth-century *Quinta da Calçada* (℡251 402 547, 🌐www.solaresdeportugal.pt; ❹), with just two rooms in a rural house 1km east of the turismo on the São Gregorio road; it also has a swimming pool.

The best **restaurant** is the *Panorama* in the Mercado Municipal, 150m northeast of the fortress (℡251 410 400), whose unexceptional decor belies excellent food (mains around €11), including roast pork leg with pineapple or lamprey cooked in rice.

Around Melgaço

Short excursions from Melgaço might include the two thirteenth-century Romanesque churches of **Paderne** (3km west, off the road to Monção) and **Nossa Senhora da Orada** (1km east, off the road to the border).

Thermal spa enthusiasts might want to stop at **PESO** – also known as Termas de Melgaço – 4km west of Melgaço. This is a tiny spa town, spread along the old main road (the new one passes just below) and looking down on a magnificent curve of the river. The spa itself is a delight, with shaded, landscaped gardens and a fountain room (baths usually open summer Mon–Sat 8am–noon

& 4–7pm), and there's a **campsite** nearby (☎251 403 282), which also has bungalows (❸) for rent. The only **hotel** is the plush, four-star *Albergaria Boavista* (☎251 416 464, ⓦwww.albergariaboavista.com; ❹) which has a swimming pool, tennis courts and a good restaurant.

A historic incident in Anglo-Portuguese relations took place on the fragile-looking bridge over the Rio Mouro just before **CEIVÃES**, another 10km west of Peso along the road to Monção. This is the spot where John of Gaunt, the Duke of Lancaster, arranged the marriage of his daughter Philippa to King Dom João I in 1386, an arrangement that resulted in the signing of the **Treaty of Windsor** between the two countries. It gave rise to an alliance lasting over six hundred years and to the naming of numerous public places in honour of "Filipa de Lencastre".

❻

The Lima valley and Parque Nacional da Peneda-Gerês

The **Rio Lima**, whose valley is one of the most beautiful in Portugal, was thought by the Romans to be the Lethe, the mythical River of Oblivion. Beyond it, they imagined, lay the Elysian Fields; to cross would mean certain destruction, for its waters possessed the power of the lotus, making the traveller forget country and home. The forces of Roman Consul Decimus Junius Brutus were so convinced of this that they flatly refused to cross, despite having trekked across most of Spain to get there. Brutus had to seize the standard and plunge into the water shouting the names of his legionaries from the far bank – to show his memory remained intact – before they could be persuaded to follow.

From Viana do Castelo, where the river meets the sea, there are roads along both banks, connecting a cluster of peaceful little settlements on the banks of the Lima and its tributaries. Regular bus services along the main IC28 stop at two highly attractive towns – **Ponte de Lima** and **Ponte da Barca** – both excellent bases for exploring the dramatic countryside. Ponte de Lima, in particular, is known for its quality rural accommodation in historic buildings and manor houses and sits near one of the north's few golf courses. Many of the small villages hereabouts, notably **Bravães**, harbour Romanesque churches of simple and rustic design, featuring naive carvings on the doorways and columns. Most were built in the twelfth and thirteenth centuries under the supervision of Cluniac monks, who brought their architecture to Spain and Portugal along the pilgrimage routes to Santiago de Compostela in Galicia; the main Portuguese route ran through Braga and so Minho has the highest concentration.

Further east, the Lima runs into the heart of the astonishingly beautiful **Parque Nacional da Peneda-Gerês**, which encompasses the dramatic mountain ranges of the Serra da Peneda to the north and the Serra do Gerês to the east. Outside summer, when the main town of **Caldas do Gerês** attracts Portuguese campers and hikers by the score, the park easily absorbs the daily visitors, and trippers and hikers alike can be sure of finding idyllic unspoilt countryside.

The Vaca das Cordas

If you're in Ponte de Lima in early June (the day before Corpus Christi), you might witness the rather odd spectacle of the **Vaca das Cordas** (literally, "Cow of the Ropes"), which involves an enraged and rather reluctant bull being dragged down through the town's streets to the beach.

Like Pamplona's famous *corrida*, this is one of many Iberian traditions that stem back to pre-Christian times, with its origins in the ancient Egyptian cults brought to the Iberian peninsula by the Phoenicians a few centuries before Christ. According to mythology, Jupiter, angry that his attempts to kidnap the beautiful Io had been repelled by her mother, turned his love into a cow and commanded a bumble bee to repeatedly sting her. Understandably perturbed, Io fled to Egypt, where she regained her human form, and promptly married the god Osiris. In her honour, the Egyptians erected altars to Isis in the image of an errant cow, a symbol which became a popular goddess of fertility in both Egypt and, later on, in Portugal. The Igreja Matriz in Ponte de Lima was presumably erected over such a temple, after which time the newly converted Christian citizens – to show their renunciation of idols – dragged their old bovine image around town until finally it fell into pieces. Since then, a live cow – actually now a bull – has been used.

Echoes of the original rite still remain. At around 3pm, the bull is led to the church, where it is stabbed with a small dart in order to madden it. At 6pm, two millers arrive, tie the bull by its horns and lead it three times around the church – a common feature of pre-Christian rituals – whilst jabbing it with goads in reference to the mythical bee described above. Following this, and depending upon whether anyone can keep a grip on its ropes, the unfortunate animal then stumbles or charges through the town's streets (mimicking Io's flight to Egypt) before finishing up at the beach. It is then led off to the abattoir, as the good people of Ponte de Lima prepare for the more sedate procession of **Corpo do Deus** the following day, which sees the streets covered with flowers carefully arranged into ornate patterns.

Ponte de Lima and around

PONTE DE LIMA – 23km east of Viana do Castelo – is a delightful place, whose pedestrianized old centre has no specific attraction other than its air of sleepy indifference to the wider world. You might disagree if you visit in July or August, when Ponte de Lima begins to show worrying signs of midsummer tourist strain, a phenomenon that the local authorities have tried to capitalize on by building an eighteen-hole golf course. Outside these times though, Ponte de Lima's lovely riverside gardens and local walks make it a great place for a night or two's stopover. The river's wide sandbank beaches provide the venue for the town's bi-monthly Monday market, the oldest in Portugal, held since a charter was first granted in 1125. A ramshackle collection of items is on sale, from mobile phone accessories to trussed chickens. Also held here is the curiously named "New Fair" (second and third weekend of Sept), a festival and market seemingly attended by half of the Minho, with fireworks, fairground rides, wandering accordionists, gigantones (enormous carnivalesque statues), and a brass band competition. More tradition is on display in early June, with the Vaca das Cordas festival.

The town

The town takes its name from the low stone **bridge** that crosses the river, rebuilt in 1368 but still bearing traces of its Roman origin. It is said to mark

the path of the first hesitant Roman crossing of the river and was part of a military route leading from Braga to Astorga. Besides the bridge, the town's main focus is the long riverside Alameda (promenade), shaded by magnificent plane trees, which threads past the rambling old convent of **São Francisco e Santo António dos Capuchos** (Tues–Sun 2–5.30pm; free), whose small museum of ecclesiastical treasures is found inside its church. Just behind here, a block inland, the lovely nineteenth-century Teatro Diogo Bernardes is the prime venue for the annual **Festival de Ópera e Música Clássical** (ⓦwww .operafaber.org), held each July and attracting some of Europe's best musicians. The performances, which include song recitals, vocal chamber music and orchestral performances of well known operas, are also held in local manor houses and on the riverside itself, attracting a delightful carnival atmosphere.

Handsome buildings in town include several sixteenth-century mansions with stone coats of arms, and the interesting remains of the old sixteenth-century keep, the **Torre da Cadeia** (Tues–Sun 2–6pm; free) now an exhibition space for temporary art displays. This was for a time the town prison, as demonstrated by its iron-grill windows. Go through the arch to one side of it to some of the town's more interesting back streets. The tower's partner, the **Torre de St Paulo** near the bridge, has marks showing the depth of historic floods, including the severe one of 1987.

Heading over the bridge you'll find the immaculately manicured **Parque do Arnada** (aka Jardims Temáticos), whose formal gardens are divided into different styles including Roman and Baroque; there's also a small hothouse. Go through the gardens to the small **Museu Rural** (Tues–Sun 2–5.30pm; free), which houses a mildly interesting collection of archaic tools and farming accoutrements.

The riverside path on this side is also idyllic, an ideal spot for a picnic. The river would offer fine swimming were it not so polluted. However, there is a municipal **pool** in Rua Francisco Sá Carneiro (Mon–Fri 10am–noon & 4–8.15pm, Sat 9am–noon), or you can take to the water on a canoe, rented from the **Centro Naútico** (☎258 944 449; €4 for 90min), 2km from the Alameda on the other side of the river by the new bridge.

Around Ponte de Lima

There's an eighteen-hole **golf course** at Feitosa, 2km to the south (☎258 743 414). If you prefer greenery to greens, wandering through some of the villages on both sides of the river is a joy, while more energetic walkers can climb to **Santo Ovídio chapel** (about an hour to the top) – a bizarre shrine to the patron saint of ears – for glorious views of the Lima valley, before ambling back to Ponte de Lima along cobbled and vine-covered lanes. The turismo has a few leaflets detailing other attractive local **walks**, including those around the protected **Lagoas de Bertiandos e São Pedro de Arcos** wildlife wetlands (Ⓦwww.lagoas.cm-pontedelima.pt), 14km to the west just off the EN202, a superb spot with riverside walks, a petting farm, bird hides and picnic areas.

Heading in the opposite direction, drivers can visit **Bravães**, 14km east on the road to Ponte de Barca. This is home of the fine Romanesque church of **São Salvador**, just to the left of the road. Its two sculpted doorways are perhaps the best in the country, with carvings of doves, griffins, monkeys and two of the local wide-horned oxen. If the church is locked ask at the cottage behind and the doors will be flung open for you, lighting up medieval murals of St Sebastian and the Virgin.

Practicalities

The **bus station** is behind the market, just a minute or so from the river. There are daily services to Arcos de Valdevez, Viana do Castelo, Barcelos, Ponte da Barca, Braga and Porto. A few minutes' walk away from the river, on Praça da República, the **turismo** is in the Paço do Marquês (Sat 9.30am–12.30pm & 2.30–5pm, Sun 10am–12.30pm; ☎258 942 335, Ⓦwww.cm-pontedelima.pt), a building which doubles as a handicrafts centre – excavations in the basement show the original town walls. During the week (Mon–Fri 9.30am–12.30pm & 2–5.30pm) the office moves to an extraordinary modern cube on a raised plinth next door. **Internet** access is available at Espaçao Internet (Mon–Fri 1–8pm, Sat 10am–noon) at Avenida Antonio Feijo 143, 100m up from the turismo.

Accommodation

The town is famous for its rural tourism properties – manor houses and the like, offering bed-and-breakfast **accommodation**. Most belong to one of several agencies promoting such accommodation, under the umbrella of the Central Nacional de Turismo no Espaço Rural (or CENTER – see "Basics", p.42), through whom you can make bookings. You can also make reservations directly with the properties concerned (see reviews below) or contact Solares de Portugal in Ponte de Lima (℡258 742 827 or 258 741 672, ⓦwww .solaresdeportugal.pt), whose office is at Praça da República, opposite the turismo. You will need your own transport to reach most of the properties. Considering Ponte de Lima's appeal, the selection of *pensões* is limited and booking ahead in peak season is a good idea. Alternatively, the turismo holds a list of private rooms, while there's also an excellent **youth hostel** out of town.

In town

Hotel Império do Minho Av Dom Luís Filipe (aka Av dos Plátanos), on the riverfront ℡258 741 510, ⓔhotelimperio@sapo.pt. The largest and most modern place in town, offering fifty en-suite rooms with three-star comforts. There's also a spacious bar and swimming pool. ❹

Pensão São João Largo de São João ℡258 941 288. The best budget option in town, near the bridge and with airy, clean en-suite rooms, though front rooms can suffer minor traffic noise. No credit cards. ❷

Casa das Pereiras Largo das Pereiras ℡258 942 939, ⓦwww.manorhouses.com. Wonderful eighteenth-century stone *solar* in a hidden square, partly built into the medieval town walls, with a pool and splendid dinners served every Fri evening. The garden is a delight, at its best when 100-year-old camellia shrubs bloom. Closed Nov–May. ❹

Outside town

Casa do Anquião Fornelas, 3km southeast of town ⓔanquiajo@solaresdeportugal.pt (no phone), ⓦwww.solaresdeportugal.pt. Right by the golf course, this seventeenth-century manor house is all bare stone, wood and low chandeliers. Facilities are far more modern, and include a Jacuzzi and outdoor pool. ❺

Casa de Crasto Ribeira, 1km east of town along the N203 to Ponte de Barca ℡258 941 156 ⓦwww.solaresdeportugal.pt A beautiful seventeenth-century property in verdant grounds, which – legend has it – was partly demolished by the owner in 1896 while looking for hidden treasure. The kitchen and tower managed to evade his attention. ❹, plus an apartment that sleeps four, ❺.

Moinho de Estorãos Estorãos, 7km northeast of Ponte de Lima ℡258 941 546 ⓦwww.solaresde portugal.pt. Low-key rustic charm in a converted seventeenth-century water mill. The location is an escapist's idyll – next to a Romanesque bridge and with walking, fishing and swimming all at hand.

Book in advance for the single double room. Closed mid-Oct to mid-May. ❹

Casa de São Gonçalo Arcozelo, 1km north of Ponte de Lima ℡258 942 365, ⓦwww .solaresdeportugal.pt. Views of the town are outstanding from this nineteenth-century house, 500m from the bridge. Although elegant and furnished with antiques, it's very much a family home, and the charming garden is a lovely place for breakfast. Since there's just one double room and a two-person apartment (same price), booking ahead is recommended. ❸

Casa da Lage São Pedro Arcos, 9km west, off N202 to Viana do Castelo ℡258 731 417 ⓦwww .solaresdeportugal.pt. Ten rooms with period features – a stone arch or antique furniture – in a magnificent seventeenth-century manor house, secluded among vineyards. Also has its own chapel, bar and indoor pool. ❺

Casa do Outeiro Arcozelo, 2km north of Ponte de Lima ℡258 941 206 ⓦwww.solaresdeportugal .pt. Stately decor in a manor house that dates from the seventeenth century – its vast kitchen fireplace is original – and is surrounded by a garden and woods by an old aqueduct. Has a swimming pool and three homely twin rooms for rent. ❹

Paço de Calheiros Calheiros, 7km northeast of Ponte de Lima ℡258 947 164, ⓦwww .solaresdeportugal.pt. A superb seventeenth-century mansion, the country retreat of none other than the Count of Calheiros, founder of the Turihab scheme. Set in beautifully landscaped gardens with views over the Lima valley, it has nine tastefully decorated bedrooms (❹), six two-bed apartments (available by the night, ❺) and one apartment sleeping six (❻), plus a swimming pool and tennis courts.

Quinta da Roseira Currelhã, Lugar da Roseira, 1km west, via N203 towards Darque ℡258 941 354, ⓦwww.solaresdeportugal.pt. Modest but charming, this lovely nineteenth-century converted farmhouse is set among vineyards and fruit trees, and offers a swimming pool and horse-riding. Views over Ponte de Lima are exceptional, though the surroundings are somewhat suburban. ❹

hostel with comfortable rooms, a kitchen and living room. Dorm beds €11, rooms with or without bath, ❶

Youth hostel

Pousada de Juventude Rua Agostinho José Taveira, 2km southeast of the centre on Viana do Castelo and Barcelos road ☎258 943 797, ⓦwww.pousadasjuventude.pt. Excellent modern

Campsite

Camping Rural e Albergue São Pedro de Arcos, 5km east of town ☎258 733 553. The nearest official site to Ponte de Lima; also offers horse-riding.

Eating and drinking

Praça de Camões, by the old bridge, is the best place to head for **cafés** with outdoor tables. Local dishes include *arroz de sarabulho com rojões* (rice cooked with blood and pieces of roast pork). To sample *vinho verde* straight from the barrel, try the characterful bar *Os Telhadinhos* at Rua Do Rosário 24, off the square (closed Tues). A more youthful clientele frequent the **bars** at the foot of Rua Formosa, while the liveliest place in town is *Lethes Bar* (till 2am, midnight Sun) on the more northern of the two alleys off Largo das Pereiras.

Alameda Largo da Feira ☎258 941 630. A snug cabin, by the bridge on the town side of the river, with splendid views, serving dishes in epic portions – there's *sarabulho* and *feijoada* for culinary explorers. Closed Wed. Inexpensive.

Bella Vitta Passeio 25 de Abril ☎258 941 090. Fashionable place with a terrace boasting grand-stand views of river. Bargain pasta, pizza and salads satisfy a young crowd. Closed all day Wed and Sun lunch. Inexpensive.

Boteca Arnado ☎258 943 962. In the riverside café-bar gardens south of the river, this inexpensive café-bar is a lovely spot by day for light lunches or drinks. At weekends it morphs into a lively late-night drink den, open till 6am.

Brasão Rua Formosa 1 ☎258 911 890. A quietly classy restaurant in an old stone building, tucked away in a back-alley. *Arroz de marisco* is delicious, the wine list long. Closed Wed. Moderate.

Parisiense Alameda ☎258 942 159. A simple *tasca* with a limited menu but a good view of the river from its first- and second-floor tables. Closed Sat. Inexpensive.

São João Largo de São João ☎259 941 288. Smarter and a touch more stylish than its neighbours, so a little more expensive – regional dishes cost around €12 – though with a bargain set lunch menu. Moderate.

Tasca d'Ouro Mercado Municipal ☎259 943 074. Friendly bar-restaurant on the corner of the bustling market building. Serves a great array of *petiscos* snacks and fine grilled meats from the neighbouring butchers. Closed Tues. Inexpensive.

Ponte da Barca

From Ponte de Lima, the N203 runs 18km east to **PONTE DA BARCA**, a smaller version of Ponte de Lima. There's not a lot to do here, but it's an attractive if sedate base from which to reach the northern stretches of the Parque Natural de Peneda-Gerês. The Barca part of its name refers to a boat that once ferried pilgrims across the Rio Lima, before the bridge was built. Nowadays the Lima is spanned by a lovely sixteenth-century bridge, beside which is the shaded Jardim dos Poetas, dedicated to sixteenth-century brothers Diogo Bernardes and Agostinho da Cruz, monastic poets who were born in the town – their statue is situated at one end of the square.

The best time to come to Ponte da Barca is for the superb fortnightly Wednesday **market** (it alternates with Arcos de Valdevez), spreading out by the river by the bridge in an almost medieval atmosphere and drawing hundreds of people from outlying hamlets. The only other time the town becomes animated is for the annual Feira de São Bartolomeu, which takes place on August 19–24, with the big day on August 24; don't expect to get any sleep once the party starts. The whole period sees a crafts fair take over Praça da República and there's a linen festival and secular parade on August 23.

Practicalities

Buses to and from all destinations drop you at the corner of Rua Diogo Bernardes and Rua Conselheiro Rocha Peixoto, around the corner from the bridge. There are regular services to Lindoso, Arcos de Valdevez and Braga. From the bridge, the main Rua Conselheiro Rocha Peixoto runs east. Just off here, on Rua Lopes da Costa, the helpful **turismo** (Mon–Sat 9.30am–12.30pm & 2.30–6pm, Sat 10am–12.30 & 2.30–5.30pm; ℡258 452 899), offers a town map and lots of brochures.

Also just off the main road, on Largo da Misericórdia is the very useful headquarters of **ADERE Peneda-Gerês** (Mon–Fri 9am–12.30pm & 2.30–6pm; ℡258 452 450, ⓦwww.adere-pg.pt), the regional development association for the Parque Nacional da Peneda-Gerês, which is a treasure chest of information on everything related to the park, from local customs and handicrafts to accommodation and activities. It also stocks free maps and walk leaflets, and can book park accommodation.

Outside festival time, you should be able to find a room easily, although the most characterful options are snapped up quickly in high season. A clutch of **restaurants** gathers on Campo do Cûrro, before the shady square by the bridge, and there are several good **bars** in town too.

Hotels and pensions

🏃 **Pensão Maria Gomes** Rua Conselheiro Rocha Peixoto 13 ℡258 452 288. Six characterful rooms and a charming owner makes this place highly recommended and worth phoning ahead for, and at around €20 for a room, it's a real bargain. An excellent breakfast is served on a balcony overlooking the river and bridge, while at the restaurant beneath the *pensão* moderately priced regional dishes are on offer. No credit cards. ❶

Casa Nobre do Correio Mor Rua Trás do Forno 1 ℡258 452 129, ⓦwww.laceme.com. The "house of the head postmaster" is a tastefully restored seventeenth-century manor house which features in a famous Portuguese novel of the same name. Its ten double en-suite rooms live up to their *nobre* (noble) billing: spacious, aristocratic and furnished with antiques. It also has a pool, sauna, games room and lovely gardens. ❸

Quinta da Prova North bank of the river, just over the bridge ℡258 452 163, ⓦwww.solaresdeportugal. Spacious two- and four-person apartments, all with kitchenette and living room available by the night, overlooking the river from a delightful terrace or set back in the woods. No credit cards. 2 people ❷, 4 people ❹

Cafés, bars and restaurants

Café Cantinho Rua Conselheiro Rocha Peixoto, corner with Rua Diogo Bernardes, no phone. Fun, rough-and-ready white-tiled bar where you can sample *vinho verde* while perched at high bar stools. Also does inexpensive food.

Doce Lima Rua Conselheiro Rocha Peixoto 69 ℡258 452 486. Bustling *pastelaria* on the main street, warm with the aroma of home-baked croissants and pastries; a great breakfast stop.

Moinho Campo de Cûrro ℡258 452 035. Pricey but excellent restaurant, with speciality dishes of octopus stew and *lampreia à la Bordalesa* (lamprey with rice in a rich sauce). Also has a children's menu. Expensive.

🏃 **Poetas** Jardim dos Poetas, by the bridge. Fashionable café-bar, open weekday evenings and all day at the weekends, with occasional live music.

Varanda do Lima Campo do Cûrro ℡258 452 035. Offers a long list of moderately priced meat; the high-quality fish and seafood tips into the expensive category. The neighbouring café serves good-value snacks. Closed Thurs. Moderate.

Arcos de Valdevez

The Rio Vez, a tributary of the Minho, is overlooked by the hillside town of **ARCOS DE VALDEVEZ**, 5km north of Ponte da Barca, another useful point of departure for the Parque Nacional da Peneda-Gerês. Despite its neat riverside gardens and pedestrianized centre, it is less attractive than Ponte da Barca, though it is certainly livelier, especially during the fortnightly Wednesday market. A seventeenth-century fire destroyed many of its older buildings, though a few survivors are worth seeking out: the Baroque Igreja da Lapa, on Largo da Lapa, and – just to the south – the Capela da Nossa Senhora da Conceição which features Manueline carving and an early fifteenth-century relief, beneath which the chapel's founder, Dom João Domingos, abbot of Sabadim, lies entombed. Look out, too, for the unusual spiral Manueline **pillory** in the Praça Municipal.

Try and coincide a visit with the three-day **Festas do Concelho**, held over the second week in August, featuring giant figures, red-caped drummers, horse races and fireworks. Traditionally these celebrations should take place on the last weekend of the holiday month, but they've been shifted to take account of local emigrants who return to work abroad at the end of August; one of the festival days is actually named the Dia do Emigrante in their honour.

Practicalities

The **bus station** is 1km northeast of town, near the river, and has regular services to Braga, Monção, Ponte de Lima and Viana do Castelo; arriving buses stop in the town centre on their way to the bus station. You can catch the Soajo and Lindoso buses at the stops along Avenida Marginal, between the bridge and *Pensão Dom António*; check in the **turismo** for latest timetables.

The **turismo** is on Rua Prof Dr Mário Júlio Almeida Costa 200m north of the bridge on the west bank of the river (June–Sept daily 9.30am–12.30pm & 2.30–6pm; Oct–May Mon–Fri 9.30am–12.30pm & 2.30–6pm, Sat 9.30am–noon & 2.30–6pm; ☎258 516 001, ⓦ www.cm-arcos-valdevez.pt). At the **national park information office** (Mon–Fri 9am–12.30 & 2–5.30pm; ☎258 515 338) on Rua do Padre Manuel Himalaia – turn uphill from the river at the fountain – you can buy a park map (around €2.50) although the turismo has just as much information, including leaflets (in Portuguese) detailing numerous walks.

Hotels and pensions

Quinta da Cortinhas Paço, 1km south of town on the Ponte da Barca road ☎258 931 750, ⓦ www.cortinhas.tripod.com. The former summer house of a politician and cousin of writer Eça de Queiroz's, with eight rooms in the lovely main house and another four in well-converted former stables. Breakfast is served in an ornate tiled dining room, and guests can also use the basement kitchens. A pool in its small leafy grounds adds to the appeal. Good value. ❸

Pensão Dom António Rua Dr Germano Amorim ☎258 521 010, ⓕ258 521 065. A friendly place at the south end of the riverside road whose rooms – all with TV, some with phones and minibars – are far brighter than the drab exterior suggests. No breakfast. ❷

Isabel Campo do Trasladário ☎258 520 380, ⓕ258 520 389. Small but up-to-date en-suite rooms on the opposite side of the bridge, above a good restaurant. Double-glazing helps reduce traffic noise in the front rooms, which boast the best views. No breakfast. ❸

Hotel Ribeira Largo des Milagres ☎258 510 240, ⓔhotelribiera@sapo.pt. A modern hotel in a rebuilt historic house on the east side of the old bridge – rooms are spacious, the finest with balconies overlooking the river. No credit cards. ❸

Bars and restaurants

Churrascaria Arco dos Caneiros Rua São João 92 ☎258 516 291. Good and cheap, offering hearty pork and *bacalhau* dishes at around €7, plus *tripas à la moda de Porto* (tripe) on Wed and a bargain €5 lunchtime *ementa turística*. Closed Sun. Inexpensive.

Floresta Campo do Trasladário Ⓣ 258 515 163. Before the bridge, and one of the few options in town for eating alfresco. Regional meats feature, as do fine garlicky beans, and generous portions

make the higher than average prices acceptable. Moderate.

Xeias Bar Largo da Valeta Ⓣ 258 523 089. Surprisingly fashionable bar for this neck of the woods, with wicker chairs on the square outside, a flat screen usually showing MTV, and occasional dance lessons if you fancy some Latino moves. Open daily till 3am.

Parque Nacional da Peneda-Gerês

The magnificent **Parque Nacional da Peneda-Gerês** divides into three regions: the central area, based around the spa town of **Caldas do Gerês**, the wilder northern section around the **Serra da Peneda** and the far eastern section of **Serra do Gerês**, which spans the border into Trás-os-Montes. Both

Park practicalities

Information, maps, brochures and walk leaflets for the **Parque Nacional da Peneda-Gerês** (ⓦ www.adere-pg.pt or ⓦ www.peneda-geres.naturlink.pt) can be obtained from the **park offices** in towns surrounding the park, most usefully at Braga (p.391), Ponte da Barca (428), Arcos de Valdevez (p.429) and Montalegre (p.484).

An invaluable series of leaflets in English detailing **footpaths** (*trilhos*) are available from the park offices and turismos in the area. There are currently nine marked trails, most around 10–16km in length. The leaflets themselves offer limited useful information, but they do describe and guide you to the starting point of the trails, which are generally well marked with red and yellow pointers. Before you start off on these, however, check with local offices as to the latest conditions, as waymarkings can get worn; landslides can also close certain sections.

The official **park map** (around €2.50), on the other hand, shows roads but omits footpaths, making it of little use to walkers, although it may suffice for drivers. A more useful alternative (with footpaths shown) are the "Série M888" 1:25,000 **topographical maps** produced by the Instituto Geográfico do Exército (ⓦ www.igeoe.pt), which you can buy online from the Institute or from shops in Portugal (see "Basics", p.69). For an excellent **guidebook** to walking in the park (mostly the area around Soajo), buy Brian and Eileen Anderson's *Landscapes of Northern Portugal* (ⓦ www .sunflowerbooks.co.uk/norport.htm).

Organized hikes and other **outdoor activities** in the park are provided by various companies, including PlanAlto in Campo do Gerês (Ⓣ 253 351 005, ⓦ www.planalto .com.pt), Clik Outdoors in Rio Caldo (Ⓣ 253 391 645, ⓦ www.clikoutdoor.net) and Trilhos in Porto (Rua de Belém 94 Ⓣ 225 504 604, ⓦ www.trilhos.pt). You can expect to pay around €15 for a simple guided walk, or more like €50 for day-long kayaking adventure.

If you want to do some hikes, you'll need good boots, warm, waterproof clothes, a compass (beware fog in spring and winter), food and a water bottle – there are plenty of streams but it's good practice to purify water with iodine or chlorine tablets. Also bear in mind that night falls a lot quicker in the mountains than on the coast, temperatures can drop quickly in fog, during rain and at night, and that in winter you're likely to find plenty of snow, which makes following trails a much riskier business. Finally, note that picking flowers and **lighting fires** are forbidden – the Portuguese have an alarming habit of lighting them whenever and wherever they picnic, with terrible consequences in the dry summers.

mountain ranges remain largely undiscovered by tourism, especially in the eastern reaches of the Serra do Gêres where the spectacular mountain terrain is still remote and often impenetrable.

The roads into the park, and to the main settlements, are pretty decent, but **bus** services are limited during the week and often non-existent at weekends. The main public transport connections are: Melgaço (on the Rio Minho) to Lamas de Mouro and Castro Laboreiro in the north; Arcos de Valdevez to Soajo and Lindoso in the centre; and Braga to Caldas do Gêres and the route east to Montalegre. Once in the park, a car is most useful, though **walking** is the best way of getting around. Waymarked trails and paths cover large areas and there are dozens of hiking opportunities, from short strolls to day treks across whole sections of the park.

Apart from in the main centre of Caldas do Gerês, **accommodation** is limited to a handful of *pensões* or *casas rural* in other villages, or **camping** at designated sites, run either by the park or by private operators. Small groups might find renting one of the ten self-catering *casas abrigos* (converted farmhouses) to be better value. Although occasionally basic, and sometimes even lacking electricity, these houses offer excellent value for money – you'll generally pay around €40 in winter and €70 in summer for a four-bed house, including firewood. They must be booked and partly paid for in advance on ☎258 452 250 or at the ADERE park office in Ponte da Barca and there is a minimum stay of two nights. The office also lists other park accommodation options, such as apartments or rooms in private *quintas*.

Caldas do Gerês

The main centre for the central section of the park is the old spa town of **CALDAS DO GERÊS** (usually referred to simply as Vila do Gerês), which can be reached easily from Braga on regular buses operated by Empresa Hoteleira do Gerês. A mountain village spectacularly sited in a densely wooded valley, the town consists of little more than a little one-way system running either side of a babbling brook and, weekends aside, when Portuguese picnickers arrive en masse, it's a relaxed base from which to explore the surrounding peaks and woodlands. "The Spa of Gerês" became fashionable in the early years of the nineteenth century – an epoch convincingly evoked by a row of grand period hotels (some now in a sorry state) along the sedate main Avenida Manuel Francisco da Costa. Old folk still queue to drink the therapeutic waters that bubble out of a rock of the little spa building at the north end of town – though only those with a prescription are supposed to drink it. A modern spa centre is currently taking shape halfway up the little high street, part of the considerable recent development that has seen a spate of guesthouses appear on the steep road above the town – each with a spectacular, almost Alpine outlook.

Gerês even has its own rather grand **Parque das Termas** (daily 9am–6pm; €1) just north of town, a wonderful tree-shaded park either side of a gushing stream. You could easily while away half a day here, picnicking on granite slabs by the waters. You can also hire boats on a little lake (€3 for 30min), play tennis (€3 an hour), table tennis (€1.50 an hour) or go swimming at the outdoor pools at the back of the park (€4; €6 at weekends).

Practicalities

Buses stop at two stops on the main drag, Avenida Manuel Francisco da Costa, which is also where you can catch local buses to Rio Caldo and also find the bank and pharmacy. The post office is at the foot of the main road, by the

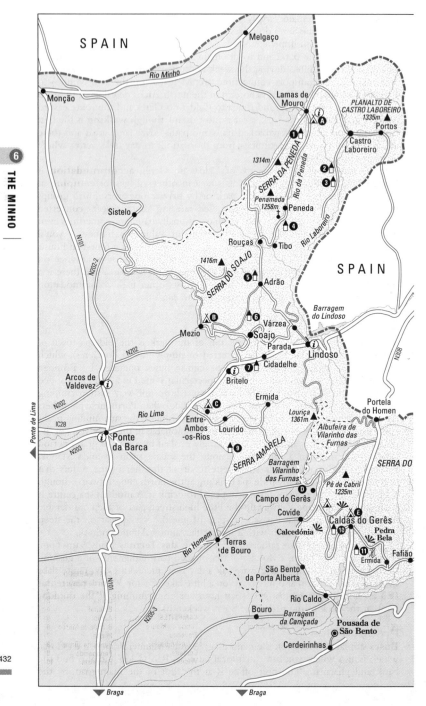

PARQUE NACIONAL
DA PENEDA-GERÊS

0   10 km

N

Celanova & Orense

SPAIN

Bande

Rio Limia

SPAIN

Tourém

Lobios

1373m

Pitões de Júnias

1545m

Montalegre   N308

Covelães

Outeiro   Paredes do Rio

1469m

Barragem de Paradela

GERÊS

Paradela

N308-4

N103

Barragem do Alto Rabagão

Rio Cabril

Pisões

Cabril

Pincães

Rio Cávado

Barragem da Venda Nova   N103

Barragem da Salamonde

N103

Venda Nova

Chaves

Chaves

CAMPSITES
Lamas de Mouro	A
Travanca	B
Entre-Ambos-os-Rios	C
Cerdeira	D
Vidoeiro	E
Outeiro Alto	F

CASAS ABRIGO
Bico de Pássaro	1
Barreiro	2
Dorna	3
Baleiral	4
Adrão	5
Branda de Murço	6
Penha	7
Pitões de Júnias	8
Penadoeido	9
Bela Vista	10
Ventuzelo	11

Life in the Parque Nacional da Peneda-Gerês

The **Parque Nacional da Peneda-Gerês** was established in 1971, not only to protect the region's landscape, archeology and wildlife, but also to safeguard the traditional rural way of life of its inhabitants.

The most common vestiges of **early human occupation** are *antas* (or dolmens), tombs constructed from upright stones that were topped with roof slabs and then covered with soil; unexcavated *anta* mounds are called *mamoas*. Less frequent are *menhirs* (tall standing stones with a phallic appearance that archeologists inevitably ascribe to fertility cults), *cromeleques* (stone circles) and *arte rupestre* (rock art, usually engraved symbols such as concentric circles, little cup-like depressions possibly used for sorting or crushing seeds, boxed crosses and hand axes). The locations of some are marked, very approximately, on the park's maps.

Unique **domestic animals** – primitive breeds long extinct elsewhere like *cachena* and *barrosa* cattle, *bravia* goats, *garrano* ponies and the powerful *Castro Laboreiro* sheepdog – continue to be the mainstay of the local economy. In distant forested corners, remnants of the **wildlife** that once roamed all Europe still survive: wild boar, otters, polecats and some of the continent's last surviving wolves exist side by side with more familiar species like badgers, foxes and roe deer. Birds are numerous in both numbers and breeds, from majestic raptors such as goshawks, eagles and kites to mountain passerines like rock buntings and aquatic dippers, while on the ground lizards and snakes, though common, are rarely seen.

The variety of **vegetation** that gives the park its lush greenness is equally impressive. A total of eighteen plant species – including the Serra do Gerês iris – are found nowhere else on earth. In the valleys oak and laurel line the riverbanks, replaced by holly, birch, pine and juniper at higher elevations.

But while the park boundaries afford some security to the natural wonders, the **traditional communities** are less easily protected. The lure of the city proves irresistibly attractive to many youngsters and village populations throughout the region are slowly shrinking. They are also ageing; in some areas as many as three-quarters of the inhabitants are of pensionable age. Tourism may go some way towards providing incentives for locals to stay in the area and thereby preserve ancient customs and traditions, but with the influx of tourists comes a responsibility to protect the delicate ecosystems and uniqueness of the environment. Time will tell if the right balance can be achieved.

roundabout. The **turismo** (Mon–Wed & Fri–Sat 9.30am–12.30pm & 2.30–6pm; ☎253 391 133) sits under the arcades at the top end of the main avenue and can handle most enquiries. The **national park office** is inconveniently sited 1.5km north on the Portela de Homem road, in an easily missed building by the entrance to the campsite (Mon–Fri 9.30am–noon & 2–5.30pm; ☎253 390 110); along with walk advice, they can arrange horse-riding with EquiCampo (☎253 357 022) for around €15 an hour.

Gerês is awash with **pensões** and some – even in the height of summer – are reasonably priced. Note, however, that many are open only from May to October; prices are often halved at those open during the winter, but their restaurants are usually closed. The best place to head first – if you don't mind the uphill walk – is to the string of large, modernized *pensões* overlooking town on Rua do Amassó, which all have parking for guests. Other good-value options are found strung out at reasonably regular intervals along the 8km down the valley to Rio Caldo. The **campsite**, *Vidoeiro* (☎253 391 289, ⓕ258 452 450, open March–Oct), is just north of town by the river – it's well maintained and has good facilities.

The **restaurants** attached to most of the *pensões* offer good-quality if unmemorable food, with portions healthy enough to satisfy the most ravenous hiker. The best places are listed below.

Hotels and pensions

Adelaide Rua do Amassó ☎253 390 020, ℱ253 390 029. Spacious and comfortable *pensão* in two separate buildings high up at the top end of the road; beg if you have to for a room with a huge balcony for grandstand views over town. Has its own lively restaurant if you can't face the trek down the hill. ❸

Águas do Gerês Av Manuel Francisco da Costa 136 ☎253 390 190, ☯www.aguasdogeres.pt. Elegant and classy modern place carved out of a grand old hotel, with the most stylish rooms in town, a pool and spa facilities. ❹

Baltazar Rua Eng José Lagrifa Mendes ☎253 391 131, ☯www.pensaobaltazar.com. Cheerful en-suite *pensão* rooms in a renovated 150-year-old stone house just behind the turismo. The moderately priced restaurant has a good-value menu, with things like grilled veal or sea bass with anchovies. ❸

Flôr de Moçambiqu ℂ Rua do Amassó ☎253 391 119, ℱ253 392 042. Clean and amiable *pensão*, with modern rooms with baths, TVs and balconies with views over Gerês. There's a decent restaurant with an fine outdoor terrace where breakfast (included) is served. No credit cards. ❶

Ponte Rua Boavista, parallel to main road ☎253 391 121. If you like the sound of running water, you'll enjoy this characterful, rambling *pensão* by the river. Simple comforts but a bit dated. No credit cards. ❷

🏃 **São Miguel do Gerês** Rua do Amassó ☎253 391 360. Very friendly, small guest house with pristine rooms each offering balconies with sweeping views over the wooded slopes. The bathrooms are showing their age but otherwise this is excellent value. ❷

🏃 **Quinta Souto-Linho** Rua Dr M. Gomes Almeida ☎253 392 000, ☯www.geocities .com/souto_linho. A picture-book *Turismo Rural* property, more central than many, uphill just east of the high street. Grand rooms come with polished floors and fine views. There's also an outdoor pool (open summer only). ❸

Restaurants and bars

Bar de Adega by the stream on the one-way system heading south. Set in a huge stone warehouse, this is the best of the limited options for nightlife. Lively sounds and a metred pool table pull in the local youth. Open daily from 8pm.

Fernandes Rua Dr Manuel Gomes de Almeida 83, on main street near bottom of town ☎253 391 109. A small, friendly place with just half a dozen tables, some by the window overlooking the river at the back. A diminutive menu too, though the portions are huge and tasty and the tourist menu is a bargain €10. Inexpensive.

🏃 **Geresiana** Rua Augusta Sérgio Almeida Maia 1 ☎253 391 226. Stone walls and crisp white tablecloths set the tone for the best eatery in town, with a decent range of starters, generous mains and fine desserts. The trout stuffed with *presunto* ham is delicious. Moderate.

A Lagôa Lugar do Vidoeiro, halfway between town and the campsite ☎253 391 918. Around 1km uphill out of town, by a cluster of cafés, this has a tranquil outside terrace by a bubbling brook and a colossal dining area where you can tuck into well-prepared fish, grills and occasionally pizzas. Moderate.

The central park: around Caldas do Gerês

With your own transport, there are some great places a short drive from **Caldas do Gerês**, though the best way to get around is to walk – you could walk the entire eastern section of the park in around three days with careful planning. Alternatively, *Hotel Universal* on Caldas do Gerês's high street (☎253 391 141) organizes daily minibus tours, open to non-guests when places are available. These vary from two hours (€5) to full-day tours (€10) and include trips to the Arado falls (see p.436) and the sanctuary at Peneda (see p.441).

The most picturesque routes into this section of the park are either north to Portela do Homem; or southeast to Ermida and on to Cabril, an easy drive or a tough two-day walk via the viewpoint at Pedra Bela. There's no public transport along these routes. From Cabril, drivers and hikers can cross the reservoirs to the eastern section of the park into the Trás-os-Montes region (see p.484).

Another option is to head south to the watersports centre of **Rio Caldo**, where the road crosses the blue waters of a beautiful reservoir. Fairly regular buses follow the dramatic route around the reservoir to the wooded campsite at Campo do Gerês, known for its adventure sports, via the pilgrimage destination of São Bento.

North to Portela do Homen

North of Caldas do Gerês, the narrow main road twists tortuously uphill into deeply wooded valleys criss-crossed by idyllic streams and bathing pools. Outside summer weekends, when the road gets busy with picnickers, this route is virtually deserted and you could easily walk or drive the 13km to **Portela do Homen** without passing a single car. After 9km or so, a left-hand forestry road offers an alternative route to Campo do Gerês (see p.438). A further 1.5km towards Portela do Homen, a small bridge marks a stream with a superb natural bathing spot just north of the road, though note that in July and August parking is strictly forbidden along this stretch. Portela do Homen itself is mountain pass with a weird deserted border post, its former customs buildings abandoned and surrounded by grazing cattle; drive right on through to enter Spain and the road to Ourense.

Pedra Bela

An hour's walk to the southeast of Caldas do Gerês, **Pedra Bela** is the destination for local Portuguese weekenders. And small wonder, with a superb *miradouro* and picnic site overlooking the vast reservoir of Caniçada and a good part of the Gerês range. You can drive here by taking the road south of Caldas and turning left (signed Ermida). To walk, the most direct approach is to take the cobbled ramp which heads steeply up opposite *Hotel Universal* on the Caldas high street – the tough climb is mostly on a dirt path which cuts off the road's corners.

Better still, follow trail **PR3** (leaflet available from the tourist office or park office), one of the region's best walks. It starts from above the picnic site opposite the campsite/park office turning, around 2km north of Caldas do Gerês on the Portela do Homen road. The ten-kilometre, half-day trail follows the summer/winter "currals" or grazing pastures for cattle ranchers. Look for the red and yellow waymarks which take you steeply uphill before levelling off to cross superb mountain pastures, framed by weird granite outcrops.

Arado waterfalls and Ermida

From Pedra Bela, another delightful four-kilometre path heads southeast to the magnificent **Arado waterfalls**, with refreshing pools for swimming. The path continues southeast to **Ermida**, a two- to three-hour walk away from Caldas do Gerês. This tiny farming community has an air of true isolation about it – if you're looking for a quiet hiking base, this is a good choice, with accommodation at the simple *Casa do Criado* (☎253 391 390; no credit cards; ❶), an orchard to camp in and a couple of cafés.

East to Cabril

The narrow eight-kilometre road from Ermida to Cabril winds through one of the most idyllic valleys in the whole of the park, with dense woodland interspersed with vineyards and little waterfalls, paradise to swim in. The stone houses that make up the farming hamlet of **FAFIÃO** make another decent hiking base: the restaurant here, *Retiro do Gerês*, has a basic rooms (☎253 658 236; no credit cards; ❶). Beyond, the countryside becomes more fertile, terraced with vines and maize, the road winding down to the slightly larger village of Cabril.

A lovely, isolated place, sat on the Rio Cabril and surrounded on all sides by mountains, **CABRIL's** centre is still sauntered through by oxen, goats and sheep. Parts of the locality have been submerged because of the Salamonde dam and, consequently, the old bridge is half under water, making for great swimming through the bridge arch. There's a **campsite**, *Outeiro Alto* (T253 659 860), 1km out on the Fafião road, which is fine provided it's not too busy – there are only two toilets and one small café. It also rents out bicycles and canoes and offers horse-riding. You can get a good **meal** at the 🍴 *Restaurante Ponte Novo* (T253 659 882), a superb spot with a terrace overlooking the new bridge, which serves a hearty meat stew along with other moderately priced grills.

East of Cabril, the road climbs through wild mountain scenery of jutting outcrops of granite, a stunningly dramatic route. Detour off the road to Sirvozelo, Lapela and Xertola to see village life at its most traditional. The narrow road then continues over the dam into Paradela in the eastern extremity of the park in Trás-os-Montes.

South to Rio Caldo and São Bento da Porta Aberta

The village of **RIO CALDO**, 8km south of Caldas do Gerês, sprawls round the two bridges that cross the west bank of the Barragem da Caniçada; change here for buses from Caldas to São Bento. Dramatically sited in a bowl surrounded by mountains, the large reservoir is a watersports centre for windsurfing and waterskiing, and the swimming is fine, too, though only in designated areas. If you want to get out onto the water, Água Montanha (T253 391 779, Wwww.aguamontanha.com) rents out canoes (€3.50/hr), and offers boat trips (€24/hr).

The best place for **food** or a drink is the swish *Finger Bar* (T253 392 023; closed Wed) by the marina; a big outdoor terrace faces the boats while the dining room offers good, mid-priced meals. There's plenty of **accommodation** – a good bet is the *Pensão Pontes do Rio Caldo* (T253 391 540, Wwww.priocaldo.web.pt; no credit cards; ③), a stone building with a garden and restaurant-bar at the road junction with the bridges. Alternatively, you could drive (or catch a bus) uphill towards Cerdrinhas to the *Pousada de São Bento* (T253 647 190, Wwww.pousadas.pt; includes breakfast; ⑥), in a superb position overlooking the reservoir from the east. This timber-beamed former hunting lodge has its own swimming pool and a superb restaurant, with great views.

Three kilometres northwest of Rio Caldo, **SÃO BENTO DA PORTA ABERTA** is a small village high above the reservoir, commanding more excellent views. Its austere sanctuary – and its modern sibling – are favourite spots with pilgrims, who gather here at the beginning of July and again a month later (and on most Sundays throughout the year) – at such times the traffic makes it a place best avoided. A former monastery, hidden under an ugly modern facade, is now the *Estalagem de São Bento da Porta Aberta* (T253 391 106, Wwww.estalagemsbento.com; ④); bag a room with a lakeside view if you can, and there's a good restaurant. It can also arrange jeep safaris and adventure sports. Cheaper **rooms** are available at *Casa dos Santos*, just north on Lugar da Seara (T253 391 212, ①), a homely place with its own patio garden full of lemon trees; there's even a bar with table tennis, and they can arrange canoeing. Incidentally, walking trail PR7 (full details from the tourist office in Caldas) ends right outside. You can eat well at the *Restaurante Mira Serra* (T253 391 362), where mid-priced meals are can be enjoyed on a breezy terrace high above the reservoir.

From São Bento, the road climbs steeply for 8km towards Campo do Gerês. A kilometre south, in quiet woodland, lies the **Museu Etnográfico de Vilarinho da Furna** (Tues–Sun 10am–noon & 2–5pm; €1), an evocative and emotive museum dedicated to the former village of Vilarinho da Furna, which was completely submerged by the building of a dam in 1972. There are farm implements, a recreated kitchen and black-and-white photos recording village life. Just beyond the museum, the Centro de Activitades (daily 9.30am–11pm; free) is a little park with picnic and play areas – the centre also organizes adventure sports in the area.

CAMPO DO GERÊS itself is a fairly mundane cluster of houses huddled around a road junction, but its location, surrounded by dense woodland, is superb and it makes a great base for hikes or adventure sports. There are daily direct buses here from Braga with Empresa Hoteleira do Gerês. You'll find a large choice of private **rooms** in Campo, while the modern *Albergaria Stop* (T253 350 040, Wwww.albergariastop.eol.pt; ●) has its own café-bar, pool table and tennis court. The well-maintained *Cerdeira* **campsite** (T253 351 005, F253 351 005; open all year ✻) also has some modern bungalows (sleep up to six; ●), bikes for rent and its own pool and restaurant; it can also arrange horse-riding and hires out bikes (€25 a day).

A great walk from the campsite (7km/90min one way) is to take the forestry track east (signed Portela do Homen). This eventually joins the road to Portela do Homen where it is a short walk to some superb natural bathing pools.

Vilarinho das Furnas **youth hostel** where the dam construction workers once stayed (T253 351 339, Wwww.pousadasjuventude.pt; ●) is a ten-minute walk from Campo do Gerês; it has bike rental and a tennis court. At the nearby Barragem Vilarinho das Furnas, you can sometimes see the ruins of the old village that was submerged by the dam poking up above the waters.

Lindoso and Soajo

Separated from the central section of the park by the towering Serra Amarela mountain range lie the traditional villages of **Soajo** and **Lindoso**, which are fine centres for hiking, as well as attractive destinations in themselves. There are fairly regular buses from Arcos de Valdevez (see p.429) and Ponte da Barca (see p.427) to Parada and Lindoso, with less frequent services to Soajo from Arcos de Valdevez. Incidentally, if you want to visit these villages from Campo or Caldas do Gerês by car, the best way is to take the road via Portela do Homen into Spain up to Lobios, entering Portugal again near Lindoso.

Lindoso

In a spectacular position, surrounded by mountains high above a glittering reservoir, **LINDOSO** – 18km from Ponte da Barca and close to the Spanish

---

The Roman columns of Via Nova

Just outside the Museu Etnográfico de Vilarinho da Furna, you'll find **Roman column XXVII**, one of a series of carved granite posts marching from Santa Cruz, south of Terras de Bouro, to the border at Portela do Homen. This section, known locally as Geira, marks out miles XIV to XXXIV of the Roman Via Nova, a military road built in the 1st century AD. The road originally linked Braga with Astorga in Spain, a distance of 344 kms.

△ Lindoso

border – is one of the most attractive villages in Peneda-Gerês. Its main sight is an extraordinary collection of some fifty nineteenth-century *espigueiros* (grain stores) spread out on the slopes around its splendid border castle. In addition to allowing drying air to pass under the grain and maize, the granite legs of these tomb-like structures offer a degree of protection from rats. Their grouping together is a vestige of the days when the isolated village depended heavily on communal effort for its survival.

Rising above the village, Lindoso's ruined **Castelo** (April–Sept Tues–Fri 10am–12.30pm & 2–6pm, Sat & Sun 10am–noon & 2.30–5pm; Oct–March Tues–Sun 2–4.30pm; €1) contains a museum chronicling the castle's military history and displays finds of local excavations. It's free to simply enjoy the guard's-eye view over the valley from the battlements, and you can also pick up general park information here.

The rest of Lindoso is a rather well-to-do border village, although a traditional lifestyle still continues for many of its inhabitants. For **accommodation**, you can enquire about staying in renovated rustic properties in the village through ADERE (☎258 452 450; most ❸) in Ponte da Barca, though a three-night minimum stay is the norm. A better bet is the friendly *Casa do Destro* (☎258 577 534; ❷), in the shadow of the castle, with nine modern rooms and two spacious suites, all with good views, plus a pool in a large terrace. This also is an excellent place for a **meal**, its restaurant (closed Wed) a surprisingly upmarket affair with a long list of starters (give the pig's ear salad a miss) and superb, if pricy, steaks and *bacalhau* dishes.

Soajo

SOAJO – 15km east of Arcos de Valdevez – has been designated as a centre for rural tourism, its stone houses scrubbed clean and linked by pristine paved alleys – even the former chapel has become a bar. Like Lindoso, its highlight is a collection of eighteenth- and nineteenth-century **espigueiros** (grain houses), over twenty of which are clumped together on a stony platform on the eastern edge of town, their roof-crosses (intended to bless the annual crop) giving them the look of a graveyard.

While the village has been spruced up for tourists, it still observes its traditions. Folkloric groups are maintained by those who stay behind, while emigrants try to inculcate a sense of *minha terra* (my homeland) into their modern-minded (and in many cases American) offspring. The local **festival** (Aug 13–15) has a playful feel, with spontaneous fun and games. Due to a lack of horses, the *corrida* is a race on foot – balancing blue plastic urns full of water on their heads, contestants compete for the honour of being ceremoniously drenched by all the others – and large, home-made fireworks are set off without warning.

The best local **walk** is a four-kilometre return route to the neighbouring village of Adrão, along a cobbled track with ruts worn into the stones over the centuries by ox carts. For details, ask at the **ADERE-Soajo** information office on Largo da Bairros (Mon–Fri 9.30am–noon & 2–7pm, Sat 9.30am–1pm; ☎258 576 427, ✉turismo.adere-soajo@sapo.pt). This can also book **accommodation** at one of the numerous private homes that have joined together in a pioneering Turismo de Aldeia scheme. Each house sleeps between two and eight people, and has its own character, although chunky stone walls, wooden ceilings and simple decor are the rule. Costs range from €45 for a night in the diminutive *Casa da Porta da Mina* (sleeps two), up to €180 for a house that sleeps eight. All prices are per night (although the minimum reservation is three days) and extra beds can be provided for €15. Also recommended (though not part of the scheme) is the stone *Casa do Adro* (☎258 576 327, Ⓦwww.casadoadroturismorural.com; ❸, 3-night minimum stay), offering rooms in a beautiful eighteenth-century house. Of the **restaurants**, best positioned is *Vidreira* (☎258 576 205, closed for lunch except Sat, Sun & throughout July & Aug) on the main square. Alternatively, *O Espigueiro de Soajo* (☎258 576 136; moderate), on the Arcos road, specializes in mountain goat and a stew of chicken and rice. You'll also find a **bank** with an ATM and a pharmacy, and there's a small **supermarket** 200m north on the main thoroughfare heading towards Arcos.

The northern section: Serra da Peneda

Thanks mainly to the limited public transport and scant accommodation, the wild **Serra da Peneda**, in the north of the park, sees far fewer tourists than the central zone, and this sense of isolation can be an advantage. You'll often have the prehistoric sites, steep forested valleys, and exposed, wind-blown *planaltos* dotted with weird rock formations entirely to yourself – not to mention the marvellous views.

Peneda

Around 28km northeast of Arcos de Valdevez, signed off the Soajo road, you arrive at the small mountain village of **PENEDA**, huddled under the towering granite summit of Penameda (1258m). The village is famous for its **Sanctuário da Nossa Senhora da Peneda**, a miniature version of the pilgrimage church at Bom Jesus near Braga. It's full of devotees at the beginning of September (especially on Sep 7 & 8), but pretty much deserted for the rest of the year. The original focus of adoration was a curious stone which natural forces had sculpted into the form of a woman, who some said was pregnant. Come Christianity, the cult and its stone was adopted as the Virgin Mary and was duly incorporated into the late eighteenth-century Church. There she remained until the 1930s, when somebody stole her; a gaudy plastic replacement now stands in place of the original.

The village itself has cafés and religious artefact shops clustered around the main square. There are plenty of inexpensive **rooms**. There's also the classy *Hotel da Peneda* (☎251 460 040, ⓔhotel.peneda@clix.pt; ❸), with its own bar and restaurant; it also lets out the attractive *turismo rural* property, the *Anjo da Guarda* (❷) in the main square.

The moderately difficult **Trilho da Peneda** (8.2km, 4hr) walking circuit (leaflets in Portuguese available from the park office in Ponte de Barca) takes you west up the side of the valley into the windblown Serra da Peneda and to the peak of **Penameda** (1258m), where there are freshwater lagoons and fine views across the whole of the park. From here, the track turns north and then east, eventually dropping back down to the Lamas de Mouro road, about 1km north of Peneda by the signpost for the same route in reverse.

Lamas de Mouro and Castro Laboreiro

From Peneda, the road continues for 8km to **LAMAS DE MOURO**, along a stunning forested valley topped on either side with vertiginous boulders. There's little to the place, but it does have a **national park visitor centre** (Mon, Tues & Thurs–Sun 9.30/10am–12.30pm & 2/2.30–5/6pm; ☎251 465 563) and a beautifully situated **campsite** (☎251 465 129; ring ahead in winter), which has hot showers, a bar, a nearby natural pool for swimming and a restaurant. There's also a good **guide** here, who covers the Trilho da Peneda circuit northwest of Peneda village (see above), in addition to several other park trails.

The left-hand fork at Lamas leads 8km up to the ancient village of **CASTRO LABOREIRO**, best known for the breed of mountain dog to which it gives its name. Once used to protect sheep from marauding wolves, the breed has become rare as wolf numbers have declined and is now hardly seen outside the region. The village itself is unexceptional, but there are superb walks in the area, especially to the east and south. The *Trilho Castrejo* leaflet (in Portuguese), available from the turismo in Melgaço, is helpful here. One of the best walks is to the ruins of the **castle**, a very steep twenty-minute walk: turn left at the roundabout on the other side of the village, then left up a path where the road drops to the right, past a large rock known as the *Tartaruga* (Tortoise), and through heather and between boulders, with sheer drops to each side and steps hacked out of the rock face.

The best **accommodation** is at the modern *Albergaria Miracastro* (☎251 460 020, ⓦwww.miracastro.com; ❷), with fine views from the balconies and a good **restaurant** serving solid mountain food such as *cabrito serrano* (mountain kid goat). Weekday **buses** to Lamas de Mouro and Castro Laboreiro leave from Melgaço on the Rio Minho (see p.421 for details).

Travel details

You can check train timetables online at Ⓦ www.cp.pt.

Trains

Barcelos to: Porto (7 daily; 1hr); Valença do Minho (7 daily; 1hr 15min–1hr 50min); Viana do Castelo (11–12 daily; 30–40min).
Braga to: Nine – change for Viana and Valença (12–15 daily; 12–28min); Porto (11–14 daily, some change at Nine; 1hr–1hr 45min).
Caminha to: Valença do Minho (8–10 daily; 20–30min); Viana do Castelo (5–8 daily; 20–40min).
Guimarães to: Porto (hourly; 1hr 10min).
Valença do Minho to: Afife (4–6 daily; 55min); Barcelos (7–8 daily; 1hr 15min–2hr); Caminha (6–8 daily; 20–45min); Nine – change for Braga (5–7 daily; 2hr 20min); Porto (3 daily, 2hr 15min); Viana do Castelo (4–10 daily; 1hr); Vigo, Spain (3 daily; 1hr 10min; connections to Santiago de Compostela and La Coruña); Vila Nova de Cerveira (8–10 daily; 13min); Vila Praia de Âncora (6–7 daily; 20min–1hr).
Viana do Castelo to: Afife (4 daily; 20min); Barcelos (12 daily; 25–45min); Caminha (7–8 daily; 20–40min); Porto (3–5 daily; 1hr 50min–2hr); Vila Nova de Cerveira (7 daily; 30min–1hr); Vila Praia de Âncora (8–10 daily; 15min).
Vila Nova de Cerveira to: Valença do Minho (8–10 daily; 13min); Viana do Castelo (6–7 daily; 30min–1hr).

Buses

Arcos de Valdevez to: Braga (10 daily; 1hr 30min–2hr); Lindoso (Mon–Fri 1–3 daily; 1hr); Monçao (4–6 daily; 45min); Ponte de Lima (5–9 daily; 50min); Porto (2–4 daily; 2hr); Soajo (Mon–Fri 1–3 daily; 45min); Viana do Castelo (5–12 daily; 1hr 30min).
Barcelos to: Braga (Mon–Fri every 30min, Sat & Sun hourly; 50min); Chaves (Mon–Fri 13 daily, Sat & Sun 3–6 daily; 6hr); Ponte de Lima (Mon–Fri 8 daily, 1–2 at weekends; 40–55min); Porto (Mon–Sat 9–12 daily, Sun 1–2 daily; 1hr 45min); Viana do Castelo (2–8 daily; 50min).
Braga to: Arcos de Valdevez (10 daily; 1hr 30min–2hr); Barcelos (Mon–Fri every 30min, Sat & Sun hourly; 30–50min); Bragança (2–6 daily; 4hr 15min–5hr); Caldas do Gerês (5–11 daily; 1hr 30min); Campo do Gerês (2–7 daily; 1hr 30min); Chaves (4 daily; 4hr); Coimbra (6–10 daily; 2hr 40min); Guimarães (every 30 min; 40min–1hr); Lisbon (9–12 daily; 4hr 30min–5hr 30min); Monçao (3–5 daily; 2hr 20min); Montalegre (4–7 daily; 2hr 40min); Ponte da Barca (4 daily; 1hr

15min); Ponte de Lima (3–10 daily; 30min–1hr); Porto (every 30min; 1hr 15min); Venda Nova (5–10 daily; 1hr 50min); Viana do Castelo (4–10 daily; 1hr 40min).
Caldas do Gerês to: Braga (5–11 daily; 1hr 30min); Rio Caldo (6–12 daily; 25min); Vila Real (3–8 daily; 2hr 40min).
Campo do Gerês to: Braga (2–6 daily; 1hr 20min).
Guimarães to: Braga (every 30min; 40min–1hr); Lisbon (4–6 daily; 4hr 30min–5hr); Mondim de Basto (2 daily; 1hr 5min); Porto (2–7 daily; 1hr); Vila Real (1–7 daily; 1hr 30min).
Melgaço to: Castro Laboreiro (Mon–Fri 1 daily; 1hr); Coimbra (1–3 daily; 5hr); Lamas de Mouro (Mon–Fri 1 daily; 40min); Lisbon (1–3 daily; 6hr); Monção (1–5 daily; 40min); Porto (1–3 daily; 3hr); São Gregório (Mon–Fri 3 daily; 30min).
Monção to: Braga (3–6 daily; 1hr 45min); Melgaço (Mon–Fri 5 daily, Sat & Sun 1 daily; 40min); Porto (2–4 daily; 2h 30min–3hr); Valença do Minho (10 daily; 20min); Viana do Castelo (1–5 daily; 1hr 20min).
Ponte da Barca to: Arcos de Valdevez (hourly; 15min); Braga (14 daily; 1hr); Lindoso (2 daily; 45min); Ponte de Lima (3–4 daily; 20–30min); Viana do Castelo (6–8 daily; 1hr 30min).
Ponte de Lima to: Arcos de Valdevez (5–9 daily; 50min); Barcelos (2 daily; 55min); Braga (3–10 daily; 30min–1hr); Ponte de Barca (3–4 daily; 20–30min); Porto (4–7 daily; 2hr 20min); Valença (1 daily; 25min); Viana do Castelo (Mon–Fri 21 daily, Sat & Sun 9 daily; 50min).
Valença do Minho to: Lisbon (4 daily; 6hr 30min); Melgaço (8 daily; 40min); Monçao (10 daily; 20min); Ponte de Lima (1 daily; 25min); Porto (2–7 daily; 2hr 30min); Viana do Castelo via Caminha (2–6 daily; 1 hr); Vila Nova de Cerveira (3–6 daily; 15min); to Spain: Sat to Vigo/Santiago (2hr/4hr 15min); Tues, Thurs and Fri via Monçao and Melgaço for Ponte Barxas.
Viana do Castelo to: Afife (6 daily; 15min); Arcos de Valdevez (3–12 daily; 1hr 30min); Barcelos (2–8 daily; 50min); Braga (4–10 daily; 1hr 40min); Caminha (roughly hourly; 30min); Esposende (4–13 daily; 25min); Lisbon (2 daily; 5hr); Moledo do Minho (5–13 daily; 30min); Monçao (1–5 daily; 1hr 20 min); Ponte da Barca (6–8 daily; 1hr 30min); Ponte de Lima (Mon–Fri 21 daily, Sat & Sun 7 daily; 50min); Porto (3–14 daily;1hr 35min); Valença (2–6 daily; 1hr); Vila Nova de Cerveira (2–4 daily; 50 min); Vila Praia de Âncora (2–16 daily; 20–30min).

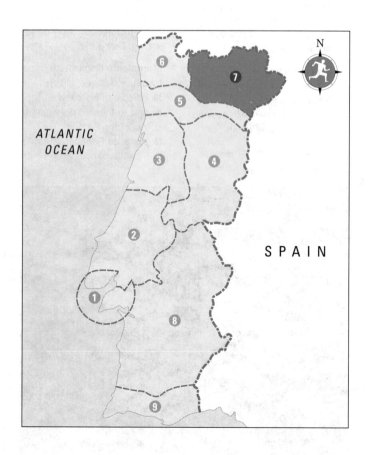

Trás-os-Montes

CHAPTER 7

Highlights

* **The Corgo train line** The narrow gauge train line from Peso da Régua to Vila Real is one of the most dramatic in the country. See p.448

* **Miranda do Douro** Take a boat trip through a craggy gorge below this attractive border village. See p.463

* **Bragança** With an ancient citadel enclosing centuries of history, Bragança is also gateway to the superb Montesinho natural park See p.466

* **Rio de Onor** One of Portugal's most authentic medieval villages, doubly fascinating as half of it lies in Spain. See p.473

* **Chaves** The Romans founded this lovely spa town which also boasts sturdy fortifications, a fine museum and a picturesque riverside setting. See p.478

* **Montalegre** Dominated by a ruined castle, hilltop Monalegre offers easy access to the wild northeast corner of the Parque Nacional da Peneda-Gerês See p.483

△ Citadela, Bragança

Trás-os-Montes

T RÁS-OS-MONTES – literally "Beyond the Mountains" – is Portugal's Lost Domain. For centuries this remote, rural province has been a place to hide and practice one's beliefs in peace: its peculiar traditions and dialects have been formed by a diversity of populations, from the prehistoric tribes who carved the enigmatic *porcas* (stone pigs) to Jews who sought refuge here from the Inquisition. For the majority, life here is hard, the landscape forcing people to eke a living from smallholdings and, as a result, emigration is high. In the more remote areas whole villages are populated by people of pensionable age as the youngsters head for the cities in search of a better life.

A sharp natural divide cuts across the province. In the south is the fertile territory officially entitled the Upper Douro, but known unofficially as the **Terra Quente** (Hot Land), which encompasses the terraced stretches of the rivers Douro, Corgo and Tua. Here the landscape, as well as the climate, is distinctly Mediterranean, peppered with olive groves and vineyards, as well as farms growing peaches, oranges, melons and almonds that flourish in the red soils. By contrast, the bitter winters of the wild and rugged north have earned it the name of **Terra Fria** (Cold Land). The extremity of the climate – "Nine months of winter and three months of hell", as the local proverb puts it – and the aridity of much of its land have kept Trás-os-Montes well apart from the mainstream. Even today, with some industry coming to the major towns, the province's population is half that of Minho in almost twice the area. But roads are continually being improved – largely thanks to European Union funding – opening up the province to such a degree that, in many areas, the traditional way of life is coming under threat; the World Bank has invested heavily in the agricultural sector; and several of the province's larger towns have undergone urban renewal projects, making them more attractive to residents and tourists alike.

One of the most accessible towns – by fast road, bus or on a dramatic train line – is **Vila Real,** a good starting point for a tour of the province, and also handy for access to the dramatic granite scenery of the **Parque Natural do Alvão**. Beyond Vila Real, main routes run up to the northern fortified frontier towns of **Chaves** and **Bragança**, two places that should feature on any itinerary of northern Portugal. The route northeast towards Bragança (the N15 or the faster IP4/E82) offers a stopover halfway at **Mirandela** in the Tua valley, from where you can access the remote southeast parts of the region via **Vila Flôr** and the medieval ruins near **Carrazeda de Ansiães**. In this corner, Trás-os-Montes comprises a succession of hardworking mountain villages and small, fortified settlements guarding the border with Spain – like workaday

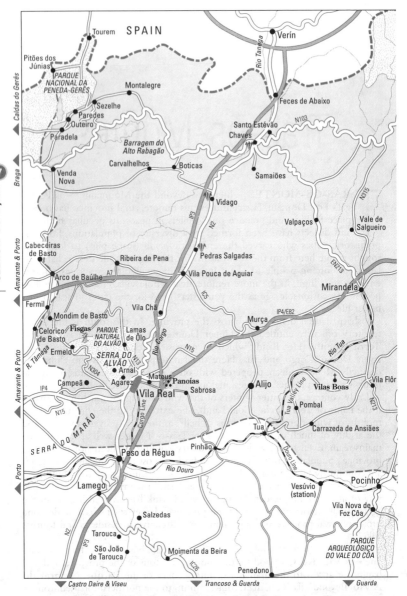

Mogadouro and **Freixo de Espada à Cinta** and historic **Mirando do Douro**. These lie within or on the fringes of the **Parque Natural do Douro Internacional** where wildlife is protected and development restricted.

Two further parks – the **Parque Natural de Montesinho** and the eastern extremity of the **Parque Nacional da Peneda-Gerês** – cover the wild and mountainous borders with Spain. Travel round these and you'll often feel like

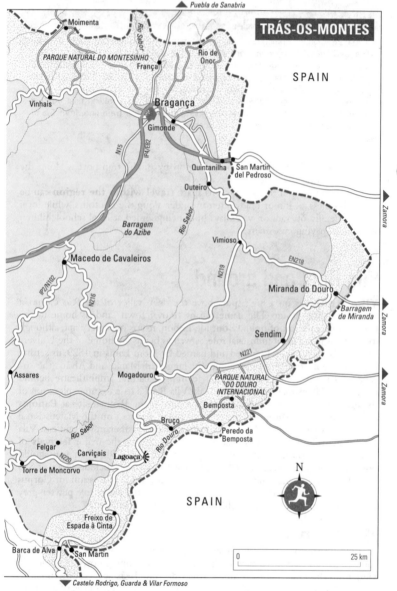

TRÁS-OS-MONTES

▲ Puebla de Sanabria

Moimenta

Rio Sabor

PARQUE NATURAL DO MONTESINHO

França

Rio de Onor

Vinhais

Bragança

Gimonde

SPAIN

► Zamora

N15

IP4/E82

Quintanilha   San Martin del Pedroso

Outeiro

Rio Sabor

Barragem do Azibe

Macedo de Cavaleiros

Vimioso

N219

EN218

► Zamora

Miranda do Douro

Barragem de Miranda

► Zamora

IP2/N102

N216

Sendim

N221

Assares

Mogadouro

PARQUE NATURAL DO DOURO INTERNACIONAL

Bemposta

► Zamora

Bruço

Peredo da Bemposta

Felgar

Rio Sabor

N220

Carviçais

Lagoaça

Rio Douro

Torre de Moncorvo

N

SPAIN

Freixo de Espada à Cinta

Barca de Alva   San Martin

0   25 km

▼ Castelo Rodrigo, Guarda & Vilar Formoso

you are the first foreign visitor to arrive, and traditional village life continues as it has done for centuries. This is where walkers and drivers can experience Trás-os-Montes at its most rural, attractive and remote.

Fast daily bus services from Porto run to the main towns of Vila Real, Chaves, Mirandela and Bragança; while Chaves can also be reached by daily buses from Braga in the Minho (near the Peneda-Gerês national park).

The narrow-gauge train lines

Two narrow-gauge branch rail lines head off from the main Porto to Pocinho Douro line, and are worth travelling for the experience alone. At Peso da Régua, 108km east of Porto, the **Corgo train line** – one of the country's joys – cuts for an hour north through a spectacular winding gorge to Vila Real. Every last vertiginous inch of the surrounding terraces is given over to vine cultivation, and tiny white villages somehow cling to the hillsides, oblivious to the small trains rattling past. Around 38km further along the Douro line, the hour-and-a-half **Tua train line**, from Tua to Mirandela, affords equally spectacular scenery.

However, the finest approach to the region by public transport is along the Douro train line (see box).

The routes between the main towns apart, **travel within the region** can be a slow business, as minor roads often meander along the contours, while local buses generally operate on weekdays only, being aimed at local schoolchildren as much as paying customers.

Vila Real and around

VILA REAL sits on a high spur above the deep valley of the Rio Corgo, a tributary of the Douro. The name means "Royal Town" and, as home to the largest concentration of nobility outside Lisbon, it was once very apt, although today it has more of an industrial role, as well as being the home of the University of Trás-os-Montes. Founded and named by Dom Dinis in 1829, its setting is magnificent, with the twin mountain ranges of Marão and Alvão (the so-called "Gateway to Trás-os-Montes") forming a natural amphitheatre behind the town. Walkers may well want to make Vila Real a base for an exploration of these ranges, while other visitors concentrate on the Roman site at **Panóias** and the **Solar de Mateus** – the country house featured on the Mateus Rosé wine label. Compared with the somnolent villages further north and east, Vila Real is actually quite a lively place – especially during the major **festivals** of Santo António (June 13–21) and São Pedro (June 28–29), when you should book your accommodation well in advance. Other *feiras* include those of São Brás (Feb 3) and Santa Luzia (Dec 13), and there's also a procession for Corpus Deus on June 3. The *feiras* are the best time to buy the distinctive pewter-grey earthenware crockery made in the nearby village of Bisalhães.

The town

The old quarter of Vila Real is built on a promontory above the confluence of the Corgo and Cabril rivers, with the main avenue running down its spine; the view from the fourteenth-century **Capela de São Brás** at its southern end is not one for vertigo sufferers. Despite its noble heritage, there's little of architectural merit in town, save the turismo building – formerly the palace of the Marquês of Vila Real, and fronted by four Manueline windows – and the **Sé**, over the way, which has modern stained-glass windows and a simple, fifteenth-century interior. At the bottom of the hill near the Câmara Municipal, a plaque on the wall of the café opposite commemorates the **birthplace of Diogo Cão**, who discovered the mouth of the Congo River in 1482. Otherwise, there's only the small **Museu de Arqueologia e Numismática** on Rua do Rossio

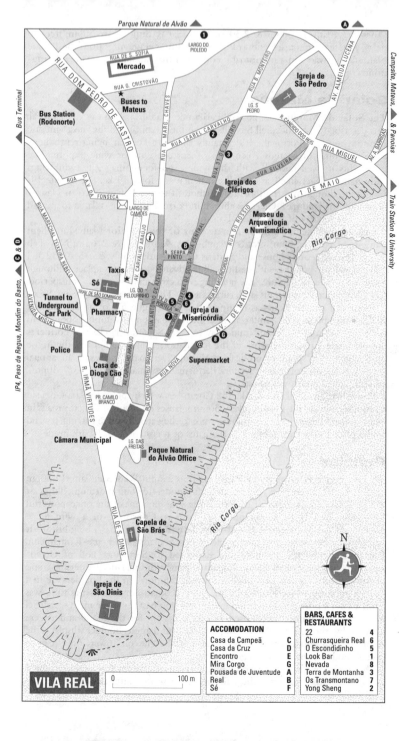

Parque Natural de Alvão ▲

A

LARGO DO PIOLEDO ❶

RUA DE S. SOFIA

Mercado

RUA G. CRISTÓVÃO

★ **Buses to Mateus**

Campsite, Mateus, ▲ & Panóias

RUA DOM PEDRO DE CASTRO

Bus Station (Rodonorte)

Bus Terminal ▲

RUA D. MARG CHAVES

RUA D ISABEL CARVALHO

RUA S MONTEIRO

LG. S PEDRO

Igreja de São Pedro ✚

AV. ALMEIDA LUCENA

R. CANDIDO DOS REIS

RUA MIGUEL

AV. A BARROSA

❷

RUA 31 DE JANEIRO

❸

RUA SILVEIRA

RUA D. AL. DA FONSECA

RUA MARECHAL TEIXEIRA REBEGO

RUA

Igreja dos Clérigos ✚

RUA CENTRAL

AV. 1 DE MAIO

✉

LARGO DE CAMÕES

Museu de Arqueologia e Numismática

Train Station & University ▲

ⓘ

R. SERPA PINTO

B

RUA DA MISERICÓRDIA

AV. CARVALHO ARAUJO

AV. DO ROSSIO

Rio Corgo

AV. MARECHAL TEIXEIRA REBEGO

G & D ▲

Taxis

E

LG. DO PELOURINHO

RUA TEIXEIRA DE SOUSA

Sé ✚

TRAV. DE SÃO DOMINGOS

F

AVENIDA MIGUEL TORGA

Tunnel to Underground Car Park

Pharmacy

RUA ANTONIO DE AZEVEDO

TV. D. PORTELA

❹

❺

❻

❼

Igreja da Misericórdia

AV. 1 DE MAIO

IP4, Peso da Regua, Mondim do Basto, ▲

Police

AV. CARVALHO ARAUJO

@

B

G

RUA CAMILO CASTELO BRANCO

Supermarket

Casa de Diogo Cão

RUA NOVA

R. IRMÃ VIRTUDES

PR. CAMILO BRANCO

Câmara Municipal

LG. DAS FREITAS

Paque Natural do Alvão Office

Rio Corgo

N

RUA DE S. DINIS

Capela de São Brás

Igreja de São Dinis ✚

VILA REAL

0   100 m

ACCOMODATION

Casa da Campeã	**C**
Casa da Cruz	**D**
Encontro	**E**
Mira Corgo	**G**
Pousada de Juventude	**A**
Real	**B**
Sé	**F**

BARS, CAFES & RESTAURANTS

22	**4**
Churrasqueira Real	**6**
O Escondidinho	**5**
Look Bar	**1**
Nevada	**8**
Terra de Montanha	**3**
Os Transmontano	**7**
Yong Sheng	**2**

(Tues–Fri 10am–12.30pm & 2.30–6.30pm, Sat & Sun 2.30–6.30pm; free) to delay you, featuring a selection of Neolithic stone engravings from the Parque Natural do Alvão and a numismatic collection that contains Roman and Visigothic coins.

Solar de Mateus

The **Solar de Mateus** (signposted "Palácio de Mateus"), 4km east of Vila Real, was described by Sacheverell Sitwell as "the most typical and the most fantastic country house in Portugal". It's certainly the most familiar, being reproduced on each bottle of Mateus Rosé, one of Portugal's major wine exports. The facade fits in well enough with the wine's soft-focus image, its twin wings "advancing lobster-like", as Sitwell put it, across a formal lake. The architect is unknown, though most authorities attribute it to the Italian, Nicolau Nasoni, who built the landmark Clérigos church in Porto. The palace is dated to around 1740 – the heyday of Portuguese Baroque.

Ticket prices include a thirty-minute **tour of the interior** (daily: June–Sept 9am–noon & 2–7.30pm; Oct & March–May 9am–1pm & 2–6pm; Nov–Feb 10am–1pm & 2–5pm; house and gardens €6.50, gardens only €3.75; ☎259 323 121), which are popular – it's best to call in advance to reserve a place. Although there are no special treasures, the building is an enjoyable evocation of its period, full of aristocratic portraits and rural scenes. The **gardens** (June–Sept 9am–7.30pm; rest of year hours as house), too, are a delight, full of ponds and box hedges; the spectacular conifer avenue forms an impressive tunnel about 50m long. On summer weekends (mid-May to early September) classical **concerts** are held here, part of the work of the foundation which administers the house and which also sponsors musical workshops, seminars and even an annual literary award for Portuguese writers. Performances usually begin late (9–10pm), so you'll need your own transport.

To get here from Vila Real, take the Corgo bus which run from Rua Gonçalo Cristovão, outside the market (every 30min). Buses drop you at the crossroads in Mateus, from where it's a five-minute walk to the gates. If you're driving, try and find a place in the square opposite the gates or it costs €3.50 to park inside.

Panóias

The fascinating Roman site of **Panóias** (Tues 2–5pm, Wed–Sun 9am–12.30pm & 2–5pm; €1.50 entry, €1.50 for an audio guide, free Sun morning), 8km east of Vila Real and 4km east of Mateus, is the sole remnant of the once-powerful settlement of Vila de Constantim de Panoyas. Consisting of a wire fence enclosing a few boulders with odd-shaped cavities, the site has a long history. It was initially the location of the temple of a particularly bloody pre-Roman cult, later adopted by the Romans and dedicated to Serapis (a god of Greco-Egyptian origin, lord of life and death – hence the sacrificial offerings), and possibly also to Jupiter. The much-eroded inscriptions on the boulders are in a strange mixture of Greek and Latin, as the Roman emperor at the time was from a Greek province. The audio guide talks you past the three main sacrificial boulders, each with a cavity used as a filter system for the blood and viscera created by the offerings. The uppermost and largest boulder displays the remnants of a temple that once stood atop it; the viewing tower above it gives you a good overview of the sight.

The site is very hard to reach by public transport. By car it is well signposted beyond Mateus – look for the left-hand turn shortly after passing under the A24 highway.

Practicalities

Vila Real is the hub of Trás-os-Montes' regional transport with frequent **buses** leaving to all major destinations. The main **bus station** is on the corner of Avenida Cidade de Orense and Rua A Valente de Fonseca – head down the latter and turn right into the main Avenida C Araújo. **Rodonorte** (ⓦwww .rodonorte.pt) services to and from Amarante, Braga, Bragança, Chaves, Coimbra, Guimarães, Porto, Peso da Régua and Viseu run from the bus station on Rua Dom Pedro de Castro, just north of the centre by *Hotel Miraneve*. The Corgo line **train station** is 500m east of the centre, on the opposite bank of the river; to reach the town centre, take the road over the bridge, and turn left. Save for the one-way system around Avenida Carvalho Araújo, driving should be fairly straightforward. There's a large underground **car park** at the southern end of the avenue, where it meets the eastern end of Avenida Miguel Torga, or try and find parking spots on Av 1° de Maio.

The central **turismo**, Avenida Carvalho Araújo 94 (June–Sept Mon–Fri 9.30am–6pm, Sat & Sun 9.30am–12.30pm & 2–6pm; Oct–May Mon–Sat 9.30am–12.30pm & 2–6pm; ☎259 322 819, ⓦwww.rtsmarao.pt), can help with local bus timetables, while anyone planning a visit to the Parque Natural do Alvão should also head for the **park headquarters** on Largo das Freitas behind the Camâra Municipal (Mon–Fri 9am–12.30pm & 2–5.30pm; ☎259 302 830, ⓦwww.icn.pt).

Accommodation

The pick of the town's **accommodation** is reviewed below but be warned-most of it is underwhelming and the more basic places can get distinctly chilly and damp in winter, and unbearably hot in summer. For directions on how to get to the various *turismo rural* properties in the area, which on the whole provide much nicer accommodation, consult the turismo.

In town

Residencial Encontro Av Carvalho Araújo 76–78 ☎259 322 532. Very central, family-run place with a mixed bag of rooms (avoid the gloomy back ones), above a restaurant, which means it can be a bit noisy at night. No credit cards. ❷

Hotel Mira Corgo Av 1 de Maio 78 ☎259 325 001, ⓔmiracorgo@mail.telepac.pt. Vila Real's swankiest hotel is an ugly modern building but beg for a room overlooking the stepped terraces of the Rio Corgo, far below, and you won't be disappointed. There's an indoor swimming pool and solarium, as well as secure parking. ❹

Residencial Real Rua Central 5 ☎259 325 879, ⓕ259 324 613. Clean, cool and fresh rooms with white walls and varnished wooden floors, sited above the *pastelaria* of the same name. Good value. No credit cards. ❷

Residencial da Sé Trav de São Domingos 19–23 ☎259 324 575. Above a café on a quiet street, this is the best budget option. Rather musty en-suite rooms, but nevertheless very popular with French and German tourists in summer, when you'd be better off booking ahead. ❶

Outside town

Casa da Campeã 10km west, 2km before Campeã, just off the IP4 ☎259 979 640, ⓔquality .vilareal@mail.telepac.pt. Modern chalet-cum-motel setup with a pool and good restaurant, which warrants inclusion for the activities offered in the nearby Vale da Campeã (Serra do Marão), including rafting, paragliding, bungee jumping and hiking. ❸

Casa da Cruz Campeã, 12km west, signposted along the road to Mondim de Basto ☎259 372 995, ⓔcasadacruz@mail.telepac.pt. Six rooms with lovely carved beds at this eighteenth-century granite farmhouse, overlooking the Vale de Campeã. There's a rustic sitting room and free use of the kitchen, although the highlight is the secluded swimming pool. Fishing and cycling trips can be arranged. No credit cards. ❹

Casa da Quinta de São Martinho Mateus, 4km east, 300m from Solar de Mateus ☎259 323 986, ⓦwww.quintasaomartinho.com. Idyllic seventeenth-century granite country house swathed in ivy and containing a comfortable clutter of old and new furniture. In addition to the two bedrooms there are also two self-contained apartments (sleeping up to four) in the garden, complete with spiral staircase and exposed stone walls. Fringe benefits include a secluded pool, and port wine tasting in the bar (the friendly proprietor being president of the Douro wine trail) ④ apartments ⑥

Youth hostel

Pousada de Juventude Av Dr Manuel Cardona, 1km northeast of the centre ⓣ 259 373 193, ⓦ www.pousadasjuventude.pt. Modern hostel with four private en-suite rooms and fourteen four-bed

dorms, as well a kitchen and common room. Dorm beds €7, rooms ①

Campsite

Parque de Campismo 700m northeast of the centre ⓣ 259 324 724. There's adequate shade at this site, and a swimming pool, but arrive early if you want a riverside pitch. Follow Av 1º de Maio and its continuations Av Aureliano Barrigas and Rua Dr Manuel Cardona, a 15min walk; if you're coming from the train station, turn right after crossing the bridge.

Eating, drinking and nightlife

Local dishes include roast kid goat and *tripas aos molhos* ("sheaves" of tripe, no less). For those with a sweeter tooth, **pastries** to ask for are *pastéis de Santa Clara* (stuffed with very sweet egg goo), and *tigelinhas de laranja* ("orange bowls"). Also worth a try is the delicious *nata do céu*, a very sweet, cheesecake-like dessert, drizzled with a sugary egg mixture. There's a weekday **market** opposite the Rodonorte bus station and a **supermarket** hidden in the shopping centre next to *Hotel Mira Corgo* on Avenida 1º de Maio.

The best **cafés** are those on Avenida Carvalho Araújo, by the town hall, with outdoor seats facing the square. On Saturday mornings, there's a small antiques market here. The liveliest nightspots are the **café-bars** along Largo do Pelourinho, although you'll have to arrive early if you're after a pavement seat. For a less family-orientated atmosphere, head to the numerous late-night drinking dens on Largo do Pioledo such as *Look Bar.*

Churrasqueira Real Rua Teixeira de Sousa 14 ⓣ 259 322 078. With mains for under €5, this little grill house is the place to fill up on the cheap. Dishes such as grilled chicken and *alheira* sausage are reliably satisfying. Closed Sun. Inexpensive.

O Escondidinho Rua Teixeira de Sousa 7 ⓣ 259 325 535. Portuguese meat and fish dishes as well as a range of pastas are served at this perennially popular wood-panelled eatery. The outdoor tables fill quickly in summer with both tourists and locals, although it's largely the latter who tuck into the chef's special tripe. Moderate.

Nevada Centro-Comercial Mira-Corgo, off Av 1º de Maio ⓣ 259 371 828. In a tile-fronted building right next to the *Hotel Mira Corgo*, this caters largely to demanding hotel guests. Seafood is pricey, but other fish and grills are surprisingly good value for quality cuisine. There's also a lively and fun bar. Moderate.

Terra de Montanha Rua 31 de Janeiro 16–18A ⓣ 259 372 075. Huge antique barrels, stacks of slowly maturing wine and stone walls set the tone for this determinedly rustic restaurant. The menu

features roast goat, steaks and traditional desserts, and there's a rotating selection of hearty *pratos do dia*. Closed Sun evening. Moderate

O Transmontano Rua da Misericórdia 37 ⓣ 259 323 540. With outdoor tables on a pedestrianized street, this is popular with big groups and can be a bit touristy. But it's good value nonetheless for standard Portuguese meals, with the *bolinhas de bacalhau* (salt cod balls) offering something slightly different. No credit cards. Moderate.

Yong Sheng Rua Isabel de Carvalho 30 ⓣ 259 322 088. Authentic, friendly and great-value Chinese restaurant which does a lovely sweet and sour pork. There's also a free after-dinner shot of fruit liquor, served in glasses that can only be described as unconventional, and probably not for the easily offended. Inexpensive.

22 Rua Teixeira de Sousa 16 ⓣ 259 321 296. Atmospheric dining on a first-floor retreat, with discerning lunchtime diners tucking into the various *bacalhau* specialities and great-value €4 omelettes. Closed Sun. Moderate.

Listings

Banks There are banks and ATMs scattered throughout the town's small centre. For exchanging

money, head to the branch of Caixa Geral de Depositos, near the turismo.

Hospital Hospital de São Pedro, 2km north of the centre ☎ 259 300 500.
Internet At Espaçao Internet (Mon–Fri 10am–2pm & 4–7pm), tucked away behind the shopping centre/supermarket off Av 1 de Maio.
Pharmacy Farmácia Almeida, Av Carvalho Araújo ☎ 259 322 874.

Police Av Miguel Torga ☎ 259 322 022.
Post office Av Carvalho Araújo (Mon–Fri 8.30am–6pm, Sat 9am–12.30pm).
Taxis Rádiotáxis Expresso ☎ 259 322 131 will take you into the Parque Natural do Alvão. There's a taxi rank by the Sé.

Parque Natural do Alvão

Parque Natural do Alvão is Portugal's smallest natural park, partly forested but mostly comprising barren outcrops of granite interspersed with patches of traditionally farmed land. Although just 5km west of Vila Real, it's not easy to see without your own transport, and there's a distinct lack of accommodation, but partly because of these limitations it's one of the few remaining places in Portugal where you really feel you're in the wild. The handful of settlements are mostly constructed on rocky terrain to conserve the little arable land that is available, and almost everywhere basks in the scent of pine. Locals remove the bark on parts of the tree trunks and use a series of channels to collect the sap in sticky plastic bags for use in solvent production. Birds to look out for include golden eagles, buzzards, screech owls and the remarkable dipper, a sparrow-sized diving bird that makes its living on turbulent rocky streams. Other wildlife isn't so easy to spot, and you'd be extremely lucky to see any of the wolves, roe deer or wild boar that live in the park, while the numerous snakes tend to disappear at the sound of approaching footsteps.

Park practicalities

The easiest access is along the N304, which connects Vila Real with Mondim de Basto, the other main gateway to the park where there is also a **park office** (see below). Three daily buses between the towns take this route (not Sun), which skirts the western tip of the park by Ermelo. There is also a regular service from Vila Real to Agarez just outside the park's southeastern boundary, and a more limited service along the minor N313 to Lamas de Ôlo (Sept–June Mon–Fri only, 3 daily), in the middle of the park. The helpful turismo in Vila Real stocks up-to-date bus timetables for all routes, or taxis are another possibility; the Vila Real to Lamas do Ôlo trip shouldn't cost more than €20.

There's little **accommodation** within the park itself, while **camping** is prohibited to avoid the very real risk of forest fires. Serious walkers intending to cross the whole reserve should obtain information and maps in advance from the park headquarters in Vila Real or Mondim de Basto. Leaflets detailing walking circuits (available from both offices) are currently available only in Portuguese. For **organized tours** or **adventure sports** in the park, contact Basto Radical (☎ 255 381 296, ⓦ www.basto-radical.pt), based in Mondim de Basto, who feature guided walks as well as a day's rafting on the Rio Ôlo (€75) and activities such as canoeing and paintball. They can also arrange accommodation in local *turismos rural*.

Mondim de Basto

The small, handsomely sited town of **MONDIM DE BASTO** provides an alternative base to Vila Real for seeing the *parque natural*; it lies on the north-western side of the park, an hour by road from Vila Real (N304) or slightly

△ Parque Natural do Alvão

closer to Amarante (see p.357), 30km back down the Rio Tâmega. There's nothing of historic interest, but Mondim has a useful range of accommodation and some good local walks.

About twenty minutes beyond the village campsite, the **Rio Cabril** – more a stream than a river – is crossed by a Roman bridge, set near a little waterfall where there's a good swimming hole. The three-hour climb up **Monte Farinha** (996m) is a tougher proposition – though you can simply drive up too – with the effort repaid by panoramic views and the summit-topping chapel of Nossa Senhora da Graça, centre of a major *romaria* on the first Sunday in September; the route starts off the N312 Cerva road east out of Mondim.

There are three **buses** a day from Vila Real (not Sun) to Mondim; to and from Amarante, you'll need to change at Fermil, 6km to the northwest, which also has connections to Guimarães and Braga. From Mondim's **bus station**, walk up to the main road and turn right for the small public gardens – facing them, at the end, on the right, is the **turismo** (daily: June–Sept Mon–Sat 9am–12.30 & 2–7pm; Oct–May Mon–Fri 9am–12.30pm & 2–5.30pm; ☎255 381 479, ⓦwww.cm-mondimdebasto.pt), where you can pick up information on local *turismo rural* properties. The local *feira* is held on the 2nd or 22nd of each month. The information office for the **Parque Natural do Alvão** (Mon–Fri 9am–12.30pm & 2–5.30pm; ☎255 381 209) is 800m down the Celorico road by the Barrio primary school. Guided walks in the park can be arranged here.

The best **accommodation** in Mondim itself is *Casa das Mourôas* (☎255 381 394 or 966 333 212; ❸), a restored granite house with just three rooms; there's no sign, but it's at the top of the gardens, facing the war memorial. The two cheaper choices provide a bed for the night, but little intrinsic charm: *Residencial Carvalho* (☎255 381 057, ⓕ255 386 633; ❶) is right by the *GALP* petrol station on the roundabout; *Residencial Arcadia* (☎255 381 410; ❶) is 100m beyond, along the avenue. The town **campsite** (☎255 381 650; closed mid-Dec to mid-Jan) is 1km from the centre along the N304 Vila Real road, near the banks of the Rio Cabril. With your own transport, you have a much better choice of local **rural tourism** properties in the vicinity, starting with the *Quinta do Fundo* (☎255 381 291, ⓦwww.quintadofundo.com), a lovely vine-shaded property 2km out of town on the N304 Vila Real road. There are five rooms (❸) and two suites (❹) in the grounds of a wine-producing estate, with pool and tennis court; dinner is available (€25). More magnificent is *Casa do Campo* (☎255 361 231, ⓦwww.casadocampo.pt), an eighteenth-century manor house at Molares, just south of Fermil, complete with outdoor pool, traditional *espigueiro* granary and an aromatic camellia garden. Accommodation is in elegant, antique-laden rooms (❹) or suites (❺), and there are also two apartments (❹); there's a two-night minimum stay.

Mondim has several chips-with-everything **restaurants**, plus a supermarket, grocers', chemist and other services. Good inexpensive choices include the *Adega São Tiago* (☎255 386 957) and the equally affable *Adega Sete Condes* (☎255 382 342; closed Mon lunch), a couple of rustic *adegas* in granite houses immediately behind the turismo.

The Terras de Basto

Mondim de Basto is one of three towns with the same suffix: the others are Celorico de Basto, just to the southwest, and the larger Cabeceiras de Basto, 25km north (in the Minho). Together, the three Basto towns and their districts form the **Terras de Basto**, a region of fertile countryside that produces a strong *vinho verde* (and some excellent food to go with it). The region's name comes from a number of life-sized Celtic warrior statues – beautifully incised with Celtic emblems on the torso and a shield on the belly – which were originally laid on warrior's graves. *Eu basto* (I suffice) was their credo, expressing a willingness to face the enemy (Romans for the most part) single-handed.

The western side of the park

ERMELO, 1km off the main N304, is a sleepy little hamlet with the proud title of "largest village in the park". Ermelo comes alive for just two days a year (August 7–8) during the Feira de São Vicente, a joint celebration also marking the annual return of Ermelo's emigrants. The place has a few cafés, but nothing more in the way of services. You can do a great day's hike from the village (5–7hr). Take the track which leads up the mountain, running high above the right bank of the Rio Ôlo – a tributary of the Tâmega – past the hamlet of **FERVENÇA**, where a three-kilometre detour takes you to **BARREIRO**, with superb views westwards. Back on the track, you cross the river at **VARZIGUETO**, before following it back westwards, crossing the Ôlo river bridge and heading back to the Ermelo junction.

A great driving circuit is to take the track 1km west of Ermelo, on the main Vila Real–Mondim road (signposted "Fisgas"), and head uphill along the forestry track, with the Rio Ôlo far below in the ravine to your right. A couple of kilometres along, a right turn takes you on a two-kilometre detour to a spectacular rocky ledge overlooking the waterfalls of **Fisgas de Ermelo,** way below in a craggy valley.

Back on the main track, continue uphill and turn right into **Pioledo**, a traditional village surrounded by *espigueiros* and fields full of oxen. Continue straight on and you can go back to Vila Real via Lamas de Ôlo (see below).

The eastern side of the park

There are occasional buses from Vila Real to **LAMAS DE ÔLO**, a quiet rural hamlet around 1000 metres above sea level, a fine base for local walks. It's notable for its peculiar granite houses (many now abandoned) with tent-like thatched roofs and, above the village, a watermill with a primitive aqueduct. Look out also for the eccentric, bus shelter-style construction where the villagers collect their post from small, individual mail boxes. The kindly old proprietress of *Café Albina de Olo* (☎250 341 950; no credit cards; reservations essential; ●) has four decent en-suite rooms to rent above the café, itself without a sign but located near the main bus stop on the edge of the village. She can also rustle up an evening meal for around €5 a head.

An attractive walking circuit (around 3hr) begins in **Agarez**, 10km northwest of Vila Real; fairly regular buses run this route. The path loops anticlockwise via the waterfall and working watermill of **Galegos da Serra** on the Arnal stream, and past a bleakly situated cottage, which was once home to forestry workers but is now used primarily by school groups. Nonetheless, it is possible to rent spartan **rooms** here for €20 per person, although you'll have to book in advance at the park office in Vila Real. The cottage has a fully equipped kitchen and a living room with open fire. From here, the path takes you upstream to **ARNAL**, where a women's cooperative produces linen clothing and sheets for sale. From Arnal, there's a minor road back to Agarez.

Mirandela

It's around 65km from Vila Real to **MIRANDELA**, a neat provincial town on the Tua river that's been making an improbable name for itself in recent years as one of the world's jet-ski hotspots, hosting the world championships in 2004 (it also hosts the annual national championships). Otherwise, the town's most striking feature is its pedestrianized **Roman bridge**, renovated in the fifteenth century and stretching a good 200m across seventeen arches. The riverside gardens and lawns are pleasant places to lounge around, while you can rent kayaks and pedaloes in summer to splash up and down the Tua.

The grandiose **Câmara Municipal** is housed in the Palácio dos Távoras, one of several flamboyant Baroque town houses associated with the Távora family, which controlled the town between the fourteenth and seventeenth centuries. The only other attraction is the modern art gallery, the **Museu Armindo Teixeira Lopes** (Mon–Fri 10am–12.30pm & 2–6pm; free), combined with the town's library, which has a section dedicated to images of Mirandela and Lisbon by local artist Armindo Teixeira Lopes.

Weekday **markets** are held in Mirandela on Thursdays. Otherwise, the best time to visit is during the **Festa da Senhora do Amparo** (July 25 to the first Sunday in August) – the Friday night is the *Noite das Bombas*, or "Night of the Drums", while the final Saturday is the big day, with a procession and fireworks.

Practicalities

Mirandela is the terminus of the **Tua train line** (departures from Tua on the Douro train line); **buses** drop you at the terminal next to the train station. To reach the town centre, turn right, then right again and, with the river on your left, it's a five-minute walk to the Roman bridge, from where the road veers into the main Rua da República. The informative **turismo** (Mon–Fri 9.30am–12.30pm & 2–6pm, Sat 10am–1pm & 2–5pm; ⊕278 200 272, ⊛www.cm-mirandela.pt) is located in a kiosk on Parque de Lazer, where there is plenty of free **parking**. Nearby, in the upper tier of the municipal market, there's free **Internet** access at Espaço Internet (daily 9am–12.30pm & 2–6pm).

Accommodation in Mirandela is pretty easy to find, except in late July during the summer *festa* and annual jet-ski championship. The local **campsite** (⊕278 263 177) is 3km north of town on the Bragança road and, as well as a restaurant and shop, has a **swimming pool** open to the public in summer (July–Sept). Mirandela is famed for both its olive oil and its delicious *alheira* **sausages**, a legacy of the Jewish community that has long since disappeared. Made primarily from chicken and bread (though pork is now also added), they're cooked quickly and served with rice or potatoes. Most restaurants in Mirandela serve them, and various shops have them draped across their windows, along with other cured meats.

Hotels and pensions

Hotel Dom Dinis Rua Nossa Senhora do Amparo ⊕278 260 100, ⊕278 260 101. Mirandela's showpiece hotel, over the river. Swanky reception area and great river views aside, the rooms really aren't much more impressive than those at the various *residenciais*, but it does have its own decent restaurant, secure parking (€10 a day) and an outside pool. ❹

Pensão Residencial O Lagar Rua da República 120 ⊕278 262 712. One of the few places in town with any character, featuring homely, comfortable rooms, some with old wooden shutters. The friendly owner serves refreshments from an ageing bar. No credit cards. ❷

Hotel Miratua Rua da República 38 ⊕278 200

140, ⊕278 200 143. Slick if unremarkable hotel on the main street, with its own little piano bar. There are some good views from the upper rooms. ❸

Restaurants

D. Maria Rua Dr Jorge Pires ⊕278 248 455. Over the bridge in a modern place below a church, this is a locally renowned restaurant that's one of the main contenders for the best *alheira*. It specializes in spruced-up traditional fare, although you can also dine on fondue and Jamaican-style pork. Closed Mon. Moderate.

Flor de Sal Parque Dr José Gama ⊕278 203 063. Across the bridge, this is a very slick, glass-fronted restaurant with a superb riverside terrace. Quality if pricey nouveau-Portuguese cuisine with mains from €15, or you can just have a drink on the terrace. Expensive.

O Jardim Rua da República 20 ☎278 262 712. Near the tourist office in a corner of the market building, you get four different types of *bacalhau* here, as well as good-value grilled chicken, beef and pork, plus a hearty vegetable soup. Closed Sun. Inexpensive.

Pizzeria Diablo Rua Vasco da Gama ☎278 263 952. A hidden gem, signposted opposite the train station and attracting a neighbourhood clientele. The mushrooms don't come from a tin, and they even provide chilli oil and freshly ground black pepper. For dessert, choose the delectable home-made chocolate mousse. Closed Mon. No credit cards. Inexpensive.

Carrazeda de Ansiães

CARRAZEDA DE ANSIÃES, 49km southwest of Mirandela, is a modern town of little intrinsic interest. However, three and a half kilometres to the south (a taxi should cost around €5 each way) are the intriguing ruins of the a medieval walled town, known as **Ansiães**. Little remains within the perimeter of walls except rocks and boulders, but two chapels stand outside, the better preserved of which – the twelfth-century **São Salvador** – has a Romanesque portal, extravagantly carved with leaves, animals and human figures. Local myth has it that a tunnel connects Ansiães to another castle beyond the Rio Douro, 12km away; a gaping, fly-ridden hole beneath an impressive slab is the principal piece of supporting evidence. What is undoubtedly true, however, is that the town was a base for five different kings, including the King of Léon and Castile, before Portuguese independence; they're listed by the gateway on a plaque unveiled by President Mário Soares in February 1987.

The last inhabitants of old Ansiães left in the mid-eighteenth century. The gradual depopulation resulted from the decision, in 1734, of a gentleman named Francisco de Araújo e Costa, to transfer the official council seat to the new town below (known by then as Carrazeda de Ansiães). In response to local protests he ordered the castle *pelourinho* to be destroyed; with this symbol gone and deprived of a sufficient supply of water, the hill community had no hope of putting up effective resistance. The medieval town went into decline and was soon totally abandoned.

A good time to visit Carrazeda de Ansiães is on January 3 for the *Cantar os Reis* (night-long music and dance in honour of the Three Kings) or, in the summer, for the **Festa de Santa Eufémia** (Aug 15–16), in which pilgrims stuff themselves with weaned sow and the local wine, the latter famed for its supposed ability to be imbibed in vast quantities without the drinker falling over. Should you still be in a fit state to drive, the most enticing **accommodation** is in the nearby village of Pombal at the *Hotel Rural Flor do Monte* (☎278 660 010, ⓦwww.flordomonte.com; breakfast included; no credit cards; ❹), where there are modern rooms and a pool, as well as activities such as hunting and fishing. Alternatively, *Pousada de Alijó* in **Alijó**, 25km west (☎259 959 215, ⓦwww.pousadas.pt; ❻) offers extremely comfortable rooms in a place with its own tennis courts, games room, restaurant and alluring outdoor pool.

Vila Flôr

VILA FLÔR (Town of Flowers), 24km south of Mirandela and 16km northeast of Carrazeda, was given its name in the thirteenth century by Dom

Dinis who, on his way to meet Isabel of Aragon, was clearly in a romantic frame of mind. His favouritism was short-lived, though, for soon Vila Flôr was forced to contribute a third of its revenue to rebuilding the walls of rival Torre de Moncorvo, 30km to the south. Vila Flôr still has a piece of old wall known as the Arco Dom Dinis as well as a so-called "Roman" fountain. Otherwise the only reason to stop here is to visit the wonderfully eccentric **Museu Municipal de Berta Cabral**, just south of the main square (daily 9am–12.30pm & 2–5.30pm; free). Three eminent Vilaflôrians donated the contents of their houses to the museum when it was founded in 1946, and the result is an incredible hodge-podge, encompassing not just local relics – like the town's first telephone – but all kinds of bizarre curios, from an embalmed Angolan rat to an ensemble of antelope-horn-and-zebra-hide furniture. Regular weekday bus services call here on the run between Torre de Moncorvo and Mirandela; there are a couple of buses on Sunday too.

For **meals** the best place by a country mile is the informal and moderately priced *Restaurante Dom Dinis* (☎278 576 696; no credit cards), with a lush garden and signposted up a side street off Avenida Marechal Carmona. There's no excuse not to delve into their renowned *posta à Vila Flor* (braised veal) and lovely table wine, a red sourced from the local Adega Cooperativa.

The main event in the region is the **Romaria de Nossa Senhora da Assunção**, which takes place every August 15 to the hilltop sanctuary of Vilas Boas, 8km northwest of Vila Flôr. Held on the site of an apparition of the Virgin in 1673, this is one of the largest *romarias* in Trás-os-Montes, where ten saintly images are carried through the multitude, headed by an image of Nossa Senhora carried on the backs of over a hundred men.

The best place to stay in the area is *Quinta do Reboredo* (☎278 516 872, ⓔarqueiroverde@clix.pt; breakfast included; ❸), just outside **Vilas Boas**, a rural retreat with comfortable rooms and horse-riding facilities. Alternatively, head for the village of **Assares**, 12km to the northeast and signposted off the main IP2, where the eighteenth-century *Quinta do Barracão da Vilariça* (☎278 536 200, ⓦwww.terra-sa.com; breakfast included; no credit cards; ❸), sits in a lovely location. There's also a **campsite** (☎278 512 350), 2km southeast of Vila Flôr on the Torre de Moncorvo road, attractively wooded and right next to the municipal outdoor pools.

Torre de Moncorvo and around

The 26-kilometre route southeast from Vila Flôr to **TORRE DE MONCORVO** is spectacular, taking you into the steep mountains round the Douro valley. The network of handsome, narrow medieval streets makes the town a pleasant place to stop off for a few hours. The imposing sixteenth-century **Igreja Matriz** – the largest church in Trás-os-Montes, took a century to build – while the turismo (see below) is housed in the yellow-and-blue **Casa da Roda**, a reconstructed dwelling complete with its own underground well. In the **Oficina Vinaria** on Travessa das Amoreiras (May–Sept Tues–Sun 10am–12.30pm & 2–6.30pm; Oct–April Tues–Sun 9am–12.30pm & 2–6.30pm; free) there's an array of ageing wine-producing equipment, while the **Museu de Ferro** in Largo Balbino Rego (May–Sept Tues–Sun 10am–12.30pm & 2–6pm; Oct–April Tues–Sun 9.30am–12.30pm & 2–5.30pm; €1), records the region's former iron industry.

That, basically, is your lot, making the town's main attraction its almond trees, the blossoming of which draws crowds of Portuguese visitors in late February and early March. Later the nuts are gathered and sugared and sold locally; a good place to try them is Flormêndoa at Largo Diogo Sá 5–7, by the Igreja Matriz. Local **festivities** include the Festa de Nossa Senhora da Assunção (second weekend of Aug), the Feira do Ano (Dec 23), and the Feira das Cerejas (May 10), in honour of Moncorvo's locally produced cherries.

Practicalities

The **bus station** is on the main road, the N220, next to the telecom building near the hospital, while the **turismo** is hidden away behind the Camâra Municipal at Travessa Campos Monteiro 21 (daily 9am–12.30pm & 2–5.30pm; ☏ 279 252 265).

For **accommodation**, *Residencial Campos Monteiro*, Rua Visconde de Vila Maior 55 (☏ 279 254 055, ℱ 279 254 280; ❷) features modern rooms with attractive balconies, plus parking and free Internet access. Better still is the lovely ⚜ *Quinta das Aveleiras* (☏ 279 258 280, ⓦ www.quinta-das-aveleiras.com; no credit cards), a wine estate 300m from the bus station on the Pocinho road, with its own pool and tennis courts. This lets out spacious rooms in four restored farmhouses, each with kitchenettes, log fires and bicycles for rent. These range from a one-room converted *pombal* (pigeon-house, ❹) to the *Casa Branca*, sleeping six for €150 a night. Further afield, at Felgar, 13km east, is the remarkable *Casa de Santa Cruz* (☏ 279 928 060, ⓦ www.casadesantacruz.com; no credit cards; ❺). Located in a corner of the village square, this eighteenth-century manor house with its own pool has been imaginatively restored, while retaining its huge old chimney and heavy oak doors; it can arrange kayaking and white-water rafting, and provide meals on request.

The best **food** can be had at the *Restaurante Regional O Lagar* (☏ 279 252 828, closed Sun evening), Rua Adriano Leandro 16, down from the Igreja Matriz, which serves very moderately priced regional food – try the stewed wild boar, washed down with a fruity table wine. Alternatively, *Jardim*, on Av Eng Duarte Pacheco (☏ 279 252 542), uphill from the church, serves fine mid-priced Portuguese and Brazilian food along with pizzas and snacks, with tables in a small garden out front.

Freixo de Espada à Cinta

The southernmost town in Trás-os-Montes is **FREIXO DE ESPADA À CINTA**, 46km south of Mogadouro in the Parque Natural do Douro Internacional (see below). The name is something of a mouthful, translating as "ash-tree of the sword of the belt" and supposedly referring to Dom Dinis hacking at a nearby ash tree as he announced the founding of the town. It feels end-of-the-worldish, as the road winds down to its valley, the town hidden on each side by wild, dark mountains, a backdrop against which you might glimpse the occasional hawk or black kite. The town was once considered so remote that prisoners who had been granted an amnesty were allowed to settle here – and it's this sense of isolation that makes the town worth a visit.

Curiously for such a remote outpost there is a very rich **Igreja Matriz** (Tues–Sun 9.30am–12.30pm & 2–5pm; free) – part Romanesque, part Manueline – with a *retábulo* of paintings attributed to famous Viseu artist, Grão Vasco. The church is at the heart of the town's **Romaria de Sete Paços**, which takes place at midnight on Good Friday; a sombre cortege of chanting, hooded penitents dressed in black, with their faces covered, proceeds from the church and wends its way through town. Across the way from the church is a magnificent heptagonal **keep** (ask for the key in the Igreja Matriz), a landmark for miles around, which affords great views from its bell tower for those who brave the very steep steps.

Practicalities

The town is served by daily Santos **buses** from Miranda do Douro, Moncorvo and Mogadouro. To the south, the N221 follows a beautiful stretch of the Douro to Barca d'Alva, 20km southwest, but there are no buses along this route. The town's small **turismo** (daily: July & Aug 9.30am–7.30pm; Sept–June Mon–Sat 9am–12.30pm & 2–5.30pm; ☎279 653 480) is on Avenida do Emigrante, just off the main Avenida Guerra Junqueira, where the buses drop you. One block northeast of Avenida do Emigrante is Largo do Outeiro, site of the regional office for the **Parque Natural do Douro Internacional** (Mon–Fri 9am–12.30 & 2–5.30pm; ☎279 658 130, ⓦ www.icn.pt), which is worth a visit if you plan to visit the park. It has route maps of the 62-kilometre two-day walk (or one day's cycle) north up through the park via Mogadouro.

The best **accommodation** option is the charming *Casa do Conselheiro* (☎279 653 439, ⓔ albusquerqus@yahoo.com; no credit cards; ❸), a lovely old house on Rua das Moreirinhas in the old part of town to the north, with lots of exposed stone and a covered patio. Alternatively, try the characterful *Hospedaria Cinta de Ouro* (☎279 652 550, ⓕ 279 653 470; ❷), on the way out of town to the south. The brightly painted walls here are hung with the owners' own artwork, and the upstairs **restaurant** (with pleasant terrace and wicker chairs) is the best place in town for quality Portuguese meals, although portions can be on the small side; try their *alheira* with egg and potato. There's also a free – if rather bleak and dusty – municipal **campsite**, the *Congida* (☎279 653 371; open all year), 4km east down a series of hairpin bends on the banks of the Rio Douro; follow the signs or take a taxi. The complex also houses the municipal swimming pool (June–Sept only; €1), a couple of cafés and a restaurant.

Parque Natural do Douro Internacional

The **Parque Natural do Douro Internacional** covers a vast tract of land along the west bank of the Rio Douro as it flows along the Spanish border from Miranda do Douro in the north to Barca d'Alva (p.373), the point at which the river officially enters Portuguese territory. It also encompasses a stretch of the Rio Águeda further south in Beira Alta. The upper Douro is ecologically important because it has a Mediterranean microclimate, in marked contrast to the harsher, mountainous terrain of the surrounding Terra Fria. The combination of mild winters and its isolation from large human populations has led to the survival of a number of animal and plant species now extinct in the south. To the visitor, this quirk of geography is most visible in the region's famous **almond trees**, explained in the legend of a Moorish prince who married a northern European princess. Though happy in summer, she grew sad and wistful in winter, and ached for the snow-clad hills of her homeland. The prince hurried to the Algarve, from where he brought back the almond trees, so that from then on, every February when the trees blossomed, the princess beheld white as far as the eye could see.

Despite some river pollution (mild in comparison with further downstream), and industrial sand extraction on the Spanish side, the area has been left largely untouched by the more damaging aspects of modern agriculture and industry. The park preserves a rich, if endangered, variety of local **fauna**, including wolves, wild cats and otters, as well as various species of bats and amphibians. It is also home to over 170 **bird species**, including rare peregrine falcons, black storks and, in summer, Europe's largest concentration of Egyptian vultures. In common with all natural parks, its success depends on achieving a fine balance between the encouragement of much-needed investment in the agricultural infrastructure on its margins, and the development of ecotourism within the park itself to benefit the local population.

The main **park office** is in Mogadouro (see p.463), which produces an excellent map (€3.50) with a brief rundown of the points of interest in the park (in Portuguese). Other offices are found at Miranda do Douro, Freixo de Espada à Cinta and Figueira de Castelo Rodrigo, any of which could be used as a base to visit the park. There are a number of waymarked **walking circuits** in the park, ranging in length and difficulty, at least two of which are accessible without your own transport, starting from Miranda do Douro and Freixo de Espada à Cinta respectively. Leaflets with detailed route maps are available from the park offices.

Scattered down the eastern side of the park are a number of viewing platforms, where you can gaze down from the canyon-like cliffs into the Douro far below, although you'll need your own transport to reach these. With a car, you can also follow the marked "Rota dos Castros", along minor roads linked by a series of fortified border posts near Bruço and Peredo da Bemposta.

Impactus (☎962 838 261, ⓦwww.impactus.pt) is an **ecotourism** outfit operating out of Castelo Melhor, near Vila Nova de Foz Côa (see p.371), offering a wide variety of nature walks and activities in the park, including eight-kilometre half-day walks, a two-day 62-kilometre hike, canoeing, jeep safaris and donkey treks. Otherwise, Torre de Moncorvo-based Sabor, Douro e Aventura (☎279 258 270, ⓦwww.sabordouro.com) organizes **adventure tours**, including walking trips, boat trips, rock-climbing and canoeing. A day's boat trip, or a day's kakaying on the Douro will set you back around €30, while guided day-walks into the park cost €17.

Mogadouro

For an unkempt and authentic picture of town life in the Terra Fria, you need look no further than **MOGADOURO**, 58km northeast of Torre de Moncorvo, on the fringes of the Parque Natural do Douro Internacional. Its main sight is a ruined twelfth-century castle, unexceptional as a monument, but the ground in front is common land where children play and farmers leave their donkeys to graze. The castle hill also commands terrific views over a long, low horizon and a patchwork of fields and traditional pigeon houses. The feeling persists of a town caught between past and present, not quite ready to embrace tourism, though it does have at least one conventional attraction in its tiny **Sala Museu de Arqueologia** (daily 9am–12.30pm & 2–5.30pm; free), a sparse display of tools, coins, ceramics, arrowheads, rock paintings and other archeological miscellany unearthed from various local sites. It's located underneath the Câmara Municipal, and signposted from the main square, Largo Trindade Coelho.

Buses drop you on Largo Trindade Coelho, where there's a Santos bus office for onward services to Freixo de Espada à Cinta, Torre de Moncorvo or Vila Real. The main tree-lined Avenida Nossa Senhora do Caminho runs off Largo

Trinade Coelho and the adjacent Praça Duarte Pacheco, with the old town and ruined castle in the opposite direction, reached via Rua Santa Marinha. At the latter you'll find the helpful information office for the **Parque Natural do Douro Internacional** (daily 9am–12.30pm & 2–5.30pm; ☎279 340 030, Ⓦwww.icn.pt), at no 4, which sells a basic park map as well as leaflets for individual walks.

Given the proximity of the Douro river, Mogadouro is one of the few places in the region where mosquitoes can seriously disrupt a good night's sleep; it's a good idea to keep your window closed from dusk onwards. The best **hotel** in town is the three-star *Hotel Trindade Coelho* (☎279 340 010, Ⓦwww.hoteltrindadecoelho .com; ❸) on the Largo. Several other inexpensive places lie just off the square: best are the reasonable balconied rooms at *Pensão Russo* on Rua 15 de Outubro (☎ & Ⓕ279 342 134; no credit cards; ❷). Alternatively, if you want to stay in the Parque Natural itself, head to the *Solar dos Marcos* (☎279 570 010, Ⓔmarcos.marcos @oninet.pt; ❹), in the little border village of Bemposta, 30km to the east. Set in an eighteenth-century former bishop's palace with its own chapel, there's a restaurant, garden, pool and eight plush rooms. The municipal **campsite** (☎936 989 213; open all year) is situated 1km or so from Mogadouro's centre, adjacent to the sports complex and **swimming pool** (June–Sept only; €1.50).

For **food**, look no further than the moderately priced *Restaurante A Lareira*, Avenida Nossa Senhora do Caminho 58–62 (☎279 342 363; closed Mon), which deserves special mention for its French-speaking chef, who personally attends to every table, and its bargain tourist menu of around €9. *Restaurante Kalifa* (☎279 342 115; closed Sun), on Rua Santa Marinha opposite the national park office, is another local favourite, with red-checked tablecloths, wood-panelled ceiling, delicious steak and superb red wine.

Be warned that the town is busy (and rooms at a premium) in August, especially during the annual **festa** in honour of Nossa Senhora do Caminho (Aug 7–23), with a special *emigrante* weekend on the last weekend of August, before they leave the country again. There's more entertainment in mid-June, with processions, music and exhibitions during the annual cultural week, the **Semana Cultural**.

Miranda do Douro

Facing Spain across the deep rocky gorge of the Rio Douro, **MIRANDA DO DOURO** – 47km northeast of Mogadouro – marked the first steps of Afonso Henriques, the future first king of Portugal, as he turned against his Spanish kinsmen and began his victorious sweep across Lusitânia at the start of the twelfth century. Some say his decision was influenced by the beauty of the Planalto Mirandês, the tableland between here and Bragança, whose blossoming almond trees in late February and early March suddenly transform the countryside. Whatever the impetus, the town played a key role in all of the country's wars subsequent to Afonso's conquest. After valiant service in the Independence, Spanish Succession and the Seven Years wars, it ended its fighting days when an explosion during a Spanish attack in 1762 destroyed the castle and the town, and killed 400 inhabitants.

After the explosion, Miranda remained a neglected outpost for nearly two centuries – sufficiently remote for its dialect, Mirandês, to flourish. It is still spoken today: local town signs are in both Portuguese and the dialect equivalent. In 1955 the huge **Barragem de Miranda** was built just below the town, breathing some new life into the place. At 528m, it is one of the largest hydroe-lectric dams in the country and the last before the Portuguese Rio Douro becomes the Spanish Rio Duero. With the border just 3km to the west, the Spanish make their presence felt in the shape of a constant stream of tourists, who frequent the rash of frontier souvenir shops.

Otherwise, Miranda is known for its famous stick dancers, the **Pauliteiros**, local men in traditional outfits who dance around clacking wooden sticks together rhythmically. It's a performance which is more often seen at large nationwide festivals than in their home town, though the *Pauliteiros* make a special appearance here every year during the Santa Bárbara *festa* on the penul-timate weekend of August. At this time you will also hear the local folk music, a tradition maintained by the recently opened *Casa da Musica Mirandês* by the ruined castle on Largo do Castelo. There's also a **feira** held on the first weekday of every month.

The town

Today, the old town of Miranda seems scarcely more than a village, although it retains the status of a city and sports a sturdy sixteenth-century **Sé** (Tues–Sun 10am–12.30pm & 2–6pm; free), which overlooks its cobbled streets and low white houses. The cathedral and the city status are the result of a decision by the Portuguese church authorities to make Miranda the capital of the diocese to counteract the feudal power of the House of Bragança in Trás-os-Montes. At the end of the eighteenth century, however, the see was transferred to the larger of the two towns, turning Miranda cathedral into a rather cumbersome memento of past glory. To the bitter comment "The sacristy is in Bragança, but the cathedral is in Miranda", the astute Bragançans reply, "If ever you go to Miranda, see the cathedral and come home."

Miranda has a certain charm, its modern sprawling outskirts to the north of its defined old town. In the latter lie the landscaped ruins of its Episcopal Palace, while the medieval facades along **Rua da Costanilha** display some of the town's best Baroque buildings. Beyond here you reach an eighteenth-century fountain, the **Fonte dos Canos**. However, the main focus of interest is the **Museu da Terra de Miranda** on Praça Dom João III, just off Rua da Costa-nilha (Tues 2–5.30pm, Wed–Sun 9.30am–12.30pm & 2–5.30pm; until 6.30pm from June–Sept; €1.50). Located in a seventeenth-century building – once the town hall and later the district prison – the museum is bursting with curiosities, reconstructed rooms in traditional Mirandês style to children's balloons made out of sheep's stomachs. Most impressive are the fearsome looking traditional masks, worn by young men during initiation rights in a ceremony remarkably similar to those practised in many African countries.

Reached by a steep hill below the new town lies the hydroelectric dam and border with Spain. It is well worth taking one of the **daily boat trips** which run along the river into Spain itself, through a dramatic rock gorge. Europarques Portugal (☎273 432 396, ⓦwww.europarques.com) operate throughout the year (Mon–Fri at 4pm; Sat & Sun and daily in Aug at 11am & 4pm; 1hr cruise €12), though there's a minimum group size of twenty – check at the turismo whether you're likely to get on or not.

Practicalities

The town is split into old and new by a central roundabout in the Largo da Moagem: uphill – along Avenida Aranda Duero – and to the southwest lies the old town; downhill to the northeast are the tourist shops and accommodation in the new town. **Buses** (to Bragança, Freixo de Espada à Cinta, Mirandela and Mogadouro) leave from a stop just to the south of the roundabout and tickets are available from the company kiosks (or the snack kiosk at weekends) across the road. Note that the only weekend service is a Sunday bus to Mogadouro. The **turismo** is located in a little cabin just above the bus stop (Mon–Sat 9am–12.30pm & 2–7pm; Sept–May closes 5.30pm; ☎273 431 132). The **Parque Natural do Douro Internacional** (see p.461; daily 9am–12.30pm & 2–5.30pm; ☎273 431 457) office is at the far end of the old town, just down from the Episcopal Ruins on Rua do Convento. This can give details of local hikes, including a nineteen-kilometre round walk into the park.

Accommodation

Given the high volume of tourists it receives, Miranda unsurprisingly boasts a sizeable range of **places to stay**, most of it clustered into a few streets in the new part of town. These are modern and good value and most command superb views over the reservoir.

Pensions and hotels

Pensão Flor do Douro Rua do Mercado Municipal 7 ☎273 431 186. Hemmed in on all sides by the tourist boutiques, the main selling point here is the view over the gorge and low prices, although the rooms are comfortable enough. No credit cards. **①**
Residencial Planalto Rua 1 de Maio 25 ☎273 431 362, ⊛www.hrplanalto.pt. A quaint and quietly ageing *residencial* 200m from the turismo, with views of the Sé and beyond. Parking. No credit cards. **②**
Estalagem Santa Catarina Largo da Pousada ☎273 431 005, ⊛www.estalagemsantacatarina .pt. Spacious, comfortable rooms with marble balconies offering dizzying views into the gorge, as does the downstairs bar and breakfast room, though whether that's worth an extra €100 a night than neighbouring guest houses is debatable. Parking. **⑤**

Residencial Santa Cruz Rua Abade Baçal 61–61A ☎273 431 374, ℗273 431 341. Miranda's oldest *residencial* with almost seventy years under its belt. It's also the only place to stay in the old town, an attraction in itself although the immaculately clean rooms, all with a/c and baths, are almost of hotel standard and the owners welcoming. Recommended. **②**
Vista Bela Rua do Mercado Municipal 63 ☎/℗273 431 054. Best of the modern guest houses on this stretch, with large rooms full of chunky furniture and uninterrupted views of the dam from its balconies. Very good value. **①**

Campsite

Santa Luzia ☎273 431 273, ℗273 431 075. It's signposted on the southern side of town by the stadium and municipal swimming pool, a 2km hike from Largo da Moagem. Closed Oct–May.

Eating and drinking

Locals maintain that Miranda is home to some of the most tender meat in Portugal, which they proudly prepare in the form of *posta à Mirandesa*, basically braised calf or veal. You can sample it at just about every **restaurant** in town, although there's the usual local debate as to which place serves the best. The liveliest café-bar is *Tri'nus,* in the Episcopal Palace gardens, open till 1am and with a flat-screen TV inside and outdoor tables under the trees.

Capa d'Honras Trav do Castelo 1 ☎273 432 699. Announced by a wrought-iron sign, this upmarket but friendly old-town restaurant takes as its theme the flowing medieval capes tradition- ally worn by local dignitaries during important events. As for the food, it's aimed at well-heeled tourists – there are no less than nine varieties of *bacalhau* on the menu, none of them under €10. Expensive.

O Mirandês Largo da Moagem ☎273 431 418. A longtime local favourite with a flurry of cooks beavering away in full view of the busy dining room. They're justly proud of their *posto à Mirandesa*, and the grilled lamb is also highly recommended. Closed alternate Sundays in winter. No credit cards. Moderate.
Miradouro Rua do Mercado 53–55 ☎273 431 259. The menu features the usual suspects – *bacalhau,*

posta steaks and grills – but portions are as expansive as the views from the outside terrace. Moderate.

O Moinho Rua do Mercado 47 ☏ 273 431 116. In the new town, with great-value pizza and pasta, plus good views of the reservoir. There's a surprising array of vegetarian options (well, at least three, which qualifies as surprising in Portugal), including a delicious *spaguetti picante* prepared with chilli and garlic. Inexpensive.

Bragança

On a dark hillock above **BRAGANÇA**, the remote capital of Trás-os-Montes, stands a circle of perfectly preserved walls, enclosing a white medieval village and rising to a massive keep and castle. Known as the **Cidadela**, this is one of the most memorable sights in Portugal, as well as the embodiment of the town's dynastic history. The Bragançans were the last line of **Portuguese monarchs**, ruling from 1640, when they replaced the Spaniards, until the fall of the monarchy in 1910. To the British, the name is most readily associated with Catherine, queen to Charles II, though for the Portuguese the town represents the defence of the liberty of the people, because the Bragançans were the first to muster a popular revolt against Junot in 1808, and always defended their power to make their own decisions.

The citadel provides the principal reason for a visit to Bragança, though the nearby Parque Natural de Montesinho is an additional draw, while the town is also a useful stop for anyone crossing the nearby border into Spain. It's certainly worth staying for a night or two, especially to experience early evening in the Cidadela, when the tourists have gone for the day and peace returns to the ancient streets. Looking out over the castle walls into Spain brings home the very real isolation that Bragança endured until recent times, something taken advantage of by the Jews in the sixteenth century, who escaped over the border from the terrors of the Spanish Inquisition. Despite the common rule by Spaniards over the two countries during this period, the Inquisition in Portugal was relatively inefficient and only spread slowly northwards with ever-decreasing zeal.

Bragança's **Festa de Nossa Senhora das Graças** (Aug 12–22) offers another very good reason to be in town, featuring lots of cultural events and traditional music. Shortly after follows the religious **Romaria de São Bartolomeu** (Aug 24), while other notable dates include the **Feira das Cantarinhas** (May 2–4), a crafts fair dedicated to the clay water jug (*cantarinha*) which was once used to store the gifts given to a bride on her wedding day. On **Ash Wednesday** (usually Feb or early March) people dressed as devils run around town whipping penitents – the origins probably lie in an ancient fertility cult, when it was believed that Pan impregnated women simply by smacking them.

The Bragança Meninas

Bragança became the focus of unwanted attention in 2003, when it featured on the cover of Time magazine because of its problem with *meninas brasileiros* – **Brazilian prostitutes**. Though the movement of sex workers is all too common in the estimated $50 billion global sex trade, it was the effect it had on the town that attracted Time. Local women made a defiant stand against the newcomers, who they accused of corrupting their men and the traditional way of life. This resulted in a few police raids and lots of unwanted publicity. Some of the prostitutes have since moved on, but plenty still remain and, in a town of under 30,000 inhabitants, they remain a visible but reluctantly accepted part of the community.

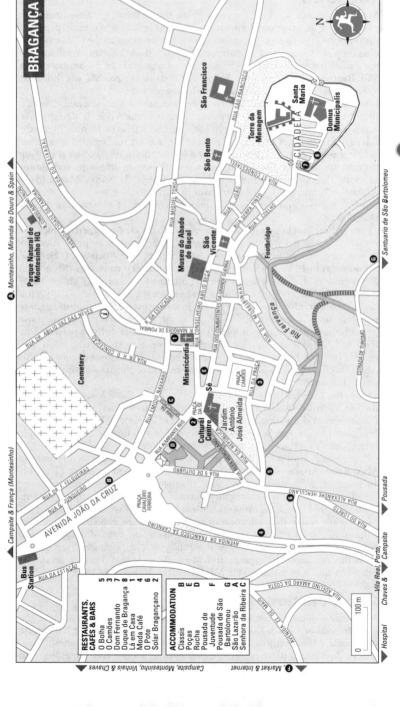

BRAGANÇA

N

RESTAURANTS, CAFÉS & BARS

O Bolha	5
O Camões	3
Dom Fernando	7
Duque de Bragança	8
Lá em Casa	1
Moda Café	4
O Pote	6
Solar Bragançano	2

ACCOMMODATION

Classis	B
Poças	E
Rucha	D
Pousada de Juventude	F
Pousada de São Bartolomeu	G
São Lazarão	A
Senhora da Ribeira	C

Bus Station

Cemetery

Parque Natural de Montesinho HQ

São Francisco

Santa Maria

Torre da Menagem

CIDADELA

Domus Municipais

São Bento

Museu do Abade de Baçal

São Vicente

Misericórdia

Sé

Cultural Centre

PRAÇA DA SÉ

Jardim António José Almeida

PRAÇA CAMÕES

Footbridge

Rio Fervença

PRAÇA CAVALEIRO FERREIRA

AVENIDA JOÃO DA CRUZ

RUA DA ESTAÇÃO

RUA 5 DE OUTUBRO

RUA ALMIRANTE REIS

RUA EMÍLIO NAVARRO

RUA DR. H. D. CONCEIÇÃO

RUA DR. ARLIQ VAZ DAS NEVES

AVENIDA CÍNLIC DE AMANGO

RUA DO SEIXAGAL

RUA MIGUEL TORGA

RUA MARQUÊS DE POMBAL

RUA CONSELHEIRO ABÍLIO BEÇA

RUA DOS COMBATENTES DA GRANDE GUERRA

RUA DA PRAÇA

RUA DAS S. MINHAS

RUA S. JOÃO

RUA SERPA PINTO

RUA T. COELHO

RUA DA ALFÂNDEGA

RUA ST CONSTÁVEL

RUA SÃO FRANCISCO

RUA DA REPÚBLICA

RUA ALEXANDRE HERCULANO

RUA DO LORETO

RUA ADELINO AMARO DA COSTA

AVENIDA 22 DE MAIO

AVENIDA DR. FRANCISCO SÁ CARNEIRO

RUA G. JUNQUEIRO

RUA DR. F. FELGUEIRAS

ESTRADA DE TURISMO

▲ Montesinho, Miranda do Douro & Spain

▲ Campsite & França (Montesinho)

▲ Santuário de São Bartolomeu

▲ Pousada

▲ Vila Real, Porto ▲ Campsite

▲ Chaves & Campsite

▲ Hospital

▲ Campsite, Montesinho, Vinhais & Chaves

▲ Market & Internet

7

TRÁS-OS-MONTES | Bragança

467

0	100 m

The town

Modern Bragança, set along the valley below the Cidadela, is a pleasant enough place, despite an eruption of concrete apartment buildings and underpasses on the outskirts. It's a twenty-minute walk from the centre up to the Cidadela – the obvious place to start your exploration of town – though for an overall view of the citadel and town, there's no beating the vantage-point of the **Santuario de São Bartolomeu**; to get there, follow the signs to the *pousada*, which is next to the church – a half-hour walk from the town centre.

At the heart of the **Cidadela** stands the fifteenth-century council chamber, the **Domus Municipalis**. Very few Romanesque civic buildings have survived, and no other in Europe has this pentagonal form. Its meetings – for solving land disputes and the like – took place on the arcaded first floor; below was a cistern. Ask around for the key at the nearby houses if peering through the keyhole isn't enough for you. Rising to one side, and almost blocking the doorway of the Domus, is the **Igreja de Santa Maria** (daily 9.30am–6.30pm; free), whose interior is distinguished by an eighteenth-century, barrel-vaulted, painted ceiling – a feature of several churches in Bragança.

Facing these buildings is the town keep, the **Torre de Menagem,** which the royal family rejected as a residence in favour of their vast estate in the Alentejo. It was one of the first works of restoration by the Society of National Monuments in 1928, and now houses a small **military museum** (Mon–Wed & Fri–Sun 9–11.45am & 2–4.45pm; €1.50, free Sun morning), collection of military odds and ends which also offers great views. At the side of the keep, a curious **pelourinho** (stone pillory) rises from the back of a prehistoric granite pig. The town's museum has three more of these crudely sculpted *porcas* (though the most famous example is to be seen at Murça, halfway between Vila Real and Mirandela). They are thought to have been the fertility idols of a prehistoric cult, and it's easy to understand the beast's prominence in this province of wild boars and chestnut forests, where the staple winter diet is smoked sausage.

From the Cidadela, the narrow, stepped Rua Serpa Pinto leads to the **Igreja de São Vicente**, where Dom Pedro I claimed to have secretly married Inês de Castro (see p.195); while a small diversion east of here, along Rua São Francisco, brings you to the **Igreja de São Bento**, the town's finest church – a simple Renaissance structure with three contrasting ceilings.

Continuing into town, along Rua Conselheiro Abílio Beça, you'll find the **Museu do Abade de Baçal**, the town's distinguished museum (Tues–Fri 10am–noon & 2–5pm, Sat & Sun 10am–6pm; €2, free Sun morning), installed in the eighteenth-century former Bishop's Palace. In its gardens Celtic-inspired medieval tombstones rub shoulders with a menagerie of *porcas*, while inside the collection of sacred art and the topographical water-colours of Alberto Souza are the highlights, along with displays of local costumes – especially the dress of the *Pauliteiros* ("stick dancers"), who hail from the area around Bragança and Miranda do Douro. Further down the street is a fine Renaissance-style **Misericórdia** dating from 1873.

Practicalities

Most buses operate from the shiny **bus station** (☏273 300 450) at the northern end of Avenida João da Cruz, where you'll find offices for Rodonorte (services to Mirandela, Vila Real, Vinhais and southern Trás-os-Montes), Auto-Viação do Tâmega (Chaves), Santos (Miranda do Douro and Mirandela) and

The Portuguese border post is 34km to the southeast at **Quintanilha. Express buses** from Bragança bus station run directly to Zamora and Valladolid, and on to Madrid, but only on Tuesdays, Fridays and Sundays (the Sunday service doesn't stop in Valladolid). There's a more minor crossing to the north, through the Parque Natural de Montesinho, via the border villages of **Portelo** (Portugal) and Calabor (Spain), and on to the Spanish town of Puebla de Sanabria, which has further bus and train services and accommodation. STUB buses from Bragança run to Portelo twice daily on weekdays, and Rodonorte has a service during term time (1–2 daily Sept–June only).

Rede Expresso (national services). **Parking** is easy up round the citadel itself.

From the bus station it's a short walk to Praça da Sé, essentially the centre of town, with the English-speaking **turismo** (May–Sept Mon–Fri 10am–12.30pm & 2–6.30pm, Sat 9am–12.30pm & 2–5pm; Oct–April Mon–Fri 9am–12.30pm & 2–5.30pm, Sat 10am–12.30pm; ☎273 381 273, ⓦwww.cm-braganca.pt) located a couple of hundred metres to the north on the wide boulevard of Avenida Cidade de Zamora. Another 200m down the avenue, in a modern development on the left, is the headquarters of the **Parque Natural de Montesinho**, Rua Cónego Albano Falcão, Lote 5, Apartado 90 (Mon–Fri 9am–12.30 & 2–5.30pm; ☎273 381 234, ⓦwww.icn.pt), where the very helpful English-speaking staff can provide you with information about visiting the park, including the ever changing accommodation situation.

Accommodation

Pensões and **hotels** are scattered around town, with generally decent standards and offering good value for money; even in summer you shouldn't find it too difficult to find a good room. There are a lot more rural options nearby, within driving distance of Bragança, particularly within the Parque Natural de Montesinho (see p.471). The two nearest **campsites** are also convenient for exploring the park.

Hotels and pensions

Residencial Classis Av João da Cruz 102 ☎273 331 631, ℗273 323 458. This slightly ageing, motel-style *residencial* is the best mid-range option, with good views from its third- and fourth-floor rooms, each with satellite TV and fridges. ❷

Residencial Poças Rua Combatentes da Grande Guerra 200 ☎273 331 428. A reliable, cheap and characterful town-centre *pensão*, though pick your room with care – some are very bare and in winter this place is freezing. Rooms with or without bathroom available. The associated restaurant is a great place for no-nonsense meat and fish dishes – family-run and popular enough to fill a couple of floors. ❶

Pousada de São Bartolomeu Estrada de Turismo ☎273 331 493, ⓦwww.pousadas.pt. South of the river, about 1km by road from the centre – drivers should follow the signs off Rua Alexandre Herculano. Purpose-built in 1959, its rooms are bright and spacious, most with great views over town. There's a good restaurant (with a reputation for wild game) as well as an inviting swimming pool; you can walk into town (steeply uphill on the way back) in around 15min. ❻

Pensão Rucha Rua Almirante Reis 42 ☎273 331 672. Run by a friendly couple, this very simple place has rooms on the first floor along corridors lined with antiques, pottery and flowers. The eight rooms (with shared bath) have a little more character than most places in town, though gloomy back ones are to be avoided. No credit cards. ❶

Residencial Senhora da Ribeira Trav da Misericórdia ☎273 300 550, ℗273 300 555. On an alley off Rua Almirante Reis, offering conspicuously spotless rooms – some with good views of the citadel – and friendly service, though the disco opposite can heighten noise levels. In the words of their own brochure, "please visit Residencial Senhora da Ribeira, the best hotel in that king, at North East of the province of Trás-os-Montes. Thank You". ❷

Youth hostel

Pousada de Juventude Av 22 de Maio ☎273 304 600, ⓦwww.pousadasjuventude.pt. Roughly 1km west of the centre, this swanky modern hostel has ten double rooms with or without bath and sixteen four-bed dorms, as well a six-bed family room (❸) and a couple of two-person

apartments with kitchen (❸). Also Internet, laundry service and bar. Open 24hr. Dorm beds €11, rooms ❶.

Campsites

Cepo Verde 8km west of town, on the N103 Vinhais road ☎273 999 371. Good facilities, plus a pool. Closed Oct–March.
Parque de Campismo Rio Sabor, 6km north of town on the França road ☎273 331 435, ℗273 327 252. The nearest campsite to town is the well-equipped municipal one, perched on the banks of the Rio Sabor, with its own bar. Closed Oct–April.

Eating, drinking and events

Bragança has a promising array of **restaurants**, most of them pretty good value. The municipal **market** is open daily for food, although its distance from town means that the central groceries are an easier option. Most of the town's **café** culture, meanwhile, unfolds along Avenida João da Cruz, where there are any number of places with pavement tables. For upcoming events, consult the monthly *Bragança em agenda* pamphlet, available from the tourist office.

Restaurants

O Camões Pr Camões 45–47 ☎273 324 040. Stylish restaurant offering alfresco dining, a tempting selection of grilled fish and seafood, and an impressive array of pasta dishes. The tourist menu is very good value. Closed Sat. Moderate.
Lá em Casa Rua Marquês de Pombal 7 ☎273 322 111. A convivial place, decked out in the kind of faux-rustic style so beloved of northern restaurateurs. The menu features a refreshingly long list of meat, fish and even shellfish, though the latter racks up the price. Moderate.
O Pote Rua Alexandre Herculano 186 ☎273 333 710. Friendly place that takes pride in its food. It specializes in game, though the other meat and fish dishes (including a prawn with whiskey dish that won't appeal to everyone) are more reasonably priced, as are the inexpensive pasta dishes. Closed Sun. Moderate.

Solar Bragançano Pr da Sé 34 ☎274 323 875. Upmarket *casa típica*, where you dine in chandelier-hung, oak-panelled rooms to the accompaniment of classical music. The food is good, although not quite as special as the prices might suggest, and it's the place to try more unusual regional dishes, like pheasant prepared with chestnuts or partridge cooked with grapes. There's a fine antique bar. Closed Mon. Expensive.

Bars

Duque de Bragança Cidadela. Nightlife in town is rather limited, though this extremely popular bar inside the walled town is always a good bet – it sometimes has live music, or magic and poetry evenings, and it's open until 3am.
Moda Café Av Dr Francisco Sá Carneiro. The place for serious dancing, where the music keeps on coming until 5am.

Listings

Banks Branches of most of the major banks are clustered on Av Dr Francisco Sá Carneiro, including Caixa Geral de Depósitos for exchanging money.
Hospital Av Abade Baçal ☎273 310 800.
Internet Cyber Centro (Mon–Sat 10am–11pm & Sun 2–8pm) in the municipal market behind the town hall.

Pharmacy Farmácia Confiança, Av João da Cruz 76 ☎273 323 226.
Police ☎273 303 400.
Post office Rua 5 de Outubro (Mon–Fri 8.30am–6pm, Sat 9am–12.30pm).
Taxis There's usually a fleet of taxis parked on Av João da Cruz, on the opposite side from the cafés, or call ☎273 322 138/273 322 065.

Parque Natural de Montesinho

Occupying the extreme northeastern tip of Portugal, the **Parque Natural de Montesinho** is the only sector of the Terra Fria where the way of life and the appearance of the villages have not yet been drastically changed by the incoming wealth of emigrant workers. That's not to say that the park is completely untouched – once-pristine villages are slowly being defaced by ugly red terra-cotta brickwork – but on the whole the Serra de Montesinho's heather-clad hills, wet grass plains and thick forests of oak look much as they have done for centuries. The park covers 751 square kilometres, and has a population of 9500 distributed between 92 villages, many of which retain their old Roman or Visigothic names. Tradition hangs heavy – though change, of course, is inevitable. Most of the curious round pigeon houses (*pombal*), a feature of the region, are now deserted, despite efforts by conservationists to entice the birds back. The pigeons, it seems, like many from Trás-os-Montes, prefer an easier existence in the cities than eking out a living in the countryside.

The two main access points for the park are Bragança and Vinhais, and there are **park information offices** in each, where you can pick up brochures on the local flora and fauna. In addition to the **walk** detailed in the box (see p.473), the park offices can also supply you with leaflets on other marked routes, including circuits around Moimenta and Quintanilha.

The **eastern section** of the park is the only one you can really see by public transport, with buses running north from Bragança along the N103-1 to the sleepy village of **França** and on to Portelo, just before which you can divert to the spectacularly situated border village of **Montesinho**. Another minor road (and irregular bus service) runs northeast from Bragança to the fascinating medieval village of **Rio de Onor**.

Obviously, having your own transport opens up many more possibilities, and that's especially true of the more remote **western section** of the park, which is home to countless little villages waiting to be discovered if you have the time and patience to negotiate the poor and often confusing road system. A fine circuit round the park is to take the Gondosende exit off the Bragança to Vinhais road, taking in the timeless villages of Vilarinho, Dines, Mofreita and Moimenta en route back to Vinhais.

Accommodation is scattered throughout the park, with fine options in Montesinho, Gimonde and França and a few rustic options at Gondosende Vilarinho, Rio de Onor, Moimenta, Travanca and Rio de Fornos. Many of these are part of the *Turismo no Espaço Rural* scheme, aimed at supplying tourists with traditional, but high-quality accommodation – check the *Turismo no Espaço* leaflet, available at the park office in Bragança for other options in the area. Wild **camping** in the park itself is prohibited, although there are two official sites located on the southern boundary (see Bragança, p.470) and another in Rio de Onor. Note that there are no credit-card facilities for accommodation payment anywhere in the park. For details of guided walks, bike rides and four-wheel jeep safaris in the park, contact Montesinho Aventura (☎273 326 080, ⓔmontesinhoaventura@mac.com).

Gimonde

Seven kilometres east of Bragança, along the N218, is **GIMONDE**, a rural village of traditional wooden houses beautifully sited on the edge of the Montesinho park, which would make a fine base should you want to stay somewhere quieter than Bragança. The rivers Onor, Sabor and Igrejas all meet

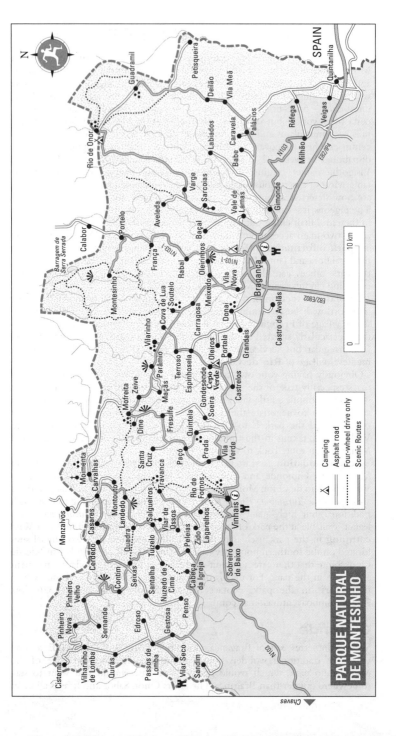

PARQUE NATURAL DE MONTESINHO

	Camping
	Asphalt road
	Four-wheel drive only
	Scenic Routes

Walking in Montesinho

The best **trail** in the park is a moderately easy two-day walk beginning and ending at França (see p.475). Start by turning left off the main road after the bridge and walk along the track which follows the Rio Sabor. This is rarely used by vehicles and winds through a steep gorge, where you can spot many species of birds and, in summer, maybe some wild boar. The track passes a hydroelectric power station and a disused trout farm (on your left), then after about 4km there's a turning off to the left marked "Soutelo". Ignore the turning and continue for about 6km along the track towards the **Barragem de Serra Serrada**, near the Spanish border, where there's a mountain hut (currently closed; check with the park office in Bragança) – just past the reservoir take a right-hand path signposted "Lama Grande". For alternative accommodation, head instead to Montesinho (p.476) – there's a signposted turning off to the left about 2km before the reservoir. It's a worthwhile detour in any case, and if you do spend a day or two here you can tackle the new **circular walk** up to the *barragem* and back (3hr, 7km), involving a climb of about 400m. The route – marked by red-and-yellow painted crosses, which are sometimes difficult to follow – takes you up from the eastern side of the village and back down the western side.

To rejoin the track to the reservoir, retrace your steps to the Montesinho junction. About 2km after the reservoir, the track splits in two; take the right-hand turning for the mountain hut (see above) and the left-hand turning to start the return journey to França. The track leads over a high plateau covered with expanses of heather and rock formations, and giving spectacular views over to Bragança in the distance. Follow the track, descending steadily for a few kilometres, then take a left-hand turning. A couple of kilometres further on, you'll see a right-hand turning – clearly signposted to França – and, if you take this, after about 4km you'll rejoin the track in França where the walk started.

here near a Romanesque bridge, a favourite spot for stork-watching in early summer. The village also boasts one of the region's most famed restaurants, the multi-prize-winning *Restaurante Típico Dom Roberto* (☎273 302 510). With a roaring log fire and a small wood-panelled bar, the menu features fine cuisine sourced from natural, chemical-free ingredients, including a bewildering array of *chouriço* and *alheira*. The various wild boar and stuffed rabbit dishes may be expensive but they're worth a splurge. Gimonde's popularity has led to the opening of a classy glass-fronted **tourist information office** (☎273 381 302, Ⓦwww.amontesinho.pt; open 24hr). This sells local produce and acts as a booking office for three local self-catering **houses** (all ❷) – *Casa da Mestre*, right behind, with spruce modern rooms and use of a communal living room and kitchen; the simpler but more secluded *Casa de Bísaro*, across the square, which sits above a sausage smoking factory; or, 2km out of town, the peaceful *Quinta das Covas* (☎273 044 000; Ⓔqcovas@amontesinho.pt; breakfast included) located in its own grounds amidst cherry trees, with homely white bed linen and simple furniture; the *azulejo*-tiled dining room is equipped with an open fire.

Rio de Onor

Reached across a bleak, Scottish-like landscape of moorland and set against wild mountains – snow-topped even into May – **RIO DE ONOR**, 25km north of Bragança, provides the most fascinating insight into village life in the Serra de Montesinho. As you wend your way here, you'll begin to realize how isolated Rio de Onor is – the road has existed for only twenty years, before which the locals had to walk across open country to and from Bragança. There are in fact two Rio de Onors – one in Spain (called Riohonor de Castilla) and one in Portugal – but two stone blocks labelled "E" and "P", and a change from cobbles on the Portuguese side to smooth concrete on the Spanish, are all that delineate the frontier.

The villagers have come and gone between the two for generations, operating essentially as an independent state and speaking, until recently, a hybrid Portuguese-Spanish dialect known as *Rionorês*. Their extreme isolation engendered a mutual cooperation that was independent of their respective nations, something considered so unusual that it inspired an anthropological study in the 1950s. In the past, communal meetings fined troublemakers and miscreants in wine, while today's ageing villagers (most of the youth have left for the cities) still share land, flocks, winepresses, mills and ovens. A steady trickle of tourists has persuaded locals to renovate some of the ancient stone houses, but it's difficult to imagine how Rio de Onor's medieval charm can survive indefinitely.

△ Rio de Onor

The two villages are set in an idyllic valley on either side of a stream: the granite steps and wooden balconies of rough schist houses line narrow alleyways, while straw creeps out across the cobbles. Hidden sheep bleat behind tattered barn doors and the ancient streets are splattered with animal dung. The old bar in the Portuguese "half" of the village – complete with an ancient, wall-mounted glass cigarette case and 1970s photographs of the local football team – contains a long stick on which locals once marked the number of cattle and sheep they owned. There's some good **hiking** to be had in the surrounding hills – if you haven't had time to pick up any routes from the park office you could try asking the locals, although don't be too surprised when they express disbelief that you want to walk anywhere rather than take your car.

Rio de Onor's **Festa dos Reis** – mainly an excuse to feast on *chouriço* – is on January 6. More traditional though is the **Lenha das Almas** ("Firewood of Souls") celebration on November 1, where the boys of the village gather firewood, which is then hauled into the village by ox carts (or, more commonly now, by tractors) and auctioned off, the proceeds going to the "souls" of the dead (ie the church). The ritual has its roots in a pre-Roman cult of ancestors, as well as marking the time when boys become adults, and ends with a communal feast and a binge on roast chestnuts.

Practicalities

STUB **buses** currently leave Bragança's bus station on weekdays only at 14.06pm and 5.41pm, returning from Rio de Onor at 2.58pm and 6.30pm, with a journey time of roughly an hour. However, the later bus will only do the full run if there are enough people; phone ahead on ☎273 300 455 to ensure it picks you up. Alternatively, a return trip by taxi from Bragança costs around €20.

There's simple **accommodation** available at the *Casa de Onor* (☎273 927 163; ❷), in an old stone building with a terrace overlooking the stream; it's on the right just before the Spanish border. The *Casa's* central location means you'll be of great interest to the villagers: dig out your Portuguese phrasebook and be ready for their earthy sense of humour. There's also a lovely leafy **campsite** (☎914 716 193; weekends only; closed Oct–April), located on the left at the entrance to the village. If you are staying the night you can pick up some supplies from Rio de Onor's sole **shop**, Tienda Casa Milin, located just over the border and down to the right in the Spanish side of the village.

França

Ten kilometres north of Bragança, up the 103-1 road, the unassuming village of **FRANÇA** – permanent population 150 – is locally famous for its chestnuts and *chouriço*, though visitors use it as a base for exploring the park. While it's not difficult to spot emigrant-inspired construction clashing with the traditional schist cottages, the village still has a number of untouched, tumbledown streets which remain rooted in the distant past. França was once home to a small gold and lead mining industry (the last lead mines at nearby Portelo closed only fifteen years ago), and was also the destination for dishonest people-smugglers during the Salazar regime in the last century. Denied passports but desperate to escape Salazar's repressive society, many labourers paid to be smuggled to the nearest safe country that would have them, France (Spain's Franco being an ally of Salazar). The smugglers duly dumped them off here at França – which means *France* in Portuguese.

There are currently three STUB **buses** daily (Mon–Fri, first departure 12.36pm) from Bragança to França/Portelo, though check timetables at Bragança's bus station. França is home to the *Promise of Portugal* (☏273 919 258, ⓦwww.promise-of-portugal.com; breakfast on request), which consists of three charmingly restored **cottages** rented out by an hospitable English couple. Both the *Casa da Montanha* (❸) and *Casa da Castanha* (❷), sleeping four and two people respectively, are tucked away up a country track at the back of the village (look for the sign), with rustic, unpretentious interiors and cheerful kitchens. Great walking and river bathing are literally on your doorstep, although if you fancy lodging in the heart of the village, they also rent out a lovingly renovated, 250-year-old cottage, *Casa Pequena* (❸), which can sleep five.

There's a small café/bar in the village down by the bridge, but for a full **meal** head to the moderately priced *Restaurante Turismo* (☏273 919 163; no credit cards) out on the left on the outskirts of the village, heading towards Portelo. It's best to give them some notice if you want to eat in the evening, when you can enjoy tasty, no-frills servings of trout, pork or omelette outside on the vine-covered patio.

The local **riding centre** (daily 9am–noon & 2.30–7pm; ☏273 919 141), signposted on the right on the road out to Portelo, offers either tuition or guided trips for €15 per hour, as well as longer expeditions into the park.

Montesinho

Flanked by wind-whipped pine plantations and dramatic granite outcrops, the border outpost of **MONTESINHO** (permanent population 35) packs centuries of history into its manure-mottled streets. The magnificently knotted chestnut tree towering over the main square is claimed by some villagers to be two thousand years old, while inscriptions on the doors of the houses date back to the sixteenth century. The village is roughly 8km northwest of França and walking alongside the **Rio Sabor** is idyllic, with wonderful deserted spots for swimming along the way.

The refreshingly rustic *Café Montesinho* (☏273 919 219) is the hub of village life and its genial, enterprising owner has **accommodation** available in a plainly fitted stone house (room ❶, whole house ❸) with kitchen and wooden balcony. If it's occupied, he can direct you to his brother who runs *Casas da Eira* (☏273 919 227; ❷–❸), a trio of traditional dwellings around a secluded, if rather scrappy, yard. The interiors are all very similar: comfortably modern-rustic with basic kitchens.

Montesinho's flagship accommodation, however, is the *Lagosta Perdida* (☏273 919 031, ⓦwww.lagostaperdida.com; dinner included; ❹), a painstaking restoration of an old granite house masterminded by a convivial Dutch/English couple. Chestnut-wood floors, an amazing central space with glass roof, vintage bread oven, ecofriendly almond husk-fired power and a heated swimming pool with bucolic views make this something special. Walking and cycling routes are on offer along with bike hire. There is in fact a marked circular hiking route from Montesinho up to the dam above the village, details of which can be found in the walking box on p.473.

The western park

The gentle chestnut- and oak-wooded hills of the central and western expanses of the park are easily accessed via the pretty five-hundred-year-old hamlet of **GONDOSENDE** (population 25), located 8km west of Bragança, just off the main N103 to Chaves. Nestled among the tranquil streets and flower-festooned

window ledges is the *Casa do Passal* (☎273 323 506, ⓦwww.casadopassal.no.sapo
.pt; no credit cards or breakfast; ❹) a rustically restored cottage. Reservations are
advised, though if this is full, just around the corner is *Casa da Bica* (☎273 999
454, ⓔcasadabica@braganca.pt; no credit cards; ❷), that's not quite as charming
as its competitors but significantly cheaper. There's also some engaging accommodation available at the 300-year-old *Casa dos Marrões* (☎273 999 550, ⓦwww
.casadosmarroes.com; ❸) in the tiny hamlet of **VILARINHO,** some 6km to the
north. While its chief attraction is the swimming pool, the house boasts some
remarkable architectural features, notably the open space in the bar/dining area.
It also has a library.

Eight kilometres or so further to the northwest is the enchanting village of
DINE, constructed on descending cobbled streets that afford sweeping views
of the valley. These lead down to an eerie, bat-inhabited *gruta* (cave), discovered,
bizarrely enough, by a Danish diplomat in 1984, with the resulting excavations
unearthing various bones, cooking implements, flints and arrowheads dating
back to 4000 BC. While there's a small museum up beside the church, ostensibly designed to display the finds, the cabinets are currently empty, with all the
exhibits languishing in museums in Brangança and Lisbon. However, there is a
series of informative panels (in Portuguese only) explaining the cave's history;
you can get the museum key from the house by the church.

For accommodation and food you'll have to head on to the equally remote
and tranquil village of **MOIMENTA**: look for the turn-off to the right just
before the village of Mofreita; the road eventually winds its way down into
Moimenta over an old Roman bridge, to the left of which there are some glori-
ously peaceful picnic spots. It's also an easy 23-kilometre drive from Vinhais (see
below). While it is marred by a lot of unsympathetic new building, Moimenta
unfolds its charms slowly and if you take the time to explore the village you'll
find parts – particularly on the western side – still filled with old granite
cottages and rows of sagging, brightly painted wooden houses perched precariously atop granite pillars. There's also a lovely, mostly seventeenth-century
Baroque church guarding the edge of the village and ringed by remote hills
stretching to the Spanish border. A marked walking circuit leads out from the
north end of the village and climbs to a height of 950m; a detailed leaflet is
available from the park office in Bragança.

The best time to visit is during the festival of Nossa Senhora do Carmo on 19–
20 August. If you fancy staying the night, enquire at the *Café Marceneiro* (☎273
649 121) for the rental of an attractive little **cottage** (❷) complete with pew-like
seats in the kitchen, a secluded, vine-draped courtyard and an old smokehouse,
still used to cure local sausages and hams. Information on the national park is
available from the *Casa do Parque* on the main street, downhill from the grocer's
(variable hours; ☎273 771 416). *Fraga dos Três Reinos* (☎273 649 174; closed Mon)
is a homely **restaurant** located on the left of the road into town, with a little
lawned garden, although any request to eat outside is likely to be met with
surprise. Persist, and you can sample some freshly caught trout from the river, or
tasty *bacalhau*, on breezy outdoor tables shaded by a young willow tree.

Vinhais

The twisting 96-kilometre white-knuckle ride from Chaves to Bragança takes
in some of the most awe-inspiring scenery in Portugal. The road passes through
broad-leaved forest, pine forest and, at its greatest altitude, rocky moorland,

blanketed by yellow gorse and purple heather at certain times of year. Interspersed amongst these are the smallholdings of traditional farmers, with tiny fields still ploughed with the assistance of reluctant donkeys.

Two-thirds of the way along the route is the pleasant village of **VINHAIS**, whose main sight is the Baroque convent of **São Francisco**, a vast building incorporating a pair of churches in its facade. It is situated at the Chaves end of the main street, which runs for 1km or more, and offers staggering views away to the south. A minor road from Vinhais leads north into the Parque Natural de Montesinho, making this a useful access point for motorists, and the town would make a good base for a few days' exploration of the park.

There is a well-stocked **turismo** (daily 9am–7.30pm; ☏273 770 309) in the centre of the village on Largo de Arrabalde, and park information available from the **Delegação do Parque** at the Casa do Povo (Mon–Fri 9am–12.30pm & 2.30–5pm; ☏273 771 416). **Accommodation** is usually easy to find except during the annual Feriado Municipal week (leading up to May 20), when various events celebrating the town being given a charter culminate in an agricultural fair on the nearest Saturday. First choice is the characterful *Pensão Ribeirinha*, Rua Nova 34 (☏2373 771 490; no credit cards; ❶), halfway between the main square and the convent, with its own good restaurant; best of the lovely en-suite rooms have balconies with superb views overlooking the valley. Upmarket but rather clinical *Residencial Cidadela Transmontana* on Rua dos Frades (☏273 770 112, ✉rescidtrans@mail.telepac.pt; ❷) 200 metres west of the *Ribeirinha*, also has an expensive restaurant that serves wild boar, rabbit and other rustic delights. Alternatively, 2km north of Vinhais in the tiny village of Rio de Fornos, the simple *Casa de Mencha* (☏934 143 171, ⓦwww.casadamench.com; no breakfast; ❹) has cosy double rooms, a little log fire and a fine balcony. In Vinhais, moderately priced **food** can be had at *Restaurante Comercial* (☏273 772 169) on the main through road, Rua da Calçada; its speciality is roast suckling pig.

Chaves and around

One of the most attractive towns in Trás-os-Montes, **CHAVES** stands just 12km from the Spanish border and its name, which means "keys", reflects a strategic history of occupation and ownership. Founded by the Romans in 78 AD, their name for the town, Aquae Flaviae, comes from a dual reference to the famous spa waters, and Flavio Vespasianus, who was emperor at the time. The town was an important point on the imperial road from Astorga, in Spanish León, to Braga. In the first century AD it served as the army headquarters under Aulus Flaviensis, who was responsible for developing the thermal stations here and elsewhere in the region, notably at Vidago, Carvalhelhos and Pedras Salgadas. Between 1128 and 1160 the town was an Islamic enclave, and in the following seven centuries it was fought over in turn by the French, Spanish and Portuguese. One of its greatest overlords, **Nuno Álvares Pereira**, was awarded the "keys" of the north by João I for his valiant service at the Battle of Aljubarrota (1385), and from him the town passed into the steady hands of the House of Bragança. However, as recently as 1912, Chaves bore the brunt of a Royalist attack from Spain – two years after Portugal had become a republic.

Today, Chaves is considerably less significant, though it's still a market centre for the villages of the fertile Tâmega plain – the richest agricultural lands in the province – and regional capital for northern Trás-os-Montes. For visitors, its principal attractions are its spa, an array of monuments in the medieval old town, and its gastronomy: Chaves is famed in Portugal for its smoked hams, delicious meat cakes (*bolas de carne*), sausages and a strong red wine. These conspire to make Chaves one of the most touristy destinations in Trás-os-Montes, or at least one of the few towns where tourists (largely French) are a visible presence.

The town hosts an important winter fair, held on November 1, as well as the annual ten-day **Feira de Artesanato**, held in the Jardim Público in mid-August,

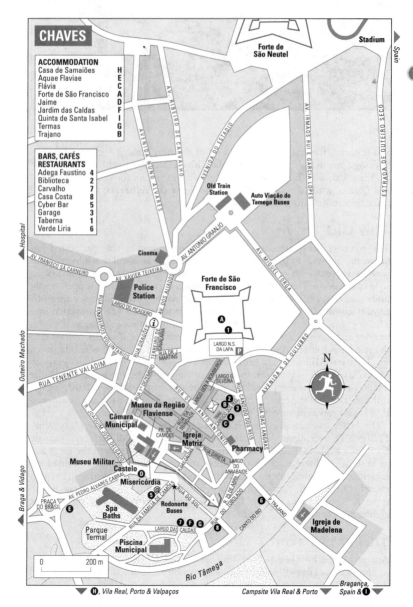

CHAVES

ACCOMMODATION
Casa de Samaiões	H
Aquae Flaviae	E
Flávia	C
Forte de São Francisco	A
Jaime	D
Jardim das Caldas	F
Quinta de Santa Isabel	I
Termas	G
Trajano	B

BARS, CAFÉS RESTAURANTS
Adega Faustino	4
Biblioteca	2
Carvalho	7
Casa Costa	8
Cyber Bar	5
Garage	3
Taberna	1
Verde Liria	6

△ Chaves

and featuring the crafts, music and food of the Alto Tâmega region and neighbouring Spanish Galicia. The **Festas da Cidade** (July 8) coincide with the Jogos do Eixo Altântico (July 6–10), a kind of mini-Olympics for northern Portugal and Galicia, while the antiquities fair, the **Feira de Velherias**, takes place one Saturday a month from May to November.

The Old Town

The compact old quarter of Chaves rises above the river, the spa located just below the old walls to the west. The town's military past is still much in evidence with two seventeenth-century fortresses, built in the characteristic Vaubanesque style of the north. The **Forte de São Neutel** is closed for visits but occasionally hosts concerts, while the **Forte de São Francisco** – originally a seventeenth-century convent fortified during the peninsular wars – has been converted into a luxury hotel (see p.481), worth visiting for a drink or meal to enjoy its beautiful interior and the magnificent views from the ramparts. The **Castelo**, overlooking the spa, has a fourteenth-century keep, the Torre de Menagem, which houses a small **Museu Militar** (daily 9am–12.30pm & 2–5.30pm; €1, includes entry to Museu da Região Flaviense). In here you can view the battle colours of the infantry regiment that repulsed the Royalist attack from Spain in 1912, but the real attractions are the castle gardens and the views from the battlements, accessed by a back-breakingly tiny door on the top floor of the museum.

The better town museum is the **Museu da Região Flaviense** (daily 9am–12.30pm & 2–5.30pm; €1, includes entry to Museu Militar) on Praça de Camões, a haphazard assortment of material tracing the history of the town and its customs, including quite an assembly of remains from the old Roman spa settlement, including coins, statuettes and fragmented mosaics. The two churches in Praça de Camões are worth a look, too: the **Igreja Matriz**, which is partly Romanesque, and the **Igreja da Misericórdia**, distinguished by vast eighteenth-century *azulejo* panels.

The river front

A new spa-fed **bathing pool** (Mon–Sat 4–7pm, Sun 8am–12.30pm; Ⓦwww
.caldasdechaves.com.pt) offers various treatments from hydromassage and

vapour baths to weekend anti-stress packages, though these do not come cheap, with treatments starting from €50. Alternatively, you can always drink the waters at the little *nascente* (spring) in a covered building in the square outside the pools, generally full of old ladies with crocheted mug-holders taking a swig. The water emerges at a piping 73°C (the hottest spring water in Iberia) and is not very tasty (loaded as it is with sodium bicarbonate). It's reckoned to be particularly good for gout, obesity, rheumatism and senility, though ironically should be only sipped if you are of a healthy disposition.

The river gardens are well kept and, though the water itself is polluted, you can take a pedalo ride to view the **Ponte Trajano** – the first-century Roman bridge – and its ancient milestones. If you feel the urge to swim, the indoor **Piscina Municipal** (daily 2.30–8pm; €2) is adjacent to the spa, a far better bet than risking the river. In summer there's also an outdoor pool (Tues–Sun 9am–7pm, Mon 2–7pm; €2.50) out of town by the campsite (see below).

Practicalities

The Auto-Viação do Tâmega **bus station** (for Vila Real, Montalegre, Mirandela and Bragança) is five minutes' walk north of the centre, around the back of the supermarket next to the old train station. Rodonorte buses (Vila Real and Braga) operate from outside their office on the central Rua da Família de Camões. If you're heading **into Spain**, catch one of the frequent services marked "Fronteira" (Border) from the Auto-Viação do Tâmega station (Mon–Fri only), and then a Spanish bus on the other side to Verin or Orense in Galicia. Although space is tight in the centre of town, there is ample **parking** in the streets around Forte de São Francisco.

A small **land train** trundles round town past the main sites, departing from Largo das Caldas (roughly hourly from 10am–noon & 2–7pm; €3). There's also a helpful **turismo** at Terreiro do Cavalaria (June–Sept Mon–Sat 9.30am–12.30pm & 2–6pm; Oct–May Mon–Sat 9am–12.30pm & 2–5.30pm; ☎276 340 661, ⓦ www.cm-chaves.pt), which has a *Circuitos Turísticos* pamphlet detailing routes to local Palaeolithic and Roman sites.

Accommodation
Accommodation is plentiful but be warned that the cheaper places can be intensely cold in winter and boiling in summer. The nearest **campsite** is *Quinta de Rebentão* (☎276 322 733; closed Dec) in Vila Nova, 5km down the Vila Real road; Auto-Viação do Tâmega buses make the short trip every two hours on weekdays.

In town

Hotel Aquae Flaviae Pr do Brasil ☎276 309 000, ⓦ hoteis-arco.com. Chaves' largest hotel – a four-star highrise with a pool (heated in winter), sauna, games room and rather shabby tennis courts. Rooms are distinctly dated, although there's a private tunnel to the spa as well as secure parking. ⑤

Hospedaria Flávia Trav Cândido dos Reis 12 ☎276 107 107. Very basic but friendly place with antiquated en-suite rooms. It's great value, around €20 for singles or doubles, although the hot water supply can be a bit erratic. No credit cards or breakfast. ①

Hotel Forte de São Francisco ☎276 333 700, ⓦ www.forte-s-francisco-hoteis.pt. A chapel with tape-recorded Mass in the reception entry hall sets the tone for this atmospheric hotel, located in a seventeenth-century fortress. The conversion is a sensitive blend of old and new, with all the trappings you'd expect of a four-star hotel – including pool, café, parking, and even occasional art exhibitions. The *Cozinha da Convento* restaurant (expensive) isn't quite as elegant as the rest of the hotel, although the service is attentive and the menu features a variety of unusual dishes, including wild boar and stewed rabbit. ⑤, or ⑥ at weekends.

481

Albergaria Jaime Rua Joaquim José Delgado ☎276 301 050, ⊛albergariajaime.com.pt. This place was operating as a *pensão* as far back as the late 1800s, although its recent makeover has placed it firmly in the hotel category. Its apricot facade and strange, often rather naughty artwork aside, rooms are plush without ever being remarkable. ❸

Residencial Jardim das Caldas Alameda do Tabolado bloc 5 ☎276 331 180. Plain, modern rooms are good value, especially the best ones overlooking the gardens of Largo das Caldas. There's a decent restaurant downstairs. ❶.

Residencial Termas Rua do Tabolado ☎276 333 280. It's a bit of a concrete hulk, but centrally located and friendly, with pleasantly cool a/c rooms with varnished wooden floors. ❶

Hotel Trajano Trav. Cândido dos Reis ☎276 301 640, ⊛www.hoteltrajano.com. Modern and comfortable, the pleasant rooms have traditional local furniture and either showers or baths (€5 extra). Best rooms have good views which they

share with the "panoramic" bar. There's a renowned restaurant (closes 9.30pm) in the basement, not too expensive and just the place for Chaves ham and local trout. ❷, rooms with bath ❸

Outside town

Casa de Samaiões Samaiões, 5km south of Chaves ☎276 340 450, ℮hotel-casadesamaioes @clix.pt. A cross between an upmarket hotel and a *turismo rural*, this combines traditional four-poster beds with contemporary furnishings, while the rural setting and landscaped grounds – complete with swimming pool and full-sized football pitch – supply all the open space and fresh air you could wish for. ❺

Quinta de Santa Isabel Santo Estévão, 7km east of Chaves ☎276 333 210, ℮lisete.sarmento @mail.telepac.pt. A traditional Trás-os-Montes country house with vineyards, 500m off the N103 to Bragança. Queen Isabel is said to have slept here the night before she married Dom Dinis. No credit cards. ❸

Eating, drinking and nightlife

Some of the *pensões* and hotels have reasonable **restaurants** attached (the *Trajano* in particular), but wherever you eat you shouldn't have any difficulty finding good Chaves smoked ham, tasty local sausages and fine red wine. Over Christmas, look out for the traditional speciality of octopus (*polvo*), brought up dried from the coast, then boiled with potatoes and greens. Despite the number of elderly spa-clients in town, there are several fashionable **bars** in Chaves, especially on Largo das Caldas and Travessa Cândido dos Reis.

Restaurants

Carvalho Largo das Caldas, Bloco 4 ☎276 321 727. Some of the region's best food is served in this modern place, as testified by the numerous awards on the walls. Service is excellent – efficient and unobtrusive – and the food uniquely prepared and presented. Try the grilled conger eel or lobster. Closed Thurs. Moderate.

Casa Costa Rua do Tabolado ☎276 323 568. Tremendously popular place serving huge portions of excellent home cooking; the speciality is *bacalhau à Costa*, ideally followed by one of their desserts. There's a pleasant vine-covered rear garden with bench-style tables. Moderate.

Adega Faustino Trav Cândido dos Reis ☎276 322 142. The best spot in town, in a high-ceilinged former wine cellar, with a cobbled floor and huge wine barrels lined up behind the bar. Great value *petiscos* include bean salads, *presunto* and *bolos de bacalhau* while main courses are also very good value. And, of course, it has terrific wines. Closed Sun. No credit cards. Moderate.

Taberna At the *Forte de São Francisco* ☎276 333 700. Built into the fort's outer walls by the main gate (go over the drawbridge for entry), this dimly lit replica of a traditional rural tavern has enough suspended hams, exposed granite and taped fado to at least get your imagination working. The food is excellent, centered on *petiscos* such as mushrooms in garlic sauce and cod balls, though there's also a small selection of main dishes. Closed Sun & Mon. Moderate.

Verde Lírio Canto do Rio ☎276 321 616. In a prime spot with an outside terrace facing the old bridge, this serves a limited but tasty array of fish and meat dishes, together with inexpensive omelettes. It also makes a good drinks spot. Moderate.

Bars and clubs

Biblioteca Trav Cândido dos Reis ☎276 325 980. The town's only central club, with a regular rotation of local and guest DJs. Packs them in after midnight.

Cyber Bar Rua da Familia de Camões, off Largo das Caldas. Groovy café-bar at the back of Albergaria

Jaime, with Internet access and pleasant outdoor tables on the square. Closed Mon Oct–May.
Bar Garage Trav Cândido dos Reis ☎276 333 172. There's no mistaking it – there are bits of cars protruding from the walls. Small and intimate bar with a happy-hour sensibly lasting to midnight every Fri.

Listings

Banks Banks and ATMs can found in the main thoroughfare of Rua de Santo António and on Largo do Arrabaide.
Hospital Av Dr F Sá Carneiro ☎276 300 900.
Pharmacy Farmácia Morais, Rua Santo António 54 ☎276 322 201.

Police Av Bombeiros ☎276 323 125.
Post office Largo General Silveira (Mon–Fri 8.30am–6pm, Sat 9am–12.30pm).
Taxis ☎276 323 803 or 276 323 804.

Vidago

The main reason to visit **VIDAGO**, 17km south of Chaves, is to sample its historic **spa** and stroll round the delightful surrounding **park** and golf course. All of these, though open to the public, are within the 40 hectares of grounds belonging to the fantastic Art Nouveau *Vidago Palácio* hotel, an opulent pile built in 1910 with 365 windows and surrounded by three small spa stations. The whole place will be closed from 2007 to 2008 while the hotel is upgraded to five stars to include modern spa facilities and an expanded 18-hole **golf course**. When open, the ninety-minute walking trails round the park are a delight, while the golf course – originally designed by McEnzie Ross and the third oldest in Portugal – hopes to host the Portuguese Open. Otherwise Vidago is a pleasant enough place on a busy through road. Buses drop you by the summer **turismo** (irregular hours; ☎276 907 470) on the main road and from here it's only a short walk to the spa and hotels – follow the flurry of signs.

Top **accommodation** choice is of course the *Vidago Palace Hotel* (☎276 990 900, @www.vidagopalace.com; closed 2007–2008), complete with outdoor pool and a sumptuous ballroom. Otherwise, *Hotel Parque*, Avenida Teixeira de Sousa (☎276 906 157, @hotelparque.vidago@clix.pt; ❹), is a decent alternative, with tennis courts and a pool. The best of the less expensive options is the ageing *Pensão Primavera* at Avenida Conde de Caria 2 (☎276 907 230, @276 909 378; ❶), facing the *Vidago Palace*, with wooden-shuttered rooms and a charming garden with its own kiosk café.

There are plenty of decent restaurants on the main through road; *Resineiro* (☎276 907 312) at its northern end is good value, with fine grills and a light white house wine. With your own transport, superb food is to be had at *Souto Velho* (☎276 999 250), in the village of the same name 3km north of town on the Boticas road. There is no menu, but the old couple who run it will rustle up the day's special from organic, home-produced meat and vegetables at a decent price; phone ahead to book a table.

Montalegre and around

The historic frontier town of **MONTALEGRE** – 45km west of Chaves, and a 10km detour off the N103 – makes a useful overnight base for exploring the eastern stretches of the Peneda-Gerês park. The dramatic ruins of a fourteenth-century **Castelo** (open daily, free); which lies open to the elements, loom up suddenly, commanding the surrounding plains. Despite its relative isolation, there's a fair amount of modern development on the steep hillside below the medieval centre, though age-old traditions remain strong here. Ask in local restaurants to sample *Vinhos dos Mortos* – Wines of the Dead – made in the nearby settlements of the Serra do Barroso. They are so called because of the practice of maturing the wine in bottles buried underground. This originated in 1809 when villagers, keen to protect their wine stocks from the invading French hordes, hid their bottles, only to find that the contents tasted considerably better when they dug them up again. Curiosities like this make the town an atmospheric stopover, especially in winter when snow covers the mountains to the north.

It's also excellent **hiking** country around Montalegre. The local turismo (see below) provides free leaflets detailing the various marked circuits, best of which are a short way to the west in the Peneda-Gerês park (see below).

Practicalities

The **bus station** is at the far end of Rua General Humberto Delgado, and a five-minute walk west brings you to the main square, Praça do Município, and the **turismo** (Mon–Fri 9am–12.30pm & 2–5.30pm; June–Sept also Sat 10am–12.30pm & 2–5.30pm, Sun 10am–12.30pm & 2–4pm; ☎276 510 200). There's also a useful **Peneda-Gerês national park office** at Rua Reigoso 17 (Mon–Fri 9am–12.30pm & 2–5.30pm; ☎276 518 320); head downhill from Largo Pelourinho, near the entrance to the castle.

Montalegre has a decent range of **accommodation**. The best option is *Casa Zé Maria* on Rua Dr Victor Branco 10 (☎276 512 457. ❷), a beautifully restored stone house in the heart of the old town. Rooms come with shiny wooden floors, bare stone walls and bags of character. Another central option is the large *Albergaria do Castelo* near the castle on Rua Ferradores (☎276 511 376; ❸) with modern, boxy rooms, some with good views of the castle ruins. The best budget choice is the comfortable en-suite rooms at the *Restaurante Hospedaria Girasol* (☎276 512 715; no credit cards; ❶), on Rua da Portela, a leafy cul-de-sac a steep ten-minute walk from the centre off the Chaves road (turn right at the roundabout).

Restaurante O Castelo (☎276 511 237), up by the castle at Terreiro do Açougue, makes for a rustic **dining** experience, strangely pitched halfway between a Mexican *cantina* and a traditional Portuguese tavern – try the grilled trout or salmon. *Restaurant Terra Fria* (☎276 512 101) on the corner of Rua do Regioso and Rua Vitor Branco, downhill from Largo Pelourinho, is a swish choice, perennially popular with locals and offering hearty, moderately priced Portuguese dishes, including an unusual seafood *feijoada*. Meat-eaters are also in for a treat – the Barroso region is famed for its smoked meats (*fumeiros*) and ham (*presunto*). There's even a whole festival dedicated to the products, the annual **Feira do Fumeiro e Presunto**, which takes place in the fourth week of January.

Into the Parque Nacional da Peneda-Gerês

The easternmost edges of the Parque Nacional da Peneda-Gerês lie just 10km west of Montalegre, cut off from the main section in the Minho district (see p.430) by the Barragem de Paradela and the towering Serra do Gerês mountain range. Close to the Spanish border, **Tourem** and **Pitões de Júnias** are two of the remotest villages in Portugal, hidden in wild terrain that offers great walking possibilities. More accessible are the delightful agricultural villages of **Paredes do Rio**, Outeiro and Paradela, set amongst neatly cultivated vineyards, which also offer fine local hikes. To the south, on the main N103 that skirts the south of the park, **Venda Nova** offers watersports on the huge reservoir of the same name.

Pitões de Júnias and Tourém

PITÕES DE JÚNIAS, 25km northwest of Montalegre, is set in one of the wildest corners of Portugal, close to the Spanish border. This is lovely walking country, with a ruined monastery and waterfall nearby, and the jagged peaks (*pitões*) of Gerês tantalizingly close to the west. The monastery was founded in the ninth century, and the following century became part of the Cistercian Order; the Romanesque facade and most of the walls still stand. There's modern family-run **accommodation** at the *Casa do Preto* (T276 566 158; no credit cards; ②), which also houses one of Pitões' two excellent restaurants, the other being the *Pitões do Gerês*.

Beyond the turning to Pitões de Júnias, it is another 10km north to **TOURÉM** across a wild plateau full of heather and roaming cattle. Tourem itself sits in a neatly cultivated valley by a reservoir, part of the River Lima, with a little bridge connecting it with Spain on the other side. It's an idyllic if startlingly remote location for a very traditional village of old stone houses. Stick around and you'll tune into the pace of village life, the liveliest moment being when local sheep are herded through the streets at the end of the day.

An easy and attractive 2.5-kilometre **marked trail** starts by the tiny chapel of Senhora do Rosário on Travessa da Caçela, at the far end of town. It heads back through the village past a stone building housing a **communal stone oven**, still used by the whole community for baking. The trail then climbs to a viewpoint above Tourém, through woodland and towards the dam before returning to the village.

There are a couple of cafés and shops to cater to your needs. If you want to stay, *Casa das Braganças* on Rua da Braganças 8–10 (T276 579 138, Wwww.casadasbragancas.com; ②) offers simple **accommodation** in an old stone house.

Paredes do Rio to Paradela

PAREDES DO RIO, 18km west of Montalegre, is an attractive little village with *espigueiros* grain stores and a small stone church. It is notable for the excellent *Hospedaria Rocha* (T276 566 147; ①), on Rua das Almas. All rooms have bathrooms, but the restaurant is the main draw, cooking meat from its own farm. Main dishes cost around €8.50: try the duck, or *cabidela de frango* – chicken cooked with blood and rice. They can also arrange four- to six-hour **walking trips** to Pitões de Júnias or lend photocopies of maps with the route marked on. If you prefer self-catering, on the hill above the *hospedaria* is the rustic *Casa da Travessa* (T276 566 121; no credit cards; ④), a stone house with one bedroom and a living room; it can also arrange bike hire, horse-riding and fishing.

The small village of **OUTEIRO**, a charming cluster of old stone houses overlooking the waters of Barragem de Paradela, 3km west of Paredes, is home to a bizarre seventeenth-century twin-towered church with a heavily decorated facade. Accommodation is just above the village at the upmarket *Estalagem Bela Vista* (T276 560 120, Wwww.estalagembelavista.co.pt; ③) with sweeping views over the dam, good meals (mains around €12) in the attached restaurant, an outdoor pool plus a sauna and games room.

PARADELA, 4km south of Outeiro via the dam (note this road is sometimes closed by rock falls, in which case it is a 20km drive via Sezelhe) sprawls downhill, offering fine views over the Barragem de Paradela. Get off the main road into the backstreets to find its cobbled alleys lined with vines and rural charm. A cluster of cafés and hotels spread uphill. Best is the characterful *Pensão Pousadinha* (T276 566 165; no credit cards; ②), set in shaded gardens with views, 200 metres down the road to Cabril, which has the feel of an English B&B, with some lovely rooms. A further 100m downhill is the friendly *Hospedaria Restaurante Dom Dinis* (☎276 566 253; no credit cards; ❷), where all rooms have views, TVs, showers and heating. The homely restaurant (closed for lunch except at weekends, and all day Wed) has a fine terrace and serves Barrosã specialities like veal and *cozido* in winter.

From Paradela, you can head over the dam and take the wild road towards Cabril in the main section of the park, or head south to Venda Nova, some 18km southeast on the main N103.

Venda Nova

The village of **VENDA NOVA** has some lovely walks in the vicinity and bracing swimming in the Barragem da Venda Nova. If you have the funds, the classy *Estalagem do Morgado*, 4km to the west at Lugar de Padrões, is *the* place to stay, on a spit of land in the reservoir (☎253 659 906, ⓦwww.hotelmorgado .com; ❺). It has a swimming pool, tennis courts, its own water-sports marina and shaded gardens. There are also lakeside cottages that sleep four for €220 a night. Alternatively, the *Motel São Cristóvão* (☎253 659 387; ❸), in an ugly modern building at the corner of the reservoir, 1km beyond Venda Nova at the junction to Salto, is a reasonable option with tennis courts and a pool.

Travel details

You can check train timetables online at ⓦwww.cp.pt.

Trains

Mirandela to: Tua (2 daily; 1hr 35min); change here for connections to Porto; (3–4hr).
Vila Real to: Peso da Régua (3–6 daily; 55min); change here for connections to Porto (3–4hr).

Buses

Bragança to: Braga (2–6 daily; 4hr 15min–5hr); Chaves (1–2 daily; 2hr 10min); Coimbra (1–3 daily; 5hr); Lisbon (6–11 daily; 6hr 30min–7hr 30 min); Miranda do Douro (Mon–Fri 1–4 daily; 1hr 30min–2hr 15min); Mirandela (7–11 daily; 1hr); Mogadouro (Mon–Fri 1–2 daily; 1hr 30min); Porto (7–20 daily; 3hr 30min); Vila Nova de Foz Côa (1–3 daily; 1hr 45min); Vila Real (8–19 daily; 1hr 30min–2hr); Vinhais (2–3 daily; 35min).
Chaves to: Braga (1–6 daily; 3hr); Bragança (1–2 daily; 2hr 10min); Coimbra (2–5 daily; 2hr 40min); Fronteira (Mon–Fri 5 daily; 1hr); Lisbon (2 daily; 6hr 30min); Mirandela (Mon–Fri 3 daily; 2hr); Montalegre (Mon–Fri 4 daily, Sun 1 daily; 1hr 20min); Porto (7–12 daily; 3hr); Vidago (12 daily; 20min); Vila Real (2 daily; 1hr 10min).
Freixo de Espada à Cinta to: Miranda do Douro (Mon–Fri 1 daily; 2hr); Mogadouro (Mon–Fri 1 daily; 1hr); Torre de Moncorvo (Mon–Fri 3 daily; 1hr).

Miranda do Douro to: Bragança (Mon–Fri 2 daily; 1hr 30min–2hr 15min); Freixo de Espada à Cinta (Mon–Fri 1 daily; 2hr); Mirandela (2 daily; 2hr–2hr 30min); Mogadouro (3 daily; 50min); Torre de Moncorvo (2 daily 1hr 45min).
Mirandela to: Bragança (7–11 daily; 1hr); Chaves (Mon–Fri 3 daily; 2hr); Miranda (2 daily; 2hr–2hr 30min); Vila Flôr (4 daily; 40min); Vila Real (14–22 daily; 1hr 10min).
Mogadouro to: Bragança (Mon–Fri 1–2 daily; 1hr 30min); Freixo de Espada à Cinta (Mon–Fri 3 daily; 1hr 15min); Miranda do Douro (3 daily; 50min); Torre de Moncorvo (2 daily; 1hr); Vila Real (Mon–Fri 3 daily, Sat & Sun 2 daily; 2hr 30min).
Montalegre to: Braga (2–4 daily; 2hr 40min); Chaves (2 daily; 1hr 20min); Venda Nova (2 daily; 1 hr).
Torre de Moncorvo Freixo de Espada à Cinta (Mon–Fri 3 daily; 1hr); Miranda do Douro (2 daily; 1hr 45min); Mogadouro (2 daily; 1 hr); Pocinho – for trains running along the Douro line (see p.371) – (1 daily; 30min); Vila Real (1 daily; 2hr 5min); Vila Nova de Foz Côa (3 daily; 35–40min).
Vila Flôr to: Carrazeda de Ansiães (Mon–Fri & Sun 2 daily; 1hr); Mirandela (Mon–Fri 4 daily; 40min); Torre de Moncorvo (Mon–Fri 1–2 daily; 30min).
Vila Real to: Braga (3–8 daily; 2hr 40min); Bragança (18–11 daily; 1hr 30min–2hr); Chaves (2 daily; 1hr 10min); Coimbra (2–4 daily; 3hr); Guimarães (1–5 daily; 1hr 30min); Lisbon (6–9 daily; 5hr–5hr 30min); Mirandela (roughly hourly; 1hr); Porto (6–12 daily; 1hr 30min).

8

Alentejo

CHAPTER 8

Highlights

* **Templo Romano, Évora**
  Enjoy a sunset drink near
  Évora's most impressive
  Roman remain. See p.494

* **Cromeleque dos Almendres**
  The Iberian peninsula's largest Neolithic stone circle,
  near Évora, is a hugely atmospheric site. See p.501

* **Saturday market, Estremoz**
  A classic Portuguese market,
  selling everything from earthenware to cheese, all locally
  made. See p.502

* **Monsaraz** Stay the night in
  one of the traditional houses
  in this fortified hilltop village.
  See p.507

* **Serpa** Defensive walls entirely
  surround one of the region's
  most delightful small towns.
  See p.526

* **Mértola** The Alentejo's best-
  kept secret – a quiet riverside
  town of great charm and
  antiquity. See p.529

* **Miróbriga** Visit the Alentejo's
  most extensive Roman
  remains. See p.534

* **Vila Nova de Milfontes**
  The Alentejo coast is quite
  distinct from that of the
  Algarve, with the estuary
  town of Vila Nova its finest
  resort. See p.537

△ Monsaraz

Alentejo

The sparsely populated plains of the **Alentejo** are overwhelmingly agricultural, dominated by vast cork and olive plantations – the two crops that are well suited to the low rainfall, sweltering summer heat and poor soil. The region covers a huge area, almost a third of the whole country, stretching south from the Rio Tejo to the northern mountain ranges of the Algarve – the very name derives from the words *além do Tejo*, beyond the Tejo river. Much of the interior landscape, it has to be said, is tedious to travel through, with long journeys the norm between the sparse population centres. However, it's a region that repays exploration, offering unexpected surprises – from superbly sited castles and remote walled towns to Roman ruins and sweeping Atlantic beaches. The Alentejo is also home to hundreds of species of birds, from black storks to great bustards, all finely adapted to the mix of varied agriculture and marginal wilderness. It's still one of the poorest parts of Europe, much of the population deriving a living from the huge agricultural estates known as *latifúndios*, which have been in place since Roman times. Handed down from generation to generation, these estates remained largely feudal in character until the 1974 revolution, when much of the land was collectivized. However, the workers possessed neither the financial means nor the technical know-how to cope with a succession of poor harvests, and increasingly the original *latifúndio* owners have been clawing back their estates at depressed prices. Moreover, mechanization has done away with much casual farm labour – a move hastened by EU grants for modernization programmes and the introduction of new agricultural methods.

For most visitors, understandably, the region's major draws are its few towns and cities, with the outstanding attraction being **Évora**, whose Roman temple, medieval walls and cathedral have put it very much on the tourist map. Elsewhere in **Alto Alentejo** (Upper Alentejo), few towns see more than a handful of visitors a day. Yet there is much to see and enjoy: the spectacular fortifications of **Elvas**; the district capital of **Portalegre**; the hilltop villages of **Monsaraz** and **Marvão**; and the marble towns of **Estremoz** and **Vila Viçosa**, where even the humblest homes are made of fine stone from the local quarries. This region is also scattered with **prehistoric remains**, including over a dozen megalithic sites with dolmens, standing stones and stone circles.

South of Évora, in the plains of **Baixo Alentejo** (Lower Alentejo), the attractions lie further apart and without a car it's difficult to construct a quick sightseeing route – limited daily bus departures mean spending nights in places you might otherwise simply stop in for a couple of hours. However, there are some

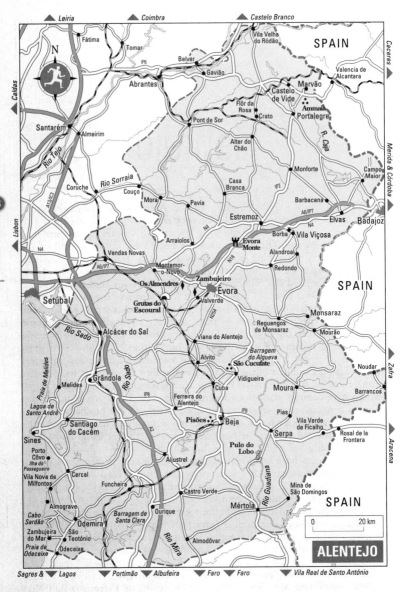

good overnight targets, including the main town of **Beja**, as well as nearby **Serpa**, **Moura** and **Mértola**, enjoyable historic towns all, with a wealth of good accommodation. To the west, the Alentejo **coastline** is almost as extensive as that of the Algarve, though it is considerably less developed. Only a few small resorts – prime among them **Vila Nova de Milfontes** – attract summer crowds, but the beaches are superb and you can reach them all by public transport.

Alto Alentejo

Évora provides the easiest starting point in Alentejo, with frequent buses and trains from Lisbon. Give yourself at least two days here if you can, and allow another day to see the surrounding sights, most notably the carpet town of **Arraiolos** and the extraordinary stone circle of **Os Almendres**. From Évora, you're within striking distance of the handsome market town of **Estremoz**, which sits at the heart of Alto Alentejo's "marble country". Here, as well as in neighbouring Borba and particularly in the regal retreat of **Vila Viçosa**, the most mundane streets and buildings are given the kind of luxurious finish you generally see only in the grandest churches and houses. South of Estremoz, the fortified village of **Monsaraz** rises from the plains, while to the east lie the superbly preserved walls of **Elvas**, close to the Spanish frontier. To the north, **Portalegre** is the capital of Alto Alentejo, though the better overnight stops are in its surroundings – either at the fine *pousada* near rural **Crato** or in the upland district north of Portalegre, whose tree-clad mountain ranges hide a series of gorgeous hilltop towns and villages. Among these, the best targets are **Castelo de Vide** and **Marvão**, the former with a historic Jewish quarter, the latter with views to rival those of Monsaraz.

Évora

ÉVORA is one of the most impressive and enjoyable cities in Portugal, full of memorable monuments. A Roman temple, Moorish alleys, a circuit of medieval walls, and a rather grand ensemble of sixteenth-century palaces and mansions are all in superb condition, spruced up by a long-term restoration programme and placed under UNESCO protection. Inevitably, they attract a great number of summer tourists but, despite the crowds, the city is far from spoiled. It's still a relatively small place – the population of 50,000 is only half its medieval number – and the streets contained within its walls are a pleasure to stroll, with none of the hustle associated with larger tourist centres. The university, re-established here in the 1970s, adds an independent side to city life, while Évora emphasizes its agricultural roots with a huge **open-air market** held on the second Tuesday of the month in the Rossio, just south of the city walls. However, Évora's big annual event is the **Feira de São João**, a folklore, handicraft, gastronomic and musical festival, whose origins date from pre-Christian times and which takes over the city during the last ten days of June.

Arrival, information and tours

Évora's **train station** is 1km southeast of the centre – if you walk up through the Rossio and follow Rua da República, straight ahead, you'll reach Praça do Giraldo, the city's main square, or it's a €4 taxi ride. The **bus station** (Terminal Rodoviaria) is five minutes' walk from the western city walls along the Lisbon road; it's a ten-minute walk in total to Praça Giraldo, or you can take one of the regular Linha Azul (blue) buses running into town. Drivers should park in one of the many (mostly free) **car parks** at the walls, as the city centre is confusing to drive around and has few parking places. There's always space on the massive Rossio (except on open-air market day). The **Linha Azul bus**

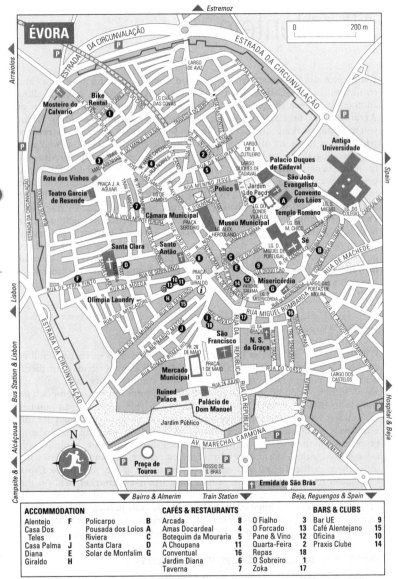

ÉVORA

Estremoz

0   200 m

Arraiolos ◀
Spain ▶
Lisbon ◀
Bus Station & Lisbon ◀
Alcáçovas ◀
Campsite & ◀
Hospital & Beja ▶
Bairro & Almerim ▼   Train Station ▼   Beja, Reguengos & Spain ▼

8 ALENTEJO | Évora

Mosteiro do Calvário

Bike Rental ❶

LARGO DE AVIZ

DA CIRCUNVALAÇÃO

ESTRADA DA CIRCUNVALAÇÃO

Antiga Universidade

Rota dos Vinhos

Teatro Garcia de Resende

Câmara Municipal

Palacio Duques de Cadaval

São João Evangelista

Jardim do Paço

Convento dos Lóios ❷

Templo Romano

Police

Museu Municipal

Sé

Santa Clara

Santo Antão

Misericórdia

Olímpia Laundry

São Francisco

N. S. da Graça

Mercado Municipal

Ruined Palace

Palácio de Dom Manuel

Jardim Público

AV. MARECHAL CARMONA

Praça de Touros

ROSSIO DE S. BRAS

Ermida de São Brás

ACCOMMODATION			CAFÉS & RESTAURANTS			BARS & CLUBS	
Alentejo	**F**		Arcada	**8**	O Fialho	**3**	Bar UE	**9**
Casa Dos Teles	**I**		Amas Docardeal	**4**	O Forcado	**13**	Café Alentejano	**15**
			Botequim da Mouraria	**5**	Pane & Vino	**12**	Oficina	**10**
Casa Palma	**J**		A Choupana	**11**	Quarta-Feira	**2**	Praxis Clube	**14**
Diana	**E**		Conventual	**16**	Repas	**18**		
Giraldo	**H**	Pousada dos Lóios	**A**	Jardim Diana	**6**	O Sobreiro	**1**		
Policarpo	**B**	Riviera	**C**	Taverna	**7**	Zoka	**17**		
		Santa Clara	**D**					
		Solar de Monfalim	**G**					

(Mon–Fri 8am–8pm, Sat 8am–2pm, every 12min; €0.50, €1 includes parking) acts as a park-and-ride service, circling all the car parks around the city walls and running into the historic centre.

The **turismo** is at Praça do Giraldo 73 (daily: April–Oct 9am–7pm; Nov–March 9am–6pm; ☎266 730 030, ⓦwww.cm-evora.pt/guiaturistico) and posts useful bus and train timetables, gives out a good city map and can help with accommodation. Guided two-hour **walking tours** of the city leave daily at 10am (book at the turismo or call ☏963 702 392, English spoken; €12), and the turismo also has information and leaflets about tours to local megaliths, vineyards and historic towns – for more on which, see "Listings". At the office of the **Rota dos Vinhos do Alentejo**, Praça Joaquim António d'Aguiar 20 (☏266 746 498, ⓦwww.vinhosdoalentejo.pt), a marketing organization for the Alentejan wine industry, there's a wine route booklet available detailing all the region's vineyards – you need to contact this office in advance to arrange vineyard visits, and they are very helpful and speak English.

Accommodation

Accommodation prices in Évora are higher than in the rest of the Alentejo, more or less comparable with Lisbon. That said, there's a more agreeable choice of places here than virtually anywhere else in the south, from simple rooms in family houses to ducal palaces. Outside the city, a large array of country houses and estates also offer accommodation, most within a short drive. In summer you're advised to book in advance to guarantee a bed anywhere, though the turismo may be able to help if you arrive without a reservation. There is a campsite reasonably close to the centre, but note that the city's youth hostel is currently closed for renovation.

In Evora

Residencial O Alentejo Rua Serpa Pinto 74 ☏266 702 903. Spacious en-suite rooms in a well-kept house, though if you want the a/c remote control you pay another €5. It's probably the best value in this category, though note there's a 1am curfew and breakfast is not included. No credit cards. ❷

Residencial Diana Rua Diogo Cão 2 ☏266 702 008, ⓕ266 743 101. Feeling its age a bit now, which means the rooms (either in the *residencial* or over the road in a dusty annexe) are adequate, not inspiring. You can save yourself €10 by taking a room with a shower cubicle but sharing a toilet. ❸

Pensão O Giraldo Rua dos Mercadores 27 ☏266 705 833. A real mix of rooms – some are far better than others – means it pays to have a good look around if possible. Prices have edged up and rooms with bath are a bit overpriced, but you'll still score a relative bargain if you're prepared to share facilities. No credit cards. ❸

Casa Palma Rua Bernardo Matos 29A ☏266 703 560. First-floor *quartos* in a scrupulously clean family house, featuring fine old pieces of furniture, polished floors and brass bedsteads. A couple of slightly cheaper rooms share a bathroom. No credit cards. ❷

Residencial Policarpo Rua Freiria de Baixo 16 ☏266 702 424, ⓦwww.pensaopolicarpo.com. The hands-down mid-range winner, this former ducal summer palace has sixteenth-century *azulejos*, a granite staircase and fine views from many rooms. Staff are helpful and English-speaking and, if the rooms

are fading a little, they still have bags of charm, while breakfast is eaten on the terrace. There's parking, but good luck trying to find the place by car. No credit cards. ❷, en suite ❸

Pousada dos Lóios Largo do Conde de Vila Flor ☏266 730 070, ⓦwww.pousadas.pt. One of the country's finest *pousadas*, housed in the former Convento dos Lóios. It really warrants its prices, as rooms are lovely – many with traditional furniture, including some dramatic four-poster beds – and there's a pool. Also elegant dining (from €45 a head; reservations required) in the cloisters, where fine Alentejan specialities (tomato soup with quails' eggs, squid with chickpeas, rabbit stew) are served. Winter rates (Nov–Feb) cut around €50 from the bill. ❼

Residencial Riviera Rua 5 de Outubro 49 ☏266 737 210, ⓦwww.riviera-evora.com. A makeover has transformed this central *residencial* into something rather special – 21 individually styled rooms with stripped wooden floors, Alentejan rugs, pretty bedspreads and little marble bathrooms. Some rooms are more attractive (and bigger) than others, but it's not a bad deal at all for the price. ❸, superior rooms ❹

Hotel Santa Clara Trav da Milheira 19 ☏266 704 141, ⓦwww.hotelsantaclara.pt. The rooms in this three-star *Best Western* are all en-suite and a/c. They are also quiet – the backstreet location, behind the convent, a real boon – and there's a little roof terrace. There's very limited reserved parking outside on Rua de Serpa Pinto. ❹

Albergaria Solar de Monfalim Largo da Misericórdia 1 ☎ 266 750 000, ⊛ www.monfalimtur.pt.
To step inside this restored summer ducal palace is
to enter an elegant, spacious and relaxed haven.
There are 25 handsome rooms, with pretty Alentejo
furniture and furnishings, while breakfast is taken
on the terrace, which has superb views. Parking
available (for a daily fee). ❹
Casa dos Teles Rua Romão Ramalho 27 ☎ 266
702 453. A nice family home with four reasonably
sized modern rooms available, sharing two clean
bathrooms. Breakfast not included. No credit
cards. ❷

Outside Évora
Quinta da Espada 4km north, Estrada da Arraiolos
☎ 266 734 549, ⊛ www.quintadaespada.com.
Seven country-style rooms in a *quinta* set in pretty
grounds, through which the Évora aqueduct runs.
There's a sun terrace and pool, and plenty of
space, and dinner is available. ❹

Estalagem Monte das Flores 5km southwest, on
the N380 (Alcáçovas road) ☎ 266 749 680. A rustic
farm offering lots of activities, including horse-
riding, as well as tennis courts, pool and a decent
restaurant. ❹
Monte da Serralheira 3km south, beyond Bairro
Almeirim ☎ 266 741 286, ⊛ www.monteserralheira
.com. Dutch-owned farm with six good-value apartments (sleeping two or four people) each with
terrace, sitting room, small kitchen and TV. It's very
peaceful, there's a nice communal pool, and you can
rent a bike or ride a horse. Breakfast also available
(€6). 2 people ❸, 4 people ❹

Campsite
Orbitur 2km southwest of town, N380 (Alcáçovas
road) ☎ 266 705 190, ⊛ www.orbitur.pt. Clean and
well equipped, with a restaurant and swimming
pool. Bus #5 from Pr do Giraldo runs nearby, or
take a taxi (around €3). Open all year.

The city

Évora was shaped by its Roman and Moorish occupations: the former is
commemorated by a temple, the latter by a characteristic tangle of alleys, rising
steeply among the whitewashed houses. Most of the city's other monuments,
however, date from the fourteenth to the sixteenth century, when Évora prospered
under the patronage of the ruling House of Avis. To them are owed the many
noble palaces scattered about the city, as is the Jesuit university and the wonderful
array of Manueline and Renaissance buildings. That the city's monuments have
survived intact is due, in large part, to Évora's decline after the Spanish usurpation
of the throne in 1580. Future Portuguese monarchs chose to live nearer Lisbon,
and the university was closed down. For the next four hundred years, Évora
drifted back into a rural existence as a provincial market centre.

Praça do Giraldo is the central hub, with the main historic kernel just to
the east. Within the surrounding city walls are several distinct old-town areas,
with another concentration of sights in the streets between the main square and
the public gardens. Meanwhile, to the north of the touristy centre you can
follow the course of the medieval **Aqueduto do Água Prata** (Silver Water
Aqueduct), into whose ever-rising arches a row of houses has been incorporated. Wherever you wander, nothing is more than a ten-minute walk from
Praça do Giraldo.

Templo Romano and Termas Romanas
The graceful **Templo Romano** stands at the very heart of the old city. Dating
from the second century AD, it is the best-preserved temple in Portugal, despite
its use as an execution-ground during the Inquisition and a slaughterhouse until
1870. The remains consist of a small platform supporting fourteen granite
columns with Corinthian capitals and a marble entablature. Its popular attribu-
tion to Diana is apparently fanciful; Jupiter is the more likely alternative. The
little garden in front of the temple has a kiosk-bar, while from the terrace you
can look north across the rooftops – and see just how small contemporary Évora
is, with the fields beginning only a few hundred metres away.

△ Templo Romano

The other significant Roman remain was uncovered beneath the nearby town hall, the **Câmara Municipal** (Mon–Fri 9am–5.30pm), where during office hours you can walk in to view the **Termas Romanas** (Roman baths), which date from a century earlier than the temple. These include an arched brick doorway, the entrance to an extraordinary room with a circular hot and steam bath that's 9m in diameter.

Convento dos Lóios and São João Evangelista

Directly opposite the temple, the magnificent fifteenth-century **Convento dos Lóios** is now a top-grade *pousada*. Hotel staff can be sniffy about allowing in non-residents (or non-diners) to look around, but those that are able to proceed beyond the doors encounter dual horseshoe arches, slender twisted columns and intricate carvings on the doorway to the chapterhouse. All are fine examples of the so-called Luso-Moorish style and have been attributed to Francisco de Arruda, architect of Évora's aqueduct and the Belém tower in Lisbon.

Adjoining the *pousada* is the former conventual church, dedicated to **São João Evangelista** (Tues–Sun 10am–12.30pm & 2–5pm; €3). This is still the private property of the Duques de Cadaval, who occupy a wing or two of their adjacent ancestral palace. You are ushered through the Gothic church doorway to see the extraordinary floor-to-ceiling *azulejos* within, the masterpiece of one António Oliveira Bernardes and created early in the eighteenth century. They show scenes from the life of São Lourenço Justiniano, founder of the Lóios order. Hidden among the pews two small trapdoors stand open to reveal both a Moorish cistern (the church and convent were built over an old castle) and a grisly ossuary containing the bones of the convent's monks. You can buy a combination ticket (€5) at the church if you also want to see the private art collection of the Cadaval dukes, housed in a few rooms of the **Palácio dos Duques de Cadaval**, but it's probably one to skip.

The Sé and around

Évora's cathedral, the **Sé** (daily 9am–12.30pm & 2–5pm; €1 or €1.50 including cloister, museum €3, combined ticket €3; entrance on Largo Miguel de

Portugal), was begun in 1186, about twenty years after the Reconquest of Évora from the Moors. The Romanesque solidity of its original battlemented towers and roofline contrasts sharply with the pointed Gothic arches of subsequent and less militaristic additions, such as the porch and central window. The interior is more straightforwardly Gothic, although the choir and high altar were remodelled in the eighteenth century by the German, Friedrich Ludwig, architect of the palace-monastery at Mafra. The cathedral museum (closed Mon) is stuffed with treasures and relics, the prize exhibits being a reliquary studded with 1426 stones and a carved statue of the Madonna, whose midriff opens out to display layered scenes from the Bible. You also shouldn't miss the marvellous Gothic cloister, or the terrace (closed Mon) above the west entrance where you can take an unusually close look at the towers.

Immediately adjacent to the Sé is the former archbishop's palace, now the **Museu de Évora**, unfortunately closed for renovations for the forseeable future – archeological excavations are holding up progress. Its important collection centres on fifteenth- and sixteenth-century Flemish and Portuguese paintings assembled from the city's churches and convents, reflecting the strong medieval trade links between the two countries. While the museum remains closed, representative selections of its art works are on display in the **Igreja de Santa Clara**, across town down Rua Serpa de Pinto (Tues–Sun 9.30am–12.30pm & 2.30-5.30pm; €1.50).

From the cathedral, a couple of other sights warrant a quick detour. In nearby Largo da Misericórdia, the **Igreja da Misericórdia** (Mon–Fri 9am–12.30pm & 2–5.30pm, Sat 9am–1pm; free) sports wooden Baroque bas-reliefs and fine *azulejos*, while at the end of the street in **Largo da Porta de Moura** there's a pretty, but well-worn, Reniassance marble fountain.

A quick stroll from here will take you to the **Antiga Universidade**, whose beautiful courtyard is entered from Rua Cardeal Rei. Founded in 1559 by Cardinal Henrique, the future "Cardinal King", the university was closed down by the Jesuit-hating Marquês de Pombal during the eighteenth century, but since reopening in the 1970s it is now one of the liveliest corners of the city. You are free to wander in and view the brazilwood ceiling, *azulejos* and double cloister of marble columns.

Igreja de São Francisco and around

Situated on the eastern side of Praça 1 de Maio, the **Igreja de São Francisco** contains perhaps the most memorable monument in Évora – the **Capela dos Ossos** (Chapel of Bones; Mon-Sat 9am–12.45pm & 2.30–5.45pm, Sun 10am–12.45pm & 2.30–5.45pm; €1). A timeless and gruesome memorial to the mortality of man, the walls and pillars of this chilling chamber are entirely constructed from the bones of more than 5000 monks. During the fifteenth and sixteenth centuries, there were 42 monastic cemeteries in town which took up much-needed space. The Franciscans' neat solution was to move all the remains to one compact, consecrated site. There's a grim humour in the ordered, artfully planned arrangement of skulls, tibias and vertebrae around the vaults, and in the rhyming inscription over the door which reads *Nós ossos que aqui estamos pelos vossos esperamos* (We bones here are waiting for your bones).

Praça 1 de Maio itself has been remodelled along with its **Mercado Municipal** (closed Mon), and several cafés and restaurants put out tables in the square. There are also farmers' and craft markets held here most weekends. A block away, off Rua da República, you might as well nip around the corner to see the exterior of the mid-sixteenth-century **Igreja Nossa Senhora da Graça**. At each of the corners of its Renaissance pediment, grotesque

Atlas-giants support two globes – the emblem of Dom Manuel and his burgeoning overseas empire.

Dom Manuel's palace stood just to the south, its reconstructed gallery – incorporating inventive horseshoe arches with strange serrated edges – now forming part of the **Jardim Público**, at the foot of Praça 1 de Maio. It was from here, historians believe, that Vasco da Gama received the commission that changed the direction of the Portuguese empire, as the explorer established the sea route to India. The resultant wealth found its expression in the flamboyant style of architecture known as Manueline – after the king – and an echo of this can be seen from the garden walls, which look out over the southern edge of the city. The **Ermida de São Brás**, visible just outside the city walls on the road to the train station, has been identified as an early work by Diogo de Boitaca, pioneer of the Manueline style. Its tubular, dunce-capped buttresses and crenellated roofline bear scant resemblance to his masterpieces at Lisbon and Setúbal, but they certainly foreshadow the style's uninhibited originality.

Eating, drinking and nightlife

Finding a place to eat is no problem, with a range of decent **restaurants** to suit most budgets located in the centre. Many are geared towards tourists, but you don't have to venture too far to find something a bit more down-to-earth. For the cheapest eats, good streets to look along are ruas Mercadores and Moeda, off Praça do Giraldo, and those around the market on Praça 1 de Maio. **Cafés** are widespread, too, though anywhere on or near Praça do Giraldo tends to hike its prices, as you might imagine. For picnic supplies, best place is the **municipal market** (Tues–Sun mornings) in Praça 1 de Maio.

Concerts and **cultural events** are advertised in the *Agenda Cultural* booklet, available from the turismo. When the students aren't around, Évora goes to bed pretty early, as if exhausted by the attentions of the tour groups, but a few **bars** can provide a bit of late-night drinking – keep an eye out for flyers for club nights. At *Café Alentejano*, Rua Raimundo 5, off Praça do Giraldo, there's **fado** on Thursday nights – you'll have to eat but the food isn't particularly expensive.

Cafés

Café Arcada Pr do Giraldo, at Rua João de Deus. The nicest perch in town, by the fountain at the top of the square, for perusing the comings and goings.

Pastelaria Conventual Rua Miguel Bombarda 56A. Excellent place to try Évora's *doces conventuais* (convent-made cakes and pastries). Opens for breakfast from 8am.

Quiosque Jardim Diana Largo do Conde Vila Flor. The outdoor kiosk by the temple is the finest place in the city for an over-the-yardarm beer, as the fading sun dapples the cathedral and temple columns. Given its location, it's amazingly low-priced. It closes by 8pm-ish though.

Gelateria Zoka Rua Miguel Bombarda 14. Lots of lovely ice cream – you can sit at tables in the pretty square outside.

Restaurants

Botequim da Mouraria Rua da Mouraria 16A ☎ 266 746 775. This tiny bar with counter-seating serves excellent regional food, mainly tapas-style dishes (scrambled eggs and wild asparagus, roast peppers, wild mushrooms in garlic) and a few market-fresh mains (say steak, or deep-fried squid with crispy potatoes). It's a place that really knows its food and drink, with a cheery owner who takes a real pride in the menu and wine list. Snack for €10 or so, or eat for €25–30 a head. Closed Sat night & Sun. Expensive.

A Choupana Rua dos Mercadores 16–20 ☎ 266 704 427. Close enough to the main square to attract tourists aplenty, but good enough to appeal to locals, too, who tend to eat at the counter rather than in the adjacent tiled dining room. Plenty of choice at middling prices and while you can eat very cheaply (dish of the day, at the counter), full meals soon add up (most mains €8–10). Closed Sun. Moderate.

O Fialho Trav das Mascarenhas 16 ☎ 266 703 079. Up a cobbled alley off Pr J. A. Aguiar, this is reckoned to be one of the best restaurants in

Portugal, and it boasts it's the "most traditional" in town. Appetizers are particularly good (spinach with prawns, stuffed crab), there's lamb, beef, game or fish to follow, and the wine list is excellent. Reservations advised. Closed Mon. Expensive.

O Forcardo Rua dos Mercadores 26 ☎ 266 702 566. A modestly priced old-town restaurant (mains €7–8) with reliable food, where the TV keeps you reassuring company. Closed Sun. Moderate.

Pane & Vino Patio do Salema 22, entrance on Rua Diogo Cão ☎ 266 749 960. Once the stables of a town house, now an amenable Italian restaurant. It's a popular local night out and, though hardly authentic, pizzas (€6–9) are filling, prices are reasonable and staff well used to tourists. Moderate.

Restaurante Repas Pr 1 de Maio 19 ☎ 266 708 540. The tables outside on the square are the big draw, opposite São Francisco church – and you can just sit down for a drink (the locals order snails as an appetizer) – but it's also a cheap place to eat a steak and chips or all the other usual standards. Inexpensive.

O Sobreiro Rua do Torres 8 ☎ 266 709 325. A bit off the beaten track, this rustic restaurant shouts its rural credentials – wood-panelling, hanging yokes, a milk pail on the a/c unit, the traditional TV in the corner. The food is good – a bargain at lunch, when a *meia-dose* will be big enough for most appetites, slightly pricier at night (mains €8–9). Closed Sun. Inexpensive.

Restaurante Taverna Trav. de Santa Marta 5 ☎ 266 700 747. Good little tavern for out-of-the-ordinary Alentejan dishes – lamb stewed with mint, *migas* with asparagus and pork, or spinach with fried pork. Dishes are all around €8–9 and, in the case of the daily changing *pratos do dia*, you can eat for €6, soup to coffee. Closed Mon. Moderate.

Taberna Tipica Quarta-Feira Rua do Inverno 16 ☎ 266 707 530. Moorish Quarter tavern with moderate prices for mostly meaty Alentejan classics – *borrego*, *bife*, *lombinhos*, *rojões*. Closed Sun. Moderate.

Bars and clubs

Amas do Cardeal Rua Amas do Cardeal 4A. Funky late-night bar, open from 10pm for a dance-crazy crowd.

BarUE Rua Diogo Cão 21. The official student union bar, tucked into a leafy courtyard near the cathedral, with a garden-terrace. The night starts here.

Oficina Rua da Moeda 27. Chilled-out cellar-style bar, open from 8 or 9pm – there's no guarantee you'll see people in black polo-neck sweaters saying "nice jazz" but it's a fair bet. Closed Sun & Mon.

Praxis Clube Rua de Valdevinos. This is it – the town's only central club, open Mon–Sat until the early hours.

Listings

Bike rental Silvano Manuel Cagado, Rua Cândido dos Reis 66 ☎ 266 703 434. Bikes from €15 a day.
Hospital Hospital do Espirito Santo, Largo Sr da Pobreza ☎ 266 740 100.
Internet Cyber Center, Rua dos Mercadores 42 (daily 9am–midnight).
Laundry Olímpica, Largo dos Mercadores 6 ☎ 266 705 293, closed Sat afternoon and Sun, does a lovely wash and iron, very cheaply.
Newspapers Foreign newspapers are sold at newsagents off Pr do Giraldo and along Rua Migeul Bombarda.

Police Police station (PSP) on Rua Francisco S Lusitano, near the Roman temple ☎ 266 702 022.
Post office Rua d'Olivença (Mon–Fri 9am–6pm, Sat 9am–noon).
Taxis You'll find them in Pr do Giraldo, or call ☎ 266 734 734.
Tours Incoming Alentejo ☎ 266 709 000 runs half-day minibus tours to the megaliths or to Monsaraz and local vineyards (€20). Other tour operators and options are posted in the turismo.

Around Évora

Évora's environs have some significant attractions, and it's worth extending your stay by a day or so to see them. Some, like the castles at **Évora Monte** or **Montemor-o-Novo**, perhaps just warrant a quick stop en route elsewhere, though the famed carpet town of **Arraiolos**, just to the north, is a popular day-trip from the city. The administrative district of Évora also contains over a dozen megalithic sites – dolmens (funerary chambers), menhirs (standing stones) and stone circles – which have their origins in a culture that flourished here before spreading north as far as Brittany and Denmark. These might seem a more specialized attraction on the face of it, but the stones of **Os Almendres**, in particular, west of the city, provide one of the country's most extraordinary sights. With your own car, you can easily combine a visit to Os Almendres with the Neolithic caves at **Escoural** and the dramatic dolmen of **Zambujeiro**.

Évora Monte

Twenty-nine kilometres northeast of Évora, along the N18 towards Estremoz, the castle at **ÉVORA MONTE** occupies a spectacular position, atop a steep mound high above the main road and modern village. It stands on fortifications going back to Roman times, and dates originally to 1306, though the current keep was constructed in the sixteenth century in Italian Renaissance style, with four robust round towers, and is adorned with a simple rope-like relief of Manueline stonework. It was here in 1834 that the regent Miguel was finally defeated and the convention signed that put Pedro IV on the Portuguese throne. Legend has it that the signing took so long that there was only stale bread left to eat, causing the invention of the well-known Portuguese dish *açorda* (a soup of bread, water, coriander, garlic and olive oil). Inside the **castle** (daily: June–Sept 10am–1pm & 2.30–6.30pm; Oct–May 10am–1pm & 2.30–5pm; €1.50) are three vaulted chambers, each displaying intricately carved granite capitals, though if you're going to pay for entrance it's really for the views obtained from the terrace.

The upper medieval village rings the castle mound and, with care, you can clamber around the walls and gate-towers, and then wander down the cobbled main street to the small church and cemetery. There's a **restaurant**, *A Convençao* (☏268 959 217; closed Mon), next to the castle, which has an outdoor terrace, and more cafés down by the modern settlement on the main road. The Estremoz bus from Évora can drop you off on the main road, but it's a long uphill hike to the castle – realistically, only drivers are going to make a halt here.

Arraiolos

ARRAIOLOS, 21km north of Évora, is famed for its superb **carpets** (*tapetes*), which have been handwoven here since the thirteenth century. Based on elaborate Persian imports, they have been much prized for centuries and adorn the interiors of any Portuguese manor or palace worth its salt – the most luxurious eighteenth-century creations hang on the walls of the Palácio de Queluz, near Lisbon. For carpet enthusiasts, Arraiolos is a dream – every second shop sells them, and you can spend €40 on a small square or €1500 or more on a fine example. The best ones are indeed expensive, but a lot less so than elsewhere.

Carpets aside, it's a very pretty small town, with a ruined hilltop castle, brightly whitewashed houses trimmed in lavender, and a sixteenth-century pillory in the paved central square, Praça Lima e Brito. Antique dye chambers, 500 years old, are preserved under glass in the square, and the **turismo** here (daily 9.30am–12.30pm & 2–6pm; ☏266 490 254, ⓦ www.cm-arraiolos.pt) can provide a map if you want to know where you're strolling and what you're looking at. A few **cafés** provide drinks and meals, while some visitors are tempted to stay longer at the lovely *Pousada Nossa Senhora da Assunção* (☏266 419 340, ⓦ www.pousadas.pt; ❼), whose contemporarily styled rooms have been inserted into a refashioned sixteenth-century convent a kilometre or so out of town on the Pavia road. There are two **buses** a day from Évora to Arraiolos, but the times are hopeless for a day trip.

Montemor-o-Novo

Thirty kilometres northwest of Évora along the N114 lies the sleepy white town of **MONTEMOR-O-NOVO**, birthplace of São João de Deus, patron saint of the sick. Its outskirts appear anything but appealing, but it's worth persevering to encounter a largely unvisited old town of cobbled streets and crumbling mansions, topped by a castle where Vasco da Gama finalized his plans for opening up the sea route to India. This was Montemor's heyday, in the fifteenth century – it's hard to resist the impression it's been all downhill since then. Climb up the steep street for the views and then wend your way back into the old town, where the main square sports a statue of São João de Deus carrying an injured beggar in need of care.

There are a couple of cafés and *tascas* in the old town, and more restaurants in the newer part of Montemor, lined along the main road through town. **Buses** drop you at the station on Avenida Gago Coutinho, with the **turismo** three minutes' walk away along the avenue and off to the left in Largo Calouste Gulbenkian (Mon–Sat 9.30am–1pm & 2.30–6pm; ☎266 898 103, ⓦwww .montemornovo.pt). There are two places to stay, a little way further down the avenue, but no earthly reason why you should. **Lunch** is another matter, either in the dining room of the *Residencial Monte Alentejano* (☎266 899 630) on the avenue – good but relatively pricey – or around the corner on Rua do Poço do Paço where *Restaurante 8 de Março* (closed Sun) is a simple diner with bargain *pratos do dia*.

Grutas do Escoural

Twelve kilometres south down the N2 from Montemor are the **Grutas do Escoural** (Tues 1.30–5.30pm, Wed–Fri 9am–noon & 1.30–5.30pm, Sat & Sun 9am–noon & 1.30–5pm; €2), a cave system discovered in 1963 and showing evidence of human habitation for the last 50,000 years. Early man would have used the caves as a mere shelter, but from around 30,000 years ago primitive rock art was being scratched out on the walls, and in Neolithic times (5000 BC) the caves were used as a burial place. A short tour (in patchy English) lights up the weird leathery interior of the caves and points out the very faint drawings. The caves are 2.5km east (signposted) of the small village of Santiago do Escoural, where a local museum has some photographs and finds from the site. There's also a café or two here.

For the Zambujeiro dolmen and stone circle of Os Almendres, you take the very minor country road from Santiago do Escoural east to São Brissos (6km) and Valverde (14km), in which case you'll pass the chapel at **São Brissos** (usually locked), built from the stones of another ancient dolmen.

Anta Grande do Zambujeiro

Brown archeological signposts at Valverde – 7km southwest of Évora, down the N380 (Alcáçovas road) – lead you through the university's agricultural faculty grounds to the **Anta Grande do Zambujeiro**, a huge burial chamber lying sheltered under a corrugated iron roof. The last 1km is along a dirt track which is usually fine for cars if it hasn't been raining, but you can always leave your vehicle and walk if you're unsure.

Zambujeiro is the largest dolmen in the country, comprising eight standing stones which lean inwards to form a chamber eight metres high, with a six-metre diameter. The capstone is missing and the chamber itself is fenced off for safety reasons, but the twelve-metre-long approach corridor is still largely intact. The moving of such enormous stones must have challenged the ingenuity of the Neolithic builders, and there's still a real sense of mystery here, the only sound that of chirruping crickets and the rustle of leaves in the ancient cork and olive trees.

Os Almendres

The Iberian peninsula's largest and most impressive stone circle lies just to the west of Évora, south of the small village of Guadalupe, 13km from the city. To get there directly from Évora, take the N114 towards Montemor/Lisbon and follow the signs from Guadalupe. If you're approaching from the south, from Escoural and Valverde, you need to turn left in Guadalupe, at the *Café Barreiros*.

You are directed out along a dirt road (largely flat and in good condition, fine for cars), reaching the **Menir dos Almendres** after 2km. This is a single, three-metre-high standing stone set in a quiet olive plantation. Despite its obvious Neolithic origins, the local legend has it that it is the tomb of an enchanted Moorish princess, who appears once a year on the eve of São João and can be seen combing her hair.

This is simply the taster, since another 2.5km along the dirt road there's a parking area beside the extraordinary **Cromeleque dos Almendres**, where no less than 92 stones are aligned in concentric enclosures for seventy metres down a dusty hillside. Placed here in several phases, between six and seven thousand years ago, they are thought to have been erected as some kind of astronomical observatory and site of fertility rituals – though no one really knows. However, what's immediately clear, even today, is the power of the site, the stones resembling frozen figures, standing impassively, gazing down across the surrounding cork plantation to Évora gleaming in the distance.

△ Os Almendres

Estremoz

ESTREMOZ, 46km northeast of Évora, is the largest and liveliest of the three so-called "marble towns" – nearby Borba and Vila Viçosa are the others. The area is so rich in marble that it replaces brick or concrete as a building material, and is used extensively in the most commonplace surroundings. This is immediately obvious in the marble streets, squares and fountains of Estremoz, a strategically sited walled market centre that in its heyday was ten times its current size (today's population is around fifteen thousand). On the hill within the star-shaped ramparts of the upper town stands the former palace of Dom Dinis, the king famous for his administrative, economic and military reforms. Meanwhile, below, on the Rossio, the vast main square of the lower town, the Saturday **market** still drives the local economy, a classic Alentejan event selling – among many other things – what are renowned as some of the best cheeses in Portugal, mainly made from ewe's and goat's milk. It starts and finishes early, so it pays to stay over on Friday night if you can. Otherwise, Estremoz's annual festival takes place in the Rossio over the first weekend in September, with bull-running, concerts, fireworks and roll-baking contests; while at the start of May it sees a cattle and handicraft fair, including displays of the earthenware pottery for which the town has been celebrated since the sixteenth century. All in all, Estremoz makes a great stopover – it's certainly the best base from which to explore the area, not least because of the number and quality of the pensions and restaurants that cater for the market crowds.

The town

Dom Dinis's palace is now a *pousada* (see "Hotels and Pensions" p.504), but you're free to wander in and look around. In particular, there's a splendid panoramic view from the thirteenth-century **Torre das Três Coroas** (Tower of the Three Crowns), so called because three kings took part in its construction, namely Afonso III, Sancho II and Dom Dinis. With its Islamic-style battlements and Gothic balconies, it bears a close resemblance to the great tower of Beja, its exact contemporary. From this part of town the castle of Évora Monte is clearly visible on the horizon, 15km to the southwest. Dom Dinis's queen, Isabel, devoted her life to the poor, giving away food and money with unseemly enthusiasm for a monarch. A famous episode saw her challenged by her husband to reveal what was beneath her skirt. The bread she had hidden there was miraculously turned into roses – as the modern statue of Isabel, in front of the tower, clearly shows.

Opposite the tower, in an old almshouse, is a small **Museu Municipal** (Tues–Sun 9am–12.15pm & 2–5.15pm; €1.50), with displays of Alentejan life and, particularly, Estremoz pottery. This is characterized by simple floral and leaf patterns, sometimes inlaid with marble chips; the most distinctive products are the porous water coolers known as *moringues*, globe-shaped jars with narrow bases, two short spouts and one handle. Although nowadays largely ornamental, the pottery used to play an important role in gypsy weddings: the procession would march into town, whereupon the bride made a sudden dash for freedom across the market place, hotly pursued by the groom. When the groom finally caught up with his bride, a fine Estremoz dish was thrown into the air. The couple were pronounced man and wife at the moment that the dish fell to the ground in pieces.

Down in the lower town, the **Rossio** – properly the Rossio Marquês de Pombal – is dominated on its southern side by the twin-towered marble facade

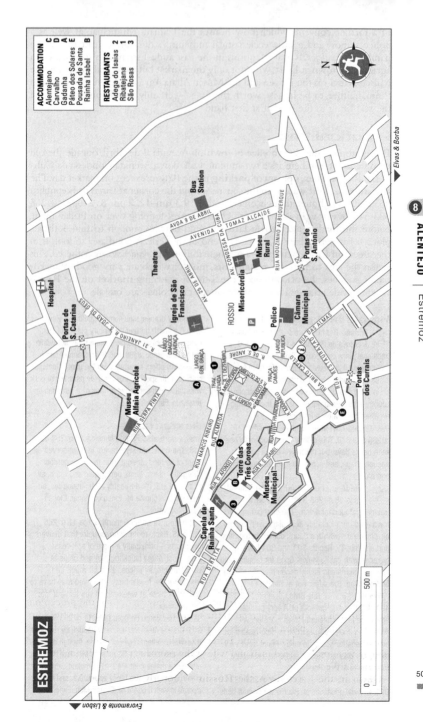

ESTREMOZ

ACCOMMODATION
Alentejano C
Carvalho D
Gadanha A
Páteo dos Solares E
Pousada de Santa
Rainha Isabel B

RESTAURANTS
Adega do Isaias 2
Ribatejana 1
São Rosas 3

N

Évoramonte & Lisbon ▲

Elvas & Borba ▲

Hospital

Portas de
S. Catarina

AV DA 9 DE ABRIL

AVENIDA

AV. CONDESSA DA CUBA

RUA TOMAZ ALCAIDE

RUA MOUZINHO ALBUQUERQUE

Bus
Station

Theatre

Museu
Rural

Portas de
S. António

Igreja de São
Francisco

Misericórdia

ROSSIO

P

Police

Câmara
Municipal

LARGO
DRAGÕES
FAIENÇA

LARGO
GEN GRAÇA

R. 31 JANEIRO

R. JOÃO DE DEUS

Museu
Alfaia Agricola

RUA SERPA PINTA

RUA NARCIS RIBEIRO

RUA D. ALMEIDA

TRAV. LENHDA

R. DE S. ANDRE

RUA S. AGOSTINHO

PRAÇA
CAMÕES

LARGO
REPÚBLICA

RUA DAS ALMAS

RUA DA REPÚBLICA

RUA BRITO CAPELO

RUA DOS CURRAIS

Portas
dos Currais

Capela da
Rainha Santa

Torre das
Três Coroas

Museu
Municipal

RUA R. S. ISABEL

RUA DA FRONTEIRA

RUA D. AFONSO III

RUA DIREITA

500 m

0

of a former convent, which now houses the Câmara Municipal, as well as a police station and a little ecclesiastical museum – duck in at least to see the handsome *azulejos*. Royal attentions in the past aside, Estremoz is still clearly an agricultural town at heart, with not only the market but two rural museums, the Museu Rural on the Rossio and the Museu Alfaia Agricola down Rua de Serpa Pinto, neither, to be honest, worth the time – certainly not if you've witnessed the real thing in the market at first hand.

Practicalities

Buses stop on the eastern edge of town on Avenida 9 de Abril, outside the old train station. From here, it's a two-minute walk down Avenida Condessa da Cuba to the Rossio. There's plenty of **parking** in the Rossio, except on market day. The **turismo** is a short walk from the square, around the corner at Largo da República 26 (unreliable hours, though officially daily 9.30am–12.30pm & 2–6pm; ☎268 333 541, ⓦ www.cm-estremoz.pt). Unless you're stopping over on Friday night, before the market, **accommodation** should be easy enough to find – there's plenty of it, particularly at the budget end of the scale. A good area to look is in the streets off Largo General Graça, where four or five *residencais* are gathered. This is also the area to hunt for **restaurants**, most of which are very good value. For picnic supplies, the place to go is the Saturday-morning **market** on the Rossio where a wide array of cheeses, spicy sausages and olives are on sale.

Hotels and pensions

Pensão-Restaurante Alentejano Rossio Marquês de Pombal 14 ☎268 337 300. A traditional place overlooking the Rossio whose dozen rooms come with flowery painted Alentejan furniture, brass beds, marble bathrooms, satellite TV and a/c. There's a bar and café downstairs and a proper old country-style restaurant on the first floor, serving excellent moderately priced food. ❷

Residencial Carvalho Largo da República 27 ☎268 339 370. This elderly tiled *residencial* has seen better days, but the rooms are in good enough shape, and some have private bathroom and a/c. ❷

Residencial O Gadanha Largo General Graça 56 ☎268 339 110, ⓦ www .residencialogadanha.com. The best bargain in town – an immaculately kept place with large air-con rooms with tile floors, decent bathrooms and satellite TV. Rooms 303 and 304 have terraces with castle views. Good for families, too, as most rooms can easily accommodate an extra bed or divan. Breakfast not available. ❷

Páteo dos Solares Rua Brito Capelo ☎268 338 400, ⓔ pateo.solares@clix.pt. A very genteel ambience in this beautiful town mansion, with a swimming pool, well-regarded terrace-restaurant, and gardens for guests to enjoy. Room rates vary (some are classed "luxo"), and drop a category from Nov to March. Parking. ❻

Pousada de Santa Rainha Isabel ☎268 332 075, ⓦ www.pousadas.pt. Rooms with grand beds

and heavy drapes, plus some scintillating views from the lavish thirteenth-century palace of Dom Dinis. The pool and gardens are a treat, set within the battlemented walls, and the restaurant (very expensive) offers a variation on the usual Alentejan cuisine, with specials like *arroz de pato*, leg of pork with garlic and coriander, or monkfish wrapped in *presunto*. Parking. ❼

Restaurants

Adega do Isaias Rua do Almeida 21 ☎268 322 318. The finest old-style tavern in town serves most of its food straight from the huge outdoor chargrill – steak, lamb, pork, squid and more, all at around €8. It's agreeably rustic inside too, an atmospheric choice for lunch or dinner. Closed Sun. Moderate.

A Ribatejana Largo General Graça 41 ☎268 323 656. Back-room *churrasqueira* that delivers the goods – principally a plate of spit-roast chicken or *leitão* (suckling pig) and chips at value-for-money prices. It's a bit rough and ready, but the food's tasty – and you may have to wait for a table at weekends if you leave it late. Inexpensive.

São Rosas Largo de Dom Dinis 11 ☎268 333 345. Once a medieval inn, now beautifully restored, it serves excellent regional cuisine, though at a price – there's a €21.50 *ementa turística*, but otherwise mains cost €12–18. Smoked salmon, or clams with garlic, are fancy appetizers, and the *açorda* is well thought of. Closed Mon. Expensive.

Vila Viçosa

Seventeen kilometres southeast of Estremoz, the ducal palace in the small town of **VILA VIÇOSA** was the last residence of the Portuguese monarchy. The dukes of Bragança were descended from the illegitimate offspring of João I of Avis and established their seat here in the fifteenth century. For the next two centuries they were on the edge of the Portuguese ruling circle but their claims to the throne were overridden in 1580 by Philip II of Spain. Sixty years later, while Spanish attention was diverted by a revolt in Catalunya, Portuguese resentment erupted and massive public pressure forced the reluctant João, eighth Duke of Bragança, to seize the throne; his descendants ruled Portugal until the foundation of the Republic in 1910. Despite a choice of sumptuous palaces throughout Portugal – Mafra, Sintra and Queluz are the most renowned – the Bragança kings retained a special affection for their residence at Vila Viçosa, a relatively ordinary country home, constructed in various stages during the sixteenth and seventeenth centuries. Dom Carlos spent his last night here before his assassination on the riverfront in Lisbon in 1908, and it was a favourite haven of his successor, Manuel II, the last king of Portugal.

It's a pretty town, dominated entirely by its palace – and by the coachloads of tourists who descend upon it for a quick visit before being whisked off again. Because of that, it's actually quite a pleasant place to spend the night, with an unhurried small-town atmosphere that survives the daily imposition of visitors. As at Estremoz and nearby Borba, marble is the dominant building material: the road from Borba, 5km away, is lined on either side with enormous marble quarries, and in town everything from the pavements to the toilets in the bus station are made of the local stone.

The town

The wide palace square, Terreiro do Paço, is backed by the **Paço Ducal** (April–Sept Tues 2.30–5.30pm, Wed–Fri 10am–1pm & 2.30–5.30pm, Sat, Sun & hols 9.30–1pm & 2.30–6pm; Oct–March Tues 2.30–5pm, Wed–Fri 10am–1pm & 2.30–5pm, Sat, Sun & hols 9.30–1pm & 2.30–5pm; €5), which can only be seen on an obligatory one-hour guided tour. This is usually in Portuguese and none too revealing – and you might well pass up on the opportunity to visit the armoury, treasury, coach museum and Chinese porcelain collection (separate charges for all) that also form part of the complex. Most of the palace dates from the sixteenth to the eighteenth centuries, and while the regal trappings of the more formal chambers are rather tedious, the private apartments and mementoes of Dom Carlos and his wife Marie-Amélia have a *Hello!* magazine fascination. Faded family photographs hang on the walls, changes of clothing are laid out, and the table is set for dinner: the whole scene seems to await the royals' return. In reality, Dom Duarte Pio, 24th Duke of Bragança and heir to the nonexistent throne, divides his time between his estate near Viseu, visiting Europe's minor royalty, opening festivals and lobbying for noble causes. The family was banned from entering Portugal until 1950, so when Dom Duarte was born (1945) it was actually in the Portuguese embassy in Berne, Switzerland, to ensure any possible future right of succession.

The old Bragança dukes were buried opposite the palace in marble tombs in the chapel of the **Mostéiro dos Agostinhos**, while the duchesses had their own mausoleum in the **Convento das Chagas**, just to the side of the palace – part of this is now the *pousada* (see below). Before you leave the square, walk a little way up the road out of town (to Borba), where on the left you can see the **Porta do Nós** – a Manueline stone gateway formed into the knot symbol of the Bragança family.

The modern town spreads back from the palace, but the original population of Vila Viçosa was based within the walls of the **old town**, whose castle was built by Dom Dinis at the end of the thirteenth century. Avenida dos Duques de Bragança runs from the palace square past the hilltop **Castelo** (same hours as the palace; €2.50), which was the seat of the Braganças before the construction of their palace. Its interior has been renovated beyond recognition, and houses an indifferent museum dedicated to hunting and archeology, but you don't need to pay to climb the outer castle walls for views over town. Behind lies the Braganças' old **Tapada Real** (Royal Hunting Ground), set within its own eighteen-kilometre circuit of walls. A few old houses and a sixteenth-century *pelourinho* are all that remain of the old town itself – if it's open, take a look at the eighteenth-century *azulejos* inside the church of **Nossa Senhora de Conceição**, the pick of Vila Viçosa's 22 churches.

Practicalities

The **bus station** is opposite the municipal market at the foot of Largo Dom João IV – cross the square and it's a two-hundred-metre walk up any of the streets ahead of you to the extraordinarily elongated Praça da República, which marks the centre of town. This slopes from São Bartolomeu church at the top to the castle mound at the bottom, with the palace another five-minute walk beyond, down either Rua Dr Couto Jardim or Rua Florbela Espança. The **turismo** is near the upper (church) end of Praça da República, in the town hall (daily 9am–7pm, restricted hours in winter; ☏268 881 101, ⓦwww.cm-vilavicosa.pt).

Budget **accommodation** can be hard to find. The *Hospedaria Dom Carlos* at Praça da República 25 (☏268 980 318; ❷), over the square from the turismo, is the most obvious choice, but rooms are pricier than they warrant. That just leaves a handful of places advertising *quartos* (❶), all found off the main square: the nicest are at Rua Dr Couto Jardim 7, around the corner from the *Dom Carlos*, but there are also some across the square, down past *Café Restauração*, at Rua Dr Gomes Jardim 19. At either, ring the bell and hope for the best. Other options in and around Vila Viçosa are far grander, starting with the *Pousada de Dom João IV*, by the palace on Terreiro do Paço (☏268 980 742, ⓦwww.pousadas.pt; ❼), which has kept intact its sixteenth-century convent cells and cloister. One kilometre out of town, there's the antique-laden seventeenth-century *Casa dos Peixinhos* (☏268 980 472; ❹), which has half-a-dozen elegant rooms available, each with a classy marble bathroom; follow the signs for Alandroal.

Cafés are found lining the lower half of Praça da República, but if you stay the night and don't eat at the *pousada*, seek out somewhere with a bit more local character. Any of the streets from the square on the turismo side lead down to Largo Dom João IV, where there are some cheap places around the market. At the top of this square, in the Mata Municipal (town gardens), *Os Cucos* (☏268 980 806) is a popular grill house with good fish and a changing list of daily specials – you'll eat well for around €15.

South to Monsaraz

The region south of Vila Viçosa is the Alentejo at its most rural, the roads running past scattered farming communities, protected at one time by the castles that still stand in places like Redondo, Alandroal and Terena. The ultimate target is the dramatic hilltop village of **Monsaraz**, close to the Rio Guadiana and the Spanish border, a 65-kilometre drive from Vila Viçosa, via the market and wine-growing town of **Reguengos de Monsaraz**. Monsaraz is one of those places that's worth the trip for the views from its walls alone, but it also has some excellent accommodation and a local circuit of megalithic stones and circles. Travelling by bus, you have to come from Évora down the N256 to Reguengos, where you change for Monsaraz.

Reguengos de Monsaraz

The small market town of **REGUENGOS DE MONSARAZ**, around 40km from either Évora or Estremoz, is known for its fine local wines, and you can visit the *adegas* outside town – though you'll need to contact the office of the *Rota dos Vinhos do Alentejo* in Évora (see p.493) to arrange this. There isn't, in fact, a great deal to delay you on your way to Monsaraz, though the **turismo** in the Câmara Municipal on Rua 1° de Maio (Mon–Fri 9am–12.30pm & 2–5.30pm, Sat & Sun 10am–12.30pm & 2–5.30pm; ☎266 508 040), just off the main Praça da Liberdade, might be able to persuade you otherwise. They can certainly give you a map of the megalithic monuments sited between São Pedro do Corval and Monsaraz (see below), and rather hopefully proffer an enormous map of Reguengos itself.

There are places to stay in town, but with Monsaraz only 17km away and regular **bus** services from Évora (as well as direct from Lisbon), plus weekday connections on to Monsaraz, it's unlikely you'd get stranded. *Pensão Gato* (☎266 502 353; ❷) on Praça da Liberdade would do the honours if it came to it, and if you're looking for lunch you can eat well at the **restaurant** here (closed Fri) or next door at the slightly pricier *Restaurant Central* (☎266 502 219; closed Tues).

The minor road on to Monsaraz passes through **São Pedro do Corval**, 5km to the east, known for its score or more ceramics workshops, many of which line the road. Some of these might tempt you to stop for a browse around – a few of the workshops and galleries also stock the hand-woven woollen scarves, rugs and blankets in which the region specializes.

Monsaraz

MONSARAZ – known locally as *Ninho das Águias* (Eagles' Nest) – is perched high above the border plains, a tiny village, fortified to the hilt and entirely contained within its walls. From its heights, the landscape of Alentejo takes on a magical quality, with absolutely nothing stirring amid a sensational panorama of neatly cultivated sun-baked fields, dotted with cork and olive trees. To the east, the Rio Guadiana, delineating the frontier with Spain, has swollen in great pools following the building of the Alqueva dam – it presents a waterlogged panorama, crossed by the snaking bridge to Mourão, at odds with the aridity to the west.

There's something peculiarly satisfying about such a small village, with a permanent population of just a few hundred people. It's entirely pedestrianized, and there are only two main streets, parallel to each other, Rua Direita and Rua de Santiago, with the **Igreja Matriz** at the heart of the village. Here in the square is the turismo (see below) and an unusual eighteenth-century **pillory** topped by a sphere of the universe. A few stepped alleys invite exploration, while *artesanato* shops hang colourful ceramics and blankets from their walls.

The **Torre das Feiticeiras** (Witches' Tower) looms from the castle at the far end of the village, part of a chain of frontier fortresses continued to the south and north. The views from the walls are magnificent. When the Moors were ejected in 1167 the village was handed over to the Knights Templar, and later to their successors, the Order of Christ. Their fort has now been converted, rather extraordinarily, into a bullring – the annual village festival, in the second week of September, features bullfights, concerts, dancing and spectacular fireworks.

Practicalities

If you time the service right from Évora to Reguengos, there are two or three **buses** a day on to Monsaraz, though there's no service at weekends. You're dropped right outside the gates. Drivers can't enter the village – use the spacious **car parks** outside the gates. The **turismo** in the square (daily 10am–1pm & 2–5.30pm; ☎266 557 136) can help with bus timetables, and has information on all the local accommodation possibilities – though by the time you reach the office, you've already passed most of them. There's not much else in Monsaraz, but amazingly there is an ATM.

Half a dozen houses along Rua Direita and its continuation advertise **rooms**, sheltered behind thick walls in traditional Alentejan homes – cool in summer, warm in winter – many with stone floors, painted furniture, terraces and balconies. Prices are broadly similar (€50 a room, breakfast included), though soften a little outside peak summer season and might be €10 less or so if you are on your own or forgo a room with a view – though the sensational panoramas are half the attraction. Good choices include our favourite, ⚡ *Casa Dom Nuno* (☎266 557 146), as well as *Casa Pinto* (☎266 557 388), *Casa Dona Antónia* (☎266 557 142, ⓦ www.casadantonia-monsaraz.com) and *Casa do Paço* (☎266 557 306), all within a few seconds' walk of the church. Booking in advance in summer is advisable – get someone to call for you if necessary, as not much English is spoken. There's also a rather fancy small **inn**, the *Estalagem de Monsaraz*, in Largo São Bartolomeu (☎266 557 112, ⓦ www.estalagemdemonsaraz.com; ❹, panoramic suite ❺), just outside the castle walls but still very close to the village, with a dozen lovely rooms, plus a garden and pool. Below the village, a few **rural tourism** places also provide comfortable accommodation, including *Monte Alerta* (☎266 550 150, ⓦ www.montealerta.pt; ❹), at Telheiro, a couple of kilometres from Monsaraz, which has eight pretty rooms, plus a pool, spa and fine gardens.

A couple of cafés and three or four **restaurants** feed the visitors. First among equals is the *Santiago* (☎266 557 188), by virtue of its outdoor terrace with the best views in Monsaraz – you can just have a drink here too. But *Casa do Forno* (☎266 557 190; closed Tues) and *O Alcaide* (☎266 557 168; closed Thurs) offer equally good food, all moderately priced (mains €8–10), with Alentejan meat specialities much to the fore – things like *borrego assado no forno* (roast lamb), pork and lamb chops, and *migas*.

Megaliths around Monsaraz

Four thousand years ago, the region around Monsaraz was an important centre of megalithic culture, and various dolmens (covered temples or tombs), menhirs (standing stones) and stone circles survive today. A good driving circuit from the village takes in four such examples, about an hour and a half's round trip.

Closest to Monsaraz, 1.5km below the village, is the most impressive, the **Cromeleque do Xerez**, a square "circle" of 49 granite stones with a towering four-metre-high central menhir, probably the site of Neolithic fertility rites. Leave Monsaraz and follow the signs at the first roundabout for the Convento do Orada, park by the low walls near the convent and it's a two-hundred-metre walk to a flat red-earth area where the stones have been re-erected – they were moved from their original site when the Alqueva dam was flooded. An archeological museum at the convent (closed Mon) may or may not be open – ring the bell and see.

Back at the roundabout, follow the sign for Telheiro and then take the Outeiro road (from Telheiro it's easiest to follow the "O Convivio" restaurant sign), where, just before Outeiro itself a blue "Menhir" sign indicates the **Menhir da Belhoa**, a five-metre-high standing stone visible from the road. It's 50m up a track, and on it you can trace zigzags, whorls and other faint symbolic markings. Next, follow the back-country road round through Outeiro, Barrada and Motrinos to the main Reguengos–Monsaraz road and turn right, towards Reguengos. Just before São Pedro do Corval, opposite the dusty football ground, there's roadside parking at the signpost for the **Rocha dos Namorados** (Lovers' Rock), a large, squat, naturally standing, mushroom-shaped stone used for thousands of years in fertility rites. If you can lob a rock on top of the stone, the stork is on its way (though you have to do it on Easter Monday to be sure).

Finally, turn back along the main road towards Monsaraz and, 7km from the fertility rock and just 1.5km from Telheiro, there's an "Anta" sign pointing 200m up a dirt road. This marks the **Antas do Olival da Pega**, a 4000-year-old dolmen nestled in an olive grove.

Elvas

The attractive hilltop town of **ELVAS**, 40km east of Estremoz, was long one of Portugal's mightiest frontier posts, a response to the Spanish stronghold of Badajoz, just 15km to the east across the Rio Guadiana. Its star-shaped walls and trio of forts are among the most complex and best-preserved military fortifications surviving in Europe. The town was originally re-taken from the Moors in 1230 and withstood periodic attacks from Spain throughout much of the following three centuries. It succumbed just once to Spanish conquest, when the garrison was betrayed by bribery in 1580, allowing Philip II to enter and, for a period during the following year, establish his court. Elvas subsequently made amends during the war over the succession of Philip IV to the Portuguese territories. In 1644, the garrison resisted a nine-day siege by Spanish troops, and in 1658, with its numbers reduced by an epidemic to a mere thousand, saw off a fifteen-thousand-strong Spanish army.

During this period, the fortifications underwent intensive rebuilding and expansion, and they were later pressed into service twice more: in 1801, when the town withstood another Spanish siege, and ten years later, during the Peninsular War, when the fort provided the base from which Wellington advanced to launch his bloody but successful assault on Badajoz. Perhaps out of tradition as much as anything, a military garrison is still stationed in the town.

These days it's much quieter in small-town Elvas. Spanish day-trippers pop over to see the steep cobbled streets and mansions, and sit in the restored central square ringed by cafés. The population is only around 25,000, all of whom appear to descend upon Elvas's **Monday market** – a vibrant, chaotic affair held just outside town behind the aqueduct. Otherwise, the town's big annual bash is its **Festa de São Mateus**, which lasts for six to eight days, starting on September 20, and encompasses a programme of agricultural, cultural and religious events, including the largest procession in southern Portugal.

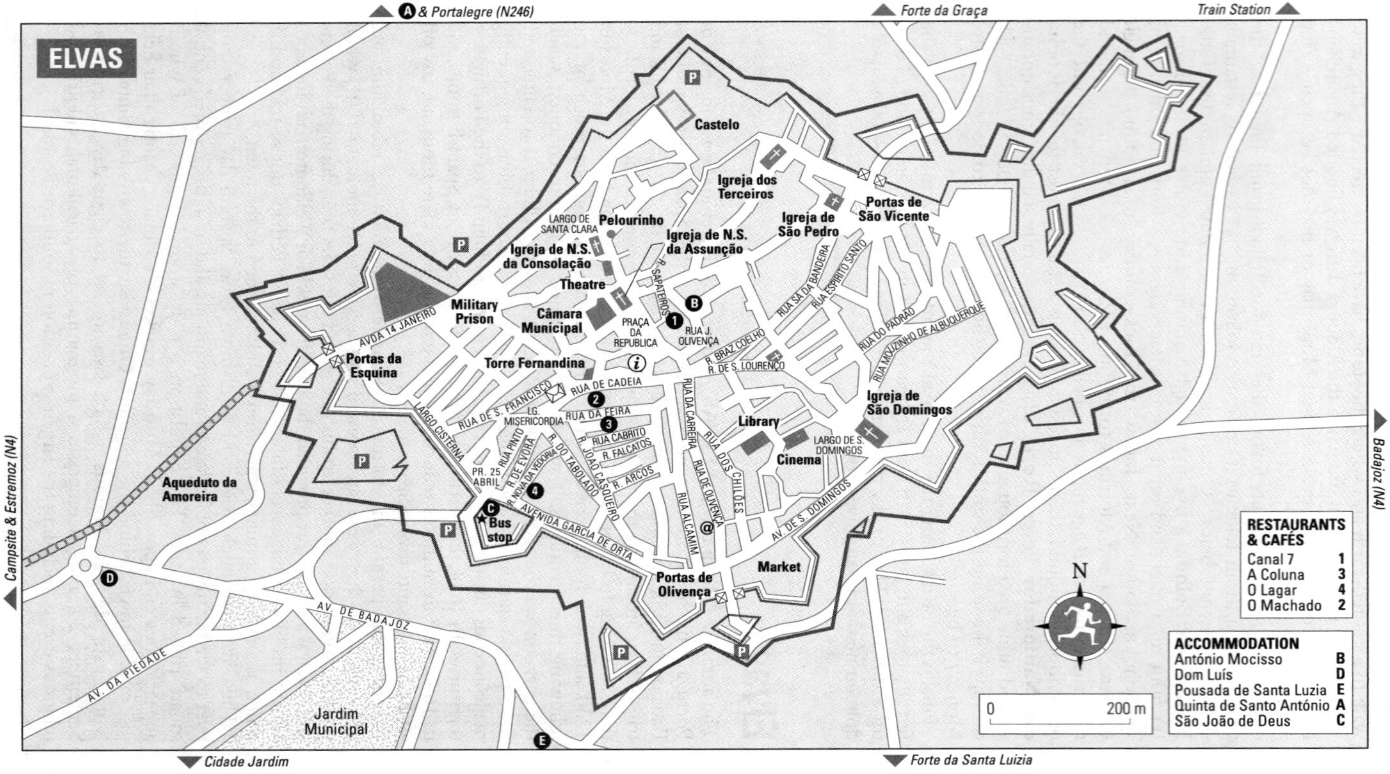
ELVAS
A & Portalegre (N246)
Forte da Graça
Train Station
Badajoz (N4)
Forte da Santa Luizia
Cidade Jardim
Campsite & Estremoz (N4)
Castelo
Igreja dos Terceiros
Portas de São Vicente
Igreja de São Pedro
Igreja de N.S. da Assunção
Pelourinho
LARGO DE SANTA CLARA
Igreja de N.S. da Consolação
Theatre
Câmara Municipal
Military Prison
PRAÇA DA REPUBLICA
R. SAPATEIROS
RUA J. OLIVENÇA
Portas da Esquina
AVDA 14 JANEIRO
Torre Fernandina
RUA DE CADEIA
RUA DE S. FRANCISCO
LG. MISERICORDIA
RUA DA FEIRA
RUA CABRITO
R. FALCATOS
R. ARCOS
R. JOÃO CASQUEIRO
R. DO TABOLADO
R. NOVA DA VEDORIA
R. DE EVORA
RUA PINTO
PR. 25 ABRIL
LARGO CISTERNA
Bus stop
AVENIDA GARCIA DE ORTA
RUA DA CARREIRA
RUA DE OLIVENÇA
RUA ALCAMIM
RUA DOS CHILÕES
R. BRAZ COELHO
R. DE S. LOURENÇO
RUA SA DA BANDEIRA
RUA ESPIRITO SANTO
RUA DO PADRÃO
RUA MOUZINHO DE ALBUQUERQUE
Igreja de São Domingos
Library
Cinema
LARGO DE S. DOMINGOS
AV. DE S. DOMINGOS
Market
Portas de Olivença
Aqueduto da Amoreira
AV. DE BADAJOZ
AV. DA PIEDADE
Jardim Municipal
N
0 200 m
RESTAURANTS & CAFÉS
Canal 7 1
A Coluna 3
O Lagar 4
O Machado 2
ACCOMMODATION
António Mocisso B
Dom Luís D
Pousada de Santa Luzia E
Quinta de Santo António A
São João de Deus C

Arrival and information

The walls make Elvas a pretty easy place to get your bearings. There's **parking** at various signposted points by the entrances to the old town, though you can also follow the "Castelo" signs up though town – the narrow streets are a bit hair-raising at times, but there's a pay car park under Praça da República and lots of free parking by the castle. **Buses** drop arrivals at the foot of town by the outer wall, at Praça 25 de Abril, where there's a hole-in-the-wall ticket kiosk. Shuttle buses (and taxis, €4) also run into the centre from the local **train station**, 4km down the Campo Maior road at Fontaínhas; the station is on the Lisbon–Badajoz line. It's easiest to cross to the Spanish city of **Badajoz**, 15km to the east, by train, as these run straight through – the local buses require a change of service at the Spanish border.

Praça da República is the main square in town, site of the **turismo** (Mon–Fri 9am–5.30/6pm, Sat & Sun 10am–12.30pm & 2–5.30pm; July & Aug stays open until 8pm; ☎268 622 236, ⊛www.cm-elvas.pt), which fails to be of much service – even the map it has to give away doesn't have a single street name marked on it. The main **post office** faces Largo da Misericordia (Mon–Fri 8.30am–6pm, Sat 9am–12.30pm), and there is **Internet** access at the *Livreiro de Elvas* bookshop, Rua de Olivença 4 (Mon–Fri 9.30am–1.30pm & 3.30–7pm, Sat 9.30am–1.30pm).

Accommodation

Good central **accommodation** is scarce, especially if you're on a budget. The bulk of the local hotels are situated on the outskirts, too far away to walk into town, but if you're really stuck you may have no choice – the N4, either towards Caia (Spain) or Varche (Estremoz) has three or four such places.

Hotels and pensions

Residencial António Mocisso Rua Aires Varela 15, off Rua de João d'Olivença ☎268 622 126 or 268 622 987. Popular "rooms" place in the jumble of streets (signposted) off the main square. They're modern and fairly compact, but you get a private bathroom, a/c and TV at the lowest rates in town. Your room could be in one of several buildings nearby. No credit cards. ❶

Hotel Dom Luís Av de Badajoz ☎268 622 756, ℗268 620 733. A few hundred metres below the walls, just outside town and right by the aqueduct. It's a modern hotel with decent rooms, restaurant, bar and terrace, but the main road location has little going for it – though you can walk up (steeply) into town in about 15min. Parking. ❸

Pousada de Santa Luzia Av de Badajoz ☎268 637 470, ⊛www.pousadas.pt. The country's first *pousada* (established 1942) is a modern building in typical Alentejan style. The location isn't great – outside the town walls, on the fume-filled N4 – though the rooms are comfortable, there's a pretty pool and it has a good restaurant serving a range of regional dishes (the renowned speciality dish is pig's trotters in coriander). Room prices are good, too – only Aug sees rates jump to €160. ❻

Quinta de Santo António Estrada de Barbacena, off the Portalegre road, 5km northwest ☎268 628 460, ⊛www.quintastoantonio .com. A relaxed, informal rural estate with rambling wooded gardens, courtyards, fountains and an excellent large swimming pool. Handsome rooms have parquet floors, marble window seats and antique beds, and there are some two- and three-bedroom apartments too, plus a moderately priced restaurant, which means it's popular with families. Rooms ❹, weekends & Aug ❺, apartments ❻

Hotel São João de Deus Largo João de Deus 1 ☎268 639 220, ⊛www.hotelsaojoaodeus.com. The finest address in the town centre is this beautifully restored four-star hotel right by the walls. Formerly a convent, it retains its grand sense of space and an interior of *azulejos* and warm colours. The rooms mix contemporary and traditional style, the restaurant occupies the old convent refectory, and there's a small terrace pool with city views. Parking. ❹

Campsite

Parque de Campismo da Piedade ☎268 628 997. The local campsite is on the outskirts of town on the N4 to Estremoz. Closed mid-Oct to April.

The town

Any exploration of Elvas has to start with its **fortifications**. The earliest stretches of the walls date from the thirteenth century, but most of what you see today is a result of the Wars of Succession with Spain in the seventeenth century. Under the direction of the great French military engineer, Vauban, the old circuit of walls was supplemented by extensive moats and star-shaped ramparts, their bastions jutting out at irregular but carefully judged intervals to maximize the effects of artillery crossfire. Echoes of these designs are to be seen at Estremoz and throughout Portugal. Further chains in the fortifications were provided by the Forte da Graça, a couple of kilometres north of Elvas, and the star-shaped Forte de Santa Luzia to the south of the town.

With its jagged and ungainly course, the **Aqueduto da Amoreira**, at the entrance to the town, looks at first like a bizarre extension of the fortifications. Despite its stark and awkward appearance, it is an imaginative and original feat of engineering: monstrous piles of masonry, distinctive cylindrical buttresses and up to five tiers of arches support a tiny water channel along its seven-kilometre course, until it is finally discharged at the fountain in Largo da Misericórdia. It was built between 1498 and 1622 to the Manueline designs of Francisco de Arruda.

Arruda was also responsible for the **Igreja de Nossa Senhora da Assunção** (daily except Tues 9.30am–12.30pm & 2.30–7pm; Oct–April closes at 5.30pm), dominating Praça da República, which was the cathedral until Elvas lost episcopal status in 1882. Alterations in the seventeenth and eighteenth centuries left a ragged hodge-podge of styles, but its original Manueline inspiration remains evident on the south portal and in the unusual conical dome above the belfry.

Behind the church lies **Largo de Santa Clara**, a tiny, cobbled square built on a slope around a splendid sixteenth-century **pelourinho**. Criminals were chained from the four metal hooks toward the top but, aside from the grisly technicalities, it's also a work of art, with a typically Manueline twisted column and rope-like decorations. Directly opposite stands the church of **Nossa Senhora da Consolação** (Tues–Sun 9.30am–12.30pm & 2.30–7pm; Oct–April closes at 5.30pm), a sixteenth-century Dominican foundation that was rededicated to Our Lady of Consolation in the nineteenth century. From the outside, it's nothing more than a plain wall with a mediocre Renaissance porch, but the interior reveals a sumptuous octagonal chapel, whose richly painted columns support a central cupola. The chapel was built on the site of a Knights Templar chapel – providing the inspiration for its octagonal design – and virtually all the surfaces are decorated with magnificent seventeenth-century *azulejos*. If it's not too busy, the custodian at the desk might lead you up the crumbling stairs to the roof for some sweeping views across the city to the two outlying forts.

Largo de Santa Clara tapers upwards to an archway flanked by fortified towers and surmounted by a loggia. Part of the city's original Moorish gate is visible through an iron gate beneath the arch, while the street beyond leads through a pretty little quarter of whitewashed mansions and cottages to the **Castelo** (daily 9am–5pm; €1.50). This was also constructed by the Moors on an old Roman fortified site, but strengthened by Dom Dinis and João II in the late fifteenth century. You can look inside at some of the restored rooms, but the best thing about the castle is its aspect – there are more magnificent views from the surrounding terraces.

Eating and drinking

Elvas has a fairly good selection of **restaurants**, covering all price ranges. Those in the old town tend to have the best atmosphere, though the most renowned local dining room is that in the out-of-town *pousada*. The best place to buy picnic supplies is the early morning food **market** held Monday to Saturday at the bottom of Rua dos Chilões, by the walls. Elvas is not a late-night kind of place, but the **cafés** overlooking Praça da República can be relied upon for daytime drinks and stay open until around midnight.

Canal 7 Rua dos Sapateiros 16 ☎ 268 623 593. A grill house that's the best of the budget places, always popular. Inexpensive.

A Coluna Rua do Cabrito 11 ☎ 268 623 728. Locally considered one of Elvas's best restaurants. Housed in restored old stables with *azulejo* tiles, it specializes in *bacalhau* dishes, but there's plenty more besides. Inexpensive.

O Lagar Rua Nova da Vedoria 7 ☎ 268 624 793. Blessedly a/c restaurant for good regional cuisine.

Clams, cuttlefish, *bacalhau*, *açordas* and *cataplanas* sit alongside the usual grills, and the *porco alentejana* is excellent. Closed Thurs. Moderate.

O Machado Rua de Cadeia ☎ 268 628 155. A bit pricier than usual but lunching locals think it's worth it – and it has the advantage of shaded streetside tables. The *pratos do dia* are always the best deal, highlighting a changing selection of regional dishes. Moderate.

Portalegre

PORTALEGRE is the capital, market centre and transport hub of Alto Alentejo. It is an attractive town of around 20,000 people, crouched at the foot of the Serra de São Mamede and endowed with a typically whitewashed old quarter that, for once, isn't dominated by a castle – only three towers and a few sections of wall remain of the thirteenth-century fortification. Instead, it's a bustling place of shops, cafés, churches, tiled houses and little squares, reached up the pedestrianized Rua 5 de Outubro, which runs steeply uphill from the main Rossio square.

Portalegre's industrial history looms large, most obviously at Robinson's cork factory, whose great twin chimneys greet you on the way into town. Originally established by an enterprising Yorkshireman, the factory has a quirky museum, the **Museu da Fábrica Robinson**, Rua 15 de Maio (Mon-Fri 9.30am-12.30pm & 2-5.30pm; free), where you'll learn something about cork harvesting and get to walk through mountains of cork bark and steam pipes. Everything in the gift shop is, naturally, made of cork. The town's major tapestry factory - last remnant of a great textile industry that peaked in the seventeenth and eighteenth centuries – was formerly housed in the Jesuit **Colégio de São Sebastião** on Rua Guilhermo Gomes Fernandes in the lower town. The building has been beautifully restored as the city council offices, but you can trace the history of local tapestry-making instead in the **Museu da Tapeçaria Guy Fino** (daily except Wed 9.30am–12.30pm & 2.30–6pm; €2), housed in a superbly adapted eighteenth-century mansion in Rua da Figueira, up in the old town. None of the background information is in English, but there are examples of old looms and a selection of the five thousand shades of wool used in the reproduction of centuries-old patterns. Exhibitions change, and there may be classical designs on show or contemporary recreations of paintings by Portuguese artists.

The wealth produced in the town's boom years, in particular from the silk workshops, has a further legacy in the collection of grand mercantile mansions and town houses. These are especially apparent as you walk along **Rua 19 de Junho** – the main thoroughfare at the top of the old town – which is lined by a spectacular concentration of late-Renaissance and Baroque mansions. Facing Praça do Municipio, and dominating the quarter, is the **Sé**, an austere building save for a flash of fancy in the pyramidal pinnacles of its towers. To one side of

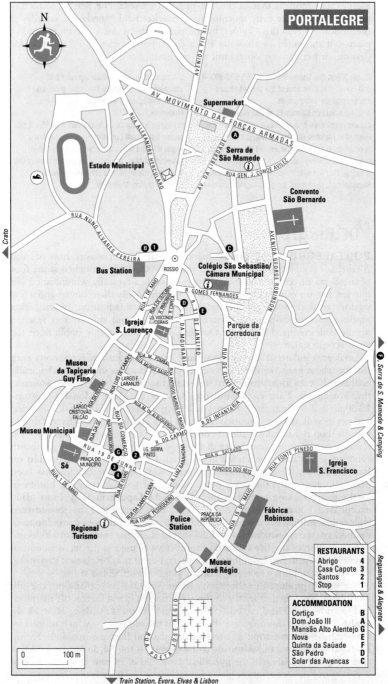

PORTALEGRE

N

Estado Municipal

AV. MOVIMENTO DAS FORÇAS ARMADAS

Supermarket

RUA ALEXANDRE HERCULANO

AVENIDA PIO XII

AV. DA LIBERDADE

A

Serra de
São Mamede (i)

RUA GEN. J. CONDE AVILEZ

Convento
São Bernardo

RUA NUNO ALVARES PEREIRA

B ❶

Bus Station

ROSSIO

C

Colégio São Sebastião/
Câmara Municipal

AVENIDA GEORGE ROBINSON

RUA GOMES FERNANDES

RUA 1 DE MAIO
RUA DE COUTINHO
R. PRIOR

D
R. 3
E
DE JANEIRO

Igreja
S. Lourenço

LG. VISCONDE
CIDRAIS

RUA DA MOURARIA

RUA DE OLIVENÇA

Parque da
Corredoura

Museu
da Tapiçaria
Guy Fino

RUA M. POMBAL
RUA MUROS BAIXOS
RUA LUIS DE CAMÕES

LARGO F.
LARANJO

RUA ANTIGOS MUROS DE BAIXO

RUA M. DE ALBUQUERQUE

RUA DE INFANTARIA

LARGO
CRISTOVÃO
FALCÃO

RUA DA SÉ
RUA WEBERLING
RUA DO COMÉRCIO

❷

RUA DO CARMO

RUA H. SALGADO

RUA FONTE PENEDO

Igreja
S. Francisco

Museu Municipal

RUA 19 DE JUNHO

LG. SERPA
PINTO

R. CANDIDO DOS REIS

Sé

PRAÇA DO
MUNICIPIO

❸
❹

RUA DE ELVAS

R. LUIZ BARAHONA

RUA 1 DE MAIO

RUA DA SANTA CLARA

RUA TORRE PESSEGUEIRO

PRAÇA DA
REPÚBLICA

RUA 15 DE MAIO

Fábrica
Robinson

Regional (i)
Turismo

Police
Station

Museu
José Régio

RUA J. POETA REGIO

RUA J. POETA REGIO

RESTAURANTS

Abrigo	4
Casa Capote	3
Santos	2
Stop	1

ACCOMMODATION

Cortiço	B
Dom João III	A
Mansão Alto Alentejo	G
Nova	E
Quinta da Saúade	F
São Pedro	D
Solar das Avencas	C

0   100 m

▶ Serra de S. Mamede & Camping

▶ Reguengos & Alegrete

this an eighteenth-century palace houses the **Museu Municipal** (closed for renovation at the time of writing), repository of some lovely ceramics and ivories as well as early Arraiolos carpets.

At the foot of the old town, all the main roads converge on the **Rossio**, the nineteenth-century square with a fountain that's at the heart of modern Portalegre. Beyond here the town **gardens** flank Avenida da Liberdade, the lower part featuring stepped polychromatic cobbled tiles and a renowned plane tree (*plátano*), planted in 1848, whose spreading branches are now so long they have to be supported by pillars.

Practicalities

The **bus station** is set just back from the Rossio on Rua Nuno Álvares Pereira. Shuttle buses to and from here (15min) meet **trains** at the Estação de Portalegre, 12km out of town to the south, on the Lisbon-Badajoz line. There's lots of **parking** by the gardens, near the Rossio, some of it free. The helpful **turismo** (Mon–Fri 10am–7pm, Sat & Sun 10am–1pm & 3–7pm; ☎245 307 445, ⓦwww.cm-portalegre.pt) is in the city council offices in the Colégio de São Sebastião on Rua Guilhermo Gomes Fernandes. There's also a regional tourist office, the **Região de Turismo de São Mamede**, Estrada de Santana 25 (Mon–Fri 9am–12.30pm & 2–5.30pm; ☎245 300 770, ⓦwww.rtsm.pt), up on the southern edge of town, while the head office for the **Parque Natural da Serra de São Mamede** is at Rua General Jorge Conde de Avilez 22 (Mon–Fri 9am–12.30pm & 2–5.30pm; ☎245 203 631), not far from the Rossio – the park spreads north and east of town and you can pick up useful pamphlets at the office on half-day waymarked walks.

Accommodation

There is only limited accommodation available in town, and it's advisable to book ahead to be sure of a bed. The well-equipped *Orbitur* **campsite** (☎245 331 736, ⓦwww.orbitur.pt; closed Nov–Feb) is at Quinta da Saúde, 3km into the hills.

O Cortiço Rua Dom Nuno Álvares Pereira 17 ☎245 202 176. The bar-restaurant opposite the bus station is usually full of good old boys, but persevere with the bar staff and you should be escorted around the corner, up Rua 1 de Maio, to an apartment building with smart, modern en-suite a/c rooms that are good-value for money. Back at the *Cortiço*, you can eat cheaply with the locals. No credit cards. ❶

Hotel Dom João III Av da Liberdade ☎245 330 192, ⓕ245 330 444. The town's only proper hotel, which means it's often busy. Reasonable rooms, three-star quality, many with balconies overlooking the gardens. ❸

Residencial Mansão Alto Alentejo Rua 19 de Junho 59 ☎245 202 290, ⓦwww .mansaoaltoalentejo.com.pt. Nicest choice up in the old town, with traditional Alentejan decor (including painted headboards) in twelve en-suite, a/c rooms. No credit cards. ❷

Pensão Nova Rua 31 de Janeiro 28–30 ☎245 331 212, ⓕ245 330 493. Friendly place with simple rooms, nicely turned out, with private bath and TV. The same management runs the nearby *Pensão São Pedro*, Rua da Mouraria 14, which offers more of the same at similar prices. No credit cards. ❷

Quinta da Saúde Estrada de São Mamede, 3km northeast of town ☎245 202 324, ⓦwww.rtsm.pt /quinta_saude. An attractive rural property with a great view over the surrounding hills, nice pool and a good restaurant. ❷

Solar das Avencas Parque Miguel Bombarda 11 ☎245 201 028, ⓦwww.rtsm.pt/solardasavencas. Five rooms in an antique-laden, eighteenth-century town mansion. It's a bit frumpy and old-fashioned, but the central location is good. ❸

Eating and drinking

There's no shortage of **cafés** and **restaurants**, mostly concentrated in the upper old town, particularly along and near Rua 19 de Junho. Three or four budget places are found near the bus station, close to the Rossio, fine if you're not too concerned about ambience. During the day the nicest place for a drink is the terrace-café at the top of the Avenida da Liberdade gardens. In the evening the action, such as it is, switches to the old town, where the *Café Central*, facing Largo Frederico Laranjo, and others in the same area, are open until late.

O Abrigo Rua de Elvas 74 ☎ 245 331 658. A favourite with local families, serving locally inspired Alentejan dishes, meat and fish. Closed Tues. Moderate.

Casa Capote Rua 19 de Junho 56 ☎ 245 201 748. Swing-door tavern on one side, typical local restaurant the other, where a full meal is likely to set you back under €10. Closes early at night sometimes, so get there before 8pm; closed Sun. Inexpensive.

Santos Largo Serpa Pinto 4 ☎ 245 203 066. Eat on the outdoor deck in a pretty square, or in the rustic dining room. The menu is

strong on *açorda* and *arroz* specials involving *mariscos* or *bacalhau*, but otherwise it's the usual grill menu in big servings, complemented by a decent regional wine list. The mention of *sobremasas* brings out a mini photo album of amateur shots of puds on tables. You'll eat for well under €15, all in. Closed Wed. Moderate.

Stop Rua Dom Nuno Álvares Pereira 11–15 ☎ 245 201 364. One of the better options just off the Rossio, serving typical Alentejan cuisine in pleasant surroundings; a slap-up meal will cost under €10. Closed Sat. Inexpensive.

Crato and around

CRATO – 21km west of Portalegre – is an ancient agricultural town that has clearly seen better days and larger populations. It's hardly an essential stop, though it is an interesting diversion, and has a terrific *pousada* just out of town to the north, set in the honey-stone convent of Flôr da Rosa. Horse enthusiasts will also want to make the thirteen-kilometre drive south of Crato to Alter do Chão, home of a prestigious *coudelaria* (stud farm).

In town, a trio of imposing, ornate churches and the elegant **Varanda do Grão Prior** in the pretty main Praça do Municipio attest, like Portalegre's monuments, to the textile boom years of the sixteenth century. The *varanda* is the most interesting of the structures – an arcaded granite balcony built for the outdoor celebration of Mass. Also worth a look is the town mansion around the corner, which houses a small **Museu Municipal** (theoretically open Tues–Sun 10am–12.30pm & 2–6pm) of Alto Alentejo handicrafts and domestic traditions. Well into the last century, alms were handed out to the local poor from a balcony-chapel upstairs.

Wind up through the streets to the town **castle**, once among the mightiest in the Alentejo, but today a pastoral ruin, overrun by farm animals, fig trees and oregano plants. There's no access, but from the cobbled square in front there is a splendid view across the countless rows of olive trees to the hills of Portalegre. On the way back into the centre you can marvel at the dominant colour scheme in town – white with mustard-yellow trim – that adorns every single house, mansion to cottage.

Buses run intermittently from Portalegre to Crato, while the **Estação de Crato**, south of town, gives access to the Lisbon–Badajoz train line. Realistically, though, Crato is a car-and-coffee stop – a kiosk in the town gardens, by the roundabout, does the honours. And if you've diverted out this way, you may as well then drive out west along the N363 towards Aldeia da Mata. After 7km you'll see the sign for the **Anta do Tapadão**, which is reckoned to be the best-preserved dolmen in Portugal. The leaning stones are visible atop a small rise in the middle of grazing land away to the left; access is along a farm track.

Flôr da Rosa

Two kilometres north of Crato lies the village of **FLÔR DA ROSA**, traditionally a centre for pottery. Off the main road, a dusty square lined with simple whitewashed cottages is overshadowed by the dour battlemented walls of the **Convento de Flôr da Rosa**, founded in the fourteenth century and much endowed over the next two hundred years. It was abandoned in 1897, due to leaking roofs and a decaying structure, and after extensive restoration (begun in 1940) the fortress monastery finally reopened in 1995 as the *Pousada de Flôr da Rosa* (T 245 997 210, W www.pousadas.pt; ❼). It's a magnificent building, marrying contemporary style with the convent buildings – there's a games room in the upper cloister and a lovely restaurant. Visitors are welcome to have a look around the main building, and trace the plan of the gardens, laid out in the insignia of the Order of Malta, in honour of the warlord **Nuno Álvares Pereira**, whose father founded the monastery. His tomb (dated 1382) is prominent in the narrow, soaring convent church.

There's a small **turismo** on the main road through Flôr da Rosa (Tues–Sun 10am–12.30pm & 2.30–5.30pm; T 245 997 341). Next door, *O Recanato* is a popular local **lunch** spot, with tables in the back dining room or on a covered outdoor terrace.

Alter do Chão

ALTER DO CHÃO, 13km to the south of Crato, is another town that did well from textiles, particularly during the sixteenth century, as indicated by its attractive Renaissance marble fountain and an array of handsome town houses. There is a castle, too, whose central tower can be climbed for an overview of the region, but the chief reason for a visit is the **Coudelaria de Alter-Real** stud farm, 3km out of town. It was founded in 1748 by Dom João V of the House of Bragança, and remained in the family until 1910 when the War Office took it over. Today, maintained by the Ministry of Agriculture, it is open for public visits (Tues–Fri 9.30am–5.30pm, Sat & Sun 10.30am–5pm; €3, Sat €5; T 245 610 060, W www.snc.pt/CA), though to see the horses in action it's best to arrive in the morning, between 10am and noon, when you can watch them filing in from the fields to feed, accompanied to the ringing of forty bells. Alter-Real horses have been sought after since the stud's foundation – one is depicted in the equestrian statue of Dom José in Lisbon's Praça do Comércio, for example – and they remain the favoured breed of the Portuguese mounted police and the Lisbon Riding School at Queluz. There's a small museum and restaurant-café at the estate, and also falconry, equestrian and coach-riding displays throughout the week – call for times or check the website.

Castelo de Vide

Twenty kilometers north of Portalegre, the small town of **CASTELO DE VIDE** covers the slopes around a fourteenth-century castle, its blindingly white cottages delineated in brilliant contrast to the greenery around. Mineral springs pepper the local hills and the town is full of public fountains and gardens, its cobbled streets and placid squares lined with well-watered pots of geraniums and two-metre-high sunflowers.

From the main road through town, half a dozen narrow parallel streets make a sharp climb up to the aptly named **Praça Alta** on the northern edge of town, from where there are sweeping views across the plain. The main road, meanwhile, peters out into a cobbled lane, descending past a tranquil Renaissance marble fountain to the twisting alleyways of the **Judairia** – the old Jewish quarter. A signpost points you up the precipitous Rua da Fonte, past cottages with Gothic doorways and windows, to the thirteenth-century **Sinagoga** (daily: June–Sept 8am–7pm, Oct–May 8am–5pm; free), the oldest surviving synagogue in Portugal. From the outside it doesn't look very different from the cottages – it's the corner building almost at the top of the street – and inside the plain room only the tabernacle survives. Keep on up Rua da Fonte for another 200m or so to the **Castelo** itself (daily: June–Sept 8am–7pm, Oct–May 8am–5pm; free), whose dour foursquare keep squats within the wider fortifications of the original medieval village.

Practicalities

Arriving by **bus** (direct from Portalegre and Lisbon, change at Portagem from Marvão) you'll be dropped right in the centre at the *pelourinho* by the town hall clocktower, on Rua Bartolomeu Álvares da Santa. A little shop, just across the road and around the corner on Rua 5 de Outubro, posts timetables in the window. The **turismo** (daily: June–Sept 9am–7pm; Oct–May 9am–5pm; ☎245 901 361, ⓦ www.cm-castelo-vide.pt) is just behind the town hall, in the middle of the large paved Praça Dom Pedro V, in the shadow of the Santa Maria church whose bulk dominates the lower town. There's ample free **parking** in clearly marked bays all around the main square and street.

Given its size, the town has a surprising amount of **accommodation**, much of it very central – there are three or four places alone by the town gardens, at the eastern end of Rua Bartolomeu Álvares da Santa. Good **restaurants** are thinner on the ground – our favourites are picked out below – but there's no shortage of **cafés** for drinks, cakes and snacks. You can sit outside those along Rua Bartolomeu Álvares da Santa and the parallel Rua de Olivença.

Hotels and pensions

Casa Amarela Pr Dom Pedro V 11 ☎245 905 878, ⓦwww.casaamarelath.com. Lovely yellow mansion, its carved stone windows overlooking the main square. Beautiful rooms with plenty of space, marble bathrooms, antiques and polished wood. Parking outside. There may be a short wait as the elderly *senhora* summons the *padron*, who arrives screeching to a halt in his car to show you in. ❺

Residencial Isabelinha Largo do Paço Novo ☎245 901 896, ⓦwww.rtsm.pt/pensao_isabelinha. Old-fashioned place virtually next door to *Melanie* with a slight smell of camphor, and plenty of knick-knackery and old furniture, but there are views onto the public gardens, and it's very clean. ❷

Casa Machado Rua Luis de Camões 33 ☎245 901 515. Three modern spotless rooms, and shared patio and kitchen, at the western (bottom) edge of town, 300m from Porta São João. No credit cards. ❶

Casa de Hóspedes Melanie Largo do Paço Novo 3 ☎245 901 632, ⓦwww.rtsm.pt/casa_melanie. Best value of the bunch at the western (town-centre) end of the public gardens is provided by this friendly, English-speaking place with five nice spacious rooms. No credit cards. ❷

Quinta do Pomarinho 4km west of town, N246 Portalegre road ☎245 901 202, ⓦwww.pomarinho.com. Pastoral, eco-friendly, Dutch-owned farmhouse – there are four rooms in the main house, accommodation in a smaller "round house" or camping under the cork and olive trees. Guests can use the kitchen, or there's breakfast (€5) or dinner available (€10) on request. You can help out around the farm, swim in the little lake or strike off on local walking trails. Free pick-ups available from Castelo de Vide. ❷

Albergaria El Rei Dom Miguel Rua Bartolomeu Álvares da Santa 45 ☎245 919 191, ⓦwww.rtsm.pt/albergaria_miguel. Seven elegant a/c rooms with polished floors and nice bathrooms, plus a baronial breakfast salon. ❸

Hotel Sol e Serra Estrada S. Vincente 73 ☎245 900 000, ⓦwww.grupofbarata.com. Just off the top of the gardens at the eastern end, it's a large three-star hotel with nicely turned out rooms with balconies over town and hills, plus pool, connections with the local golf course (10min drive away), bar and restaurant. Prices are very reasonable too. ➍

Restaurants

O Alentejano Largo Mártires da República ☎ 245 901 355. Simple budget meals, in a little restaurant at the top of a sloping square next to the town gardens. Closed Wed. Inexpensive.

Dom Pedro V Pr Dom Pedro V ☎ 245 901 236. A good place for quality regional dishes, with mains costing €8–10. Moderate.

Marino's Pr Dom Pedro V ☎ 245 901 408. Tucked away at the back of the main square, and specializing in Italian dishes (pastas, grilled veg and carpaccio) as well as regional food. You'll be able to eat well for €25. Closed Sun, & Mon lunch. Expensive.

Marvão

Beautiful as Castelo de Vide is, nearby **MARVÃO** surpasses it. The panoramas from its remote eyrie site are unrivalled and the atmosphere even quieter than a population of less than a thousand would suggest. No more than a handful of houses – each as scrupulously whitewashed as the rest – lies outside the seventeenth-century walls, which encircle a dramatically sited rocky outcrop high above the undulating *serra*. There was a Roman settlement on the plains below, later abandoned in the face of the Moorish advance in around 715, under whose rule the first fortifications were built – and named after Marvan, the Moorish Lord of Coimbra. Marvão fell to the Christians in 1166, and the castle was rebuilt by Dom Dinis around 1229 as another important link in the chain of outposts along the Spanish border.

The **castle** (always open; free) stands at the far end of the village, its walls blending into the slopes of the *serra*. It's dauntingly impenetrable, and was provided with a huge *cisterna*, just inside the main entrance, still full of water, designed to supply the entire village. Indeed, the castle was captured only once, in 1833, when the attackers entered through a secret gate. In the village, stepped and cobbled streets switchback along the contours, the terraces planted with impeccably kept gardens and the houses sporting granite windows and pitched red roofs. Just walking around is enjoyment enough, though there is a **Museu Municipal** (daily 9am–12.30pm & 2–5.30pm; €1), in the Igreja de Santa Maria, which has an interesting range of Roman remains and other local finds.

Some of the archeological exhibits come from the **Cidade Romana de Ammaia** (Tues–Fri 9am–1pm & 2–5pm, Sat & Sun 10am–1pm & 2–5pm; €2.50), around 7km south of the village on the Portalegre road; follow the signs for São Salvador de Aramenha from the Portagem junction. It's a beautiful site in a wooded hollow, Marvão high on its bluff in the distance. Sheep graze across the Roman remains, which include parts of the south gate, a bath complex, forum and temple, while a small museum occupies the kitchen and basement of an old Roman house.

Practicalities

Marvão is 12km from Castelo de Vide and 17km from Portalegre. There are buses from both places, though only a couple a day (Mon-Fri only) in each direction – and coming from Castelo de Vide, you may have to change at the road junction of Portagem. At Marvão, **buses** stop just outside the main village gate, the Portas de Rodão. You can park here as well, or drive further into the village, where there's more **parking** in the first square you come to. You can drive onwards and upwards, too, following signs for the turismo and castle, but it's narrow, cobbled and unnerving – you might want to park early and get your bearings first.

The village makes a superb night's stop, as several houses within the walls are rented out under a scheme organized by the **turismo**, in Largo de Santa Maria, very near the museum and castle (June–Sept Mon–Fri 9am–7pm, Sat & Sun 10am–12.30pm and 2–7pm; Oct–May daily 9am–12.30pm & 2–5.30pm; ☏245 993 886, ⓦwww.cm-marvao.pt). In some of these you can get just a room, while others are rented out as a unit; prices, consequently, are extremely varied. Otherwise, **accommodation** is pricier than in Castelo de Vide, but includes the characterful *Dom Dinis* on Rua Dr António Matos Magalhães (☏245 993 957, ⓦwww.casaddinis.pa-net.pt; ❸), on the corner across from the turismo – pay the extra €5 for room 15, with its own terrace with extensive views; or, two doors, down, *Casa do Arvore*, a gleaming private house flanking Largo de Camões (☏245 993 854; ❸), whose genteel rooms have wooden floors, carved pine beds and great views. Up a rung there's the *Albergaria El Rei Dom Manuel*, Largo do Terreiro (☏245 909 150, ⓦwww.turismarvao.pt; ❹) – in the first square through the gate – whose appealing rooms have more expansive views, tasteful decor and monogrammed towels. Top choice is the superb *Pousada de Santa Maria* at Rua 24 de Janeiro 7 (☏245 993 201, ⓦwww.pousadas.pt; breakfast included; ❻), converted from a couple of former village houses – not all the rooms have views, but those that do are blessed.

For budget **meals**, you can eat well at the *Varanda do Alentejo* (☏245 993 272), in the middle of the village in Praça do Pelourinho, and less well at *Casa do Povo* (☏245 993 160), just down Rua da Cima off the square – though the latter does have an outdoor terrace. The more upmarket choices are the restaurants at the *albergaria* (moderate) and the *pousada* (expensive), both good and with menus that venture from the standard. The occasional little **bar** and café tucks into quiet corners and old town houses: at *O Castelo* (marked "Café-Bar"), opposite *Dom Dinis*, you can snack on scrambled egg or smoked ham *petiscos*, and sit outside under the spreading trees.

Baixo Alentejo

There are two main routes south into the Baixo Alentejo. From Évora, the main highway runs down to **Beja**, 80km away, which is arguably the most interesting southern Alentejo town, and certainly the only one of any real size. If you're not in any hurry, you could always follow the minor roads instead and head for Beja via **Viana do Alentejo** and **Alvito**, both small towns of some charm. Beja sits at the heart of the Baixo Alentejo and from here there are easy routes to the old Moorish town of **Moura**, close to the **Alqueva** dam, and to the classic walled town of **Serpa**, while further south – en route to the western Algarve – riverside **Mértola** really demands a night of its own.

Approaching the Alentejo from Lisbon and Setúbal, however, the obvious route south loops around the Rio Sado estuary via the old port of **Alcácer do Sal** and runs on through the agricultural town of **Grândola**, 25km further south – the latter not worth a stop, though legendary in Portugal through the song *Grândola vila morena*, the broadcasting of which was the prearranged signal for the start of the 1974 revolution. From here, Beja is a straight run to the east, while motorway and highway speed south through interminable parched tracts of wheat fields towards the central Algarve. The highlight of this side of the Alentejo, though, is its long Atlantic coastline, which begins in earnest just to the west of **Santiago do Cacém**. Resorts like **Porto Covo**, **Vila Nova de Milfontes** and **Zambujeira do Mar** provide an attractive alternative to the summer crowds on the Algarve. Their only disadvantage – and the reason for a very patchy tourist development – is their exposure to the Atlantic winds, which at times create huge breakers and dangerous swimming conditions.

South from Évora

While it's temping to take the fast road to Beja and the south, there's an attractive detour to be made into deepest rural Alentejo, via the small historic towns of **Viana do Alentejo** and **Alvito** and the Roman ruins of **São Cucufate**. From Évora the first stop, Viana do Alentejo, is a simple twenty-minute drive down the ruler-straight N254. There's no public transport along this route – at least, none that makes any sense in terms of jumping off for a quick look around and heading swiftly on. You'll need a car.

Viana do Alentejo

VIANA DO ALENTEJO is a typically dozy southern Alentejan town – village really – which nonetheless preserves a highly decorative castle, full of Mudejar and Manueline features. The walls were built on a pentagonal plan by Dom Dinis in 1313, and the interior ensemble of buildings was expanded under Dom João II and Dom Manuel I in the late fifteenth century. To this latter period belong a sequence of elaborate battlements, with their witch's hat towers and pinnacles, and the beautiful parish church which has a superbly carved door, mottled with lichen. You can grab a quick coffee down the street from the castle in the Praça da República before moving on.

Alvito

ALVITO, 10km further south, has altogether more to delay you, being a small town of great charm with an abundance of Manueline features. It's dominated, as is the way, by its castle – now a *pousada* (see below) – but in the few streets between here, the parish church and the town hall clocktower is plenty of interest. The castle itself (built in 1494) is a curious Manueline-Mudejar hybrid, a style seen also in the much smaller Ermida de São Sebastião, on the edge of town, from where there are fine views across the cultivated plains below. In addition, many of the houses have carved sixteenth-century windows and door-frames, and if you seek out the town gardens, small market and typical *pelourinho* in the handsome main square, Praça da República, you've easily occupied an hour or two.

There's no need to stay longer though there's a feeling that the presence of the *Pousada do Castelo de Avito* (☎284 480 700, ⓦ www.pousadas.pt; ⓺) – and the money it brings in – has raised the town's game. Certainly, it's a pleasant night's stop and, if you can't run to **accommodation** at the *pousada*, then *Hospedaria A Varanda* (☎284 485 135, ⓦ http://avaranda-hospedaria.planeta-clix.pt; ⓷), right opposite the castle on Praça da República, has much the same outlook. Who could resist a drink in its "Lady Di" bar in any case? The **turismo** (Tues–Sun 9.30am–12.30pm & 3–7pm; ☎284 485 440) in Largo do

Relógio, behind the town hall, next to the market, can also point you in the direction of rural guest houses, like *Horta da Lameira* (☎284 475 286, ⓦwww .hortadalameira.com; ⊕), 7km northwest of town near Vila Nova da Baronia, which has pretty rooms and a pool. Dinner can be arranged here, and it's much better value if you stay more than one night.

São Cucufate

Heading east from Alvito to the Beja road, you'll pass the **Ruinas Romanas de São Cucufate** (Tues 2.30–5pm, Wed–Sun 9am–12.30pm & 2–5pm; €2.50), 19km from Alvito and around 1km before Vila de Frades. It's a peaceful, rural spot, shrouded in landscaped grounds of rosemary, thyme and lavender, where the history of three separate Roman villas is laid bare in a series of extensive excavations and reconstructions. The first villa was built here in the middle of the first century AD, but replaced by two successively grander constructions, with baths, grain stores, oil presses and servants' quarters. The third villa was abandoned in the fifth century and later reoccupied in medieval times as a monastery – the old wine cellar was eventually decorated with frescoes in the late sixteenth century, after which the whole complex was abandoned once more. There is a small exhibition detailing the site's history, but it's all in Portuguese – you'll need to buy the English-language leaflet to make much sense of the ruins, though they are atmospheric enough without explanation.

Beja

On the inland route through southern Alentejo, **BEJA** appears as a welcome oasis amid the sweltering, featureless wheat fields. Commanding a strategic position in the centre of the plains, it has long been an important and prosperous city. Founded by Julius Caesar in 48 BC it was named Pax Julia, in honour of the peace accord signed here between Rome and the Lusitanians, but later became Pax Augusta and then just Pax, from which it gradually corrupted to Paca, Baca, Baju, and finally Beja.

South of Évora, it's the only major town en route to the Algarve, but it's still hardly a teeming metropolis, with a population of only around 25,000. Once past the modern suburbs Beja reveals an unhurried old quarter with a cluster of churches, a beautiful convent and a thirteenth-century castle. You can take in the sights in the compact historic centre in half a day, though in summer the heat will slow you down – and it's not a bad night's stopover in any case, with plenty of good cafés and restaurants. Annual events and **festivals** include Ovibeja (March), a big agricultural and handicrafts fair, and the *feira* for São Lourenço and Santa Maria (second week of August).

The town

In Portugal Beja is best known for the love affair of a seventeenth-century nun who lived in the **Convento de Nossa Senhora da Conceição**, right in the centre of today's town. Sister Mariana Alcoforado is believed to have fallen in love with Count Chamilly, a French cavalry officer, and is credited with the notorious (in Portugal anyway) *Five Love Letters of a Portuguese Nun*, first published in Paris in 1669. The originals have never been discovered, and a scholarly debate has raged over the authenticity of the French "translation".

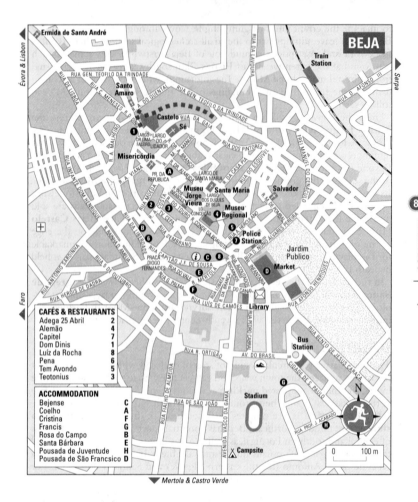

CAFÉS & RESTAURANTS

Adega 25 Abril	2
Alemão	4
Capitel	7
Dom Dinis	1
Luíz da Rocha	8
Pena	6
Tem Avondo	5
Teotonius	3

ACCOMMODATION

Bejense	C
Coelho	A
Cristina	F
Francis	G
Rosa do Campo	B
Santa Bárbara	E
Pousada de Juventude	H
Pousada de São Francsico	D

Mertola & Castro Verde

Nonetheless, English and Portuguese editions soon appeared and the letters became internationally famous as a classic of romantic literature.

The convent is an impressive building, first founded in the fifteenth century, and has an array of Manueline fripperies, including elaborate portals and a rhythmic roofline decorated with balustrades and pinnacles. Dissolved in 1834, the convent today houses the excellent **Museu Regional** (Tues–Sun 9.30am–12.30pm & 2–5.15pm; €2, free on Sun morning, also includes entry to Museu Visigótico), entered from Largo de Conceição. Rescued church art and Flemish paintings are gathered in the galleries of the cloister, but it's the convent's sumptuous tilework that first catches the eye - the walls of the cloisters and chapterhouse are completely covered with sixteenth- and seventeenth-century *azulejos*, and present one of the finest examples of this art form. The other highlight is a magnificent Rococo chapel, dripping with gold and embellished with flying cherubs. A stunning fifteenth-century Mujedar terracotta grille once linked the convent to the neighbouring palace – it's hopelessly romantic to imagine the errant nun first glimpsing her lover through the delicate tracery. Before you leave, nip upstairs to the small archeological section, where Roman stonework and inscriptions remind you of Beja's erstwhile importance. Much was found at the extensive site of **Pisões**, 7km southwest of town (signposted from Aljustrel road; closed Mon & Tues morning), where the walls of a Roman dam and the remains of rural buildings of the first to fourth century AD can still be seen.

From the convent, walk up Rua do Touro into the old town, passing the **Museu Jorge Vieira** (Tues–Sun 1.30-11pm; free) en route. It's a quirky private showcase for the work of Jorge Vieria, whose surreal terracotta sculptures – part feminine, part grotesque – show a clear Cubist lineage from Picasso and Braque. Beyond lies attractive **Praça da República** and its *pelourinho*, while at the head of the square is the distinctive mid-sixteenth-century **Igreja da Misericórdia**. Its huge projecting porch served originally as a meat market and the stonework is deliberately chiselled to give a coarse, rustic appearance; handicrafts are sold just inside the entrance. Beyond, past the unassuming cathedral, Beja's **Castelo** (Tues–Sun 10am–1pm & 2–6pm; tower €1.35) rises decoratively on the edge of the old quarter. It was built – yet again – by Dom Dinis and is remarkable for the playful battlements of its Torre de Menagem. A Saturday market is held beneath the walls.

In the shadow of the keep stands the small, whitewashed, Visigothic **Igreja de Santo Amaro** (Tues–Sun 9.30am–12.30pm & 2–5.15pm), today a small archeological museum. The building is a rare survival from pre-Moorish Portugal; the interior columns are carved with seventh-century geometric motifs.

Practicalities

The old quarter is a circular tangle of streets, enclosed within a ring road that has largely replaced the town walls. You can get fairly close to the historic centre by car, and there's signposted **parking** at various points (some of it metered, free at the weekends) – anywhere around the gardens or bus station is convenient.

The **bus station** is five minutes' walk southeast of the old centre, the **train station** five minutes northeast. Beja has good transport connections to the rest of central and southern Portugal, as well as a bus link to Seville. For Lisbon and the western Algarve, it's usually quickest to take the train, whereas for Évora, Vila Real de Santo António (for the eastern Algarve) and Santiago do Cacém (for the Alentejo coast) it's better by bus.

The **turismo**, right in the centre at Rua Capitão João Francisco de Sousa 25 (Mon–Sat: May–Sept 9am–7pm; Oct–April 10am–1pm & 2–6pm; ☎284 311 913, Ⓦwww.cm-beja.pt, Ⓦwww.rt-planiciedourada.pt), is fairly useless, though you'll get a nice big map with everything marked on it.

Accommodation

Most of the town's accommodation is to be found within a few blocks of the turismo, and in summer it's worth booking ahead to make sure of a room at the better places. Parking near your hotel is often difficult as many of the central streets and squares are pedestrianized.

Hotels and pensions

Residencial Bejense Rua do Capitão J.F. de Sousa 57 ☎284 311 570, ℮residencial-bejense@sapo.pt. The best budget choice in town, clad in inviting bougainvillea and nicely tiled within, has tasteful, high-ceilinged, a/c rooms with newish bathrooms and satellite TV. It's a welcoming place, which hangs its family photos on the landings and serves breakfast in a rustic first-floor dining room. ❷

Residencial Coelho Pr da República 15 ☎284 324 031. It's a lovely square, and some rooms have balconies opening directly onto it, but they have all seen lots of better days. Rooms are plain and worn, with functional shower-rooms, but would do for the night. No credit cards. ❷

Residencial Cristina Rua de Mértola 71 ☎284 323 035, ℱ284 329 874. Rooms (en-suite, a/c) are disappointingly austere, but spacious enough – and there are views from those on the fourth floor. If you like padded leather, the 1970s period piece of a bar will delight. Some parking available. ❸

Hotel Francis Pr Fernandes Lopes Graça ☎284 315 500, ⓦwww.hotel-francis.com. Flashy in the public areas – in the way of Portuguese three-stars – not quite so grand in the rooms, but still nice enough, with colour-coordinated rooms, many with big balconies. Best of all, there's a sauna, Turkish bath, gym and hot tub, plus parking (and a pizzeria) right outside. It's right by the bus station, down the steps off Rua da Conde São Paulo – driving, follow the signs. ❹

Pousada de São Francisco Largo Dom Nuno Álvares Pereira ☎284 313 580, ⓦwww.pousadas .pt. Imposing *pousada* inside a former convent, where rooms have been fashioned from the monastic cells. They are, of course, extremely comfortable, while the public areas make the same enterprising use of the space – an enclosed cloister with grand restaurant (high-quality Portuguese cuisine with Alentejan specialities; expensive), bar

and esplanade, attractive gardens and pool, and your very own Gothic chapel. Parking. ❻

Hospedaria Rosa do Campo Rua da Liberdade 12 ☎284 323 578. Eight decent rooms in a good location – furnishings are traditional, but facilities are up-to-date, including a/c, cable TV and private bathrooms. No credit cards. ❷

Residencial Santa Bárbara Rua de Mértola 56 ☎284 312 280, ℱ284 312 289. Trim, good-value, a/c rooms with tile floors and a small en-suite shower/toilet. Rooms either overlook the street, with pocket-sized balconies, or are internal, a bit quieter and with perhaps a glimpse of the sky. Check out the bar – a veritable wooden pulpit. ❷

Youth hostel

Pousada de Juventude Rua Prof Janeiro Acabado ☎284 325 458, ⓦwww.pousadasjuventude.pt. Close to the bus station, with a good-sized common room, Internet facilities and bike rental. Dorms are four-bedded, though there are also six en-suite doubles. Dorm beds €11, rooms ❶

Campsite

Parque de Campismo Av Vasco da Gama ☎284 311 911. The municipal site, on the south side of town, past the stadium. It's fairly pleasant and shaded, and adjoins the local swimming pool.

Eating and drinking

Beja has a lot of **cafés and restaurants**, all signposted at every turn by the enthusiastic city authorities. There are plenty of places where you can sit outside with a coffee, while meals tend to be of the traditional variety – big portions, meat-orientated. The nicest **bar** in town is *Esplanada O Capitel*, in the gardens opposite the Tribunal building.

Adega 25 Abril Rua da Moeda 23 ☎284 325 960. There's an Alentejan farmer somewhere missing his tools, because they're all on the walls in this huge rustic *adega*. The menu is big on grills – mostly Alentejan pork – and with a *meia dose* from €5 it's very affordable. Closed Mon. Inexpensive.

Churrasqueira O Alemão Largo dos Duques de Beja 11 ☎284 311 490. The queues out the door at lunch are for the takeaway side of the operation – slip though into the simple tiled dining room for cheap charcoal-grills, sausages to steaks, though the chicken is in a league of its own. Closed Sun. Inexpensive.

Restaurante Dom Dinis Rua Dom Dinis ☎284 325 937. An upmarket grill house where meat is very definitely the thing – the butcher's is right next door. It's pretty good, but with mains at €10 or 11 the bill soon mounts up. Closed Wed. Expensive.

Luíz da Rocha Rua do Capitão J.F. de Sousa 63 ☎284 323 179. In business for over a century, the café and tearoom downstairs is one of Beja's big meet-and-greet destinations, popular with elderly matrons, garrulous blokes and giggling teenagers. Pop in for a *bica* and a pastry or an evening brandy, or head upstairs for the cheap meals. July–Sept closed Sun. Inexpensive.

Restaurante Pena Praça de Diogo Fernandes de Beja 19A ☎284 323 714. Come here if you fancy fish – there's more choice than on most local menus (mackerel, sardines, bream, squid) and the prices aren't too high. Closed Sun & Sept. Moderate.

Tem Avondo Rua Alexandre Herculano 25A ☎284 328 956. A typical *casa de pasto* of the old school, where local families queue up to eat on Sun. It's easy to see why – the food is extremely good value (most things available in a *meia dose*

525

for €4.50–6), concentrating on the likes of *arroz de pato, porco alentejana*, or grilled meat and fish. Closed Sat. Inexpensive.
Restaurante Teotonius Rua do Touro 8 ⑦284 328 010. Grills a speciality in this old-town restaurant –

the *picanha a Teotonius* is the house-recipe veal steak, though there are also good lamb cutlets and game in season. There's a chatty owner and an outdoor patio. Closed Mon & 2 weeks in Aug. Moderate.

Listings

Bikes Available for free use around town – you'll see the racks – though you have to go through a tortuous form-filling procedure first (take ID) at the turismo, the Câmara Municipal or the Casa da Cultura.
Hospital Rua Dr António F.C. Lima ⑦284 310 200.

Internet At the Biblioteca Municipal, Rua Luís de Camões (Mon 2.30–10.30pm, Tues–Fri 10.30am–12.30pm & 2.30–10.30pm, Sat 3–7.30pm).
Police PSP, Largo Dom Nunes Álvares Pereira ⑦284 322 022.
Post office Largo dos Correios (Mon–Fri 8.30am–6.30pm).

Serpa

Thirty kilometres east of Beja, on the road to Spain, the small market town of **SERPA** offers the classic Alentejan attractions – a walled centre, a castle and narrow, whitewashed streets of handsome bougainvillea-clad houses and lush gardens. The town has at various times been occupied by Celts, Romans and Moors, and its highest point is inevitably dominated by the remnants of its **Castelo** (Tues–Sun 9am–12.30pm & 2–5.30pm; free), blown up by the Spanish, whose surviving battlements you can climb for spectacular vistas of the plain to the north and the hills to the south. There is a tiny archeological museum in the keep and, close by, the thirteenth-century church of **Santa Maria**, containing an altarpiece of intricate woodcarving, surrounded by seventeenth-century *azulejos*. From the castle battlements you can track the course of the well-preserved eleventh-century **aqueduct** (closed to the public), which retains an antique chain-pump at one end. You can see this best from just outside the walls, on Rua dos Arcos.

Beyond these few attractions, the delight of Serpa is in wandering its quiet, little-visited streets that spread for just a few hundred metres within the encircling walls. Centre of the settlement is the **Praça da República**, with its two palm trees and two cafés. Arched gates provide access to the more modern town beyond – equally sleepy – with a **Museu Etnográfico** (Tues–Sun 9am–12.30 & 2–5.30pm; free), flanking the eastern walls at Largo do Corro. This offers an interesting account of the changing economic activity of the area, with exhibits of agricultural implements, olive presses and local costumes. To the south, just a couple of minutes from the walls, the **public gardens** provide shade in the hottest part of the day.

Practicalities

Cars can enter the walled town for access only, but you wouldn't want to risk the narrow streets in any case. There's plenty of **parking** all around the walls, with nothing more than five minutes' walk from wherever you stop. The **bus station** is off Avenida de Paz in the modern southwest of town, ten minutes' walk from the old centre. The **Spanish border** is 37km to the east, at Vila Verde de Ficalho, and a daily bus service runs out this way. Serpa's **turismo** is within the walls, just off Praça da República at Largo Dom Jorge de Melo 2 (July & Aug daily 9.30am–1pm & 3.30–7pm; otherwise daily 9am–12.30pm & 2–5.30pm;

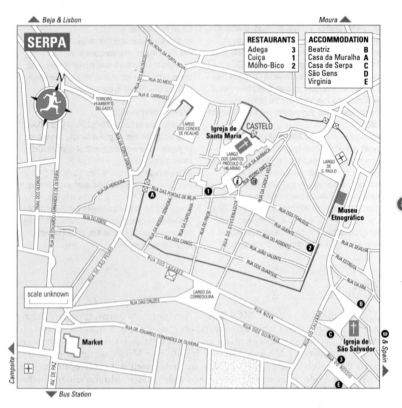

☎ 284 544 727, ⓦ www.cm-serpa.pt), and hands out a useful map of town. Close by on Rua Pedro Anes there's free **Internet access** at Espaço Internet (Mon-Fri 9.30am-7pm, Sat 11am-7pm, Sun 1-7pm).

There's plenty of **accommodation**, all (bar one) modest, though there's only one place sited within the walls. Otherwise, there's a concentration of pensions just beyond the southeast corner of the walls, near São Salvador church. There are also lots of inexpensive **restaurants**, particularly outside the walls around Largo São Salvador and Largo 25 de Abril. While you're here, try the delicious local cheese, *queijo de Serpa*. There are big celebrations each Easter (in honour of Nossa Senhora de Gaudulupe) and a full cultural calendar throughout the year. As well as the annual *feira* (closest weekend to 24 August), summer events include the **Noites na Noura** (first week July to first week Aug), when late-night concerts, cabaret, theatre productions and circus acts are held in an atmospheric courtyard by the aqueduct.

Pensions and hotels

Residencial Beatriz Largo do Salvador 10 ☎ 284 544 423, ⓦ www.residencialbeatriz.com. The smartest of the places near the church, all rooms here have private bath and a/c, and there's parking. Also three small apartments with kitchen, good for families. ❷, apartments ❷–❸

Casa da Muralha Rua das Portas de Beja 43 ☎ 284 543 150, ⓦ www.casadamuralha .com. The only place actually within the walls is right by the aqueduct gate, with lovely rooms opening on to a tree-shaded courtyard garden. There are two in the main house and two more in the garden, with painted Alentejan furniture, traditional cane ceilings and cool tile floors. Breakfast is a good spread of local cheese, ham, fruit, fresh bread, home-made preserve and coffee. Stay more than one night and the price drops €10. ❹

Casa de Serpa Largo do Salvador 28 ☎284 549 238, ⓦ www.casadeserpa.com. Pretty town house with patio and courtyard, offering half-a-dozen comfortable rooms and a warm welcome. No credit cards. ❸

Estalagem São Gens Alto de São Gens, 2km south, signposted from town ☎284 540 420, ⓦ www.estalagemsgens.com. Modern resort-style property, on a hill with wonderful views. All the rooms have balconies to take advantage of the position, and there's a pool and tennis court. ❹

Casa de Hóspedes Virginia Rua do Rossio 75, on Largo 25 Abril ☎284 549 145. Pretty basic, but pretty cheap too, and it's on an attractive square near some good restaurants. No credit cards. ❶

Campsite
Parque de Campismo Eira de São Pedro ☎284 544 290. Serpa's well-equipped municipal campsite is at the southwest corner of town, a bit closer in than the bus station, near the swimming pool complex (to which there's free access).

Restaurants
A Adega Rua do Rossio 76 ☎284 544 308. Does good pizzas (as well as grilled meats), and you can sit outside for a welcome breath of night air. Closed Thurs. Inexpensive.

O Cuiça Rua das Portas de Beja 18 ☎284 549 566. Locals come here for the good-value Alentejan dishes. Closed Sat night & Sun. Inexpensive.

Adega Mólho-Bico Rua Quente 1 ☎284 549 264. The weekend family favourite – a rustic grill house with a wide-ranging menu, fish as well as meat. Closed Wed. Moderate.

Moura

The thermal spa town of **MOURA**, 29km north of Serpa, springs another Alentejan surprise – highly agricultural on the outskirts, but in the centre an opulent place full of grand mansions and pretty squares. It's also the closest town to the controversial Alqueva dam (see p.530). The Moors occupied the town from the eighth century until 1232 – an Arabic well still survives in the old town – and Moura is named after a Moorish maiden, Moura Saluquia, who ostensibly threw herself from the castle tower in despair when Christians murdered her betrothed and overran the town.

Be that as it may, it was the discovery of thermal springs that prompted Moura's eventual prosperity. These are located beside the pretty public gardens, the **Jardim Doutor Santiago**, and are still in use (Mon–Sat 10am–5pm) – a euro gets you a brief soak in a marble bath. Just outside the gardens stands the sixteenth-century Manueline **Igreja de São João Baptista**, with a typically exuberant sculpted doorway and unusual (for Portugal) interior seventeenth-century Sevillian *azulejos*.

Behind the gardens rises the **Castelo**, built by Dom Dinis over a Moorish citadel and largely destroyed by the Spanish Duke of Osuna in 1701. One Moorish tower survives, plus a few sections of wall and a forlorn clocktower topped by a stork's nest, but the castle grounds have been attractively landscaped and form the background for the summer "enchanted nights" of music, dance and other events held here. From the green lawns and slate terraces within the walls are expansive views across the surrounding land – a telescope is trained on the Alqueva dam wall, clearly visible 12km to the north.

The **Moorish quarter** is just to the west of the castle, off the elongated main square, Praça Sacadura Cabral. Once a teeming hive of alleys, it's now a quiet residential neighbourhood, whose few narrow cobbled streets only spring to life once the heat of the day diminishes and people congregate to chat or share a drink. The surviving Moorish-era well – signposted "Poço Arabe" – forms part of a small collection of Arabic artefacts in the **Núcleo Árabe**, Rua da Mouraria 11 (Tues–Sun 9.30am–12.30pm & 2.30–5.30pm; free). This is an outpost of

Moura's municipal museum, whose main building is at Rua da Romeira 19, behind the Igreja de São João Baptista. There's not much to grip you here, though you might want to stroll up to the museum's other outpost, the **Lagar de Varas** (Tues–Sun 9.30am–12.30pm & 2.30–5.30pm; free), at Rua São João de Deus 20, just around the corner from the *Hotel de Moura*. This is the old municipal olive-oil plant, a beautifully cool, dark building featuring the restored wooden presses, vats, storage areas and various utensils plus a small exhibition about the production of olive oil.

Practicalities

Fairly regular buses run from Beja to Moura, via Serpa, and also once daily from Lisbon via Évora. If you're not dropped at Praça Sacadura Cabral, by the castle, then you'll end up at the **bus station**, outside the old train station, at the top end of Moura. You can see the castle tower from here, and follow your nose into town, unless you want the **turismo** first (Mon–Fri 9am–1pm & 2–5pm, Sat & Sun 10am–1pm & 2.30–5.30pm; ☎285 251 375, ⓦ www.cm-moura.pt), in which case turn left at the top of the gardens and then first right – it's in a little yellow building further down the avenue, on your left. Keep straight on down from here for the old town and castle.

Accommodation is easy to find, unless you coincide with the two big annual fairs, in May and September (both second weekend). Best value is *Residencial Alentejana*, Largo José Maria dos Santos (☎285 250 080, ⓦ www .residencialalentejana.com.pt; ❷), a block down from the bus station – on the right-hand side of the gardens – which has modern, air-conditioned rooms with tile floors, good bathrooms and a buffet breakfast. Another couple of blocks down towards the centre, *Hotel de Moura*, on the peaceful Praça Gago Coutinho (☎285 251 090, ⓦ www.hoteldemoura.com; ❸), has a facade completely covered with *azulejos* and, within, updated rooms, patios, wrought-iron balconies, mirrored doors and a rambling garden. Or there's the *Pensão Residencial Santa Comba*, right on Praça Sacadura Cabral (☎285 251 255, Ⓕ285 251 257; breakfast included; no credit cards; ❷), by the castle, which is the cheapest of the lot, but as it's right on a road junction front-facing rooms can be noisy.

A few pleasant **cafés** face the gardens and castle on Praça Sacadura Cabral, and there are plenty of **restaurants** in the streets running back from here. *O Trilho*, Rua 5 de Outubro 5 (☎285 254 261; closed Mon), serves moderately priced regional dishes, while *O Túnel*, Rua dos Ourives 13 (☎285 253 384; closed Sat night & Sun), is more in the way of an inexpensive neighbourhood bar and grill house. It's popular at lunchtime, though you may find yourself eating in splendid isolation at night.

Mértola and around

MÉRTOLA is as beautifully sited as any town in the south, set high on a spur above the confluence of the Guadiana and Oeiras rivers, guarded by the ruins of a Moorish frontier castle. It makes a fine place to stay the night, or longer – either en route to the Algarve, or just as a destination in its own right – sporting a compact, somnolent old town full of discoveries and quiet back-country surroundings that form part of the **Parque Natural Vale do Guadiana**. The region is home to the rare black stork and other endangered species, and the local hills, riverbanks and valleys have some excellent walks.

The Barragem de Alqueva

In February 2002 the floodgates opened on the controversial **Barragem de Alqueva (Alqueva Dam)**, a project started decades ago under the Salazar regime. At 250 square kilometres (of which 69 square kilometres is in Spain), it's created Europe's largest reservoir from the waters of the Rio Gaudiana and several tributaries, which – the government claims – will provide reliable irrigation in this arid region, satisfy the increasing need for domestic water supplies in the neighbouring Algarve and provide jobs in the agricultural and tourism industries. There are many who still dispute these claims and strongly decry the destruction of over a million oak and cork trees, the threats to the habitats of golden eagles and the even rarer Iberian Lynx, plus the submerging of over 200 prehistoric sites. The World Wildlife Fund has described the project as an ecological disaster, while the inhabitants of the former village of Luz on the east bank of the Guadiana, now submerged, have had to be relocated to a facsimile village above the waterline.

The government, in turn, points to the benefits of the dam, not least the hydroelectric plant, switched on in 2004, which will provide enough electricity to supply the Évora and Beja districts combined. The dam is also designed to irrigate vast tracts of land which can then be exploited by farmers, while tourism projects in this previously underdeveloped area of Portugal are also underway now that a secure source of water is on hand. Primarily, of course, this means resort hotels and golf courses, something Alentejan farmers seem to have managed well without for hundreds of years.

You can drive right on to the **dam wall** from Moura – just follow the signs from town for 12km. Whatever you think of it, it's an extraordinary engineering project, whose viewing platforms offer sweeping vistas of the now-submerged river valley. The road continues up to Portel, on the Beja–Évora highway, while there's another road-bridge crossing, much further north, at Mourão, just south of Monsaraz, where the rising waters have completely changed the Guadiana river's environs.

Mértola's history goes back as far as Phoenician times, when it was an important river port, and it was later fortified and expanded by both Romans (as Myrtilis) and Moors (Martulah), before being taken by Dom Sancho II in 1238 as part of the Christian Reconquista. With the walled town occupying such a small area, successive conquerors and settlers simply built on what they found, which provides Mértola with its current fascination – the evidence of thousands of years of habitation visible in almost every building and street.

The town

The archeological finds from the various sites around Mértola could simply have been placed in a municipal museum, but instead, the whole town has been imaginatively designated a "vila museu", allowing you to trace its art and history in a series of small, well-designed **exhibitions**. They are all open roughly the same hours (Tues–Sun: May–Oct 9.30am–12.30pm & 2–6pm, Nov–April 9am–12.30pm & 2–5.30pm, unless otherwise stated) and a single ticket (€5) gets you in them all, or you can pay €2 to visit a single exhibition.

If you start with the **Castelo** the layout of the walled old town and modern settlement beyond becomes clear. The arched main door and winding entrance lead into the central keep (daily 9am–5.30pm), which is Moorish in origin, though the rest of the castle dates from the thirteenth-century Christian Reconquest, when for a century it became the headquarters of the Order of Santiago. The earlier Islamic inhabitants lived within the castle walls and, later, in the Moorish quarter, just outside, which is still being excavated. The parish church at the foot of the castle, the **Igreja Matriz** (Wed–Sun 10am–1pm & 3–7pm; free), started life as a mosque and was barely altered after the Reconquest. Its Moorish arched doorways are still visible and it retains its *mihrab* (prayer niche) behind the altar on the eastern wall.

The various exhibitions each deal with a single facet of the town's history, like the **Núcleo Romano** (Mon–Fri 9am–12.30pm & 2–5.30pm, Sat & Sun 10am–1pm & 3–7pm), showing the foundations of a Roman house discovered under the Câmara Municipal. In the **Museu Islâmica** are gathered the inscribed funerary stones, glazed tableware and decorated urns discovered within the Moorish quarter, while the tiny **Museu de Arte Sacra** concentrates on religious art, notably the three retables from the parish church depicting Sancho's ousting of the Moors. A cooperative set up to revive the traditional weaving industry showcases its methods and products in the **Oficina de Tecelagem**, while even the town's former blacksmiths' workshop, the **Forja do Ferreiro** (key available from adjacent cottage if locked), is open for visits. All these lie in the old walled town, signposted and easily found, though the most moving exhibit is five minutes' walk away in the modern part of town, where the **Basilica Paleocristã**, in Largo do Rossio do Carmo, preserves thirty funerary stones in a partial reconstruction of an early Christian temple. These inhabitants – a "servant of God", "a man of social standing", or simply "son" or "daughter of" – were buried here, outside the city walls, over 1500 years ago.

Around Mértola

Cross the old bridge south of town (the Vila Real road), spanning the Ribeira de Oeiras, and it's a fifteen-minute walk up to the former **Convento de São Francisco** (Fri–Sun 2–6pm; €2.50; ℡286 612 119, ⓦwww.conventomertola .com), whose Dutch owners have turned it into an artistic retreat, with organic gardens, bird sanctuary, open-air art and a water museum demonstrating historic irrigation techniques; there's also a contemporary art gallery in the old church. You can also stay here (see "Practicalities" p.532).

North of town, across the new bridge, the road to Serpa winds for 17km to **Mina de São Domingos**. The copper mines here were once the principal source of the town's employment, and until World War II they were owned by a British company, which employed a private police force and treated the workers with appalling brutality. The mines closed in 1965 and there's little left of the old mining machinery, though its industrial heritage will live on – there are plans to build one of Europe's largest solar "parks" here to generate electricity. In the meantime, there's a swish hotel (see below) and a very attractive river beach on the small reservoir, with plenty of shade, very popular on summer weekends.

Practicalities

Mértola is around 50km from Beja or Serpa, an easy drive, and only 72km north of Vila Real de Santo António on the eastern Algarve, which means it sees progressively more tourist traffic. If you're heading south to Vila Real afterwards, you won't want to miss Alcoutim on the way. Don't, incidentally, even think of driving into the walled town – **park** anywhere you like close to the walls or by the bus stops.

Buses come either from Beja, or stop in Mértola on the express run between Lisbon and Vila Real, with a limited local service on to Vila Real via Alcoutim. You're dropped at the bus stops by the main Serpa/Beja traffic circle in the new town – follow the signs for "Mértola/Vila Real" for the five-minute walk down the road to Largo Vasco de Gama at the foot of the old town. The **turismo** (daily May–Oct 9.30am–12.30pm & 2–6pm, Nov–April 9am–12.30pm & 2–5.30pm; ☎286 610 109, ⓦwww.cm-mertola.pt) is just inside the walls (signposted), and hands out a very useful map, plus accommodation and restaurant lists. You can access the **Internet** for free here too.

Although the walled town is handsome in the extreme, most services are in the modern town, not unattractive itself, which sits in a tight clump between the castle walls and traffic circle. For **accommodation**, it's hard to conceive of a better – or friendlier – budget choice than the *Residencial Beira Rio*, Rua Dr Afonso Costa 109 (☎286 611 190, ⓦwww.beirario.co.pt; ❷) down the left-hand fork as you come towards the old town, whose best rooms (all modern and en-suite, most air-conditioned) have balconies directly overlooking the peaceful river. A good buffet breakfast can be eaten on the terrace, and there's parking. The *Oásis*, immediately adjacent at number 104 (☎286 612 404; no credit cards or breakfast; ❶), is a budget standby, but isn't half the place. Some prefer the only choice within the walls, *Casa das Janelas Verdes*, Rua Dr Manuel Francisco Gomes 38–40 (☎286 612 145; ❸), up from the turismo, a town house of some character, though it only has three rooms available. Just out of town, you can stay in tasteful, rustic surroundings at the *Convento de São Francisco* (☎286 612 119, ⓦwww.conventomertola.com), either in a pretty room with verandah (❸) or a former monk's cell (❷) with a river view. They also let out a bucolic cottage (sleeps two; €150 a week) in the grounds. At Mina de São Domingos, the old mining company HQ has been converted into the flash five-star *Estalagem São Domingos* (☎286 640 000, ⓦwww.hotelsaodomingos .com; ❻), whose smart rooms all have terrace or balcony with views over the pool and garden or river beach.

The best local **restaurants** are all ranged along Avenida Aureliano Mira Fernandes, the garden-avenue beyond the traffic circle in the modern town. First choice is the *Alengarve* (☎286 612 210; closed Wed), run by an affable bunch of young guys, serving a varied menu at highly reasonable prices. You'll eat very well for around €15 (try the *atum cebolada*), and can sit outside on the raised terrace. A bit grander – though no more expensive – is *O Nautico*, Rua Dr Serrão Martins (☎286 612 596; closed Sun), the sailing club restaurant, with panoramic windows and terrace. It's just before you get to Largo Vasca de Gama. In the old town, *Migas*, by the market building (☎965 782 159, closed Mon) is a cosy place with mains from €8; the speciality, not surprisingly, is *migas*, a heavy corn-bread and pork dish that's a bit of an acquired taste.

Alcácer do Sal

Coming from Lisbon and the west, **ALCÁCER DO SAL** is the first town of the Baixo Alentejo, just 52km from Setúbal. It is one of Portugal's oldest ports, founded by the Phoenicians and made a regional capital under the Moors – whence its name (*al-Ksar*, the town) derives. The other part of its name, *do Sal*, "of salt", reflects the dominance of the salt industry in these parts; the Sado estuary is still fringed with salt marshes.

Few stop longer than to stretch the legs – either Beja or the coast are less than an hour away – but it's an attractive enough place to do just that, particularly along the waterfront promenade. A couple of roads back from the promenade, at its western end, lies a charming quarter of medieval houses. Further uphill,

△ Pousada, Alcácer do Sal

above the town, stands the part-ruined Moorish **castle**, from where there are striking views of the lush green paddy fields which almost surround the town, and of the storks' nests on the church rooftops. The castle is now home to the fabulous *Pousada Dom Afonso II* (☎265 613 070, ⓦwww.pousadas.pt; ❼), whose contemporary rooms, swimming pool and pricey restaurant make dramatic use of the buildings. For a good meal down by the river instead, there's *A Descoberta*,

Av João Soares Branco 15 (☎265 623 877; closed Mon), which offers regional *terras do Sado* food and wines at moderate prices.

There are more modest hotels in town, but none provide as good a reason to stop as the *pousada*. However, for quieter country surroundings, you could always drive the 30km east along the minor N5 to Torrão, past the **Barragem de Vale do Gaio**, whose *Pousada de Vale do Gaio* (☎265 669 610, ⓦwww .pousadas.pt; ⑥) – sited on the edge of the reservoir – is a fairly simple conversion of the lodge used by the dam engineers.

Santiago do Cacém

South of Alcácer, the only place that might tempt you to stop before the Alentejo coast is **SANTIAGO DO CACÉM**, a pleasant little provincial town overlooked by a castle, with the fascinating Roman ruins of Miróbriga on its outskirts. You certainly don't need to stay the night, even travelling on public transport – there are regular bus services west and south to the local beaches.

The modern town centres on its market, with what's left of the old town (not much) spreading up one of the hills to the **Castelo** (April–Sept Mon–Sat 8.30am–7pm, Sun 8.30am–12.30pm; Oct–March Mon–Sat 8.30am–4.30pm, Sun 8.30am–12.30pm; free), Moorish in origin but later rebuilt by the Knights Templar. It now does rather odd duty as a cemetery for the neighbouring church, but you can climb up to the battlements for distant views to the coast. The castle is a steep fifteen-minute walk up from town. Back down in the centre, it's worth having a look around the covered market, before making your way to the **Museu Municipal**, facing the municipal gardens off Avenida Álvares Pereira (Tues–Fri 10am–noon & 2–5pm, Sat 2–6pm; free). Housed in one of Salazar's more notorious prisons, one of the spartan cells has been preserved while two others have been converted into a "typical country bedroom" and "a rich bourgeois bedroom".

Miróbriga

The archeological section in Santiago's museum should whet your appetite for a visit to the **Ruinas Romanas de Miróbriga** (Tues–Sat 9am–12.30pm & 2–5.30pm, Sun 9am–noon & 2–5.30pm; €3). It's a short drive from town or around half an hour's walk – follow the Lisbon road, Rua de Lisboa (N120), as far as the windmill on the hill, turn sharp right at the signpost and keep on down the country lane for another ten minutes. The site, which lies isolated amid arcadian green hills, was first inhabited during the Iron Age, but the Roman city here dates from the first century AD. For 200 years Miróbriga thrived on trade, a planned town set around its forum and temple, with recreational zones and residential areas – a "new town" of its era. By the fourth century AD it was in decline, and was then lost to history until the sixteenth century, and only first excavated in the nineteenth century.

The ruins are extensive, scattered over the gullies and hills below the small interpretation centre. At the highest point a **Temple of Jupiter** has been partly reconstructed, overlooking the forum with a row of shops built into its supporting wall. A house below here retains some second-century **wall paintings**, protected by a wooden hut. A paved street descends to a huge **bath complex** whose underground central heating system is still intact, while alongside sits a beautifully preserved Roman **bridge** from the first century AD.

Practicalities

The **bus station** is in the square just above the market, and there are regular services from Lisbon, as well as south to Porto Covo and Vila Nova de Milfontes. There's also a regular summer (May–Sept) service west to the lagoon beach at Lagoa de Santo André, the nearest sands to town, though this becomes less reliable out of season. The **turismo**, 100m from the station, in the side of the market building, (Mon–Fri 9am–7pm, Sat 9am–1pm & 2–6pm; ☎269 826 696, Ⓦwww.cm-santiago-do-cacem.pt), hands out a useful town map.

There really is no need for **accommodation**, though the *Pousada da Quinta da Ortiga* (☎269 822 871, Ⓦwww.pousadas.pt; ❻), 1km out of town on the Lisbon road, attracts some – set on a typical Alentejan rural estate, with a pool and a decent restaurant. If you were stuck in town, the best budget choice is *Residencial Gabriel*, Rua Professor Egas Moniz 24 (☎269 822 245; ❷), on the main road through Santiago. There are simple **restaurants** between the bus station and market where you can get an inexpensive meal, though if you're heading out to Miróbriga you might as well combine seeing the ruins with lunch at the moderately priced *Restaurante Refúgio do Mirante* (☎269 826 622; closed Sun & Dec), opposite the entrance to the site. It excels for fish – *massa do peixe*, a soupy dish of minted macaroni and mixed poached fish is recommended.

The Alentejo coast

The long **Alentejo coast** stretches for over 150km, from Setúbal bay to the western Algarve. For the most part it's undeveloped, as its beaches can seem pretty wild – whipped by the Atlantic winds, many are strictly local in character, often only reached on minor roads or tracks. The northern section has really only one realistic target, the lagoon beach of **Lagoa de Santo André**, northwest of Santiago do Cacém. South of the lagoon, the industrial town of **Sines** dominates the coast for some distance around, its oil refinery, towers and pipelines adding more than just an unattractive smell to the air – the sea in the vicinity is polluted as well. The centre of Sines is actually better than you'd imagine, but there's no reason to visit – not even on the trail of Vasco da Gama, who was born here but left no trace. Buses instead run directly from Lisbon and Santiago do Cacém to **Porto Côvo**, the first place on the coast you could call a resort, with its low cliffs backed by a rash of villas.

It's further south that things really improve, particularly at **Vila Nova de Milfontes**, the main – and by far the nicest – Alentejan resort. **Almograve** and **Zambujeira do Mar**, further south, are both much less developed seaside villages with stupendous beaches, while **Odemira** – about 15km from the coast – is the only inland stop worth making. Zambujeira is the southernmost Alentejo beach, and an attractive road twists its way into the hills of the Algarve from the river crossing at Odeceixe. For the most dramatic approach, however, take the road from Odemira through the Serra de Monchique, descending to the Algarve coast at Portimão.

All the resorts are accessible by local **buses** from Santiago do Cacém or Odemira, but you can also simply head straight for them from Lisbon on the daily express routes – in which case it's wise to buy your ticket in advance. From Vila Nova de Milfontes and Zambujeira do Mar there's a daily express bus service on to the Algarve (to Sagres, Lagos or Portimão).

Lagoa de Santo André

Fifteen kilometres northwest of Santiago do Cacém a beautiful sand beach separates the **Lagoa de Santo André** from the sea. The wide lagoon itself, only a couple of metres deep, is backed by an extensive *reserva natural* of pinewoods and reeds, and development is consequently limited, at least adjacent to the lagoon and beach. There's a beach café and a couple of restaurants at the road's end, while beyond is the sand – miles and miles of it. The sea is very enticing with high waves and good surf, but be warned: the undertow can be fierce and people drown here every year.

In summer, up to five **buses** a day run out here from Santiago do Cacém (30min), stopping right at the road's end. You can stay, but there's only one **hotel**, the apartment-style *Al Tarik* (☎269 708 600, ⓦwww.hotelaltarik.com; ❹, Oct–May ❸), and a large, well-equipped **campsite**, the *Parque do Campismo* (☎269 708 550), both found on the road in, but set well back from the beach on the northern side of the lagoon, where some development has been allowed. Otherwise, it's the kind of place Portuguese families come to rent villas and apartments – you may find "*quartos*" advertised – but as there's no real village centre, it's not the greatest overnight stop.

Porto Côvo

The coast south of Sines is undeniably pretty, with a minor road hugging the coves and high dunes as far as **PORTO CÔVO**, a former fishing village now entirely surrounded by modern holiday villas. However, the centre – just a few cobbled, whitewashed streets around a restored square – remains highly attractive, while boats still bob around in the minuscule deep cove harbour. It's very crowded in August – when it turns into a sort of Lisbon-on-Sea – but there are still recognizable elements of the old-fashioned village it once was, and for most of the year the predominant sounds are the whistle of the Atlantic breeze and the crashing of the waves. Clifftop paths run north and south of town providing access to the coves and beaches. **Praia do Somouqueira** just to the north is named after the extraordinary rock formations and is popular at low tide when temporary new beaches are created.

The pedestrianized Rua da Vasco da Gama runs from the cliffs above the sea up to the main Largo Marquês de Pombal. There's an bank with ATM along here, as well as most of the village's dozen cafés and restaurants, plus various shops selling beach gear, souvenirs, postcards and Peruvian jewellery. **Buses** connect Porto Côvo with Santiago do Cacém, Vila Nova de Milfontes, Almograve and Zambujeira. There's a **turismo** (Mon–Sat 10am–1pm & 3–7pm; may close in winter; ☎269 959 124, ⓦwww.freguesiadeportocovo .com) at the car park above the square, next to the small daily **market** (mornings only).

The turismo has a list of local **accommodation**, but it's just a matter of strolling the few central streets and checking out the options. You'll see "*quartos*" and "*apartamentos*" signs all over town, and more posted in the turismo windows. Prices given below are for July and August – you'll get much better deals everywhere out of season. For simple whitewashed rooms with tile floors and private bathrooms, *Quartos Abelha*, Rua Vasco da Gama 44 (☎269 905 108; no credit cards; ❷), can be recommended – *Pensão Zé Inácio*, next door (☎269 959 136; ❸), is smarter but overpriced. A cheaper, more old-fashioned place is *Pensão Boa Esperança*, Rua Conde Bandeira (☎269 905 109; no credit cards; ❷), two blocks west, which offers no-frills accommodation with shared bathrooms. A block over from the *Boa Esperança*, basic **apartments** are available by the night at

Port wine

If ever a drink was synonymous with a country it's port – the fortified wine from the Douro region of Portugal. For three centuries wine has been shipped down the Douro river to Vila Nova de Gaia, whose famous wine lodges (Sandeman, Graham's, Cockburn, Taylor's) reflect the early British influence on its production. A tour and a tasting form an integral part of any visit to Portugal's second city, Porto, while you can also follow the wine trail right along the Douro by car and cruise boat. The country's port wine institute, the Instituto dos Vinhos do Douro e do Porto (ⓦwww.ivdp.pt), has a useful English-language website, while the Rota do Vinho do Porto (ⓦwww.rvp.pt) details the region's wine estates, attractions and events.

Developing a taste – the early days

Wine has been produced in the Douro valley since Roman times, but the clear distinction between port wine (*vinho do porto*) and other Portuguese wines wasn't made until the beginning of the eighteenth century. British merchants living in Porto were already familiar with the local wine, and when Britain prohibited the import of French wines during the War of the Spanish Succession, Portuguese wines quickly filled the void. Boosted by favourable trading terms established under the **Methuen Treaty** (1703), the wine trade became so profitable that inferior wines (often adulterated and artificially coloured) were soon being passed off as the genuine article. This led to the creation of a regulatory body in 1756, the **Companhia Geral da Agricultura das Vinhas do Alto Douro**, and, the following year, the declaration of the world's oldest **demarcated wine region**. Port wine could now only legitimately be produced in this area, and the boundaries in the Douro valley were marked with granite pillars. Yet it was only in the mid-nineteenth century that port wine began to resemble the fortified wine of today, when the addition of grape brandy to stop fermentation became widespread, enabling the wines to be transported over even longer distances.

The Douro wine route

The grapes for making port wine are grown in a 250,000-hectare demarcated region along both banks of the **Rio Douro** (see p.321), stretching from Mesão Frio to the Spanish border. Sheltered by the Marão and Montemuro ranges, around fifteen percent of the region is under vines which benefit from cold winters and hot, dry summers. The characteristic vineyard terraces can be seen along the length of the Douro, and they form a particularly beautiful backdrop to the small port-producing town of **Pinhão** (p.370). The grapes are harvested at the

▼ Traditional port wine boats

quintas (vineyard estates) from September to October and crushed. The juice ferments for a few days and then fermentation is arrested by the addition of brandy – exactly when this is done determines the wine's sweetness – with the wine subsequently stored in casks until the following March. Various *quintas* offer tours of the process at the depot town of **Peso da Régua** (p.361), which is also the destination of many Douro river cruises (p.362). The final stage in the wine route is the transportation downstream to the shippers' lodges, where the wine is blended and matures. The traditional *barcos rabelos* (port wine boats) have been replaced by cistern lorries, but you'll still see the boats tied up on the quayside at **Vila Nova de Gaia** (p.342), across the river from Porto city centre – here, the leading port-wine producers, some of them two centuries old, offer fascinating tours of their cellars culminating in a tasting of their famous wines.

What's in the bottle?

Port wine is either Ruby (ie deep red) in style, Tawny (made from a blend of differently aged wines) or white – the first two are generally drunk at the end of a meal, or with cheese or dessert, the last served chilled as an aperitif. The finest and most expensive reds are known as **Vintages**, wines from a single year that are bottled two to three years after harvest and left to mature. A vintage is only declared in certain years (just fourteen times between 1901 and 1999), and the wine is only ready to drink at least ten to fifteen years after bottling, when the flavours

are at their most complex, the wine deep purple and full-bodied. Late Bottled Vintage (LBV) is not of vintage quality, but is still good enough to mature in bottles, to which it's transferred after four to six years in the cask. All other ports are blended and are kept in the cask for between two and seven or more years, with the colour developing into various shades of tawny and with a flavour of intense fruit and wood – they are ready to drink when bottled. Of these, a **Colheita** ("Harvest") is a Tawny port made from grapes from a specific year and aged at least seven years in the cask; other fine wines are **superior Tawnies** dated 10, 20, 30 or 40 years old (the average age of the wines in the blend), while **Reserve** ports (both Tawny and Ruby) are decent blended wines, the best being the Tawny Reserve ports which have to spend at least seven years in the cask.

Drinking up – six of the best

Solar do Vinho do Porto, Lisbon. Start your night in the Bairro Alto in refined surroundings. See p.133.

Vinologia, Porto. Porto's best wine bar is entirely dedicated to port, especially from small producers. See p.349.

Barão de Fladgate, Vila Nova de Gaia. Taylor's panoramic restaurant is just the place to sip a chilled white port as the sun goes down. See p.348.

Solar do Vinho do Porto, Porto. The bar at the Port Wine Institute HQ is set in the gardens of the city's most attractive park. See p.348.

▼ Port wine shop

Vintage House, Pinhão. Enjoy the river views over a glass of port on the terrace of the Douro's most glamorous hotel. See p.371.

Solar do Vinho do Porto, Peso da Régua. Once simply known as "Warehouse 43", Régua's impressive *solar* is both tasting bar and exhibition hall. See p.361.

The 10 best port wine lodge tours

Around thirty port wine lodges in Vila Nova de Gaia are open for tours. There's a map and more information about visits on p.343–344.

Barros, Almeida Ⓦwww.porto-barros.pt. One of only a handful of remaining family-owned companies makes an interesting contrast to the larger producers.

Cálem Ⓦwww.calem.pt. A small Portuguese lodge, especially informative about the port-production process.

Cockburn Ⓦwww.martinez.pt. Now owned by Spanish combine Martinez, Cockburn – established in 1815 – is the most English of the lodges, offering tours of its supremely atmospheric cellars.

Graham's Ⓦwww.grahams-port.com. A lodge with an impressive stone-arched reception and a splendid tasting terrace overlooking the river.

Kopke Ⓦwww.kopkeports.com. The world's oldest port wine company (1638), now owned by Barros, retains some venerable wooden casks in its cellars.

Ramos Pinto Ⓦwww.ramospinto.pt. The famous advertising posters of this Portuguese company did much to popularize port in the 1900s – there's a good museum with photographs, trinkets and posters.

Real Companhia Velha Ⓦwww.realcompanhiavelha.pt. Founded (1756) to lead the Portuguese challenge to the British port monopoly, Velha features a 6km tunnel originally intended to form part of a rail link – having been built at the wrong angle it now serves as storage for the wines.

Rozès Ⓦwww.rozes.pt. Founded in 1855 by a Bordeaux-based trader (and French-owned ever since), this has one of the best tours, with several different ports to savour.

Sandeman Ⓦwww.sandeman.com. The black-hat-and-cape cut-out provides the most recognisable of company logos and the lengthy tour includes a good museum.

Taylor, Fladgate & Yeatman Ⓦwww.taylor.pt. Founded in 1692, and still an independent family firm, Taylor's has panoramic views from its salon, terrace and restaurant.

Apartamentos Rosa, Rua da Farmacía 6 (☎269 905 510; no credit cards; ❷), and over the road at *Apartamentos Campos*, Rua da Farmacía 11 (☎269 905 144; no credit cards; ❷), though you may have to get the turismo to call as there's often no one at the actual addresses. There's a bit more comfort all round at *Aparthotel Porto Côvo*, Rua Vitalina da Silva (☎269 959 140, ⓦwww.hotelportocovo.com; ❸, August ❹), a little way inland, above the turismo – the air-conditioned studios and one-bed apartments come with kitchen and the use of a pool. There's also a good year-round **campsite**, *Parque de Campismo* (☎269 905 136), on the Vila Nova road out of town.

Restaurants, on the whole, are aimed at well-to-do Portuguese holidaymakers. The two in the square, and others, specialize in seafood and are not a cheap night out. However, they are good, particularly the *Marquês* (☎269 905 036; open for drinks until 1am), which is more like a classy Lisbon *cervejaria* than a local restaurant, with stand-at-the-bar beers, oysters, fresh-from-the-tank lobsters and other delights. They also have a good cakes-and-ice cream **café** across the square.

Ilha do Pessegueiro

The next beach south of Port Côvo is at **Ilha do Pessegueiro** (Peach Tree Island), reached by car off the Porto Côvo–Vila Nova de Milfontes road. However, it's much nicer to walk, following the coastal path south from Porto Côvo. It's only a couple of kilometres and en route you'll pass the remains of a Bronze Age burial site.

The name actually applies to the mainland beach, another typically duned stretch of sand sitting below a small sixteenth-century fort. The island itself – with the matching ruins of another fort – is a few hundred metres offshore, clearly visible from Porto Côvo and reachable from there on local fishing **boats**. Between mid-June and mid-September these run to a schedule (daily at 9am, 11am, 2pm & 4pm; €8) from Porto Côvo harbour, though you might persuade someone to take you over at other times of the year too.

At the dusty car park by the beach there's the *Restaurante A Ilha* (☎269 905 113), while the **campsite** (☎269 905 178) is a fair way inland, back up the road to Vila Nova de Milfontes.

Vila Nova de Milfontes

VILA NOVA DE MILFONTES – 20km south of Porto Côvo – lies on the estuary of the Rio Mira, whose wide sandy banks gradually merge into the coastline. It is an advantageous spot for sailors (the port is reputed to have harboured Hannibal and his Carthaginians during a storm) and, while the resort is not exactly undiscovered, it remains an attractive place – at least it does below the sprawl of the new town that has developed since the 1980s. Portuguese families on holiday from the big cities of the north give it a homely atmosphere quite distinct from that of the cosmopolitan Algarve. The few whitewashed streets of the old town huddle around a striking, ivy-wreathed castle, with the long river beach just a few minutes' walk to the west. The beach road, Avenida Marginal, ends at a lighthouse, fifteen minutes from the centre, from where you can see the full force of the Atlantic crashing waves down onto the rocks below. Even though the beach is spacious, it gets busy in July and August, when you might want to take the **ferry** (every 30min, daily 10am–7pm; €2 return) instead from the town jetty at the foot of the castle. This runs to the far side of the estuary, to another long duned swathe of river beach. Swimmers in the river need to be aware of the strong currents – the town beach has a roped-off swimming area that you should heed.

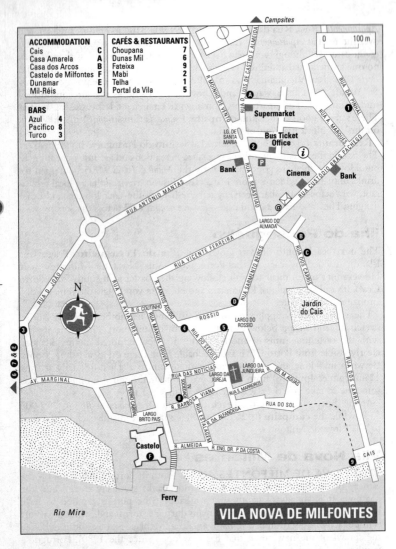

Campsites

ACCOMMODATION	
Cais	C
Casa Amarela	A
Casa dos Arcos	B
Castelo de Milfontes	F
Dunamar	E
Mil-Réis	D

CAFÉS & RESTAURANTS	
Choupana	7
Dunas Mil	6
Fateixa	9
Mabi	2
Telha	1
Portal da Vila	5

BARS	
Azul	4
Pacifico	8
Turco	3

Supermarket

Bus Ticket Office

Bank

Cinema

Bank

LARGO DO ALMADA

Jardin do Cais

ROSSIO

LARGO DO ROSSIO

LARGO DA IGREJA

LARGO DA JUNQUEIRA

LARGO BRITO PAIS

Castelo

Ferry

Rio Mira

VILA NOVA DE MILFONTES

Practicalities

Buses come in down the main Rua Custódio Brás Pachego in the newer, upper part of town, and drop you off in a small lot near the **turismo** on Rua António Mantas (July & Aug daily 10am–7pm; Sept–June 10am–1pm & 2–6pm; ☏283 996 599). There's a daily morning service to the Algarve, several express services to Lisbon, and local connections to Odemira, Porto Côvo and Zambujeira do Mar, with times posted on the ticket office door. Apart from providing a range of useful lists and brochures, the turismo is the place to find out about local **activities and tours**, from river trips and kayak rental to scuba-diving and horse-riding. Or you can check out the local **surf scene** with Surf

Milfontes (℡919 922 193, ⓦwww.surfmilfontes.com), who do board rental, lessons and surf trips. There's **Internet access** at Cyber House, Rua Custódio Brás Pachego 2 (daily 10am–2am, restricted hours in winter).

Accommodation is spread all over town, with a few traditional *pensões* in the centre and lots of apartments along the beach road and in the surroundings. Prices peak in August, but are far more reasonable in low season (Sept–June), when you should be able to do better than the rates indicated below. There are two **campsites** just north of town, both also with bungalows for rent as well as tent space: the *Parque Campismo de Milfontes* (℡ & ⓕ283 996 104) has excellent facilities, while the nearby *Parque Campismo Campiférias* (℡283 996 409; closed Dec) is more modest.

Hotels and pensions

Casa Amarela Rua D Luís de Castro e Almeida ℡283 996 632 or 934 204 610, ⓦwww.casaamarelamilfontes.com. The "yellow house" is the highly personal project of a gregarious backpacking owner, who has decorated seven stylish en-suite rooms (some with terrace) with art from his trips. Some rooms sleep up to four, and there's a kitchen and lounge, with free Internet access for guests. A separate mews-style block a couple of minutes' away has eight more en-suite rooms (one of them a dorm; €10–15 a bed, depending on season) arranged around a large terraced area and kitchen. Laundry facilities available. Breakfast not included. No credit cards. ❷

Pensão Casa dos Arcos Rua dos Carris ℡283 996 264, ⓕ283 997 156. A very pleasant small pension with crisp tiled bathrooms and stand-up balconies on most of the modern-looking rooms – however, the views are only partial. No credit cards. ❸

Pensão do Cais Rua dos Carris 9 ℡283 996 268. This is the first choice in town for *pensão* rooms, primarily because of the estuary views – even if your room (fairly spacious with traditional furniture and modern bathrooms) doesn't have the best aspect, there's always the lovely vine-covered patio or first-floor terrace. No credit cards. ❸

Castelo de Milfontes Largo do Brito Pais ℡283 998 231, ⓕ283 997 122. Vila Nova's finest lodgings, inside the fortress – cross the drawbridge to enter. The seven rooms have terrific views, while surroundings are baronial to say the least. Dinner is available. ❺

Apartamentos Dunamar Rua dos Médos 2, off Av Marginal ℡283 998 208, ⓦwww .dunamarmilfontes.com. In a prime location, high above the estuary, these smart a/c studio and one-bedroom apartments (with balconies and kitchenette) have great views and are just a few minutes' walk from the beach and town, with the *Dunas Mil* restaurant on your doorstep. There's parking, but breakfast isn't available. ❸, July & Aug ❹

Residencial Mil-Réis Largo do Rossio 2 ℡283 998 233, ⓕ283 998 328. Smart, clean, central rooms with TV, looked after by kindly owners. No credit cards. ❷

Cafés and restaurants

Restaurante A Choupana Av Marginal ℡283 996 643. Beachcomber-style bar and restaurant, down the cliff steps at the far (lighthouse) end of the beach road. An outdoor barbecue dishes up fish and meat grills, but while the food's fine it's not really the main event – the views and the sunsets are the thing. Moderate.

Restaurante-Marisqueira O Dunas Mil Av Marginal ℡283 996 420. The best fish restaurant in town, five minutes' along the coast road and high up on the right. There's a big outdoor terrace, and they specialize in *arroz* dishes, *açordas* and *cataplanas*, as well as excellent shellfish, but none of this comes cheap. Grilled fish and meat are more reasonably priced. Expensive.

Restaurante A Fateixa Rua dos Carris ℡283 996 415. A superb location on the riverbank below town, and a shady terrace, makes this a good bet for lunch. It's pretty fair value too – platters of squid, sardines, mackerel, swordfish and tuna, all cost around €8. Closed Wed. Moderate.

Mabi Largo de Santa Maria 25A. A great choice for breakfast – filled croissants, sandwiches, pastries and fresh orange juice. It's busy from opening at 8am and is a funky, young kind of place, open late. Inexpensive.

Churrasqueira A Telha Rua da Pinhal 3 ℡283 996 138. Simple grill-house menu at reasonable prices, especially the charcoal-grilled chicken. Inexpensive.

Portal da Vila Largo do Rossio ℡283 996 823. With every internal inch covered in tiles, and the ceiling dripping in greenery, it doesn't look much like a local restaurant – and you're unlikely to find many Portuguese in here. But the kebabs suspended on hangers and the sizzling hot-stone dishes (*da pedra*) of pork and veal are different enough to attract a tourist crowd for an enjoyable night out. Around €25 a head for a full meal and drinks. Closed Mon. Expensive.

Bars

Café Azul Rossio 20. Relaxed bar playing a mix of jazz, rock and blues, washed down with frozen tequila margaritas. Busy Fri and Sat and open from 9pm till 4am.

Bar Pacífico Rua Barbosa Viana. Dance-bar playing a mixture of chart, techno and reggae music. Open 10pm–6am (closed Oct & Nov).

Café Turco Rua Dom João II. Mock-Moorish café-bar, a favourite with Lisboans, featuring live music at the weekend. Open 10pm–4am, though weekends only in winter.

Almograve

The coast south of Vila Nova de Milfontes becomes ever more rugged and spectacular. At the tiny resort of **ALMOGRAVE**, 10km south of Vila Nova (west of the Odemira–Vila Nova de Milfontes road), huge waves come crashing down on the rocks and for most of the day swimming is impossible. It can get very crowded at high tide, too, when the beaches are reduced to thin strips with occasional waves drenching everybody's belongings; but, for all that, it's an exhilarating place. There are miles of high dunes to north and south, riddled with tracks, where – according to the local tourist brochure – "flora and fauna meet in perfect harmony".

Buses stop in the modern village, basically just a block of houses and villas which sits back from the beach – a road and boardwalk runs over the dunes to a huge car park above the sands. There are several bars and restaurants by the roundabout in the village, while the beach road passes the *Residencial Duna Praia* (☎283 647 115; ❸), which has a terrace and grill. There's also an increasingly popular **youth hostel** (☎283 640 000, ⓦwww.pousadasjuventude.pt; dorm beds €11, July & Aug €16, rooms ❶–❷), sited close to the beach and with private rooms as well as dorms.

South of Almograve, drivers can make for the promontory of **Cabo Sardão**, a dead-end road that culminates in a cliff-top lighthouse, from near where there are magnificent panoramas of the rocky coastline.

Zambujeira do Mar

The southernmost Alentejan resort is the small village of **ZAMBUJEIRA DO MAR**, which is 29km south of Vila Nova de Milfontes and slightly less from the inland town of Odemira (see p.541). The main street stops at the top of the cliff, which provides a dramatic backdrop to the handsome beach below, whose rocky outcrops give some shade during the day. If you find the main beach too crowded, then there are good alternatives less than three kilometres' walk north or south, reached by clifftop paths. Zambujeira is a much smaller, more laidback place than Vila Nova de Milfontes, attracting a largely foreign, backpacker crowd – in fact, it has more in common with the surfer hangouts of the western Algarve not far to the south. It's a profile that fits the **Festival Sudoeste** (ⓦwww.festivalsudoeste.pt), Portugal's best summer music festival, which rocks the joint for four days early every August.

New villas have been tacked on to what was a tiny fishing village at one time, and facilities are adequate but sparse: a small market, a bank, a few shops and half a dozen restaurants, all within a couple of hundred metres or so. The **bus** stops near the end of the road; timetables are posted in the newsagent's window. There's an enthusiastic **turismo** just up the road (Tues–Sat 10am–1pm & 2.30–6.30pm; possibly closed in winter; ☎283 961 144), who will positively insist you stay and, if you can track down a decent **room**, you might be persuaded. There are two places right on the village road, best the *Residencial Mar-e-Sol* (☎283 961 171; no credit cards; ❷), though for more modern rooms and quieter surroundings just walk a couple of blocks north into the residential zone to Rua da Palmeira, where *Residencial Onda Azul* (☎283 961 450; ❸) and *Pensão Rita* (☎283 961 330; ❸) stand almost adjacent – rooms everywhere will be cheaper once August has gone. The turismo also has details of private rooms, and can check on space at the numerous **rural tourism** properties in the surroundings – with your own car, you might prefer to stay out of the village and have the use of a pool and kitchen. The local **campsite**, *Parque Campismo da Zambujeira* (☎283 961 172, ❻www.campingzambujeira.com.sapo.pt), is back up the village road, about 1km from the cliffs, and has a café-bar and also apartments (❸) to rent.

The **restaurants** along the main street provide the evening's entertainment, and you can eat inexpensive grilled sardines and chicken at most of them. Seafood, as always, comes at a price, but *Taberna Ti Vítório* (☎283 961 130; closed Mon) has a good reputation – it's been grilling fish and chicken for the locals for over fifty years.

Odemira and the Barragem de Santa Clara

The main town hereabouts is **ODEMIRA**, 27km southeast of Vila Nova de Milfontes and about 15km inland. It's pretty enough, set around the River Mira which is crossed by an antique iron bridge – there are good views from the *miradouro* at the top of town. Buses run from here to both Zambujeira do Mar and Vila Nova, but they're not that frequent – in any case, you've no need to come here first if it's the beach you want, since there are direct services to all the nicest places on the coast.

If you are stuck for whatever reason, there's the *Residencial Rita* (☎283 322 531; ❷), just off to the left when you come out of the bus station. The **turismo** is up the hill in Praça da República (Mon–Fri 10am–1pm & 2–pm; ☎283 320 900, ❻www.cm-odemira.pt). More to the point, especially for touring drivers, is **lunch**. Look no further than *O Escondidinho*, Largo Brito Pais (☎283 322 558; closed Sun), just over the road and around the corner from the *residencial*, where an outdoor grill caters for seemingly half the town. After the inflated prices on the coast, you're in for a treat.

From Odemira, the main road (N120) heads south towards the western Algarve resorts – Odeceixe is just 25km away. But there's an attractive minor route (N123) which first runs east and then south to the **Barragem de Santa Clara**, a dam and reservoir 30km from town. These are very pretty surroundings, best enjoyed from the terrace and pool of the *Pousada de Santa Clara-a-Velha* (☎283 882 250, ❻www.pousadas.pt; ❻), which overlook the sparkling blue waters. The Algarve mountain town of Monchique is another 30km to the south.

Travel details

Trains

You can check train timetables online at ❻www.cp.pt.

Alcácer do Sal to: Lisbon (3 daily; 1hr 45 min–2hr 45 min).

Beja to: Évora (3 daily; 1hr 30min); Faro (3 daily; 3hr 10min); Lisbon (3–6 daily; 2hr 30min–3hr 15min).

Elvas to: Lisbon (3 daily; 4hr 50min–5hr 10min); Portalegre (3 daily; 50min).

Évora to: Beja (4 daily; 1hr 30min); Faro (2 daily; 4hr 40min); Lisbon (4–6 daily; 2hr 30min–4hr).

Portalegre to: Crato (3 daily; 15min); Elvas (3 daily; 50min); Lisbon (3 daily; 3hr 30min).

Buses

Alcácer do Sal to: Lisbon (3 daily; 1hr 30min).

Almograve to: Lisbon (1–2 daily; 4hr 10min); Porto Côvo (3 daily; 40min); Vila Nova de Milfontes (2 daily; 15min).

Beja to: Elvas (1 daily; 2hr 50min); Évora (3–5 daily; 1hr 10min); Faro (4 daily; 3hr 10min); Lisbon (3–6 daily; 2hr 40min); Mértola (1–3 daily; 1hr 15min); Moura (3–5 daily; 1hr 15min); Portalegre (2 daily; 4hr); Serpa (3–6 daily; 45min); Zambujeira do Mar (Mon–Fri 1 daily; 2hr 50min).

Borba to: Elvas (8 daily; 30min); Estremoz (3–4 daily; 15min); Évora (3 daily; 50min); Lisbon (3 daily; 3hr); Vila Viçosa (3–4 daily; 10min).

Castelo de Vide to: Lisbon (2 daily; 4hr); Marvão (Mon–Fri 2 daily; 30min); Portalegre (3 daily; 25–40min).

Elvas to: Borba (8 daily; 30min); Estremoz (hourly; 1hr–1hr 30min); Évora (3 daily; 1hr 30min); Lisbon (6 daily; 2hr 45min); Portalegre (2 daily; 1hr 15min); Vila Viçosa (2 daily; 35min).

Estremoz to: Borba (3–4 daily; 15min); Elvas (hourly; 1hr–1hr 30min); Évora (4–5 daily; 45min); Lisbon (5 daily; 2hr 30min); Portalegre (5–7 daily; 1hr).

Évora to: Arraiolos (2 daily; 25min); Beja (3–5 daily; 1hr 10min); Coimbra (2 daily; 4hr 30min); Elvas (3 daily; 1hr 30min); Estremoz (2–3 daily; 45min); Faro (3 daily; 4hr); Lisbon (hourly; 1hr 45min); Montemor-o-Novo (3–7 daily; 30min); Moura (1 daily; 1hr 30min); Portalegre (2–3 daily; 1hr 25min–1hr 45min); Reguengos de Monsaraz (5–7 daily; 35min–1hr); Santarém (2 daily; 2hr); Vila Viçosa (3 daily; 1hr).

Mértola to: Alcoutim (2 weekly; 1hr); Beja (1–3 daily; 1hr 15min); Lisbon (1–2 daily; 4hr); Vila Real de Santo António (1–2 daily; 1hr 30min).

Moura to: Beja (3–5 daily; 1hr 15min); Évora (1 daily; 1hr 30min); Lisbon (1 daily; 3hr 45min); Serpa (3–5 daily; 40min).

Odemira to: Lisbon (4 daily; 3hr 30min); Vila Nova de Milfontes (2 daily; 20min); Zambujeira do Mar (2–4 daily; 40min).

Portalegre to: Alter do Chão (1–2 daily; 40min); Beja (2 daily; 3hr 50min); Castelo de Vide (1–4 daily; 30min); Crato (1–2 daily; 25min); Elvas (2 daily; 1hr 15min); Estremoz (5–7 daily; 1hr); Évora (2 daily; 1hr 45min); Lisbon (3 daily; 4hr); Marvão (Mon–Fri 2 daily; 1hr); Portalegre train station (3 daily; 15min); Viseu (2 daily; 5hr).

Porto Côvo to: Almograve (3 daily; 40min); Lisbon (6 daily; 2hr 30min); Santiago do Cacém (4 daily; 1hr); Vila Nova de Milfontes (7 daily; 30min); Zambujeira do Mar (2 daily; 1hr 15min).

Reguengos de Monsaraz to: Monsaraz (Mon–Fri 3–5 daily; 35min) – though not all connect with Évora services.

Santiago do Cacém to: Lisbon (8 daily; 2hr 15min); Porto Côvo (5 daily; 1hr); Vila Nova de Milfontes (6 daily; 1hr 25min); Zambujeira do Mar (3 daily; 2hr).

Serpa to: Beja (3–6 daily; 45min); Lisbon (3 daily; 4hr), Moura (3–5 daily; 40min).

Vila Nova de Milfontes to: Almograve (2 daily; 15min); Lisbon (4 daily; 3–4hr); Odemira (2 daily; 20min); Portimão (July–Sept 1 daily; 2hr); Porto Côvo (7 daily; 30min); Sagres (July–Sept 1 daily; 2hr); Zambujeira do Mar (1–2 daily; 40min).

Vila Viçosa to: Borba (3–4 daily; 10min); Elvas (2 daily; 35min); Estremoz (3–4 daily; 35min).

Zambujeira do Mar to: Aljezur (July–Sept 1 daily; 35min); Almograve (2 daily; 25min); Beja (Mon–Fri 1 daily; 2hr 50min); Lisbon (1–2 daily; 3hr 40min–4hr 30min); Porto Côvo (2 daily; 1hr 15min); Sagres (July–Sept 1 daily; 1hr 20min); Santiago do Cacém (1–2 daily; 2hr 15min); Vila Nova de Milfontes (1–2 daily; 40min).

The Algarve

CHAPTER 9 # Highlights

* **Olhão** Highly atmospheric old town with a superb market and boats to offshore beaches. See p.556

* **Ilha de Tavira** Sandspit island with an enormous stretch of dune-backed beach – the best in the eastern Algarve. See p.564

* **Rio Guadiana** The river marking the border with Spain offers some of the region's least spoilt scenery. See p.569

* **Silves** The historic Moorish capital of the Algarve is overlooked by the grandest of castles. See p.588

* **Serra de Monchique** The woods around Monchique's mountains offer superb walking terrain. See p.591

* **Boat trip, Lagos** Explore the extraordinary rock formations and grottoes on a boat trip from Lagos. See p.597

* **Sagres** Iberia's most south-westerly point, complete with fortress, lighthouse and great surfing beaches. See p.603

* **West coast beaches** A stunning variety of wave-battered sandy swathes between Sagres and Odeceixe. See p.608

△ Tavira

The Algarve

W ith its spectacular sandy beaches and picturesque rocky coves, it is not surprising that the **Algarve** is Portugal's most popular region for holidaymakers. This has inevitably led to some heavy development. Large segments of the coast from Faro west to Albufeira have suffered most, with endless villa complexes creating a rather depressing Mediterranean-style suburbia. But at least the facilities are first rate, as are the beaches. Elsewhere in the Algarve, especially around Sagres and Tavira, the surroundings are far more attractive, with relaxed, small-scale resorts located near superb beaches or island sandbanks.

The coastline in fact has two quite distinct characters. To the west of Faro you'll find the classic postcard images – namely a series of tiny bays and coves, broken up by weird rocky outcrops and fantastic grottoes. They're at their most exotic around the major resort towns of **Lagos, Armaçao de Pêra** and **Albufeira**, while attractive smaller resorts include the former fishing villages of **Salema** or **Burgau**, or the historic cape of **Sagres** – site of Henry the Navigator's naval school. The string of villages along the rougher west (Atlantic) coast, as far as **Odeceixe**, are quieter still, with limited facilities but fantastic wild beaches.

East of Faro, there's a complete change as you encounter the first of a series of sandy offshore islets, the **ilhas**, which front the coastline virtually all the way to the Spanish border. The resorts here have a more Portuguese feel than those in the central stretch, and first-choice bases here would be **Faro** itself – capital of the entire region – **Olhão, Fuzeta** or **Tavira**, all of which offer access to the sandbank islands.

Inland Algarve is still relatively undeveloped, especially around **Alcoutim** on the Spanish border, and there are other scattered attractions in the Roman ruins of **Estói** and the market town of **Loulé**, both north of Faro, and the old Moorish town of **Silves**, easily reached from Portimão. The outstanding area, however, is the **Serra de Monchique**, the highest mountain range in the south, with cork and chestnut woods, remote little villages and a beautiful old spa in **Caldas de Monchique**.

The Algarve is a year-round destination, and in many respects the region is at its best in **spring** or **winter**, when the sunshine is still warm and there are far fewer visitors. Indeed, off-season travel in the Algarve will get you some of the best deals in the country, with luxury hotels offering all-in packages at discounts of up to seventy percent; check out the latest deals at the local tourist offices. But if you come in high **summer** without an advance booking, finding accommodation can be a real struggle, though you'll usually find something. It's

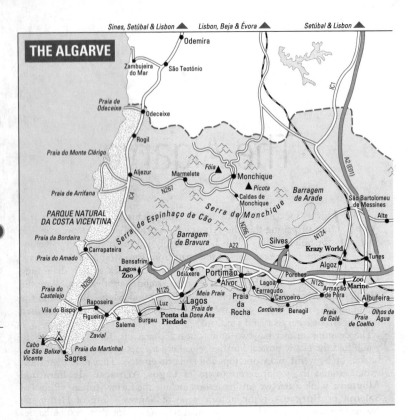

THE ALGARVE

PARQUE NATURAL
DA COSTA VICENTINA

essential to reserve in advance if you want to stay at a particular establishment, and you should also be prepared for very high summer prices relative to the rest of the country – pensions and hotels can cost up to twenty percent more on the Algarve.

Getting around by public transport is easier here than anywhere else in Portugal and, since the coastline is only 240km long from east to west, you can see an awful lot in just a few days. The **Algarve rail line** (timetables on ☎808 208 208, ⓦwww.cp.pt) runs from Lagos in the west to Vila Real de Santo António on the Spanish border, calling at most major towns en route (you may have to change at Tunes, Faro or Tavira, depending on your destination); while **buses** link all the resorts and main inland villages. With a car, you'll be able to reach the more out-of-the-way inland villages and inaccessible cove beaches.

The Algarve's best beach restaurants

Restaurante O Farol Albufeira p.577	**Restaurante Restinga** Alvor p.587
Estrela do Mar Armação de Pêra p.581	**O Poço** Luz p.601
	Beach Bar Burgau Burgau p.602
Rei das Praias Praia da Caneiros p.582	**Mira Mar** Salema p.603
	Raposo Sagres p.607

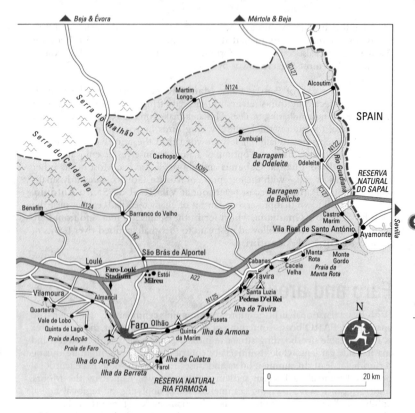

The main east-west A22 highway from Lagos to the Spanish border offers fast and easy access to the region, linking with the A2/E01 motorway to Lisbon just northeast of Albufeira.

Finally, a comprehensive calendar of **cultural events** can be found in *Agenda*, available free from tourist offices, cultural centres and larger hotels – the biggest affair is the Algarve International Music Festival (early summer), hosting major artists. For information in general, try Ⓦ www.algarvenet.com or the information hotline (☏ 808 781 212).

The eastern Algarve

All flights to the Algarve land at **Faro**, the administrative capital of the region since 1776 and by far the largest town along the coast. The centre of town is considerably more attractive than the concrete suburbs might suggest, and there are some fine beaches within easy reach, as well as possible day-trips inland to the Roman remains at **Estói** and the small country town of **São Brás de Alportel**. Faro is also a useful transport hub, connected to Lisbon by fast express coaches and to most Algarve towns by bus or – a little slower – on the Algarve rail line.

The coastline east of Faro as far as **Manta Rota**, en route to the Spanish border, is protected by thin stretches of mud flats, fringed in turn by a chain of magnificent long sandbanks, or *ilhas*. This area makes up the Reserva Natural da Ria Formosa, the shores thick with wading birds in winter and spring. The sandbank beaches are usually far less crowded than the resorts of the western Algarve and visitors have the option of basing themselves at enjoyable little towns like **Olhão**, **Fuzeta**, **Cabanas** and, above all, **Tavira**. Most of the other resorts on this stretch – with the exception of **Monte Gordo** – are fairly small-scale, while the Portuguese coast peters out at **Vila Real de Santo António**, a historic small town that preserves a fair bit of character. Vila Real lies near the mouth of the **Rio Guadiana**, which forms the Spanish border, and from here there's a fine route to be followed upstream to the small fortified river towns of **Castro Marim** and **Alcoutim**.

Faro and around

With its international airport, impressive shopping centre and ring of high-rise apartments, **FARO** boasts something of a big city feel. However, the central area is a manageable size, boasting attractive mosaic-paved pedestrianized streets and marina-side gardens, while its university contributes to a lively nightlife, during termtime at least. In summer, boats and buses run out to some excellent local beaches. Originally a Roman settlement, the city was named by the Moors, under whom it was a thriving commercial port, supplying the regional capital at Silves. Following its conquest by the Christians, under Afonso III in 1249, the city later experienced a series of conquests and disasters. Sacked and burned by the Earl of Essex in 1596, and devastated by the Great Earthquake of 1755, it is no surprise that modern Faro has so few historic buildings. What interest it does retain is contained within the pretty **Cidade Velha** (Old Town), which lies behind a series of defensive walls overlooking the mudflats.

Arrival, information and transport

Flights land at Faro's international **airport** (flight information ☎289 800 800), 6km west of town, where there's a bank, ATMs, post office and tourist office (daily 8am–11.30pm; ☎289 818 582), as well as shops and restaurants. A number of car rental companies also have offices at the airport. There are no direct public transport services to other resorts from the airport, which means heading first into central Faro.

A **taxi** into the centre of town (15min) should cost about €9–10, plus €1.50 for any luggage that goes in the boot; there's also a twenty-percent surcharge between 10pm and 6am, and at weekends. Local **buses** #14 and #16 also run from the airport to the centre (25min), costing €1.50 (departures roughly every 45min, 7.15am–8pm; buy tickets on board). Both stop outside the bus terminal in town (see below) and, further on, at the Jardim Manuel Bivar ("Jardim" on the timetables) by the harbour.

Faro's **bus terminal** (☎289 899 760) is on Avenida da República, behind and beneath the *Hotel Eva*, just back from the marina. There's an English-speaking

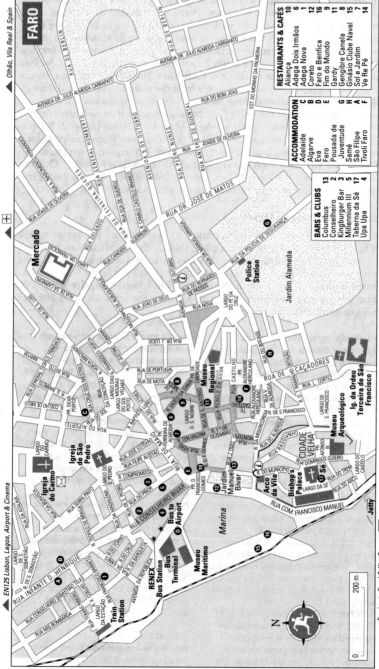

FARO

▲ Olhão, Vila Real & Spain

RESTAURANTS & CAFÉS
Aliança	10
Adega Dois Irmãos	6
Adega Nova	1
Coreto	12
Faro e Benfica	16
Fim do Mundo	9
Gardy	11
Gengibre Canela	8
Ginásio Clube Naval	15
Sol e Jardim	7
Ve Re Pé	14

ACCOMMODATION
Adelaide	C
Algarve	B
Eva	D
Faro	E
Pousada de Juventude	G
Samé	H
São Filipe	A
Tivoli Faro	F

BARS & CLUBS
Columbus	13
Conselheiro	2
Kingburger Bar	5
Millennium III	17
Taberna da Sé	3
Upa Upa	4

EN125 Lisbon, Lagos, Airport & Cinema ▲

Mercado

Igreja do Carmo

Igreja de São Pedro

Museu Regional

Police Station

Jardim Alameda

Museu Arqueológico

Ig. da Ordeu Terceira de São Francisco

CIDADE VELHA

Arco da Vila

Bishop's Palace

Sé

Jardim Manuel Bivar

Marina

Museu Marítimo

Bus Terminal

RENEX Bus Station

Train Station

Bus to Airport

N

0   200 m

Ferries to Farol & Ilha Deserta ▶

Ferries to Farol & Ilha Deserta ▶

information office inside, though it is not always staffed. The RENEX bus terminal (for express buses to Lisbon, Porto and the Minho) is opposite. The **train station** is a few minutes' walk further north up the avenue, facing Largo da Estação. The compact town is simple to negotiate on foot, and all the *pensões*, hotels, restaurants and bars are extremely central. There is a **town bus service**, but you'll only need it to get to the beach (for which, see p.552) and back to the airport. More fun is to take the **Comboio Turístico** (land train, hourly 10am–midnight; €2.50) which trundles from the marina to the Sé and through the modern town before skirting back to the marina via the market.

Faro's **turismo** is at the end of the town gardens at Rua da Misericórdia 8 (May–Sept daily 9.30am–7pm; Oct–April Mon–Fri 9.30am–1pm & 2–5.30pm; ☎289 803 604, ⊛www.cm-faro.pt), and provides town maps and posts local and long-distance bus, boat and train timetables. The regional tourist office – **Região de Turismo do Algarve** – east of the old town at Avenida 5 Outubro (Mon–Fri 9.30am–12.30pm & 2–5.30pm; ☎289 800 400, ⊛www.visitalgarve .pt) is a better source of information on the area as a whole.

Accommodation

If you arrive without a room reservation, it's worth asking the airport tourist office to try and help you book a place, though it's not officially part of their job and you'll have to pay for any calls they make on your behalf. Most of the city's *pensões* and hotels – the best of which are picked out below – are concentrated in the area just north of the harbour. Faro's basic **campsite** at Praia de Faro was closed at the time of writing – call for the latest details (☎289 817 876) or check with the turismo.

Hotels and pensions

Residencial Adelaide Rua Cruz das Mestras 7–9 ☎289 802 383, ℗289 826 870. The friendly owner offers the best-value rooms in town, with attached bathrooms and cable TV, and there's an airy breakfast room-cum-snack bar. Some rooms sleep three or four, and in summer the roof is opened for dorm beds at €15 per person. ❷

Residencial Algarve Rua Infante Dom Henrique 52 ☎289 895 700, ⊛www.residencialgarve .com. Very popular *residencial*, with bright rooms on several floors (there's a lift). Bathrooms are spotless, the rooms have a/c and cable TV, while breakfast (included) is served in the downstairs dining room or on the little internal patio. Parking on nearby streets is usually easy. ❸

Hotel Eva Av da República 1 ☎289 001 000, ⊛www.tdhotels.pt. The town's top hotel offering slightly fusty rooms with balconies looking across to the old town or the marina. There's a rooftop pool and restaurant, and a courtesy bus to the local beach. Parking. ❻

Hotel Faro Praça Dr. Francisco Gomes 2 ☎289 830 830, ⊛www.hotelfaro.pt. Modern four-star above (and accessed via) a shopping centre. Rooms are functional and geared to business travellers – with mini bar, cable TV and a/c. The

main attraction is the sunny roof terrace with its own restaurant and fine marina views. ❻

Residencial Samé Rua do Bocage 66 ☎289 824 375, ⓔsamefaro@mail.telepac.pt. Small rooms in a neat, modern hotel just outside the old town. Some have balconies and front ones can be noisy; all come with bathrooms and TV. There's an appealing lounge downstairs. ❸

Pensão São Filipe Rua Infante Dom Henrique 55-1° ☎ & ℗289 824 182. Smart rooms, each with cable TV and en-suite facilities. Rooms are small but have high ceilings with spinning fans, though the front ones contend with the traffic of a busy through road. ❸

Pensão Tivoli Faro Praça Alexandre Herculano 6 ☎289 829 825, ⊛www.tivoli-faro.net. Welcoming English-run pension with a mixed bag of airy, bright rooms with high ceilings and cable TV. Some have showers and small balconies and you can use the communal kitchen and lovely roof terrace. There's also a ground-floor annexe with backpacker rooms for €12.50 per person. All rooms have 10 percent discount for Rough Guide users. No breakfast. ❶

Youth hostel

Pousada de Juventude Rua da Policia de Segurança Pública ☎289 826 521,

www.pousadasjuventude.pt. A quiet place next
to the gardens, on the left past the police station.
Book well in advance as it's often filled with

groups. Dorms sleep four or six people (€13),
and twin rooms, with and without bath, also
available. ❶

The town

The only part of town to have survived the various violent historic upheavals
is the **Cidade Velha**, or Vila-Adentro ("town within"), an oval of cobbled
streets and bright–white buildings set within a run of sturdy walls. The houses
are fronted by decorative balconies and tiling, with the odd one serving as an
antique shop, café or art gallery. The most central entry is through the eighteenth-century town gate, the **Arco da Vila**, next to the turismo. From here,
Rua do Município leads up to the majestic Largo da Sé, flanked by the cathedral
and a group of palaces – including the former bishop's palace – and lined with
orange trees. The **Sé** itself (Mon–Sat 9am–12.30pm & 1.30–5pm, Sun open for
Mass at 10am & noon; €1.50) is a squat, white mismatch of Gothic, Renaissance and Baroque styles, all heavily remodelled after the 1755 earthquake.
However, there's fine eighteenth-century *azulejo* tiling inside, while you can
climb the bell tower for views over the old town and the mud flats beyond.

More impressive is the **Museu Arqueológico** (March–Oct Tues–Fri 10am–
6pm, Sat & Sun noon–6pm; Nov–Feb Tues–Fri 9.30am–5.30pm, Sat & Sun
11.30am–5.30pm; €2) in nearby Largo Afonso III, installed in a sixteenth-
century convent with a beautiful cloister – one of the oldest in Portugal. In
front of the building stands a forthright, crucifix-carrying statue of the
conqueror Afonso himself, king between 1249 and 1279. The most striking of
the museum's exhibits is a superb third-century AD Roman mosaic of Neptune
surrounded by the four winds, unearthed near the train station. Other items
include a collection of Roman statues from the excavations at Estói (see p.554),
exquisite Moorish lamps, vases and bowls, and a variety of Baroque and Renaissance paintings. There are also Futurist works by Carlos Porfirio, one of the
country's leading twentieth-century artists.

South of the Cidade Velha and marked by an impressive fountain, **Largo de
São Francisco** serves as a giant car park for most of the year, but is cleared in
late October for the Feira de Santa Iria, an enormous market-cum-fairground
with live entertainment over the best part of a week. The square is overlooked
by the **Igreja da Ordeu Terceira de São Francisco**, rebuilt in the eighteenth
century on the site of an earlier church. It's plain on the outside, but the interior
contains Baroque tiles and some beautiful Rococo woodwork.

At the **marina**, the town gardens and a cluster of outdoor cafés overlook the
rows of sleek yachts and at the end of the day much of Faro gathers to
promenade here. Continuing around the harbour to the west you'll pass the
small **Museu Marítimo** (Mon–Fri 2.30–4.30pm; free), a modest maritime
museum with displays of model boats and local fishing techniques. Heading
southwards on Rua Comandante Francisco Manuel, you can follow the railway
line for an attractive walk along the seafront, with the town walls on one side
and the mud flats on the other. A small arch through the old town walls offers
another approach to the Cidade Velha, while from the jetty opposite here, ferries
depart to the local sandspit beaches (see below). Most of the town centre is
devoted to shops, bars and restaurants, though there are a couple of other sights.
At the end of Rua de Santo António, on Praça de Liberdade, the **Museu
Regional** (Mon–Fri 9am–12.30pm & 2–5.30pm; €1.50) has a display of local
crafts and industries, including reconstructions of typical cottage interiors, and
models of the net systems still used for tuna fishing.

9

THE ALGARVE | Faro and around

Churches

By far the most curious attraction in town is the twin-towered, Baroque **Igreja do Carmo** (Mon–Fri 10am–1pm & 3–6pm, Oct–April until 5pm, Sat 10am–1pm, Sun only for Mass at 9am; free), near the central post office on Largo do Carmo. A door to the right of its altar leads to the sacristy where you buy a ticket (€1) to view the macabre **Capela dos Ossos** (Chapel of Bones), set in an overgrown garden at the rear, its walls decorated with human bones disinterred from the adjacent monks' cemetery. Nearby, in Largo de São Pedro, the sixteenth-century **Igreja de São Pedro** is infinitely more attractive as a church, its finest decorative work an altar (to the left of the main altar) whose central image is a gilded, wooden *Last Supper* in relief.

The beaches

Faro's "town beach" – **Praia de Faro** – is typical of the sandspit *ilha* beaches of the eastern Algarve; a long sweep of beautiful sand with both a sea-facing and a more sheltered lagoon-facing side. However, as it's so close to both airport and Faro, it is rather overdeveloped, with bars, restaurants and villas jammed onto a sandy island almost too narrow to cope – though out of season you'll probably have the sands to yourself. The beach is situated on the Ilha de Faro, southwest of town; buses #14 and #16 run from the marina gardens, or the stop opposite the bus station, calling at the airport en route (every 45 min, 7.15am–8pm), stopping just before the narrow bridge to the beach itself. In July, the area between here and the airport hosts the **Faro Bike Concentration** (Ⓦwww.motoclubefaro.pt), Europe's largest meeting of bikers, with plenty of live entertainment. Ageing rockers Nazareth and Peter Frampton have appeared in recent years.

Alternatively, in summer, **ferries** shuttle from Faro through narrow marshy channels to a great sandbar beach, between Faro and Olhão. They depart from the jetty below the old town to **Farol** (described on p.559) on the Ilha da Culatra (June to mid-Sept 4 daily, first boat 9.30am, last return 7pm; €4 return; Ⓣ917 634 813). You can also take two-and-a-half-hour boat trips to the so-called **Ilha Deserta** (daily at 11am & 3pm, weather permitting; €20; Ⓣ917 811 856, Ⓦwww.ilha-deserta.com), part of the Parque Natural da Ria Formosa. The island's official name is Ilha da Barreta, the most southerly point of mainland Portugal. Once there, you'll find one pricey café and a great beach.

Eating, drinking and nightlife

The heart of the town is an attractive pedestrianized shopping area on either side of Rua de Santo António, where you can find innumerable **restaurants**, **cafés** and **bakeries** – the latter stocked with almond delicacies, the regional speciality; try *Gardy* takeaway at Rua de Santo António 33. Most of the pavement restaurants have similar menus and similar prices; if you're prepared to scout around the back streets, you can often find cheaper, better food, though without the accompanying streetlife that makes central Faro so attractive. As you'd expect, the cuisine is predominantly seafood-based, the highlight the ubiquitous *arroz de mariscos* (a stew of shellfish and rice).

The best of Faro's nightlife is concentrated along two or three central pedestrianized streets – in particular Rua Conselheiro Bivar, with its café-bars with outdoor seating, and the parallel Rua do Prior, where many of the **bars and clubs** feature DJs, live bands and video screens; there are rarely cover charges, though there is a high turnover of places. Few places open much before 11pm and things get going around midnight; soon afterwards, as the bars fill up, drinkers spill out onto the cobbled alleys to party. Faro also occasionally hosts big-name rock and pop **gigs** at the football stadium – check posters around town, or ask at the turismo.

Cafés

Café Aliança Rua Dr F. Gomes 6–11 ☎ 282 458 860. Once the favoured haunt of the literary set – including Simone de Beauvoir – this faded coffee house is said to be one of the oldest cafés in Portugal, dating from 1908, as the photos on the wall testify. It has seats outside, and a full menu of breakfasts, burgers, salads, omelettes, pastries and ice cream.

Café do Coreto Jardim Manuel Bivar ☎ 289 822 964. Glass kiosk café-bar with prime seating facing the marina. Serves everything from croissants to ice cream, cakes, beers and light meals.

Gardy Rua de Santo António 16 ☎ 289 824 062. Popular local *pastelaria* whose seats are always at a premium – excellent cakes, pastries and coffee. Closed Sun.

Restaurants

Adega Dois Irmãos Largo Terreiro do Bispo 14 ☎ 289 823 337. Opened in 1925 by two brothers (*dois irmãos*) in a former welder's shop, this attractive tiled place is one of the oldest of the city's fish restaurants. The day's catch can be expensive (around €15), though the *pratos do dia* are usually better value. Despite the number of tourists passing through, service remains courteous and efficient, and there's a pleasant garden. Expensive.

Marisqueira Faro e Benfica Doca de Faro ☎ 289 821 422. One of the town's best spots for a splurge on fish and seafood, with tables facing across the harbour. The pricey specialities include *cataplana*, *feijoada* and various rice dishes. Closed Tues & all Nov. Expensive.

Fim do Mundo Rua Vasco da Gama 53 ☎ 289 826 299. A bustling place mostly filled with locals enjoying good-value grilled fish and meat dishes – *frango piri-piri* is the house speciality. Closed all Tues & Mon lunch. Inexpensive.

Gengibre Canela Rua de Mota 10 ☎ 289 822 424. Neat, cosy vegetarian restaurant – a rarity in these parts – with good-value dishes including salads, great fruit juices and shakes. Closed Mon evening. Moderate.

Restaurante Ginásio Clube Naval Doca de Faro ☎ 289 823 869. Set on a raised terrace right on the harbour, this is one of the few restaurants in town where you can dine with a sunset view over the tidal mud flats. There are well-priced fish dishes and grilled meats. Closed Mon. Moderate.

Sol e Jardim Pr Ferreira de Almeida 22–23 ☎ 289 820 030. Characterful place with a barn-like "garden" dining room serving moderately priced Portuguese food. Live folk music on Fri. Closed Sun. Moderate.

Adega Nova Rua Francisco Barreto 24 ☎ 289 813 433. This old-fashioned *adega* seats diners along long shared benches. It's a buzzy place, serving big portions of traditional Portuguese food and jugs of local wine or sangria. Order *bife na pedra* and you can cook your own steak on a sizzling stone, brought to your table. Moderate.

Ve Re Pé Trav Castilho 6 ☎ 968 904 193. Characterful family-run bar-restaurant with one meat and one fish dish each day – always good value and well prepared. Darts, good music and a TV add to the attraction. Closed Sun evening, unless there's a big soccer game on. Inexpensive.

Bars and clubs

Columbus Jardim Manuel Bivar, corner with Rua João Dias ☎ 289 813 051. Jazzy local haunt with outdoor seats under the arcades facing the marina. There's a dartboard and some lethal sangrias and caipirinha cocktails. Closed Sun.

Conselheiro Rua Conselheiro Bivar 72–78 ☎ 966 488 531. Disco bar with a large bar area, two dance floors and three games rooms, complete with snooker and videos. Minimum consumption policy most nights.

Kingburger Bar Rua do Prior 40. A small and relaxed bar, one of the first to open up along here, and one of the last to close. Closed Sun–Tues.

Millennium III Rua do Prior 23 ☎ 289 823 628. Large club with an industrial-warehouse feel, playing dance and Latin sounds. There are good DJs and occasional performances by local bands. Open 1am–7am; closed Sun–Tues.

Taberna da Sé Largo da Sé 26 ☎ 965 827 662. Arty tavern in the old town with outdoor tables attracting a friendly, young crowd. A popular spot for spontaneous jamming sessions on a summer's evening. Closed Sun.

Upa Upa Rua Conselheiro Bivar 51 ☎ 289 807 832. Laid-back and relatively early opening music bar with a mixed clientele spilling onto outdoor tables on the widest stretch of this pedestrianized street. Closed Sun Oct–April.

Listings

Car rental The following agencies have offices at the airport: AutoJardim ☎800 200 613, ⓦwww.auto-jardim.com; Avis ☎800 201 002; Hertz ☎800 238 238.

Cinema There's a multiplex (☎289 889 300) at the Fórum Algarve shopping complex, on the airport road (N125), a brisk fifteen-minute walk from town up Rua Infante Dom Henrique.

Consulate The only British consulate in the Algarve is in Portimão (p.585). In Faro itself, there are the following: Canada, Rua Frei Lourenço Santa Maria 1-1º, Apt 79 ☎289 803 757; Denmark, Rua Conselheiro Bívar 1-10º ☎289 805 561; and Netherlands, Largo Francisco Sá Carneiro 52 ☎289 820 903.

Football/Live music International games are sometimes played at the 30,000-seater Algarve stadium (☎289 990 360, ⓦwww.parquecidades-eim.pt), the centrepiece of a cultural, sports and medical park called Parque das Cidades, 6km north of Faro on the Loulé

road. This also hosts the Summer Festival in June, which attracts international bands – Lenny Kravitz and Da Weasel have appeared previously.

Hospital Hospital Distrital de Faro, Leão Penedo ☎289 891 100/289 892 820. In emergencies call ☎112.

Left luggage At the bus terminal (Mon–Fri 9am–1pm & 3–7pm); €2.50 per item per day.

Police Rua da Policia de Segurança Pública 32 ☎289 822 022.

Post office Largo do Carmo (Mon–Fri 8.30am–6.30pm, Sat 9am–12.30pm). It has *poste restante* facilities, and you can make international telephone calls from here too.

Taxis There's a rank in Pr Dr Francisco Gomes, by the town gardens, otherwise call ☎289 822 275 or 289 895 795.

Travel agencies Abreu, Av da República 124 ☎289 870 900; Top Tours, Edifício Hotel Eva, Doca de Faro Av da República ☎289 895 340.

Around Faro: Estói and São Brás de Alportel

Apart from the beach, other worthwhile day trips from Faro are to the couple of villages in the gentle hills to the north. At **Estói**, you can divide your time between the gardens of a delightful eighteenth-century country estate and the remains of a Roman settlement at **Milreu**, just below the village. Further north is the hilltop town of **São Brás de Alportel**, whose *pousada* provides a more refined base for the region than staying in Faro. Travelling by bus, unless you make a fairly early start it's difficult to see both villages on the same day. However, it's perfectly feasible to take the bus to São Brás and walk the 7km down to Estói, catching the late-afternoon bus back to Faro from there.

Estói

Regular buses make the twenty-minute journey 11km north of Faro to **ESTÓI**, which basically consists of a main street, a little square and a small white church. Buses drop you in the square, just off which you'll find the delightful peach-coloured **Palácio do Visconde de Estói**, a diminutive version of the Rococo palace of Queluz near Lisbon. It's currently being converted into a *pousada* (ⓦwww.pousadas.pt), but the attractive grounds are still open to the public (Mon–Sat 9am–12.30pm & 2–5.30pm; free), the terraces lined with spectacular *azulejos* and tropical plants.

The main reason for a visit to Estói, however, is the Roman site at **Milreu** (pronounced *mil-rio*; ☎289 803 633, Tues–Sun: April–Sept 9.30am–12.30pm & 2–6pm; Oct–March 9.30am–12.30 & 2–5pm; €2), a ten-minute walk downhill from the square. Known to the Romans as Ossonoba, the town that once stood here predated Faro and was inhabited from the second to the sixth century AD. The surviving ruins are associated with a peristyle villa – one with a gallery of columns surrounding a courtyard – and dominated by the apse of a temple, which was converted into a Christian basilica in the third century AD, making

△ Milreu

it one of the earliest of all known churches. The other recognizable remains are of a bathing complex southwest of the villa, with its fragmented fish mosaics, and the *apodyterium*, or changing room, sporting stone benches and arched niches below for clothes. The site was finally abandoned in the eighth century AD, after which date the Moors founded Faro to the south.

Back in the village, there's good **food** at *Casa do Pasto Victor*, Rua Vasco da Gama 41 (closed Sun), just off the square on the Olhão road, where you'd be hard pushed to spend more than €12 a head. There are also no fewer than eleven **café-bars** along and around the main street; the two on the main square are good bets.

São Brás de Alportel

Seven kilometres north of Estói, the only reason to visit the otherwise dull town of **SÃO BRÁS DE ALPORTEL** is to see its great museum. Buses pull up in the main square and, just off it, at Rua Dr José Dias Sancho 61, lies the **Museu Etnográfico do Trajo Algarvio** (W www.museu-trajo-algarve.web.pt; Mon–Fri 10am–1pm & 2–5pm, Sat 2–5pm; €1), housed in a nineteenth-century palacette. The museum's alcoves and corridors are full of traditional costumes, and farming and domestic equipment. A series of buildings around an outside courtyard shelter cork-cutting equipment, ancient donkey carts and looms, while in the courtyard itself you can walk down a partially excavated traditional well. From the museum, cut down Rua Nova de Fonte to the **Jardim da Verbena** (May–Sept 8am–8pm; Oct–April 8am–5pm; free), a wonderful little garden with an open-air swimming pool (hours as park; free). Just west of here lie the narrow streets of the oldest part of town, clustered round the **Igreja Matriz**, from where there are lovely views of the surrounding valleys.

There's a small **turismo** on the main square (Mon–Fri 10am–1.30pm & 2.30–6pm; T 289 843 165). There's not much cause to stay here, but if you are stuck the *Residencial São Brás*, just off the square at Rua Luís Bivar 27 (T & F 289 842 213; ❸), has large if musty rooms in a fine old town house. However, if you have the funds, there is every reason to stay at the very comfortable *Pousada de São Brás* (T 289 845 171, W www.pousadas.pt; ❻) a few kilometres to the north. The views from the comfortable rooms' balconies are splendid, and there's a pool, tennis courts, games room and (expensive) restaurant. Advance booking is essential in summer. **Restaurants** back in town are sparse but try the *Savoy*, Rua Luís Bivar 40 (closed Wed), past the *Residencial São Brás*, which offers well-cooked international cuisine and a children's menu. There are also plenty of café-bars round the main square.

Olhão and around

OLHÃO, 8km east of Faro, is the largest fishing port on the Algarve and an excellent base for visiting the surrounding sandbank **ilhas** of Armona and Culatra or the Quinta da Marim environmental centre. There are few sights in town, but with a vibrant market, attractive riverfront gardens and atmospheric back streets, it makes a great place to visit on a day trip or to stop for a night or two. The largely pedestrianized old town is punctuated with some superb tile-fronted buildings, quirky shops and bars. The flat roofs and narrow streets are striking and give a North African look to the place. No surprise, then, that Olhão has centuries-old trading links with Morocco, as well as a small place in history for its uprising against the French garrison in 1808. Following the French departure, the local fishermen sent a small boat across the Atlantic to Brazil to transmit the news to the exiled king, João VI. The journey, completed without navigational aids, was rewarded after the king's restoration to the throne by the granting of a town charter.

The old town's most prominent building is the seventeenth-century parish church of **Nossa Senhora do Rosário** (Tues–Sun 9.30am–noon & 3–6pm), right in the middle of town. Outside, at the back of the church, an iron grille protects the chapel of **Nossa Senhora dos Aflitos**, where townswomen traditionally gathered when there was a storm at sea to pray for their sailors amid candles and curious wax ex-voto models of children and limbs.

Opposite, the back of the church of Nossa Senhora da Soledade hosts the small **Museu da Cidade** (T 289 700 184, Tues–Fri 10am–12.30pm & 2–5.30pm, Sat 10am–1pm; free), with a small collection of archeological finds from the region, from bronze-age pots to Islamic vases. Upstairs there are relics

OLHÃO

Railway Station

N

Bus Station

★ Taxi Rank

Nossa Senhora do Rosário

Museu da Cidade

N. S. da Soledade

Porta da Pesca

AVENIDA DAS FORÇAS ARMADAS

Police Station

AVENIDA 5 DE OUTUBRO

Mercado

Marina

0   200 m

Ferry to Ilhás

ACCOMMODATION

Bela Vista	C
Bicuar	B
Boémia	A

RESTAURANTS, CAFÉS & BARS

A Bote	3
Faz Gostos	1
Gelvi	5
Kinkas	4
Sociedade Recreativa Olhanense	2

of Olhão's industrial heritage, with model fishing boats, oil presses and old black-and-white photos.

The other obvious focus of the town is the **market**, held in the two modern redbrick buildings on the harbourside. Open from the crack of dawn (Mon–Sat), there's meat, fruit and vegetables on one side, fish on the other, the latter hall full of tuna steaks the size of hubcaps and alarmingly large octopus and squids. In August, the gardens either side host the Festival do Marisco (seafood festival; Ⓦ www.festivaldomarisco.com) with food stalls and nightly entertainment over five days.

Practicalities

The **train station** is at the northern edge of town, off Avenida dos Combatentes da Grande Guerra, with the **bus terminal** a few minutes away on Rua General Humberto Delgado. From either, it's a quick walk down to the main Avenida da República, a wide boulevard which leads into the town centre, a further five minutes' walk away. At the parish church, the avenue forks: follow Rua do Comércio to find the **turismo** on Largo Sebastião Martins Mestre

(June to mid-Sept daily 9.30am–7pm; mid-Sept to May Mon–Fri 9.30am–1pm & 2–5.30pm; ☎289 713 936, ⓦwww.cm-olhao.pt), which can provide sailing times of boats to the *ilhas*.

Accommodation options are limited, though there are plans to build a new hotel complex to the west of town. There are plenty of inexpensive cafés and bars around the market buildings, while the riverfront Avenida 5 de Outubro is lined with more expensive **fish restaurants**. Up by the ferry stop is another clutch of budget cafés and fast-food restaurants, while **nightlife** is liveliest round the back of the market buildings, where various bars play dance music till late.

Hotels and pensions

Pensão Bela Vista Rua Dr Teófilo Braga 65–67 ☎ & ⓕ289 702 538. A longstanding favourite, with a range of simple, bright rooms – some completely tiled – arranged around a tiled, flower-filled courtyard. No breakfast. ❷, also lets out apartments sleeping 2–4 from €50.

🏃 **Pensão Bicuar** Rua Vasco da Gama 5 ☎289 714 816, ⓦwww.pension-bicuar.net. Very central English-run *pensão* on a quiet pedestrianized street, with a variety of rooms, including family rooms and dorms sleeping up to four. All are well furnished with cable TV, most with private showers and balconies overlooking the old town. From the roof terrace there are great views. No breakfast. Recommended. ❷

Pensão Boémia Rua da Cerca 20 ☎ & ⓕ289 714 513. A friendly, quiet choice in a residencial part of town. Rooms come with shower and balcony. ❷

Campsite

Camping Olhão Pinheiros de Marim, 3km east of town, next to Quinta da Marim ☎289 700 300, ⓦwww.sbsi.pt/camping. The upmarket site, served by regular bus from Olhão, is set in substantial grounds with use of its own pool (for a small fee), playground, tennis courts, mini-market, restaurant and bars.

Cafés and bars

Café Gelvi Mercado, Av 5 de Outubro. Bustling *pastelaria* and *geladaria* in the corner of the fish market, with outdoor seats facing the water.

Sociedade Recreativa Olhanense, Av da República 35. The local cultural centre has its own small bar – enjoy a beer in its extensive back patio. The centre also has a theatre, video room and exhibition centre, with live fado on Sat nights in summer.

Restaurants

🏃 **A Bote** Av 5 de Outubro 122 ☎289 721 183. The best place for a lively meal, serving superb grilled meat and fish dishes. Closed Sun. Moderate.

Faz Gostos Av da República 148 ☎289 701 900. Making waves on the culinary front with top-notch fusion cuisine – roast duck, shrimp crepes and traditional desserts such as *tocinho do céu* egg pudding. Closed Sat evening. Expensive.

Kinkas Av 5 de Outubro 46–48 ☎289 703 333. Opposite the market, this is known for its fine steaks, though it also does some fine *cataplanas*, rice dishes and a few vegetarian options. Moderate.

Armona and Culatra

Separate **ferries** leave for the *ilhas* of Armona and Culatra from the jetty at the eastern end of Olhão's municipal gardens, five minutes' walk from the market. There's a timetable posted at the kiosk; if it isn't open, you can buy tickets on the ferries. The **Ilha da Armona** (15min) is accessible all year round, as are the villages of Culatra (35min) and Farol (45min) on the **Ilha da Culatra**. Note that in summer you can also get the boat to Farol from Faro (see p.552).

Ilha da Armona

Ferries (June & early Sept 9 departures daily; July & Aug first departure 7.30am, then hourly 9am–8pm; late Sept to May 4 daily; €2.60 return) drop their passengers at the southern end of the single settlement on **Ilha da Armona** – a long, crowded strip of holiday chalets and huts that stretches right across the island on either side of the main path. It's a fifteen-minute walk to the ocean, where the beach disappears into the distance. A short walk will take you to attractive stretches of sand and dune – the further you go, the greater the privacy. Continue east for two hours up the beach and you end up at Praia da Fuzeta opposite Fuzeta town (see below).

There are a few **bar-restaurants** by the jetty, though most are closed once summer is over. There are no *pensões* or hotels on Armona, and camping on the beach is frowned upon, but *Orbitur* (☎289 714 173, ⓦ www.orbitur.pt) operates a series of beachside holiday **bungalows** sleeping up to six (❹; closed Nov–March; reservations advised; one-week minimum stay in high season).

Ilha da Culatra

The **Ilha da Culatra** (ferries June & Sept 6 daily; July & Aug 7 daily; rest of year 4 daily; €2.60 return to Culatra, €3 to Farol) is another huge sand spit, though quite different in character from Armona. Its northern shore is dotted with a series of fishing settlements, mixed with an incongruous sprinkling of holiday chalets. The ferry's first port of call, **Culatra**, is the largest settlement, though **Farol**, the second stop, is far more agreeable, with its fishermen's huts and holiday homes gathered below a lighthouse, edged by beautiful tracts of beach on the ocean side – the mainland-facing beach is rather grubby. If you're considering staying, the best you can do is to ask around in Farol's market where you might be able to pick up a private **room** for around €35; camping is not allowed. In Farol, *À-do-João Restaurant* (Oct–April weekends only) serves good seafood dishes, including *cataplana*, as well as less expensive snacks and sandwiches.

Quinta da Marim

Three kilometres east of Olhão, just off the N125 Olhão-Tavira road (and served by regular bus from Olhão and Fuzeta), **Quinta da Marim** (☎289 704 134; daily: centre 9am–12.30pm & 2–5.30pm; park Mon–Fri 8am–7pm (Oct–May until 6pm), Sat & Sun 8am–3pm; €1.50) is an environmental educational centre within the **Parque Natural da Ria Formosa**. It's a lovely quiet spot, set amid scrubby dunes and mud flats dotted with pines and gorse, well worth a half-day's visit. You can follow a three-kilometre-long **nature trail** that leads from the car park past the visitor centre, along which you'll also be able to view storks' nests, and the remains of Roman salt pans. The highlight is one of the country's last remaining tidal mills, complete with a rooftop organic café; there's also a restaurant at the visitor centre.

The reserve is also known for being the refuge of bizarre **aquatic poodles** that were formerly bred to dive into the water to help chase fish into the local fishermen's nets. More modern, less enterprising, methods were adopted in the 1950s, though the shaggy dogs still thrive here in their pure-bred form in the **park kennels** (ⓦ www.caodaguapt.com; Mon–Fri 11am–1pm & 2–4pm, Sat & Sun 10am–noon).

Fuzeta

Around 10km east of Olhão, and served by regular bus as well as the main Algarve rail line, the fishing town of **FUZETA** (or Fuseta) is one of the Algarve's least "discovered" resorts, probably because of its shortage of accommodation. It is not the region's most beautiful town, but it does retain some character as a working fishing port. Indeed its daily routine revolves around the fishermen, whose colourful boats line up alongside the river in town, though in summer Fuzeta also attracts a lively community of backpackers. The two communities usually mingle at the line of lively kiosk-cafés spreading down from the ferry stop towards the river beach.

The town's back streets straddle a low hill facing the lagoon, sheltered by the eastern extremity of the Ilha da Armona. Many of the local fish find their way to the small covered **market** on Largo 1º de Maio, on the road running parallel to the river; the quayside behind the building is often lined with drying octopus. On Saturdays the market expands into a weekly flea market that lines the adjacent pedestrianized Rua Tenente Barrosa. Continue up this road to reach the town's little palm tree-lined central square and Rua da Liberdade.

The waterfront of modern shops and apartments faces broad gardens that are largely taken over by the campsite (see below). Beyond this is the **river beach**, a fine stretch of white sand that weaves up to a wooden lifeboat house. Many people splash about in the calm waters of the river, though more exhilarating and cleaner waters are found over the river on the Ilha da Armona (see p.558). Regular **ferries** (April–Oct roughly every 15min, 9am–7pm and often later; Nov–March 4 daily; €1.50 return) shuttle from the fishing quay at the back of the campsite across the lagoon to **Praia da Fuzeta** on the eastern end of the Ilha da Armona. The beach immediately opposite the ferry stop gets fairly crowded in high summer, but you only have to walk ten minutes or so either way from the holiday beach huts and seasonal drinks kiosks to have beautiful, low dune-backed sands all to yourself. You can also reach the sands by Aquataxis (☎962 539 810) for €2 per person.

Practicalities

Buses drop you at the waterfront gardens, opposite the campsite. There are **rooms** (*quartos*) advertised in private houses, but most visitors stay at the waterside **campsite**, the *Parque de Campismo da Fuzeta* (☎289 793 459, ⓕ289 794 034), beautifully positioned under the trees. It gets pretty full in high summer. Around 2km northwest of Fuzeta – signposted Bias Sul – *Monte Alegre* (☎289 794 222, ⓔmonte.alegre@iol.pt; ④) consists of three well-equipped apartments sleeping up to five, and a superb studio with its own terrace. It's set in countryside with great coastal views, there's an outdoor swimming pool, stables for horse rides and a pond full of resident frogs; rooms all have satellite TV and kitchenettes.

There are plenty of **cafés and restaurants** on and around the ferry terminal and the main Rua da Liberdade. First choice is *Skandinavia,* on Rua Tenente Barroso 11 near the market (☎289 793 853; closed Tues) with moderately priced fish and friendly service; outdoor tables spill onto the pedestrianized street. Nearby *Capri*, at Praça da República 4 (☎289 793 165; closed Wed) is a lively bar-restaurant with tables on the main square, serving inexpensive fish dishes and reliable grills. Out on Praia da Fuzeta, just back from the sands, *Restaurante Caetano* (☎919 962 048; daytime only) is open from April to October for excellent salads, snacks and full meals.

Tavira and around

Situated 30km east of Faro, **TAVIRA** is one of the most beautiful towns in the Algarve and a clear winner if you are looking for a base on the eastern stretch.

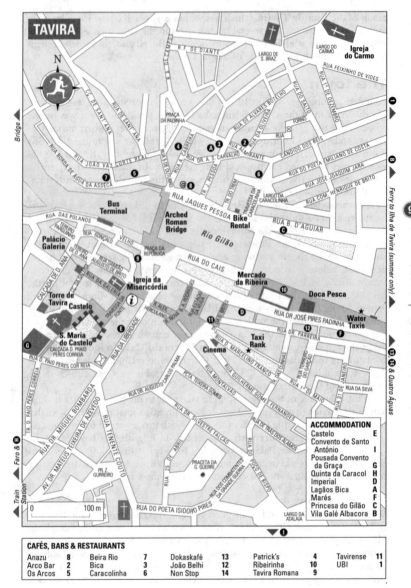

TAVIRA

N

Bridge
Ferry to Ilha de Tavira (summer only)
13, 14 & Quatro Águas
Faro & 13
Train Station

ACCOMMODATION

Castelo	E
Convento de Santo António	I
Pousada Convento da Graça	G
Quinta da Caracol	H
Imperial	D
Lagôas Bica	A
Marés	F
Princesa do Gilão	C
Vila Galé Albacora	B

CAFÉS, BARS & RESTAURANTS

Anazu	8	Beira Rio	7	Dokaskafé	13	Patrick's	4
Arco Bar	2	Bica	3	João Belhi	12	Ribeirinha	10
Os Arcos	5	Caracolinha	6	Non Stop	14	Tavira Romana	9

Tavirense	11
UBI	1

It's sited on both sides of the broad Rio Gilão, which is overlooked by balconied houses and straddled by low bridges, one of Roman origin. Despite ever-increasing numbers of visitors and encroaching development Tavira continues to make a living as a fishing port, and its seafood restaurants along the palm-lined river are a powerful incentive to stop. Indeed, many stay longer than planned – particularly those intent on lounging around on the superb island beach of the **Ilha de Tavira**, which lies within easy reach of the town by year-round ferry. There are also several quieter spots in the area, such as the holiday village of **Pedras d'el Rei** and nearby beach at **Barril** and, for some excellent seafood, the tiny fishing village of **Santa Luzia**.

The town

Founded as long ago as 400 BC, Tavira was an important port trading with North Africa until the Great Earthquake of 1755, when the town was largely rebuilt with the graceful eighteenth-century town houses and mansions that you see today. The old bridge was mostly built in 1667 on the foundations of a Roman structure; the other central bridge was put up by the army in 1989 as a temporary structure, but has held firm ever since. In the old-town streets on both sides of the river, numerous houses retain fine old doorways with traditional knockers in the shape of hands.

From the arcaded **Praça da República**, with its little modern amphitheatre by the river, it's a short climb up into the old town following Rua da Galeria. Ahead stands the **Igreja da Misericórdia** with its fine stone doorway carved by master-mason André Pilarte (1551) depicting a series of mermaids, angels and saints. Inside there's a striking *azulejo* interior showing scenes from the life of Christ, below a wooden vaulted ceiling, but unfortunately the church is almost always locked. Turn left here and a couple of hundred metres up the cobbled street are the ruins of the **Castelo** (Mon–Fri 8am–5pm, Sat & Sun 9am–5.30pm; free), half hidden amid landscaped gardens on a low hill in the centre of town. From the walls you can look down over the peculiarly hipped terracotta rooftops and the town's numerous church spires. Adjacent to the castle, the impressive, whitewashed **Santa Maria do Castelo** is open daily, and contains the tomb of Dom Paio Peres Correia, who reconquered much of the Algarve, including Tavira in 1242, from the Moors. Fittingly, the church stands on the site of the former mosque.

On the other side of the castle, you can take a lift to the top of the 100m-high **Torre de Tavira** (daily every 30min, 9.30–5pm; €3) a former water tower that now acts as an interesting Câmara Obscura – with images of the town projected onto a white disk, together with commentary in English. Just below here, on Calçada da Galeria, the **Palácio Galeria** (Tues–Fri 10am–12.30pm & 2-6pm, Sat 2–6pm; free) is a sixteenth-century palace with sixteen rooms and sixteen roofs – now hosting a modest collection of contemporary arts.

The riverfront

With its tranquil vistas and palm-lined gardens, the **riverfront** is the best part of Tavira for a wander. There are no sights as such north of the river, though the old streets hide many of the town's best restaurants. South of the river, the former town market building, **Mercado da Riberia**, has become a "cultural centre" – actually a handful of small boutiques and waterfront cafés. The old market walls are also used for temporary exhibitions, usually the work of local artists and photographers.

Beyond the market lies the fish market (for the trade only) and the fishing boats, lined up as far along as the flyover – this part of the river is also where most of the touristy fish restaurants are. In summer, you can catch direct ferries to the Ilha da Tavira (see p.564) from here. Head under the bridge and you'll see the large new town **market** (Mon–Sat 8am–1.30pm), whose bustling interior is filled with an array of fruit and vegetables. The bars alongside are the current in places to spend the evening.

Practicalities

Tavira's **bus terminal** is by the river, from where it's a two-minute walk to the old bridge and Praça da República. The **train station** is 1km from the centre of town, straight up the Rua da Liberdade and at the end of Avenida Dr Mateus Teixeira de Azevedo. Up the steps just off Praça da República is the **turismo**, at Rua da Galeria 9 (May–Oct Mon & Fri–Sun 9.30am–1pm & 2–7pm, Tues–Thurs 9.30am–7pm; Nov–April Mon & Fri–Sun 9.30am–1pm & 2–5.30pm, Tues–Thurs 9.30am–5.30pm; ℡281 322 511, 🖰www.cm-tavira.pt). Drivers will encounter a complicated one-way system in the central area; there's metered parking in and around Praça da República so it's probably best to head for the free **car park** under the flyover – follow signs to Quatro Águas. A fun way to get your bearings is by taking the **road train**, which does a circuit from Praça da República out to Quatro Águas (daily every 45min, 10am–dusk; €4). Alternatively, **horse and carriages** tour town from outside the cinema (15min for €10 for up to five people). Sport Nautica, Rua Jacques Pessoa 26 (℡281 324 943), offers **bike rental** from €5 a day. **Taxis** line up opposite the cinema.

The town has a growing number of places to stay and finding **accommodation** is only a problem in high season. The tourist office can help with **private rooms** (❸) if you have no luck at any of the places listed below. The nearest campsite is on the Ilha de Tavira, for which see p.564. There are **cafés and restaurants** all over town; the seafood restaurants on the partly pedestrianized Rua José Pires Padinha have tables that edge out on to the riverside, though they are pricey and largely frequented by tourists.

Hotels and pensions

Quinta do Caracol ℡281 322 475, 🖰www .quintadocaracol.pa.net.pt. Just over the railway line opposite the station, this lovely farmhouse is set in attractive gardens with a small plunge pool and tennis courts. The grounds have a series of self-catering apartments sleeping 2–5 in taste-fully converted outbuildings. Great for families. ❺

Pensão do Castelo Rua da Liberdade 22 ℡281 320 790, ℻281 320 799. Very centrally located, this rambling place has spotlessly clean en-suite rooms with TVs. There's also disabled access. No breakfast. ❸

Convento de Santo António Rua de Santo António, 1km southeast of town ℡281 321 573, ℻281 325 632. Book well ahead (by fax only) for one of the seven elegant double rooms in this converted convent with swimming pool and roof terrace. It's located just out of town in a residential suburb. There's a minimum four-night stay in summer, two in winter. Closed Jan. ❽

Residencial Imperial Rua José Pires Padinha 24 ℡ & ℻281 322 234. Small *residencial* above a decent restaurant. Opt for one of the rooms overlooking the gardens and river.❷

Residencial Lagâos Bica Rua Almirante Cândido dos Reis 24 ℡281 322 252. On the north side of the river, this has simple but attrac-tive rooms clustered round a rooftop patio. It's

above the top-notch budget restaurant, *Bica* (see p.564). ❷

Residencial Marés Rua José Pires Padinha 134–140 ℡281 325 815, ℮maresresidencial @mail.telepac.pt. Extremely pleasant rooms, some facing the river, with tiled floors and *azulejos* in the bathrooms; there's also a roof terrace and sauna. ❹

Pousada Convento da Graça Rua D. Paio Peres Correia, ℡281 442 001, 🖰www.pousadas.pt. Set in a sixteenth-century convent around beautiful cloisters and with its own church, the Algarve's newest *pousada* is hard to fault. Most of the plush rooms look down over the old town or a rural hillside, while the swimming pool nestles inside Tavira's old town walls. During renovation work, the remains of Moorish settlement were found and these can be viewed through a glass partition in the bar, and there's also a highly rated restaurant that uses local ingredients. ❼

Residencial Princesa do Gilão Rua Borda d'Àgua de Aguiar 10–12 ℡ & ℮residencial-gilao @hotmail.com. A white modern building with *azulejo*-decorated interior, located right on the quayside. The rooms are small, and fairly simply furnished, but the front ones are enhanced by balconies overlooking the river. ❹

Vila Galé Albacora 2km east of town, opposite Quatro Águas ℡281 380 800, 🖰www.vilagale.pt.

This former tuna-fishing village has been tastefully converted into a four-star hotel, with rooms in the old houses either facing the river estuary or the enormous central courtyard (though some face the car park). The flower-filled courtyard also contains a large pool, games room, restaurant and bar; inside there's another pool and health club. The downside of its riverside position is a colony of voracious mosquitoes. Parking. ⑥

Restaurants

Os Arcos Rua João Vaz Corte Real 15 ☎281 324 392. Good-value local tavern serving fine grills, soups and salads. In summer, tables are placed in a superb riverfront position facing the old bridge. Full meals around €10. Inexpensive.

Beira Rio Rua Borda da Àgua de Assêca 46–48 ☎281 323 165. Arty and airy riverside bar-restaurant set in a former girls' school, with tree-shaded tables. It's a tranquil venue for pizza, pasta and salads; evenings only; closed Nov. Moderate.

Bica Rua Almirante Cândido dos Reis 22–24 ☎281 323 843. Excellent-value Portuguese meals in a bustling little restaurant on the north side of the river. Mains around €7. Inexpensive.

Caracolinha Largo da Caracolinha 9 ☎281 381 069. A bargain takeaway joint Portuguese-style: mountains of pork steaks or chicken, chips, salad and rice for around €7 which is enough for 2–3 people. Inexpensive.

🏃 **João Belhi** Rua José Pires Padinha 94–96 ☎965 449 557. There are no outdoor tables, but this is less expensive and more locally inclined than most of the restaurants on this stretch. The menu features the usual fish and meat dishes and there's good house wine. Moderate. Closed Tues.

Quatro Águas Quatro Águas ☎281 325 329. Out by the ferry stop, this highly rated seafood restaurant specializes in dishes such as açorda and cataplana de marisco, or try the bife de frango com molho roquefort (chicken with roquefort sauce). Closed Mon. Expensive.

Ribeirinha Mercado da Ribeira, Loja 3 ☎965 384 464. One of the best positioned of the old market café-restaurants, a fine spot for a beer or a simple

meal overlooking the river. Closed Thurs Oct–May. Inexpensive.

Cafés

Anazu Rua Jacques Pessoa 11–13 ☎281 381 935. A lovely, tiled riverfront café, which seems to catch the sun all day – a good place for breakfast or a sunset drink. There's a games-room/cyber café attached. Inexpensive.

Tavira Romana Pr da República ☎281 323 451. The café by the pedestrianized bridge does superb ice creams.

Tavirense Rua Marcelino Franco 19. For some of the best cakes in town, try this old-fashioned pastelaria opposite the cinema.

Bars and clubs

Arco Bar Rua Almirante Cândido dos Reis 67 ☎918 504 200. One of a few fashionable spots north of the river, attracting a laid-back crowd. Open from 9pm. Closed Mon.

🏃 **Dokaskafé** Mercado Municipal Loja 2 ☎966 340 739. Rated one of the best of the row of music bars along the front of the market building – this one is the furthest from the flyover. Contemporary dance sounds and a bit of jazz plus a friendly, mixed crowd. Open from 9pm.

Non Stop Mercado Municipal ☎281 325 162. Bills itself as a "music café" with dance and Latin sounds until the small hours. Also does toasted sandwiches. Open from 10pm; Fri and Sat only from Oct–March.

Patrick's Rua Dr António Cabreira 25–27 ☎281 325 998. A welcoming adega-style English-run bar-restaurant where, along with some familiar beers, you can enjoy bar food such as piri-piri prawns and curries. Closed Sun, Mon & Nov.

UBI Rua Almirante Cândido dos Reis ☎281 324 577, ⑬www.ubidisco.web.pt. Follow Rua Almirante Cândido dos Reis to the outskirts of town. Tavira's only club is housed in a huge former factory. The locals warm up with a few pre-clubbing drinks in the Bubi Bar in the same building, open from 10pm. Club open July–Sept Tues–Sun 11pm–6am; Oct–June Fri & Sat only.

Ilha de Tavira

The Ilha de Tavira stretches southwest from Tavira almost as far as Fuzeta, some 14km away, and the beach is enormous, backed by tufted dunes. In summer you can catch ferries direct from the riverfront in town (July–Sept daily 8.30am–8pm, roughly hourly; €1.50 return). Otherwise, you get there by ferry from the jetty at **Quatro Águas**, 2km east of town – it's a thirty-minute walk, or you can take the road train from Tavira (see "Practicalities", p.563) or a bus from the terminal (July to mid-Sept Mon–Fri roughly hourly). There's a huddle of cafés and restaurants next to the ferry terminal, while the **ferries** themselves (daily: Easter–June 8am–8pm; July–Sept 8am–9pm; Oct–Easter 9am–dusk; €1 return) take just five minutes to cross to the island. In high season they run every fifteen minutes or so, often until much later than 9pm; at other times they run roughly hourly – always check with the ferryman what time the last boat returns. Alternatively, **aquataxis** (daily from 8am; ⓣ964 515 075 or 917 035 207) from Quatro Águas do the ride for €15 (for up to six people).

On the **Ilha de Tavira**, the main path on the island runs from the jetty through a small chalet settlement to the beach, where there are umbrellas and pedaloes for rent, and half a dozen bar-restaurants. In high summer this part of the beach is packed with families and beach dudes, though you only have to walk fifteen minutes or so to be clear of the crowds, and out of season you'll probably have the place entirely to yourself. Alternatively, pick up an attractive path heading west from the ferry stop, parallel to the coast, where there are picnic tables dotted under fragrant pines.

The **campsite** (ⓣ281 321 709, ⓦwww.campingtavira.com; closed Oct–Easter) is just a minute from the sands, with a well-stocked mini-market. Between here and the beach *Pavilhão da Ilha* (ⓣ281 324 131; closed Nov–Feb) is the best place on the island for a full **meal**, with moderately priced fish and grills and a lively bar area.

Santa Luzia, Pedras d'el Rei and Barril

Along the coastal road from Tavira, regular weekday buses (three on Sat) run the 3km west to the fishing village of **SANTA LUZIA**, which bills itself as the "King of the Octopus". It's an earthy working fishing village with a number of seafood restaurants catering to day-trippers, who saunter around the palm-lined waterfront and small fishing harbour. Having admired the octopus traps on the jetty, and the bright, whitewashed buildings, most people settle for a leisurely meal. Best bet is *Capelo* (ⓣ281 381 670; closed Wed), a slightly pricey joint on the main Avenida Engheneiro Duarte Pacheco, with a spacious *azulejo*-lined interior and an outdoor terrace. You can also take boat trips from near the jetty. Santa Luzia Boats (ⓣ969 523 629, ⓦwww.santaluziaboats.com) run two-hour trips into the lagoon for €25 for two people.

A kilometre west down the river, 4km from Tavira, **PEDRAS D'EL REI** is served by six buses daily from Tavira's bus station (Mon–Fri only). This is a fairly upmarket holiday complex, which offers access to another stretch of the Ilha da Tavira at Barril (see below). The **apartments and villas** here (⚐ ⓣ281 380 600, ⓦwww.pedrasdelrei.com; from ❻) are perfect for families, set in beautifully landscaped grounds. There's a central lawned area focused on an outdoor pool and overlooked by a café, bar and restaurant. Facilities include a playground, children's club, aviary and well-stocked shop, and residents have free passes for the train to the beach.

From the bus stop and car park next to Pedras d'El Rei, you cross the causeway to the terminal of a rather ancient-looking **miniature train** (daily, except in bad weather, 8am–dusk, roughly every 15–30min; €1 one-way). This shuttles across the mud flats, past thousands of fiddler crabs, to the beach of **Barril** on the Ilha de Tavira. You can also walk alongside the tracks (10–15min). At the beach, attractive former fishermen's houses have been turned into a cluster of slightly pricey café-restaurants; there's also a small shop, showers and toilets. A few minutes' walk right or left of the terminus – past lines of anchors wedged into the dunes – there are miles of peaceful, dune-fringed beach.

East of Tavira: to Monte Gordo

Just to the east of Tavira, beyond the resort of **Cabanas**, the sand spit that protects much of the eastern Algarve from the developers starts to thin out and merges with the shoreline beach at **Manta Rota**, 12km away. Manta Rota itself and neighbouring **Altura** have been intensively developed, although the beaches are still alluring, and there are more sandy stops further to the east at **Praia Verde** and the resort of **Monte Gordo**. However, there is one surprise on this part of the coast: for some reason, the small hamlet of **Cacela Velha** (not to be confused with Vila Nova de Cacela, 2km inland) is barely touched by tourism.

You can reach Cabanas, Altura and Monte Gordo by bus from Tavira; for Manta Rota, the only services are from Vila Real (or Monte Gordo); and for Cacelha Verde and Praia Verde, the best you can do is get off any bus to Vila Real on the highway and walk down the side roads. You can of course always **walk** along the beach: from Manta Rota it's around thirty minutes to Altura, another twenty minutes to Praia Verde, and forty more to Monte Gordo.

Cabanas

Six kilometres east of Tavira – past the golf course at Benamor – lies **CABANAS**, named after the fishermen's *cabanas* (huts) that were the original settlement. Today a kernel of back streets is still made up of pretty fishermen's houses along with a line of low-rise shops, cafés and bars facing a picturesque river estuary lined with mimosa trees. Moored fishing boats testify to the village's former mainstay, though nowadays the economy is largely driven by tourism thanks to the glorious sands on **Praia de Cabanas** over the estuary and to the ruins of an old sea fort just east of town. Ferries shuttle passengers to the beach from a small jetty at the eastern edge of town (April–Oct, every 15min; €1 return). Cross the dunes and you're faced with miles of golden sand, plus a couple of seasonal beach cafés.

Eight weekday **buses** (only two on Sat) run from Tavira to Cabanas, stopping at the west end of the waterfront. The town is also just 1km south of Conceição on the Tavira to Vila Real **train** line, though you'll have to walk into the centre from the station. **Accommodation** options are mainly limited to apartments and villas, although you can always ask at bars and cafés for private **rooms**. *Pastelaria Jerónimo*, on Avenida 28 de Maio (☏281 370 649; ❸), opposite the ferry jetty, rents out decent apartments with sea-facing balconies; there's no breakfast but the café does great pastries. On the sloping main road into town, *Pedras da Rainha* (☏281 380 680, ⓦwww.pedrasrainha.com; from ❺) has apartments and villas (sleeping up to ten) clustered around pleasant lawns, tennis courts and a large pool, all with disabled access. **Cafés**, **bars** and **restaurants** spread along the riverfront and a block or two inland, best being *Pedro* on Rua Capitão Batista Marçal 51 (☏281 370 425) on the way to the jetty, with an outdoor terrace and moderately priced fish and seafood.

Cacela Velha

Ten kilometres from Cabanas, and perched on a low cliff facing the estuary, the whitewashed village of **CACELA VELHA** is a reminder of how the Algarve must have looked half a century ago. Apart from a couple of simple café-restaurants, there are no tourist facilities, just a pretty church and the remains of an eighteenth-century fort, and even that is a GNR station and closed to the public. Surrounded by olive groves, and offering exhilarating views from its clifftop, it is spectacularly pretty and, despite the Quinta da Ria/Quinta da

Cima golf courses just to the west, rarely overrun by visitors. The only time the place gets busy is during the July **Moorish Nights** festival, with four days of Arabic food and Moorish-inspired events, including a souk.

The beach below the village is a delight. To get to it, follow signs to "Fábrica", just west of the village, around 1km downhill. Here a ferryman can take you over to the beach for €1 return (daily in summer but only during good weather the rest of the year).

To reach Cacela Velha by public transport, ask to be let off the Tavira-Vila Real bus on the highway, just before Vila Nova de Cacela, from where it's a fifteen-minute walk down a side road to the village. There are a few private rooms that get snapped up quickly in summer, or try *Cantinho da Ria Formosa* in Ribeira de Junco (℡281 951 837, ⓦwww.cantinhoriaformosa.com; breakfast included; ❹), around 1km from the beach and the golf course. Eight rooms in this blue-edged *residencial* have satellite TV and air conditioning, and have views over the garden or fields. There are stables attached, and horse rides are on offer for around €20 an hour.

Manta Rota, Altura and Praia Verde

Two kilometres further along the coast at **MANTA ROTA**, a group of half a dozen restaurants, all serving platters of sardines and grilled swordfish or tuna, cluster at the entrance to a superb, broad beach. There's not much else to hang about for; the main road is a fifteen-minute walk up from the beach. The next resort east, **ALTURA**, is more developed, backed by white villas and apartments facing another fantastic beach, Praia de Alagoas. Here, there's a line of beach umbrellas and beach bars, drinks kiosks and water sports on hand. Further east, towards Monte Gordo, the beach becomes more unkempt, backed by scrubby dunes, but the sands are much less likely to be crowded in summer. Four kilometres east of Altura, **PRAIA VERDE** is the nicest stretch, with just one beach café.

Monte Gordo

MONTE GORDO is the last resort before the Spanish border and the most built-up of the eastern holiday towns, with its own casino. In June expect to see a profusion of Harley Davison riders who descend for an annual biker's meet. White hotels overlook the wide, clean sands, on which are scattered a profusion of café-restaurants with studiously similar menus and inflated prices; *O Firmo* (℡281 513 280) is a good choice, with mid-priced grills and salads and a fine beachside terrace, *Jaime* (℡281 512 361) further west up the beach, serves lunchtime snacks and is a great spot for a beer overlooking the fishing boats.

Buses from Vila Real and Tavira pull up on Rua Nova de Lisboa, by the parish church. Take a right and it's a short walk to the seafront and casino. Just east of the casino is the **turismo** (May–Sept Mon & Fri–Sun 9.30am–1pm & 2.30–7pm, Tues–Thurs 9.30am–7pm; Oct–April Mon–Fri 9.30am–1pm & 2.30–5pm; ℡281 544 495), which has details of private rooms in town. However, if you want **accommodation** right on the beach, look no further than the *Vasco da Gama*, Avenida Infante Dom Henrique (℡281 510 900, ⓦwww.vascodagamahotel.com; ❺) a highrise with tennis courts and kids' facilities, where some of the large en-suite rooms have sea views (❻). A simpler choice is *Pensão Promar*, Rua Dr Francisco de Almeida 73 (℡281 542 250; ❷) a block back from the beach west of the casino, with bright rooms. Meals served on request. Monte Gordo is also the site of the last – and largest – **campsite** (℡281 510 970, ⓕ281 510 003) on this stretch of the Algarve, a huge place set under pines near the beach on the Vila Real road.

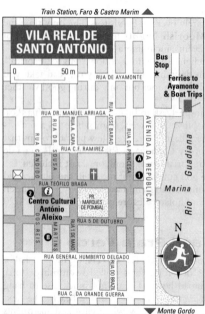

Train Station, Faro & Castro Marim ▲

VILA REAL DE SANTO ANTÓNIO

0   50 m

RUA DE AYAMONTE

Bus Stop ★

Ferries to Ayamonte & Boat Trips

RUA DR. MANUEL ARRIAGA

RUA C.F. RAMIREZ

RUA TEÓFILO BRAGA

RUA JOSÉ BARAO

AVENIDA DA REPÚBLICA

Rio Guadiana

Marina

❷ ⓘ
Centro Cultural António Aleixo

PR. MARQUÊS DE POMBAL

RUA 5 DE OUTUBRO

RUA DR. SOUSA MARTINS

RUA GENERAL HUMBERTO DELGADO

RUA DO BRASIL

RUA C. DA GRANDE GUERRA

N

▼ Monte Gordo

ACCOMMODATION		CAFÉS & RESTAURANTS	
Guadiana	A	Arenilha	2
Matos Pereira	B	Caves do Guadiana	1

Vila Real de Santo António

The border town and harbour of **VILA REAL DE SANTO ANTÓNIO** is one of the more architecturally interesting towns in the Algarve. The original settlement was demolished by a tidal wave following the earthquake of 1755 and the current town was rebuilt on a grid plan by the Marquês de Pombal, using the same plans he had already pioneered in the Baixa quarter of Lisbon. Remarkably, the whole project only took five months.

The central grid built by Pombal radiates out from the handsome square that bears his name, ringed by orange trees and low, white buildings, a couple of which are pleasant outdoor cafés. On the north side of the square is Rua Teófilo Braga, the pedestrianized main drag that leads inland from the riverfront Avenida da República. The former market building along here has been reborn as the **Centro Cultural António Aleixo** (Mon–Fri 10am–1pm & 3–7pm; free), an innovative space used for temporary exhibits, installations and occasionally even films. The surrounding streets have a certain low-key charm, bristling with linen shops, electrical retailers and grocers, and the riverside **gardens** offer fine views across to the splash of white that is Ayamonte in Spain. The town used to be the main crossing point into Spain and the ferry terminal still has a grand arched entrance; its importance has declined since the opening of a road bridge over the Rio Guadiana, 4km to the north, but it's well worth taking a boat trip from here up the river (see opposite).

Practicalities

Vila Real is the eastern terminal of the Algarve railway, and **trains** pull up at the station, five minutes north of the riverfront. **Buses** either stop by the river or at a terminus just north of the train station, while the **turismo** (Mon–Fri 9.30am–1pm & 2.30–5pm; ☎281 542 100) is situated in a corner of the Centro Cultural on Rua Teófilo Braga. If you wish to stay, the *Hotel Guadiana* at Avenida da República 94–96, overlooking the gardens and river (☎281 511 482, ⓦwww.hotelguadiana.com.pt; breakfast included ❹), is a National Monument with a fine old Art Deco frontage, an ornate breakfast room and river views, though the rooms are nothing special. Alternatively, *Residencial Matos Pereira*, Rua Dr Sousa Martins 57 (☎281 543 325; ❷) offers decent rooms

❾

with TV and bath in a tall townhouse with marble floors and family clutter. Best rooms are those on the top floor with a shared terrace.

Half-a-dozen similarly priced **cafés and restaurants** line the riverfront, all with outdoor seats. *Caves do Guadiana*, Avenida da República 89–90 (☎281 544 498; closed Thurs), has long been considered the best in town. It's got a tiled and vaulted interior, and you'll pay around €16 for a full meal. For less expensive fish and grilled meats try the *Churrasqueira Arenilha* on Rua Cândido dos Reis 89 (☎281 544 038), which specializes in *cozido* (stew) on Sundays.

Crossing the border: Ayamonte

Daily buses run from Vila Real across the bridge to **Ayamonte** in Spain (15min), which has onward connections to Huelva (1hr) and Seville (4hr). There are timetables posted at the Vila Real bus terminus, and remember that Spanish time is one hour ahead of Portuguese. If you just want to make a day trip to the Spanish border town – with its tapas bars and palm-lined squares – it's more fun to use the **ferry** from Vila Real's harbour (daily every 40min from 8.20am, last return 7pm, which is 8pm Spanish time; €1.30 each way). This is a lovely twenty-minute ride across the Rio Guadiana, with the forts of Castro Marim visible to the west and the impressive bridge to the north.

Inland: along the Rio Guadiana

North of Vila Real, the **Rio Guadiana** forms the border with Spain and provides a little-travelled diversion. There are regular weekday bus services from Vila Real to **Castro Marim** and less frequent services to **Alcoutim**, both with impressive castles and historic interest. Best of all, though, is a **boat trip** up the river itself. These go up to Foz de Odeleite (with Viagens, Ⓦ www.riosultravel .com) or Alcoutim (Peninsular, Ⓦ www.peninsular.cjb.net); prices start at around €40 per person, which includes food and drinks.

Castro Marim

The little village of **CASTRO MARIM**, 5km north of Vila Real, was once a key fortification protecting Portugal's southern coast. Marim was the first headquarters of the Order of Christ (1319) and is the site of a huge **castle** (daily: April–Oct 9am–7pm; Nov–March 9am–5pm; free), built by Afonso III in the thirteenth century. The massive ruins are all that survived the earthquake of 1755; it's a pretty place with fine views of the bridge to Spain. The castle is the centrepiece of the village's Medieval Days Festival over the last weekend in August, with recreations of medieval life and plenty of entertainment.

There's also the smaller fort of São Sebastião across the village, also with fine views. The **turismo** is in Praça 1 de Maio (Mon–Fri 9.30am–1pm & 2–5.30pm; ☎281 531 232), on the main street. There are several **cafés** on Rua de São Sebastião, west of the turismo, or eat at the simple *Eira Gaio* (☎281 351 358; closed Sun evening) on Rua 25 de Abril opposite the turismo.

The marshy area around Castro Marim forms the **Reserva Natural do Sapal**, a reserve where flamingoes stop off to feed. One of the area's most unusual and elusive inhabitants is the ten-centimetre-long, swivel-eyed, opposing-toed, Mediterranean **chameleon** – a harmless, slow-moving lizard that's severely threatened elsewhere by habitat destruction. The village turismo (see above) can direct you to the remote **park headquarters** (Mon–Fri 9am–12.30pm & 2–5.30pm; ☎281 510 680) which has details of local walks.

Alcoutim

Some 40km north of Vila Real – and best approached by car along the road that hugs the Guadiana river – **ALCOUTIM** is extremely attractive. It has a long history as a river port, dominated in turn by Greeks, Romans and Arabs who all fortified the heights with various structures; the **castle** (daily 9am–1pm & 2–5.30pm; €2.50) dates from the fourteenth century and offers fine views over the town and the Rio Guadiana. The entrance fee includes access to a small archeological **museum** by the main gates, which traces the history of the castle, its active service in the War of Restoration and the Liberal Wars, and the remnants of earlier structures on the site. The fee also covers entry to the so-called Núcleos Museológicos, tiny craft museums that have been set up in many of the villages in the region; details from the tourist office (see below). For further diversion, a ferry (daily 9am–1pm & 2–7pm; €1 single) crosses the river to the Spanish village of **Sanlúcar**, a mirror image of Alcoutim, with its own ruined castle.

Alcoutim is also the starting point of the Via Algarviana **walking route**, itself part of trans-European route E4 from Greece. The Portuguese part heads 240km across the Algarve to Cabo de São Vicente. Full details can be obtained from Almargem (☎289 412 959, ⓦwww.algargem.org).

A couple of buses a day (not weekends) run back down to Vila Real, and there's a twice-weekly service north to Mértola and Beja in the Alentejo. A small **turismo** (May–Oct Mon–Fri 9.30am–1pm & 2.30–7pm; Nov–April closes at 5.30pm; ☎281 546 179) is located in the main Praça da República, right in the centre of the village. They're helpful people and can point you in the right direction for private **rooms**, or try at the modern *Pensão Afonso*, Rua João Dias 10 (☎281 546 211; ❷), just uphill from the main square, which has some pleasant en-suite rooms. The smart fifty-bed **youth hostel** (☎281 546 004, ⓦwww.pousadajuventude.pt; dorm beds €16, rooms ❷) is around 1.5km north of the village, across the Ribeira Cadavais; cross the bridge beyond Praça da República and follow the signs. It has its own canteen, bar, swimming pool and laundry, as well as disabled access. It also hires out bikes (€2/hr) and arranges kayaking and canoeing on the river. For upmarket lodgings next to the youth hostel, head north out of Alcoutim and follow the signs to the *Estalagem do Guadiana* (☎281 540 120, ⓦwww.grupofbarata.com; breakfast included; ❹), a very swish modern inn with its own pool, tennis court and restaurant. The spacious rooms come with satellite TV, baths and fine river views.

Alcoutim's inexpensive **cafés** cluster around the square, though the best positioned place in town is *O Soeiro* (☎281 546 241), with outdoor tables facing the river, a bustling downstairs café (closed Sun) and an upstairs restaurant serving fine local specialities such as lamprey (lunch only, closed weekends). For **nightlife**, *Riverside Tavern* up the riverside on Av Duarte Pacheco 3 (☎281 547 314; closed Wed) is a swish bar-restaurant with ambient sounds and an attractive terrace (meals from €7); it only gets packed when the weekly boat trips call by.

The western Algarve

The western Algarve stretches for a hundred kilometres from Faro to Sagres, and encompasses some of the region's best beaches but also Portugal's most intense tourist development. Much of the stretch between Faro and Albufeira, for example, consists of purpose-built resorts that feature marinas, golf links and tennis centres – "Sportugal" – as the tourist board promotes the leisure complexes – which are fine if you've booked a package holiday, but with little promise for anyone simply in search of a quiet beach and a local meal.

Albufeira itself is one of the biggest – and *the* most enjoyable – resorts, while other decent stops include **Alvor**, **Ferragudo** and **Lagos**, which still retain some character close to fine beaches. All the resorts are packed to the gills in summer and, particularly if you have transport, you might do better to seek a base inland at the interesting old market towns of **Loulé** or **Silves** and drive down to the nearest beach for the day. **Caldas de Monchique**, a nineteenth-century spa town, and the neighbouring market town of **Monchique** are other inland options, though these are a good forty-minute drive from the sea.

West of Lagos beyond Luz, development has been restricted by the Parque Natural do Sudoeste Alentejano e Costa Vicentina, which embraces most of the coastline. As a result, erstwhile fishing villages such as **Burgau** and **Salema** still retain a fair amount of charm, while beyond the road cuts high above the sea across a cliff-edged plateau and down to **Sagres**, with its dramatic scenery and busy nightlife. The coast north of Sagres, heading towards the Alentejo, is the least developed part of the Algarve – partly because this stretch of the Atlantic is distinctly cold and often pretty wild. Low-key villages such as **Vila do Bispo**, **Carrapateira**, **Aljezur** and **Odeceixe** all have magnificent local beaches that attract a rather more "alternative" crowd than resorts on the Algarve proper, with plenty of beach parties, nude sunbathing and surfing.

Loulé

LOULÉ, 18km inland of Faro, has always been an important market town and has recently grown to a fair size, though its compact centre doesn't take long to look around. Its most interesting streets, a grid of whitewashed cobbled lanes, lie between the remains of its Moorish castle (now a museum) and the thirteenth-century Gothic **Igreja Matriz**, with its palm-lined gardens in front. Here you'll see traditional craftsmen labouring in workshops, producing copper *cataplanas* (cooking vessels) and leatherwork for the region's restaurants and souvenir shops.

The remains of Loulé's castle enclose a mildly interesting **Museu Arqueológico** (Mon–Fri 9am–5.30pm, Sat 10am–2pm; €1.20), housing a range of Roman, Moorish and early Portuguese finds from Loulé and the surrounding area. The largest exhibit is a giant sixteenth-century stone urn, retrieved from the castle itself. Loulé's most atmospheric sight, however, is the covered fruit and vegetable **market** (Mon–Sat 8am–3pm) on Rua José Fernandes Guerreiro, a couple of minutes' walk southeast off the main Praça da República, set in a red onion-domed building with Moorish-style windows. Try and visit on a Saturday morning, when the market spreads into the surrounding streets – a medley of stalls selling everything from pungent cheese to cages of live chickens and rabbits. Equally atmospheric is the Saturday **morning market** (from 9.30am), which takes place around fifteen minutes' walk northwest of the centre – follow the signs to IP1/Boliquieme – on a patch of ground beautifully framed by a pair of dazzling white churches, including the curious modern beehive-shaped **Nossa Senhora da Piedade**. At Easter, the church is the starting-point of a procession into town for *Mãe Soberana*, one of the Algarve's most important religious festivals.

Practicalities

The **bus station** is on Rua Nossa Senhora de Fátima, a couple of minutes' walk north of the old town area; there are regular services from Quarteira and Faro. The **turismo** (May–Sept Mon–Sat 9.30am–1pm & 2–7pm, until 5.30pm; ☏289 463 900, ⓦ www.cm-loule.pt) is on Avenida 25 de Abril, close to the bus station. For **accommodation**, try *Casa Beny*, at Rua São Domingos 13 (☏289 417 702; ❸), on the main through road. It's not the quietest of spots, but the tastefully renovated town house offers neat rooms with mini-bar and bathroom. Better is the comfortable *Loulé Jardim Hotel* at Praça Manuel de Arriaga 23 (☏289 413 094, ⓦ www.loulejardimhotel.com; ❹), a block south of Rua Nossa Senhora da Piedade, which boasts a bar, a small pool and comfortable rooms with cable TV.

Just around the corner from the castle, *Café Calcina* (closed Sun) is a great traditional **café** with outdoor tables, dark wood fittings, and black-and-white photos of old Loulé on the walls. Downhill below the castle, *A Muralha*, Rua Martim Moniz 39 (☏289 412 629; dinner only except Sat; closed Sun) is housed in a former bakery, and has an attractive flower-filled patio and pleasant interior – the meat and seafood dishes are elaborate if pricey. For simpler local fare, try *Flôr da Praça*, Rua José Fernandes Guerreiro 44 (☏289 462 435; closed Sun), opposite the food market.

Quinta do Lago, Vale do Lobo and around

Around 12km northwest of Faro, right on the Almancil turn-off from the N125, the church of **São Laurenço** (Mon 2.30–6pm, Tues–Sat 10am–1pm & 2.30–6pm; €1.50) comes as a surprise amid the development. Built in the eighteenth century, it survived the earthquake of 1755 and retains its superb tiled interior depicting the life and martyrdom of St Laurence.

Almancil itself is served by regular buses from Faro, and is also the turn-off point for the first of the resorts west of Faro, **QUINTA DO LAGO**, which is a vast, luxury holiday village with its own golf courses and sports complex. One or two daily buses run here directly from Loulé and Almancil. The *Hotel Quinta do Lago* (☏289 350 350, ⓦ www.quintadolagohotel.com; ❾) is typical of what's on offer, popular with celebrities who appreciate the privacy offered by its sprawling wooded grounds. The rooms are truly splendid, and there are restaurants, bars, an indoor and outdoor pool, and spa and sports facilities, though a night here will set you back close to €500. Most day visitors, however, head straight for the great beach, the **Praia do Ançâo**, reached over a wooden bridge from the car park at the end of Avenida André Jorge, the main drag. The bridge heads across the western extremity of the Parque Natural da Ria Formosa; it also marks the start of two marked nature trails that lead either side of the inland waterways.

Facilities are similar at **VALE DO LOBO**, just to the west, where a great beach is backed by more serious-money hotels; there are even plans to build a Dubai-style offshore island in the shape of a shell, complete with underwater hotel. For the time being, the resort makes do with a 24-hour reception as you enter the complex (℡289 353 000, ⊛www.valedolobo.com), which can help with booking accommodation. Nearby are golf courses, a riding school, and the **Vale de Lobo Tennis Academy** (℡289 357 850, ⊛www.premier-sports.org), the most famous in the country. You can book lessons and coaching sessions, though as even Tim Henman comes here to practise, courts do get booked up well in advance.

Quarteira

QUARTEIRA, 22km west of Faro, has a very different feel to the deluxe resorts on either side. It was one of the first fishing villages to be developed in the Algarve, and remains high-rise and downmarket. Stick to the palm-lined seafront promenade and the attractive stretch of beach – Praia de Quarteira – and it's a pleasant enough destination, and at least it remains largely Portuguese in character. The main attraction is the bustling fish and vegetable **market** (Mon–Sat 8am–3pm, Sun vegetable market only 8am–2pm) by the working fishing harbour, to the west end of town, though there's also a good weekly flea market each Wednesday, a couple of blocks east of the bus station. You can also tour Quarteira on a **road train** which trundles along the seafront to Vilamoura (see below) every hour or so (daily 10am–11pm; €4). Heading a few kilometres inland, **Aquashow** (⊛www.aquashowpark.com; daily April–Oct 10am–5.30pm; €18, children €15) at Semino, out on the Loulé road, makes a change from the beach, with water slides, pools and crazy golf along with tropical birds and Europe's largest "watercoaster".

The **bus terminus** is a couple of blocks back from the beach, on Avenida Dr Sá Carneiro, with the **turismo** right by the beach on Praça do Mar (May–Sept Mon & Fri–Sun 9.30am–1pm & 2–7pm, Tues–Thurs 9.30am–7pm; Oct–May same hours until 5.30pm; ℡289 389 209). They should be able to help with finding **accommodation** if there's no room at the very pleasant *Pensão Miramar*, Rua Gonçalo Velho 8, off the seafront (℡289 315 225, ℻289 314 671; ❸) – some rooms here have sea views, while others face a charming plant-lined internal terrace. There's also a well-equipped **campsite** (℡289 302 821, ⊛www.orbitur.com) 1km east of town, with a pool, shop and restaurants; any bus to or from Faro will stop outside it.

Quarteira boasts one of the Algarve's top seafood **restaurants**, *O Jacinto* at Avenida Dr Sá Carneiro (℡289 301 887; closed Mon), which is on the north side of the main road through town; it's the best place to try Quarteira prawns, rated as some of the best in the world. For something decidedly less expensive, *Rosa Branca* (℡289 314 430), at the market end of the seafront, has decently priced fish and grilled meats and outdoor tables facing the sands.

Vilamoura

Now virtually merged with Quarteira, **VILAMOURA** is a complete contrast, a constantly expanding resort (which will eventually cater to over half a million visitors) with a bewildering network of roads signposted to upmarket hotels and exclusive leisure facilities, including five renowned **golf courses**. It's perhaps *the* place in the Algarve to come and practise your swing, while another indication of the kind of clientele Vilamoura attracts is the ritzy **marina**, bristling with yachting hardware and lined by pricey international cafés. Various stalls offer **boat trips** which range from local excursions (from €15 for a two-hour trip) to dolphin-watching (up to €50 for a full-day excursion).

The only historical sight in Vilamoura is just to the northwest of the marina, where the **Museu Cerra da Vila** archeological site and museum (☎289 312 153; May–Sept Tues–Sun 10am–1pm & 3–8pm; Oct–April Tues–Sun 9.30am–12.30pm & 2–6pm; €2) displays the vestiges of a late Roman, Visigothic and Moorish colony. You can make out the foundations of a Roman mansion, baths and a fish-salting tank, together with well-preserved Roman mosaics laid out in a scrubby field.

The bus drops you next to the casino, one block from the impressive beach, the **Praia da Marina**. The land train from Quarteira also stops here (see p.573). The enormous *Tivoli Marinotel* (☎289 303 303, ⓦ www.tivolihotels.com; breakfast included; ❾) is typical of the accommodation here, a five-star place with every conceivable comfort, overlooking the marina. For a drink, meal or late-night action, *Sete* (☎289 313 625) in the marina is a fashionable chrome-and-steel **café-bar** part-owned by Portuguese soccer star Luís Figo, and named after his shirt number (*sete*, seven). Plasma TVs show the latest soccer action and guest DJs and karaoke nights feature. Even livelier, on the outskirts, opposite the Mobil garage on the Vilamoura-Albufeira road, *Kadoc* (ⓦ www.kadok.pt; 11pm–6am: June–Sept daily; Oct–May Sat only) – the Algarve's biggest **club** – pulls in up to four thousand revellers a night, and often hosts guest DJs from all over Europe.

Albufeira and around

ALBUFEIRA tops the list of package-tour destinations in the Algarve – and it's easy to see why. The old centre remains an unusually pretty village, with narrow, twisting lanes of whitewashed houses crisscrossing the high ochre-red cliffs above a beautiful spread of beaches. But beyond, hundreds of apartment buildings lie strung across the hillsides that spread east and west, around the town's marina. If you're looking for unspoiled Portugal, this isn't it. Nevertheless, Albufeira is undeniably a fun resort, attracting a varied mix of holidaymakers, notably a well-heeled clientele that frequents the more expensive restaurants, and a younger contingent who devote themselves to consuming as much alcohol as is humanly possible.

Although the 1755 earthquake did for much of the town, there's still a Moorish feel to parts of central Albufeira – the original Arabic name of the town, *Al-Buhera*, means "Castle-on-the-Sea". There are some fine beaches either side of the town, too. **Praia da Oura** and those further east towards **Praia da Falésia** are the more developed, while the cove beaches to the west, up to the swathe of sands at **Praia de Galé**, tend to be quieter. Inland, Albufueira is the nearest base for a couple of the Algarve's best family-orientated **theme parks**, while day-trips also run north into the hills to the pretty village of **Alte**.

Arrival and information

Albufeira's **bus terminal** is around 2km north of town. A red route shuttle bus runs to Avenida da Liberdade at 10 and 40minutes past each hour (from 7am to midnight; until 10pm from Oct–April; €1), which is a five-minute walk from

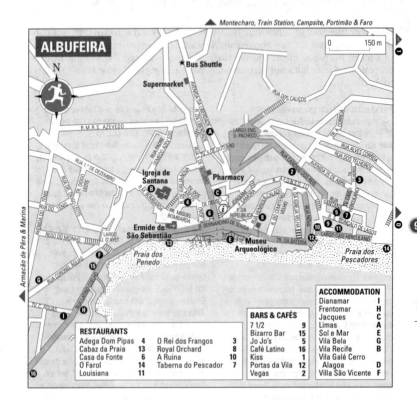

ALBUFEIRA

0   150 m

N

★ **Bus Shuttle**

Supermarket

Igreja de Santana

Pharmacy

Ermide de São Sebastião

Praia dos Penedo

Museu Arqueológico

Praia dos Pescadores

Armação de Pêra & Marina

THE ALGARVE | Albufeira and around

BARS & CAFÉS	
7 1/2	9
Bizarro Bar	15
Jo Jo's	5
Café Latino	16
Kiss	1
Portas da Vila	12
Vegas	2

RESTAURANTS			
Adega Dom Pipas	4	O Rei dos Frangos	3
Cabaz da Praia	13	Royal Orchard	8
Casa da Fonte	6	A Ruina	10
O Farol	14	Taberna do Pescador	7
Louisiana	11		

ACCOMMODATION	
Dianamar	I
Frentomar	H
Jacques	C
Limas	A
Sol e Mar	E
Vila Bela	G
Vila Recife	B
Vila Galé Cerro Alagoa	D
Villa São Vicente	F

the central square, Largo Engenheiro Duarte Pacheco. Albufeira's nearest **train station** is 6km north of town at Ferreiras; a bus connects it with the bus terminal every 45 minutes or so (daily 7am–8pm), or a taxi will set you back about €10. Central Albufeira is not an easy place to find a parking spot; it's best to follow signs to the out-of-town **car parks**.

If you're in Albufeira on a package holiday, you might well be staying in one of the handful of resort-villages on either side of town. The blue bus route serves many of these, going from the bus station via Areias de São João, Oura and Santa Eulalia to **Montechoro,** a downmarket suburb to the northeast, known as "the strip", with a gaudy Eurotrashy appeal. If you plan to use the buses a lot, consider a *bilhete turístico* day pass for €3, or buy a *cartão recarregável* rechargeable charge-card on which you can load ten journeys for €5. Otherwise it is €1 a ride.

You can also get round town on the **road train** which circles Albufeira and runs out to Montechoro (every 20min, 9am–1am; 24hr in Aug; €2 a trip, or €3 for a day pass).

The **turismo** (Oct–May Mon–Fri 9.30am–1pm & 2–5.30pm; June–Sept same hours until 7pm; ☎289 585 279, Ⓦwww.cm-albufeira.pt) is on Rua 5 de Outubro, close to the tunnel to the beach.

Accommodation

In high season most of the hotels and *pensões* are block-booked by package holiday companies. Those listed below may have "independent" vacancies, otherwise the tourist office can help you find a **private room** (❸), though they'll charge you for any phone calls they make. Alternatively, accept the offer of a room from one of the touts at the bus station; you can always look around on your own later if it's not up to scratch. Note many places close from October to April.

Hotels and pensions

Pensão Dianamar Rua Latino Coelho 36 ☎289 587 801, ⓦwww.dianamar.com. Well-run Swedish-owned *pensão* in the nicest part of town, near the cliff above the beach. The simple en-suite rooms are pristine and breezy, and those at the top have great sea views, as does the communal roof terrace. Recommended. ❸

Pensão Residencial Frentomar Rua Latino Coelho ☎289 512 005, ⓔfrentomar@sapo.pt. Simple, clean rooms on a quiet side road. Get one with a sea view and you won't be disappointed, though these are usually snapped up quickly. Closed late Oct to April. No breakfast. ❸

Jacques Accommodation Rua 5 de Outubro 36 ☎969 584 933. Lovely town house with large, airy rooms – each with their own bathrooms – right on the main street to the beach. No breakfast. ❸

Residencial Limas Rua da Liberdade 25–27 ☎289 514 025. Ten decent en-suite rooms with TVs in an attractive, yellow-faced building. Avoid the front ground-floor rooms or it'll feel as if you're sleeping on the street. No breakfast. ❷

Hotel Sol e Mar Rua Bernardino de Sousa ☎289 580 080, ⓦwww.grupofbarata.com. In a great position, with its entrance above the tunnel to the beach, though somewhat characterless, this four-star hotel stretches down five floors to exit right on the beach. The balconies overlook the sands, while there's live entertainment and a small covered swimming pool. Parking. ❺

Residencial Vila Bela Rua Coronel Águas 32–34 ☎289 512 101, ⓔctr@mail.telepac.pt. Attractive *residencial* with its own bar and balconied rooms overlooking a small swimming pool and the bay. Breakfast included. April–Oct. ❹

Residencial Vila Recife Rua Miguel Bombarda 6 ☎289 583 740, ⓔvila.recife@iol.pt. This rambling *residencial* has its own garden and small pool. The communal areas are lined with *azulejos*, and while the en-suite rooms are on the small side they are comfortable, and the best have fine views. Closed Nov–April. ❹

Vila Galé Cerro Alagoa Apartado 2155 ☎289 583 100, ⓦwww.vilagale.pt. Large, somewhat bland four-star 1km uphill from Praia dos Pescadores, near the town hall. Good for families, with two outside pools and a jungle-themed indoor pool by the health club. There's also a restaurant and English-style pub, with nightly entertainment. ❻

Villa São Vicente Hotel Largo Jacinto d'Ayet 4 ☎289 583 700, ⓦwww.hotel-vila-sao-vicente .com. A modern three-star hotel built in traditional style with tiled floors and whitewashed walls. It has its own small pool and a terrace facing the beach. You pay less for rooms facing the street, but it is worth the extra for the sea views. All rooms are en suite with TVs and a/c. ❹

Campsite

Camping Albufeira Estrada de Ferreiras, 2km to the north of town, off the N396 ☎289 587 629, ⓕ289 587 633. Expensive but well appointed, complete with swimming pools, restaurants, bars, shops and tennis courts. There are regular red-bus route connections from the bus station.

The town

The focus of Albufeira is the main square, **Largo Engenheiro Duarte Pacheco**, a pretty, pedestrianized space with a small fountain and benches beneath palms and exotic trees. After dark, it's a magnet for families and promenaders, often serenaded by live performers and buskers. From the square, Rua 5 de Outubro leads – through a tunnel – down to the town **beach**, as good as any in the region, flanked by strange tooth-like rock formations, though avoid the exit to the storm drain by the tunnel after heavy rains. If it's too crowded here, a relatively short bus (or taxi) ride can open up a number of other good beaches, the best of which are detailed on pp.578–579.

Just above the tunnel to the beach, in the old town hall, the **Museu Arqueológico** (Tues–Sun: mid-Sept to May 10am–5pm; June to mid-Sept 2.30–8pm; free) presents a rather sparse but well laid out collection of artefacts gathered from the area from Neolithic times to the present. There are fragments of mosaics from a Roman villa, Visigothic rock tombs and jars, and even an Islamic silo excavated *in situ* beneath the museum.

Albufeira's other historic sites lie up the steps to the west of the tunnel, around Praça Miguel Bombarda. The **Ermide de São Sebastião** is one of the region's oldest churches with a distinctive Manueline door, though most of the building was constructed in the early eighteenth century. The church houses the **Museu Arte Sacra** (July–Oct daily 10am–midnight; free), a picturesque if uninspiring museum containing plaster images of saints; its most valuable items are a silver crown and chalice for Nossa Senhora Ourada, a local saint. Nearby, from the patio at the front of the whitewashed, domed **Igreja de Santana**, there are lovely views over the distinctive filigree chimneys of the old town and across the other church spires to the sea.

Eating

Albufeira has **restaurants** to match every budget – and most tastes. As well as Portuguese restaurants, there's also a whole range of places serving pizzas, Chinese and Indian food, even fish and chips. The morning-after-the-night-before is well catered for in most restaurants and bars, with massive **English-style breakfasts** available until the sensible hour of 3pm.

Cabaz da Praia Pr Miguel Bombarda 7 ☎289 512 137. With a roof terrace overlooking the beach, this French-inspired place has an excellent menu – feast on things like duck breast with apricot sauce, or monkfish with rosemary, and finish off with one of the long list of desserts. Expensive.

Adega Dom Pipas Trav dos Arcos 78 ☎289 588 091. The mock olde-worlde decor and standard Portuguese menu are nothing special, but there are outdoor tables in an attractive narrow alley often strung with coloured ribbons. Closed Tues. Moderate.

Restaurante O Farol Praia dos Pescadores ☎289 513 552. Simple beachside cafe-restaurant right behind the boats on the fisherman's beach. It's refreshingly unpretentious – though service can be excessively laid back – and the fresh fish and grilled meat come in generous portions. Closes at 6pm from Oct–April. Moderate.

Casa da Fonte Rua João de Deus 7 ☎289 514 578. A popular spot set around a beautiful Moorish-style courtyard complete with *azulejos* and lemon trees – get there early if you want a courtyard table. There's a long menu but it boils down to the usual range of fish and meat. Moderate.

Louisiana Cais Herculano ☎289 587 018. In a prime position overlooking the beach. As the name suggests, it is not particularly local, but the Portuguese staples are well presented and as tasty as the international and vegetarian options. Moderate.

O Rei dos Frangos Trav dos Telheiros 4 ☎289 512 981. A first-rate *churrasqueira* – the chicken comes smothered in *piri-piri* and there's grilled steak, swordfish and a speciality meat *cataplana*. Inexpensive.

Royal Orchard Beco Bernardino de Sousa ☎289 502 505. Thai restaurant with sumptuous decor and tables laid out in a leafy courtyard. The long menu features noodle and rice dishes with fish, meat or seafood, though there's also a range of vegetarian options. Moderate.

A Ruina Largo Cais Herculano ☎289 512 094. Superb old restaurant built into the cliffs over the beach – there are rooms and terraces at various levels. The lower, beachside area is the best place for those with kids, as they can play in the sand while you have a meal. The waiter will show you the latest fish catch, but check the price when ordering. Expensive.

A Taberna do Pescador Trav Cais Herculano ☎289 589 196. A genuinely authentic Portuguese *taberna* that attracts as many locals as tourists, with an outdoor terrace where most of the barbecuing takes place. The fish, seafood and meats are grilled to perfection and portions are huge. Inexpensive.

Drinking and nightlife

At night, the focus switches to Albufeira's pedestrianized streets. **Rua Candido dos Reis** is the focal point of a writhing mass of humanity parading past handi-craft and souvenir stalls, or sitting at bars and cafés which vie with each other to play the loudest music and offer the most over-the-top cocktails. Like the restaurants, Albufeira **bars** and **clubs** are into promotion and, since there's not much to choose between them, you may as well frequent those offering the cheapest drinks at the time – Happy Hour is an extremely flexible concept here. The other main areas for carousing are along Rua São Gonçalo de Lagos, around Largo Engenheiro Duarte Pacheco and on Rua Alves Correira. Most bars stay open until around 3am, the clubs until 6am or later in summer.

7 ½ Rua São Gonçalo de Lagos 5. Serves meals until 7pm, then turns into a vibrant dance club until the small hours. Often has live bands, karaoke sessions and guest DJ.

Bizarro Bar Esplanada Dr. Frutuosa Silva 30. This attractive bar is high above the eastern end of the beach, with superb views over the sands from its front terrace. Closed Sun.

Jo Jo's Rua São Gonçalo de Lagos 1. Friendly family-run pub with British soccer and other sports on satellite TV – the owner proudly recalls the day Paul Gascoigne and his mates got hopelessly drunk here. The bar food always includes a vegetarian option.

Café Latino Rua Latino Coelho 59. A superb spot to start off an evening with a cocktail – the back terrace has fantastic views over the town

and the beach, while inside the modern bar has hip music, spinning ceiling fans and a snooker table. Good crepes and snacks. Closed Mon.

Kiss Rua Vasco da Gama, Areias de São João ☏ 289 515 693. With five bars and two dance floors, this glitzy place is regarded as the best club around. It often hosts foreign guest DJs (keep an eye out for flyers), but tends to be overcrowded. It's 2km east of town; green and blue bus routes pass nearby. Open from 11pm.

Portas da Vila Rua da Bateria. High-ceilinged cocktail and sangria bar, just above the old fish market, next to the site of the old gates to the castle.

Vegas Rua Candido dos Reis 22–26. Café, bar and club offering everything from milkshakes to rudely named cocktails, live soccer to thumping dance sounds.

Listings

Banks and exchange Banks and ATMs are grouped around Largo Eng. Duarte Pacheco and along Av da Liberdade.

Bike/motorbike rental Vespa Rent ☏ 289 542 377, ⓦ www.vesparent.com will deliver to your hotel; scooters from around €60 for 3 days.

Bookshop Julie's, Rua Igreja Nova 6 (closed Sun afternoon and weekends from Oct–April) stocks a large range of English-language books, most of them secondhand.

Bullfights ☏ 289 519 280. Take place weekly from May to October, usually on Sat. The bullring is a five-minute taxi ride to the east or on the blue bus route. Tickets (available from travel agents round town or at the arena) start at around €30.

Car rental Avis, Rua Igreja Nova 13 ☏ 289 512 678; Hertz, Rua Manuel Teixeira Gomes Bloco 1, Areias de São João ☏ 289 542 920.

Health Centre Urbanização dos Caliços, 2km north of the centre ☏ 289 588 770 or 289 587 550 (open 24 hours). The nearest hospital is in Faro or Portimão.

Internet access Daimler's Bar, Rua Latino Coelho 24–26 (☏ 289 588 480) is a friendly café-bar with Internet access in a side room (daily 9am–3pm & 4pm–midnight).

Markets A lively flea market takes place to the north of the centre at Urbanização dos Caliços, 2km north of the centre, on the first and third Tues of each month.

Pharmacy Farmácia de Sousa, Rua 5 de Outubro 40.

Police Contact the local police on ☏ 289 513 203.

Post office Rua 5 de Outubro (Mon–Fri 8.30am–5.30pm).

Supermarket Alisuper, Av da Liberdade (daily 8am–8pm).

Taxi There's a taxi rank on Av da Liberdade. To order a cab call ☏ 289 583 230.

Travel agents Rua 5 de Outubro has row upon row of travel agents offering everything from tickets to bullfights to tours (inland Algarve, Lisbon, Spain or Gibraltar).

The local beaches east

Immediately **east of Albufeira**, ochre-red cliffs divide the coastline into a series of bays and beaches, all reached on local buses (8–12 daily) from the bus station. Also reached on the green bus route, you can walk to the first, **PRAIA DA**

OURA, just 2km away, by heading down Albufeira's beach and up along a rocky bluff along a coastal path. This, though, has been extensively developed and you might want to push on by bus to **OLHOS DE ÁGUA** or neighbouring **SANTA EULALIA** (on the blue bus route) 7km further east, to visiterstwhile fishing villages with attractive beaches. If this, too, is crowded, there is generally space at **PRAIA DA FALÉSIA**, 10km east of Albufeira, which is one tremendous stretch of sand backed by unbroken red cliffs topped with sprawling villa complexes.

Albufeira marina and local beaches west

Reached on the red bus route, Albufeira's marina sits downhill 2km west of the centre, a collection of brightly coloured lego-like modern shops, bars and apartments clustered round in-your-face yachts and speedboats. Daily boat trips depart from here up and down the neighbouring coastline from around €15 per person. Most of the development behind the headlands further **west of Albufeira** is set back from a series of cliff-backed cove beaches. There are no direct buses to these resorts, though the Albufeira-Portimão service drops passengers on the main road, a steep two-kilometre walk away. Busy **SÃO RAFAEL**, 3km west of Albufeira, and slightly quieter **CASTELO**, 1km further, spread back from small beaches with craggy, eroded rock faces. A delightful clifftop path links the two resorts via the best cove of this stretch, **PRAIA DA COELHA**, reached down a sandy track, with no development apart from a seasonal beach café. Five kilometres west of Albufeira, at **PRAIA DE GALÉ**, one of the Algarve's most exclusive hotels, the boutiquey *Estalagem Vila Joya* (☎289 591 795, ⓦwww.vilajoya.com; ⓪), sits right above the beach. Its luxurious rooms and suites will set you back around €400 a night; there is also a spa. The hotel is renowned for its two-Michelin-star restaurant for which reservations are essential.

Local theme parks

Around 7km northwest of Albufeira, off the N125, **Zoo Marine** (April–June & Sept–Oct daily 10am–6pm; July & Aug daily 10am–7.30pm; Nov–March Tues–Sun 10am–5pm; €20.50, children €12.50; ☎289 560 300, ⓦwww.zoomarine .com) is part zoo and part theme park, and makes a great day out for families. Tickets allow entry to the swimming pools, fairground rides, aquarium and animal enclosures, and various shows are staggered throughout the day, including performing parrots, sea lion performances and a spectacular dolphin show. Special buses are laid on to Zoo Marine from Albufeira and other resorts.

Krazy World (March–May & Sept daily 10am–6pm; June–Aug daily 10am–7.30pm; Oct–Feb Sat–Wed 10am–6pm; €17, children €10; ☎282 574 134, ⓦwww.krazy-world.com; some attractions closed in winter when prices are reduced), around 13km north, is also a sizeable zoo-cum-theme park. Buses from Albufeira to São Bartolomeu de Messines stop near the entrance. Low-key and set in attractive farmland, the neatly landscaped park has a mostly traditional rides, such as a ferris wheel, a mini zoo-cum-petting farm and "Amazonia", a reptile zone complete with enormous pythons, crocodiles and a turtle city. There is also a swimming pool (summer only) and crazy golf passing life-size mock dinosaurs.

Alte

Around 30km northeast of Albufeira along the winding N124, **ALTE** makes a fine day trip – though there is no direct public transport here. Local tourist literature calls the village the prettiest in the Algarve and it is certainly attractive, consisting of a series of narrow, cobbled streets gathered on the hillside. It is a short walk up to the local springs, Fonte Pequena and Fonte Grande, where there's a small rocky pool, a stream and an old mill, now converted into a **restaurant**, *Fonte Pequeno* (✆289 478 509; closed Mon, & Oct–March closed evenings) – a delightful spot, though perhaps not when it's full with visiting tour groups. The springs also make a pleasant picnic stop. The **turismo** is located on the main road just below the village on the Estrada da Ponte (Mon 9am–12.30pm & 2–5.30pm, Tues–Fri 9am–5.30pm, Sat 9.30am–11.30pm & 2–4.30pm; ✆289 478 666), and hands out local maps and information about private rooms. For a drink or snack you have the choice of the *Café Central* or the *Café Regional*, both just down from the church. The *Alte Hotel* at Moninho (✆289 478 523, ⓦwww.altehotel.com; ❹) is a modern hotel in rural surroundings, 1km out of Alte, with its own restaurant, pool and superb views from most of the comfortable en-suite rooms.

Armação de Pêra and around

ARMAÇÃO DE PÊRA, 15km west of Albufeira, fronts one of the largest beaches in the Algarve, which spreads east all the way to Galé (see p.579). Beach aside, it is not the greatest looking of resorts by any means; modern high-rise buildings and apartments straggle along the town's main through-road, tempered only by the terraced gardens and cafés overlooking the central part of the sands. The remains of the town's fortified walls are at the eastern end of the seafront road; a terrace in front of a little white chapel provides sweeping views. But the town beach is fine and if the main section is crowded, just head further east, beyond the cluster of traditional boats on the fishermen's beach towards Galé, where things are quieter.

To the west, the coast changes, boasting fine caves and strange rock formations around **Praia da Senhora da Rocha**, which can be visited on daily boat trips (April–Oct only; around €15 for 90min) from the fisherman's beach. The 10km or so of coast between here and **Centianes** is flat and scrubby, fronting a series of delightful cove beaches that have somehow escaped any large-scale development (see below). The other local attraction is 4km up the main N125 at **Porches**, where the most famous of the Algarve's hand-made pottery comes from. It's thick, chunky and hand-painted, and has a good, heavy feel, so if you're looking for ceramics to take home this is the place to stop. There are various shops along the main road.

Practicalities

Armação de Pêra's **bus terminal** is on Via Dorsal – to reach the sea, head down Rua J.P. Vieira, turn first left and head right down Rua R. Santa. There are regular services from Albufeira, Portimão (via Porches), and Silves. Head right for five minutes along the seafront Avenida Marginal, where you'll find the **turismo** (Mon–Fri 9.30am–1pm & 2–5.30pm; ✆282 312 145).

For **private rooms**, ask at *O Serol* restaurant, Rua Portas do Mar 2 (✆282 312 146, shared bath, no breakfast; ❷), overlooking the beach near the fishing boats. For something more upmarket, there's the *Hotel Garbe* at Avenida Beira Mar 1 (✆282 320 260, ⓦwww.hotelgarbe.com; ❺ sea-view rooms ❻), just up the seafront road from the turismo, which has a pool and terrace overlooking the beach. There's also a public Internet terminal in reception. If you don't mind high-rise living, the spacious apartments in *RosaMar* on Rua Dom João II

△ Benagil

(☎282 312 377, ✉paraizo@gawab.com; ❹), a block back from the tourist office, are good value, with sitting rooms, kitchenettes and heavy Portuguese decor, some with sea-facing balconies. There's a bar downstairs. The nearest **campsite**, the shady *Parque de Campismo Armação de Pera* (☎282 312 904, ℱ282 315 379), faces mudflats 1km out of the centre, back up the N269-1 towards highway N125. It's well equipped, with its own pool, supermarket, restaurant and gardens. A **road train** trundles from here to the seafront roughly hourly 10am–6pm (€2.50).

There are countless **bars and restaurants**, most with some fine seafood. The moderately priced *O Serol* (see above; closed Wed) sees a fair number of local people tucking into its daily fish specials. Top budget choice is *Estrela do Mar*, Largo 25 de Abril (☎282 313 775; closed Mon), a simple shack right on the fishermen's beach offering bargain Portuguese staples; the grilled sardines are superb.

West to Centianes

PRAIA DA ALBONDEIRA, 5km west of Armação, marks the start of a superb coastal footpath that runs for 4km along clifftops all the way to Benagil. Next along, **PRAIA DA MARINHA** nestles below a craggy red sandstone cliff, with the only trace of development being a seasonal beach restaurant and a tasteful villa complex a little up the hill. By car, these beaches can be reached from a turning south off the main N125, 8km west of Armação, opposite the International School.

A couple of kilometres further west, the road winds round to the next bay at **BENAGIL**, a tiny village consisting of a cluster of buildings with a couple of cafés above a narrow gully. The road loops down over a dried up river valley, at the bottom of which is a fine beach under high cliffs. Fishing boats can take you out to an amazing seacave, as large as a cathedral, with a hole in its roof. You can also walk to the top of it on the path that starts uphill by the restaurant *Algar* just above Benagil; take care of deep drops. Best place to stay is *Vila Linda Mar* (☎282 352 812, ⓦwww.algarve-paradise.com; ❹) 1.5km back from the beach, a tasteful, traditionally decorated guest house with gardens, a small pool and a highly rated restaurant.

West of Benagil, the scenery changes again with coastal development crowding in around another appealing beach at **PRAIA DE CENTIANES**, 3km away. From here, the road is lined with villas and apartments all the way to Carvoeiro.

Carvoeiro and around

Cut into the red sea cliffs, the small resort of **CARVOEIRO** must once have been an attractive fishing village, but now its small cove beach has to support the prostrate bodies of hundreds of tourists shipped in to what has become an overblown resort. The beach is pleasant enough, though it's rockier and less impressive than many along this stretch, and most accommodation is in the form of block-booked apartments. Out of season, perhaps, the town has more appeal, and at least it is within range of some superb neighbouring beaches, Praia de Centianes and Benagil (see above). Accessible by the coast road, and by a road train that trundles out every 20 minutes or so (€3 round trip) a kilometre east, are the impressive rock formations of **Algar Seco**, where steps lead down low cliffs to a series of dramatic overhangs above blow holes and grottoes.

The **turismo** (mid-Sept to May Mon & Fri–Sun 9.30am–1pm & 2–5.30pm, Tues–Thurs 9.30am–5.30pm; June to mid-Sept daily 9.30am–7pm; ☎282 357 728), just behind the beach, can help with **private rooms**. *Hotel Carvoeiro Sol* (☎282 357 301, ⓦcarvoeirosol.com; ❻) is the most comfortable hotel, a four-star property right by the beach. Rooms come with small balconies, and there's also a pool, courtyard bar and a babysitting service. The best budget option is *O Castelo*, Rua da Casino 59–61 (☎ & ⓕ282 357 416, ⓔcasteloguesthouse @net.pt; ❷, no breakfast), which has modern rooms, the best with a superb view over the beach (❸) – take the road that overlooks the beach uphill above the tourist office and it's a five-minute walk. Restaurants are generally bland, though *Oasis,* on Rua do Barranco (closed Sun), gets good reports for its moderately priced steaks and tuna, and has an outdoor terrace with wicker chairs.

West of Carvoeiro

There are two superb cove beaches a few kilometres to the west of Carvoeiro, though you'll need your own transport to reach them. First up is **Praia da Caneiros**, with a rock stack off some fine sands and a superb beachside restaurant, *Rei das Praias* (☎282 461 006; daily March–Oct). A couple of kilometres further, **Praia Pintadinho** is almost as nice, with a simpler café-restaurant.

Another couple of kilometres west lies the broad sands of **Praia Grande** at the mouth of the Rio Arade and with a scattering of restaurant-bars. A large **campsite**, the *Parque Campismo de Ferragudo* (☎282 461 121), is just beyond here, a short walk from the beaches, but it is only open to members of the International Camping Club. It has a pool, kids' play area, large supermarket and restaurant.

For slides, pools and aquatic fun, **Slide & Splash** theme park (daily April–Oct 10am–5pm, till 6pm in Aug; €16.50, children €13.50; ⓦwww.slidesplash .com) is just a short drive just outside Estômbar, signposted off the N125 at Vale de Deus.

Ferragudo

Surprisingly, **FERRAGUDO**, facing Portimão across the estuary, has made relatively few concessions to international tourism. It is centred on a strip of palm-fringed gardens which spread alongside a narrow riverlet up to the cobbled main square, **Praça Rainha Dona Leonor**, a wide space dotted with cafés. The riverlet ends at the Rio Arade estuary, where there is a small fishing harbour and a few fish restaurants backed by a waterfront promenade. South of here, the old town spreads up the side of a hill, a warren of atmospheric cobbled backstreets gathered around the town church; from its terrace there are great views over the estuary. Below the church – accessible from the fishing harbour or by taking the road that skirts the old town – lies the town beach, which gets progressively more appealing as it approaches the **Castelo de São João do Arade**, one of the only forts in Portugal that lies right behind a sandy beach. The fort (closed to the public), a partner to that in Praia da Rocha, is a tremendous site – built in the sixteenth century to defend Portimão against attack.

The town is connected to Portimão by a regular **bus** service (hourly 7.30am–7.30pm), which drops you on the main road by Praça Rainha Dona Leonor. The travel agent Beroli at nearby Rua 25 de Abril 40 (T282 461 100, Wwww.algarve.tourismus.com) is the best source of local information, and can arrange tours and boat trips. **Accommodation** is somewhat limited; if you aren't fussed about nudity, the best option is the naturist *Quinta da Horta* (T282 461 395, Wwww.naturist-holidays-portugal.com; ④) just out of town – follow the concrete riverlet east for ten minutes and it is on the right. It sports a series of tasteful studios, as well as a two-room apartment, set round a hacienda-style garden full of tropical plants. There's also a small plunge pool, sauna, TV room and tennis court; the owners can also arrange bike hire and horse-riding.

There are a number of lively cafés and bars on and around the main square – including *O Barril,* on Travessa do Caldeirão 1–5 which has live fado on Monday and Wednesday – while *Sueste* on the riverfront Rua da Ribeira (T282 461 592; closed Mon) is the most arty and buzzy of a row of fish **restaurants** facing the harbour. Better value, though far more basic, is *O Velho Novo*, Rua Manuel Teixeira Gomes 2 (dinner only), where good-value fish and meat is grilled on an outside barbecue. It's five minutes' walk from the main square – cross the riverlet along the road signed to Belavista and it's on the left.

Portimão and around

Portimão is the second largest town in the Algarve, with a population of nearly forty thousand. Sited on the estuary of the Rio Arade, it has made its living from fishing since pre-Roman times and today remains a sprawling port. Most visitors are just here for a day's shopping, taking time out from the full-blown resort of **Praia da Rocha**, 3km south of Portimão. The coast road west of Praia da Rocha, towards Lagos, has been engulfed by a series of massive and graceless tourist developments fronting more sweeping beaches – with further development in the pipeline part-financed by leading footballers, including Cristiano Ronaldo, Deco and Ricardo Carvalho; only **Alvor**, slightly inland, retains its original charm.

The town

As a town, **PORTIMÃO** is fairly undistinguished – most of the older buildings were destroyed in the 1755 earthquake. Its most historic building is the **Igreja da**

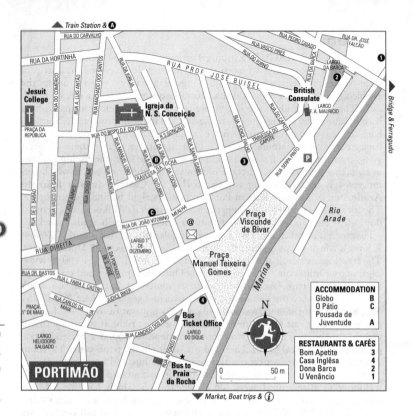

Nossa Senhora da Conceição, rebuilt after the earthquake, but retaining a Manueline door from the original fourteenth-century structure; the interior is more impressive, covered in seventeenth-century *azulejos*. The encircling streets are pleasant enough, filled with shops selling lace, shoes, jewellery, ceramics and wicker goods; the main shopping streets are around the pedestrianized Rua Diogo Tomé and Rua da Portades de São José. Just off the latter street lies Largo 1° de Dezembro, an attractive square with seats inlaid with *azulejos* depicting historical scenes.

However, the best part of town is undoubtedly the **riverfront**, where a series of squares – Largo do Dique, Praça Manuel Teixeira Gomes and Praça Visconde de Bivar – are filled with outdoor cafés by gushing fountains. You'll be approached by people offering **boat trips** along the coast to see the grottoes (2hr; €15), while three-hour trips (around €25) also go up the Rio Arade to Silves (departure times depend on the tides).

Heading up the river and under the road bridge you'll find a series of open-air restaurants serving inexpensive grilled sardine lunches. The streets just back from the bridge – off **Largo da Barca** – are Portimão's oldest: narrow, cobbled and with more than a hint of their fishing-quarter past. Other reasons to come to town are the huge **market** on the first Monday of each month, selling secondhand clothes, ceramics, CDs and junk; it's held near the riverfront on Estrada da Rocha, just southwest of town towards Praia da Rocha. On the morning of the first and third Sunday of each month, a **flea market** spreads out past the railway station in the Parque das Exposições.

Practicalities

The **train station** is inconveniently located at the northern tip of town but a bus runs into the centre every 45 minutes (Mon–Fri only); a taxi costs about €4 or it's a fifteen-minute walk. **Buses** (including those to and from Praia da Rocha) pull up in the streets around Largo do Dique, close to the river. The **turismo** (May to mid-Sept daily 9.30am–7pm; mid-Sept to April Mon–Fri 9.30am–1pm & 2.30–5.30pm; ℡282 470 732) is on Avenida Zeca Afonso, on the way to Praia da Rocha, opposite the football stadium. There's a **post office** in Praça Manuel Teixeira Gomes while the Algarve's only **British consulate** is further up the quayside at Largo Francisco A. Mauricio 7-1° (℡282 490 750).

Portimão has a good *Pousada de Juventude* at Lugar do Coca, Maravilhas (℡282 491 804, ⓦwww.pousadasjuventude.pt; currently being renovated, call for prices), a large modern place with its own small swimming pool, bar, canteen and sports facilities – it's a twenty-minute walk out of the centre. Otherwise, the better-value **accommodation** options include the modern *Hotel Globo*, Rua 5 de Outubro 151 (℡282 416 350, Ⓕ282 483 142; ❻) and the *Residencial O Pátio*, Rua Dr. João Vitorino Mealha 3 (℡282 424 288, Ⓕ282 424 281; ❸), with simpler rooms but a groovy bar. *U Venâncio* (℡965 095 158) is the best of the row of inexpensive fish **restaurants** north of the old bridge, on the riverfront – they all specialize in grilled sardines, though other fish and meat dishes are available. Nearby are some more expensive fish restaurants: best is the highly rated ⚓*Dona Barca* with outdoor tables on Largo da Barca (℡282 484 189), or try friendly *Bom Apetite*, Rua Júdice Fialho 21 (℡919 133 829; closed Sun lunch), which serves authentic Portuguese cuisine, including a splendid *arroz de marisco* and has a great little graffitied bar area. Finally, *Casa Inglêsa* in the riverside Praça Manuel Teixeira Gomes is a thoroughly pleasant café with outdoor tables.

Praia da Rocha

PRAIA DA ROCHA, five minutes' south of Portimão by bus, was one of the first Algarve tourist developments and it's easy to see why. The beach is one of broadest of the entire coast, the wide expanse of sand framed by jagged sea cliffs and the walls of an old fort built in 1691. The **Fortaleza da Santa Caterina** once protected the mouth of the Rio Arade and its terrace offers splendid views at sunset – beach and ocean on one side, Ferragudo, river and marina on the other. Sadly, the effect is totally spoiled by the high-rise hotels, discos and casino that sit on the clifftop behind the beach, all but swamping the town's original *fin-de-siècle* villas. Most of the development lies channelled in a strip just two blocks wide, with the beach reached down steep steps from the elevated main street, Avenida Tomás Cabreira – but at least that means that from virtually every bar, restaurant and hotel terrace the views are of the sands and sea. There's little that is traditionally Portuguese, of course, but it is lively enough to be fun at whatever time of year you visit.

Practicalities

There's a **bus** from Portimão every 45 minutes (7am–8pm) and it stops in front of the *Hotel da Rocha* on Avenida Tomás Cabreira. If you plan to do much to-ing and fro-ing, buy a block of ten tickets from the bus-stop kiosk in Portimão, which will save you around fifty percent. Drivers should note that the main coast road is one-way west to east; it is best to **park** on the main drag in from Portimão. The **turismo** (May to mid-Sept daily 9.30am–7pm; mid-Sept to April Mon–Fri 9.30am–1pm & 2.30–5.30pm; ℡282 419 132) is opposite the bus stop by the beach.

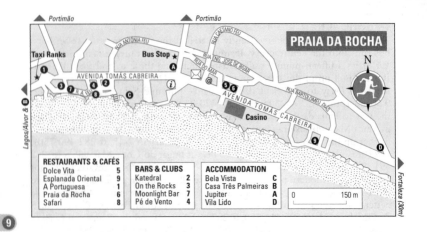

Finding **accommodation** can be expensive and you may want to commute here from Portimão; the following *pensões* or more expensive hotels are the best bets. **Restaurants** are plentiful if largely uninspiring. For a civilized **drink**, the lovely bar of the *Hotel Bela Vista* is open to the public, though there are plenty of far less sophisticated places showing live soccer before switching to dance sounds.

Hotels and pensions

Hotel Bela Vista Av Tomás Cabreira ☎ 282 450 480, ⊚ www.hotelbelavista.net. The most stylish place to stay on the seafront, a pseudo-Moorish mansion built in 1903 by the wealthy Magalhães family as a wedding gift. The rooms and communal areas are an exquisite mixture of carved wood, stained glass, and yellow, white and blue *azulejos*. Breakfast included. Parking. ⑤

Hotel Jupiter Av Tomás Cabreira ☎ 282 415 041, ⊚ www.hoteljupiter.com A modern hulk on the wrong (land) side of the Avenida, but with all mod cons including a bar and swimming pool. ⑤

Casa Três Palmeiras Praia do Vau, 2km west of Praia da Rocha ☎ 282 401 275, ⊚ www.casatrespalmeiras.com. In a sublime position on a clifftop above a little beach, this sleek villa is a superb example of 1960s' chic. Glass-fronted rooms curve around a terrace with a pool, where breakfast is served in summer. Rooms and communal areas are spacious and tastefully furnished in traditional Portuguese style. Services available include manicures, reflexology and massages, and discounts are available for local golf courses. Parking. Closed Dec & Jan. ⑥

Residencial Vila Lido Av Tomás Cabreira ☎ 282 424 127, ⊚ www.hotelvilalido.com. Beautiful blue-shuttered building with original decor in its own small grounds facing the fort. Front rooms have superb views over the beach. Closed Jan–Feb. ⑤

Restaurants and cafés

La Dolce Vita Av Tomás Cabreira ☎ 282 419 444. Owned and run by Italians, so the home-made pastas and pizzas are authentic and pretty good value; set lunch €8. There's live music at weekends. Inexpensive.

Cervejaria Praia da Rocha Edifício Colunas, off Av Tomás Cabreira ☎ 282 416 541. With an outdoor patio and bustling interior, this attracts a largely Portuguese crowd for excellent good-value daily specials, though seafood is expensive (try the clams).

Esplanada Oriental Av Tomás Cabreira (by the *Oriental Hotel*). Small terrace café serving snacks amongst Oriental style chimney pots; great sea views. Inexpensive.

A Portuguesa Av Tomás Cabreira ☎ 282 424 175. Good for Portuguese grills and pasta, together with a children's menu. Bright decor backed by gentle jazzy sounds. Closed Sun. Moderate.

Safari Rua António Feu ☎ 282 423 540. In a wonderful position overlooking the beach and while it's a mainly Portuguese menu, there are a few decent international dishes. Closed Mon. Moderate.

Bars and clubs

Katedral Av Tomás Cabreira ☎ 282 417 268, ⊚ www.katedraldisco.com. Housed in a futuristic cube on the clifftop, this is the largest and highest-profile club in town, with a lightshow and the latest dance sounds. The downstairs bar, *Nicho*, is a good place to start the evening. Open daily from midnight.

Moonlight Bar Rua António Feu. Bright decor, lively sounds and a superb terrace facing the beach to while the night away. Open until 4am.

On the Rocks Av Tomás Cabreira, Lojas B & C ☎282 416 144, ⊛www.discobarontherocks.com. A modern dance bar with a sunset terrace. Live soccer on TV sometimes vies for attention in the bar; there's also a dance floor and live music on Fri. Daily 4am.

Pé de Vento Av Tomás Cabreira, Loja A ☎282 424 1822. Popular disco-bar on two floors. The upstairs bar has a beach-facing terrace, next to a large dance floor which features live music on Wed. Daily 3pm–4am.

Alvor and Quinta da Rocha

The resorts immediately west of Praia da Rocha – Vau and Praia Três Irmãos – have good beaches but little else going for them, and it is better to push on to historic **ALVOR**, 6km west of Praia da Rocha. The ancient port briefly achieved fame as the place where Dom João II died in 1495 and, though much of the town was razed in the 1755 earthquake, it still boasts a sixteenth-century Igreja Matriz with Manueline doors, arches and pillars carved into fishing ropes and plants. It remained a sleepy fishing village until the 1960s, when tourism began to take hold, and today the old town has been outgrown by a sprawl of modern – though largely low-rise – buildings. Nevertheless, the old core around the church and the central Praça da República retains its character, while the harbour itself is a delight, lined with colourful fishing boats and aromatic fish restaurants.

The town's **turismo** is in the centre of town at Rua Dr. Alfonso Costa 51 (daily: July–Sept 9.30am–7pm; Oct–June 9.30am–1pm & 2–5.30pm; ☎282 457 540). From here it is a short walk uphill to the leafy ruin that is Alvor's **castle**, which dates back to the thirteenth century but now houses a children's playground. From here, Rua Padre David Neto leads onto Rua Dr Frederico Romas Mendes, the main drag lined with bars and restaurants. This stretches down to the riverside **Largo da Ribeira**, marked by a modern statue of a fish, where you'll find the former market building. Half a dozen fish restaurants here, most with outdoor seating, overlook the picturesque estuary of the Rio Alvor. Head right as you face the river and a path leads up the estuary for a tranquil walk; bear left and it is a ten-minute stroll past fishermen's huts and riverside cafés to the **Praia de Alvor**, an enormous beach backed by café-bars.

Rooms can be hard to come by, though there are plenty of expensive **hotels** around 1km east of Alvor, facing the beach. The best bet in town is *Hospedaria Buganvilia*, Rua Padre Mendes Rossio de 5 Pedro (☎282 459 412; ❸, no breakfast) just down the hill from the turismo, a modern place with flouncy decor above a decent restaurant. *Campismo da Dourado* (☎282 459 178, ℗282 458 002) lies around 1km north of Alvor, near the N125, a pleasant, leafy **campsite** with a small shop.

The best of the decently priced fish **restaurants** on the harbourfront is the inexpensive *Tasca do Margadinho* at Largo da Ribeira 9 (☎282 459 144; closed Thurs), an atmospheric place with outdoor tables. Up near the castle, *O Alcaide* on Rua do Castelo 17 (☎282 459 330) is more intimate, with fine *cataplanas* and moderately priced grills. Down on the sands, *Restaurante Restinga* (☎282 459 434; closed one month in winter) sits on the cusp of a large dune and offers great views to go with its moderately priced fish and grills; Robert de Niro was a recent satisfied customer.

Quinta da Rocha lies on the peninsula between the mouths of the rivers Alvor and Odiáxere, northwest of Alvor's huge beach. It is an extensive area which, in the parts not given over to citrus and almond groves, consists of copses, salt marshes, sandy spits and estuarine mud flats, forming a wide range of habitats for different species of animals and birds – including twenty-two species of wading bird. You can follow paths and tracks around the reserve by taking the turning off the main N125 opposite Mexilheira Grande; there are no marked trails, but follow any of the tracks into the wetlands.

Silves and around

Eighteen kilometres northeast of Portimão, **SILVES** – the medieval residence and capital of the Moorish kings of the al-Gharb – merits a half-day's detour. It has a superb castle and a highly dramatic approach, with its red ring of walls gradually revealing their course as you emerge from the wooded hills. Under the Moors, Silves was a place of grandeur, described in contemporary accounts as "of shining brightness" within its three dark circuits of guarding walls. Such glories and civilized splendours came to an end, however, in 1189, with the arrival of **Sancho I**, at the head of a mixed army of Portuguese and Crusaders. Sancho, desperately in need of extra fighting force, had recruited a rabble of "large and odious" northerners, who had already been expelled from the holy shrine of St James of Compostela for their irreligious behaviour. The army arrived at Silves toward the end of June and the thirty thousand Moors retreated to the citadel. There they remained through the long, hot summer, sustained by huge water cisterns and granaries, until September when, the water exhausted, they opened negotiations.

Sancho was ready to compromise, but the Crusaders had been recruited by the promise of plunder. The gates were opened after Sancho had negotiated guarantees for the inhabitants' personal safety and goods; all were brutally ignored by the Crusaders, who duly ransacked the town, killing some six thousand Moors in the process. Silves passed back into Moorish hands two years

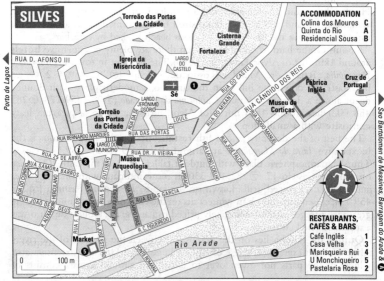

△ Silves castle

later, but by then the town had been irreparably weakened, and it finally fell to Christian forces in 1249.

The town

The **Moorish Fortaleza** (daily: mid-July to mid-Sept 9am–7pm; mid-Sept to mid-July 9am–6pm; last entry 30min before closing; €1.25) remains the focal point of Silves, dominating the town centre with its impressively complete set of sandstone walls and detached towers. It is currently undergoing extensive renovation, which will eventually recreate a Moorish-style garden, a traditional well and the governor's palace, but this is unlikely to be completed until 2008. Renovation also restricts access to the wonderful vaulted thirteenth-century water cistern, the **Cisterna Grande**, which once served the town. Some 10m in height and supported by six columns, the cistern is said to be haunted by a Moorish maiden who can be seen sailing across the underground waters during a full moon. However, you can still clamber onto the castle walls for impressive views over the town and surrounding hills.

Silves's **Sé** (Mon–Sat 8.30am–6.30pm, limited hours on Sun; free) sits below the fortress, built on the site of the Grand Mosque. Flanked by broad Gothic towers, it has a suitably defiant, military appearance, though the Great Earthquake and centuries of impoverished restoration have left their mark within. The tombs lining the cathedral walls are of bishops and of Crusaders who died taking Silves back from the Moors. Opposite the Sé, it is worth a quick look in the newer **Igreja da Misericórdia** (Mon–Fri 9.30am–1pm & 2–5.30pm; free), a sixteenth-century church with a fine Manueline doorway and hung with seven impressive religious paintings, some of them dating back to the seventeenth century.

Below the Sé, in Rua das Portas de Loulé 14, is the town's **Museu Arqueologia** (☎282 444 832; Mon–Sat 9am–6pm; €1.50). It's engaging enough, despite a lack of English-language labelling, and romps through the history of

Silves from the year dot to the sixteenth century with displays of local archeological finds. At the centre of the museum is an Arab water cistern, which boasts a ten-metre-deep well.

Silves's other main attraction is the **Fabrica de Inglês** (Tues–Sun 12.30–3pm & 7–10.30pm; free except during special events; ⓦwww.fabrica-de-ingles .com), near the riverfront, five minutes' walk east of the road bridge. A series of cafés, bars and fountains are clustered round a large central courtyard filled with outdoor tables below scented orange trees. It is a lovely space, most animated when it hosts the annual summer **Silves Beer Festival**, usually in July. At this time – and on Friday evenings in summer – the cafés and bars are heaving, and a spectacular light show illuminates the fountains. The one permanent attraction is the **Museu da Cortiças** (daily 9.30am–12.45pm & 2–6.15pm; €2), a cork museum in the northwest corner of the complex, which won the European Industrial Museum Award in 2001. But unless you have a keen interest in the cork industry, its displays are unlikely to get your pulse going.

Silves's **market** (Mon–Sat 8am–1pm) on the riverfront, near the narrow thirteenth-century bridges is fronted by some of the town's best café-restaurants – fine places to sit outside and watch life go by.

Practicalities

The **train station** – an easy approach from either Lagos or Faro – lies 2km out of town; there is a connecting bus. **Buses** stop on the main road, near the riverfront at the foot of town. The **turismo** is at Rua 25 de Abril 26–28 (Mon–Fri 9.30am–1pm & 2–7.30pm; ⓣ282 442 255, ⓦwww.cm-silves.pt), on the road up to the castle.

Apart from **private rooms** (ask at the town turismo), there are a couple of basic **pensões**, including the friendly family-run *Residencial Sousa*, Rua Samora Barros 17 (ⓣ282 442 502; ❷, shared bath and no breakfast), with large, high-ceilinged rooms. A more upmarket option is *Hotel Colina dos Mouros* (ⓣ282 440 420, ⓔcolinadosmouros@hotmail.com; ❹), a prominent modern hotel over the road bridge opposite the fortress, which has an outdoor pool, and rooms with superb views over the town. For rural tranquility drive out to the lovely *Quinta do Rio*, at Sitio São Estevão (ⓣ & ⓕ282 445 528; ❸), around 5km out of town off the road to São Bartolomeu de Messines, a country inn with six rustic-style rooms with shaded terraces facing orange groves and grazing horses. The Italian owners can supply evening meals on request.

In town, ⁂ *Café Inglês* on Rua do Castelo 11 (ⓣ282 442 585; closed Mon evening & Sat lunch), by the fortress, is a fashionably restored town house which sells delicious home-made snacks, ice cream and fruit juices, as well as full meals, including pizzas on the roof terrace in summer; it also has seats outside, live music at weekends and the occasional art exhibition. Also recommended is the pricey *Restaurante Marisqueira Rui*, Rua Comendador Vilarinho (ⓣ282 442 682; closed Tues), one of the Algarve's finest seafood **restaurants**. *Casa Velha*, near the tourist office on Rua 25 de Abril 13 (ⓣ282 445 491) is a lively *marisqueira* in a fine pink-tiled building with well-prepared and moderately priced fish and seafood in bubbling tanks. Alternatively, *U Monchiqueiro* (closed Wed) is one of the best of a handful of inexpensive grill-cafés on the riverfront road in front of the market. For something simpler, *Pastelaria Rosa*, in Largo do Município, is a superb old *pastelaria* with a cool *azulejo*-lined interior and a counter smothered in cakes and goodies. Outdoor tables spill onto the pretty main square next to a small fountain.

A walk around the Rio Arade

You'll need a car or bike to reach the start of this pretty three-hour circular walk above the Rio Arade – and save it for a spring or autumn day when it's not too hot. Drive out of Silves on the N124 (Monchique road) and after about 2.5km there's a turn-off to the left at two large white domes (a sewage station) and by a bus stop and small makeshift house-café. An unmade road (fine for cars) runs for 1km down to the **Clube Náutico de Silves**, where there's a bar and parking – the cruise boats from Portimão sometimes put in here too. Here, you can pick up the path alongside the raised concrete irrigation channel, the *levada*, which runs above the **Rio Arade** and out to the confluence with the Ribeira de Odelouca – the path is under trees for the most part, and wading birds are visible on the mudbanks. Always stick with the *levada* path and eventually it swings around and inland, away from the river. Where it crosses a small tarmac road you leave the *levada* and climb up a road to the right (past the "Stop" sign and a few houses). This road heads towards the N124, which you'll soon see, and a path then swings around to the right, parallel with the main road. It eventually joins the track from the main road down to the *Clube Náutico*, where you turn right for the final stretch to the *Clube* car park – the only drawback here is the indescribable smell from the run-off from the sewage station, which you'll have to brave for a minute or so as you scurry past.

Barragem do Arade

Around 8km northeast of Silves, signed off the road to São Bartolomeu de Messines, the **Barragem do Arade** makes a good excursion for a picnic. This is one of the area's main sources of water, set amongst rolling, tree-lined hills, popular with campervanners and migrating birds. There's a pricey café here, *Coutada*, which can organize boat trips (€8 per person) to a scraggy, tree-lined offshore islet known as **Paradise Island**; the fee covers the return trip together with use of canoes, sunloungers and swimming in a cordoned-off area of the reservoir. You can also hire jet skis at the café.

The Serra de Monchique

Frequent weekday buses – fewer at weekends – leave Portimão for the 24-kilometre journey north to the market town of **Monchique** via the spa town of **Caldas de Monchique**. These both lie in the **Serra de Monchique**, a green and wooded mountain range of cork, chestnut and eucalyptus that provides the western Algarve with a natural northern boundary. This area bears the brunt of summer fires that seem to rage annually, but the woodland is generally quick to recover and it remains ideal hiking country. Cyclists or drivers have the option of cutting across afterwards to the wilder reaches of the western Algarve coast, along the minor N267, which passes through the little mountain village of Marmelete and continues all the way to Aljezur (see p.609). It's a fine route, heading through tranquil countryside before swinging down through the hills and forests to the west coast.

Caldas de Monchique

CALDAS DE MONCHIQUE, set in a ravine and surrounded by thick woods, has been a celebrated spa since Roman times. In 1495 Dom João II came here to take the waters (though he nevertheless died soon afterwards in Alvor), and in the nineteenth century the town became a favourite resort of the Spanish bourgeoisie. In 2000, virtually the entire village was purchased by the Monchique Termas company, which set about sympathetically restoring the run-down buildings round the main square into hotels and guest houses, revitalizing the cafés and shops and completely modernizing the spa itself. In doing so they have transformed a somewhat ramshackle spa resort into a tourist village – but the results, so far at least, have been fairly successful.

Caldas is 19km north of Portimão, and the centre is reached by a looping, one-way side road off the main Monchique road. Halfway down the hill on the left you'll see the cobbled, tree-shaded main square, fronted by the pseudo-Moorish windows of the former casino – now an exhibition hall – and surrounded by lovely nineteenth-century buildings. The setting is as beautiful as any in the country, though the tiny village's peace and quiet is shattered daily by busloads of day-trippers.

Head downhill and you pass the modern **thermal spa** (Mon 9am–1pm, Tues 10.30am–1pm & 3–7pm, Wed–Sun 9am–1pm & 3–7pm; €25; Ⓦwww .monchiquetermas.com), flaunting its well-kept gardens and housing various specialist water treatments on the ground floor of a modern hotel. The entrance fee gives access to the sauna, steam room, gym, water massage facilities and pool, with extra sessions ranging from "jet-showers" (€10) to full body massages from €50. Discounts are available to hotel guests.

Climbing up from the spa, above the square, you can follow the stream to sit under giant eucalyptus trees – a wonderful spot for a picnic. Take along some of the local drink – *medronho* – a kind of schnapps made from the arbutus (or strawberry tree) that grows on the surrounding hills.

Practicalities

Not all **buses** from Portimão call into the centre of Caldas, some stopping instead on the main road just out of town before continuing up to Monchique. Still, it's only a minute's walk downhill to the main square. There's a four-star **inn** just above the main square, the *Albergaria do Lageado* (☎282 912 616, Ⓦwww.albergariadolageado.com; closed Nov–March; ❸), which has tiled floors, white walls and elderly bathrooms (not all rooms a/c), though it's set in restful stepped gardens with a good pool; the restaurant has adequate meals for around €20. Apart from this, the rest of the **accommodation** is owned by the Monchique Termas company (reception office on left as you enter town; ☎282 910 910), including the *Hotel Central* (❻), a very comfortable three-star partly set in the former casino building on the main square; and *Estalagem Dom Lourenço* (❻), opposite, a four-star inn in another converted nineteenth-century building, with hardwood floors and contemporary decor. Monchique Termas also rents out apartments (sleeping up to four people; ❻) overlooking the main square, with small living rooms and kitchenettes. Guests at any of the above can use an outdoor pool.

An obvious but very pricey place to eat is *Restaurante 1692* (☎282 910 910), named after its year of construction, with tables set out under the square's trees. Better value is *O Rouxinol* on the main road above Caldas (☎282 913 975, closed Sun & Dec–Jan) in an old hunting lodge, with fine local and international dishes from around €20. For something simpler, *O Tasco*, on the far side of the main square, below the path up to the picnic tables, is a darkened **bar** set in sixteenth-century stables, the oldest building in the village. Specialities include bread rolls with sausage meat inside, baked in the traditional exterior oven, though it closes at 7pm.

Omega Parque

A couple of kilometres south of Caldas de Monchique – and served by the same buses – **Omega Parque** (ⓦ www.omegaparque.com; daily 10am–7pm; until 5.30pm Oct–April; €8, children €5) is a small zoo set in steep woodlands dedicated to preserving endangered species. Well cared-for residents include cheetahs, pygmy hippos and red pandas. Rare birds include the Bali starling and blue-necked cassowary. There's also a decent café and shop.

Monchique

MONCHIQUE, 6km to the north of Caldas de Monchique, and 300m higher up the range, is a hill town whose large market on the second Monday of each month (by the helipad) is famous for smoked hams and locally made furniture – especially the distinctive x-shaped wooden chairs. There's also a weekly Sunday market on the main square, Largo 5 de Outubro, though the town is liveliest during the March Traditional Sausage Fair, when restaurants lay on special menus and there's live jazz and folk round town.

The most impressive building in town is the **Igreja Matriz** (Mon–Sat 10am–5.30pm; free), up a steep cobbled street from Largo 5 de Outubro, but the rest of Monchique is worth a wander too – it's dotted with beautifully crafted metal sculptures of local characters made by a contemporary Lisbon artist. The most evocative local sight, though, is the ruined seventeenth-century monastery of **Nossa Senhora do Desterro**, which you can walk to up a wooded track – brown signs point you up here from Rua do Porto Fundo, the road leading uphill from the bus station. Only a rickety shell of this Franciscan foundation survives, apparently quite uncared for, but it's in a great position overlooking the town and shows a beautiful blend of classical Renaissance facade with Moorish-influenced vaulting.

Practicalities

Buses arrive at the terminal in the main Largo 5 de Outubro. Monchique's helpful **turismo** (Mon–Fri 9.30am–1pm & 2–5.30pm; ☎282 911 189, ⓦ www.cm-monchique.pt) sits 100m up the steep Fóia road on Largo de S. Sebastião – there's plenty of free parking here. There are a couple of budget **places to stay** in town, first choice the very welcoming *Estrela de Monchique*, Rua do Porto Fundo 46 (☎282 913 111; no breakfast, ❷), a stone's throw to the right of the bus terminal. Otherwise, facing the main Largo 5 de Outubro, the *Bela Vista* (☎282 912 252; no breakfast, ❶) offers basic comforts above a decent café. The front rooms have balconies facing the square, but these can be noisy. The Irish-owned *Albergaria Bica-Boa*, Estrada de Lisboa 266 (☎282 912 271; ❸) is a few hundred metres out of town, up the Lisbon road (signposted), with a lovely garden, vine-covered terrace and pool. Its restaurant serves veggie dishes, piri-piri chicken, tuna salad, pasta and the like, though the location is better than the food. If you have your own transport, you may prefer to stay at the excellent places on the Fóia road (see p.594).

Monchique itself also has a handful of **restaurants** that soak up the passing tourist trade. *A Charrete*, Rua Samora Gil 30–34 (☎282 912 142; closed Wed), is recommended, specializing in award-winning "mountain food" – meat and fish cooked with beans, pasta and rice and the like – while *Restaurante Central*, near the church at Rua da Igreja 5 (☎282 913 160), offers basic but inexpensive Portuguese cuisine. It's a tiny place virtually smothered under the weight of thousands of photocopied notes and postcards detailing past visitors' comments – most of them complimentary.

Nightlife centres on the well-signed *Barlefante,* on Rua João Deus 13 (⊕282 912 774), a cavernous and fashionable café-bar offering tapas, drinks and occasional live music.

Fóia

Fóia, 8km west of Monchique, is – at nearly 900m – the highest of the *serra*'s peaks, though you'll need your own transport to get here: it's a beautiful winding drive. Bristling with antennae, and capped by an ungainly modern complex sheltering a café-restaurant and shop, the summit itself can be an anticlimax, especially if clouds obscure the views or you have to share the experience with the midsummer crowds. Get here early if you can. On a clear day, the panoramic view of the Algarve takes in Portimão, Lagos, the foothills stretching to the Barragem da Bravura, and west across to Cabo de São Vicente.

You may also want to spend the night on the wooded slopes leading up to it. The *Estalagem Abrigo da Montanha*, a couple of kilometres from the centre of Monchique (⊕282 912 131, ⓦwww.abrigodamontanha.com; ❹), has a lovely garden, a pool and views, as well as a fine dining room; while 4.5km from Monchique on the same road, the *Quinta de São Bento* (⊕ & ⓕ282 912 700; ❹) has just five rooms stuffed with period antiques in a home owned by the Bragança family, the former monarchs of Portugal. It is also one of the best places in this part of the Algarve for high-quality, but reasonably priced Portuguese cooking, featuring traditional recipes (restaurant closed Mon).

Lagos and around

LAGOS is one of the Algarve's most attractive and historic towns, its historic centre enclosed in largely fourteenth-century walls at the mouth of the Ribeira de Bensafrim. It was from here that many of Portugal's great explorers set off for the New World, including Gil Eanes, who was born here. In 1577, Lagos became the administrative capital of the Algarve, though much of the town was destroyed in the 1755 earthquake and Faro took over as capital in 1776. Lagos went into long decline, until tourism revived the town in the 1960s, since when it has developed into a major resort – though it also remains a working fishing port and local market centre. For all its historical significance, Lagos's main attraction is its proximity to some of the best beaches on the Algarve coast. To the east of the town is the long sweep of **Meia Praia**, while to the west – from **Praia de Dona Ana** to **Porto do Mós** – is an extraordinary network of coves, pierced by tunnels and grottoes and studded by extravagantly weathered outcrops of purple-tinted rock. Popular boat trips run along the west coast all year round, while other popular side trips are inland to the **Barragem de Bravura**, a pretty hillside reservoir, or to **Lagos Zoo**.

Arrival and information

Lagos is the western terminal of the Algarve railway line and its **train station** is across the river, a fifteen-minute walk from the centre via a swing bridge in the marina; taxis are usually available if you can't face the walk. The **bus station** is a bit closer in, a block back from the main estuary road, Avenida dos Descobrimentos, and almost opposite the bridge to the train station. The **turismo** (May–Sept Mon–Fri 9.30am–7pm, Oct–April same hours until

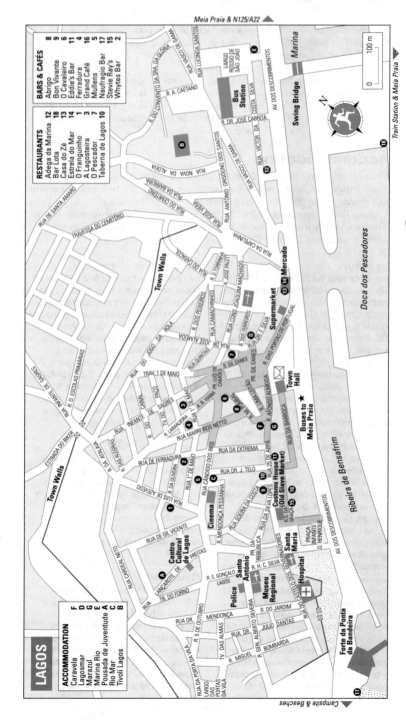

ACCOMMODATION
Caravela	F
Lagosmar	D
Marazul	G
Marina Rio	E
Pousada de Juventude	A
Rio Mar	C
Tivoli Lagos	B

RESTAURANTS
Adega da Marina	12
Bar Lota	18
Casa do Zé	13
Estrela do Mar	14
O Franguinho	1
A Lagosteira	3
O Pescador	7
Taberna de Lagos	10

BARS & CAFÉS
Abrigo	8
Bon Vivante	9
O Cavaleiro	6
Eddie's Bar	11
Ferradura	4
Grand Café	16
Mullens	5
Naufragio Bar	17
Stevie Rays	15
Whytes Bar	2

Meia Praia & N125/A22

Train Station & Meia Praia

Campsite & Beaches

THE ALGARVE | Lagos and around

5.30pm; ☎282 763 031, ⓦwww.cm-lagos.pt) is inconveniently positioned at Sítio de São João, which is the first roundabout as you come into the town from the east. From the centre, it's a twenty-minute walk; keep going down Rua Vasco da Gama, past the bus station.

Most of Lagos can be explored comfortably on foot, but the best way to see the outlying sights in summer is on the **road train** (May–Sept hourly, 10.30am–7pm; €3), which trundles from the marina along Avenida dos Descobrimentos and out via the beaches of Praia de Dona Ana and Porto de Mós to the headland at Ponta da Piedade.

Accommodation

Most of the town's hotels and *pensões* are fully booked through the summer so if you turn up without a reservation, your best chance of a bed will be a **room** in a private house (❸). The tourist office may phone around and try to find you a space, though you'll probably be met by touts at the bus or train station. There's a **youth hostel** in town, while Lagos also has a **campsite**, to the west of the centre, near Praia de Dona Ana.

In town

Pensão Caravela Rua 25 de Abril 16 ☎282 763 361. Unspectacular but well-placed rooms on the town's main pedestrianized street. Doubles come with or without bath. ❷

Pensão Lagosmar Rua Dr. F. Silva 13 ☎282 763 523, ⓔdfhoteis@inoxnet.com. Upmarket *pensão* on a quiet street, where some rooms have small balconies. ❹

Residencial Marazul Rua 25 de Abril 13 ☎282 770 230, ⓦwww.pensaomarazul.com. Beautifully decorated *residencial*, with bright rooms and communal areas tiled in *azulejos*. The en-suite bedrooms vary in size, but all come with TVs and some have terraces with sea views. Closed Oct–March. ❷

Albergaria Marina Rio Av dos Descobrimentos 388 ☎282 769 859, ⓦwww.marinario.com. A large, modern four-star inn facing the harbour (though back rooms face the bus station). Bland but good facilities, including satellite TV, a games room and rooftop pool. ❹

Hotel Rio Mar Rua Cândido dos Reis 83 ☎282 763 091, ⓔhotel.riomar@clix.pt. Smart, medium-sized hotel with its own bar, tucked into a central street. Most rooms have a balcony – the best overlook the sea at the back of the hotel, others overlook a fairly quiet main street. Good value. ❸

Tivoli Lagos Rua Nova da Aldeia ☎282 790 079, ⓦwww.tivolilagos.com. Lagos's most upmarket central hotel (5min from the market) is built round a central garden area with its own pool. Not all the rooms are spacious, and some overlook a busy street, but the best have terraces with fine views. There are two restaurants, bar, indoor and outdoor pool, and health club, plus a courtesy bus to its own beach club at Meia Praia. Parking available. ❻

At the beaches

Meia Praia Beach Club Meia Praia ☎282 789 400, ⓦwww.dompedro.com. A 10min drive from Lagos, just back from one of the best stretches of beach, this tasteful three-star is set in attractive grounds; the best rooms have sea-facing balconies. Apartments for 4–6 people are also available, there are tennis courts and a pool, while guests are entitled to discounts at the Palmares Golf Course. Parking. ❺

Sol e Praia Praia de Dona Ana ☎282 764 462, ⓦwww.dfhoteis.com. The best option on this stretch, close to the steps down to the beach and with a pool, gym and games room. Most rooms have coastal-facing balconies. ❺

Youth hostel

Pousada de Juventude Rua de Lançarote de Freitas 50 ☎282 761 970, ⓦwww.pousadasjuventude.pt. Modern, well-designed youth hostel, just up from the Centro Cultural de Lagos, with several dorms plus a few en-suite doubles (book in advance for these). There's a pleasant courtyard plus Internet access, laundry facilities and currency exchange. Dorms €16, rooms ❷

Campsite

Campismo da Trindade Rossio da Trindade ☎282 763 893, ⓕ282 762 885. Wedged up by the Clube de Futebol Esperança de Lagos on the way to Praia de Dona Ana, this is a basic and cramped campsite with a small shop. In season a bus marked "D. Ana/Porto de Mós" runs to the site from the bus station. On foot, follow the main Sagres road around the old town and it's 10–15min from the Forte Ponta da Bandeira to the site.

The town

Lagos was a favoured residence of Henry the Navigator, who used the town as a base for the new African trade, to which is owed the town's least proud relic – Europe's first **slave market**. This opened in 1444, and its arcades survive alongside the old **Customs House** in Praça da República near the waterfront. It was from this part of town that the youthful Dom Sebastião is said to have roused his troops before the ill-fated Moroccan expedition of 1578. Fired up by militant Catholicism, the dream-crazed king was to perish on the battlefield of Alcácer-Quibir (modern Ksar el Kbir, between Tangier and Fez) along with almost the entire Portuguese nobility. It was a disaster that enabled the Spanish to absorb Portugal for sixty years, but it did Dom Sebastião's reputation a world of good among the aggressively devout. He's commemorated in the centre of Lagos, in Praça Gil Eanes, by a fantastically dreadful modern statue – pink, ridiculous and looking like a flowerpot man.

Much of the old town was devastated by the 1755 earthquake, though one rare and beautiful church that survived is the **Igreja de Santo António**. Decorated around 1715, its gilt and carved interior is wildly obsessive, every last inch filled with a private fantasy of cherubic youths struggling with animals and fish. The church forms part of a visit to the **Museu Municipal** (☎282 762 301; Tues–Sun 9.30am–12.30pm & 2–5pm; €2.10) next door, worth a look if only to discover the true meaning of the word eclectic. Alongside barrowloads of Neolithic axeheads, pottery shards, statuary and local religious art are jars containing misshapen animal foetuses, a display of models of Algarvian chimneys, straw hats, lobster pots and fossils, the 1504 town charter, and assorted muskets, swords and cannonballs.

Stroll along the waterfront Avenida dos Descobrimentos to see the remains of Lagos's once impregnable walls and fortifications, which include the squat seventeenth-century **Forte Ponta da Bandeira** (Tues–Sun 9.30am–12.30pm & 2–5pm; €2.10), guarding the entrance to the harbour. The fort sits opposite Lagos's small but attractive sandy town beach. The other end of the palm-lined Avenida dos Descobrimentos, leading up to the small marina and neighbouring fishing harbour, is usually lined with stalls offering dolphin "seafaris" and **boat trips** to the amazing grottoes and sea caves along the surrounding coast. It's worth shopping around for the best deal, but most cost around €10 per person for a 45-minute trip up to around €30 for half-day excursions; some of them include a soft or alcoholic drink. Bom Dia (☎282 764 670, ⊛www.bomdia.info) is one of many operators, but unlike the others its grotto trips are on a former cargo schooner (they transfer you to a motorboat for the fun part, skipping in and out of the grottoes); they also have longer half-day trips to Sagres. Also recommended are Dolphin Seafaris (⊛www.dolphinseafaris.com) which can whisk you out to see local dolphin colonies in a rigid inflatable dinghy for €30.

The beaches

The promontory south of Lagos is fringed by eroded cliff faces that shelter a series of postage stamp-sized cove beaches, within easy walking distance of the old town. Follow Avenida dos Descobrimentos up the hill (toward Sagres) and turn left just opposite the fire station, where you see signs to the tiny **Praia do Pinhão**. This is the first of the coves – around a twenty-minute walk from town. Five minutes further, across the cliffs, is the **Praia de Dona Ana** – one of the most photogenic of all the Algarve's beaches, with a restaurant, the *Mirante*, built into the cliffs. Out of season the beach is superb, though in summer the crowds can get overwhelming.

△ Praia de Dona Ana

Beyond here, you can follow a path around the cliffs and coast to **Praia do Camilo** – sometimes a bit less crowded – and right to the **Ponta da Piedade**, a headland where a palm-bedecked lighthouse makes a great vantage point at sunset. This marks the final point of call for the road train from Lagos.

Beyond the point, the coast sweeps west again and you can continue to follow paths close to the cliff's edge to the beach of **Porto do Mós**, another 45 minutes' walk away, a nice enough beach though development has spoilt the surroundings. The path then moves on as far as Luz (see p.601), another hour away; it's a splendid stretch, high above the ocean, until the obelisk above Luz comes into sight, from where you scramble down the hillside and into town.

To the east of Lagos, across the river and flanked by the railway line, is **Meia Praia**, a vast tract of sand that extends for 4km to the delta of the rivers Odiáxere and Arão. It's particularly popular with backpackers who congregate at the beach bars dotted along the sands. You can walk to the beach via the marina and fishing harbour in around twenty minutes, or there's a regular bus service from Avenida dos Descobrimentos which travels the length of the beach.

Barragem de Bravura and Lagos Zoo

Around 15km north of Lagos, the **Barragem de Bravura** is one of the most picturesque of the Algarve's reservoirs. There's no public transport but, with a car, the drive is a delight, either along the IC4 up the Ribeira da Bensafrim valley towards Aljezur – from where the *barragem* is signed off to the right – or along the coast road towards Portimão, where the *barragem* can be reached by taking the N125-9 from Odeáxere. Both roads pass through bucolic countryside, flower-filled in spring and early summer. The road stops at the top of the dam over the Rio Bravura; to the south, the deep valley is little more than an overgrown stream fed by a waterfall from the dam, while behind the dam lies the deep, still green waters of the reservoir, filled with huge carp. It's an idyllic spot, and you can walk right over the top of the dam and around the edge of the reservoir on the other side along a dirt trail. Swimming, fishing and water sports, however, are prohibited.

Around 8km north of Lagos, just off the main N120 to Aljezur and close to the village of Barão de São João, **Lagos Zoo** (Ⓦwww.zoolagos.com; daily: April–Sept 10am–7pm; Oct–March 10am–5pm; €8, children €5, family ticket €21) makes an interesting hour or two's detour (though you'll need a car to get here). The large, leafy complex houses flamingoes, toucans, ibis, parrots and emus, as well as a few wallabies, monkeys and farm animals in a special children's enclosure. There's also a shop, restaurant and an exhibition centre.

Eating

The centre of Lagos is packed with **restaurants**, most found along Rua Afonso d'Almeida and its continuation Rua 25 de Abril. Where Avenida dos Descobrimentos meets Rua das Portas de Portugal, there's a diverting **fish and vegetable market** (Mon–Sat 8am-2pm), in front of which is a line of good, unpretentious fish restaurants. Menus are of a similar standard and price almost everywhere, though Lagos does also have a couple of highly regarded places where it's worth pushing the boat out.

Estrela do Mar Mercado Municipal, off Av dos Descobrimentos ☎282 769 250. Atop the main *mercado* and boasting fine views from its terrace, this swish place serves fresh fish straight from the market along with speciality *cataplanas*. Live music every other Sat completes its attractions. Expensive.

O Franguinho Rua Luís de Azevedo 25. Bustling *churrasqueira* with a tiny first-floor dining room. This is the place to come for barbecued chicken or *febras de porco* (grilled pork steaks). There are daily changing specials, too. Closed Mon. Inexpensive.

Taberna de Lagos Rua 25 de Abril ☎282 084 250. Lovely, high-ceilinged 400-year old mansion converted into a sophisticated bar-restaurant that attracts a laid-back, arty crowd. Fresh organic dishes include steaks, pasta and fish while the fruit and ice cream desserts are also superb. If you don't fancy a full meal, pop in for shots or a cocktail. Expensive.

A Lagosteira Rua 1 de Maio 20 ☎282 762 486. Upmarket, blue-tiled restaurant specializing in *camarão flambé* (flambéed prawns), fish cooked in a *cataplana* and, of course lobster. Daily specials too. Expensive.

Bar Lota Doca Pesca ☎282 764 048. At the station end of the fishing harbour over the bridge past the marina. Very much a local haunt with wooden benches as rough-looking as the clientele, but the fresh fish is, as you'd expect, hard to beat. Tables inside and out. Inexpensive.

🍖 **Adega da Marina** Av dos Descobrimentos 35 ☎282 764 284. A great barn of a place with rows of tables like a giant wedding party. Very good-value food, with stonking portions of charcoal-grilled meat and fish; the house wines are great. Inexpensive.

O Pescador Rua Gil Eanes 6–10 ☎282 767 028. Unglamorous modern decor is compensated for by friendly service and excellent fish and grills. Closed Sun. Moderate.

Casa do Zé Av dos Descobrimentos. On the corner with the market, and open until 2am, where filling fish dishes are served at very fair prices. It's very much a locals' choice at lunchtime, with the outdoor seating soaking up a brisk trade – daily specials cost around €7. Inexpensive.

Drinking and nightlife

There is no shortage of **bars** around town, many of them owned by expatriates – in particular Irish and British. **Cocktails** are extremely popular in Lagos and measures are almost universally generous; look out for the places offering two-for-one deals and special events. Most bars stay open until at least 2am, some even later if the party is in full flow.

Cervejaria Abrigo Rua Marquês de Pombal 2. Laid-back place with outdoor tables under scented orange trees – beer, cocktails, snacks and meals all day. Closed Sun.

Bon Vivante Rua 25 Abril 105. This late-night den at the top of the street has drinking on three floors, gaudy marble "cactus" pillars and a superb roof terrace, that's a great spot to watch the sun go down. Open till 4am.

O Cavaleiro Rua Garret 23. Just off the Praça Luís Camões and open 22 hours a day, it makes a pleasant place to sit outside during the day and welcome refuelling stop in the small hours. There's a long menu of drinks, meals, snacks and pizzas. Inexpensive.

Eddie's Bar Rua 25 de Abril 99. Small, friendly bar with good selection of sounds. Attracts a surf/bike/skate dude kind of crowd. Live soccer also shown on a large screen.

Cervejaria Ferradura Rua 1 de Maio 26A. Atmospheric *cervejaria* with stools around a horseshoe-shaped bar, walls covered in soccer scarves and posters and stacks of inexpensive shellfish *petiscos*. Closed Sun.

Grand Café Rua Senhora da Graça 7. In a fine high-ceilinged building bedecked in gold-leaf and velvet, this is one of the town's coolest hangouts, with an outside terrace, guest DJs and lively crowd. Daily from 9pm, weekends only from Oct–March.

Mullens Rua Cândido dos Reis 86. This cavernous *adega* is the most appealing late-night choice in town. The drinks are inexpensive – there's Guinness, sangria and *vinho verde* on tap – while excellent, moderately priced meals are served to a jazz and soul soundtrack. Live music at weekends.

Naufragio Bar Av dos Descobrimentos. Pleasant bar with a youthful clientele, jazzy sounds and moderately priced bar snacks. Out the back there's a great terrace facing the town beach and the Forte da Ponta da Bandeira.

Stevie Ray's Rua Senhora da Graça 9 ⓦwww .stevierays.com. Lagos's premier jazz club, with live music every Sat and cool sounds other nights from 8.30pm. Closed Sun.

Whytes Bar Rua do Ferrador 7A. Positively thrives on drunken behaviour and offers a dodgy combination of darts, cocktails and lethal measures of spirits. The brave commit the "Nine Deadly Sins" in the downstairs bar to win a free T-shirt.

Listings

Banks and exchange Banks and ATMs are grouped around Pr Gil Eanes, and you can exchange money in almost every travel agency.
Bullfights These take place most Sat throughout the summer, usually at 5.30pm (€35) at the Praça de Touros de Lagos, out on the Portimão road.

Car/motorbike rental Auto Jardim, Rua Vítor da Costa Silva 18 ☎282 769 486, ⓦwww .auto-jardim.com; Avis, Largo das Portas de Portugal 11 ☎282 763 691; Hertz, Rossio de São João ☎282 769 809; LuzCar-Sociedade, Largo das Portas de Portugal 10 ☎282 761 016, ⓦwww.luzcar.com (also does motorbikes).

Hospital Rua do Castelo dos Governadores, adjacent to the Santa Maria church ℗ 282 770 100.

Internet Império do Mar, Rua Cândido dos Reis 199 (Mon–Sat 10am–4am, Sun 2pm–4am), opposite the cinema.

Police Rua General Alberto Silveira ℗ 282 762 930.

Post office Next to the town hall, just off Av dos Descobrimentos (Mon–Fri 8.30am–6pm).

Taxis There are ranks in front of the post office or call Lagos Central Taxi ℗ 282 762 469.

Telephones It's easiest to make long-distance calls at the Telecom office, next to the post office.

Travel agency Tickets (including bus tickets) and tours from Tourlagos, Rua Infante de Sagres 31 ℗ 282 767 967.

Supermarket São Roque, Rua das Portas de Portugal 62 (Mon–Fri 9am–8pm, Sat 9am–7pm).

West to Sagres

The coast west of Lagos, to Vila do Bispo and Sagres, remains one of the least spoiled parts of the Algarve, largely thanks to the Parque Natural do Sudoeste Alentejano e Costa Vicentina which prohibits large-scale building on the coastline west of Burgau. As a result, the resorts – certainly west of **Luz** at **Burgau** and **Salema** – remain largely low-rise and low key.

In summer there are frequent **bus** services from Lagos to Luz and Burgau, and a regular service to Salema. Connections are less frequent during the winter, but you should always be able to get to at least one of the villages and back in a day-trip, even if it means walking to the highway on occasion to pick up the bus. You could also plan a day that involved walking between the villages: Salema to Luz or Luz to Lagos, in particular, are beautiful walks. Other local beaches, near **Figueira** and **Raposeira**, can't be reached by public transport, but they are much less visited as a consequence – great if you're looking for some solitude.

Luz

Five kilometres west of Lagos, the mass of white chalets and villas that is the resort of **LUZ** pile up behind a fine, sweeping beach set below towering cliffs. There's not much of a centre to Luz, but there's a palm-lined beachside promenade that leads from the sands to a *miradouro* beneath the village's old fort – now a restaurant – and the church. Along the promenade there are any number of bar-restaurants with advantageous terraces, including *O Poço* (℗ 282 789 189), which serves moderately priced fish and seafood, including a tasty *espadarte de tamboril* (monkfish kebab). *Fortaleza da Luz* (℗ 282 789 926), above the west end of the beach at Rua da Igreja 3, is a pricier choice for Algarvian and international cuisine, served inside the old fort or on a lovely sea-facing terrace. There's live music on Thursdays. Best value hotel accommodation is *Belavista da Luz* (℗ 282 788 655, ⓦ belavistadaluz.com; ⓞ), around 1km uphill on the road out of town towards Sagres – four-star facilities include tennis, health club, restaurant and pool, but there's little in the way of character. The rest of Luz's accommodation consists of **apartments** and villas, often block-booked in summer, though you can try the main agency, *Luz Bay Club*, Rua do Jardim (℗ 282 789 640, ⓦ www.lunahoteis.com; ⓞ), some of whose apartments have balconies and views of the sea. **Campers** like the *Valverde* site (℗ 218 789 211), close to the highway but a good 1.5km or so from the seafront, which has a restaurant, bar, supermarket and kids' playground.

Walkers should take the **path to Lagos** which starts at the eastern end of the beach. At the Algarve Sports Club, follow the private road uphill and make the steep scramble up to the obelisk on the cliffs, from where a gentle path careers along the tops to Porto do Mós, Ponte das Piedade and Lagos.

Burgau

It's another 5km or so to **BURGAU**, a resort that still displays vestiges of its former fishing village life. The cobbled main street retains some charm, running right through the village and tumbling down to a wide sweep of sand backed by crumbling cliffs and colourful fishing boats. In July and August the village is somewhat mobbed, but at other times it retains a distinct character, with locals grilling fish on tiny grills outside their homes. Note that not all the **buses** from Lagos and Sagres call into Burgau itself, though all pass the turn-off on the highway, from where it's a two-kilometre walk to the village through arid farming country.

Unless you're here on a pre-booked holiday, you'll find it tough to locate **accommodation** in summer, though signs scattered around the village advertise rooms in private houses. The best choice is *Casa Grande* (☎282 697 416, ⓔcasagrande@yahoo.com; ❷–❹ depending on size of room), at the top end of town on the road towards Luz, which is a characterful old manor run by Brits. Set in its own grounds, the rooms have soaring ceilings; you can also hire a barn sleeping six from €165. There's also a fine restaurant attached, the *Adega Casa Grande* (evenings only, closed Nov) which serves veggie dishes and weekend pizza and pasta. Failing that, *Hotel Praia do Burgau* (☎282 690 160, ⓔimulagos@sapo.pt; ❺), on a hillside to the east of town, is a friendly three-star place with a small pool. The top rooms with balconies have superb views (€10 extra).

Burgau is well served with **bars and restaurants**, including the *Beach Bar Burgau* with a splendid terrace-bar (closed Mon & evenings Oct–April) and good, if pricey, food in the restaurant. Slightly less expensive, *A Barraca*, Largo dos Pescadores 2 (☎282 697 748), sits on the clifftop and does fine *cataplanas*, while above it, *Bar Varanda* on Largo dos Pescadores 4 (☎942 443 363) is a lively café-bar with an outdoor terrace, boppy music and English breakfasts.

Salema

SALEMA remains one of the most popular resorts along this stretch, certainly for independent travellers who have numerous accommodation options. Just 20km west of Lagos, the turn-off from the N125 snakes down a delightful semi-cultivated valley, the sea creeping ever closer. The bus parks just above the beachside promenade, much of it cluttered with brightly coloured boats. The fairly homogenous white splodge of apartment and villa construction spreads back up the valley, leaving the old village to the east of the harbour largely untouched. The beach – a wide, rock-sheltered bay – is magnificent: in winter, the sea comes crashing right up to the edge of the village.

There are plenty of **rooms** to let round the old town (just look for the signs: you should be able to secure something with a terrace and kitchen). There's also the central *Hotel Residencial Salema* (☎282 665 328, ⓦwww.hotelsalema.com; closed Nov–March; ❺), whose small rooms have skewed sea views; there's also a bar. There are cheaper rooms at *A Mare* (☎282 695 165, ⓦwww.algarve.co.uk; ❹) on the hill above the main road into town, where the small rooms have bath, sea views and terraces with sun loungers. More upmarket – and steeply uphill – is the *Estalagem Infante do Mar* (☎2282 690 100, ⓦwww.infantedomar.com; ❻), around 1km from the seafront on the road to Figueira, a smart four-star inn with many rooms offering panoramic views over the coast; there's also a restaurant, bar and pool. The pleasantly landscaped **campsite**, *Quinta dos Carriços* (☎282 695 201, ⓔquintacarrico@oninet.pt), is 1.5km back up towards the main highway – the bus passes it on the way into the village.

Best of the **restaurants** is *Mira Mar*, Travessa Mira Mar 6 (℡919 560 339), with a sea-facing terrace and excellent fresh fish at moderate prices; try the bream. The nearby *Boia Bar Restaurante*, Rua das Pescadores 101 (℡282 695 382; closed Tues), is a swish place with snappy service; *caldeirada* (fish stew) is the speciality and full meals here cost around €18. *Bar Aventura*, Rua das Pescadores 80, is an attractive bar with Internet access (open until 2am).

Figueira and Raposeira

At the village of **FIGUEIRA** on the N125, around 3km northwest of Salema, there's the very welcoming *Bar Celeiro* by the bus stop. Opposite here, a rough farm track (signed Forte da Figueira) leads off to the isolated sands of **Praia da Figueira** (a 20–30min walk through lovely countryside), one of the least-visited beaches along this stretch, below the ruins of an old fort.

Between Figueira and Raposeira, a sign points off the main N125 to the chapel of **Nossa Senhora de Guadalupe**, reached down the old road which runs parallel to the highway. Built in the thirteenth century by the Knights Templars, and said to have been frequented by Henry the Navigator, the chapel stands in rural solitude. It is usually kept locked, but it's a pleasant place to stroll around or have a picnic.

Two other little-visited beaches are accessible by road from the village of **RAPOSEIRA**, 3km further west, sliced through by the speeding highway. The turn-off to the beach ("Ingrina") is signposted at the traffic lights on the highway: go through Hortas do Tabual and take the left fork, and after 3km you'll reach **Praia do Zavial**, a rocky beach popular with surfers and with a decent café-restaurant (closed Mon). Another couple of kilometres around the bay, **Praia da Ingrina** is more sheltered and sandy, good for beachcombing amid the rock pools, with another beachside café (closed Tues). There's also a rural **campsite** (℡/℗282 639 242) here, 1km up from the sea, with its own bar-restaurant. There are no public transport connections with either beach from the main road.

West of Raposeira the road passes Vila do Bispo and the turn-off for the west coast, before heading across the flattened landscape for Sagres.

Sagres and Cabo de São Vicente

Sagres and its wild and windswept cape were considered by the Portuguese as the far limit of the world. It was on these headlands in the fifteenth century that Prince Henry the Navigator made his residence and it was here, too, that he set up a school of navigation, gathering together the greatest astronomers, cartographers and adventurers of his age. Fernão de Magalhães (Magellan), Pedro Álvares Cabral and Vasco da Gama all studied at Sagres, and from the beach at Belixe – midway between the capes of Sagres and **São Vicente** – the first long caravels were launched, revolutionizing shipping with their wide hulls, small adaptable sails, and ability to sail close to the wind. Each year new expeditions were dispatched to penetrate a little further than their predecessors, and to resolve the great navigational enigma presented by the west coast of Africa, thereby laying the foundations of the country's overseas empire.

After Henry's death here in 1460, the centre of maritime studies was moved to Lisbon and Sagres slipped back into the obscurity from which he'd raised it. These days, Sagres attracts a growing number of families, young backpackers, divers and surfers, drawn by warm waters, surf schools and the string of magnificent local

beaches. It's not a handsome town, but it can still be a great place to stay, with an ever-growing array of rooms, restaurants and bars, along with a smart *pousada*, which overlooks the village. Its liveliest day is August, 15 with celebrations and fireworks to celebrate the local saint's day.

Sagres

SAGRES village, rebuilt in the nineteenth century over the earthquake ruins of Henry's town, is the most southwesterly harbour in mainland Europe. Its small sixteenth-century Fortaleza de Baleeira was damaged by Francis Drake in 1587 and further ruined in the 1755 earthquake; the rest of the town is little more than a main road – Rua Comandante Matoso – connecting the lively fishing harbour and Praia da Baleeira at one end with the main square at the other, all backed by a new town of white villas and apartments. The small square, **Praça da Républica**, is the main focus of town, an attractive cobbled space lined with squat palms and whitewashed cafés, swooped over by swallows. From here, it's a short walk southeast to Sagres's best beach, Praia da Mareta (see p.606).

Henry the Navigator's **Fortaleza** (daily: May–Sept 10am–8.30pm; Oct–April 10am–6.30pm; €3) dominates the whole village, with Rua da Fortaleza running directly up the headland towards its massive bulk; it is better to walk this way than to follow the road signs which take you on a detour to a giant car park set well back from the fort. An immense circuit of walls – only the north side survives intact – once surrounded the vast, shelf-like promontory, high above the Atlantic.

After the formidable tunnel entrance is spread a huge pebble **Rosa dos Ventos** (wind compass), unearthed beneath a church in 1921. Wind compasses are used to measure the direction of the wind, but most are divided into 30 segments. This is unusual in that its 43-metre diameter is divided into 40 segments. No one is sure whether the compass dates back to Henry's time, though the simple, much-restored chapel of **Nossa Senhora da Graça** besides the compass is accepted as dating from the fifteenth century.

The only other buildings inside the walls are a shop, café and exhibition space showing maps of Portugal and other nautical memorabilia – but, gracelessly

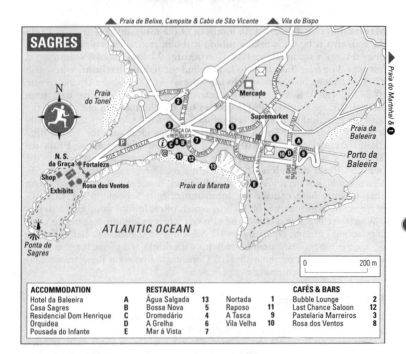

ACCOMMODATION		RESTAURANTS				CAFÉS & BARS	
Hotel da Baleeira	A	Água Salgada	13	Nortada	1	Bubble Lounge	2
Casa Sagres	B	Bossa Nova	5	Raposo	11	Last Chance Saloon	12
Residencial Dom Henrique	C	Dromedário	4	A Tasca	9	Pastelaria Marreiros	3
Orquidea	D	A Grelha	6	Vila Velha	10	Rosa dos Ventos	8
Pousada do Infante	E	Mar á Vista	7				

constructed with concrete, they have done little to enhance the beauty of the site. Still, it's pleasant enough to wander around the walls or out to **Ponta de Sagres**, a headland with a small lighthouse beacon offering fine views along the coast, past fishermen dangling lines suicidally off the immense cliffs.

Local beaches and the harbour

Most people's days in Sagres are spent on one of the excellent beaches, five of which are within easy walking distance of the village. Three of them are on the more sheltered coastline east of the fortress, with the nicest, **Praia da**

Sagres surfing

The Algarve is gaining a reputation as being one of Europe's best **surfing** destinations, with Sagres as its surfing capital. Its position at the bottom corner of Portugal means that there are nearly always excellent surfing conditions, whatever the weather. The swell "wraps" round Cabo de São Vicente, giving relatively gentle waves in the bays between Sagres and Lagos, ideal for the less experienced. With swell sizes of up to 5 metres, the beaches north of Cabo de São Vicente face the full brunt of the Atlantic so are ideal for experienced surfers – legs of the World Surfing Championships are held at nearby Praia do Amado. Indeed, it can be decidedly dangerous and inexperienced surfers are best off going with a surf school – which can give one-off lessons or courses – or a surf camp, which throws in accommodation and transport to the best beaches. Top surf camps in the region include ⓦwww.freeridesurfcamp .com, ⓦwww.algarvesurfschool.com, ⓦwww.surferdream.com/Algarve and ⓦwww .surf-experience.com.

Mareta, just five minutes' walk southeast of the main square. The small **Praia da Baleeira** is by the working fishing harbour, around fifteen minutes' walk from the main square along Rua Comandante Matoso, though swimming is less appealing here. Take time to look round the **fishing harbour**, where you can also arrange boat trips and **diving** courses – try the Scuba Diving Centre (T282 624 594, W www.scubado-algarve.com) which offers dive trips from around €35 or four-day PADI courses for €280. From the cliffs above the harbour it's another five- to ten-minute walk to the longest, and generally least crowded, beach, **Praia do Martinhal**, an ideal spot for windsurfing (there's a rental outfit here; T282 624 147). West of the fortress, **Praia do Tonel** is a wilder location, popular with surfers. It's a longer walk to the beautiful **Praia de Belixe**, 2km down the road from Sagres to Cabo de São Vicente, which is overlooked by a small fortress (currently closed). If you want **surf lessons** here contact the International Surf School (T914 482 407, W www.internationalsurfschool.com) which offers lessons from €35 a day.

Whichever beach you choose, be cautious when swimming – there are some very strong currents, especially on the west side of the fortress. Before setting off for the more distant strands, stock up with drinks and picnic supplies at the village supermarket on the main Rua Comandante Matoso as there are virtually no beach facilities, especially out of season.

Practicalities

Buses from Lagos stop just by Praça da República and then continue to the harbour. The **turismo** (Tues–Sat 9.30am–12.30pm & 1.30–5.30pm; T282 624 873) is by a dusty square just up from the *praça*, while on Praça da República, in the *Residencial Dom Henrique*, there's also a privately run information office, **Turinfo** (daily 8am–midnight; T282 620 003, F282 620 004), which can arrange room rental, book you on a boat tour, organize surf lessons or mountain bike rental, and provide Internet access.

There is no shortage of **accommodation**. In summer, you'll be approached by people offering **rooms** (❸) often with access to a kitchen too; prices come down considerably out of season. The nearest **campsite**, *Parque de Campismo de Sagres* (T282 624 351, F282 624 445), is 2km northwest of the village, along (and off) the main road; it sits in rural solitude, so the bike hire can come in handy.

Hotels and pensions

Hotel da Baleeira Porto da Baleeira T282 624 212, W www.sagres.net/baleeira This smart hotel is the spot for harbour views, complete with pool, gardens, restaurant and tennis courts. Parking. Closed winter 2006 for renovation. ❺

Residencial Dom Henrique Pr da República T282 620 000, W www.domhenrique.com. In a great position right on the square – there's a terrace and bar, while the front rooms have superb sea-facing balconies (which you pay €8 more for). ❹

Orquídea Porto da Baleeira T282 624 257, W www.velozplus.com. An ungainly block with its own small pool on the clifftop above the harbour; most rooms have fine views. Spacious apartments for two or double rooms are good value, though breakfast costs extra. ❸

Pousada do Infante T282 620 240, W www .pousadas.pt. The best choice in town – an attractive clifftop mansion with Moorish elements and splendid views of the fortress from its bar-terrace. Rooms are large and comfy with luxurious bathrooms. There are also tennis courts, a restaurant and a games room. Parking. ❼

Casa Sagres Pr da República T282 624 358. Behind the main square, on the road down to Praia da Mareta, this is primarily a restaurant that also lets out decent en-suite rooms. The best ones have sea-facing balconies (€10 extra). ❹

Restaurants

Bossa Nova Rua Comandante Matoso, corner with Rua da Mareta T282 624 566. Lively place just off the main drag with a little courtyard, noted for its pizzas, pasta, salads and imaginative vegetarian meals. Closed Tues. Inexpensive.

Dromedário Rua Comandante Matoso ☎ 282 624 219. Fashionable little bar-bistro with Egyptian-inspired decor, serving pizzas, great breakfasts and a mean range of cocktails and juices. Live jazz on Mon. Closed Tues. Inexpensive.

A Grelha Rua Comandante Matoso. At the fishing harbour end of the road, this is a simple place with a modest menu of grills which attracts a largely local crowd. Inexpensive.

Mar á Vista Sítio da Mareta ☎ 282 624 247. On a scrubby patch of ground just off the road to Praia da Mareta, this pleasant eatery serves a long list of good-value fish, omelettes and salads (around €15 for a full meal), with fine views from its outdoor tables. Closed Wed. Moderate.

Nortada Praia da Martinhal ☎ 282 624 147. Jazzy bar and restaurant with a beach terrace. Serves a good range of international dishes and baguettes along with the usual Portuguese fare. Closed Tues Sept–April. Moderate.

Raposo Praia da Mareta ☎ 282 624 168. Lovely wood and chrome beach bar-restaurant right on the sands. Food is good value if you steer clear of the pricey seafood. By day it's full of surfers enjoying a drink. Moderate.

A Tasca Porto da Baleeira ☎ 282 624 177. Sagres's best fish restaurant, with a few meat dishes but superb fish straight from the harbour. Tables outside face the Atlantic, though it's just as fun in the barn-like interior, its walls encrusted with pebbles and old bottles. Expect to pay upwards of €20. Closed Wed Oct–April. Expensive.

Vila Velha Rua Patrão António Faustino ☎ 282 624 788. Excellent upmarket restaurant. The Dutch owners gives an international twist to Portuguese ingredients in a rustic-style interior. Has vegetarian options and a children's menu. Has live music on the first Thurs of each month. Evenings only, closed Mon. Expensive.

Cafés and bars

Água Salgado Rua Comandante Matoso 8650 ☎ 282 624 297. Bright bar with a happening feel to it, with cool sounds, a TV and table football. Also does crepes and pizzas and offers Internet access. Open till 3am.

Bubble Lounge Rua Nossa Senhora da Graça 1 ☎ 282 624 497/938 632 302. Laid-back surfers' bar with comfy chairs, a screen showing the day's surf moves, games, books and ambient sounds. Occasional live music. Closed Mon Oct–April.

Last Chance Saloon Sítio da Mareta ☎ 282 624 113. In a wooden shack overlooking the beach, this is a laid-back place to down an early evening beer or two, and also has Internet access. Closed Mon.

Pastelaria Marreiros Pr da República 12 ☎ 282 624 861. Very popular tourist spot, thanks to the attractive outside tables on the main square. There's a good range of snacks, including croissants, *tostas* and sandwiches.

Rosa dos Ventos Pr da República ☎ 282 624 480. Atmospheric bar in an old town house on the main square, which also does simple food.

Cabo de São Vicente

The exposed **Cabo de São Vicente** – Cape St Vincent – across the bay from Sagres, was sacred to the Romans, who called it Promontorium Sacrum and believed the sun sank hissing into the water beyond here every night. It became

St Vicent

St Vicent was born in Zaragoza in Spain in the fourth century AD and became the town's deacon during the early days of Christianity in Iberia. He was later imprisoned in Valencia and sentenced to death in 304 during the days of Christian persecution. It is said that while he was being burned alive, the room filled with flowers, light and the voices of angels, and he was proclaimed a martyr and then a saint. In the eighth century, his remains – which had somehow survived the fire – were miraculously washed up in an unmanned boat piloted by ravens at what is now Cabo de São Vicente. Perhaps more credible is the theory that Christians took whatever was left of Vincent with them to flee invading Moors, arriving at the safe outpost of the Cape where they later built a chapel to house his remains. In 1173, Afonso Henriques, Portugal's first Christian monarch, had the saint's remains moved to Lisbon. Legend has it that the faithful ravens followed to the capital, and guarded over him in the cloisters of Lisbon's Sé (cathedral), until the last one died in 1978. Today São Vicente remains Lisbon's patron saint.

a Christian shrine when the relics of the martyred St Vincent arrived in the eighth century (see box, p.607). Today the sea off this wild set of cliffs shelters the highest concentration of marine life in Portugal, including rare birds such as Bonelli's eagles, white storks, white herons, kites and rock doves.

It was almost certainly at the cape that Henry established his School of Navigation, founded a small town, and built his Vila do Infante. Today only a **lighthouse** – the most powerful in Europe – flanked by the ruins of a sixteenth-century Capuchin convent, are to be seen. The other buildings on the cape, already vandalized by the piratical Sir Francis Drake in 1587, came crashing to the ground in the Great Earthquake of 1755, the monks staying on alone until the Liberal suppression of the monasteries in 1834.

Two daily buses from Sagres (Mon–Fri only) go out here, or it's a dramatic and exhilarating 6-kilometre (2hr) walk on a path skirting the cliffs for much of the way. In spring and early summer you should be able to spot blue rock thrushes and peregrines nesting on the cliffs. Walking on the road is easier – it'll take less than an hour and a half, with glorious views all the way. Try to be at the cape for sunset, which is invariably gorgeous.

The west coast

Unlike the southern stretches of the Algarve, the west coast, stretching north from Sagres to Odeceixe, is almost totally undeveloped. There are several reasons: the coast is exposed to strong Atlantic winds; the sea can be several degrees cooler than on the south coast; and swimming can be dangerous. In addition, the designation in 1995 of the stretch of coast from Burgau to Cabo de São Vicente and up through the Alentejo as a nature reserve – the Parque Natural Sudoeste Alentejano e Costa Vincentina – largely protects this dramatic and rugged scenery from potentially harmful development. The nearest bases to the beaches are at the uneventful villages of **Vila do Bispo** and **Carrapateira** or the livelier **Aljezur** and **Odeceixe**, all of which have an inexpensive network of private rooms and accommodation options. Like Sagres, these resorts attract a predominantly young crowd of surfers and campervanners.

Vila do Bispo

VILA DO BISPO, at the junction of the west and south coast roads, is a fairly scrappy traditional little town whose kernel of old white houses centres on a lovely seventeenth-century parish **church** (Mon–Sat 10am–1pm & 2–6pm; free), every interior surface of which has been painted, tiled or gilded. The town has no other sights, but it makes a pleasant spot for a coffee or a meal in one of the bars and restaurants by the town garden.

If you have your own transport, the town could make a reasonable accommodation base, ideally suited for day trips to the surrounding beaches. The nearest stretch of sand, **Praia do Castelejo**, is reached via the bottom of town – from the main square, take the road downhill past the post office, turn left and then bear right – along a narrow road leading 5km west. The beach is a huge swathe of sand (though covered in high tides) lashed by heavy waves below dark grey cliffs, with a fine café-restaurant (closed Wed & Oct–April) to add a touch of civilization.

Buses from Sagres or Lagos drop you right at the bottom of the village, five minutes' walk from the church. There are **rooms** advertised here and there, or try the simple *Pensão Mira Sagres*, Rua 1º de Maio 3 (☎282 639 160; Ⓔsantos .patricia2@netc.pt; ❶ with shared facilities, or ❷ in annexe with en-suite rooms) – opposite the church – which has its own basic bar-restaurant downstairs. There are several other places to **eat**: the best is *Restaurante Correia* (closed Sat), on Rua 1º de Maio 4 next to the post office, with a decent inexpensive menu and a friendly, local feel. *Tasca do Careca* next door (T282 639 478; closed Sun) is also good. The village also has a small supermarket, bakery and even a couple of **bars** that see some late-night action; the *Convivio* on the central square, Praça da República (closed Sun), serves a wicked range of cocktails until 2am.

Carrapateira and its beaches

Fifteen kilometres to the north (connected by 1–2 weekday buses from Vila do Bispo) is the low-key village of **CARRAPATEIRA**, which is better positioned for the beach, a kilometre's walk from the village. **Praia da Bordeira** is a spectacular strand with dunes, a tiny river and crashing surf. The sandbanks provide shelter from the wind for a sizeable unauthorized campervan community, who seem to be tolerated by the local police. There is a moderately priced restaurant just back from the beach, *O Sitio do Rio* (T282 973 119; closed Tues & Nov), which uses largely organic produce – fresh soup, simple grills or stir-fried veggies offer a change from usual Portugese seaside food.

Four kilometres south of Praia da Bordeira, along the coast road, lies **Praia do Amado**, which is also signed off the main road just south of Carrapateira. This fantastic, broad sandy bay backed by low hills with a couple of seasonal cafés is particularly popular with surfers. There's also a **surf school** here (T & F282 624 560) which offers equipment rental and surf courses from €35.

It's possible to get **accommodation** in Carrapateira in a private room (look for *quartos* signs on the way to the beach) or try for space at the best budget place, *Pensão das Dunas*, Rua da Padaria 9 (T & F282 973 118; ❶), a very pretty building on the beach side of the village, which has a number of simple rooms overlooking a flower-filled courtyard; there are also two apartments sleeping two or four (❷). With your own transport, the best option if you like solitude is *Monte Velho* (T282 973 297; Wwww.wonderfulland.com/montevelho; ❺), reached down a bumpy track 5km south on the road to Vila do Bispo (follow signs to Vilarinho/Herdade do Beiçudo stables). Set in wild countryside on a breezy hill, all rooms (some of which can sleep up to five) come in contemporary styles and have terraces. The owners can arrange donkey rides, quad/mountain bike hire, surf lessons and massage.

Aljezur and around

Fairly regular buses run from Lagos and Portimão to the village of **ALJEZUR**, 16km north of Carrapeteira, which is the liveliest town along the west coast of the Algarve, though some way inland from any beaches. The main coast road passes through a prosaic, modern lower town where you find banks, the post office and a range of cafés and restaurants. The more interesting historic centre spreads uphill beyond the bridge over the Aljezur river, a network of narrow cobbled streets reaching up through whitewashed houses to the remains of a tenth-century Moorish **castle**. It's a lovely walk with sweeping views over the valley, via a trio of dull museums; the only one worth a visit is the **Casa Museu Pintor José Cercas** (T289 991 011; Tues–Sat 10am–12.30pm & 2–4pm; free) on Rua do Castelo 2, which displays the works and collections of local artist José Cercas, who lived in the house until his death in 1992. His well-observed landscapes and religious scenes are complemented by the attractive house and pretty garden.

At the foot of the old town, the **turismo** (Mon & Fri–Sun 9.30am–1pm & 2–5.30pm, Tues–Thurs 9.30am–5.30pm; ☎282 998 229) in Largo do Mercado, by the river, does its best to help with private **rooms**. Most places to stay are in the suburb of Igreja Nova, 1km from the tourist office, just off the Monchique road – the bus from Lagos loops through Igreja Nova on its way out of Aljezur. Best bet is the modern *Residencial Dom Sancho*, Largo Igreja Nova 1 (☎282 997 070, Ⓔturimol@mail.telepac.pt; ❸), which overlooks a pedestrianized street. Rooms are large and comfortable and come with bath and TV. The local **campsite**, *Parque de Campismo do Serrão* (☎282 990 220, Ⓔcamping-serrao @clix.pt), has its own pool, supermarket and tennis courts amongst dense trees; it's 7km northwest of Aljezur, and 4km from the lovely beach of Praia Amoreira.

There are several inexpensive **cafés and restaurants** in Aljezur, most of them along the main through-road, Rua 25 de Abril. *Restaurante Ruth* at no. 14 (☎282 998 534; closed Sat) is highly regarded, specializing in regional dishes such as goose barnacles and sweet potatoes. Also moderately priced, but in a better position, *Pont'a Pé*, near the tourist office on Largo da Liberdade 16 (☎282 998 104; closed Sun), offers grills in a cosy diner or on the riverside terrace. Live music most weekends competes with the sound of the resident frogs.

Arrifana and Monte Clérigo

From May to September, two buses daily run to a couple of superb beaches within a few kilometres of Aljezur. The largest of these is **Praia da Arrifana**, 10km to the southwest, a fine, sandy sweep set below high, crumbling black cliffs. The beach is excellent, and surf competitions are sometimes held here – several simple café-restaurants lie along the road above the beach, all serving grilled fish at moderate prices. *Oceano* (☎282 997 300; ❷) will cater to most of your needs, with a café, restaurant and guest house on the clifftop above the beach. The simple rooms come with shower and fine views, while the upstairs restaurant (closed Tues) does fine mid-priced fish and grills. Even better for food is the last building along here, closest to the headland – *Fortaleza* (☎282 998 474), with expensive mains (€9-14) but it has a contemporary menu you rarely see elsewhere – shrimps with couscous, pineapple with seafood and wild mushrooms – as well as a terrific *arroz de marisco*, stuffed with lobster.

At the end of the road – at the headland, **Ponte da Arrifana** – there are the remains of an old fort and a clifftop restaurant, while a fine coastal walk runs north, via the Ponte da Atalaia to the superb beach and small village of **Espartal** (2hr walk). It's not marked or signposted, but keep the sea on your left – you can hardly get lost and the views are excellent, down into the deep, green waters and along the fragmented coast. There are some superb deserted strands below – not easily accessible – while the clifftop path, 100m up, runs through the brush- and herb-carpeted dunes.

MONTE CLÉRIGO, 8km northwest of Aljezur, is a pretty little holiday village of pink- and white-faced beach houses. A cluster of café-restaurants face a superb, family-oriented beach tucked into the foot of a river valley.

Odeceixe and around

ODECEIXE tumbles down a hillside opposite the broad valley of the Odeceixe river, below the winding, tree-lined main coast road. Sleepy out of season, its character changes in summer when it attracts a steady stream of backpackers, surfers, campervanners and families, lured by a superb beach and a very laid-back atmosphere. The beach, the **Praia de Odeceixe**, is 4km west of the village, reached down a verdant river valley, the fields either side neatly cultivated with corn. A road-train trundles back and forth during July and August, but it's a lovely walk as well, following the river to a broad, sandy bay framed by low cliffs. It is one of the most sheltered beaches on this stretch of coast, offering superb surfing and relatively safe swimming, especially when the tide is out. There's lots of parking above the south end of the bay, as well as a cluster of houses and cafés, some offering *quartos*.

Back in Odeceixe, everything centres on the single main street and a small square, Largo 1° de Maio, where you'll find plenty of cafés and restaurants, a couple of mini-markets, post office, bank, and a few beach and souvenir/craft shops. Even so, it's not over-developed by any means and is still very attractive. **Rooms** are advertised everywhere, most obviously at *Residência do Parque* (℡282 947 117; ❷), on the main street by the post office, a backpackers' haunt with a mixed bag of en-suite rooms – the best are on the top floor with small balconies overlooking the valley, and there's also a hammock lounge downstairs. You'll pass rooms signs and a couple of other formal pensions as you follow the road down in the direction of the beach; there's a particularly good deal at *Pensão Luar*, Rua da Várzea 28 (℡282 947 194; ❷, August ❸), on the beach road at the edge of the village, where the en-suite rooms are big, bright and light and you can park outside.

The top choice for **eating and drinking** is the very cheery *Tasca da Saskia* (℡919 433 367; open 8am–midnight, closed Mon; restricted opening in winter), a contemporary bar-restaurant on the beach road (by the *Pensão Luar*) with great breakfasts, plus pasta, pizza and veggie meals (€6–8). It used to be a club, hence the open-plan, multi-level interior and roof terrace, and the German owner, Saskia, has filled it with her large-scale paintings – there are theme nights, gigs and cinema during the year. In the village, *Chaparro* (℡282 947 304; closed Sun), opposite *Residência do Parque*, is the best place for barbecued fish and meat (€8–9) – there's a blackboard menu for the catch of the day, and you can sit outside at wooden benches. Nearby *O Retiro do Adelino* (℡282 947 352; closed Mon) is also good, with tables in a covered courtyard.

Travel details

Trains

Along the Algarve train line, the IC (Intercidades) trains are considerably faster than the stopping IR (Interregional) and snail-like R (Regional) trains. Fast Alfa trains serve stations to Lisbon. You can check train timetables online at ⓦ www.cp.pt.

Faro to: Albufeira (14 daily; 15–45min); Alcácer do Sal (2 daily; 2hr 25 min); Lagos (7 daily; 1hr 40min); Lisbon (4 daily; 3–4hr); Monte Gordo (3–4 daily; 1hr–1hr 15min); Olhão (16 daily; 10min); Portimão (7 daily; 1hr 15min–1hr 35min); Setúbal (3 daily; 3hr); Silves (7 daily; 1hr–1hr 15min); Tavira (12–17 daily; 35–45min); Vila Real de Santo António (10–13 daily; 1hr–1hr 20min).

Lagos to: Albufeira (8 daily; 1hr 10min); Faro (7 daily; 1hr 40min); Loulé (8 daily; 1hr 25min); Portimão (10–13 daily; 15–20min); Silves (13 daily; 30–50min); Tunes (13 daily; 50min–1hr).

Tunes to: Lisbon (4 daily; 2hr 35min–3 hr 30min, add on 1hr 30min or so for connections from Vila Real, 1hr from Lagos); Beja (3 daily; 3hr).

Local buses

Full timetables on ⓦ www.rede-expressos.pt and ⓦ www.eva-bus.com/uk or ⓦ www. eva- bus .com.net

Albufeira to: Armação de Pêra (Mon–Sat 12 daily, Sun 5 daily; 15–20min); Faro (8 daily; 40min–1hr 15min); Olhos d'Água (hourly; 10min); Portimão (Mon–Fri 11 daily, Sat & Sun 4 daily; 45min); Quarteira (Mon–Fri 15 daily, Sat & Sun 9 daily; 40min); Silves (3–7 daily; 45min); Vila Real (1 daily; 3hr).

Faro to: Albufeira (8 daily; 40min–1hr 15min); Estói (Mon–Fri 14 daily, Sat & Sun 9 daily; 25min); Évora (3–4 daily; 4hr–4hr 30min); Huelva (for connections to Sevilla, Spain; 2–4 daily; 3hr 30 min); Loulé

(Mon–Fri hourly till 7.30pm, Sat 8 daily, Sun 6 daily; 40min); Monte Gordo (Mon–Fri 9 daily, Sat & Sun 4 daily; 1hr 35min); Olhão (Mon–Fri every 15–30min, Sat & Sun roughly hourly; 20min); Quarteira (Mon–Fri hourly, Sat & Sun 3 daily; 25min); Tavira (7–11 daily; 1hr); Vilamoura (Mon–Fri hourly, Sat & Sun 9 daily; 30–40min); Vila Real (6–9 daily; 1hr 40min).

Lagos to: Albufeira (12 daily; 1hr 15min); Aljezur (2–5 daily; 50min); Alvor (6 daily, Sat & Sun 4 daily; 15min); Armacão de Pêra (12 daily; 45min–1hr); Burgau (8–11 daily, 4 daily on Sun; 25min); Faro (8 daily; 1hr 45 min); Luz (8–11 daily, 4 daily on Sun; 15min); Odeceixe (Mon–Fri 4 daily, Sat 1 daily; 1hr 20min); Portimão (hourly; 15min–35min); Sagres (7–11 daily; 1hr); Salema (2–5 daily; 40min); Vila do Bispo (7–11 daily; 45min).

Portimão to: Albufeira (Mon–Fri 11 daily, Sat & Sun 4 daily; 45min); Alvor (Mon–Fri hourly, Sat & Sun roughly every 2hr; 20min); Caldas de Monchique (Mon–Fri 9 daily, Sat & Sun 5 daily; 30min); Faro (8 daily; 1hr 25min–1hr 45min); Ferragudo (hourly; 10min); Lagos (hourly; 15–35min); Monchique (Mon–Fri 9 daily, Sat & Sun 5 daily; 45min); Praia da Rocha (every 15–20min; 5min); Silves (Mon–Fri 9 daily, Sat & Sun 7 daily; 35–45min).

Sagres to: Cabo de São Vicente (Mon–Fri 2 daily, 15min); Lagos (Mon–Fri 7–11 daily; 1hr); Salema (Mon–Fri 7–9 daily, Sat & Sun 3–4 daily; 35min); Vila do Bispo (hourly; 15min).

Vila Real de Santo António to: Albufeira (1 daily; 3hr); Alcoutim (Mon–Sat 1 daily; 50min); Ayamonte, Spain (2–4 daily; 15min); Castro Marim (Mon–Fri 12 daily, Sat & Sun 2 daily; 15min); Faro (10 daily; 1hr 20min); Huelva, Spain (2–4 daily; 1hr); Manta Rota (Mon–Fri 4–5 daily, Sat 2 daily; 30min); Monte Gordo (Mon–Fri at least half-hourly, Sat & Sun in winter 10–13 daily; 7min); Olhão (10 daily; 1hr); Tavira (9–10 daily; 40min).

Long-distance buses

Several companies operate regular daily express buses between Lisbon and the Algarve. Ask at any travel agency or bus terminal for details, though note that the Rede Expressos buses (ⓦ www .rede-expressos.pt) are slightly cheaper than EVA buses (ⓦ www.eva-bus.com.net). EVA also runs a number of international buses from the Algarve, the most useful being the service from Lagos to Seville (€18).

Lagos to: Seville (2 daily, at 6.30am and 1.45pm; 5hr 30min), via Faro (1hr 20min). Connections from Seville to Malaga, Cádiz, Algeciras and Grenada.

Linha Litoral express service: runs from Lagos to Vila Real/Ayamonte (Mon–Fri 2 daily; 3hr 30min); on the Lagos–Albufeira leg of the route, there are more like seven weekday departures and four at weekends.

Lisbon to: Albufeira (2hr 40min–3hr 20min); Faro (3hr 15 min–4hr); Lagos (4hr 15min); Olhão (4hr 15min); Tavira (4hr 15min–4hr 30min); Vila Real (4hr 30min–5hr).

Contexts

Contexts

History

The early history of Portugal – as part of the Iberian Peninsula – has obvious parallels with that of Spain. Indeed, any geographical division is somewhat arbitrary, since independent development only really occurred following Afonso Henriques' creation of a Portuguese kingdom in the twelfth century. Border skirmishes and territorial disputes were common during the following centuries, and Spanish rule briefly reasserted itself between 1581 and 1640, before the Bragança family assumed the throne. They ruled until 1910, since when Portugal has been a republic.

Early civilization

The human presence in Portugal dates back at least 30,000 years, when ice covered much of northern and central Europe. Some time around 22,000 years ago, Palaeolithic hunter-gatherers, concentrated in the sheltered river valleys of the upper Douro and Tejo, began to leave **animal engravings** on the rocky river flank, most famously around Vila Nova de Foz Côa. The purpose of the etchings remains a mystery, although their unerringly lifelike nature suggest that shamanic ritual may have been involved. Over the following millennia as the ice receded, through the Mesolithic and **Neolithic** era, early man extended his range further into Portugal. The first man-made stone structures made their appearance 6000 to 7000 years ago in the form of communal tombs or **antas** (dolmens), most of which follow a basic design of a circular stone-walled chamber, roofed with flat slabs and originally covered with soil and rubble. Associated with the *antas* is a fertility cult, whose most obvious remains are a series of vertically planted stone **menhirs** (heavy cylindrical stones, some carved into unarguably phallic forms) – egg-shaped boulders bearing vaginal symbols are believed to be the female equivalents. The largest surviving dolmen in the country is the Anta Grande do Zambujeiro, near Évora, though there are scores of others sited across the Alentejo and Beira regions. There's also a series of Neolithic **stone circles** (most dramatically at Os Almendres, near Évora) whose exact purpose is still unclear, though they may have had religious or even time-keeping significance.

How long this so-called "granite civilization" lasted is unknown, though certainly by 2000 BC it was well integrated into a broader western European megalithic culture, as testified by the development of symbolic rock art. Particularly fine examples of Neolithic art are the carved shale funerary plaques from Alentejo and Algarve, mostly in the form of stylized owls or other birds of prey, probably a divinity; the plaques may also have been symbols of tribal power or affiliation.

The end of the Neolithic era, roughly around 1000 BC, saw the development of northern Portugal's **Cultura Castreja**, based around fortified hilltop towns – called **citânias** – and villages (*castros*). The potential for new trading outlets and the quest for metals, in particular tin for making bronze, attracted a succession of peoples from across the Mediterranean but most of their settlements lay on the eastern seaboard and so fell within "Spanish" history. The **Phoenicians**, however, established a series of outposts along Portugal's Atlantic coastline around 900 BC, and there were contacts, too, with Mycenaean Greeks: a curious testament to this cultural mingling is found at Panóias, close to Vila Real, where an engraved text next to a massive sacrificial altar bears a bilingual Latin and Greek inscription dedicated to the Greco-Egyptian deity of Serapis.

The Cultura Castreja was further developed and refined after the arrival of **Celtic peoples**, between 700 and 600 BC. The most impressive remains are at the Citânia de Briteiros, near Braga, and Citânia de Sanfins de Ferreira, north of Porto, both of which reveal paved streets, drainage systems and circuits of defensive walls; like many of the *citânias* they survived, remarkably unchanged, well into the Roman era. Remains from settlements in neighbouring Trás-os-Montes reveal more clues about the nature of this pastoral society: crude granite statues – *berrões* or *porcas* – of wild sows and boars, and some bulls, have been found throughout the area, and may have been venerated as objects of a fertility cult; there are particularly visible examples at Bragança and Murça. From both Minho and Trás-os-Montes are life-sized statues of Celtic warriors, whose popular name – *figuras de basto* – alludes to their bravery: *eu basto*, "I suffice" (in defending the people), was their motto.

Romans, Suevi and Visigoths

In the mid-third century BC, the Phoenicians were followed by Carthaginians, who recruited Celtic tribesmen for military aid against the Roman empire. Once again, though, their influence was predominantly on the eastern seaboard and in the south; with defeat in the Second Punic War (218–202 BC) they were to be replaced by a more determined colonizing force. Entering the peninsula in 210 BC, the **Romans** swiftly subdued the Mediterranean coast and the south of Spain and Portugal. In the interior, however, they met with great resistance from the Celtiberian tribes and in 193 BC the **Lusitani** rose up in arms. Based in central Portugal, between the Tejo and Lima rivers, they were, in the words of the Roman historian Strabo, "the most powerful of the Iberian peoples, who resisted the armies of Rome for the longest period". For fifty years they held up the Roman advance, under the leadership of **Viriatus**, a legendary Portuguese hero and masterful exponent of the feigned retreat who, on several occasions, brought the Romans to accept his autonomous rule. He was betrayed after a successful campaign in 139 BC and within two years the Lusitani had capitulated as the legions of Decimus Junius Brutus swept through the north. Still, over a century later, their name was given to this most westerly of the Roman provinces, while in the northern Celtic villages Roman colonization can scarcely have been felt.

Integration into the **Roman Empire** occurred largely under Julius Caesar, who in 60 BC established a capital at Olisipo (Lisbon) and significant colonies at Ebora (Évora), Scallabis (Santarém) and Pax Julia (Beja). In 27 BC the Iberian provinces were further reorganized under Augustus, with all but the north of Portugal being governed – as Lusitánia – from the great Roman city of Merida in Spanish Extremadura. The Minho formed part of a separate province, later added to northwest Spain to create Gallaecia, with an important regional centre at Bracara Augusta (Braga). In general, though, it was the south where Roman influence was deepest. Here they established huge agricultural estates (*latifundia*, which still survive in the Alentejo) and changed the nature of the region's crops, as they introduced wheat, barley, olives and the vine to the area.

There are no great **Roman sites** in Portugal – at least nothing to compare with Spanish Merida, Tarragona or Itálica – though the city of Évora and the excavated sites of Conímbriga, Milreu and Miróbriga have a real interest. The mark of six centuries of Roman rule consists more in a network of roads and bridges, many still in use today, and a series of ruins of small towns and villas, found largely in the Alentejo. There is a more basic legacy, too, the Portuguese language being very heavily derived from Latin.

The decline of the Roman Empire in Portugal echoes its pattern elsewhere, though perhaps with greater indifference, the territory always being something of a provincial backwater. **Christianity** reached Portugal's southern coast towards the end of the first century AD and by the third century bishoprics were established at Braga, Évora, Faro and Lisbon. But the Roman state was already disintegrating and in 409 the first waves of barbarian invaders crossed the Pyrenees into Spain. Vandals, Alans, Suevi and Visigoths all passed through Portugal, though only the last two were of any real importance.

The **Suevi**, a semi-nomadic people from Germany's Rhine valley, eventually settled in the area between the Douro and Minho rivers, establishing courts at Braga and Portucale (Porto). They seem to have coexisted fairly peacefully with the Hispano-Roman nobility and were converted to Christianity by St Martin of Dume, a saint frequently found in the dedications of northern churches.

Around 585 AD, however, the Suevian state disappeared, having been suppressed and incorporated into the **Visigothic** empire, a heavily Romanized yet independent force which for two centuries maintained a spurious unity and rule over most of the peninsula. The Visigothic kings, however, ruled from Toledo, supported by a small and elite aristocratic warrior-caste, so in Portugal their influence was neither great nor lasting. And by the end of the seventh century their divisions, exacerbated by an elective monarchy and their intolerance (including the first Iberian persecution of the Jews), resulted in one faction appealing for aid from Muslim North Africa. In 711 a first force of **Moors** crossed the straits into Spain and within a decade they had advanced and conquered all but the mountainous reaches of the Asturias in northern Spain.

The Moors and the Christian Reconquest

In Portugal, Aveiro probably marked the northernmost point of the **Moorish advance**. The dank, green hills of the Minho held little attraction for the colonizers and most of the Moors were content to settle in the south: in the Tejo valley, in the rich wheat belts around Évora and Beja, and above all in the coastal region of **al-Gharb**: Algarve, or "the west". Here they established a capital at Shelb, modern Silves, which, by the middle of the ninth century, was an independent kingdom, detached from the great Muslim emirate of al-Andalus which covered most of Spain.

The Moors in Portugal were a mix of ethnic races – for the most part consisting of Berbers from Morocco, but also considerable numbers of Syrians and, around Faro, a contingent of Egyptians, some of them probably Coptic Christians. In contrast to the Visigoths, the Moors were tolerant and productive, their rule a civilizing influence. Both Jews and Christians were allowed freedom of worship and their own civil laws, while under Muslim law small landholders continued to occupy and cultivate their own land. For most of these **Moçárabes** – Christians subject to Moorish rule – life must have improved. Roman irrigation techniques were perfected and the Moors introduced the rotation of crops and cultivation of cotton, rice, oranges and lemons. Their culture and scholarship led the world – though less from al-Gharb than from Córdoba and Seville – and they forged important trade links, many of which were to continue centuries after their fall. Perhaps still more important, urban life developed, with prosperous local craft industries: Lisbon, Évora, Beja and Santarém all emerged as sizeable towns.

The Christian Renconquest, the **Reconquista**, began – at least by tradition – at Covadonga in Spain in 718, when Pelayo, at the head of a small band of Visigoths, halted the advance of a Moorish expeditionary force. The battle's significance has doubtless been inflated but from the victory a tiny kingdom of the Asturias does seem to have been established. It expanded over the next two centuries to take in León, Galicia and the "lands of Portucale", the latter an area roughly equivalent to the old Swabian state between the Douro and the Minho.

By the eleventh century **Portucale** had the status of a country, its governors appointed by the kings of León. In 1073 Afonso VI came to the throne. It was to be a reign hard-pressed by a new wave of Muslim invaders – the fanatical Almoravids, who crossed over to Spain in 1086 after appeals from al-Andalus and established a new Muslim state at Seville. Like many kings of Portugal after him, Afonso was forced to turn to European Crusaders, many of whom would stop in at the shrine of St James in Compostela. One of them, Raymond of Burgundy, married Afonso's eldest daughter and became heir-apparent to the throne of León; his cousin Henry, married to another daughter, Teresa, was given jurisdiction over Portucale. With Henry's death Teresa became regent for her son, **Afonso Henriques**, and began to try to forge a union with Galicia. Afonso, however, had other ideas and having defeated his mother at the battle of São Mamede (1128), he established a capital at **Guimarães** and set about extending his domains to the south.

The Reconquest of central Portugal was quickly achieved. Afonso's victory at Ourique in 1139 was a decisive blow and by 1147 he had taken Santarém. In the same year Lisbon fell, after a siege in which passing Crusaders again played a vital role. Many of them were English and some stayed on; Gilbert of Hastings became Archbishop. By now Afonso was dubbing himself the **first King of Portugal**, a title tacitly acknowledged by Alfonso VII (the new king of León) in 1137 and officially confirmed by the Treaty of Zamora in 1143. His kingdom spread more or less to the borders of modern Portugal, though in the south, Alentejo and the Algarve were still in Muslim hands.

For the next century and a half Afonso's successors struggled to dominate this last stronghold of the Moors. **Sancho I** (1185–1211) took their capital, Silves, in 1189, but his gains were not consolidated and almost everything south of the Tejo was recaptured the following year by al-Mansur, the last great campaigning vizier of al-Andalus. The overall pattern, though, was of steady expansion with occasional setbacks. Sancho II (1223–48) invaded the Alentejo and the eastern Algarve, while his successor **Afonso III** (1248–79) moved westwards, taking Faro and establishing the kingdom in pretty much its final shape.

The Burgundian kings

The reconquest of land from the Muslims also incorporated a process of **recolonization**. As it fell into the king's hands, new territory was granted to such of his subjects that he felt would be able to defend it. In this way much of the country came to be divided between the church, the Holy Orders – chief among them the **Knights Templar** – and a hundred or so powerful nobles (*ricos homens*). The entire kingdom had a population of under half a million, the majority of them concentrated in the north. Here, there was little displacement of the traditional feudal ties, but in the south the influx of Christian peasants blurred the distinction between serf and settler, dependent relationships coming instead to be based on the payment of rent.

Meanwhile a **political infrastructure** was being established. The land was divided into municipalities (*concelhos*), each with its own charter (*foral*). A formalized structure of consultation began, with the first **Cortes** (parliament) being held in Coimbra in 1211. At first consisting mainly of the clergy and nobility, it later came to include wealthy merchants and townsmen, a development speeded both by the need to raise taxes and by later kings' constant struggles against the growing power of the church. The capital, which Afonso Henriques had moved to Coimbra in 1139, was transferred to **Lisbon** in about 1260 by Afonso III.

The Burgundian dynasty lasted through nine kings for 257 years. In the steady process of establishing the new kingdom, one name stands out above all others, that of **Dom Dinis** (1279–1325). With the Reconquest barely complete when he came to the throne, Dinis set about a far-sighted policy of strengthening the nation to ensure its future independence. Fifty fortresses were constructed along the frontier with Castile, while at the same time negotiations were going on, leading eventually to the Treaty of Alcanizes (1297) by which Spain acknowledged Portugal's frontiers. At home Dinis established a major programme of forest planting and of agricultural reform; grain, olive oil, wine, salt, salt fish and dried fruit became staple exports to Flanders, Brittany, Catalunya and Britain. Importance, too, was attached to education and the arts: a **university**, later transferred to Coimbra, was founded at Lisbon in 1290. Dinis also helped entrench the power of the monarchy, forcing the church to accept a much larger degree of state control and, in 1319, reorganizing the Knights Templar – at the time being suppressed all over Europe – as the **Order of Christ**, still enormously powerful but now responsible directly to the king rather than to the pope.

Despite Dinis's precautions, fear of **Castilian domination** continued to play an important part in the reigns of his successors, largely owing to consistent intermarrying between the two royal families. On the death of the last of the Burgundian kings, Fernando I, power passed to his widow Leonor, who ruled as regent. Leonor, whose only daughter had married Juan I of Castile, promised the throne to the children of that marriage. In this she had the support of most of the nobility, but the merchant and peasant classes strongly opposed a Spanish ruler, supporting instead the claim of João, Grand Master of the House of Avis and a bastard heir of the Burgundian line. A popular revolt against Leonor led to two years of war with Castile, finally settled at the **Battle of Aljubarrota** (1385) in which João, backed up by a force of English archers, wiped out the much larger Castilian army.

The great abbey of **Batalha** was built to commemorate the victory. **João I**, first king of the **House of Avis**, was crowned at Coimbra the same year, sealing relations with England through the 1386 Treaty of Windsor and his marriage to Philippa of Lancaster, daughter of John of Gaunt, the following year.

Dom Manuel and the maritime empire

Occupying such a strategic position between the Atlantic and the Mediterranean, it was inevitable that Portuguese attention would at some stage turn to **maritime expansion**. When peace was finally made with Castile in 1411, João I was able to turn his resources toward Morocco. The outpost at Ceuta fell in 1415, but successive attempts to capture Tangier were not realized until the reign of Afonso V, in 1471.

At first such overseas adventuring was undertaken partly in a crusading spirit, partly to keep potentially troublesome nobles busy. The first real advances in exploration, however, came about through the activities of **Prince Henry "The Navigator"**, third son of João and Philippa. As Grand Master of the Order of Christ, he turned that organization's vast resources towards marine development, founding a School of Navigation on the desolate promontory of Sagres (then regarded as the end of the world) and staffing it with Europe's leading cartographers, navigators and seamen. As well as improving the art of offshore navigation, they redesigned the caravel, making it a vessel well suited to long ocean-going journeys. **Madeira** and the **Azores** were discovered in 1419 and 1427 respectively, and by the time of Henry's death in 1460 the **Cape Verde Islands** and the **west coast of Africa** down to Sierra Leone had both been explored.

After a brief hiatus, overseas expansion received a fresh boost in the reigns of João II, Manuel I and João III. In 1487 **Bartolomeu Dias** finally made it around the southern tip of Africa, christening it "Cabo da Boa Esperança" in the hope of good things to come. Within ten years **Vasco da Gama** had sailed on past it to open up the **trade route to India**. This was the great breakthrough and the Portuguese monarchy, already doing well out of African gold, promptly became the richest in Europe, taking a fifth of the profits of all trade and controlling important monopolies on some spices. The small cargo of pepper brought back by Vasco on his first expedition was enough to pay for the trip three times over. Meanwhile Spain was opening up the New World and by the **Treaty of Tordesillas** in 1494 the two Iberian nations divided the world between them along an imaginary line 370 leagues west of the Cape Verde Islands. This not only gave Portugal the run of the Orient but also, when it was discovered in 1500, Brazil (though its exploitation would have to wait nearly 200 more years). By the mid-sixteenth century Portugal dominated world trade; strategic posts had been established at Goa (1510), Malacca (1511), Ormuz (1515) and Macau (1557), and the revenue from dealings with the East was backed up by a large-scale **slave trade** between West Africa and Europe and Brazil.

The reign of **Manuel I** (1495–1521) marked the apogee of Portuguese wealth and strength. It found its expression at home in the extraordinary exuberance of the **Manueline** style of architecture. Notable examples can be seen in the Convento de Cristo at Tomar, and the monastery and tower of Belém in Lisbon, while decorations and motifs are to be found on churches and civil buildings throughout the country.

Enormous wealth there may have been, but very little of it filtered down through the system, and in the country at large conditions barely improved. The practice of siphoning off a hefty slice of the income into the royal coffers effectively prevented the development of an entrepreneurial class and, as everywhere else in Europe, financial matters were left very much in the hands of the Jews, who were not allowed to take up most other professions.

Portugal had traditionally been considerably more tolerant than other European nations in its treatment of its **Jewish citizens** (and towards the Moorish minority who had been absorbed after the Reconquest). However, popular resentment of their riches, and pressure from Spain, forced Manuel – who had initially welcomed refugees from the Spanish persecution – to order their expulsion in 1496. Although many chose the pragmatic course of remaining as "New Christian" converts, others fled to the Netherlands. This exodus, continued as a result of the activities of the **Inquisition** (from 1531 on), created a vacuum that left Portugal with an extensive empire based upon commerce, but deprived of much of its financial expertise. By the 1570s the economy was beginning to collapse: incoming wealth was insufficient to cover the growing costs of maintaining an empire against increasing competition, a situation exacerbated by foreign debts, falling prices and a decline in the productivity of domestic agriculture.

Spanish domination

In the end it was a combination of reckless imperialism and impecunity that brought to an end the dynasty of the House of Avis and with it, at least temporarily, Portuguese independence. **Dom Sebastião** (1557–78), obsessed with dreams of a new crusade against Morocco, set out at the head of a huge army to satisfy his fanatical fantasies. They were crushed at the battle of **Alcácer-Quibir** (*Ksar el-Kebir* in Arabic; 1578), where the Portuguese dead numbered over eight thousand, including Sebastião and most of Portugal's nobility. The aged **Cardinal Henrique** took the throne as the closest legitimate relative and devoted his brief reign to attempting to raise the crippling ransoms for those captured on the battlefield.

The Cardinal's death without heirs in 1580 provided Spain with the pretext to renew its claim to Portugal. **Philip II** of Spain, Sebastião's uncle, defeated his rivals at the battle of Alcántara and in 1581 was crowned Filipe I of Portugal, inaugurating a period of Habsburg rule which lasted for another sixty years. In the short term, although unpopular, the union had advantages for Portugal. Spanish wheat helped alleviate the domestic shortage and Spanish seapower helped protect the far-flung empire. Philip, moreover, studiously protected Portuguese autonomy, maintaining an entirely separate bureaucracy and spending long periods in Portugal in an attempt to win popular support. Not that he ever did – throughout his reign pretenders appeared, claiming to be Sebastião miraculously saved from the Moroccan desert, and tapping a strong vein of resentment among the people. In the long run, Spanish control proved disastrous. Association with Spain's foreign policy (part of the Armada was prepared in Lisbon) meant the enmity of the Dutch and the British, Portugal's traditional allies, losing the country an important part of its trade which was never to be regained.

Philip's successors made no attempt to protect Portuguese sensibilities, attempting to rule from Madrid while raising heavy taxes to pay for Spain's wars. The final straw was the attempt by Philip IV (Filipe III of Portugal) to conscript Portuguese troops to quell a rising in Catalunya. On December 1, 1640, a small group of conspirators stormed the palace in Lisbon and deposed the Governor of Portugal. By popular acclaim and despite personal reluctance, the Duke of Bragança, the senior member of the family which had long been the most powerful in the country, took the throne as **João IV**.

The house of Bragança

Although the status of the newly independent nation looked pretty shaky at first, as it turned out, the Spanish were so preoccupied with wars elsewhere that they had little choice but to accept the situation, though they did not do so formally until the 1668 **Treaty of Lisbon**. Relations with Britain had been strained during the establishment of that country's Commonwealth, especially by Oliver Cromwell's particular brand of Protestant commercialism, but were revived by the marriage of Charles II to Catherine of Bragança in 1661. The **discovery of gold and diamonds in Brazil** during the reign of Pedro II (1683–1706) made the crown financially independent and did away with the need for the Cortes (or any form of popular representation) for most of the next century. It was **João V**, coming to the throne in 1706, who most benefited from the new riches, which he squandered in an orgy of lavish Baroque building. His massive convent at Mafra, built totally without regard to expense, virtually bankrupted the state. The **Methuen Treaty**, signed in 1703 to stimulate trade with Britain, only made matters worse: although it opened up new markets for Portuguese wine, it helped destroy the native textile industry by letting in British cloth at preferential rates.

The accession of João's apathetic son, **José I** (1750–77), allowed the total concentration of power in the hands of the king's chief minister, Sebastião José de Carvalho e Melo, better known by his later title, the **Marquês de Pombal** (1699–1782), who became the classic enlightened despot of eighteenth-century history. It was the **Great Earthquake of 1755** that sealed his dominance over the age; while everyone else was panicking, Pombal's policy was simple – "bury the dead and feed the living".

Pombal saw his subsequent mission as to modernize all aspects of Portuguese life, by establishing an efficient and secular bureaucracy, renewing the system of taxation, setting up export companies, protecting trade and abolishing slavery within Portugal. It was a strategy that made him many enemies among the old aristocracy and above all within the Church, whose overbearing influence he fought at every turn. Opposition, though, was dealt with ruthlessly and an assassination attempt on the king in 1758 (which some say was staged by Pombal) gave him the chance he needed to destroy his enemies. Denouncing their supposed involvement, Pombal executed the country's leading aristocrats and abolished the Jesuit order, which had long dominated education and religious life in Portugal and Brazil.

Although Pombal himself was taken to trial (and found guilty but pardoned on the grounds of old age) with the accession of Maria I (1777–1816), the majority of his labours survived him, most notably the reform of education along scientific lines and his completely rebuilt capital, Lisbon. Further development, however, was soon thwarted by a new invasion.

French occupation and the Miguelite years

With the appearance of **Napoleon** on the international scene, Portugal once more became embroiled in the affairs of Europe. The French threatened to invade unless the Portuguese supported their naval blockade of Britain, a demand that no one expected them to obey since British ports were the destination for most of Portugal's exports. Only the protection of the British fleet, especially after the victory at Trafalgar in 1805, kept the country's trade routes open. General Junot duly marched into Lisbon in November 1807.

On British advice the royal family had already gone into exile in Brazil, where they were to stay until 1821, and the war was left largely in the hands of British generals **Beresford** and **Wellington**. Having twice been driven out and twice reinvaded, the French were finally forced back into Spain in 1811 following the Battle of Buçaco (1810) and a long period of near starvation before the lines of Torres Vedras.

Britain's prize for this was the right to trade freely with **Brazil**, which, together with the declaration of that country as a kingdom in its own right, fatally weakened the dependent relationship that had profited the Portuguese treasury for so long. Past roles were reversed, with Portugal becoming effectively a colony of Brazil (where the royal family remained) and a protectorate of Britain, with General Beresford as administrator. The only active national institution was the army, many of whose officers had absorbed the constitutional ideals of revolutionary France.

In August 1820, with King João VI still in Brazil, a group of officers called an unofficial Cortes and proceeded to draw up a new **constitution**. Inspired by the recent liberal advances in Spain, it called for an assembly to be elected by universal male suffrage and for the abolition of clerical and noble privilege. The king, forced to choose between Portugal and Brazil, where his position looked even more precarious, came back in 1821 and accepted its terms. His queen, Carlota, and younger son **Miguel**, however, refused to take the oath of allegiance and became the dynamic behind a reactionary movement which drew considerable support in rural areas. With João VI's death in 1826, a delegation was sent to Brazil to pronounce Crown Prince Pedro the new king. Unfortunately Pedro was already Emperor of Brazil, having declared its independence some years earlier. He resolved to pass the crown to his infant daughter, with Miguel as regent provided that he swore to accept a new charter, drawn up by Pedro and somewhat less liberal than the earlier constitution. Miguel agreed, but once in power promptly tore up any agreement, abolished the charter and returned to the old, absolutist ways. This was a surprisingly popular move in Portugal, certainly in the countryside, but not with the governments of Britain, Spain, or France who backed the liberal rebels and finally put Pedro IV (who had meanwhile been deposed in Brazil) on the throne after Miguel's defeat at Évora-Monte in 1834.

The death of the monarchy

Pedro didn't survive long. The rest of the century – under the rule of his daughter Maria II (1834–53) and his grandsons Pedro V (1853–61) and Luís (1861–89) – saw almost constant struggle between those who supported the charter and those who favoured a return to the more liberal constitution of 1822. In 1846 the position deteriorated virtually to a state of **civil war** between Maria, who was fanatical in her support of her father's charter, and the radical constitutionalists. Only a further intervention by foreign powers maintained peace, imposed at the Convention of Gramido (1847).

In the second half of the century, with relative stability and the two warring factions to some extent institutionalized into a revolving two-party system, the economy began at last to recover, with the first signs of widespread industrialization and a major public works programme under the minister Fontes Pereira de Melo. The monarchy, however, was almost bankrupt and its public humiliation over possessions in Africa – Britain and Germany simply ignored the Portuguese claim to the land between Angola and Mozambique – helped strengthen growing Republican feelings.

Republicanism took root particularly easily in the army and among the urban poor, fuelled by falling standards of living and growing anger at government ineptitude. **Dom Carlos** (1898–1908) attempted to rule dictatorially after 1906, alienating most sectors of the country in the process, and was assassinated, along with his eldest son, following a failed Republican coup in 1908. Finally, on October 5, 1910, the **monarchy was overthrown** once and for all by a joint revolt of the army and navy. Dom Manuel went into exile and died, in Britain, in 1932.

The "Democratic" Republic

After a provisional government of Republican Unity, elections took place in 1911, showing a marked swing towards Afonso Costa's **Democratic Party**, which remained the most dominant political force in the country until 1926. However, the divisions among the Republicans, the cyclical attempts at violent overthrow of the new regime by the monarchists, and the weakening of the country's economic, social and political structures kept the Republic in permanent turmoil. Political life was in chaos and the hopes, perhaps unrealistically high, of the Republic's supporters never began to be realized. There were 45 changes of government in sixteen years and several military uprisings.

The forces that had brought the Republic were supported largely by the urban and rural poor, yet new electoral laws based on a literacy test led to a smaller electorate than under the monarchy, disenfranchising most of the Republic's strongest supporters. Successive governments failed to fulfil the least aspirations. Anticlericalism had been a major plank of Costa's platform, arousing massive hostility in the countryside. Legalizing the right to strike merely gave workers a chance to voice their discontent in a massive wave of work stoppages, but the new regime proved to be less than responsive to workers' rights and the repression of union activities was a constant theme. Further fuel was given to the reaction by Portugal's economically disastrous decision to enter **World War I** on the side of the Allies in 1916 and by the vicissitudes of the postwar recession. By 1926 not even the trade unions were prepared to stand by the Republic, preferring to maintain "proletarian neutrality" in the face of what at first seemed no more significant a military intervention than any other.

Salazar and the "New State"

While the military may have known what they wanted to overthrow in 1926, they were at first divided as to whether to replace it with a new Republican government or a restored monarchy. From the infighting, a Catholic monarchist, **General Carmona**, eventually emerged as president (which he remained until his death in 1951) with the Republican constitution suspended.

In 1928 one **Dr António de Oliveira Salazar** joined the Cabinet as Finance Minister. A professor of economics at Coimbra University, he took the post only on condition that he would control the spending and revenue of all government departments. His strict monetarist line (helped by a change in the accounting system) immediately balanced the budget for the first time since 1913 and in the short term the economic situation was visibly improved. From then on he effectively controlled the country, becoming Prime Minister in 1932 and not relinquishing that role until 1968.

His regime was very much in keeping with the political tenor of the 1930s and while it had few of the ideological pretensions of a fascist state, it had many of the trappings. Members of the National Assembly were chosen from the one permitted political association, the National Union (UN); "workers' organizations" were set up, but run by their employers; education was strictly controlled by the state to promote Catholic values; and censorship was strictly enforced. Opposition was kept in check by the PIDE – a secret police force set up with Gestapo assistance – which used systematic torture and long-term detention in camps on the Azores and Cabo Verde Islands to defuse most resistance. The army, too, was heavily infiltrated by PIDE and none of the several coups mounted against Salazar came close to success. Despite remaining formally neutral throughout the **Spanish Civil War**, Salazar had openly assisted the plotters in their preparations and later sent unofficial army units to fight with Franco. Republican refugees were deported to face certain execution at Nationalist hands.

At home Salazar succeeded in producing the infrastructure of a relatively modern economy but the results of growth were felt by only a few and agriculture, in particular, was allowed to stagnate. Internal unrest, while widespread, was apparently easily controlled; the New State's downfall, when it came, was precipitated far more by external factors. Salazar was an ardent imperialist who found himself faced with growing **colonial wars**, which proved costly and brought international disapprobation. India seized Goa and the other Portuguese possessions in 1961 and at about the same time the first serious disturbances were occurring in Angola, Mozambique and, later, in Guinea-Bissau.

The government's reign came to an end in 1968 when Salazar's deck chair collapsed, and he suffered brain damage. Incapacitated, he lived for another two years, deposed as premier – though such was the fear of the man, no one ever dared tell him. His successor, **Marcelo Caetano**, attempted to prolong the regime by offering limited democratization at home. However, tensions beneath the surface were fast becoming more overt and attempts to liberalize foreign policy failed to check the growth of guerrilla activity in the remaining colonies, or of **discontent in the army**.

It was in the African-stationed army especially that opposition crystallized. There the young conscript officers came more and more to sympathize with the freedom movements they were intended to suppress and to resent the cost – in economic terms and in lives – of the hopeless struggle. From their number grew the revolutionary **Movimento das Forças Armadas** (MFA).

Revolution

By 1974 the situation in Africa was deteriorating rapidly and at home Caetano's liberalization had come to a dead end. The **MFA**, formed originally as an officers' organization to press for better conditions, and which had become increasingly politicized, was already laying its plans for a takeover. Dismissal of two popular generals – Spínola and Costa Gomes – for refusing publicly to support Caetano, led to a first chaotic and abortive attempt on March 16. Finally, on April 25, 1974, the plans laid by **Major Otelo Saraiva de Carvalho** for the MFA were complete and their virtually bloodless coup – known as the **Revolution of the Carnations** – went without a hitch, no serious attempt being made to defend the government.

The next two years were perhaps the most extraordinary in Portugal's history, a period of continual **revolution**, massive politicization and virtual anarchy, during which decisions of enormous importance were nevertheless made – above all the granting of independence to all of the overseas territories. At first there was little clear idea of any programme beyond the fact that the army wanted out of Africa. Though the MFA leadership was clearly to the left and at first associated with the PCP (Portuguese Communist Party), the bulk of the officers were less political and **General Spínola**, whom they had been forced to accept as a figurehead, was only marginally to the left of Caetano and strongly opposed total independence for the colonies. Spínola's dream was clearly to share the conservative nationalist policies that General de Gaulle had imposed in France, while the army was above all determined not to replace one dictator with another.

In the event their hands were forced by the massive popular response and especially by huge demonstrations on May Day. It was clear that whatever the leadership might decide, the people, especially in the cities, demanded a rapid move to the left. From the start every party was striving to project itself as the true defender of the "ideals of April 25". Provisional governments came and went but real power rested, where it had begun, with the MFA, now dominated by Saraiva de Carvalho and Vasco Gonçalves. It was a period of extraordinary contradictions, with the PCP, hoping to consolidate their position as the true revolutionary party, opposing liberalization and condemning strikes as counter-revolutionary, while ultra-conservative peasants were happily seizing their land from its owners.

Sudden **independence** and the withdrawal of Portuguese forces from the former colonies did not always work so well for the countries involved. Guinea-Bissau and Mozambique experienced relatively peaceful transitions, but **Angola** dissolved into full-scale civil war. The situation was even worse in **East Timor**, where more than ten percent of the population was massacred by invading Indonesian forces following Portuguese withdrawal. In Portugal itself the arrival of more than half-a-million colonial refugees – many of them destitute – came to be a major problem for the regime, though their eventual integration proved one of its triumphs.

At home, the first **crisis** came in September 1974, when Spínola, with Gonçalves and Saraiva de Carvalho virtual prisoners in Lisbon's Belém Palace, moved army units to take over key positions. The MFA, however, proved too strong and Spínola was forced to resign, General Costa Gomes replacing him as president. By the summer of 1975 more general reaction was setting in and the country was increasingly split, supporting the Revolution in the south, while remaining deeply conservative in the north. The Archbishop of Braga summed up the north's traditional views, declaring that the struggle against communism should be seen "not in terms of man against man, but Christ against Satan". Nevertheless, a coup attempt in March failed when the troops involved turned against their officers. The Council of the Revolution was formed, promptly nationalizing banking and private insurance; widespread land seizures went ahead in the Alentejo; and **elections** in the summer resulted in an impressive victory for Mário Soares' Socialist Party (PS).

On November 25, 1975, elements of the army opposed to the rightward shift in the government moved for yet another **coup**, taking over major air bases across the country. Otelo Saraiva de Carvalho, however, declined to bring his Lisbon command to their aid; nor did the hoped-for mass mobilization of the people take place. Government troops under Colonel Ramalho Eanes moved in to force their surrender and – again virtually without bloodshed – the Revolution had ended.

Democracy and Europe: the 1980s

In 1975, the ruling Socialist Party helped to shape the post-revolutionary constitution – a mildly Socialist document, though providing for a fairly powerful president. Early fears of a right-wing coup led by Spínola failed to materialize, helped by the election of **Colonel Eanes**, a man whom the army trusted, as president. He above all was a figure of stability, with enormous popular support and happy to concentrate on developing Portugal's links with Africa, Asia and Latin America and overseeing a gradual normalization process. The Socialists had effective control until 1980 when Dr Sá Carneiro managed to create the **Democratic Alliance**, uniting the larger groupings on the right. But within a few months he died – some say suspiciously – in a plane crash.

In elections held on the ninth anniversary of the Revolution, April 25, 1983, Mário Soares' Socialist Party again became the largest single party in the national assembly. Soares' premiership was dogged by the unpopularity of his economic austerity measures and by constant breakdowns in the talks over Portuguese and Spanish **entry into the European Community**. These problems did have one positive result, however, namely closer relations with the traditionally hostile government in Madrid. But the government's economic problems led eventually to the withdrawal of Social Democratic support and to the collapse of the coalition.

Soon after the inconclusive elections of October 1985, the revolutionary leader Otelo Saraiva de Carvalho was arrested and put on trial in Lisbon accused of being the leader of 73 suspected terrorists in the **FP-25** urban guerrilla group. Proceedings were postponed following the shooting of one of the key witnesses and it was not until 1987 that Saraiva de Carvalho was sentenced to 15 years' imprisonment. He was later conditionally released after a Supreme Court ruling that there had been irregularities at his trial. In February 1990 he renounced the armed struggle and requested an amnesty.

President Eanes, meanwhile – the other great figure at the end of the Revolution – had been forced to resign the presidency on completion of his second term in January 1986. He was replaced by former Socialist Prime Minister **Mário Soares** who, with the reluctant support of the Communists, narrowly defeated the candidate of the centre-right, becoming the first **civilian president** for sixty years.

Portugal's entry into the **European Community** in 1986 brought with it the most important changes since the Revolution. With the help of a massive injection of funds and increased foreign investment, Portugal enjoyed unprecedented economic growth, though behind the trappings of the new prosperity remained pockets of deeply entrenched poverty. Prime Minister Aníbal Cavaco Silva's early attempts to introduce an economic reform programme were hampered by his lack of a majority, but in 1987 his PSD (Social Democrats) party won the first absolute majority since the 1974 Revolution, and with it the strength to implement real change.

However, the centre-right government's free enterprise drive did not run unchallenged and the late 1980s were marked by **industrial unrest**. In 1989 the socialist opposition gained control of the capital, Lisbon, the northern industrial centre, Porto, and other significant cities during municipal elections. Four years of economic growth had benefited a new aspirant class, but voters were aware of accentuated social inequality and the continued inadequacy of health and education structures. Despite this, Cavaco Silva won a convincing mandate in the 1991 elections, when the PSD was returned to government.

Politics into the new millennium

The 1990s saw Portugal assume the **presidency of the European Community** in 1992, the year when (on December 31) all remaining trade and employment barriers were removed and the EC became the European Union (EU). On the domestic front, the PSD continued with privatization and forged plans for the conversion of state-run banks in preparation for joining the European Monetary System. Dealing with inflation remained at the top of the government's agenda, but there was increased discontent over social issues like infant mortality and illiteracy rates, while wages failed to increase in real terms in spite of impressive economic growth.

General elections in 1995 brought ten years of conservative rule to an end and the moderate Socialists assumed power under the enthusiastic leadership of **António Guterres**. Cavaco Silva's surprise defeat in the presidential elections of January 1996, ushered in leftwing former mayor of Lisbon, **Jorge Sampaio**, giving Portugal a head of state and prime minister from the same – Socialist – party for the first time since the 1974 Revolution. Guterres' programme differed little from that of his conservative predecessors. He offered a touch more sympathy towards the social welfare budget and a tougher stance towards the European Union, but otherwise pledged to continue to liberalize and privatize the economy. In the **1999 general elections**, stability seemed the order of the day, with Guterres and the Socialists Returned for a second consecutive mandate – the first since the Revolution.

On a broader stage, the late 1990s saw a huge boost in Portuguese self-esteem. Lisbon's **Expo 98** was an enormous success, and in the following year, 1999, Portugal's last colony – **Macau** – was handed back to Chinese rule without the problems encountered by the UK with Hong Kong. Portugal also played a large part in the fate of former colony, **East Timor**. Following the 1974 Revolution, Indonesia's bloody 24-year rule had resulted in the genocide of over a third of the population, which only came to an end after a UN-organized referendum in August 1999 – which saw an overwhelming vote in favour of independence. The Portuguese had been pushing for this for two decades, and the sense of relief was palpable – the feeling was of a long-standing obligation which had finally been fulfilled.

Following the 2002 general election, a right-of-centre Social Democrat PSD government, ruling in **coalition** with the minor CDS-PP party, was elected on the promise to cut government spending and tighten immigration laws. The economic problems facing the country were clear – notably a negative balance of trade and a steadily rising national debt – but not all were home-made, as global recession and spiralling oil prices also took their toll. Prime Minister **Manuel Durão Barroso** looked uncomfortable in the international spotlight, doing himself no favours by agreeing to host the 2003 Azores Iraq War Conference between Bush, Blair and Spain's Aznar. This did little to bolster Barroso's standing within Portugal, so when the post of European Commissioner within the EU became vacant, Barroso was only too glad to oblige, and resigned the premiership in July 2004. His replacement, former mayor of Lisbon, **Pedro Santana Lopes**, failed to lift the economy and called fresh elections in February 2005. The PS (Socialists) won a surprising absolute majority, as new Prime Minister **José Sócrates** set about the task of reinvigorating a country that a survey in early 2004 determined was Europe's second-most pessimistic nation (after Slovakia).

Portugal today

Portugal might be at something of a crossroads, but it's hard to deny that the country has progressed immensely since the Revolution. The installation of democracy has been an unmitigated success, and whilst excesses, corruption and other kinks remain, they are minor and hardly unique, even in Europe. The country's **infrastructure** has developed beyond recognition, particularly the roads, but there have also been ambitious bridges, new transport systems in Lisbon and Porto, a series of stadiums built for the successful **2004 European Football Championships**, and many other local developments, from new concert halls to revitalized public buildings. A high-speed train line connecting Lisbon, Porto and Madrid is in the pipeline, and a new Lisbon airport at Ota planned along with new bridges over the Tagus estuary. There is a heavy emphasis on developing alternative energy – from enormous wind farms to wave-turbines – and there's also been considerable investment in communications technology. Not only does Portugal have one of the world's highest densities of mobile phone use, it's also one of the few European countries with virtually complete high-speed Internet coverage.

However, Portugal still finds itself at the bottom of many comparative lists of economic factors, even after the **enlargement of the European Union** (2004) from fifteen to twenty-five member states. This in particular hailed the end of the "free lunch" period of EU structural funding, which has played a dominant role in Portugal's recent development. Worse, the bulk of Portugal's industries remain small or medium in scale, and have now to compete with eastern European enterprises which have the advantage of lower labour costs and new EU funding.

Many of the country's biggest challenges – ones that each government since 1974 has failed adequately to address – remain unanswered. Despite massive social change and economic restructuring, the economy remains ill-equipped to compete successfully in the international arena. The Portuguese earn much less than their more industrialized European partners – official GDP per capita figures currently put Portugal below every major Western European country, as well as Greece, Slovenia, Cyprus and even Malta. Personal and family debt levels are rising, unemployment is relatively high, and education remains a slumbering catastrophe, with Europe's highest school drop-out rates. The country is overly dependent on oil, which an alternative energy programme is only now starting to address. The country is also vulnerable to drought, especially in the south, affecting both agriculture – still a significant employer – and tourism.

Unforeseen developments have even damaged traditional industries like cork production: Portugal produces up to half the world's cork, but the shift by wine-makers to plastic stoppers has threatened livelihoods. Tourism, of course, is a major earner and, though there are plenty of pile-em-high and get-rich-quick developments, a more sensible approach to planning does seem to be taking hold. Environmental issues are at least given lip service, and if the ambitious project at the Mata de Sesimbra, south of Lisbon, is a success, Portugal could be at the forefront of sustainable tourist development.

Chronology of monuments and arts

22,000–8000 BC ▶ **Palaeolithic** hunter-gatherers sheltering from the Ice Age in the tributaries of the Douro and Tejo rivers leave behind thousands of engravings of animals, some of the world's oldest art.

7000–2000 BC ▶ **Neolithic** "granite civilization". Portugal's first man-made stone structures, belonging to a fertility cult; rock art spreads across country, beginning of metal ages.

1000–700 BC ▶ **Cultura Castreja** based around fortified hilltop settlements; Phoenicians establish first Atlantic trading posts around 900 BC; culture begins to adopt elements of classical mythology, including veneration of bulls.

700–200 BC ▶ **Celtic migrants** along Europe's Atlantic seaboard intermingle with locals; impressive towns at Briteiros and Sanfins. Local religion centred on wild sows and boars, of which statues remain.

210 BC ▶ **Romans** begin colonization; Conímbriga, 4th century BC Celtic town near Coimbra, adapted to Roman occupation (survives until 5th century AD).

193 BC ▶ **Lusitani uprising**, led by Viriatus, against Roman occupation; Viriatus is betrayed in 139 BC; northern Portugal not pacified until 19 BC.

60 BC ▶ **Julius Caesar** establishes a capital at Lisbon and towns at Beja, Braga, Évora, Santarém, etc. Walls and other remains at Idanha, in Beira Baixa; temple and aqueducts of Évora; bridges at Chaves, Ponte de Lima, Leiria and elsewhere.

1st to 4th century AD ▶ **Christianity** reaches Portugal's southern coast towards the end of the first century AD; bishoprics founded at Braga, Évora, Faro and Lisbon.

5th to 7th century AD ▶ Declining Roman Empire unable to resist **Barbarian invasions**. The Suevi establish courts at Braga and Porto in the north. Visigoths incorporate Suevian state into their Iberian empire in 585. Isolated churches, mainly in the north: São Pedro de Balsemão, near Lamego, and São Frutuoso at Braga.

711 ▶ **Moors** from North Africa invade and conquer peninsula within seven years. Christian **Reconquista** begins in 718, but will take more than 500 years to retake all Portugal. Moorish fortresses/walls survive at Silves, Lisbon, Sintra, Elvas, Mértola and Alcácer do Sal. Portuguese language emerges, heavily influenced by Arabic.

9th century ▶ **Al-Gharb** (Algarve) becomes an independent Moorish kingdom, governed from Silves. Porto reconquered by the Christian kings of Asturias-León in 868.

11th century ▶ Country of **Portucale** ("the sheltered port") emerges and in 1097 is given to Henry of Burgundy. Cluniac monks, administering pilgrimage route to Santiago, bring Romanesque architecture from France: 12th-century churches at Bravães, Tomar and around Penafiel, and council chamber at Bragança.

12th century ▶ **Afonso Henriques** recognized as first king of Portucale at the Treaty of Zamora of 1143. Guimarães castle built. In 1147, Afonso takes Lisbon and Santarém from the Moors; followed in 1162 by Beja and Évora. Fortress-like Romanesque cathedrals of Lisbon, Coimbra, Évora, Braga and Porto constructed.

13th century ▶ First assembly of the Cortes (parliament) at Coimbra in 1212. **Gothic architecture** enters Portugal at the Cistercian abbey of Alcobaça and several churches, most notably in Coimbra, and Porto's Sé. In 1249, **Afonso III** completes Reconquest of the Algarve.

1279–1325 ▶ Reign of **Dom Dinis** sees construction of chain of fortresses along Spanish border.

1385 ▶ Battle of Aljubarrota: **João I** defeats Castilians to become first king of House of Avis. The great triumph of mature Portuguese Gothic – the abbey of Batalha – is built in celebration. Paço Real built at Sintra.

1415 ▶ **Infante Henriques** (Prince Henry the Navigator) active at the Navigation School in Sagres. Madeira discovered in 1419, and Azores in 1427. Flemish-influenced "Portuguese Primitive" painters include Nuno Gonçalves.

1434–1487 ▶ The **Portuguese Discoveries**: Gil Eanes opens the sea route around Africa. Cape Verde Islands discovered 1457; Ghana 1475; Congo 1482; and Cape of Good Hope rounded in 1487 by Bartolomeu Dias. Development of *Romanceiro* ballads.

1495–1521 ▶ Reign of **Dom Manuel I** ("The Fortunate"). Two years into his reign, the flotilla of **Vasco da Gama** reaches India; Cabral discovers Brazil in 1500; and in 1513, Portuguese reach China. New riches finance **Manueline** architectural style, with greatest examples at Tomar, Batalha and Belém. By 1530s Renaissance forms are introduced and merged.

1521–57 ▶ Reign of **João III**. Celebrated contemporary painters include Grão Vasco.

1557–78 ▶ Reign of boy-king **Dom Sebastião**. Important sculptural school at Coimbra (1520–70) centred on French Renaissance sculptors Nicolas Chanterenne, Filipe Hodart and Jean de Rouen. **Luís de Camões** publishes *Os Lusíadas* (1572), Portugal's national epic in verse.

1578–1640 ▶ Sebastião's disastrous expedition to Morocco, loss of king and mass slaughter of nobility at Alcácer-Quibir. **Philip II** steps into the void in 1581 and brings Spanish occupation under Habsburg rule.

1640 ▶ **João IV**, Duke of Bragança, restores independence. Severe late-Renaissance style: eg São Vicente in Lisbon designed by Felipe Terzi.

1706–50 ▶ Reign of **Dom João V**. Gold and diamonds discovered in Brazil, reached peak of wealth and exploitation in the 1740s, reflected in opulence of **Baroque** style. Highlights include Porto's church and tower of Clérigos, the palace-monastery of Mafra, Queluz palace, Coimbra university library, and the more rustic Baroque style at Lamego and Bom Jesus.

1755 ▶ **Great Earthquake** destroys Lisbon and parts of the Alentejo and Algarve. "Pombaline" Neoclassical style employed for rebuilding of Lisbon (Baixa) and Vila Real de Santo António in the Algarve. Regulation of port wine industry by Pombal guarantees Porto's success and flourishing of the arts.

19th century ▶ Maria II (1843–53) holds throne with German consort, Fernando II. Pena Palace folly built at Sintra. Extensive mercantile construction throughout the country in Neoclassical and Renaissance styles. Birth of fado music in Lisbon's popular *bairros*.

1900–10 ▶ Assassination of Carlos I in Lisbon in 1908; exile of Manuel II ("The Unfortunate") two years later marks end of Portuguese monarchy.

1910–26 ▶ "Democratic" Republic. Works by writer **Fernando Pessoa**. Fado's popularity spreads, particularly among Coimbra's students.

1932–68 ▶ Salazar dictatorship. Goa is seized by India; colonial wars in Africa. Traditional music, bearer of North African and Celtic heritage, recorded by Michel Giacometti and composer Fernando Lopes Graça from 1950s onwards; influences Lopes Graça's own choral output.

1974 ▶ April 25 Revolution. "New Song" movement of singer-songwriters associated with the change, but trashy "Pimba pop" replaces fado – scarred by Salazar's support – as the nation's most popular music. **European Community** (1986) kicks off massive road-building programme.

1994–1998 ▶ Lisbon is European Capital of Culture (1994). Permanent gallery of modern Portuguese artists opens at Lisbon's Gulbenkian Foundation. Lisbon hosts Expo 98; becomes a showcase for the work of national and international architects.

1999 ▶ Porto's Serralves Museum of Contemporary Art opens, the work of architect Álvaro Siza Vieira. Death of fado singer **Amália Rodrigues** sees three days of national mourning and marks revival of the genre.

2001–2007 ▶ Porto is European City of Culture (2001); signals massive programme of urban regeneration, including new metro system and Casa da Música concert hall. Portugal hosts the 2004 **European Football Championships**, losing the final in Lisbon. In the same year, fado music celebrates the centennial of its first recording.

C

Music

Musically, Portugal is best known as the home of the passionate and elegant vocal and instrumental fado of Lisbon and Coimbra but, away from the cities, a rich variety of regionally distinct music and a wide range of traditional instruments can still be encountered. Even though social and economic change has diminished its role in everyday life, you are still likely to come across traditional music during local festivals. This inheritance invests much of what is distinctively Portuguese in the music coming out of the country today, as it did in the "new song" movement of singer-songwriters associated with the political change of the 1974 Revolution. Portuguese democracy has matured to an eclectic soundtrack: vibrant music from the country's former colonies and Lusophone variants of pop, rock, rap, electronic dance music and jazz have developed alongside the home-grown kitsch known as *pimba*.

Portuguese instruments

Portugal is home to a remarkable variety of instruments, most of them associated with particular regional traditions.

Guitarra Portuguesa

The best-known Portuguese music is fado, and be that the Lisboa or Coimbra tradition its dominant instrument is the **guitarra**. Though sometimes called the Portuguese guitar, its body isn't "guitar-shaped", but that of an Arabic lute (*ud* or *'aoud*), introduced over a thousand years ago during the Moorish conquest. Two designs evolved – the Lisbon *guitarra*, usually used for accompanying singers, and the larger body and richer bass of the version more suited to Coimbra fado, with its strong *guitarra*-virtuoso strand. Both have six pairs of steel strings tuned by knurled turn-screws on a fan-shaped metal machine head.

Violas

In fado, the *guitarra* is usually accompanied by a six-string guitar of the Spanish form which, like all fretted instruments of that waisted body-shape, is known in Portugal as a *viola*. Though the **viola de fado** is usually a normal Spanish guitar, there is a remarkable range of other specifically Portuguese *violas*. They are virtually always steel-strung, and most have soundboards decorated with flowing tendril-like dark wood inlays spreading from the bridge, and soundholes in a variety of shapes.

The version encountered most often, particularly in the north, is the **viola braguesa**, which has four pairs of strings and is usually played *rasgado* (a fast intricate rolling strum with an opening hand). A slightly smaller close relative, from the region of Amarante, is the **viola amarantina**, whose soundhole is usually in the form of two hearts. Other varieties include the ten- or twelve-stringed **viola campanica alentejana** which has a very deeply indented waist, almost like a figure of eight; a notable modern player is **José Barros** of the Alentejo duo **Cantesul**. Another version is the **viola beiroa**, which is distinctive in having an extra pair of strings which are played in a way similar to the high fifth string on an American banjo.

Cavaquinhos and bandolims

One popular Portuguese stringed instrument has taken root across the world. The **cavaquinho** looks like a baby viola with four strings, and is played with an ingenious

Regional traditions

Each region of Portugal has its own characteristic songs, ensembles and instruments but the vocal and instrumental traditions survive most strongly in the rural areas away from the sea – regions like Trás-os-Montes, Beiras and Alentejo. Villages and towns throughout Portugal have folklore troupes known as **ranchos folclóricos** who perform at festivals and sometimes on concert stages and help perpetuate the musical traditions of the country. These were encouraged by the dictatorship as exemplars of the happy colourful peasantry, and were therefore somewhat disapproved of by musicians who were opponents of the regime, but emerging from those associations some continue to exist. Recently there has also been an increase in the number of musicians and bands performing traditional material, making new music with a roots heritage.

Portuguese tradition is rich with song, some of it drawing on the **oral ballad** repertoire that was once widespread across Europe. Iberia has its own specific

fast strum akin to the braguesa's *rasgado*. It spread from Portugal to the Azores and Madeira, and travelled onwards with Portuguese migrants from the Atlantic islands to Hawaii, where it became, with very few changes, the ukulele. The Portuguese form of mandolin, the **bandolim** or *banjolim*, is much used; a particularly fine player is **Júlio Pereira** (ⓦwww.juliopereira.pt), who is also an expert exponent of *cavaquinho* and the range of *violas*.

Pipes
The *gaita-de-foles* is the Portuguese bagpipe, in form similar to the Scottish Highland war-pipe but closest to the *gaitas* of Spanish Galicia and Asturias, all of which are drawn from the Moorish tradition (*ghaita* being the Moroccan word for a pipe), itself perhaps evolved from Celtic influence two thousand years ago. It is the main melody instrument of Trás-os-Montes music, accompanied by *bombo* and *caixa*. Each *gaita* has the tuning its player chooses, the scale in which he sings, rather than the fixed, mathematical scale developed for classical harmony that has come to prevail in much of the western world.

Percussion
A feature of Beira Baixa music, and found elsewhere too, is the *adufe*. Introduced by the Arabs a millennium ago, it is a square double-headed drum usually containing pieces of wood or pebbles which rattle. Held on edge and tapped with the fingers, it's played by women, often in groups, to accompany their singing. Also found in several traditions is the clanking *ferrinhos* (triangle), played pretty much as in Cajun music.

Bombo, *caixa*, *adufe*, *pandeiro* (small drum) and *pandeireta* (tambourine) or occasionally *cântaro com abano* (a clay pot struck across its mouth with a leather or straw fan) provide the thump of Portuguese traditional music, while the clatter comes from the likes of the *cana* (a split cane slap-stick), **trancanholas** (wooden "bones"), *castanholas*, *reco-reco* (a scraped serrated stick), *conchas* (shells rubbed together), *zaclitracs* (a form of rattle) and *genebres* (a wooden xylophone hung from the neck (a feature of the *dança dos homens* (men's dance) in Beira Baixa).

group of ballads – the *Romanceiro* – which were sung in the royal courts from the fifteenth until the seventeenth century, but continued in the fields and villages long after that. Many other traditional songs – of love, religion or the cycles of nature – remained part of life until the 1970s, but with migration, changing ways of work, and mass media, the need and occasions for singing them have dwindled. Many now exist only in field recordings or in the repertoire of the revival folk bands.

Singers are sometimes joined by others in a refrain, perhaps accompanied by a stringed instrument or percussion. In the south, particularly **Alentejo**, there is a long tradition of *a cappella* vocal groups, a vibrant Mediterranean sound comparable to that of the vocal ensembles of Corsica and Sardinia. These are generally single-sex with a lead singer who delivers the first couple of verses before being joined by harmonizing lines from a second singer and then full-group vocal. Performing and recording ensembles exist, such as **Ensemble Vidigueira**, **Cantadores de Redondo**, **As Ceifeiros de Pias** or the female group **As Camponesas de Castro Verde**. **Vozes do Sul**, a group led by Alentejo singer-songwriter **Janita Salomé**, combines the singers from some of these groups and from his own family with new arrangements on acoustic instruments. An unexpected commercial success in 2004 was the Alentejan-style *As Meninas da Ribeira do Sado*, performed by folk group **Adiafa** (ⓦ www.adiafa.com).

Trás-os-Montes in the northeast is the heartland of *gaita-de-foles* (bagpipes), and the old tradition – inherited from both Celtic times and Moorish occupation – survives principally in the easternmost tip, Miranda do Douro, hard up against the Spanish border. Of the surviving handful of traditional Mirandês *gaiteiros*, two of the best are in the quartet **Galandum Galundaina**, fine musicians and singers whose activity shows signs of creating new interest. They play regularly for the *dança dos paulitos*, a stick dance for men which is strongly reminiscent of an English morris dance. Its music is provided by the standard Trás-os-Montes line-up of a *gaita-de-foles* accompanied by a *bombo* (bass drum) and *caixa* (snare drum), or sometimes by a solo musician playing a three-hole whistle (*flauta pastoril*) with one hand and a small snare drum (*tamboril*) with the other.

Bombos and *caixas* also feature in other northern and central regions as the thud and snap driving various ensembles playing for ceremony or celebration, such as the *zés-pereiras* of the **Minho** region, where they join flutes and sometimes clarinets and *gaitas*. Another style of Minho ensemble is the *rusga*, a variable line-up of stringed instruments such as *viola braguesa*, *cavaquinho* and perhaps violin, with accordion, flutes, clarinet, perhaps ocarina, and a clattering rhythm section.

Every region of Portugal has its own traditions – songs and ways of singing them, instruments, types of ensemble – and social or festival events at which they occur. Wherever you are, you might well stumble across something interesting. For more detail, sound samplers, festival listings and links, take a look at these websites: ⓦ www.attambur.com, run by the group At-Tambur, and ⓦ www.juliopereira.pt.

Roots revival

In the 1970s, young performing groups began to form to devote their attention either to the performance of traditional music, or to the construction of new music with folk roots. They used material that was still being sung or played, or could be enticed from the memories of their elders. Another source of inspiration was the material preserved in the **field recordings** made by enlightened individuals earlier in the twentieth century, notable among them being Michel Giacometti (1929–90), a Corsican-born Frenchman who together with Fernando Lopes Graça made field recordings throughout Portugal that were released on various labels from the late 1950s onwards.

The number of new revival bands appears to be increasing, while several of the pioneers are still around, including **Brigada Victor Jara** (@www .brigadavictorjara.pt), formed in Coimbra in 1975, which, while containing none of its original members, continues to be a major force. A particularly innovative recent arrival is **Gaiteiros de Lisboa**, which makes dramatic new music with deep roots, using raw percussion, voices, *gaitas* and other reeds plus quirky invented instruments. Another such inventive project is the group **Adufe**, inspired by Japanese Taiko drumming and formed by José Salgueiro, which makes a dramatic show focused on four giant *adufes*.

Well worth tracking down, too, are performances by accordion group **Danças Ocultas**, who – fed up with the accordion's usual fairground repertoire – reinvented the genre and, some would say, the instrument, with some extraordinarily atmospheric and at times haunting sounds. In similarly uncategorizable vein is the flute playing of **Rão Kyao**, fusing the formal beauty of Indian *raga* with frequent collaborations with Moroccan drum and lute players, and classical fado guitar.

Fado

Portugal's most famous musical form, **fado** ("fate") is currently experiencing a boom in popularity at home and abroad. It's an urban music, a thing of night-time and bars, the origins of which are debatable but certainly involve influences from Portugal's overseas explorations. The essence of fado is *saudade* (inadequately translatable as "yearning" or "beautiful melancholy"), which is carried in the lyrical and sentimental expression of a solo singer, usually accompanied by the *guitarra* and *viola de fado*. There are two distinct traditions of fado: Lisbon, which is very much a vocal form, male and female, and Coimbra, which in addition to its songs has a purely instrumental, *guitarra*-led aspect and is a male-only preserve. Portuguese are often mystified as to what a non-Portuguese speaker could get from fado, since so much of its meaning is in the poetic lyrics, but the beauty of the soaring vocals over the silvery *guitarra* is certainly seductive.

By far the most famous of the fado singers, and arguably its greatest performer, was **Amália Rodrigues** who had an immeasurable impact upon the direction of the fado through her recordings. Born in 1920 in the Alfama district of Lisbon, her death in October 1999 saw three days of official mourning announced in Portugal. Though in the course of her long singing career she ventured into other musical forms, her style and most celebrated recordings have become a central reference point in what people mean by fado.

Two working-class districts of Lisbon – Mouraria and Alfama – are considered the birthplace of fado, and **fado** clubs can still be found in the latter, along with the Bairro Alto (see pp.135–137). Some are expensive, some are tourist-traps, some are both; as with the elusive *duende* of Spain's flamenco, you may find the most memorable fado of all is performed by an unadvertised performer and, whether the performer is famous or not, when you're present at a special, real moment of fado you'll know it. Fado clubs are social places, with eating, drinking and informality, but during a song set in a good club the waiters don't serve, and the music is treated with due reverence. It's also not unusual for well-known fadistas to run their own clubs. **Maria da Fé** owns the Lisbon fado house *O Senhor Vinho*, where she and other notables perform. Seated at the long tables in the Clube de Fado in Alfama, you might well hear the owner **Mário Pacheco** himself, a fine **guitarrista** and the last to play with Amália, accompanying **Ana Sofia Varela**.

Contempoary fadistas start with world-music star **Mariza** (⊕www.mariza .org), the statuesque singer who won the BBC's Radio 3 European award for world music in 2003 and who frequently tours the globe. Also listen out for **Mísia** (⊕www.misia-online.com), **Cristina Branco** (⊕www.cristinabranco .com), **Kátia Guerreiro** (⊕www.katiaguerreiro.com), **Mafalda Arnauth** and male singers **Helder Moutinho** and **Camané** (⊕www.camane.em.pt). At the same time, **Dona Rosa**, a blind former busker and unaccompanied save for her gently tinkling triangle, is now receiving international acclaim after years of performing her very personal fado on the streets of Lisbon.

Many performers move in and out of fado, or mix aspects of it with other genres. For example **Dulce Pontes** (⊕www.dulcepontes.net) began in the world of rock-pop ballads, then for her second CD, *Lágrimas*, she performed fado and while she explores other genres it has remained a strong thread in her music. The music of longstanding Lisbon band **Madredeus** (⊕www .madredeus.com) – a manicured blend of classical guitars and keyboards surrounding the songbird vocals of **Teresa Salgueiro** in songs largely by band leader Pedro Ayres Magalhães – while not fado as such is, nevertheless, replete with the reflective melancholy of *saudade*.

Coimbra fado has a very different style: reflecting that city's ancient university traditions, and typically performed by students and Coimbra graduates, it's an exclusively male domain. As well as more formal songs that are less personally expressive than in Lisbon fado, there is also a strong aspect of *guitarra*-led instrumentals. The most famous Coimbra *guitarra fadista* of the latter half of the twentieth century was **Carlos Paredes**, who combined enviable technical mastery with genuine feeling and expression, placing the fado guitar centre-stage alongside the singers it traditionally accompanied. Coimbra's instrumental fado continues to evolve in skilled hands in both traditional and new combinations: most of **Pedro Caldeira Cabral**'s compositions aren't fado as such, but they and his immense virtuosity on the *guitarra* can be seen as part of the legacy of Coimbra fado.

For an excellent and detailed introduction to fado, "the people's soul", see ⊕http://paginas.fe.up.pt/~fado.

Nova Canção and música popular

It was an attempt to update the Coimbra fado that resulted in the modern Portuguese **ballad** (the term in this context meaning a set of poetic – usually contemporary – lyrics set to music, rather than the epic story-song that is the traditional folk-ballad).

The great figure in this movement was **José Afonso**. He had a classic, soaring fado-style voice and his first recording, with Luís Góes in 1956, comprised fados from Coimbra together with a couple of his own songs. It was principally

Afonso's songs, his choice of those by others, and his music drawing on regional traditional musics and fado that, during the last years of the dictatorship, became known as **nova canção** (new song). Together with the songs and performances of a gathering cast of others such as **Fausto**, **Luís Cília**, **Sérgio Godinho** and **Vitorino**, this provided a rallying point in the development not only of new Portuguese music but also of a new democratized state. In the final years of dictatorship, censorship and the restriction of performing opportunities caused some songwriters to move and record abroad, but Afonso remained, when necessary masking social and political messages with allegory.

In the years after the 1974 Revolution *nova canção* broadened to a movement known as **música popular** – essentially contemporary singer-songwriter music with folk roots. As in fado, the lyrics were as significant as the music, but unlike the more personal and emotional subject matter of fado they dealt with contemporary social and cultural issues. The music drew on popular tradition, both rural and urban, as well as reflecting Latin American, European and North African influences. Though he died in 1987, Afonso's albums keep his music and ideas very much a touchstone in Portuguese musical thinking, and many of his contemporaries are still performing. Other singers and songwriters, such as **Amélia Muge**, continue in a similar spirit of drawing on a mixture of rural and fado traditions, and you'll frequently hear songs by Afonso, Godinho and other *nova canção* leaders in the repertoire of fado singers.

Rock, pop, dance and indie

The acknowledged "father of Portuguese rock" is guitarist and singer-songwriter **Rui Veloso** (ⓦwww.ruiveloso.net), now into his third decade of performing. Combining elegant bluesy guitar sounds in the manner of Eric Clapton and Bob Dylan, he remains popular across the generations. Jazz-trained singer and musician **Pedro Abrunhosa** (ⓦwww.abrunhosa.oninet.pt) – who never takes his shades off in public – is the other major star. His first release, *Viagens* (1994), broke all sales records in Portugal; he's subsequently recorded in the States with musicians from Prince's band, collaborated with Rui Veloso and many others, written for films and musicals and toured widely. Far more off the wall is **Paulo Furtado**, better known as The Legendary Tiger Man (ⓦwww.legendarytigerman.com), a wiry, weird one-man band who takes his show around Europe's festivals – expect a Cramps-style blend of swamp-blues and rock and roll, to an indie-movie backdrop.

These three, alongside some of the contemporary fadistas, at least have an international profile on the world-music scene, but most Portuguese pop and rock bands are little known. In Portugal, however, there's a big following for venerable rockers like the Delfins (ⓦwww.delfins.pt), Xutos e Pontapés (ⓦwww.xutos.pt) and GNR, the mixed pop-rock of Clã, and Pluto, the rock band born out of the split of Porto's 90s alt-rockers Ornatos Violeta. More mainstream is Ronalda (ⓦwww.ronaldaonline.com), Euro-popster who sang Portugal's 2006 World Cup song and who has made a name for herself on the back of her Manchester United star brother, Cristiano Ronaldo.

Bands that sing in English are a more obvious commercial proposition, and the domestic rock scene was blown wide open by the success of the REM-influenced Silence 4, formed in Leiria in the mid-1990s. They released two best-selling albums before splitting in 2002. The band's founder, David Fonseca (ⓦwww.davidfonseca.com) has since launched a successful solo career, citing acts as diverse as Jeff Buckley, Roy Orbison, Pixies and B52s as influences. Along with fado star Camané he's also one of the voices with Portuguese "supergroup" Humanos, formed to sing the songs of the late, lamented António Variações – their 2004 release, Humanos, was a huge hit.

Also off-the-wall are Blasted Mechanism (⊛www.blastedmechanism.com), experimental world fusion rockers who are rapidly acquiring an international reputation for their theatrical shows and mutant-alien costumes. Dead Combo (⊛www.deadcombo.net) are similarly edgy, though here we're talking jangly Shadows-style guitars cutting across flamenco, tango and even fado infuences. If boy bands are your thing, this year's model is D'ZRT, a spin-off from the enormously popular teen-soap Morangos com Açucar. Most Portuguese are also happy to claim eclectic songstress Nelly Furtado as one of their own – Canadian-born to Portuguese parents from the Azores, her song Força was the official anthem for the Euro 2004 football championships held in Portugal.

Lisbon DJs like DJ Vibe and Rui da Silva were at the vanguard of the 1990s club scene – Rui da Silva is still the only Portuguese to have a UK number-one hit (2001's Touch Me). Although imported sounds dominated, Portuguese rap and hip-hop from the likes of Da Weasel and Boss AC soon began to make inroads into the club scene – Brazil-born American producer Mario Caldato Jr (best known for his work with the Beastie Boys) captured the best on his 1999 *Tejo Beat* compilation. More recently, the international dance scene has embraced the trip-hoppy likes of Coldfinger, the dub-electro fusion of Space-boys and especially the avant-garde electronica of Micro Audio Waves (⊛www .micraudiowaves.com), who take festivals like Barcelona's Sónar by storm.

Pimba

You're unlikely to get through a visit to Portugal without hearing some **música-ca pimba** – unrepentantly tacky music of the sort that usually enters the charts around Christmas time. Despite the wholesale snubbing of this style by the Portuguese media and intelligentsia, *pimba* – which has its roots in a popular oom-pa-pah brand of music played at fairs and festivals – has succeeded in conquering the whole country, as well as being big in countries with large Portuguese communities. Its success was previously limited to rural areas, but the introduction of satirical jokes and sexual references in the lyrics found new support among college students, and endless performances on morning and afternoon TV shows means *pimba* is now firmly established. The origin of the word lies in a mid-1990s song by acknowledged "King of Pimba" Emanuel, whose Nós Pimba! roughly translates as "We give it to them!" – which pretty much tells you all you need to know about the double-entendres that are the mainstay of the music. **Quim Barreiros** packs more into his scurrilous lyrics than most – the word *bacalhau* (salt-cod), slang for vagina, crops up again and again – while other names to watch out for are the microphone-juggling **Marco Paulo**, the raunchy **Ágata** and **Roberto Leal**.

Music from former colonies

Touring musicians and bands from all over the world perform in Portugal, but naturally it's a good place to encounter those from the world's biggest

Lusophone country, **Brazil**. An exciting and relatively recent development in the Portuguese music scene has been the appearance of groups from the **former colonies** of Angola, Mozambique, Cabo Verde, Guinea-Bissau and São Tomé e Príncipe. Following the colonial wars and independence many African musicians settled in Lisbon, while some spend part of the year based in Portugal while they tour Europe or record.

Cabo Verde music in particular has achieved great acclaim, with the reflective, melodic fado-like *morna* – whose most internationally famous exponent is **Cesária Évora** – and the more danceable *moradeira*. Another fine Lisbon resident Cabo Verdean singer is **Celina Pereira**. Among the **Lisbon Cabo Verdean** community, some women, such as the twelve-strong group **Voz de África**, gather on Sundays and at celebrations to play, sing and dance *batuc* – a social music banned in colonial times in which lively singing is accompanied by clapping, slapping on plastic-covered pillows and a dance in which two women circle and bump hips. Taking some influences from *batuc* **Sara Tavares**, who made a reputation in her teens as a pop singer, is now turning to what she describes as her personal tradition, with roots in Cabo Verde, Portugal and elsewhere, delivering live performances of freshness, beauty and subtlety.

Soft-voiced Angolan singer-guitarist **Waldemar Bastos** was imprisoned in his native country in the 1970s, and defected to Portugal in 1982. Now an internationally esteemed performer with influences from Brazilian and Portuguese as well as Angolan forms, he runs a small restaurant with his wife in Lisbon's Barrio Alto (*Água do Bengo*; see p.129) where you can dine to an Angolan-inspired soundtrack. New resident African-rooted formations arise and visiting bands arrive frequently, so it's worth keeping an eye on the posters and papers for promising-looking live shows and festivals.

Discography

This list is just a pointer to some of the recordings available, many of them internationally. Investigation of small music shops and chain stores in Portugal will turn up the many CDs that don't have international distribution, and there's a steady stream of new releases and re-issues too. In particular, there are a large number of Lisbon fado CDs – new and historic recordings, single artist releases and compilations (which often include tracks from great singers, particularly from the past, who have no whole album extant). Better than any CD, though, go and experience the music live – follow that sound echoing down the street.

Traditional

Ensemble Vidigueira *Portugal: Voices of Alentejo* (Auvidis)

Various *Musical Traditions of Portugal* (Smithsonian/Folkways)

Various *Musical Travel: Portugal and the Islands* (Auvidis)

Various *Portugal: Sons da Tradição* (BMG Classics/RCA)

Various *Portuguese Folk Music*, several volumes. Field recordings by Giacometti and Lopes Graça (Strauss) covering every Portugese region.

Various *Women's Voices of Portugal* (Auvidis)

Roots revival and development

Brigada Victor Jara *Danças e Folias* (Farol)

Danças Ocultas *Ar* and *Danças Ocultas* (both EMI Valentim de Carvalho)

Gaiteiros de Lisboa *Bocas do Inferno*, *Invasões Bárbaras* and *Dançachamas* (all Farol)

Né Ladeiras *Traz os Montes* (EMI Valentim de Carvalho)

Realejo *Cenários* (Movieplay)

Sétima Legião *Sexto Sentido* (EMI Valentim de Carvalho)

Vai de Roda *Polas Ondas* (Alba)

Various *Novas vos Trago* – a modern interpretation of medieval *Romanceiro* ballads, with Amélia Muge, Brigada Victor Jara, Gaiteiros de Lisboa, João Afonso and Sérgio Godinho (Tradisom)

Fado

Lisbon fado

João Braga *Cantar ao Fado* (Strauss)

Camané *Pelo Dia Dentro* (EMI Valentim de Carvalho)

Cristian Branco *Sensus, Ulisses* **(Universal)**

Katia Guerreiro *Fado Maior* (Ocarina), *Tudo ou Nada*

Mafalda Arnauth *Esta Voz Que Nos Atrevessa* (EMI Valentim de Carvalho)

Mariza *Fado em Mim* (World Connection), *Fado Curvo* (EMI), *Transparente* (Times Square Records), *Concerto em Lisboa* – live versions of best-known songs from the first three albums

Mísia *Ritual, Fado: Garras dos Sentidos, Canto, Drama Box* (all Erato)

Helder Moutinho *Sete Fados e Alguns Cantos* (Ocarina)

Amália Rodrigues *The Art of Amália* (EMI Hemisphere), *The First Recordings* (EPM), *Clássicos da Renascença* (Rádio Renascença/Movieplay)

Dona Rosa *Histórias da Rua* (Jaro)

Various *Portugal: The Story Of Fado* (EMI Hemisphere)

Various *Arquivos do Fado* (Heritage) – series of CDs; recordings from the 1920s and 1930)

Coimbra fado

Fernando Machado Soares *The Fado of Coimbra* (Auvidis) – vocal fado

Carlos Paredes *Guitarra Portuguesa* (EMI Valentim de Carvalho), *O Melhor de Carlos Paredes e Rão Kyao* (Universal Music Portugal) – instrumental fado

Pedro Caldeira Cabral *Variações - Guitarra Portuguesa* (World Network)

Fado-influenced developments

Carlos Paredes & Charlie Haden *Dialogues* (Antilles)

Dulce Pontes *Caminhos* (Movieplay)

Fernando Lameirinhas *Live* (Munich)

Filipa Pais *L'Amar* (Strauss)

Júlio Pereira *Acústico* (Sony)

Madredeus *Antologia* and *Movimento* (both EMI Valentim de Carvalho)

Nova canção and música popular

Amélia Muge *Todos os Dias* (Columbia)

José Afonso *Cantigas do Maio* (Movieplay), *Fados de Coimbra e Outras Canções* (Movieplay), *Best of José Afonso* and *José Afonso* (Movieplay)

Sérgio Godinho *Lupa* (EMI Valentim de Carvalho)

Vitorino *Alentejanas e Amorosas* (EMI Valentim de Carvalho), *Clássicos da Renascença* (Rádio Renascença/Movieplay)

Rock, pop, dance and indie

Blasted Mechanism *Avatara* (Toolateman)

Coldfinger *Lefthand* (Nortesul/EMI)

David Fonseca *Our Hearts Will Beat As One* (Universal)

Dead Combo *Quando a Alma Não e Pequena* (Dead & Company/Universal)

Micro Audio Waves *No Waves* (N-Records)

Pedro Abrunhosa *Viagens* (PolyGram)

Rui Veloso *O Melhor de Rui Veloso* (EMI) – a best-of compilation, *O Concerto Acústico*; (EMI) – unplugged

Silence 4 *Only Pain is Real* (Universal)

Spaceboys Sonic Fiction (Nylon)

The Legendary Tiger Man Masquerade (NorteSul/BMG)

Xutos & Pantapés 78/82, Mundo ao Contrário

Music from former colonies

Waldemar Bastos *Pretaluz* (Luaka Bop)

Justino Delgado *Casamenti D'Haos* (Lusafrica)

Cesária Évora *Miss Perfumado* and *Cesária* (Lusafrica/Melodie),

Anthologie: Mornas & Coladeras (BMG)

Celina Pereira *Nôs Tradições* (Lusafrica)

Various *The Soul of Cape Verde* (Tinder)

Compilations

Various *Music from the Edge of Europe: Portugal* (EMI Hemisphere) – compiled from EMI Valentim de Carvalho's catalogue; *Fado, guitarra, nova canção/música popular, guitarra* and jazzish, but no rural traditional music.

Various *The Rough Guide to the Music of Portugal* (World Music Network). Compiled from Movieplay's catalogue: *fado, nova canção, guitarra*, roots revival but again no traditional rural music.

Various *Café Portugal* (Union Square Music). Includes Amália Rodrigues, Maria Da Fé, Argentina Santos, Anabela, Filipe Duarte and Tereza Tarouca.

Books

T here are plenty of books available in English covering Portuguese history and society, and also lots of fiction in translation. It's always worth checking the latest output from UK publisher Carcanet Press (☎0161/834 8730, ⊛www.carcanet.co.uk), which has a fiction series entitled "From the Portuguese" and a non-fiction series entitled "Aspects of Portugal". Publishers are given below for books published only in Portugal; everything else you'll be able to track down on Amazon (⊛www.amazon.co.uk or ⊛www.amazon.com).

General travel writing

William Beckford *Recollections of an Excursion to the Monasteries of Alcobaça and Batalha; Travels in Spain and Portugal (1778–88).* Highly eccentric and enormously rich, Beckford lived for some time at Sintra and travelled widely in Estremadura. His accounts, told with a fine eye for the absurd, are a lot of fun.

Lord Byron *Selected Letters and Journals.* Only a few days of Portuguese travel but memorable ones – beginning with romantic enthusiasm, ending in outright abuse.

Almeida Garrett *Travels in My Homeland.* A classic Portuguese writer, Garrett was exiled to Europe in the 1820s, came into contact with the Romantics and later returned to play a part in the liberal government of the 1830s. This is a witty, discursive narrative ramble around the country.

Manfredi Hamm and Werner Radasewsky *Lisbon.* The strength of this book is its wonderful photographs, which capture the atmosphere and light of the city, its people and its surroundings through all its varying moods.

Paul Hyland *Backwards Out of the Big World.* A fascinating and sympathetic account of a journey through Portugal by a man who knows the country's people, history and literature as few foreigners do.

Marion Kaplan *The Portuguese: the Land and its People.* A readable, all-embracing volume, covering everything from wine to the family, poetry and the land. The style is a bit old-fashioned, but it's the best general introduction to the country available.

Rose Macaulay *They Went to Portugal.* The book covers British travellers to Portugal from the Crusaders to Byron, weaving an anecdotal history of the country in the process. There was a follow-up volume, *They Went to Portugal, Too.*

Fernando Pessoa *Lisbon: What the Tourist Should See (O que o turista deve ver)* (Livros Horizonte, Portugal). A somewhat dull insight into the city as Pessoa saw it. Written in English and Portuguese (but only available in Portugal), Pessoa's 1925 guidebook describes a Lisbon that is largely recognizable today.

José Saramago *Journey to Portugal.* Portugal's best-known novelist describes his journey round the country towards the end of the last century. The book is a strangely pedestrian plod which reveals little about himself or the places he visits; Saramago proves himself to be better at fiction than travel writing.

Anne de Stoop *Living in Portugal.* A glossy coffee-table tome filled with beautifully evocative photographs of Portugal's sights and architectural gems, from palaces and manor houses to rural houses, *pastelarias* and restaurants.

History and politics

David Birmingham *A Concise History of Portugal*. Recommended for the casual reader; concise but providing straightforward and informative coverage from the year dot.

António de Figueiredo *Portugal: Fifty Years of Dictatorship*. An illuminating study which takes as its starting-point the 1926 military coup that brought Salazar to power and goes through to the 1974 Revolution.

Peter Russell *Prince Henry "the Navigator": A life*. Fascinating, if academic, biography of the fifteenth-century prince.

José Hermano Saraiva *Companion History of Portugal*. The most recent of its kind, this is an accessible, generously illustrated and concise history of the country written especially for non-specialist foreigners by the author of the best-selling Portuguese original. Includes useful easy-reference glossaries of historical figures and places.

Ronald Watkins *Unknown Seas: How Vasco da Gama Opened the East*. The fascinating story of Vasca da Gama's voyage and triumphant return, which paved the way for the runaway expansion of the Portuguese empire. It's a well-told tale that rattles along.

Patrick Wilcken *Empire Adrift*. The Portuguese royal family fled from the French to Brazil in 1807 and established a court in exile there for 13 years. It was a move that was to change both Brazil and the path of the monarchy in Portugal, as this lively account of the fluctuating fortunes of João VI and his family shows.

Art, culture and biography

Jorge Barros and Soledade Martinho Costa *Festas e Tradições Portuguesas* (Círculo de Leitores, Portugal). A lavishly illustrated eight-volume set covering the country's major *festas*, *feiras* and *romarias*, some as strange as they are beautiful, and many with roots in pre-Christian traditions.

Helder Carita and Homem Cardoso *Portuguese Gardens*. A huge, beautiful tome, lavishly illustrated with photographs and plans, with a scholarly text.

Miles Danby *The Fires of Excellence*. Magnificent and detailed study of the Oriental architecture of Spain and Portugal, illustrated with specially commissioned photographs.

Júlio Gil and Augusto Cabrita *The Finest Castles in Portugal*. A superb illustrated survey of Portuguese castles, let down a little by a highly pedestrian translation/text.

Luís Lourenço and José Mourinho *Made in Portugal*. The authorized biography of Portugal's most successful football manager José Mourinho, tracing his career path from translator with Bobby Robson to manager of European Champions Porto, and onwards to a multi-million pound salary with Chelsea (see also box feature p.164).

C

CONTEXTS | Books

645

Fiction

Monica Ali *Alentejo Blue.* Best known for Brick Lane, which looked at the difficulties Asian immigrants face in London, Monica Ali here turns her gaze to ex-pat immigrants and would-be emigrants in a small, rural Alentejan village. Ali, who has a holiday home in the region, creates an atmospheric but ultimately inconsequential world where nothing actually happens – perhaps apt for the Alentejo, but far from riveting to read.

António Lobo Antunes *An Explanation of the Birds, The Natural Order of Things, Act of the Damned, The Return of the Caravels* and *South of Nowhere.* Psychologically astute and with a helter-skelter prose style, Antunes is considered by many to be Portugal's finest contemporary writer after Saramago. *The Return of the Caravels*, a modern "take" on the Discoveries, is a good place to start.

Maria Isabel Barreno, Maria Teresa Horta and **Maria Velho da Costa** *New Portuguese Letters: The Three Marias.* Published (and prosecuted) in 1972, pre-Revolution Portugal, this collage of stories, letters and poems is a modern feminist parable based on the seventeenth-century "Letters of a Portuguese Nun".

José Cardoso Pires *Ballad of Dog's Beach* (o/p). Ostensibly a detective thriller but the murder described actually took place during the last years of Salazar's dictatorship and Pires' research draws upon the original secret-police files. Compelling, highly original and with acute psychological insights, it was awarded Portugal's highest literary prize and made into a film.

Mario de Carvalho *A God Strolling in the Cool of the Evening.* Set in the third century AD, this fascinating novel traces the life of a Roman magistrate whose Luitanian town is threatened by subversive Christians and the prospect of attack from the Moors. Summing up the circumstances that ultimately destroyed the Roman Empire, the book won the Pegasus Prize for Fiction in 1996.

Lídia Jorge *The Migrant Painter of Birds.* Born near Albufeira in 1946, Lídia Jorge is one of Portugal's most respected contemporary writers. This beautifully written novel describes a girl's memories as she grows up in a small village close to the Atlantic, and in doing so poignantly captures a changing rural community.

Ray Keenoy, David Treece and **Paul Hyland** *The Babel Guide to the Fiction of Portugal, Brazil and Africa.* A tantalizing introduction to Portuguese literature, with a collection of reviews of the major works of Lusophone fiction since 1945.

Eugénio Lisboa (ed) *The Anarchist Banker and Other Portuguese Stories* and *Professor Pfiglzz and His Strange Companion and Other Portuguese Stories.* A fabulous two-volume collection of twentieth-century short stories, which gives more than a taste of the exuberance and talent currently proliferating in Portuguese literature. Stories by old favourites – Eça de Queirós, Pessoa, José Régio and Miguel Torga – are included too, mostly for the first time in English.

Eugénio Lisboa and **Helder Macedo** (eds) *The Dedalus Book of Portuguese Fantasy.* A rich feast of literary fantasy comprising short stories by the likes of Eça de Queirós and José de Almada Negreiros.

José Rodrigues Miguéis *Happy Easter.* A powerful and disturbing account of the distorted reality experienced by a schizophrenic, whose deprived childhood leads him to a self-destructive and tragic life in Lisbon; evocatively written and a gripping read.

🏃 **Fernando Pessoa** *Book of Disquiet, A Centenary Pessoa, The Education of the Stoic: The Only Manuscript of the Baron of Teive*. The country's best-known poet wrote *The Book of Disquiet* in prose; it's an unclassifiable text compiled from unordered fragments, part autobiography, part philosophical rambling. Regarded as a Modernist classic, the Penguin edition is the most complete English version. *A Centenary Pessoa* includes a selection of his prose and poetry, including his works under the pseudonym of Ricardo Reis. *The Education of the Stoic* was compiled in 1999 from the Pessoa archives in Lisbon. Written under the heteronym the *Baron of Teive*, it is a bleak work exploring the impossibility of producing perfect art by an artist who bins all his output before destroying himself. See also box on p.108.

🏃 **Eça de Queirós** *The Sin of Father Amaro; The City and the Mountains; Cousin Bazilio; The Maias; The Illustrious House of Ramires; To the Capital; The Yellow Sofa* and *Three Portraits*. One of Portugal's greatest writers, Eça de Queirós (or Queiroz; 1845–1900) introduced realism into Portuguese fiction with *The Sin of Father Amaro*, published in 1876. It was recently given contemporary treatment in a successful Mexican film, *The Crime of Father Amaro*. Over half a dozen of his novels have been translated into English; always highly readable, they present a cynical but affectionate picture of Portuguese society in the second half of the nineteenth century. His *English Letters*, written during his long stint as consul in England, is also well worth investigating (see also box on p.103).

José Régio *Flame Coloured Dress*. Like Eça de Queirós, Régio examines how society imposes restrictions on everyday life. *Flame Coloured Dress* is a series of vivid short stories, each one about the struggles of a woman but in very different circumstances, from a society woman to one suffering abject poverty.

Erich Maria Remarque *The Night in Lisbon*. Better known as author of *All Quiet On The Western Front*, German author Remarque writes with a similar detachment in this tale of a World War II refugee seeking an escape route from Europe. One night in Lisbon, he meets a stranger who has two tickets, and within hours their lives are inextricably linked in a harrowing and moving tale.

Mário de Sá-Carneiro *The Great Shadow* and *Lucio's Confessions*. *The Great Shadow* is a collection of short stories set against the backdrop of Lisbon in the early 1900s as the author describes his obsession with great art. Sá-Carneiro, who committed suicide at 26, writes with stunning intensity and originality about art, science, death, homosexual sex and insanity. Similar themes appear in *Lucio's Confessions*, in which a menage-a-trois between three artists ends in a death.

🏃 **José Saramago** *All the Names; Baltasar and Blimunda; Blindness; The History of the Siege of Lisbon; The Year of the Death of Ricardo Reis; The Gospel According to Jesus Christ; The Stone Raft; The Tale of the Unknown Island; Manual of Painting and Calligraphy; The Cave; The Double* and *Seeing*. Saramago won the Nobel prize for literature in 1998 and is Portugal's most famous living writer. His novels have come thick and fast and are mostly experimental, often dispensing with punctuation altogether; *Blindness* even avoided naming a single character in the book. The one to start with is *Ricardo Reis*, a magnificent novel whose theme is the return of Dr. Reis, after sixteen years in Brazil, to a Lisbon where the Salazar dictatorship is imminent and where Reis wanders the streets to be confronted by the past and the ghost of the writer Fernando Pessoa. In *Baltasar and Blimunda*, Saramago mixes fact with myth in an entertaining novel set around the building of the Convent of Mafra and the construction of the world's first flying machine.

Antonio Tabucchi *Declares Pereira, Requiem: A Hallucination* and *Fernando Pessoa* (with Maria José de Lancastre). Tabucchi is a highly regarded Italian author and biographer of Pessoa, who lived in Portugal for many years. In *Declares Pereira* he has re-created the repressive atmosphere of Salazar's Lisbon, tracing the experiences of a newspaper editor who questions his own lifestyle under a regime which he can no longer ignore. The book has recently been made into a film by Roberto Faenza. *Requiem: A Hallucination* is an imaginative and dreamlike journey around Lisbon. The unifying theme is food and drink, and the book even contains a note on recipes at the end.

Miguel Torga *The Creation of the World* and *Tales from the Mountain*. Twice nominated for the Nobel Prize before his death in 1995, Torga lived and set his stories in the wild Trás-os-Montes region. His pseudonym "Torga" is a tough species of heather which thrives in this rural, unforgiving landscape, where the fiercely independent characters of his

books battle to survive in a repressed society. Torga's harsh views of rural life in *Tales from the Mountain* led to the book being banned under the Salazar regime.

Gil Vicente *Three Discovery Plays: Auto da Barca do Inferno, Exortação da Guerra, Auto da Índia*. Three plays from the sixteenth-century scribe whom some consider the Portuguese equivalent of Shakespeare, with the original archaic Portuguese versions alongside English translations, and copious notes.

Robert Wilson *A Small Death in Lisbon*. A policeman attempts to find the murderer of a girl found dumped near a beach on the train line to Cascais, opening up a can of worms stretching back to the last World War. The novel presents an evocative account of the seedier side of contemporary Lisbon, though its potted summary of the last War is less convincing. A gripping page-turner from a British author who lives in Portugal.

Richard Zimler *The Last Kabbalist of Lisbon*. Kabbala is a magical art based on an esoteric interpretation of the Old Testament. American author Zimler, now a resident of Porto, writes an intense and compelling story of a Jewish kabbalist attempting to discover the mystery behind his uncle's murder during the massacre of New Christians in Lisbon in 1506. Based on historical fact, the story has been a bestseller in Portugal, Italy and Brazil.

Poetry

Luís de Camões *The Lusiads, Epic and Lyric, Selected Sonnets*. *The Lusiads* (Os Lusíadas) is Portugal's great national epic, written in 1572. Modelled on Virgil's *Aeneid*, it celebrates his ten-month voyage with Vasco da Gama, which opened

the sea route to India. The Oxford Classics is a good verse translation by Landeg White. *Epic and Lyric* includes extracts from *The Lusiads* together with other shorter poems, while *Selected Sonnets* shows the development of his remarkable lyrical poetry both before and after his experiences in Africa and India.

Sofia de Mello Breyner *Breyner Log Book: Selected Poems*. Evocative selection of translated poems from one of the country's foremost writers, winner of the 1999 Prémio Camões.

🏃 **Fernando Pessoa** *Pessoa: Selected Poems*. Pessoa wrote his poetry under several different identities, which he called heteronyms. Those wanting a brief introduction to the range of his different "voices" are well served by Jonathan Griffin's elegant translations of four of them. *A Centenary Pessoa* – this superlative anthology of poems, prose, letters and photographs is the most comprehensive selection of Pessoa's output yet published in English. *Fernando Pessoa*, available only in Portugal (Hazan, Portugal), is a revealing collection of documents and photographs of the author at work, with an introduction by Antonio Tabucchi.

Pedro Tamen *Honey and Poison: Selected Poems*. Lisbon law graduate Tamen is regarded as one of Portugal's leading contemporary poets; his poems of passion capture the distinctive sights and emotions of a country which has moved from dictatorship to democracy during his lifetime.

Food and wine

Jean Anderson *Food of Portugal*. The best of the cookbooks by non-Portuguese writers, a wonderful tour of the gastronomic horizon with easy-to-follow recipes.

Rainer Horbelt and Sonja Spindler *Algarve Country Cooking* (Vista Ibérica, Portugal). A series of regional recipes based round local anecdotes and the four seasons; well translated from German and a charming insight into rural Algarve traditions.

Richard Mayson *The Wines and Vineyards of Portugal*. A wide ranging, award-winning account of all you need to know about Portuguese wines by a passionate expert in the field.

Ana Patuleia Ortins *Portuguese Homestyle Cooking*. All the classics: easy-to-follow regional recipes collected by a first-generation Portuguese American, peppered with fun anecdotes, stories and photos.

🏃 **Edite Vieira** *The Taste of Portugal*. A delight to read, let alone cook from. Vieira combines snippets of history and passages from Portuguese writers (very well translated) with anecdotes to illustrate her dishes; highly recommended.

Guides

Brian and Eileen Anderson *Landscapes of Portugal* (Sunflower Books online only; ⊛www.sunflowerbooks.co.uk). Regional books with maps and small photos detailing walks – covering the Algarve and Lisbon areas, and northern Portugal; there are also car tours and some practical information.

Bethan Davies and Ben Cole *Walking in Portugal*. Dependable guide to trekking in the national parks of Gerês, Serra da Estrela, Montesinho and Serra de São Mamede.

Chris Nelson and Demi Taylor *Surfing Europe*. A glossy tome for the dedicated surfer, with tips on how to find and surf the best Atlantic waves from Orkney to Morocco. The Portugal section is detailed and comprehensive, backed up by some fine colour photographs.

Oleg Polunin and B.E. Smythies *Flowers of South-West Europe: A Field Guide.* The best available guide to the Portuguese flora.

Laurence Rose *Where to Watch Birds in Spain and Portugal.* Comprehensive guide to some of Europe's finest and most environmentally sensitive wildlife sites, with practical information on how to get there and when to go. Interesting reading for amateurs as well as being invaluable for ardent ornithologists.

Language

Language

Language

I f you have some knowledge of Spanish you won't have much problem reading Portuguese. Understanding it when it's spoken, though, is another matter: pronunciation is entirely different and at first even the easiest words are hard to distinguish. If you're stuck, people may understand spoken Spanish (albeit reluctantly) and in the cities and tourist areas English and French are also widely spoken. Even so, it's well worth the effort to master at least the rudiments; once you've started to figure out the words it gets a lot easier very quickly.

The **pronunciation guide** below and the words on pp.654–657 will equip you with the basics, and there's also a full **menu reader**, so you shouldn't ever be stuck for choice in a restaurant. For more detail, purchase the *Rough Guide Portuguese Phrasebook*, set out dictionary-style for easy access.

Pronunciation

The chief difficulty with pronunciation is its lack of clarity — consonants tend to be slurred, while vowels are nasal and often contracted to the point of being ignored.

Consonants

The **consonants** are, at least, consistent:

C is soft before E and I, hard otherwise unless it has a cedilla – açucar (sugar) is pronounced "assookar".

CH is somewhat softer than in English; chá (tea) sounds like "shah".

J is pronounced like the "s" in pleasure, as is

G except when it comes before a "hard" vowel (A, O and U).

LH sounds like "lyuh" (Batalha is pronounced "Batalyuh").

M as in English, except at the end of a word when it's more like a nasal "-ng" – com (with) is pronounced "kong" (without sounding the G).

Q is always pronounced as a "K".

S before a consonant or at the end of a word becomes "sh", otherwise it's as in English – Cascais is pronounced "Kashkaish", adeus (goodbye) is "a-day-ush".

X is also pronounced "sh" – caixa (cash desk) is pronounced "kaisha".

Vowels

Vowels are often difficult for English-speaking tongues to get around. The only way to learn is to listen: accents, ã, ô or é turn them into longer, more familiar sounds.

When two vowels come together they continue to be enunciated separately except in the case of **EI** and **OU** – which sound like the "ay" in day and the "oh" in dough respectively.

E at the end of a word is virtually silent unless it has an accent, so that *verde* (green) is pronounced "verd", while *café* is pronounced "ca-feh" (with the emphasis on the accented vowel).

The tilde over **Ã** or **Õ** renders the pronunciation much like the French -an and -on endings only more nasal.

More common is **ÃO** (as in *pão*, bread – *são*, saint – *limão*, lemon), which sounds something like a strangled yelp of "Ow!" cut off in midstream.

Portuguese words and phrases

Greetings and questions

olá; bom dia	hello; good morning	de nada	you're welcome
boa tarde/noite	good afternoon/night	fala Inglês?	Do you speak English?
adeus, até logo	goodbye, see you later	sou…	I am…
tudo bem?	everything all right?	Americano/a; Inglês /Inglesa	American/English
está bem	it's all right/OK		
não sei	I don't know	Australiano/a; Neozeelandês/ Neozeelandesa	Australian/ New Zealander
não compreendo	I don't understand		
como?	sorry/pardon me?		
como se diz isto em Português?	What's this called in Portuguese?	Canadiano/a	Canadian
		Irlandês/Irlandesa; Escocês/Escosesa; Galês/Galesa	Irish/Scottish/ Welsh
pode escrever isso?	can you write it down?		
sabe…?	do you know…?		
pode…?	could you…?	Como se chama? (chamo-me…)	What's your name? (my name is…)
não faz mal	it doesn't matter		

Useful words

sim; não	yes; no	aqui; ali	here; there
por favor/se faz favor	please	perto; longe	near; far
obrigado/a*	thank you	este/a; aquele/a	this; that
desculpe; com licença	sorry; excuse me	agora; mais tarde	now; later
		mais; menos	more; less
hoje; amanhã; ontem	today; tomorrow; yesterday	grande; pequeno	big; little
onde; que	where; what		
quando; porquê	when; why	* Obrigado agrees with the sex of the person speaking – a woman says obrigada, a man obrigado.	
como; quanto	how; how much		
com; sem	with; without		

Signs

aberto; fechado	open; closed	elevador	lift
empurre; puxe	push; pull	perigo/perigoso	danger/dangerous
entrada; saída	entrance; exit	pré-pagamento	pre-payment required
fecha a porta	close the door	senhoras; homens	women; men
dormidas/quartos	rooms	lavabo(s)/casa de banho	toilet(s)/bathroom
ar condicionado	air-conditioned		

Public transport

Onde é...	Where is...
a estação de camionetas/ terminal rodoviária?	...the bus station?
...a paragem de autocarro para...	...the bus stop for...?
...a estação de comboios	...the railway station?
Há uma camioneta para...?	Is there a bus to...?
Donde parte o autocarro para...?	Where does the bus to ... leave from?
Paragem	Bus stop
Pare aqui por favor	Stop here please
Qual é o destino deste comboio?	What is the destination of this train?
É este o comboio para...?	Is this the train for...?
A que horas parte?	What time does it leave?
(chega a...?)	(arrive at...?)
Queria um bilhete para...	I'd like a ticket to...
ida e volta	return/round trip

Driving and directions

Qual é a estrada para...?	Which is the road to...?
Para ir a...?	How do I get to...?
esquerda, direita	left, right
sempre em frente	straight ahead
ar; pneu	air; tyre
óleo	oil
gasolina; gasóleo (sem chumbo)	petrol; diesel (unleaded)
Encha, se faz favor	Fill it [the tank] please
desvio	diversion
obras	(road)works
passagem proibida	no entry
(rua) de sentido único	one-way (street)
proibido estacionar /estacionamento proibido	no parking
Posso estacionar aqui?	Can I park here?
autoestrada	motorway
portagem	tollbooth
bomba de gasolina	petrol station
carta de conduçao; documentos	driving licence; documents

Finding accommodation

Há uma pensão/ aqui perto?	Is there a pension/ campsite near here?
Queria um quarto	I'd like a room
...para uma pessoa	...for one person
(duas pessoas)	(two people)
...com duas camas/ um casal	...with two beds/a double bed
...com duche/casa de banho privado	...with a shower/ private bathroom
É para uma noite (semana)	It's for one night (week)
Posso ver?	May I see?
Quanto custa?	How much is it?
Está bem, fico com ele	OK, I'll take it
É caro,	It's expensive,
Há um quarto mais barato?	Is there a cheaper room?
chave	key
Pode-se acampar aqui?	Can we camp here?

Shopping

O que é isso?	what's that?	peso/pesar	weight/to weigh
Quanto é?	how much is it?	quilo	kilo
Queria um saco	I'd like a bag	unidade	unit
fatias/fatiado	slices/sliced	padaria	bakery
fresco	fresh	talho	butcher
lata, em lata	can, tinned	banco; câmbio	bank; change
litro	litre	correios	post office
mercado	market	(dois) selos	(two) stamps
mini-mercado/ mercearia	mini-market/grocery	farmácia	pharmacy/chemist
supermercado	supermarket	incluído IVA	includes VAT
biológico/produtos biológicos	organic/organic produce		

Days of the week

domingo	Sunday	quinta-feira	Thursday
segunda-feira	Monday	sexta-feira	Friday
terça-feira	Tuesday	sábado	Saturday
quarta-feira	Wednesday		

Months

janeiro	January	julho	July
fevereiro	February	agosto	August
março	March	setembro	September
abril	April	outubro	October
maio	May	novembro	November
junho	June	dezembro	December

The time

Que horas são?	What time is it?	uma e dez	ten past one
A que horas?	(At) what time?	uma e quinze	quarter past one
à/às...	at...	uma e vinte	twenty past one
meio-dia	midday, noon	uma e meia	half past one
meia-noite	midnight	quinze para as duas/duas menos um quarto	quarter to two
uma da manhã	one in the morning (1am)		
uma da tarde	one in the afternoon (1pm)	dez para as duas /duas menos dez	ten to two
sete da tarde	seven in the evening		

Numbers

um/uma	1	dezoito	18
dois/duas	2	dezanove	19
três	3	vinte	20
quatro	4	vinte e um	21
cinco	5	trinta	30
seis	6	quarenta	40
sete	7	cinquenta	50
oito	8	sessenta	60
nove	9	setenta	70
dez	10	oitenta	80
onze	11	noventa	90
doze	12	cem	100
treze	13	cento e um	101
catorze	14	duzentos	200
quinze	15	quinhentos	500
dezasseis	16	mil	1000
dezassete	17	dois mil	2000

Menu reader

See "Food and drink" in Basics, pp.45–52, for a full explanation of where to eat what, and the drinks to accompany your meal. The lists below should help you figure out what you're ordering.

Basics

Açucár	Sugar
Arroz	Rice
Azeite	Olive Oil
Azeitonas	Olives
Broa	Cornbread
Farinha	Flour
Manteiga	Butter
Massa	Pasta
Molho de tomate /piri-piri	Tomato/chilli sauce
Óleo	Oil (except olive oil, *azeite*)
Omeleta	Omelette
Ovos (cozidos /escalfados /mexidos/quentes /estrelados)	Eggs (hard-boiled /poached/scrambled /soft-boiled/fried)
Pão (trigo/centeio /caseiro/intégral)	Bread (wheat/rye /rustic/wholemeal)
Pimenta (preta /branca)	Pepper (black/white)
Queijo	Cheese
Sal	Salt
Salada	Salad
Vinagre	Vinegar

In a restaurant

Ementa (turística /do dia)	Menu (set menu)	Acepipes	Appetizers
Prato do dia	Dish of the day	Entrada	Starter
Especialidades	Specialities	Sobremesa	Dessert
Carta dos vinhos	Wine list	Prato	Plate
Dose (uma dose /meia dose)	Portion (full/half)	Chávena	Cup
Pequeno almoço	Breakfast	Copo	Glass
Almoço	Lunch	Garrafa	Bottle
Jantar	Dinner	Faca	Knife
Comidas	Snacks	Garfo	Fork
Petiscos	Snacks	Colher	Spoon
		Conta	Bill

Cooking terms

A vapor	Steamed	Guisado	Stewed
Assado/no espeto	Roasted/spit-roasted	Mexido	Scrambled
Bem passado/mal passado	Well done/rare	Molho	Sauce
		Na brasa	Char-grilled, braised
Caril	Curry	No churrasco	Char-grilled
Caseiro	Home-made	No forno	Baked
Cozido	Boiled/stewed	Panado	Bread-crumbed and pan-fried
Empada	Pie		
Ensopado de...	Soup or stew of...	Picante	Spicy/hot
Estrelado	Fried	Piri-piri	With chilli sauce
Frio	Cold	Quente	Hot
Frito	Fried	Recheado	Stuffed
Fumado	Smoked	Salgado	Salted
Fundido	Melted	Salteado	Sautéed
Gratinado	Gratin	Temperado	Marinated
Grelhado/na grelha	Grilled		

Snacks

Amendoins	Peanuts	Pastéis de carne	Puff pastries stuffed with sausage meat
Bifana	Slice of grilled or fried pork on bread	Pastéis/bolinhos de bacalhau	Codfish-and-potato cakes
Chamuça	Samosa	Prego no pão/prato	Steak sandwich; with a fried egg on top
Croquete	Deep-fried meat patty		
Empada de frango/ atum	Chicken/tuna pie	Sande(s)	Sandwich(es)
Isca de bacalhau	Battered cod fishcake with egg	Tosta mista	Grilled ham-and-cheese sandwich
Lanches	Sweetish bread stuffed with ham	Tremoços	Pickled lupin seeds, to go with your beer

Soups (Sopas)

Caldo de castanhas	Chestnut soup
Caldo verde	Cabbage/potato broth (with or without *chouriço*)
Canja de galinha	Chicken broth with rice and boiled egg yolks
Gaspacho	Chilled vegetable soup, a summer dish in the south
Sopa à alentejana	Garlic/bread soup with poached egg on top
Sopa de feijão verde /grão/legumes /marisco/peixe	Green bean/chickpea /vegetable/shellfish /fish soup
Sopa de tomate	Tomato soup, in the Alentejo often made with quails' eggs or beaten egg

Fish (peixe) and shellfish (mariscos)

Ameijoas	Clams
Anchovas	Anchovies
Atum	Tuna
Besugo	Bream
Camarões	Shrimp
Caranguejo	Crab
Carapau	Mackerel
Cherne	Sea bream
Chocos	Cuttlefish
Congro	Conger eel
Dourada	Bream
Enguia	Eel
(Peixe) Espada	Scabbard fish (absolutely not be confused with…)
Espadarte	Swordfish
Gambas	Prawns
Garoupa	Grouper
Lagosta	Lobster
Lagostim	Giant prawns
Lampreia	Lamprey (similar to eel)
Linguado	Sole
Lulas	Squid
Mexilhões	Mussels
Ostras	Oysters
Pargo	Snapper
Peixe Gale	John Dory
Perceves	Goose barnacles
Pescada	Hake
Polvo	Octopus
Robalo	Sea bass
Salmão	Salmon
Salmonete	Red mullet
Santolas	Spider crabs
Sapateiras	Common crabs
Sarda	Mackerel
Sardinhas	Sardines
Tamboril	Monkfish
Truta	Trout
Vieiras	Scallops

Meat (carne), poultry (aves) and game (caça)

Almôndegas	Meatballs
Bife	Steak
Borrego	Lamb
Bucho	Haggis
Cabrito	Kid goat
Carne de porco	Pork
Carne picada	Mince meat
Carneiro	Mutton
Chouriço	Cured sausage
Coelho	Rabbit
Cordeiro	Lamb
Cordoniz	Quail
Costeleta	Chop/cutlet
Dobrada	Tripe
Enchidos	Smoked sausages
Entracosto	Spare rib
Escalope	Escalope
Farinheira	Floury sausage
Febras	Thin pork steaks

Fiambre	Boiled ham	Pata/Pé	Hoof/foot
Fígado	Liver	Pato	Duck
Frango	Chicken	Perdiz	Partridge
Fumeiros	Smoked meats	Perna	Leg
Javali	Wild boar	Perú	Turkey
Leitão	Suckling pig	Picanha	Sliced rump steak, Brazilian-style
Linguiça	Cured sausage		
Lombo	Loin, fillet or tenderloin	Pomba	Pigeon
		Presunto	Smoked ham
Medalhão	Medallion	Rim	Kidney
Miolos	Brain	Salpicão	Smoked sausage
Moela	Gizzard	Salsicha	Sausage
Morcela	Black pudding, blood sausage	Tripas	Tripe
		Vitela	Veal
Paio	Cured sausage		

Ⓛ Vegetables (legumes or hortaliças) and salad (salada)

Abacate	Avocado	Couve-flor	Cauliflower
Abóbora	Pumpkin	Ervilha	Pea
Agriões	Watercress	Espargos	Asparagus
Aipo	Celery	Espinafre	Spinach
Alcachofra	Artichoke	Fava	Broad bean
Alface	Lettuce	Feijão	Bean
Alho	Garlic	Feijão-frade	Black-eyed bean
Alho Francês	Leek	Feijão-verde/ -vermelho	Green bean/kidney bean
Batatas (fritas /cozidas/a murro)	Potatoes (French fries /boiled/jacket)	Grão(-de-bico)	Chickpea
Berlingela	Aubergine	Lentilha	Lentil
Cebola	Onion	Nabo	Turnip
Cenoura	Carrot	Pepino	Cucumber
Coentro	Coriander	Pimento	Sweet pepper
Cogumelo	Mushroom	Salsa	Parsley
Couve	Cabbage	Tomate	Tomato

Fruit (fruta)

Ameixas	Plums	Laranja	Orange
Ananás/Abacaxi	Pineapple	Limão	Lemon
Castanha	Chestnut	Maçã	Apple
Cerejas	Cherries	Manga	Mango
Damascos	Apricots	Maracujá	Passion fruit
Figo	Fig	Melancia	Water melon
Framboesas	Raspberries	Melão	Melon
Frutas silvestres	Berries	Meloa	Cantaloupe or Carmargue melon
Goiaba	Guava		
Groselhas	Red currants	Morangos	Strawberries

Pêra	Pear	Tangerina	Tangerine
Pêssego	Peach	Toranja	Grapefruit
Romã	Pomegranate	Uvas	Grapes

Desserts (sobremesas), sweets (doces) and pastries (pastéis)

Arroz doce	Rice pudding	Pudim, Pudim flan	Crème caramel
Bolinho	Bun	Queijadas	Cheese cakes
Bolo	Cake	Sorbet	Sorbet
Broa de mel	Soft cornflour and honey cake	Suspiro	Meringue
		Tarte	Tart
Doces conventuais	Sweet egg-based "Convent desserts"	Torta	Roll
		...de arroz/feijão /cenoura/chila	...with rice/beans /carrot/pumpkin
Gelado	Ice cream		
Maçapão	Marzipan	...de amêndoa /amendoim/noz /nata/mel	...with almonds /peanuts/walnuts or nuts/pumpkin/cream or custard/honey
Mel	Honey		
Mil-folhas	Puff pastry (mille feuille)		
Pastel de nata	Custard tart		

Portuguese specialities

Açorda (de marisco)	Bread-based stew (with shellfish, garlic and coriander)	na brasa	roasted with sliced potatoes
Alheira	A fried pork-free "sausage" from Trás-os-Montes, traditionally of minced chicken and bread – more like a rissole than a sausage	à Gomes de Sá	sliced, baked with potatoes, served with boiled eggs and olives, speciality of Porto, named after a 19th century cod merchant turned chef
		à lagar (lagareiro)	roasted in lots of olive oil (a *lagar* is an olive-oil press), served with roast potatoes
Ameijoas à Bulhão Pato	Clams sautéed with garlic and coriander (named after a 19th century Portuguese poet)		
		com natas	baked with cream
Arroz de...	Rice...	com todos	"with everything", ie boiled potatoes, cabbage and eggs, (a Christmas dish)
...cabidela/pato/ polvo	enriched with chicken blood/with shredded duck/with octopus		
Arroz de mariscos	A thick, soupy seafood rice	Bife de atum de cebolada	Tuna steak with stewed onions, cooked in an earthenware dish
Bacalhau...	Dried salt cod, soaked and then cooked...		
com batatas e grão	with boiled potatoes and chickpeas	Bife à Portuguesa	Beef steak, topped with mustard sauce and a fried egg
à brás	fried, with egg, onions and potatoes		

Cabrito assado no forno	Oven-baked kid goat
Caldeirada de peixe	Fish stew, with a base of onions, tomatoes and potatoes
Cataplana	The name of the copper cooking vessel – most commonly used to cook shellfish, particularly clams (*ameijoas*), with smoked ham, pepper and onion
Chanfana	Goat/kid stew, braised in red wine, a Beiras dish
Coelho à caçadora	"Hunter's rabbit", a stew with tomatoes and garlic
Cozido à portuguesa	Boiled casserole of pork, beef, blood sausage, offal, beans, cabbage and carrots, served with rice
Ensopado de borrego	Lamb stew
Espetada mista	Mixed meat kebab (usually pork and beef, with onion and green pepper); *espedatas* of squid/shrimp are also common
Feijoada	White bean stew, reminiscent of a cassoulet. *à moda de Trás-os-Montes* (with root vegetables, cabbage, beef and *chouriço*); *à moda do Porto* (with *chouriço* and tripe)
Filetes (de pescada)	"Fillets", nearly always battered or bread-crumbed fish fillets, usually served with tomato rice

Francesinha	The "little French thing", a Porto speciality – a grilled steak, ham and sausage sandwich, smothered in melted cheese, doused in spicy beer-and-tomato sauce
Frango no churrasco	Barbecued chicken; sometimes with piri-piri (chilli) sauce
Frango na púcara	Chicken casserole made with wine, port and brandy (a *púcara* is the earthenware pot it's cooked in)
Leitão assado	Roast suckling pig
Lulas recheadas	Stuffed squid (with meat and herbs)
Massa(da) de…	Soupy pasta dish, usually with *peixe* (fish)
Migas (à Alentejana)	Fried maize-bread-based dish (with pork, garlic and spices)
Papas de sarrabulho	Thick blood- and bread-based stew with herbs and spices
Pescada com todos	Poached hake, with potatoes, boiled eggs and greens
Porco à alentejana	Pork cooked with clams, served with fried potatoes and often topped with a few pickled vegetables (originally from the Alentejo)
Rodizio	Beloved of Brazilian restaurants every where – a fixed-price buffet of barbecued meats, sliced from skewers at the table, served with black beans, rice and salad

| Rojões (à Minho) | Cubed pork (marinaded in wine, cumin and garlic), roasted with chunks of blood sausage and potato (from the Minho) | Tripas à moda do Porto | Tripe stewed with beans and vegetables |
| | | Truta com/recheado com presunto | Trout stuffed with smoked ham |

Glossary of Portuguese words

Architectural, historical and religious terms

Anta	Prehistoric megalith tomb	Infanta	Princess
		Infante	Prince
Azulejo	Glazed, painted tile	Manuelino	Flamboyant, marine-influenced style of late Gothic architecture developed in the reign of Manuel I (1495–1521)
Capela	Chapel; *capela-mor* is a chancel or sanctuary		
Capela dos ossos	Ossuary		
Castelo	Castle		
Citânia	Prehistoric/Celtic hill settlement	Moçárabe	Moorish-Arabic (usually of architecture or a design)
Claustro	Cloister		
Convento	Convent, though just as often an old church	Mosteiro	Monastery, or just as often an old church
Coro	Central, often enclosed, part of church built for the choir	Mudéjar	Moorish-style architecture and decoration
		Nossa senhora (N.S.)	Our Lady – the Virgin Mary
Dom, dona	Courtesy titles (sir, madam) usually applied to kings and queens	Retábulo	Altarpiece – usually large, carved and heavily gilt
Ermida	Remote chapel, not necessarily a hermitage	Sala do capítulo	Chapterhouse
		Sé	Cathedral
Fortaleza	Fort	Torre de menagem	Keep of a castle
Igreja	Church; *igreja matriz* is a parish church		

General terms

Adega	Wine cellar or winery, often also a wine bar or restaurant
Alameda	Promenade
Albufeira	Reservoir or lagoon
Aldeia	Small village or hamlet
Artesanato	Handicraft shop
Bairro	Quarter, area (of a town); *alto* is upper, *baixo* lower
Baixa	Low; used to mean commercial/shopping centre of town
Barragem	Dam
Cachoeira	Waterfall
Caldas	Mineral springs or spa complex
Câmara municipal	Town hall
Campo	Square or field
Centro comercial	Shopping centre
Centro histórico	Historic centre
Chafariz	Public fountain
Cidade	City
Correios	Post office, abbreviated CTT
Cruzeiro	Cross
Eléctrico	Tramcar
Elevador	Elevator or funicular railway
Espigueiro	Grain shed on stilts, common in the north
Esplanada	Seafront promenade
Estação	Station
Estrada	Road; Estrada Nacional is a main road
Farmácia	Pharmacy
Feira	Fair or market
Festa	Festival or carnival
Fonte	Fountain or spring
Freguesia	Parish (*Junta da Freguesia* is the local council)
Grutas	Caves
Ilha	Island
Jardim	Garden
Lago	Lake
Largo	Square
Miradouro	Belvedere or viewpoint
Paço	Palace or country house
Paços do concelho	Town hall
Palácio	Palace or country house; *palácio real*, royal palace
Parque	Park
Parque nacional /natural	National/Natural Park or Reserve
Pelourinho	Stone pillory
Poço	Well
Pombal	Pigeon house
Ponte	Bridge
Praça	Square
Praça de touros	Bullring
Praia (fluvial)	Beach (river beach)
Quinta	Country estate, farm or villa
Ria	Narrow, open-ended lagoon where sand bars block a river's mouth
Ribeiro	Stream
Rio	River
Romaria	Pilgrimage/festival
Serra	Mountain or mountain range
Solar	Manor house or important town mansion
Termas	Thermal springs or spa complex
Tourada	Bullfight
Vila	Town

Avoid Guilt Trips

Buy fair trade coffee + bananas ✓

Save energy - use low energy bulbs ✓

   - don't leave tv on standby ✓

Offset carbon emissions from flight to Madrid ✓

Send goat to Africa ✓

Join Tourism Concern today ✓

Slowly, the world is changing.
Together we can, and will, make a difference.

Tourism Concern is the only UK registered charity fighting exploitation in one of the largest industries on earth: people forced from their homes in order that holiday resorts can be built, sweatshop labour conditions in hotels and destruction of the environment are just some of the issues that we tackle.

Sending people on a guilt trip is not something we do. We know as well as anyone that holidays are precious. But you can help us to ensure that tourism always benefits the local communities involved.

Call 020 7133 3330
or visit **tourismconcern.org.uk** to find out how.

A year's membership of Tourism Concern costs just £20 (£12 unwaged) - that's 38 pence a week, less than the cost of a pint of milk, organic of course.

Fighting Exploitation in Tourism

TourismConcern

Small print and
Index

A Rough Guide to Rough Guides

Published in 1982, the first Rough Guide – to Greece – was a student scheme that became a publishing phenomenon. Mark Ellingham, a recent graduate in English from Bristol University, had been travelling in Greece the previous summer and couldn't find the right guidebook. With a small group of friends he wrote his own guide, combining a highly contemporary, journalistic style with a thoroughly practical approach to travellers' needs.

The immediate success of the book spawned a series that rapidly covered dozens of destinations. And, in addition to impecunious backpackers, Rough Guides soon acquired a much broader and older readership that relished the guides' wit and inquisitiveness as much as their enthusiastic, critical approach and value-for-money ethos.

These days, Rough Guides include recommendations from shoestring to luxury and cover more than 200 destinations around the globe, including almost every country in the Americas and Europe, more than half of Africa and most of Asia and Australasia. Our ever-growing team of authors and photographers is spread all over the world, particularly in Europe, the USA and Australia.

In the early 1990s, Rough Guides branched out of travel, with the publication of Rough Guides to World Music, Classical Music and the Internet. All three have become benchmark titles in their fields, spearheading the publication of a wide range of books under the Rough Guide name.

Including the travel series, Rough Guides now number more than 350 titles, covering: phrasebooks, waterproof maps, music guides from Opera to Heavy Metal, reference works as diverse as Conspiracy Theories and Shakespeare, and popular culture books from iPods to Poker. Rough Guides also produce a series of more than 120 World Music CDs in partnership with World Music Network.

Visit www.roughguides.com to see our latest publications.

Rough Guide travel images are available for commercial licensing at www.roughguidespictures.com

Rough Guide credits

Text editor: Helena Smith
Layout: Ankur Guha
Cartography: Amod Singh
Picture editor: Mark Thomas
Production: Aimee Hampson
Proofreader: Helen Castell
Cover design: Chloë Roberts
Photographer: Eddie Gerald, Demetrio Carrasco
Editorial: London Kate Berens, Claire Saunders, Ruth Blackmore, Polly Thomas, Richard Lim, Alison Murchie, Karoline Densley, Andy Turner, Keith Drew, Edward Aves, Nikki Birrell, Alice Park, Sarah Eno, Lucy White, Ruth Tidball, Jo Kirby, James Smart, Natasha Foges, Joe Staines, Duncan Clark, Peter Buckley, Matthew Milton, Tracy Hopkins; **New York** Andrew Rosenberg, Steven Horak, AnneLise Sorensen, Amy Hegarty, April Isaacs, Sean Mahoney, Ella Steim, Anna Owens, Joseph Petta
Design & Pictures: London Scott Stickland, Dan May, Diana Jarvis, Jj Luck, Harriet Mills, Nicole Newman; **Delhi** Umesh Aggarwal, Ajay Verma, Jessica Subramanian, Pradeep Thapliyal, Sachin Tanwar, Anita Singh, Madhavi Singh

Production: Katherine Owers
Cartography: London Maxine Repath, Ed Wright, Katie Lloyd-Jones; **Delhi** Jai Prakash Mishra, Rajesh Chhibber, Ashutosh Bharti, Rajesh Mishra, Animesh Pathak, Jasbir Sandhu, Karobi Gogoi, Alakananda Bhattacharya, Athokpam Jotinkumar
Online: New York Jennifer Gold, Kristin Mingrone, Cree Lawson; **Delhi** Manik Chauhan, Narender Kumar, Rakesh Kumar, Amit Kumar, Amit Verma, Rahul Kumar, Ganesh Sharma, Debojit Borah
Marketing & Publicity: London Niki Hanmer, Louise Maher, Jess Carter; Anna Paynton, Nikki Causer; **New York** Geoff Colquitt, Megan Kennedy, Katy Ball; **Delhi** Reem Khokhar
Special Projects Editor: Philippa Hopkins
Manager India: Punita Singh
Series Editor: Mark Ellingham
Reference Director: Andrew Lockett
Publishing Coordinator: Megan McIntyre
Publishing Director: Martin Dunford

Publishing information

This twelfth edition published April 2007 by **Rough Guides Ltd**,
80 Strand, London WC2R 0RL
345 Hudson St, 4th Floor,
New York, NY 10014, USA
14 Local Shopping Centre, Panchsheel Park,
New Delhi 110017, India
Distributed by the Penguin Group
Penguin Books Ltd,
80 Strand, London WC2R 0RL
Penguin Group (USA)
375 Hudson Street, NY 10014, USA
Penguin Group (Australia)
250 Camberwell Road, Camberwell,
Victoria 3124, Australia
Penguin Books Canada Ltd,
10 Alcorn Avenue, Toronto, Ontario,
Canada M4V 1E4
Penguin Group (NZ)
67 Apollo Drive, Mairangi Bay, Auckland 1310,
New Zealand
Cover concept by Peter Dyer.

Typeset in Bembo and Helvetica to an original design by Henry Iles.

Printed in Italy by LegoPrint S.p.A

680pp includes index

A catalogue record for this book is available from the British Library

ISBN: 9781843537380

Help us update

We've gone to a lot of effort to ensure that the twelfth edition of **The Rough Guide to Portugal** is accurate and up to date. However, things change – places get "discovered", opening hours are notoriously fickle, restaurants and rooms raise prices or lower standards. If you feel we've got it wrong or left something out, we'd like to know, and if you can remember the address, the price, the time, the phone number, so much the better. We'll credit all contributions, and send a copy of the next edition (or any other Rough Guide if you prefer) for the best letters. Everyone who writes to us and isn't already a subscriber will receive a copy of our full-colour thrice-yearly newsletter. Please mark letters: "**Rough Guide Portugal Update**" and send to: Rough Guides, 80 Strand, London WC2R 0RL, or Rough Guides, 4th Floor, 345 Hudson St, New York, NY 10014. Or send an email to **mail@roughguides.com**
Have your questions answered and tell others about your trip at
www.roughguides.atinfopop.com

Acknowledgements

Jules Brown and Matthew Hancock would like to thank Teresa Ventura at ICEP for her help, and Helena Smith, Ankur Guha, Amod Singh, Mark Thomas, Joanna Kirby and Helen Castell at Rough Guides for their hard work on this edition.

Jules would also like to thank Carine Batista at Turismo do Alentejo and Luisa Azevedo at ADETURN for their kind assistance. Zé told me all sorts of helpful things about Portuguese politics, media and music, while John's specialist subjects (football terrace chants, moscatel, bathroom plumbing) came in very useful too. I had one great walk in Peneda-Gerês (thanks Matthew), another in the Serra da Estrela (thanks Yves) and a completely hopeless time following non-existent tracks in the Algarve (thanks a lot Capt. I. Little). Mum, Dad, Chris, Simon, Michael, Toby, Stacey, Linda, Alison and the Two Marks have all been good company in Portugal at various times. Kate, as usual, has borne with good grace

my absences on "work trips" to beaches, bars and restaurants, for which I'm eternally grateful – meanwhile, Lyn and Rowl, Andy and Yves, and Hannah and Derek have helped make living in Portugal a pleasure. And finally, where would I be without the constant attentions of my two best boys Fox and Rips? In the Bahamas, drinking cocktails, that's where.

Matthew would also like to thank Joe Budd for Lisbon nightlife and Amanda Tomlin, Alex and Olivia for ideas and support. Also Júlio Pires and Manuel Cabral Morais (members of ILGA Portugal); Vitor Carriço at the Lisbon Tourist Board; Luisa Azevedo, Carlos Oliveira, José Arragão and Luís Pinto at ICEP; Carla Rosa Fernandes; Luís Coelho at the Algarve Tourist Board; Julie Jarratt at Magellan; Maria do Céu Sá Lima at Turihab; Jules Brown for ideas and walks; Luke and Paula for their usual assistance; everyone who helped me with accommodation.

SMALL PRINT

Readers' letters

Thanks to all those readers of the eleventh edition who took the trouble to write in with their amendments and additions. Apologies for any misspellings or omissions.

Evangelos Aktsalis, Maureen and Lorne Anton, Guy Archer, Theresa Arnold and Teresa Pereira, Robert Asher, James Aston, Alina Badus and John Parejko, Garth Baker, M. Bazany, J Beatson, Rosie Belcher, Richard Bennett, Asier Berra, Caroline Bolhoven, Alan Bolister, J. Carpenter, Jonathan and Chris Chapman, Judy Consden, Mary Cox and John Hopkins, Sandra Cunha, Paddy Dolan, Beryl and Dave Frost, Susie Hargreaves, Victor and Hellena Gallant, H Greer, Red Hunter, Peter Jørgensen, Mark Judd, Sadiq Kassamo, Nick Kennedy, Geralya Kitov, Mats Kullstedt and Eva Noble, Beatrice Lönnkvist, Paulo Lopes, Jonas Ludvigsson,

Terence Maguire, Muriel and Andr Mandi, Kaye and Richard Morton, Knut Roald Myhre, Timothy Nodder, Claire O'Connor, Peter and Mary-Rose O'Grady, Dave Owen, John Owens, Jean and Michael Pooley, Johnny Pring, Kevin Protheroe, RE Prout, N Raposo, Adriana Rendon, David Robertson, Philippe Do Rosaria, Barry Sheldon, Andrew Sheppard, Alan Sinclair, Marian Smith, Margaret Taylor, Lilia Teixeira, Tony Titchener, Barbara Tyson, Bjorn Wahlin and Ylva Svensson, Haydn Walker, Henry Warren and family, Eve Watkins-Buskirk, John Weldon, Henrik Wigestrand, Derek Wilde.

Photo credits

Index

Map entries are in colour.

I

INDEX

Map symbols

maps are listed in the full index using coloured text

-----	International boundary		⌂	Casa abrigo
----	Chapter boundary		∩	Arch
▬▬▬	Motorway		⊥	Gardens
═══	Road		⊙	Statue/monument
▬▬▬	Pedestrianized road		✈	Airport
⊓⊓⊓⊓	Steps		★	Bus stop
::::::::::	Unpaved road		Ⓜ	Metro station
}::::::::{	Underpass		🅿	Parking
⇒)(⇐	Tunnel		@	Internet access
- - - - -	Path		⊞	Hospital
━━━━	Railway		ⓘ	Tourist office
,,,,,,,,,,,,,	Funicular		ⓒ	Telephone
— — —	Ferry route		✉	Post office
———	Waterway		♜	Castle
●----●	Cable Car		🏛	Stately home
‿	Bridge		⛫	Abbey
▬▪▬▪▬	Wall		+	Chapel
⊠—⊠	Gate		⛪	Monastery
⧫	Point of interest		✡	Synagogue
◉	Accommodation		⚲	Church (regional maps)
⌃⌃	Mountains		⚡	Skiing
▲	Peak		⛳	Golf course
⚲⚲⚲	Cliff		⊛	Swimming pool
rocks	Rocks		⬭	Stadium
⚐	Viewpoint		▭	Market
⌂	Cave		■	Building
♨	Waterfall		⊞	Church (town maps)
⚶	Spring		⊞	Cemetery
∴	Ruins		▦	Park
⚑	Lighthouse		⸛	Forest
▮	Tower		▦	Beach
⚠	Campsite			

MAP SYMBOLS

The **Rough Guide** to

Portugal

written and researched by

Jules Brown, Mark Ellingham, John Fisher, Matthew Hancock and Graham Kenyon

ROUGH GUIDES

NEW YORK • LONDON • DELHI

www.roughguides.com